Pro Visual Studio 2005 Team System Application Development

Steve Shrimpton

Apress®

Pro Visual Studio 2005 Team System Application Development

Copyright © 2006 by Steve Shrimpton

ISBN-13 (paperback): 978-1-59059-682-1

ISBN-13 (electronic): 978-1-4302-0217-2

Lead Editor: Ewan Buckingham

Technical Reviewer: Riley Perry

Editorial Board: Steve Anglin, Ewan Buckingham, Gary Cornell, Jason Gilmore, Jonathan Gennick, Jonathan Hassell, James Huddleston, Chris Mills, Matthew Moodie, Dominic Shakeshaft, Jim Sumser, Keir Thomas, Matt Wade

Project Manager: Beth Christmas

Copy Edit Manager: Nicole LeClerc

Copy Editor: Liz Welch

Assistant Production Director: Kari Brooks-Copony

Senior Production Editor: Laura Cheu

Compositor and Artist: Kinetic Publishing Services, LLC

Proofreader: Lori Bring

Indexer: John Collin

Cover Designer: Kurt Krames

Manufacturing Director: Tom Debolski

Distributed to the book trade worldwide by Springer-Verlag New York, Inc., 233 Spring Street, 6th Floor, New York, NY 10013. Phone 1-800-SPRINGER, fax 201-348-4505, e-mail orders-ny@springer-sbm.com, or visit http://www.springeronline.com.

For information on translations, please contact Apress directly at 2855 Telegraph Avenue, Suite 600, Berkeley, CA 94705. Phone 510-549-5930, fax 510-549-5939, e-mail info@apress.com, or visit http://www.apress.com.

The source code for this book is available to readers at http://www.apress.com in the Source Code section. You will need to answer questions pertaining to this book in order to successfully download the code.

I dedicate this book to all people throughout the world,
from many ethnic backgrounds,
working together as a team to increase the achievement,
knowledge, and wisdom of all humanity.

Contents at a Glance

Contents

About the Author

 **STEVE SHRIMPTON** was born and educated in the UK and obtained a master's degree in physics from Southampton University. After two years of teaching high school, he worked as a scientist with the UK Ministry of Defence and quickly became involved in airborne computing systems. He migrated to the United States and worked in defense and automotive systems in California for 12 years as a systems engineer, circuit designer, and software developer. He also developed a plug-in digital storage oscilloscope product for DOS 1.1. After a period of time in New Zealand teaching in a university, he settled in Sydney, Australia, where he operates as a contract software architect (www.steveshrimpton.com), undertaking assignments in banking, finance, medical, and many other businesses. Steve considers himself very much a hands-on architect and a programmer's programmer!

About the Technical Reviewer

 **RILEY PERRY** is an Australian-born computer enthusiast currently living in Thailand. He has a degree in IT (software engineering) from the Australian National University and a master's degree in computer science from The University of Technology, Sydney. He also holds several Microsoft certifications (including an MCSD) and is a CCNA (Cisco Certified Networking Associate). Riley's first attempt at programming was on a TRS-80 model 1 level II, and he has been programming ever since. After many years of being a hobbyist and then working professionally in the industry, Riley is now the director of Distributed Development Thailand and Distributed Development Australia (www.disdev.com). Distributed Development specializes in .NET development, business-to-business and application-to-application integration, and Visual Studio Team System.

Acknowledgments

I am grateful to my technical reviewer, Riley, for ideas and encouragement, and to the friendly folks at Apress for their valuable advice and assistance, particularly Beth, Ewan, Laura, and Liz.

Introduction

Microsoft Visual Studio 2005 Team System is an important step in the development of tools for software projects; here the premier .NET development tool has been extended to encompass the software development life cycle. Visual Studio 2005 Team System brings together almost all facets of the project and makes process and development natural partners.

This book goes beyond describing the features of Team System and providing examples. I show how Team System works in a realistic organization with employees interacting as a team to undertake a major project. The characters and companies are of course entirely from my own imagination, and no resemblance to any real individual or organization is intended.

The book essentially does three things. First, it illustrates the use of Team System in the kind of project for which it was designed. Second, it demonstrates how Microsoft Solution Framework for CMMI Process Improvement can work in this kind of project. Third, it illustrates an architecture and design that uses many of the new features of Visual Studio 2005 in developing an enterprise system. But Team System isn't just about process; it's full of tools to make architecture, development, and testing fun and effective. Many of these tools relate to code quality, testing, and performance; you see them in use throughout the project.

To benefit from this book, you should be familiar with programming in C# with some knowledge of ASP.NET, ADO.NET, and SQL. However, I do describe things quite thoroughly and include many illustrations and code listings. You can also do the exercises available from the Apress website (www.apress.com) in the Source Code section, to understand each chapter better.

I begin the book with an introduction to Team System features and introduce the technologies used in the book. Chapter 2 describes the business case for the new project with a survey of an existing enterprise system, and you become familiar with the company's business and jargon. Chapter 3 covers managing the early stages of the new project. Chapter 4 deals with requirements—I provide some detailed descriptions of use cases and scenarios. In Chapter 5, you'll see how the new features of Team System for Architects are used, but in Chapter 6 the detailed design of the implementation begins and the team figures out what planning an iteration really means. Prototyping begins in Chapter 7, where the new developer features of Visual Studio 2005 come into their own.

From here on, the work becomes more formal as the team proceeds through iteration 1, testing as they go, and using the work item and source control features to coordinate the work. Chapters 8 and 9 describe this process, showing check-in and merging. While the majority of the project uses C#, Visual Basic .NET is used for a significant amount of the work. Chapter 10 demonstrates web and performance testing, and Chapter 11 shows change and risk managed by branching.

Next the project moves into the consolidation track. Chapters 12 and 13 concentrate on how Team System is used to manage the later stages, where the details are being completed and bugs found and corrected. Finally in Chapter 14 the new system is deployed.

This book is very broad in scope. I include topics ranging from project management and requirements through architecture, detailed development, and testing. I describe a complex project, and the descriptions of iteration 1 are very detailed, whereas the detail decreases as the project progresses; I found this is an inevitable consequence. Please do not expect to see complete and accurate code. The code will be useful and the architecture fairly realistic, but I do not claim it is anywhere near a fully working system. For that I would need a gigantic book and a team of architects, developers, and testers, as well as managers and business leaders.

A kingdom for a stage, princes to act and monarchs to behold the swelling scene!

Without those extras, I need you, the reader, to extend the project technically with your imagination. *For 'tis your thoughts that now must deck our kings.* Anyway, I think you will find it a useful read. I'll welcome comments or inquiries by email at enquiries@steveshrimpton.com.

CHAPTER 1

Introducing Microsoft Visual Studio 2005 Team System

Software development today seems both easier and more difficult than ever before. It is easier because the tools now available provide developers with the ability to construct complex applications more quickly, yet it is more difficult because defining what those complex applications do, how they are architected, how they interact with other complex applications, how they can be tested, and how they can be consistently deployed and maintained still seems an unrelenting problem.

The Need for Team System

Software development is more than ever a team pursuit, and each of these difficult areas is often the responsibility of different members of the team. Inevitably members see things from their own point of view, and it is rare to find a team member with the experience and perception to see across all the boundaries. Teams can easily become compartmentalized, and in the absence of a concerted approach, the development part of the team is sometimes left to its own devices, because management does not have a clear view of its activities.

One can take the view that only the code really matters in the end, and when push comes to shove, this view often prevails. After all, the customer usually does not see or appreciate the use cases, architectural designs, detailed designs, class structure, test plans, project schedules, or anything else concerned with the process; they usually only experience the finished product and judge it based on its ability to do the job for which they buy it. As long as the code works, the customer is almost always happy. Of course, we all know that this simple statement does not really imply that we can neglect the other traditional parts of the software development life cycle. Indeed, for some customers, such as government defense departments, delivery of documents is as much a contractual requirement as delivery of working code.

But the views of the whole team really are needed. Clear statements of requirements will provide the basis for good design and testing. Thorough and clear design will usually lead to accurate code, leaving fewer bugs to be found by testing and fewer trivial issues to be tracked around the code-test cycle. This provides everyone with more time to concentrate on the difficult issues that justifiably could not have been foreseen. Good, readily understandable architecture and code design also lead to easier modification and better maintainability. Adequate test coverage at the unit, integration, and system levels will provide confidence that the code does what is required and properly implements each component of the design, allowing true progress through the project to be more visible. Repeatable unit tests and system tests will also enable modifications and refactoring to proceed, where needed, with the confidence that undetected defects will not creep in. Good, enlightened project management, in contact with the pulse of the project, will bring the right forces to bear at the right time, minimize risk, and optimize the chances of a successful outcome.

Nevertheless, most people would agree that good code is the most important end product, and this book is about how the limited view of each team member can be successfully combined using Microsoft Visual Studio 2005 Team System. This is a book that gets deeply into the code development, yet emphasizes that the development occurs in a broader team context.

Perhaps the central importance of good code is why the first and primary software development life-cycle tool to come from Microsoft was Visual Studio, in all its variations through all the versions of Visual Basic and Visual C++ prior to .NET, the watershed of .NET and those versions coming afterward, right up to Visual Studio 2005. All of these evolutions of the product, including the new .NET languages, allow the developer to do a better job of producing, in a more efficient manner, code that implements increasingly ambitious functionality. Visual Studio is a highly complex developer's product and is unfamiliar to many other important members of the software development team. Nevertheless, tools have always been needed to perform the tasks of other team members, such as project management, requirements definition, and testing, leaving the developers to use Visual Studio to its best effect.

In Figure 1-1, the ongoing activities involved in the software development life cycle of a typical Microsoft project are summarized with an indication of the tools often being used prior to adopting Team System. Project managers use Microsoft Project to organize the project's work and Excel to organize project data. Business analysts use Excel and Visio to document and visualize the requirements. Architects use Visio to draw class diagrams, data center diagrams, network diagrams, data models, data flow diagrams, and so forth. Testers use Microsoft Application Center Test, a variety of third-party products, and manual methods to perform tests at different levels. The whole team uses Microsoft Word to generate documents. Such documents, along with the source code, are stored in a version control repository such as Visual SourceSafe or a third-party product with richer features. A variety of third-party products are employed to track progress of the project by maintaining a database of requirements, defects, and other work items. Various freeware and shareware products or homemade programs are used to perform formal controlled builds from the source code repository. Since this book concentrates on Microsoft technology, I have not listed the variety of good third-party products currently used in the software development process. To mention only the ones I have experienced would be unjust to those I have not met. Good though these tools may be, used together in the software development cycle they still do not provide an optimal suite that supports an effective process, for reasons that I will now discuss.

Visual Studio Team System represents a departure from the previous evolution of Visual Studio in that it attempts to bring under one umbrella all of the activities shown in Figure 1-1. By activities, I mean a responsibility area of the project performing a particular function to achieve a successful project outcome. These do not necessarily involve people. Source code versioning, for example, I call an *activity* under this definition since it is an ongoing job that continues for most of the duration of the project, and is implemented by some sort of tool. Project management is another example of an activity, one that involves one or more people and some tools. Software development involves a number of people and tools. Figure 1-1 also attempts to show roughly the interactions among these activities. For example, software

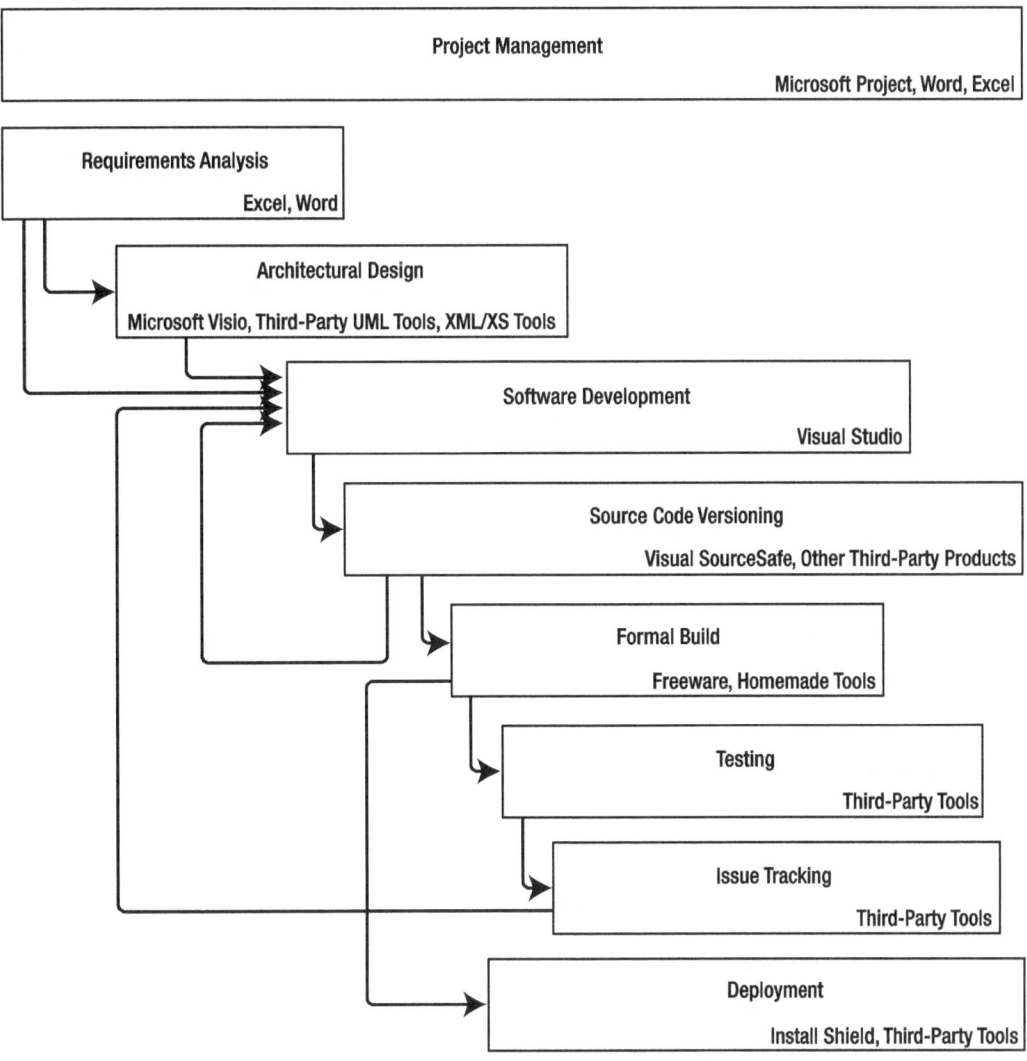

Figure 1-1. *Before Team System: the activities involved in the software development life cycle and their associated tools*

development delivers code to source version control and obtains code from it. Formal build obtains code from version control, and so forth. Not all of the interactions are shown in the figure.

Why would bringing these activities under one umbrella be a desirable thing to achieve? There are a number of reasons. In the current multiple-tool, multiple-vendor environment, all these tools need to be purchased, licensed, installed, and maintained on the team members' machines. Some third-party tools have expensive and complicated licensing requirements. The team members need to learn to use each of these tools and see how they fit into the project and project development process. This can take weeks for new team members, and inadequate knowledge often leads to confusion and inconsistency across the team in the way the tools are applied. In my experience there is an accumulation of project "folklore" that has to be picked up by new team members when learning how to do such things as performing a formal build, interpreting coding standards, checking in modified or new code, or tracking defects.

The process followed by the project is often another source of confusion and inconsistency. The process is usually described in documents or in a set of process guidance web pages, but is typically described in a general manner rather than in terms of the tools that are actually used to carry out the steps it defines. Thus, it is left up to the team members to interpret the process guidelines and determine the way in which they use the tools to carry out their everyday tasks.

Lack of integration is a third problem with the multiple-tool environment. This affects both the efficiency of the team members and the visibility of the management. Too often in projects, the metrics used by the management to track progress are not really effective, since they are too far removed from the development process and are too difficult to keep up to date. A Microsoft Project report is only as accurate as the data typed into it, which is often communicated verbally by the team members, who will provide such statements as "Feature X is 60 percent complete." Such statements are obviously subjective because seldom does anybody define what 60 percent really means. Does it mean 60 percent of the code is written, 60 percent of the code is working, 60 percent of the scenarios have been demonstrated, or 60 percent of the allocated time and budget have been consumed? Even if we make our statements more precise by saying, for example, that 60 percent of the documented scenarios have been demonstrated, the possibility is still left open that the developer has left the most difficult ones until last! To make such statements meaningful requires not just an integrated tool, but a more precise management discipline among all concerned, for example, to consider each of the scenarios thoroughly, assess their level of difficulty, break them into quantifiable units, and ensure that they are properly demonstrated. This takes a greater level of commitment to management overhead than many project budgets and schedules are able to tolerate, but the cost and time of achieving effective management visibility at the micro level will be lessened by the use of integrated tools. This is because these tools relate code changes, as they are added to version control, to tasks that have been scheduled to implement functionality and fix defects. Up-to-date reports can then be generated quickly from this source of low-level data so that the tracking of task completion against the schedule can be followed more easily.

Consideration of requirements and tasks brings us to one of the key features of Team System: the concept of *work items*. Defects, tasks, requirements, issues, and so forth are recorded in Team System using work items, and they allow the related code to be tracked as it is written and tested. This is the way in which the "Issue Tracking" activity in Figure 1-1 is brought under the Team System umbrella and integrated with the development product. Work items are central to everything in Team System, and I will show their relevance and use throughout this book.

To summarize, in this section I have surveyed the background of Microsoft Visual Studio 2005 Team System and indicated the reasons why a more integrated system of software development life-cycle tools is desirable. It is my task in the chapters that follow to show you how this new integrated system of tools will make your life as a software development team member so much easier. First, however, I must introduce Team System as a product.

Microsoft Visual Studio 2005 Team System

Visual Studio 2005 Team System (VSTS) is aimed at development teams ranging from 5 to 500 members and consists of a set of editions of Visual Studio 2005, each with features intended for use by a particular role in the development team, together with a server application called Team Foundation Server (TFS). The three roles covered are architect, developer, and tester, and there are separate versions for each. Also, a full version is available that has the features of all three roles. Team members who are not involved with the code development are supported by the client application of Team Foundation Server, called Team Explorer, and by the ability of some Microsoft Office applications, such as Project and Excel, to integrate with TFS. Team System therefore integrates the whole team, not just the developers. All editions of Team System provide all of the features of Visual Studio 2005 Professional but the role-based versions have additional features as described in the next three sections.

Visual Studio 2005 Team Edition for Software Architects

Additional features in this version are tools that assist the architect in designing distributed applications and the hardware infrastructure to support them. The tools come in the form of the "Distributed System Designers," which support the design of distributed applications—that is, applications made up of interacting component applications. They are particularly aimed at service-oriented architectures, but can support other kinds of applications using their "generic" features and can be customized to support other specific types of distributed applications more fully. There is an Application Designer, a System Designer, a Logical Data Center Designer, and a Deployment Designer.

The use of these tools is studied in detail in Chapter 5 of this book. Essentially though, the Application Designer allows the architect to design distributed applications in terms of component applications, such as Windows applications, web service applications, websites, generic applications, and database applications. The designer allows you to place endpoints on the application symbols, which can be connected to other applications to show how the distributed application is composed of its interacting component applications.

A distributed application, in this sense, is actually a somewhat general concept for which there can be various deployed configurations, called *Systems,* and the System Designer is the tool that allows these configurations to be designed from an existing application.

The Logical Data Center Designer allows you to design a configuration of logical server and client machines, together with their interconnections. You can then use the Deployment Designer to simulate a *deployment* by selecting one of the systems and deploying it on a logical data center, assigning each component application to a logical server. Various constraints on applications and data centers can be defined that are checked for mutual agreement during deployment.

Visual Studio 2005 Team Edition for Software Developers

This edition is intended for developers and includes a set of tools designed for them, containing a static code analyzer similar to FxCop, unit-testing tools similar to NUnit, as well as code-coverage and code-profiling tools.

For those unfamiliar with FxCop, it is a free tool from Microsoft that checks your code against a set of more than 200 rules that avoid known defects and poor design in areas such as library design, localization, naming conventions, performance, and security. The static code analysis tool in Visual Studio 2005 Team Edition for Developers performs a similar check and is fully extensible; it allows you to easily add new rules. You can enable or disable rules according to whether you regard them as important. When enabled, the static analyzer runs after the build, and you can specify that each rule produce an error or a warning, so you can define rules that require compliance for a successful build. Check-in to the source code repository can then be made conditional upon a successful build and also upon the running of the static code analysis tool.

NUnit is an open source, freely available unit-testing framework, which was developed from a similar framework for Java called JUnit and has had widespread use by developers for several years. The unit-testing capability included in Visual Studio allows you to create a test project simply by right-clicking on a class or member function and selecting Create Tests. The project and unit-testing framework is automatically constructed, and you can immediately write the code to implement the required set of tests. The unit tests are collected together under the Test View window. From here you can select tests for execution and review the results.

Once you've written your unit tests, it is important to evaluate the degree of code coverage of these tests. The code-coverage tool will do this for you by giving a percentage indication of the code that has been covered by a set of unit tests; the covered code is also identified in the text view by a green color (the code not covered is indicated by red). Of course, "covered" simply means executed, and it remains for the developer to determine whether the unit tests adequately test the logic of the code. There is a figure called the *cyclomatic complexity*, which is a measure of the number of linearly independent paths through the code, and although all the code may have been executed by a set of tests, this does not mean that all paths have been exercised. Generally the higher the cyclomatic complexity, the more unit tests you need to properly test it, and you also need to verify the correct handling of a range of data values, to ensure that problems such as overflow are avoided.

The code profiler provides the capability to obtain data about the dynamic behavior of the code by determining the frequency at which each function is executed as well as how long it takes, and thus enables developers to make decisions about performance tuning. For example, if a function within the code is executed very rarely, it makes little sense to spend a great deal of time optimizing it, whereas a function in which the code spends a great deal of its time should be made as efficient as possible. The profiler can operate in two modes: sampling and instrumentation. In the sampling mode, the profiler interrupts execution at regular intervals, determines which function the code was executing when interrupted, and maintains a count of the number of times each function was detected. Statistical data is maintained, which over a period of time gives a reasonable profile of where the code spends most of its time. When the instrumentation method is used, the profiler inserts enter and exit probes in each function, which allows it to detect not only each and every time that function is entered, but also how long it takes to execute on each occasion. Although this method is more intrusive and makes the code execute much more slowly, it gives a very accurate profile of the dynamic behavior of the code.

A class designer is also included that provides graphical UML-style class diagrams, which are maintained in a synchronized state with the code. You can modify either the class diagram or the code and they remain in agreement. This feature is actually included in the other versions of Visual Studio 2005 and you do not have to buy a Team Edition to obtain it; however, this feature forms such an important part of the development described in this book that I will discuss it frequently. The unit-testing and code-coverage tools are also included in the edition for testers since it is not always clear where the responsibility lies for this kind of testing.

Visual Studio 2005 Team Edition for Software Testers

This edition is intended for software testers and includes tools for developing various kinds of tests and for managing them, running them, and reporting the results.

The unit-testing, code-coverage tools, and Test View are the same as those included in the edition for developers, but in the edition for testers, there is an extra feature called Test Manager that allows tests to be categorized into multilevel lists. The version for software testers provides the capability to define test projects that are placed under version control on Team Foundation Server in the same way as any other piece of code. The types of tests that can be included in a test project are unit tests (as in the developer version), manual tests, generic tests, web tests, load tests, and ordered lists of tests.

Manual tests are implemented either as plain-text or Microsoft Word documents, and Word can be automatically launched when a new manual test is created with a standard test format. There is a Manual Test Runner, launched from Test Manager, that enables the tester to record the result of the test. The failure of the test is associated with a new work item. Thus, manual tests are included in the overall testing structure and are integrated into the Team System environment.

Generic tests can be used to wrap around existing third-party automatic tests or test harnesses written as part of the project. To be able to be integrated into Test Manager as a generic test, such a test must conform to a certain data or return code interface.

Web tests allow for the functionality of web pages to be tested by recording a sequence of navigation through the pages. Web tests allow you to validate the results returned in web pages and are thus a functional rather than a load test.

Load tests allow you to simulate an environment where multiple users are interacting with an application simultaneously. A wizard lets you define your included tests and load profile, which specifies how the load varies with time. You can then run the load test and obtain selected information about performance.

An ordered test is simply a list of tests, excluding load tests, that must be run in a specified order.

I will describe the use of these various tests in detail as the book progresses through the various development and testing stages of the project.

Visual Studio 2005 Team Suite

This edition includes all of the features of the editions for architects, developers, and testers in one package, which is useful for team members or consultants who play more than one role.

Visual Studio 2005 Team Foundation Server

Team Foundation Server is the server system that ties the architects, developers, testers, and other team members together into a team. Visual Studio 2005 Team Editions communicate with TFS as a centralized repository for source control, work item tracking, builds, and other project artifacts such as Visio or Word documents. It consists of two tiers:

- A data tier consisting of a set of databases hosted within SQL Server 2005

- An application tier providing a set of web services that are used by the various instances of Visual Studio 2005 Team Edition installed on the workstations of the team members, and by instances of Team Explorer (which we see in a moment), as well as Excel and Project

The application and data tiers of TFS may be installed either on one machine or on separate machines. TFS also contains a project web portal implemented by Windows SharePoint Services (WSS). This portal acts as a place where team members can disseminate information to each other in the form of announcements; list and view useful websites; obtain reports of the project's status; and view development process guidelines. It also provides a repository for documents under control of WSS to provide versioning, check-in, check-out, and integration with Microsoft Office applications such as Word, Excel, PowerPoint, and Project.

Included with TFS is Team Explorer, which is a lightweight client for TFS that enables team members not directly involved in architecture, development, or testing to access documents on the server and create and manage work items. As an alternative to this, such team members can also use Excel and Project to access and manage work items. We will study all of these tools in detail later in this book.

How Team System Is Described in This Book

This book will do more than describe the features of Team System; it will show how it can be used in a real project that involves developing a significant distributed, service-oriented application that forms the core enterprise system of a sizable business. This is exactly the kind of project for which Visual Studio 2005 Team System is intended, and I will trace the project through its various stages and show how the features of Team System are used. For example, I will show how the project management tools are used to plan and track the progress of work items. I will also show how the architecture tools—the distributed system designers—are used during the architectural design phase of the project. As the project moves through the build phase, you will see how the code development, code analysis, and test features can be utilized to achieve stability.

The project, of course, is imaginary, as is the company and characters, but I will use their business and staff members to illustrate the interactions among team members, project tasks, and artifacts as the development moves along. The project is fairly straightforward and is typical of many kinds of applications that are developed across the world. I think a completely innovative project, using new techniques, would be too complex to describe in the depth necessary, and you would doubtless become too involved in understanding the complexities of the code to appreciate the bigger picture. Nevertheless, I have included some challenging areas that I hope will illustrate the iterative and risk-reducing way in which I have shown the management of the project.

This brings me to my second aim, which is to show how Microsoft Solution Framework (MSF) can work in a real project. MSF is Microsoft's framework for the software development process. Currently two variants ship with Team System: MSF Agile and MSF for CMMI Process Improvement, which I discuss in Chapter 3. I have chosen MSF for CMMI Process Improvement since this more formal approach, based on the Software Engineering Institute's Capability Maturity Model Integration (CMMI), is more appropriate to a project of the type illustrated, where the company's business is very dependent on the success of the project and risk must be kept to a minimum. Of course, I have been unable to show every detail and document produced by the team as they follow the process—such an approach would bore my readers and be beyond the capability of my one pair of hands—so I have tried to give a representative picture of how the process is applied by examining selected artifacts at various critical points in the development.

Similarly, I have not been able to generate all of the requirements, design, and code for the project but have included a representative sample. I do not expect you will want to check every line and verify that the project is complete! However, I have shown the complete implementation and testing of certain critical areas of functionality, which you should be able to build, test, and run at the end of each stage of the project. Indeed, a third aim of this book is to illustrate an architecture that can be used for a typical distributed service-oriented application. I have tried where possible to use architectural techniques that are recommended by Microsoft, but I have also been inventive in certain areas—which, I claim, is how a good architect should work—and of course I show only the architectural technique that I have chosen with limited time available, which works in the scenario illustrated. I have attempted to choose architectural techniques that illustrate the new features of ASP 2.0 and Visual Studio 2005, and also show some diversity; for example, I have included both browser-based and smart clients, for convincing architectural and business reasons, I think. You may well be able to think of better techniques and indeed in a real project, you should invest time in evaluating alternative architectures to find the best. However, remember to invest such time in areas that matter, where the architecture choice impacts a key feature of the system such as performance or security. In many places in the code, a suboptimal design may be quite acceptable as long as it is clear and works in a satisfactory manner.

I have used the terms distributed application, service-oriented architecture, and smart client in this section, and these concepts will permeate this book. I daresay you are familiar with them to some extent, but I will spend the remainder of this introductory chapter reviewing their meaning and placing them in the right context for the ongoing discussions.

Distributed Applications

The idea of a distributed application is not new, and has appeared in many forms ever since computers became cheap enough for the move away from the centralized mainframe model to take place. I'm going to define it this way: a distributed application is a collection of software components, working together to implement some defined business capability; each of these software components has some degree of autonomy in that each is either physically or logically separate. The whole distributed application may use a number of applications that can be considered complete in themselves, which we can call component applications. I'm sorry to use the word "component" here because that word has a special meaning under COM and DCOM that I will mention later. I do not imply that meaning here, and I could just as well use the term "building block" as I simply mean applications that work together to make bigger applications.

To constitute a distributed application, the software should be under some degree of management as a whole. A set of component applications that just happen to work together one day but fail later because one of them has been changed could not be considered a distributed application. An example of this is an application that uses a number of uncontrolled websites to obtain trading information about securities by screen scraping. *Screen scraping* is a technique used to extract information from the HTML presented by a website intended for viewing by users. If the distributed application no longer works because of an arbitrary change to the screen appearance by one of the websites, then the application cannot be considered a distributed application under this definition.

The point, then, about a distributed application is that the component applications must be controlled in some manner so that they can always be relied on to work properly together. This does not mean that they must be developed by the same team, or managed by the same managers, or even owned by the same company. All that is required for a distributed application to operate properly is that the interfaces exposed by the component applications must be agreed on and maintained. What does the phrase "exposing an interface" mean? It is rather like offering goods for sale. The component application advertises a contract that may be entered into by a purchaser. The purchaser does something and the vendor does something in return; the contract is agreed on and both sides know what they are getting into. If I go into a grocery store and buy onions, I expect to have onions in my basket—I do not expect them suddenly to be replaced by mangoes; similarly, a software contract must be clearly defined and unchanging.

Those who are familiar with service-oriented architectures may see that we are moving along toward defining providers, consumers, WSDL, SOAP, and so on, but let's not jump ahead. Distributed applications are not necessarily service-oriented architectures; there are other forms, and I'm going to mention some of them in order to give a wider illustration of the software world.

Let's start with something completely different. Military aircraft in the Western world contain various computers that are manufactured by different vendors and perform part of the job of flying the plane and doing battle. Examples are Mission Computer, Fire Control Computer, Stores Management System, Inertial Navigation System, and so on. I won't describe what these do, other than to say that *stores* are things like bombs and rockets, but you can get an idea from the names. In the 1980s, these computers used to communicate with each other using something called a serial data bus, which transferred data between one computer and another according to a predefined schedule. For example, every so often a message would be initiated that would transfer data from the Inertial Navigation System to the Mission Computer, which would update information about the location of the airplane and be used to update navigation displays. The system is shown in Figure 1-2.

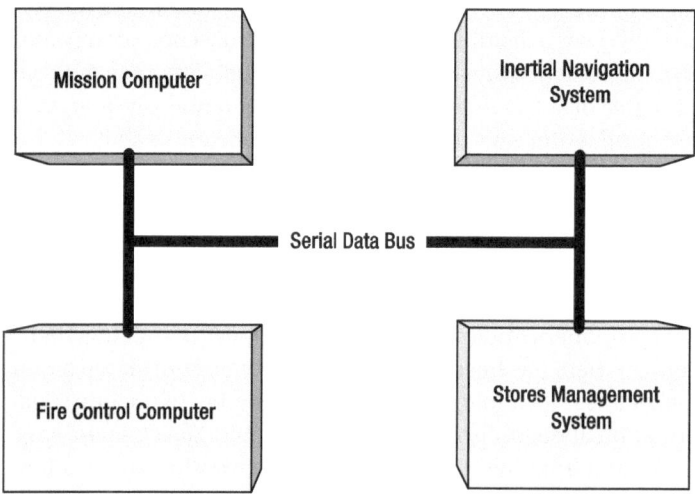

Figure 1-2. *A distributed application on a military airplane*

Is this a distributed application according to our earlier definition? Yes, it certainly is. The whole set of component applications in the various computers combine to form an application whose job is to allow the crew to perform their mission. The component applications are not under the control of one management team or one company, and each can be modified independently. The only criterion is that they support the contract between them. Think of the Inertial Navigation System; it must always respond to a predefined command in the same manner, giving the location of the airplane in an agreed format that the other component applications can interpret correctly. There is another side to the contract, though, which we can call nonfunctional requirements, such as the requirement that the application in the Inertial Navigation System always responds within an agreed time.

Can you use Microsoft Visual Studio 2005 Team System for this distributed application? Well, theoretically I think you could, but you would have to customize the Application Designer and you probably would not be using managed code such as C# or Visual Basic for these embedded systems. So it's a bit of an extreme example!

Let's move on to something closer to home and consider a different kind of distributed application. Before .NET was invented, people used to write applications using Component Object Model (COM) and DCOM. COM is a scheme that allows components of an application, perhaps written in different languages, to work together by exposing interfaces containing member functions. DCOM is a variant that allows the components to reside on different machines and expose their interfaces across a network. The code for the components may be contained either within dynamic link libraries (DLLs) or within separate executables. Either way, they can be constructed and maintained independently and can come from different vendors. The component applications can work together, provided contracts are maintained between them. These contracts consist of the defined interfaces that each component exposes for use by other components making up the distributed application. The components are really objects and the interfaces define methods. This is called *component-based distributed computing*, and a distributed application built in this way is a *component-based distributed application*.

Let's imagine an example. Suppose I'm writing a Microsoft Word document and I want to include within it some UML class diagrams. I also want a few mathematical equations and a couple of spreadsheets. First, I open Word 2000 and create a new document and type some text. Then I decide to draw a Visio UML class diagram. I can do this by selecting Insert ➤ Object from the main menu and choosing Microsoft Visio Drawing from the list of objects available, as shown in Figure 1-3. I then get a dialog box, as shown in Figure 1-4, and if I choose a UML diagram and click OK, I see the screen shown in Figure 1-5. I can now add classes to the UML diagram embedded in the Word document just as if I had opened the Visio application independently. If I click somewhere else in the document, the embedded Visio drawing will close but will still show the passive image of the drawing. I can edit the drawing again by double-clicking on it.

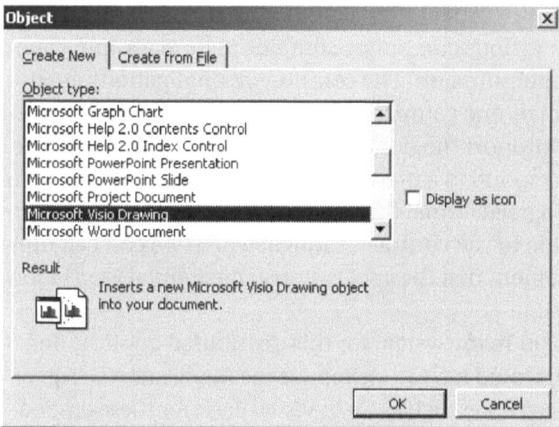

Figure 1-3. *Inserting a Visio drawing into a Word document: choosing the object type*

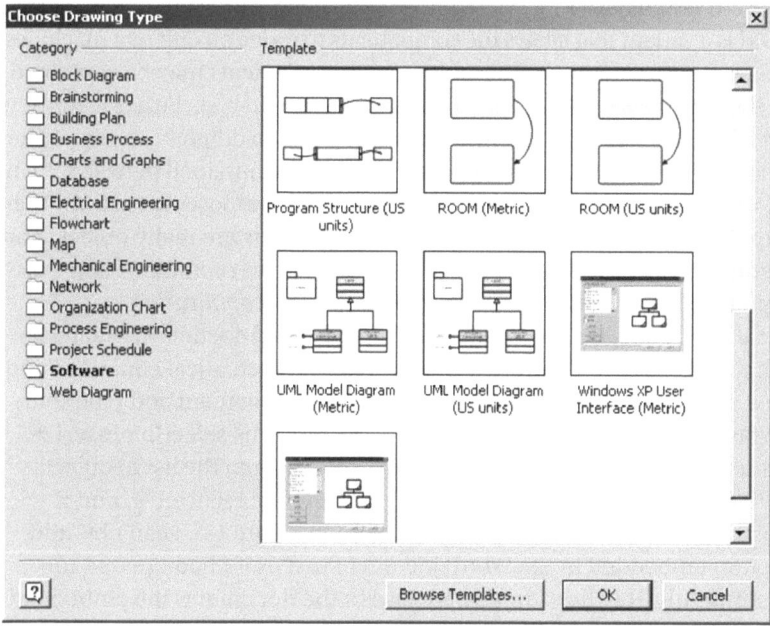

Figure 1-4. *Inserting a Visio drawing into a Word document: choosing the drawing type*

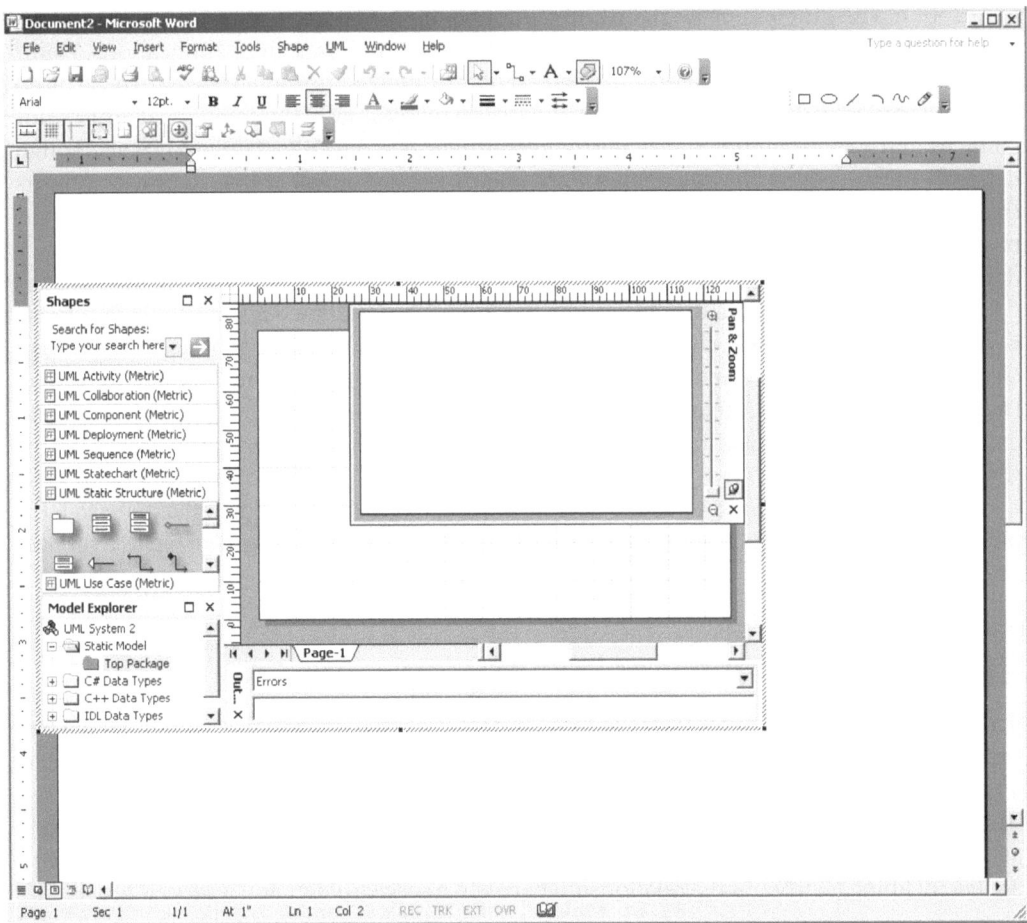

Figure 1-5. *A Visio UML diagram embedded in a Word document*

How does this work? It is all done by a technology called Object Linking and Embedding (OLE), which is a variation of the COM technology that we have been discussing (though OLE 1.0 actually predates COM). It defines the capability of applications—in this case executables called COM servers—to link or embed within other objects, instances of the objects they can manufacture. In the example, the Visio document object is embedded in the Word document object. If you look at Task Manager while the embedded diagram is being edited, you will see that both WINWORD.EXE and VISIO.EXE are running. Winword communicates with Visio and delegates to it all the work of editing the Visio diagram within the Word document. It does this by calling member functions on a whole host of interfaces that are defined as part of the OLE standard and are implemented by the embedded object. A similar thing happens if we go through the same procedure but insert a mathematical equation object, by selecting Microsoft Equation 3.0 in the Insert Object dialog box. In this case, the application EQNEDT32.EXE acts as a COM server, and will start up. A similar process happens when a Microsoft Excel spreadsheet is inserted.

I do not want to get into the details of OLE and COM, although these are still in use and can be included in a .NET application using COM Interop, except to say that these four component applications working together form an example of a component-based distributed application. The function of the distributed application is to provide the capability to write documents with diagrams, equations, and spreadsheets. The component applications, Word, Visio, Excel, and Equation 3.0, are completely separate applications, but they all expose interfaces that comply with the COM and OLE standards. In this case all of the component applications come from the same vendor, but that is not essential since the OLE standard is well enough defined to allow vendors to write applications, knowing that they will be able to provide objects that can be embedded into other documents. Notice that these applications run on the same machine, so they are not geographically distributed. However, as mentioned earlier, DCOM does allow for that geographically separated case as well.

Can we use Team System to help us write these kinds of distributed applications? The answer is yes, but we would have to customize the Application Designer or use generic applications. Generic applications are catchall applications in addition to those defined in the Application Designer and cannot be implemented—that is, their code cannot be generated, or reverse-engineered—by the Application Designer. We will see how generic applications are used in Chapter 5.

By now you should have a good idea of what I mean by a distributed application, so let's now move on to discuss a particular variety that is built around the concept known as a service-oriented architecture.

Service-Oriented Architectures

Service-oriented architectures (SOA) are component-oriented architectures modified to suit the Internet. An SOA is a distributed application that separates its functional areas into smaller applications that provide or use services. An application that makes available a service to be used by other applications is called a provider, and an application that uses a service made available by another application is called a consumer. To use a service is to consume it. There are two defining features of the relationship between a service client and a service provider:

- Services are loosely coupled to their consumers so that the consumer makes a request of the service, the service responds, and the connection is closed.

- Service providers are stateless, which means that each request to the service is treated as a completely independent operation, and the service has no memory of any sequence of requests.

Service-oriented distributed applications have many of the characteristics of component-based distributed applications. For example, the service applications that are integrated to form the one distributed application may be developed on different platforms by different teams under different schedules, as long as the interfaces by which the services are accessed are agreed on. The difference is in the degree of coupling. A provider and a consumer in a component-based architecture, as in COM and OLE, have a much tighter coupling, which is connection oriented. The provider maintains state, the consumer can make multiple calls on the provider during the connection, and the connection can be maintained for as long as is required. The provider can even make return calls on the consumer, in the form of events, for example. This is the case in the OLE example in the previous section and results in a great deal of complexity.

Also COM, OLE, and the newer .NET Remoting all involve the provision of *objects* to the consumer, which the consumer can hold between function calls and which retain state. In the service-oriented approach objects may certainly exist on the client and server, but these are simply encapsulations of the message transmission and receipt functionality and do not survive on the provider beyond the transmission of the response message to the consumer. Clearly the movement to a looser coupling is a natural response to the demands of the Internet, where there may be a low bandwidth and unreliable connection between provider and consumer.

The stateless nature of a web service does not, of course, imply that any business entities that are processed by the service have no state. For example, a service may provide a method to modify the details of a business entity, such as a customer held on a database to which the service provider has access. For instance, a request is received by the service to change the customer's telephone number, the request is processed, the data is changed in the database, and a response message is sent. The state of the customer as an entity in the database has certainly changed, but the service itself has no memory of the transaction—there cannot be a sequence of messages that together cause the customer data in the database to change. This is what we mean by stateless. Furthermore, we can regard the customer existing in the database as an object, but that object is not exposed to the consumer as such, other than perhaps implicitly via the message interactions defined in the web service.

These statements define a service-oriented architecture, but there are further characteristics applicable to .NET web services. The first is that the services are accessed via the sending and receiving of messages. A service provider exposes a service interface to which all messages are sent, the consumer sends a message to the provider requesting the service, and the provider responds with a message containing the results of the request. The second is that the "web" in the name web service implies that HTTP will be used since this is the ubiquitous protocol of the Internet and is invariably passed by firewalls. The third characteristic applying to most .NET web services is that the data included in the request and response messages is formatted according to the Simple Object Access Protocol (SOAP), which is defined in terms of XML structures.

Although the concept can be interpreted more generally, in this book I will treat an SOA as a collection of applications that are loosely coupled as either providers or consumers (or both) of web services and distribute the functions of the application among those providers and consumers in such a way that the data relating to a particular service is encapsulated locally with that service. In many applications, though, it is not true to say that any given service exclusively uses the data tables in the database that it accesses. This might be an ideal, but in practice the database often forms the central part of a large distributed application and many services access the same tables for various reasons. Care must then be taken to set up a mechanism of transactions to ensure that the integrity of the database is maintained.

A further feature of web services that needs to be mentioned is that their details can be *discovered* by a consumer. Each service can give to a consumer details of the service it provides in the form of a Web Service Definition Language (WSDL) file. A potential consumer can request this file, which provides complete details of the services offered, as well as the request and response message structures, including definitions of any parameters, and their complex types if applicable.

Figure 1-6 shows an example of an SOA implementing a sales website. The client is browser based, running on a customer machine. The browser client accesses the Sales Website Application, which accesses a database to keep a record of customer orders, and also uses the functionality provided by the Catalog Web Service, giving a listing of the company's products and their prices. The Catalog Web Service also uses a database that contains tables listing the products offered for sale, and uses another web service, the Currency Conversion Web Service, which provides information to convert prices into the currency requested by the customer. This web service makes use of a third database that contains currency conversion factors, which are updated daily.

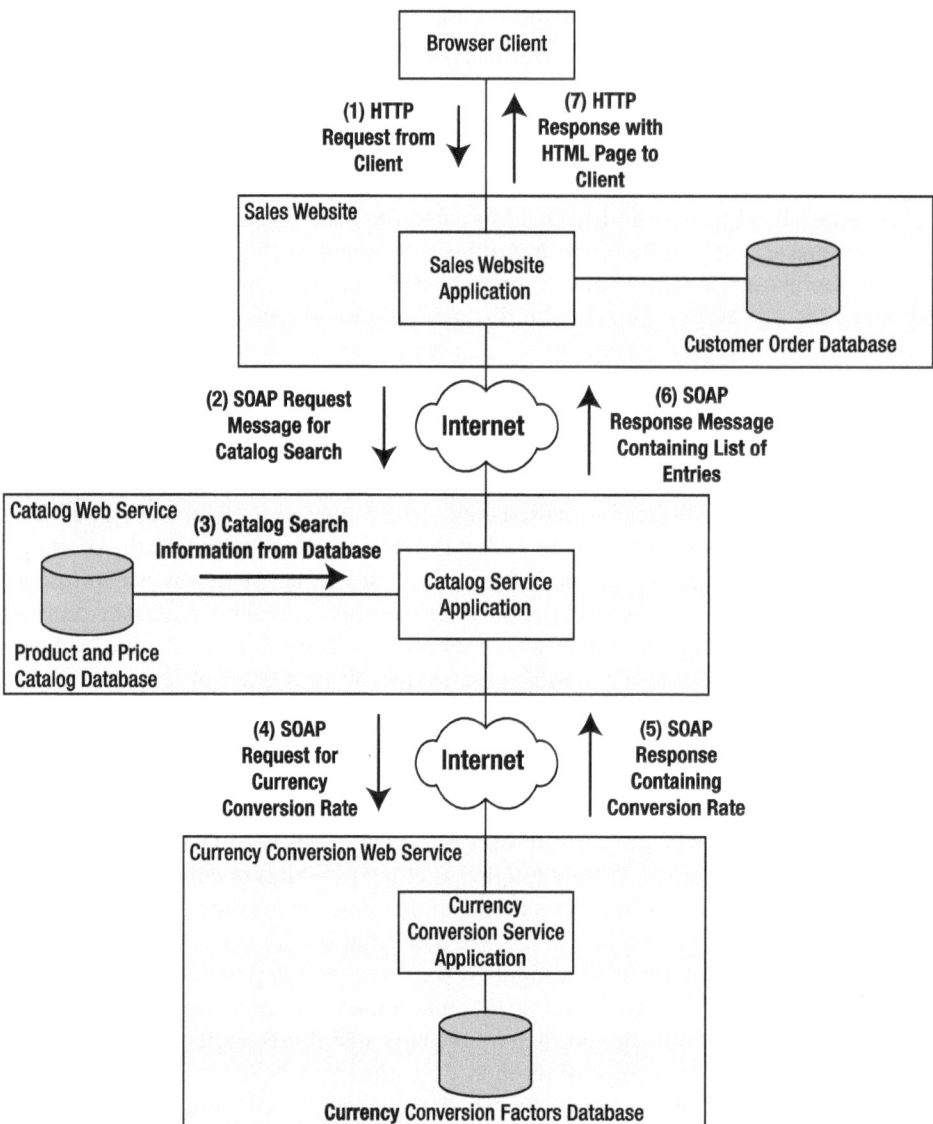

Figure 1-6. *A typical service-oriented architecture distributed application: a sales site using a catalog web service and a currency conversion web service*

Figure 1-6 shows the message flow for a typical search of the catalog initiated from the browser client:

1. The browser client posts a page to the Sales Website Application to initiate a catalog search.

2. The Sales Website Application processes the post and determines that a call to the Catalog Web Service is required.

3. The Catalog Web Service receives a request message for a catalog search and calls a stored procedure in the Product and Price Catalog Database to execute the search. The stored procedure returns a list of catalog entries, each with a price in U.S. dollars.

4. The Catalog Service Application makes a call to the Currency Conversion Web Service to request a conversion rate between U.S. dollars and the user's currency preference, which happens to be Indian rupees.

5. The Currency Conversion Web Service returns a message containing the required currency conversion factor.

6. The Catalog Service Application converts all of the prices in the list of items from the catalog to rupees and returns the list of items in a response message back to the Sales Website Application.

7. The Sales Website Application populates a Web Forms page with the data and returns an HTML page to the client browser.

The Smart Client Approach

The architecture of enterprise applications has evolved over time. Client-server architectures have given way to browser-based, thin-client designs, and now the *smart client* is gaining vogue. Let's now examine this evolutionary story and explore the reasons behind it.

Evolution of the Client-Server Architecture

During maybe the last 10 to 15 years, the architecture of enterprise applications has moved through various stages. We won't discuss small-scale single-user applications running on a single machine, where all of the data and software is contained within that one machine. Here we'll focus on the Microsoft array of technologies; I want to trace the reasoning behind their evolution, although actually the evolution of these technologies seems to be fairly representative of the evolution of the industry as a whole, since there has been such a degree of exchange of ideas between say, the Java and .NET schools of thought.

Once multiuser enterprise applications moved away from centralized mainframe-based applications using terminals such as 3270, and Microsoft solutions began to be adopted as well as others, two common categories of architecture emerged. Both of these can be considered client-server in a manner of speaking.

One type of application uses a file server as the server side and places all the application's software on each client machine. An example is a Microsoft Access application where the database files reside on a server and are opened by the clients. Another is an application in which flat files are stored on the server and each instance of the application opens the file to read, or opens and locks it to write. These are called "thick-client" applications, where all of the business logic is duplicated on each client machine.

The other type of client-server application uses a relational database on the server with stored procedures and triggers. The stored procedures can be very simple, or they can be complex and include business logic. An example of a stored procedure that includes business logic might be called AddSalesOrder. AddSalesOrder can receive raw textual information taken straight from that entered by the user on the client screen. This stored procedure checks the data for validity, and then performs multiple inserts into various tables to add a sales order, perhaps obtaining more data by making joins across other tables or even attaching to other databases. A simple stored procedure might just add a row to the SALESORDER table and be given the exact values for each column. You could design this kind of client-server application either with most of the business logic on the client or most of it on the server. Both approaches have advantages and disadvantages. Putting the business logic on the server means that the number of times the client accesses the database is usually minimized, and it also means that the client can be made much simpler. It probably reduces network traffic at the expense of making the database server do much more programmatic work in running the stored procedures, but if the database server is a big, powerful machine, this may not be a problem.

Most people would agree, however, that while a good SQL programmer can make the language do almost anything, SQL is not intended to perform logic but to access data. So if there is a lot of decision making to be performed in the business logic, it is better written in the language of the client, such as Visual Basic or Visual C++. If you are prepared to accept business logic written in SQL, though, this kind of architecture can separate the business logic from the display logic, and thus represents a two-tier system.

The client is still what we consider to be "thick" in the sense that, in the Microsoft world, it is a Visual Basic or Visual C++ application running as an executable on the client and has a set of DLLs that will be required for it to operate properly. Here is the problem! The well-known phrase "DLL Hell" describes the situation in which several applications installed on a client expect different versions of a given DLL. You could install a client application that uses various DLLs that come with the operating system and everything works fine, but then later someone installs another application that overwrites those DLLs with different versions—maybe earlier ones—and suddenly the first application breaks. The first application is reinstalled, but it still does not work because it relied on DLLs that were installed with the operating system. The only answer is to reinstall the operating system—what a nightmare!

Another scenario is that the developer builds an application, installs it on his own machine, and it works fine, but when someone else installs it on a different machine, it does not work. This is because the developer happened to have DLLs installed on his machine as a result of installing Visual Studio. So now the team has to try to find which DLLs are on the developer's machine but missing from the client machine. This situation is made worse by the fact that DLLs load other DLLs in a chain so that even though an application may have access to the correct version of a required DLL, that DLL may require a second DLL that also must be the correct version. The task of solving this problem then becomes more complicated as a chain of DLL versioning requirements must be satisfied.

In all these examples, careful control of client machines is needed to ensure that the suite of applications installed is compatible. When there are several client machines in a company, this becomes a serious expenditure of time and labor. Even leaving aside the "DLL Hell" problem, installation of a complex application on client machines together with possible hardware implications is still a significant task. The same rationale applies to any Windows application built using technology from other vendors such as Borland's Delphi or Sybase's PowerBuilder, since these use many DLLs installed with the Windows system and are subject to versioning. Thus, there is a justification to move away from the idea of having large Windows applications on client machines, and thin-client applications have become a popular alternative.

Thin Clients and the N-Tier Architecture

The World Wide Web began with websites supplying textual and pictorial data, which was displayed by users on their client machine using an application called a web browser. Thin clients developed as websites grew from simply supplying data for display, to permitting customer input via HTML forms, with controls such as drop-downs, text input, and buttons rendered by an enhanced browser. A telephone directory site is a good example of a website that allows simple customer data entry in the form of search criteria. Gradually the concept of e-commerce came into being, with customers placing orders for goods and services via the Internet using their browsers. The web browser, when displaying HTML forms that form part of the graphical user interface to an application, is called a thin client. One of its chief features is that the architect of the server part of the application neither needs nor has much control over the client configuration.

It became clear to architects of enterprise applications that this technique could be used within the bounds of the corporate intranet. Employees responsible for processing company data could be connected to a web server using only their browsers. A range of corporate applications could then be hosted on that server and be operated by employees with a very simple and standard client machine configuration.

Thin clients then, are characterized by the use of some kind of general-purpose display application, invariably a web browser, and receive all the formatting and display detail from the server. The web browser accesses a sequence of URLs on one or more servers to obtain the screens that the user will see when using the application to perform its business functions. Since Microsoft Internet Explorer is such a ubiquitous application, and is installed as part of the Windows operating system, we can usually assume it is available. Provided the application that sends the HTML to the client for each screen does not use any features that are specific to a particular version of Internet Explorer, the application will always work. This technique has the advantage that a home user—over whose computer the architect has no control—can also run the application.

The server that delivers the business application to the client can run an ASP, or more recently an ASP.NET application, and becomes a *middle tier*, with the browser client forming the top, or client tier, and the database forming the bottom, or data tier. In a simple ASP application, there are two possible places to write the code that implements the business logic. One is to program it into stored procedures in the database in a similar manner to the client-server application described previously. The other is to implement it using JavaScript or VBScript embedded in the HTML pages stored on the server, and enclosed within special tags. The web server includes a script engine that executes this code on the server before delivering the HTML to the client browser.

For more complex ASP applications, the middle tier is broken into more than one tier (the n-tier model) and the business logic is encapsulated in COM components in the form of objects delivered by COM servers in response to create requests from the script in the ASP pages. Various member functions of these objects can then be called by the ASP script to execute business logic and database operations that are coded in the language of the COM components—either VB or C++. The set of ASP pages then becomes known as the presentation tier and the COM components are called the business tier. In a good design, the ASP pages consist of only simple script and the HTML that produces the required appearance, while all of the business functionality of the application is placed in the COM components or the stored procedures in the database.

With the advent of .NET, COM components have become unnecessary for this type of application, and the business logic can be separated from the presentation code quite well by placing it in the code-behind classes in the form of C# or VB.NET code. For a simple application, this is very good, but suffers from the disadvantage that areas of business logic needing to process data relating to more than one web page must be duplicated in the aspx.cs files, and thus become more difficult to maintain and test. It is better therefore to reintroduce a form of n-tier by placing business logic in appropriate classes that can be unit-tested independently, and that can be used by many code-behind classes corresponding to many web pages. It is also a good idea to place the data access code either in these business object classes or, as a much better option, in a separate tier again called the data access tier or data access layer (DAL). This separation of presentation, business, and data access functionality is usually seen as good practice.

OK, so why do we need anything else? There are a few problems with thin clients; for one thing, it is seldom possible to avoid putting some sort of logic on the client in the form of client-side scripting executed by the web browser. This scripting on the client, of course, is not installed on the client like a thick-client application, but is delivered by the web server with each page, and executes for various reasons on the client browser before the page is posted back to the server. One example is when the options in one drop-down control depend on the setting of another—like a list of states in an address depending on the selection of a country—so that when one is changed, the collection of options in the other needs to be updated. This script is never easy to debug and maintain, and its success often depends on a particular version of the browser.

As well as these problems with scripting, the display features that can be presented on a browser client are rather limited. To provide a richer client experience, the designer is invariably drawn back to using a Windows application as the client tier.

Smart Client Applications

A "smart client" application is the name that Microsoft uses to define a client that is a compromise between a thick client and a thin client. It is a full Windows Forms application that makes use of both local resources and network resources, and can operate as part of a service-oriented architecture. It is distinguished from the old-fashioned thick client in that it usually does not interface directly with a database but with a server that exposes one or more web services or other network resources. The smart client application is intended to take the presentation tier away from the server and combines it with the client tier, formerly implemented with a browser, to provide a richer client experience.

Figure 1-7 shows how a smart client is used in a service-oriented architecture. The smart client is a Windows Forms application installed and running on the client machine. Here's how it might work. It might look like a multiple-document application (an application in which several documents can be open on the screen at one time), although the "documents" will probably not be documents stored on the local drive but represent entities stored in the remote database. Let's suppose it's a customer relationship management system. It might have a File menu that has an Open Customer option that allows the user to view the details of a customer by choosing that customer from a list. Imagine the user clicks the Open Customer menu item, which brings up a dialog box listing the available customers. To populate the list in the dialog box, the application calls a function on one of the web services exposed by the ASP.NET application in Figure 1-7. There is a web service, perhaps called Manage Customers, which will have a set of functions defined. One of these functions, ListCustomers, returns a list of customer names that the smart client application can display in a list box on the Open Customer dialog box.

When the user has selected the required customer from the list and clicked OK—or maybe just double-clicked the name in the list—the dialog box disappears and the customer details are obtained from the server to be displayed in the application as an opened customer. To do this, the smart client needs to make another call on the Manage Customers web service, this time perhaps calling a function called GetCustomerDetails. In each call to a web service function, an XML SOAP document is sent to the server and another SOAP response document is returned containing the required information. Code within the smart client is responsible for populating the various controls on the screen, such as the list box displaying the customers and the various labels, text boxes, and combo boxes displaying the data fields representing the customer details.

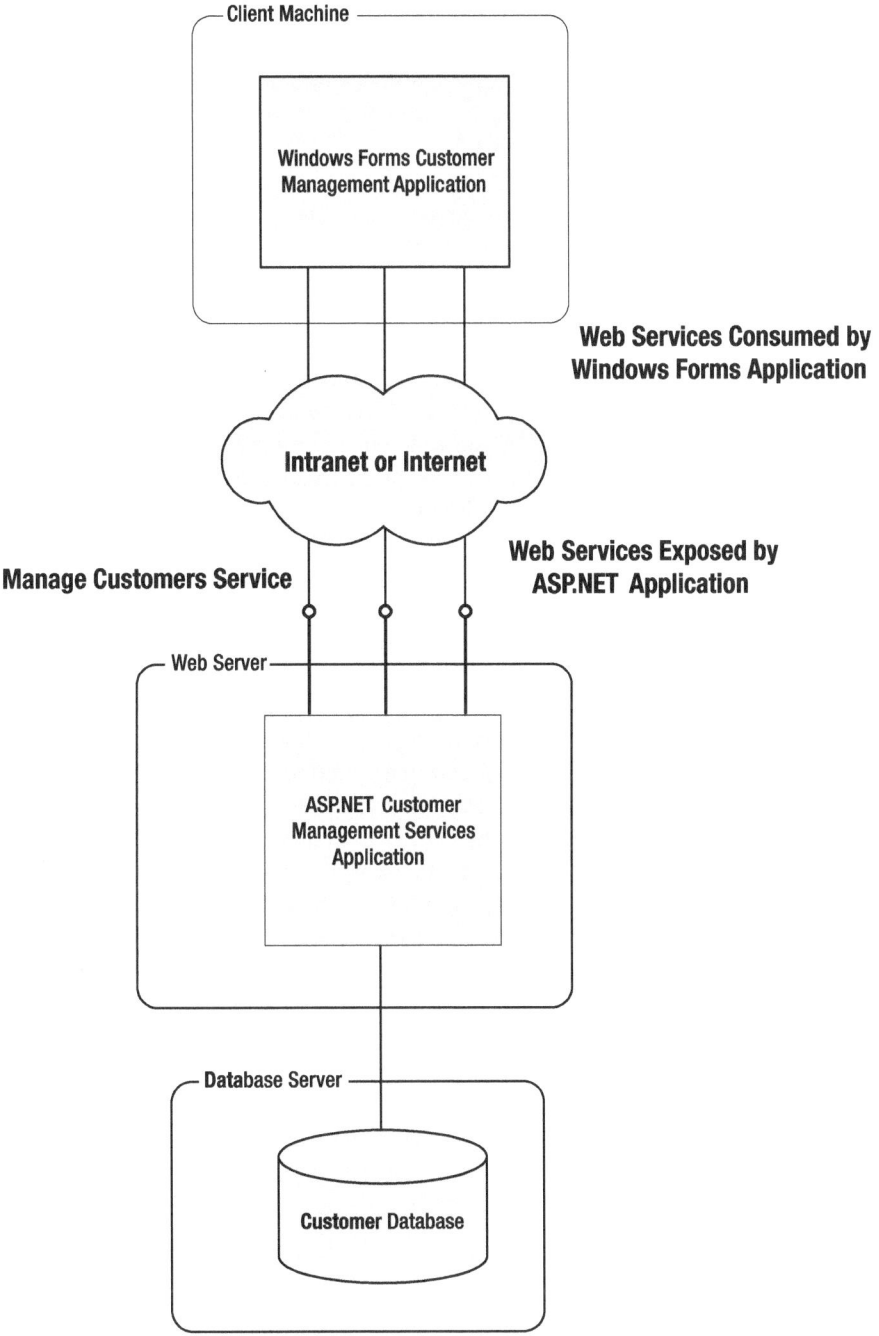

Figure 1-7. *Architecture of an application using smart clients*

Why is it that full-function clients are now acceptable and the DLL Hell described earlier is no longer a problem? The main reason is because .NET assemblies in DLLs are better managed than old-style DLLs. Not only does the global assembly cache (in which .NET assemblies intended to be shared by applications reside) allow for multiple versions of shared assemblies to coexist using the "strong naming" feature, it also introduces the concept of *private assemblies*. When a private assembly needs to be loaded by an executing application, probing takes place in the local folder and any subfolder that is specified by a `.config` file in the local folder. Thus, a whole set of assemblies required only by a particular application may be installed without interfering with those installed for another application. Furthermore, under .NET, unlike COM, there is no longer any need to place details of assemblies in the Registry; it can all be done using copying—known as the "XCopy install."

Let's reconcile these ideas about assembly location with the way that the code creates an object that is an instance of a class defined within an assembly. There are two ways to create an object. The first is when the .NET project references the assembly, which we see clearly in Solution Explorer under the project references. In this case, instances of the class can be created within the code for the referencing project using the new keyword. The second way does not require a reference to the assembly to be defined within the project. Instead, the assembly is loaded explicitly by name (and possibly location), and instances of its classes are created using the features of the System.Reflection namespace. In either case the probing rules for public or private assemblies apply. This different approach to assemblies makes the installation and upgrade of complex applications much simpler and greatly reduces the management overhead of smart clients compared to old-style thick clients.

There are a couple of other features of smart clients to be considered. One is that they are capable of implementing some sort of disconnected or offline capability. How much capability a client can implement when disconnected from the server depends on the application. It may be possible to produce full functionality, with data synchronization occurring when the client is reconnected, or it may be impossible to provide any functionality at all, other than a polite message indicating disconnection.

The other feature is the ability to perform click-once deployment. Click-once deployment avoids the need to place an executable for an application on each user's machine. Instead, the executable is placed on a common web page from which users can launch it. As part of the launch process, a copy of the application is retrieved to the client's hard drive so that in the future, the application can be launched locally. Applications deployed by the click-once technology can be self-updating and appear in the Start menu and the Add/Remove Programs list. They are deployed in a special location on the client machine, are self-contained, and are kept separate from other installations, but they must be installed separately for each user as they cannot be installed for use by multiple users of the machine.

There are alternatives to click-once deployment. You can use the Windows Installer by packaging all the files needed for deployment into an .MSI file, but regardless of whether smart clients are installed by click-once installation or using the Windows Installer, they can always be self-contained and avoid the DLL versioning problems described earlier.

Summary

The goal of this chapter was to introduce Visual Studio 2005 Team System; explain its reason for existence, including the problems it addresses; and give a summary of its features. This chapter also introduced some concepts related to the architecture of enterprise systems; these concepts will be used later in the book. At this point you should

- Understand the purpose of Visual Studio 2005 Team System

- Be familiar with the features it makes available to architects, developers, and testers

- Understand the concept of a distributed application

- Understand the concept of a service-oriented architecture

- Have a picture of the evolution of enterprise system architecture in the past 10 to 15 years and the reasoning behind it

- Be familiar with the way in which smart clients and web clients fit into a service-oriented architecture

We continue our discussion by introducing an imaginary company and describing its project plans. The remainder of this book follows the progress of this project and explains in detail how Visual Studio 2005 Team System is employed throughout.

CHAPTER 2

The Business Case and Project Scope

As explained in Chapter 1, this book uses Microsoft Visual Studio Team System in a fairly complex, realistic project and provides some insight into the way this kind of project can be organized and managed. Along the way, I look at the architecture, coding, and test techniques available to you. In this chapter I introduce a fictitious company called Icarus Travel Services, Inc., and describe their business and management teams. I also introduce a team of stalwart consultants and their small company Guru's Nest, which will be undertaking most of the project. You will see how the team of consultants investigates the existing system, how the case for the upgrade project Icarus Enterprise 3.1 develops, and how the team arrives at the proposed solution. Details of this new solution will be developed in the next three chapters, but in this fairly short chapter, I will set the scene. Without dwelling on the details of the existing system, my intent is to give enough detail to provide a flavor of the features currently available so that you can follow the thinking that goes into developing the solution.

The Business Justification

Icarus Travel Services, Inc. is an organization that manages sales of worldwide travel resources offered by a range of vendors, large and small, to customers wishing to arrange holiday or business travel. The resources listed for sale by Icarus's vendors include various kinds of hotel accommodations, rental cars, and travel packages via bus or train. Icarus also offers reservations for tours, such as day trips to tourist sites in countries such as Greece and Italy. The company currently sells both through travel agents and directly to the general public, using online sales and a call center. A software package called Sales Manager, written in Visual Basic 6, is installed on operator machines at the call center and provides rich client features, while the Icarus Sales website provides a basic online sales capability. Another VB6 application called Resource Manager gives staff the capability to respond to information from vendors and update the listings database.

Icarus plans an interesting new business expansion to provide sales capability for training courses to be held at various exotic locations around the world, and it is currently completing negotiations with an enterprise called World Wide Chefs (WWC) that offers courses on ethnic cuisine delivered by local chefs in authentic surroundings. World Wide Chefs' most successful offerings are currently the weeklong courses held on the islands of Corfu and Crete in which dishes such as moussaka, souvlaki, and Greek salads are covered. However, WWC is thinking of expanding its course offerings into China and Mexico.

Per Icarus's agreement with World Wide Chefs, which allows them sole Internet marketing rights for two years, Icarus must upgrade its present software to handle the reservation and sales for WWC's courses. A major area requiring upgrade is the Resource Manager application, since WWC wishes to have the capability to manage their offerings themselves rather than work through one of Icarus's vendor administrators. WWC wants much greater control of how their course offerings are presented to potential customers, such as the layout of pages and the inclusion of images on the Icarus Sales website. They also want to be able to adjust the availability of courses and introduce special promotions in a timely manner. In addition, the new contract requires that Icarus upgrade their web-based sales capability by introducing better categorization and search capability for listing data.

Other considerations have also prompted Icarus to undertake a large upgrade. Neither Icarus's existing vendors nor their travel agents find the current system easy to use. Icarus has therefore formed an alliance with several agents in order to gain their help in defining the requirements for the redesigned system, and they hope the project will pave the way for a substantial increase in their market share and give them a considerable edge over their competitors.

Under the advice of their consultant architect, Peter Sage, Icarus is also going to take this opportunity to begin migrating their current system—which has evolved over six years and is a mixture of old technologies—to Microsoft .NET and SQL Server 2005. Peter has also been reading a lot about Microsoft Team System and has managed to convince Icarus's IT manager, Tony Woods, that their software development has not been nearly as well organized as it could be. Marcia Polo, the CEO, is anxious to grow the business and keep costs down, and is not happy with the recent work managed by Tony; in fact, she is beginning to see the IT department as a weak point. Thus the upgrade of Icarus's sales system, dubbed Icarus Enterprise 3.1, is extremely critical to both the company and various careers, and is highly visible to upper management. It would not be overstating the importance to call the project a "make or break" situation for Icarus, since their enterprise system is currently holding them back and an improved system will count as an impetus toward forward progress.

The requirements of WWC are only the latest in a sequence of events that have underlined the inadequacy of Icarus's current system, but have finally prompted Marcia to allow a far-reaching and somewhat risky upgrade to Icarus's business system.

The High-Level Requirements

In a nutshell, Icarus needs to be able to sell the various travel resources on their website and via their call center, accepting payment in a limited set of currencies by credit card or sending out invoices and accepting payment by check or other forms of funds transfer. They need to keep track of the money paid by their customers, extract their commissions, and account for money owed to vendors. As part of the sales process, they must provide an online catalog of courses offered by their vendors, with pictures of the local attractions; support customer inquiries; and provide email and printed confirmation of orders. They must also make regular reports to vendors such as WWC and their own management and marketing personnel. Icarus would like to sell local tours as supplementary items when they sell accommodation, and so they wish to keep records of customer purchases in the hopes of selling those customers other travel products listed by their worldwide clients.

Existing Enterprise System Architecture

Of course, there is already an infrastructure in existence that must be analyzed by the consultant team before plans can be made. Peter has spent a month studying it, and this section summarizes his findings. He has made some screen shots containing old vendors, customers, and orders, to help with documentation, and some of these are reproduced here. The core of the system is a SQL Server 2000 database that contains details of vendors, their resources listed for sale by Icarus, and Icarus's customers and their orders. Another database contains accounting information and is used to keep track of sales monies earned, commissions, and money owed to vendors. Vendors, resources, customers, and reservations are maintained in the SQL 2000 database by various applications, which are shown with their interactions in Figure 2-1 and are described in the following sections. The sales and resource management applications also initiate asynchronous actions via an application called the orchestration service, also shown in Figure 2-1. These actions occur when it is necessary to initiate a downstream process, such as sending a confirmation email or printing an itinerary to be mailed to a customer. The orchestration service receives documents and forwards them to three downstream services: the document, accounting, and email services.

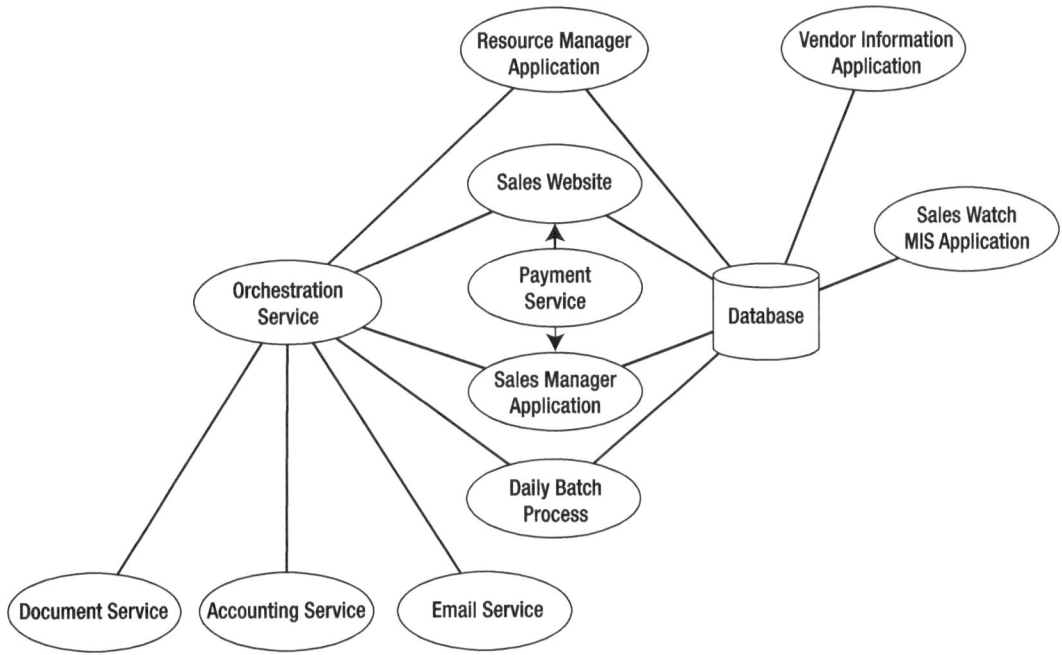

Figure 2-1. *The main applications making up the Icarus Enterprise System*

Resource Manager

This existing application is written in Visual Basic 6 and runs on administrative or call center client machines, allowing operators to manage both vendors and the resources they offer. For example, various small hotels sell reservations for their rooms through Icarus, and an operator will use Resource Manager to set up a hotel owner as a new vendor. The operator will enter the resources available from this vendor, including the number and type, the availability dates, the costs, various options, and so on. Once resource data entry has been completed, the resources will be available for reservation by Icarus's customers. Resource Manager can also be used to modify or withdraw resources, change availability dates, modify information about resource providers, update contact or billing information, and so on.

User Interface

The main screen of the Resource Manager application, shown in Figure 2-2, provides an alphabetical listing of vendors. The operator may select any vendor and click the Vendor Details button to the right of the vendor list to bring up the Vendor Details dialog box shown in Figure 2-3. This dialog box has three tabs: one containing basic information about the vendor; another containing contact information, such as addresses and telephone numbers; and a third containing billing and payment information, enabling financial transactions to take place between Icarus and the vendor. Depending on the financial arrangements made at the time of the reservation, Icarus may receive payment in full from the customer or they may receive a deposit. In some situations no payment is received. Thus money may be owed in either direction, since Icarus may owe deposits or full sales amounts to the vendor, or the vendor may owe commissions to Icarus. Therefore, billing information for commissions as well as deposit information for money owed to vendors is included in this page.

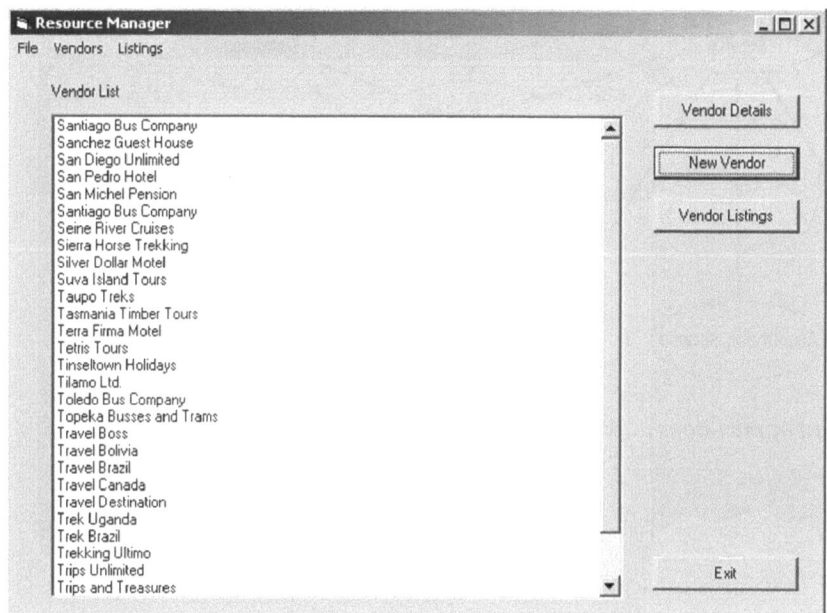

Figure 2-2. *Main screen for the Resource Manager application*

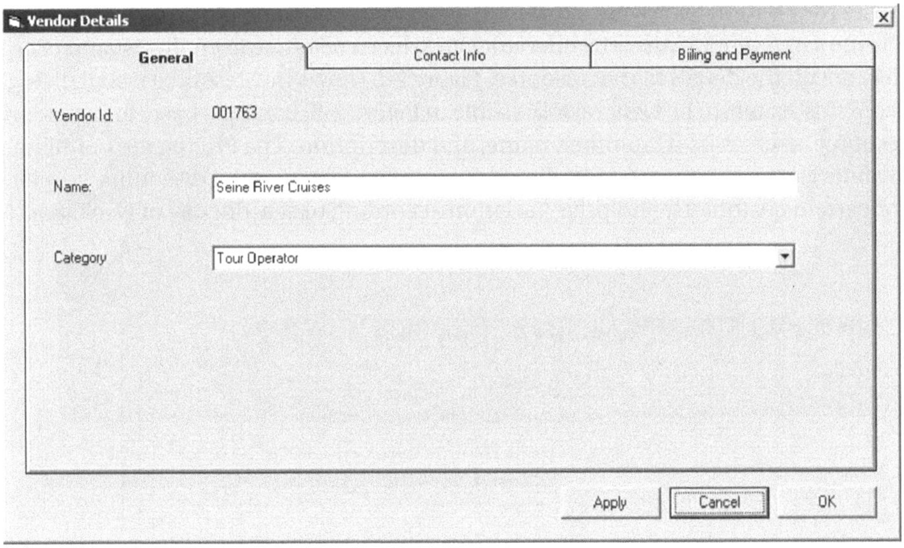

Figure 2-3. *The Vendor Details dialog box*

From the dialog box shown in Figure 2-2, the operator can also select a vendor and click the Vendor Listings button. The resulting dialog box, shown in Figure 2-4, lists the resources offered for sale by the vendor through Icarus. Resources include any item listed for reservation such as hotel rooms, tours, rail travel, bus travel, teaching courses, seats at shows, and so forth. Figure 2-4 shows the resources offered by a vendor called "Croisières De Fleuve De Seine" (Seine River Cruises), a company operating a fleet of small tour boats on the River Seine in Paris, France. This small company offers a choice of three cruises: Morning, Afternoon, and Dinner cruises. This dialog box allows the operator to add new resources or delete existing ones. In fact, existing resources are never deleted in the database but are simply marked as unavailable for reservation. Deletion would result in referential integrity issues for the historical data in the database.

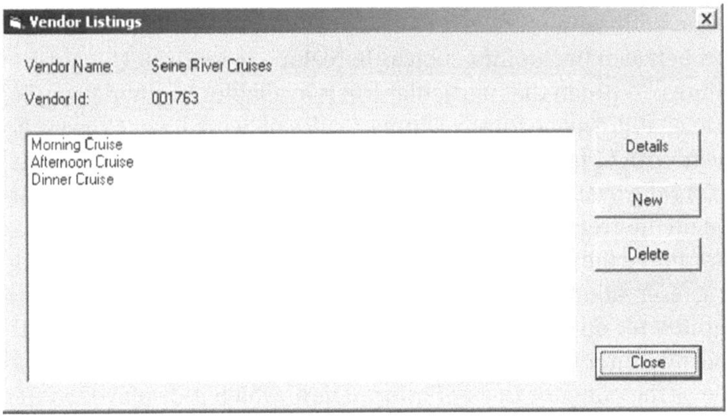

Figure 2-4. *The Vendor Listings dialog box*

Clicking the New button allows the operator to insert a new resource into the database as an offering by the same vendor. Also, the operator can select a resource from the list and click Details to view or edit the details of that resource. Figure 2-5 shows the Resource Detail dialog box, which contains six tabs. The General tab, visible in Figure 2-5, contains basic information about the resource, such as its ID number, name, and description. The Pricing tab contains information about the pricing structure of the resource, including quantity discounts, special discounts for certain customers, and price variation according to season, day of week, and time of day.

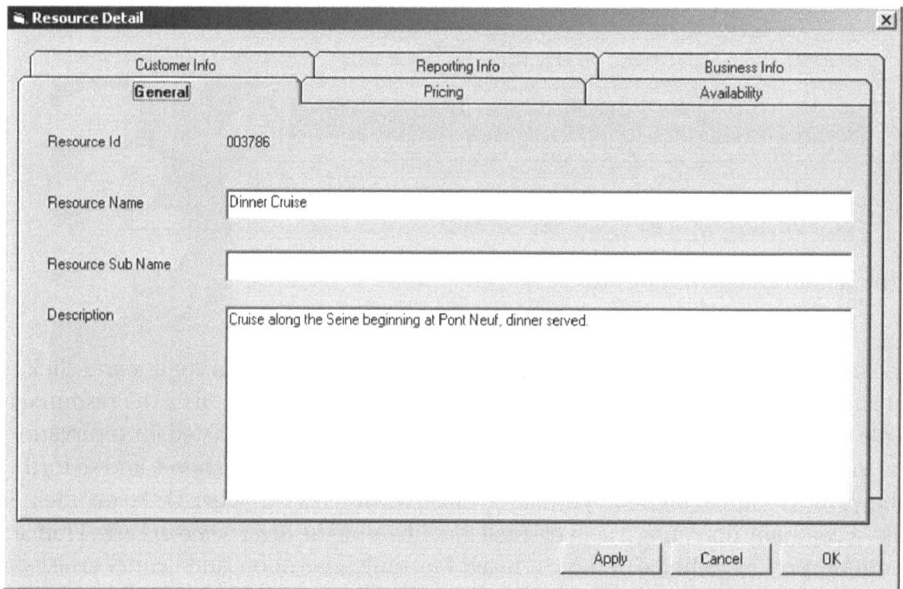

Figure 2-5. *The Resource Detail dialog box, with the General tab displayed*

The Availability tab contains information about the availability of the resource. The information provided depends on the definition of the resource. For example, bus or train travel resources are described as trips between two points, such as Barcelona to Madrid. The Availability tab lists the dates and times on which that particular trip is available. Another example, shown in Figure 2-6, gives the availability page for the Dinner Cruise of Seine River Cruises. It was available every day for the month of January 2004 at either 6:00 PM or 6:30 PM. For each cruise a total number of 10 units were available, a number referred to as the *capacity*. A *unit* in this case obviously means a seat on the cruise boat, but for other resources it could mean a room in a hotel, a seat on a bus, or a seat in a theater. Remember that Resource Manager has nothing at all to do with actually making reservations of these resources. The application only concerns itself with providing the capability for operators to define or alter the resource details and numbers available on each date and time.

The Customer Info tab allows the operator to enter information, which is displayed to the customer when they browse resources in Icarus's catalog prior to making a purchase. This information appears in a standard web page describing the resource. It includes a URL provided by the vendor, which will take the potential customer to more specific information about the resource. So when viewing the standard information on Icarus's site for a particular resource, say a hotel, the customer can click a link that will open the URL mentioned previously in a new window. This may take the customer to an external site provided by the vendor and not under control of Icarus. However, Icarus provides hosting for custom sites as an option to vendors, and a custom site may contain multiple pages that give information about the resources offered.

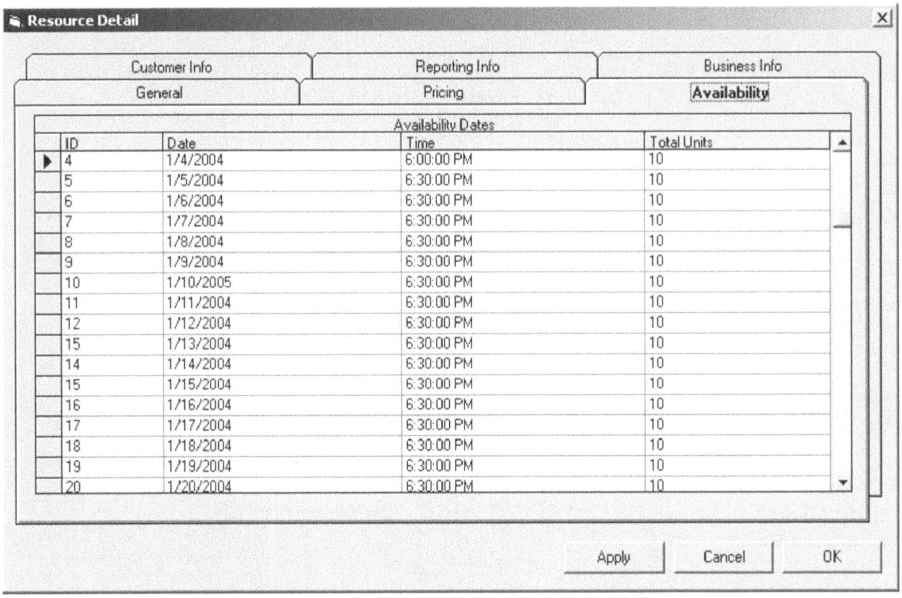

Figure 2-6. *The Availability tab*

The Reporting Info tab provides information that is available to customers when they make reservations, in order to allow them to go to the correct place at the right time to make use of their purchase, such as join a tour or check into a hotel. This information will be used to produce the email and written confirmation that is sent to the customer, combined with specific information, such as the customer's name, address, and reservation reference number.

Finally, the Business Info tab contains information describing the business relationship between Icarus and the vendor that is specific to that particular resource. This includes such details as commissions and exclusivity arrangements.

Implementation and Data Model

To understand the existing system, Peter has produced the data model diagrams shown in Figure 2-7 and Figure 2-8. Figure 2-7 shows the tables relating to the vendor management part of the application. In the table called VENDOR, each row represents a separate vendor. As well as the fields ID and NAME, there are a set of addresses and a set of contacts. Addresses and contacts are contained in separate tables referenced by foreign key fields in the VENDOR table. Each address in the ADDRESS table has two street address fields, LINE1 and LINE2; a REGION field; and foreign key fields into the CITY, STATE, and COUNTRY tables. The STATE table has a fully prepopulated set of states for the United States, Canada, and Australia along with their codes. Other regions, such as UK counties or Chinese provinces, are held in the REGION field. The COUNTRY table is fully prepopulated with the countries of the world and their codes.

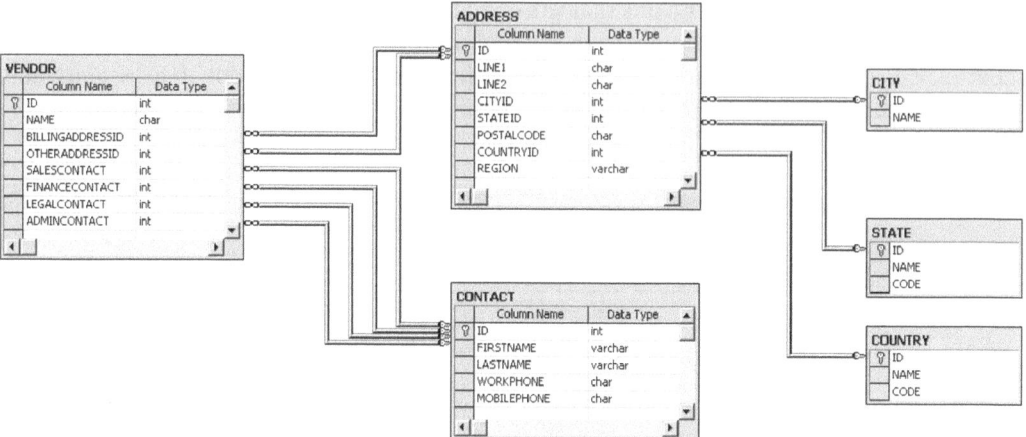

Figure 2-7. *Simplified data model for the existing vendor management capability*

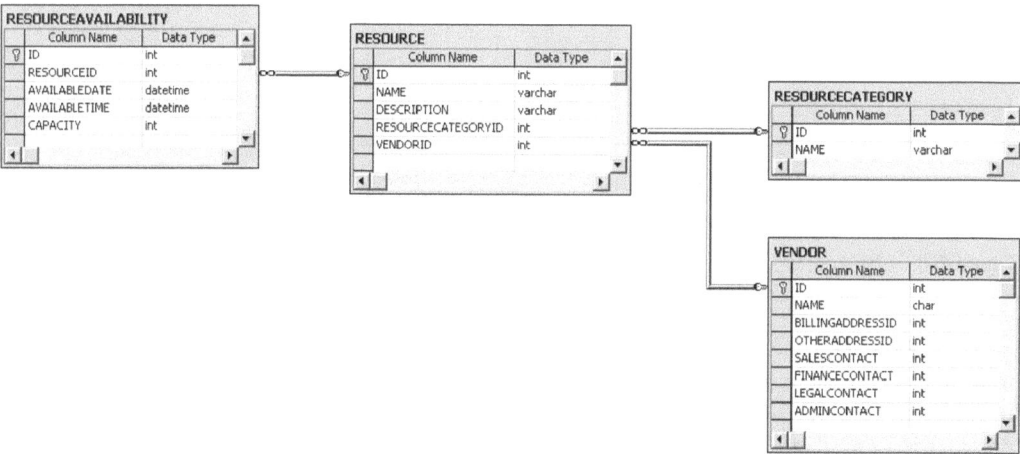

Figure 2-8. *Simplified data model for the existing resource management capability*

Figure 2-8 shows the resource portion of the Resource Manager data model. The RESOURCE table contains one row for each resource holding the basic data pertaining to the resource. Each row contains a foreign key into the RESOURCECATEGORY table, which contains a set of categories under which the resources are classified. There is also a foreign key into the VENDOR table, allowing each row representing a resource in the RESOURCE table to be associated with a row in the VENDOR table. This is a many-to-one relationship, as in general many resources will be associated with a given vendor. The RESOURCEAVAILABILITY table contains rows that each define a period of time when the resource is available for sale. These rows contain the date and time of the availability as well as capacity.

The architecture of the existing Resource Manager application is very simple, consisting of a Visual Basic 6 client implementing the Windows screens described earlier and containing all of the business logic. This client application is connected via the intranet to the SQL Server 2000 database containing the data model and some simple stored procedures. Multiple instances of the Resource Manager client application are installed that all connect to the same database. Transactions enclose all writes to the database to ensure data integrity, and optimistic concurrency is used on shared information that is presented to the clients. For those unfamiliar with this concept, it simply means that multiple clients are allowed to display the same data on their machines in the hope that the chances of two clients viewing and modifying that same data is a rare occurrence. If a second user has modified the data between the time a first user reads the data and the time the first user attempts to write modified data back, the modification is detected and the first user's changes are rejected and lost.

Sales Manager

This existing application is also written in Visual Basic 6 and runs on call center client machines. It allows call center operators to make and manage orders on behalf of customers who contact Icarus by telephone. Operators can provide customers with information about resources and their availability, make reservations for customers, accepting payment by credit card or check, and provide them with confirmation or other information about their orders.

User Interface

Figure 2-9 shows the main screen for the Sales Manager application, which contains a list of customers ordered alphabetically. The operator can select a customer, then click the Details button to open the Customer Details dialog box in Figure 2-10.

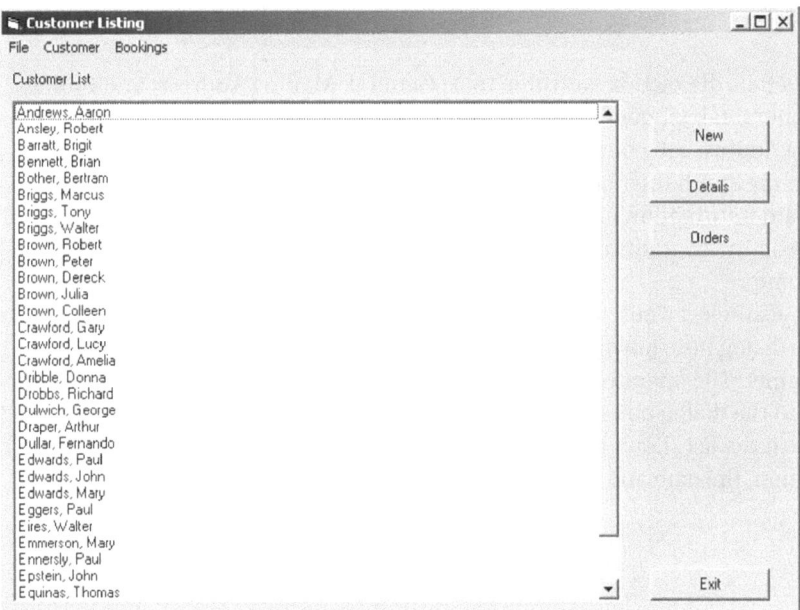

Figure 2-9. *The main screen of the Sales Manager application*

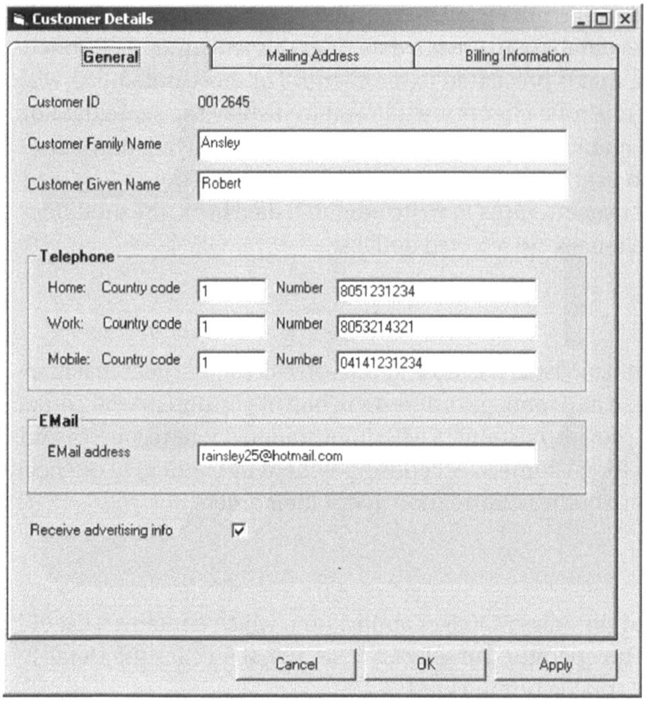

Figure 2-10. *The Customer Details dialog box*

The Customer Details dialog box has three tabs: General, Mailing Address, and Billing Information. The General tab (shown in Figure 2-10) contains name, telephone, and email contacts. The Mailing Address tab contains the customer's residence address and any alternative address to which they wish their confirmation details sent. The Billing Information tab contains the credit card information used in transactions. While talking to a customer, the call center operator can edit the contents of this dialog box and save it, to update database information for that customer.

An operator can also select a customer from the main screen and then click the Orders button to display the dialog box shown in Figure 2-11, which simply lists the orders that exist for the selected customer. The operator can select an order in the data grid, and then click the Details button to open the dialog box shown in Figure 2-12, which lists the items included in the order. Each entry in the list shows the item number, the name of the vendor, the product number and description, the date and time, and the number of units reserved.

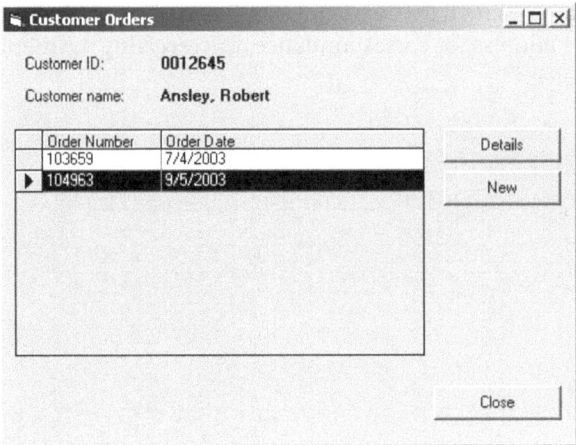

Figure 2-11. *The Customer Orders dialog box*

Item No.	Vendor	Product No.	Description	Date	Time	Number
▶ 1	San Michel Pension	4863	Double Room	5/11/2004	2:00:00 PM	1
2	San Michel Pension	4863	Double Room	5/12/2004	2:00:00 PM	1
3	Seine River Cruises	1693	Dinner Cruise	5/11/2004	6:30:00 PM	4

Figure 2-12. *The Customer Order Detail dialog box*

To create new customer orders, the operator clicks the New button in the Customer Orders dialog box, which takes the user through a wizard sequence creating a new order. One of the screens in the wizard, shown in Figure 2-13, allows resource reservations to be added or removed from the order. To add a new resource at this point, the operator clicks the Add Resource button, which displays the dialog box in Figure 2-14. This dialog box allows the operator to select a vendor from the left-hand list box, and the Resource list box automatically displays the resources available from the selected vendor. The operator can then select one of these resources and click on a day in the calendar display. The number of places available (seats, rooms, etc.) is then displayed. Figure 2-14 shows that for the Dinner Cruise offered by Seine River Cruises, eight places are available on May 12, 2004. The operator has been asked to book four seats, so she types "4" into the Number to Book box and clicks the Add to Order button. This closes the dialog box and returns to the Select Resources screen in the wizard. The next screens in the wizard (not shown) deal with verifying the address for correspondence and receiving payment either by credit card or by sending an invoice.

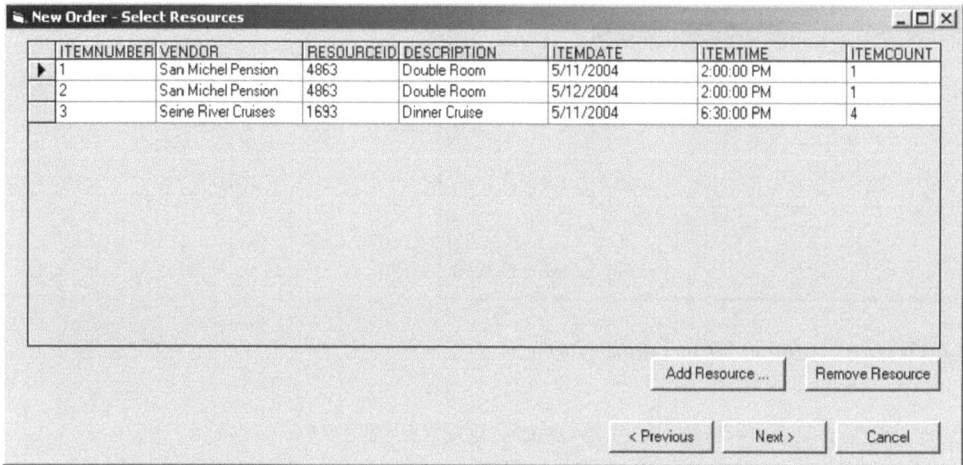

Figure 2-13. *The Select Resources screen in the New Order wizard*

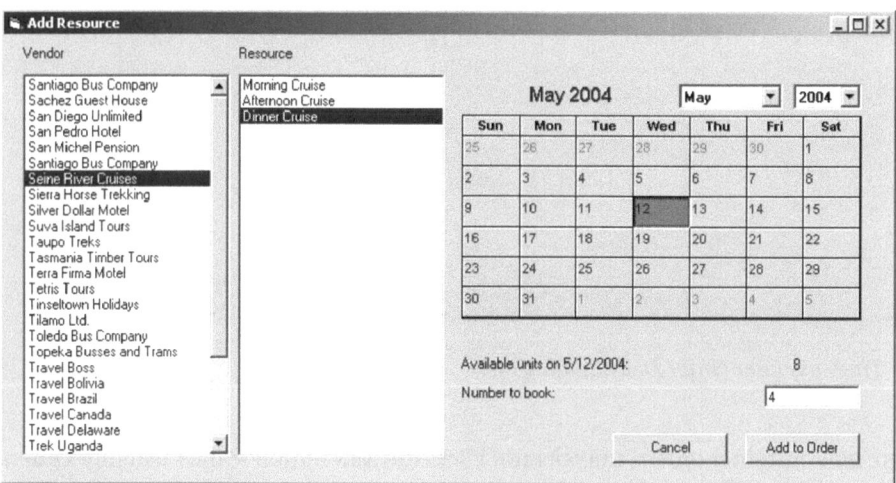

Figure 2-14. *The Add Resource screen, which allows resources to be selected and added to the order*

I could spend a great deal more time describing the details of the Sales Manager application, but the previous description should provide some indication of what the new project will replace. One point to note is that Icarus's business managers would like to see the inclusion of an improved vendor and resource browsing capability, and also an ability to search by region and category. This will make it much easier for operators to assist customers in selecting suitable resources to add to an order. The present screen in Figure 2-14 does not allow users to search or browse resources by geographic region or category. It is simply an alphabetic list, and the call center operator must rely on the customer to provide the vendor name (which the customer has obtained either from the catalog that the company publishes or by browsing the website).

Implementation and Data Model

Figure 2-15 shows part of the data model for the existing reservation system. A table called ORDER contains a row for each separate customer order; the CUSTOMERID field is a foreign key pointing into the CUSTOMER table, so that each order can have only one customer but there can be many orders that all point to the same customer. The RESERVATION table contains a row for each order line item in Figure 2-12, and each row contains a foreign key into the ORDER table to indicate the order to which the line item belongs. Each row also contains a foreign key into the RESOURCEAVAILABILITY table so that each line item references one instance of resource availability.

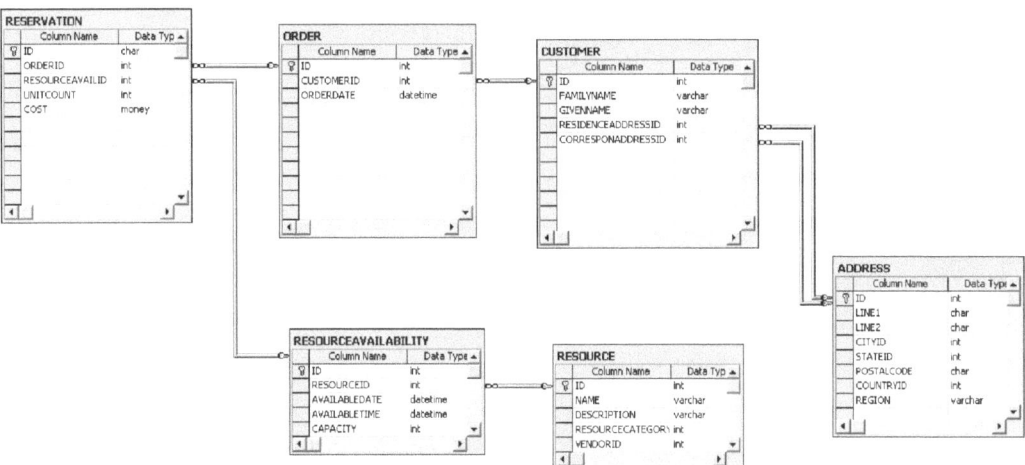

Figure 2-15. *Simplified data model for the reservation system*

However, each RESOURCEAVAILABILITY row contains a capacity element, which might be, say 10, and a reservation row may only be using perhaps 4 places out of the total capacity of 10. Think back to the Seine cruises case. The customer might have reserved 4 seats out of a total of 10, so 6 remain. Therefore, the row in the RESERVATION table contains a field to indicate how many are taken by that reservation, 4 in our example, and there may be more reservation rows belonging to different orders but referencing the same resource availability row. The number taken by all the reservations must of course be less than or equal to the capacity. Thus there is a many-to-one relationship between the RESERVATION table and the RESOURCEAVAILABILITY table. A row in the RESERVATION table also contains a monetary cost field, which is calculated when the reservation is made according to pricing information associated with the RESOURCEAVAILABILITY row, not shown in the data model for simplicity. The RESOURCEAVAILABILITY, RESOURCE, and ADDRESS tables are the same tables as are shown in Figure 2-7 and Figure 2-8, because that part of the data model is shared between the two applications.

Icarus Sales Website

This application provides capability for the sale of Icarus's resources directly to customers via the Internet. The application is currently written in ASP, without the use of COM components (except for payment processing and other back-end services, as explained later), with the business logic scripted in the ASP code. This code accesses the SQL Server 2000 database to obtain and deliver all the data for resources and reservations, and essentially does the same thing as the Sales Manager application, except that it only allows viewing of the orders made by a single authenticated user.

The Icarus website is quite extensive, but the Sales portion is rather simple and badly needs improvement. Figure 2-16 shows the My Orders web page, which allows a user, who has already logged in with their username and password, to view their existing orders. The user may click on the order number (e.g., 103659 in the figure) to navigate to the page shown in Figure 2-17, which shows the detail of a particular order and is similar to the order detail displayed by the Sales Manager application.

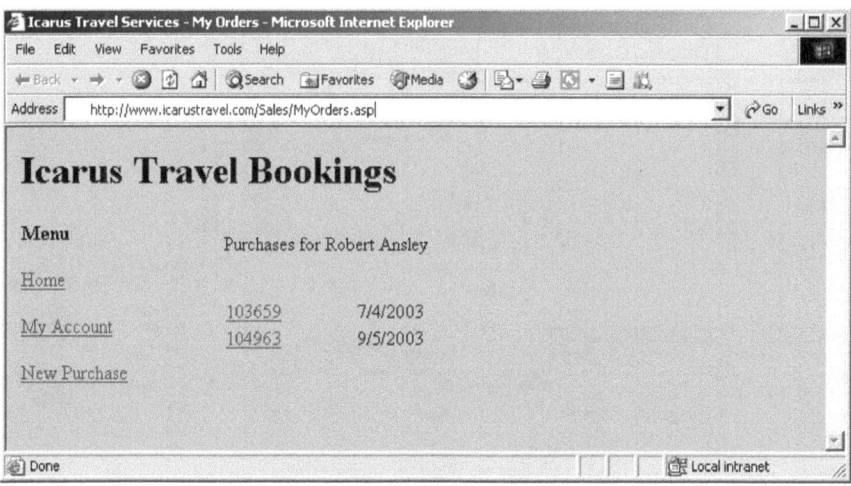

Figure 2-16. *The My Orders page of the Icarus Sales website*

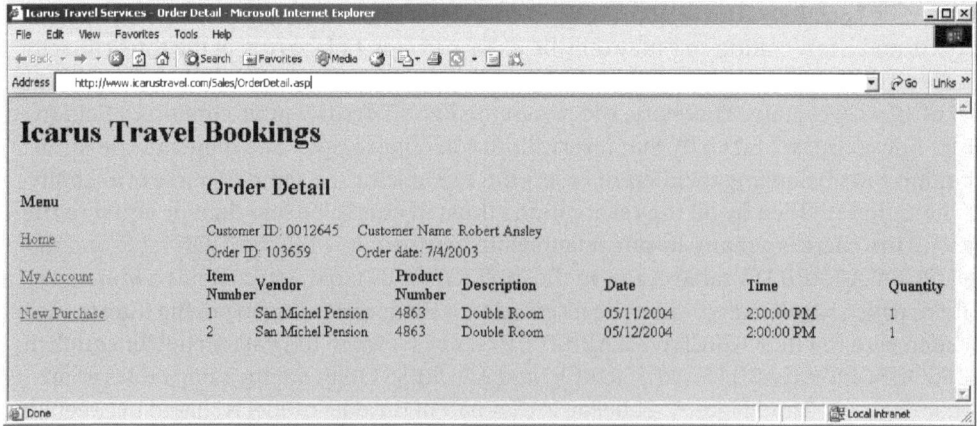

Figure 2-17. *The Order Detail page of the Icarus Sales website*

To make a new order, the user navigates through a sequence of screens, also similar to Sales Manager. Figure 2-18 shows an example from the sequence, the page where resources may be added to those included in the new order. The user chooses a provider from the left-hand list, chooses a resource type from the list in the center, selects a desired date from the calendar control, and views the number of places available. If this is satisfactory, the user may enter the number of places to reserve and click the Add button to include the reservation in the new order.

Users of the sales site may also manage their account details, but users who want to make changes to existing reservations must contact the Icarus call center.

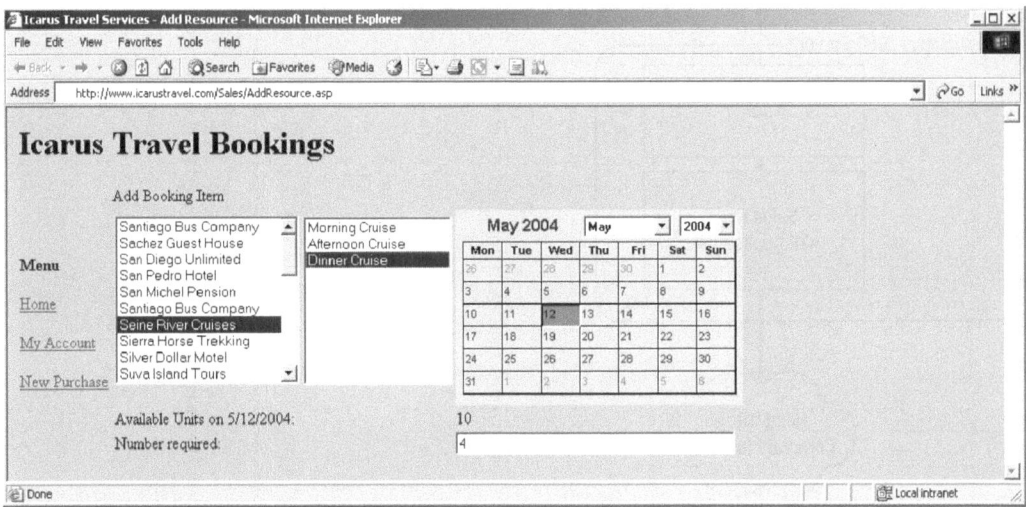

Figure 2-18. *Users can use this page to make reservations.*

Implementation and Data Model

The data model that goes with the Icarus Sales website is the same data model as that of the Sales Manager application, so I won't describe it again. The architecture of the application is shown in Figure 2-19. As you can see, there are three tiers: the client tier, which is simply the browser; the presentation/business tier, which is the ASP application; and the data tier, which is the data model hosted on the SQL Server 2000 database. The data tier contains simple stored procedures that return RecordSet objects needed to populate the screens and also save new and modified information from the screens to the database.

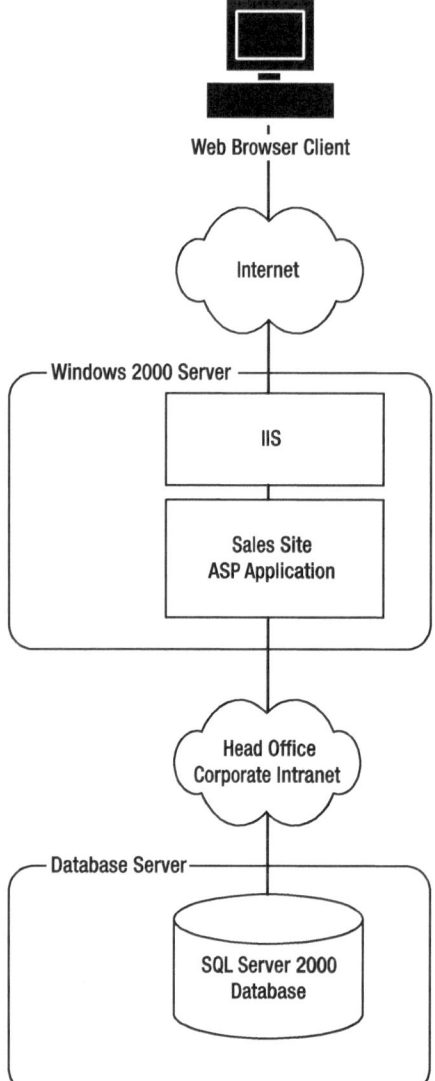

Figure 2-19. *Architecture of the Icarus Sales website*

Vendor Information Website

This application, written in ASP and running on Windows 2000, provides information to vendors about the status of the reservations of their resources. The application is relatively simple; it allows authenticated vendors to review reservations applicable to each of their resources offered for sale through Icarus. This application uses a simple set of business objects written in Visual Basic 6 to represent resources and reservations, which are populated from the SQL Server 2000 database.

This site is an information-only site in that providers cannot make changes to their resources, modify their availability, or add new resources. They must call or send an email to a vendor administrator, who will make the changes on their behalf.

Sales Watch MIS Application

This application, written in Crystal Reports and communicating directly with the SQL Server 2000 database, provides various reports containing management information about the status of Icarus sales.

Periodic Batch Process

This process contains a number of tasks that are run daily as an automatic chronological process and some that are started on a weekly basis. Some of the tasks are

- Generation of weekly status reports to vendors

- Generation of daily reports to management

- Generation of weekly reports to management

- Generation of reminder emails to customers and vendors for overdue payments

- Generation of printed reminder notices for mailing to customers and vendors

- Generation of reminder emails to staff members

Orchestration Service

The orchestration service, which consists of BizTalk Server 2000 and a number of custom applications, acts as a central point through which various XML documents pass that are involved in the business processes. Documents typically originate from the Sales Manager application, the Icarus Sales website, or the Resource Manager application. From the Sales Manager application and the Sales website, they result from a sale, a cancellation, or an amendment of a reservation. From Resource Manager, they result from the addition or modification of a resource, or its availability. The orchestration service receives XML documents from the Sales Manager and Resource Manager applications via Microsoft Message Queue (MSMQ), and from the Sales website ASP application via Distributed Component Object Model (DCOM). It is then responsible for generating and directing the resulting documents to other services. For example, when a reservation is made, the orchestration service receives a reservation confirmation document and performs the following:

1. It generates an XML document and places it in a share on the document server to generate a confirmation letter to be sent to the customer.

2. It passes a document to the email server using DCOM, which causes that server to send an email to the customer.

3. It calls a web method on the SAP Ledger web service, passing it a sales journal entry XML document.

The Ledger web service is a fairly recent addition. It uses more modern technology than the document and email servers, and the orchestration service has recently been upgraded to accommodate it.

Similarly, a change to a resource availability requested by a phone call from a vendor to a vendor administrator in the call center results in an MSMQ message to the orchestration service from the Resource Manager application. This in turn results in downstream action by the document and email services to generate confirmation documents to be sent to the vendor.

Document Service

This application is written in C++ and is responsible for taking various kinds of XML documents (such as confirmation notices, cancellation notices, and reminders) and rendering them as printable documents. They are then sent to a set of printers to be mailed to customers. The input documents are written by an upstream application to a file share and picked up by the document service, rendered into printable format, and placed in one of the print queues.

Email Service

This application is responsible for receiving email notices in the form of XML documents, converting them to email documents, and sending them to the specified email address via an installation of Microsoft Exchange Server.

Payment Service

Credit card payments either coming from the sales site or from the call center Sales Manager application are currently handled via the payment service, which is written in C++, exposes its services through DCOM objects and accesses a payment gateway service via the Internet. Secure sockets are used between the browser client and the Sales website when credit card details are being transferred. Secure sockets are also used between the payment server and the payment gateway site. Currently the ASP Sales website creates instances of DCOM objects on the payment server, and calls their member functions to initiate payment processing via a synchronous call to the payment gateway. The Sales Manager application handles payments in a similar manner.

General Ledger Service

This is a SAP application that hosts the company's accounts. It exposes a web service to allow sales journal entries to be posted in order to keep track of money in accounts receivable and payable as well as commission earnings. The general ledger server also hosts other SAP applications for the company that are not relevant to this project.

Enter the Consultants

A company such as Icarus does not undertake a project of this scale very often, and they do not want to employ permanent staff capable of managing, architecting, and implementing such a major revamp of their system. Icarus management has therefore hired the services of

Guru's Nest, a consulting group, to provide them with the expertise needed. I have already mentioned that Peter Sage, a member of the senior staff of Guru's Nest, has been working at Icarus for a month, examining their existing system and producing tentative high-level plans for the new system.

The Architectural Vision

Peter's tentative plan for the new enterprise system has the following features:

- The Icarus Sales website will move from the current ASP implementation on Windows 2000 to Windows 2003 IIS, using ASP.NET, and will be completely rewritten. The sales business functionality will be taken out of the presentation layer and moved into business logic components.

- This server will also expose the sales functionality provided by these components as web services that can be consumed by a rewritten Sales Manager smart client, called "Sales Wing," which will be hosted on both travel agent client machines and on call center clients. This replacement for Sales Manager will give travel agents and call center operators a richer experience and also allow for some degree of offline work by travel agents.

- The web server will also expose web services providing access to a set of listing business logic components. A second smart client called "List Wing" will consume these services to provide resource management capability both directly to providers and to administrator and call center clients.

- A third Windows Forms smart client application called "Sales Status" will be written to provide similar information to the current Sales Watch Crystal Reports application. This application will access the database directly.

- The new reservation system will interface via the existing orchestration service with the accounting system, document server, and email server, but it is expected that these systems may themselves need small changes to accommodate the increased functionality. Ultimately the orchestration service will be exposed via new web services, rather than the combination of DCOM, MSMQ, and file share inputs that it currently supports.

It is known that Icarus's business managers have several ideas about the features of the new system, and certainly the company will not want to undertake this project simply to change technology. Some of these new features relate to the agreement with WWC and other vendors, but many are improvements across the board and need to be elaborated by the business analysts.

This is Peter's vision for the new Icarus enterprise architecture, supported generally by Tony and Marcia. Marcia has misgivings about the risk in developing a new reservations system and while she wants her IT manager and other software staff to be involved, she prefers the project management to be in the hands of Guru's Nest. There is also a likelihood of a long-term outsourcing arrangement to this company for maintenance. Guru's Nest has provided a project manager, Clare Green, of whom Derek has heard excellent reports. Clare and Peter have been gaining experience with the new Microsoft Team System and think that this would be an ideal project in which to apply it. Guru's Nest business analyst Susan Drivewell has also joined the team and has been working at Icarus with Peter and Clare for several days reviewing the requirements for the new system.

The Kickoff Meeting

A kickoff meeting is held at the corporate offices of Icarus on March 12, 2006. The attendees are as follows.

For Icarus:

- Marcia Polo—CEO
- Tony Woods—IT manager
- James Ruff—Listing manager
- William Fairways—Sales manager

For Guru's Nest:

- Clare Green—Project manager
- Peter Sage—Architect
- Susan Drivewell—Business analyst

James and William, who manage the listing and sales sections of the business, have been called in to get the business management involved with the requirements at an early stage. Some informal discussions have already taken place between Peter, Susan, James, and William.

After Marcia explains the importance of the project and introduces Clare and Susan, Clare takes the floor and discusses the project drivers and the business needs. She also provides an idea of the timeframe, which as usual is very aggressive. Her presentation is shown in Figure 2-20.

Next Peter goes through a presentation that contains much of what is included in the early part of this chapter and gives a high-level description of the component applications and how they interact. He ends with Figure 2-21, which shows the existing applications described earlier in this chapter installed in client and server machines at the various Icarus sites around the world. Peter explains that the chart in Figure 2-21 is simplified in that it does not show the network security zones and firewalls.

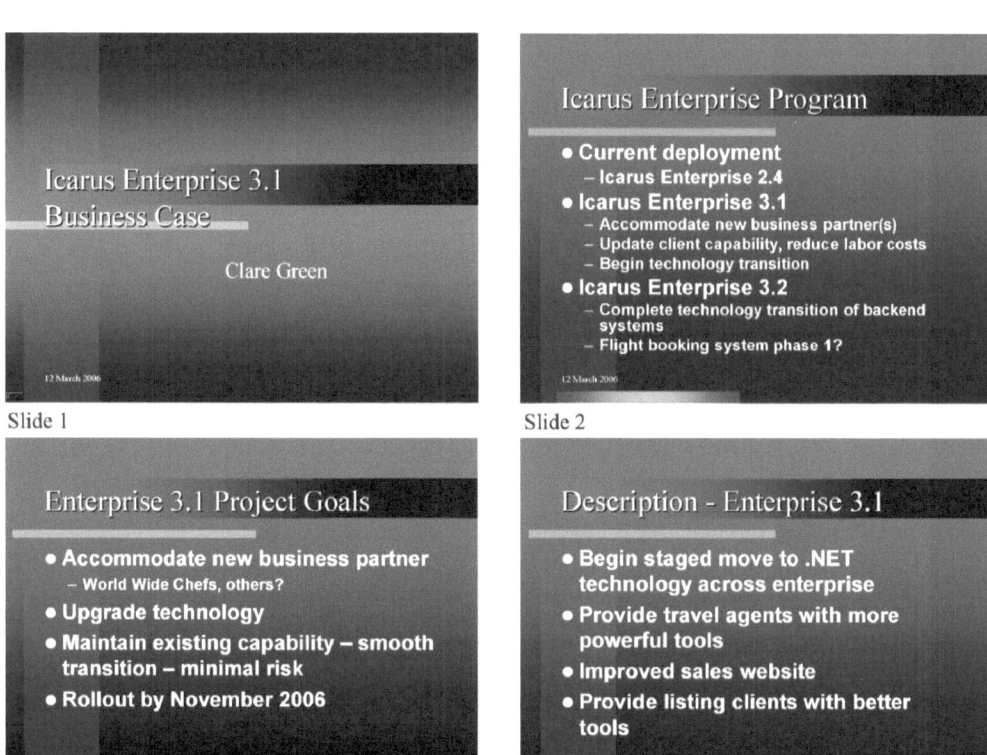

Figure 2-20. *Clare's presentation at the kickoff meeting*

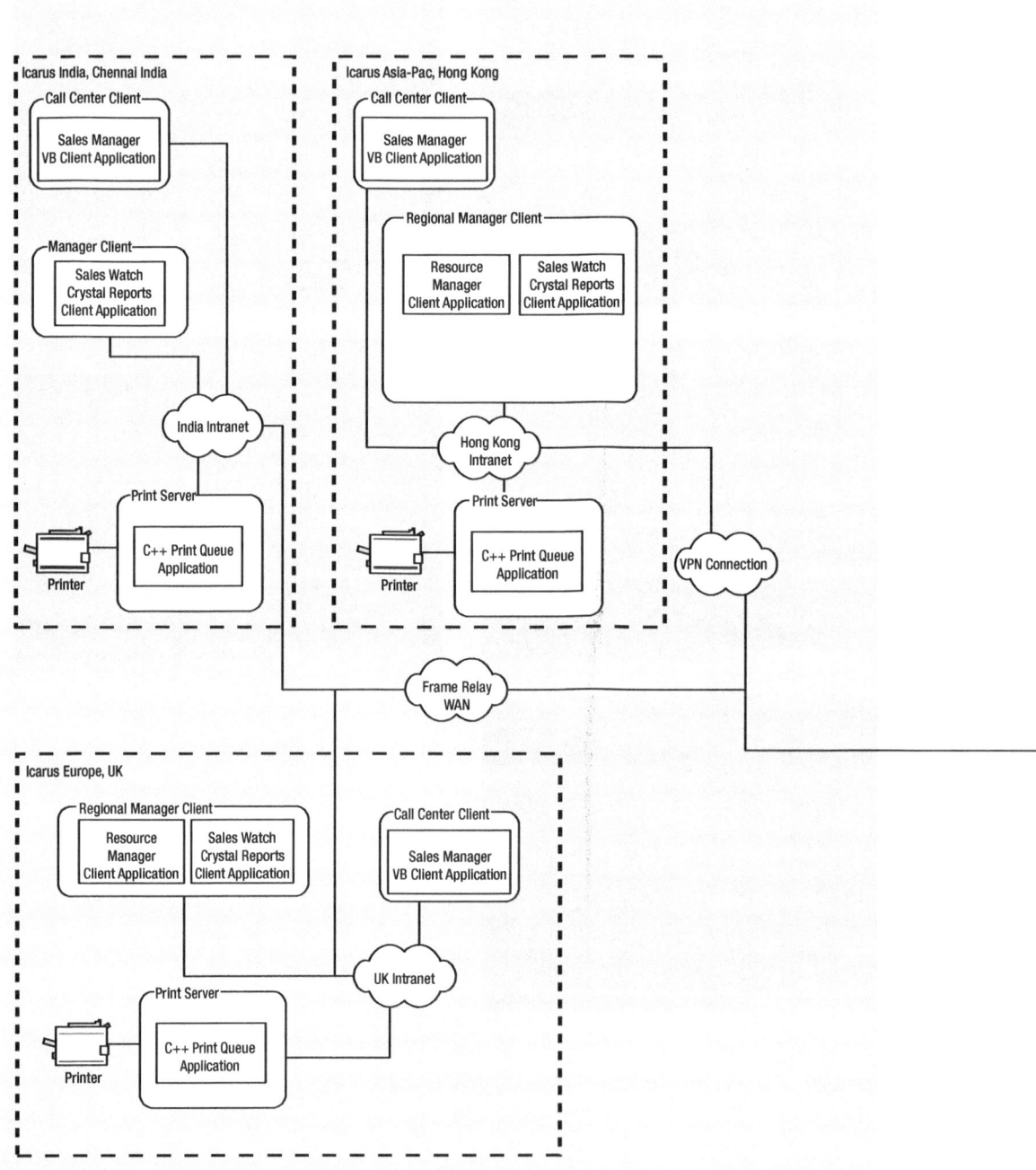

Figure 2-21. *Simplified existing Icarus Enterprise 2.4 distributed application*

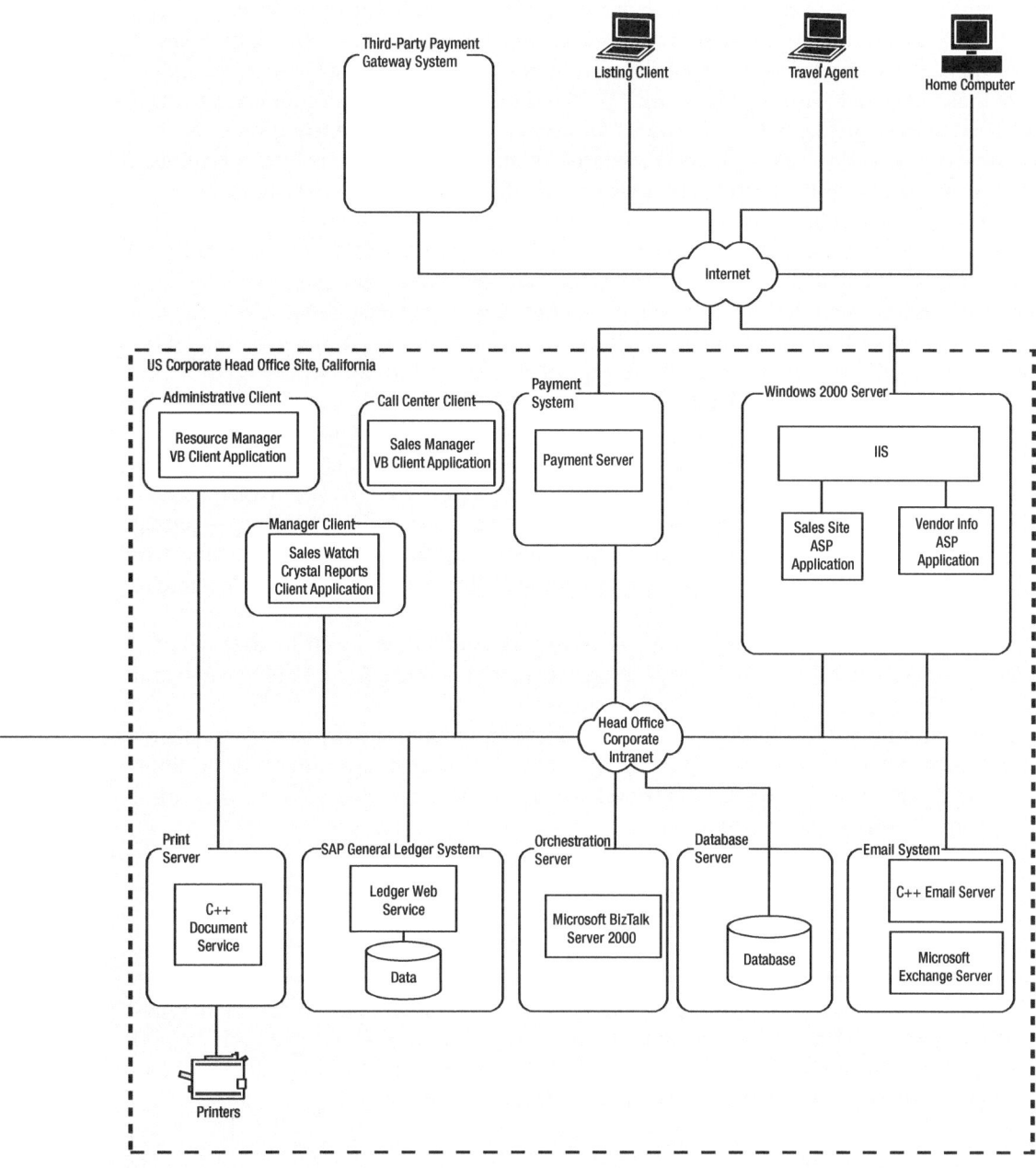

The main site in California contains all the server applications, including the database, the orchestration server, and the downstream services as well as the web servers hosting the Sales website. This site also contains numerous call center client machines running Sales Manager, admin clients running Resource Manager, and manager clients running the Sales Watch application. There are three overseas sites: Icarus Asia-Pac in Hong Kong; Icarus India in Chennai, India; and Icarus Europe in the UK. The UK and India sites are connected to the California site via a private frame relay wide area network (WAN), but the Hong Kong site is accessible via a virtual private network (VPN) over a high-bandwidth public Internet connection. The overseas sites host call center clients and admin clients with the same client applications as California.

"Resource Manager needs to be completely rewritten," says Peter. "World Wide Chefs want to be able to update their course offerings on their own. They're not happy with having to email Icarus information about changes, or discuss them on the telephone. Also, many of the other vendors feel the same, and there have been a lot of errors lately with availability dates. Then the salespeople have to back off some of the reservations and work with the customers to sort out the mistakes. That's really a nightmare—right, Bill?"

William grimaces painfully, as Peter goes on. "Then we have to rewrite Sales Manager because it's costing you far too much money to cope with travel agents via the call center. If this application can run on agents' own machines they can look after everything themselves, and they'll be a lot happier. Besides, you need to move on technically. That VB 6 app is getting hard to maintain and sometimes there are problems because of the number of users. Tony tells me that he has lost most of the original developers and his new staff have really been afraid to touch it.

"Having rewritten Sales Manager, we then have to rewrite the Sales website so that it can use business logic common with Sales Manager. Also, we need to add far better search and browse capability for customers choosing resources."

Peter continues, describing how the new applications should use Microsoft smart client technology, which will make them much simpler to install and update, and will also allow offline work. "This is really important for travel agents—some of those folks still use dial-ups—and they like to work on laptops at home."

Peter then displays the diagram in Figure 2-22, which shows the proposed configuration at the completion of Enterprise 3.1 deployment. A new Windows application, Sales Wing, has been placed on both the call center client and the travel agents' client, both communicating with the Sales web service. This will be written in C# by Guru's team of developers and replaces Sales Manager. A new application, List Wing, has been placed on both the administrator client and the vendor client and communicates with a new Listing web service. This will be written in India where Guru's Nest has developers who are more experienced in Visual Basic. The ASP Sales website application will be phased out and replaced by an ASP.NET application that services home-based Internet clients to maintain the direct sales capability.

Discussion continues about some of the features of these clients and problems with the existing system. Peter also clarifies some points about web services and smart clients.

"I like those new names, guys," says Marcia. "Sales Wing's one side of the company and List Wing's the other—sounds good. Somebody needs to make up a nice icon for the applications so it looks good for the vendors and agents."

Next, Tony describes the changes that will take place in the back-end systems, which include the orchestration service, document service, and email service. In essence, these services will be upgraded to expose web services to their clients. The orchestration server will be upgraded to BizTalk Server 2006. The C++ services, print and email as well as the payment server, will be fitted with web service front-ends accessing their existing code via COM Interop. This part of the project will be handled internally by Icarus and will be managed by Tony. Icarus has succeeded in retaining a fairly effective group of developers in the C++, scripting, and database areas. Tony suggests that his group's schedule may run behind the schedule for the front-end systems managed by Guru's Nest, so the system integration should be carefully managed.

The talk then turns to methodologies. Clare and Peter have been discussing Microsoft Visual Studio 2005 Team System at some length since they began their involvement with Icarus and are convinced that it is the way to go. They recommend the product to the others, explaining how it integrates the various tasks of software life-cycle management and will avoid many of the difficulties that have occurred in past Icarus projects.

The meeting ends with the delegation of action items. Peter is to begin design of the architecture, conditional on management approval to move ahead, and James and William are to nominate knowledgeable people from their departments to work full time with Susan in order to begin putting together detailed business requirements. Clare takes an action item to set up Team System, write a vision document, and begin work on a project plan.

Two days later another meeting takes place with the same attendees, and after some clarifications, everyone agrees to proceed as planned. At this meeting, there is some discussion about which development process to use within Team System, and the merits of MSF Agile and MSF for CMMI Process Improvement are discussed. The Guru's Nest people feel that MSF for CMMI Process Improvement is probably appropriate, but the decision is put off until the first project planning meeting. You can follow this in the next chapter.

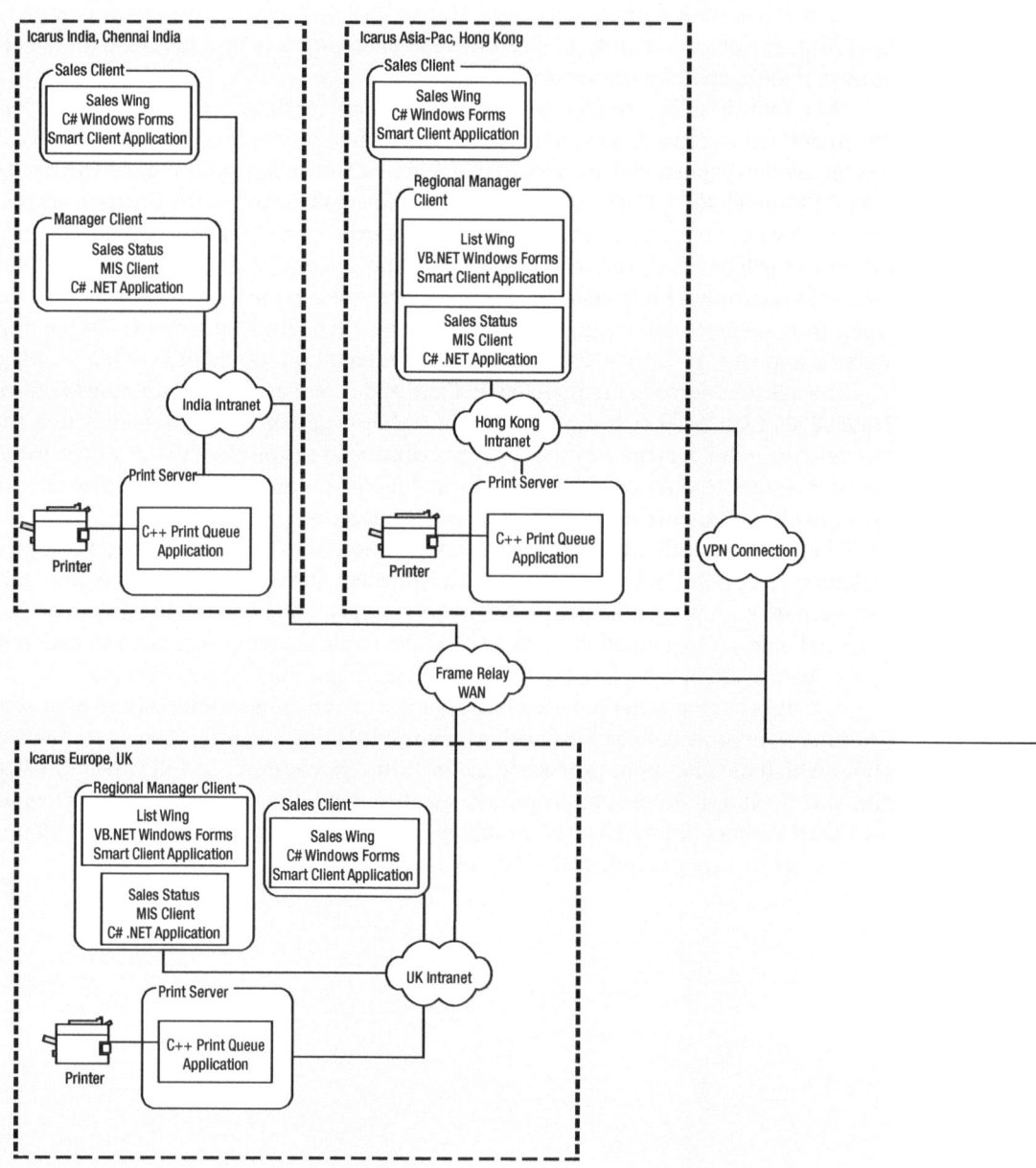

Figure 2-22. *Proposed Icarus Enterprise 3.1 distributed application*

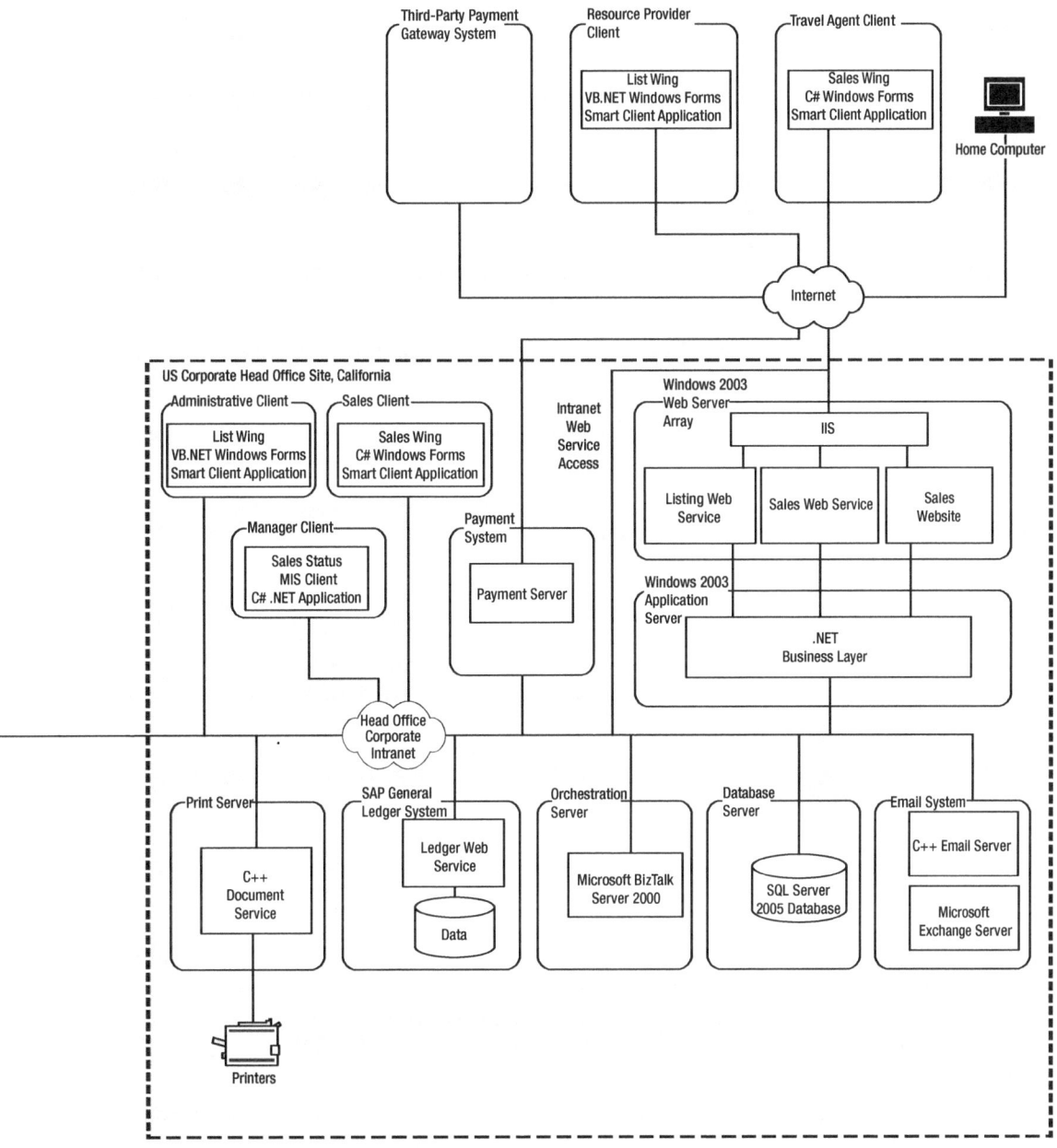

Summary

In this chapter you were introduced to Icarus Travel Services and its business. Icarus sells many kinds of travel resources—hotel rooms, bus and train travel, tours, and educational courses, for example. These services are listed for sale by vendors, such as hotel owners and tour operators.

Icarus sells these resources in two ways: through call center operators who sell by phone to travel agents and customers, and via its Sales website, where customers can make reservations directly for the various travel services.

The vendors that list their services for sale through Icarus contact Icarus by phone or email, and a vendor administrator working for Icarus adds the services to the system.

The applications are currently in use at Icarus are as follows:

- The Sales website is the ASP website where customers can make reservations for the travel services listed for sale.

- Sales Manager is the Visual Basic application that call center operators at Icarus use to make sales over the telephone.

- Resource Manager is the Visual Basic Application that vendor administrators use to update vendors' listings as a result of phone calls or emails.

- The Vendor Information website provides information for vendors about how their resources have been booked.

- An application called Sales Watch provides management information systems (MIS) information for management.

- An orchestration service and several downstream applications handle asynchronous operations such as sending out emails, sending printed confirmation, and adjusting accounting information.

- A synchronous payment server carries out credit card transactions via a third-party payment gateway.

Pressure from their vendors and travel agents has forced Icarus into a major upgrade project. Peter, the architect for the project, has proposed that the Sales Manager, Resource Manager, and Sales website applications be redesigned to use a great deal more common business logic code and to utilize new smart clients called Sales Wing and List Wing. These applications are to be installed on travel agent and vendor machines, respectively, as well as on machines used by operators in the call center.

In the next chapter you will see how the team chooses a development process and begins planning the project using the project management Team System features.

The Project Manager: Initial Tasks and Project Planning

This chapter concentrates on Team System features for the project manager and here I will describe the initial management tasks associated with setting up and beginning the Icarus project under Visual Studio Team System. Before a team project can begin, a development process must be selected; I will discuss the development process in general and summarize the two choices available in Microsoft Solution Framework (MSF). As mentioned in Chapter 1, central to Team System is the concept of work items, among them *task work items*. When the project is created, a number of task work items are automatically generated according to the selected development process. I will discuss the meaning of these tasks and examine in detail the performance of some, while leaving the rest to subsequent chapters. Finally in this chapter, you will see how the master or overall schedule of the project is determined, how it is broken down into iterations, and how the features to be developed are divided roughly among those iterations. First, let's meet some more team members.

Innovation from the Subcontinent

"So will this flight simulator you're developing take into account the effects of wind?" asks Charles.

Two of the senior developers, Angela and Charles, together with Peter and Ron, their team leader, are sitting in one of the conference rooms at the Guru's Nest office, waiting for Clare. Angela is expected to do most of the development of the .NET business layer for the Sales Wing and Sales website applications. They have just welcomed Bangalore, India, native Rahul Singh to the United States. He is spending two weeks here in the Pacific Northwest to learn about the MSF process and Team System, before returning to India to work with his team on the List Wing application and its supporting business objects. The team is impressed with his knowledge of .NET, and now he seems to be demonstrating an expertise in aviation technology.

"Oh, definitely," Rahul replies. "And the air temperature, as well as uneven wear on the ball."

"The ball?" says Angela. "What ball?"

"Well, of course the cricket ball," says Rahul, surprised.

"So it's a cricket ball flight simulator!" bursts out Peter, laughing. "I thought it was an airplane simulator."

Rahul looks very serious. "Certainly it is a cricket ball simulator. It is very important to better understand the flight of the ball. There is much painstaking research yet to be done. The combined effects of spin and surface wear on the transition between lamina and turbulent flow is not well understood, and the influence of the Magnus effect on the ballistic motion..."

"You know, I don't really understand the game of cricket," interrupts Peter enthusiastically, "but when I was in college I played a bit of baseball and I bet that's all similar to pitching a curve ball. The size of the ball would be different but..."

"Good morning, guys," says Clare as she enters the room, and the meeting turns to the much less important matter of discussing the choice of a development process.

Choice of a Development Process

It is certainly possible to develop high-quality software without having any defined process in place—some companies have become successful by starting in just that way. If you have no process, however, success or failure depends completely on the individuals and is likely to swing wildly in one direction or the other as developers join or leave the company. Even an individual developer working alone is likely to have some sort of process, although it may reside completely in his or her head. This kind of development seems more akin to the work of an artist, and works of genius are often created in this way. There is a place for individual talent, and the process should not stifle it, but complete reliance on the abilities of one individual usually leads to disappointment. When companies need to provide satisfactory results consistently, they must put some sort of process in place to provide a framework to ensure that the creative work of individuals is consolidated into a successful team achievement.

The big danger, unfortunately, is that processes are only as good as the people who participate in them, and their success or failure also seems to depend heavily on the type of application being developed. A process can work well with one type of development but fail with another. For example, the waterfall methodology—which demands a rigid sequence of requirements definition, design, development, and testing—can work well when a team is developing an application similar to others they have implemented in the past. They are just repeating a well-known formula with different parameters. On the other hand, when an organization is venturing into an area beyond their experience, perhaps beyond anyone's experience, they need to explore as they proceed, establishing their hold on new territory before reaching further; in this case, a waterfall approach can be disastrous. You don't order the iron for the railroad until you have explored the mountain pass on foot. The process should help rather than be a burden, and encourage rather than inhibit innovative thought. I've seen processes that seem like a set of actions that have to be done as an afterthought, once a particular stage in the development has been successfully accomplished—rather like laying a paper trail once the real work has been done!

In this book, I will show how a relatively straightforward distributed application development project can successfully follow a fairly rigorous process. I'll show how the features of the process can help guide the development in a useful way and be adapted as necessary. As an example of such adaption, in Chapter 4 I have added use cases because they are helpful in breaking down the requirements into manageable portions. Use cases are not mentioned in MSF for CMMI Process Improvement, but that does not mean they cannot be added to the process. If you deny yourself a useful technique just because you don't find it mentioned in the process, you may be forcing yourself to use the wrong tools for the job. Certainly MSF allows tailoring the process up front, but at that stage you often do not know what you will need, and so it may be better not to be too rigid as things move along. You can't just sidestep the process, though, which often is a result of underestimating the human resource, budget, and schedule impact of following a rigid process. Teams sometimes seem to become bogged down in producing document after document, and suddenly there is a big panic because no software has been written. When this happens, the process is quietly abandoned and people begin coding. So a whole lot of time and money has been wasted to no avail, because management lacked the experience and foresight to see that their process decision was incompatible with business realities.

Microsoft Solution Framework

The Microsoft Solutions Framework (MSF) was first introduced in 1994 and is a collection of software development processes, principles, and proven practices. It is based on well-known industry best practices that enable developers to achieve success in the software development life cycle (SDLC). Notice the word *collection* here—it's not a pronouncement of the "one true faith" but more a selection of "proven practices," some of which are more applicable to certain circumstances than others.

At the present time, Microsoft provides two process templates with Team Foundation Server: MSF for Agile Software Development and MSF for CMMI Process Improvement. I'm going to abbreviate these throughout this book as MSF Agile and MSF CMMI, respectively. MSF Agile is a new process intended for small software development organizations and is based on the work of a team called the Agile Alliance. The Agile Alliance agrees on the following tenets:

- Individuals and interactions are more important than processes and tools.

- Customer collaboration is more important than contracts.

- Working software is more important than comprehensive documentation.

- Responding to change is more important than following a plan.

MSF CMMI is a more formal process that has its roots in the Capability Maturity Model developed by the Software Engineering Institute (SEI) at Carnegie Mellon University. This model is used to assess prospective government contractors, and the U.S. Department of Defense funded its development by the SEI in 1984. CMMI stands for Capability Maturity Model Integration, an amalgamation of maturity models for different kinds of activities, and is a model for improving the ability of an organization to produce high-quality software within budget and on schedule. One of the major advantages of CMMI is that it is an established standard by which software vendors can be compared. Companies anxious to improve their standing among their competitors can benefit from increasing their CMMI rating. There are five levels of CMMI rating, beginning at level 1, Initial, which describes a company where there is little stable process, and the ability to show consistent success depends on individuals rather than the company. The fifth level, Optimizing, describes a company that has reached a state where the entire company is focused on continuous process improvement. I cannot help but smile when I read this—if the whole company is focused on process improvement, when do they find the time to develop any software? But of course the reality, as I described earlier, is that process is an evolving thing and must continually improve, because software as a discipline changes with the technology and market.

Special cause variation and *common cause variation* are terms that come from process improvement terminology. Essentially, a special cause is one particular thing that caused a departure from the expected process flow and that impacts quality and schedule. Common cause variation is a more random or statistical set of causes that occur frequently and in an unpredictable manner. Reduction of both of these variations improves the process. As projects come and go, and the process is applied in varying situations, a variety of special and common cause variations can be identified and corrected and the process thus improved. The scenario I described in the previous section—where management failed to properly match the process to the schedule and business environment—is an example of special cause variation, but if it happened repeatedly, it would be regarded as a common cause variation.

MSF CMMI aims to provide a process by which a company can reach level 3 in the CMMI rating, that is, "The organization uses a defined software process and software quality is tracked." Do not think that, because SEI dates back to 1984, MSF CMMI is a rigid, old-fashioned process; it is definitely not. MSF CMMI includes such principles as customer partnership, open communications, shared vision, pride of workmanship, frequent delivery, and early specifics, which are fairly self-explanatory. MSF CMMI is focused on delivering flow of value to the customer in short bursts of limited requirements, just like agile methods.

CMMI certainly has its critics. It has been criticized as being overly bureaucratic, and some claim that it provides little guidance as to how to set up an effective software organization. It strongly encourages the establishment of a team of auditors to which the organization will be accountable for delivering the various documents and other artifacts prescribed. A concern is that this might cause the IT department to become overly focused on generating documents rather than effectively producing software and being attuned to the needs of the customer and the marketplace. Another concern is that the level reached in the CMMI maturity model by a contracting software development company bidding for a contract might skew the judgment of those awarding the contracts in favor of those companies adhering to bureaucratic process, compared to those with genuine skills and knowledge. Having pointed out some of the advantages and disadvantages of CMMI, I intend in this book to try to demonstrate how MSF CMMI can be used effectively, without getting bogged down in bureaucratic process and without generating unnecessary documents.

Nevertheless, this is not a book on process and I am not a process expert. Like many of my readers, I am a software developer trying to see how the process will help my project achieve success. The project described in this book pushes few boundaries in that it is a fairly straightforward architecture implementing the sort of requirements that are quite common in various guises throughout many industries. I believe that agile processes are more suitable for very innovative projects, typical of many smaller start-up companies, whereas the example company described here, Icarus, is a mature business that requires a controlled upgrade of an existing, working system. It cannot afford to take too much risk, and those risks must be controlled. It is thus a good example for the application of a low-bureaucracy example of MSF CMMI. This is not to say that MSF CMMI cannot be used for more innovative projects, but I think the management would be more difficult and costly and the delivery date would stretch out. There seems to be a very clear trade-off between tightly planned and controlled projects with reduced risk and more speculative projects showing a high level of innovation.

Many of these points were discussed at length in the meeting that you glimpsed earlier in the chapter—they did get down to business when Clare arrived! Some of the team felt that MSF CMMI was too complicated and wanted to use the customizing features of Team System to define their own process, but Clare would not hear of it, maintaining that the schedule was much too tight, and I think she was right. Instead, a compromise was reached that the documentation would be kept at a light level and the emphasis would be on prototyping, at least in the first iterations. Thus, the Icarus development team decided, based on their business environment, that they would follow MSF for CMMI Process Improvement.

Installing Team System

I am only going to make the briefest comments here on installation. To install Team System for a group of team members, you need to install SQL Server 2005 and Team Foundation Server (TFS) on server machines, and then install a suitable team client suite on each of your team members' machines. For the server side, you can choose either a single-server or a dual-server installation, where dual-server involves putting the application server (TFS) on one machine (with Windows SharePoint Services) and SQL 2005 on another. If you have fewer than 100 users, you can probably use single-server deployment; Microsoft suggests in the documentation that the limit for a dual-server deployment is about 500 users. If you have more users and you have multiple team projects, you can put different projects on different servers, but you cannot scale by splitting any one project across servers. The servers should be dedicated to TFS and not used as mail servers or file servers, or for some other application—certainly not as test servers for your application!

When trying out the system, you can install SQL Server 2005, TFS, and Team Suite on one machine, but you will need a lot of memory—you should regard 1GB as the minimum. Both SQL Server 2005 and Team Suite take a lot of memory. I've found that, with the full Team Suite client and the servers on one machine, you can expect to see a lot of paging unless you have 2GB. When you install, to set up an environment for your architect, developers, testers, business analysts (BAs), and project manager, the configuration you use depends very much on the number of users you expect. The documentation gives you some useful guidelines. Certainly for your developer, tester, and architect clients, you will find Visual Studio 2005 slow if you don't have 1GB of RAM.

The Icarus development team has installed a single-server configuration of TFS, as shown in Figure 3-1. For the BA and project manager client machines, they are using Microsoft Office and Team Explorer as the client applications. You install the TFS client applications from the TFS CD and include the Team Explorer, Document Explorer, .NET Framework 2, VS 2005 Tools for Office Runtime, and Office 2003 Primary Interop Assemblies on these machines.

The developers are using Visual Studio 2005 Team Edition for Developers, the testers are using Visual Studio 2005 Team Edition for Testers, and the architect is using Visual Studio 2005 Team Suite, which includes everything, since that individual will need to create prototype code and explore some areas of testing as well as the architectural work. The developers also need to install Team Explorer, Document Explorer 2005, and Tools for Office Runtime from the TFS CD. Team Explorer does not appear as a separate application on machines with any of the Visual Studio 2005 Team Editions since it is integrated into them. You can also install Team Explorer on machines that have Visual Studio 2005 Professional or Standard Edition by installing on top of those applications. This may be a cost-saving option for team members who do not need to use the advanced features of Team System, such as Unit Test, Static Code Analysis, Code Coverage, and Code Profiler.

Casual stakeholders, who occasionally need to check in or view files such as graphical images or documents, can use Team Explorer as their sole TFS client. Alternatively, they can use the project portal, described later, to upload and view files.

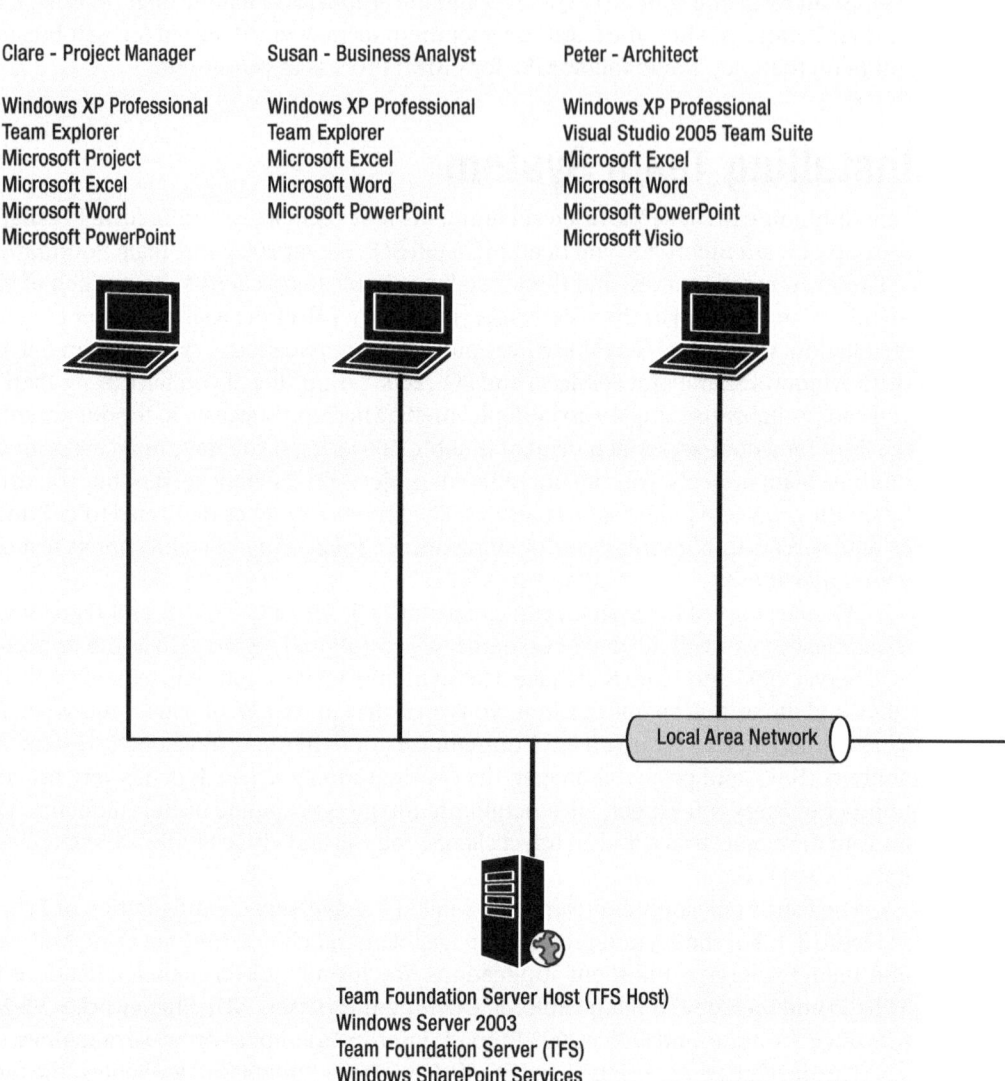

Figure 3-1. *Team System installation for Enterprise 3.1. The development and test servers for the application are not shown.*

Angela, Rahul - Senior Developers

Windows XP Professional
Visual Studio 2005 Team System for Developers
Microsoft Excel
Microsoft Word
Microsoft PowerPoint
Microsoft Visio

Developers

Windows XP Professional
Visual Studio 2005 Team System for Developers
Microsoft Excel
Microsoft Word
Microsoft PowerPoint
Microsoft Visio

Testers

Windows XP Professional
Visual Studio 2005 Team System for Testers
Microsoft Excel
Microsoft Word
Microsoft PowerPoint
Microsoft Visio

Project Manager: Creating the Team Project

Since our project team is planning to use Team System right from the start of the project, they must begin by creating a new team project so that they can start adding artifacts to it long before they start writing any code. The afternoon following the kickoff meeting, Clare, the project manager, performs the task of creating the team project. To do this, she starts her copy of Team Explorer and connects to the TFS by selecting Tools ➤ Connect to Team Foundation Server. When she does this, she can browse for servers or connect to servers that are listed, and she can choose which team projects she wants to see in the Team Explorer window.

If you are using Team Explorer for the first time, you will need to go through the sequence shown in Figure 3-2. In the Connect to Team Foundation Server dialog box, click the Servers button and then the Add button, which displays the Add Team Foundation Server dialog box. Type the Team Foundation Server name, in this case ICARUS-TFS, and make sure you enter the correct port number and select either HTTP or HTTPS. Then click OK, and the server will appear in the list in the Add/Remove Team Foundation Server dialog box. Click Close to connect to the server and view a list of team projects (if any) on the server.

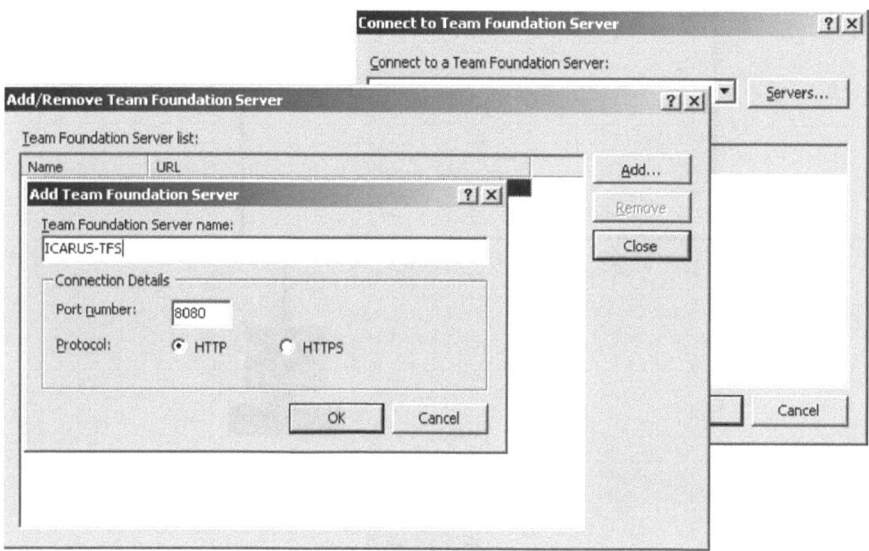

Figure 3-2. *Connecting to the Team Foundation Server*

To create a team project, Clare right-clicks on the server in the Team Explorer window and selects New Team Project, which takes her into the wizard that creates the project; the various screens of this wizard are shown in Figures 3-3 through 3-7. In the first wizard screen, Clare names the project Enterprise 3.1 and clicks Next. The next screen allows her to choose which methodology she wants to use. At the time of this writing, Microsoft ships MSF for Agile Software Development and MSF for CMMI Process Improvement. The Icarus team has decided to use MSF for CMMI Process Improvement, so Clare selects this option and clicks Next.

The next screen prompts Clare to name the project portal—not particularly important, so she could be imaginative—but the team will have to look at it for six months, so she chooses something simple, Enterprise 3.1 Portal; types a line of brief description; and clicks Next. She then can choose whether there will be a new source control folder, or if this will be a branch from an existing folder—this might be useful for Enterprise 3.2, thinks Clare—but at the moment the project is starting off with new code or possibly code copied from another source control system, so she elects to create an empty source control folder and clicks Next. The final screen shows Clare the Team Project settings she has entered. Always review these settings carefully before clicking Finish—these values cannot be changed later, so if you've made a silly typo in the name, now's your chance to fix it. Clare checks the information and clicks Finish.

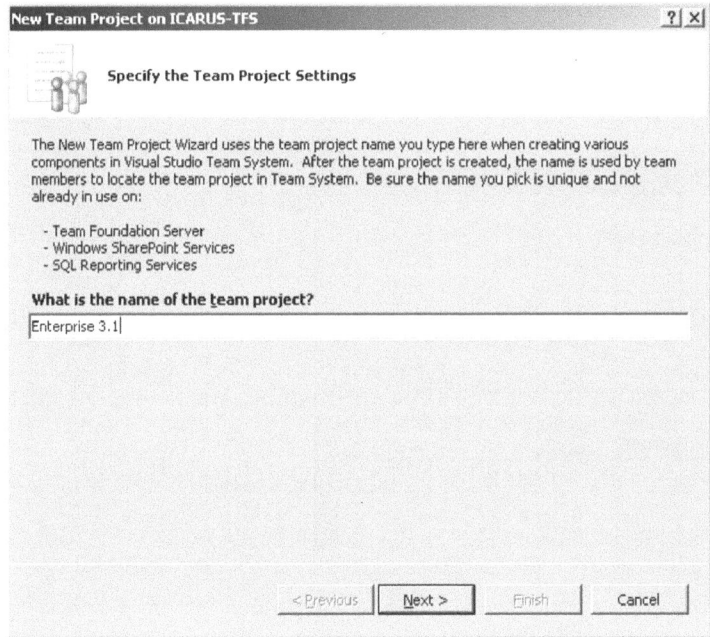

Figure 3-3. *New Team Project Wizard—naming the project*

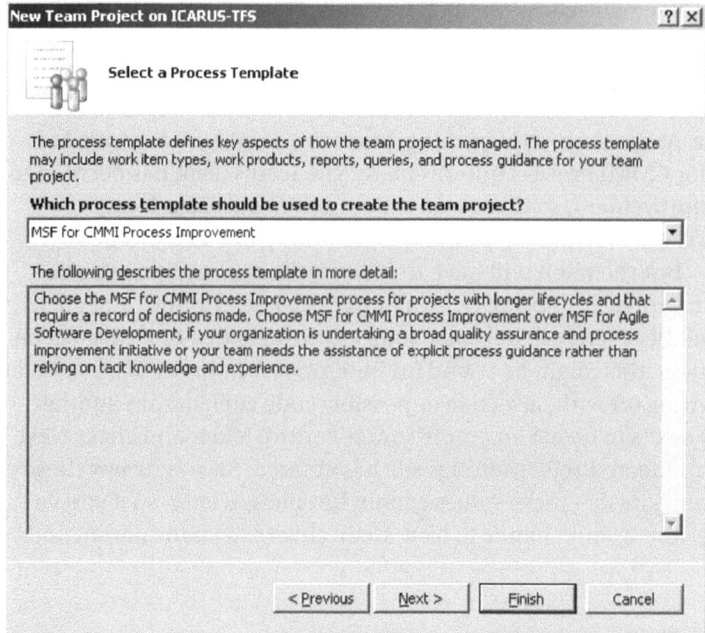

Figure 3-4. *Choosing the process template*

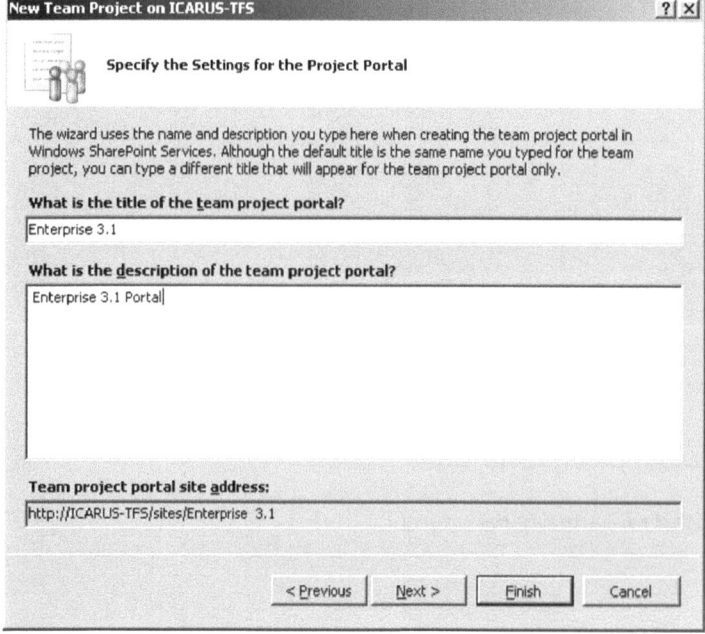

Figure 3-5. *The project portal*

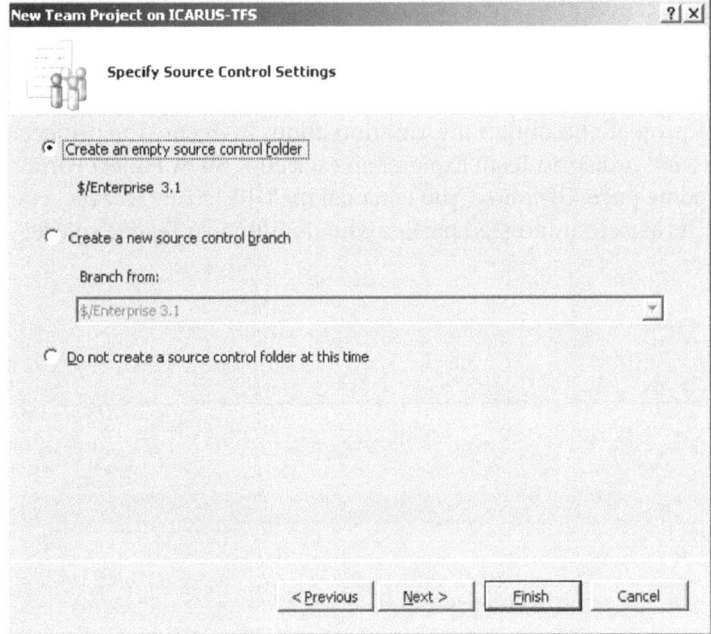

Figure 3-6. *Source control settings*

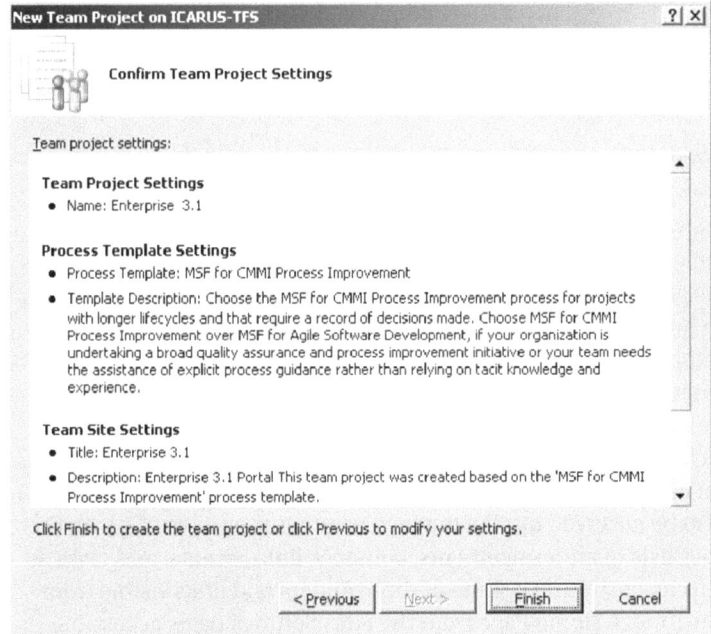

Figure 3-7. *Confirming settings*

The Project Portal

TFS requires that Windows SharePoint Services be installed prior to its own installation. It uses SharePoint to provide a project portal through which team members and other interested parties can participate in the project and obtain information about it. Access the project portal by right-clicking on the team project in Team Explorer and selecting Show Project Portal. Figure 3-8 shows the portal's home page. Of course, you can mail the URL http://Icarus-tfs/sites/enterprise 3.1/default.aspx to interested parties who do not have Team Explorer installed.

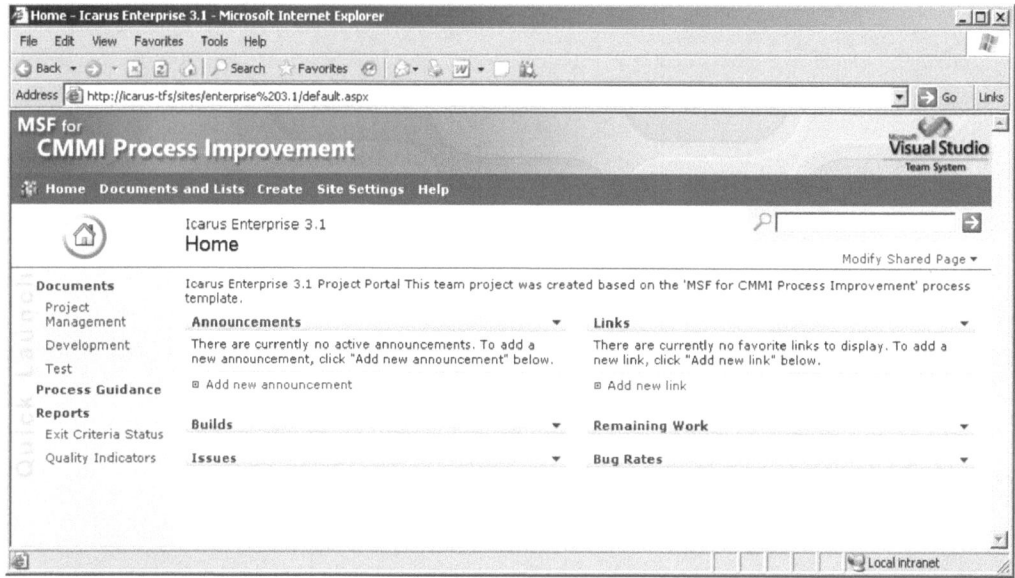

Figure 3-8. *The project portal home page, just after the project has been created*

The home page features several sections. The announcements section lets you add new entries, optionally with attachments. A Links section allows you to add links to any useful URLs, which could be external web pages that provide useful tips such as Microsoft forums and blogs, information about or links to internal test machines, hosts containing software downloads, and so forth. There are also report generators for Builds, Remaining Work, Issues, and Bug Rates, which I will illustrate later in the book as they become relevant.

The portal also includes a hierarchy of pages accessible from the Documents link in the side Quick Launch menu, which organizes into folders the documents placed in TFS. The same folder structure is accessible in the Documents folder in the Team Explorer window (Figure 3-9). The document folders may also be accessed by clicking the Documents and Lists link on the home page, which also includes lists of announcements, contacts, links, events, and tasks as well as a discussion board. You can easily make some of these folders and links visible from the home page by selecting Customize Home Page from the Sites Settings page, accessible from the main menu at the top.

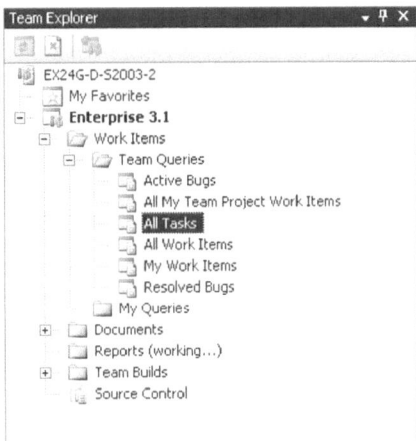

Figure 3-9. *Team Explorer, showing work item queries that are automatically added when a team project is created*

The alerts feature allows users to specify that they receive an email when, for example, a new document is added or a new entry is posted on the discussion board. This is configured on the Site Settings page under Manage My Information ➤ My alerts on this site. Before alerts can be set up, they must be configured for the virtual server under Windows SharePoint Services using the SharePoint Central Administration tool. Consult the Windows SharePoint Services Help to find out how to do this.

Another important feature of the project portal is known as Process Guidance. Click this link on the left side of the home page to access a collection of HTML documents stored on the server in the \Documents\Process Guidance folder. It is very helpful to be able to refresh your memory as to what the various activities mean in the process being followed by your project.

Lastly, the portal offers an extensive report feature that allows you to generate a variety of reports on the project's status. Once again, I'm going to postpone discussion of this feature since our example project does not yet have very much on which to report.

Automatically Generated Tasks for the MSF for CMMI Process Improvement Project

When Clare created the Enterprise 3.1 team project, Team System automatically added some task work items appropriate to the methodology. You can see work items in a project selectively by running one of the queries listed under the Work Items ➤ Team Queries node of the team project in the Team Explorer pane, as shown in Figure 3-9. A set of useful queries are added automatically when the project is created, but you can create your own. For now we can use the All Tasks query to see the tasks automatically created. Figure 3-10 shows what happens when you right-click on this query and select Open. All the tasks are currently assigned to Clare, since she created the team project.

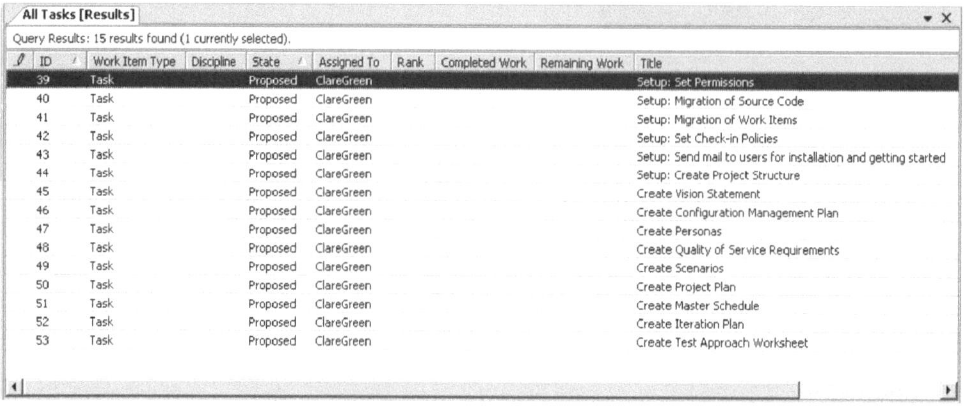
All Tasks [Results]
Query Results: 15 results found (1 currently selected).
ID | Work Item Type | Discipline | State | Assigned To | Rank | Completed Work | Remaining Work | Title
39 Task Proposed ClareGreen Setup: Set Permissions
40 Task Proposed ClareGreen Setup: Migration of Source Code
41 Task Proposed ClareGreen Setup: Migration of Work Items
42 Task Proposed ClareGreen Setup: Set Check-in Policies
43 Task Proposed ClareGreen Setup: Send mail to users for installation and getting started
44 Task Proposed ClareGreen Setup: Create Project Structure
45 Task Proposed ClareGreen Create Vision Statement
46 Task Proposed ClareGreen Create Configuration Management Plan
47 Task Proposed ClareGreen Create Personas
48 Task Proposed ClareGreen Create Quality of Service Requirements
49 Task Proposed ClareGreen Create Scenarios
50 Task Proposed ClareGreen Create Project Plan
51 Task Proposed ClareGreen Create Master Schedule
52 Task Proposed ClareGreen Create Iteration Plan
53 Task Proposed ClareGreen Create Test Approach Worksheet

Figure 3-10. *Work items automatically added by Team System for a new MSF for CMMI Process Improvement project*

The First Planning Meeting

MSF CMMI defines an iterative approach, and most of the work in iteration 0 is concerned with planning the project and putting together initial high-level architectural designs and customer requirements. It is expected to last a month, but Clare has yet to plan the iteration and publish a schedule. Clare, Susan, Peter, and Ron agree to hold planning meetings every day for a week during iteration 0 to help Clare with this task. They are joined by Herman Muller, who is to be the test manager assigned to the project. Herman is based at the Guru's Nest U.S. office, but also has the responsibility of supervising, via Rahul, quite a large test team in Bangalore, India. The first of these planning meetings occurs just after Clare has created the team project; the purpose is to discuss which of the set of automatic tasks shown in Figure 3-10 are relevant, whether any should be added, and who will take responsibility for each one.

It is agreed that these initial tasks will be assigned to the team members as illustrated in Table 3-1.

Table 3-1. *Task Assignment*

Iteration	Work Item	Responsibility
Iteration 0	Set Permissions	Clare
Iteration 1	Set Check-in Policies	Ron
Iteration 0	Setup: Send Mail to Users for Installation and Getting Started	Ron
Iteration 0	Setup: Create Project Structure	Clare
Iteration 0	Create Vision Document	Clare
Iteration 1	Create Configuration Management Plan	Ron
Iteration 0	Create Personas	Susan
Iteration 0	Create Quality of Service Requirements	Susan
Iteration 0	Create Scenarios	Susan
Iteration 0	Create Project Plan	Clare
Iteration 0	Create Master Schedule	Clare
Iteration 0	Create Iteration Plan, Iteration 0	Clare
Iteration 1	Create Test Approach Worksheet	Herman

There is no source code and there are no work items to be migrated to the project, so the work items 40 and 41 in Figure 3-10 will be set to state Closed, with reason Rejected. The group also agrees to add the task-type work items shown in Table 3-2.

Table 3-2. *Additional Work Items*

Iteration	Work Item	Responsibility
Iteration 0	Create Solution Architecture	Peter
Iteration 1	Create Product Requirements	Peter
Iteration 1	Establish Environments	Peter

After the meeting Clare will set the permissions for the team members on the project since at present she is the only one permitted to do that. In the next sections we'll talk about these tasks and what they mean to the project as the team members carry them out. Figure 3-11 shows how these tasks interrelate during iterations 0 and 1.

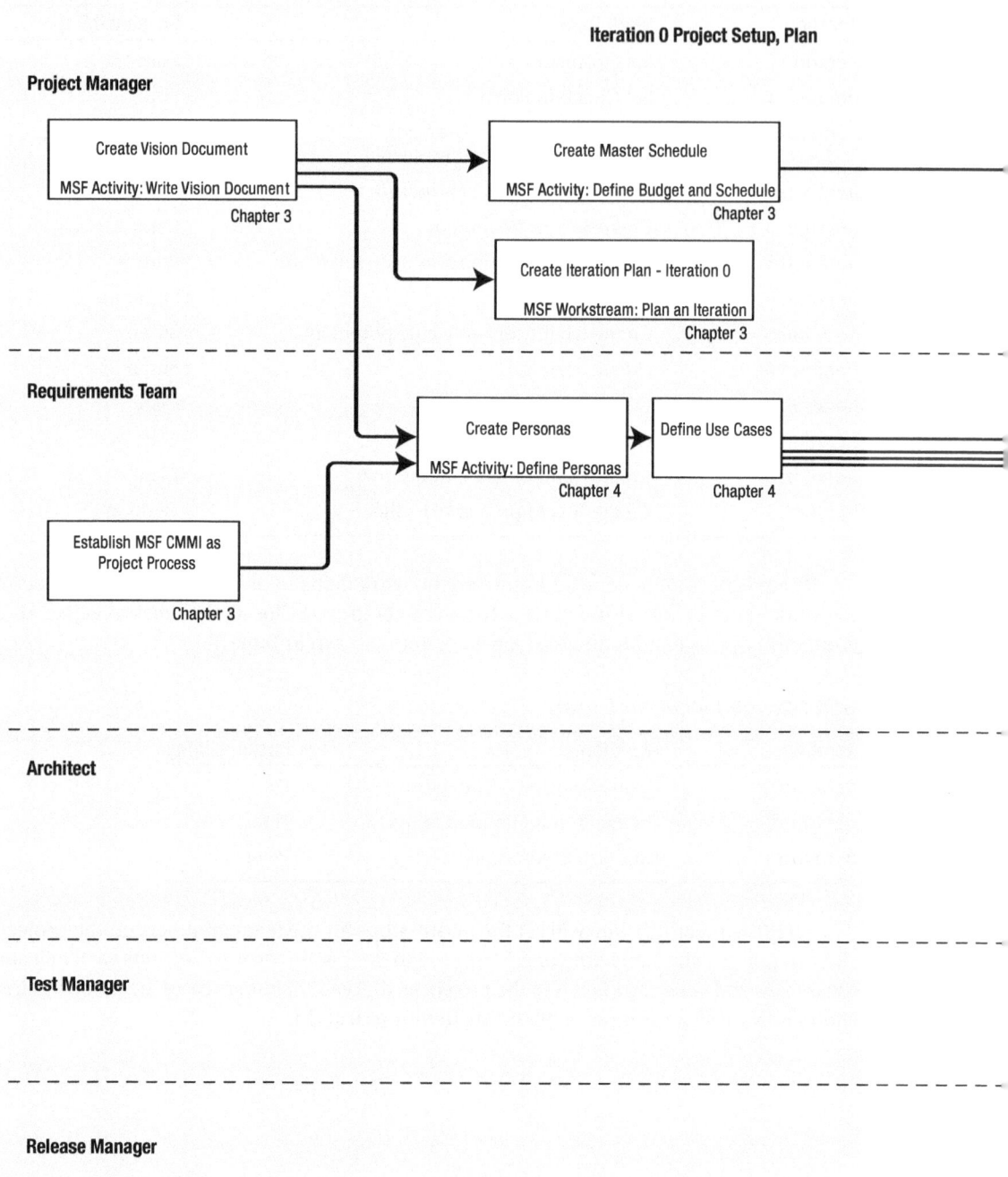

Figure 3-11. *Process flow for the major workflows and activities in iteration 0 and 1*

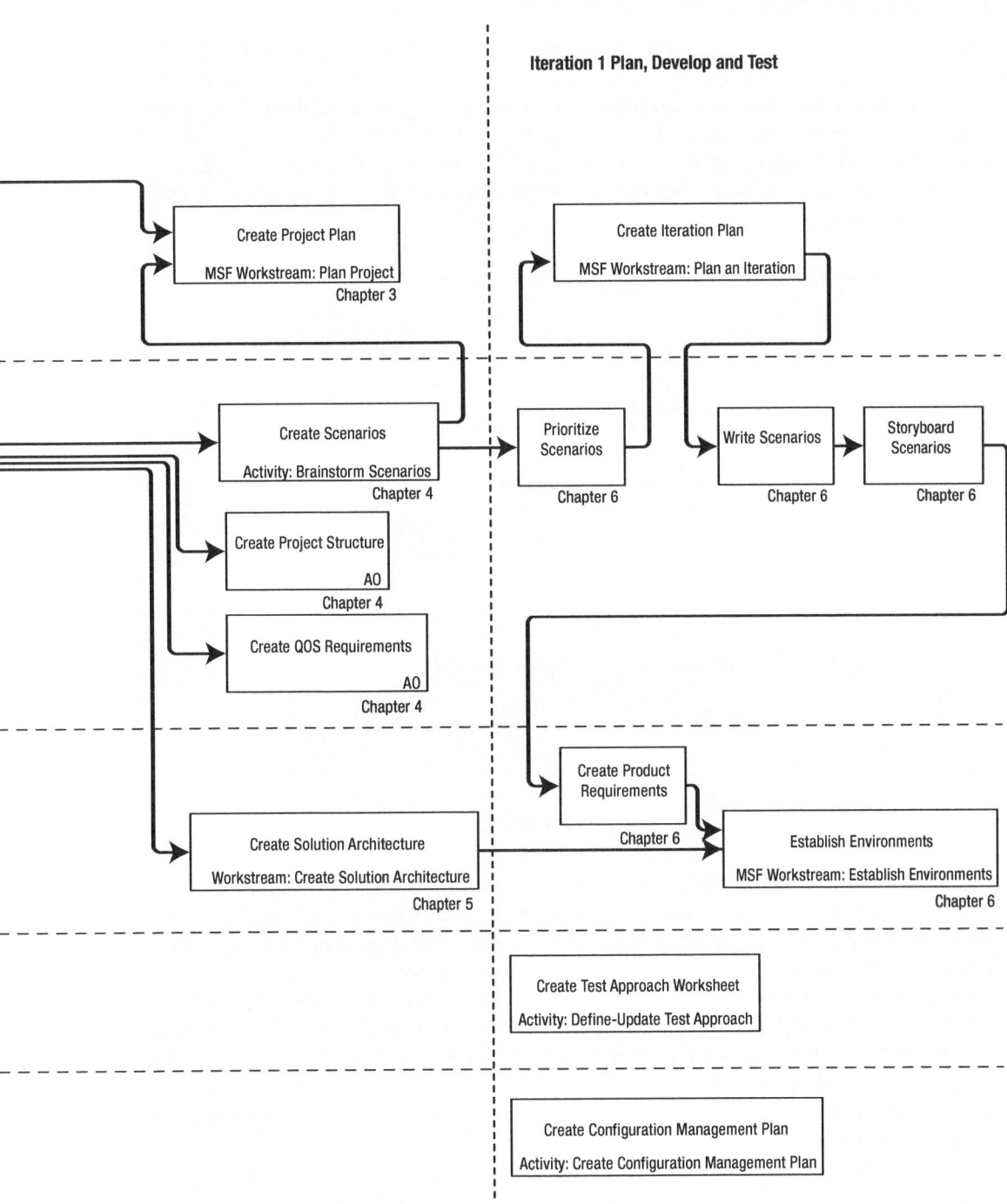

Iteration 1 Plan, Develop and Test

Create Project Plan

MSF Workstream: Plan Project
Chapter 3

Create Iteration Plan

MSF Workstream: Plan an Iteration

Create Scenarios

Activity: Brainstorm Scenarios
Chapter 4

Prioritize
Scenarios

Chapter 6

Write Scenarios

Chapter 6

Storyboard
Scenarios

Chapter 6

Create Project Structure

AO
Chapter 4

Create QOS Requirements

AO
Chapter 4

Create Product
Requirements

Chapter 6

Create Solution Architecture

Workstream: Create Solution Architecture
Chapter 5

Establish Environments

MSF Workstream: Establish Environments
Chapter 6

Create Test Approach Worksheet

Activity: Define-Update Test Approach

Create Configuration Management Plan

Activity: Create Configuration Management Plan

Setting Permissions

To set the permissions on a project requires adding users to groups and then assigning the security permissions on those groups. You can assign users to groups by right-clicking on the project in Team Explorer and selecting Team Project Settings ➤ Group Membership from the context menu. In the resulting dialog box shown in Figure 3-12, seven default groups are defined by Team Foundation Server. The lower three in the figure are server groups, while those above are groups that have been created for the specific project. The descriptions in Figure 3-12 are fairly self-explanatory.

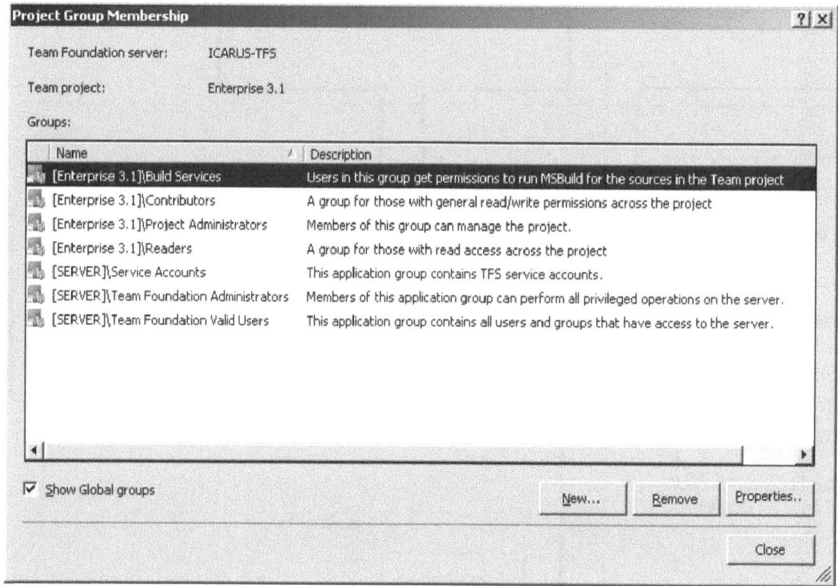

Figure 3-12. *The Project Group Membership dialog box*

It has been agreed that, in addition to Clare, Peter and Ron will be placed in the Project Administrators group and that Susan, Herman, and all the developers and testers will be placed in the Contributors group. Project administrators are able to administer the project whereas Contributors have read/write access to all of the contents.

To add members to the Project Administrators group, you select the group name and click the Properties button. This brings up the dialog box shown in Figure 3-13, which has an Add button that lets you add members to the group. Icarus is using Windows-defined users rather than TFS users; therefore, users that are defined locally, or in Active Directory, can be added to groups. The dialog box that lets you select users is similar to the one you'd use to add users to any ordinary Windows group.

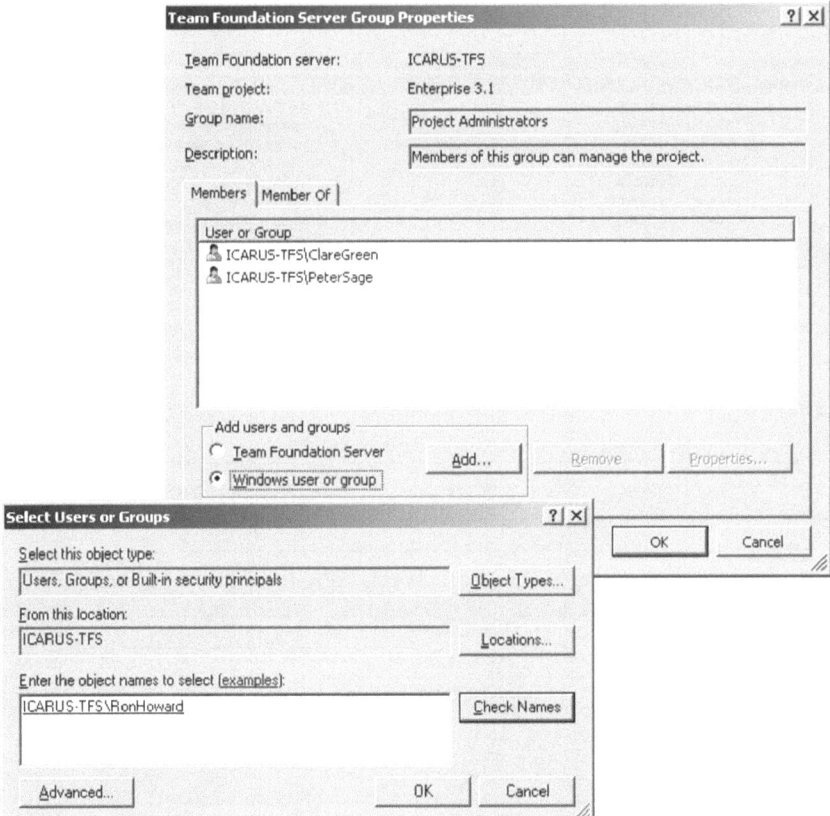

Figure 3-13. *The Team Foundation Server Group Properties dialog box and the Select Users or Groups dialog box*

Assigning Tasks

To assign the initial tasks as agreed, Clare runs Team Explorer, right-clicks on the All Tasks query, and selects Open from the context menu. In Figure 3-14 you can see how selecting one of the tasks in the list also displays the details in a pane below. To reassign the tasks as agreed, Clare simply selects each task from the list at the top and then selects the new assignee from the Assigned To drop-down box. Clare also marks her Setup: Set Permissions task as Closed, reason Complete; marks each assigned task as Active, reason Approved; and marks the unneeded migration tasks as Closed, reason Rejected. This is done in each case by selecting the required new state and reason from the values available in these drop-down boxes on the work item detail in Figure 3-14. There is a definite set of state transitions that a task can make, and in any given state the possible transitions are limited by the alternatives displayed in these two drop-down boxes. I will show the detailed life history of tasks in a later chapter. You cannot delete work items once they have been created, so if you've made a mistake, you must close them with the Reason field set to Rejected.

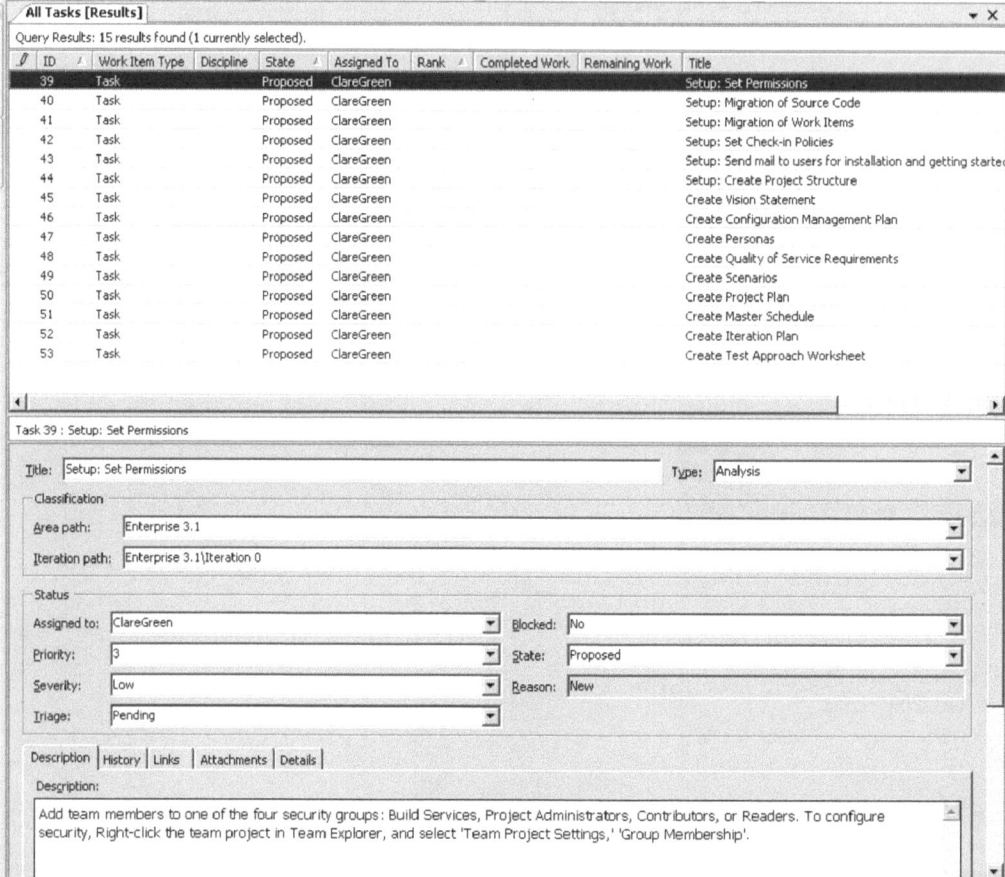

Figure 3-14. *The work items automatically added by Team System that need to be reassigned*

Clare also adds the three new work items that were agreed on. She does this by right-clicking on the Work Items folder of the project in Team Explorer and selecting Add Work Item ➤ Task. The new task for Peter, Establish Environments, is shown in Figure 3-15, and the final list of work items is shown in Figure 3-16. Clare must run the query again to update this page, so she right-clicks on the page itself and selects Run Query from the context menu. Figure 3-16 shows the updated list of task work items.

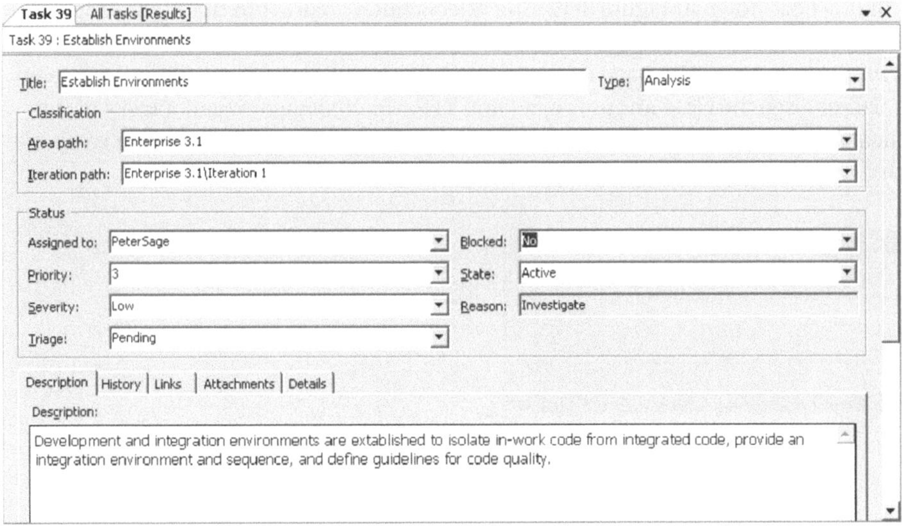

Figure 3-15. *Creation of the Establish Environments task*

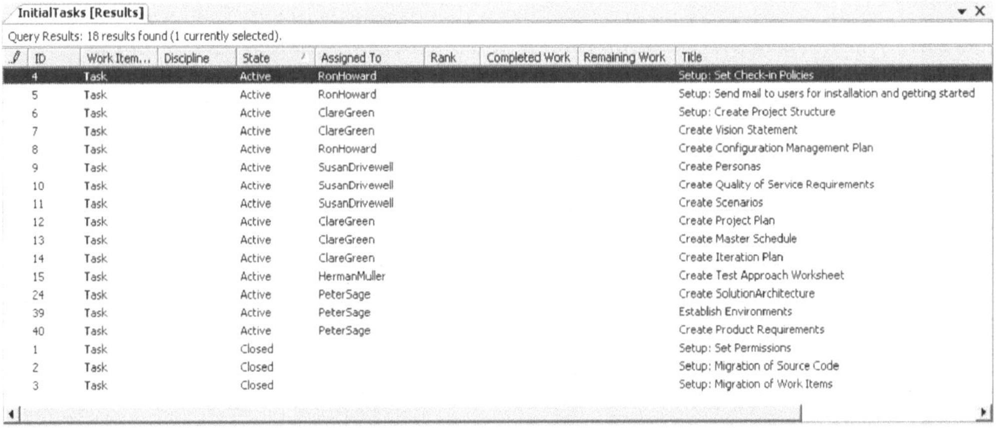
InitialTasks [Results]

Query Results: 18 results found (1 currently selected).

ID	Work Item...	Discipline	State	Assigned To	Rank	Completed Work	Remaining Work	Title
4	Task		Active	RonHoward				Setup: Set Check-in Policies
5	Task		Active	RonHoward				Setup: Send mail to users for installation and getting started
6	Task		Active	ClareGreen				Setup: Create Project Structure
7	Task		Active	ClareGreen				Create Vision Statement
8	Task		Active	RonHoward				Create Configuration Management Plan
9	Task		Active	SusanDrivewell				Create Personas
10	Task		Active	SusanDrivewell				Create Quality of Service Requirements
11	Task		Active	SusanDrivewell				Create Scenarios
12	Task		Active	ClareGreen				Create Project Plan
13	Task		Active	ClareGreen				Create Master Schedule
14	Task		Active	ClareGreen				Create Iteration Plan
15	Task		Active	HermanMuller				Create Test Approach Worksheet
24	Task		Active	PeterSage				Create SolutionArchitecture
39	Task		Active	PeterSage				Establish Environments
40	Task		Active	PeterSage				Create Product Requirements
1	Task		Closed					Setup: Set Permissions
2	Task		Closed					Setup: Migration of Source Code
3	Task		Closed					Setup: Migration of Work Items

Figure 3-16. *The updated set of work items*

Create Iteration Plan—Iteration 0

Iteration 0 represents the first stage of the plan track of the project and contains some of the tasks that have been mentioned earlier. You can see the concept of *tracks* described in the Governance page of the process guidance. The first iteration is rather a special case, but I show it here to illustrate how Clare uses Microsoft Project early on to begin to plan the project schedule.

Microsoft Project and Excel are Clare's favorite tools, so the integration of these Microsoft Office tools with Team Foundation Server is very important to her. Clare begins by running the Microsoft Project application and selecting Team ➤ Choose Team Project from its main menu to open the dialog box shown in Figure 3-17. She selects Enterprise 3.1 in the Team Projects list box and clicks OK, which configures the project to display a set of TFS work items as tasks in the usual Project window. (The page is empty until the work items are retrieved from Team Foundation Server—see the Note about Project and TFS.) To create a new set of tasks in the Project application, Clare must now specify the work items by selecting Team ➤ Get Work Items, which displays the dialog box shown in Figure 3-18.

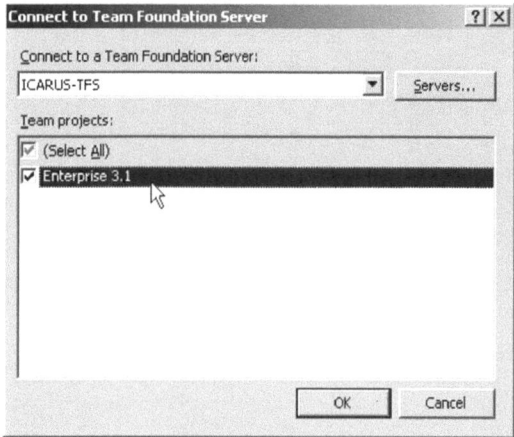

Figure 3-17. *The dialog box in Microsoft Project that allows connection to a team project*

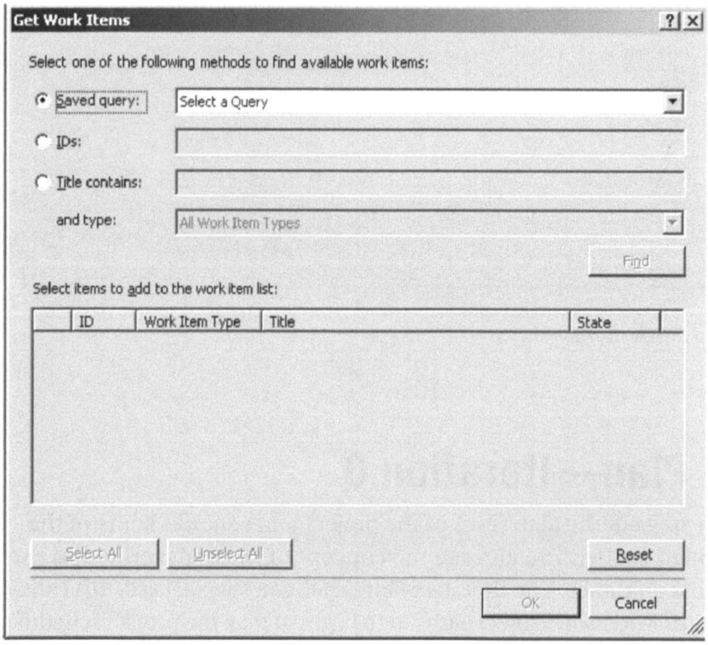

Figure 3-18. *The Get Work Items dialog box in Microsoft Project*

In Figure 3-18, you can see several ways to select work items from a team project: by running a query that has already been saved, by specifying an item's ID or type, or by searching for a string contained in the title. Clare chooses to use one of the queries that are added to the project automatically on creation, so she makes sure the Saved Query radio button is selected and selects the All Tasks query from the drop-down. This activates the Find button, which she clicks so that a list of tasks appears in the dialog box. By default, all the tasks are checked for retrieval from the server, but she deselects those that are closed and those not to be included in iteration 1, as shown in Figure 3-19. Then Clare clicks OK. The Project screen is updated to display all of the checked tasks, as shown in Figure 3-20. (Clare has tidied up the column widths to display all of the information.)

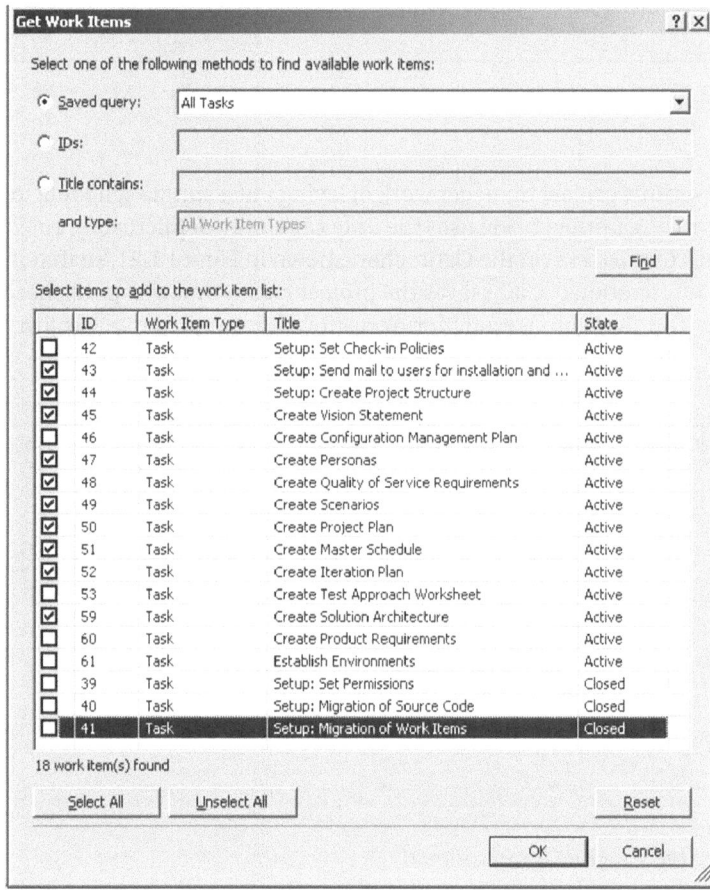

Figure 3-19. *The work items returned by the All Tasks query*

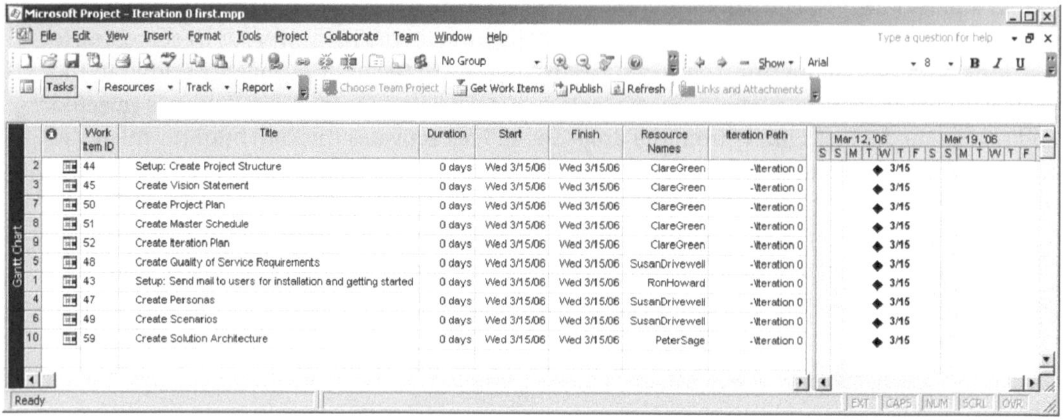

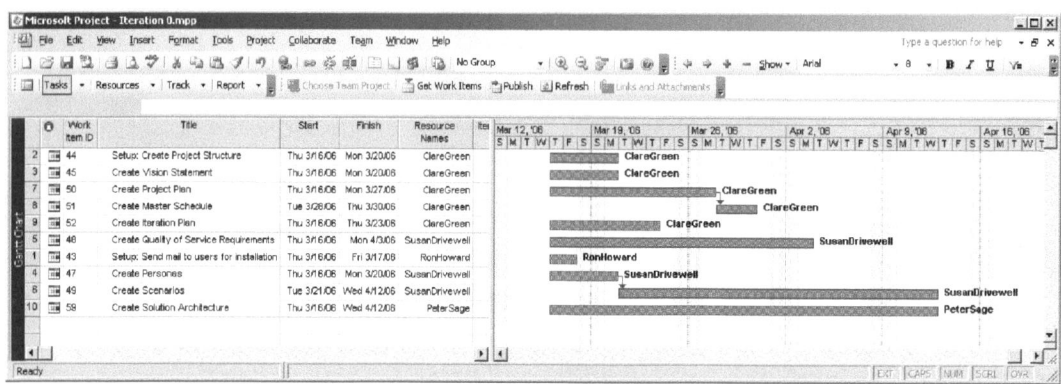

Figure 3-20. *Microsoft Project screen display after the work items have been retrieved*

She can now begin some serious project manager work of laying out a simple schedule for iteration 0 of the Icarus Enterprise 3.1 project. She uses the drag capability of Microsoft Project to move the start and end dates of the tasks on the Gantt chart shown in Figure 3-21, so that it represents a simple schedule for iteration 0. Clare saves the project locally and also publishes the changes to the team project on the Team Foundation Server by choosing Team ➤ Publish Changes.

Figure 3-21. *Project screen showing the schedule for iteration 0*

Note I want to clarify the relation between TFS and Microsoft Project. The Microsoft Project application has the concept of a "project," which consists of a set of tasks with start and end dates and resources allocated to them, that can be saved in a project (`.mpp`) file and displayed in various ways; the Gantt chart is perhaps the most well known. In the work described previously, the tasks themselves have been downloaded from the team project on Team Foundation Server, which is a different concept of a project from that supported by Microsoft Project. The integration of Project with TFS requires that there be an association between tasks in Project and work items in TFS including a mapping of fields in work items to fields in the Project task. Once the association is made, each can be updated from the other in a limited way; the only thing exchanged between TFS and Project is the set of work items and their attributes. The start and end dates and many other things concerning the tasks within the Project application are not retained when the project is published to TFS and then reopened from TFS in the Project application. Thus, it is essential to retain a copy of the project created by the Microsoft Project application in an `.mpp` file, separately from the tasks held as work items in TFS. If you do not do this, you will be very disappointed to discover that all of your Microsoft Project information such as Gantt chart layout, links between tasks, and hierarchical organization of tasks has been lost. Of course, once you have saved the project locally, you can publish it in TFS as a document for others to view.

"Good," thinks Clare. "It's not much of a schedule, but at least it's a start, and now I understand how to convert task work items into a Gantt chart." She glances across to Peter's desk, alerted by a sudden commotion. Peter and Rahul are involved in a highly animated conversation. There is a great deal of technical jargon in which she catches the words "Bernoulli's Theorem" repeated over and over, and Rahul keeps swinging his arm over his head for some reason. Suddenly Peter lifts one leg, gyrates around as though throwing something, and sends his full cup of coffee from the edge of his desk flying across the cubicle. She walks across, as he furiously tries to mop up the mess.

"Oh, Peter," she says tersely, "I've put together a rough schedule for iteration 0. There's a very big task on there for you, you know." She suppresses a smile as she shuts down her computer and heads for the parking lot.

Summary of the Tasks in Iteration 0

It will help to set the scene for the coming chapters if I briefly summarize the tasks that are scheduled for this stage of the project. Some will be described completely in this chapter, while other, longer ones will be left until the next chapters. Since the emphasis of this book is on Team System, I will not dwell on those tasks that are mainly concerned with budget and other project management issues. The interrelationship between these tasks is shown in Figure 3-11.

Create Vision Document

The vision document is a statement of what has been decided in Chapter 2. Typically it is written by product or program managers—one person or a group of people responsible for the business area or market that the project seeks to address. For an enterprise application such as Icarus Enterprise 3.1, it will be a statement of the business opportunity, needs, goals, timelines, and so forth. For a project involving a piece of software to be launched as a product on the market, the vision document would contain similar elements but would relate to the sale of the software itself rather than the service provided by the company using the software.

Clare and other business representatives will write a detailed vision document. I am not going to present that document here since Chapter 2 includes a detailed description of the vision and that gives a good indication of what Icarus's vision document contains.

Create Personas

Creation of personas is a precursor to creating scenarios and corresponds to the Define Personas activity in the process guidance. The *personas* are the individual users of the system; each character named as a persona represents an example of a category of persons that interact with the system. It is a concept within MSF Agile or MSF CMMI, rather than within Team Suite itself. The business analyst (BA) will write the scenarios in terms of the interaction of one or more of the personas with the software system. Susan, the BA, will perform this task, in consultation with the representatives from the business, William and James. You can watch her do this in Chapter 4.

Create Scenarios

This task corresponds to the MSF CMMI activity Brainstorm Scenarios. As defined in the process guidance, it consists of these subactivities:

- Determine Scenario Goals

- Determine Scenarios

This task takes place at the beginning of each iteration, but the instance of it in iteration 0 is intended more to get an overview of the scenarios in the whole project. In other iterations, the task defines in detail the scenarios that will be implemented during that iteration. We'll call the iteration 0 scenarios "Top-Level Scenarios," and in Chapter 4 you can accompany our BA Susan as she works to produce the list of these scenarios that will act as input to the tasks in iteration 1.

Create Project Structure

The project area structure is a hierarchy of names that you can build, starting with Area as the root and branching downward. For example, you might choose to break down your project area functionally by customer or product requirements, by department responsibility, by iteration, or by something else. It's just a tree structure of names that you can arrange in any way you like and with which you can associate work items. Probably the most obvious idea is to organize the project structure according to the functional breakdown. So in the case of Icarus Enterprise 3.1, it can be organized by the project functionality, as it is known at the end of the Envision track.

You add project structure by right-clicking on the project in Team Explorer and selecting Team Project Settings ➤ Areas and Iterations, which brings up the dialog box shown in Figure 3-22. The nodes in this tree view have the alternative names of *project nodes* or *project areas.* The project begins with just the root node in the tree, called Area. You can add subnodes by right-clicking on any node and selecting New from the context menu. You can also use the menu and buttons in the dialog box to change the position of nodes in the hierarchy and change the order. It's also possible to set security on individual nodes in the structure so that specified groups are given defined rights at each node level. As I said earlier, the whole point of this structure is to be able to attach your work items to a node in the tree. On the detail display of all work items, there is a combo box called Area Path that allows you to select a node in the project structure with which to associate a work item. For example, if you organize your project functionally, as in Figure 3-22, some work items will be associated with the Listing area, some with the Sales area, and some with the Sales Status area. There is no reason why you should not have trees other than the functional tree—you might have a set of performance areas for instance, or architectural study areas or areas relating to the overall management, such as the iteration plan. When using the Team System reporting feature to show status of work items, remaining work, quality indicators, etc. (see Chapters 12 and 13), you can filter the information by the project area with which the work item is associated, so it's worth thinking about how the project structure is organized because it determines how you can organize your reporting.

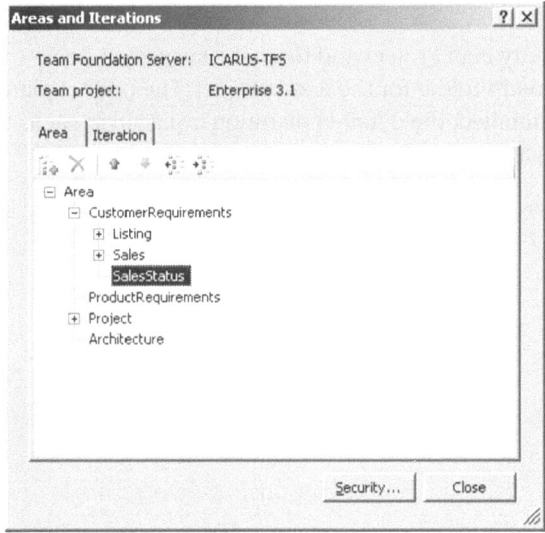

Figure 3-22. *Areas and Iterations dialog box*

As you can see in Figure 3-22, this dialog box also contains an Iteration tab. This tab allows you to define the iterative structure of the project in a similar tree-like manner to represent the Project plan discussed later in this chapter.

Create Quality of Service (QOS) Requirements

This task corresponds to the MSF CMMI activity Brainstorm Quality of Service Requirements. As defined in the process guidance, it consists of these subactivities:

- Determine Quality of Service Goals

- Determine Quality of Service Requirements

Quality of service requirements will be described in Chapter 4.

Create Master Schedule

This task corresponds to the MSF CMMI activity Define Budget and Schedule. As defined in the process guidance, it consists of these activities:

- Determine Whether Date or Scope Driven

- Define Delivery Date

- Define High-Level Dependencies

- Divide Schedule into Iterations

- Divide Functionality Across Iterations

- Determine Budget

Create Project Plan

This task corresponds to the MSF CMMI activity Plan Project and there is a suggested document format in the Documents\General Documents folder for the team project. The project plan defined in this activity is not intended to be detailed; the detailed planning is placed at each iteration. The Plan Project work stream consists of the following list of activities:

- Determine Risk Sources and Categories

- Define Risk Parameters

- Determine Risk Management Strategy

- Estimate Project

- Plan Project Resources

- Plan Project Knowledge and Skills

- Form Project Team

- Establish Project Team Charter

- Define Project Roles and Responsibilities

- Define Project Life Cycle

- Define Project Communication Plan

- Identify Project Stakeholders

- Define Budget and Schedule

- Plan Project Stakeholder involvement

- Review Project Plan

- Integrated Project Management Office Review

- Hold Project Launch

- Obtain Project Commitments

You can consult the process guidance to see these described fully.

Create Solution Architecture

This task, the Create Solution Architecture work stream in the process guidance, is Peter's largest job in the planning stage of the project, and we will join him in Chapter 5. This task will make use of the range of new tools provided in Visual Studio 2005 Team Edition for Architects, so it is a good place to get involved with the practical use of Team System and see many of its important new features.

Summary of Tasks—Iteration 1

The tasks in iteration 1 are typical of the work that takes place in the other iterations. Describing these forms a large part of this book, as I take you through the decisions made in designing and testing the code. This section summarizes those tasks.

Prioritize Scenarios

Looking at the scenarios that exist, the team will prioritize them into those that should be included in iteration 1 and those that will be considered later.

Create Iteration Plan

This task will be carried out once as part of iteration 1 of the project, and then again at the beginning of each subsequent iteration. At the start of each iteration, the exercise of performing the iteration plan defines the scope, schedule, and responsibilities for that iteration. Do not confuse this task with the Create Master Schedule task, which involves planning the sequence of iterations that make up the whole project and is performed only once for the project, during iteration 0.

Write Scenarios

Detailed step-by-step descriptions of each scenario will be written. Some scenarios will need to be split into more than one scenario as variations are discovered.

Storyboard Scenarios

The graphical screens that go with the scenarios will be created and the exact controls used in each step identified. The sequence of screens presented to users as they move through each scenario will be described graphically. You can see this in Chapter 6.

Create Product Requirements

Susan and Peter will work together to carry out this task. In MSF CMMI, product requirements are derived from customer requirements. Customer requirements describe what the product will do from the user's viewpoint, but product requirements specify, from an engineering viewpoint, what needs to be designed to support those customer requirements. This effort is therefore driven by the architecture and the scenarios, and defines what each component application will do functionally, as well as the interfaces that it must support. It also will include nonfunctional requirements such as performance and security needed to meet the quality of service requirements defined by the BA team.

This task will occur once in iteration 1 (described in Chapter 6), and then again in some of the other iterations. This is because requirements will increase when more scenarios are added as the iterations progress, and the requirements for the product will need to be augmented.

Establish Environments

Peter must define the development and integration environments and physically establish these environments so that code that is *in-work* is kept separate from integrated code. He must also provide a unit test, integration, and functional test environment; define sequences and procedures; and provide guidelines for code quality and coding standards. Peter can define these environments using the tools in the Visual Studio 2005 Team Edition for Architects. You will see this in Chapter 6.

Create Configuration Management Plan

This plan describes the configuration management, strategies, policies, and activities for the project's life cycle.

Create Test Approach Worksheet

This task defines the test strategy and quality objectives for the project.

The Project Plan: Defining the Budget and Schedule

Earlier I talked about Create Project Plan as a major task, involving many activities, that the project manager must do during iteration 0. Much of this work involves project issues that are not particularly relevant to Team System. However, I will spend the remainder of this chapter showing how the schedule is established and then divided into iterations and how the functionality is divided between iterations. The process guidance page applicable to this activity specifies that the result of this activity is the project plan, which is described in MSF CMMI thus:

The project plan identifies resources and budget against each life-cycle track. It lays out a sequence of iterations, identifying key scenarios to be completed in each one. The project plan is not intended to be detailed or specific. Detailed plans are postponed to each iteration.

There is an important point here: at the time this plan is put together, the team does not know enough to make a detailed plan—to lay out each person's tasks, for example. Team members do not know the detailed tasks or how they will interrelate, so they leave that kind of detailed planning until the beginning of each iteration.

Date Driven or Scope Driven?

A project is date driven if it needs to deliver working functionality by a certain date, but usually there is some variability within a market window, and compromise is acceptable. Sometimes implementing new and innovative functionality is far more important than delivery date, but a truly open-ended research project with no particular delivery date is unlikely to use Team System!

High-Level Dependencies

By *high level* here we mean mainly functional dependencies, but there might be other dependencies that are obvious right at the start. Dependencies can be established from the work of the Icarus requirements team, but at this point in the project, the use case analysis and scenarios to be described in Chapter 4 are not yet available. Thus, only the vision document and early architectural work exists like Figure 2-22, and dependencies will need to be established from that. We imagine, though, that during iteration 0 the project management, architecture, and requirements tasks are happening in parallel and that the people are talking to one another. In this book, it is a bit difficult to decide which to place first, but in general I'll try to find a path along which the story logically evolves. However, if you have a pretty clear idea of what the project is about from Chapter 2, it would not do any harm, as you read through the next three sections, to have a sneak preview of a few parts of Chapter 4.

Figure 3-23 shows the dependencies that we expect at this time between the new functional areas of the project that need to be developed as well as the existing orchestration service. To remind yourself of what these areas mean, have another look at Chapter 2. The early plans include a completely new database to contain resource information for all of the vendors with which Icarus works, as well as order information for all of Icarus's customers. The Listing business objects, which provide the low-level capability to do things like create and modify resources and vendors, depend entirely on the enterprise database and cannot be developed and tested without that database. Similarly, the Sales business objects, which provide the low-level capability to do things like create, modify, and delete orders, have the same database dependency. We can call these two groups of business objects, together with the database, the business logic system, and we will examine in Chapter 5 how these systems can be described in Visual Studio Team Edition for Architects.

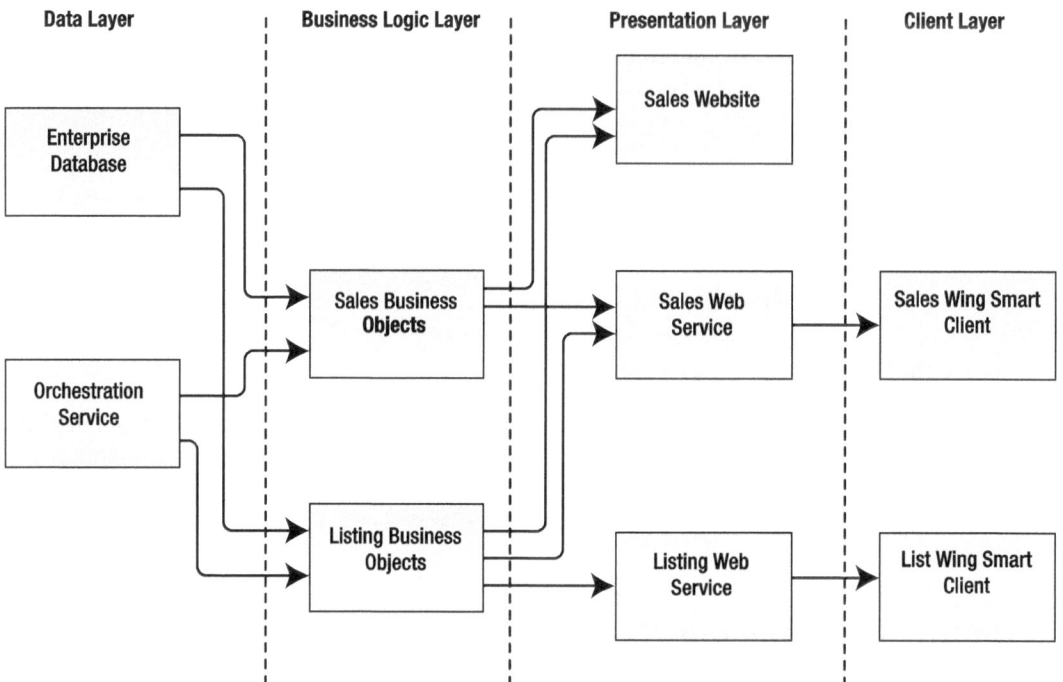

Figure 3-23. *High-level dependencies between the functional areas of Icarus Enterprise 3.1. The arrows show the natural flow of development, from the independent to the dependent.*

The Sales website contains ASP.NET 2.0 code that displays screens to home customers to allow them to view resources and make reservations. This software provides a presentation layer over the top of the Sales business objects and Listing business objects, and so is heavily dependent on both of those. The Sales web service that provides the capabilities of the business objects in the form of web services is in the same position, as is the Listing web service.

The smart client applications, Sales Wing and List Wing, are heavily dependent on the Sales web services and cannot be developed or tested without these components. There are high-risk areas of functionality involved in the offline working capability of the Sales Wing client that need to be developed and tested early on. These dependency issues are a critical problem for successful management of the project, and considerable discussion is necessary to come to a solution. How can these dependencies be managed?

One approach would be to carefully design the system, defining all of the functionality and interfaces, and then develop it starting from the database and working from left to right in Figure 3-23. Provided the design is thorough, the database will have all of the necessary tables, the business objects will have the capability required by the web services, and finally the smart clients will be written to make use of them. This would be following a kind of waterfall approach, in the sense that the design would need to be complete before code was written—and it might work. It would take quite a lot of work, using UML to lay everything out in Visio. It would be necessary to define sequence diagrams for all of the critical scenarios of the use cases described in Chapter 4, particularly the difficult areas included in the offline working capability. The less critical ones could be left until later, but there would surely be some surprises that would require modification of the database and business logic layer during the development of the smart clients. Test harnesses would need to be written for the business logic layer and presentation layer, so that their operation could be verified in the absence of the smart clients.

An obvious modification of this approach would be to finish the design phase, then develop the data layer and business logic layer, presentation layer, and client layer simultaneously using stubs and test harnesses to allow each to be unit tested at the same time. The last phase of the project would be to bring them all together for system integration. At least, this strategy has the advantage of making things happen in parallel, which will lead to a shorter schedule.

The major disadvantage with this modified approach, of course, is risk. It's a bit like digging two ends of a tunnel under a river and hoping they will meet. Of course, tunneling engineers do this regularly with success; they do their sums very carefully and check them many times. I suppose there's no alternative with tunneling. However, with any complex project, mistakes do occur, and such mistakes can be very costly to correct later. It therefore behooves us to minimize risk as far as possible. You can point a finger of blame late in the project, but this will not avoid huge delays and a lost business opportunity. So let's try to reduce risk early on!

We need to document a risk mitigation plan—but let's make it mean something—and that means having risk management as a key ingredient of the project plan, not something that's being done out on the fringes, just to satisfy a documentation requirement. How can we mitigate most of the risks? We have to show that something works, before it's too late to do anything about it. It's a bit like digging a very narrow tunnel and making sure both ends meet before widening it to full size. We need iterations in our development of the functionality, and then our risk management plans can show how we will mitigate risks by showing things starting to work as early as we can. Then management can identify problems early on and the development team can change the design as needed, or the requirements team can change functionality accordingly.

Of course, iteration is part and parcel of all modern software development processes; certainly it is a key ingredient in both MSF Agile and MSF CMMI, and my comments only echo what are now well-known practices. Let's examine in the next section how our project team can make iteration a meaningful part of the plan and succeed in reducing risk and providing greater visibility of progress.

Dividing the Schedule into Iterations

MSF for CMMI Process Improvement prescribes an iterative development within a series of tracks: Envision, Plan, Build, Stabilize, and Deploy. At this point, the team must decide how many iterations the project should include and how long they should be. Iterations cost money and take up team members' time, so there is a clear trade-off between just letting the developers get on with it, with their heads down for six months and trusting them, at the one extreme, and at the other, forcing them to account for themselves by generating a delivery at such frequent intervals that they spend nearly all their time with release procedures and have no time to consider the long-term view.

The iteration length also has an effect on testing. If the iterations are too frequent, the testers spend a great deal of time performing regression testing on the same functionality and reporting bugs that the developers have no time to fix (and that may be irrelevant in the next iteration).

At the end of the Envision track, we'd like to be able to answer the question "Are we doing the right thing?" Certainly management will have something to say about what they would like to see first; to respond positively to this question, they need to know that what is being developed will fulfill their needs. In reality, I think that this question can be answered broadly at the end of the Envision track but continues in narrower terms through the Plan track and into the Build track. By this I mean that, although the general requirements may be agreed on and accepted by management early on, there will always be features of the user interface, work process flows, ease of use, and so forth that will become apparent when the end users experiment with the iteration releases. So when the iterations are being planned, the users should be asked to identify those features that pose the biggest risk of changing the project's functional requirements. For example, for Icarus, there may be a big cloudy piece of functionality, say "Forward Planning of Resource Usage," which allows vendors to predict resource usage over the next six months based on extrapolation from the previous six months—or is it the corresponding six months in the previous year? See what I mean? If this is important to the success of the project but nobody is sure of the exact requirements, then the team needs to start working those ideas into iterations early on. End users' requests may be impossible to implement, or they may turn out to be unnecessary once they gain experience with the early implementations.

At the end of the Plan track, management should be able to answer the question "Can we do it in the right time frame and budget? Is the business case justified?" So at the end of the Plan track, there should not be too many unanswered questions—most of the uncertainties in requirements and architecture should have disappeared. How many iterations does it require to reach the level of confidence necessary to mark the end of the Plan track? MSF CMMI suggests between two and six weeks is a reasonable length of time for iterations. There's a lot to do early in the project, and management needs to see a fair sampling of end-to-end capability working. Let's look at the factors driving what kind of functionality should appear at the end of each iteration.

Major Risk Areas

Now that you know the iterations should be chosen to reduce risk, what are the risk areas? The basic idea of managing listings and sales does not appear particularly risky unless we have a very inexperienced team. We have to be concerned about how these concepts interact, though, and be sure there are no large areas of functionality we are not aware of yet.

Performance is certainly an issue. The team needs to demonstrate that the architecture is capable of reaching the performance targets and that it can be scaled successfully so that the servers deliver the response times that we specify under the required load. They will need to make sure that the split of implementation across the database, business logic, presentation, and client does not upset this scalability and performance.

The team will need to think carefully about the balance of function between the client and the business layer. They must avoid the trap of a traditional "thick-client, client-server approach" where the business logic has surreptitiously crossed the boundary between layers and ended up on the client. It's easy to slip into this trap by placing table adapters on forms—as you'll see later. The team has to reconcile the aim of having business logic in the business layer against the aim of offline working. Here is a real issue—how do they obtain offline working with the business logic on the servers? It looks as if there will have to be some sort of business layer on the client—but at least this should be designed to be identifiable and self-contained.

This brings us to the risky area of the offline working and synchronization, which needs to be demonstrated to be able to deliver the capability required. The requirements for this are discussed in Chapter 4.

Divide Functionality Across Iterations

Project management will want to see iterations whose results indicate whether the project is succeeding, so that they can report to upper management that their money is being well spent. The team should therefore choose iterations that address the risks in the project early on—in Icarus's case, the provision of offline working for travel agents. Will this really work out? How will travel agents synchronize with the database when they come back online? Suppose two travel agents have reserved the same resource at the same time? The requirements team at Icarus has a vague concept that there will be *tentative reservations* that can be made when agents are working offline, and those reservations will be automatically confirmed when synchronization takes place, but there may be unforeseen problems that will have to be resolved. It's no good leaving the whole offline concept until the last phase and then discover huge structural changes are needed to implement it. In such a case, the whole idea will probably have to be dropped, and management, who might have been regarding it as one of the main reasons for funding the project, will be most upset!

The architect and senior developers must have input into this decision, since they will also have a feeling for risks and uncertain requirements. Typically the architect will have a good understanding of how the different parts of the application interrelate from the development point of view. Will it really be possible to implement a certain piece of functionality in an early iteration? An example from the Icarus project illustrates this; the team won't be able to demonstrate the Sales Wing Windows application working right through to the database until the Sales web service and Sales business objects applications are working. Therefore, it's not practical to demonstrate offline working too early in the development, whereas the developer working on the Sales Wing application could perhaps demonstrate its basic functionality as a Windows Forms application quite well using a Sales web service stub.

Here we can also think about the split of responsibilities between the architect and the team leader. On some projects the architect works at a high level, defining applications and interfaces and specifying a framework of some sort before moving on to another project. It's then up to the team leader to make all the technical decisions that are needed later. The architect is available for consultations, but in reality has lost touch with the details and therefore can only make a few wise-sounding pronouncements before rushing off to the next meeting. This does not sound very good, but it's not entirely bad. In a large organization, it may be much more important for the architect to keep track of all the interactions between the applications across the enterprise than to worry about the design of individual applications. In that case, this individual should perhaps be called an *enterprise architect* or *integration architect*, whereas an *application architect* might assume more responsibility for the design of individual applications. There certainly should not be an architectural vacuum at the application level, where the developers are left to make it up as they go along!

Let's look back at Icarus for clarification. Peter's job is clearly the architecture of the distributed application that runs Icarus's business. Team leader Ron Howard's job will be to concentrate on the success of developing the individual applications. There will be lots of things for Ron to worry about, such as mentoring team members, helping them set up their environments, chasing them to get code checked in for builds, maintaining coding conventions—the list goes on. Thus, Ron won't have too much time to think about the architecture of each component application.

In some projects, where perhaps the methodology is more relaxed, the team leader might also be the architect—certainly in projects of two or three developers, this would almost certainly be the case. In the case of Icarus Enterprise 3.1, where does the responsibility for the design of each component application lie? The answer in this example is between Peter the architect and the developer or senior developer responsible for the component application, and this is why I've chosen to call Ron the team leader rather than the technical leader. A lot bigger projects exist out there in the world than Icarus Enterprise 3.1, but I've chosen one of this size so that it's not too big to understand fairly easily. In a larger project a team would be allocated to each component application, maybe with a project manager. I could have made Icarus Enterprise 3.1 look like that, even though the functionality of the components is quite small, but I chose to allocate the project team realistically because I want to portray the usage of Team System in terms of moderate projects as well as large projects.

So returning to the planning of Enterprise 3.1, both the architect Peter and the team leader Ron will have some input. Ron will be more concerned with issues of build and organization, whereas Peter will be more concerned with technical issues at this stage. Last but certainly not least, Herman will have something to say about the iteration planning, since he has to test each one.

After much discussion, the Icarus team decides to allocate functionality across the iterations as shown in the sidebar "Allocating Functionality."

ALLOCATING FUNCTIONALITY

Envision Track, Plan Track

Iteration 0—Four Weeks

- Initial tasks, plan project, establish initial requirements, create architecture.

Plan Track

Iteration 1—Six Weeks

- Data model containing resources, orders, vendors, and customer tables. Vendors and customers are added via scripts for test purposes.

- Design to include capability for offline working for resource browsing and sales, but not to be demonstrable.

- Establish end-to-end operation of basic elements of listing management: create resource, list resources, edit resources.

- Establish end-to-end operation of basic elements of order creation: create order, list orders, edit orders.

- No authentication or authorization included.

- Above functionality includes elements in database, business logic, presentation, and client layers.

- Demonstrate performance and scalability for sales capabilities as above.

Iteration 2—Six Weeks

- Demonstrate basic offline working for resource browsing and sales capability.

- Demonstrate basic authentication and authorization capability for privileged users (travel agents and Icarus employees) to access multiple customers.

Plan Track, Build Track

Iteration 3—Four Weeks

- Demonstrate basic working of Sales Status application.

- Added listing functionality (detailed scenarios to be added at start of iteration).

- Added sales functionality (detailed scenarios to be added at start of iteration).

- Added authentication and authorization functionality (detailed scenarios to be added at start of iteration).

- Added offline functionality (detailed scenarios to be added at start of iteration).

Iteration 4—Four Weeks

- Added Sales Status application functionality (detailed scenarios to be added at start of iteration).

- Added listing functionality (detailed scenarios to be added at start of iteration).

- Added sales functionality (detailed scenarios to be added at start of iteration).

- Added authentication and authorization functionality (detailed scenarios to be added at start of iteration).

- Added offline functionality (detailed scenarios to be added at start of iteration).

Iteration 5—Four Weeks

- Complete Sales Status application functionality.

- Complete listing functionality.

- Complete sales functionality.

- Complete authentication and authorization functionality.

- Complete offline functionality.

Iteration 6—Two Weeks

- System test.

- Bug fix.

Iteration 7—Two Weeks

- System test.

- Bug fix.

Iteration 8—Two Weeks

- Bug fix.

- User acceptance test, staging.

- Deployment to production.

Total Duration 30 Weeks (Approx. 7 Months)

Clare uses Microsoft Project to make a schedule setting out the top-level plan, showing these iterations as a set of task work items. One way to do this is to create a place in the project structure called Schedules and then a subnode called Master, to contain all tasks that are part of the master schedule. You can then open Microsoft Project, select Team ➤ Choose Team Project, and select your project name—Enterprise 3.1 in this case. You can then type in the iterations as tasks, assign them the durations given earlier, and link all the iterations by dragging from the predecessor to the next iteration in the Gantt chart. You then must set the area path on each to Schedules\Master, specify the work item type as Task, and then click Publish on the Team toolbar. This will send the project to TFS and create work items of Task type for each of the tasks in the project.

You must also save the Microsoft Project file locally; otherwise you lose the start and end dates from the view seen in Project. Actually, the start and end dates are published to the server, but are not returned to Project when you retrieve the tasks. You can see the exact mapping between TFS Work Item fields and Project fields by choosing Team ➤ View Column Mappings, but you cannot modify these mappings once you have created the team project. Having saved the project file locally, you can then upload it to the TFS documents area using Team Explorer or the project portal. When you need to modify it, you must first open it locally in Project, and then click Refresh on the Team toolbar. This will update your local copy with any changes that have been made to the TFS version of the work items, but leave the fields that are not retrieved from TFS in their original state. When you have finished editing the file in Project, you can publish to TFS and save it locally.

When you consider it, this makes sense. TFS only knows about work items; it does not have the capability to store all the information that is in a Microsoft Project file, so the only thing exchanged between TFS and Project is the work items. Their start dates and finish dates are sent from Project to TFS but appear on lists of work items returned from queries only if you define the query to include those columns. The start and finish dates do not appear on the detail pane of the Query Results View. You can edit them as work item fields in Excel and save them back to TFS, but they will not be returned to Project. So the bottom line is that Project holds most scheduling information and forms the master copy of it as it applies to work items, but the master copy of the other aspects of the work items (such as the status and assignee) stays with TFS.

Clare uses this approach and produces the schedule shown in Figure 3-24. Of course, she can use features of Microsoft Project to add a lot more information to this schedule, such as budget, resource utilization, and so on.

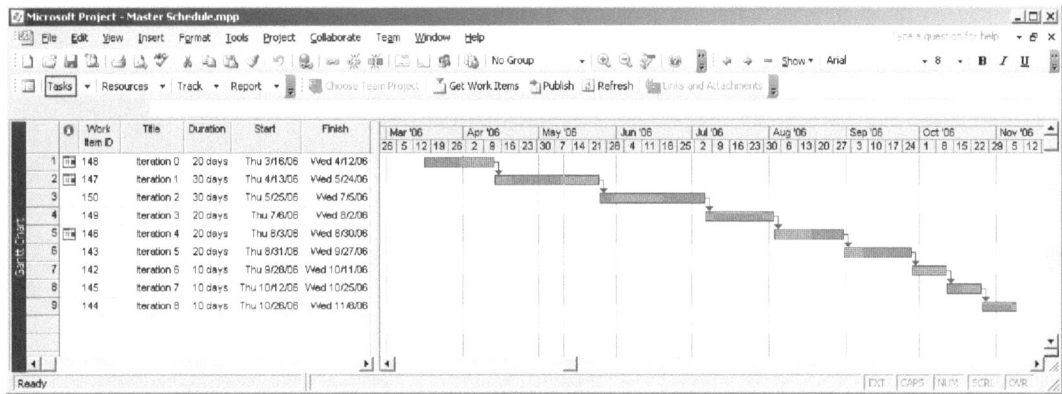

Figure 3-24. *Microsoft Project schedule for the iteration plan*

Summary

This chapter covered the beginning phase of the project and emphasized Team System features for the project manager.

I discussed the development processes included with Team Foundation Server, and you saw the reasons for the choice of MSF for CMMI Process Improvement for the Icarus project. We discussed briefly the installation of Team Foundation Server and its client machines, and you saw the creation of the Icarus Enterprise 3.1 Team project. I also summarized the project portal and its features.

For a new project, TFS generates a number of tasks automatically, according to the process selected. I described the meaning of these tasks within the chosen process, and you saw how the Icarus team allocated those tasks to team members. I showed how Microsoft Project can be used to organize task work items into a schedule and present them in the form of a Gantt chart.

We considered the planning of the project, with particular emphasis on reducing risk. I showed how the Icarus team divided the project into iterations, again using Microsoft Project, and allocated major areas of development to iterations.

The next chapter will follow the efforts of Susan, the requirements manager, as she works with Icarus stakeholders to put together the high-level customer requirements of the project.

CHAPTER 4

The Business Analyst: Creating the Personas, Use Cases, and Scenarios

I have already introduced Icarus, its business, and its rationale for pursuing the development of Icarus Enterprise 3.1. The purpose of this chapter is to describe how the early ideas about the proposed capability of the new system, described in Chapter 2, are refined in the development of the customer requirements documentation within Visual Studio Team System. At the end of this chapter, you should have a clear idea of the planned requirements of the new system and the features of Team System that support the activity of their definition. The chapter will show how the Icarus team follows the process of MSF for CMMI Process Improvement (MSF CMMI) in moving through their task. This is a large process suitable for very large projects—larger than Icarus Enterprise—and so the team will not need to use all of its features. This is not a book about process alone, and if I were to attempt to describe every document that may be included I would swamp the reader in the details and lose sight of my purpose. Rather, my intent is to give a view of the project from several angles, focused mainly on Team System, with sufficient detail in selected areas to be illustrative of a real project. Thus I will not present in this chapter every use case and every scenario, but only enough to demonstrate the process that is being followed and to give some insight into the technical challenges the project presents. Generally speaking, those functional areas that are treated in detail in this chapter will be treated in similar detail throughout the book as architecture, design, code, unit tests, and functional tests are examined.

The Requirements Process

Susan, William, and James, as the requirements team, agree to hold a series of meetings to come up with the set of personas and scenarios that will define the customer requirements for the Icarus Enterprise 3.1 project.

MSF CMMI specifies that the early requirements artifacts of a project will include a vision document, and a definition of the personas that will use the system with their lifestyle descriptions. The term *lifestyle descriptions* here refers to the characteristics of the personas that might affect their interaction with the product and upon which the design of the product might depend. For example, the requirements team could seek to understand the way travel agents might interact both with their customers and with the software, and how the customer-related events in their workday might affect their interaction with the product. You can see that this effort is all about understanding the human environment in which the proposed software is to provide benefit.

From there, MSF CMMI requires that customer requirements be developed in the form of *scenarios* and *quality-of-service (QoS) requirements*. From these, the team passes through a process of solution architecture and product requirements creation to arrive at *functional*, *interface*, *safety*, *security*, and *operational* requirements for the software product itself. This second set is intended to be the requirements of the product, as it is designed to meet the business requirements that were expressed only in the form of scenarios and QoS requirements. In a nutshell, this is how the requirements definition process in MSF CMMI is intended to work. Some of these terms are fairly obvious in their meaning, and the customer requirements terms will become clearer as you read through this chapter. The product requirements terms will be clarified more fully in Chapters 5 and 6, which cover solution architecture and product requirements.

What About Use Cases?

Anyone who is familiar with business analysis using Unified Modeling Language (UML) will be familiar with the concept of a use case and use case diagrams. These diagrams provide a tool for documenting the dynamic behavior of a system by defining use cases and showing their relationships. A *use case* is a collection of functionality that the system provides for use by an *actor*. An actor is an entity, usually a human, that interacts with the system and uses its capability. A use case diagram shows use cases, their interaction with actors, and their relationships with other use cases. For instance, it can show one use case as a *generalization* of another use case, so that an example use case Buy Car would be a generalization of Buy New Car. It can also show "extend" and "include" associations between use cases. An extended use case is one that has the functionality of the original but with more added, whereas an include relationship implies that one use case makes use of the functionality of another use case in implementing a larger piece of functionality.

Figure 4-1 shows an example. A use case called Make Purchase includes functionality such as Browse Catalog, Select into Basket, Proceed to Checkout, Make Payment, and Update Delivery Details. All the ellipses on the diagram represent use cases, and one "actor" (called a persona in MSF CMMI) is shown who represents a certain class of people who interact with the system described by the diagram. This actor, Customer, is shown using the Make Purchase use case, and this is the only use case on the diagram with which that individual interacts. Why are the other five displayed? The answer is that they give more information about the Make Purchase use case in that they describe certain parts of it independently. The diagram shows, by the include relationships, that for example Make Purchase *includes* another piece of functionality called Browse Catalog, and that piece of functionality is sufficiently self-contained to have an ellipse of its own and be regarded as a separate use case—similarly with Select into Basket. The Browse Catalog use case does not have to be used only as part of Make Purchase; it could be used on its own—the customer could browse the catalog without making a purchase. This diagram therefore provides a very good way of describing the overall functionality of the system and breaking it down into smaller pieces of component functionality. This process, known as functional decomposition, serves to identify manageable chunks of capability that can be designed, developed, and tested one at a time.

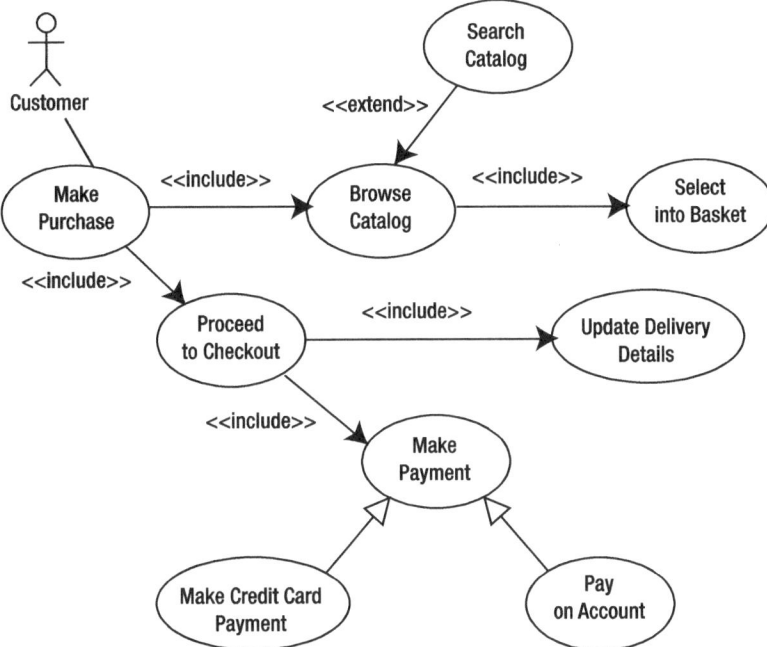

Figure 4-1. *An example use case diagram showing the use of the include, generalize, and extend relationships between use cases*

In this example, generalization and extension is also shown. The Make Payment use case is a generalization of the more specific Make Credit Card Payment and Pay on Account use cases. The Search Catalog use case extends the Browse Catalog use case by providing additional capability, over and above manual search capability, to automatically look through the catalog to find possible items that match the user's requirements.

Notice that the diagram does not say anything about the way in which the use cases will be implemented or their order of execution. A use case is just a piece of capability, an encapsulation of some things the system can do for the actor.

A use case can be described completely by a set of scenarios. Each of these is one unique, clearly defined path through the use case, identified by a finite, defined number of steps leading to an end result required by the actor. Scenarios can, however, be *success* or *failure* scenarios; a failure scenario includes some exception situation that arises for a reason that is defined and repeatable. It is also a valid response of the system that can be specified and tested. Here is an example related to Figure 4-1.

1. The user opens the catalog.

2. The user selects Widgets from the menu, and the system displays a list of many different sorts of widgets: cheap widgets, expensive widgets, pocket widgets, widgets that hang on the wall, widgets that stand on the floor, and so on!

3. The user selects a nice-looking widget from the list that appeals to his or her artistic tastes and clicks Add to Cart.

4. The system displays the user's shopping cart with the chosen widget listed in the cart, the price displayed, and the total calculated.

This scenario is one that belongs to the Browse Catalog use case, but it also belongs to the Make Purchase use case because of the include relationship. Obviously, each of the use cases in Figure 4-1 contains many scenarios.

In UML, a set of use cases is defined and displayed in this manner on use case diagrams, and their realization is designed in terms of their scenarios, as just described. Classes of objects that will act together to implement these scenarios are then defined and their interactions represented on class diagrams. The implementation of each scenario using objects of these classes is then represented in UML either by composite structure diagrams (a UML-2 concept), collaboration diagrams (called communication diagrams in UML-2), or sequence diagrams, so that realization of a particular use case will involve a set of such diagrams. The sequence diagrams and collaboration diagrams represent unique paths through the system, corresponding to the use case scenarios that will need to be tested.

UML has always been a rich modeling tool, and with UML-2 it has become even richer, so it is beyond the scope of this book to explore it much further. Composite structure, communication, and sequence diagrams are not currently supported by Team System, but that does not mean you should not create them using Visio and include the documents within the team project as part of the design process.

Team System and MSF CMMI do not deal with use cases either, but this is not to say that we should assume Microsoft sees the scenarios defined in Team System as being a replacement for use cases in UML. There is no capability in Team System for scenarios to be defined that extend, include, or generalize other scenarios. There is a capability for scenarios to be linked to a set of other scenarios, but no indication that Microsoft intends this linking to imply any of the three relationships shown in use case diagrams. Indeed, the definition of a scenario is quite clearly "a type of work item that records a single path of user interaction through the system." Use cases are a more general concept; each needs a set of scenarios to define it fully, so I do not believe scenarios are a replacement for use cases. It's also perhaps arguable whether a set of requirements can ever be described by a finite set of scenarios, whereas with use cases, you are at liberty to describe them in prose and diagrams, so you can use any conceptual definition that is appropriate. One thing it's safe to assume is that actors in use case diagrams are much the same concept as the personas we define for MSF CMMI.

So the bottom line is that scenarios, as defined in Team System, are the things we track as work items and associate with iterations, code check-in, and tests. They represent the user requirements but are an end result of whatever other method of analysis our BAs are following. In this chapter I will show how the BA team at Icarus utilizes use case methods with Visio to arrive at a set of scenarios.

There is, however, another end result set of requirements from the business analysis, the QoS requirements, which must also be associated with iterations and tests. The derivation of these from the business is, in a sense, a different dimension of the requirements process, or another view of the requirements.

At the first meeting, the requirements team discusses and agrees on the general process of requirements definition that will follow MSF CMMI, with the addition of use case analysis. Susan feels that use cases are a necessary precursor to scenarios for the reasons described earlier: that they set down the functional breakdown of the project and lead to easy division of the scenarios into groups and priorities. The planned set of requirements activities is shown in Figure 4-2 and is a portion of the iteration 0 activities shown in Figure 3-7 in Chapter 3.

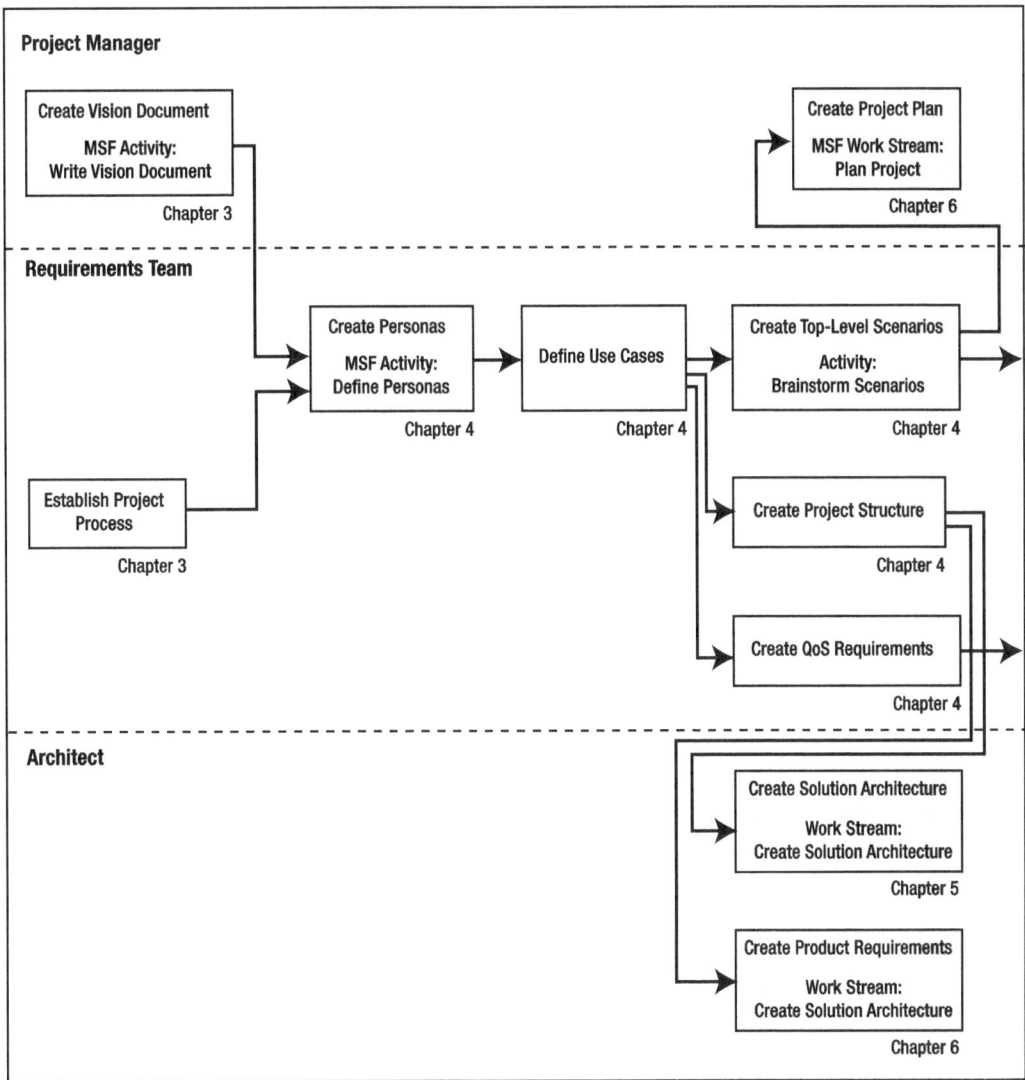

Figure 4-2. *Approximate sequence of activities making up the requirements definition phase.*

Define Personas

The Define Personas activity from the MSF CMMI process guidance is shown in Figure 4-3, but let's first review what is meant by the term *persona*. If you look in the index of the process guidance for MSF CMMI, under Work Products, you'll find *persona* defined thus:

> *A persona describes the typical skills, abilities, needs, desires, working habits, tasks, and backgrounds of a particular set of users. A persona is fictional reality, collecting together real data describing the important characteristics of a particular user group in a fictional character. By doing so, it becomes easier to talk and reason about the whole user*

group, since we can relate to, and understand individuals more easily than we can a group. Each time we refer to a persona, we feel like we are addressing an individual, but we are in effect addressing the group that the persona represents.

Figure 4-3. *The process guidance page for the Define Personas activity supplied with MSF for CMMI Process Improvement*

So there you have it: each persona is an example from a group of individuals who are going to interact with the system. In the case of Icarus, we can immediately see three main groups of personas:

- Employees who work in the call centers; answer calls from customers, vendors, and travel agents; and use the Sales Wing application in responding to those calls

- Customers who use the Sales website, talk to the call center, or deal with travel agents

- Vendors and their employees who list their services, either by talking with Icarus employees or by using the List Wing application

The definition of personas certainly allows us to wax creative and let our imaginations have free rein. Maybe this is a point in the project to have a bit of fun—we could even hang pictures or cartoons of our personas around the office and invent all kinds of details about their imaginary lives. OK, but before our team members all turn into scriptwriters for daytime soaps, let's think what's important about persona definition for these three groups.

Really, for Icarus's employees, we are only interested in their work lives—that is, what they do during their workday at Icarus. We're interested in the tasks they need to perform and how they do those tasks, what problems and issues they face, which tasks take up a lot of time, how the software can improve these, and so forth.

For Icarus's customers, we *are* a little more interested in their personal lives, because Icarus wants to sell them products that will fit in nicely with their travel aspirations, the way they like to travel, their interests, and the things they want to do. We are also interested in their lives when they are not traveling since this might dictate how they choose to interact with Icarus when they make their orders. For example, a person who is familiar with computers (I'm not going to use the words "wiz," "geek," or "techie" on principle, but you know what I mean) might naturally feel at home ordering Icarus's products online. On the other hand, he or she may be too busy to spend the time. Just because a person is able to do something does not mean that individual does not want to use other people to do time-consuming tasks, such as sorting through hotels on the Internet. Certainly, though, a person who does not have a computer or cannot cope with the Internet will want to work through either a travel agent or Icarus's call center. Of course, the idea of personas is important to Icarus's business plans and advertising, but here we must limit ourselves to how those personas will interact efficiently and pleasantly with Icarus—and of course come back time and again.

Turning to the people at Icarus's vendors, as with Icarus's employees, we are only interested in aspects of their work lives. Of course, they may be customers as well, but then they become a different persona. We should remember that people involved with vendors may be employees of a business owner, or perhaps they may be business owners themselves, since many of Icarus's providers are small hotel owners and similar owner/operators.

Personas: Icarus Employees

The requirements team meets to discuss the subject of personas. They decide on a format for the persona documents similar to that suggested by MSF CMMI and identify personas that apply to the project as described in the next sections. William and James agree to use their own names for the executive personas—a good indication of their commitment and enthusiasm for the project! Remember that, although MSF CMMI suggests giving names to personas, each persona represents a group. The name simply identifies an *example* member of that group. Indeed, some people might find the use of a person's name confusing and prefer to use names such as Customer, Vendor Employee, Call Center Operator, and so on.

Rajiv: Call Center Sales Operator

This person is employed by Icarus to work in a call center handling direct sales to Icarus's customers. He will answer telephone calls from customers who wish to make, modify, cancel or seek information about ordering resources offered by Icarus.

This persona will deal pleasantly with customers and be familiar with Icarus's business policy, but generally will perform a routine job using the system in repetitive ways. This persona is at the forefront of Icarus's business and will be well trained to deal with customers and use the system efficiently and quickly.

Julie: Vendor Administrator

This person is employed by Icarus to work in a call center handling sales of Icarus's service to vendors. She will answer telephone calls from vendors who wish to add to, modify, delete or seek information about the resources they are currently offering for sale by Icarus. Julie will also deal with potential vendors who want to open accounts with Icarus and with inquiries from vendors about payment and other business matters.

She is also in the forefront of Icarus's business and will deal pleasantly and efficiently with vendors and be familiar with Icarus's business policy, but also will perform a routine job using the system in a repetitive manner.

Jill: Call Center Sales Supervisor

Jill is one of the supervisors at the California call center, but the call centers overseas have the same personas. There are three supervisors who look after the day-to-day, middle management of about 30 call center sales operators. As well as general supervision, they handle difficult customers or nonstandard requirements from customers—anything for which the call center operators are not trained or that is not routine. They also handle administration of the call center operator user accounts, such as creating new accounts and assigning privileges. Jill and her peers report to William.

William: Sales Executive

William reports directly to Icarus's CEO and has the responsibility for management of Icarus's sales operation worldwide. He will be interested in reports of sales and their breakdown into geographic regions, categories, and providers. He will be a participant in the long-term planning of Icarus's business, in particular the choice of vendors and negotiations regarding pricing and margins. He will also work with his supervisors to identify which sales staff are most effective, so he will be interested in sales figures arranged by call center sales operators.

James: Vendor Executive

James reports directly to Icarus's CEO and has the responsibility for management of the listing side of Icarus's business. His job is that of providing listed products and services from vendors for William's team to sell. He will be interested in the same reports as William, in particular sales broken down by vendor, and will provide feedback personally to the larger vendors and negotiate with them regarding business matters. He supervises the team of vendor administrators worldwide.

Personas: Customers

In the customers group the team includes people who buy travel services from Icarus and also the travel agents who make reservations on behalf of customers.

Sam: Internet Customer

Sam is a typical twenty-something, computer-savvy customer of Icarus. He has his own home computer and installs various software products, using it for both work and games. Travel is one of his passions, and he browses the Internet regularly looking for his next trip destination and arrangements. He has a fair amount of disposable income, but lives in a city with high costs and so is quite budget conscious.

Mrs. Gentle: Call Center Customer

Mrs. Gentle is a 73-year-old widow, living in Pasadena. She owns a 350-cubic-inch 1973 Chevrolet Camaro, with an odometer reading of only 8,000 miles. She is quite familiar with using the telephone but is terrified of computers. Despite her age, she is healthy and active, and is fond of travel. She has made several orders with the Over 50s Adventure Trekking Company of Kathmandu, a veteran vendor with Icarus.

Mr. Lightly: Travel Agent Customer

Mr. Lightly is a self-employed painting contractor living in a suburban area of London. He owns a computer, which he uses for printing his business invoices with the help of his son. His computer skills are patchy and he intends to brush up on them one day. A colorful character, he typically enjoys two holidays a year in various parts of the world, often reserving his hotel accommodations through Icarus.

Rose: Travel Agent

Rose is a travel agent with a business in South London, UK. She owns the business and employs three other staff members, all of whom use computers for a variety of uses concerned with the business. She has learned quite a lot about computers, but prefers to concentrate on the "people" side of her business.

Personas: Vendors

In the vendors group the team includes owners and employees of businesses that list services for sale by Icarus.

Dominic: Resource Business Owner

Dominic owns a hotel with 15 rooms in Naples. He is a very busy small businessman with little time to spare. His English is rather limited. His computer skills are quite good and he uses Microsoft Word for all of his letters, uses an accounting package for his books, and takes advantage of the Internet regularly for business needs.

Maria: Resource Business Employee

Maria works as a receptionist and administrator at Venice Water Excursions, a business that offers gondola tours of the canals of Venice, water taxi services, and one larger tour boat traveling to the outlying islands. Maria has many duties in the business, part of which is sales and advertising. She is knowledgeable about computers and has taken on the role of keeping the listings on Icarus up to date for the tours and taxi reservations available from the business for which she works.

Use Case Analysis

In their next meeting, the requirements team begins to determine the use cases. They start by defining high-level use cases that describe in general terms the things that will be needed from the main areas of functionality in Enterprise 3.1. At the end of the meeting, they have put together a top-level use case diagram for the application on the whiteboard, which Susan later adds to a Visio document, shown in Figure 4-4.

Note Exercise 4-1 applies to this section.

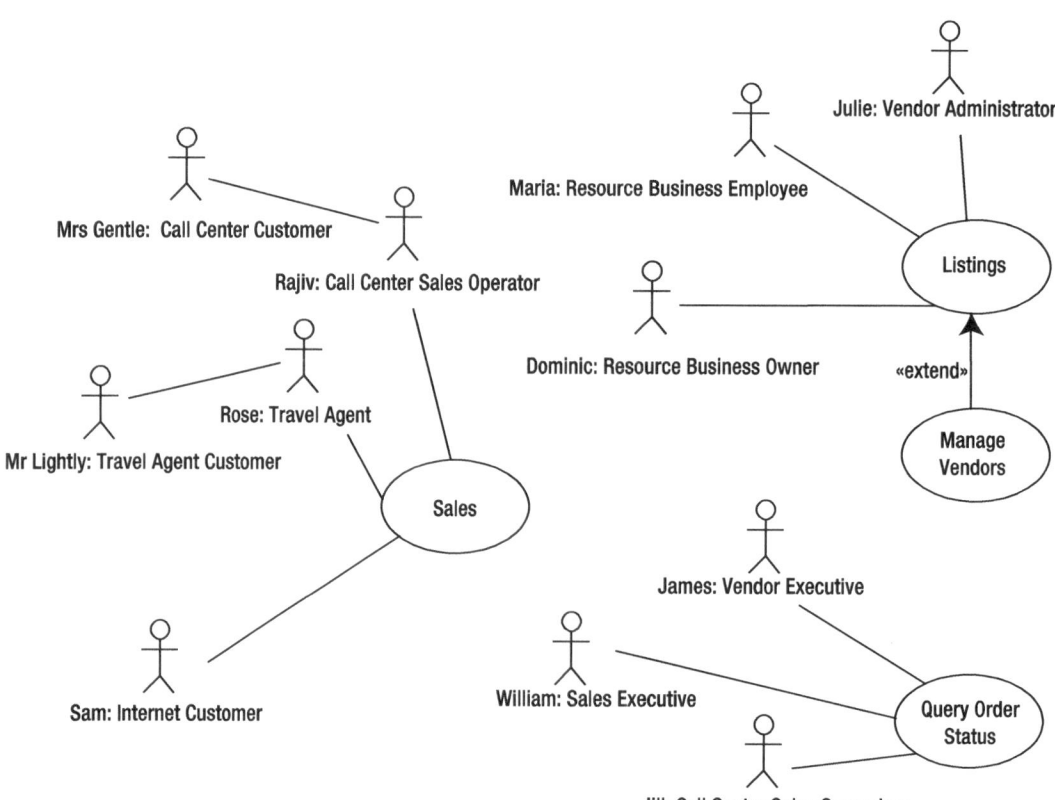

Figure 4-4. *Top-level use case diagram for the Icarus Enterprise 3.1 application*

It's important to add these documents, which are essential software artifacts, to the team project, so Susan opens Team Explorer, right-clicks on the Requirements folder under `Documents` in the Enterprise 3.1 project, and selects Upload Document from the context menu. A dialog box opens that allows Susan to select a file from anywhere on her machine. She selects the Visio document `Enterprise 3-1 Use Case Diagram.vsd` in My Documents and clicks Open. This copies the document to Team Foundation Server and it becomes part of the project.

You can do the same thing by dragging a file from a Windows Explorer window to the desired location in Team Explorer. Once you've uploaded a document to Team Foundation Server, you can open it to view by simply double-clicking or by right-clicking and selecting Open. To edit the document, you must select Edit from the context menu, in which case you can save your changes back to Team Foundation Server.

The top-level use case diagram in Figure 4-4 shows all of the defined actors and the parts of Enterprise 3.1 with which they will interact. Actually, the team has been a bit loose with the UML definition; the diagram shows actors interacting with other actors, just to remind us that some customer personas interact with travel agent personas and call center personas rather than directly with the software. I never mind bending rules in diagrams if it gets the point across.

The diagram shows the Sales use case with actors Rajiv, the call center sales operator, and Rose, the travel agent, interacting with it. The actor Sam, the Internet customer, also interacts with the Sales use case. This will need further elaboration, but for now, the team knows that it includes everything to allow the call center sales team to sell reservations for the listed resources, including managing customer accounts. It also allows Internet customers to buy, modify, and view reservations, as well as handle their own customer accounts.

Next the diagram shows a Listings use case that contains all of the things that the actors need to manage listings—that is, resources like hotel rooms, tours, and educational courses that vendors offer for sale. The actors interacting with this use case are Julie, the vendor administrator; Maria, the vendor business employee; and Dominic, the vendor business owner. The use case is extended by Manage Vendors, which allows authorized operators to view, add, and modify vendors as well as manage the resources they provide. At this level in the design, the team has not yet had time to elaborate the Listings use case into its included functions, but they know that this will include the features needed for vendors to add, modify or delete resources. The Manage Vendors extension will allow Julie to add or remove vendors and also perform such tasks as resetting their passwords when they forget them.

The Query Order Status use case contains everything that the executive actors William and James need to obtain reports of order activity, by period, by geographic location, by category, and by provider. They will also be able to view orders made by individual staff in order to monitor performance.

Sales Use Case

The Sales use case is broken down into its component parts in Figure 4-5, which shows how the actors or personas interact with its included use cases. Remember, we could put a ring around all but the actors in Figure 4-5 and label it "Sales." The Internet customer actor, Sam, interacts with three use cases, Browse Catalog, Manage Orders, and Manage Customer Account. As a customer or potential customer, he arrives at the company's site and browses the resources that are offered for sale by various vendors, looking through an online catalog organized by geographic location, by category and by provider. He may also perform a search according to specific criteria and inquire about availability of particular resources on particular dates. He does not need to be a registered customer with Icarus, or be authenticated in order to do this.

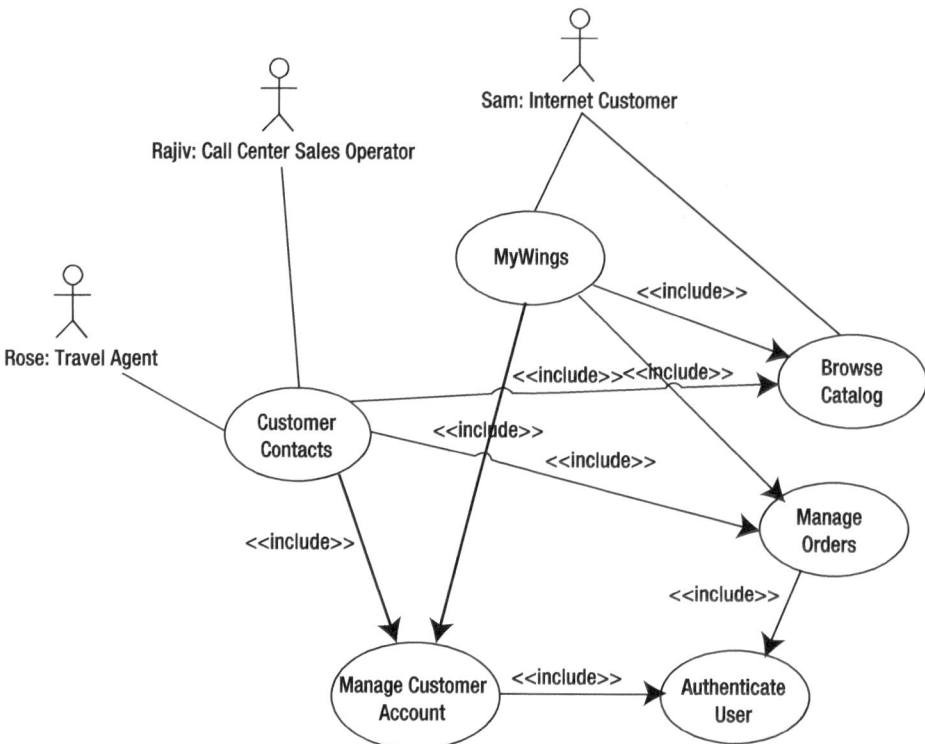

Figure 4-5. *Top-level use case diagram for the Sales use case*

Sam may also interact with the Manage Orders use case, which involves things like making a new order, viewing details of his existing orders, modifying or canceling an existing order—within allowable limits according to the business. To perform these functions he will need to be a registered customer with Icarus and to have been authenticated as genuinely being that registered customer. Thus in Figure 4-5, the Manage Orders use case includes the Authenticate User use case, since an attempt to go through part of the Manage Orders functions will involve either performing a new authentication or checking that the user is authenticated.

The third use case that forms part of the Sales use case is Manage Customer Account. This allows Sam to manage the details of his account with Icarus, such as his password, his mailing and email addresses, his credit card, and so forth. This use case also includes Authentication, as obviously he needs to be authenticated before he can view or change his personal details.

The Browse Catalog, Manage Orders, and the Manage Customer Account use cases form part of a main use case offered to registered Icarus users. Called My Wings, this is the basic use case with which authenticated Internet users interact, and forms a personalized home page on the website.

Both Rajiv, the call center operator, and Rose, the travel agent, also interact with the Manage Orders use case, but we can consider their highest level of use case as being Customer Contacts. This is the use case that represents a sequence of events, each consisting of an interaction with a customer and use of the system to meet the customers' needs during the interaction. The customer, say Mr. Lightly, could be sitting in Rose's office while she uses the Sales Wing software to search for hotel accommodations in, say Rome, and then make an order, print out the receipt, and pay for the order from the agent's account, accepting a check from Mr. Lightly.

Rajiv could be speaking to Mrs. Gentle and be checking her reservation for whitewater rafting on the Dudh Kosi, perhaps modifying her order to include her daughter. On the other hand, Rajiv could be talking to a new customer and accepting information to create an account for that individual. The use cases Browse Catalog, Manage Orders, and Manage Customer Account are therefore included in the Customer Contacts use case.

Authentication works a little differently for Rajiv and Rose compared to Sam, since they need to authenticate once during their session and then deal with many customer accounts during that one authenticated session.

This brings us to the subject of authorization, the job of checking if a particular user is permitted to do the action they are attempting. Though Sam is authenticated using the same use case as Rose and Rajiv, his rights are much more limited. He can only access orders that belong to his account, and he can only access details of his account. Similarly Rose can access orders belonging to any of her customers, but she cannot access the orders of other travel agents that sell Icarus offerings. Rajiv is much more powerful in that he can access orders of any of Icarus customers, including those of any travel agent. However, Jill, the call center supervisor, has all of Rajiv's rights, but also the ability to modify the privileges of other system users and add privileged accounts.

The Browse Catalog, Manage Orders, and Manage Customer Account use cases need to be taken down to a lower level before scenarios can be identified. The requirements team develops the use cases using Visio, and adds the specification for each in the description text included in each use case symbol on the Visio diagram.

As we split up the functionality into these use cases, we can start to get a little insight into how this will look in practice. We leave the storyboarding of the scenarios of these use cases until later, but it does help to have a few thoughts as to how the client Windows applications might be designed to present these use cases to the operators. For example, it is quite clear from Figure 4-5 that the Customer Contacts use case is only required by the travel agent Rose and call center operator Rajiv and not by the home customer, Sam. This difference in functionality might nicely match the difference in implementation. Peter's initial plans include Windows Forms applications for the call centers and travel agents, and a web forms, browser-based application for the home customer. The main window of the Windows Forms application can perhaps be built around the Customer Contacts use case, which is required by Rose and Rajiv but not by the home customer, Sam. We might consider the Windows Forms, Sales Wing application a multiple document interface application, and think of each document as representing a customer. So, for example, Rose might be working privately on Mrs. Gentle's travel reservations, when Mr. Lightly calls on the telephone, so she leaves Mrs. Gentle as an open customer contact, and opens Mr. Lightly's travel plans. Perhaps the main window should be a master-detail screen showing the customers on the left and their details on the right. Browsing resources, searching, and adding orders could then be implemented as modal dialog boxes.

When drawing use case diagrams using Visio, a specification of the use case can be included in the symbol itself. Here is the specification for the Customer Contacts use case:

USE CASE: CUSTOMER CONTACTS

General Description

The user will be able to keep track of customer contacts organized by customer, date, and time of contact and resource reservation.

There will be a list of customers on the left of the screen, with customer detail on the right for the customer selected on the left.

The right side of the screen will consist of a set of tabs as follows:

1. Customer Details: Name, Address, Telephone, Email, etc.

2. Customer Orders: A list of orders ordered by date

3. Billing information for the customer

Each customer order will have detail represented in a page, which will display as a **modal** dialog box and may be accessed by double-clicking on an order.

In a similar vein, we see that the My Wings use case can form a tidy home page that the home user will arrive at after authentication, from which they can navigate to other activities they will require, such as checking current orders, placing new orders, or changing their account details. So the web-based Manage Orders functionality can be built around this as the home base. The team will need to look at this more when the storyboard phase is reached and when the product requirements—as opposed to the customer requirements—are established.

Browse Catalog Use Case

Figure 4-6 shows the Browse Catalog use case expanded to show its included use cases—remember, all this is ultimately included in the Sales use case. Navigate Catalog allows navigation of lists within catalogs ordered by geographic location, by category and by provider. Each catalog is a hierarchy of lists ending with a single resource page showing details of the resource. Navigation by each of these methods represents a different use case. Another use case, View Resource Details, is entered when the user has drilled down to a resource, and displays individual pages showing the detailed information that is available about any one particular resource listed for reservation. The View Resource Details use case also forms part of the main Browse Catalog use case, since a user can enter a resource number and go directly to the detail page.

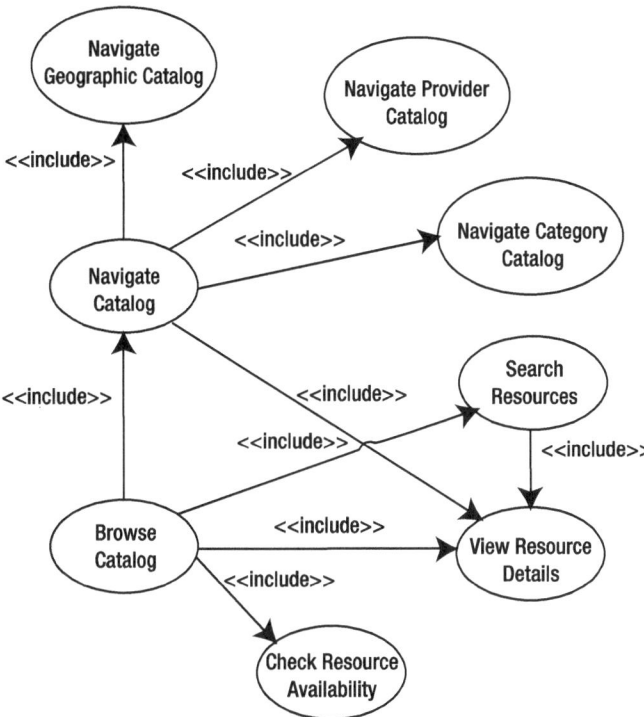

Figure 4-6. *Use case diagram for the Browse Catalog use case*

Figure 4-7 illustrates the structure of the resource catalog. The specification of the Browse Catalog use case is:

USE CASE: BROWSE CATALOG

The user may browse through the catalog in various ways to find a suitable resource. Access may be obtained via

1. Navigating through a hierarchical set of catalogs

2. Searching for resources meeting certain criteria

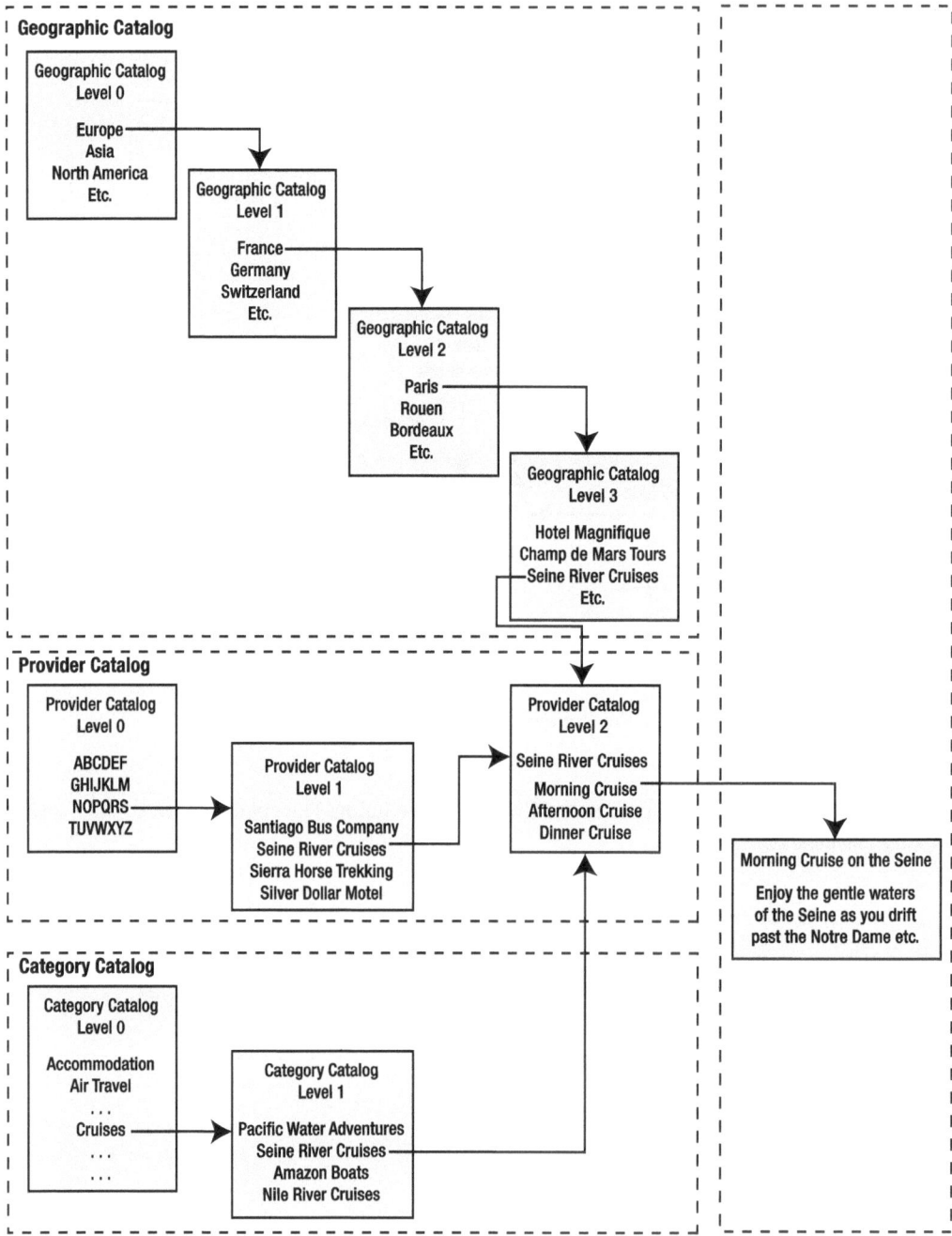

Figure 4-7. *The structure of the resource catalog*

The options for viewing the catalog, included in the Browse Catalog use case, form separate included use cases, as in Figure 4-6. These included use cases are specified next:

USE CASE: NAVIGATE CATALOG

The user will have the capability to navigate a catalog of resources available from Icarus's vendors via Icarus. There will be three ways of navigating the catalog to find a suitable resource:

1. Navigate by geographic area.

2. Navigate by alphabetic listing of provider names.

3. Navigate by resource category.

Again the three ways of navigating are separate included use cases as in Figure 4-6, specified next:

USE CASE: NAVIGATE GEOGRAPHIC CATALOG

The user will be able to navigate a catalog that is organized by geographic region to narrow down available vendor choices to a particular country or city.

Each level in the catalog will represent a geographic region, the highest being the entire world, and display a list of regions within that region. At the lowest level in the catalog, the vendors in that region will be listed.

At any screen during the navigation, the user will be able to page up or down if there are more geographic regions at that level than can be displayed on the screen.

The user will also be able to click on a listed geographic region to navigate to a lower level in the hierarchy and see the regions at that lower level displayed. The user will also be able to move up a level by clicking a special button or link on the page that indicates up.

At the lowest level, the list of geographic regions will be replaced by a list of vendors within that region.

Clicking on a vendor in the list will enter the Navigate Provider Catalog use case and display the list of resources offered by that provider.

The default entry point to this use case will present the user with a top-level list of the geographic regions in which Icarus's vendors offer resources.

There will also be an entry point that allows entry direct to a particular region at its level by specifying a region.

The entire hierarchy of regions will be configurable by tables in the database.

USE CASE: NAVIGATE PROVIDER CATALOG

The user will be able to navigate a catalog that is organized by vendor name to narrow down available vendor choices to a particular named provider. The catalog will be organized into sections according to the letters of the alphabet.

At any screen during the navigation, the user will be able to page up or down, if there are more provider names or resource names in the displayed set than can be displayed on the screen.

Clicking on a vendor in the list will display the list of resources offered by that provider.

The default entry point to this use case will present the user with a set of alphabet letters A–Z. Clicking on any of these will navigate to a page listing all of the providers whose names begin with that letter.

There will also be an entry point that allows entry direct to a particular provider's resource list by specifying a provider name at entry.

The entire grouping of providers will be configurable by tables in the database.

USE CASE: NAVIGATE CATEGORY CATALOG

The user will be able to navigate a catalog that is organized by resource category to narrow down available resource choices to a particular type of resource. Each level in the catalog will represent a category of resource or subcategory, the highest being the list of the broadest categories available. At the lowest level in the catalog, the resources of a particular vendor will be listed.

At any screen during the navigation, the user will be able to page up or down if there are more categories or resources in the set at that level than can be displayed on the screen.

The user will be able to click on a listed category to navigate to a lower level in the hierarchy and see the categories at that lower level displayed. The user will also be able to move up a level by clicking a special button or link on the page that indicates up.

At the lowest level, the list of categories will be replaced by a list of resources offered by a particular vendor.

Clicking on a resource in the list will enter the View Resource Details use case and display the details of the resource selected.

The default entry point to this use case will present the user with a top-level list of the categories of resource available.

There will also be an entry point that allows entry direct to a particular level by specifying a category.

The entire hierarchy of categories will be configurable by tables in the database.

USE CASE: SEARCH RESOURCES

The user will be able to search a catalog of resources by specifying any or all of the following criteria:

- Resource name, or partial name entered in a text box

- Vendor name, or partial name entered in a text box

- Resource geographic region, selected from a set of available regions

- Resource type, selected from a list of available resource types

- Resource availability date

After clicking a search button, the user will be presented with a list of resources satisfying the search criteria, with the above five fields listed in columns.

The user may page up or down in the list if there are too many returned from the search to be displayed on the screen.

The user will be able to click on a listed resource, which will cause entry into the View Resource Details use case displaying the details of the selected resource.

The entire list of geographic regions and resource types that may be selected for the search will be configurable in the database.

USE CASE: VIEW RESOURCE DETAIL

This use case will allow the user to view the details, including pictures of a particular resource.

USE CASE: CHECK RESOURCE AVAILABILITY

The user will be able to display availability dates and times for a specified resource.

The display will depict a calendar, each page showing a month. Each day in the month will indicate by color if the resource is available or not. If there are multiple units of a resource, say rooms in a hotel or places on a tour, a numeric indication will be provided.

Some resources may be available at various times of the day. In these cases the user may click on the day in the calendar, which will display a day showing times that the resource is available.

The user may page from month to month, or day to day, by clicking next and previous buttons.

Manage Orders

The Manage Orders use case is expanded in Figure 4-8 to show five included use cases: View Orders, Make New Order, Modify Order, and Cancel Order. View Orders allows a customer to view his or her orders, that is, those that are associated with the customer's account. It also allows travel agents to view orders of any of their customers, and it allows call center operators to view all the orders. View Orders includes several use cases: Browse Orders by Customer, Browse Orders by Provider, and Search Orders. Manage Orders also includes the Authenticate User use case since it will sometimes be entered by an unauthenticated user, from the catalog. It also includes a use case called Authorize User, which determines if the authenticated user is authorized to perform defined actions such as viewing orders that are not their own or attached to them as an agent, or to modify or cancel any specific order.

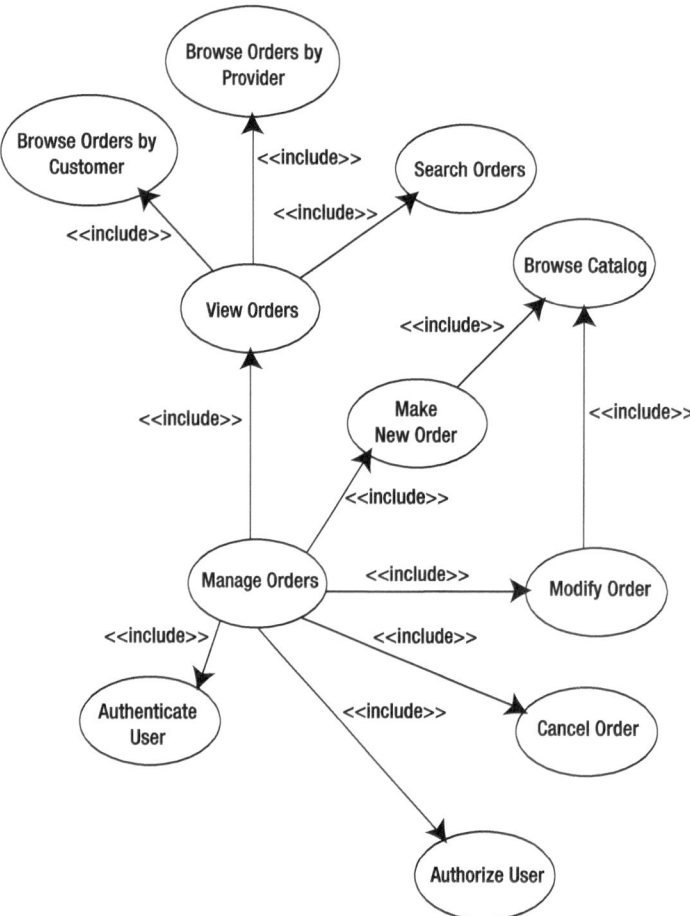

Figure 4-8. *Included use cases for Manage Orders*

The Make New Order use case includes the various ways in which a new order can be made, either by searching the resources or by being entered with a specific resource number defined. It provides a sequence of screens that allow the user to specify dates, numbers of people, and other information about their order, and finally requires payment. The sequence allows for the user to add more resources to the order before proceeding to payment.

Modify Order is entered from View Orders or Search Orders, or by specifying an order number. It displays the detailed information relating to a specific order, page by page, and allows the information to be changed, within limits determined by the conditions attached to the particular resource.

Cancel Order is entered in the same way and allows cancellation of the order within the limits of business rules attached to the resource.

Offline Working for Travel Agents

One of the features of Windows smart clients is the ability to provide some degree of offline working, which means that the client application can operate and provide some level of the functionality when disconnected from the servers providing the business web services and the database. The amount of offline working functionality available depends, of course, on the definition of the system. If for example it is absolutely necessary that the clients always see the most up-to-date record of the status of the database, offline working is clearly impossible. Nevertheless, even in this situation, we can at least provide to our clients a graceful indication that the connection is down and normal functionality is not available. The help system can certainly be available even then. This is much better than simply throwing an unrecognizable exception.

Sales Wing Offline Working Capability

The requirements team holds an offline working brainstorming session. It includes for the first time a representative from Trendy Travel, a company in Sydney, Australia, that has agreed to be a beta site for Icarus. Ian McKenzie works as an agent-partner with Trendy Travel, has worked with Icarus via their call center and website for two years, and is enthusiastic about making the search and order process more efficient by having a richer, customer-centric interface for the client application. The customer-centric nature of the user interface is brought out by the existence of the main use case, Customer Contacts in Figure 4-5.

Ian has been brought to California for a two-week period to help define the requirements for the Sales Wing smart client, and it being February, he is looking forward to a weekend of good skiing while he is here. Ian thinks that to have any value at all, an individual travel agent's list of clients should be stored entirely locally, along with their current orders. This does not seem to be a very large amount of data and no more than a travel agent would expect to store in maintaining their client database. It enables an agent to respond to a client's inquiries about their current orders and lets the agent review this information when they are not connected to the Internet. Situations in which disconnection occurs are mainly through the use of laptops, when traveling or at home. Ian travels on a train to work each day and finds it very useful to review his clients or think of suggestions during this period. Also, although Ian has a DSL connection at home, he is not particularly technical, does not have a home network, and often likes to use his laptop in the living room away from his home computer—which his children use for their schoolwork.

Ian would really like to be able to browse through available resources and make orders for his clients while on the train. This poses a much more difficult problem since

a. It requires much of the Icarus database of resources (possibly all) to be available on the client machine, causing a problem both with disk space and with data bandwidth during download.

b. There is a problem of synchronization as the Icarus resource database may change while the client is offline, and resources may be added or deleted or become unavailable through other reservations.

c. There is a possibility that a client may make changes to their own orders via the website or call center while the travel agent is offline, so that the travel agent's copy of their orders is out of date, or the Icarus database copy is out of date.

d. Icarus management is concerned about the security aspects of allowing so much of their database to be on client sites.

After some discussion, a compromise solution is reached regarding points (a) and (d). The results of a limited number of the most recent searches will be stored locally on the client.

There will also be an overall limit of a specified number of resources that can be stored locally and a limit on the size of the data. This solution sounds very reasonable since data from searches is downloaded as the search proceeds and thus would impose no additional bandwidth issues. However, this is not quite true because a search will typically list all the hotels in, say, Barcelona, but will not usually download the resource detail page for every item in the list. Doing this might well make presentation of the search results slower, so the download of detail pages should take place in the background. It is expected that some of the detail pages will contain a lot of data—images in particular—so again, to keep the data transfer reasonable, a *summary* detail page will be defined for each resource that will not contain images, but it will contain enough information to allow the travel agent to suggest and make tentative orders for the client.

The synchronization issue, point (b), poses some difficulty, since there is absolutely no way that a travel agent can make an order offline and be sure that the resource is still available. In many ways you can view this as an extended case of an optimistic concurrency (or optimistic locking) arrangement. In optimistic concurrency, users of a system download information and make changes in the knowledge that other users may be doing the same thing and that their changes may clash. If this happens, then an optimistic concurrency exception is raised when a user tries to save his modified data, only to be told that the system has discovered that it has been changed and saved by someone else before he could attempt to save his modified data. Usually the system simply discards his changes and presents a curt message. The first user to open in this example is actually the last user to save, and the first user to save "wins" under the optimistic concurrency arrangement. This tough-luck approach is only acceptable if it happens rarely, and so optimistic concurrency is used when this kind of clash is likely to be a rare event.

Why is this similar to the problem with the offline travel agent? Well, Agent A could place an order having been told that resources are available on a given date and, before Agent A saved the data, Agent B could have made and saved an order using those same resources. In a normal optimistic concurrency situation, Agent A would receive the exception as he tried to save the order. In the offline situation, the save occurs when the agent goes back online and the data held locally is really data that has not been committed to the database. Agent B in the scenario could have been online, in which case that agent will win. However, if both users are offline when they save their orders, the "winner" will be the first user who goes back online and allows synchronization to take place.

Naturally, this situation will only be acceptable if the exception occurs fairly rarely. This will depend on two things: the level of demand on a particular resource and how long travel agents typically spend offline. Ian thinks that in some cases clashes could be quite frequent for high-demand resources at popular times of the year. Also, he makes the point that he would feel unprofessional if he made an order for a client and later had to tell the client that the order did not really exist. In the end, the team agrees that orders made in this way should be indicated as Tentative and then everyone can be straight with one another.

Point (c) is very similar to (b) except that its effects could be more complex—for example, the client could have actually added or deleted orders while the travel agent was offline. The client could also have made changes to other data, such as their address or phone number details. The simplest solution is to invalidate all of the offline agent's work if information has been changed *for that client* while the agent also made offline changes. The team feels that there is a possibility for a merge to be carried out, but that this is difficult to define and presents a high level of risk at this stage of the project.

The use case diagram of Figure 4-5 has been extended in Figure 4-9 to show Offline Customer Contacts, which extends the Customer Contacts use case. Keep in mind that an extend relationship in use case diagrams, where a second use case extends a first, means that an actor interacting with the first use case—here Customer Contacts—sees both use cases together. The second use case—here Offline Customer Contacts—is not an optional add-on but is part of Customer Contacts. The only real reason for showing it as a separate use case is for ease of understanding and to allow staged development.

Figure 4-9. *Use case diagram of Manage Orders extended to show offline working for travel agents*

Offline Customer Contacts includes the Offline Browse Catalog, Offline Manage Orders, and Offline Account Management use cases. A number of important scenarios will need to be identified in these three functional areas. These use cases are specified next.

USE CASE: OFFLINE CUSTOMER CONTACTS

This use case will extend the Customer Contacts use case to cover offline working. The detail of this is contained within the included use cases.

USE CASE: OFFLINE BROWSE CATALOG

This use case provides capability to allow browsing of the resource catalog when the client installation is offline. Normally browsing of the resource catalogs and searching for resources would not be available. This use case provides for the maintenance of a local set of offline catalogs that have the same structure as the online catalogs and whose entries duplicate part of the online catalog entries.

Detailed functionality is provided by the two included use cases:

- Catalog Augmentation

- Catalog Synchronization

USE CASE: CATALOG AUGMENTATION

This use case provides capability to add content to the offline catalog in a manner that reflects the past interests of the user in browsing the online catalog.

Entries are added to the offline catalogs both at the level of the hierarchical catalog pages and at the resource detail level. Entries are provided in the geographic, alphabetic, and category catalogs in the form of pages at a particular level. When a page from the online catalogs is viewed on the client, that page will be automatically added to the offline catalogs.

Resource detail pages will be added to the offline catalogs when they appear in a catalog page at the next lowest level down. The downloading of resource detail will occur as a background task that is scheduled when a page containing a list of resources is viewed.

Lists of resource entries displayed as a result of a search will also cause a similar background task to be scheduled.

USE CASE: CATALOG SYNCHRONIZATION

General Description

This use case provides capability to synchronize the entries in the offline catalog with the corresponding entries in the online catalog.

Listings

During the next meeting, the requirements team concentrates on the Listings use case and draws the use case diagram on the whiteboard, as shown in Figure 4-10.

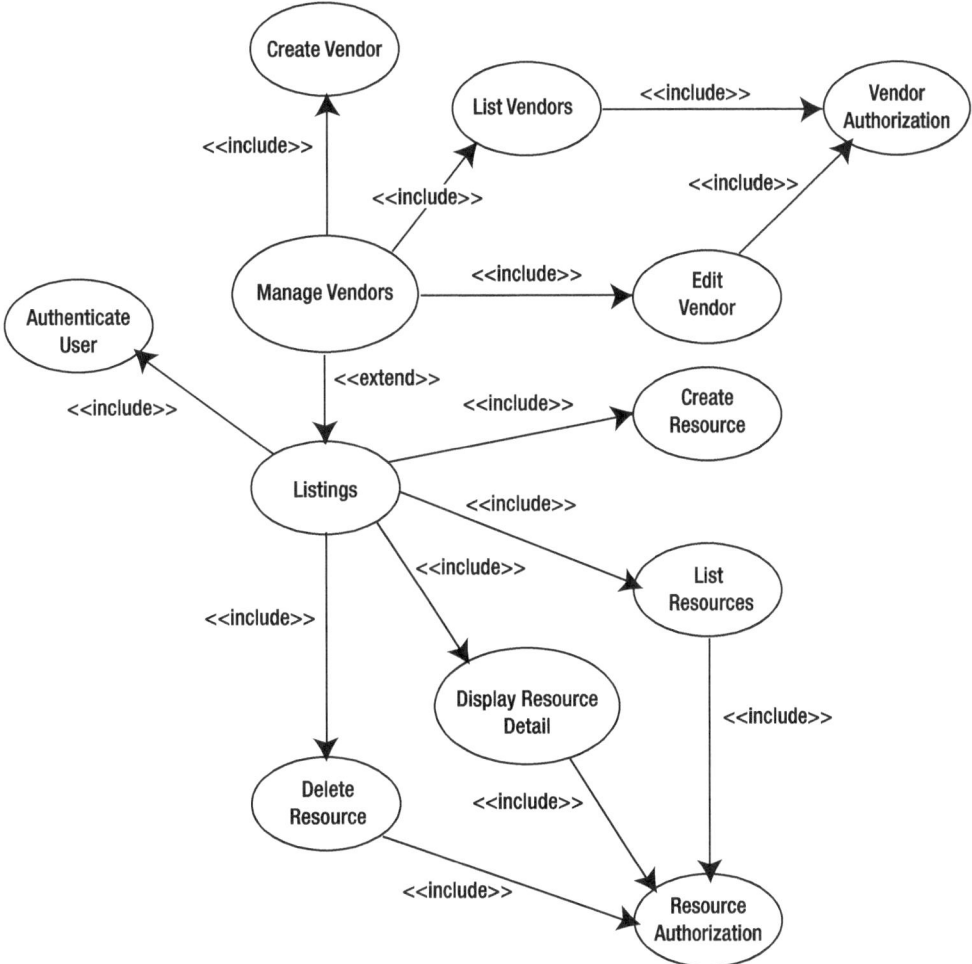

Figure 4-10. *Use case diagram for the Listings functionality*

The Listings use case includes six separate use cases: Create Resource, List Resources, Display Resource Detail, Delete Resource, Authenticate User, and Resource Authorization. There are various paths through each of these, which become the scenarios, consisting of alternative success paths as well as exception paths resulting in failure. Each of these will become a scenario that will need to be entered as a work item.

List Resources allows the user to list resources in various ways, alphabetically by name or vendor, by category, or by geographic location.

Create Resource allows the creation of a new resource listing offered by an existing vendor. The actor will be presented with a wizard, which takes them through several pages that describe the resource, name, type, description, and so forth, as well as the availability dates, costs, and quantities available. Finally, the user will be able to upload pictures of various aspects of the resource and other files that may be provided by the vendor.

Display Resource Detail allows the user to display and edit the detail of a particular resource that has been selected from the lists. The information that may be edited is the same information that was entered in the Create Resource use case.

Delete Resource allows the user to "delete" a resource from the system. In actuality, no resources are ever deleted but are marked as unavailable and do not appear in normal listings. It will be possible to undelete a resource that was deleted accidentally.

The Authenticate User use case allows for users to log on to the system and be authenticated by username and password. Once users are authenticated, they may carry out many actions during their session. Some users are privileged to access the resources of many vendors, while others can only access resources belonging to them.

The Resource Authorization use case provides the capability to determine if users are permitted to access a particular use case concerned with a resource. For example, only users granted that privilege will be able to access the resources of other vendors.

Manage Vendors Use Case

The Manage Vendors use case extends the listings use case by providing the capability to perform actions concerned with management of vendor details stored in the system. It has four included use cases: List Vendors, Create Vendor, Edit Vendor, and Vendor Authorization. Vendors cannot be deleted from the system.

- List Vendors allows a user to list the vendors alphabetically or search by name.

- Create Vendor provides a wizard via which an operator can create a new vendor in the system.

- Edit Vendor allows the user to display and edit the details of a vendor.

- Vendor Authorization checks the authority of the user to access these use cases, for example, preventing ordinary vendors who are logged in as vendors from accessing details of other vendors or creating new vendors. Only Icarus's administrative staff will be permitted to do that.

Query Orders

There are a set of use cases defined by the team that define the functions of what will become the Sales Status application. These use cases are concerned with obtaining reports on order history for various financial periods, various vendors, geographic areas, and so on. This is a significant piece of functionality in its own right. I'm not going to describe all of the use cases here, but you can imagine the way in which the use cases can be divided into a set of included use cases—report by financial period, report by geographic region, and so forth.

Identifying the Top-Level Scenarios

Figure 4-11 shows the process guidance for the Brainstorm Scenarios activity, which the requirements team must tackle next. This activity in MSF CMMI process guidance is described as taking place at the start of each iteration and is followed by scenario prioritization, at which time detail and storyboarding are included. This then leads to the functional requirements for the product and the solution architecture design necessary as part of each iteration. The allocation of the development tasks arising from that architecture is then possible, followed by the coding, unit test, integration, and delivery of the functionality included in the iteration. For iteration 0, though, a scenario list must be started for the whole project where the scenarios are described at a high level and follow on, in Icarus's situation, from a use case analysis. So the scenarios that Icarus requirements team now describe are a representative sample of the critical functionality, to give a starting point to the solution architecture design and product requirements activities, as shown in Figure 4-2.

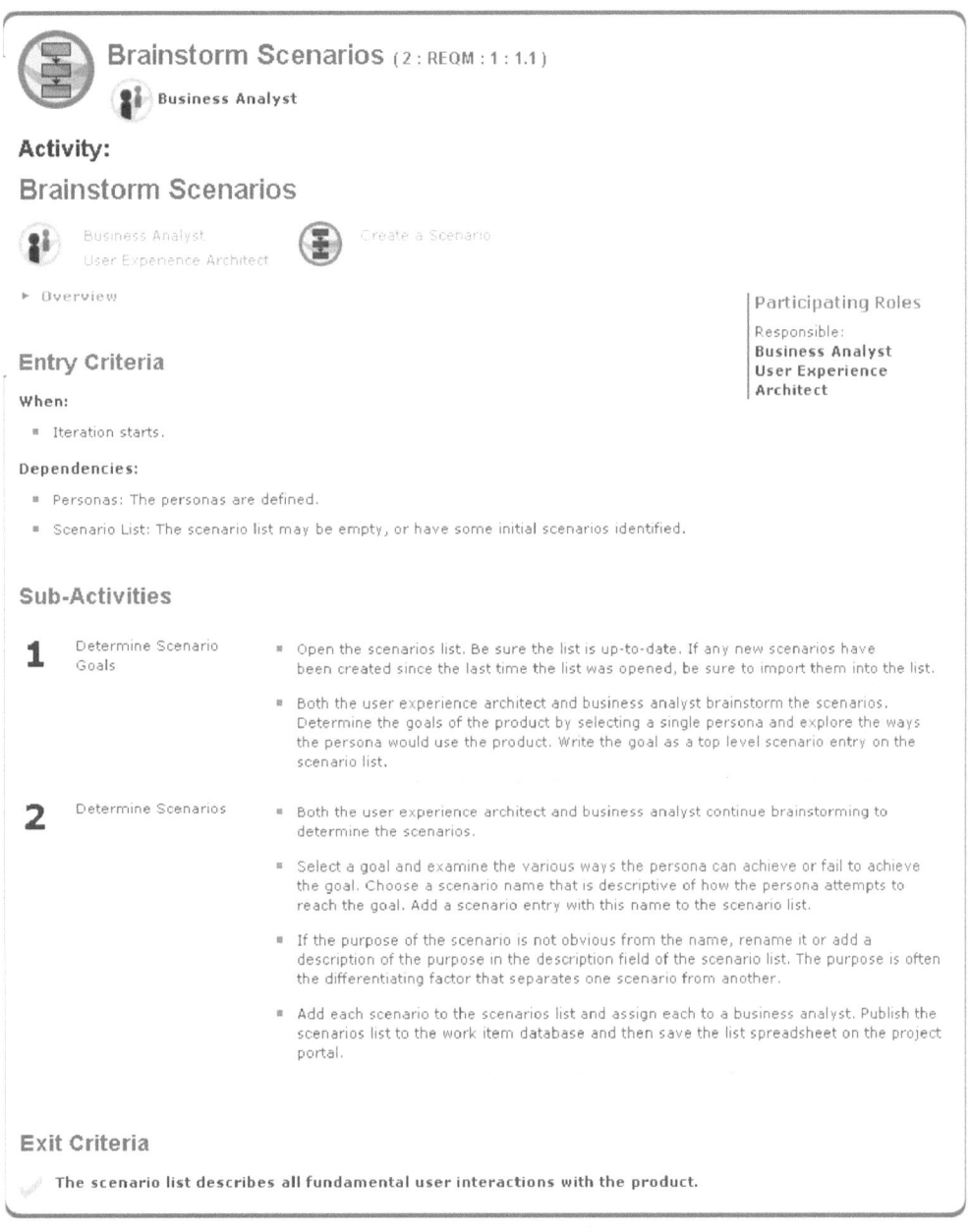

Figure 4-11. *The process guidance page for the Brainstorm Scenarios activity supplied with MSF CMMI*

Moreover, since I am showing you only what is an instructive glimpse of the Icarus project, I cannot list all the scenarios, so in the remainder of this chapter I briefly describe a sample and concentrate on using Excel and Team System to create and manage those scenarios.

Order Scenarios

The requirements team enters the Create Top-Level Scenarios activity on Figure 4-2 for the Manage Orders use case and holds an all-day session with the intention of coming up with a list of scenarios for the entire order capability. Another member has joined the requirements team, developer Angela Cheung. Angela is primarily a senior-level C# developer but has a good deal of experience with requirements definition and is thoroughly familiar with use case modeling. She will assist the requirements team by prototyping some of the screens that will be needed to develop the storyboards that will be the next stage of elaborating the requirements of the Order Management functionality. For this meeting, the team has brought two laptops along. Susan operates one, which is being used to write the scenarios into Excel, connected to Team Foundation Server, while Angela uses the other to display the use cases that have already been developed. The team has only one projector, but a video switch has been set up in the conference room to alternate between the two machines on its screen. The team expects to continue this approach during the storyboarding of scenarios and development of product requirements to come later, when Angela will actually use Visual Studio to develop the graphical user interface screens.

The Sales use case seems like a good place to start. Having viewed the resource options available, selected those most suitable, and identified which are available on their required dates, customers would probably navigate to the Make New Order use case right after using the View Resource Detail use case. The use case diagrams of Figure 4-6 and Figure 4-8, of course, just represent a breakdown of functionality requirements. They do not indicate how navigation between screens takes place within use cases or when transition takes place from one use case to another. This is to be determined during the Write Scenarios and the Storyboard Scenarios activities.

When you think about writing scenarios for a piece of functionality described by the Navigate Geographic Catalog use case, you must consider carefully what a scenario means. It is clearly defined in MSF to be a unique, step-by-step sequence that achieves a defined goal. It may also fail to reach a goal if the scenario being documented is an exception scenario, but still acts in a predictable manner. The point is that it cannot be general—it must be specific and repeatable, which makes it readily testable. So how do you use this concept to describe a general piece of functionality? You cannot say that the user navigates up and down in a hierarchy, pages up and down, and finally makes a selection. This is a great way to test something in an ad hoc test—where knowledgeable users play with the system—and often find unexpected bugs and missing functionality. So such ad hoc testing has its place; a finite number of scenarios cannot identify every application bug, and there are always scenarios that have not been thought of, so I like it. Nevertheless, a good set of scenarios forms a framework that ensures the application implements a known baseline of capability. Thus, to define scenarios for this kind of functionality, you have to break it down into identifiable steps. Then you can either describe your scenarios as these small steps, or write scenarios that are longer and are designed, collectively as a group, to encompass all the steps.

Remember that scenarios are used as work items in MSF CMMI, and so they define pieces of capability that will go into each iteration and are tested. Therefore, it may make sense to join small scenarios into longer ones if each represents functionality that must obviously be grouped together in development. On the other hand, perhaps short scenarios are readily identifiable with pieces of functionality, whereas a long one that encompasses everything may hide the things being tested under a confusing sequence, for which there is no documented explanation other than in the writer's mind at the time of writing. Taking these things into account, the requirements team decides to break down the functionality into rather small steps for the Navigate Resource Catalog use case and come up with the set of top-level scenarios in Figure 4-18. As an example, I will describe the creation of these catalog navigation scenarios using Team System in some detail.

Creating the Browse Resource Catalog Scenarios—In Detail

The team agrees the scenarios for Browse Resource Catalog use case and its included use cases. It's a good idea to tie the scenarios in Team System to the documented use cases in some way, and there are various ways in which this can be accomplished.

Note Exercise 4-2 applies to this section.

For example, the team could add requirements of type Functional that each described in words a particular use case, attach a Visio document to them, and then link each scenario belonging to that use case to the use case's Functional Requirement work item. This is not a good idea, since it is not really in keeping with the way requirements are intended to be used in MSF CMMI. Customer requirements are supposed to be represented as scenarios, and functional requirements are intended to represent engineering requirements that are defined for the product as a result of the customer requirements. In other words, functional requirements come about as a result of figuring out how the product will implement the scenarios defined by the business analysts (BAs).

Another approach might be to write brief documents describing the use cases for which scenarios are to be written and attach them to each of the scenarios. Yet another would be to add Use Case as a work item type by customizing the process template.

However, for the moment a good strategy is to use the concept of the project structure to represent the use case functional decomposition. All work items can be linked to a node in the project structure, which is called the area path field in the work item detail. The project structure was described in Chapter 3, and it is a downward-branching tree of names beginning at a root node with the name Area. You can define a project structure in whatever way seems suitable, so why not define it as a functional decomposition, following the use cases? Then you can link scenarios to use cases by means of the Area Path field in the work item. There's no reason why, when you get to the functional or product requirements (as opposed to the user requirements) you should not add a separate project structure to represent the design breakdown. You could also have another part to represent QOS Requirements. The project structure can contain whatever nodes you find appropriate places on which to hang work items.

Icarus's requirements team plans to do it that way, and Clare has updated the project structure in Figure 4-12 to represent the use case diagram in Figure 4-6. It's also a good idea to attach a use case document to each scenario as well, and the Icarus team plans to do this with Visio documents describing all their use cases.

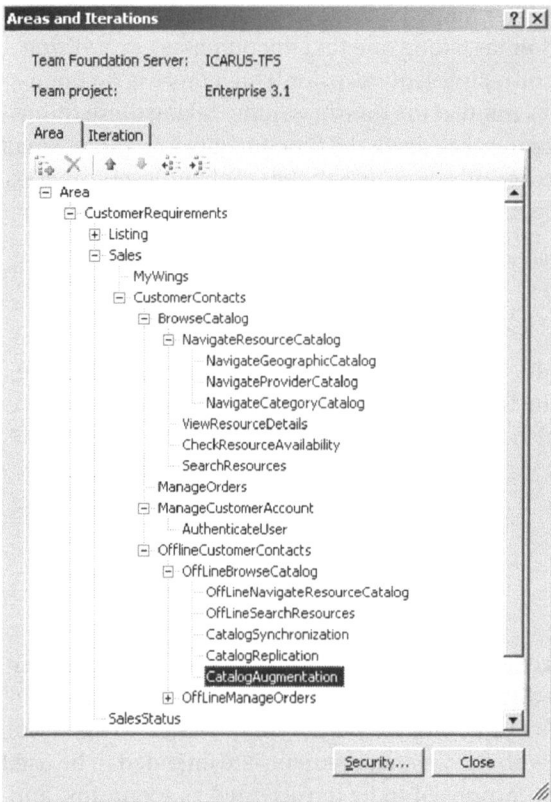

Figure 4-12. *Project structure with the Browse Catalog use cases added to it*

During the meeting Susan enters the scenarios as work items of type Scenario. I will quickly review work items as they appear in Team System. Work items in MSF CMMI come in seven different flavors: Task, Change Request, Risk, Review, Requirement, Bug, and Issue. All of these represent an item of work. Work items can relate to each other, so that a Change Request, for example, might have a number of tasks associated with it, the first perhaps being a task called Analyze Change Request. Notice that there is *no* parent-child relationship between work items and there is no way to associate specific meaning to links, except perhaps by adding a comment to a link. For example, you might wish to define a convention that each scenario has various implementation tasks associated with it, and you could comment each of those links with the word Implementation or Analysis. Sometimes the name of the linked work item would itself be sufficient to show the reason for the link. There is also no way in Team System for an *order* to be defined among work items, so you cannot set up links to imply that one task comes before another. This information should be retained within Microsoft Project files, since Project can take task work items and impose project planning on them. The Microsoft Project files must be retained as separate documents within Team System to preserve the project information, as you saw in Chapter 3.

As a result of the analysis of a change request, more tasks, risks, or requirements might be added. At the moment we are concerned with the Requirement type of work item. Requirements come in seven varieties: Scenario, Quality of Service, Safety, Security, Functional, Operational, and Interface. We have mentioned earlier that customer requirements take the form of either scenarios or quality of service requirements. The others are defined when we specify features of the product that are designed to satisfy these customer requirements.

Susan is a BA, of course, and does not use Visual Studio like the developers, but Team System is designed to also accommodate team members who are more at home with Microsoft Office applications. At present, TFS integrates with Office and Excel, so BAs who are familiar with spreadsheets can work happily in Excel with the knowledge that they are simply getting a different view of the same team project to that of the developers. Susan begins by opening Excel, her favorite application, and selects New List from the Team menu. The resulting dialog box, shown in Figure 4-13, allows Susan to select the server and project. She selects Enterprise 3.1 and clicks OK, which opens the dialog box shown in Figure 4-14. This dialog box allows Susan to select an existing query to populate the spreadsheet with work items, or to enter a new list to produce a blank worksheet. Susan is going to enter a set of new requirement work items of type Scenario, so she selects the Input List radio button and clicks OK.

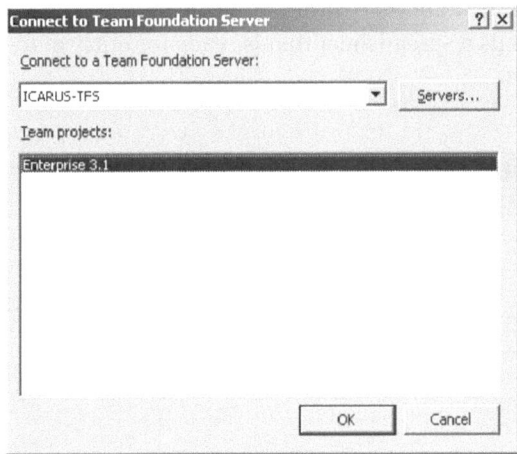

Figure 4-13. *Connecting to Team Foundation Server from Excel*

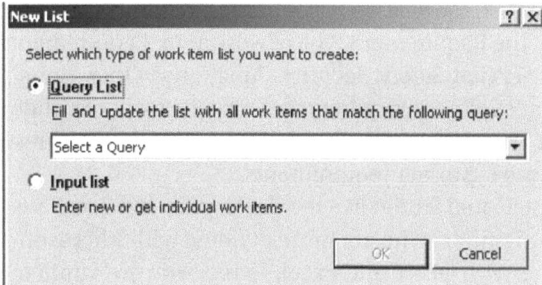

Figure 4-14. *New List dialog box*

This new spreadsheet, shown in Figure 4-15, is set up for entry of work items in general, but does not allow for the special fields required in Scenario-type work items, so Susan must adjust the columns by clicking the Choose Columns button on the Team toolbar. This brings up the dialog box shown in Figure 4-16. Susan now selects Requirement in the Work Item Type drop-down and clicks the Add Required button. This will add only those fields from the left-hand pane that are *required* for the selected work item type. She also selects the Description field in the left-hand pane and clicks the > button, since she wants to type descriptions of each scenario. Figure 4-17 shows the results. Clicking OK opens a spreadsheet that is ready for entry of the scenarios as they are identified in the discussion.

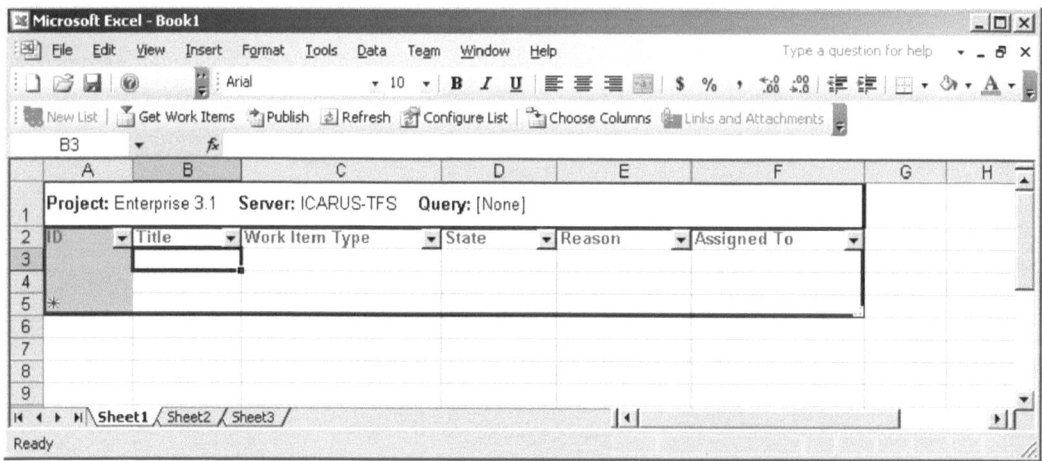

Figure 4-15. *Empty spreadsheet for entering a new set of work items using Excel*

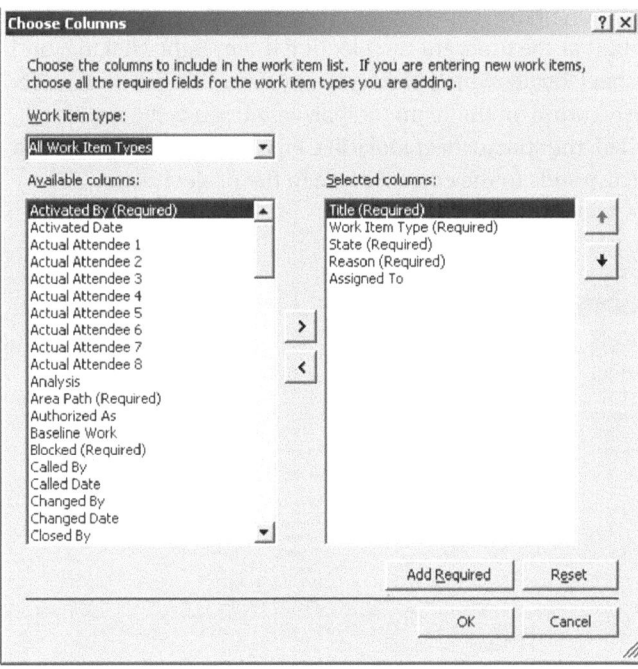

Figure 4-16. *This dialog box allows the user to choose the required columns.*

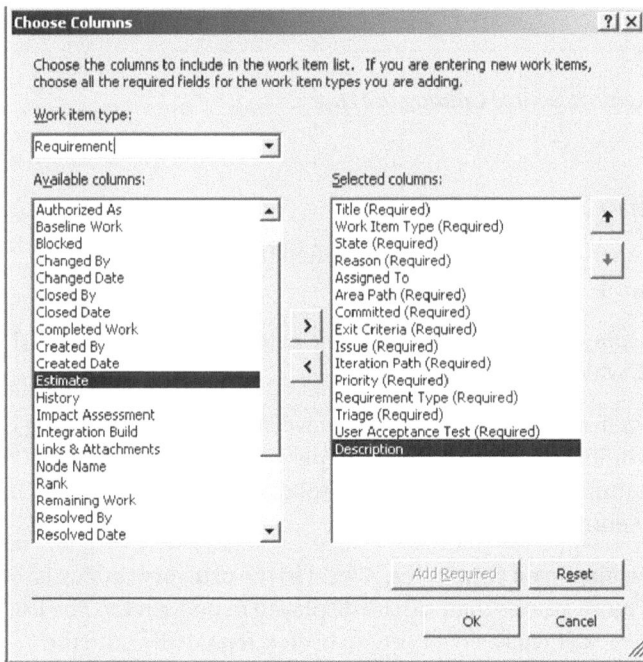

Figure 4-17. *The Choose Columns dialog box with the required columns added*

Susan types the summary information of the scenarios into the spreadsheet. She hides the columns in Excel that are not important at the moment by selecting them, right-clicking, and choosing Hide. She saves the spreadsheet locally, which preserves any formatting she has added to the cells, and then clicks the Publish button on the Team toolbar, which sends the results to the team project. When she has finished, the spreadsheet looks like Figure 4-18. Notice that the Area Path field for each scenario corresponds to the correct place in the project structure of Figure 4-12. Brief descriptions of the scenarios follow.

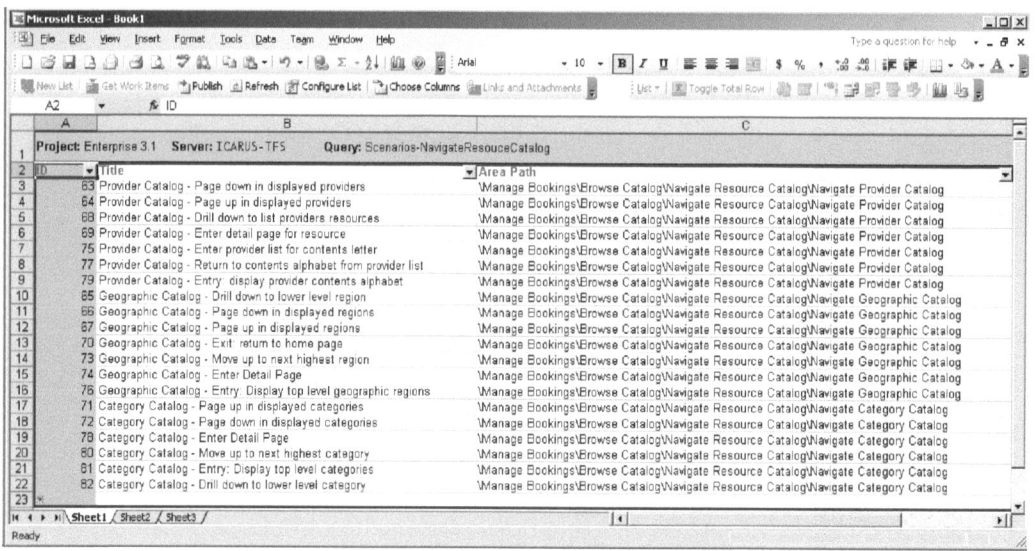

Figure 4-18. *The scenarios for the Navigate Resource Catalog use case*

Navigate Resource Catalog Scenarios

Here are brief descriptions of the scenarios that have been identified for the Navigate Resource Catalog use case (see Figure 4-18):

- **Category Catalog - Entry: Display top level categories**. The category catalog is entered and displays the default level, which is the highest level.

- **Category Catalog - Page down in displayed categories**. A level in the category catalog is displayed, in which there are more entries than can be displayed in one screen. The user clicks on a Page Down button and the next page is displayed. The user continues to click Page Down until the last entries are displayed.

- **Category Catalog - Page up in displayed categories**. A level in the category catalog is displayed, in which there are more entries than can be displayed in one screen. The last page of entries is displayed. The user clicks on a Page Up button repeatedly until the first entries in the level are displayed.

- **Geographic Catalog - Entry: Display top level geographic regions**. The geographic catalog is entered and displays the default level, which is the highest level.

- **Geographic Catalog - Drill down to lower level region**. The geographic catalog is displayed at the default (highest) level. The user clicks on regions that are displayed until the lowest level is reached and the resources offered by one vendor are displayed.

- **Geographic Catalog - Enter Detail Page**. The geographic catalog is displayed at the level showing the resources offered by a single vendor. The user clicks on one of the resources and the resource detail page for that resource is displayed.

- **Geographic Catalog - Move up to next highest region**. The geographic catalog is displaying at the level showing the resources offered by a single vendor. The user clicks an Up button and the list of vendors at the next highest level appears. The user clicks Up until the highest-level region is displayed.

- **Geographic Catalog - Page down in displayed regions**. A level in the geographic catalog is displayed, in which there are more entries than can be displayed in one screen. The user clicks a Page Down button and the next page is displayed. The user continues to click Page Down until the last entries are displayed.

- **Geographic Catalog - Page up in displayed regions**. A level in the geographic catalog is displayed, in which there are more entries than can be displayed in one screen. The last page of entries is displayed. The user clicks a Page Up button repeatedly until the first entries in the level are displayed.

- **Geographic Catalog - Exit return to home page**. Anywhere in the catalog, the user clicks an Exit button, which causes exit to the home page. Note that there is more than one scenario here, since exit could take place from any page.

- **Provider Catalog - Entry: Display provider contents alphabet**. The provider catalog is entered and displays the default level, which is the highest level.

- **Provider Catalog - Drill down to list providers resources**. The provider catalog is displayed at the default (highest) level. The user clicks on an alphabetic letter, then clicks the providers that are displayed, until the lowest level is reached and the resources offered by one vendor are displayed.

- **Provider Catalog - Enter detail page for resource**. The provider catalog is displayed at the level showing the resources offered by a single vendor. The user clicks on one of the resources and the resource detail page for that resource is displayed.

- **Provider Catalog - Return to contents alphabet from provider list**. The provider catalog is displayed at the level showing the resources offered by a single vendor. The user clicks an Up button and the list of vendors at the next highest level is displayed. The user clicks Up until the contents alphabet is displayed.

- **Provider Catalog - Page down in displayed providers**. A level in the provider catalog is displayed, in which there are more entries than can be displayed in one screen. The user clicks a Page Down button and the next page is displayed. The user continues to click Page Down until the last entries are displayed.

- **Provider Catalog - Page up in displayed providers**. A level in the provider catalog is displayed, in which there are more entries than can be displayed in one screen. The last page of entries is displayed. The user clicks Page Up repeatedly until the first entries in the level are displayed.

Search Catalog Scenarios

The team also generates scenarios for the Search Catalog use case. I will not describe these scenarios in detail, but they cover the various kinds and combinations of searches that can be made for suitable resources.

Offline Browse Catalog

Offline Browse Catalog is part of Offline Customer Contacts, which extends the Customer Contacts use case. This defines the same features as the Browse Catalog use case—including navigation and search—but works when the user is offline and is limited to the catalog entries that are retained locally. There are thus no new scenarios to be added to describe this capability, but for development and test purposes, the operation of these scenarios when offline will need to be coded and tested. It is expected that there will be a great deal of common code, but there will certainly be some differences; therefore, we must add all duplicates of the scenarios listed in Figure 4-18 with the proviso that the sequence is carried out when the user is offline.

The Catalog Synchronization and Catalog Augmentation use cases, however, do include additional scenarios, which must be identified. This functionality represents a good deal of risk since it is breaking new ground and needs to be prototyped early on. The requirements team at this stage has only a tentative idea of how these use cases will eventually work. We will spend a little time in the next section seeing how these scenarios are written, while demonstrating the Work Item Query capability of Team System.

Writing a New Scenario Query—Offline Catalog Synchronization

In adding the catalog augmentation and synchronization scenarios, you will see a slightly different way to using Microsoft Excel to enter scenarios. First, Susan selects the Team Queries folder under Work Items in Team Explorer, right-clicks, and selects Add Query from the context menu. This opens the window shown in Figure 4-19, which contains the beginnings of the definition of a new query. Queries are intended to retrieve lists of work items and contain a set of clauses that specify constraints for the set of work items to be retrieved. The default clause, automatically added in Figure 4-19, simply ensures that the set of work items returned will belong to the project that is currently open when the query is defined. A second clause will ensure that the work items returned are only the Requirement type. Another clause will ensure that, from those Requirement work items, only those of type Scenario will be returned. Yet another clause will ensure that all returned work items will have their area path field set to Manage Orders\Browse Catalog\ Synchronize Offline Catalog. You can see that, if area paths in the project correspond to functional areas and use cases, it is easy to select scenarios corresponding to a particular use case, by specifying the required Area Path field in the query.

Note Exercise 4-3 applies to this section.

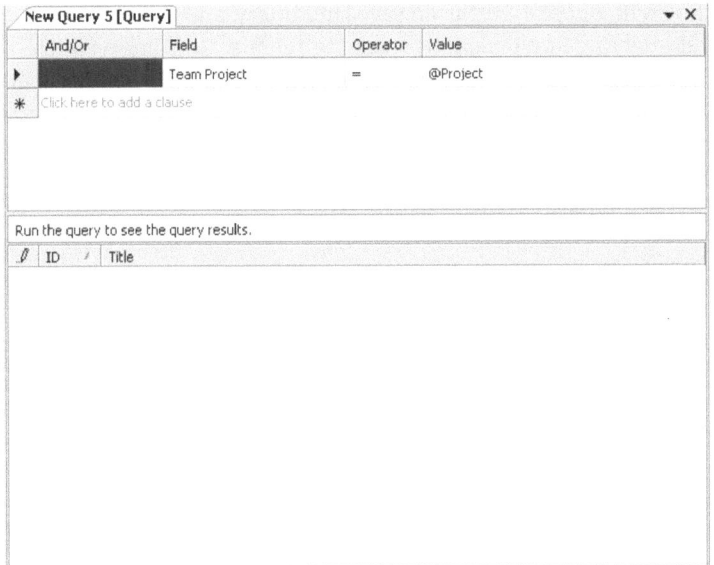

Figure 4-19. *The View Query window for a newly created query*

You add a new clause by clicking "Click here to add a clause," and then selecting either And or Or to link the clause into the whole Boolean query statement. In this case, Susan requires all of the clauses to be satisfied by queries to be returned, so she selects And for each one. Next on the clause line, Susan must specify the field to be tested from the defined set of fields of work items. For the second clause, Susan selects Work Item Type for the field to be tested. The operator can also be selected, and a whole range of operators are available for comparing field contents for the Work Item Type field. In this case a simple equals is needed. In the Value field, Susan chooses Requirement from the set of options. For the third clause, she specifies that the Requirement Type will be equal to Scenario. For the fourth clause, she wishes to select only those work items in which the area path is equal to the Manage Orders\Browse Catalog\Synchronize Offline Catalog path, so she selects that path from the drop-down.

Note The Area Path drop-down contents do not always update if you change the Project Areas and Iterations settings in the middle of writing a query. You need to refresh the project by right-clicking on the team project in Team Explorer and selecting Refresh, but you may also need to reopen or run the query to get the area paths available in the drop-downs to update.

The operations available in the query clause that references the Area Path field are different from those for the other fields. Susan selects Under rather than = since she might add sublevels under the area path that she has specified and she would like all work items in those sublevels to be returned as well as those in the specified level.

The completed query is shown in Figure 4-20. Susan saves her query, and then she can run it by right-clicking on it and selecting Run Query; by selecting Team ➤ Run Query; or by pressing F5. Of course, no scenarios are returned since Susan has not yet defined any. She can at this point define the columns that the query will return for the work items that meet the criteria that she has just defined. To do this, with the query open, she right-clicks anywhere on the query design surface and selects Column Options or chooses Team ➤ Column Options. This opens the dialog box shown in Figure 4-21.

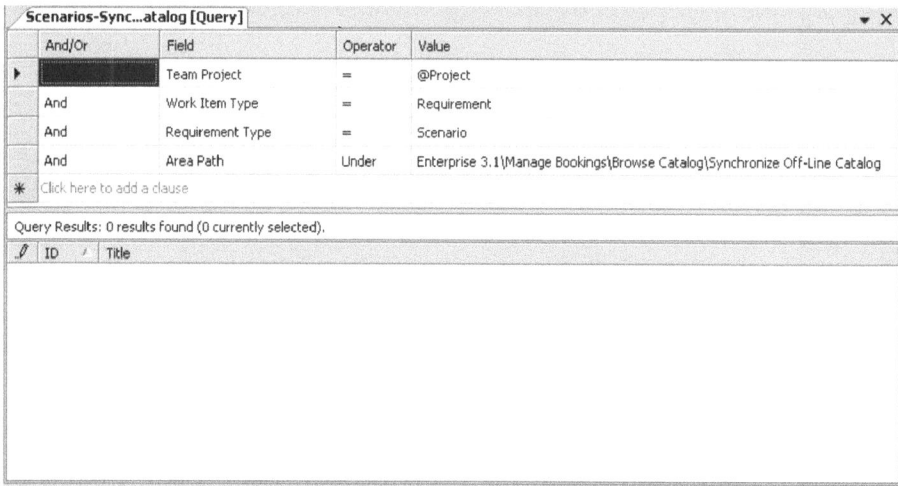

Figure 4-20. *The completed query for viewing the scenarios for the Synchronize Offline Catalog use case*

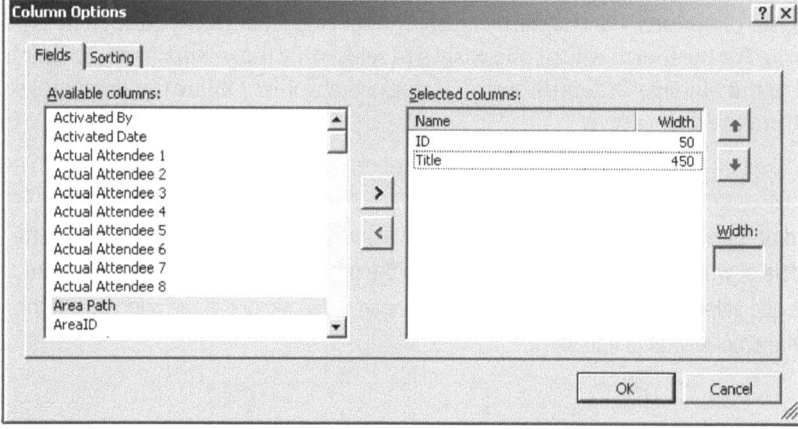

Figure 4-21. *The Column Options dialog box for a query*

Susan can select columns from the left-hand pane and add them to the set of displayed columns in the right-hand pane. For a valid scenario, these columns are required:

ID

Title

Area Path

Committed

Exit Criteria

Issue

Iteration Path

Priority

Reason

Requirement Type

State

Triage

User Acceptance Test

Work Item Type

Susan saves and closes the query. Now she can use Excel to open the query and type work items into the list that is created by the query. To do this, she opens Excel, which creates a new spreadsheet, and clicks in the top-left cell to define where the list generated by the query is to be placed—it will be placed with its top-left corner on the selected cell. Then she clicks the New List button on the Team toolbar or selects Team ➤ New List. In the resulting dialog box, she selects the required team project and clicks OK. In the next dialog box, she selects the new query, Scenarios-SynchronizeOfflineCatalog, and clicks OK. The resulting list within the spreadsheet is shown in Figure 4-22.

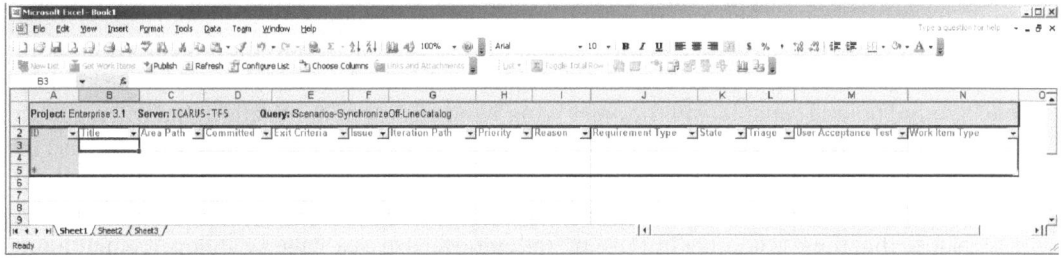

Figure 4-22. *An empty spreadsheet generated from a query*

Susan first sets the Work Item Type field to Requirement from the drop-down for that cell in the first row, which causes many of the other fields to be populated with default values. (The drop-downs for the field values are not populated until this is done.) Susan also sets the Requirement Type field equal to Scenario, and sets the Area Path field to \Manage Orders\Browse Catalog\

Synchronize Offline Catalog (available as an option on the drop-down list). Now Susan is ready to enter a list of scenarios for the Scenarios-SynchronizeOfflineCatalog use case. The complete set of scenarios defined by the team is shown in Figure 4-23.

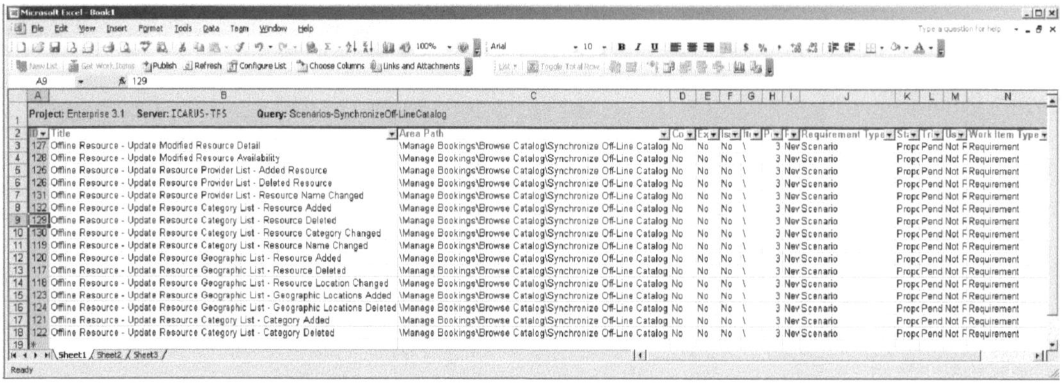

Figure 4-23. *The scenarios for the offline resource catalog synchronization*

At this point, Susan clicks Publish on the Team toolbar and the new queries are written back as work items in Team Server. She can create queries for all of the use cases that are defined in the project structure by simply copying and pasting this one several times into the Team Queries folder, changing the name, and editing the conditional clause that specifies the Area Path value. This might be a useful technique for a lead BA to define the work for several assistants, providing them with empty lists of scenarios, placed at defined places in the project structure, to be completed as the details are worked out.

Let's now look at the scenarios that the team has defined related to the Catalog Synchronization use case. This use case was first shown in Figure 4-9 and described briefly in the use case specification. It enables the system to keep the offline resource catalog synchronized with the one stored in the main database. The scenarios in Figure 4-24 identify the cases when the offline resource needs to be updated, such as when some detail of the resource is changed, when its availability is changed, or when new resources are added to the list available from a particular vendor. It is not clear at this stage in the project exactly how the system will achieve this capability, but the requirements team has some ideas. One possibility is some kind of background polling capability in the Sales Wing Windows client application that will regularly request that the server provide details of any changes to resources. The client can then use the report obtained to determine whether any of its offline information needs to be refreshed. If that's the case, the client can then request the new information from the server.

Notice that there is another important, rather novel use case called Catalog Augmentation, shown in Figure 4-9 and specified in the text following it, for which the team also defines scenarios. This will certainly need early prototyping.

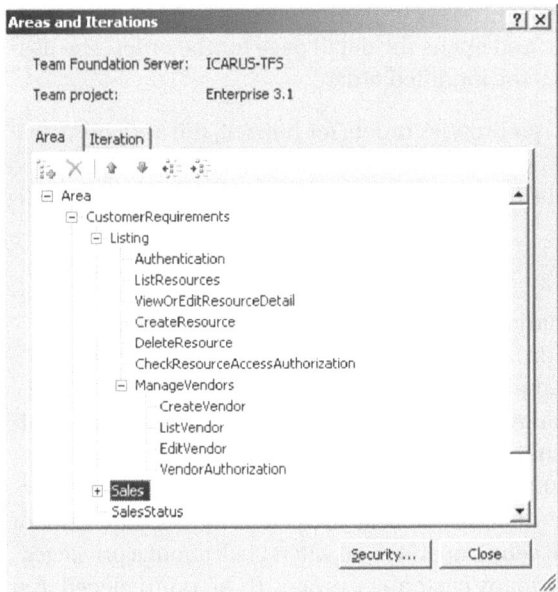

Figure 4-24. *Project structure with the resource management use cases added to it*

Manage Orders Scenarios

The requirements team follows a similar process in creating the scenarios that describe the Manage Orders use case shown in Figure 4-8. Some of the scenarios are summarized here:

- **Manage Orders - Make new order**. The user selects a resource from the catalog, navigates to the resource detail page, and then clicks a Make Order link, which takes the user through a sequence of pages and results in creation of a new order for the authenticated user. At some point in the sequence, the user is given the option to add more resources, which he declines.

- **Manage Orders - Make new order, multiple resources**. The user selects a resource from the catalog, navigates to the resource detail page, and then clicks a Make Order link, which takes the user through a sequence of pages and results in creation of a new order for the authenticated user. At some point in the sequence, the user is given the option to add more resources, which she accepts and adds two more resources chosen from the catalog. The user then completes the order.

- **Manage Orders - Make new order for specified customer**. The user selects a resource from the catalog, navigates to the resource detail page, and then clicks a Make Order link, which takes the user through a sequence of pages and results in a new order being made for a specified customer. At some point in the sequence, the user is given the option to add more resources, which he declines. Only a privileged user is permitted to make orders for a specified user rather than for himself.

- **Manage Orders - Modify order**. The user browses orders for herself, the authenticated user as the customer, selects an order, and opens the detail page for the order. The user makes a change to the order and saves the modified order.

- **Manage Orders - Cancel order**. The user browses orders for himself, the authenticated user as the customer, selects an order, and clicks the Cancel button. The user is presented with a cancellation conditions page. The user accepts the conditions and cancels the order.

View Orders Scenarios

The requirements team creates a list of scenarios for the View Orders use case in Figure 4-8. Again we summarize some of them to get a flavor of how the system will behave. Remember that the behavior is complicated by the fact that the Manage Orders functions are to be used not only by travel agents and call center operators when they are handling the orders for multiple customers, but also by the customers themselves for their own orders using the website. At this stage in the project, the team hopes that the same code can be used for each, with constraints applying according to whether the authenticated user is an ordinary customer user or a privileged user, such as a travel agent or call center operator. So when I talk about a privileged user here, I mean a user privileged to handle many customers' orders. By an unprivileged user, I mean an ordinary customer who is only permitted to see or modify his or her own orders.

- **Browse Orders by Customer - Authenticated user as customer**. An unprivileged user is authenticated and selects to browse orders. He is presented with a list of his own orders.

- **Browse Orders by Customer - Choose customer**. A privileged user is authenticated and selects to browse orders by customer. She is presented with a list of customers, clicks on one, and is presented with a list of the orders for that customer.

- **Browse Orders by Provider - Privileged user**. A privileged user is authenticated and selects to browse orders by provider (or vendor). He is presented with an alphabetic index, selects a letter, and is presented with a list of vendor names beginning with that letter. He selects one and is presented with a list of orders that apply to that vendor.

- **Search Orders by Customer Name - Privileged user**. A privileged user is authenticated and selects to search orders. She is presented with a search specification page, enters a particular customer name, and clicks Search. She is presented with a list of orders for that customer.

- **Search Orders by Vendor Name - Privileged user**. A privileged user is authenticated and selects to search orders. He is presented with a search specification page, enters a particular vendor name, and clicks search. He is presented with a list of orders for that vendor's resources.

- **Search Orders by Resource Name - Privileged user**. A privileged user is authenticated and selects to search orders. She is presented with a search specification page, enters a particular resource name, and clicks Search. She is presented with a list of orders for that resource.

- **Search with customer name and vendor name**.

- **Search with customer name and resource name**.

- **Search with vendor name and resource name**.

- **Search with all three of customer name, vendor name and resource name**.

Listings

Finally, the team agrees on the top-level scenarios of the Listings use case shown in Figure 4-10 and its included use cases. All these scenario work items have their Area Path values set to nodes in the project structure as before; the Listing portion of the use case hierarchy in the project structure appears earlier in Figure 4-24. The new set of scenario work items is shown in Figure 4-25. Here are some brief descriptions of each.

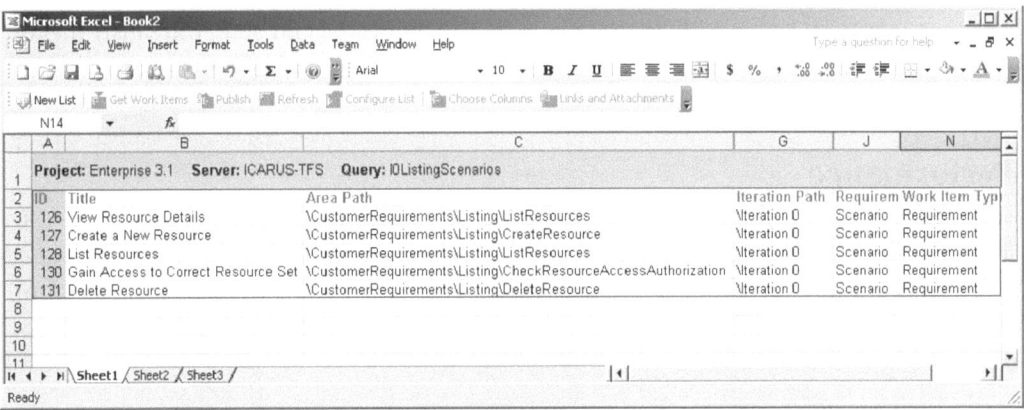

Figure 4-25. *A set of scenarios entered into an Excel spreadsheet, ready to be published to the team project.*

- **List Resources**: The user accesses the Resource List screen for a particular vendor, and the available resources are listed correctly on the screen.

- **Create a New Resource**: The user opens a wizard that creates a new resource and follows the wizard step by step to create a new resource as part of the collection offered by a particular vendor.

- **View Resource Details**: From the Resource List screen, the user selects a resource and either by double-clicking or clicking an Edit button, displays the resource detail page(s). The user modifies a detailed feature of a resource and saves the detail page, causing the resource detail information to be successfully updated.

- **Gain Access to Correct Resource Set**: A user authenticates as a vendor, with vendor privileges, chooses the Resource List page, and sees only those resources that belong to the vendor.

- **Authenticate User**: The user logs on to the system and is authenticated with username and password.

- **Delete Resource**: From the Resource List screen, the user selects a new resource and then clicks the Delete button. A warning appears; the user clicks OK, and the resource is marked as deleted, which means that it is no longer visible in searches and catalogs. The resource is not actually deleted in the database, since that would cause referential integrity problems, as previous orders may have been made against that resource.

Create Quality of Service Requirements

Quality of service requirements are those requirements on a system that do not specify functionality. Examples include performance, load, availability, stress, accessibility, serviceability, and maintainability. Like functional requirements, they need to be tested, or at least theoretical arguments must be made that the application, as architected and built, will satisfy them. Many of these QoS requirements are satisfied by the application and infrastructure together, and thus both work together in the design of the solution.

Performance

Performance is usually specified in response time for a set of critical functional features under a specified user load. It may also be necessary to specify such things as the number of instances of the various entities in the database since this will often affect the performance. For example, Icarus's system is required to work at its specified performance under the conditions in Table 4-1.

Table 4-1. *Database Population Assumed for Performance Testing*

Description	Value
Number of vendors	10,000
Total number of resources	100,000
Number of registered customers	10,000,000
Total number of orders	50,000,000
Average line items per order	3
Average orders per customer	5
Average resources per provider	10

The figures in Table 4-1 are based on an optimistic projection of Icarus's growth over the next five years. In specifying test data, it is important to avoid data that will satisfy the requirements but that will be completely unrealistic. For example, you can put test data into the database in which all the customers had the same name, or all of the orders reserve the same resource. You can be as scientific as you feel necessary. The performance specifications are shown in Table 4-2 and Table 4-3. The figures in Table 4-3 do not include delays due to limited Internet bandwidth at the home customer's end.

Table 4-2. *Performance Requirements for Sales Wing*

User Operation	Average Response Time (sec.)	Standard Deviation (sec.)	Number of Concurrent Users
Update of Customer List	4	2	1,000
Update of Customer Details	4	2	1,000
Update of Customer Contacts List	4	2	1,000
Update of Customer Order List	4	2	1,000
Browse Resource Geographic—any page update	6	3	1,000
Browse Resource by Provider—any page update	4	2	1,000
Browse Resource by Category—any page update	6	3	1,000
Search Resource Catalog—any criteria	8	4	1,000
Resource Details Display	4	2	1,000
Save order—new or modified	8	4	1,000
Authenticate User	10	10	1,000

Note: Concurrent users make similar access at 30-second intervals to provide parallel load.

Table 4-3. *Performance Requirements for Sales Website*

User Operation	Average Response Time (sec.)	Standard Deviation (sec.)	Number of Concurrent Users
Update of My Wings	6	3	10,000
Browse Resource Geographic—any page update	8	4	10,000
Browse Resource by Provider—any page update	6	3	10,000
Browse Resource by Category—any page update	8	4	10,000
Search Resource Catalog—any criteria	12	6	10,000
Resource Details Display	6	3	10,000
Display order	10	5	10,000
Save order—new or modified	10	5	10,000
Authenticate User	10	10	10,000

Note: Concurrent users make similar access at 30-second intervals to provide parallel load.

Load

The required load for Icarus's system is specified as follows:

- Sales Wing Client Installed at travel agent site—1,000 concurrent users, with performance as specified in Table 4-2.

- 5,000 concurrent users with response time permitted to degrade by 100 percent, i.e., double.

- Sales Site accessed from home Internet browser—10,000 concurrent users with performance as specified in Table 4-3

- 20,000 concurrent users with performance degraded by 100 percent

Availability

The Icarus system is to be available 24 hours, seven days a week. Scheduled maintenance will be 4 hours once per month when the system will be down and also 24 hours per month when the system will operate at 50 percent of normal performance.

The mean time between unscheduled outages is not to be less than 30 days.

Serviceability

The mean time to restore after an unscheduled outage is to be no greater than 4 hours.

Maintainability

All code and infrastructure is to be fully documented and maintainable by qualified personnel after six weeks training.

The mean time to fix code bugs discovered after production is to be as defined in Table 4-4.

Table 4-4. *Performance Requirements for Sales Website*

Severity	Mean Time to Fix
Severity 1	1 Week
Severity 2, 3	1 Month
Severity 4–6	3 Months

Summary

In this chapter we explored some of the initial work of the Icarus requirements team in identifying the high-level requirements for their project, Enterprise 3.1. You learned the meaning of personas, and we described them for this project. The section on use case analysis examined that technique and showed how it can lead to the definition of high-level scenarios. The requirements team defined the main use cases for Icarus Enterprise 3.1.

You saw how Microsoft Excel, combined with Team Foundation Server, is a useful tool with which to document scenarios and enter them into a team project. You learned how to write queries in Team Foundation Server that retrieve defined groups of scenarios for display and editing.

The requirements team defined the main top-level scenarios for the project as well as the quality of service requirements in terms of performance, load, availability, serviceability, and maintainability.

The next chapter follows Peter Sage, the project's architect, as he creates the solution architecture.

CHAPTER 5

The Architect: Creating the Solution Architecture

In Chapter 1, I introduced the tools that Visual Studio Team System provides for the architect. Now we'll follow Peter Sage, the architect for the project, as he proceeds with his task of creating the solution architecture. His first job is to create an initial, *high-level* solution in the team project since, unlike the requirements and project management artifacts, the diagrams he will use must be part of a solution. Peter uses Team System for Architects, so most of his work will be performed using that environment as his Team System client.

Creating the Solution

From Peter's perspective, at this point in a project there's a product vision from Icarus's management but nobody is quite sure whether these tentative, high-level requirements are right or complete. If you look at the governance chart shown in Figure 5-1, you can see that the team should expect to start the Plan track before completion of the Envision track. This is desirable since a look at the planning aspects will help with the approval of vision and scope that concludes the Envision track. You can also see from Figure 5-1 that, at the end of the Plan track, we should have an answer to the question "Can we do it within the right time frame and budget?"

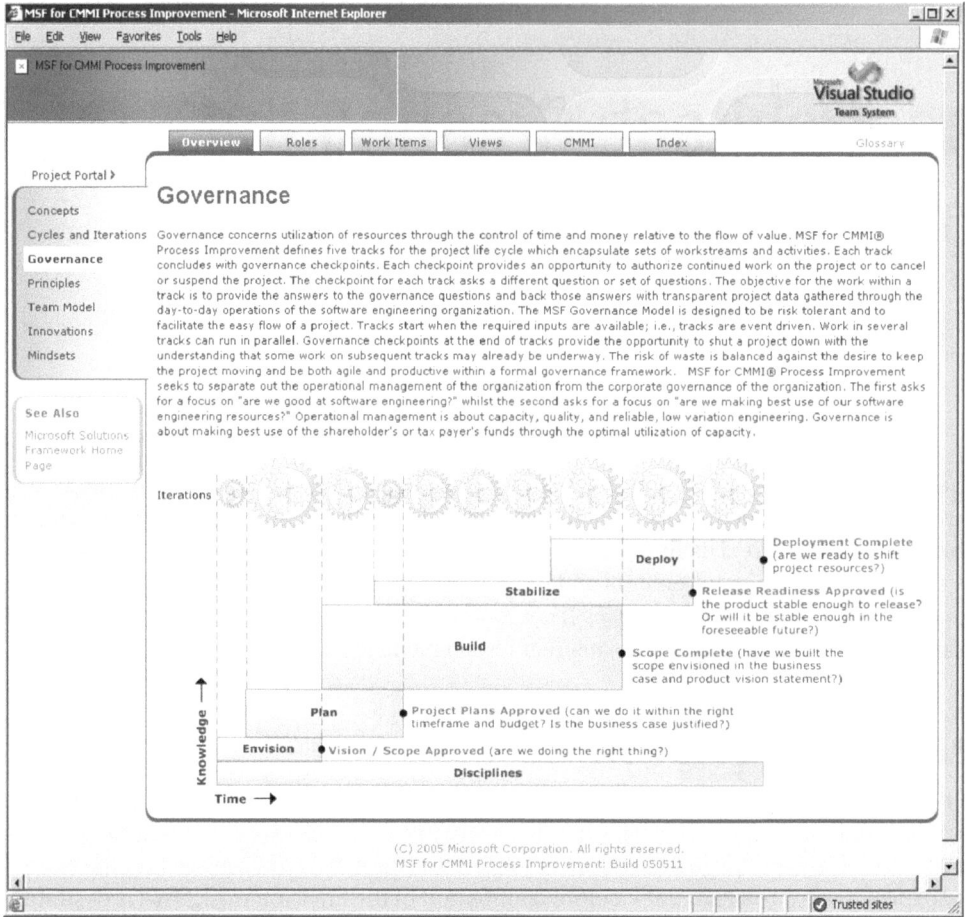

Figure 5-1. *The tracks specified in MSF for CMMI Process Improvement*

So to make the planning phase a success, it's important that Peter start drawing up his architectural ideas early. The initial, high-level solution is where Peter will put his first designs for the entire distributed application. It is a first attempt to design the entire enterprise application to be delivered. Later (you will see this in Chapter 6) he will create a *proof-of-concept* solution and create the first diagrams and projects for iteration 1, in which he and the senior developers will write code to prototype their detailed ideas. Prototyping reduces risk and is thus an important part of the Plan track. As he thinks about the application design, various risks and uncertainties will come to mind and he will create risk work items to keep track of these. Later he or the senior developers can think about how these risks can be mitigated— researching the literature, analyzing, or prototyping. A branch of the solution can be added during the project—preferably not too late—for someone to try some experiments to determine how things will work out. Branching is a feature of the Team Foundation Server version control capability; a branch is a separate path along which some of the code can develop before being merged back into the main code later.

Note Exercise 5-1 will help you understand this section.

Before creating the high-level solution, Peter ensures that he is connected to the Enterprise 3.1 Team Project in the Icarus-tfs Team Foundation Server in the same way as Clare in Chapter 3. To create the solution, Peter then chooses File ➤ New ➤ Project, which brings up the New Project dialog box shown in Figure 5-2. He chooses Blank Solution from the Visual Studio Solutions group under Other Project Types, then browses to find the place on his developer machine where he should locate the project. He also clicks the Add to Source Control checkbox as he wants all his work to be included in the team's source control. Once he clicks OK, the dialog box shown in Figure 5-3 appears. This allows Peter to select the team project in which he wants to insert the solution. He chooses the Enterprise 3.1 team project that you saw Clare create in Chapter 3, gives the solution the name Enterprise 3.1, and clicks OK. Peter then saves the solution.

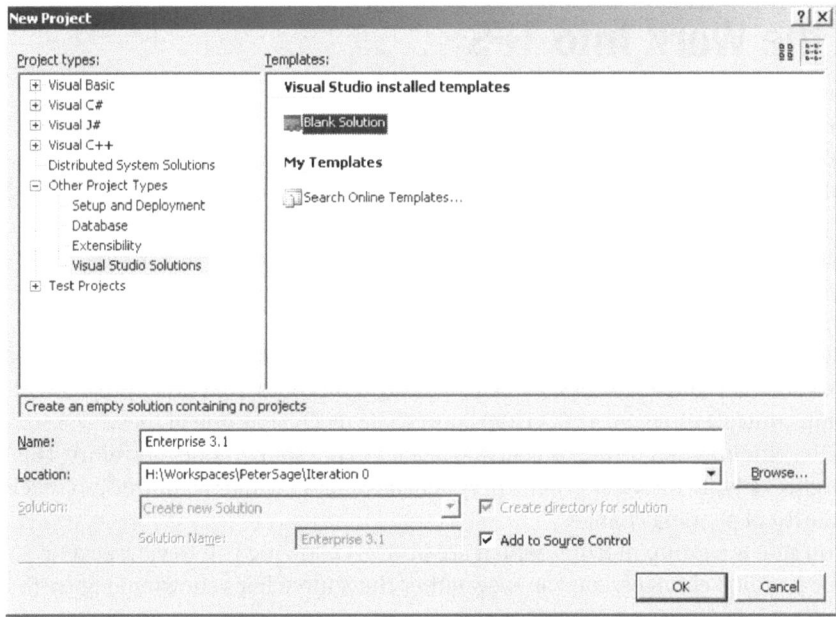

Figure 5-2. *New Project dialog box*

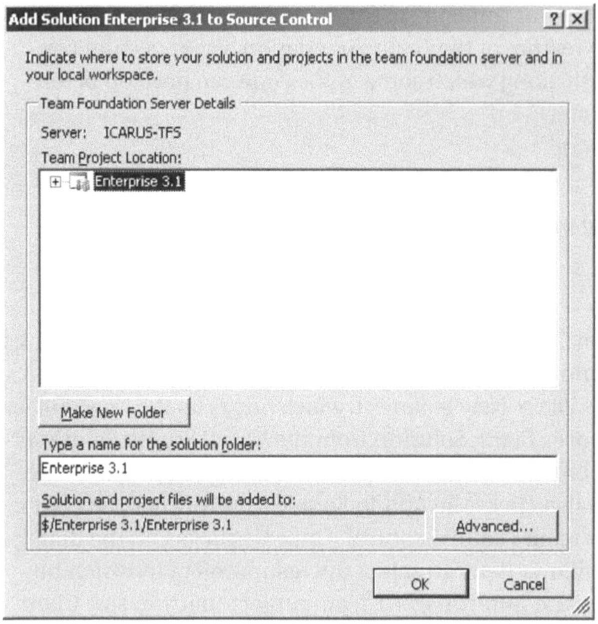

Figure 5-3. *Add Solution to Source Control dialog box*

Checking the Work Into TFS

The solution for Enterprise 3.1 is now created, and Peter can think about how to design the new application. But first, it's a good idea to check the new solution into TFS. We mentioned the source control capabilities of Visual Studio Team System in Chapter 1, and at this point in the project those capabilities will be used for the first time. Although only a solution has been created, this is an important step, as Peter and others will now add folders and various files to the solution. There are various ways of checking in, and various windows that are useful in working with source control. Figure 5-4 shows the Pending Changes window (select View ➤ Other Windows ➤ Pending Changes). This window can display either the flat view in Figure 5-4 or a view organized by folder, which gives you a better idea of where the files belong. As expected, there are only two changes, the new solution file and its .vssscc file. I'll mention at this point that every project that is bound to a version control system such as Visual SourceSafe or TFS has one of these .vssscc files. They contain the bindings that tie the project and its files to the source code repository. The .vssscc file itself is checked into the version control system as well as the files it controls, so that is why it appears in the list of pending changes.

At the left-hand side is a group of icons, which are buttons allowing you to view several other aspects of the pending changes. You can view either the Source Files shown in Figure 5-4 or the Work Items, Check-In Notes, or Policy Warnings.

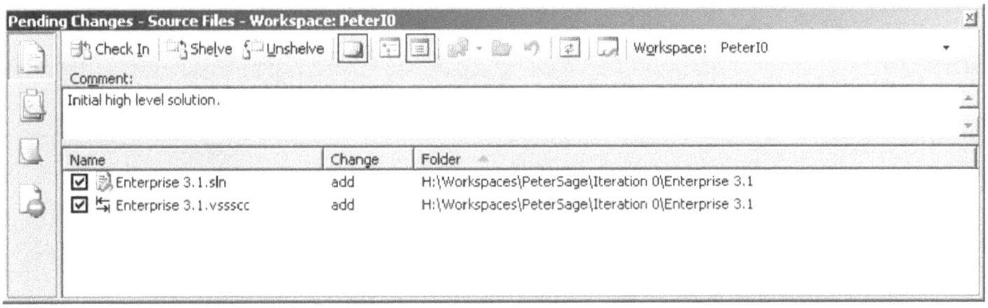

Figure 5-4 shows the Pending Changes window.

Figure 5-4. *The Pending Changes window*

The Work Items view is provided so that you can associate a check-in operation with a set of work items. Before the work items in this view will be visible, however, Peter needs to select a suitable query that will return a set of work items relevant to his work. He first clicks on the ellipsis to the right of the Query drop-down at the top of the window, which opens the browse window in Figure 5-5. Here Peter can select the correct team project and an appropriate query.

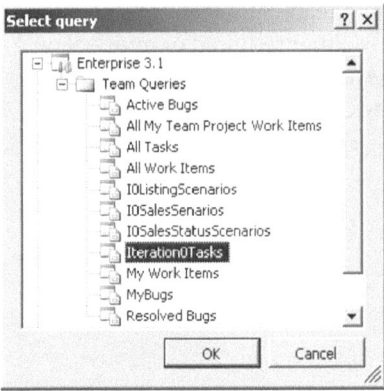

Figure 5-5. *Select a query to fetch the work items to populate the Work Items view.*

Peter selects a query that was written to show the iteration 0 tasks (you learned how to write queries in Chapter 4), and clicks OK to produce the list of work items that now populates the window shown in Figure 5-6. He wants to associate his check-in of the new solution with Create Solution Architecture, his major task during iteration 0, and he does this by checking the box beside that task.

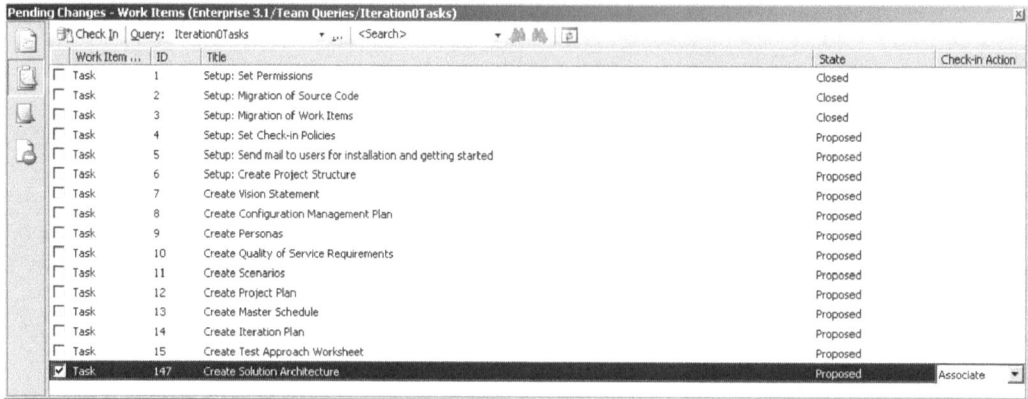

Figure 5-6. *The Pending Changes window—Work Items view*

Clicking the third button on the left (the one that looks like a stack of yellow sticky notes), Peter displays the Check-in Notes dialog box for the pending changes, as shown in Figure 5-7. Default notes are included that allow explanations from the three named reviewers in Figure 5-7 to be added, but a user in the Project Administrators Team System group can define more check-in notes and specify whether their completion is either required or optional on check-in. To do this, the user right-clicks on the team project in Team Explorer and selects Source Control to open the Source Control Settings dialog box.

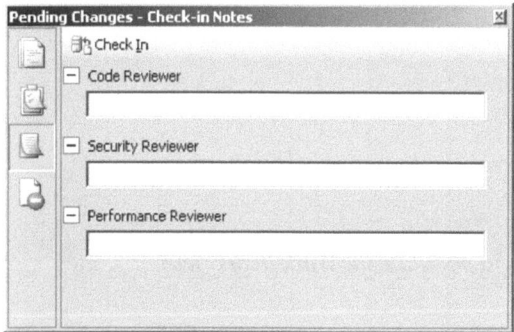

Figure 5-7. *The Pending Changes window—Check-in Notes view*

The fourth button on the left allows the user to view any policy warnings prior to attempting a check-in operation. Check-in policies may be defined to require successful builds, unit tests, and so forth. None have been defined on the project yet, so this view will be empty. I'll show you that in Chapter 8.

Peter can now click the Check-In button at the top left to check his changes into TFS. The Pending Changes window should then be empty. Checking in work is part of the configuration aspects of TFS, and we will return to that topic again and again.

Application Diagrams

Now that Peter has a solution, he can start putting some useful files in it. Visual Studio 2005 Team Edition for Architects lets you create application diagrams, which assist the design of distributed applications. These applications, discussed in Chapter 1, are distributed over an enterprise, often with each functional area communicating with others via service-oriented architecture (SOA) concepts. The component parts of the entire distributed application are themselves applications and may be scattered geographically, with each hosted on different machines in different parts of the world, or they may all be hosted on the same machine. An application diagram defines one distributed application in terms of those applications that are part of it, along with their interconnections. The entire set of component applications makes up a certain defined functionality for the total application. The application diagram reveals nothing about where the applications are deployed, but it can indicate constraints that determine where these component applications *may* be deployed.

Application diagrams do much more than just help you design and visualize the application; they can also implement parts of it, and the diagram itself can be created by reverse-engineering existing applications. For the rest of this chapter, I'll concentrate on the design and visualization side of things. I'll discuss implementation later, when our architect Peter has thought things through well enough and is ready to start the ball rolling by creating code.

What Is an Application?

When I first read the documentation on Application Designer, I felt a little confused. What does the word *application* mean in this instance? Well, the whole diagram generally represents one application in the sense of providing a certain amount of functionality for an enterprise, but then each box on the diagram also represents an application in that it provides some functionality that is used by the whole application. So I settled on this definition: anything represented by a whole diagram is a *distributed application* and anything represented by one box on the diagram is a *component application*. That's the terminology I'm going to use in this book. Remember also, however, that a component application as it appears on one diagram might just be the distributed application for another diagram. In other words, one distributed application might consist of several other distributed applications.

Let's look at an example—suppose we consider a bank. Its entire enterprise system—all its desktop applications, server applications, mainframe CICS (Customer Information Control System) regions, maybe the customers' browsers too—can be thought of as one huge application: the First National Bank of Hootersville Enterprise Application version 7.35. Now that vast distributed application—which nobody has ever fully described—is made up of smaller distributed applications that themselves consist of various bits and pieces of software—the component applications. Examples might be the Home Loans Processing Application, the Internet Banking Application, and the Customer Relationship Management Application. Each of these might well have one or two databases, several web services, client applications of various kinds, mainframe applications, collections of files, and who knows what else. However, Home Loans Processing, Internet Banking, and so forth are the component applications of the bank's whole application.

Notice that I've not mentioned *systems* at all; this is because the word *system* is reserved for another concept, a particular configuration of an application, which I'll discuss later. It's important to notice, though, that an application isn't necessary one definite set of component applications connected in a particular way. The concept is more general than that. A distributed application, as shown in an application diagram, represents all the components and all the possible ways they can be connected.

But the application diagram definitely does *not* represent the physical way the applications are deployed. Don't start thinking that the boxes represent host computers, or you're going down the wrong track! That sort of thing is represented by a logical data center diagram, which again I'll discuss later in the "Deployment" section.

One final example: I once designed a product consisting of components that used a publish/subscribe interaction between them. The component set that was included at any one time was configurable and each type of component had its own set of ASP.NET pages and database tables. I think that system would make a very good distributed application on an application diagram. All those little component applications ran on the same computer and they did not use web services, but it was still a distributed application. Microsoft may be thinking mainly of distributed applications as being designed under the SOA umbrella, but it's always fun to extend the concept, isn't it? That's what developers will be doing, you can bet on it!

Application Prototypes Available in Team System

When adding an application to your diagram, you choose from a set of prototypes that represent types of applications. Microsoft provides a set of application prototypes in Team System that will get you started. They cover the basic application types that you can develop with Visual Studio, as well as some catchall types.

- **WindowsApplication**—This application prototype is intended to represent a Windows application, a console application, or a Windows service on your application diagram.

- **ASP.NETWebService**—This prototype represents a web service on your diagram.

- **ASP.NETWebApplication**—This represents an ASP.NET web application that delivers Web Forms to a browser.

- **OfficeApplication**—This represents an Office application: an Excel workbook, an Excel spreadsheet, an Outlook add-in, a Word document, or a Word template.

- **ExternalWebService**—This represents a web service that is external to the application and is defined by a single Web Service Definition Language (WSDL) file.

- **ExternalDatabase**—This represents a database that is external to the solution; it is not built as part of the solution. This applies to any database that your application uses.

- **BizTalkWebService**—This represents an external web service that is known to be a BizTalk web service.

- **GenericApplication**—This represents any unsupported or unspecified application. It exists for documentation purposes only; you can't implement code with it or reverse-engineer code to generate it.

If there's an application type that's not represented by a prototype, you can either develop a custom application or use the generic one. It's easy to make a custom application prototype from one of the existing ones: simply select an application that you have configured with endpoints, settings, and constraints on the design surface and add it to the toolbox. You will see this in the section on using legacy applications as prototypes.

Note You can also create custom applications using the System Definition Model (SDM) SDK. I don't have space in this book to describe how to use the SDM SDK.

Connecting Applications

Displaying the component applications of a distributed application together on a diagram is a great idea, but to make it useful we want to show how they interact. In the application diagram concept, applications interact through *endpoints*. Provider and consumer endpoints are defined; two applications can only be connected by connecting a consumer endpoint to a provider endpoint. The Toolbox contains a selection of provider endpoint prototypes. You can add provider endpoints to any application by dragging them from the Toolbox onto the application—but only if the application is defined as being able to accept the kind of provider endpoints you're trying to add. To add consumer endpoints, you first click on the connector in the Toolbox and then drag from the application you choose as consumer to a provider endpoint on another application. You can also drag in the opposite direction, from a provider endpoint to the consumer application. This will do two things: it will create a consumer endpoint on the consumer application, and then place a connection between the new consumer endpoint and the selected provider endpoint.

Note Exercise 5-2 will help you understand this section.

Consumer endpoints that have been created like this will have attributes that make them specific to the provider endpoint. To see this, you can select a new connection that you've added this way, right-click, and select Delete from the context menu. This deletes the connection but leaves the consumer endpoint that you added. Now you can try to add a new connection from the new consumer endpoint to another provider. You'll find that it will only accept a provider that is compatible with the consumer endpoint. This can be a bit confusing if you start using Application Designer without taking the trouble to understand endpoints properly. However, you can always add a connection from that consumer endpoint back to the original provider endpoint or some other compatible endpoint. Experimenting a little with applications and connections will help you get the idea and avoid confusion. You can also right-click on any endpoint and select Properties to see its detail in the properties window, which can be helpful if you can't figure out why two endpoints can't be connected.

Application Designer defines four preconfigured endpoint prototypes; all are available in the Toolbox except `DatabaseEndpoint`, and each can take the form of either providers or consumers.

WebServiceEndpoint

When used as a provider endpoint, this represents a point on a component application where a web service is exposed. It is possible to use a WSDL or `.disco` file to define characteristics of the web service that is provided by the application. When used as a consumer, it indicates a point in a component application where the application uses a web service. You can only add this endpoint prototype to an `ASP.NETWebApplication` or `ASP.NETWebService` application.

WebContentEndpoint

When used as a provider endpoint, this represents the point on a component application where web content is available, which could be HTML files or Active Server Pages (ASP) and their associated images, scripts, and so forth. When used as a consumer, it represents a point where a component application can act as a client and receive the same kind of web content. You can only add this endpoint prototype to an `ASP.NETWebApplication` or `ASP.NETWebService` application.

DatabaseEndpoint

When used as a provider, this represents a point where another application can connect to a database. As a consumer, it represents a place in an application where that application uses a database. A `DatabaseEndpoint` appears automatically on an `ExternalDatabase` application and you cannot add more of them.

GenericEndpoint

As a provider, this represents a connection point where another application can obtain some kind of service that is unspecified. As a consumer, it represents a place where the application obtains unspecified services from another application. Of course, you can use the name of the endpoint to indicate the type of services that are provided or consumed. You can add this type of endpoint to any application.

Customizing Endpoints

Having defined features specific to a particular endpoint such as hosting constraints, URL names, namespaces, and binding names, you can save an endpoint to the Toolbox as an endpoint prototype and reuse it. For example, you might want to define a very specific web service consumer endpoint that will only bind to a provider with a certain URL and only be hosted in a logical server with equivalent endpoint characteristics.

Application Settings

Application Designer exposes to the architect a model of the application's settings via Settings and Constraints Editor. The application settings are values set in the application's environment that control the behavior of the application. Many of the settings go into the application's XML `.config` file; these are shown in the Settings and Constraints Editor arranged into groups called *resources* under a folder called Configuration, which is under a folder called Directory. In addition, there are custom settings that you define yourself. Depending on the type of application, the `.config` file could be `Web.config` or `App.config`. Its settings override any defined for the machine environment in `machine.config`, according to the normal rules of .NET. A defined set of resources exists for each application type, any of which may be added in the Settings and Constraints Editor by right-clicking on the Configuration folder and selecting from the resources available from the context menu.

As I said, the settings configured via these resources in the Settings and Constraints Editor translate to XML elements in the appropriate `.config` file. A good example is the addition of a group of app settings, which would normally be done by editing either the `Web.config` or the `App.config` file for an ASP.NET or Windows Forms application, respectively. Using the Settings and Constraints Editor, the architect can enter the application settings together with their values early in the design. Of course, the values of these settings may change at deployment and be different for various usages of the application, so it is possible to select a checkbox for each setting to indicate that it can be overridden. Override can take place in System Designer and implies physical configuration of `.config` files at install time. In other words, each system could have different overridden values of some of the settings whose default values were defined in the application.

As well as at the architecture stage, additions and modifications to the `.config` files may take place during coding, after the applications designed in Application Designer have been implemented. Any changes made in the `App.config` or `Web.config` after implementation will appear back in the Settings and Constraints Editor. Similarly, changes made in the editor after implementation will appear in the appropriate `.config` file.

A great many settings are available for some application prototypes. You reference these settings via constraints in logical servers to control which applications may be hosted within them. I have briefly summarized in the next section the settings applicable to the available prototype applications, but it is beyond the scope of this chapter to explore how all of these can be used. If you're interested, consult the Visual Studio documentation to learn the details. The custom settings can be whatever you like and appear in the `.sdm` file for the application and other documents, but they do not go into the `.config` file and you cannot set constraints that refer to them.

Settings Available for the Prototype Applications

Figure 5-8 shows the settings for a typical application. Table 5-1 summarizes the settings available for the various standard application prototypes.

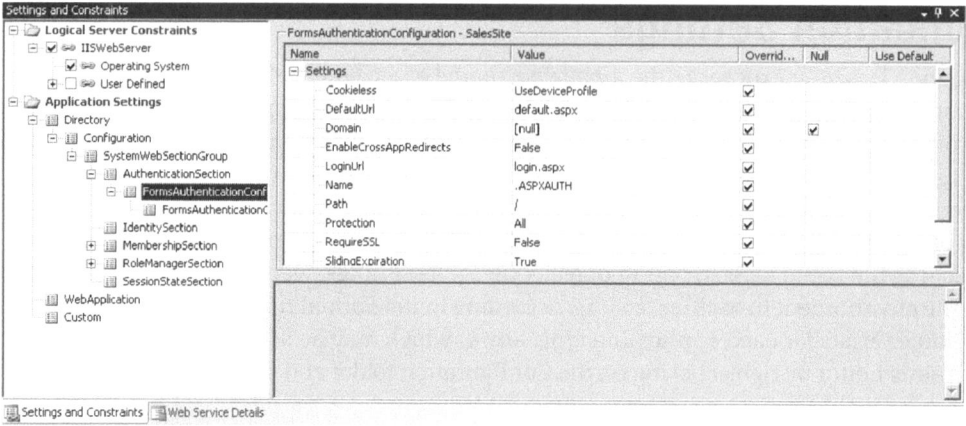

Figure 5-8. *Example of settings available for the ASP.NETWebApplication prototype*

Table 5-1. *Summary of Settings for the Standard Application Prototypes*

Application Prototype	Settings Available
WindowsApplication	Settings for the file containing the application; custom settings
OfficeApplication	Settings for the file containing the application; custom settings
ASP.NETWebApplication	Settings for the file containing the application; custom settings; settings related to authentication, identity, membership, role management, and session state
ASP.NETWebService	Settings for the file containing the application; custom settings; settings related to authentication, identity, membership, role management, and session state
ExternalWebService	Custom settings
ExternalDatabase	Custom settings
BizTalkWebService	Custom settings
GenericApplication	Custom settings

Application Constraints

Constraints are requirements that a configuration value be set in a certain way. A constraint set at the application layer provides a requirement on the data center layer on which the application is to be hosted. Alternatively, a constraint applied at the data center layer puts a requirement on all applications that expect to be hosted on it. Thus the idea of settings and constraints results in a set of mutual requirements between layers of the architecture that must be met at deployment time, but that can be verified using Deployment Designer long before the application has been built. The word *layer* is used here to illustrate a general concept across which constraints may be applied, but in the distributed system designers, it means constraints between the application layer and the hosting layer.

Note Exercise 5-3 will help you understand this section.

The constraints that applications can impose on their environment are summarized in Table 5-2 and fall into three categories:

- **Implicit constraints**: Those automatically associated with a particular type of application prototype, such as a web service, a Windows application, or a database

- **Predefined constraints**: A set of constraints that are predefined and from which you may choose

- **User-defined constraints**: Constraints that you make up yourself and for which you define matching settings on servers

Implicit constraints are authored by the person who defined the application prototype and are not displayed or editable by the Settings and Constraints Editor. Application prototypes can be produced using the SDM SDK, and someone designing a new application prototype would probably want to define some implicit constraints. One example of an implicit constraint is a requirement that defines where an application can be hosted. For example, a web service application must be hosted on a web server.

Predefined constraints are displayed and can be selected in the Settings and Constraints Editor to enable you to select which constraints, for a particular application, you wish to specify. Here are some examples, some of which are specific to the IIS web server:

- Operating system, which specify the operating system requirements of the application

- Authentication settings

- Reliability settings

- Multiple processor configuration

The constraints available to be set for each of the application prototypes are summarized in Table 5-2.

Table 5-2. *Constraints That Can be Specified on Standard Application Prototypes*

Application Prototype	Constraints Available
WindowsApplication	Constraints on the type of logical server, operating system, common language runtime.
OfficeApplication	Constraints on the type of logical server supported, operating system, common language runtime.
ASP.NETWebApplication	Constraints on the type of logical server supported, operating system, common language runtime, IIS configuration.
ASP.NETWebService	Constraints on the type of logical server supported, operating system, common language runtime, IIS configuration.
ExternalWebService	None.
BizTalkWebService	None.
ExternalDatabase	Constraints on the type of logical server supported.
GenericApplication	Constraints on the type of logical server supported. Also, depending on the type of logical server supported, operating system, common language runtime, IIS configuration.

Application Diagrams for Icarus Enterprise 3.1

Peter has the task of creating the solution architecture for Icarus Enterprise 3.1, and the project team has made the decision to use Visual Studio 2005 Team System, which allows the architect to design and implement applications as we have just discussed. How can Peter best use those features to steer Enterprise 3.1 in the right direction? In this project, Peter is beginning with a legacy distributed application, and he needs to remove some of its component applications and replace them with new ones. Some of the retained applications may have to be modified to accommodate the new capabilities, while others will stay the same. Peter must plan for the developers to be able to test the new applications with some confidence before production rollout.

Also, integration testing must take place without disturbing the live system, and deployment must occur over a weekend with the minimum of risk. By Monday after deployment, they must either have the new application in place, or have reliably rolled back to the old system, with a plan to try again at a subsequent date. Thus, system testing must take place in a configuration that is as close as possible to production. Unfortunately, cost prevents the company from having more than two installations of the orchestration service, one that is in production and one that is used for staging. The staging system will be available for one week prior to deployment to production, which allows some time for correcting last-minute problems—but not a lot! Peter therefore feels he must system-test the new application thoroughly using some kind of stubbing of the orchestration service.

With this in mind, Peter decides that his first task will be to use Application Designer to model the existing application. He plans to include on the new application diagram those legacy applications that the new ones must work with. In Team System, it is only possible to have one application diagram per solution. The application diagram is solution scoped, so that if you require a hierarchy of application diagrams, you will need to have different solutions for each application diagram in the hierarchy. Similarly, if you want to model an existing distributed application before you start modeling the new one, you must create a solution for the old application. Peter therefore opens Visual Studio again and creates a new solution called Enterprise 2.4.

Creating an Application Diagram for the Existing Application

To create an application diagram for the existing system, Peter right-clicks the solution Enterprise 2.4 in Solution Explorer and selects Add ➤ New Distributed System Diagram. This displays the Add New Item dialog box, which lets users add three kinds of distributed system diagrams: application diagrams, logical data center diagrams, and system diagrams. Peter will use all three of these in the planning of Enterprise 3.1, but for the moment he's working with application diagrams. So to create one, he selects Application Diagram and names it `Enterprise 2.4.ad`, as shown in Figure 5-9.

Note Exercise 5-4 will help you understand this section.

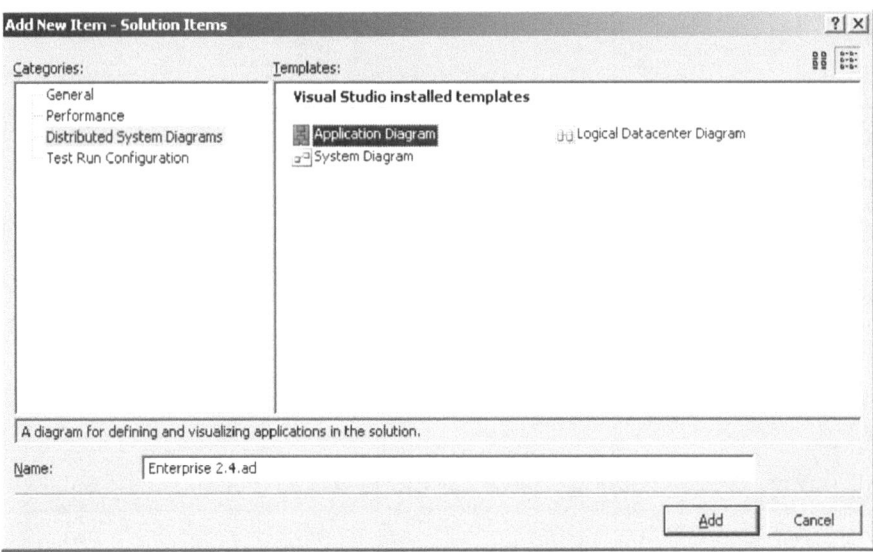

Figure 5-9. *The Add New Item dialog box*

Once Peter clicks Add, Application Designer adds a folder automatically to the solution and the solution diagram is created within it, as shown in Figure 5-10. At this point, Peter brings the Toolbox to the screen by hovering over it and then clicking its pushpin. The Application Designer window now looks like Figure 5-11.

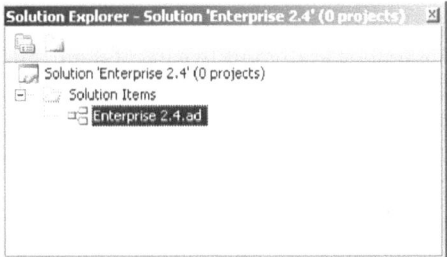

Figure 5-10. *Solution Explorer after the new application diagram has been added*

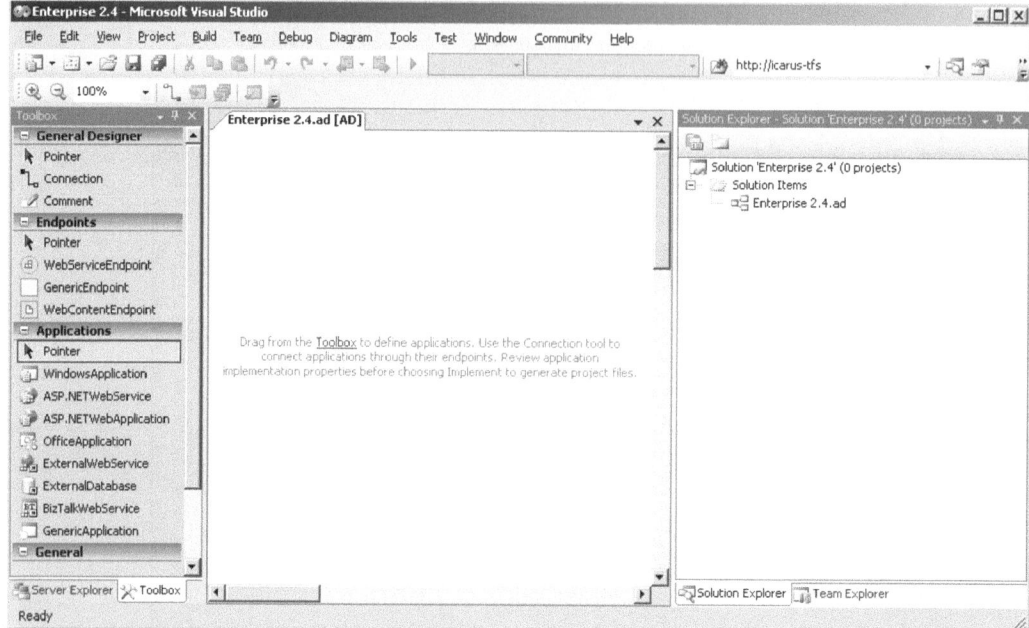

Figure 5-11. *The development environment after creating a new application diagram*

Peter refers back to his Visio drawing (Chapter 2, Figure 2-22) and begins adding the applications to the diagram. The completed diagram (shown in Figure 5-12) represents the entire distributed application that the Enterprise 2.4 solution implements; let's see how Peter created it.

Peter starts by adding the existing database as an external database. To do this, he drags that application prototype from the Toolbox to the empty diagram and labels it SQL2000Database.

Next, he drags four generic application instances from the Toolbox onto the diagram; labels them EmailService, DocumentService, AccountingJournalService, and OrchestrationService; and lays them out as shown in Figure 5-12. Then he adds generic endpoints to each of them and labels them as shown in the figure. Peter then connects the generic provider endpoints on EmailApplication, DocumentService, and AccountingJournalService to the orchestration service by clicking the connection in the Toolbox and dragging from the OrchestrationService application to the generic endpoints on each of the other three in turn. This automatically creates three consumer endpoints on the OrchestrationService application. You can also do this by simply holding down Alt and dragging, without bothering to select the connection in the Toolbox, either from the OrchestrationService application to the provider endpoints on the other applications or from the provider endpoints to the OrchestrationService application. Either way, you will create new consumer endpoints on the OrchestrationService application.

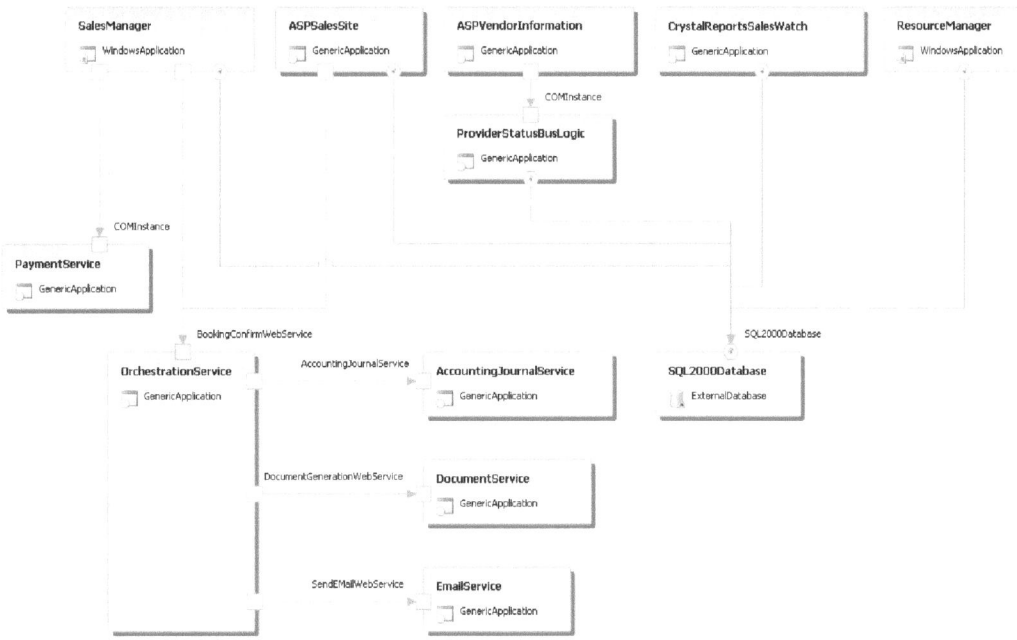

Figure 5-12. *The completed application diagram of the legacy application, Enterprise 2.4*

Next Peter adds a generic application to represent the Visual Basic COM (Component Object Model) server that acts as the middle tier in the existing Vendor Information website, labels it ProviderStatusBusLogic, drags a generic endpoint from the Toolbox to the top of the application, and labels the endpoint COMInstance. Then he connects this application to the database provider endpoint by holding down the Alt key and dragging from the provider endpoint on SQL2000Database to the ProviderStatusBusLogic application.

He adds the two Windows applications next, to represent the existing thick clients SalesManager and ResourceManager, connecting SalesManager both to the database and to the orchestration service by holding down Alt and dragging from the provider endpoints on SQL2000Database and OrchestrationServer to each of the new applications. ResourceManager is connected directly to the database.

Finally, Peter depicts the applications, ASPSalesSite, ASPVendorInformation, and also the Crystal Reports application, by three more generic applications and connects them as shown, using the same technique. Keep in mind that the sales applications, both ASPSalesSite and SalesManager, are connected to the orchestration server as well as the database. This is because they need to access information and save data in the database to represent new sales, but they also need to kick off asynchronous actions via the orchestration server to generate printed receipts, accounting records, and confirmation emails.

Using the Legacy Applications As Prototypes

Having drawn this diagram of the existing application, Peter knows that he will use some of its component applications in the new distributed application, i.e., those that will not be replaced as part of the Enterprise 3.1 project. To help with this, he can make those component applications into custom application prototypes in the Toolbox. To do this, Peter right-clicks on the application that he wants to use as a prototype and selects Add to Toolbox. There are always multiple ways of doing things in Visual Studio; you can also click Diagram ➤ Add to Toolbox. Either approach opens the dialog box shown in Figure 5-13, which prompts you to type a name for the application; here, Peter has used "OrchestrationService", though you might sometimes want to make a prototype based on an existing application but with a more general name. Names must not contain spaces or other undesirable characters such as hyphens, periods, and colons—but you can use underscores if you must simulate spaces just like names in your code.

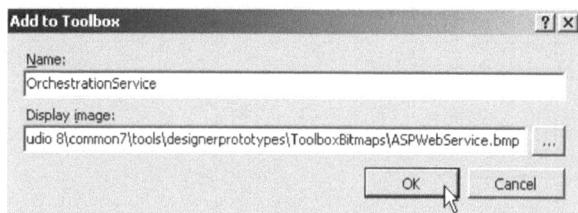

Figure 5-13. *This dialog box lets you add an application as a prototype to the Toolbox.*

At this point, Peter clicks OK to open the Save File dialog box. Peter specifies the name and location of the file that contains the prototype application, as shown in Figure 5-14. This file is saved in a proprietary format so you cannot edit it.

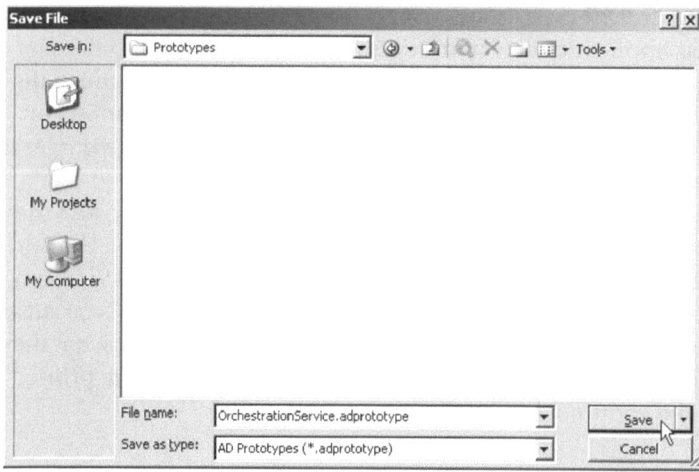

Figure 5-14. *Specify where the application prototype file will be saved.*

Custom application prototypes saved in this manner will be automatically loaded into the Toolbox, which is organized into tabs as shown in Figure 5-11. The new prototypes will be loaded under the tab that you happen to have selected in the Toolbox. It's a good idea to create a new tab for custom applications; Peter, for example, creates one called "Enterprise 2.4 Applications" and makes sure all of the prototypes made from the legacy applications go there. To create the new tab, he simply right-clicks on the Toolbox and selects Add Tab. If you accidentally save the prototypes in the wrong place, you can easily drag them from one tab to another.

Creating the Application Diagram for the New Solution

Peter now needs to create an application diagram for the new solution. To do this, he opens the Enterprise 3.1.sln solution again in Visual Studio and creates another application diagram as before, this time calling it "Enterprise 3.1". The Toolbox now looks like Figure 5-15, with all of the legacy application prototypes listed under the Enterprise 2.4 Applications tab.

Note Exercise 5-5 will help you understand this section.

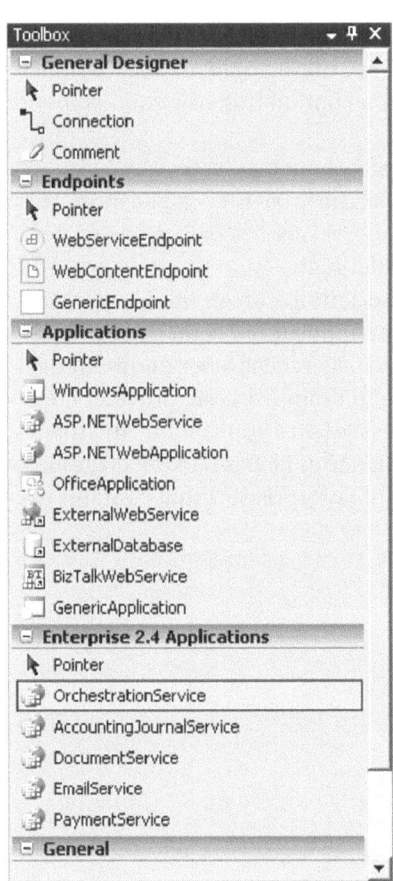

Figure 5-15. *The Application Designer Toolbox after adding the legacy applications as prototypes*

The legacy applications were connected when they were saved; therefore, if Peter drags them from the Toolbox in the order of providers first, the connections actually happen automatically, so he drags EMailService, DocumentService, PaymentService, AccountingJournalService, and then OrchestrationService onto the drawing. The connections are automatically restored, and he lines up the applications neatly. A word about formatting: you can drag applications around the diagram to lay them out neatly, and position their connections by dragging the handles that appear on them in an intuitive manner. You can also move endpoints around on the perimeter of an application box and drag their labels to position them relative to the endpoint symbols. Finally, choosing Redraw Connection from the right-click menu will move the endpoints to a location chosen automatically and then reroute the connection.

These are the only legacy applications to be included—it's all new stuff from now on—so next Peter places two GenericApplication applications on the drawing; these will become the SalesBusinessObjects and ListingBusinessObjects middle-tier applications. He names them and then opens the Settings and Constraints Editor for SalesBusinessObjects. This application should specify a constraint—the server on which it can be installed can only be GenericServer. Peter therefore deselects DatabaseServer, IISWebServer, and WindowsClient. There are no more constraints that can be set for a generic application, so he clicks the ListingBusinessObjects application and sets its constraints in the same manner.

Next Peter adds an ExternalDatabase application, calls it Enterprise, and drags the DatabaseServer endpoint to the top. He holds down Alt and drags from this endpoint to first the SalesBusinessObjects application and then to the ListingBusinessObjects application, creating database consumer endpoints automatically on both these applications. He right-clicks on each new consumer endpoint, selects the Show Label option from the context menu, and then changes their names to EnterpriseDB.

Finally, he adds a connection by holding down Alt and dragging from BookingConfirmWebService on the legacy OrchestrationServer application to the SalesBusinessObjects application. This is because the SalesBusinessObjects application will need to use BookingConfirmWebService to trigger downstream action as a result of a sale being made; such actions include printing a confirmation slip, entering a journal in the accounts, and sending an email. These asynchronous events will be handled by the OrchestrationServer application. Peter selects Show Label again from the right-click menu for the newly created GenericConsumer endpoint on SalesBusinessObjects. Finally, he holds down the Alt key and drags from the provider endpoint on the PaymentService application to the SalesBusinessObjects application, and then renames the consumer endpoint to make it more meaningful. After he has laid the diagram out neatly, it looks like Figure 5-16. This completes the part of Enterprise 3.1 that contains the business logic.

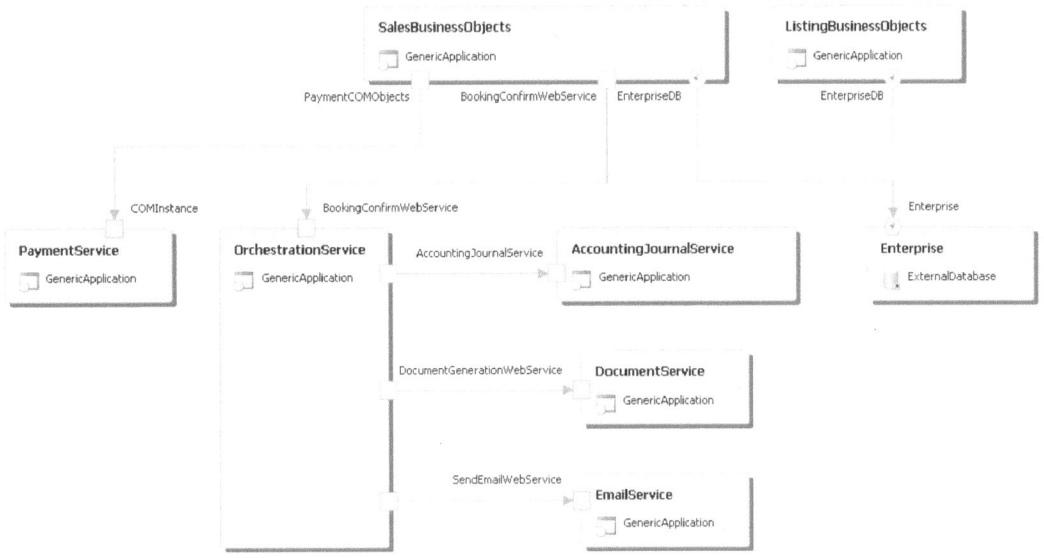

Figure 5-16. *The business logic part of the Icarus Enterprise 3.1 application*

In this kind of n-tier application, the business logic is placed on a middle tier and consists of classes that encapsulate business processes and business entities. The business processes can be called upon to do various tasks, such as create, delete, or modify an order. In carrying out their work, the functions in these classes will create instances of business entity classes, each of which will represent some sort of persistent business object, such as an Order object. By *persistent*, I mean that the object exists for a long period of time in the database and can, for example, be brought into the memory of the application, modified, and returned to the database. I will describe these concepts in the next few chapters, which deal with the Build track of the project.

Next Peter turns his attention to the presentation layer, in which the services provided by the business layer—resident in the business logic, and exposed via .NET Remoting—are presented to loosely coupled smart clients and browser clients via web services and a website, respectively. I explored the concepts of the browser client and smart client in Chapter 1.

A browser client is nothing more than a general-purpose web browser such as Microsoft Internet Explorer and can implement an application on a client machine only because the server sends it HTML page by page. The presentation layer on the server that supports this kind of client consists of a set of ASP.NET pages that are delivered to the client in a defined sequence as the user navigates through a business process. In ASP.NET, these display pages have *code behind* that deals with the business logic layer via .NET Remoting to do the real work of the process. Data is obtained from the business layer objects to populate screens sent to the browser, and data is received from the browser to be relayed back to the business layer. In this way, an ASP.NET application *presents* the business processes implemented in the business logic middle tier to the user.

An alternative presentation layer is a web service. In this case a smart client, which will be a Windows Forms application, provides all of the screens for the user and contains a great deal more capability than a browser. The smart client usually deals with a server that exposes business functionality based on the business logic, but offers it in the web service format. In the case of Icarus Enterprise 3.1, both methods are required for the sales capability; hence there are two separate presentation layer applications: SalesWebService and SalesSite. There is no requirement for resource management to be carried out via a browser client, and so in this case only ListingWebService is required.

Peter now adds the presentation layer applications. He adds two ASP.NETWebService applications by dragging the prototype twice from the Toolbox and labeling them SalesWebService and ListingWebService. He also drags an ASP.NETWebApplication from the Toolbox and names it SalesSite. He drags the provider endpoints to the top and gives them meaningful names. Next he opens the Settings and Constraints Editor, checks Operating System as a constraint imposed by these applications, and defines the permitted operating system as Windows 2003, with Server Type: Server, and Suite Type: Enterprise.

Next he drags a GenericEndpoint from the Toolbox to the top of first SalesBusinessObjects and then ListingBusinessObjects. He gives the endpoints the same name as the applications. He opens the Settings and Constraints Editor for each endpoint, checks UserDefined under the endpoint hosting constraints, and then enters ".NET Remoting" as the Protocol Value setting. He also enters ".NET Remoting" as the Protocol Value setting for the application endpoints. The constraints and settings are thus the same for the endpoints on top of SalesBusinessObjects and ResourceBusinessObjects. Both require .NET Remoting as the protocol supported by the endpoint to which they are bound on a logical server. They also have a protocol setting of .NET Remoting so their protocol will satisfy a similar constraint applied to them by a server endpoint.

For each of these application endpoints, Peter also deselects the Overridable checkbox in the Settings and Constraints Editor for the Communications, Protocol setting, which is under the Application Endpoint Settings (now set to .NET Remoting). If this Overridable option is enabled, the setting can be overridden when this particular application is included as part of a System. I'm really jumping ahead a little with all this discussion involving endpoint constraints and settings and how they relate to systems and logical servers as I have not yet described those two concepts. You might want to read on through this chapter and look back at this paragraph when you better understand systems and logical data centers.

Next, Peter Alt-drags from each endpoint to the SalesSite and SalesWebService applications so that two consumer endpoints are added on each. Then he drags from the endpoint on the top of ListingBusinessObjects to ListingWebService to create a consumer endpoint. He sets the characteristics of all the new endpoints on the presentation layer applications to be the same as the .NET Remoting endpoints on SalesBusinessObjects and ListingBusinessObjects.

Finally, Peter adds the client layer by dragging three WindowsApplication prototypes onto the drawing, placing them at the top, and then labels them SalesWing, SalesStatus, and ListWing. He also adds a GenericApplication and labels it WebBrowser. Peter connects the web services and website presentation endpoints to the applications, creating the consumer endpoints automatically. The SalesWing and SalesStatus applications both require connection to the SalesWebService application, while the ListWing application requires connection to the ListingWebService application. The WebBrowser application needs to be connected to the SalesSite application. This completes the diagram of the Icarus Enterprise 3.1 application; see Figure 5-17.

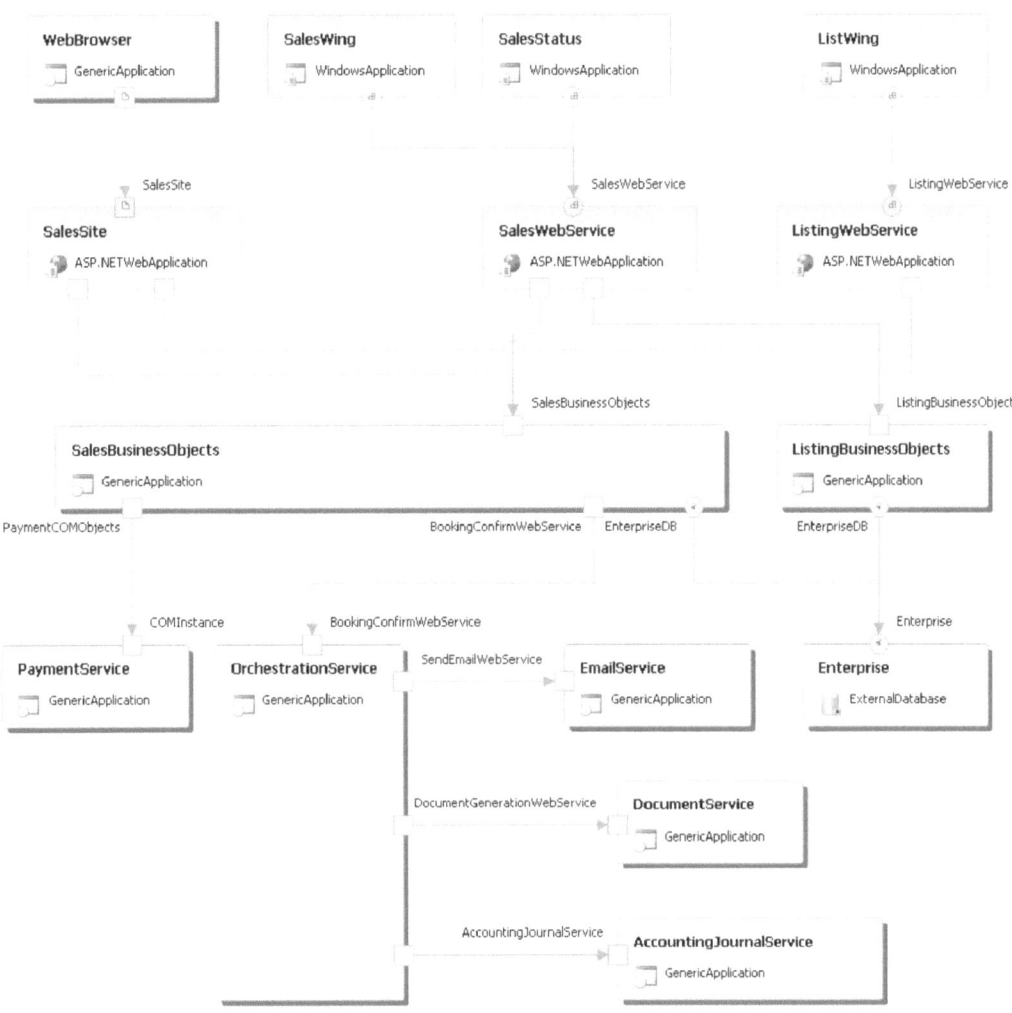

Figure 5-17. *The complete Icarus Enterprise 3.1 application*

Stub and Test Harness Applications for the New Solution

In Chapter 3, the team put together an iteration plan that showed development of limited end-to-end capability in the first six-week iteration and further capability in the second iteration. In order to meet these goals, work on the Sales Wing Windows Forms smart client application will need to begin immediately at the start of the iteration. It cannot wait until the database, business objects, and web service applications are working before the developers are able to run it. The developers of the Sales Wing application will therefore need a stub that simulates, in a limited way, the functions in the web service so that they can get their screens working. As architect, Peter must define these interfaces carefully during the early part of the iteration so that the Windows Forms smart client can work with the real web service when integration begins—perhaps in about the last two weeks. The developers of the List Wing smart client have the same problem.

Peter therefore drags two more `ASP.NETWebService` applications from the Toolbox and names them `SalesWebServiceStub` and `ListingWebServiceStub`. He connects these to the `SalesWing` and `ListWing` Windows applications, and creates another web service consumer endpoint on each of these.

A different situation exists for the developers of the Sales Web Service and Listing Web Service; they may need a way of testing their applications in the absence of the Windows application smart clients. Peter keeps these in mind as possibilities but leaves them off the diagram for simplicity. These would act as consumers for the web services and allow testing prior to the integration with the real clients, but it may be possible to test the web services using Internet Explorer. We will see more of the planning for this in Chapter 6 when Peter begins to define the requirements for these individual applications and specify their interfaces. We expect these designs to change from iteration to iteration since the requirements will be added in a piecemeal manner through the iterations, as described in Chapter 3.

Finally, Peter adds a generic application called `OrchestrationServiceStub`. This stub will be needed for a much longer period of time since the real orchestration service will not be available for integration with the new distributed application until staging. This, of course, is a major risk to the project, brought about because of the unacceptable cost of duplicating the orchestration server in the development environment. The completed diagram for the new application is shown in Figure 5-18.

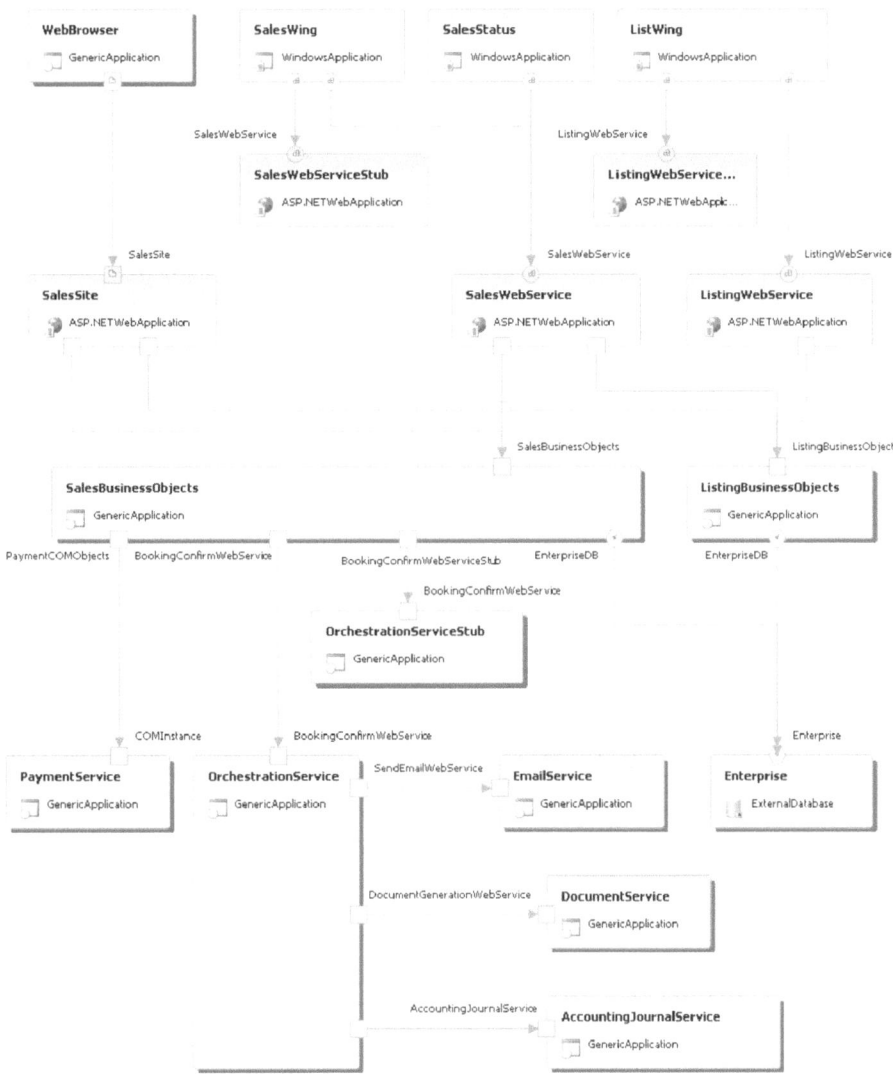

Figure 5-18. *The completed application diagram of the new project*

Multiple Instances of the Same Web Service

The diagram in Figure 5-18 shows the SalesWing application with two consumer endpoints that both consume a web service with the same name: SalesWebService. One is the real one; the other is a stub. The ListWing and SalesBusinessObjects have a similar problem. What does this mean for the application? We know that the real code for the SalesWing application only consumes one of them. That is, there will be code within the implementation that accesses the web service and expects it to always be the same one. The URL of the web service will be determined by a .config file that will be set up at install time, so at install time, the application may be configured to consume either the real web service or the stub. Thus, we can conclude that the consumer endpoints shown on an application do not represent what the application always consumes, but what it *can* consume.

However, you could look at it a different way. Suppose you just drew the one provider application for the orchestration service in our diagram and you regarded the stub and the real one as two different *implementations* of the same application. Maybe you could consider an application as having multiple implementations.

But wait a minute. The point about application diagrams is that you can implement the code of your applications from them, so that settles it—the application is tied to generating some sort of code, and you might customize the template to make it quite specific. You still might adjust the implementation's behavior at install time by way of .config files, but it seems as if the difference between a stub web service and a real one is so great that they should be considered to be different applications (particularly as the web service might be implemented in a technology other than .NET, such as BizTalk 2000 or SAP). So, generally speaking, this means that stubs and real providers should be treated as separate applications; in this book, consumer endpoints shown in an application indicate what the application *can* consume, not necessarily what it *does* consume.

Designing the Production Systems

Earlier in this chapter I mentioned *systems* as a specific concept in the distributed system designers. I explained that an application diagram describes all the ways that its component applications can work together to form one distributed application. The diagram does not define any particular configuration that would be installed—it's a more general concept than that. So now let's talk about systems, and how they relate to Peter's job of architecting Icarus's new enterprise system.

The Concept of a System

A system is a *configured usage* of a set of applications from the application diagram. The application diagram describes how the applications *can* be connected, whereas the system diagram shows how they *will* be connected in a particular usage configuration.

As an example, let's consider a service-oriented application designed to manage systems within a building. There is a master control application, an application controlling the heating system, and another application controlling the security system. The latter two each expose a web service to be used by the master control application. The application diagram would display three applications. Now some buildings might not have a security system, so some configurations might only have the master control application and the heating control application. Only these two would appear on a *system* diagram for that specific building. Moreover, there might be different kinds of heating control applications, some for different makes of hardware. The application diagram could therefore include many different heating control applications and be quite large. The company might produce a different system diagram for each building using the application, with only two or three applications shown on each.

The Production Systems

Returning again to Icarus Enterprise 3.1, Peter must document the systems to be deployed into production. It makes sense to consider Icarus's entire production system as a set of systems rather than just one. For example, Icarus's U.S. telephone sales system—with its call center applications that work with the server applications and databases—can be considered as one system. The overseas office telephone applications, together with the U.S. servers and databases, form other systems. The two systems have some things in common—for example, the servers and databases in the United States are shared between the U.S. office system and the overseas office systems. How do we handle that?

Note Exercise 5-6 will help you understand this section.

Well, system diagrams can include other systems as well as applications, so we can consider the whole of the business logic applications: `SalesBusinessLogic`, `ListingBusinessLogic`, and the `Enterprise` database plus some others, to be one system, called `BusinessLogic`. This system when deployed on servers forms the core of the business and needs be kept in a secure location. We can then include this `BusinessLogic` system in another system called `USTelephoneSalesSystem`; however, it might be a good idea to use an intermediate system called `Presentation`, since this system will be common to other larger systems. We will see this in the system diagrams that Peter now develops.

BusinessLogic System

The `BusinessLogic` system consists of the business logic server applications, together with their associated database, orchestration service, and payment service. The final diagram does not show the services behind the orchestration server (downstream services) that are unchanged in the Enterprise 3.1 development, but they could easily be added to it.

To create this system diagram, Peter right-clicks on the `Solution Items` folder in Solution Explorer and selects Add ➤ New Solution Folder. He names the new folder `Production Systems`. Then he right-clicks on this folder and selects Add ➤ New Distributed System Diagram. In the resulting dialog box, he selects System Diagram, types the name `BusinessLogic.sd`, and clicks Add. The blank system diagram appears, with the System View pane on the left, as shown in Figure 5-19. He then drags all the applications he requires onto the drawing page one by one, positioning them in suitable places. Next he connects them, as shown in the completed diagram in Figure 5-20. Notice that Peter does not include any of the stubs, since this diagram shows only applications that will be deployed in production to form this system.

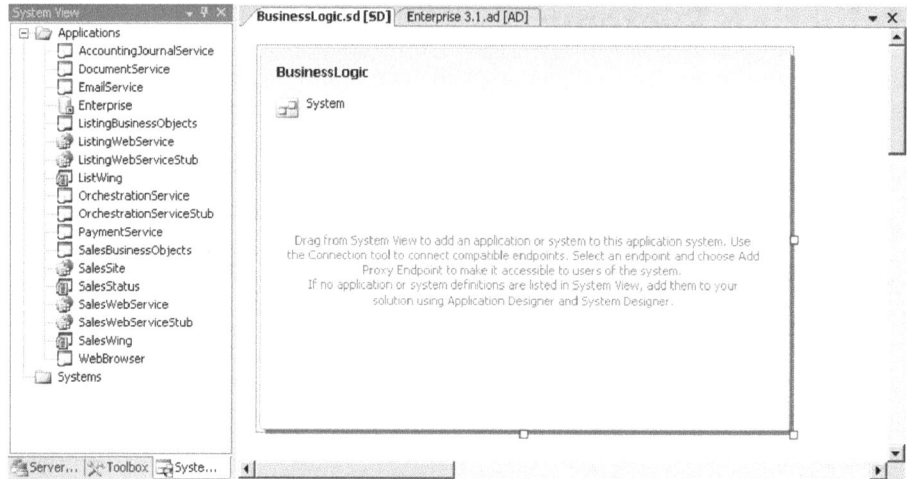

Figure 5-19. *The System Designer showing the new empty system diagram*

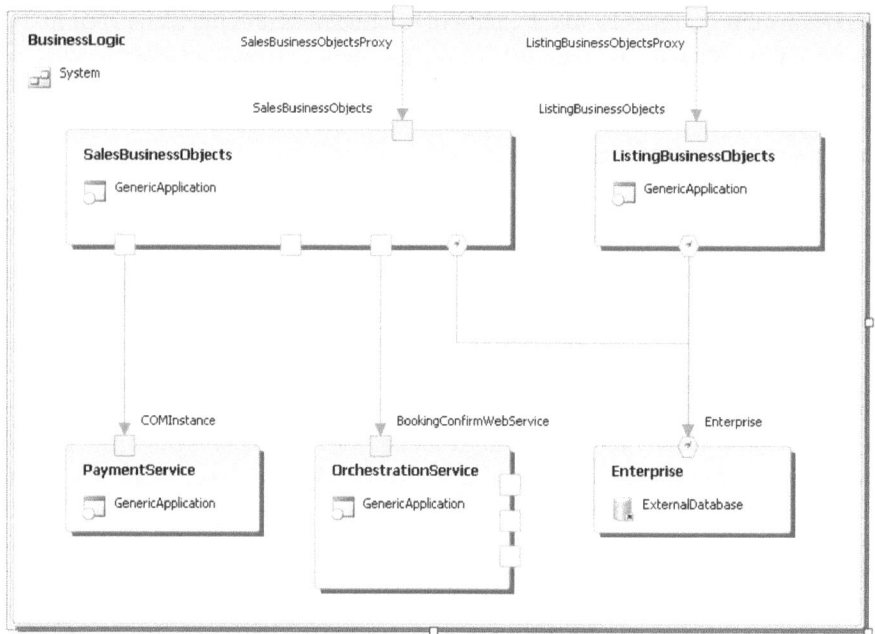

Figure 5-20. *System diagram representing the BusinessLogic system*

System diagrams can include *proxy endpoints*, which represent endpoints that exist on applications within the system that need to be exposed at the edge of the system. The concept is an essential feature that allows you to build systems out of smaller systems. To form a proxy endpoint, simply Alt-drag from an endpoint on the application to the edge of the system diagram box. Peter has added two proxy endpoints to Figure 5-20 for the sales and listing business objects.

When you do this sort of work, you need to move the endpoints around to suitable positions on the boxes and resize the boxes as necessary to lay the diagram out neatly. Once the applications are there, you can start connecting them. Although selecting the connection in the Toolbox and dragging from one endpoint to another is the most obvious way, you'll soon get used to the shortcut of holding down the Alt key to start dragging connections around.

Presentation System

Having defined the `BusinessLogic` system, we can now add another layer around it and define the system that exposes the services offered to the outside world by the secure business logic and the databases in the `BusinessLogic` system. We can call this the `Presentation` system, because it presents the business capabilities of the inner system to the clients in the form of either web services or a website. The boundary between the `Presentation` system and the `BusinessLogic` system is a tightly coupled boundary using .NET Remoting of business logic objects, whereas the boundary between the presentation layer and the clients that use its services is a more loosely coupled SOA boundary.

The `Presentation` system is made up of the `BusinessLogic` system and instances of the `SalesWebService`, `ListingWebService`, and `SalesSite` applications. By *instances*, I mean particular installations of the same application. In a system, it is permissible to install the same application more than once, and each instance must be given a different name. In the `Presentation` system in Figure 5-21, there are two instances of the `SalesWebService` application and two instances of the `ListingWebService` application, with the instance names prefixed by *Intranet* and *Internet* to distinguish them. If the name of the instance differs from the name of the application, System Designer helpfully adds the name of the application underneath the name of the instance. This is just like object-oriented design, where the application in the application diagram represents a class of applications and an instance on a system diagram is like an object of that class.

One pair of services are used to provide sales and listing services via the company's intranet to client applications in the call center and admin areas, while the other pair are used to provide the same services to the Internet for use by resource providers and travel agents. The `SalesSite` application only has one instance as website sales are only made via the Internet.

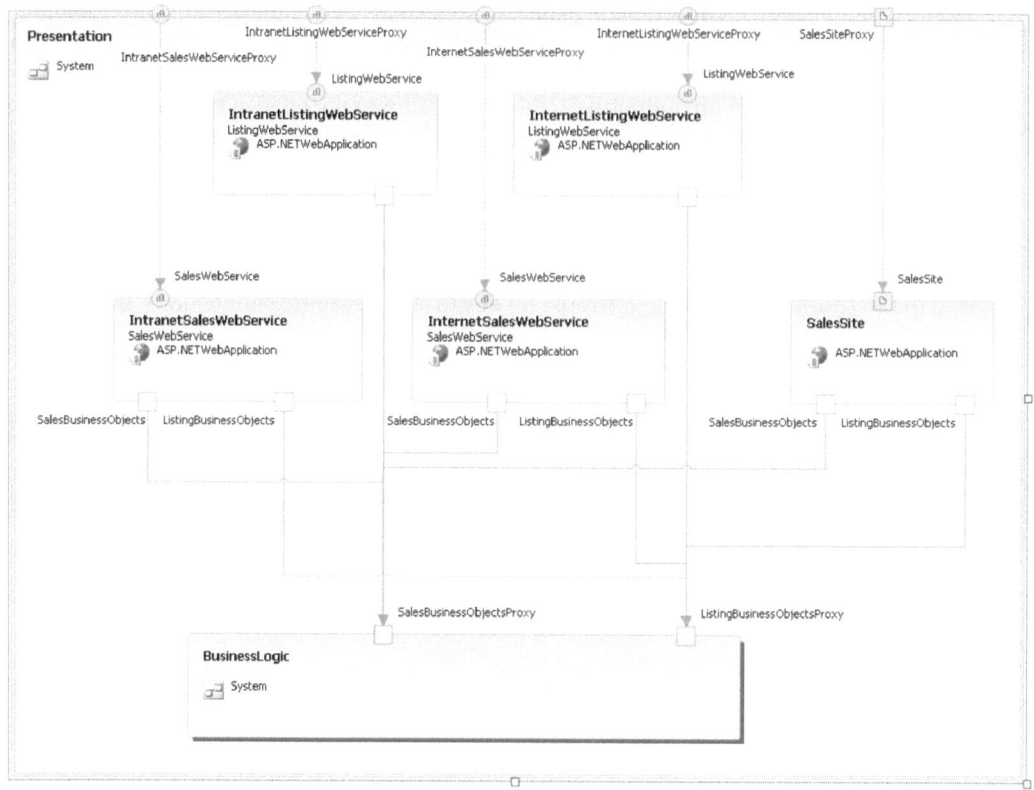

Figure 5-21. *Diagram representing the Presentation system*

California Office System

Figure 5-22 shows the entire system called `CaliforniaOffice`. It includes the three client applications, `SalesWing`, `SalesStatus`, and `ListWing`, which consume web services exposed by the `Presentation` system. Peter draws this diagram by creating a new system diagram called `CaliforniaOfficeSystem` in the same folder, and then drags these three applications onto it from the System View. Then he drags the `Presentation` system onto the diagram from the `Systems` folder in the System View pane. The applications and the system can now be connected in the same way as before. It is also necessary to drag the Internet endpoints of the `Presentation` system to the boundary of the `CaliforniaOffice` system to form proxy endpoints so that the client applications on the Internet can be connected to them.

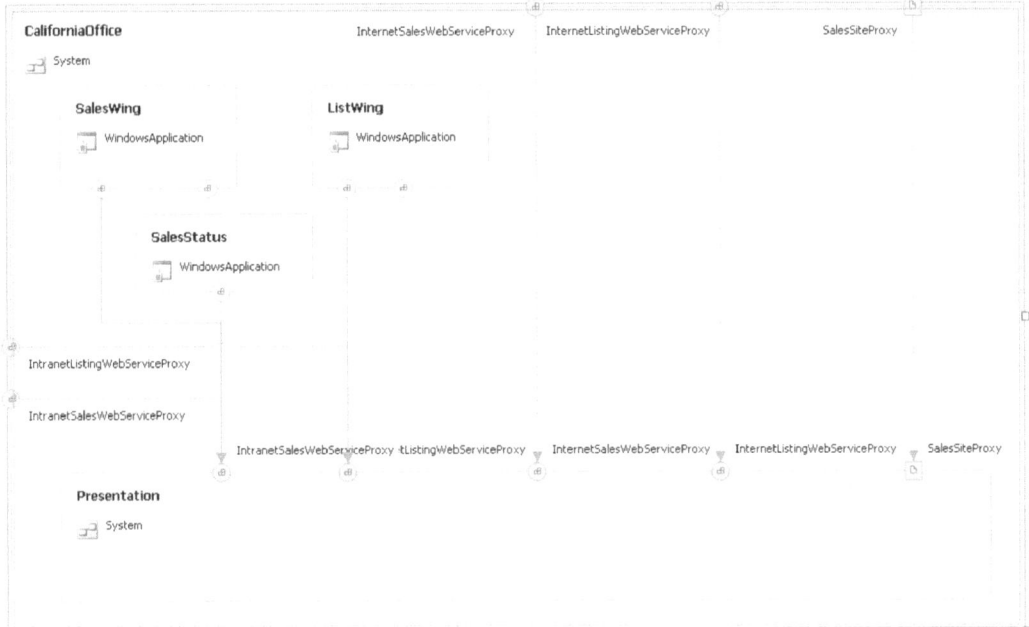

Figure 5-22. *The CaliforniaOffice system*

The Icarus Global System

The system called IcarusGlobal is shown in Figure 5-23. It is built around interfaces to the CaliforniaOffice system. It consists of the overseas offices and the Internet access clients, which I describe next.

Overseas Offices

Icarus has offices in the United Kingdom (UK), Hong Kong, and Chennai, India, as shown at the left in Figure 5-23. All of these offices have a similar function in that they have call centers, in which operators make sales for customers, and administrative areas in which managers keep track of Icarus's business and vendor administrators deal with vendors and update resource availability and information. Each overseas office client has endpoints that are attached to the IntranetSalesWebService and IntranetListingWebService, which are exposed by the Presentation system.

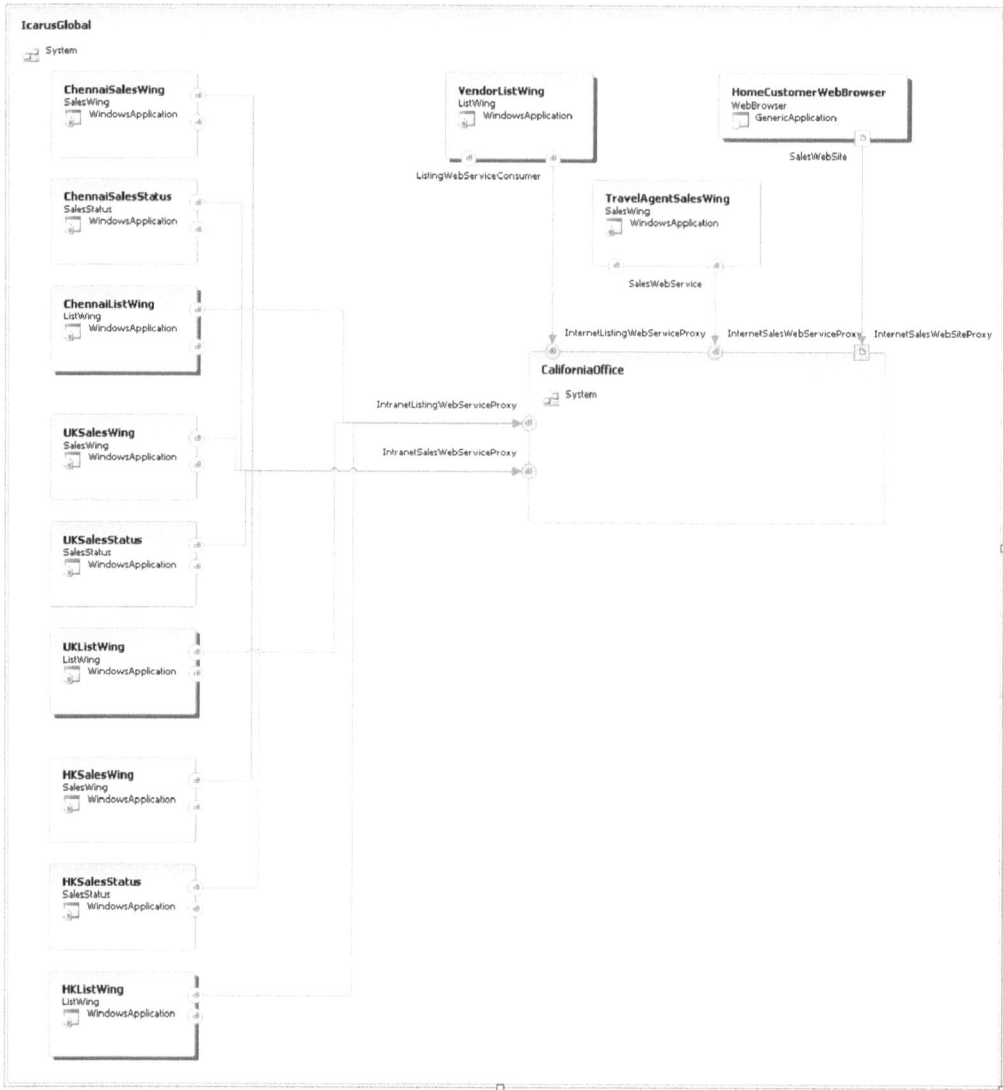

Figure 5-23. *Icarus's complete global system*

Internet Access Clients

The global system diagram must also show the part of the system that provides the capability for Internet-connected users to access the business capabilities. There are three categories of these clients, shown at the top of Figure 5-23.

Some vendors that sell their services through Icarus will install the `ListWing` application on their own machines and access the `ListingWebService` application in the `Presentation` layer via the Internet. These are represented by the instance of the `ListWing` application called `VendorListWing`.

Some travel agents will want to install instances of the `SalesWing` application on their own machines, which will access the `SalesWebService` via the Internet. These are represented by the instance of `SalesWing` called `TravelAgentSalesWing`.

Lastly, the home-based Internet customer, who reserves resources offered by Icarus via the Internet using a web browser, will also access the `Presentation` system and is represented by the instance of `WebBrowser` called `HomeCustomerWebBrowser`.

Vertical Slices and Systems Containing Other Systems

A very useful ability of system diagrams is to allow systems to be built out of application instances and other systems. It is important to realize, however, that when a system is added to a system diagram, effectively all of its applications are added. Thus, if the system is added twice all of the applications will be added twice, resulting in two instances of each. Sometimes this may be what is required, but often you will want to view a large system as consisting of smaller systems in different ways. For example, you might want to view the business systems vertically—that is, you might want to include, for example, the `ListWing`, `ListingWebService`, and the `ResourceBusinessObjects` applications as well as the `Enterprise` database application on one system diagram. You can do this by using the System Designer and then explore deploying these systems on logical data center designs.

However, you would want to do the same for the vertical slice that represented the Sales capability as well and then both of these vertical slice systems would include the `ListingBusinessObjects` and the `Enterprise` database. Now, to build up the global system, you would want to include both of these vertical slice subsystems, *but* when you deployed the entire system you would see multiple instances of the database and the business objects applications being deployed, which is *not* what you wanted to show. Thus, you have to build a large system from the inside out in the way I have done in this chapter, or just as one large conglomeration of applications, which is confusing. Should there be some way of indicating that systems can *reference* other systems and show them in their individual diagrams, but allow these referenced parts to be deployed independently rather than being contained and deployed as a hard-and-fast part of each subsystem? I don't know the answer to this.

Deployment

Team System addresses another important aspect of architecture: the design of an infrastructure and the deployment of systems to operate in that infrastructure. Team System distinguishes between tools that support the application architect and those that support the infrastructure architect. *Application architect* refers to the person who designs the distributed application software, and *infrastructure architect* refers to the person who designs the server, workstation, and network infrastructure. So far in this chapter, I have concentrated on discussing the use of the application architecture tools to design applications, and then systems that are configurations of those applications for a particular use. In the remainder of this chapter, I will explain the infrastructure tools, and how they assist with designing an application for deployment, using Icarus Enterprise 3.1 as an illustrative example.

The infrastructure architect designs and documents the data center and network structure. Earlier in this chapter, I spent a good deal of time describing what is meant by applications and systems. Now I must explain the term logical data center. First, a *data center* is a place that hosts applications and makes them available to users in one way or another. This includes hosting database applications, server applications, and client applications, and also allowing them to communicate. The data center includes the entire infrastructure needed to make that possible. Physically the infrastructure, as we define it here, means the servers, workstations, routers, hubs, network cabling, load balancers, firewalls, and anything else used to implement the collection of hardware that allows our distributed application software to operate. However, it also includes the system software such as the operating systems, .NET Frameworks, protocol stacks, database provider layers, system configuration files (like `machine.config`), and any other software components that are not considered part of the application.

Now what about a *logical* data center? What's the difference between the physical and logical varieties of data center? The logical data center describes servers that are available, their properties, how they are connected, and what constraints they and their connections apply on the applications they host. It does not describe how many servers are working in a farm in parallel to represent a server in a logical data center, or how the storage is organized, such as what kind of RAID system is used, or what kind of WAN system is in place connecting physically separated parts of the network. It *does* describe limitations applied by a firewall to the protocols that are permitted to pass across a particular logical connection and the ports that may be accessed through the firewall. But it *does not* describe the firewalls and routers as units in the diagram. So, for example, in a logical data center description, it would be wrong to represent all the machines in a web server farm. The array of servers works as one logical unit, so we regard it as one logical server. The array of routers and firewalls provides one or more logical links between logical servers, so we show the logical links on the diagram rather than the physical components that make up that link. The logical data center describes security mechanisms in terms of authentication mechanisms involving applications rather than such things as encryption at wire level.

In summary, then, a logical data center describes all the server and client hosts and their links in terms of what they look like from the point of view of providing the requirements of the applications and satisfying their communication requirements.

Logical Data Center Designer and Its Concepts

Visual Studio 2005 for Architects allows you to design logical data centers using the Logical Data Center Designer. It uses the concepts of zones, logical servers, endpoints, and connections. There is a Toolbox that contains a collection of prototype logical servers, zones, and endpoints that you can drag onto your diagram and connect together. You can also assign settings and constraints to these objects once they are on your diagram and then place them back in the Toolbox to use as prototypes of your own. So it's possible to define data center components that have very specific constraints, and then save them in the Toolbox to be used in various parts of the same data center design or in different data center designs. You can also do operations such as copy and paste if you want to duplicate parts of your data center design that will have the same or similar characteristics. I'll now describe what these components of the logical data center mean.

Zones

We can consider zones first, since they would be a good point to start in a complex data center diagram, but of course in a simple diagram you might not need them and you can always connect clients and servers first to get an idea, then start moving them into zones later.

Zones can be used to define communication boundaries in data centers, or they might be used just to group servers together to make the arrangement more intuitive. They can represent physical boundaries such as computers in a different site or building, they can represent different subnets, or they can represent regions separated by a firewall. Examples of zones are a company's internal network, a peripheral network—often called a demilitarized zone (DMZ)—or the public Internet.

If you start with a blank data center diagram, you can add zones simply by dragging from the zone in the Toolbox onto any point on the drawing. You can change the name of the zone in the properties window and set its other properties, such as what kinds of servers are allowed in it. You'll see that the default zone has two circular blobs on its perimeter, one with an arrow going in and one with an arrow going out. These are the zone endpoints, which enable the logical servers that you will place inside to have communications pathways with the outside world. You can delete one of these blobs if you don't need it, drag more endpoint blobs from the Toolbox onto the zone, and move them around to convenient places on the zone's perimeter. You can also change the name of a selected zone in the properties window or by double-clicking on its name, just as you would a filename in Windows Explorer.

Zone Constraints

Constraints can be defined to exist in zones. These are constraints that are applied by the zone to the servers that might be located within it—the types of logical server (including clients) that can be in a zone. You can select any set from `DatabaseServer`, `GenericServer`, `IISWebServer`, or `WindowsClient`. You can also allow other zones. You can be more restrictive by specifying features about the logical servers permitted to be in a zone, such as specifying the operating system and Common Language Runtime (CLR) characteristics for `IISWebServer` and `WindowsClient`. For `IISWebServer` you can also specify features of its IIS installation that must apply if it is allowed in a given constrained zone. You cannot, though, define custom constraints on logical servers and specify constraints on zones that refer to them. It's also not possible to define custom logical server prototypes in the Toolbox and then constrain a zone to allow only those types of logical server. Figure 5-24 shows how the constraints are set that a zone will enforce.

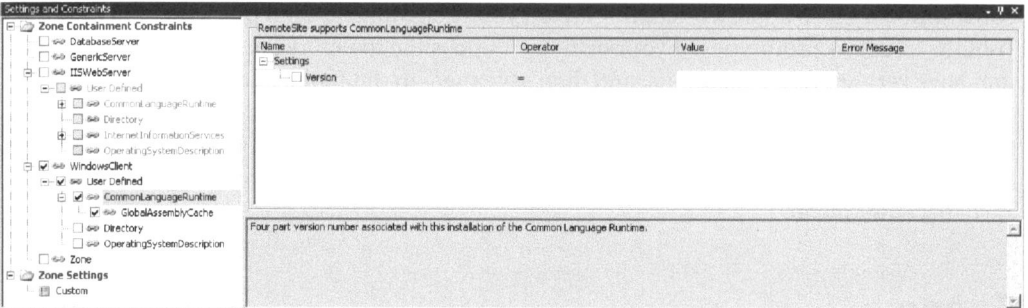

Figure 5-24. *Constraints that may be selected to specify the types of logical servers permitted in a particular zone. The operating system, CLR, and IIS settings may also be specified as constraints for some types of server.*

Zone Endpoints and Their Constraints

When you add endpoints to a zone, you can also apply a limited set of constraints to them, which will be applied to the endpoints of logical servers that will be permitted to connect to them:

- The direction of allowable traffic—in, out, or bidirectional.

- The protocol that's allowed in the communication—specify by selecting one or more of `HTTPClientEndpoint`, `GenericClientEndpoint`, and `DatabaseClientEndpoint`, shown in Figure 5-25.

You can't specify any more detail than that. You can assign custom settings to zones and endpoints, but you cannot refer to them in constraints.

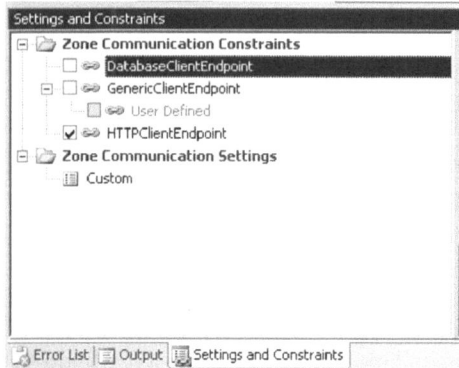

Figure 5-25. *The Zone Communication Constraints available for zone endpoints.*

Logical Servers

Once you have created zones on your logical data center diagram, you can add servers to them by dragging the logical server prototypes from the Toolbox onto the diagram within or outside one of the zones. Each logical server prototype already has endpoints on it, appropriate to its definition, but you can add more by dragging endpoints of the required type from the Toolbox onto the logical server symbol on your diagram. There are some rules about where you can drop endpoints; for example, you cannot drop a WebSiteEndpoint onto a WindowsClient logical server or a DatabaseServer logical server. You can give the endpoints appropriate names and add custom settings that will appear in the deployment report.

Connections can be added between endpoints on the logical servers and endpoints on other logical servers or the zones in which the servers have been placed. To add a connection, you hold down Alt and drag the mouse between two compatible endpoints in the same way as you would when connecting applications on application and system diagrams.

Logical servers can have constraints attached to them, which means that the logical server will apply those constraints on any applications that it hosts. When you try to deploy an application to the server, you will get an error if the server imposes constraints that cannot be met by the application.

Table 5-3 summarizes the constraints that may be defined on each of the prototype logical servers provided with Logical Data Center Designer. Constraints are organized in a hierarchical manner, so for example on WindowsClient prototype logical servers, the first thing you need to decide is which of a selection of prototype applications they will allow to be installed. Once you have selected the checkbox to make the server support that kind of application prototype, there are a whole range of features in that application type that you can constrain.

Table 5-3. *Constraints Available for WindowsClient Type Logical Servers*

Logical Server Prototype	Constraints Available
WindowsClient	Type of application supported: GenericApplication, WindowsApplication, and/or OfficeApplication. For Office and Windows applications, many of the settings in the .config file may be constrained.
IISWebServer	Type of application supported: ASP.NETWebApplication, ExternalBizTalkWebService, ExternalWebService, and/or GenericApplication. For an ASP.NETWebApplication, a wide range of settings for the application may be constrained.
DatabaseServer	Type of application supported: ExternalDatabase and/or GenericApplication.
GenericServer	Type of application supported: ExternalWebService and/or GenericApplication.

The Icarus Production Data Centers

Having spent time describing the features of the Logical Data Center Designer, let's now return to the Icarus Enterprise 3.1 project. Peter now needs to define the logical data centers on which the distributed application will be hosted.

■**Note** Exercise 5-7 will help you understand this section.

California Data Center

This logical data center includes all the zones and logical servers (including clients) that exist in the company's headquarters site. Remember it is a *logical* data center, so all the clients are not shown, just a representative one for each type.

High Security Zone

Peter begins his design of the logical data centers with the company's main site in California. Since Icarus is a very security-conscious company, there are a number of zones across which traffic is restricted. The most secure zone, called High Security Zone, is where the database servers and application servers are located. A firewall is located at the boundary of the zone and limits traffic into it to .NET Remoting from only two web servers located in peripheral zones. The two peripheral zones are called the Internet peripheral zone and the Intranet peripheral zone. The Internet peripheral zone contains the web servers that host the Sales website, the Sales web service, and the Listing web service. These are accessible from the public Internet and are thus most likely to suffer attack. The Intranet peripheral zone contains the web servers that host the same server applications for use by company employees. Icarus has separated these zones to ensure that an attack on the Internet-facing servers (perhaps a denial-of-service attack) will not affect the intranet web services and thus will allow the company to keep operating. The California call center, which services only the U.S. market, is within a zone that only allows access to the Intranet peripheral zone to maintain integrity of the client workstations used by the call center operators (these employees do not need to access the public Internet). The last zone is the Administrative zone, which is less restricted and includes management staff, developers, accounting, and others.

Peter begins by creating a new solution folder in the Enterprise 3.1 solution, calling it Data Centers. He then right-clicks on the new folder and selects Add ➤ New Distributed System Diagram. In the resulting dialog box, he selects Logical Datacenter Diagram, calls the diagram CaliforniaDataCenter, and clicks Add. The empty diagram is shown in Figure 5-26 with the Toolbox at the left. There are three tabs of interest on the Toolbox: the General Designer tab, with connections and comments; the Endpoints tab, showing various endpoints, including ZoneEndpoint; and the Logical Servers tab, with four kinds of logical servers and the zone.

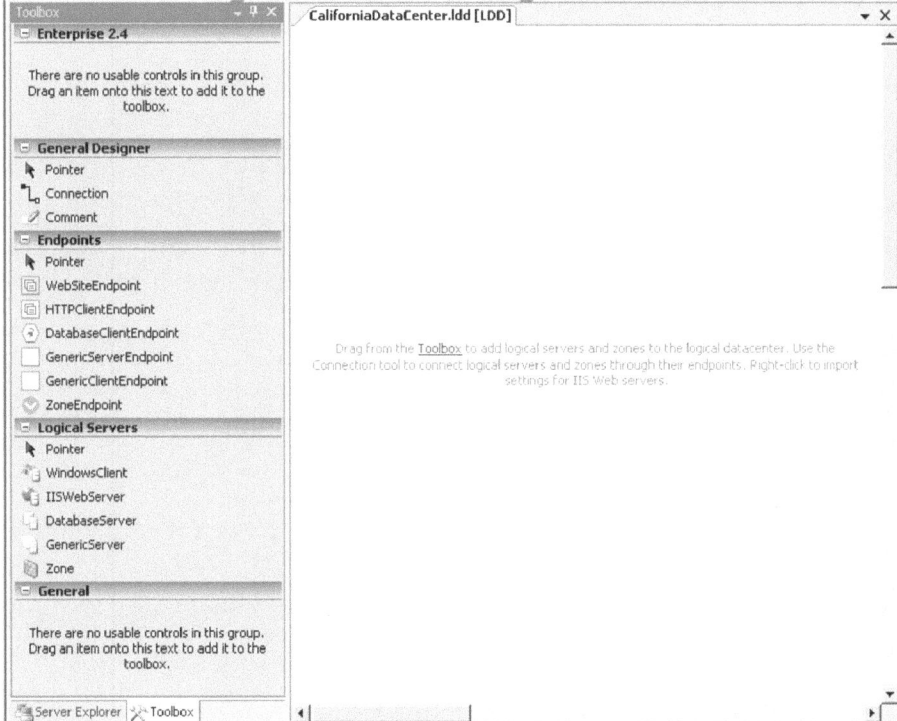

Figure 5-26. *Beginning a new logical data center diagram*

Peter begins by dragging a zone from the Toolbox onto the drawing tablet. It has the default name of Zone1; he changes this by double-clicking on the name and typing "HighSecurityZone". Notice that you cannot have spaces in the names of any objects in the distributed system designers—they are like names in a programming language and it is a good idea to use Pascal case. There are initially two zone endpoints on this zone, and Peter only requires one, for *incoming* traffic. He therefore clicks on the endpoint blob with the arrow pointing out of the zone and presses the Delete key. Peter also moves the incoming traffic zone endpoint to the top of the zone by selecting and dragging, and then renames it.

The servers that need to go into the zone are the application, orchestration, and database servers. These can be modeled using the GenericServer and DatabaseServer logical server prototypes. To do this Peter drags two instances of GenericServer and one of DatabaseServer from the Toolbox, changes the labels of the servers and the endpoints, resizes the zone and servers, and lays them out neatly. He also adds an additional GenericClientEndpoint to OrchestrationServer to allow communication with the downstream web services. The result is shown in Figure 5-27.

Figure 5-27. *Design of the California Data Center logical data center. Some zones and servers have been placed on the diagram but not yet connected.*

Next Peter Alt-drags from the endpoint on DatabaseServer to anywhere on ApplicationServer, which creates a connection and adds a new client endpoint to ApplicationServer. He right-clicks on this client endpoint and selects Show Label to make the label of the client endpoint visible. On the properties page of the selected endpoint, Peter also changes the name to DatabaseClientEndpoint. He then takes similar steps to connect BookingConfirmWebServiceEndpoint on the OrchestrationServer to the application server and renames the new client endpoint to OrchestrationServerClientEndpoint. Lastly, he draws a connection between the provider endpoint at the top of ApplicationServer and the zone endpoint; the resulting diagram appears in Figure 5-28.

Peter also adds some constraints to the definition of HighSecurityZone. Figure 5-29 and Figure 5-30 shows diagrams that indicate how the constraints look in the Settings and Constraints windows for the logical servers and the endpoints in the high security zone. To make these diagrams, I have taken a lot of screen shots of the Settings and Constraints window and drawn arrows onto an image of that part of the data center. In reality, of course, you can only look at them one at a time.

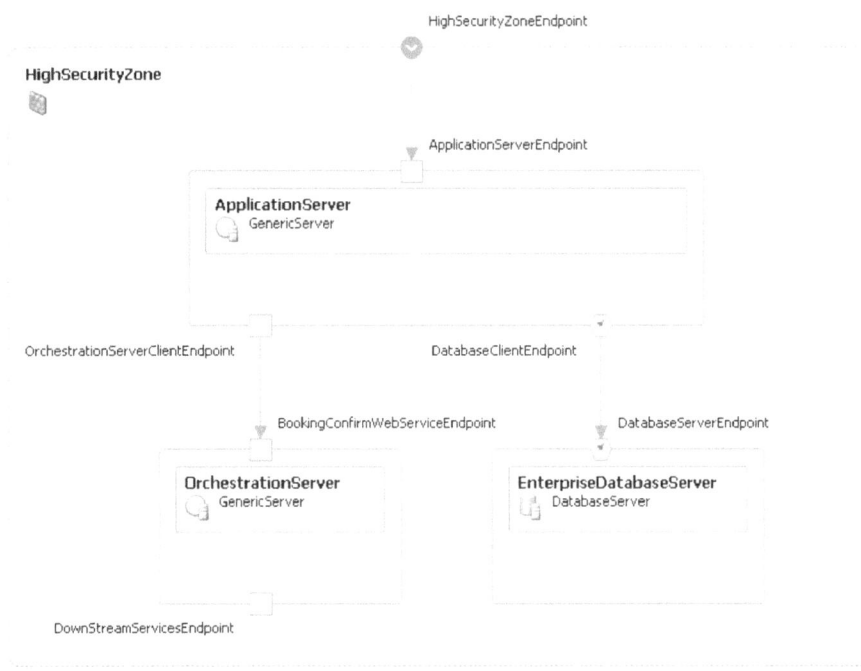

Figure 5-28. *Complete drawing for the high security zone*

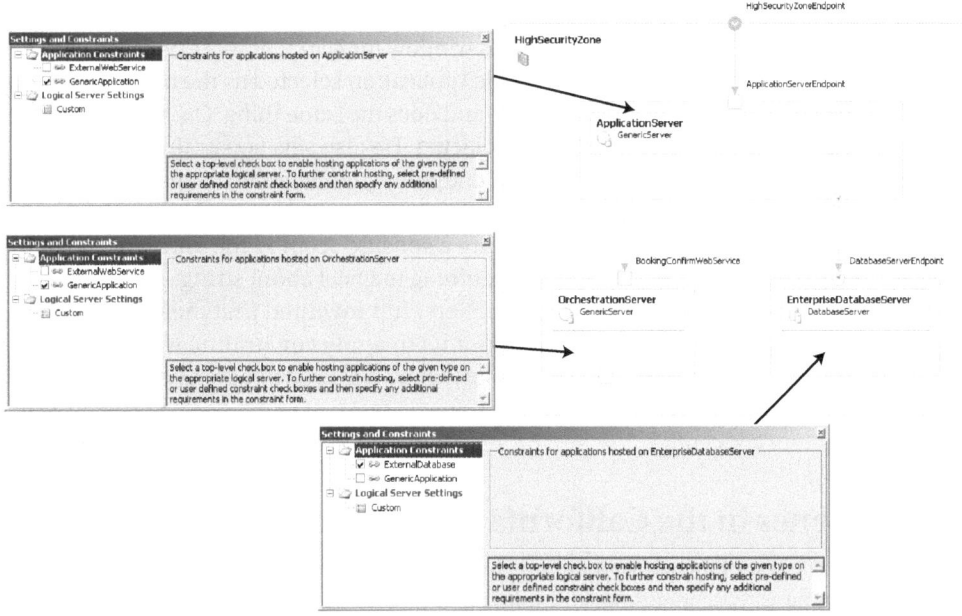

Figure 5-29. *How the Settings and Constraints Editor shows the constraints for the servers in the High Security Zone. This diagram is made from screen shots of the Settings and Constraints window and the image of the logical data center.*

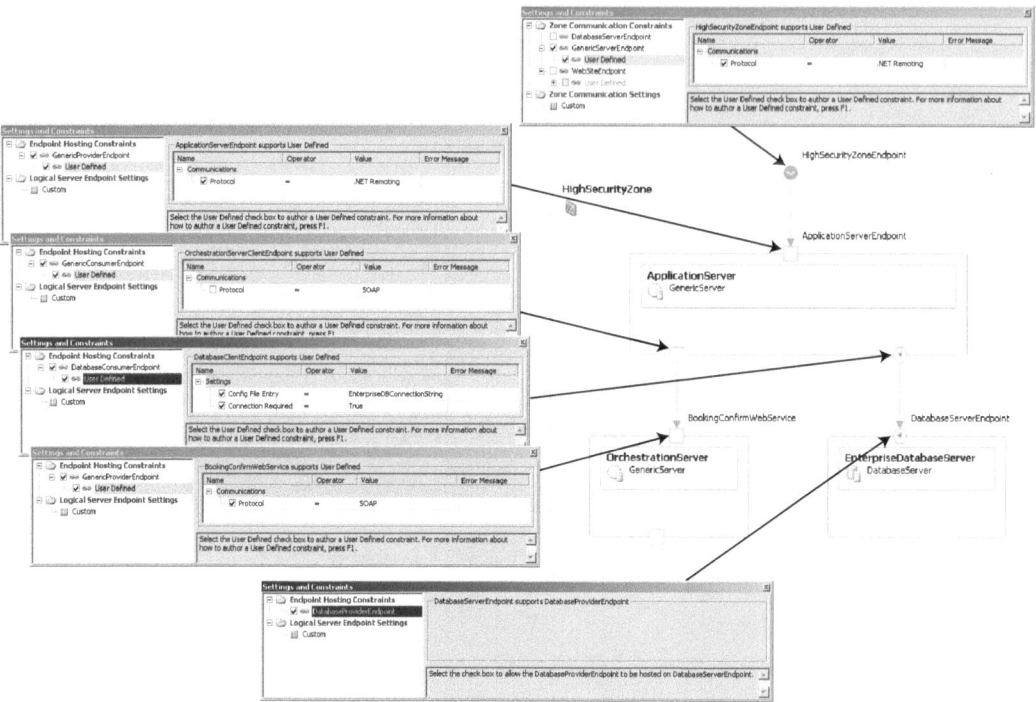

Figure 5-30. *The window of the Settings and Constraints Editor shown for each endpoint in the HighSecurityZone diagram*

First Peter opens the Settings and Constraints window for ApplicationServer and clears the ExternalWebService checkbox, leaving GenericApplication selected as the only application permitted. Then he clicks on OrchestrationServer and does the same thing. On DatabaseServer, he leaves only the ExternalDatabase checkbox selected. He also sets constraints for the two client endpoints on ApplicationServer. The client endpoint connected to OrchestrationServer is set to allow only the Simple Object Access Protocol (SOAP) protocol, while the client endpoint connected to the database is configured to require a specific .config file entry for the database connection. I should point out that there is nothing magical about strings such as SOAP and .NET Remoting. They are simply strings that Peter has invented that mean something within the architecture and allow the zone endpoints to apply constraints when the Team System architectural tools are used to simulate deployment. They need not even be real protocols; the idea is to ensure that the architecture is self-consistent in terms of its defined application, system, and infrastructure concepts.

The Other Zones in the California Data Center

Figure 5-31 shows the rest of the zones that Peter adds to the California data center. The Internet peripheral zone contains three incoming endpoints allowing traffic from the public Internet, and one outgoing entry point allowing access to the application server via .NET Remoting. The outgoing endpoint of this zone is set up with constraints, as shown in Figure 5-32. The web server placed in this zone, InternetWebServer, is constrained to allow only an application type of ASP.NETWebApplication. It will host the ASP.NET Web Forms pages of the SalesSite application as well as the SalesWebService and ListingWebService applications.

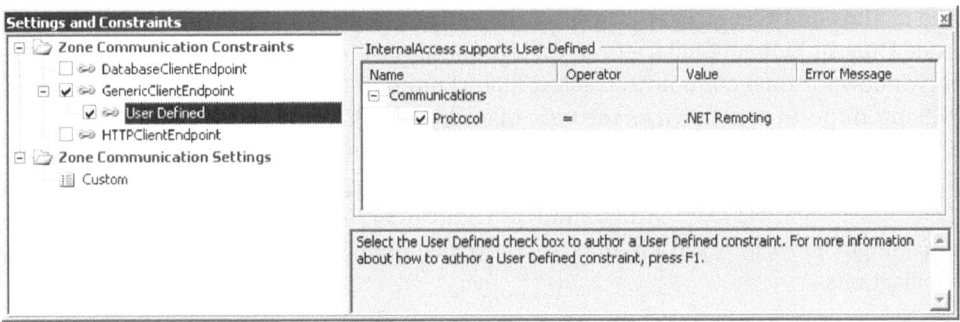

Figure 5-31. *The completed California Data Center logical data center diagram*

Figure 5-32. *Settings and constraints for the InternalAccess endpoint of the Internet peripheral zone*

The Intranet peripheral zone is similar to the Internet peripheral zone except that its web server must host only the web services. These web applications will be accessed via three separate URLs, as outlined in Table 5-4.

Table 5-4. *URLs for Access of the Web Applications*

Web Service or Site Name	URL
SalesWebService	http://services.prod.icarus.com/sales.asmx
ListingWebService	http://services.prod.icarus.com/listing.asmx
SalesSite	http://www.icarussales.com/

These URLs are placed in the settings for the website endpoints on InternetWebServer and IntranetWebServer. However, since the zone communication constraints in the zone endpoints for the Internet and Intranet peripheral zones only allow one URL to be added (in the user-defined constraints), it is necessary to add three separate zone endpoints on the Internet zone and two on the Intranet zone. Figure 5-33 shows the constraints on one of these, the PublicSalesSiteAccess zone endpoint of InternetPeripheralZone.

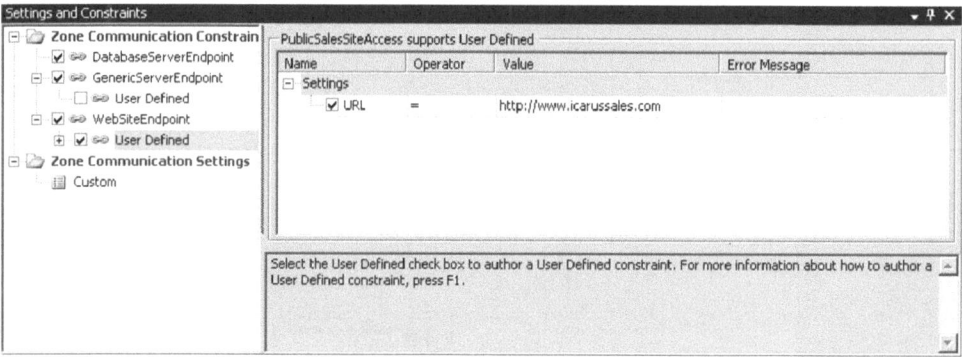

Figure 5-33. *Settings and constraints for the PublicInternetAccess endpoint of the Internet peripheral zone*

The two client zones, CallCenterZone and AdminZone, are constrained to contain only WindowsClient-type logical servers. Their endpoints are set to constrain traffic to outbound only and to allow only HTTP client traffic. Zone endpoints are set to allow Inbound Only, Outbound Only, or Bidirectional traffic in their properties windows. In the Settings and Constraints window for zone endpoints, GenericClientEndpoint, DatabaseClientEndpoint, or HTTPClientEndpoint are shown as the type of endpoints that the zone endpoint may be specified to support or not support for logical servers connected to it. Remember that a client machine as modeled in a logical data center diagram is still regarded as a logical server. In this case, Peter selects only HTTPClientEndpoint, as Figure 5-34 shows. Other endpoints on these zones that might allow access to a mail server or to the public Internet have not been included in these diagrams.

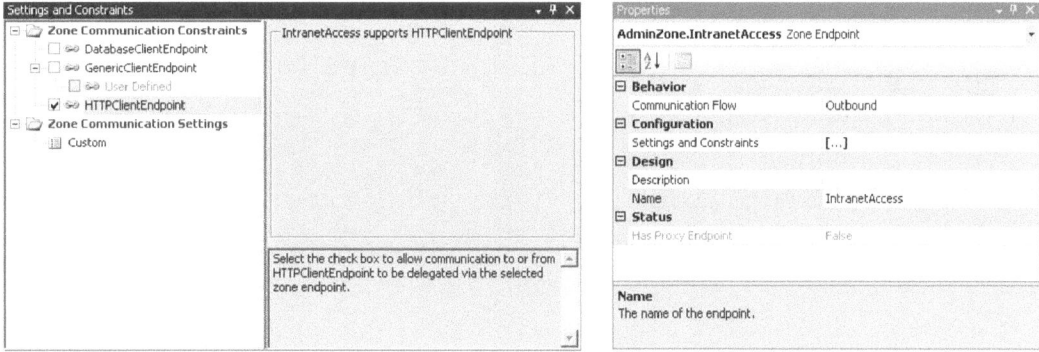

Figure 5-34. *Constraints on the IntranetAccess endpoint of AdminZone*

Deployment in the California Data Center

Now let's look at how the systems are deployed into the logical data center. Team System for Architects allows you to simulate deployment of the systems you have built from your applications to your logical data centers. To see how this works, let's watch as Peter attempts to do this for the BusinessLogic system.

Note Exercise 5-8 will help you understand this section.

First, he double-clicks on the BusinessLogic.sd file in the Solution Explorer window, which shows the system diagram that was drawn in Figure 5-20. To simulate a deployment, Peter right-clicks anywhere on the system diagram, but outside any of the applications, and selects Define Deployment. In the dialog box shown in Figure 5-35, Peter selects the CaliforniaDataCenter diagram from the drop-down and clicks OK. He then sees the screen shown in Figure 5-36, which is the starting point for deployment of the system. On the left is a System View window that lists the applications present in the system being deployed. It is now necessary to allocate the applications (perhaps strictly application usages instances) within that system to logical servers. Peter does this by dragging them from the System View and dropping them on logical servers.

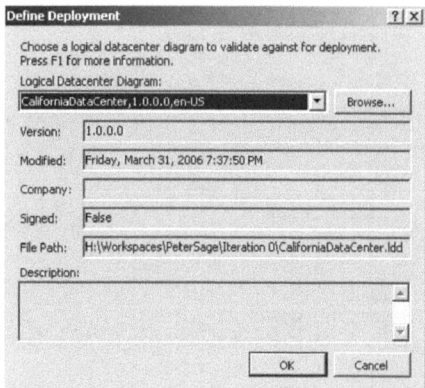

Figure 5-35. *The Define Deployment dialog box*

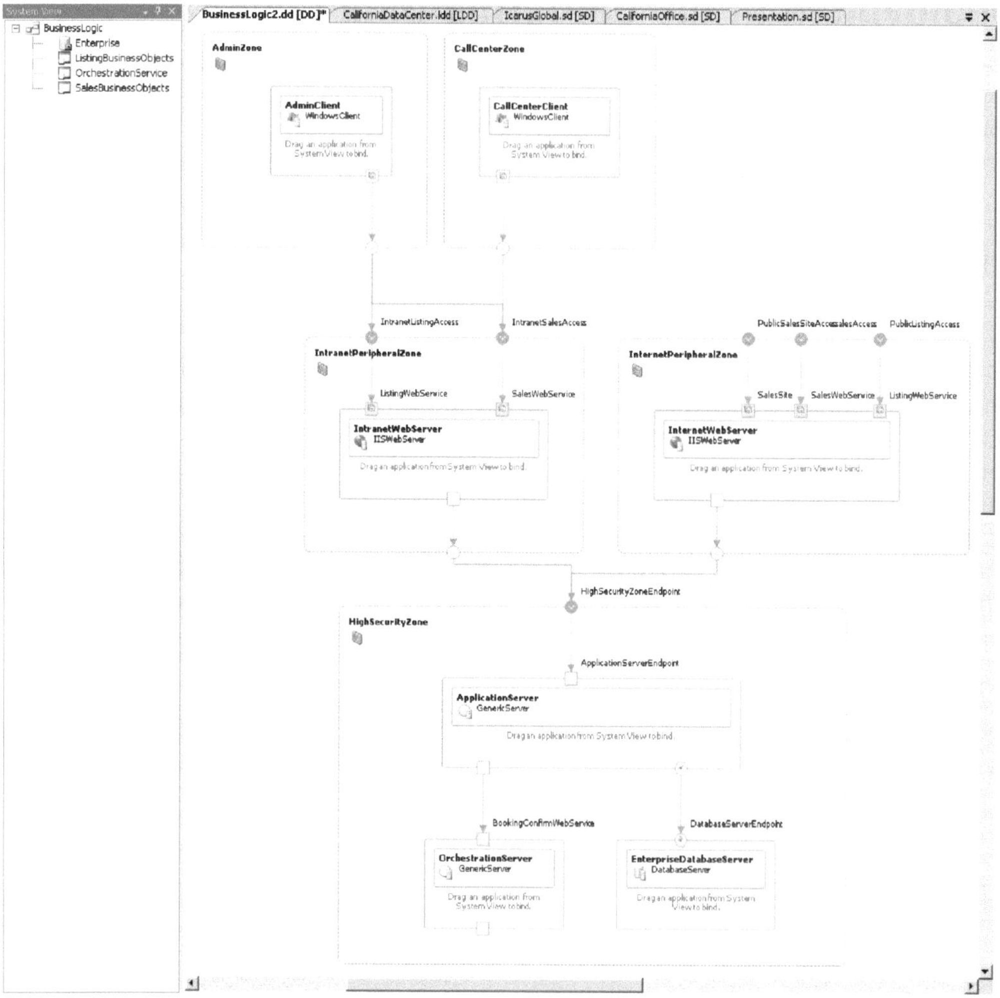

Figure 5-36. *The initial deployment diagram for the deployment of the BusinessLogic system to the California data center*

Peter performs the following drag-and-drop operations:

1. Drags the Enterprise database application from the System View and drops it on the DatabaseServer logical server

2. Drags the OrchestrationService generic application from the System View and drops it on the OrchestrationServer logical server

3. Drags the SalesBusinessObjects generic application from the System View and drops it on the ApplicationServer logical server

4. Drags the ListingBusinessObjects generic application from the System View and drops it on the ApplicationServer logical server

This completes the deployment. We can check that all is OK by right-clicking on a blank part of the diagram and selecting Validate Diagram. If all is well, you will see this message:

```
Validation of BusinessLogic2.dd complete.  0 errors/warnings found.
```

One thing that's quite instructive at this point is to right-click on an application that has been deployed such as SalesBusinessObjects in ApplicationServer and select Binding Details. The resulting dialog box (Figure 5-37) shows how the endpoints defined on the SalesBusinessObjects application have been automatically allocated to endpoints on the ApplicationServer logical server. This automatic binding takes place as long as there's no ambiguity—if the binding is ambiguous this dialog box will pop up when you drag the application onto a logical server and you'll be asked to resolve it. If you have an unexplained error on some part of a deployment diagram, however, it's always possible that another application that you deployed earlier might not have been bound the way you intended it—so it's often worth checking.

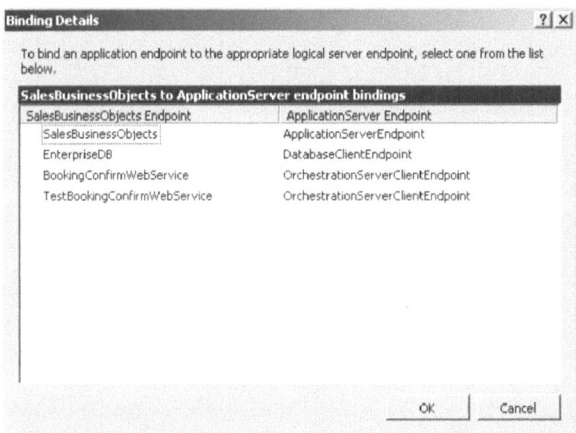

Figure 5-37. *Binding details for the BusinessObjects application deployed in the ApplicationServer logical server*

At this point you can also generate a deployment report by right-clicking on any blank part of the diagram and selecting Generate Deployment Report. I've extracted some content from Peter's deployment report and reproduced it in Figure 5-38. The report also includes the deployment, data center, and system diagrams, which you've already seen. It contains links that make navigating easy. The first section contains the deployment details and is shown in

Figure 5-38. The section is broken down into zones—in this report there is only one—and each zone is broken down into its logical servers. Each logical server is broken down by the applications deployed on it; for each application, the bindings are listed between the application endpoints and the logical server endpoints. To see the details of the bindings you click on the link, which takes you to the binding information for systems at the end of the document. The document also contains listings of logical servers and systems.

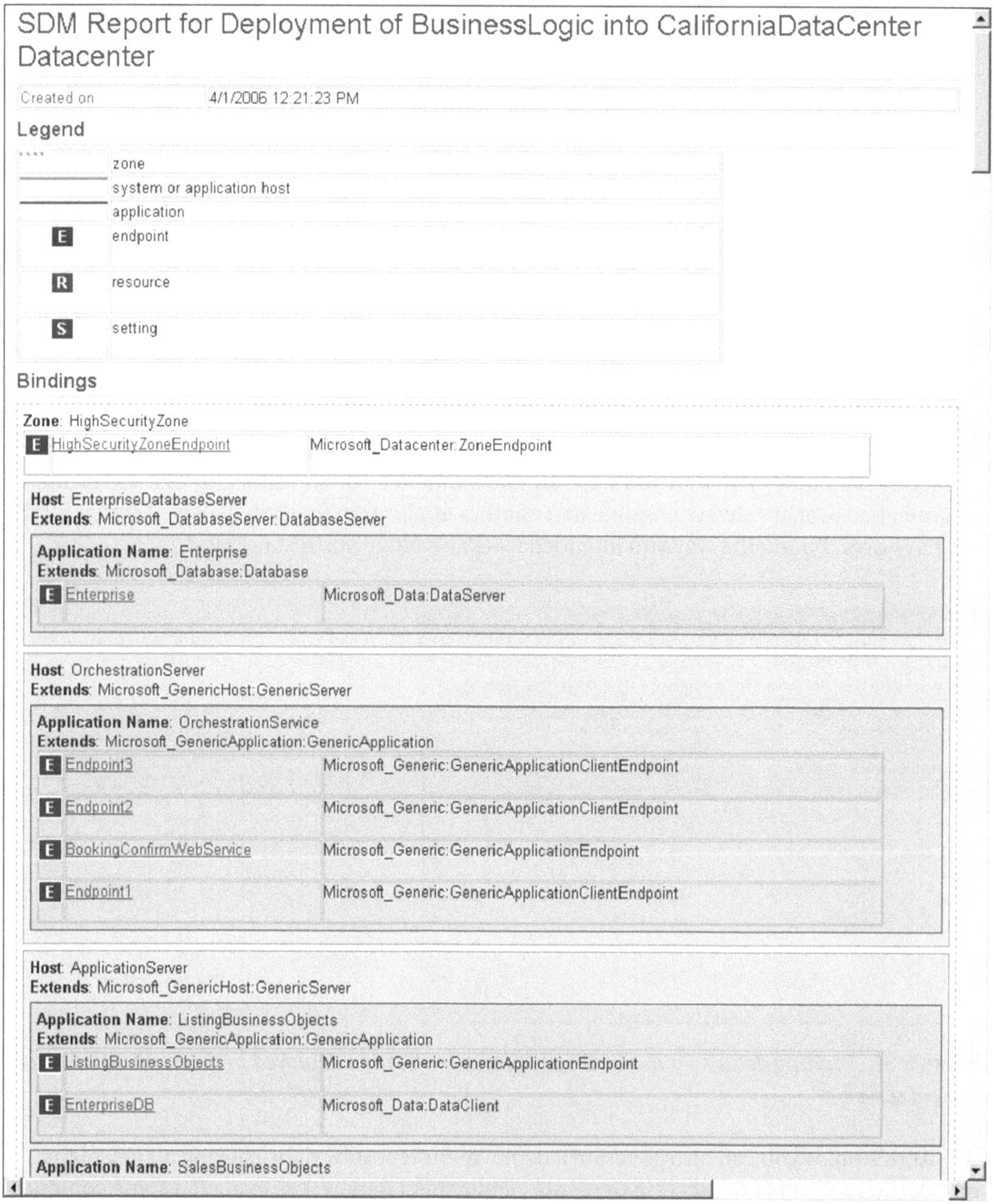

Figure 5-38. *The first section of the deployment report for BusinessLogic system deployed in CaliforniaDataCenter*

Global Data Center

The Icarus global data center representing the entire collection of logical servers, zones, and connections that must host the Icarus global system is shown in Figure 5-23. In addition to the California data center, the following local data centers must be added:

- UK

- Hong Kong

- Chennai (India)

Also, there are parts of the global data center that do not belong to Icarus and are not under its full control. Nevertheless, Icarus can expect to exert some control or make some assumptions that will enable it to plan deployment of its applications on these sites:

- Resource provider sites, for example, the World Wide Chefs office in Athens

- Travel agent sites

- Home Internet customer sites

Peter makes the global data center, shown in Figure 5-39, by adding the remote Icarus sites and the customer sites. These sites are pretty simple; the clients are all just copies of the call center and admin clients, and the three remote Icarus sites—UK, Hong Kong, and Chennai—are all exactly the same.

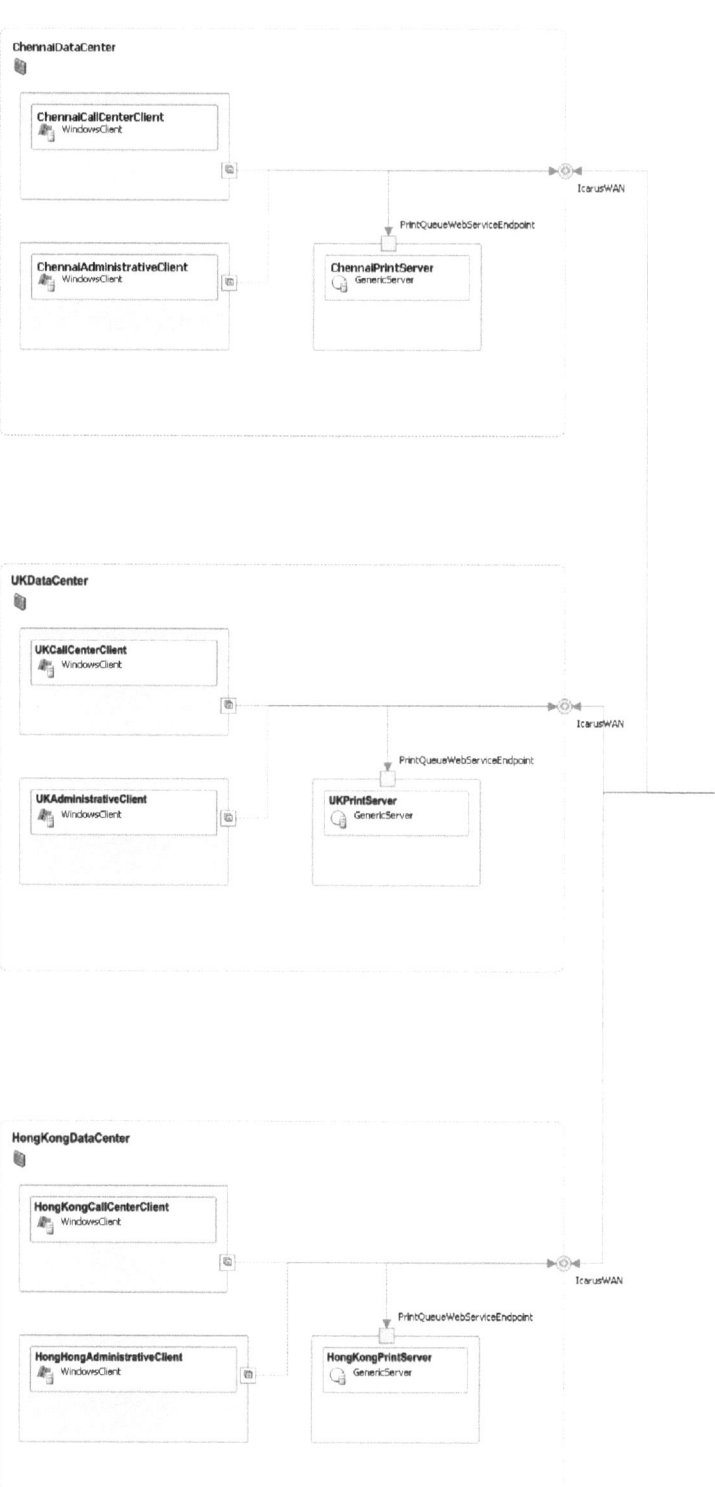

Figure 5-39. *Icarus's global data center*

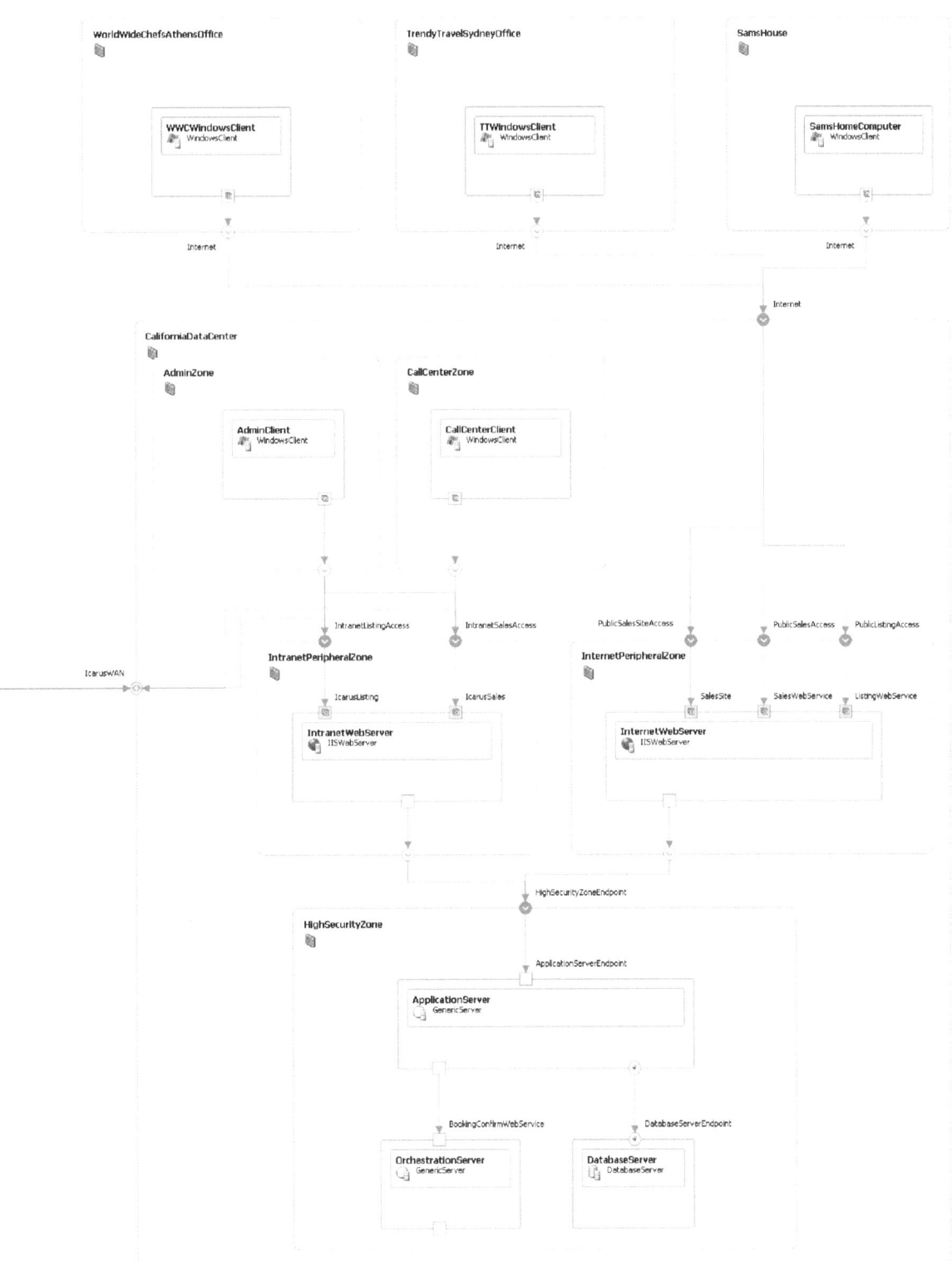

He then carries out a deployment of the Icarus global system to the global data center in the usual manner by opening the system diagram and selecting Define Deployment. If you don't like doing this from the context menu, you can use the Diagram menu in the main menu at the top, or set up shortcuts. Peter selects the GlobalDataCenter as the logical data center diagram for deployment and gets the usual deployment diagram, with the System View on the left (Figure 5-40) and all of the logical servers and zones on the right.

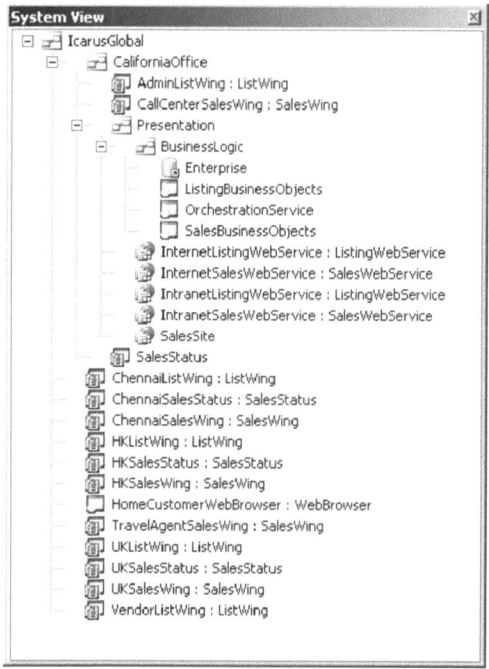

Figure 5-40. *System View of the Icarus global system, as seen in the deployment diagram*

Since the diagram is now rather complicated, it may be easier to use an alternative technique to bind the applications to the servers. The Icarus global system has several instances of the same application, particularly SalesWing, with different names, and these are intended to be deployed in different zones. Therefore, Peter has to be careful in assigning each application to the right server. He can deploy an application by right-clicking on it in System View and selecting Bind Application. If, for example, Peter selects IntranetListingWebService (which is the instance of the application ListingWebService that is intended to be hosted on the web server servicing the company's *intranet* rather than the Internet) and selects Bind Application, he will see the dialog box shown in Figure 5-41. Notice that the Show Only Logical Servers checkbox is selected by default so that only compatible logical servers are listed.

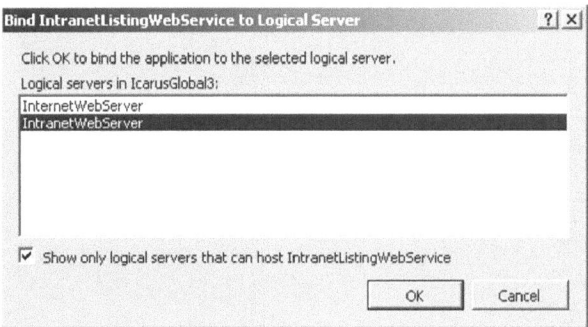

Figure 5-41. *The logical servers available to bind the IntranetListingWebService application instance*

Peter selects IntranetWebServer and clicks OK. The Binding Details dialog box, shown in Figure 5-42, then appears. Why has this happened? Well, if you look again at the definition of IntranetWebServer in the CaliforniaDataCenter diagram, you will remember that two website endpoints were added, both of which supported only web services according to the constraints defined on them to be applied to application endpoints. These differ only by the URL that was defined in their constraints and settings. The Deployment Designer sees that both of these will be suitable endpoints to bind the website endpoint of the ListingWebService application and does not know which one to choose. So Peter has to be careful to choose IcarusListing as the endpoint to use, or he will get verification errors later because of the mismatched URLs.

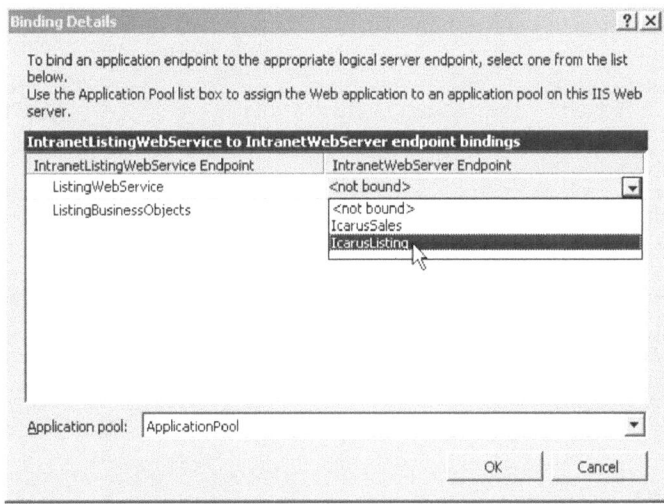

Figure 5-42. *Binding details for IntranetListingWebService. The binding cannot be determined automatically, so the user is asked to select an endpoint for the ListingWebService application endpoint.*

So our intrepid architect goes through the binding procedure for each application in IcarusGlobalSystem, making the correct decisions each time, and finally arrives at the diagram in Figure 5-43.

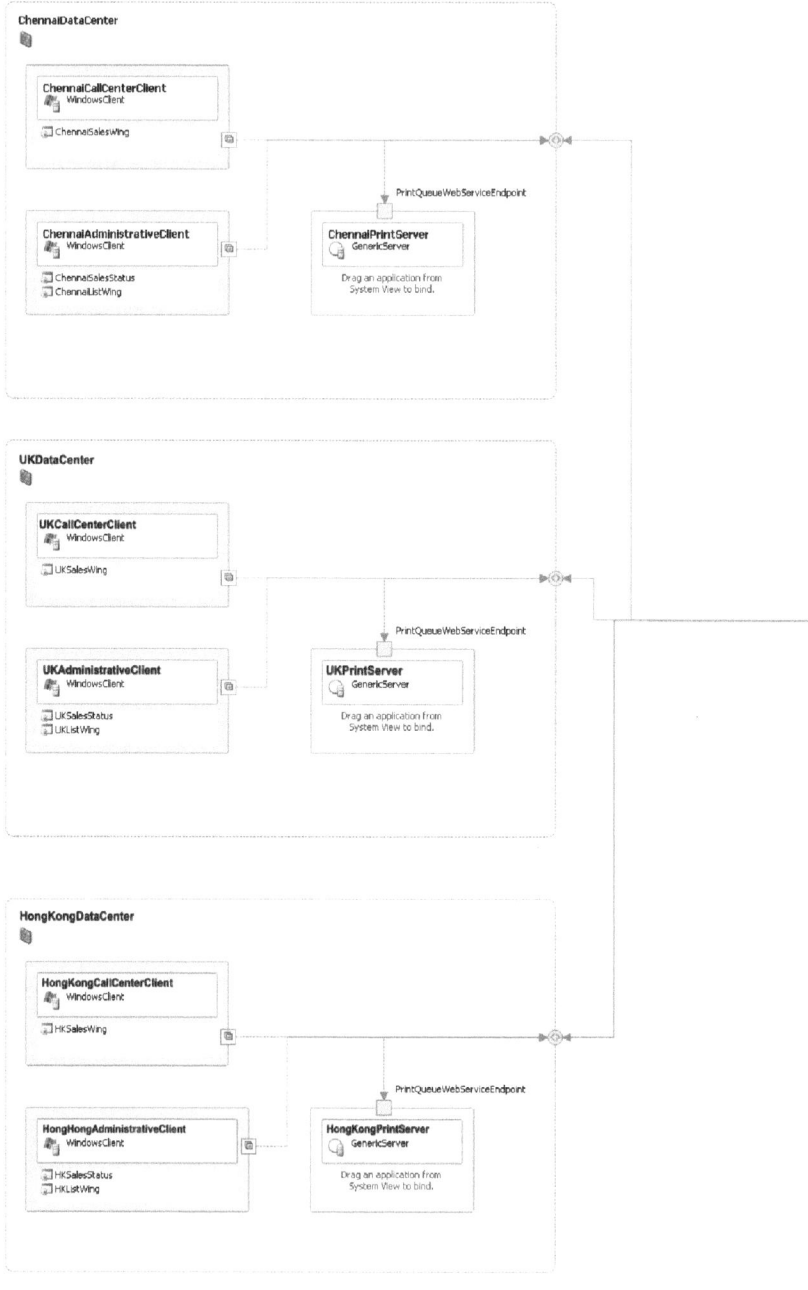

Figure 5-43. *Deployment of the system IcarusGlobalSystem to the data center GlobalDataCenter*

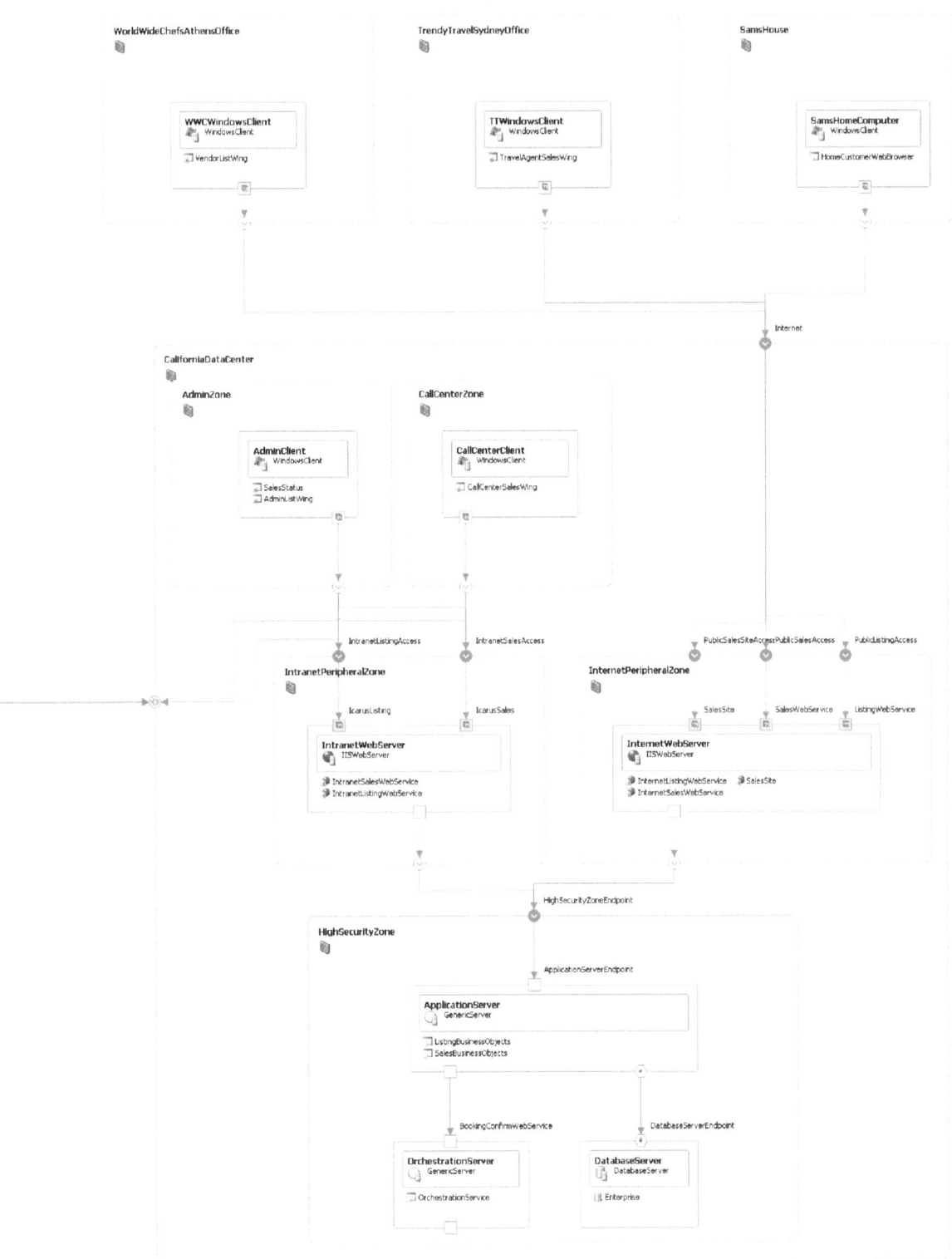

Summary

The main goal of this chapter was to show you how to use the distributed system designers in Visual Studio 2005 Team Edition for Architects. Along the way, we developed the high-level architecture for our example project, Icarus Enterprise 3.1.

This chapter introduced to you the concepts of application diagrams, with prototype applications and constraints, and we drew an application diagram for the legacy Icarus Enterprise 2.4 application. You learned how to add custom applications to the Toolbox as prototypes. You saw the creation of the application diagram for the new project.

You learned about the concept of systems and watched the development of the system diagram for the new worldwide Icarus system.

We discussed the meaning of logical data centers and examined the logical data center diagram for the Icarus worldwide network of servers and clients.

Finally, you learned how the Team System Deployment Designer can simulate deployment of the global system to this global data center.

In the next chapter we leave consideration of the whole system at a high level to begin the detailed planning and design of the software to be delivered during iteration 1.

CHAPTER 6

Business Analyst and Design Team: Designing the Application

We now move from the high-level approach in iteration 0 to the detailed development in iteration 1. As you'll recall, in Chapter 3 the functionality was roughly divided across the iterations and now the management, requirements, and architectural effort switches to the details of the iteration 1 deliveries. If you refer back to Figure 3-11, you will see how the initial activities of iteration 1 involve writing the scenarios to be implemented in iteration 1 and storyboarding them. Once that step is completed, the team will need to determine product requirements for iteration 1 and create the solution architecture.

Work Streams, Activities, Work Products, and Iterations

MSF CMMI introduces some unfamiliar concepts such as constituencies, roles, work streams, activities, and iterations. *Constituencies* represent views on the software development life cycle. MSF CMMI defines seven of these: Program Management, Product Management, Architecture, Development, Test, Release Operations, and User Experience. Each of these constituencies requires advocacy within the team in order to provide a balanced viewpoint and avoid lopsided decisions. One example is to contrast the viewpoints of the development and test constituencies. Developers may be more than ready to make a quick change to the code that will result in a major change to its function. The test constituency, however, may find that verifying that the new function operates correctly is a much bigger job and means rewriting a large number of test cases. The User Experience constituency may have reservations about such a change because it may introduce capability in the product that is outside the user's experience and may require additional training. Another example is the relationship between architecture and development. Developers may often see a quick solution to implementation of a requirement that falls outside the architectural structure that the architect is trying to apply across the product. Using the approved architectural methods may seem cumbersome in the short term but lead to more consistency and easier maintenance in the long term.

Each *role* falls into one of the constituencies and therefore advocates a particular viewpoint. Examples of roles are shown in Table 6-1; this information is taken straight from the process documentation. A great deal can be said about what these roles mean; you can read the process guidance to learn more, but I will try to illustrate their viewpoints throughout this book.

Table 6-1. *Roles and Their Constituencies*

Constituency	Role Name
Program Management	Sponsor, Project Manager
Architecture	Architect, Subject Matter Expert
Development	Developer, Development Manager, Build Engineer
Test	Tester, Test Manager, Auditor, Quality of Service Specialist
Release/Operations	Release Manager, Integrated Program Management (IPM) Officer
User Experience	User Experience Architect, User Education Specialist
Product Management	Product Manager, Business Analyst

One role does not necessarily map to one individual in the team. In small teams, one individual may take responsibility for several roles, whereas for large projects multiple people may be responsible for each role. Team members take on roles and perform *activities*, which are grouped into *work streams*. Activities generate *work products,* which are artifacts of one kind or another such as documents and code. Table 6-2 shows some examples of work streams and the activities that they include.

Table 6-2. *Examples of Work Streams and Activities*

Work Stream	Activities
Plan an Iteration	Select Iteration Backlog, Iteration Analysis, Plan Knowledge and Skills, Plan Iteration Resources, Form Iteration Team, Define Iteration Roles and Responsibilities, Identify Iteration Stakeholders, Plan Iteration Stakeholder Involvement, Estimate Iteration, Define Iteration Budget and Schedule, Iteration Plan Review, IPMO Iteration Review, Obtain Iteration Commitments, Define Communications Plan
Create Solution Architecture	Create Alternative Application Partitioning Diagrams, Design System Architecture and Deployment, Create Proof of Concepts, Assess Alternatives, Select Architecture, Architecture Control Board Meeting, Develop Threat Model, Develop Performance Model
Create a Scenario	Brainstorm Scenarios, Prioritize Scenarios, Write Scenarios, Storyboard Scenarios, Validate Scenarios, Write User Acceptance Tests
Create Product Requirements	Develop a User Interface Flow Model, Develop a Domain Model, Define Functional Requirements, Define Interface Requirements, Define Security Requirements, Define Safety Requirements, Define Operational Requirements, Allocate Product Component Requirements, Prioritize Functionality, Validate Requirements

Iterations are stages in the incremental completion of the project. Each iteration may involve product definition, development, and testing, and results in a stable portion of the overall system. Iteration plans, storyboards, product requirements, and the solution architecture are examples of groups of work products resulting from work streams; some are specific to an iteration, and some can be evolving artifacts that are enhanced at each iteration as more scenarios are added. The generation of the work products within these groups will be illustrated in this chapter. For example, the work stream Create Solution Architecture involves a set of activities such as Create Alternative Application Partitioning Designs, Design System Architecture and Deployment, and Create Proof of Concepts. These activities create work products such as Application Connection Diagrams, Logical Data Center Diagrams, System Diagrams, Deployment Diagrams, and Proof of Concepts. Following MSF CMMI can generate a huge amount of work and documentation, but "stretch to fit" is one of the concepts of the team model, and the level of work and documents should be adjusted as appropriate to the project. Where one team member can perform several roles, one document can represent more than one work product. The important thing is that the activities and work products described in the process guidance for the work streams are important reminders of what you should be thinking about, even on a fairly small project. In this chapter, though, I want to show these activities and work products arising naturally out of the development rather than just because the process guidance says they should be there. You tend to feel a process is right if the documents and activities seem appropriate to meet the needs of the project as they arise, as well as being reminders of aspects that you might have omitted.

Iteration Sequence Is Goal Oriented

Of course, the functionality was divided across the iterations in Chapter 3, so that the product requirements and solution architecture will evolve in the right direction. It obviously would be no good adopting an approach where customer scenarios to be added in later iterations were completely ignored in the early ones. This would be a recipe for disaster, since the architecture might have to be completely redesigned late in the project because of some late feature that could not be implemented in the existing architecture. This applies to quality-of-service requirements as well as customer functional requirements in the form of scenarios.

Iteration 1 was defined, at the end of Chapter 3, as containing the following functionality:

- Data model containing resources, orders, vendors, and customer tables. Vendors and customers are added via scripts for test purposes.

- Design to include capability for offline working for resource browsing and sales, but not to be demonstrable.

- Establish end-to-end operation of basic elements of listing management: create resource, list resources, edit resources.

- Establish end-to-end operation of basic elements of order creation: create order, list orders, edit orders.

- No authentication or authorization included.

- Order and listing functionality includes elements in database, business logic, presentation, and client layers.

- Demonstrate performance and scalability for sales capabilities.

The topics have been chosen to include demonstration of the basic functionality with its performance, and the risky area of the offline working, in design only. The product requirements and solution architecture will then reflect these early in the project. The system to be demonstrated at the end of iteration 1 could be called a proof of concept for the system, even though there may be more limited proof of concepts developed by the architect or developers when evaluating the suitability of architectural techniques. The practical coding work will probably be done by the architect and maybe two or three senior developers. Notice, however, that the iteration plan at the end of Chapter 3 out of necessity left until iteration 2 some important areas, such as security and actual demonstration of offline working. So there is still risk remaining in the architectural decisions at the end of iteration 1.

We will begin our look at iteration 1 activities with the Planning an Iteration work stream.

Planning Iteration 1

As part of the iteration plan, Clare will generate work items and assign them to the various members of the team. The tasks in iteration 1 were described briefly in Chapter 3 and have already been defined as work items in Team System. As a result of the prioritizing, writing, and storyboarding of scenarios, the product requirements and the architecture for this iteration will be defined. The MSF process guidance shows the Create Architecture work stream as a complex, multistep process. It's this process that will occupy most of this chapter, and I will focus on two aspects of it in particular: Storyboard Scenarios and Design System Architecture. In Chapter 7 I will concentrate on Create Proof of Concepts, and we will get into the detailed use of Visual Studio 2005 for development. It is not always easy to reconcile the somewhat idealistic process flow from Chapter 3 (see Figure 3-11) with the realities of developing a new and innovative system.

You met Clare, the project manager, in Chapters 2 and 3, spent a long time looking at Susan's requirements in Chapter 4, and watched Peter design the high-level architecture in Chapter 5. Today is April 13 and these people have now joined Ron, the development team leader, at the start of iteration 1 to discuss the iteration planning.

"I really want to put together a rather detailed schedule for iteration 1," says Clare at the start of the meeting. "I'd like to see all the development tasks for each scenario on it." She notices a frown from Peter and, looking at him questioningly, adds as an afterthought, "But I'm really not sure if that's going to be possible."

"I don't see how we can do that," he answers. "We haven't even defined the scenarios for iteration 1 yet. And besides, some of the tasks are going to be dependent on the architecture and so far I've only designed that at a high level."

"Yes, I know," Clare agrees but continues to press the point. "The Plan Iteration task in the process guidance requires me to identify all the development tasks. So I do need those now as I've got to make a schedule and allocate staff resources before we can begin the work. Really I need to do that today."

"Well, we can throw something together," says Ron. "But I don't think it will be very accurate. Peter's right; we don't really know what the tasks will be at the moment."

Clare isn't happy. "Well, it's no good if it's not accurate," she sighs. "The point of following MSF CMMI is that I keep a pretty tight control on everything. How can I give Icarus's upper management a report on the schedule if nobody's really following it? This is the first time we've used this process and we really need to make it work."

"As I understand the process guidance," suggests Peter, studying the process guidance page, "some of the inputs Clare needs require quite major analysis, and also some prototyping. Surely activity 2, Iteration Analysis, in the guidance for Plan an Iteration requires input from the whole team."

The Plan an Iteration work stream, which the group considers, is shown in Figure 6-1, and consists of a sequence of activities. Activity 2, the iteration analysis, is described in the process guidance as involving a Solution Architect, a Tester, a User Experience Architect, and a User Education Specialist, which are all examples of *roles* defined in the process. Clearly for this project, Peter will assume the role of Solution Architect and Susan the role of User Experience Architect. However, that role will be shared with the developers, who will have some experience of what constitutes a usable application gained from their work with other customers, as well as Icarus personnel such as the department managers, William and James, and one or two experienced operators from their teams. The concept of a role in MSF CMMI does not necessarily have to be identified with just one individual. The process guidance also includes the Tester role in this activity since establishing the testability is essential to inclusion of a particular product feature and understanding of these features is needed by the test team to define their approach—in itself another activity. Again, a product feature is useless if no one can understand how to use it! Can you think of a feature in your favorite application that you think would be great if only you had the time to figure it out? The User Education Specialist therefore becomes involved in this activity as well, and again this is a role to be assumed by Susan in the early stages of the project.

"Well, I suppose the Plan Iteration work stream ought to be a fairly extended thing then," says Ron. "It's something that involves quite a few members of the team and needs to go on while Peter and his people are doing their analysis."

"So how long would that take, Peter?" asks Clare.

Figure 6-1. *The Plan an Iteration process guidance page showing the activities involved*

"Two to three weeks, I think," Peter replies. "I need to prototype at least one of the Customer Management scenarios before I can say that I am confident in the architecture to go ahead with the rest of the scenarios in iteration 1."

"And what about me?" protests Susan. "I have to go through and define the detailed scenarios for iteration 1. We've—"

"But I thought you'd done the scenarios!" interrupts Clare.

"No," continues Susan patiently, drawing the word out to its full length. "We've only worked on the top-level scenarios for the whole system so far. Now I need to work with the developers to define exactly what they will produce for iteration 1. That's Write Scenarios and Storyboard Scenarios."

"I agree with that," says Ron. "That's how it works."

"Me too," says Peter.

Clare looks frustrated. "I don't know how I can convince Icarus that we're on top of this unless I can show them a detailed schedule," she says with a note of finality. There is silence for few moments. Clare wonders whether as project manager she should insist on having her way, but she feels that she cannot override the objections of Peter and Ron. She is not at all sure whether she has a charter that allows her to lay down the law. In any case, she needs the support of Peter and Ron since she very much respects their technical knowledge, even if she is a little impatient with Peter's apparent lack of organization.

Finally Ron breaks the silence as he shuffles through his papers. "Well," he says, "we can't start this project by disagreeing and breaking up into separate camps. I've been reading MSF for CMMI Process Improvement quite carefully and one thing I notice is that it has some underlying principles."

He reads from a printout of the process guidance that he has made. "One of them reads like this. It says 'A team of peers with clear accountability, shared responsibility and open communications. Each role is accountable for a specific share of the quality of the overall solution.' In another place it says 'Partner with Customers. The customer is the consumer at the end of the value chain. In order to maximize customer value, everyone in the value chain must partner by seeking to better understand customer value and share that information back up the value chain.' Maybe I can suggest how you should handle Icarus, Clare."

Clare catches on quickly. "You're going to say that I should bring them into the scenario definition phase and make it clear to them that the exact development tasks aren't clear until that's done," she interjects somewhat doubtfully.

"Yes, getting them involved will make them understand," says Ron. "Make it clear it's a partnership."

There is some discussion about this idea before Clare agrees that it's possible, but Clare is feeling relieved that other members of the team understand her predicament and are contributing helpful ideas. "I think that point about everyone in the value chain being responsible to the customer is a great idea," she says with a wry grin. "Not just me as project manager!"

Everyone laughs. The atmosphere is a good deal lighter.

Peter adds, "I think it's easier to involve the customer in the scenarios than the architecture and prototyping, since it relates better to their view of the project. Anyway, I think you *are* right; we need to put together some sort of schedule, and the tasks involved in iteration planning form the early activities. Then we can put in some placeholders for the later activities. We know that we have to develop business objects for the Customer Management, Resource Management, and Sales parts of the application because those are the deliverables we've set for iteration 1. But we just can't be very specific in that area yet."

Clare is regaining her confidence. "OK, I've got an idea. Let's consider iteration 1 as having two phases, an analysis phase and an implementation phase. In the analysis phase we define the scenarios, product requirements, and architecture, and your group, Peter, does whatever prototyping is necessary in support of that. With support from you all, I gradually put together a plan for the second phase. Then in the second phase we formally implement the scenarios, test, and deliver. Maybe this pattern will continue for the other iterations in the project."

"I think that's a good idea," says Ron. "And we keep the customer from getting impatient by involving them in the scenario work."

"I believe this kind of phase one analysis will get shorter as we get to the later iterations," says Peter. "The whole project will become more clearly defined as we move from innovation into bug fixing. But you know, there's still this kind of analysis phase where we evaluate the code or design changes for a bug or change request."

"Of course, if a serious change comes through it would throw us into another longer analysis phase," murmurs Susan darkly. Everyone looks at her questioningly but she says no more.

The Plan for Iteration 1

To summarize the previous discussion, iteration 1 will consist of an analysis phase and a development phase. The analysis phase will involve tasks that are in support of the Create Iteration Plan task, and will consist of a good deal more than just meetings and paper planning. For example, the Storyboard Scenarios activity will involve developers generating façade-type applications that show the screens to be included in the scenarios and allow them to determine which Visual Studio 2005 features can best be used to implement the screens. This is far better than simply sitting down with pencil and paper to define the screens, and then giving the drawings to the developers to implement. Similarly, the Create Architecture work stream will involve generating proof-of-concept applications, since only by experimenting with the new technologies in Visual Studio 2005 will the architect and his team gain confidence that the architecture can move forward successfully through the iteration. Phase two will be a more formal development of the deliverables at the end of iteration 1, more closely tied to work items and involving some degree of unit test, application test, and performance test.

Later that day, Clare talks to Peter and Ron, and they decide to form two working groups for the analysis phase. Susan, Charles, Rahul, and another developer, Ed, will concentrate on storyboarding the scenarios for Customer Contacts, Reservation Sales, and Resource Management, which are the functional areas to be demonstrated at the end of iteration 1. Ed, who is very good with ASP.NET, will work on the sales screens for the Sales Site application, while Charles will tackle the Sales Wing Windows Forms for customer management. Rahul, in India, will work on prototyping the resource management screens in Visual Basic .NET.

Peter, Angela, and Alberto, a database administrator (DBA), will concentrate on the architectural design and prototyping of the proof-of-concept code. Angela is very good at ADO.NET and works with object-oriented concepts applicable in the business logic area. Alberto is an expert on SQL Server and will help out with the design of stored procedures and aspects of database efficiency. Also, since the customer management screens are quite limited in scope, Charles will move on to integrating his screens with Angela's business objects. The proof-of-concept code will consist of working end-to-end customer management code and will be checked into Team System and operating by the end of the three-week phase one period. Then, in the development phase of iteration 1, most of the development team will work toward delivering the complete iteration 1 functionality, while Peter and one or two other senior developers will work on the performance aspects. The team is thus performing most of the tasks identified in this chapter and Chapter 7 pretty much at the same time. At the end, the results need to show dependencies, but it would not be practical to try to isolate the tasks so that one does not begin until the other is complete. Such an approach might require the team members to work in too abstract a manner and miss the chance to draw on the experience of other team members.

Here are the members of the iteration 1 team and their responsibilities:

THE ITERATION 1 TEAM

- Clare Green, Project Manager

- Susan Drivewell, Requirements Manager, responsible for writing and storyboarding scenarios

- Linda Brown, Business Analyst, assisting with scenarios and storyboards

- Jill Drake (Icarus) Call Center Sales Supervisor, assisting with scenarios

- Peter Sage, Architect, responsible for overall architecture

- Ron Howard, Team Leader, responsible for team environment, procedures, check-in rules, builds

- Angela Cheung, Senior Developer (C#), responsible for (1) business object prototyping and (2) Sales business objects development

- Rahul Singh (India), Senior Developer (VB.NET), responsible for (1) prototype List Wing screens and (2) Listing business objects development

- Manish Patel (India), Developer (VB.NET), responsible for List Wing development

- Charles Hodges, Developer (C#, Windows Forms specialist), responsible for prototype Sales Wing customer management screens, development of Sales Wing application

- Ed Marshall, Developer (C#, ASP.NET specialist), responsible for (1) prototype Sales website screens and (2) Sales website application

- Alberto Morrelli, Database Administrator (SQL Server expert), responsible for data model, stored procedures, and general database efficiency and security

Clare adds the following new work items to Team System using Excel, then opens all of the iteration 1 work items in Microsoft Project by opening a query that she has written called Iteration1Tasks. You learned how to write queries in Chapter 4.

Phase 1

Develop customer management screens and storyboard

Develop sales screens and storyboard (order creation, display, edit)

Develop resource management screens and storyboard

Design iteration 1 application

Design iteration 1 system

Design iteration 1 deployment

Design data model

Design business logic component architecture

Design offline architecture

Prototype customer business entity components

Prototype end-to-end customer management system

Phase 2

Develop listing business entity components

Develop order and reservation business entity components

Develop sales system—orders and reservations

Develop listing system

Clare then allocates the tasks to the team members in Project and uses that program to organize the tasks into groups. This makes it much easier to see how the tasks relate to each other. She also sets the start and end dates of each task to produce a Gantt chart and links the tasks together. The result is shown in Figure 6-2. She saves this file locally, publishes to TFS, and then closes Project.

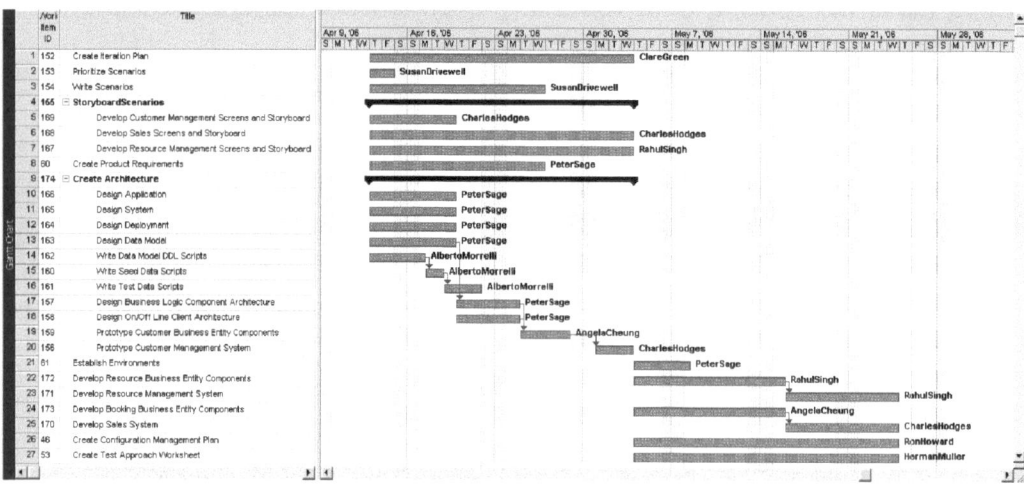

Figure 6-2. *The schedule for iteration 1*

She then uploads the schedule to the documents folder in Team Explorer in the Project Management subfolder. This will now be available on the project portal for all the team to see. Figure 6-3 shows the tasks involved in iteration 1 and how they interrelate.

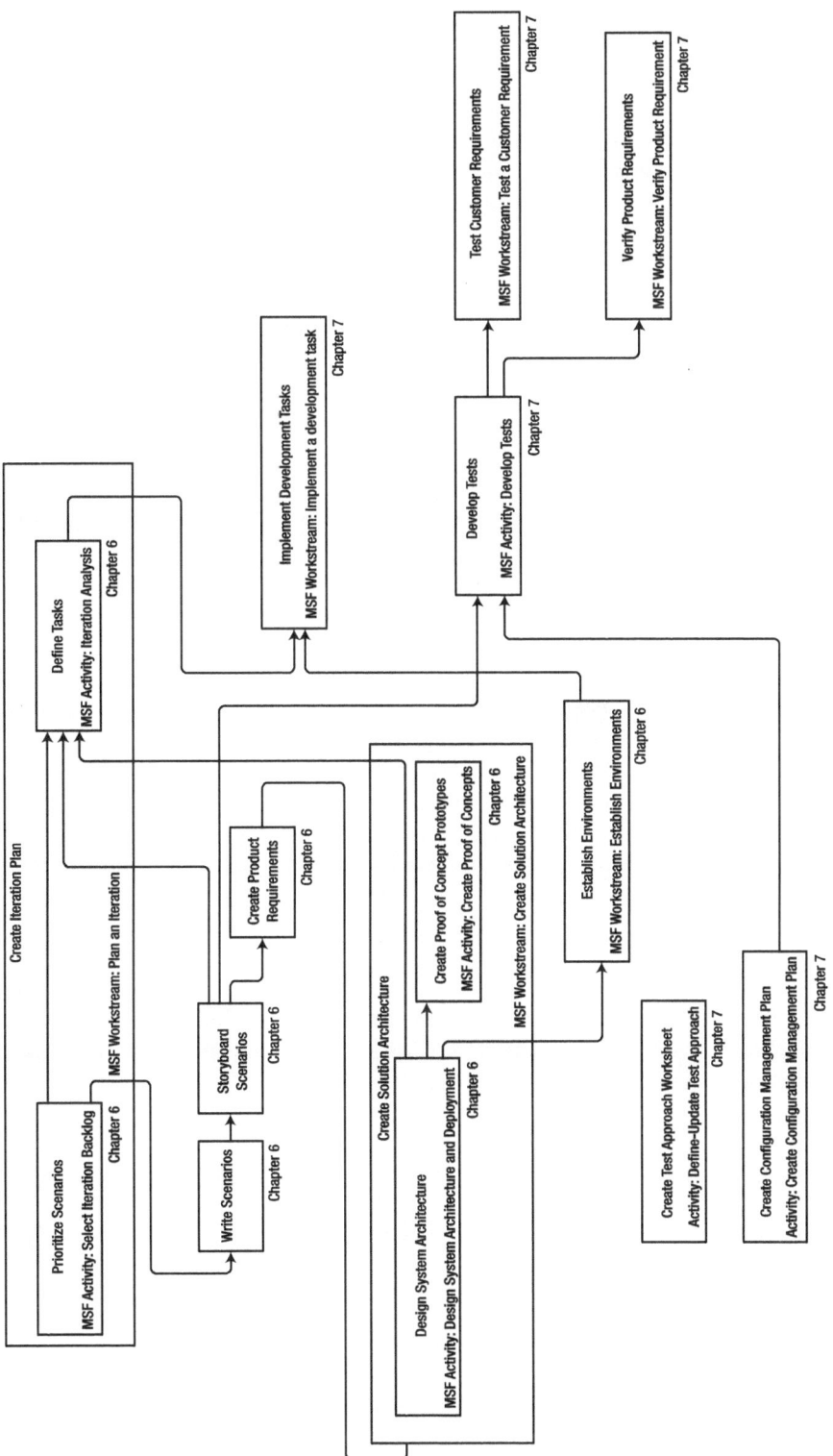

Figure 6-3. *Tasks involved in iteration 1*

Writing the Scenarios

MSF CMMI describes the Write Scenarios activity as occurring at the start of each iteration, after a set of scenarios have been chosen from the list. Writing a scenario means creating a written description of the scenario, step by step, following a single train of thought. Each step in the scenario should be a separate paragraph with more detail regarding the actions of the user and less about the actions of the software; many of those details are left until the storyboarding scenarios activity. Often, scenarios will have a great deal of commonality, with many of their steps identical. These areas can be described in detail in the first scenario, and then outlined in subsequent scenarios where steps are the same. An example is one where some activity is performed and there is more than one way of navigating between certain screens, such as using a context menu item, a main menu item, or a shortcut key. It is necessary to consider these as separate scenarios; otherwise the alternative techniques will not be tested. However, in the second and third scenarios, it is only necessary to describe the actions on the part of the user that are different from the first scenario.

It is pretty clear that, even for a modest project, the team must write an enormous number of scenarios. I'm not going to list them all in this chapter; I'll move straight on to the storyboarding task, since that will indicate to the reader what kind of scenarios need to be written and also give some more insight into the kind of functionality the team is developing. I'll make an exception for one group, the offline scenarios, since their consideration is essential for the design of iteration 1.

For the first three weeks, the task of the team is to produce the scenario storyboards, the product requirements, and architecture design, which will together support the functionality to be formally delivered at the end of iteration 1. During the first meeting the team will perform the Prioritize Scenarios task and identify most of the scenarios to be implemented in iteration 1. During the next few days, Susan will work with her BA assistants and the developers to write the scenarios. The developers will generate the screens as part of their prototypes, and provide screenshots for Susan's group to include in the storyboards, which her group will produce.

Offline Critical Scenarios

These are the first scenarios that Susan and Peter write, so that Peter can work on designing the architecture that will support them. There is an assumption in these scenarios that an offline cache exists on the client that contains portions of the Enterprise database application described in Chapter 5. The implementation of this cache is not yet defined.

BROWSE BY CATEGORY—CORRECT OFFLINE CACHE UPDATE WHEN RESOURCE IS MODIFIED

This scenario begins with a clear offline cache.

1. While online, the user browses by category down to viewing a specific resource summary page.

2. The user goes offline and verifies that the same page can be viewed.

3. A change is made to the page while the user is offline.

4. The user goes back online and verifies that the changed page is viewed.

5. The user goes offline and verifies that it is the changed page that is viewed and not the old one.

BROWSE BY CATEGORY—CORRECT OFFLINE CACHE UPDATE WHEN RESOURCE DELETED

in the first scenario, but while the user is offline, the resource is deleted. It is removed from all of the category catalogs.

When the user comes online again, the resource does not appear in any catalog page and is therefore inaccessible. Verify that this is still the same when the user goes offline a second time.

BROWSE BY CATEGORY—CORRECT OFFLINE CACHE UPDATE WHEN RESOURCE CATEGORY CHANGED

Same as the first scenario, but while user is offline, resource is moved from one category to another. Verify that when the user comes back online the resource is accessible through the new category and not the old one. Verify that this is still the case when the user goes offline a second time.

BROWSE BY CATEGORY—CORRECT OFFLINE CACHE UPDATE WHEN RESOURCE ADDED

Same as the first scenario, but a new resource is added while the user is offline. When the user comes back online, the user sees the resource in the correct place in the category catalog. When the user goes offline a second time, the new resource is still visible in the correct place in the category catalog.

Other scenarios relate to the need for customer information and orders for customers of an agent to be held offline on an agent's computer. If the agent makes a change to a customer's orders, these changes need to be held offline until the agent's computer is reconnected; then they must be synchronized with the server database. Any conflicts must be detected and warnings issued to the user.

The List Wing application also has offline scenarios describing the ability of a vendor to read and update that vendor's resource information while offline. When the vendor reconnects, the application must also update on the server database any resources that were modified locally.

Storyboarding the Scenarios

Storyboarding the scenarios means creating visual representations of the screens that will be displayed, and identifying their sequences and the actions users take in order to progress through them. Screens can be drawn using a graphics program or just described in words, but another technique is to develop façade screens using Visual Studio. By façade screens, I mean screens that simply display the Windows Forms or web forms that will be used in the complete application, but have no functionality other than perhaps to provide basic navigation between the screens and some contrived representative data. The developers will get involved at this time, and since iteration 1 is not very long—only six weeks—the team has decided that storyboarding and prototyping will go pretty much hand in hand, so that the storyboards will follow the screens that the developers are prototyping.

The prototyping team is responsible for delivering a proof-of-concept system at the end of iteration 1. They hold their first meeting in the offices of Guru's Nest. I have already introduced many of the team members, but it will do no harm to remind you that the team now consists of Peter Sage, Susan Drivewell, Angela Cheung, Charles Hodges, Ed Marshall, Rahul Singh, and Alberto Morrelli. Peter will be responsible for the overall prototyping, assisted by Angela for the business objects, Charles for the Sales Wing sales application, Ed for the Web Sales application, and Rahul for the List Wing application. Alberto is involved as the DBA. Mention was made of customer involvement during the planning meeting discussions described earlier in this chapter, and Icarus Sales Manager William Fairways has also joined in the meeting. Susan has two other assistants who will help her with the more formal work in the later phase.

Let's look now at the work of the team in storyboarding the scenarios. Sets of scenarios were described in Chapter 4 for the Browse Catalog and Manage Reservations parts of this use case. There are also scenarios for the Customer Contacts and Manage Customer Account parts of the sales use case, but in iteration 1 the team does not have to implement all of these. The team only has to demonstrate the basic functions of end-to-end creation of reservations. They must also demonstrate the end-to-end working of the basic scenarios of the Listings use cases in Chapter 4 (Figure 4-23) that form part of the capabilities of the List Wing application.

Customer Management Scenarios

The customer management use cases are not included in iteration 1, but the team decides that, in order to demonstrate the sales orders and reservation capability, it will be necessary to implement some elementary customer management function. This capability will form the basis of the Sales Wing application. Let's look in on the team to see how they are storyboarding this set of scenarios. Some discussion is taking place about the way in which the customer management capability is to be organized. The Sales Wing application needs a main screen on which to place the menu bar, and there are a number of ways in which this screen can be organized.

Charles suggests that the screen should have a master-detail format, with a list of customers on the left and a panel on the right showing the customer details, including the orders and their reservations. He sketches this on the whiteboard.

"There's a problem with that," says William. "We've got a huge number of customers and that list on the left is going to have to be populated with all the customers from the database when the application starts up."

"Wouldn't some kind of document concept be better? " says Rahul's voice from the speak-erphone. "Couldn't we make it like an MDI and treat each customer as a separate document?"

Note An MDI is a multiple-document interface application. It is an interface scheme that embodies the concept of a document, which is usually a file on a disk, which may be opened and edited, then saved and closed again. This concept can also be used for a single-document interface, where the application can only open one document at a time, like Notepad. In an MDI application, all the open documents are displayed in separate windows that are child windows of the main window of the application. Microsoft Word is an example of an application that can open many documents at a time, and the user can switch from one to the other, but they are completely separate windows and appear as separate applications even though they all belong to the same process. Others, like Visual Studio, require all of the open documents (such as code files) to be placed in windows within the application's main window. Within this window each one can usually be minimized, or made to take full screen; alternatively the application windows can be tiled or cascaded. Another approach, which is used in Visual Studio, is to arrange the windows displaying the multiple documents as a collection of tab pages.

Some discussion takes place to enable all of the team members to get the same picture in their minds of what Rahul is suggesting.

"I don't think you mean that the multiple documents are *real* documents stored on the disk drive, do you, Rahul?" says Peter. "You mean that the documents would be clusters of data gathered from the database and displayed as a details screen, using a set of controls, right?"

"Yeah of course, I'm not talking about a text type of document. It's really an idea of a virtual document. Each user is represented by a document, in the form of Name, Address, Credit info, etc. plus, of course, a list of their current orders with Icarus. We can show the individual customer documents as separate tab pages in a tab control."

"So then you open a customer as a document using a selection from a File menu?" says Angela. "And you need some way of selecting the customer—maybe have an Open Customer dialog box that allows you to select the customer to open—but you don't want to list *all* the possible customers there..."

"Yeah, well, we should have some way to filter them on that dialog box, like maybe just enter the first few letters of the name," prompts Rahul.

"And we need to search for customers by first name and last name too," points out Susan.

Peter takes up the idea and draws the display on the whiteboard, as in Figure 6-4. "So the Open Customer dialog box can have a set of text boxes to type in search information, and a data grid that shows the results of the search, plus OK and Cancel buttons," he suggests. "And if you just type the first letter, A for example, you get all the customers listed that begin with A, then you select one and hit OK to open that customer."

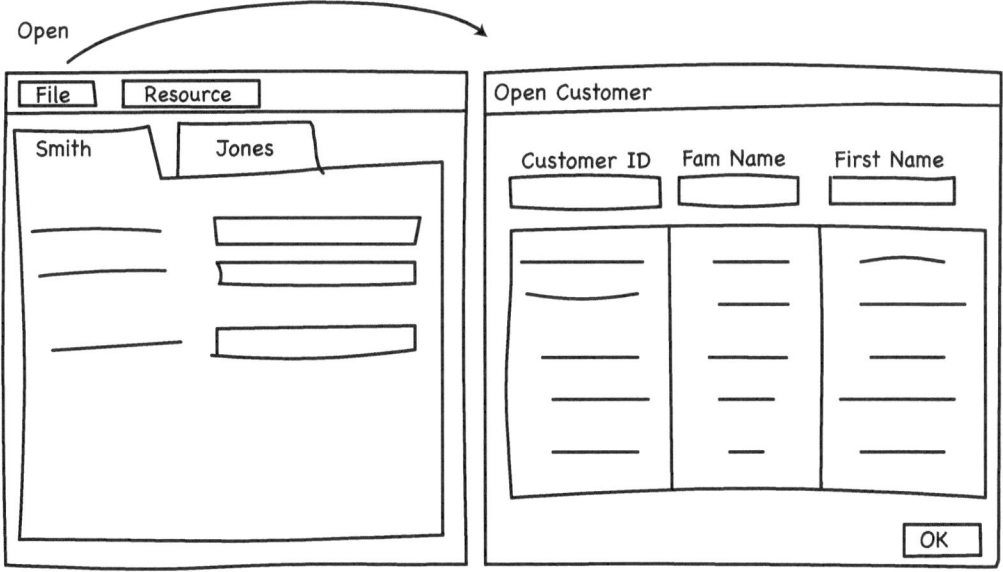

Figure 6-4. *Peter's whiteboard drawing of the main screen for Sales Wing*

"Or double-click on the row in the dialog box," adds Susan.

"Right. Do you know how to implement that, Angela?" asks Peter.

"Mmm," she considers, "I'll use a data-bound DataGridView control for the collection of customers, but how does that work with the web services and the business objects on the server? I'd be OK if it was dealing directly with the database of course, but it will need to work with business objects in this case."

"OK, we need to think about that. Or maybe that's my job," admits Peter. "Anyway, you go ahead and implement the screens so we can take screen shots. And Susan, you can make the scenario document. What is there? Open Customer, Close Customer—that's about it, eh? We can worry about creating and deleting customers later, right?"

"Yes, I agree," says Susan.

Peter starts to get up. "So are we done with this then?"

"There could be a problem with having many customers open at once," says Charles. "When the user changes the details of a customer, like their address for instance, they could leave the customer document open all day, without saving the change whereas with a modal approach that can't happen. If customers sit open, modified for a long time, there's more chance of optimistic-locking exceptions."

"Yes, that's true," agrees Peter, sitting down again. "How can we mitigate that? Maybe modifications, like adding orders, should be modal so that they get saved at the end of the new order sequence, even though the customer remains open."

Note A modal dialog box is one that requires completion of an operation, such as creating a new order and a final OK, before any other screen of the application can be activated—so you have to finish one thing before doing anything else. A wizard is usually modal although it involves several successive screens.

"We're going to have to watch out for those sorts of problems, though," points out Charles. "It's not just orders, it's changes to customer data, which we plan to implement in iteration 2."

"Probably we should prevent switching to a different customer tab until any changes are saved then," says Peter and they get up to leave.

After the meeting, Charles creates some screens using Visual Studio 2005 and Susan puts the screen shots into a document describing the customer management scenarios for iteration 1. We will see in the next chapter exactly how Charles creates the screens—there is a lot to say—but for the moment we'll concentrate on observing how the functionality of the application is defined and look at the technicalities when we have time to do them justice.

Open Customer

The Open Customer storyboard is shown in Table 6-3 and its associated figures.

Note Most people in the world have two or more names. My name is Steve Shrimpton. Steve is my first name and Shrimpton is my last name, but Shrimpton is also my *family* name—the same last name as my father and grandfather—whereas Steve is my *given* name, the name my parents gave me. In Asia, people in some countries, such as China, put their family name first, so if my family name was Shi and my given name was Tian, I would be called Shi Tian. Icarus is a global company and they have sales in Asia, so they adopt the use of Given Name and Family Name to keep everything consistent. In the United States, Given Name is First Name and Family Name is Last Name.

Table 6-3. *The Open Customer Scenario Storyboard*

Step	User Action	System Response
Initial State	**The Sales Wing application is running without any customers open, as in Figure 6-5.**	
1.	The user clicks the File ➤ Open Customer main menu option.	The system displays the Open Customer dialog box (Figure 6-6). Since all search strings are empty, all the customers are displayed in the data grid.
2.	The user types characters, e.g., "an", into the Family Name text box.	The system displays in the data grid only those customers whose family name begins with "an". The qualification is not case sensitive.
3.	The user selects one of the customers listed in the data grid, and then clicks the Open button.	The system closes the Open Customer dialog box and displays the main Customer Contacts screen with one tab added (Figure 6-7). The tab will contain a complete multi-tab user control (called the CustomerDetails control) populated with the data for the selected customer, retrieved from the database.

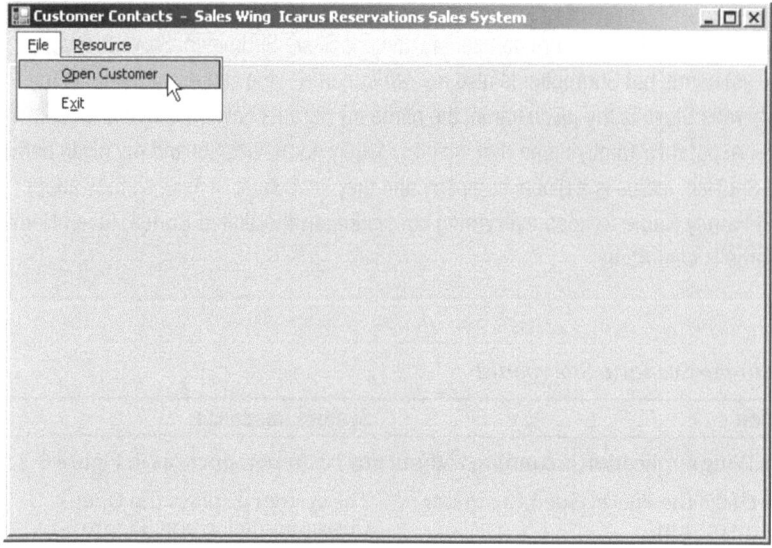

Figure 6-5. *Customer Contacts, the main screen of the Sales Wing application*

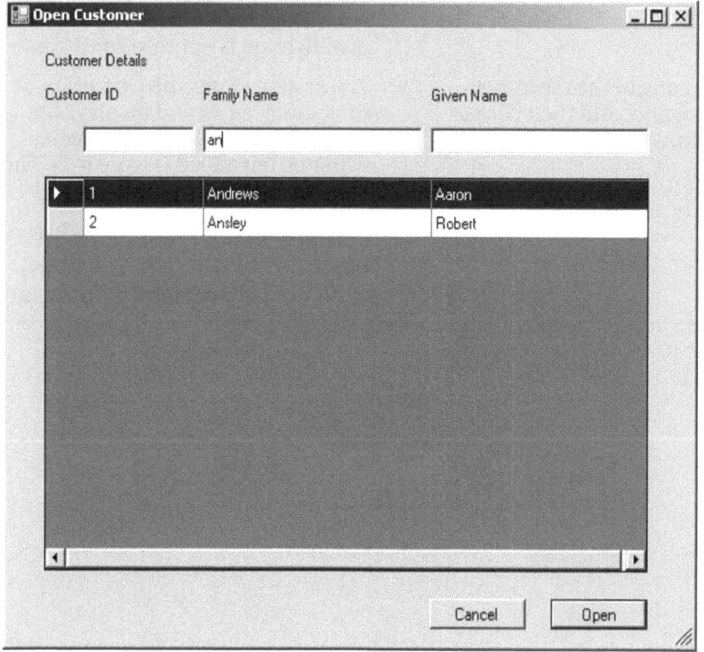

Figure 6-6. *The Open Customer dialog box*

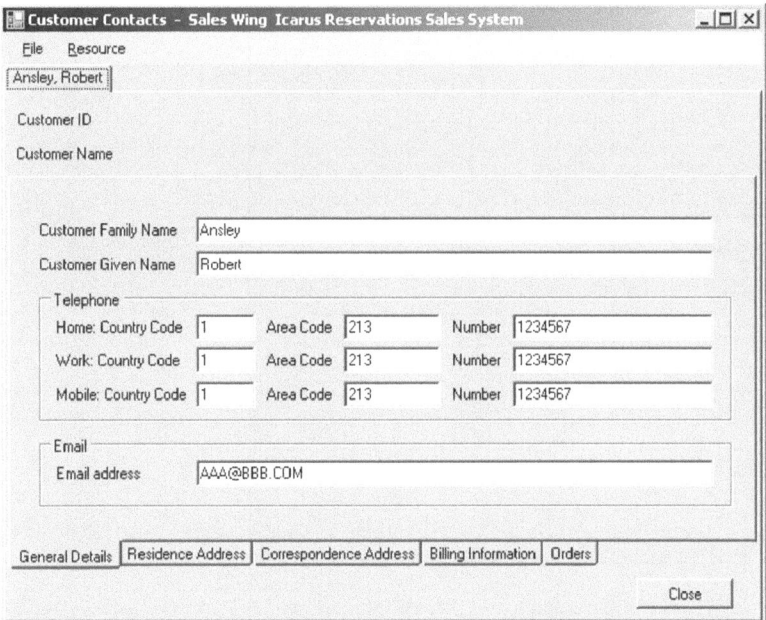

Figure 6-7. *The customer details tab page. It is itself also a tab page with these tabs: (a) General Details, (b) Residence Address, (c) Correspondence Address, (d) Billing Information, and (d) Orders.*

Open Customer—Variations

Variations are identified in which the user types strings into the other two search string boxes, Customer ID and Customer Given Name, or a combination of any pair or all three. The user may type no search string at all and select from the initial display in the data grid. The user may change the search strings that are entered, adding, deleting, or modifying characters. The user may abort the Open Customer operation by clicking Cancel. The user may enter the scenario when there are already one or more customers open.

Close Customer

The Close Customer scenario appears in Table 6-4 (and Figure 6-8).

Table 6-4. *The Close Customer Scenario Storyboard*

Step	User Action	System Response
Initial State	**The Sales Wing application is running with two customers open, as in Figure 6-8. Two tabs are visible.**	
1.	The user selects the tab of the customer that is to be closed and clicks the Close button.	The system removes the tab containing the details of the selected customer from the screen, leaving the other customer displayed in a single tab.

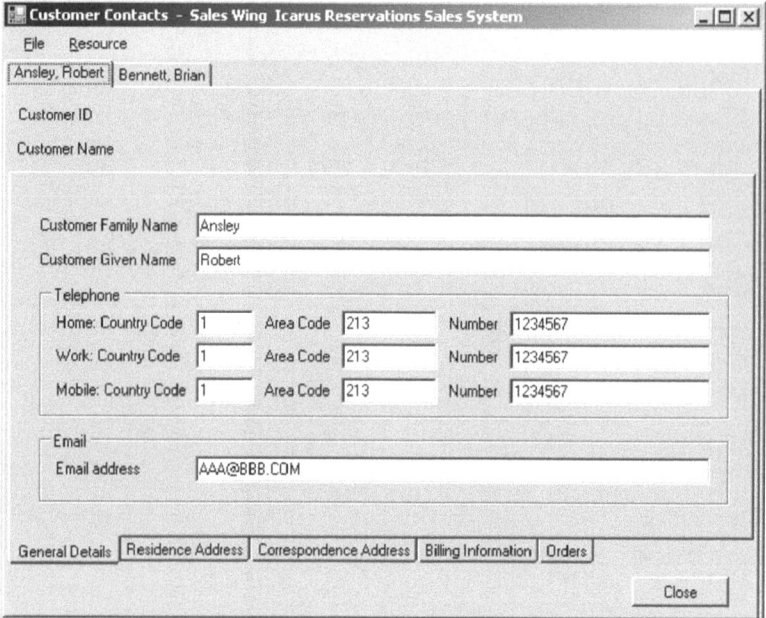

Figure 6-8. *Close Customer, step 1. The main window shows a customer display open. The user clicks the Close button.*

Close Customer—Variations

There may be various numbers of customers already open and the user may select from any of them. The other customers should remain open, displaying the correct data.

Manage Reservations Scenarios

The discussion about these scenarios is mainly concerned with how to create the order and add reservations. Susan thinks it would be nice if a user could be working on more than one customer's order at a time, but all agree that if the process of creating or editing an order is not modal, then half-created orders could hang around on users' machines for a long time, which increases the chance that someone else might create an order that conflicts with that one, resulting in an optimistic lock exception. Although it is unlikely that more than one operator will work on the same customer at the same time, it could be that an operator reserves a resource that has limited capacity, then takes a long time saving the order, so that another operator has booked the same resource and used up the capacity before the first operator saves the order. It's all debatable, since agents would come to know that it is necessary to save their orders to be sure they are confirmed.

Chapter 4 described a browse resource use case, which would allow the user to approach the reservation of a resource by browsing by region or by category. However, the sales scenarios that are agreed on for iteration 1 are to be based on a search sequence, in which the user can specify geographic region, category, vendor, date, and quantity, or any subset and see displayed the alternative options in a data grid view. Also, the plan is that, as the user selects the resource, by choosing first the region and then the category, the selections available for the rest of the criteria will be reduced to include only those that are compatible. For example, if the user selects Madrid as the geographic region, only those vendors that list resources in Madrid will appear in the Vendor combo box drop-down.

The technical members of the team are not sure how this will work, and Susan is not entirely sure whether this will be the best approach for the users, but that is the reason for an iterative development.

Charles has produced Windows Forms screens to illustrate the scenario in the storyboard. Again there is a lot to be said about the controls that are used—things that are new in Visual Studio 2005—but again we will reserve discussion of this until Chapter 7.

Create Order

The Create Order scenario is shown in Table 6-5 and its associated figures.

Table 6-5. *The Create Order Scenario*

Step	User Action	System Response
Initial State	**The customer for whom the order is to be created is opened in the Customer Contacts page and the Order tab selected, as in Figure 6-9.**	
1.	The user clicks the New button.	The system displays the Order Detail dialog box.
2.	The user selects a geographic location (e.g., Mexico) from the locations that are listed alphabetically in the Location combo box.	The system displays the same page but updates the contents of the Category and Vendor combo box item collection to contain only the categories of resources and vendors of resources that are available within the selected geographic location. The system updates the Alternative Options data grid view to list all the resources available in the selected location.
3.	The user selects a resource category (e.g., Hotel) from the Category combo box.	The system displays the same page but updates the contents of the Vendor combo box item collection to contain only the vendors of resources that are available within the selected geographic location *and* the selected category. The system updates the Alternative Options data grid view to list all the resources available in the selected location and of the selected category.
4.	The user selects a vendor (e.g., Sanchez Guest House) from the Vendors combo box.	The system displays the same page but updates the contents of the Alternative Options data grid view to list all the resources available in the selected location, in the selected category, and that are offered by the selected vendor.

Continued

Table 6-5. *(Continued)*

Step	User Action	System Response
5.	The user selects the date on which the reservation is required in the Date date/time picker control.	The system displays the same page but limits resources displayed in the Alternative Options data grid to those available on that particular date.
6.	The user enters a quantity (e.g., 2) in the Quantity: text box.	The system displays the same page but limits the resources displayed in the Alternative Options data grid to those for which there are at least the number available that the user has requested.
7.	The user selects one of the resources listed in the Alternative Options data grid view and clicks the Add Reservation button.	A reservation is created (but not saved to the database) and a row is added to the list box at the top of the screen. The list view entry contains all the columns shown in Figure 6-10.
8.	The user clicks OK on the Order Detail dialog box.	The system creates a new order with the reservation added as shown and saves it to the database. The Order Detail dialog box is closed and the Customer Contacts screen is updated so that the selected customer's Orders tab shows the new order.

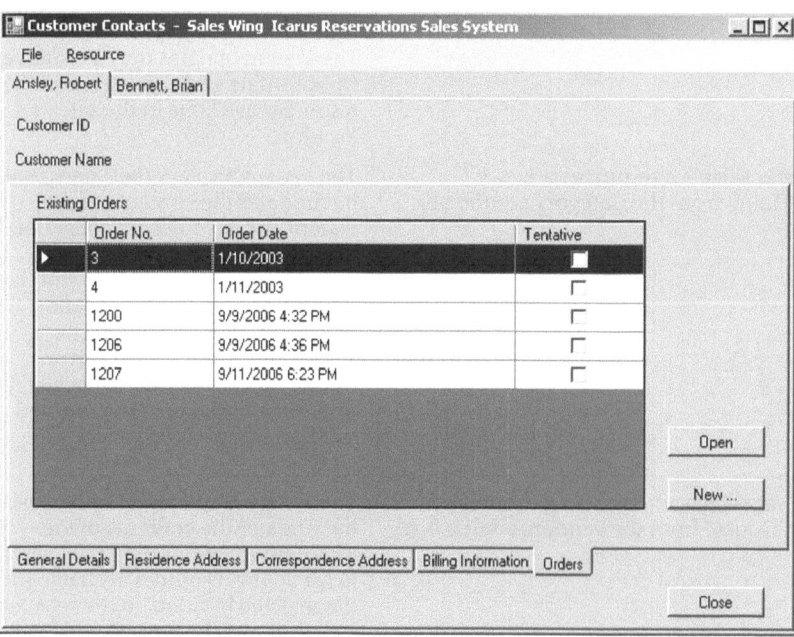

Figure 6-9. *Create Order, step 1: the Sales Wing main screen, Customer Contacts*

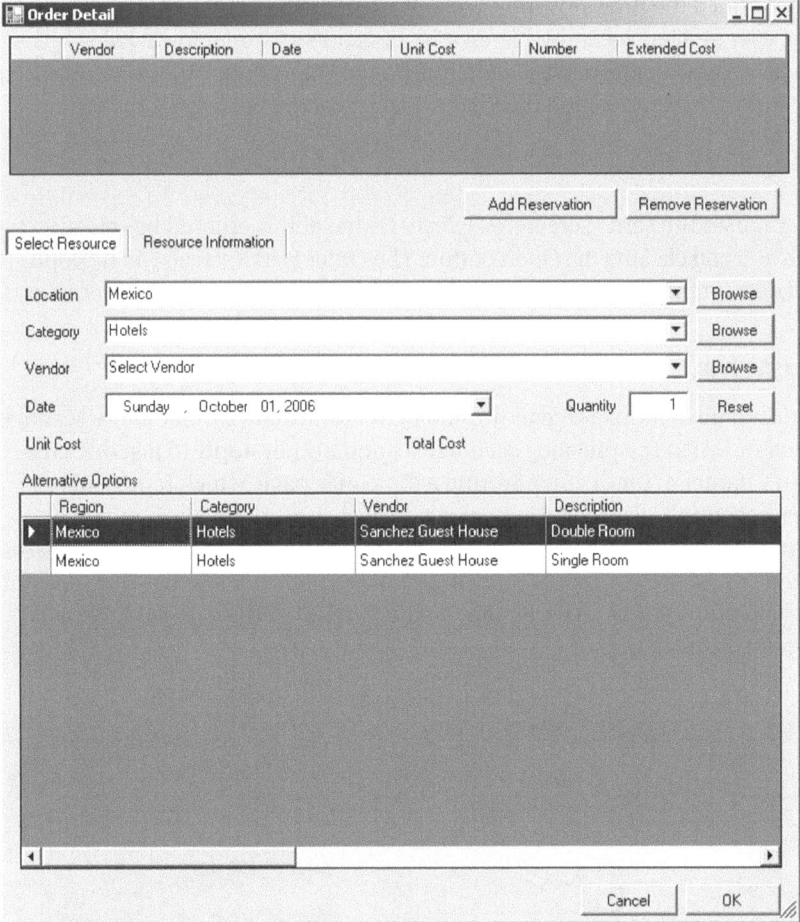

Figure 6-10. *Create Order, step 2, the Order Detail dialog box*

Create Order Variation—Two Reservations Made

In this variation the user creates a second reservation in the order, by repeating steps 2 through 7, before saving it.

Create Order Variation—Delete Reservation

In this variation a reservation is added, then deleted. Then a different reservation is added before the order is saved.

More Create Order Scenario Variations

The team thinks of a few more variations, which I will not take the space to list here, covering situations where the user has selected a location and a category, then goes back and changes the location. In this case the alternative values available in the location are the same as if the user had selected the category first. To get all the locations back, the user will have to click the Reset button, or return all the combo boxes to None. There are a number of scenario variations like this.

I have also not mentioned the Browse buttons, which are not to be implemented in iteration 1. These allow the user to select locations, categories, or vendors by opening a dialog box in which the user may select a larger category and then drill down. For example, the user could first select Europe as a location, then France, and then Paris. The rest of the behavior is the same.

Edit Order

The Edit Order scenario uses the same screens as Create Order, and is entered by selecting an existing order in Figure 6-9 and clicking the Open button. The Order Detail screen will be populated with the original data for the order and the user may delete or add one or more reservations.

Web Sales Scenarios

The web sales scenarios to be demonstrated at the end of iteration 1 are similar to the Manage Reservations scenarios shown in the previous section except that they apply to just one customer. As described in Chapter 4, they center around a My Wings page, which represents the customer's own Icarus account. Customers can browse the website, but to create or edit an order, they must log in. They then see the page shown in Figure 6-11 as their base in the Icarus site. Ed has put together a basic web application using Visual Studio 2005 but has only taken it far enough to show some prototype screens, as shown in Figures 6-11 through 6-14. We will study his work fully in the next chapter.

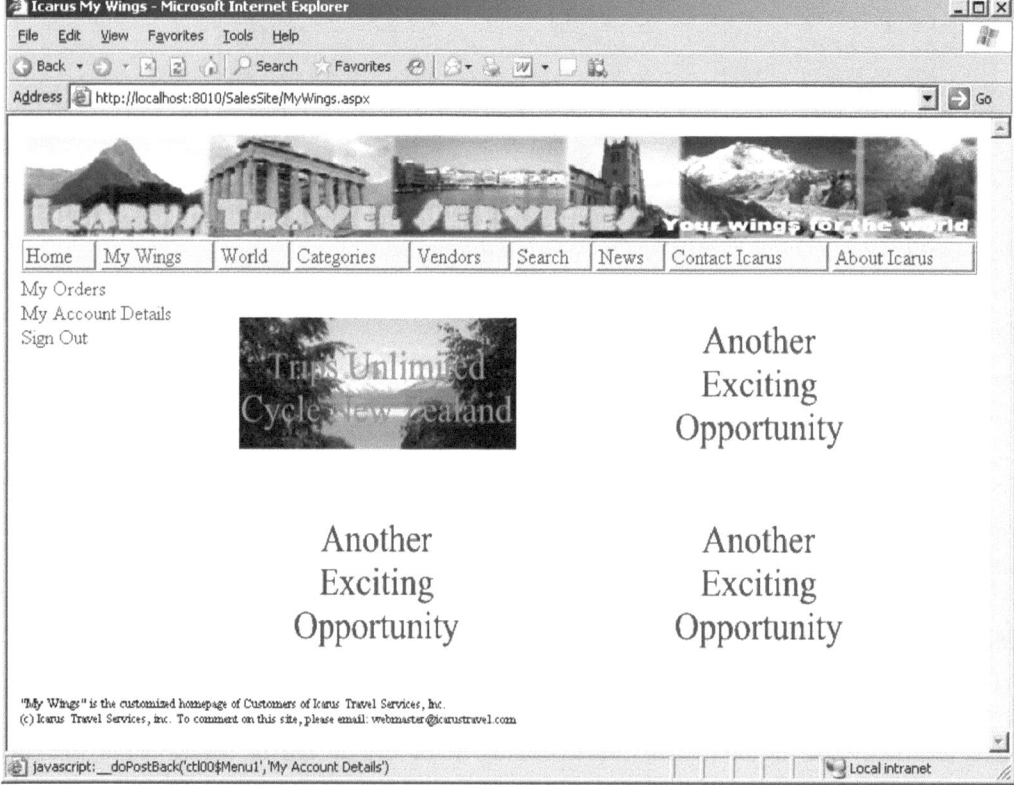

Figure 6-11. *The draft My Wings web page*

The My Wings page has a heading section common to most of the Icarus site, a menu section on the left and a main section that includes a set of panels containing some advertising pictures showing attractions offered by Icarus vendors. The details are to be determined in a later iteration of the project.

Create Order

The Create Order scenario is shown in Table 6-6. It is similar to the equivalent scenario in the Windows Forms application, but the screens are a little simpler.

Table 6-6. *The Create Order Web Sales Scenario*

Step	User Action	System Response
Initial State	**The customer is currently viewing his personalized My Wings page (Figure 6-11).**	
1.	The customer clicks the My Orders link.	The system displays the My Orders page showing the orders that the customer has already made with Icarus (Figure 6-12).
2.	The customer clicks the New Order link.	The system displays the Order Details page (Figure 6-13), initialized to allow a new order to be defined.
3.	The customer clicks the Add Reservation link.	The system displays the Make Reservation page, initialized to allow a new reservation to be defined.
4.	The user selects a geographic location (e.g., France) from the locations that are listed alphabetically in the Location drop-down list.	
5.	The user selects a resource category (e.g., Water Tours) from the Category drop-down list.	
6.	The user selects a vendor (e.g., Seine River Cruises) from the Vendors drop-down list.	
7.	The user selects the date on which the reservation is required in the Date picker control. This control consists of day, month, and year drop-down lists.	
8.	The user enters a quantity (e.g., 2) into the Quantity Required text box.	
9.	The user clicks the Search button.	The system updates the Alternative Options GridView control on the page to show all the resources that meet the criteria specified by the user (Figure 6-14).
10.	The user selects one of the resources listed in the Alternative Options data grid view and clicks the Add Selected Reservation to My Order link.	A reservation is created, attached to the order and saved to the database. The system displays the Order Details page modified to show a row added to the Reservations data grid.

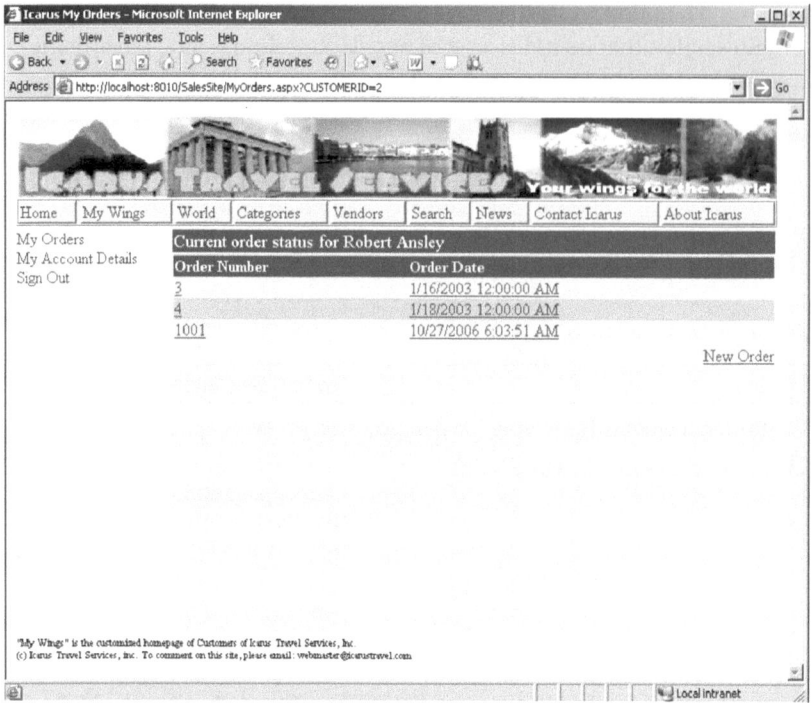

Figure 6-12. *The draft My Orders web page*

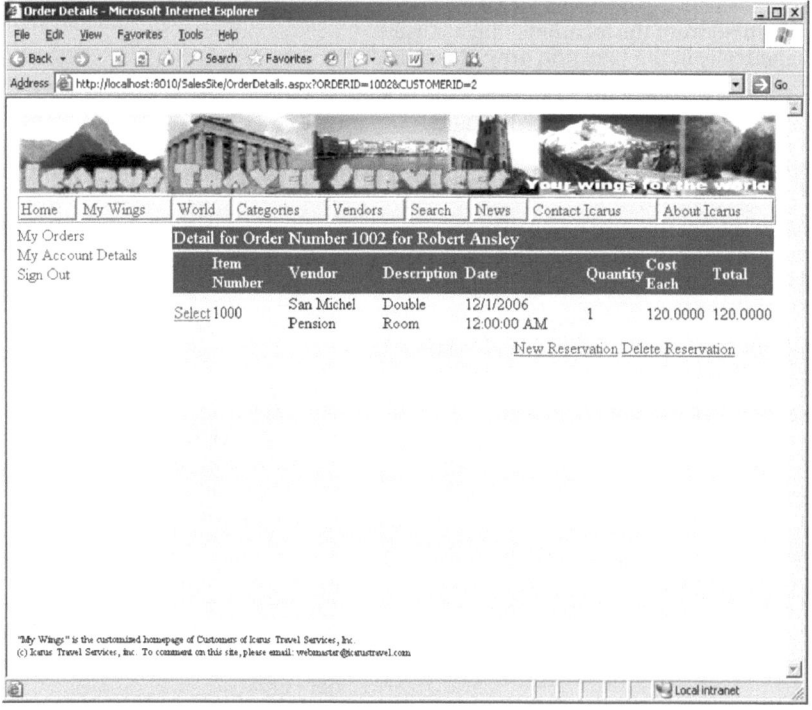

Figure 6-13. *The draft Order Details web page*

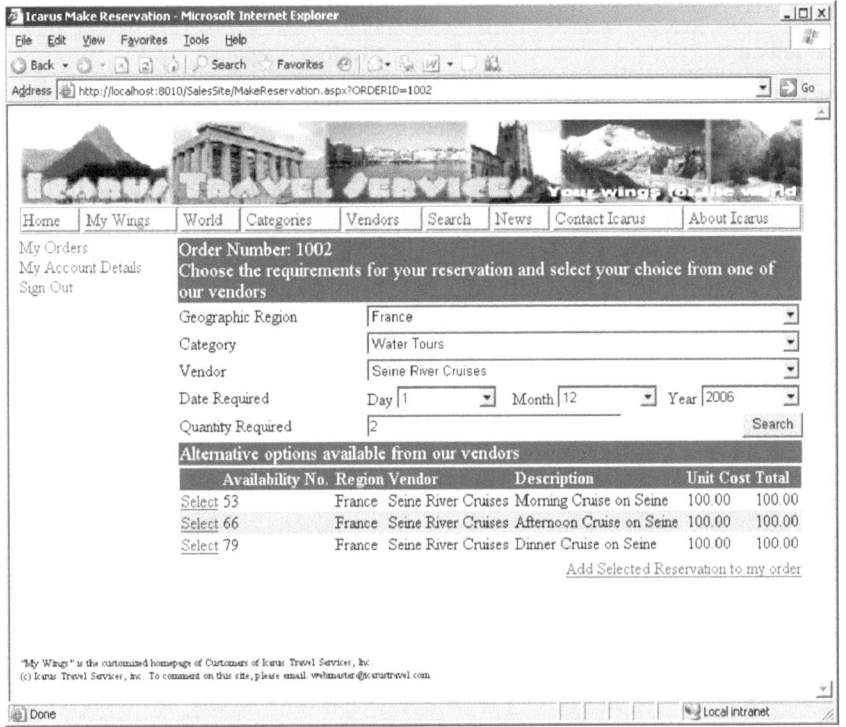

Figure 6-14. *The draft Make Reservation web page*

Listing Scenarios

The listing scenarios will be implemented by the List Wing application using VB .NET in Visual Studio 2005. The screens have been put together by Rahul, and there is a set of vendor management screens that are very similar to the customer management screens.

Open Vendor

The Open Vendor scenario is shown in Table 6-7. It is very similar to the Open Customer scenario and needs little explanation.

Table 6-7. *The Open Vendor Scenario*

Step	User Action	System Response
Initial State	**The List Wing application has been started and the empty Vendor Contacts screen, shown in Figure 6-15, is displayed.**	
1.	The user selects Open Vendor from the File menu.	The system displays the Open Vendor dialog box shown in Figure 6-16. The data grid view is populated by an unconditional list of vendors.
2.	The user enters the first letter of the Vendor Company Name in the Company Name text box.	The system reduces the vendors displayed in the data grid view to only those with business name beginning with the letter typed in the Company Name text box.
3.	The user selects one of the vendors in the data grid view, and clicks the Open button.	The Open Vendor dialog box is closed, the vendor details are retrieved from the database, and a new tab is added to the Vendor Contacts screen populated with the data from the database as in Figure 6-17.

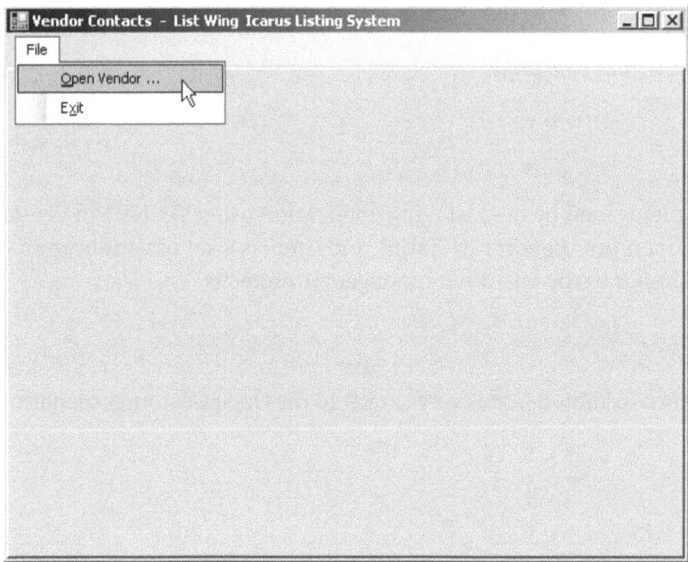

Figure 6-15. *Vendor Contacts, the main screen of the List Wing application*

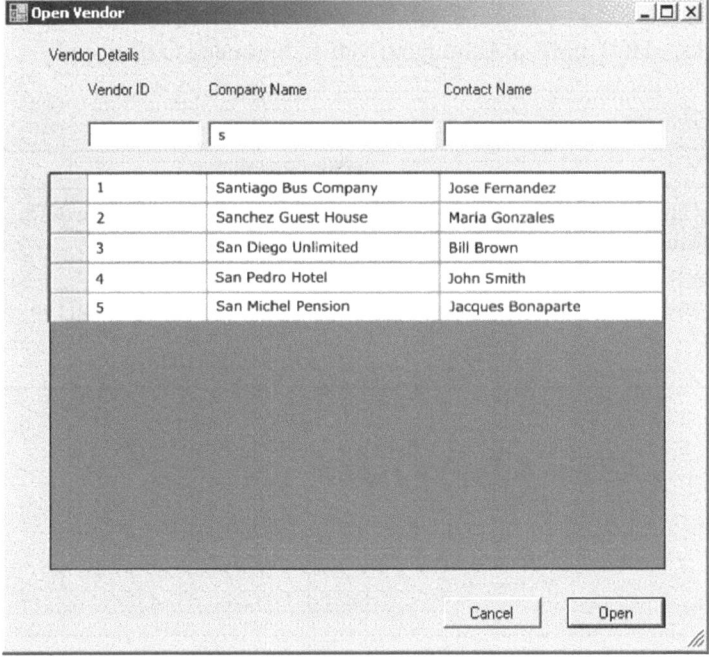

Figure 6-16. *The Open Vendor dialog box*

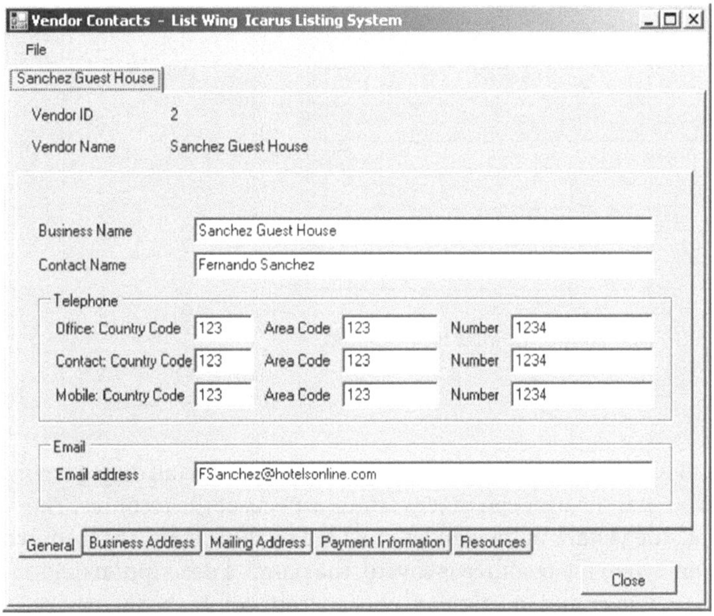

Figure 6-17. *Vendor Contacts with a vendor details tab opened*

Close Vendor

The Close Vendor scenario is listed in Table 6-8. Although trivial, it does need to be tested.

Table 6-8. *The Close Vendor Scenario*

Step	User Action	System Response
Initial State	**The Sales Wing application is running with two vendors open, as in Figure 6-18. Two tabs are visible.**	
1.	The user selects the tab of the vendor that is to be closed and clicks the Close button.	The system removes the tab with the selected vendor from the screen, leaving the other vendor displayed in a single tab.

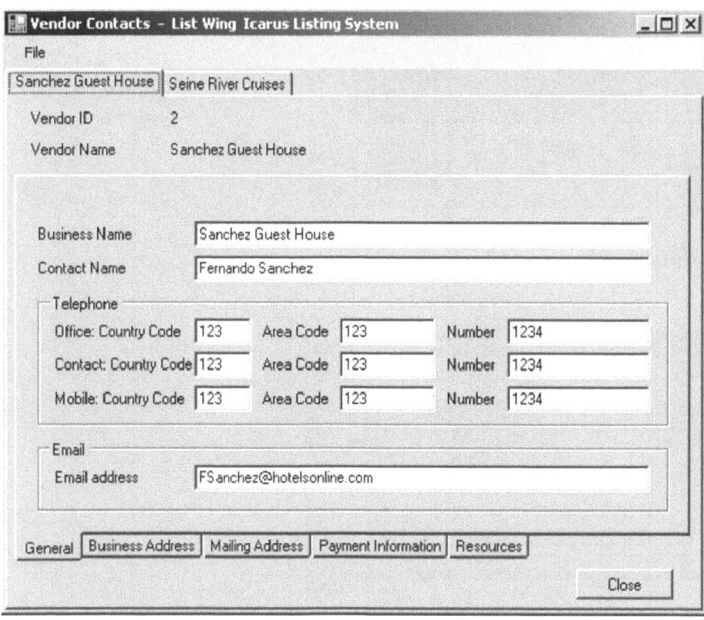

Figure 6-18. *Vendor Contacts with two vendor details tabs opened*

Create Resource

This scenario involves the Vendor Contacts main screen and the Resource Detail dialog box, which will have two tab pages so that the user can enter various aspects of the resource. The first tab will have general detail, the vendor name and ID provided by the system, the resource ID (also generated by the system when the resource is saved), the name, a description field, the category, and location. The category and location are chosen from combo boxes, whose item collections are to be populated from data in the database. New locations and categories can be added using a different scenario of the Listings use case, not included in iteration 1. For iteration 1, all locations and categories are to be entered using SQL scripts.

The second tab will have details of the resource availability. When a reservation is added to an order—as described in the Create Order scenario—part of the process of creating the reservation is to specify a date and quantity. The system must verify that the required quantity is available on that date. In this tab, the user can specify, when adding a resource, periods of time when it is available and the capacity available. It is assumed that the resource may be reserved on a daily basis; however, some resources may be reserved on an hourly or some other basis, so there is some functionality here that will need to be thought out in a later iteration.

The Create Resource scenario is described in Table 6-9 and its associated figures. The Vendor Contacts page (Figure 6-19) contains a tab page for each vendor that is open—another multiple-document interface—and each tab contains a Vendor Details control, which in turn contains multiple tabs. Most of the tabs are similar to those for the customer, except the rightmost tab, which contains a list of the resources that this vendor has listed for sale by Icarus. All the resources appear in the Listed Resources data grid on that tab. When creating a new resource, the user must complete the Resource Detail dialog box. The first tab (Figure 6-20) displays general information, and the second tab (Figure 6-21) displays a set of availability entries specifying a start and end date and capacity. The bottom section allows the user to define new availability periods and add them to the set.

Table 6-9. *The Create Resource Scenario*

Step	User Action	System Response
Initial State	**The Sales Wing application is running with a vendor open, as in Figure 6-19.**	
1.	The user selects the Resources tab at the bottom of the vendor details, and then clicks the New button.	The system displays the Resource Detail dialog box. The Resource ID field is blank but the Vendor ID and Vendor Name fields are populated with values for the open vendor. The Resource Location and Resource Category combo boxes have their item collections populated from all the available locations and categories in the database.
2.	The user ensures that the General tab is selected.	
3.	The user enters resource name text in the Name text box.	
4.	The user enters resource description text in the Description text box.	
5.	The user selects a location for the resource from the Resource Location combo box.	
6.	The user selects a category from the Resource Category combo box.	
7.	The user clicks the Availability tab.	
8.	The user selects an availability start date.	
9.	The user selects an availability end date.	
10.	The user types an integer as an availability capacity.	

Continued

Table 6-9. *(Continued)*

Step	User Action	System Response
Initial State	**The Sales Wing application is running with a vendor open, as in Figure 6-19.**	
11.	The user clicks the Add Availability Period button.	The system displays the new availability period in the Availability Periods data grid view showing the start date, end date, and capacity.
12.	The user clicks the OK button.	The system closes the Resource Detail dialog box and creates a new resource in the database. The Listed Resources data grid view in the Resources tab of the vendor details is updated to show the new resource.

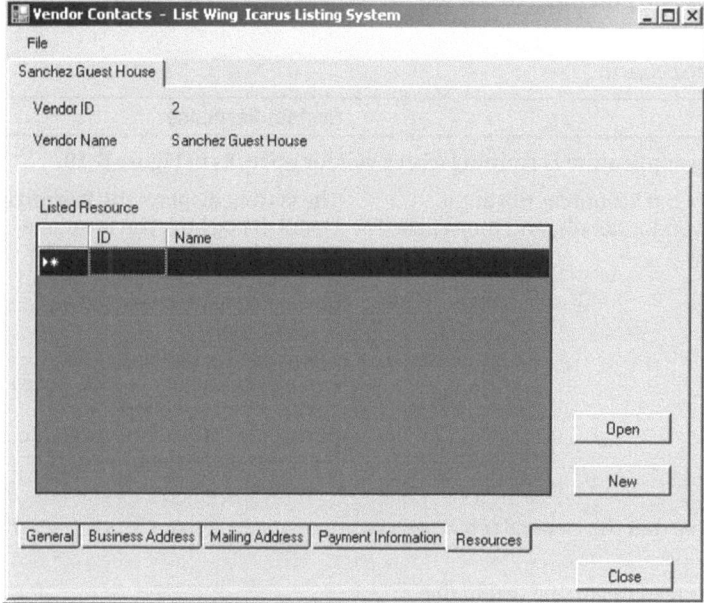

Figure 6-19. *Vendor Contacts with a single vendor opened and the Resources tab selected*

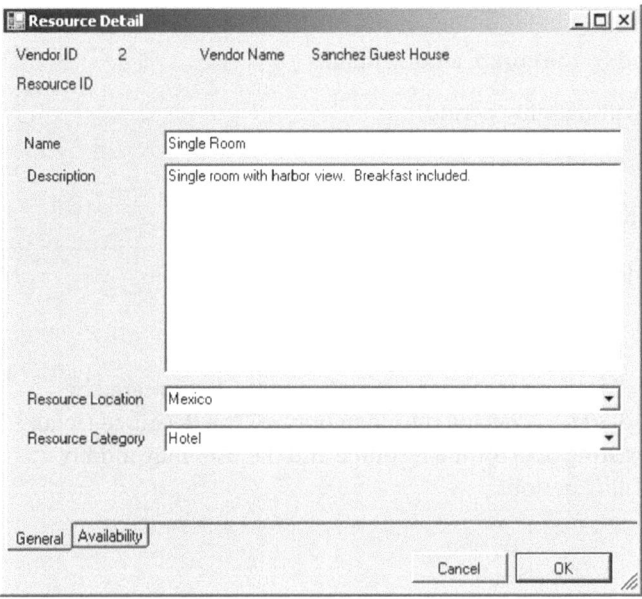

Figure 6-20. *The Resource Detail dialog box, showing the General tab*

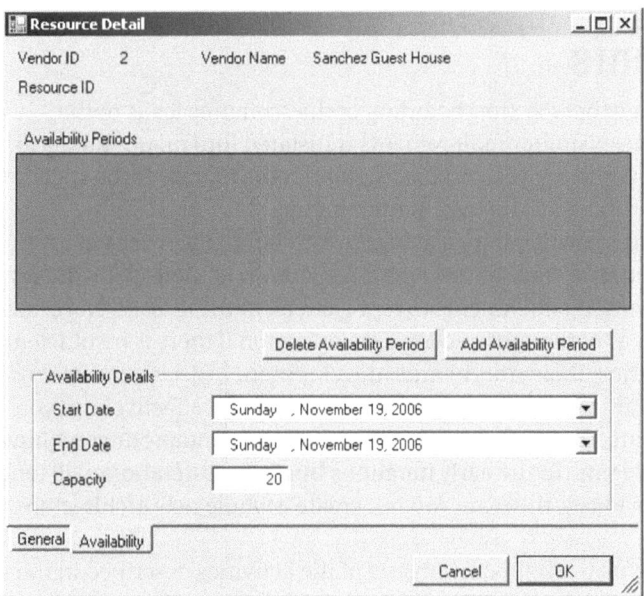

Figure 6-21. *The Resource Detail dialog box, showing the Availability tab*

Create Resource—Variations

A number of variations are identified by the group, among them:

- The user adds more than one availability period.

- The user adds and deletes availability periods.

- The user attempts to enter more than three digits in the Capacity field.

- The user attempts to enter a non-numeric character in the Capacity field.

Edit Resource

The Edit Resource scenario involves the same screen as Create Resource. It is entered by selecting a listed resource in Figure 6-19 and clicking the Open button. The Resource Detail screen is then populated with the existing data for the resource and the user may modify it, including adding or deleting availability periods.

Edit Resource—Variations

Again the group identifies many variations. The user can modify various combinations of fields. There may be a succession of additions and deletions of availability periods during the scenario before the user makes up his mind.

Product Requirements

Going back to Figure 6-3, you can see that the storyboarding of the scenarios leads to the product requirements, which are the customer requirements translated into requirements for the product and its various parts. In other words, product requirements represent the specification of the design of the product that meets the user requirements.

According to MSF CMMI, all the activities shown in Figure 6-3 should take place at each iteration. In the Icarus project, however, the iterations are rather short and there is no time to go through a formal process of generating documents to represent all of these tasks. Nevertheless, they are real and constitute areas of thought and logical steps, even if there is insufficient time to formalize them. The scenarios, their storyboards, development tasks, and tests do indeed need formal control, and Team System provides the means to do so effectively, as you will see in Chapter 12 where a later iteration is followed. The architecture and product requirements tasks, however, will take more time in the early iterations but in later iterations will tend to consist of small adjustments. Obviously, the team will not create a whole new architecture at each iteration.

The Create Product Requirements work stream consists of the activities described in the next subsections. I will review briefly these activities to identify how they match the activities described in this and the next chapter. Icarus Enterprise 3.1 is not a very large project and the schedule is quite ambitious, so generally, the documents will be produced over several of the early iterations, but will evolve as the project moves forward. A larger project occupying several years with longer iterations might produce a formal set of documents at each iteration.

Develop a User Interface Flow Model

The user interface flow model is the result of storyboarding the scenarios as described in the previous section. It can be documented more fully in the form of diagrams that show the flow between screens, but for iteration 1, the team considers the storyboards sufficient.

Develop a Domain Model

The domain model is an object-oriented analysis model that translates into the object-oriented design of the software to be developed. We will see in the next chapters how the Visual Studio 2005 Class Designer can be used to develop this model. All class diagrams have a Copy Image option in the context menu that enables you to prototype your detailed class structure in Visual Studio 2005 and export the diagrams to a document.

However, depending on the project, there may be a need to develop domain models at a higher level. For instance, the domain model may be an analysis model, representing the objects that exist in the business, as a precursor to translating the business model into a high- and low-level object model for the solution. Therefore, you can't view Class Designer as a substitute for UML or other analysis methods in modeling and design; using Visio and other tools to develop class, sequence, activity, and state diagrams is still a justifiable approach to this activity. This activity requires a considerable investment in resources and the design artifacts produced can quickly get out of date. Perhaps having undertaken such an effort and gained understanding from it, it is better to set it aside as completed work. Then, once coding has begun, the class diagrams available from Visual Studio can become the as-built documentation, augmented with other Visio diagrams where necessary. I wonder if we will see any other UML style diagrams in the next version of Visual Studio!

Develop Functional Requirements

In a more complex system, it may well be necessary to write requirements documents for the various interacting systems. At this stage, since the iteration is quite ambitious, the team decides to take the scenarios as their requirements and move quickly through the prototyping to the proof of concept.

Develop Interface Requirements

These include requirements such as the format of the SOAP messages supported by the web services. These need to be documented, and Peter takes this as an action item to be completed at the end of iteration 1. He will use the experience gained in the prototyping phase and make the requirements apply to iteration 2.

Develop Security Requirements

Security requirements are not required for iteration 1. Peter will begin working on these requirements as they apply to the authentication to be implemented in iteration 2.

Develop Safety Requirements

The team does not anticipate any safety issues as part of this application.

Develop Operation Requirements

Operation requirements are not applicable at this stage since they consist of the requirements to be specified for administering the product when it is in operation.

Allocate Product Component Requirements

Product component requirements will be developed during the design and prototyping of the business objects and other components. Peter will include these requirements in a design document; the first draft will be available for iteration 2, and will take into account the experience of the prototyping phase but with iteration 2 requirements in mind.

Prioritize Functionality

For iteration 1, these priorities are set:

1. Open and close customers.

2. Display orders on Sales Wing.

3. Create an order from Sales Wing.

4. Display orders on Sales Site.

5. Create order from Sales Site.

6. Open and close vendors in List Wing.

7. Display vendors' resources in List Wing.

8. Create a resource.

Validate Requirements

At the end of the first three weeks of iteration 1, the team presents its requirements and design to the business managers and CIO of Icarus. The entire team is in attendance since everyone should be satisfied that the product requirements are valid. The senior members of the team use Microsoft PowerPoint to explain how the product will meet customer requirements.

Exploring Alternative Architectures

Product requirements, according to Figure 6-3, lead to creation of the architecture. In Chapter 5, I showed how the new solution was designed using application, system, and data center diagrams, and examined the new Team System for Architects tools. However, the Create Solution Architecture work stream, as described in MSF for CMMI Process Improvement, includes investigating alternative architectures using the Distributed System Designers, building proof of concepts, and assessing alternatives, and finally deciding on one architecture from several alternatives. According to MSF CMMI, each iteration includes the Create Solution Architecture work stream, but of course you would not normally expect to create a new architecture at each iteration; rather, you can expect to tweak the existing architecture a bit to take account of the requirements of the iteration. Exploring alternative architectures is a very sound approach but relies on sufficient time being available to evaluate alternatives, and the ability to base the evaluation on the critical scenarios. Such time can be well spent, and perhaps it is a good idea to make the first iteration long enough to do this thoroughly, but it really depends on the nature of the project. Sometimes, the architecture—at least at the high level—is fairly clear immediately, perhaps dictated by the existing business; other times it may not be at all obvious and investigating alternatives fully is essential. It may also be possible to move between alternative approaches as the iterations progress if the alternatives are not very different; in that way, decisions can be made with the benefit of experience learned. The main objective is to arrive at an architecture that will work, and this is not always the most optimal. You could always do better a second time around. Again I stress the need to evaluate the critical requirements—including performance—early; otherwise, you cannot be sure that the architecture will indeed work. Notice that our Icarus team has put performance demonstration in iteration 1. It may not be possible to complete a full performance test then, but some demonstration at least is desirable so that the team and the customer feel satisfied that they are following a reasonable path.

Having said this, though, part of investigating alternatives concerns the way in which the functionality is partitioned among the component applications. For example, how much business logic should be put on the smart client and how much in the server business logic components? How much business logic is in the stored procedures? It may seem that Chapter 5 has pressed ahead with defining the architecture of the entire Icarus distributed application before the critical scenarios have been properly written and storyboarded. But partitioning among the component applications defined in Chapter 5 has not really been carried out. All the architect has done is define that certain applications exist and are hosted on particular servers. Now the team needs to add flesh to the bones.

In Chapter 5 the team decided to use smart clients and web services. They have not yet defined what those web services do, other than in the most general of terms—by naming them Listing and Sales. What alternatives could have been explored? They could perhaps consider placing the business logic entirely on the clients for the List Wing and Sales Wing applications, which would mean that they would deal directly with the database—like traditional client-server applications. This seems to be a reasonable alternative architecture, particularly when we consider the requirement for offline working.

When the Sales Wing client is working offline, it will need to store its data somewhere. A good approach is to use a smaller version of the main database. This raises the possibility of using the same code in the offline client and the online client; the only difference is that a different connection string would be used. However, this approach is not desirable because it requires coupling between database and client over the Internet using the database native communication protocol rather than HTTP. The point about web services is that they are a loosely coupled service-oriented concept that allows communication to occur via HTTP, which is easily passed by firewalls. SQL Server 2005 can, in fact, respond to native HTTP SOAP requests, which makes it possible for the database itself to expose web services and possibly allow for the elimination of the middle tier when dealing with smart clients. However, then we must consider the effect on scaling of having much business logic in the database.

It boils down to determining the functionality of the various tiers in the architecture defined in Chapter 5—and for that we must bite the bullet and start to examine implementation of the critical scenarios in detail. So hold on tight; here we go!

Solution Architecture Design

In this section we create the architecture that will support the product requirements. The decisions at this stage concern where to place the functionality in the various components described in Chapter 5. We join the team as they begin discussion of the architecture at a point when most of the Sales scenarios have been storyboarded. The meeting consists of Peter, Angela, Charles, Rahul (telephone), and Alberto; so we have three developers, an architect, and a DBA.

Offline Working Architecture

Peter leads the meeting and begins by reminding everyone of the architecture defined in Chapter 5 for the Sales Wing (SalesWing) windows application and the Sales Site (SalesSite) web application. The storyboards for the scenarios have been written (and described earlier in this chapter), and now the question of how they will work needs to be determined. It is clear to all in the meeting that the offline working requirement is going to have a big impact. The List Wing and Sales Wing applications, introduced in Chapter 2 and described in Chapter 4 and 5, are examples of *occasionally connected clients*. This means that they are client applications that cannot always access services or data over a network in a timely manner. Disconnection could occur because the client machine is disconnected from the network, because one or more servers are down for maintenance, or because access to servers is too slow and unreliable due to temporary degradation of network performance.

Peter explains that Microsoft suggests two approaches for occasionally connected clients: *service oriented* and *data centric*. A service-oriented approach stores up service requests to the server in a queue during offline periods and sends them when the client is connected. This might be fine for something like an email application or an application that uses email as a part of its functionality; the application could perform a lot of tasks and simply store up the email service requests in a queue. Another example would be an order processing system, in which a request is made for asynchronous processing—like shipping the order. Again each service request goes into a queue. The point with those examples is that they don't require an immediate response. "But that's not us," Peter concludes. "We are driven pretty much into the data-centric approach as the client can't do anything without being able to access customers or browse resources. So unless a travel agent at least has that travel agent's customers on the local machine they can't do anything."

"And what can they do if they don't have the database tables containing orders? They couldn't display the reservations that were contained in the client's order. And to make a new reservation they need the resource tables and information about the availability," adds Charles. "And anyway we've already defined the scenarios for offline working, so we're definitely committed to a data centric approach with a subset of the server data cached on the client."

"The question is how we represent the local data on the client, given that it's a subset of the data on the server database?" says Peter.

"Well, surely it's obvious," says Alberto. "We can have the same data model on the client as on the database server. The only difference is that there is less data. We can use SQL Server 2005 Express Edition for each client. It's available free."

Angela objects to this idea. "Is that really the best thing? That means that each client has to go through the process of installing a whole database engine. I wonder if some sort of flat file system might be better. There are database providers that work with flat files, so we could still use the same SQL statements."

"That means that we can't use stored procedures, if we want to use common code for the data access layer," points out Alberto. "Also it would be good to be able to use the same SQL scripts to install and update from one version to another."

"It would be really good to have as much commonality as possible. If we have to duplicate functionality on the client, we might as well do it in such a way as to reduce the amount of code," observes Peter.

"Well, what about putting the same business logic on the client?" suggests Angela. "Why don't we use the same classes on the client as on the server? Then the client can work independently, and we've only got to write and test the business logic and data access layer code once."

There is a lengthy pause as everyone takes this in. Peter sits back in his chair, smiling, and eventually responds: "You know, that is a darn good idea." He looks around the room. "What do you all think?"

"Well, I don't know," says Charles. "It seems like if we do that we might as well just write a thick client. The client might as well access the database directly. Why do we then need the business objects on the server?"

"No," says Peter. "The business logic must still execute on the server—for security reasons, at least—the idea is that the business logic would be delegated to the client temporarily when the client is offline. Then when the client goes back online everything has to be confirmed by the server business logic."

"I don't quite understand that," says Charles.

"No," says Peter, "I think it will be a lot clearer when we consider specific examples, because we really don't know yet exactly what business logic there will be. I think we need to make all this a lot clearer in a document. How about you and Alberto writing that, Angela? We'll call it *Offline Architectural Concept* and make it part of the Product Requirements."

Angela and Alberto work on the document. I'm not going to reproduce it here, but I'll explain its contents carefully, as they are crucial to understanding the architecture that the team is using. Let's take as an example the business objects that support the customer management scenarios. These are called *business entity objects* and are represented by classes whose names end in BE, like CustomerBE shown in Figure 6-22. The customer details, like name, addresses, telephone contact numbers, email addresses, and so on, are displayed by a class called CustomerDetails, which is actually a user control placed on a Windows Forms page. This control has controls within it that are bound to columns in tables of a dataset, called CustomerDS, which is exposed as a property of the CustomerBE class. When a customer is opened, an instance of the business entity class CustomerBE will be created and populated from one of the databases. The dataset that is obtained as a property of the CustomerBE instance, and is a representation of its data, is then bound to the controls in the CustomerDetails control, and its fields are used to update the displayed data about that customer. We'll go through the code for all of this in Chapter 7, by the way.

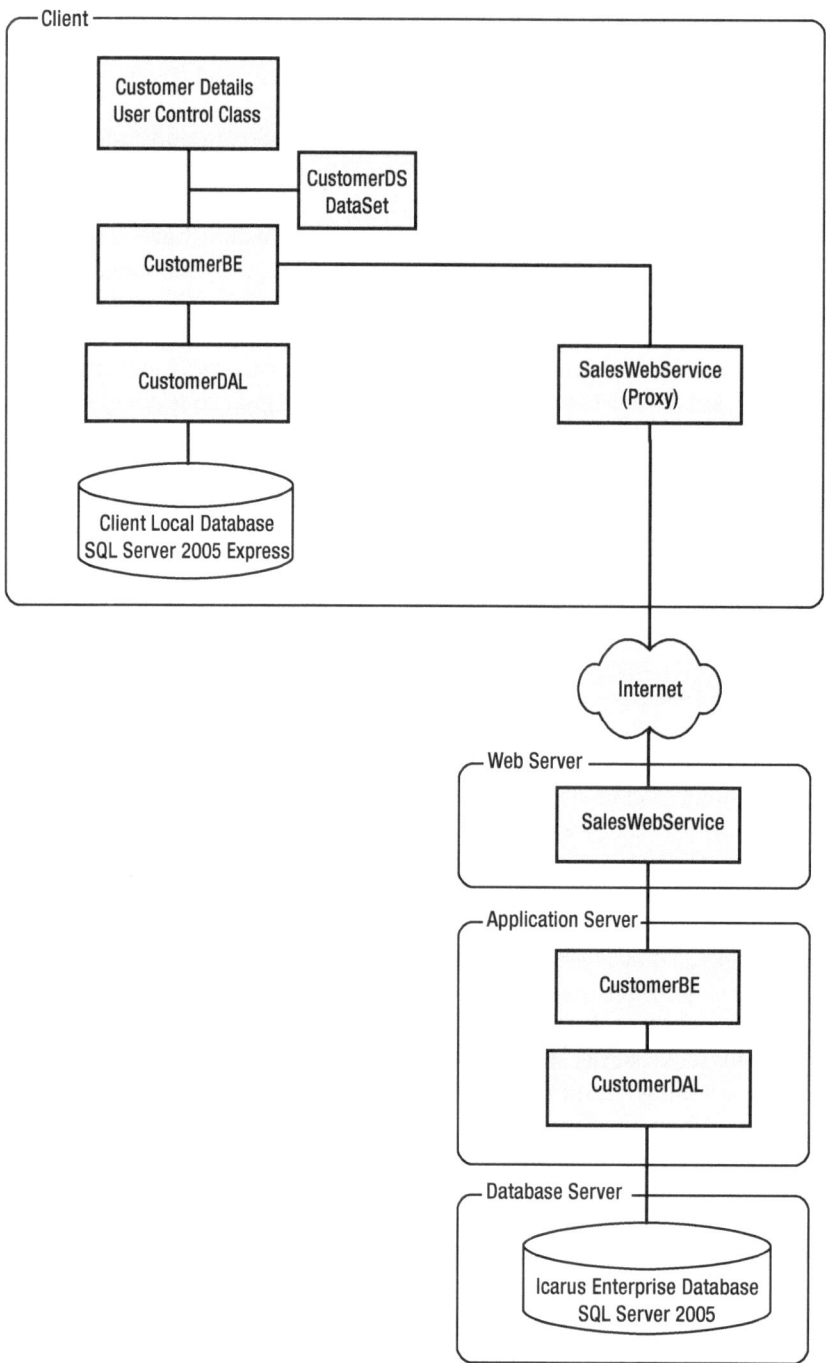

Figure 6-22. *Block diagram in Angela and Alberto's document showing the layers involved in the offline working architecture*

I'll explain how in this design, the instance of CustomerBE gets populated with its data for the particular customer that it represents. The CustomerBE class will expose a static method

```
CustomerBE Get(int id)
```

that returns an instance of CustomerBE populated with the data for the particular customer specified by its ID passed as the parameter. This method needs to get the data either from the Client Local Database or from the Icarus Enterprise Database, as shown in Figure 6-22. It's a good idea to separate the code that accesses the database from the code that represents the business entity, and the database access code is represented in Figure 6-22 by the block labeled CustomerDAL, where DAL stands for data access layer. However, Figure 6-22 shows the instance of CustomerBE on the client accessing both an instance of CustomerDAL on the client and an instance of the SalesWebService proxy. The idea is that, if the client is online (i.e., able to access the web service that provides access to customer data), the CustomerBE Get(int id) method will use the web service; however, if the client is offline, it will use the local instance of CustomerDAL to access the local database.

The SalesWebService proxy class exposes a method called

```
public CustomerDS GetCustomer(int id)
```

This is the proxy access to a method of the same name on the real web service class located on the web server and is the mechanism by which the customer data is passed across the Internet. It is easy to use dataset objects since they are automatically serialized to XML; it takes very little effort to write the web service classes, and the web service proxy classes can be generated automatically by Visual Studio.

Looking now at the server in Figure 6-22, we see that the SalesWebService class also accesses an instance of the CustomerBE class, which also uses CustomerDAL. Actually CustomerDAL is not one single class but a project containing many classes. When the GetCustomer(int id) member function is called on the web service, it calls the static Get(int id) function of CustomerBE, which creates an instance of various classes within CustomerDAL and calls functions to obtain the data from the database. If this is hard to follow, don't worry. Remember that we will be going through the prototype code for this in Chapter 7.

Many details remain to decide on this scheme, and these details can be worked out during the prototyping. For example, how do entities that are created or modified in one database get replicated onto the other? For the moment, however, the idea is to show how the same business entity class, data access layer class, and database schema can be used on both the client and the server.

The Application Diagram for Iteration 1

Creating application and system diagrams are part of the Create Solution Architecture work stream. In Chapter 5, Peter designed an application diagram as part of the iteration 0 architectural design of the whole distributed application. Now this diagram needs to be enhanced and modified to show the results of the architectural discussions that have taken place, and moreover, it needs to be made specific to the current iteration. So Peter will use the Team System architectural tools to produce an application diagram applicable to iteration 1 as well as system diagrams that will take into account the more detailed decisions that have taken place. The diagrams will include only those features to be demonstrated at the end of iteration 1.

Peter generates a new solution called Enterprise 3.1POC (proof of concept) and adds an application diagram to it, shown in Figure 6-23. The main difference from his original application design in Chapter 5 (Figure 5-17) is that the SalesWing and ListWing applications communicate with the SalesBusinessObjects and ListingBusinessObjects applications rather than directly with the web services on the server. This means that the sales and listing business objects have now become part of the original SalesWing and ListWing applications as they were shown in Figure 5-17 as well as appearing in Figure 5-17 in their own right, on the server. The SalesBusinessObjects application now has a connection with the SalesWebService as well as with the Enterprise database application and similarly, the ListingBusinessObjects application has a connection to the ListingWebService application as well as to the Enterprise database application. Notice that in the iteration 1 application, there is no connection between the SalesWing application and ListingBusinessObjects to correspond to the connection between the SalesWebService and the ListingBusinessObjects in Figure 5-17. This is because the ability to browse resources in the Sales use case, and make a reservation directly from a view of a resource, is not to be included in iteration 1. Thus, the two applications can be kept separate. The web service stubs have been included in Figure 6-23 as alternative web service connections for the business objects applications.

Figure 6-23. *The application diagram for the prototype sales architecture*

The Proof-of-Concept System and Its Deployment

Peter must define the systems that the team will demonstrate at the end of iteration 1. There are three of them: the Agent Sales system for the call center operators and travel agents, the Web Sales system that sells directly to customers, and the Listing system used by vendor administrators to respond to vendor requests and by the vendors themselves.

Agent Sales System

Figure 6-24 shows the Agent Sales system. There are two instances of the SalesBusinessObjects application called ClientSalesBusinessObjects and ServerSalesBusinessObjects. ClientSalesBusinessObjects delivers sales business objects such as CustomerBE and OrderBE to the Windows application and populates them with data obtained from a remote server via SalesWebService. ServerSalesBusinessObjects delivers the same objects to the SalesWebService and populates them from the database on the server. Notice the assumption that this system always works in online mode, where the client is connected to the server. Offline working will not be demonstrated in iteration 1, so that feature is not included in the system to be delivered at that stage, though of course it has been incorporated into the design of the distributed application in Figure 6-23. To make this clear, the system in Figure 6-24 demonstrates the occasionally connected client when it is in its *connected state*, which is the iteration 1 configuration. At iteration 2, shown in Figure 6-25, the system will have a second instance of Enterprise database called ClientLocalDatabase connected to the database client connection called Enterprise on ClientSalesBusinessObjects. At iteration 2, the system will be able to switch between online and offline operation—connected and disconnected.

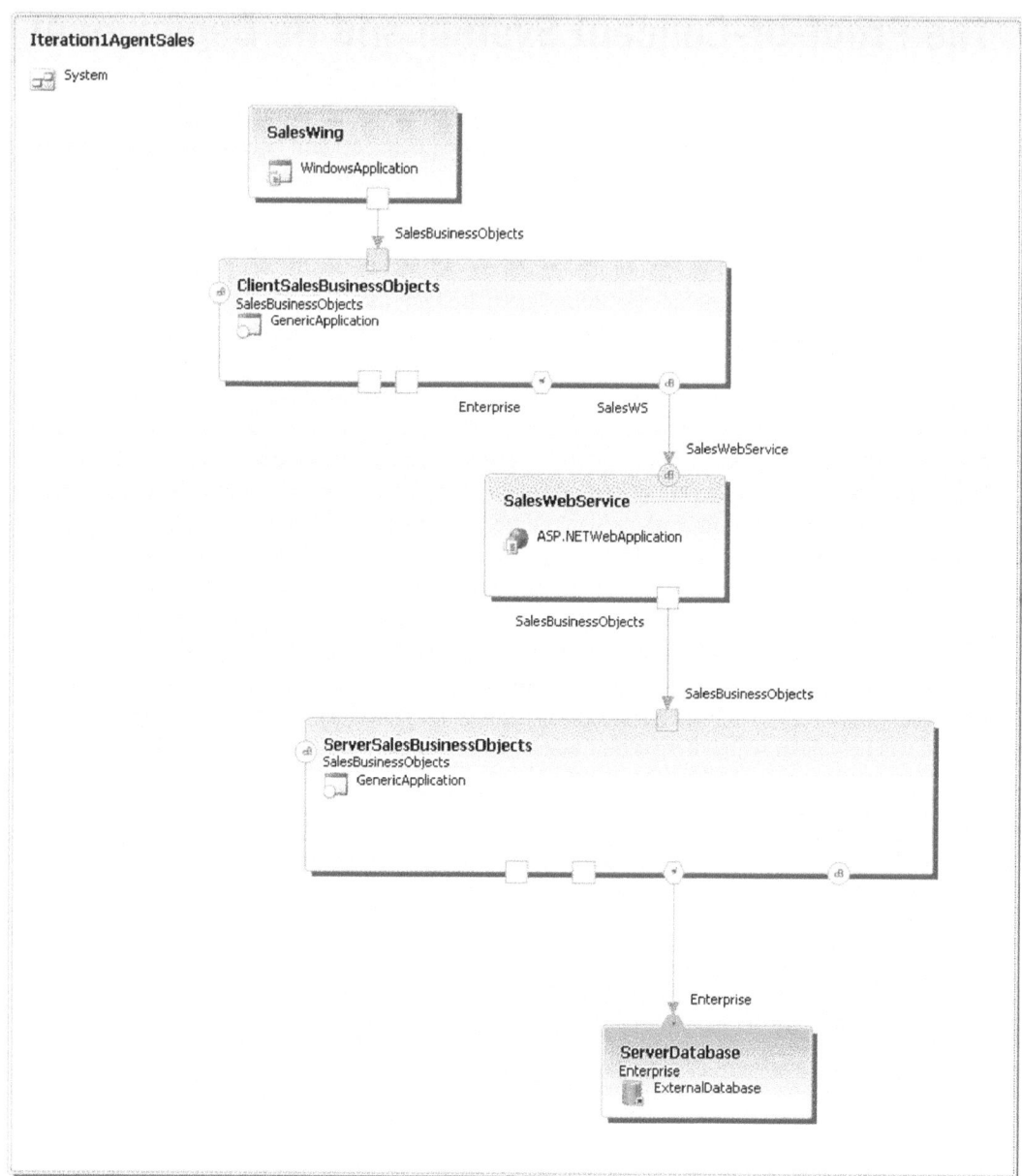

Figure 6-24. *System diagram for the Agent Sales part of iteration 1*

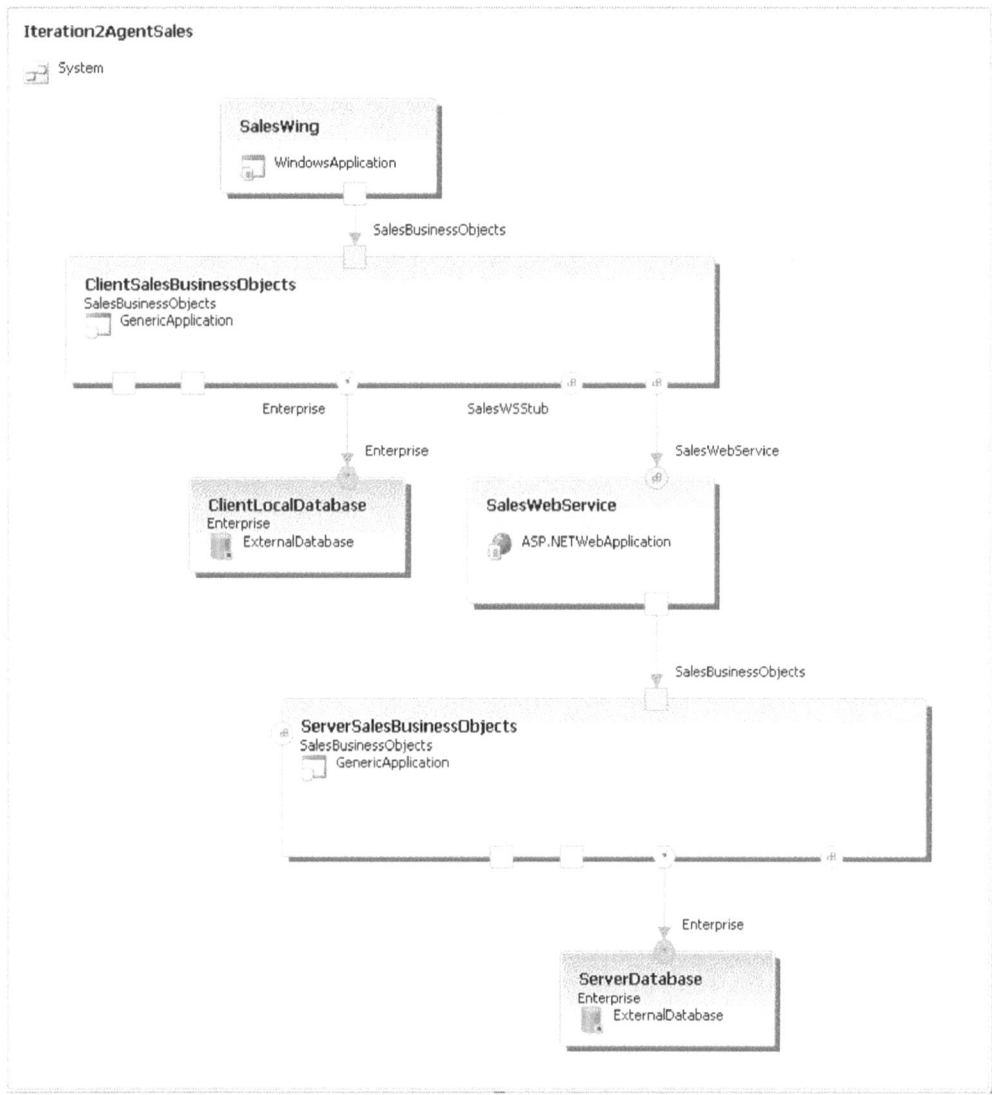

Figure 6-25. *System diagram for the Agent Sales part planned for iteration 2*

Direct Sales System

Figure 6-26 shows the web-based direct sales system, in which the ASP.NET SalesSite uses an instance of SalesBusinessObjects to deliver to it the same CustomerBE and OrderBE objects as were delivered to SalesWing in the previous section, populated from the server database. In this case there is no offline working to consider, and therefore only one instance of SalesBusinessObjects.

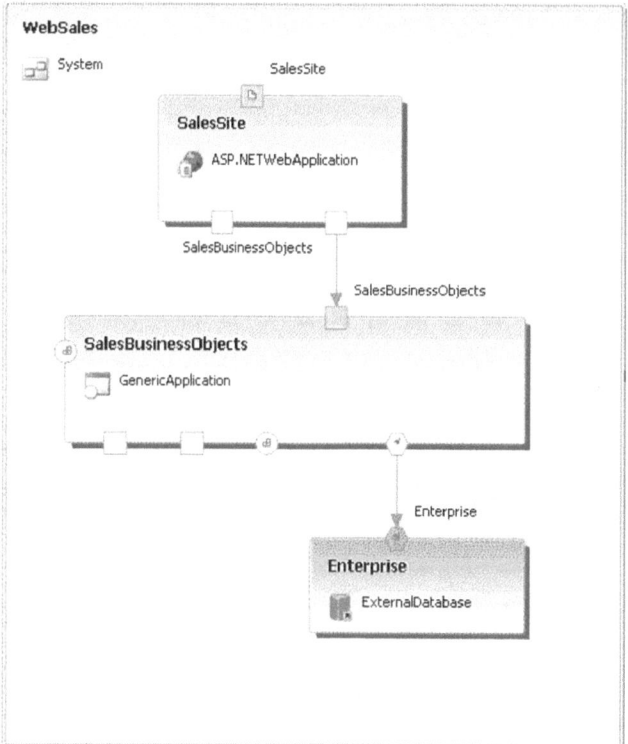

Figure 6-26. *System diagram for the Direct (Web) Sales part of iteration 1*

Just to remind you, SalesBusinessObjects is the .NET application that contains classes that encapsulate the business logic mainly as business entities. Business entities are classes that represent persistent objects such as a customer, order, and reservation for which there is a corresponding set of rows in one or more tables in the database. Business entity classes can also represent *collections* of business objects, such as all the customers whose family name begins with A. These classes also contain code implementing the logic of business operations that are to be performed involving one or more of these entities. Mainly for security reasons, the SalesBusinessObjects application may be hosted on a different machine from the SalesWebService and SalesSite applications, in which case the business entity objects will be made available to these web applications by .NET Remoting.

Listing System

Figure 6-27 shows the Listing system, in which there are two separate instances of ListingBusinessObjects, one on the client and one on the server. When the Listing system is working entirely online as in iteration 1, the objects on the client are populated from and saved to the server database via the ListingWebService. On the server, this web service uses the second instance of ListingBusinessObjects to obtain instances of the same objects populated from and saved to the server database.

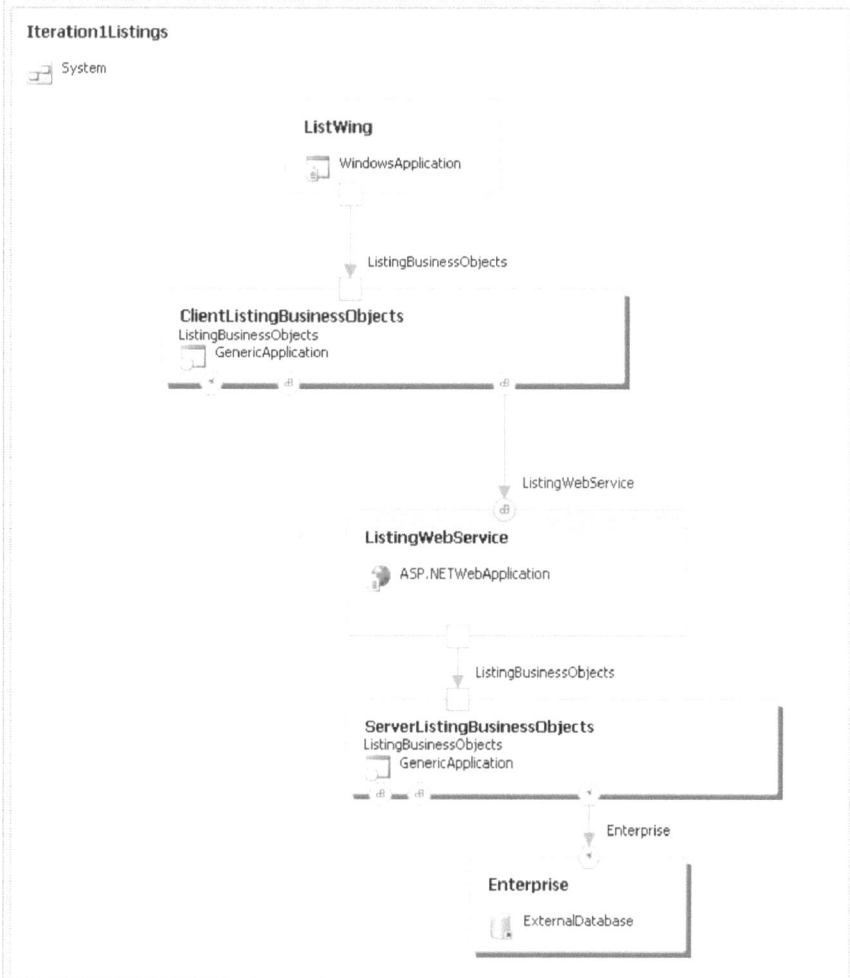

Figure 6-27. *System diagram for the Listing part of iteration 1*

The Development and Test Environment Treated As a Data Center

The concept of the logical data center, which we explored in Chapter 5 when planning the future production deployment, can also be applied to planning the development and test environments. Peter is assigned an MSF CMMI work stream called Establish Environments, and by planning the development, unit test, and integration environments as logical data centers on which the iteration 1 systems are deployed, he can envisage better how the developers and testers will actually work. One of the features to be remembered about logical data center diagrams is that the servers shown on the diagrams are indeed *logical servers* and a physical server can actually fulfill the function of more than one logical server. Don't forget also that logical servers that are not servers in the "usual" sense; as you'll recall, desktop workstations are still called logical servers on data center diagrams. The developer machines will certainly be expected to fulfill the function of many of the logical servers shown in Figure 6-28.

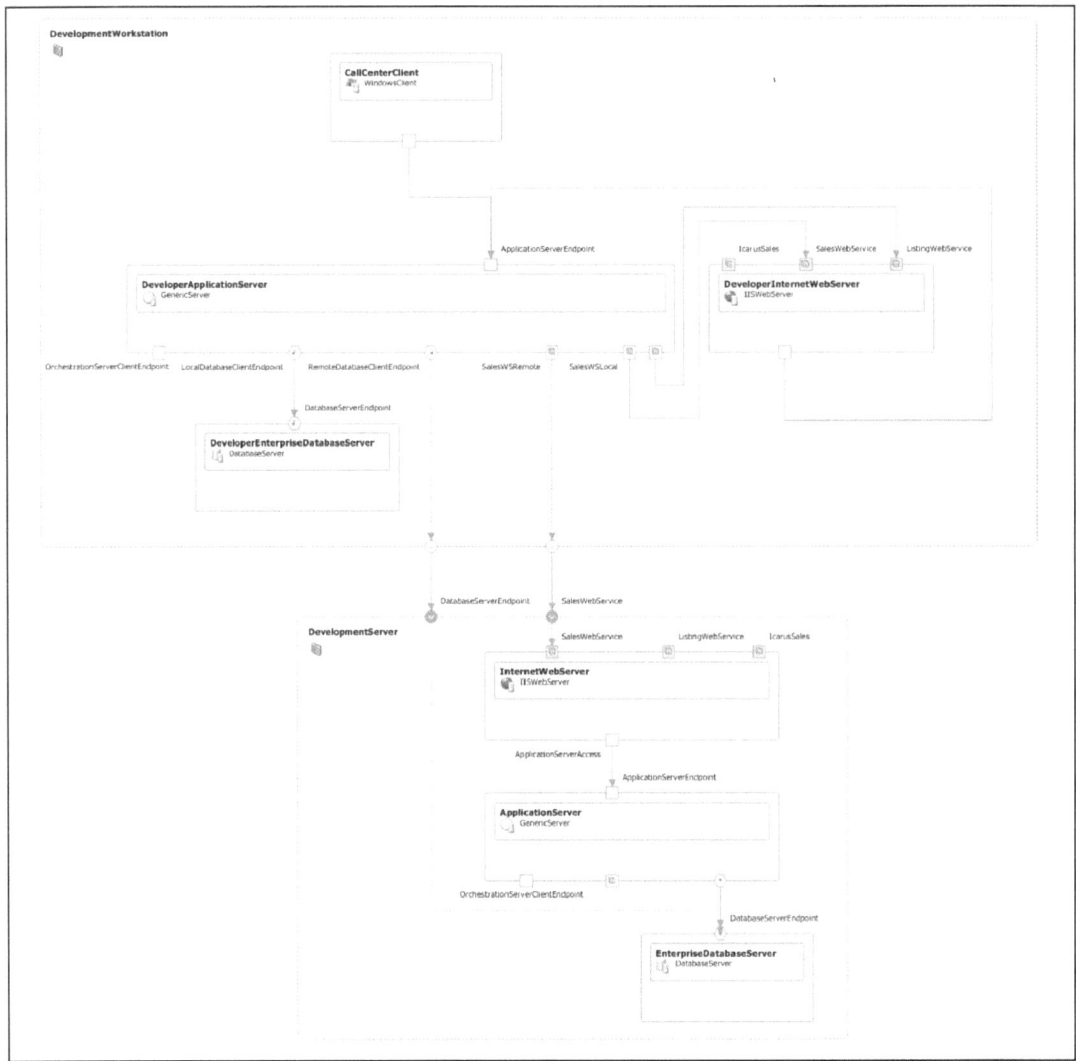

Figure 6-28. *Development data center diagram*

The physical developer workstation is in fact represented in Figure 6-28 by a zone called DeveloperWorkstation, another use for the zone concept. This zone contains an instance of four of the logical server types that were defined in Chapter 5: CallCenterClient (also serving as the AdminClient), ApplicationServer, InternetWebServer, and EnterpriseDatabaseServer. The reason for this is that developers will need to run all parts of the application locally so that the code can be debugged and tested. Running the database locally has a lot of advantages, as does running the server code locally. Developers can work with the data model, stored proce-dures, triggers, and the test data without affecting other members of the team. There is no cost involved since SQL Server 2005 Express Edition is available at no charge. In addition to devel-opers running all of the software on their own machine, they will sometimes want to run part on their own machine with the rest on a server. Therefore, the diagram in Figure 6-28 also shows a development server represented as the zone DevelopmentServer, which as a physical server also hosts more than one logical server, the InternetWebServer, the ApplicationServer, and the EnterpriseDatabaseServer. We expect the logical data center used for testing to be similar to this except that the InternetWebServer will be missing, since the testers will never deploy the web services on their local machines.

Figures 6-29 through 6-31 show the deployment of the three iteration 1 systems to the development logical data center in the case where all the applications are deployed locally. These will be the deployments used by the developers during the proof-of-concept develop-ment in iteration 1. Angela and Charles will use Figure 6-29, Ed will use Figure 6-30, and Rahul will use Figure 6-31. Peter (and perhaps Angela too) will probably need to deploy all the three systems on their machines. A deployment diagram can easily be generated for this case.

Figure 6-29. *Local deployment of the Agent Sales system in the development data center*

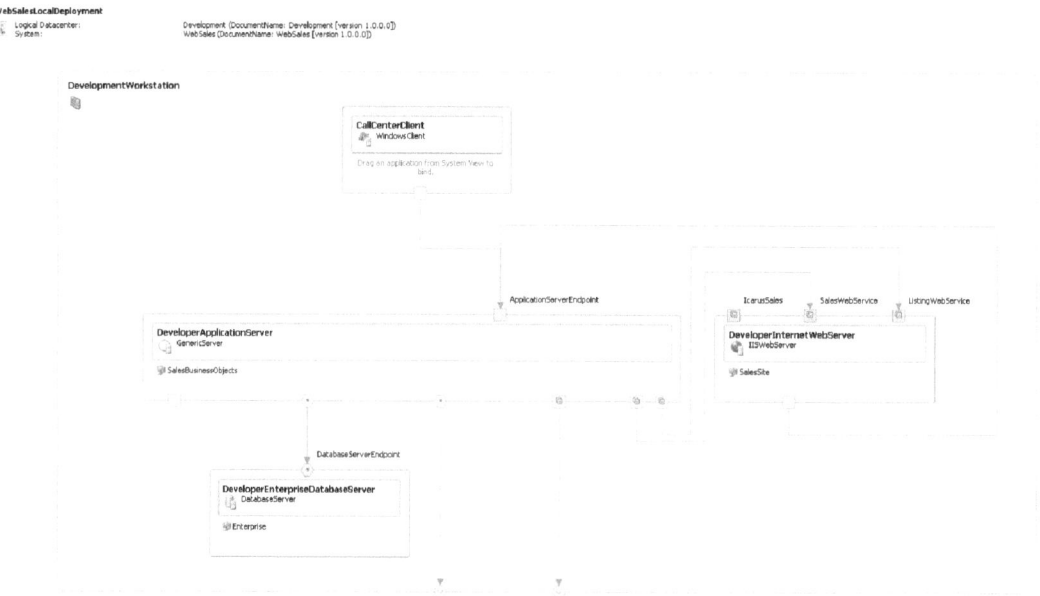

Figure 6-30. *Local deployment of the Direct (Web) Sales system in the development data center*

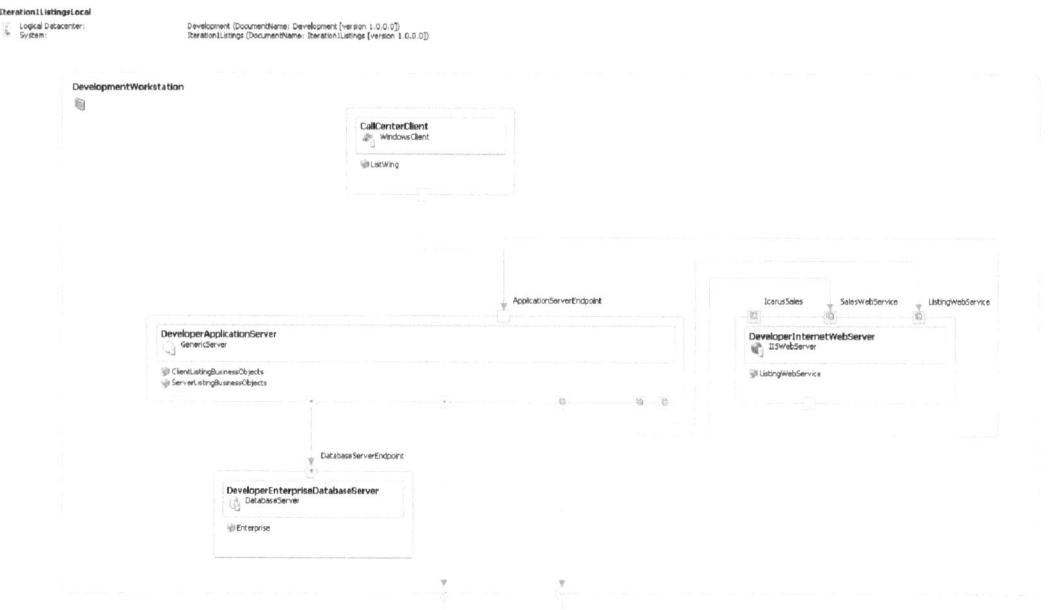

Figure 6-31. *Local deployment of the Listing system in the development data center*

Data Model

The afternoon after the discussion about offline working, the team meets again to discuss the data model. Designing the data model is important to the customer management, sales, and listing scenarios, and Rahul is on the phone again.

Alberto has his laptop with Visual Studio 2005 running on it, with the proof-of-concept project Enterprise 3.1POC, and has added a database project called EnterpriseDatabase in a folder called DataLayer. I'll just digress for a moment to show how he did this. First he obtained from the team project on Team Foundation Server, the Enterprise 3.1POC solution that Peter created. Then he created a DataLayer solution folder and added the EnterpriseDatabase database project by right-clicking on that folder and selecting Add ➤ New Project. As you can see in Figure 6-32, the Add New Project dialog box allows you to add a database project by selecting Other Project Types, then Database. The EnterpriseDatabase project Alberto added will contain various scripts concerned with installing and maintaining the ExternalDatabase application called Enterprise in Figure 6-23.

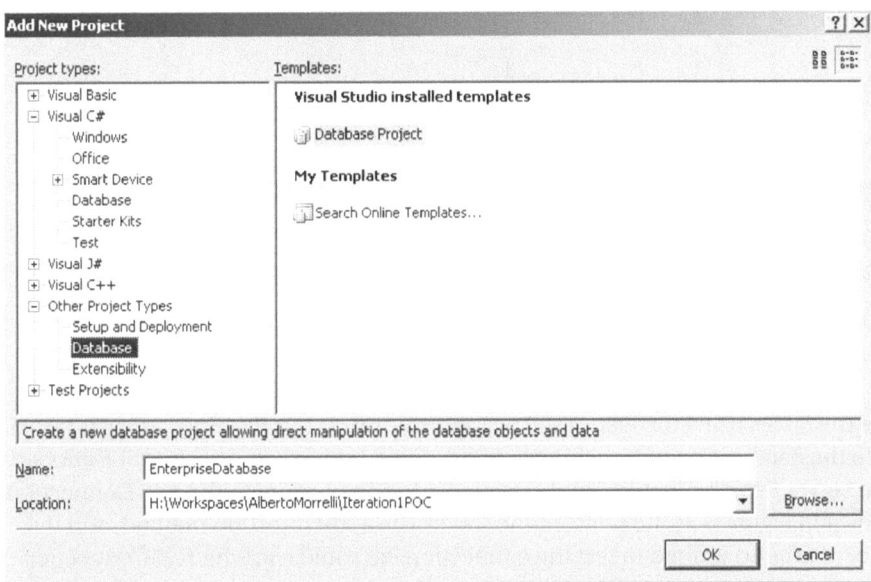

Figure 6-32. *The Add New Project dialog box when adding a database project*

After Alberto clicked OK in the Add New Project dialog box, Visual Studio opened another dialog box, asking him to either choose an existing connection to a database or define a new connection. Alberto connected to an installation of SQL 2005 Express on his machine, in which he had created an empty database called Enterprise.

It's a good idea to start right away with a project in the solution like this that represents your database because you can place the project under source control and include all the scripts necessary to generate the database—tables, stored procedures, triggers, and so forth. Then you can always generate the right version of the database when installing any version of the system. You can also include scripts to generate seed data or test data.

Once he provided the name "EnterpriseDatabase" and selected the location, Alberto clicked OK to add his project. Some folders are created automatically in the project and Alberto right-clicked on the new EnterpriseDatabase project in Solution Explorer and selected New Folder to create a folder to hold seed data scripts. He called this folder "Seed Data Scripts"; then he generated another called "Test Data Scripts". The resulting project appears in Solution Explorer as shown in Figure 6-33.

As you can see in Figure 6-32, database projects are also listed under Visual Basic and Visual C# projects. However, these are SQL Server projects, and are not covered in this book.

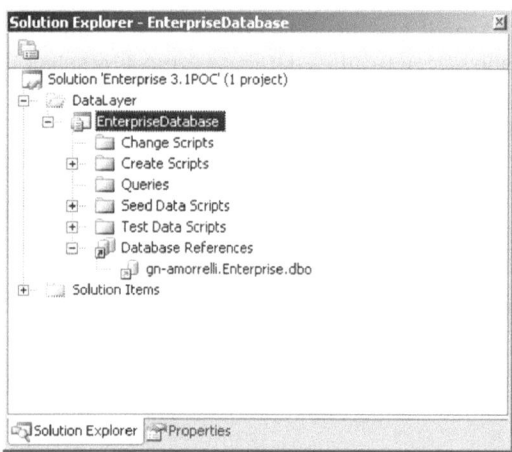

Figure 6-33. *Solution Explorer showing a new database project, EnterpriseDatabase*

As we mentioned, a database project can contain scripts that you can run against the database, and you can generate all your tables by writing scripts. However, there is an easier way: designing the tables using the features of Server Explorer. In this example, Alberto added a connection to the database on his machine in Server Explorer by right-clicking on Data Connections in the Server Explorer window and selecting Add Connection. In the Add Connection dialog box, shown in Figure 6-34, he selected the server, the authentication method, and the database name. (If Alberto wanted to test the connection, he could click the Test Connection button in the lower-left corner.) At this point, Alberto clicked OK to add a connection to the specified database in the Server Explorer window, as shown in Figure 6-35.

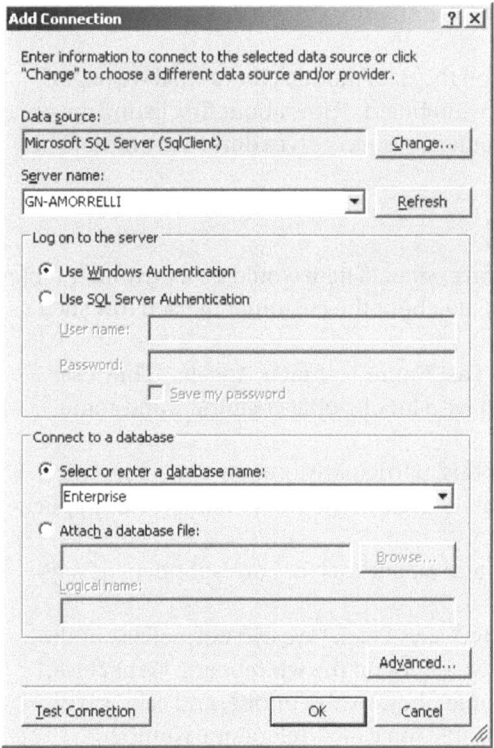

Figure 6-34. *The Add Connection dialog box, which allows you to add a connection to Server Explorer*

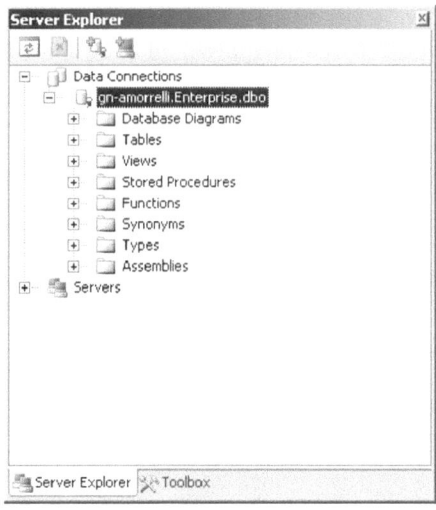

Figure 6-35. *Server Explorer after a database connection has been added*

Let's return now to the data model meeting, where Alberto will be adding tables to the database as the meeting proceeds.

"Well, hello again, we're here to make a start on the data model. Where shall we begin?" Peter opens the meeting as usual and goes to the whiteboard. "How about first listing the areas that need to be included in the data model? Customers, resources, vendors—Any more?" he says as he writes.

"Sales?" ventures Charles.

"And reservations go with sales," adds Angela.

"OK, let's start with customers as an entity," says Peter. "There would be a Customer table with an ID number for a primary key, then some data about the customer in each row such as First Name and Last Name."

"Actually Icarus does not use First Name and Last Name," remarks Angela. "They use Given Name and Family Name. It's because they have a lot of global customers and some countries put family name first."

There is some discussion about the merits of this, particularly on how to decide which name to put first on an address, but apparently this is done in the Document Service application—which is not their responsibility!

"The current system has a residence address and an address for correspondence," says Charles, as the discussion turns to addresses.

"So that's two addresses for each customer row," says Peter. "We can normalize out the addresses in a separate table then." He sketches two tables on the whiteboard. "What else?"

"There are three possible phone numbers: home phone, work phone, and cell," says Charles. "They can be normalized into a separate table too called Telephone Number."

"And also an email address," adds Angela.

"What about the fields in the address and telephone number table?" inquires Peter.

"Mmm—for the telephone—country code, area code, and number," responds Charles.

Peter adds all this to his sketch, so that the whiteboard now looks like Figure 6-36. "Is 50 characters enough for these?" he asks. Nobody responds and he answers himself: "I guess it'll do for now, but we may have to increase it."

After a while Alberto mentions something important: "There's a requirement to be able to do sales reports by country and by city. Doesn't that mean we will have to have tables of cities normalized out from the Address table."

"It would sure help a lot if we do," Charles acknowledges.

"And States as well," points out Rahul.

"Yep, all that then," Peter agrees. He presses the print button on the whiteboard, and then erases the three tables.

He quickly draws the Address table again and adds a State table, a City table, and a Country table.

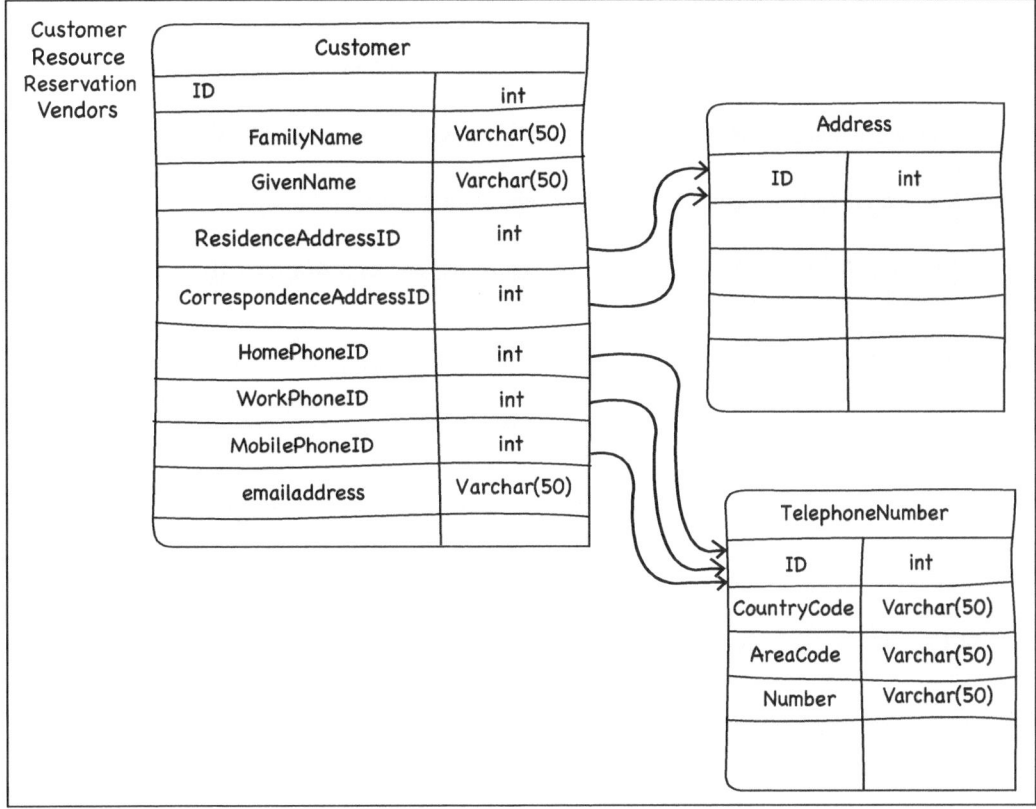

Figure 6-36. *Peter's whiteboard drawing, showing the first three tables in the Customer data model*

"We need street address and zip, or postal, code," says Charles.

"And a region field for countries that don't have states like India," says Rahul. "But actually the regions in India could be treated like states."

"And China provinces, like Guangdong and Fujian," says Angela. "Nobody seems to do that, though—U.S. states are always preloaded into a table and can be selected by combo box, whereas other countries regions are usually typed in as text. If we had other countries regions prepopulated into tables we could do reports based on other regions as well as U.S. states."

"Too much geography—maybe next version!" laughs Peter. "But what about the City table—are we going to prepopulate that with all of the world's cities? We can't do that!"

"We'll have to have some sort of algorithm that populates them as they are added—when customer addresses are added," suggests Charles.

"How will we recognize if they are already there?" asks Angela. "Oh yes—probably just do a select based on the name in a stored procedure and insert it if it does not exist."

"But then different spellings or alternative names will appear as different cities," points out Charles. "I suppose we can't help that."

"Is this algorithm a risk, do you think?" asks Peter.

"No, it can wait till the iteration in which we do the Add Customer scenarios," says Angela.

"And the Add Vendor scenarios," says Rahul. "They have addresses with cities as well."

While they have been talking, Peter has scribbled the data model on the whiteboard, so that it looks like Figure 6-37.

"We need a second street address column," points out Charles.

"Of course—but there's no room on my drawing," says Peter. "Don't forget to include two street address columns, Alberto."

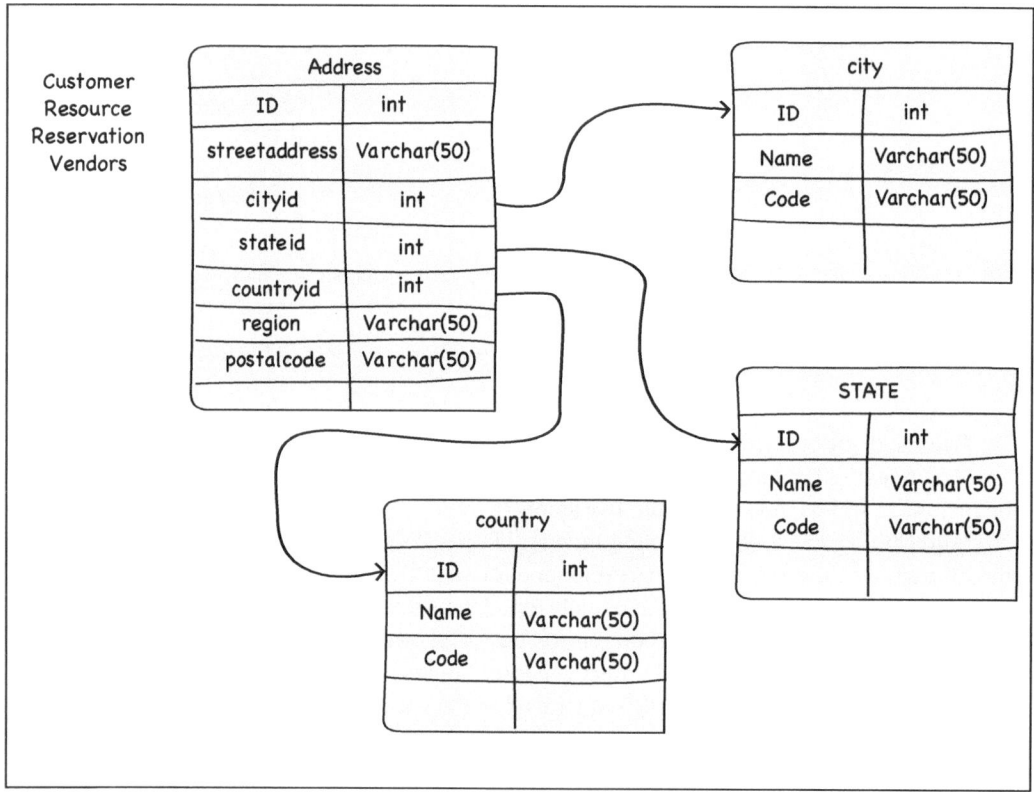

Figure 6-37. *Peter's whiteboard drawing, showing the address tables*

While Peter has been drawing, Alberto has been busily typing and moving the mouse around—in fact, he has been doing that all through the meeting, stopping only to speak. Let's see what he has been doing and examine ways to create the tables in a database using Visual Studio 2005.

In the Enterprise database in the Server Explorer window, Alberto right-clicks on the Tables folder and selects Add New Table, which displays the Table Definition window empty of all rows. In the left-hand column, Alberto types the names of all the fields in the CUSTOMER table and in the accompanying column, he selects the type of the field from the drop-down. The third column contains the Allow Nulls checkbox; he selects this checkbox for all fields except the ID field, as this will make it easier to enter temporary test data to the tables. When he has finished entering the definition for the CUSTOMER table, the Table Definition window looks like Figure 6-38. Alberto then clicks the Save button in the Visual Studio Toolbar and names the table "CUSTOMER" in the dialog box that opens (Figure 6-39). He clicks OK to complete the creation of the CUSTOMER table and closes the Table Definition window.

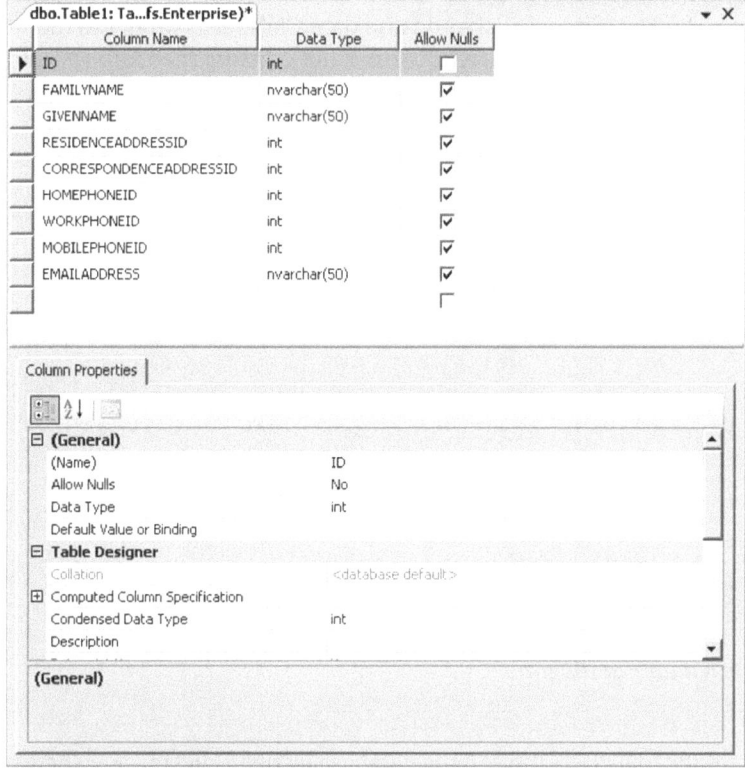

Figure 6-38. *Table definition for the CUSTOMER table*

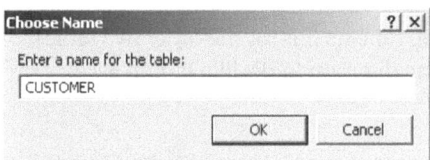

Figure 6-39. *Saving the CUSTOMER table*

This is one way to create a table using Server Explorer, but Alberto also likes to use diagrams since they also show relationships between tables. He right-clicks on the Database Diagrams folder under the Enterprise database in Server Explorer and selects Add New Diagram.

Note Sometimes when you create a database diagram for the first time, the server will warn you that certain database objects are absent and offer to create them for you. If this happens, simply click OK.

This opens up a new Database Diagram window and also opens the Add Table dialog box shown in Figure 6-40. There is only one table in the database at the moment: the CUSTOMER table that Alberto just added. He selects it and clicks Add and then Close. This produces the diagram shown in Figure 6-41. Remember that here Alberto is not creating the CUSTOMER table a second time; he is creating a new diagram and adding the CUSTOMER table as the first table on the diagram.

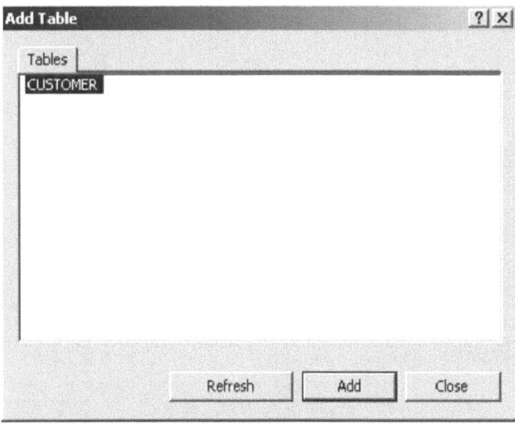

Figure 6-40. *Adding tables to a database diagram*

This time Alberto creates the ADDRESS table in the database by right-clicking anywhere on the diagram shown in Figure 6-41 and selecting New Table. First he is prompted to name the table; then the new table appears on the diagram and he can add rows to it. He adds all the rows that were defined for the ADDRESS table, then adds the TELEPHONENUMBER table in the same manner. Next Alberto must define the primary keys. On the ID field in the CUSTOMER table, he right-clicks and selects Set Primary Key, and then repeats this for the other two tables, selecting the ID field as the primary key in each case. The diagram looks like Figure 6-42.

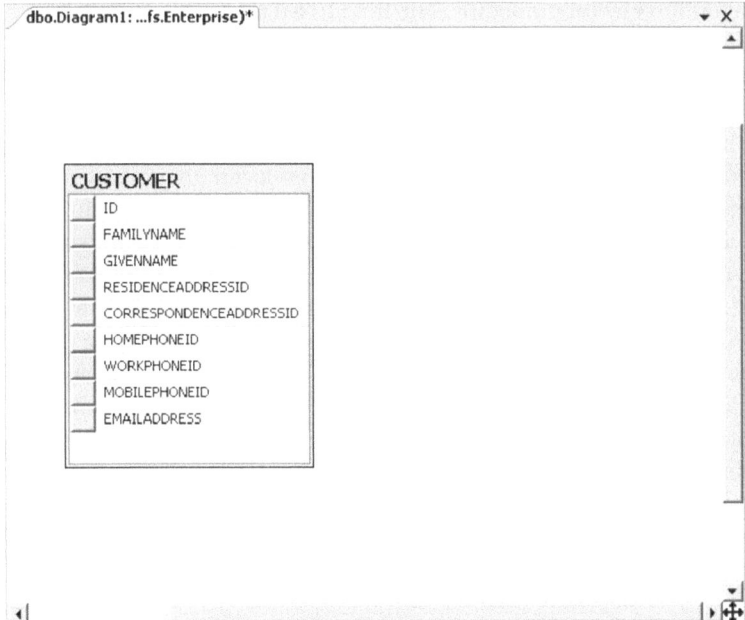

Figure 6-41. *Customer database diagram—just begun*

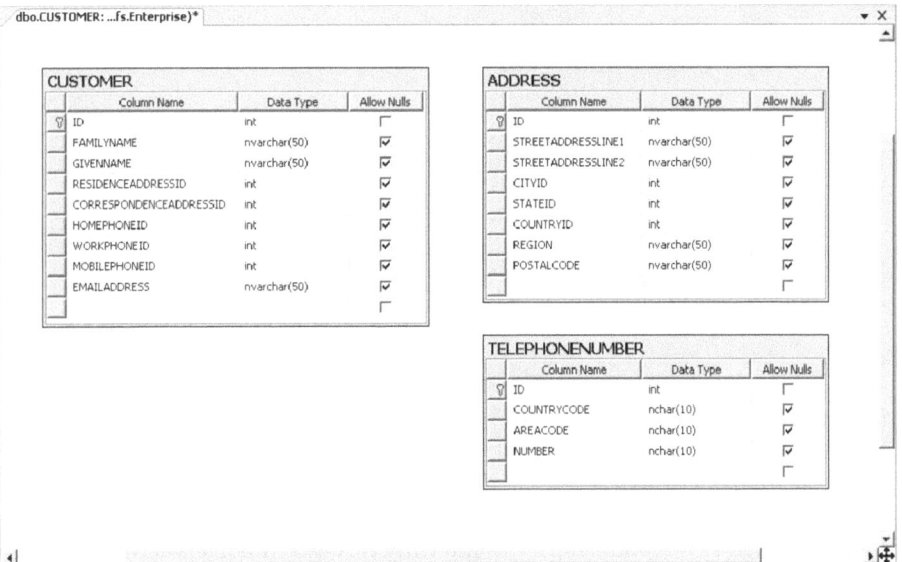

Figure 6-42. *Customer database diagram, with tables added*

Next Alberto adds the foreign key relationships. The field RESIDENCEADDRESSID is intended to be a foreign key that specifies one row in the ADDRESS table. This means that the integer value in the RESIDENCEADDRESSID field in each row of the CUSTOMER table must be equal to the ID value of one of the rows in the ADDRESS table. This is what foreign key relationships are about. To set up this first one, Alberto clicks on the row header to the left of the RESIDENCEADDRESSID column name in the CUSTOMER table to select it, then presses the left mouse button and drags to anywhere on the ADDRESS table. The Tables and Columns dialog box, shown in Figure 6-43, opens. A default value appears in the Relationship Name text box. ADDRESS is shown in the Primary Key Table text box, with the ID field (the defined primary key) set as the default. CUSTOMER appears in the Foreign Key Table text box, with the field RESIDENCEADDRESSID selected. It's always a good idea to check this when using the drag method in case you have dragged from the wrong field. Alberto clicks OK, which closes the Tables and Columns dialog box and causes another dialog box to open, displaying more foreign key relationship details. He clicks OK on this dialog box, which completes the process of setting the first foreign key for the RESIDENCEADDRESSID field. He follows the same steps to add foreign key relationships for the fields CORRESPONDENCEADDRESSID, HOMEPHONEID, WORKPHONEID, and MOBILEPHONEID in the CUSTOMER table. The last three are foreign keys that specify rows in the TELEPHONENUMBER table.

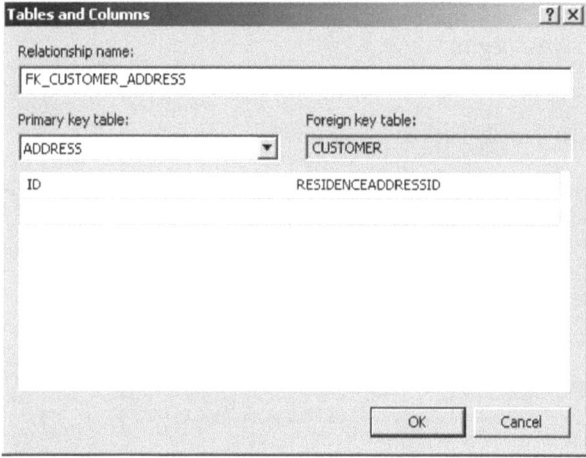

Figure 6-43. *The Tables and Columns dialog box allows you define a foreign key relation in a database diagram.*

The resulting diagram is shown in Figure 6-44. Alberto has dragged the tables and relationship connections around so that the links are positioned to indicate which fields on the tables are linked by foreign key relationships; the end with the key symbol lies at the primary key, ID field, and the end with the chain symbol lies at the foreign key field. It's a pity that the diagrams don't do that automatically as it makes it clear at a glance which fields are related. The trouble is, if you move anything, you mess up the diagram and have to adjust the field positions again.

Alberto clicks the Save button on the Visual Studio Toolbar and is prompted to provide a name for the database diagram; he types the name "CUSTOMER". When he clicks OK, Visual Studio displays a warning dialog box, shown in Figure 6-45, which indicates that his changes to the diagram will change the database tables and asks him to confirm. Alberto clicks Yes.

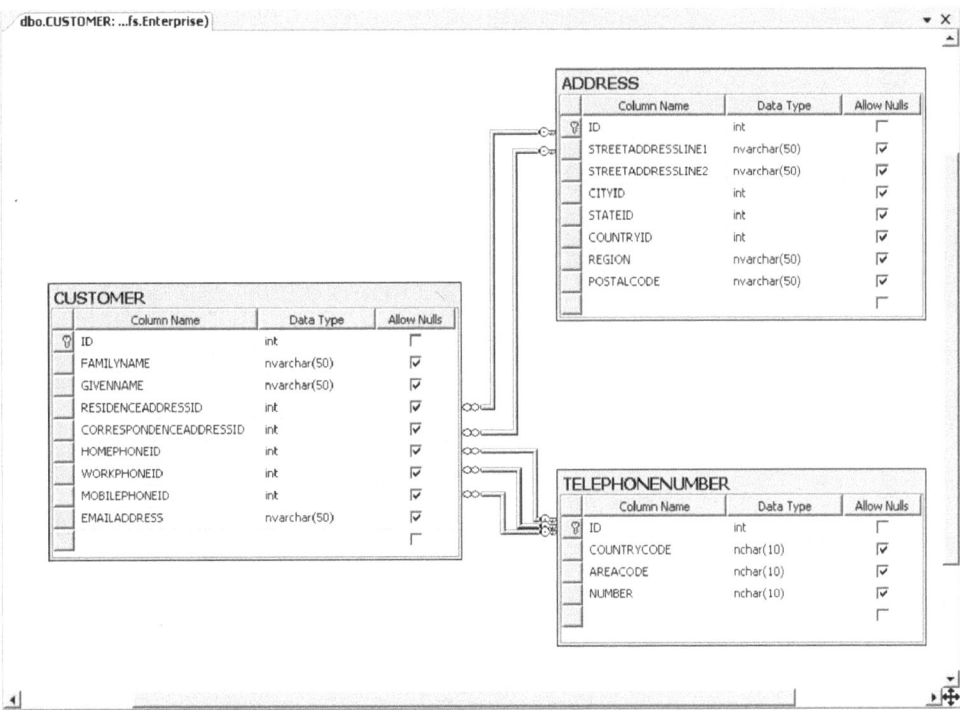

Figure 6-44. *The Customer database diagram, with the foreign and primary keys added*

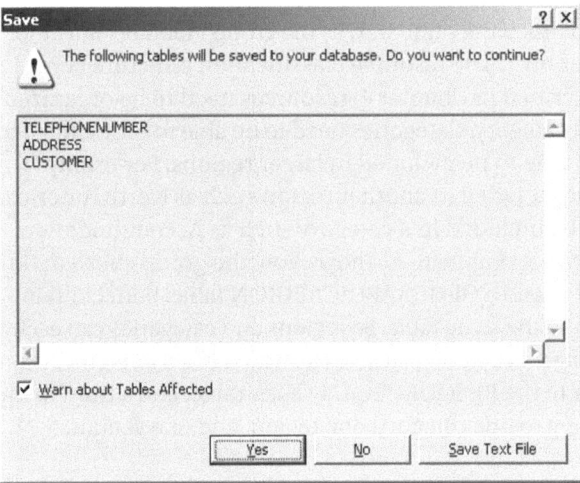

Figure 6-45. *Table update warning dialog box*

Because addresses might be used for vendors as well as customers, Alberto decides to add the tables that form the definition of addresses, STATE, CITY, and COUNTRY, in a separate diagram. The diagram he produces is shown in Figure 6-46.

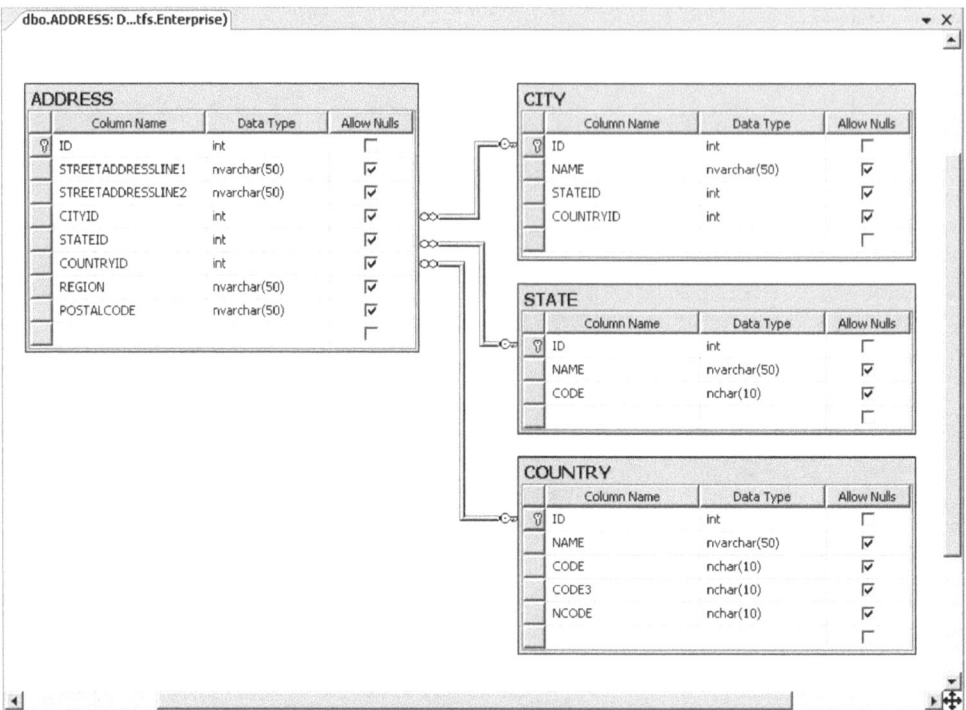

Figure 6-46. *Database diagram for the address model*

The data model meeting continues in much the same way, as the group identifies the other tables and relationships needed for iteration 1. The resource classification structure comes next. According to the requirements described in Chapter 4, resources need to be organized under two groups: geographic region and category. Categories need to be able to be included in larger categories and regions need to be able to be included in larger regions. For example, a region such as the United States will be included in another region such as North America. Similarly, a category such as Hotels will be included in a category such as Accommodation. Each resource can belong to only one vendor. Figure 6-47 shows how the group chose to do this. There is a RESOURCECATEGORY table and a GEOGRAPHICREGION table; both contain foreign key fields that reference other rows in the same table. So regions and categories can each be included in others of the same kind. There is a RESOURCE table, which has a foreign key to the GEOGRAPHICREGION table, another to the RESOURCECATEGORY table, and a third to the VENDOR table. Thus, a resource can belong to one category, one region, and one vendor.

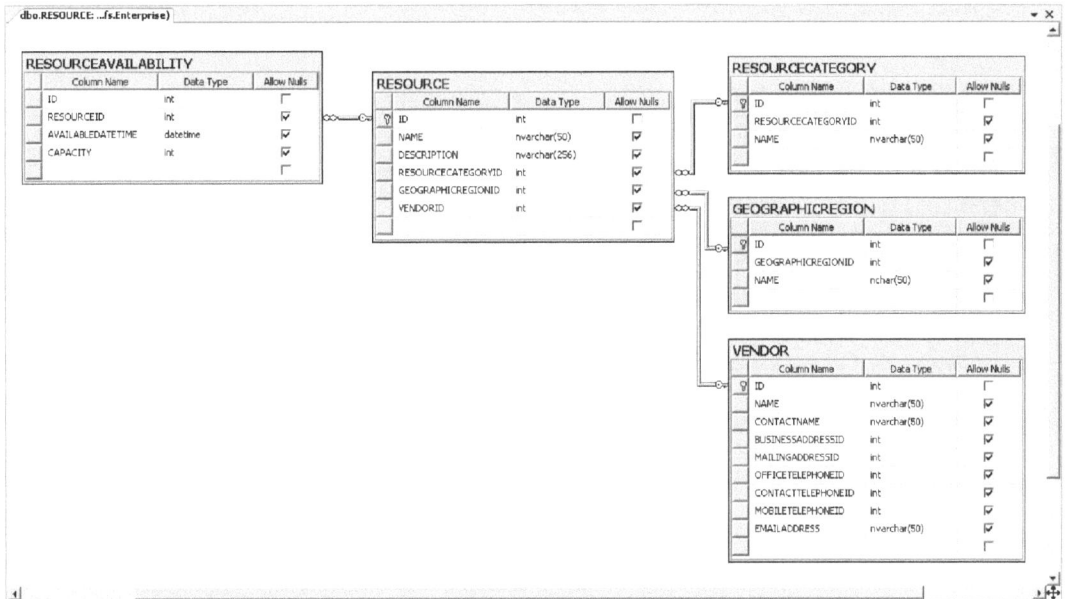

Figure 6-47. *Database diagram for the resource model*

"But couldn't a resource come into more than one category?" asks Angela suddenly.

"Maybe," says Peter. "That might be a change that comes later."

Considerable discussion ensues about the way resource availability is to be implemented. You saw the resource availability concept when the scenario team defined the Add Resource scenario—a resource must define its available capacity on a particular date. In the end, the team decides that there will be a table called RESOURCEAVAILABILITY of Resource Availability Entries and that each of these will have a date and a capacity. One or more entries covering a particular day will allow the user to determine the available capacity on that day by adding the capacity values for all the entries, although the user would expect to see only one entry for a particular date.

The vendor structure is very much like that for customers since vendors have several addresses and phone numbers. The model is shown in Figure 6-48.

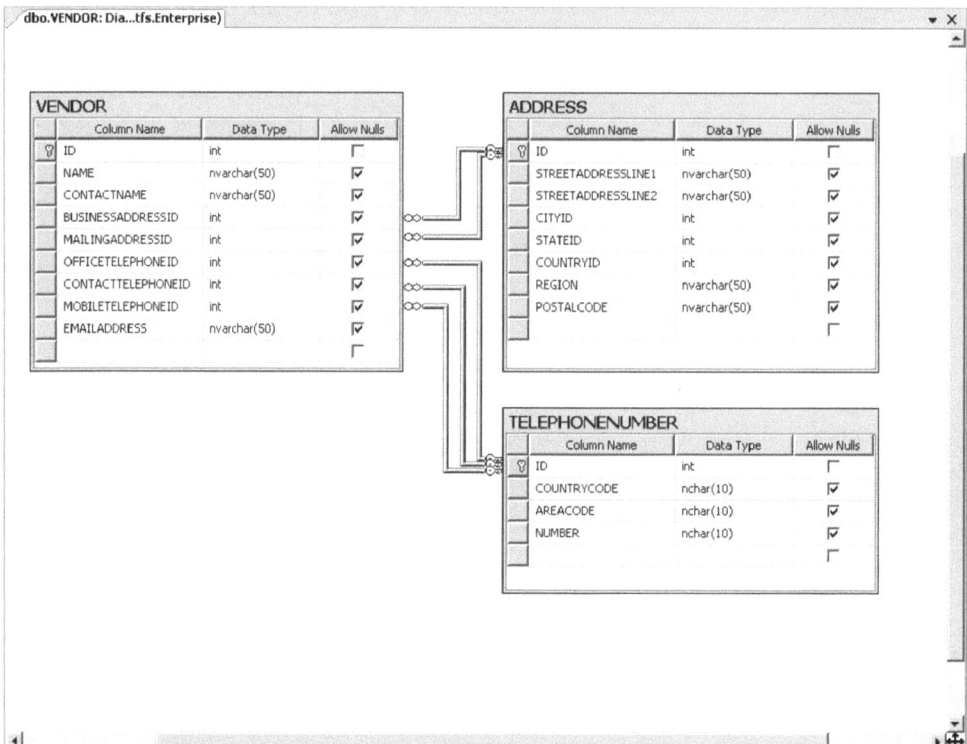

Figure 6-48. *Database diagram for the vendor model*

Finally the group decides on the order and reservation part of the model. It is agreed that a customer can have many orders, so there will be an ORDER table with a foreign key, CUSTOMERID, to the CUSTOMER table. The order has an ID and a Date; that will be all for iteration 1. Orders have multiple line items, each of which is a reservation of some resource. However, resources have limited capacities, so a reservation must reference a resource availability entry, not the resource directly. Many RESERVATION rows will have foreign keys pointing to the same RESOURCEAVAILABILITY row, but the business logic will have to make sure that the number of reservation rows that point to a given availability row are such that the sum of the quantity fields of all the reservation rows does not exceed the capacity on the availability row. The diagram for the order and reservation model is shown in Figure 6-49. In this figure, only the new tables have the Data Type and Allow Nulls fields shown; it's possible to select the view by right clicking on the table in the diagram and selecting either Table View ➤ Standard or Table View ➤ Column Names.

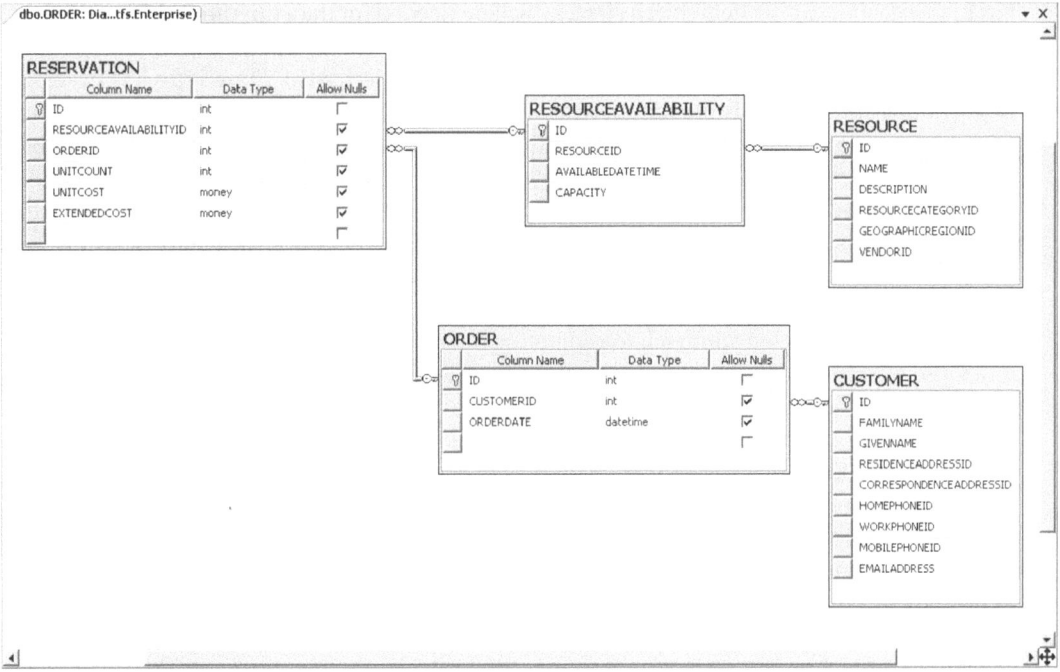

Figure 6-49. *Database diagram for the order and reservation model*

"Is there likely to be a multiuser problem with that?" asks Charles. "If two users make a reservation around the same time using the same resource, the user who saves first might use up the availability before the first user can save."

"I think we'll have to put that check in a stored procedure within a transaction," warns Alberto. "And indicate to the user that the resource is no longer available."

Peter makes a mental note to keep an eye on that issue.

They also plan to include the unit cost and extended cost as well as the quantity in the reservation row. These will have to be calculated from some sort of pricing structure when the order is actually made. The details of pricing are to be decided in a later iteration.

Generating the Database DDL Scripts

After the data model meeting Alberto has an action item to generate scripts that will form part of the Enterprise database data layer project that he added to the solution. He has created the database tables and relations using Server Explorer, but has not yet put anything into the database project that will allow the database to be re-created. The scripts therefore will consist first of ones that create the database, tables, stored procedures, and triggers; these are the Data Definition Language (DDL) scripts. Second, there will be scripts that add the constant seed data to the database, such as the countries and states. Third are the scripts used only for adding test data. The first two sets of scripts will be used to create the databases for deployment on the development logical data center (as in Figure 6-28) as well as the test logical data center, and also to deploy the database to the production data center during rollout.

As a DBA, Alberto is also aware of the need to maintain the database, which in production will contain a large amount of data that is essential to the company's business. Icarus already has in place a backup strategy, but a strategy will be needed for data migration of the existing database of vendors and customers to the new SQL Server 2005 as the 3.1 project goes to deployment; this will have to be considered later in the project. Also, sometimes it is necessary to provide scripts to modify the database as the project goes through various release versions; these scripts must not delete any data from the tables, particularly if there are a large number of manually entered test cases, or other projects depend on the database. Remember that often, large enterprise databases are not the custody of just one project but are shared by many; thus the DBA must consider many requirements. With Icarus Enterprise 3.1, the database is only used for this project, and it seems best for test purposes if the entire database can be re-created each time a new iteration release goes into testing. To make this effective, the developers and testers need to take an organized approach to generating their test case data in the form of scripts. They must also take into account the need to clean up after a test is run, so that any table entries created or deleted as part of the test are restored to a condition so that the test can be rerun.

So Alberto's first task is to create the DDL, which it turns out is a very easy thing to do with Visual Studio 2005. During the meeting, he has created the tables using Server Explorer and established the relationships between them, as you saw earlier. Server Explorer can also generate the DDL scripts to re-create those tables in an empty database. To do this, Alberto expands the database connection in Server Explorer, expands the Tables node, selects a table (let's say COUNTRY), right-clicks, and selects Generate Create Script to Project from the context menu. This action does not require any further settings and immediately generates a SQL script file called `EnterpriseDev.dbo.COUNTRY.SQL`, in the Create Scripts folder of the `EnterpriseDatabase` project in the solution. He double-clicks on the file in Solution Explorer to view its contents:

```
/****** Object:  Table [dbo].[COUNTRY]    Script Date: 04/17/2006 11:02:55 ******/
IF  EXISTS (SELECT * FROM sys.objects
WHERE object_id = OBJECT_ID(N'[dbo].[COUNTRY]') AND type in (N'U'))
DROP TABLE [dbo].[COUNTRY]
GO
/****** Object:  Table [dbo].[COUNTRY]    Script Date: 04/17/2006 11:02:55 ******/
SET ANSI_NULLS ON
GO
SET QUOTED_IDENTIFIER ON
GO
IF NOT EXISTS (SELECT * FROM sys.objects
WHERE object_id = OBJECT_ID(N'[dbo].[COUNTRY]') AND type in (N'U'))
BEGIN
CREATE TABLE [dbo].[COUNTRY](
  [ID] [int] NOT NULL,
  [NAME] [nvarchar](50) NULL,
  [CODE] [nchar](10) NULL,
  [CODE3] [nchar](10) NULL,
  [NCODE] [nchar](10) NULL,
 CONSTRAINT [PK_COUNTRY] PRIMARY KEY CLUSTERED
(
   [ID] ASC
)WITH (IGNORE_DUP_KEY = OFF) ON [PRIMARY]
) ON [PRIMARY]
END
GO
```

The script first drops any existing table with the same name (of course, any data in it will be lost), then sets a couple of options. The ANSI_NULLS option makes the table comply with the ANSI SQL-92 treatment of nulls in that a field may not be compared with NULL in any expression. With this option on, you can still use the IS NULL or IS NOT NULL syntax in a where clause. Since this is the default SQL Server 2005 option, Alberto leaves this option on. Setting QUOTED_IDENTIFIER to ON also follows ANSI SQL-92 in that it requires single quotes as character string delimiters and does not allow double quotes. Double quotes or brackets ([]) may be used to delimit identifiers when they are required, such as when an identifier has the same name as a reserved word but not literal strings.

The script then creates the table (if it does not already exist), setting the names of the fields, their types, and the option to allow or disallow nulls. The constraints on the fields are included in the CREATE statement, in this case just CONSTRAINT [PK_COUNTRY] PRIMARY KEY CLUSTERED ([ID] ASC) that defines the ID field as a clustered primary key with the records arranged in ascending order. Only one clustered primary key is allowed in a database since this means that the table's data will be held in memory in the order of ascending values in the ID field. The IGNORE_DUP_KEY option is set to OFF, which causes the entire INSERT transaction to fail if an attempt is made to insert a row with the same value for the ID field as an existing row.

Alberto can continue to generate the create scripts for all the tables in the same way. Let's look at a more complicated one, such as CUSTOMER:

```
/****** Object:  Table [dbo].[CUSTOMER]    Script Date: 04/17/2006 11:29:07 ******/
IF  EXISTS (SELECT * FROM sys.objects
WHERE object_id = OBJECT_ID(N'[dbo].[CUSTOMER]') AND type in (N'U'))
DROP TABLE [dbo].[CUSTOMER]
GO
/****** Object:  Table [dbo].[CUSTOMER]    Script Date: 04/17/2006 11:29:08 ******/
SET ANSI_NULLS ON
GO
SET QUOTED_IDENTIFIER ON
GO
IF NOT EXISTS (SELECT * FROM sys.objects
WHERE object_id = OBJECT_ID(N'[dbo].[CUSTOMER]') AND type in (N'U'))
BEGIN
CREATE TABLE [dbo].[CUSTOMER](
  [ID] [int] NOT NULL,
  [FAMILYNAME] [nvarchar](50) NULL,
  [GIVENNAME] [nvarchar](50) NULL,
  [RESIDENCEADDRESSID] [int] NULL,
  [CORRESPONDENCEADDRESSID] [int] NULL,
  [HOMEPHONEID] [int] NULL,
  [WORKPHONEID] [int] NULL,
  [MOBILEPHONEID] [int] NULL,
  [EMAILADDRESS] [nvarchar](50) NULL,
 CONSTRAINT [PK_CUSTOMER] PRIMARY KEY CLUSTERED
(
  [ID] ASC
)WITH (IGNORE_DUP_KEY = OFF) ON [PRIMARY]
) ON [PRIMARY]
END
```

```
GO
IF NOT EXISTS (SELECT * FROM sys.foreign_keys
  WHERE object_id = OBJECT_ID(N'[dbo].[FK_CUSTOMER_ADDRESS]')
    AND parent_object_id = OBJECT_ID(N'[dbo].[CUSTOMER]'))
ALTER TABLE [dbo].[CUSTOMER]  WITH CHECK ADD  CONSTRAINT
  [FK_CUSTOMER_ADDRESS] FOREIGN KEY([RESIDENCEADDRESSID])
REFERENCES [dbo].[ADDRESS] ([ID])
GO


-- Additional foreign key constraints omitted for brevity.
```

The first part of this SQL script is similar to the previous one. It creates the CUSTOMER table in the same way and sets the ID field as the clustered primary key. Five similar statements follow that create the foreign key constraints in the database that include the CUSTOMER table. The first statement, provided the relationship does not already exist in the sys.foreign_keys view, executes an ALTER TABLE statement to add the foreign key constraint that the RESIDENCEADDRESSID field of the CUSTOMER table references the ID field of the ADDRESS table.

These foreign key constraints are added one after another, including the CORRESPONDENCEADDRESSID field, which also references the ID field of the ADDRESS table, and the three telephone number fields for residence, work, and mobile (cell phone), which all reference the ID field of the TELEPHONENUMBER table.

Well, this is very nice, but to generate all of the tables in an empty database, it will be necessary to run each of the scripts in turn in a specific order. This is because SQL Server cannot create, for example, the foreign key constraints that are required in the script that generates the ADDRESS table until the CITY, STATE, and COUNTRY tables have been created, and it cannot create the CUSTOMER table with its foreign key constraints until the ADDRESS and TELEPHONENUMBER tables have been created. Running these manually is therefore an error-prone procedure. It occurs to Alberto that he can create a batch file called CreateTables.bat and put in commands such as these:

```
osql -E -d %1 -i EnterpriseDev.dbo.COUNTRY.SQL
osql -E -d %1 -i EnterpriseDev.dbo.STATE.SQL
osql -E -d %1 -i EnterpriseDev.dbo.CITY.SQL
osql -E -d %1 -i EnterpriseDev.dbo.ADDRESS.SQL
osql -E -d %1 -i EnterpriseDev.dbo.TELEPHONENUMBER.SQL
osql -E -d %1 -i EnterpriseDev.dbo.CUSTOMER.SQL
```

where he has assumed a trusted connection and parameterized the database name as %1. Running this batch file will fail if the tables already exist, however, because the script will try to delete the COUNTRY table first, which cannot be done until the foreign key constraints that apply to that table have been removed. Code can be written to do all this, and it is a standard way that DBAs and developers tend to do things, but there is a better way.

If you use Ctrl-click to select all the tables that define an address—ADDRESS, CITY, STATE, COUNTRY—in the database using Server Explorer, and then right-click and select Generate Create Script to Project, you'll generate a DDL script that creates all of those tables. Here is the script:

```
IF  EXISTS (SELECT * FROM sys.foreign_keys
  WHERE object_id = OBJECT_ID(N'[dbo].[FK_ADDRESS_CITY]')
    AND parent_object_id = OBJECT_ID(N'[dbo].[ADDRESS]'))
ALTER TABLE [dbo].[ADDRESS] DROP CONSTRAINT [FK_ADDRESS_CITY]
GO


/* Script to drop other foreign key constraints - omitted for brevity.*/


/****** Object:  Table [dbo].[ADDRESS]    Script Date: 04/17/2006 13:23:19 ******/
IF  EXISTS (SELECT * FROM sys.objects
WHERE object_id = OBJECT_ID(N'[dbo].[ADDRESS]')
  AND type in (N'U')) DROP TABLE [dbo].[ADDRESS]
GO


/* Script to drop other tables - omitted for brevity.*/


/****** Object:  Table [dbo].[ADDRESS]    Script Date: 04/17/2006 13:23:20 ******/
SET ANSI_NULLS ON
GO
SET QUOTED_IDENTIFIER ON
GO
IF NOT EXISTS (SELECT * FROM sys.objects
  WHERE object_id = OBJECT_ID(N'[dbo].[ADDRESS]') AND type in (N'U'))
BEGIN
CREATE TABLE [dbo].[ADDRESS](
  [ID] [int] NOT NULL,
  [STREETADDRESSLINE1] [nvarchar](50) NULL,
  [STREETADDRESSLINE2] [nvarchar](50) NULL,
  [CITYID] [int] NULL,
  [STATEID] [int] NULL,
  [COUNTRYID] [int] NULL,
  [REGION] [nvarchar](50) NULL,
  [POSTALCODE] [nvarchar](50) NULL,
 CONSTRAINT [PK_ADDRESS] PRIMARY KEY CLUSTERED
(
   [ID] ASC
)WITH (IGNORE_DUP_KEY = OFF) ON [PRIMARY]
) ON [PRIMARY]
END
GO


/*  Script to create other tables - omitted for brevity.*/

IF NOT EXISTS (SELECT * FROM sys.foreign_keys
  WHERE object_id = OBJECT_ID(N'[dbo].[FK_ADDRESS_CITY]')
    AND parent_object_id = OBJECT_ID(N'[dbo].[ADDRESS]'))
ALTER TABLE [dbo].[ADDRESS]  WITH CHECK ADD  CONSTRAINT
  [FK_ADDRESS_CITY] FOREIGN KEY([CITYID])
```

```
REFERENCES [dbo].[CITY] ([ID])
GO

/*  Script to create other foreign key constraints - omitted for brevity.*/
```

Looking briefly at this SQL, you can see that it first deletes all of the constraints. Then it deletes all of the tables. Next, it creates all four tables and adds the constraints. Generating the script in this way saves a lot of editing compared to manually merging all of the create scripts into one. Alberto selects all of the tables in Server Explorer and generates a create script for the whole set. He names this script "GenerateTables.sql". Compared to the batch file, this approach has the advantage that the script can be run from the Visual Studio database project itself. To do this, you right-click on the file in the database project in Solution Explorer and select Run. This will run the script on the default database for the database project EnterpriseDatabase, which will probably be the one that you created the script from. Of course, you might want to run the script on another database—a test database, for example, so as not to lose all your test data in your development database. To do this you select Run On, which opens a dialog box that allows you to select a different database connection. You can, in fact, have more than one database connection in a database project and nominate any one of them as the default, or select the one you want using the Run On option.

The Seed Data Scripts

Seed data scripts are needed for the COUNTRY and STATE tables. There is no alternative but to type the data in manually for these tables. Some typical rows for these tables are as follows:

```
DELETE STATE;

INSERT INTO STATE (ID, NAME, CODE) VALUES ('1', 'Alabama', 'AL');
INSERT INTO STATE (ID, NAME, CODE) VALUES ('2', 'Alaska', 'AK');
...

DELETE COUNTRY;

INSERT INTO COUNTRY (ID, NAME, CODE, CODE3, NCODE)
  VALUES ('1', 'AFGHANISTAN', 'AF', 'AFG', '004');
INSERT INTO COUNTRY (ID, NAME, CODE, CODE3, NCODE)
  VALUES ('2', 'ALBANIA', 'AL', 'ALB', '008');
INSERT INTO COUNTRY (ID, NAME, CODE, CODE3, NCODE)
  VALUES ('3', 'ALGERIA','DZ', 'DZA', '012');

/* etc. */
```

It's a boring job, but someone has to do it! Alberto spends a couple of hours typing in the INSERT statements for the STATE and COUNTRY tables. He obtains the original state and country data, in table form, from websites like these:

http://worldatlas.com/aatlas/ctycodes.htm

www.usps.com/ncsc/lookups/abbreviations.html#states

and then uses the replace feature of the editor to add in the rest of the SQL.

The Test Data Scripts

These scripts are similar to the seed data scripts in that they do simple INSERTs into the various tables. It is a case of building the data from the independent entries up to those that are dependent, so entries in RESOURCECATEGORY and GEOGRAPHICREGION come first, followed by VENDOR, RESOURCE, and RESOURCEAVAILABILITY, then CITY, ADDRESS, TELEPHONENUMBER, and CUSTOMER, and finally ORDER and RESERVATION. These are the test data scripts that Alberto writes:

- `DeleteTestData.sql`

- `PopulateGeographicRegions.sql`

- `PopulateResourceCategories.sql`

- `PopulateVendors.sql`

- `PopulateResources.sql`

- `PopulateCustomers.sql`

- `PopulateOrders.sql`

together with a `CreateTestData.bat` file to run them:

```
osql -E -d %1 -i DeleteTestData.sql
osql -E -d %1 -i PopulateGeographicRegions.sql
osql -E -d %1 -i PopulateResourceCategories.sql
osql -E -d %1 -i PopulateVendors.sql
osql -E -d %1 -i PopulateResources.sql
osql -E -d %1 -i PopulateCustomers.sql
osql -E -d %1 -i PopulateOrders.sql
```

Summary

In this chapter we explored some of the issues that occur during the early part of the first iteration of the project. The team interpreted the work streams and activities defined in MSF for CMMI Process Improvement into a plan for a rapid first iteration.

You saw in some detail the writing and storyboarding of the scenarios for customer management, sales, and listing. This will help in understanding the code to be developed and tested in later chapters.

You watched Peter and his developers discuss and design the architecture and object model to support the requirements of the project and in particular, the offline operation. The team again used the distributed system designers to refine the application diagram from Chapter 5. Peter also designed systems to represent the code to be developed in iteration 1 and the logical data center for development, and verified the deployments for the developers. The team designed the data model for iteration 1 and the DBA, Alberto, created a database project to hold scripts for generating the database and the test data within it.

In the next chapter, we will join the team as they begin detailed coding of the proof of concepts that they need to continue the analysis phase of iteration 1.

CHAPTER 7

Prototype Group: Proof of Concept Development

This chapter is about prototyping the project. It concentrates on getting the design right and using new features of Visual Studio 2005 to implement what is required for the Icarus Enterprise 3.1 project. The formal aspects of check-in and work items are left until the next chapter.

Sales Business Objects—The Customer Business Entity

One morning in the second week of iteration 1, Clare walks into Peter's cubicle to find him on his knees with his head half under the lowest shelf of a bookcase. "Good morning, Peter," she says cheerily. "Are you busy?"

"Hey! Finally—here it is!" Peter exclaims in triumph as he pulls out a dusty document consisting of 20 or so torn pages stapled together. "Oh, hello," he says, turning around. "I've been looking for this for nearly an hour. It's a really good article on data adapters in .NET 2.0."

"Yes, I thought you might be looking for something. You know, Peter, it would be a good idea to tidy your work area one of these days, don't you think?"

"Well, certainly!" he says rather shortly. "But I really don't have time at the moment."

She gives a half-smile and retreats, shaking her head as she passes Angela in the hallway.

"But he has time to spend an hour searching for things," she murmurs, half to Angela and half to herself. Angela gives a silent grin and nod simultaneously. Peter follows Clare out and hands the paper to Angela.

"Here, Angela, this describes the new data adapters very well," he says.

"Oh, thanks, I'll have a look at it right away," she says and walks on to her cubicle, which she shares with Charles. Charles always wears headphones and she can faintly hear high-pitched twittering that presumably must be the treble end of something he calls music as he reads something on the Internet about his favorite soccer team. Charles is of English origin and she once made the mistake of asking him about soccer—or "football" as he calls it. The twittering is not loud enough to be annoying and she allows herself a two-minute look—not longer—at a Chinese horoscope website, then opens up Peter's document.

After half an hour she has a basic idea of `DataSet` and `TableAdapter` classes in Visual Studio 2005 and is ready to try out some ideas. She starts by creating a couple of folders in the iteration 1 solution called `SalesBusinessObjects` and under that, `DataAccessLayer`. She will begin by developing the data access layer.

The Data Access Layer

The Data Access Layer, as we saw in Chapter 6, is the code layer that handles persistence of the business objects to the database. I tend to use the term *persistence* to mean both reading of the data from the database to populate the object and the writing of modified data in an object back to the database. The data access layer (DAL) consists of a set of datasets with associated table adapters. Actually, table adapters make up the DAL and the datasets are used in the architecture to hold the data in the business objects and to provide the means by which the data is communicated from the business entity objects to the ASP. NET pages and Windows Forms in the presentation layer.

The CustomerDS Dataset

Angela right-clicks on the `DataAccessLayer` folder under `SalesBusinessObjects` in Solution Explorer and selects Add ➤ New Project. In the Add New Project dialog box, under Project Types she selects Visual C#, then Windows. Then, under Visual Studio Installed Templates, she selects Class Library. In the Name text box, she types in the name "CustomerDAL", as shown in Figure 7-1, and then clicks OK.

Note You can find the source code at this point in the folder `Chapter 7\Chapter7Start`. Exercise 7-1 will help you understand this section.

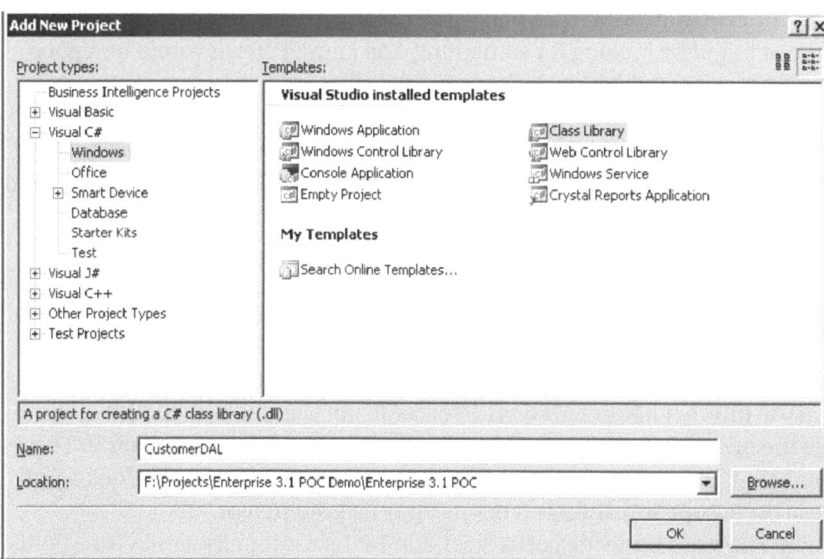

Figure 7-1. *Creating the CustomerDAL project*

Angela deletes `Class1`, which Visual Studio has automatically added. Namespaces in projects are often left until last, but it's a good idea to set the project namespace right away—that way, all the classes will have a consistent namespace. Angela right-clicks on the new `CustomerDAL` project in Solution Explorer and selects Properties. She types "com.icarustravel. enterprise31.Customer" into the Default Namespace box and closes the Properties dialog box.

Now she is ready to create a dataset. She right-clicks on the `CustomerDAL` project and selects Add ➤ New Item. She selects the DataSet icon in the Add New Item dialog box, and types "CustomerDS.xsd" as the name (Peter asked her to give all typed datasets in the solution a name ending in `DS`). Once Angela clicks Add, Visual Studio opens the Dataset Designer window for the new dataset, and she can now drag items from the Toolbox onto the surface of the designer. The screen looks like Figure 7-2; Angela has closed Solution Explorer to give herself more room.

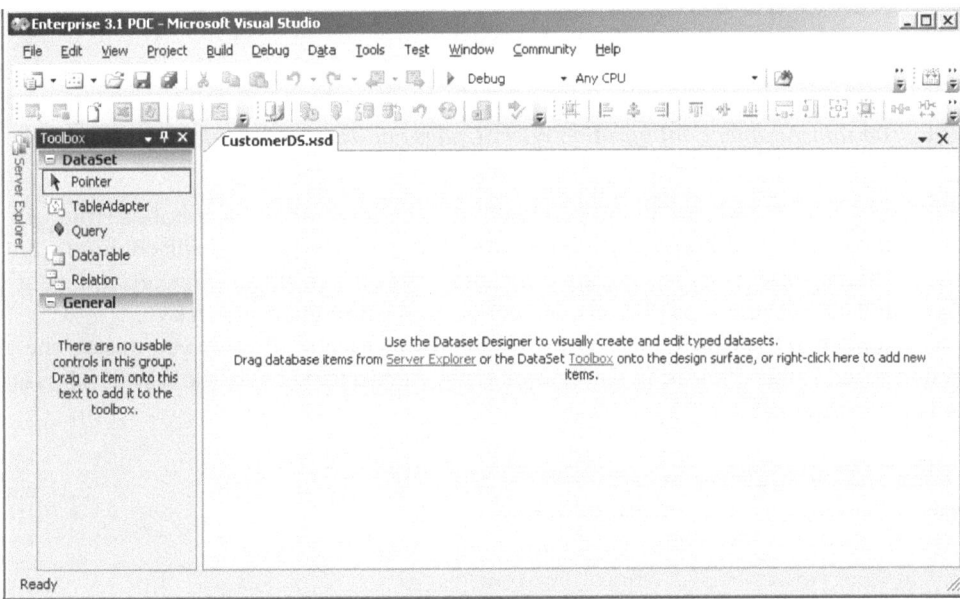

Figure 7-2. *The Dataset Designer*

Angela begins by dragging onto the design surface a `TableAdapter` from the Toolbox. Visual Studio opens the TableAdapter Configuration Wizard, as shown in Figure 7-3. Table adapters provide the means by which tables of data in a dataset can be loaded from a database by running SQL queries or stored procedures. They also provide the capability to save updated or new rows back to the database and delete rows in the database corresponding to rows in a table of the dataset marked as deleted. They therefore form a channel of communication between an application and the database. The concept is not new and corresponds somewhat to a data adapter and connection object in Visual Studio 2003, but it has been improved greatly in Visual Studio 2005 and saves a huge amount of code compared to doing the whole thing manually. The configuration wizard allows you to configure the new table and adapter to work either with inline SQL or with stored procedures. You can write the stored procedures as you go, as you'll see, or you can use existing ones in the database.

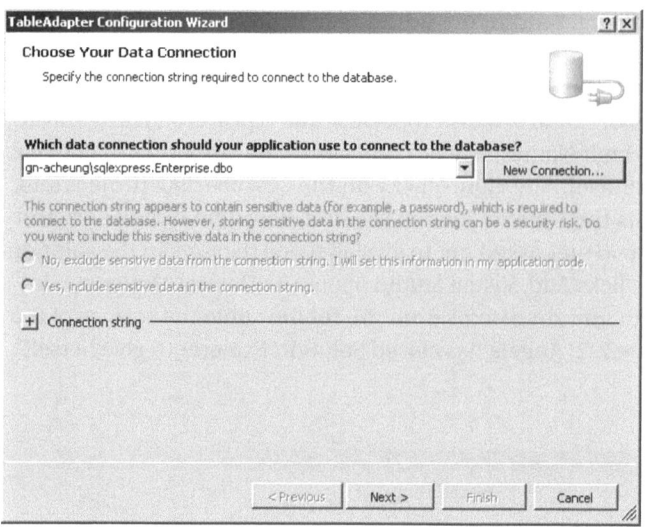

Figure 7-3. *The TableAdapter Configuration Wizard, page one. Here you define the connection.*

The first page of the wizard allows you to define a connection to the database that will contain the data tables and stored procedures with which the table adapter will communicate. It is easy to change this when the software is installed, so at the start you can work with your development database or a copy of it on your workstation without any worries.

The next page of the wizard (see Figure 7-4) confirms this by allowing you to save the connection string in the application configuration file. Angela makes sure the Yes checkbox is checked before clicking Next.

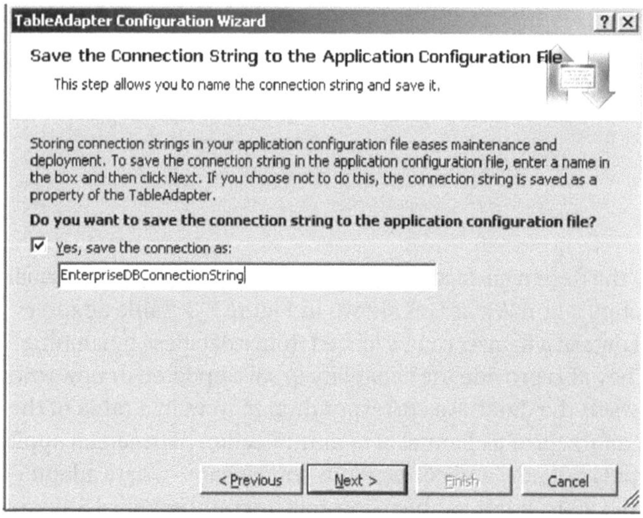

Figure 7-4. *The TableAdapter Configuration Wizard, page two. Here you can save the connection string in the application configuration file.*

The third page of the wizard (see Figure 7-5) allows you to choose SQL statements in the code, create new stored procedures, or use existing stored procedures to access the database. Angela checks the Create New Stored Procedures option before clicking Next again, which brings up the fourth page in the wizard (see Figure 7-6).

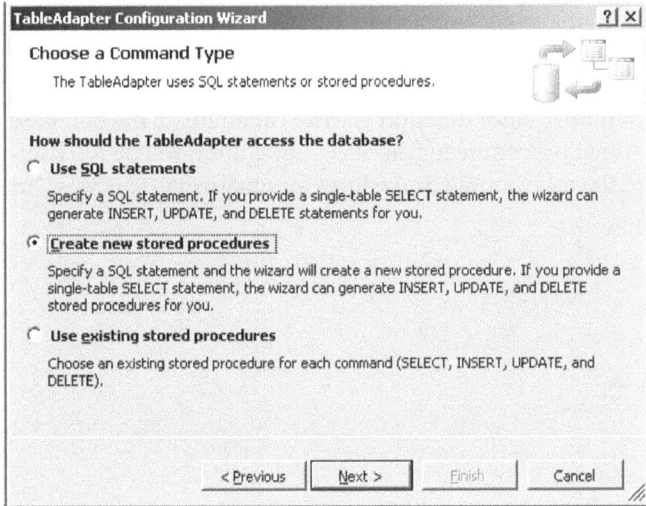

Figure 7-5. *The TableAdapter Configuration Wizard, page three. Here you select the way in which the table adapter will access the database.*

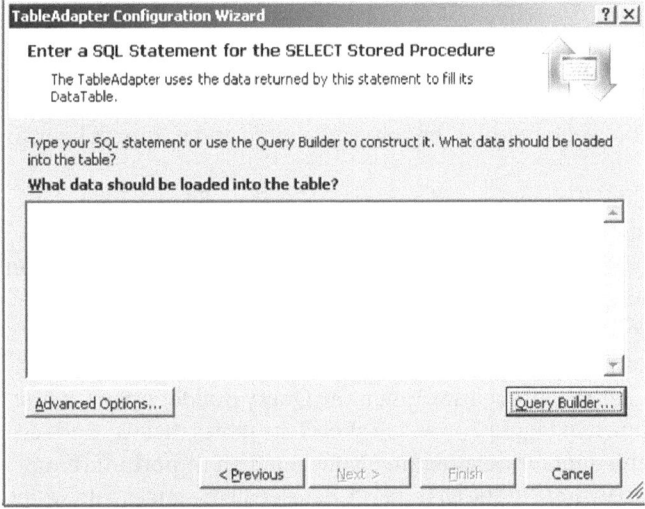

Figure 7-6. *The TableAdapter Configuration Wizard, page four. Here you define the new SELECT stored procedure.*

This page allows you to define the stored procedure that will be used to populate a table in the dataset from the database. This is called the SELECT stored procedure; it is the only one that you can define explicitly in the wizard, so the wizard has to use its own internal rules to attempt to generate stored procedures for INSERT, UPDATE, and DELETE, if those are required. Angela clicks the Advanced Options button first, which displays the Advanced Options dialog box, shown in Figure 7-7. These options will be important later in the project, but for the moment she deselects the first option, which automatically forces the other two to be deselected. In this dataset, she will eventually want to generate INSERT, UPDATE, and DELETE statements, since she plans for this dataset to contain the information for a single customer entity. Some of this information may be modifiable by the operator, but for iteration 1, write capability to the database is not required. As you will see, the stored procedure for the SELECT operation will be too complicated for Visual Studio to generate the other stored procedures automatically. This was why Angela deselected the top checkbox.

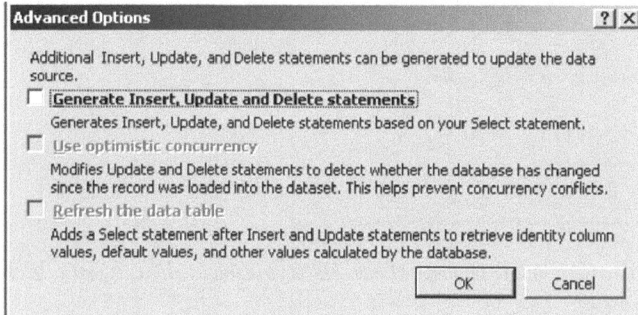

Figure 7-7. *The Advanced Options dialog box for the SELECT stored procedure*

The Use Optimistic Concurrency option will be important later when the team takes multiple users into account. Selecting this option allows the user to detect modifications of a row in the database that have occurred between reading the row to the table and writing it back to the database.

The Refresh the Data Table option, if checked, will generate SQL that will read back data that was written, particularly so that identity column values—values that are generated automatically in a sequence by the database—are read back. Again, this will be important later when the team decides on the mechanism for generating the ID fields.

After clicking OK in the Advanced Options dialog box, Angela clicks the Query Builder button in the TableAdapter Configuration Wizard, which will allow her to build a query that will form the basis of the new SELECT stored procedure. When the Query Builder opens, it first displays the Add Table dialog box, shown in Figure 7-8, which shows the tables that were added to the database by Alberto during the data model meeting. Now here's an important thing: Angela does not think it's necessary to include in the CustomerDS dataset all the tables into which the customer data is normalized in the data model. She is planning to denormalize the addresses, phone numbers, and city fields into one CUSTOMER table. So the CUSTOMER table in the dataset will have a lot more fields than the corresponding table in the database. She is planning to include the STATE and COUNTRY tables as read-only tables in the dataset as these will be needed to populate the combo box item collections for the State and Country controls in address tabs on two of the hidden tab pages of the Customer Details Windows Form in Figure 6-7.

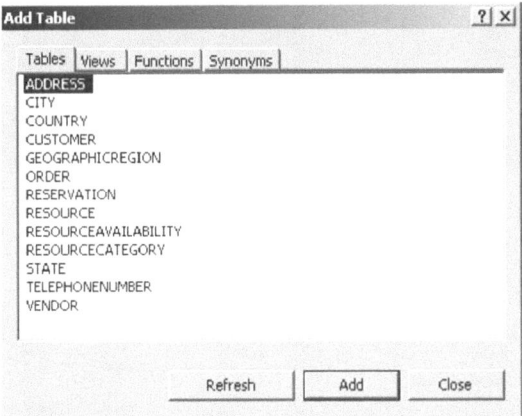

Figure 7-8. *The Add Table dialog box for the Query Builder*

Angela selects the CUSTOMER table and clicks Add. Next she selects ADDRESS and clicks Add twice, which adds two instances of that table into the query. Then she selects CITY and clicks Add twice. There are now two instances of ADDRESS and two instances of CITY, as well as the one instance of CUSTOMER, in the query. Her aim is to return the denormalized residence address and correspondence address together with city name for each. Let's see how she does this.

First, Angela closes the Add Table dialog box. By default, the Query Builder puts in all the foreign key relationships as inner joins, which is not quite what she wants. So she repositions the tables in the Diagram pane of the Query Builder so that she can see what she is doing. She then gives new aliases to the ADDRESS and CITY table instances in the diagram. Angela does this by right-clicking on each table, selecting Properties, and typing the new alias names in the Alias field. Next she deletes four of the links, leaving only the joins

CUSTOMER. RESIDENCEADDRESSID to RESIDENCEADDRESS.ID

CUSTOMER.CORRESPONDENCEADDRESSID to CORRESPONDENCEADDRESS.ID

RESIDENCEADDRESS.CITYID to RESIDENCECITY.ID

CORRESPONDENCEADDRESS.CITYID to CORRESPONDENCECITY.ID

Next she checks the fields in the tables that she requires in the output of the SELECT statement and types alias names for output fields with the same names from different tables. Finally, she adds a condition, =@ID, in the Filter column of the Criteria pane for the CUSTOMER.ID field.

Before she adds the logic to the SQL that will return the customer's three telephone numbers, Angela decides to test it by clicking the Execute Query button in the Query Builder. She enters the ID of one of the test customers in the database. The Query Builder is shown in Figure 7-9. As you can see, the SQL that has been automatically generated is visible.

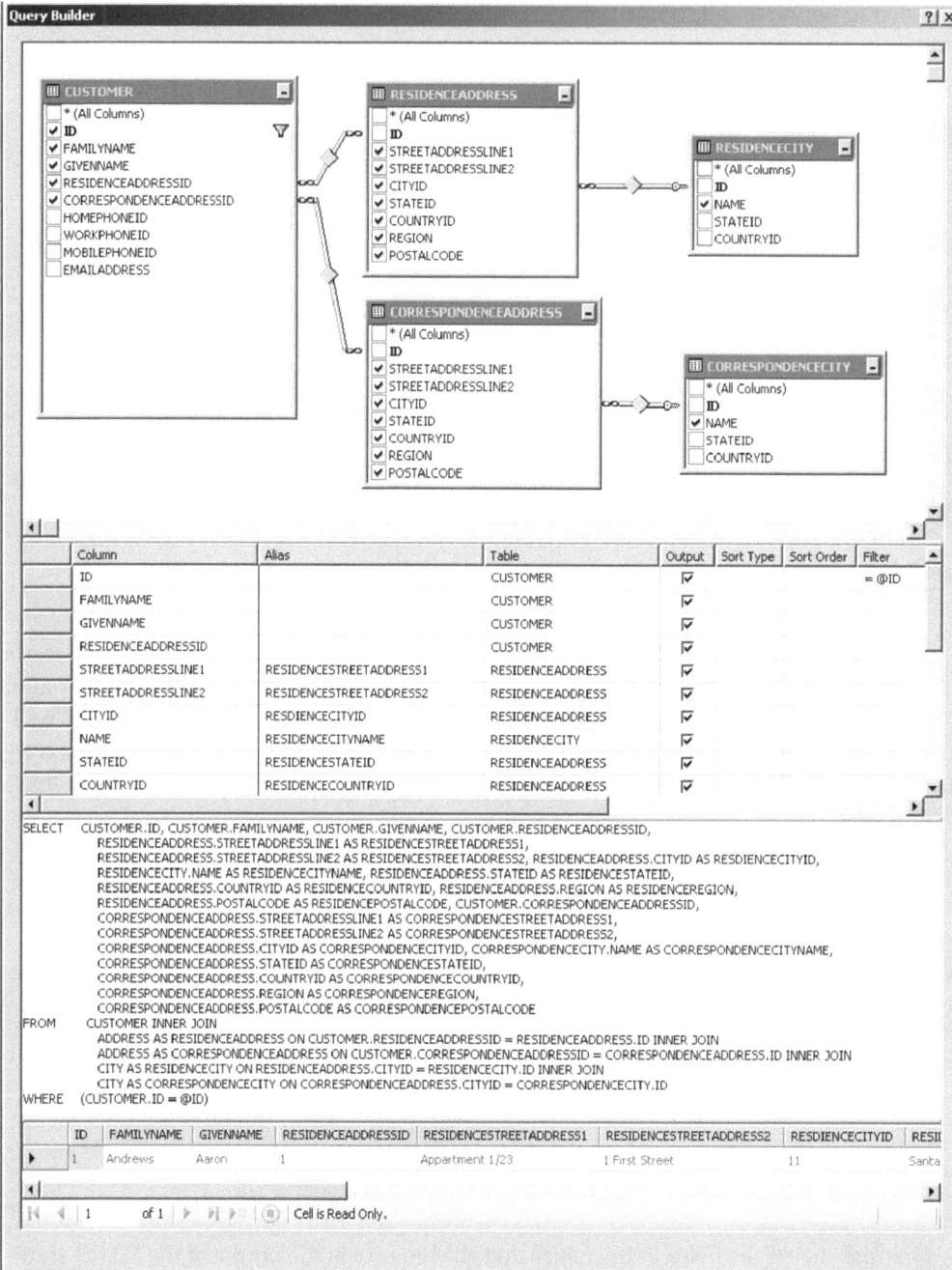

Figure 7-9. *The Query Builder after the address portion of the query has been entered and tested*

Now Angela adds the tables for the home, work, and cell (mobile) phones. This is done in a similar manner; she adds multiple tables with aliases. This time she deletes all the links that are inserted automatically and creates the joins on the design surface, by dragging from the appropriate ID in the CUSTOMER table—say the HOMEPHONEID field to the ID key in the table aliased as HOMETELEPHONENUMBER. She also checks the CUSTOMER.EMAILADDRESS field in the CUSTOMER table so that it appears in the output. The resulting Query Builder windows are shown in Figures 7-10 through 7-12. She runs the query again to check it, and then clicks OK in the Query Builder.

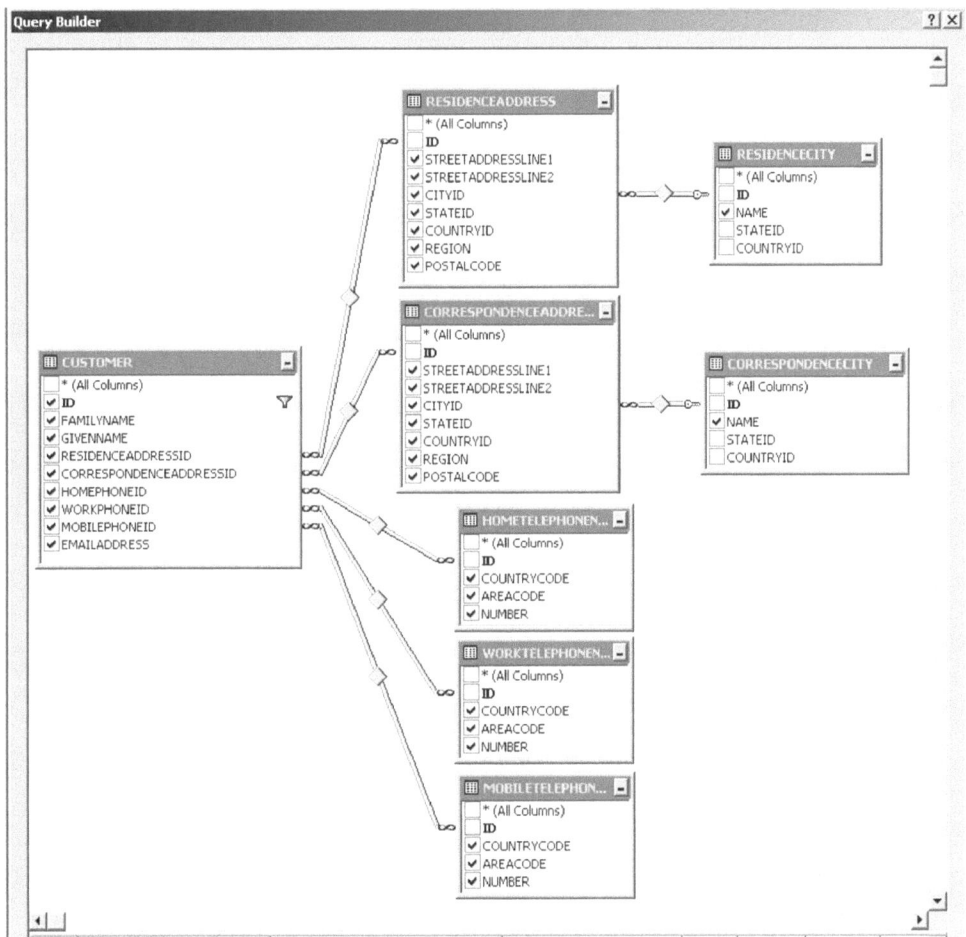

Figure 7-10. *The final query generator Diagram pane*

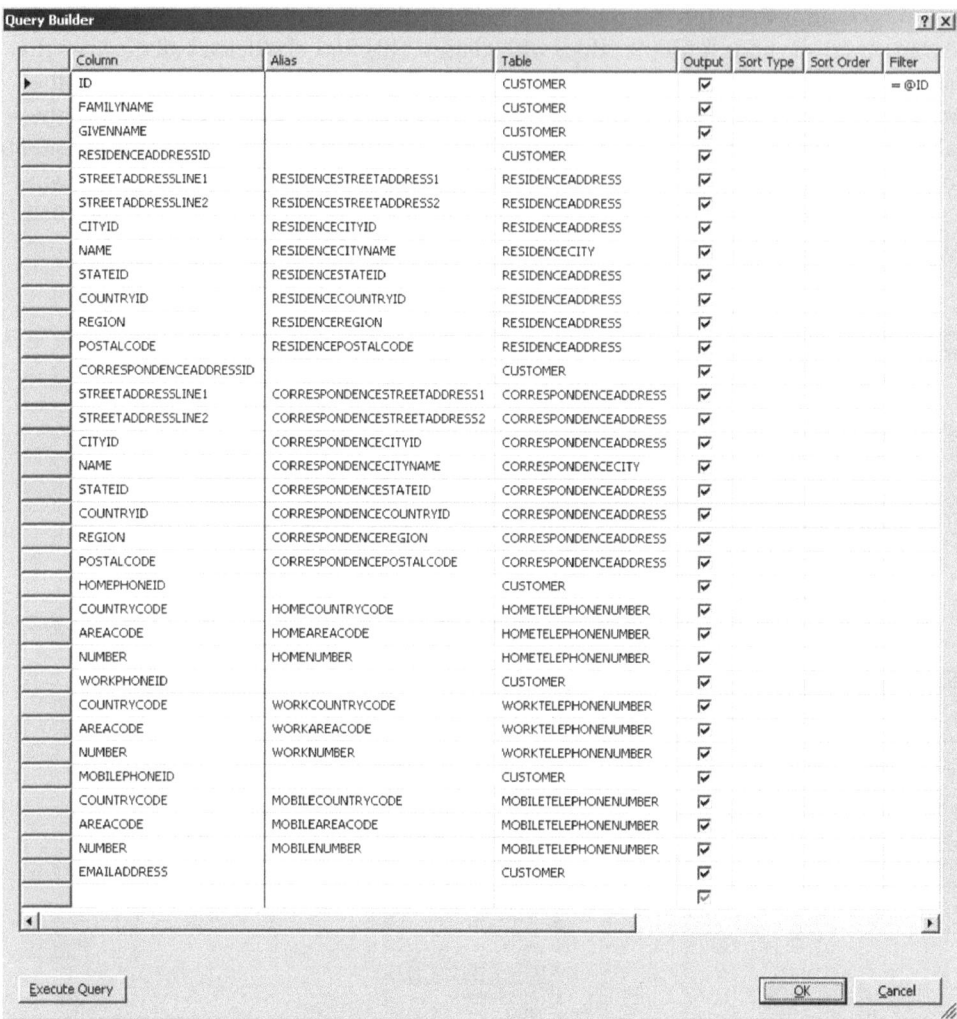

Figure 7-11. *The final query generator Criteria pane*

```
SELECT   CUSTOMER.ID, CUSTOMER.FAMILYNAME, CUSTOMER.GIVENNAME, CUSTOMER.RESIDENCEADDRESSID,
         RESIDENCEADDRESS.STREETADDRESSLINE1 AS RESIDENCESTREETADDRESS1,
         RESIDENCEADDRESS.STREETADDRESSLINE2 AS RESIDENCESTREETADDRESS2, RESIDENCEADDRESS.CITYID AS RESDIENCECITYID,
         RESIDENCECITY.NAME AS RESIDENCECITYNAME, RESIDENCEADDRESS.STATEID AS RESIDENCESTATEID,
         RESIDENCEADDRESS.COUNTRYID AS RESIDENCECOUNTRYID, RESIDENCEADDRESS.REGION AS RESIDENCEREGION,
         RESIDENCEADDRESS.POSTALCODE AS RESIDENCEPOSTALCODE, CUSTOMER.CORRESPONDENCEADDRESSID,
         CORRESPONDENCEADDRESS.STREETADDRESSLINE1 AS CORRESPONDENCESTREETADDRESS1,
         CORRESPONDENCEADDRESS.STREETADDRESSLINE2 AS CORRESPONDENCESTREETADDRESS2,
         CORRESPONDENCEADDRESS.CITYID AS CORRESPONDENCECITYID, CORRESPONDENCECITY.NAME AS CORRESPONDENCECITYNAME,
         CORRESPONDENCEADDRESS.STATEID AS CORRESPONDENCESTATEID,
         CORRESPONDENCEADDRESS.COUNTRYID AS CORRESPONDENCECOUNTRYID,
         CORRESPONDENCEADDRESS.REGION AS CORRESPONDENCEREGION,
         CORRESPONDENCEADDRESS.POSTALCODE AS CORRESPONDENCEPOSTALCODE, CUSTOMER.HOMEPHONEID,
         HOMETELEPHONENUMBER.COUNTRYCODE AS HOMECOUNTRYCODE, HOMETELEPHONENUMBER.AREACODE AS HOMEAREACODE,
         HOMETELEPHONENUMBER.NUMBER AS HOMENUMBER, CUSTOMER.WORKPHONEID,
         WORKTELEPHONENUMBER.COUNTRYCODE AS WORKCOUNTRYCODE, WORKTELEPHONENUMBER.AREACODE AS WORKAREACODE,
         WORKTELEPHONENUMBER.NUMBER AS WORKNUMBER, CUSTOMER.MOBILEPHONEID,
         MOBILETELEPHONENUMBER.COUNTRYCODE AS MOBILECOUNTRYCODE, MOBILETELEPHONENUMBER.AREACODE AS MOBILEAREACODE,
         MOBILETELEPHONENUMBER.NUMBER AS MOBILENUMBER, CUSTOMER.EMAILADDRESS
FROM     CUSTOMER INNER JOIN
         ADDRESS AS RESIDENCEADDRESS ON CUSTOMER.RESIDENCEADDRESSID = RESIDENCEADDRESS.ID INNER JOIN
         ADDRESS AS CORRESPONDENCEADDRESS ON CUSTOMER.CORRESPONDENCEADDRESSID = CORRESPONDENCEADDRESS.ID INNER JOIN
         CITY AS RESIDENCECITY ON RESIDENCEADDRESS.CITYID = RESIDENCECITY.ID INNER JOIN
         CITY AS CORRESPONDENCECITY ON CORRESPONDENCEADDRESS.CITYID = CORRESPONDENCECITY.ID INNER JOIN
         TELEPHONENUMBER AS WORKTELEPHONENUMBER ON CUSTOMER.WORKPHONEID = WORKTELEPHONENUMBER.ID INNER JOIN
         TELEPHONENUMBER AS MOBILETELEPHONENUMBER ON CUSTOMER.MOBILEPHONEID = MOBILETELEPHONENUMBER.ID INNER JOIN
         TELEPHONENUMBER AS HOMETELEPHONENUMBER ON CUSTOMER.HOMEPHONEID = HOMETELEPHONENUMBER.ID
WHERE    (CUSTOMER.ID = @ID)
```

Figure 7-12. *The final query generator SQL pane*

The SQL that we have seen in these screens now appears in the TableAdapter Configuration Wizard, page four. Angela could have pasted the SQL directly into this pane after creating it using any other SQL tool, like SQL Server 2005 Management Studio. She clicks Next and sees the page shown in Figure 7-13. If she wanted to preview the SQL she just generated, together with the rest of the SQL needed to generate a stored procedure in the database, Angela could click the button Preview SQL Script. On this page she names the SELECT stored procedure to be generated "GETCUSTOMER" and clicks Next.

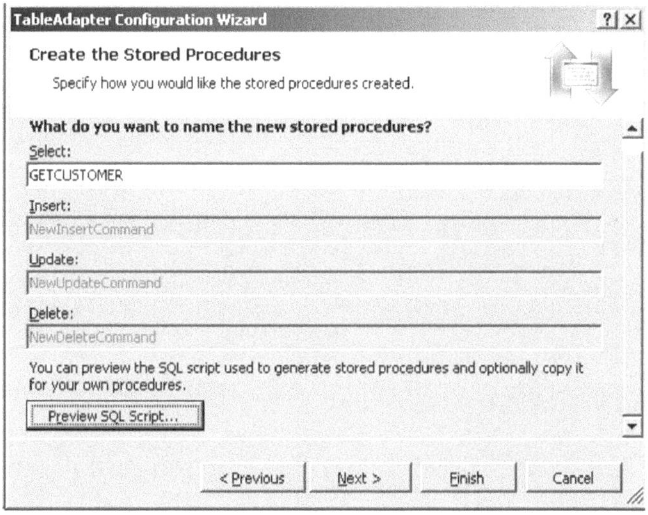

Figure 7-13. *The fifth page of the TableAdapter Configuration Wizard*

The sixth page allows Angela to specify whether she wants to generate a method that simply fills a `DataTable` and/or creates and returns a new `DataTable`. There will be several tables in the `CustomerDS` dataset and Angela expects the code to first create an instance of this dataset, then pass one of the tables within it to each of the table adapters in turn via their `Fill` function. So she selects the Fill a DataTable checkbox, as shown in Figure 7-14, and deselects the others.

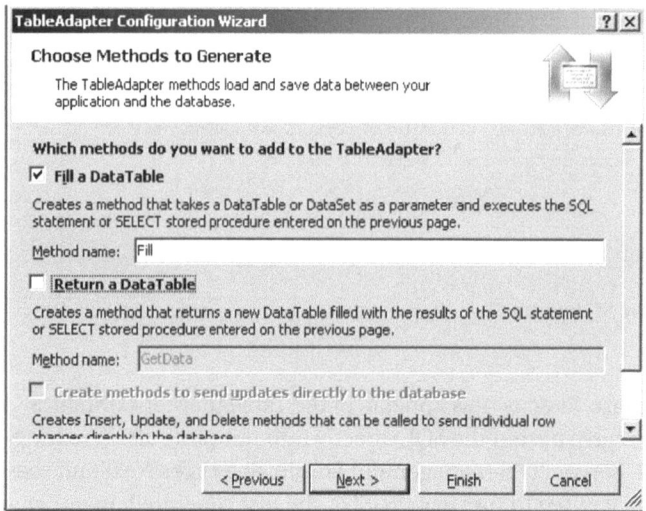

Figure 7-14. *The sixth page of the TableAdapter Configuration Wizard*

Figure 7-15 shows the wizard's last page, which summarizes what has been done. (The figure says it has generated `UPDATE` methods but the Generate Update, Insert and Delete SQL Statements option was not selected in the Advanced Options dialog box [Figure 7-7] and no `UPDATE` method is actually generated. I assume this is a bug.) Angela clicks Finish to complete the generation of the new table adapter.

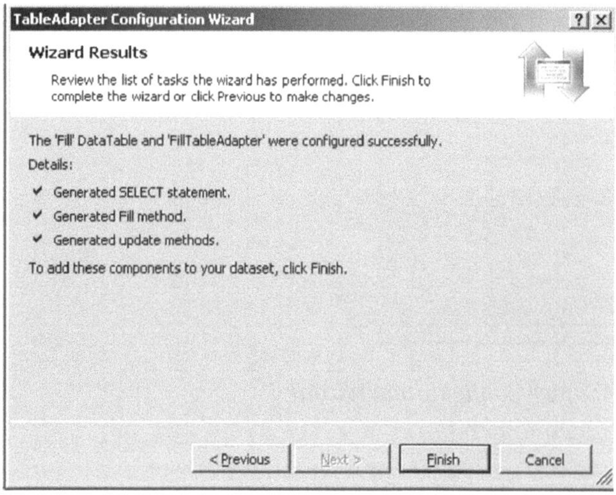

Figure 7-15. *The last page of the TableAdapter Configuration Wizard*

Angela has not yet finished with CustomerDS. In the architecture she and Peter designed, the CustomerDS dataset class will be used to bind to the controls on each tab page of the CustomerDetails control for each customer that is opened in the main Sales Wing screen. These controls will eventually allow the user to edit customer details (such as addresses, phone numbers, and orders) and save them back to the database. Although orders will be edited in a different dialog box bound to a different dataset, the orders belonging to a particular customer must be listed on one of the tabs in the CustomerDetails control.

As I mentioned, one aspect of customer details that may be edited is the addresses. As you saw in Chapter 6, those will contain combo box drop-down controls so that the user can select the state and country from a fixed list of states and countries prepopulated into the STATE and COUNTRY tables in the database. It is therefore necessary to have in the CustomerDS dataset two tables containing the state and country options. These are read-only tables. Of course, this is constant data and it would be nice to not have to transfer it over the Internet each time a new customer is opened and a CustomerDetails control populated. Peter should probably give some thought to caching this information on the clients somehow; perhaps it can be included within the offline working capability in some way, although it would definitely not be good practice to populate these combo box lists from constant data held within the code! For the moment, Angela is going to include STATE and COUNTRY tables in the CustomerDS dataset.

Angela still has CustomerDS open with the one table on it called by default GETCUSTOMER. She changes this to CUSTOMER by right-clicking, selecting Properties, typing the new name in the Name field, and pressing Enter.

Next, Angela drags another table adapter from the Toolbox onto the design surface and goes through the same wizard as before. This time the database connection is already present in the settings and is the default on the first page. On the second page, she selects the Create New Stored Procedures option again. On the third page, in the advanced options, she again deselects them all since this table is going to be populated with read-only lists of states. The query for the SELECT stored procedure is very simple—she only needs to add the STATE table— then on the Diagram pane she checks each of the three fields to be included in the output: ID, NAME, and CODE. That's all there is to it. She clicks the Execute Query button in the Query Builder, and sees all the states in the table come up before closing the Query Builder by clicking OK.

On the next wizard page, she names the SELECT stored procedure "GETSTATES". On the one after that she chooses to generate only the method called Fill to fill a DataTable. Again she changes the name of the table adapter from GETSTATES to STATES.

In a similar way, Angela adds a COUNTRY table adapter and creates a stored procedure called GETCOUNTRIES, which populates the table with all the fields of the COUNTRY table in the database.

The last table needed in the CustomerDS is a table called ORDER that contains a list of the orders that have been placed by that customer. There is a little more to this one. Angela drags another table adapter from the Toolbox onto the design surface and the wizard opens as usual. On page one, she accepts the same connection; on page two she clicks the Create New Stored Procedures option; and on page three she clicks the advanced options, clears all of the check-boxes as before, and opens the Query Builder. She selects just the ORDER table, and then checks the ID and ORDERDATE fields in the ORDER table in the Diagram pane. These columns will appear as output columns from the query in the Criteria pane. In the next empty column in this pane, she selects CUSTOMERID; in the first column of this pane, she types "=@ID" in the Filter column and unchecks the Output checkbox. She also selects ascending for the Sort Type column of the ORDERDATE field in this pane. The resulting query, shown in Figure 7-16, simply obtains all of the orders, in ascending order of date, whose CUSTOMERID field is set to a specified value passed in the parameter @CUSTOMERID.

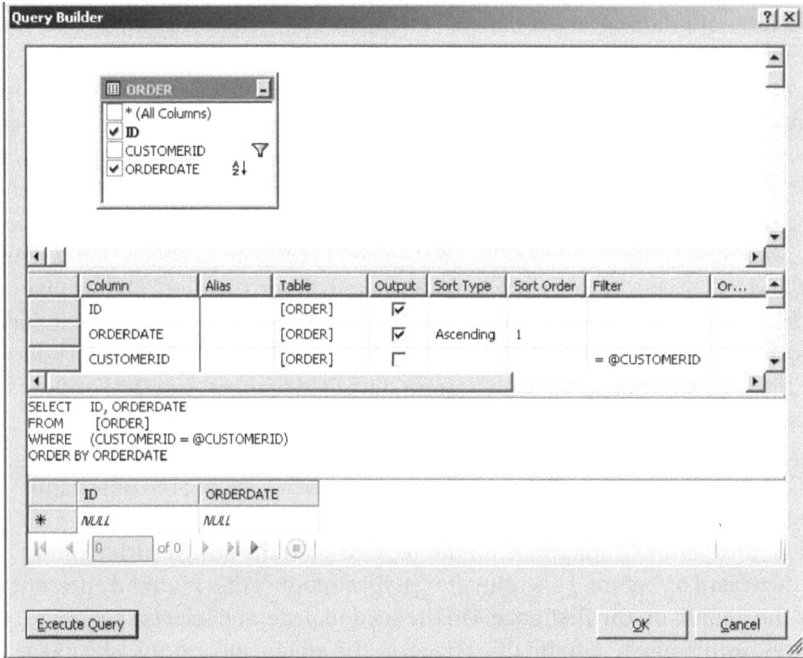

Figure 7-16. *Query Builder screen showing the ORDER select query*

On the next page of the TableAdapter Configuration Wizard, she names the SELECT stored procedure "GETORDERSFORCUSTOMER" and on the following page specifies that she wants to create only the Fill a DataTable method. She completes the wizard, changes the last table name to ORDER, and looks at the design surface of the completed CustomerDS dataset (which looks like Figure 7-17). Angela saves the dataset, then gets herself a well-earned cup of her favorite tea.

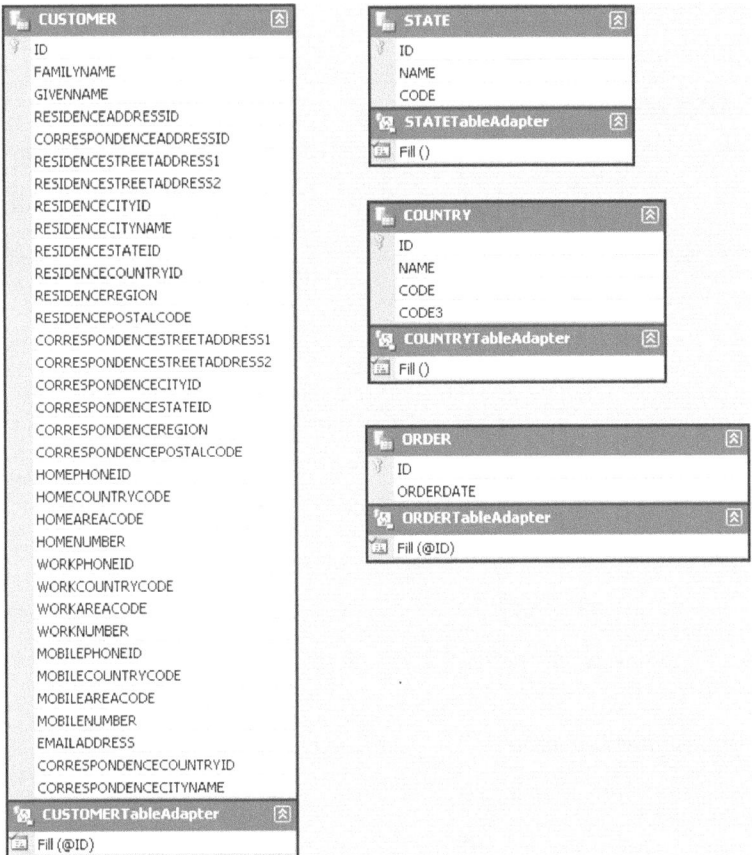

Figure 7-17. *The completed CustomerDS dataset*

What has Angela accomplished by all this work? Figure 7-18 shows the class view of the code that has been added to the CustomerDAL project by creation of the CustomerDS dataset. The project namespace is

com.icarustravel.enterprise31.Customer

and there have been two more namespaces created under that one:

com.icarustravel.enterprise31.Customer.CustomerDSTableAdapters
com.icarustravel.enterprise31.Customer.Properties

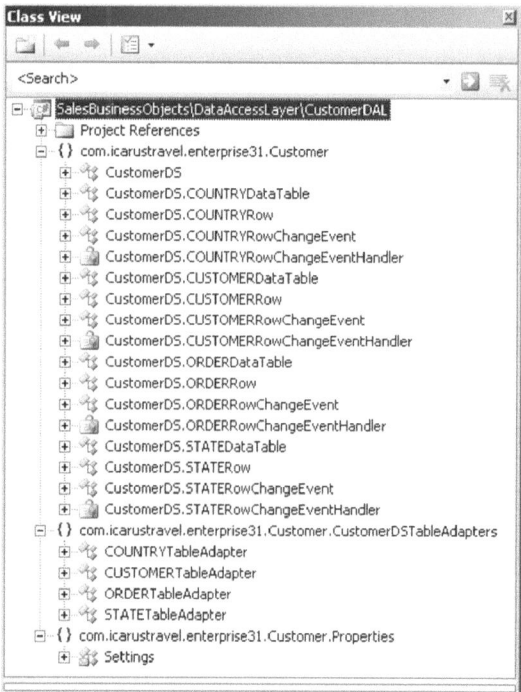

Figure 7-18. *Class view of the CustomerDAL project*

The classes in the project namespace begin with the CustomerDS class itself, but there are also specific classes for each of the three data tables and for the rows of each table. CustomerDS is derived from DataSet, the table classes are derived from DataTable, and the row classes are derived from DataRow. These specific classes have properties and methods that allow access to the named fields directly via similarly named properties. These are the characteristics of typed datasets. For example, Figure 7-19 shows the properties of the CUSTOMERRow class, which represent all of the fields in the row corresponding to columns in the CUSTOMER table that accept and return strongly typed values. From this we can see that typed datasets generated in this way make an excellent repository for the persistent data contained within a business entity class such as CustomerBE.

Figure 7-19. *Properties of the CustomerDS.CUSTOMERRow class*

The creation of the typed dataset has also resulted in a set of TableAdapter classes: COUNTRYTableAdapter, STATETableAdapter, CUSTOMERTableAdapter, and ORDERTableAdapter. Examining the class view, as shown in Figure 7-20, we can see that the only public methods on these classes aside from the constructors are their Fill functions, like

```
public virtual int Fill(CustomerDS.CUSTOMERDataTable dataTable, int ID)
```

By exposing the Fill functions, the table adapter classes provide the means of transferring the persistent data from the database to the in-memory representation of a business entity and therefore make up the data access layer, as I explained earlier.

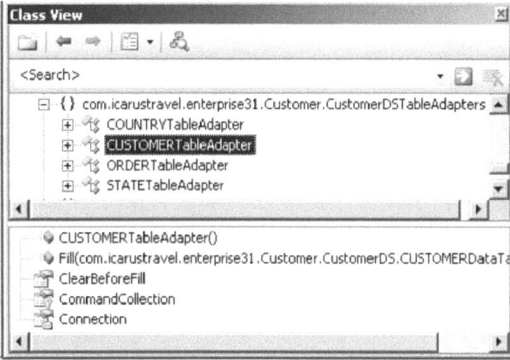

Figure 7-20. *Public properties and member functions of the CUSTOMERTableAdapter class*

Note The source code at this stage is in the folder Chapter 7\Exercise 1.

The CustomerSearchDS Dataset

A second dataset is needed for the open customer scenario, and will be called CustomerSearchDS. This dataset contains only one data table called CUSTOMERSEARCH, with an associated table adapter. This table will contain a list of customers found by the search that occurs when the Open Customer dialog box (see Chapter 6, Figure 6-6) is displayed and refreshed. Angela creates the dataset in the same way; its design looks like Figure 7-21.

Note The source code at this stage is in the folder Chapter 7\Exercise 1. Exercise 7-2 will help you understand this section.

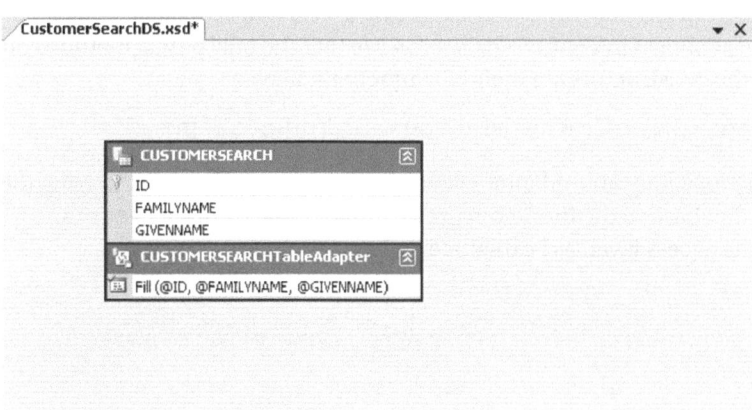

Figure 7-21. *The CustomerSearchDS dataset*

CUSTOMERSEARCHTableAdapter will only be used to read data and to populate the OpenCustomer Windows Form; therefore, CUSTOMERSEARCHTableAdapter only needs a Fill function, which uses a stored procedure called CUSTOMERSEARCH defined as follows:

```
CREATE PROCEDURE dbo.CUSTOMERSEARCH
(
  @ID nvarchar(10),
  @FAMILYNAME nvarchar(50),
  @GIVENNAME nvarchar(50)
)
AS
  SET NOCOUNT ON;
  SELECT ID, FAMILYNAME, GIVENNAME
  FROM CUSTOMER
  WHERE (CAST(ID AS CHAR(10)) LIKE @ID + N'%')
    AND (UPPER(FAMILYNAME) LIKE UPPER(@FAMILYNAME) + N'%')
    AND (UPPER(GIVENNAME) LIKE UPPER(@GIVENNAME) + N'%')
  ORDER BY FAMILYNAME, GIVENNAME
```

This procedure performs a wildcard search based on the ID, FAMILYNAME, and GIVENNAME parameters that are passed to it. A Fill function is automatically generated on the CUSTOMERSEARCHTableAdapter class.

Note The source code at this stage is in the folder Chapter 7\Exercise 2.

Problems with Web References

Angela next turns to the design of the business entity classes. When Peter creates the projects from the application diagram, those representing the SalesBusinessObjects and ListingBusinessObjects will have to be created manually. This is because they are represented on the application diagram as generic applications and this type of application cannot be implemented automatically by Application Designer. These projects will therefore be created as a set of class library projects, one for each area of business logic functionality. Let's first look in on the implementation of the CustomerBE class that Angela is working on.

"There's a bit of a problem with this architecture, Peter," Angela says as she wanders into Peter's cubicle.

"Oh," he replies, "what's that?"

"Well, it has to do with the web services. In the document that we put together describing the architecture, we have the business entity classes, like CustomerBE, calling the web service member functions as an alternative to using the data access layer to populate them from the local database."

"Yes, that's right. They are populated from the data access layer when coming from the client local database and from the Sales web service when coming from the remote server."

"Well," Angela says, "the Sales web service also needs to access the same business entity classes to respond to calls on its member functions. Suppose a Sales Wing user opens a customer.

That application then needs to call a static `Get` function on the `CustomerBE` class that will return a populated instance of `CustomerBE` for a specified ID."

"Right . . ."

"Well, if the user is online, the static `Get` function will call a function called `GetCustomer (int id)` on the web service and that function, running on the web server, will call the same static method on its own copy of the same `CustomerBE` class."

"Yes . . ."

"Well, the problem is that we've got a circular dependency at build time because the web service needs to reference the project containing the `CustomerBE` class and the `CustomerBE` class needs a web reference to the web service."

"Mmm, that's right," agrees Peter. They both think for a while. Peter lifts his coffee cup, finds it empty, and puts it down again. "But you know it's only a circular reference because you need to update the web reference in the `CustomerBE` project. You would not do that on every build. You'd check the code file that's generated when the reference is added—the proxy class— into TFS. Then when a team build is done, all the code is available."

"Yes, but what about when you add a member function to the Sales web service and call that function from the `CustomerBE` class? You can't build `CustomerBE` because the web refer- ence proxy class hasn't got the new function in it, and you can't update the web reference to `SalesWebService` since it won't build as it needs `CustomerBE`. This is how I found the problem!" she explains, exasperated.

"Of course, you can do the thing piecemeal," suggests Peter. "Build `CustomerBE` without the call to the new function, build the web service with the new function, update the web ref- erence, then add the call to the new function into `CustomerBE` and build again. That will work."

"Yes—well, that's what I've been doing actually," says Angela. "But it's not very good, is it? I mean we ought to define the project so the build process is straightforward." She thinks for a while. "I suppose generating the proxy classes is not *really* part of the build process. I mean, these proxy classes are based on an interface that ought to be defined as part of the architec- ture. We shouldn't forget that web services are really defined by WSDL and the web reference mechanism is only a convenient method for generating the proxy classes."

"Yes, that's true. Maybe we should define the web services using raw WSDL and generate the proxy classes from that. Or, of course, we could write the proxy classes from scratch."

WSDL (Web Service Definition Language) is a complete description of a web service written in XML and defines first the types, then the messages, and then the operations, the bindings, and the services. It's extremely wordy and not the sort of thing that humans want to look at very often—computers love it of course! There are graphical tools that will allow you to define a web service interface and generate the WSDL—so this is a possible way to go. In a sense it's a nice pure system architect's approach where the interfaces are defined first.

"I suppose the WSDL really should define the interface rather than the code," agrees Peter reluctantly. "And I really should maintain that WSDL. For the time being, though, to get us along quickly, I've got an idea. Do you remember that in my first application diagram, I included stub applications, `SalesWebServiceStub` and `ListingWebServiceStub`? Why don't we base the WSDL on those applications? They can build without using the Sales business objects, so they can be early in the build order, and then we can update the web references based on WSDL generated from them."

"That means we have two web services with the same name hosted on our development machines. I'm not sure how that will work," says Angela. "But I think I should try it that way and see how it goes."

Let's get a bit ahead of Angela and Peter and see how this works out in Visual Studio 2005. First, what happens when you want to debug a web service project in a solution? The easiest way to do this is to use the ASP.NET Development Server, which is built into Visual Studio 2005 and is designed to serve pages that are requested locally, using a URL beginning with something like `http://localhost:12345/`. Each web application is assigned a randomly numbered port on the development server (or you can specify a fixed one), and instances of the Development Server servicing that port will start up when you run the debugger. There is therefore nothing to stop you from defining a stub web service and a real web service in the same solution since they will have different ports under the Development Server. You can then add to projects web references to either one or the other, and when the web references are updated, an instance of the Development Server will start up servicing the port required.

In this solution, however, the team wants to use the stubs to define the web reference and then make that reference actually access a different URL when the application runs. To do this, the user can change the settings for the URL after the web reference has been updated. The setting to change is the `CustomerBE_SalesWS_SalesWebService`, which is generated automatically from the web reference and is in the `App.config` file for the class library project. It can be accessed via the `Settings.settings` file in the Properties folder of the project. After build, though, these settings are included in the assembly containing the class library project and cannot be modified during deployment. Another problem is that every time the user updates the web reference from the stub web service, this setting is changed back to point to the stub web service.

A better way is to write code such that the web service URL property of the proxy is set when an instance of the proxy is created and used to access the web service. The setting to be used can then be placed in a `.config` file for the application and its value adjusted during deployment.

The Sales Web Service Stub

Peter needs to create the web services by implementation from the application diagram. They were defined on his application diagram for the entire project (Chapter 5) and then updated (Chapter 6) to be specific to the iteration. The diagram Peter uses is `Enterprise 3.1.ad` in the Enterprise 3.1 POC solution, which he created in Chapter 6. First, he verifies that the properties of the web services applications are correct, in particular (and most important) that the language that defaults to VB .NET has been changed to C#. Implementation is a simple matter of right-clicking on the application in the application diagram and selecting Implement Application from the context menu. Peter implements both the `SalesWebService` and the `SalesWebServiceStub` applications, shown in Chapter 6, Figure 6-23, as file system websites.

Note The source code at this stage is in the folder `Chapter 7\Exercise 2`. Exercise 7-3 will help you understand this section.

Working in the Enterprise 3.1 POC solution, Angela writes the code for the `SalesWebServiceStub`, first adding a reference to the `CustomerDS` project that she wrote earlier in this chapter. That way, she can define the web methods as returning this typed dataset. Then she adds two methods:

```csharp
using com.icarustravel.enterprise31.Customer;

namespace com.icarustravel.enterprise31.SalesWebService
{
    [System.Web.Services.WebServiceBinding(Name = "SalesWebService",
        ConformsTo = System.Web.Services.WsiProfiles.BasicProfile1_1,
        EmitConformanceClaims = true,
        Namespace = "http://webservices.enterprise31.icarustravel.com/"),
     System.Web.Services.Protocols.SoapDocumentService(),
     System.Web.Services.WebService(
        Namespace = "http://webservices.enterprise31.icarustravel.com/")]
    public class SalesWebService : System.Web.Services.WebService
    {
        // Get a customer defined by ID
        [System.Web.Services.WebMethod()]
        public CustomerDS GetCustomer(int id)
        {
            return new CustomerDS();
        }

        // Get a collection of customers defined by search criteria
        [System.Web.Services.WebMethod()]
        public CustomerSearchDS GetCustomerBySearch(
                               string id, string familyName, string givenName)
        {
            return new CustomerSearchDS();
        }
    }
}
```

The real web service will define these web methods so that they create instances of the CustomerBE and CustomerSearchBE and call static Get functions on them, as we will see later.

Note The source code at this stage is in the folder `Chapter 7\Exercise 3`.

Business Entities and Datasets

The team plans to make Sales Wing a Windows Forms application with a set of forms that allow the user to step through its various business processes. Each form will contain an assortment of controls such as labels, text boxes, combo boxes, and data grid view controls. There are two ways of populating these controls from the data retrieved from the database for a business entity such as a customer. One method is to write code that explicitly writes values to the various properties of the controls on the forms for display to the user, and reads the values of these properties back to pick up values entered by the user. The other method is to use "bound" controls. Data binding means that the one or more properties of the control are associated with a data source, which can take a variety of forms, the most general of which is an object. A data member string added to the binding specifies the path within the object to the property whose value is to be bound to the specified property of the control. The value of the property on the control is, by default, updated from the property on the object when the value of that property changes. Similarly, the value of the property in the object is, by default, updated from the control when the value of the control property is validated. Many controls such as `ListBox`, `ComboBox`, and `DataGridView`, require that the data source implement the `IList` or `IListSource` interface, since these controls require a list of values to which they can be bound.

Whether or not data binding is used in an application such as Sales Wing is a matter of choice. People debate whether the use of data binding is really simpler than explicitly setting the value of a property from code. Data binding is an implicit thing that takes place behind the scenes, established by the setting of a number of properties on the Design view of the Windows Form, and it can be more difficult to track down problems when data binding is used compared to when properties in controls are set explicitly. Nevertheless, data binding can accomplish a lot on the screen with a very small amount of work on the part of the developer and requires a small amount of code to maintain.

Some applications contain `DataSets` on the Windows Forms, which can be populated directly from a database when the form loads. This has been a feature of .NET (and before that, VB6 and Visual C++) applications for a long time. This approach is essentially a client-server approach, as described in Chapter 1, since it requires all of the business logic to be either on the client or in the database. This approach is not being used in the project described in this book.

For a long time now, the idea of encapsulating business logic into some kind of *entity*, *business process*, or *session* class has been a popular architectural concept in both the .NET and the Java J2EE environments. Some business objects mainly store data with little or no actual coded logic, whereas others need a great amount of functionality coded into them. As an example, in this application it will be necessary to calculate the cost of a reservation and then the cost of an entire order. Although the team has not yet explored this area, it is likely that there will be a fair amount of code required to do this under different discounting arrangements, commission agreements, and taxation environments as well as the need for conversion between currencies.

Datasets, implemented by the `DataSet` class, or inheriting this class, are an important concept in .NET and we have already discussed their use with table adapters to form the data access layer. They are like databases in miniature in that they can contain tables and relations between the tables in the same way as relational databases. They are therefore an excellent means of storing the data held within a business entity such as a customer, where there might be one row of data containing the fields relating to the customer as a person—family name, given name, residence address, etc.—and a set of rows containing summary information about the orders that exist that were placed by that customer. We also might elect to contain within such a Customer business entity the line items of each order—the reservations, in fact; or we might only retrieve those rows from the database when an individual order belonging to a customer is to be displayed in detail. These scenarios have been set out in the previous chapter. So you can see that business entities typically have a tree-like structure, with a base collection of data and sets of other identically structured collections of data that are well suited to being held in the form of a `DataSet`. Remember that I am talking here about the in-memory representation of a business entity, the Customer business entity, which we now assume will be encapsulated within a class called `CustomerBE`.

When there is considerable programmed logic to be contained in the business entity, it may be better to store the data in a form suited to the processes to be performed. For example, storing collections of data in a hash table or array may facilitate access of the data by the algorithms making up the business logic. If for instance, we need a table within a business entity containing a long list of vendors and we wish to access them quite frequently by name, it might be better to store the vendor objects in a hash table rather than a table in a DataSet. Although we can pick a row from a table easily in a DataSet using the DataTable.Select() function, it may be much more efficient to access the data if it is stored in a hash table because the data in a hash table is organized to be quickly accessible by means of a key. However, an object of the DataView class can be defined for a DataSet, to which indexes may be added to make access using the Select member function quicker. Thus, the issue is not clear-cut and each case has to be examined for its own merits. DataSet classes are so convenient that it's often hard not to use them!

A business entity object is an instance of a class of business entities of a particular type, like customers, vendors, orders, and so forth. When we speak of an *entity* we mean an instance of a class of objects that exists over a long period of time—in other words, it is a *persistent* object. Of course, we may use a class to represent a customer in some software that exists only while the software runs, or maybe just while a particular function executes, and when its purpose has been accomplished it is lost by going out of scope. A business entity is more than this; it has an in-memory representation and also a *persistent* representation, which could be a row in a flat file or a single row in a table in a database. Certainly, for the customer business entity that we have been talking about, there will be a representation in the main database that may look very much like the DataSet described in the previous paragraph. However, the CUSTOMER table that the Icarus team defined in their data model meeting will have not just one customer but many rows representing many customers. The ADDRESS and TELEPHONENUMBER tables will have multiple rows *for each customer* as the TELEPHONENUMBER table will contain three telephone numbers for each customer, foreign-keyed to a single row in the CUSTOMER table. The ADDRESS table will have two rows for each customer foreign-keyed to a single row in the CUSTOMER table.

Thus, we might say that the in-memory representation of a business entity such as this has a *footprint* in the database, and if we represent the data within the in-memory entity in a DataSet, the tables in that dataset can be the same as the tables in the database and contain a very small subset of the rows in the database tables. It is a pretty routine task in these circumstances to write the code to transfer the necessary rows between the database tables and the in-memory dataset tables, and this of course is the job done by the table adapters and their stored procedures.

The Business Entity Layer

Angela spent the morning reading the document Peter found for her about adapters and developing typed datasets. In the afternoon, a discussion takes place between Angela, Peter, and Charles about the form the business entities should take. Angela has suggested that they should be derived from the typed datasets so that, for example CustomerBE would inherit from CustomerDS. Then the web service member functions would return classes like these. Peter has some concerns about the serialization of these classes and feels that there would be confusion about what would be transferred over the Internet. Some objects within the business entity classes would not be serializable to XML, and these members would need to be marked as nonserialized. This would lead to confusion about how much of the object was being passed over the Internet and also feels too much like .NET Remoting or DCOM, rather than a service-oriented architecture. He thinks that it may be advantageous to derive the entity classes from a common base, which would provide other useful inherited capability—such as perhaps something in support of the offline working. This will be impossible if they derive the classes from the typed datasets.

Note The source code at this stage is in the folder `Chapter 7\Exercise 3`. Doing Exercise 7-4 will help you understand this section.

In the end they agree, as a starting point, that the business entity objects will communicate their entire persistent data in the form of their typed datasets (although they may in some circumstances hold the data in a different form internally). A constructor may be defined for each business entity object that will take its corresponding typed dataset and the typed dataset will also be exposed as a read/write property:

```
public CustomerBE(CustomerDS data)
{
    ....
}
```

and

```
public CustomerDS Data
{
   Get{ ... }
   Set{ ... }
}
```

This enables business entities to be readily populated with data from the dataset and also for their data to be easily extracted.

Business Entity Base Classes

After this discussion, Angela gets back to work. She wants to write the business entity base classes first, since all business entity classes must inherit from them, so she creates a new solution folder and calls it `Framework`. She right-clicks on this folder and selects Add ➤ New Project. In the Add New Project dialog box, under Project Types she selects Visual C#, then Windows. Then, under Visual Studio Installed Templates, she selects Class Library. Angela types in the name "BusinessEntity" and clicks OK. She deletes the `Class1` class automatically created, goes into the project properties, and sets the namespace to

`com.icarustravel.enterprise31.BusinessEntity`

She then creates a class, `BusinessEntityBE`, and types in the following code:

```
namespace com.icarustravel.enterprise31.BusinessEntity
{
    public abstract class BusinessEntityBE
    {
        public enum InstallMode
        {
            SERVER = 0,
            CLIENT = 1
        }

        private static InstallMode installedMode = InstallMode.SERVER;

        public static InstallMode InstalledMode
        {
            get { return installedMode; }
            set{ installedMode = value; }
        }

        DataSet data;
    }
}
```

This class contains some base functionality. First, it contains a DataSet that will hold a typed dataset containing the instance data for the object. Second, it contains a flag, installedMode, to indicate whether this particular instance of the business entity is installed on a client or a server. The flag is static, so it will only need to be set once for all the different derived classes and their instances. This flag can be used to determine whether the persistence action is via a web service URL, for a client business entity, or to a database for a server entity instance. An enum is defined called InstallMode with two values, and a public property is added to access it. The installedMode variable is initialized so it defaults to SERVER mode.

Customer Business Entity

Angela now right-clicks on the SalesBusinessObjects folder and selects Add ➤ New Project. In the Add New Project dialog box, under Project Types she once again selects Visual C#, then Windows. Then, under Visual Studio Installed Templates, she selects Class Library. She types in the name "CustomerBE" and clicks OK, and then goes into the project properties and sets the namespace to

com.icarustravel.enterprise31.Customer

She adds a reference to the CustomerDAL project and then creates a class, CustomerBE. She intends CustomerBE to inherit from BusinessEntityBE, so she adds a reference to the BusinessEntity project and a using directive for its namespace:

using com.icarustravel.enterprise31.BusinessEntity;

She can then make CustomerBE derive from BusinessEntityBE:

```
public class CustomerBE : BusinessEntityBE
{
}
```

She knows pretty much what she wants to do. She needs a static function in `CustomerBE` that will take an integer ID and return a populated instance of `CustomerBE`:

```
public static CustomerBE Get(int id)
{
  CustomerBE customerBE = new CustomerBE();

  // (Code to fill it from the database)

  return customerBE;
}
```

The code to fill the object from the database will do one of the following:

- Create a copy of `CustomerDS` and populate it from the database table by table using the table adapters that were created for each table.

- Call a web service that will return a `CustomerDS` dataset. Having obtained the populated `CustomerDS`, it will then store it in the instance of `CustomerBE` before returning the `CustomerBE` instance.

The business entity object instances, created by a web service that acts as the remote server source for the data, will always use the first option. Business objects on the client, however, can use either option. If the client is disconnected, it will have to use the first option, but if it is connected, it will use the second method. The code that does this ought to be similar for most types of business entities, such as `OrderBE`, `ResourceBE`, and so on, so it would be nice to put it into the base `BusinessEntityBE` class. Angela could write a `Fill` function something like this:

```
protected void Fill(int id)
{
    if (InstalledMode == InstallMode.CLIENT)
    {
        SalesWS.SalesWebService salesWebService = new SalesWS.SalesWebService();
        data = salesWebService.GetCustomer(id);
    }
    else
    {
        CustomerDS customerDS = new CustomerDS();
        new COUNTRYTableAdapter().Fill(customerDS.COUNTRY);
        new STATETableAdapter().Fill(customerDS.STATE);
        new ORDERTableAdapter().Fill(customerDS.ORDER, id);
        new CUSTOMERTableAdapter().Fill(customerDS.CUSTOMER, id);
        data = customerDS;
    }
}
```

where the function `SalesWebService.GetCustomer(int id)` looks like this:

```
namespace com.icarustravel.enterprise31.SalesWebService
{
    [System.Web.Services.WebServiceBinding(
                Name = "SalesWebService",
                ConformsTo = System.Web.Services.WsiProfiles.BasicProfile1_1,
                EmitConformanceClaims = true,
                Namespace = "http://webservices.enterprise31.icarustravel.com/"),
     System.Web.Services.Protocols.SoapDocumentService(),
     System.Web.Services.WebService(Namespace =
                    "http://webservices.enterprise31.icarustravel.com/")
    ]
    public class SalesWebService : System.Web.Services.WebService
    {
        [System.Web.Services.WebMethod()]
        public CustomerDS GetCustomer(int id)
        {
            return CustomerBE.Get(id).Data;
        }
    }
}
```

For iteration 2, there will need to be some other logic in the `Fill` function to determine whether the client is offline and to access the local database via the `else` clause if that is the case. Angela cannot place this function in the base class `BusinessEntityBE` because it uses classes and functions that are specific to `CustomerBE`—that is, `SalesWebService`, `GetCustomer` (`int id`), `CustomerDS`, and the four table adapters.

There is another problem that Peter mentions when she talks to him about it. "Actually, you're going to have two different classes derived from `DataSet` stored in the base class `data` field, depending on whether that function uses the local or remote branch to fill the dataset," he points out.

"Why?" asked Angela in surprise. "Surely the web method returns `CustomerDS` and the `else` clause that fills it locally creates an instance of `CustomerDS`."

"Well, but if we generate the web service proxy classes from the `SalesWebService` stub class like we said earlier, the proxy will generate its own version of the `CustomerDS` class. That class will have a different namespace depending on the name you give to the web reference," explains Peter. "If you call the web reference `SalesWS`, the class in the proxy will have this name." He writes on the whiteboard.

```
com.icarustravel.enterprise31.Customer.SalesWS.CustomerDS
```

"Whereas the other has this name," he continues.

```
com.icarustravel.enterprise31.Customer.CustomerDS
```

"And so with that 'SalesWS' string added into the namespace, it's a totally different class. The proxy is created from the WSDL definition of the types used in the messages—that's all it has to go on. Of course, you can create your own proxy class—it just has to unpack the XML in the SOAP message and populate an instance of `CustomerDS`—but we don't really want to have to bother with that right now."

"Besides, it's useful to generate them automatically as we will want to modify the web service and data model, I expect," adds Angela. "So CustomerDS will then need to change. Can't I just do a cast in the Fill function?" She writes this on the whiteboard:

```
CustomerDS data = (CustomerDS)salesWebService.GetCustomer(id);
```

"No that won't compile," says Peter. "But this will work."

```
CustomerDS data = new CustomerDS();
data.Merge(salesWebService.GetCustomer(id));
```

"I see," says Angela. "We are copying the tables and rows into a DataSet of the correct type, which we know has the same structure. But won't that degrade the performance?"

"We'll need to investigate that," says Peter. "Maybe there's a better way, but this will make it work for iteration 1."

Angela goes back to her desk and modifies her Fill function code to look like this:

```
protected void Fill(int id)
{
    if (InstalledMode == InstallMode.CLIENT)
    {
        SalesWS.SalesWebService salesWebService = new SalesWS.SalesWebService();
        data = new CustomerDS();
        data.Merge(salesWebService.GetCustomer(id));
    }
    else
    {
        CustomerDS customerDS = new CustomerDS();
        new COUNTRYTableAdapter().Fill(customerDS.COUNTRY);
        new STATETableAdapter().Fill(customerDS.STATE);
        new ORDERTableAdapter().Fill(customerDS.ORDER, id);
        new CUSTOMERTableAdapter().Fill(customerDS.CUSTOMER, id);
        data = customerDS;
    }
}
```

■ **Note** The source code at this stage is in the folder Chapter 7\Exercise 4. Doing Exercise 7-5 will help you understand the remainder of this section.

"Why bother to have a base class, if there's nothing in it but one dataset?" says Angela to herself. "And I've not even added the logic yet to detect an offline situation. This really should go into the BusinessEntityBE class!"

Suddenly the word *generics* flashes into her mind. Maybe she can write the base class so that it can be parameterized to handle whatever type of DataSet is used by the specific business entity class. It will still need to use specific code in the derived class to access the table adapters and the web service, but the basic mechanism of the Fill function can be inherited. She spends the next hour thinking and typing, and here are the results:

DualPersistBE Class

```
namespace com.icarustravel.enterprise31.BusinessEntity
{
  public abstract class DualPersistBE
  {
    public enum InstallMode
    {
      SERVER = 0,
      CLIENT = 1
    }

    private static InstallMode installedMode = InstallMode.SERVER;

    public static InstallMode InstalledMode
    {
      get { return installedMode; }
      set{ installedMode = value; }
    }
  }
}
```

BusinessEntityBE Class

```
namespace com.icarustravel.enterprise31.BusinessEntity
{
  public abstract class BusinessEntityBE<LocalDSType, RemoteDSType> : DualPersistBE
    where LocalDSType : DataSet, new()
    where RemoteDSType : DataSet, new()
  {

    protected LocalDSType data;
    protected static string wSURL = null;

    public LocalDSType Data
    {
      get { return this.data; }
      set { this.data = value; }
    }

    protected BusinessEntityBE()
    {
    }

    protected BusinessEntityBE(LocalDSType data)
    {
      this.data = data;
    }
```

```
static BusinessEntityBE()
{
  if (InstalledMode == InstallMode.CLIENT)
  {
    Configuration exeConfiguration =
        ConfigurationManager.OpenExeConfiguration(ConfigurationUserLevel.None);
    if (exeConfiguration != null)
    {
      ConfigurationSectionGroup settingsSectionGroup =
          exeConfiguration.SectionGroups["applicationSettings"];
      if (settingsSectionGroup != null)
      {
        ConfigurationSection settingsSection = settingsSectionGroup.Sections[
            "com.icarustravel.enterprise31.BusinessEntity.Properties.Settings"];

        if (settingsSection != null)
        {
          SettingElement settingElement =
            ((System.Configuration.ClientSettingsSection)
            (settingsSection)).Settings.Get(
                                "BusinessEntityBE_SalesWS_SalesWebService");

          if (settingElement != null)
          {
            wSURL = settingElement.Value.ValueXml.InnerText;
          }
        }
      }
    }
  }
}

protected void Fill(int id)
{
  data = new LocalDSType();

  if (InstalledMode == InstallMode.CLIENT)
  {
      data.Merge(GetRemoteData(id));
  }
  else
  {
      GetLocalData(id);
  }
}
```

```csharp
    protected virtual RemoteDSType GetRemoteData(int id)
    {
      return new RemoteDSType();
    }

    protected virtual void GetLocalData(int id)
    {
    }
  }
}
```

CustomerBE Class

```csharp
namespace com.icarustravel.enterprise31.Customer
{
  public class CustomerBE : BusinessEntityBE<CustomerDS, SalesWS.CustomerDS>
  {
    private CustomerBE() : base()
    {
    }

    protected override SalesWS.CustomerDS GetRemoteData(int id)
    {
      SalesWS.SalesWebService salesWebService = new SalesWS.SalesWebService();
      if (wSURL != null)
      {
        salesWebService.Url = wSURL;
      }

      return salesWebService.GetCustomer(id);
    }

    protected override void GetLocalData(int id)
    {
      new COUNTRYTableAdapter().Fill(data.COUNTRY);
      new STATETableAdapter().Fill(data.STATE);
      new ORDERTableAdapter().Fill(data.ORDER, id);
      new CUSTOMERTableAdapter().Fill(data.CUSTOMER, id);
    }

    public static CustomerBE Get(int id)
    {
      CustomerBE customerBE = new CustomerBE();
      customerBE.Fill(id);
      return customerBE;
    }

    public static DataTable GetData(int id, string tableName)
    {
      return Get(id).data.Tables[tableName];
```

```
        }
    }
}
```

The three classes defined here are shown in Figure 7-22 (which incidentally is the first Visual Studio 2005 class diagram that we've seen so far in the book; we'll be using them more later on). First there is a new ultimate base class, DualPersistBE, which represents the most general concept of a business entity that can be persisted both locally and remotely. Second, there is the BusinessEntityBE, which has become a generic class, and third, there is the specific business entity class CustomerBE. We will see other derived classes, like CustomerSearchBE, later.

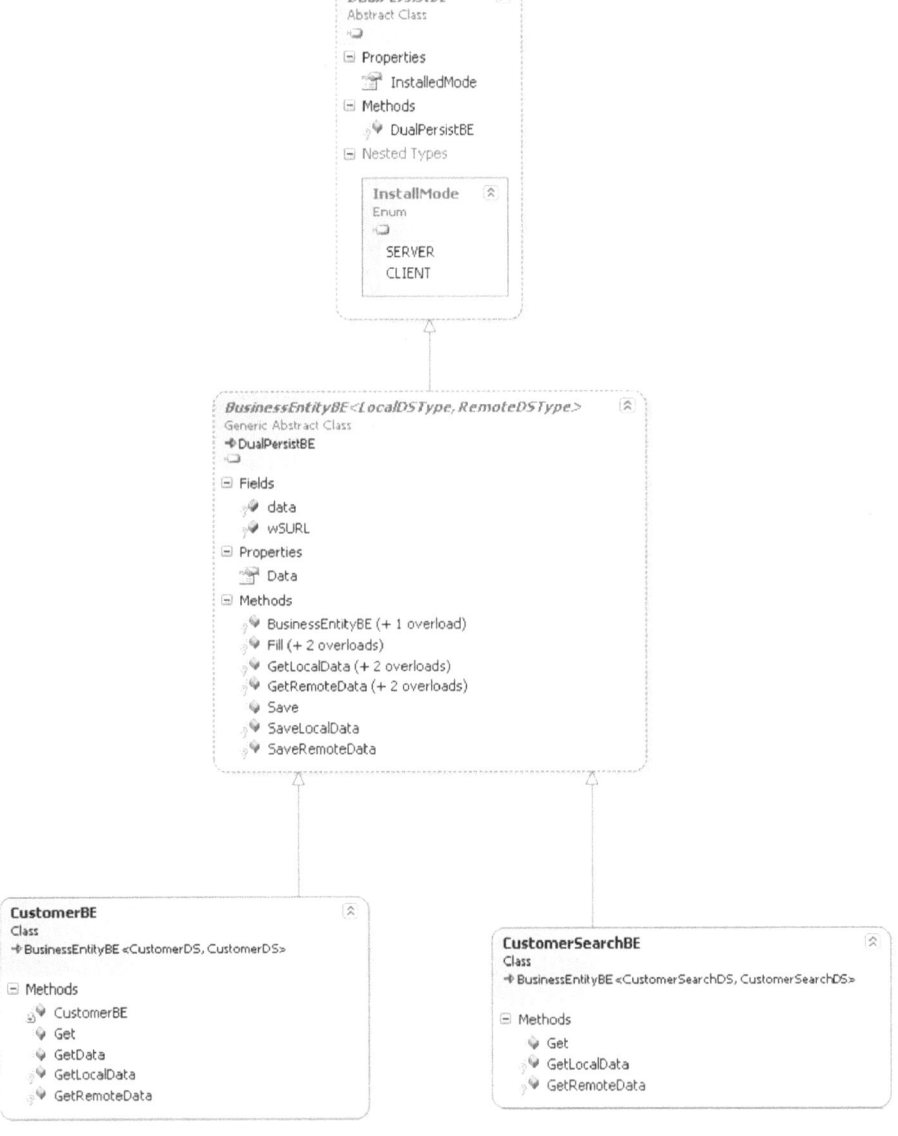

Figure 7-22. *Class diagram of the CustomerBE class structure*

Generic classes combine reusability and type safety in a way that nongenerics cannot. They do this by allowing the class definition to specify *type parameters*, which allow the class to take on specific features when it is used rather than when it is designed. Type parameters allow one or more types within the class to be passed to the class when a reference to an instance of it is declared and when the constructor is called. In the definition of the class, the type parameters appear within angle brackets after the name of the class. When an instance of the class is created, the types that are to be the values of those parameters are passed in similar angle brackets in the code.

The class as written with its type parameters is generic in the sense that it can perform actions that deal with objects that may have a type that is unknown when the class is written. Sometimes, however, the code in the generic class needs to make assumptions about the types that will be given when an instance of the generic class is created so that it will compile. For this reason, *constraints* can be applied to the type parameters that specify these assumptions. Only a certain set of constraints is allowed by the language. For instance, a type parameter can be constrained so that it always must be a particular class or a class derived from that class. The code within the generic class can then make that assumption and it will compile. Let's suppose that there is a class Dog that has a member function Bark(); a type parameter could be constrained that it must be a class derived from Dog, such as Greyhound. Since Greyhound is derived from Dog, it will always have the function Bark() so the code in the generic class can call Bark() on instances of the class represented by the type parameter and the code will compile.

Also, a type parameter may be constrained to be a type for which a public parameterless constructor is present. In this case the code within the generic class may use the new keyword to create an instance of the class represented by the type parameter.

This idea is used in the BusinessEntityBE class, which is parameterized as a generic class in two ways by the definition of two type parameters, LocalDSType and RemoteDSType, constrained to be derived from DataSet, as shown in the definition repeated here:

```
public abstract class BusinessEntityBE<LocalDSType, RemoteDSType> : DualPersistBE
        where LocalDSType : DataSet, new()
        where RemoteDSType : DataSet, new()
{
```

The parameters are also both constrained to support the new keyword and must therefore both have a public, parameterless constructor. The LocalDSType parameter allows BusinessEntityBE to define the field variable data and its accessor in terms of the strong type. The Fill function has been moved to the BusinessEntityBE class and defined in terms of the type parameters. To perform the actual remote and local parts of the fill, virtual functions have been defined, again using the type parameters:

```
protected virtual RemoteDSType GetRemoteData(int id)
{
    return new RemoteDSType();
}

protected virtual void GetLocalData(int id)
{
}
```

These are expected to be overridden by inheriting classes such as CustomerBE. Although BusinessEntityBE is abstract and we do not intend to create instances of it, none of its member functions are actually abstract; default functions are provided for these two virtual functions that return empty, but valid, DataSets of the type specified. Thus, it is possible to derive a class that does not provide both local and remote persistence.

The new CustomerBE, however, does override both of these virtual functions. For the remote case, the overriding function

```
protected override SalesWS.CustomerDS GetRemoteData(int id)
```

calls the correct web service and returns an instance of the RemoteDSType class—of course derived from DataSet. In the local case, the overriding function

```
protected override void GetLocalData(int id)
```

simply populates all the tables in the data field variable, which it knows to be of the correct type CustomerDS.

We need to look at one other thing in the BusinessEntityBE code. Earlier discussions between Peter and other members of the team concerned the use of the stub web service to generate the proxy. This results in the URL for the stub web service being placed in the proxy, and this is not correct for testing with the real web service, even locally on the developer's machine. In any case, the URL that is placed in the proxy when it is generated for the web reference is seldom correct for the production or test installations. It therefore must be supplied in a .config file at install time. Unfortunately, class library assemblies do not have application .config files, so the settings that can be added to a class library project cannot be modified in a .config file at install time. We must devise a method to allow these classes to extract such settings as the web service's URL for various types of business entities from the application .config file. Thus, code has been included in a static constructor for the BusinessEntityBE class, which uses a call to the .NET ConfigurationManager class to open the configuration file for the executable

```
Configuration exeConfiguration =
    ConfigurationManager.OpenExeConfiguration(ConfigurationUserLevel.None);
```

and then reads the value of a setting called

```
CustomerBE_SalesWS_SalesWebService
```

This setting contains the URL of the web service required by the CustomerBE business entity.

Note The source code at this stage is in the folder Chapter 7\Exercise 5.

Customer Search Business Entity

This business entity represented by a class CustomerSearchBE has a similar class inheritance structure; it also appears in Figure 7-22.

Note The source code at this stage is in the folder `Chapter 7\Exercise 5`. Doing Exercise 7-6 will help you understand this section.

The static `Get` function for this class needs to specify search parameters—rather more than just an integer id value. To implement the static `Get` function for this class, Angela therefore needs to extend the base class functionality somewhat. A new generalized `Fill` function must be defined in the base class `BusinessEntityBE` and corresponding virtual functions `GetRemoteData` and `GetLocalData`, as shown next. The new `Fill` function in the base class takes an array of objects, which can be any set of objects that specifies the identity of the entities to be returned. In this case it is the three strings representing the first characters of the ID, the family name, and the given name of the customer. It is up to the derived class to interpret them as it defines them. Of course, this is not quite type safe and there is some further scope for the use of generic capabilities here, to perhaps define a third type parameter in the `BusinessEntityBE` class to define some sort of qualifier object class (which could be an integer for a simple get by ID or a more complex object for a search operation such as this). Anyway, for iteration 1, this is the code Angela wrote:

```
protected void Fill(object[] objects)
{
  data = new LocalDSType();

  if (InstalledMode == InstallMode.CLIENT)
  {
    data.Merge(GetRemoteData(objects));
  }
  else
  {
    GetLocalData(objects);
  }
}

protected virtual RemoteDSType GetRemoteData(object[] objects)
{
  return new RemoteDSType();
}

protected virtual void GetLocalData(object[] objects)
{
}
```

The code for the derived class, `CustomerSearchBE`, is shown here:

```
namespace com.icarustravel.enterprise31.Customer
{
  public class CustomerSearchBE
      : BusinessEntityBE<CustomerSearchDS, SalesWS.CustomerSearchDS>
```

```
{
  protected override SalesWS.CustomerSearchDS GetRemoteData(
                                    object[] searchStrings)
  {
    SalesWS.SalesWebService salesWebService = new SalesWS.SalesWebService();
    if (wSURL != null)
    {
      salesWebService.Url = wSURL;
    }

    return salesWebService.GetCustomerBySearch((string)searchStrings[0],
      (string)searchStrings[1], (string)searchStrings[2]);
  }

  protected override void GetLocalData(object[] searchStrings)
  {
    new CUSTOMERSEARCHTableAdapter().Fill(
          data.CUSTOMERSEARCH, (string)searchStrings[0],
          (string)searchStrings[1], (string)searchStrings[2]);
  }

  public static CustomerSearchBE Get(string id,
                  string familyName, string givenName)
  {
    CustomerSearchBE customerSearchBE = new CustomerSearchBE();
    customerSearchBE.Fill(new string[] { id, familyName, givenName });
    return customerSearchBE;
  }
}
}
```

This concludes our examination of Angela's work in designing the business entity classes needed for the open and close customer scenarios.

Note The source code at this stage is in the folder `Chapter 7\Exercise 6`.

The Sales Web Service

The Sales web service at iteration 1, needed to demonstrate the open and close customer scenarios, exposes two web methods, as shown in the code that follows.

Note The source code at this stage is in the folder `Chapter 7\Exercise 6`. Exercise 7-7 will help you understand this section.

```
namespace com.icarustravel.enterprise31.BookingWebService
{
  [System.Web.Services.WebServiceBinding(Name = "SalesWebService",
      ConformsTo = System.Web.Services.WsiProfiles.BasicProfile1_1,
      EmitConformanceClaims = true,
      Namespace = "http://webservices.enterprise31.icarustravel.com/"),
   System.Web.Services.Protocols.SoapDocumentService(),
   System.Web.Services.WebService(
      Namespace =   "http://webservices.enterprise31.icarustravel.com/")]
  public class SalesWebService : System.Web.Services.WebService
  {
    [System.Web.Services.WebMethod()]
    public CustomerDS GetCustomer(int id)
    {
      return CustomerBE.Get(id).Data;
    }

    [System.Web.Services.WebMethod()]
    public CustomerSearchDS GetCustomerBySearch(string id,
                                          string familyName, string givenName)
    {
      return CustomerSearchBE.Get(id, familyName, givenName).Data;
    }

  }
}
```

The first one, the `GetCustomer(int id)` web method, which is used to return the typed DataSet needed to populate the `CustomerBE` object on the client, creates an instance of `CustomerBE` on the server, calls its `Get(int id)` function, and returns its `DataSet` which it obtains from the `Data` property on `BusinessEntityBE`.

The second one, `GetCustomerBySearch(string id, string familyName, string givenName)`, creates an instance of `CustomerSearchBE`, calls its more complicated `Get(id, familyName, givenName)` method, and again returns its typed `DataSet` for use in populating a `CustomerSearchBE` object on the client.

This completes the discussion of the business object layer on the client and server. The remainder of this chapter deals with the prototyping of the smart client Windows Forms applications and the Sales website.

Note The source code at this stage is in the folder Chapter 7\Exercise 7.

Prototyping the Sales Wing Windows Forms Smart-Client Application

We now move from the business objects to the prototyping of the Sales Wing smart-client application.

Note The source code at this stage is in the folder Chapter 7\Exercise 7. Exercise 7-8 will help you understand this section.

Creating the Main Screen

Charles has been attending all of the storyboarding sessions. It is his task to create the proto-type Windows Forms application that will form the proof of concept at the end of the analysis phase. To begin this development, Peter uses his Architect version of Visual Studio 2005 Team System to create the application corresponding to the SalesWing application on the diagram in Chapter 6, Figure 6-23. He first makes sure the implementation properties are correct: the project name is SalesWing, and the language is C#. Peter then right-clicks on the application in the diagram and selects Implement Application. This displays the Confirm Application Implementation dialog box shown in Figure 7-23. Peter checks the details and clicks OK to continue. Visual Studio creates a new Windows Application project in the solution. Peter checks it in to TFS and Charles can begin work.

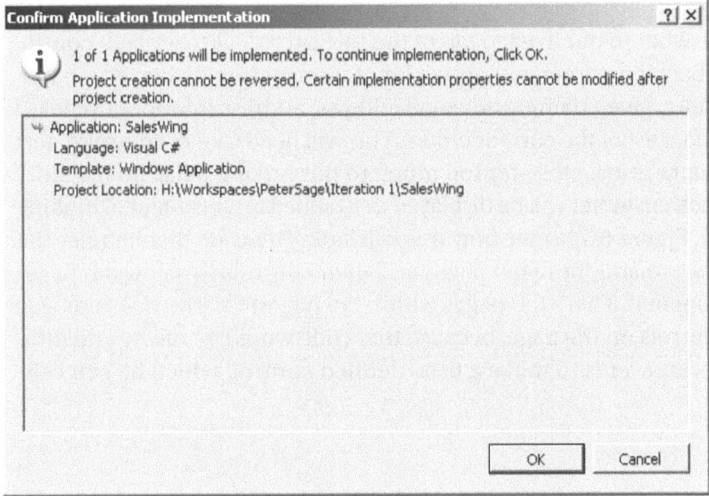

Figure 7-23. *Confirm Application Implementation dialog box*

Charles first sets the namespace of the project in the project properties to

com.icarustravel.enterprise31.SalesWing

He then corrects the namespace declaration in the Program.cs file and deletes and re-creates the default Form1 Windows Form. Charles then verifies that the project builds. Next he renames the Form1 form to "CustomerContacts". This will be the main form of the application. He does this by simply renaming the Form1.cs file in the Solution Explorer to "CustomerContacts.cs"; this automatically renames the class within and all references to it. This is one of the neat features of Visual Studio 2005—the refactoring feature. Sometimes refactoring occurs automatically; other times you get it as an option when you change the name of something in the code. In this case refactoring occurs as part of the operation of the Windows Forms Designer. There's an option in the Windows Forms Designer section of the Options dialog box called Enable Refactoring on Rename to turn this feature on or off.

Charles next modifies the text for the form to "Customer Contacts - Sales Wing Icarus Reservations Sales System"; at some point the team will need to make a nice-looking icon to go on the top of the form. The main form will need a menu, so he drags a MenuStrip control from the Menus and Toolbars tab of the Toolbox and renames it "menuStripMain". He adds two menu items to the menu script by typing in the Type Here location: "&File" and "&Resource". The ampersand character defines the next character as the one to be used with the Alt key to select the menu. By clicking on the File menu he sees the items within that menu and can add two new ones by typing in the Click Here location: "&Open Customer" and "E&xit". This is all very similar to Visual Studio 2003.

Of course, the final application will need toolbars, status bars, and so forth, but for the moment the team is concentrating on the bare essentials. As described earlier, this form is to be a multiple-document interface, with each open customer represented by a tab. So the next control Charles adds is a tab control from the Containers tab in the Toolbox; he sets the Dock property to Fill, names it "tabControlCustomers", and deletes all of the tab pages from it. To do this, he goes to the Tab Pages property, clicks on the ellipsis button to display the Tab Pages dialog box, and then removes each tab page. Charles will write code a bit later that will add a new tab page to the tab control each time a new customer is opened and delete it when that customer is closed.

Next Charles must decide what to put in each tab of the tabControlCustomers tab control when a customer is opened. Each customer will have a lot of information displayed—basic information such as family name, given name, and email address; address information; telephone contact information; and a list of the current orders. This will need a lot of controls—text boxes, combo boxes, labels, data grids, etc.—far too much to put on one page. So the storyboarding group decides that each customer will be displayed as a tabbed arrangement of multiple pages. Look back at Chapter 6, Figure 6-7, to see how this will look. The code that handles the opening of a customer will have to add these tab pages and their controls to a new tab page each time a new customer is opened. That's tab pages within tab pages! Charles does not want to write code to lay out the controls on the page, because that code would be messy and difficult to maintain. The obvious answer is to make a user-defined control, which he can call

CustomerDetails. Charles can design this user control just as if he were laying out an ordinary Windows Form; that's much better than writing code to add all the controls. When a new customer is opened, the code can simply create a new instance of this control and place it in a new tab page. We have already mentioned this control earlier in this chapter—now is the time to explain it.

Note The source code at this stage is in the folder Chapter 7\Exercise 8.

The CustomerDetails User Control

You can create three kinds of user-defined Windows Forms controls in .NET: the composite control, the extended control, and the custom control. Composite controls, as their name implies, are user-defined controls made up of a set of other controls. Extended controls are controls inherited from another control. Custom controls are controls made completely by the user that inherit directly from the Control class.

Note The source code at this stage is in the folder Chapter 7\Exercise 8. Exercise 7-9 will help you understand this section.

It is clear that the CustomerDetails control should be a composite control since the aim is to collect together a set of controls to contain the information about a customer that can be included as a whole on each customer tab page. To create this control, Charles right-clicks on the project and selects Add ➤ User Control. He types the name "CustomerDetails.cs" in the Add New Item dialog box and clicks Add. This creates a basic user control and opens the User Control Designer, a resizable design surface on which you can drag controls from the Toolbox and lay them out. The first control he adds is a tab control that is sized to fill most of the screen, but with room at the top for controls to display the customer ID and name and at the bottom to allow a Close button. The tab control is anchored to all four sides so that it will resize to follow the user control itself. He increases the tab page collection to five and defines the tabs in the Tab Page Collection Editor dialog box. On each tab page, he places a set of controls so that the user control has the appearance shown in Figure 7-24. It is important to anchor the controls so that they resize suitably as the control resizes. For example, in the first tab page, the family name, given name, email address, the group boxes, and all of the number text boxes are anchored top, left, and right so that they resize horizontally. The Close button is anchored bottom, right so that it stays in the bottom-right corner. All the other controls are anchored top, left.

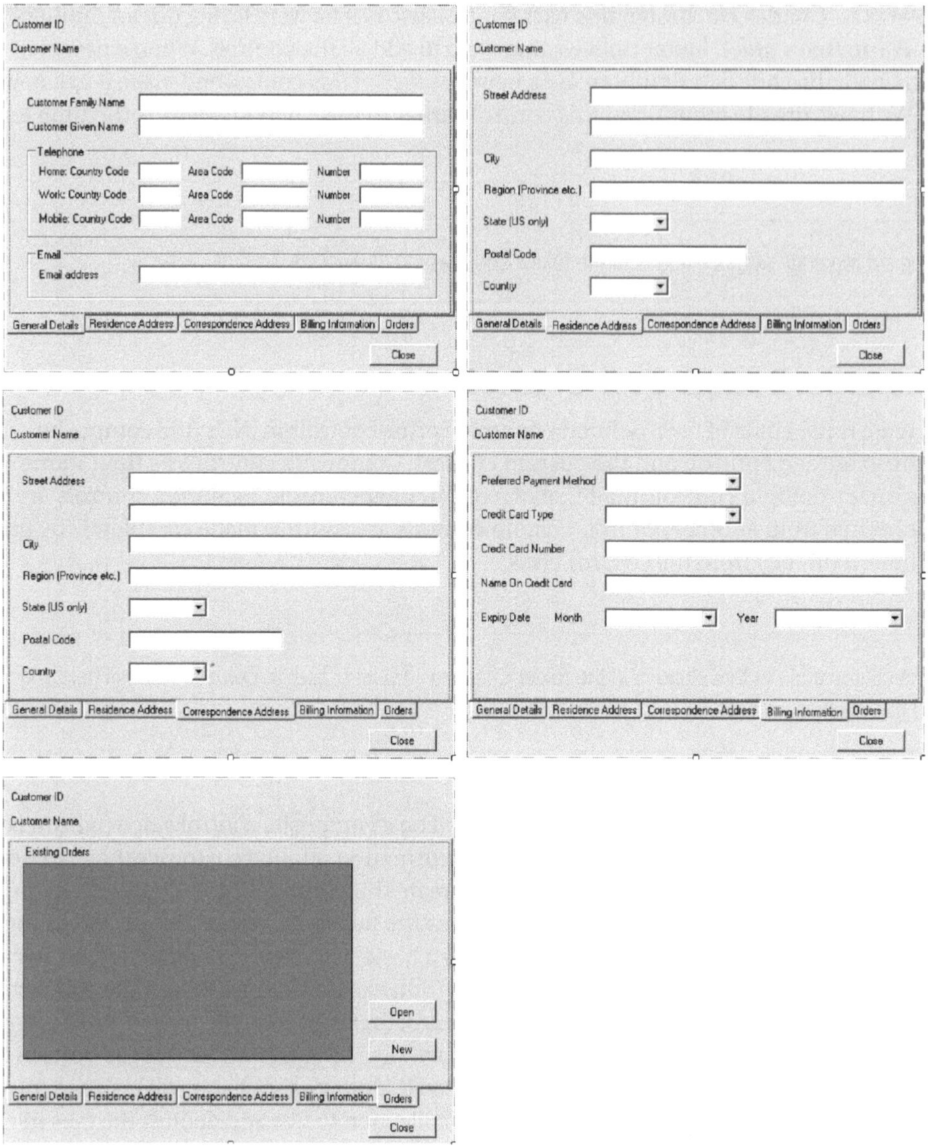

Figure 7-24. *UserDetails composite control—the appearance of each tab at design time*

Now Charles writes the code to open a customer; he does this in the Click event handler of the Open Customer menu item. He generates this event handler function by double-clicking on this menu item in the Design view of the CustomerContacts form; then he types in code so that the event handler function looks like this:

```
private void openCustomerToolStripMenuItem_Click(object sender, EventArgs e)
{
    // Create a CustomerDetails User Composite Control
    CustomerDetails customerDetails = new CustomerDetails();
    customerDetails.Dock = DockStyle.Fill;      // Dock style to fill all of tab page
```

```
    // Create a new Tab Page, place the new customer details control in it
    // and add it to the TabPages collection of the customers tab control.
    TabPage newTabPage = new TabPage();
    newTabPage.Text = "Customer Name";          // Temporary name for test
    newTabPage.Controls.Add(customerDetails);
    this.tabControlCustomers.TabPages.Add(newTabPage);
}
```

Note The source code at this stage is in the folder `Chapter 7\Exercise 9`.

Binding the Typed Datasets to the CustomerDetails Control

Now Charles has to consider how to populate the data in the page from the data model in the database. Here he will need to use Angela's `CustomerBE` business entity together with its `CustomerDS` typed dataset class.

Note The source code at this stage is in the folder `Chapter 7\Exercise 9`. Exercise 7-10 will help you understand this section.

First, it is necessary to add a reference in the `SalesWing` project to the `CustomerDAL` project so that the `DataSet` classes in that project will be available. Then from the Data tab in the Toolbox, Charles drags a `DataSet` onto the design surface of the `CustomerDetails` user control, which opens the Add Dataset dialog box, shown in Figure 7-25. To select the right type of `DataSet`, since `CustomerDS` is in another project, he selects Referenced Datasets from the Name drop-down, and then selects `com.icarustravel.enterprise31.Customer.CustomerDS` (Figure 7-26), also from the Name drop-down. If you try this and can't see the required dataset, it probably means that you have not added a reference to the project containing the dataset. Charles adds an instance of `CustomerDS` in this way and changes the default name to "customerDSCustomerData".

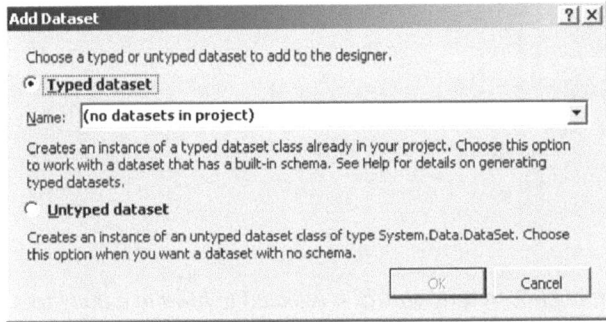

Figure 7-25. *The Add Dataset dialog box as it appears when you drop a dataset from the Toolbox*

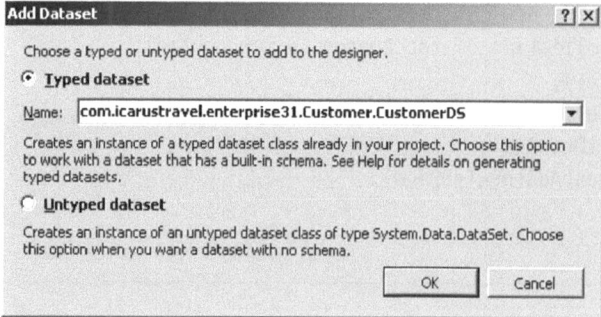

Figure 7-26. *The Add Dataset dialog box after selecting CustomerDS as a referenced Dataset*

Next, Charles needs to bind many of the controls to this dataset. He does this by going through control by control and setting the binding properties. For example, starting with the General Details tab page, he selects the textBoxFamilyName control and in the Data section in the Properties window, expands the (Data Bindings) field. He opens the Text drop-down, which shows a tree view of the data sources available in the form, and he expands the nodes until the Properties window looks like Figure 7-27. He then clicks on the FAMILYNAME field of the CUSTOMER table in the instance of CustomerDS that he added to the form.

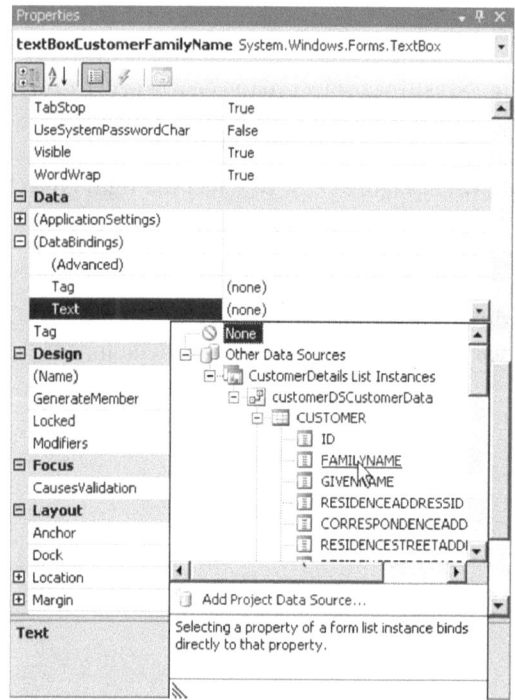

Figure 7-27. *The Properties window, showing how a data source is selected to bind to a text box*

The binding process continues in this way until all the text boxes on all the tab pages have been bound. The combo boxes on both of the address tabs are a little different. Here, it is necessary to bind both the selection in the text box part and the list of items. To bind the selection, it is only necessary to bind the Selected Value field in the (Data Bindings) group of the Data properties. For the State combo box, this needs to be bound to the RESIDENCESTATEID field of the CUSTOMER table. To bind the collection of items in the combo boxes, you need to select a Data Source, a Display Member, and a Value Member in the Data group of properties, outside of the (Data Bindings) set. The data bindings for the combo boxes should look like those shown in Figure 7-28. The bindings for the Orders data grid view on the last tab are very simple. It is just necessary to set the Data Source property to the same instance of `CustomerDS` called `customerDSCustomerData` and the Data Member field to the ORDERS table. To make the columns fill the space available as the `CustomerDetails` control is resized, you need to go to the Columns property of the data grid view control and set the Width properties of the columns in the Edit Columns dialog box as shown in Figure 7-29. The width of the Order ID field can be left at 100 pixels, but the Order Date column should have its `AutoSizeMode` property set to Fill.

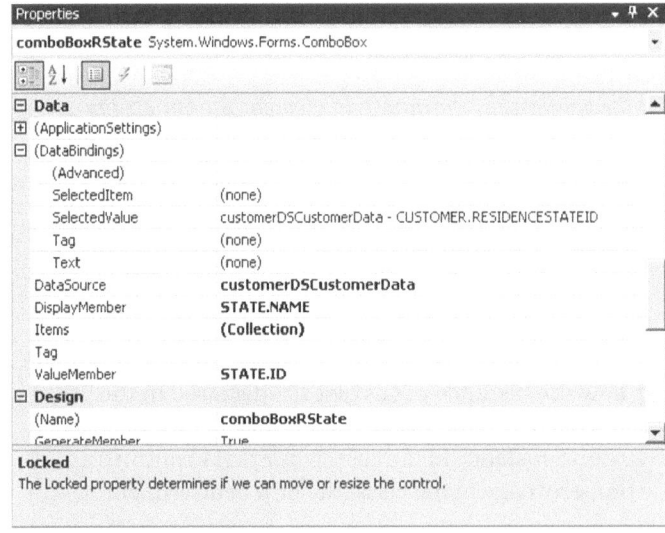

Figure 7-28. *Data bindings for the combo boxes*

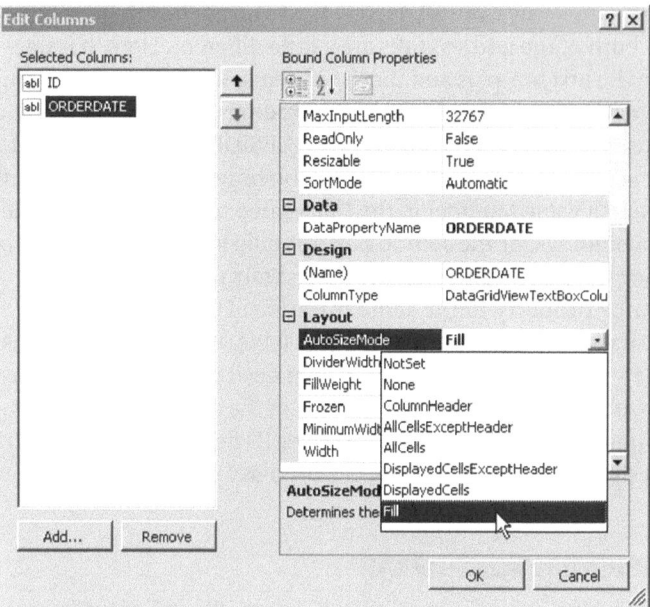

Figure 7-29. *Setting the properties for the columns in the data grid view for the Orders list*

■ **Note** The source code at this stage is in the folder `Chapter 7\Exercise 10`. Doing Exercise 7-11 will help you understand the rest of this section.

Now Charles needs to consider how the instance of `CustomerDS` declared in the `CustomerDetails` control will be loaded with data from the `CustomerBE` object that Angela has coded. First he has to expose the `CustomerDS` instance in the `CustomerDetails` control class as a read/write property by placing the property code in the class (the new code is in bold):

```
using com.icarustravel.enterprise31.Customer;
namespace com.icarustravel.enterprise31.SalesWing
{
    public partial class CustomerDetails : UserControl
    {
...

        public CustomerDS Data
        {
            set { this.customerDSCustomerData = value; }
            get { return this.customerDSCustomerData; }
        }
    }
```

Then he needs to add more code to the Open Customer menu item `Click` event handler function so it now looks like this, with the new code in bold:

```
private void openCustomerToolStripMenuItem_Click(object sender, EventArgs e)
{
    // Get the populated CustomerBE instance for the specified ID.
    CustomerBE customerBE = CustomerBE.Get(1);

    // Create a CustomerDetails User Composite Control
    CustomerDetails customerDetails = new CustomerDetails();
    customerDetails.Dock = DockStyle.Fill;  // Dock style to fill all of tab page

    // Merge the data from the customer business entity into the control's
    // CustomerDS  dataset
    customerDetails.Data.Merge(customerBE.Data);

    // Create a new Tab Page, place the new customer details control in it
            // and add it to the TabPages collection of the customers tab control.
            TabPage newTabPage = new TabPage();
            newTabPage.Text = "Customer Name";          // Temporary name for test
            newTabPage.Controls.Add(customerDetails);
            this.tabControlCustomers.TabPages.Add(newTabPage);
        }
```

The main function needs to initialize the business object base class to indicate a CLIENT
installation of the business entities, as we saw in the section on the DualPersistBE class:

```
static void Main()
{
    DualPersistBE.InstalledMode = DualPersistBE.InstallMode.CLIENT;

    Application.EnableVisualStyles();
    Application.SetCompatibleTextRenderingDefault(false);
    Application.Run(new CustomerContacts());
}
```

An App.config file needs to be added to the SalesWing project containing the following XML:

```
<?xml version="1.0" encoding="utf-8" ?>
<configuration>
  <configSections>
    <sectionGroup name="applicationSettings"
        type="System.Configuration.ApplicationSettingsGroup, System,
        Version=2.0.0.0, Culture=neutral, PublicKeyToken=b77a5c561934e089" >
      <section name=
                "com.icarustravel.enterprise31.BusinessEntity.Properties.Settings"
          type="System.Configuration.ClientSettingsSection, System, Version=2.0.0.0,
              Culture=neutral, PublicKeyToken=b77a5c561934e089"
              requirePermission="false" />
    </sectionGroup>
  </configSections>
```

```
  <applicationSettings>
    <com.icarustravel.enterprise31.BusinessEntity.Properties.Settings>
      <setting name="BusinessEntityBE_SalesWS_SalesWebService" serializeAs="String">
        <value>http://localhost:8020/SalesWebService/SalesWebService.asmx</value>
      </setting>
    </com.icarustravel.enterprise31.BusinessEntity.Properties.Settings>
  </applicationSettings>
</configuration>
```

Finally, a reference must be added in the SalesWing project to the CustomerBE and
BusinessEntity projects; and using directives placed in the Program.cs file:

```
using com.icarustravel.enterprise31.BusinessEntity;
```

and in the CustomerContacts.cs file:

```
using com.icarustravel.enterprise31.Customer;
```

Charles now finds he can run the project and open a customer (the code currently always
opens the customer with ID = 1) and all the fields are populated except those on the billing
tab, where the tables have not yet been added to the CustomerDS dataset (the description of the
billing tab is not included in this book).

He now needs to make the Close button work. It's easy to add an event handler to the Close
button Click event, and that is what Charles does first, simply by double-clicking on the Close
button on the CustomerDetails user control in Design view. Then he needs to add something
to let the CustomerDetails control communicate to the outside world that the Close button
was clicked. The way to do that is to define an event that can be invoked and will be expected
to be delegated to an event handler function by the form containing the CustomerDetails control. The following code added at the top of the CustomerDetails control class defines an event
and a delegate. The event handler function for the Close button click is shown at the bottom,
and this is where the Close event is invoked:

```
public partial class CustomerDetails : UserControl
{
    public event CloseEventDelegate Close;
    public delegate void CloseEventDelegate(Control control);

    // Other code

    private void buttonClose_Click(object sender, EventArgs e)
    {
        Close.Invoke(this);
    }
}
```

Yet another line of code must be added to the Open Customer menu item Click function
to assign a delegate to the event that will reference the CustomerDetailsClose event handler
function. Remember that this function lies in the code for the CustomerContacts form that will
create multiple instances of the CustomerDetails control and listen for Close event invocations
from each one:

```
private void openCustomerToolStripMenuItem_Click(object sender, EventArgs e)
{
    // Get the populated CustomerBE instance for the specified ID.
    CustomerBE customerBE = CustomerBE.Get(1);

    // Create a CustomerDetails User Composite Control
    CustomerDetails customerDetails = new CustomerDetails();
    customerDetails.Dock = DockStyle.Fill;  // Dock style to fill all of tab page
    customerDetails.Close += new
        CustomerDetails.CloseEventDelegate(CustomerDetailsClose);

    // Merge the data from the customer business entity into the control's
    // CustomerDS dataset
    customerDetails.Data.Merge(customerBE.Data);

    // Create a new Tab Page, place the new customer details control in it
    // and add it to the TabPages collection of the customers tab control.
    TabPage newTabPage = new TabPage();
    newTabPage.Text = "Customer Name";          // Temporary name for test
    newTabPage.Controls.Add(customerDetails);
    this.tabControlCustomers.TabPages.Add(newTabPage);
}
```

The event handler function must also be added in the code for the CustomerContacts form:

```
private void CustomerDetailsClose(Control customerDetailsControl)
{
    // The CustomerDetails controls are always placed in the Control collection
    // of a tab page on this form.  When the CustomerDetails control in a tab
    // page fires the control event, the tab page must be deleted from
    // the tab control on this form.
    Control parent = customerDetailsControl.Parent;

    if (parent is TabPage)           // Safety code
    {
        this.tabControlCustomers.TabPages.Remove(parent as TabPage);
    }
}
```

Charles tests this manually by opening ten tabs (each of course will have the same customer details) and then closing them in random order. All of them seem to work perfectly!

Note The source code at this stage is in the folder Chapter 7\Exercise 11.

The Open Customer Dialog box

Now that this part is operational, Charles needs to provide a means of selecting which customer is to be opened. To do this, he must implement the Open Customer dialog box shown in Chapter 6 (Figure 6-6).

Note The source code at this stage is in the folder `Chapter 7\Exercise 11`. Doing Exercise 7-12 will help you to understand this section.

The development of this dialog box is generally unremarkable, and its appearance is exactly as was anticipated in Chapter 6, Figure 6-6. The `DataGridView` control is bound to an instance of the `CustomerSearchDS` dataset as its data source, with its data member set to CUSTOMERSEARCH (which is that dataset's only table). The column widths in the data grid view are set manually to match the horizontal locations of the text boxes above them in the form. The code in the `OpenCustomer.cs` file is shown here:

```
using System;
using System.Collections.Generic;
using System.ComponentModel;
using System.Data;
using System.Drawing;
using System.Text;
using System.Windows.Forms;

using com.icarustravel.enterprise31.Customer;

namespace com.icarustravel.enterprise31.SalesWing
{
    public partial class OpenCustomer : Form
    {
        public OpenCustomer()
        {
            InitializeComponent();
        }

        public int SelectedId
        {
            get
            {
                return (int)dataGridViewCustomerSearchResults.SelectedRows[0].Cells[
                    "iDDataGridViewTextBoxColumn"].Value;
            }
        }
    }
```

```
private void OpenCustomer_Load(object sender, EventArgs e)
{
    UpdateCustomerSearchData();
}

private void textBoxCustomerId_TextChanged(object sender, EventArgs e)
{
    UpdateCustomerSearchData();
}

private void textBoxFamilyName_TextChanged(object sender, EventArgs e)
{
    UpdateCustomerSearchData();
}

private void textBoxGivenName_TextChanged(object sender, EventArgs e)
{
    UpdateCustomerSearchData();
}

private void UpdateCustomerSearchData()
{
    this.customerSearchDSSearchData.Clear();
    this.customerSearchDSSearchData.Merge(CustomerSearchBE.Get(
        this.textBoxCustomerId.Text, this.textBoxFamilyName.Text,
        this.textBoxGivenName.Text).Data);
}
    }
}
```

Notice that event handlers are added to the Text Changed events for all three of the text boxes, and each of these, as well as the Load event handler, call a common function:

UpdateCustomerSearchData();

which clears the instance of CustomerSearchDS, then merges into it an instance of CustomerSearchDS returned from a Get function on another business entity class called CustomerSearchBE, which Angela has written.

Once the Open Customer dialog box is complete, a further change needs to go into the event handler function for the Open Customer menu item in CustomerContacts.cs:

```csharp
private void openCustomerToolStripMenuItem_Click(object sender, EventArgs e)
{
    OpenCustomer openCustomer = new OpenCustomer();
    if (openCustomer.ShowDialog() == DialogResult.OK)
    {
        // Get the populated CustomerBE instance for the specified ID.
        CustomerBE customerBE = CustomerBE.Get(openCustomer.SelectedId);

        // Create a CustomerDetails User Composite Control
        CustomerDetails customerDetails = new CustomerDetails();
        customerDetails.Dock = DockStyle.Fill;  // Dock style to fill all of tab page
        customerDetails.Close += new
            CustomerDetails.CloseEventDelegate(CustomerDetailsClose);

        // Merge the data from the customer business entity into the control's
CustomerDS dataset
        customerDetails.Data.Merge(customerBE.Data);

        // Create a new Tab Page, place the new customer details control in it
        // and add it to the TabPages collection of the customers tab control.
        TabPage newTabPage = new TabPage();
        newTabPage.Text = customerDetails.CustomerName;
        newTabPage.Controls.Add(customerDetails);
        this.tabControlCustomers.TabPages.Add(newTabPage);
    }
}
```

The additional code executes the ShowDialog() function to display the new dialog box prior to the code that creates the new tab page executing, and also makes that code conditional on the return value of the ShowDialog() function being DialogResult.OK, meaning the user clicked the OK button and not the Cancel button. There is also a change required to pass to the Get function on CustomerBE, the customer ID value that the user selected in the dialog box instead of the constant "1". This selected ID is made available through the SelectedId property of the dialog box. Also the temporary name for the tab has been replaced by a call to a new property added to the CustomerDetails control:

```csharp
public string CustomerName
{
    get
    {
        if (this.customerDSCustomerData.CUSTOMER.Rows.Count == 1)
        {
            CustomerDS.CUSTOMERRow customerRow =
                this.customerDSCustomerData.CUSTOMER[0];
            return customerRow.FAMILYNAME + ", " + customerRow.GIVENNAME;
        }
```

```
        else
            return "";
    }
}
```

The basic open customer and close customer scenarios are now operational and demonstrate the architecture that was defined in the previous chapter in this simple end-to-end scenario of the Sales Wing application.

Note The source code at this stage is in the folder `Chapter 7\Exercise 12`.

Prototyping the Sales Site Application

Ed Marshall's first responsibility is the development of the façade screens for the `SalesSite` ASP.NET web application, and his second is development of the full iteration 1 functionality integrated with Angela's business objects. Peter first needs to create the website project using his Architect version of Visual Studio 2005 Team System. Many of the improvements included in Visual Studio 2005 relate to web development. For example, in earlier versions all web projects had to have their files in a virtual folder under either a local IIS installation or remote IIS installation. This is no longer necessary as now you have the additional project choices of a file system website or an FTP-based website. In the file system website, all the files for the site are stored in a simple folder; it is no longer necessary to use IIS to access and run them. The FTP-based website allows files in the site to be accessed in Visual Studio using the FTP protocol.

Note The source code at this stage is in the folder `Chapter 7\Exercise 12`. Exercise 13 will help you understand this section.

The team is going to use a file system website project. Peter sets the language to C# and the default class namespace to "com.icarustravel.enterprise31.SalesSite". Before the `SalesSite` application is implemented from the application diagram, the properties are as shown in Figure 7-30; after implementation, the project appears in Solution Explorer as shown in Figure 7-31.

Figure 7-30. *Properties for the SalesSite application before implementation by the architect*

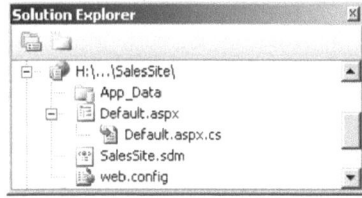

Figure 7-31. *The new website project in Solution Explorer*

The Master Page and the "My Wings" Page

Now Ed can begin the work of developing the web pages. One of the important new features of Visual Studio 2005 web development is the introduction of *master pages*, which allow shared features of web pages to be placed in one common location. The end-product pages that the user sees, based on this scheme, are called *content pages*, and specify one master page that defines the overall layout of the page. The master page contains *content placeholder* controls and the content pages contain *content* controls, each of which corresponds to a content place-holder in the master page. The HTML markup within these content controls is placed in the content placeholder controls on the master page to make up the final page delivered to the viewer. Let's watch Ed to see how this is done.

He first deletes the default.aspx page, which Visual Studio created automatically with the project. Then he right-clicks on the SalesSite project in Solution Explorer and selects Add New Item. In the resulting dialog box, Ed selects Master Page under Visual Studio Installed Templates and types the name "SalesSite.master", as shown in Figure 7-32.

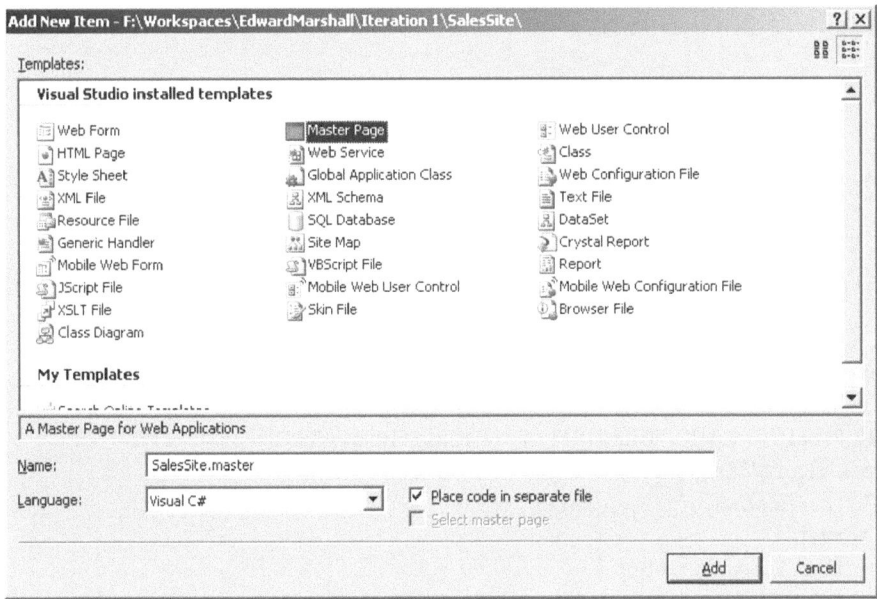

Figure 7-32. *The Add New Item dialog box*

Visual Studio automatically adds a control called a content placeholder, which he deletes—he'll add another one later. Most ASP.NET pages are based on a table to establish the overall layout, so he selects Layout ➤ Insert Table from the main menu. The Insert Table dialog box provides a selection of table templates. Ed clicks the Template radio button; selects the Header, Footer and Side option in the template drop-down (as shown in Figure 7-33); and clicks OK. He looks at the markup code that has been generated in the Source tab of the Web Page Designer.

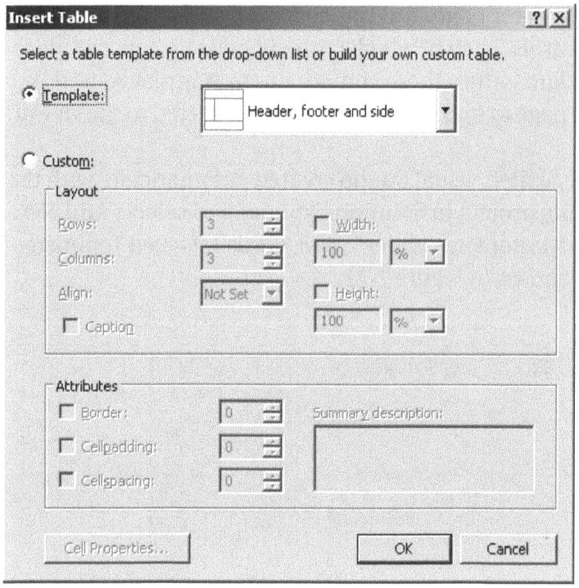

Figure 7-33. *The Insert Table dialog box*

```
<%@ Master Language="C#" AutoEventWireup="true" CodeFile="SalesSite.master.cs"
Inherits="SalesSite" %>
<!DOCTYPE html PUBLIC "-//W3C//DTD XHTML 1.0 Transitional//EN"
    "http://www.w3.org/TR/xhtml1/DTD/xhtml1-transitional.dtd">
<html xmlns="http://www.w3.org/1999/xhtml" >
<head runat="server">
    <title>Untitled Page</title>
</head>
<body>
    <form id="formSalesSite" runat="server">
    <div>
         <table border="0" cellpadding="0" cellspacing="0" style="width: 100%;
            height: 100%">
            <tr>
                <td colspan="2" style="height: 200px">
                </td>
            </tr>
```

```
        <tr>
            <td style="width: 200px">
            </td>
            <td>
            </td>
        </tr>
        <tr>
            <td colspan="2" style="height: 200px">
            </td>
        </tr>
    </table>
    </div>
    </form>
</body>
</html>
```

First, notice at the top of the file there is a @Master directive rather than the usual @Page directive and that the page inherits from the SalesSite class, which is the code-behind class placed in the file SalesSite.master.cs. However, there is a significant improvement between Visual Studio 2005 and previous versions. In previous versions the ASP.NET web page was compiled into a class that inherited from the code-behind class. The code-behind class contained all of the declarations of the controls included in the web form, together with a great deal of generated code to initialize those controls. In Visual Studio 2005, the concept of *partial classes* has been introduced. The code-behind file now contains a partial class from which the web form class will inherit. The remainder of this inherited code-behind class is generated when the page is compiled, and all of the declarations of the controls and initialization code is inferred from the markup code in the .aspx file. This means that Visual Studio no longer needs to maintain synchronization between the code in the .aspx file and that in the .aspx.cs code-behind class (or .aspx.vb in VB, where the concept is the same).

The bold code shows the markup inserted by Visual Studio to define the table. You can see that the table is specified to take up 100 percent of the containing division. Icarus uses fixed-size web pages, so Ed changes the style so that the size of the outer table is 770px wide and 600px high. There are three rows: the first and last have a colspan of 2 and a specified height, the middle row is left at automatic height and split into two <td> elements; the left has a specified size; and the right is left automatic. Ed wants the top portion to contain a standard Icarus banner with a horizontal overall menu below it. The left-hand pane will contain the menu specific to the functions being carried out. He needs to add another row to this table so that the horizontal menu can be placed in a cell of its own, separate from the banner. He does this by clicking in the top cell of the table in Design view and selecting Layout ➤ Insert ➤ Row Below from the main menu. He then adjusts the height and width of each cell by setting styles on each and sets the positioning of the contents. Finally, Ed places an image in the top table cell to act as the banner. The resulting code follows:

```
<body>
    <form id="formSalesSite" runat="server">
    <div>
        <table border="0" cellpadding="0" cellspacing="0" style="width: 770px;
        height: 600px; background-color: #ffffcc;">
            <tr>
                <td colspan="2" style="height: 80px" align="left" valign="top" >
                    <asp:Image ID="Image1" runat="server" Height="100%"
                        ImageUrl="~/Image/Icarus Banner.gif" Width="100%" /></td>
            </tr>
            <tr>
                <td colspan="2" style="height: 30px" align="left" valign="top"></td>
            </tr>
            <tr>
                <td style="width: 20%" align="left" valign="top"></td>
                <td style="width: 80%; background-color: #ffffff" align="left"
                valign="top"></td>
            </tr>
            <tr>
                <td colspan="2" id="TD1" style="font-size: x-small; color: black;
                height: 30px">"My Wings" is the customized homepage of Customers of
                Icarus Travel Services, Inc.<br/>
                (c) Icarus Travel Services, inc. To comment on this site, please
                email: webmaster@icarustravel.com</td>
            </tr>
        </table>
    </div>
    </form>
</body>
```

So there is a very simple master page, which will serve as the basis for all the pages of the sales site. Ed will need to add more features to it, such as the common menus, but first he wants to create a web form that will use this master page. The first form will be the My Wings form that will act as the main page for customers who have logged into their Icarus account.

To do this, Ed right-clicks on the project and selects Add New Item. This time in the Add New Item dialog box he selects Web Form under Visual Studio Installed Templates, types the name "MyWings.aspx", and checks the Select Master Page checkbox, as shown in Figure 7-34. After clicking Add, Ed sees the Select Master Page dialog box, shown in Figure 7-35, which allows him to select a master page. Since there is only one present in the project so far, Ed selects SalesSite.Master and clicks OK.

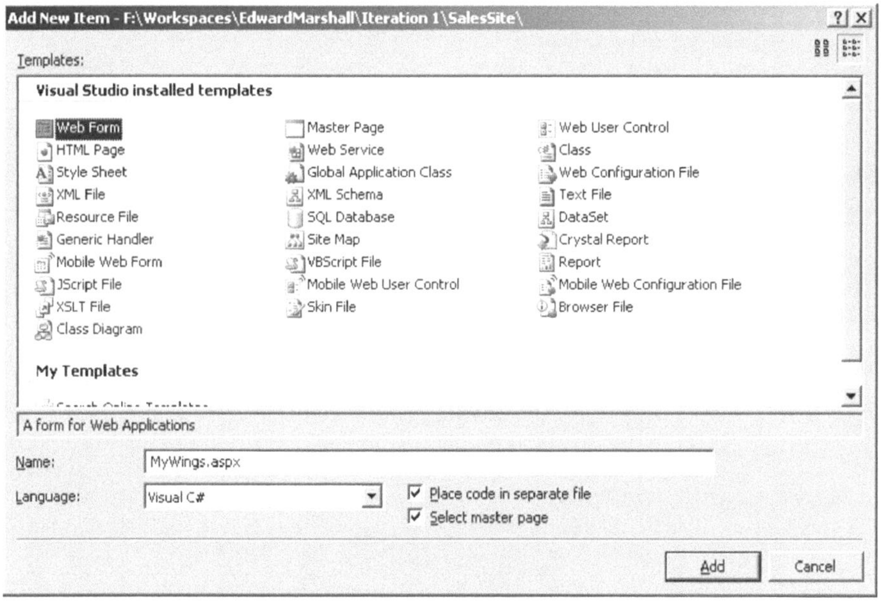

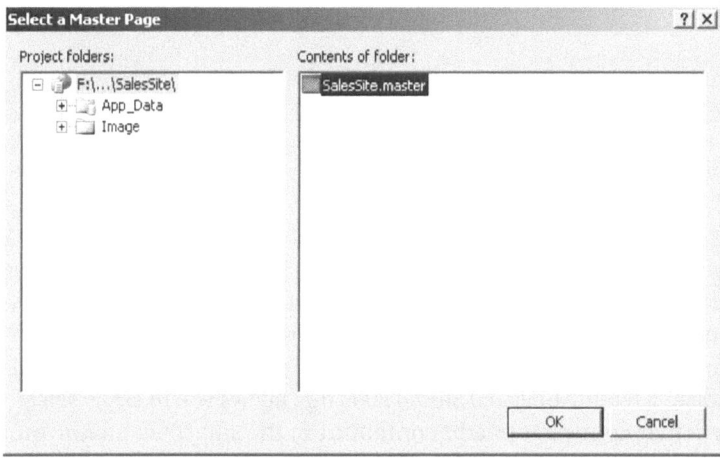

Figure 7-34. *The Add New Item dialog box, used to add a web form with a master page*

Figure 7-35. *The Select a Master Page dialog box*

The new My Wings web form comes up in the Designer in Source view. Before he does anything else, Ed runs the form by right-clicking on it and selecting View in Browser. Figure 7-36 shows the result—he sees just what is on the master page. Now he needs to provide the capability for the pages that use the master page to add their own content. To do this, he goes back to the master page and drags a `ContentPlaceholder` control from the Toolbox into the idle right-hand cell in the table. Then Ed goes back to the My Wings page and looks at Design view. The content placeholder is visible in the correct place on the form. This is where the My Wings page, which is a content page, will place its specific content.

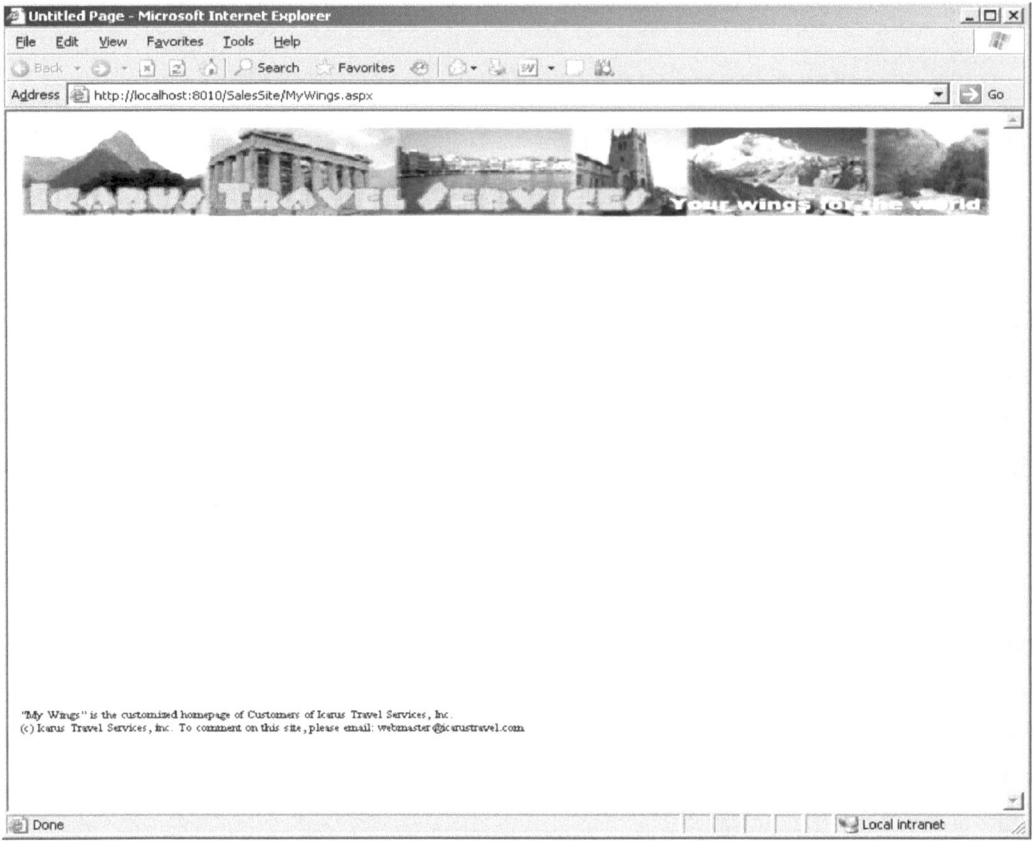

Figure 7-36. *The MyWings.aspx content page—all we see is what is on the master.*

While it is perfectly possible to add the content control directly into the Source view of the My Wings page, the easiest way is to choose the Design view; select the box labeled Content—Content1 (Master), which represents the content control; and click on the smart tag glyph to bring up the smart tag menu. (The smart tag glyph is the little arrow just beyond the top-right corner of the control and accesses a feature of Visual Studio 2005 that allows you to easily select tasks that are specific to particular controls.) To add content from the smart tag menu you select Create Custom Content, which creates a content control in the markup source for the content page. You can then begin typing text or markup into the content control in the Design view. Ed does this, and, to be sure it is working, he drags an HTML Div control from the Tool-box, types "My Wings content" into this control, and sets the style for the Div control to width 100 percent and height 300px.

Before Ed views it in the browser, he goes back to the SalesSite.master form and drags a menu control into the left-hand cell and another one into the second cell down from the top. He applies no formatting to these, but adds some menu items using the smart tag menu. Then in the Properties window for the left-hand menu, he sets the Layout, Orientation property to Vertical.

At this point Ed needs to remove the height field from the outer table property so that the total height of the page is determined by the contents rather than being fixed. So

```
<table border="0" cellpadding="0" cellspacing="0" style="width: 770px;
    height: 600px; background-color: #ffffcc;">
```

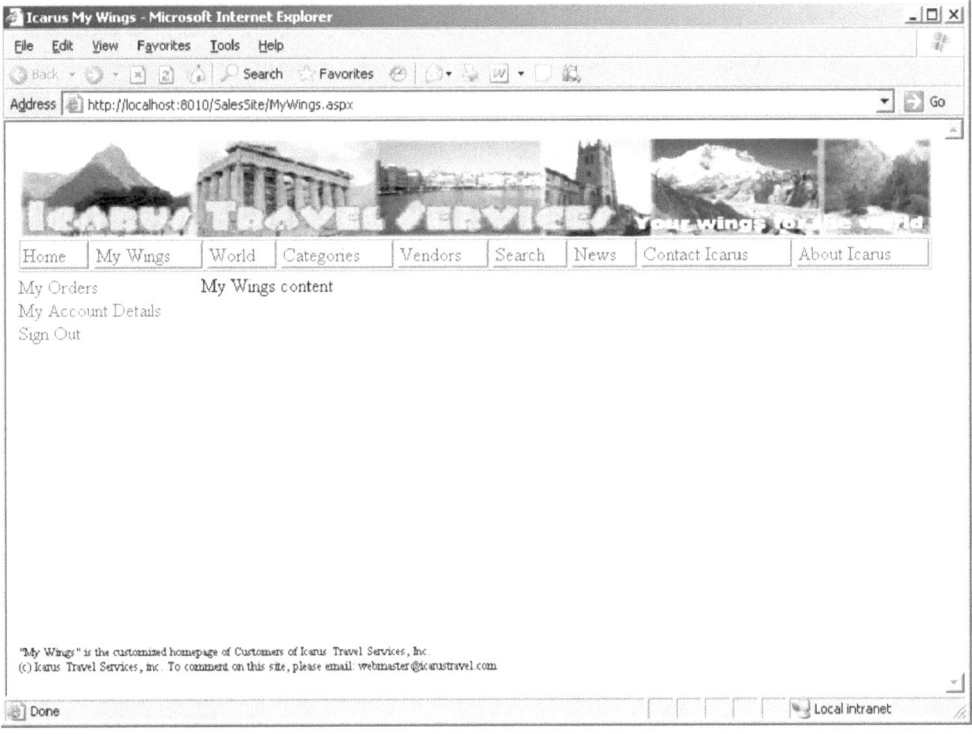

Figure 7-37. *The MyWings.aspx content page—the menus have been added and the content page is displaying its test content in the right place.*

becomes

```
<table border="0" cellpadding="0" cellspacing="0" style="width: 770px;
    background-color: #ffffcc;">
```

He can then view the My Wings form in the browser, as shown in Figure 7-37.

Finally, in the My Wings page, Ed adds some representative pictures that look like advertisements. He views the MyWings web form in Design view again and removes the "My wings content" text, being careful to leave the <div> tag in place. Then with the cursor in the content control and also within the <div> tag, he selects Layout ➤ Insert Table from the top-level menu. This time in the Insert Table dialog box, he selects the Custom radio button and sets the Rows to 4 and the Columns to 4. He also checks the Width and Height checkboxes, leaving them set at 100 percent. This will make the table fill the <div> element within the content control. The <div> element was set to a fixed height and 100 percent width, so it should determine the height of the content control. The height and width of the rows and columns in the table are adjusted so that there are four large cells with small spacer cells between them.

Now it is necessary to provide some ad pictures for the table cells. In each of the four large cells, Ed drags an image control, and then sets its Image URL property to point to an image. This completes the My Wings page, which is shown in Figure 7-38.

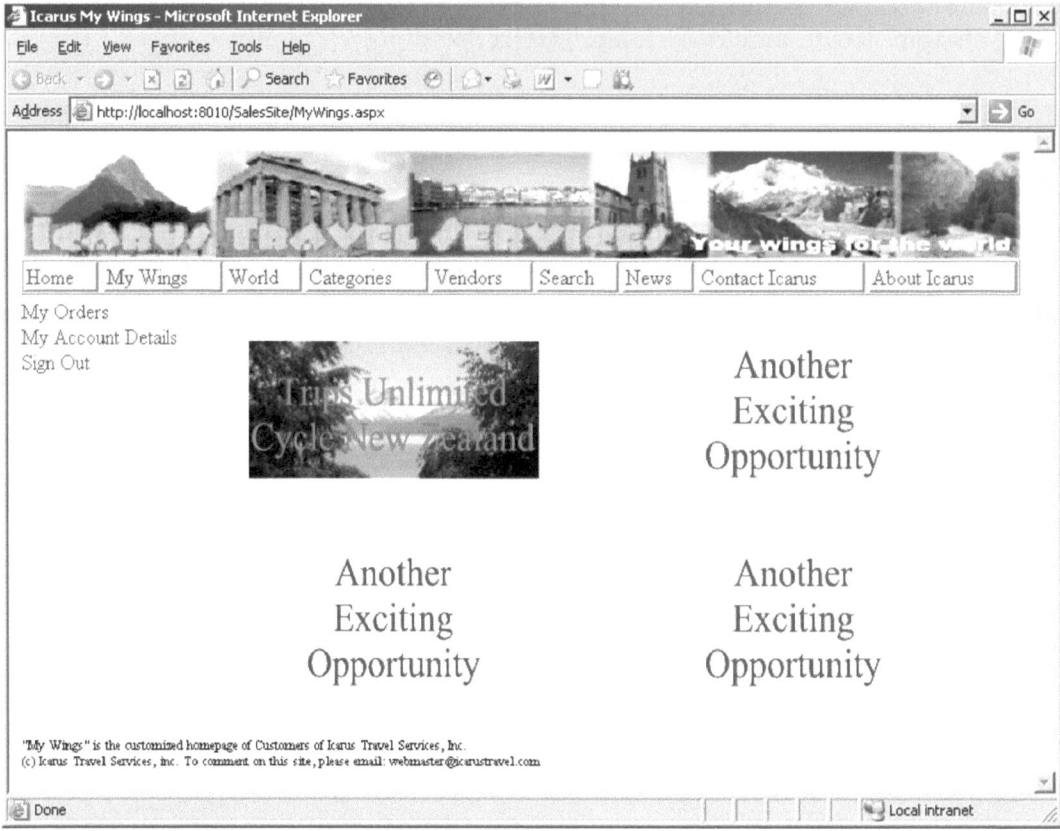

Figure 7-38. *The completed MyWings.aspx content page*

Note The source code at this stage is in the folder Chapter 7\Exercise 13.

The My Orders Page

Next, Ed creates the MyOrders.aspx page in the same way. He creates a new web form and chooses SalesSite.master as the master form. He adds a table with three rows: one for the introductory/instruction text, one to contain the list of orders, and one to contain buttons to make things happen.

Note The source code at this stage is in the folder Chapter 7\Exercise 13. Exercise 14 will help you understand this section.

He then drags a GridView control from the Data tab of the Toolbox into the middle cell of the new table. He ignores the smart tag menu that appears, since he is not ready yet to configure the GridView control. He also drags a LinkButton control from the Toolbox into the lower cell of the table and sets the text to "New Order". He makes quite a few adjustments to the styles and other attributes. The HTML markup code for this page now looks like this:

```
<%@ Page Language="C#" MasterPageFile="~/SalesSite.master" AutoEventWireup="true"
    CodeFile="MyOrders.aspx.cs" Inherits="MyOrders" Title="Untitled Page" %>
<asp:Content ID="Content1" ContentPlaceHolderID="ContentPlaceHolder1"
        Runat="Server">
  <div style="width: 100%; height: 400px; background-color: #ccffcc;">
    <table style="width: 100%">
      <tr>
        <td style="height: 20px;">
          <asp:Label ID="Label1" runat="server"
                Text="Current order status for Robert Ansley"></asp:Label></td>
        <td style="height: 20px">
        </td>
      </tr>
      <tr>
        <td colspan="2">
          <asp:GridView ID="GridView1" runat="server" Height="100%" Width="100%"
              AutoGenerateColumns="False" DataSourceID="ObjectDataSource1">
            <Columns>
              <asp:BoundField DataField="ID" HeaderText="Order Number" />
              <asp:BoundField DataField="ORDERDATE" HeaderText="Order Date" />
            </Columns>
          </asp:GridView>
        </td>
      </tr>
      <tr>
        <td style="height: 20px;" colspan="2" align="right" valign="middle">
             <asp:LinkButton ID="LinkButtonNewOrder" runat="server">
            New Order</asp:LinkButton></td>
      </tr>
    </table>
  </div>
  <asp:ObjectDataSource ID="ObjectDataSource1" runat="server" SelectMethod="GetData"
      TypeName="com.icarustravel.enterprise31.Order.CustomerOrdersBE">
    <SelectParameters>
      <asp:Parameter DefaultValue="1" Name="id" Type="Int32" />
      <asp:Parameter DefaultValue="ORDER" Name="tableName" Type="String" />
    </SelectParameters>
  </asp:ObjectDataSource>
</asp:Content>
```

Ed has to perform quite a bit of fiddling with the styles here to make the form look right. He can either edit the HTML code in the Source view of the page, or he can select a control in Design view, go to the Style entry in the Properties window, and click on the ellipsis button. This brings up the Styles dialog box, from which Ed can choose the styles that apply to the selected control or HTML tag. At this point I must mention another really useful feature of Visual Studio 2005 Visual Web Developer: the Document Outline, which applies both to Windows Forms and web forms. This feature allows you to see at a glance the hierarchical structure of your form and in particular to select the control or tag that you want to modify.

For example, to set the styles on the <div> tag that encompasses all of the content, Ed can select it in the document outline (Figure 7-39) and then click on the ellipsis in the Style property (Figure 7-40), which brings up the Style Builder dialog box (Figure 7-41).

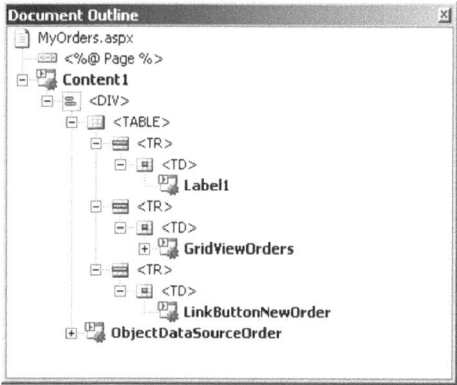

Figure 7-39. *The document outline for the My Orders web form*

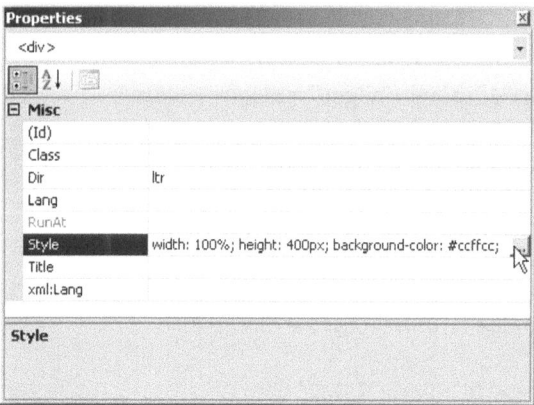

Figure 7-40. *The Style entry in the Properties window for the <div> tag in the My Orders web form*

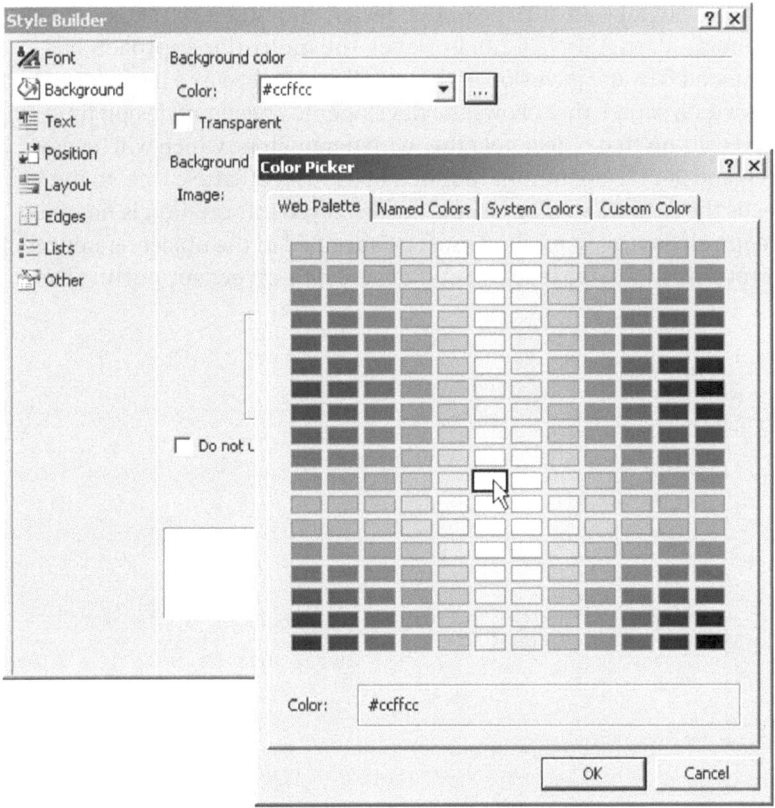

Figure 7-41. *The Style Builder dialog box for the <div> tag in the My Orders web form. The background color is being changed.*

In this dialog box, you can select things like the font, background color, positioning, and so on. In the figure, light green is being selected as the overall background color for the content provided by the My Orders form. I always find laying out web forms a tricky job, and I think these features make the process a lot easier. Of course, I have not mentioned the use of style sheets (I've left them out of this book), but in some ways I think perhaps the use of master forms makes style sheets a little bit redundant. Nevertheless, you are likely to have quite a few master forms on a company website, and notice that Visual Web Developer only supports one level of master and content forms—you cannot set up an *inheritance* chain of master forms. So you could achieve some commonality across master forms by using style sheets.

Ed must now turn his attention to how he will populate the GridView control that will display the list of orders that the customer has placed with Icarus. GridView controls, which replace the DataGrid controls in earlier Visual Studio versions, need to be bound to a DataSet or DataTable object, and there are various ways in which this can be done. Before Visual Studio 2005, you had two choices. You could place a data connection object and DataSet object on the web form page and bind the DataGrid to the DataSet object obtained from a specified database; in other words the web form could act as a part of the client of a two-tier system. Alternatively, if you wanted the controls to work with data provided from a middle tier, you could generate DataSet objects in the business object tier and bind them to DataGrid controls on the forms programmatically. In the second case you could not really take advantage of the design-time tools and a good deal of repetitive code was generated. In ASP.NET 2.0, however, the multi-tier approach has been much better accommodated by the inclusion of the new ObjectDataSource (Figure 7-42). ObjectDataSource defines a data source that allows the developer to specify, at design time, an object and a set of method calls on that object, together with parameters, which will be used for SELECT, UPDATE, INSERT, and DELETE operations required of the ObjectDataSource. In the My Orders form, Ed only needs the SELECT operation since the displayed information is not to be edited in the Grid View control. For this, a method must be specified in the object referenced by the data source that returns a DataTable, DataSet, DataView, or object supporting the IEnumerable interface.

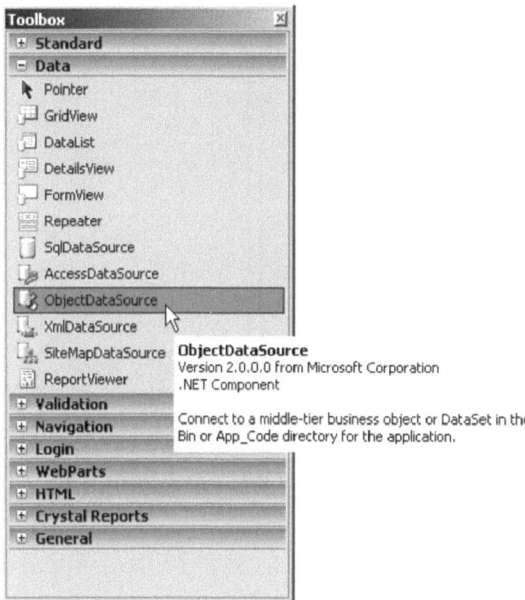

Figure 7-42. *The ObjectDataSource control in the Toolbox*

Let's see how Ed uses this control in the My Orders web form. If you recall the work that was being done by Angela in developing the business entity objects, the CustomerBE class, as an example, had a static member function Get(int id) that returned an instance of CustomerBE. The DataSet object embedded in that class, the CustomerDS strongly typed object, was then visible as a property of that returned instance of the class. Ed therefore needs Angela to provide him with a business entity class, perhaps called CustomerOrdersBE, which will expose a CustomerOrdersDS that will contain a table of orders obtained from the database for the specified customer. Angela has not written those objects yet, but Ed wants to see what his forms will look like, so he decides to write some simple stubs that will deliver one of these CustomerOrdersBE objects.

Unfortunately, if a dataset is returned by the call to the function named as the SELECT function in configuring the ObjectDataSource, the GridView will automatically bind to the first table in the dataset. If the developer defines a dataset with multiple tables, such as CustomerDS for example, it is a little risky to rely on the one that happens to be first in the XML definition of the dataset to be the correct one to use for binding. Moreover, the developer might use the same dataset to contain several tables that need to bind to different GridView controls on the form.

Thus, a better approach appears to be to not return an object of the DataSet class from the business entity class but to return a DataTable and to specify which DataTable is to be provided by a parameter in the function call. It is this approach that Ed decides to use. He first creates a folder called SalesBusinessObjectsStubs and, within that, creates a project called OrderBEStub. He then creates a dataset by right-clicking, selecting Add New Item, and choosing DataSet in the Add New Item dialog box. Then, onto the dataset design surface, he drags a DataTable from the Toolbox (not a TableAdapter like Angela, since this is part of a stub and will not connect to a database). He adds two columns to it by right-clicking on it and selecting Add Column; he then names the columns "ID" and "ORDERDATE" and changes the types to int32 and DateTime, respectively. He makes these name and type changes in the properties page for each column, which he views by right-clicking on a column in the data table and selecting Properties.

Next he creates a class in the OrderBEStub project called OrderBE and types in the following code:

```
using System;
using System.Collections.Generic;
using System.Text;
using System.Data;

namespace com.icarustravel.enterprise31.Order
{
  public class CustomerOrdersBE
  {
    CustomerOrdersDS data;

    public CustomerOrdersDS Data
    {
      get { return data; }
    }

    public static CustomerOrdersBE Get(int id)
    {
      CustomerOrdersBE customerOrdersBE = new CustomerOrdersBE();
      customerOrdersBE.data = new CustomerOrdersDS();

      customerOrdersBE.Data.ORDER.LoadDataRow(new object[] { 1, DateTime.Now },
          true);
      customerOrdersBE.Data.ORDER.LoadDataRow(new object[] { 2, DateTime.Now },
          true);
      customerOrdersBE.Data.ORDER.LoadDataRow(new object[] { 3, DateTime.Now },
          true);
      customerOrdersBE.Data.ORDER.LoadDataRow(new object[] { 4, DateTime.Now },
          true);
```

```
        return customerOrdersBE;
    }


    public DataTable GetDataTable(int id, string tableName)
    {
        return Get(id).Data.Tables[tableName];
    }
  }
}
```

This includes a stubbed version of the Get(int id) type of function that just fills the object's dataset with some dummy data, and a new function called GetDataTable(int id, string tableName) that simply calls the Get function and then returns the specified table from the dataset obtained via the Data property.

Going back the MyOrders.aspx web form and selecting the ObjectDataSource control, which he calls ObjectDataSourceOrders, Ed now clicks on the smart tag glyph and in the smart tag menu, clicks Configure Data Source, which opens the Configure Data Source wizard, shown in Figure 7-43.

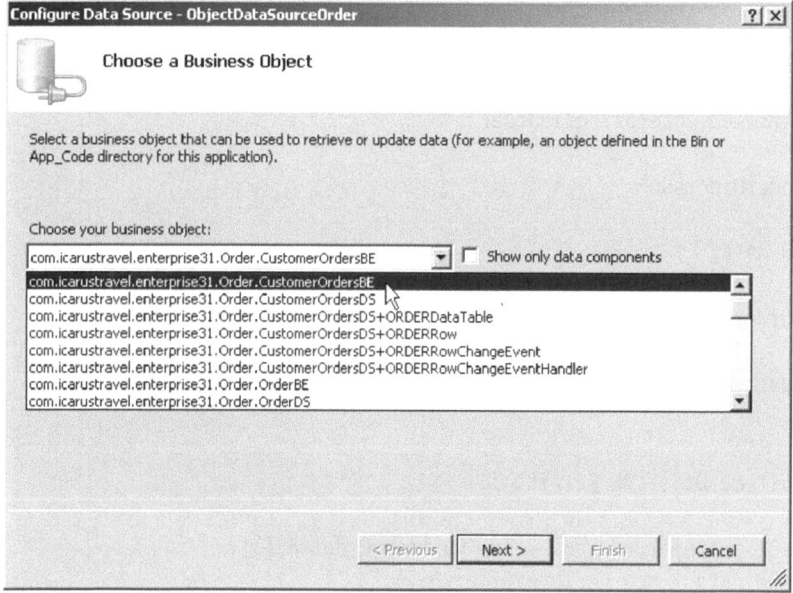

Figure 7-43. *The Configure Data Source wizard, page 1*

This first page of the wizard prompts the user to choose the class on which the method is to be named that will return the data table for binding. Ed leaves the checkbox Show Only Data Components deselected since the CustomerOrdersBE class is not a data component, even though it has a method to return one. He selects the `CustomerOrdersBE` class of course—this is the stub class—but when he builds the project with the real business entity class, he will change the reference in the `SalesSite` project to the nonstub project. The website should then compile with the correct code for deployment.

Figure 7-44 shows the next page of the wizard, which allows the user to select the method to be called for each of the `SELECT`, `UPDATE`, `INSERT`, and `DELETE` operations. Since Ed intends this page to be read-only, he only selects a function name for the `SELECT` operation (i.e., the one to use when the `ObjectDataSource` control is retrieving data for display) and then selects the `GetDataTable` function that he just defined.

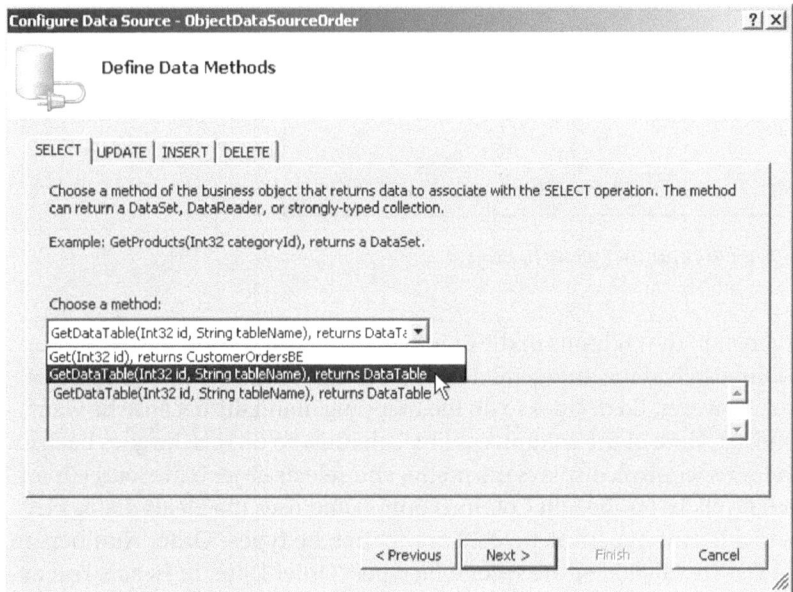

Figure 7-44. *The Configure Data Source wizard, page 2*

Figure 7-45 shows the next wizard page, which allows the user to define parameters that will be passed to the named function. The first is the ID integer value of the customer, which in this case will be the ID of the customer who is currently logged onto the site and viewing the page. Ed has not yet decided where this will come from—he will probably use forms authentication and the ID will be saved in the cookie. The wizard page allows for this option to be selected, but for the moment, ED selects None for the source and types "1" as the default value. For the `tableName` parameter, the value will always be "ORDER", so again he leaves the source at None and types "ORDER" into the default value. Ed clicks Finish to complete the wizard.

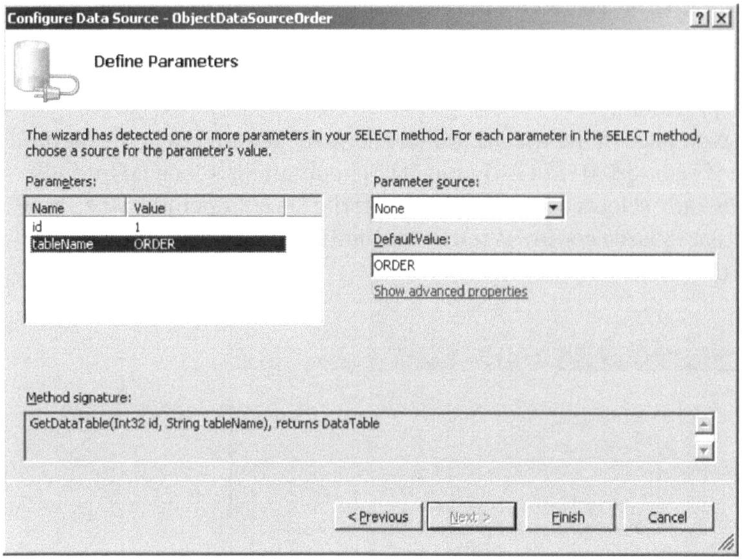

Figure 7-45. *The Configure Data Source wizard, page 3*

It is now necessary to map the columns in the GridView to the columns in the DataTable, which can be done automatically if the AutogenerateColumns option is set in the properties for the GridView control. However, Ed decides to do the mapping manually because he wants to name the headers and set some of the columns as link columns. To do this, he goes back to the smart tag for the GridView control, displays the menu, and selects objectDataSourceOrder as the data source. Then he clicks on the Edit Columns option and uses the Fields dialog box, shown in Figure 7-46, to add two hyperlink fields. For the first, he types "Order Number" in HeaderText and "ID" in DataTextField; for the second he types "Order Date" in HeaderText and "ORDERDATE" in DataTextField. He leaves NavigateURL blank for the moment.

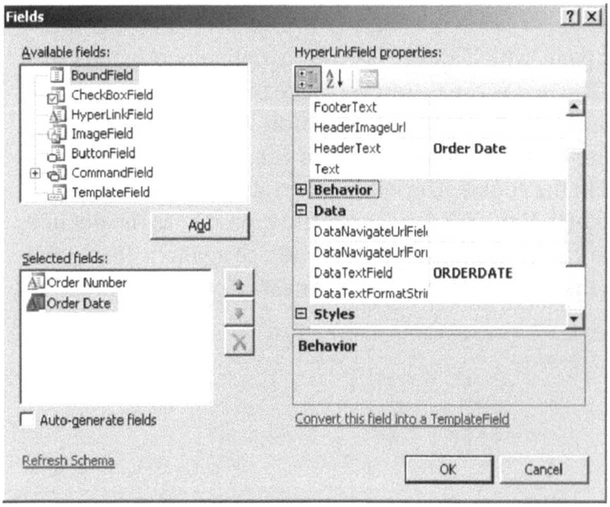

Figure 7-46. *The Fields dialog box*

Note The source code at this stage is in the folder `Chapter 7\Exercise 14`.

The Order Detail Page

The `OrderDetail.aspx` web form is very similar to the `MyOrders` form. Ed builds it by copying the entire `<div>` element from the `MyOrders` form and making a few changes.

Note The source code at this stage is in the folder `Chapter 7\Exercise 14`. Exercise 15 will help you understand this section.

Ed creates a dataset called `OrderDS` and an `OrderBE` class to add to his stub project. He sets up the `ObjectDataSource` control in almost the same way. He adds two tables to `OrderDS`, ORDER and RESERVATION, with the intention that ORDER will contain just one row for a specific order and RESERVATION will contain a row for each reservation in the order. The `GridView` has its `AutoGenerateDeleteButton` property set to true, and Ed adds a `void Delete( int id )` function to the `OrderBE` class so that the `DELETE` operation of the `ObjectDataSource` control can be configured. As the business entity class is a stub, it does nothing—the deletion of a reservation will be designed later. Figure 7-47 shows the complete `OrderDetail.aspx` page as viewed in a browser.

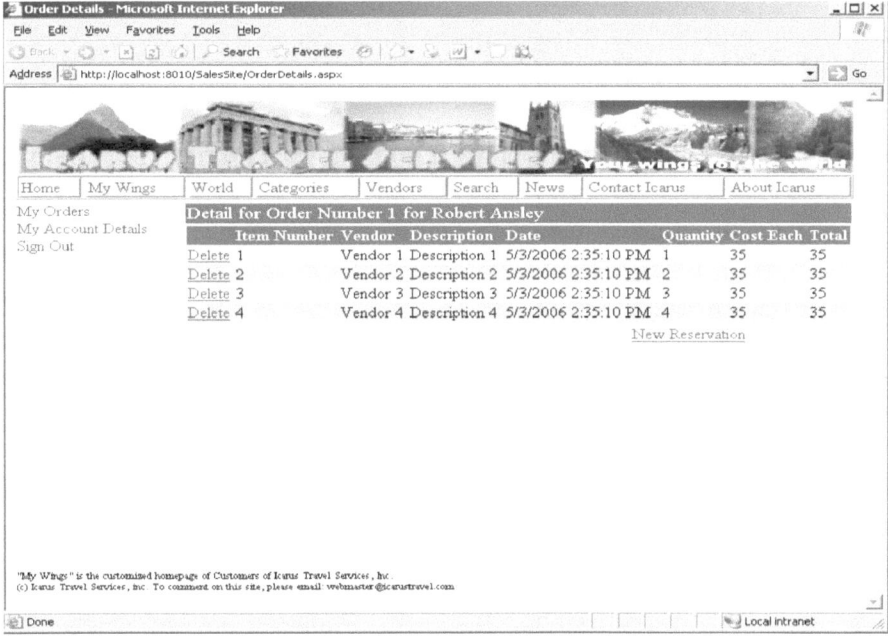

Figure 7-47. *The OrderDetail.aspx web form*

Note The source code at this stage is in the folder `Chapter 7\Exercise 15`.

The Make Reservation Page

The `MakeReservation.aspx` web form is a good deal more complicated. The page is seen in
Design view in Figure 7-48, where Ed has added many rows and columns to the main table in
the content control. Three `DropDownList` controls have been added for selection of the Geographic
Region, the Category, and the Vendor in narrowing choices for the resource that the customer
wishes to reserve.

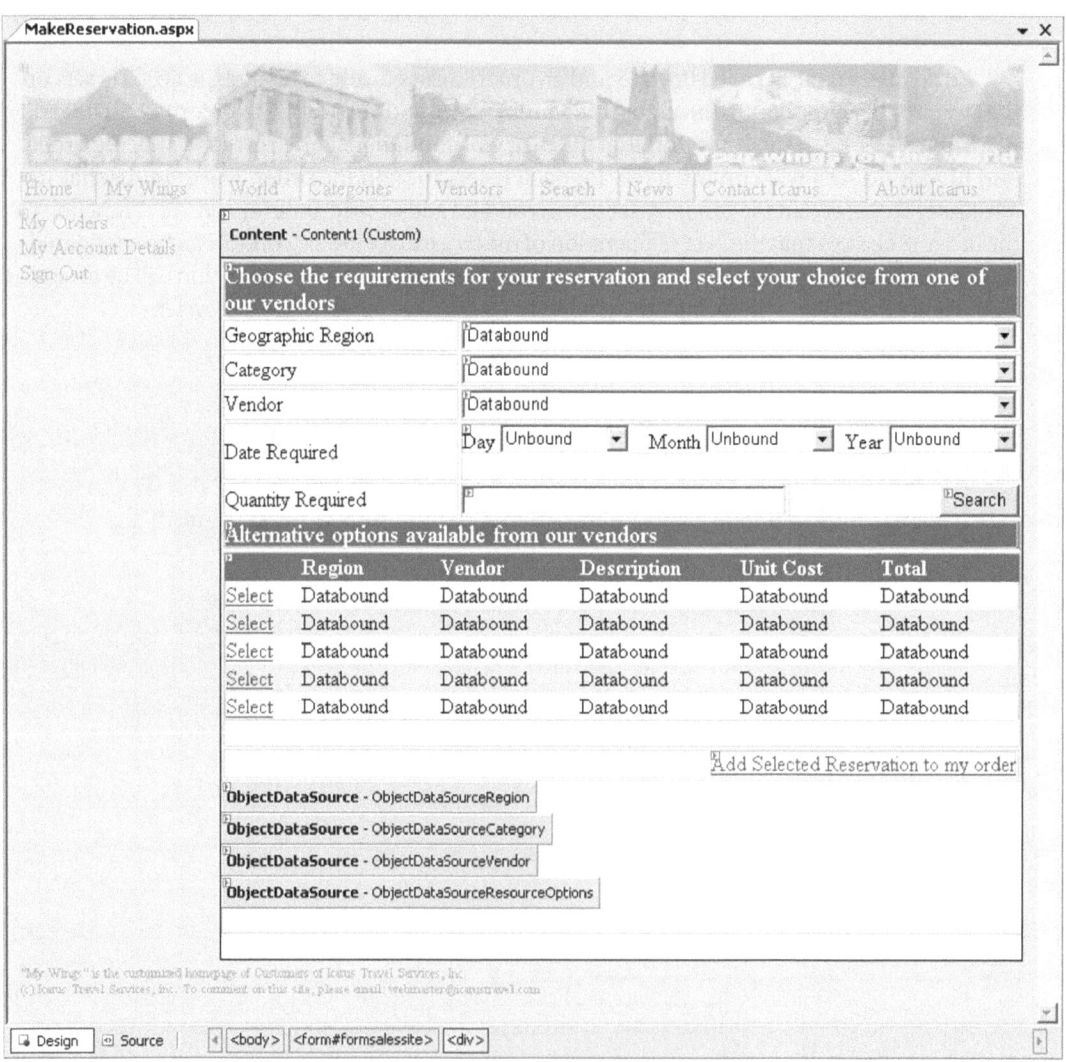

Figure 7-48. *The MakeReservation.aspx web form in Design view*

Note The source code at this stage is in the folder `Chapter 7\Exercise 15`. Exercise 16 will help you understand this section.

There are also three controls for selecting the day, month, and year on which the reservation is to be made and a text box where the user will enter the quantity. There is a `GridView` control that will show the options that meet the five selection criteria: location, category, vendor, date, and quantity. At this point, Ed has not bound this grid view to an `ObjectDataSource` control but he has placed four `ObjectDataSource` controls on the page. Why four? Because `ObjectDataSource` controls do not allow more than one function to be specified that returns a `DataSet` or `DataTable` object, and the controls that bind to an `ObjectDataSource` cannot specify a data member (i.e., a table in a dataset) to which they should bind. Therefore, Ed must include an `ObjectDataSource` for each control and each will reference a different table in a data source. It's then a straightforward task to bind the region, category, and vendor `DropDownList` controls and the options `GridView` control to the `ObjectDataSource` controls.

DropDownList controls in web forms do not have an obvious way to bind the selected value to a data source. This is the value appearing in the top box of the `DropDownList` control. Once the user selects an item, this selection will be retained through posts by being held in view state, which is fine for this form. However, if Ed wanted to initialize the selection from data in the database passed via a dataset, he would have to do it programmatically by catching, for example, the `DataBound` event. He could click the Events button (the little lightning streak) in the Properties window for one of these `DropDownList` controls and double-click on the `DataBound` event, which would create an event handler. He could then set the `SelectedValue` to a string that matches one of the values bound to the Value field of the items in the list.

```
protected void DropDownListGeographicRegion_DataBound(object sender, EventArgs e)
{
  this.DropDownListGeographicRegion.SelectedValue = "3";
}
```

This pretty much completes the series of screens that Ed has to produce for the storyboarding described in the previous chapter. It's not bad for a start, and we will see if it works out functionally when he integrates with the business entity objects that Angela is writing. I can see one problem right away—can you?

Well, each time the `DropDownList` controls bind, they will cause the static member function `GetDataTable(int id, string tableName)` to be called on the `ReservationSelectionBE` class. This is fine when that class is a stub, but in fact, that member call will create an instance of `ReservationSelectionDS`, which will be populated from the database each time by calling four separate stored procedures. The problem is that only one table will be used each time it is called, so we will be wasting six stored procedure calls. It's nice to put all the data needed for the page into one `DataSet` class, but then we want to use it all at the same time and not throw away the biggest part! So we might as well split `ReservationSelectionDS`, the `DataSet` that supports this page, into four separate ones. It's tidy to have them together, though—and at the moment, the team is not thinking much about performance—they just want to get it working.

Finally, Ed needs to address the way in which the day, month, and year `DropDownList` control collections can be populated. The contents of the item collections in each case need to be populated with values that are consistent with the calendar, including leap years. There is a web forms CalendarControl but Ed does not want to take up that amount of room on this web form, and since the Windows Forms DateTimePicker is not available as a web form control (at the time he is working), he is forced to use three DropDownList controls to select the year, month, and day for the reservation.

This seems like the ideal opportunity to create a user control. User controls are similar to composite controls on Windows Forms in that they can contain a set of controls configured as a group that can be treated on a web form as a single control. To create a user control you add a new item to the project; be sure to choose Web User Control from the Add New Item dialog box and give it a suitable name—in this case, DatePicker—and type in the filename DatePicker.ascx. Then you can lay out controls on the page as though you're constructing a web form. When the user control is complete, you can drag it from its place in Solution Explorer onto the form that needs to use it, in this case MakeReservation.aspx. The DatePicker control needs to have a number of features. First, it needs to display only days that are included in the displayed month—only 1 to 28 in a non-leap-year February, for instance. Second, it needs to limit dates to a range of acceptable dates for Icarus, such as not allowing dates before the present time— or actually not before one week after the present time—and it must not allow dates in the far future, probably no more than two years. The control in Design view is shown in Figure 7-49. The corresponding HTML markup is as follows:

```
<%@ Control Language="C#" AutoEventWireup="true" CodeFile="DatePicker.ascx.cs"
    Inherits="DatePicker" %>
<table border="0" cellspacing="0" cellpadding="0" style="width: 100%">
  <tr>
    <td style="width: 33.33%" align="left">
      Day <asp:DropDownList ID="DropDownListDay" runat="server"
        Width="70%"></asp:DropDownList>
    </td>
    <td style="width: 33.33%" align="right">
      Month <asp:DropDownList ID="DropDownListMonth" runat="server"
        Width="70%" ></asp:DropDownList>
    </td>
    <td style="width: 33.33%" align="right">
      Year <asp:DropDownList ID="DropDownListYear" runat="server"
        Width="70%" ></asp:DropDownList>
    </td>
  </tr>
</table>
```

Most of the detail in this HTML is involved in laying out the control so that it resizes correctly and displays properly when placed on a page.

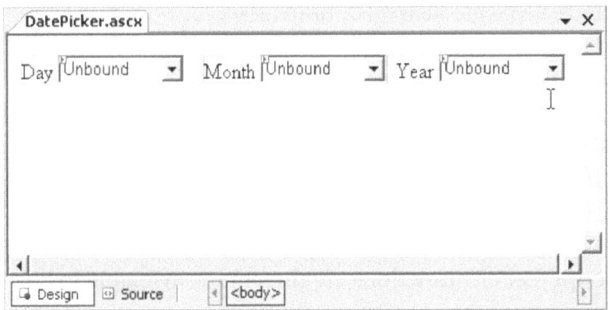

Figure 7-49. *The DatePicker web user control in Design view*

When the year or the month is changed, the available days must be updated in the Day drop-down. The Month drop-down also needs to update if the available months are limited by the acceptable date rules described earlier. This can be done either on the server or as client-side script. It is quite simple to do it on the server, but it is preferable (although more difficult) to do it as client-side script since this will avoid postbacks when the month or year drop-downs change, which may involve delay on a slow connection.

The client-side JavaScript (SalesSite\DatePicker.js) that accomplishes this is quite long. There are five separate JavaScript functions:

```
function InitializeDatePicker( clientIDDay, clientIDMonth,
    clientIDYear, minDay, minMonth, minYear )
```

```
function FillDatePicker( clientIDDay, clientIDMonth, clientIDYear, minDay,
    minMonth, minYear, selectedDay, selectedMonth, selectedYear )
```

```
function UpdateDatePicker( clientIDDay, clientIDMonth, clientIDYear, minDay,
    minMonth, minYear )
```

```
function DaysInMonth(month,year)
```

```
function IsLeapYear(year)
```

The InitializeDatePicker function will be called each time the page is first sent to the browser. The function needs the ID of the DropDownList controls for the day and month, as well as the minimum day month and year values as integers starting at one. This function initializes the DatePicker and allows it to display the default values, which will be the initial entry in the items list for each control.

The FillDatePicker function will be called when the page is sent back to the browser after a postback, so that it will be displayed with the same settings selected by the user when it was posted. It contains three extra arguments to supply the item indexes to be the selected indexes in the DropDownList controls.

The UpdateDatePicker function will be called whenever the month or year control is changed by the user on the form displayed in the browser.

The DaysInMonth and IsLeapYear are utility functions that will be called by the others.

ASP.NET 2.0 contains a feature called the ClientScriptManager that makes it easier to handle client-side script in ASP.NET pages. An instance of this class exists for each ASP.NET page, and your code can obtain a reference to it from the System.Web.UI.Page.ClientScript property. You can then call the ClientScriptManager member function RegisterClientScriptInclude in, for example, the Page_Load function of a code-behind file to register a script such as the DatePicker.js file as an included JavaScript file. The functions are then made available to be called by the HTML markup code. You can also use the ClientScriptManager member function RegisterStartupScript to register a script that will run when the page is displayed by the browser.

In the case of the DatePicker control, to make sure these functions get called at the right times, Ed needs to add some C# code in the code-behind file. First, here is the code used when the form is initially sent to the client browser:

```
string parameters =
    "'" + this.DropDownListDay.ClientID + "','"
    + this.DropDownListMonth.ClientID + "','"
    + this.DropDownListYear.ClientID + "',"
    + this.minimumDate.Day.ToString() + ","
    + this.minimumDate.Month.ToString() + ","
    + this.minimumDate.Year.ToString();


this.DropDownListMonth.Attributes.Add(
                        "OnChange", "UpdateDatePicker( " + parameters + " )");
this.DropDownListYear.Attributes.Add(
                        "OnChange", "UpdateDatePicker(" + parameters + " )");


this.Page.ClientScript.RegisterClientScriptInclude(
                        "DatePickerJS", "DatePicker.js");
this.Page.ClientScript.RegisterStartupScript(
                        this.GetType(),
                        "StartJS",
                        "InitializeDatePicker( " + parameters + " );\n", true);
```

In this case, the code adds OnChange attributes to the DropDownListMonth and DropDownListYear controls containing script that calls the UpdateDatePicker function and passes the necessary parameters. The file DatePicker.js is registered as an included file, and a call to InitializeDatePicker with the same parameters is registered as a start-up script.

The following code is used when the form is sent to the client after a postback:

```
DatePicker datePicker = sender as DatePicker;

int dayIndex = int.Parse(datePicker.DropDownListDay.SelectedValue);
int monthIndex = int.Parse(datePicker.DropDownListMonth.SelectedValue);
int yearIndex = int.Parse(datePicker.DropDownListYear.SelectedValue);
```

```
string parameters =
    "'" + this.DropDownListDay.ClientID + "','"
    + this.DropDownListMonth.ClientID + "','"
    + this.DropDownListYear.ClientID + "',"
    + this.minimumDate.Day.ToString() + ","
    + this.minimumDate.Month.ToString() + ","
    + this.minimumDate.Year.ToString();

string parameters1 = parameters + ","
    + dayIndex.ToString() + ","
    + monthIndex.ToString() + ","
    + yearIndex.ToString();

this.DropDownListMonth.Attributes.Add(
                        "OnChange", "UpdateDatePicker( " + parameters + " )");
this.DropDownListYear.Attributes.Add(
                        "OnChange", "UpdateDatePicker( " + parameters + " )");

this.Page.ClientScript.RegisterClientScriptInclude(
                                        "DatePickerJS", "DatePicker.js");
this.Page.ClientScript.RegisterStartupScript(
        this.GetType(), "StartJS", "FillDatePicker( " + parameters1 + " );\n", true);
```

The difference between this code and the code that runs when the form is first loaded is that the `FillDatePicker` function is registered as a start-up script so that the `DatePicker` control will be initialized with the values that were posted. A separate parameter string, `parameters1`, is used so that the three additional parameters can be passed. In the `Page_Load` function the decision can be made to run the correct piece of code on the basis of the familiar `if (!this.IsPostBack)` call.

Another piece of code has to be added to the `Page_Load` function that will run when the page is initially sent to the browser to avoid postback validation error exceptions. This populates the Items collections of the `DropDownList` controls with the maximum number of entries that they can have.

```
// Initialize the drop-down Items collection with the maximum number of
// elements possible.  This information will be overridden by the client-side
// script, but this initialization is needed to avoid invalid arguments in postback
// validation.
for (int i = 1; i <= 31; i++)
    this.DropDownListDay.Items.Add(i.ToString());
for (int i = 1; i <= 12; i++)
    this.DropDownListMonth.Items.Add(i.ToString());
for (int i = minimumDate.Year; i <= minimumDate.Year + 10; i++)
    this.DropDownListYear.Items.Add(i.ToString());
```

Note The source code at this stage is in the folder `Chapter 7\Exercise 16`.

Prototyping the List Wing Windows Forms Application

Rahul, who is working in India, has the responsibility of creating the List Wing Windows Forms application. He has a team of three people who will work with him to build and unit-test this application, but for the prototyping stage he is working alone and is responsible for delivery of the façade screens at the end of the second week of iteration 1 so that their visual images can be integrated into the storyboard document.

Rahul's team consists of Visual Basic developers. The List Wing Windows Forms application will be developed in Visual Basic .NET using Visual Studio 2005 Team System for Developers.

Before Rahul can begin work, Peter must use his Architect version of Visual Studio Team System to implement the ListWing project. He selects Visual Basic for the language in the implementation properties of the application in the application diagram, then right-clicks on the ListWing application in the application diagram and selects Implement Application. He then deletes the default form and changes the root namespace to

com.icarustravel.enterprise31.ListWing

The List Wing Windows Forms

Rahul can now begin adding forms, first as façades to support the storyboarding effort and then in detail so that they can be integrated with the ListingBusinessObjects classes that he and one of his team members, Manish, will be writing, beginning week 4 of iteration 1.

Note The source code at this stage is in the folder Chapter 7\Exercise 16. Exercise 17 will help you understand this section.

In the early discussions about storyboarding the List Wing application, the team has decided that resource management will be based around a main form that will act as a multiple document interface for vendors. Each vendor will be opened into a page of a tab control and displayed on a VendorDetails user composite control. This is very similar to the CustomerDetails control, and it is rather lucky that Rahul's team members are VB specialists because now you will see how to do this in VB as well as C#. First Rahul adds a new Windows Form to the application by right-clicking on the ListWing project and selecting Add ➤ Windows Form. He names the new form "VendorContacts.vb". Next he sizes the form and adds a MenuStrip control from the Toolbox. He adds a File menu item by typing "File" in the Type Here location on the MenuStrip control, then adds an "&Open Vendor" and an "E&xit" menu item under the File menu item. He quickly implements the Exit function by double-clicking on that menu item to generate its event handler function and types "Me.Close()" in that function.

Then Rahul goes to the MyProject folder under the solution and double-clicks to open the tabbed dialog box that represents the view of the code and settings within it. The Startup Form combo box must be adjusted to show VendorContacts as the startup form. He runs the application to be sure that the Exit menu item works.

Next, Rahul drags a TabControl from the Toolbox onto the design surface of the form, and adjusts it to take up the whole form. He opens the TabPages collection and deletes both of the tab pages, since he will write code to add them programatically each time a vendor is opened.

Now Rahul can create the user control VendorDetails, which will be placed in a tab page for each open vendor. This is similar to the C# implementation of the CustomerDetails user control; in fact, he even copies and pastes the sets of controls, within each tab, from the CustomerDetails user control in the SalesWing Windows Forms project in C# to the new VB user control. He only needs to rename a few of them; this is how similar C# and VB have become! The VendorDetails.vb control ends up looking like Figure 7-50 (the General tab) and Figure 7-51 (the Resources tab). The Business Address and Mailing Address tabs are the same as for the CustomerDetails control.

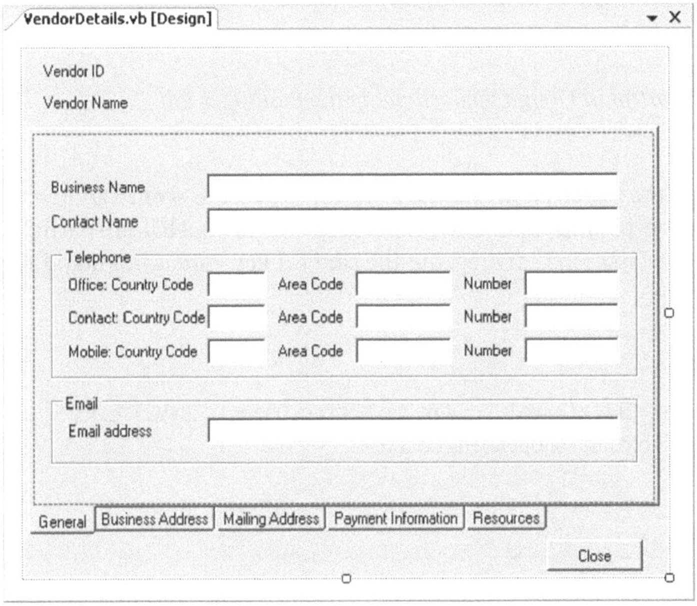

Figure 7-50. *The Vendor Details control in Design view showing the General tab*

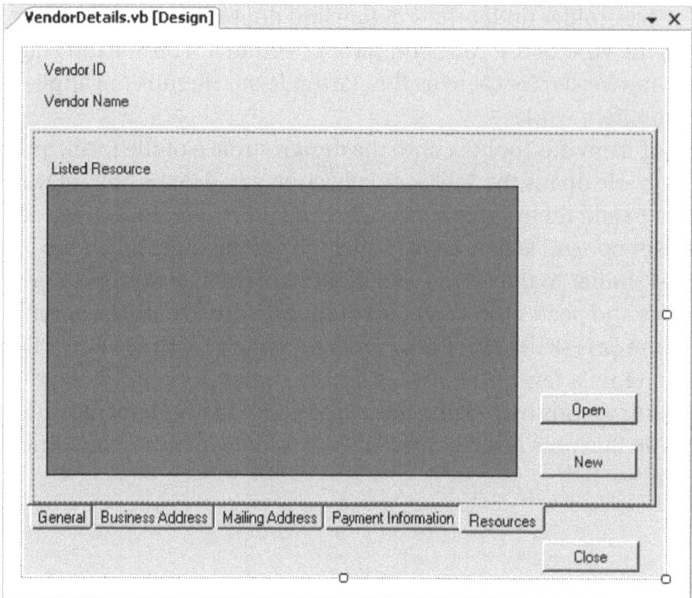

Figure 7-51. *The Vendor Details control in Design view, showing the Resources tab*

Next Rahul double-clicks on the Open, New, and Close buttons to create event handlers for them. He then looks at the code-behind class. Code-behind classes in VB .NET are partial classes in the same way as the C# classes in ListWing, but the partial keyword is not mandatory in VB. The code is shown here:

```
Public Class VendorDetails

    Private Sub buttonOpenOrder_Click(ByVal sender As System.Object, ByVal e As
        System.EventArgs) Handles buttonOpenOrder.Click
    End Sub

    Private Sub buttonNew_Click( _
        ByVal sender As System.Object, _
        ByVal e As System.EventArgs) Handles buttonNew.Click
    End Sub

    Private Sub ButtonClose_Click( _
        ByVal sender As System.Object, _
        ByVal e As System.EventArgs) Handles ButtonClose.Click
    End Sub

End Class
```

Certainly the event handler functions are there, but they don't do anything yet. The user control needs to either handle the action itself or communicate to its parent form that a button has been clicked. Actually, Rahul plans that the code that implements the creation of a new resource or displays and edits the details of an existing resource will be within this control, so it is only the clicking of the Close button that must be communicated to the parent form. To do this, he defines an event and a delegate; the principle is the same as in C# even though the syntax is different. Rahul adds code so that the VendorDetails class now looks like this:

```
Public Class VendorDetails

    Public Event CloseVendor As VendorDetailsEventHandler

    Public Delegate Sub VendorDetailsEventHandler(ByVal sender As VendorDetails)

    Private Sub buttonOpenOrder_Click(
                ByVal sender As System.Object, ByVal e As System.EventArgs)
                Handles buttonOpenOrder.Click
    End Sub

    Private Sub buttonNew_Click(
                ByVal sender As System.Object, ByVal e As System.EventArgs)
                Handles buttonNew.Click
    End Sub

    Private Sub ButtonClose_Click(
                ByVal sender As System.Object, ByVal e As System.EventArgs)
                Handles ButtonClose.Click
        RaiseEvent CloseVendor(Me)
    End Sub

End Class
```

The first two new lines add an event called CloseVendor and a delegate called VendorDetailsEventHandler that will represent a function that takes an instance of the VendorDetails form as an argument. The last line fires the CloseVendor event and passes this form as the argument to the event handler function.

Now that Rahul has created the VendorDetails user control, he must write the code that will add instances of it to the main VendorContacts Windows Form inside new tabs added to the tab control. To do this, he goes to the main menu in the VendorContacts form and double-clicks on the Open Vendor menu item to create the event handler for that menu item. Visual Studio generates the following code:

```
Private Sub OpenVendorToolStripMenuItem_Click(
                ByVal sender As System.Object, ByVal e As System.EventArgs)
                Handles OpenVendorToolStripMenuItem.Click

End Sub
```

The next step is to create the OpenVendor dialog box (shown in Chapter 6, Figure 6-16), which is similar to the OpenCustomer dialog box. Then Rahul can add VB code to the Open button event handler that will allow the vendor to be selected and a new populated tab page to be created. The following code performs these actions:

```
Private Sub OpenVendorToolStripMenuItem_Click(
            ByVal sender As System.Object, ByVal e As System.EventArgs)
            Handles OpenVendorToolStripMenuItem.Click

    If OpenVendor.ShowDialog() = Windows.Forms.DialogResult.OK Then

        Dim newPage As TabPage
        Dim vendorDetails As VendorDetails

        newPage = New TabPage()
        vendorDetails = New VendorDetails()
        vendorDetails.Dock = DockStyle.Fill
        AddHandler vendorDetails.CloseVendor, AddressOf OnCloseVendor
        newPage.Controls.Add(vendorDetails)
        Me.TabControl1.TabPages.Add(newPage)

    End If

End Sub

Public Sub OnCloseVendor(ByVal vendorDetails As VendorDetails)
    Me.TabControl1.TabPages.Remove(vendorDetails.Parent)
End Sub
```

If the Open Vendor dialog box returns DialogResult.OK, a new TabPage object is created together with a new instance of the VendorDetails user control. The Dock property of the VendorDetails user control is set to DockStyle.Fill so that it will fill the tab page area and resize with it. The code also adds a handler for the CloseVendor event that was just added—in VB, it is necessary to use the AddressOf operator when referring to the function OnCloseVendor. Finally, the new tab page is added to the control collection of the TabControl on the VendorContacts form. Of course this code does not actually obtain the vendor data from the database since only a façade project is being created at this time.

The OnCloseVendor function simply removes the parent of VendorDetails from the TabControl. The parent of the VendorDetails control that is passed in the argument is, of course, a TabPage control.

There is one more form in the façade set used for storyboarding the List Wing application: the ResourceDetail Windows Form, which allows the user to create new resources that belong to a particular vendor and view and edit details of existing resources. This form appears in Chapter 6 (Figures 6-20 and 6-21). The construction of it is straightforward, so I will not describe the details here.

Note The source code at this stage is in the folder Chapter 7\Exercise 17.

The Listing Business Objects Stubs

Defining the Listing business objects as stubs at this stage allows the team to define and test the details of the DataSet classes to which the forms will bind. Later the team will augment these forms with table adapters to communicate between the DataSet classes and the database table model.

Note The source code at this stage is in the folder Chapter 7\Exercise 17. Exercise 18 will help you understand this section.

Rahul first defines a ListingBusinessObjectsStubs folder and a Visual Basic class library project within it called VendorBEStub in which he can define the necessary DataSet classes and business entity classes. He then adds a new DataSet item to it and defines four DataTable objects (not TableAdapters): VENDOR, STATE, COUNTRY, and ORDER. He uses fields very similar to those used in CustomerDS. (You can look at this dataset in the source code.) He then goes back to the ListWing project and adds a reference to the VendorBEStub project. He does so by first right-clicking on the project and selecting Properties. The properties page for a VB project has a set of tabs, and references are controlled on the References tab. On the same tab it is also helpful to check the namespace com.icarustravel.enterprise31.Vendor in the Imported Namespaces, which is similar to a using statement in C#. On the VendorDetails user control, Rahul can now drag a DataSet from the Toolbox and select Referenced DataSets and VendorDS—exactly the procedure used in the SalesWing C# project.

Now comes the job of mapping all of the controls on the VendorDetails user control to fields on tables in the DataSet. This is again very similar to the process described for the CustomerDetails user control.

Then, Rahul must add the stub class VendorBE to the VendorBEStub project and write the code to implement the Get function in stub form:

```
Public Shared Function [Get](ByVal id As Integer) As VendorBE

  Dim vendorFields As Object() = {1, "Company1", "Contact1", _
  1, "Bus Address Line 1", "Bus Address Line 2", 1, _
  "BusCity1", 1, 1, "BusRegion1", "12345", _
  1, "Mail Address Line 1", "Mail Address Line 2", 1, _
  "MailCity1", 2, 2, "MailRegion1", "54321", _
  1, "12", "123", "1234", _
  1, "12", "123", "1234", _
  1, "12", "123", "1234", _
  "mail@mail.com"}

  Dim vendorBE As VendorBE

  vendorBE = New VendorBE
  vendorBE.data = New VendorDS
```

```
    vendorBE.data.VENDOR.LoadDataRow(vendorFields, True)

    Dim stateFields1 As Object() = {1, "Arkansas", "AK"}
    Dim stateFields2 As Object() = {2, "California", "CA"}
    Dim stateFields3 As Object() = {3, "Washington", "WA"}

    vendorBE.data.STATE.LoadDataRow(stateFields1, True)
    vendorBE.data.STATE.LoadDataRow(stateFields2, True)
    vendorBE.data.STATE.LoadDataRow(stateFields3, True)

    Dim countryFields1 As Object() = {1, "Australia", "", "", ""}
    Dim countryFields2 As Object() = {2, "Canada", "", "", ""}
    Dim countryFields3 As Object() = {3, "Zambia", "", "", ""}

    vendorBE.data.COUNTRY.LoadDataRow(countryFields1, True)
    vendorBE.data.COUNTRY.LoadDataRow(countryFields2, True)
    vendorBE.data.COUNTRY.LoadDataRow(countryFields3, True)

    Dim orderFields1 As Object() = {1, DateTime.Now}
    Dim orderFields2 As Object() = {2, DateTime.Now + New TimeSpan(1, 0, 0, 0)}

    vendorBE.data.ORDER.LoadDataRow(orderFields1, True)
    vendorBE.data.ORDER.LoadDataRow(orderFields2, True)

    Return vendorBE

End Function
```

This is a Shared function (the equivalent of a static function in VB). The Shared function creates an instance of VendorBE, gives it an instance of VendorDS as its DataSet, and then populates the tables of VendorDS with test data.

Rahul writes a similar stub for the ResourceDetail screen called ResourceBE with a dataset called ResourceDS. It is very similar to the VendorBE stub and can be seen in the ListingBusinessObjectsStubs\ResourceBE project. Rahul carries out the mappings to the controls in a similar manner. Upon testing, the ListWing application now has a ResourceDetail page populated with stub data, as shown in Figure 7-52.

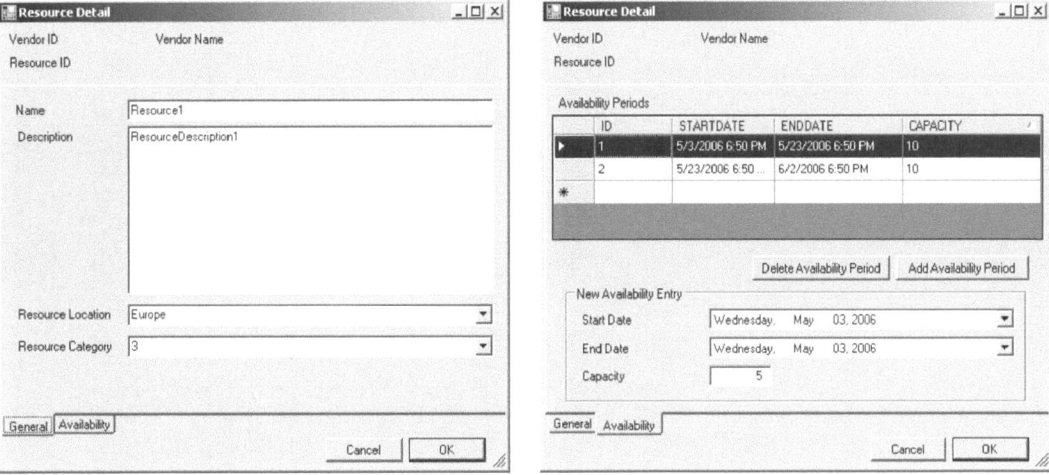

Figure 7-52. *The Resource Detail page populated with stub data, showing the General and Availability tabs*

Summary

This chapter has concentrated on coding various parts of the application using some of the new features of Visual Studio 2005. You followed the first stage of code development for the project, in which the prototyping needed for the analysis phase of iteration 1 was performed. The group focused mainly on constructing a prototype system implementing some degree of initial functionality, and you saw how the architect and prototyping group arrived at the initial proof-of-concept design. Only the display of customer details was made to operate right through to the database; other areas were completed as façade screens only.

Peter generated all the applications, other than the generic ones from the application diagram.

Angela and Peter prototyped part of the `SalesBusinessObjects` application, and you followed the code development in C#. Angela used generics to construct a base class for business entities that could be parameterized according to the type of datasets needed by the derived classes. You learned how to use typed dataset classes and their associated table adapter classes.

You saw the prototyping of the Sales Wing smart client application and learned how to define data binding between Windows Forms controls and `DataSet` classes. You also observed the prototyping of the Sales website. I explained the new concepts of master pages and partial classes, and showed how they can be used. We then focused on the `ObjectDataAdapter`, which is new to ASP 2.0, and how it can be used in binding web forms to business entity classes. Finally, this chapter outlined the prototyping of the List Wing smart client application in Visual Basic.

In the next chapter we will become more formal as we watch the team move into the second phase of iteration 1, with an emphasis on unit testing, code quality, and check-in controls.

CHAPTER 8

Development Team: Sales Business Layer Development

This chapter describes the more formal development phase in which the defined functionality for the `SalesBusinessObjects` application for iteration 1 is completed. We will follow Angela as she completes and consolidates the work on the sales business objects begun in the previous chapter. In that chapter we saw the prototyping of some of the classes in this application, `CustomerBE`, `CustomerDS`, and `CustomerDAL` classes, in a high level of detail. Here we will see the development of some of the rest of the business objects in support of the sales capability that implement reservation sales and management.

Adding the Prototype Code to Source Control

At the beginning of the development phase of iteration 1, all the developers working on the façade applications and business objects check all of the code into Team Foundation Server (TFS) version control to form a prototype baseline, which implements the storyboard screens and the capability to open and display detailed information for customers.

Note The source code for this section is in the folder `Chapter 8\Chapter8Start`. Exercise 8-1 demonstrates how to add a solution to source control.

Opening the Project from Source Control

Angela begins the development of the order business objects by opening the solution from source control to get the latest code onto her machine. Before she can do this, she will need to set up a *workspace*. Workspaces are the copies on the developer client machine of the files and folders on the source control server; they contain the files the developer is working on. Those files may differ from the corresponding versions on the server, or they may be newly created or deleted and therefore constitute *pending changes*. A defined workspace contains a definition of a location on the client in which to put these working files, as well as a corresponding folder in source control. It is thus a mapping between the two.

Note The source code for this section is in the folder `Chapter 8\Chapter8Start`. Exercise 8-2 applies to this section.

Angela starts Visual Studio 2005 and makes sure she is connected to the correct project in TFS; then she creates a workspace by selecting File ➤ Source Control ➤ Workspaces (Figure 8-1). The resulting Manage Workspaces dialog box will allow her to define a set of workspaces that associate particular folders within the team project with specified folders on her local machine. She clicks the Add button in the Manage Workspaces dialog box and sets up a workspace, as shown in Figure 8-2. Angela then clicks OK and closes the Manage Workspaces dialog box.

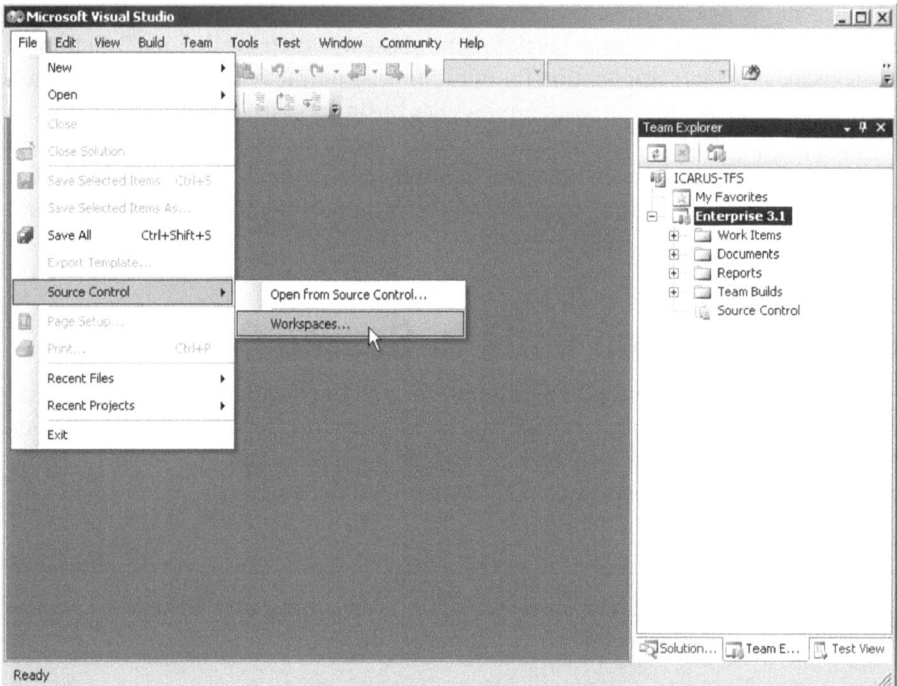

Figure 8-1. *Setting up workspaces for projects from source control*

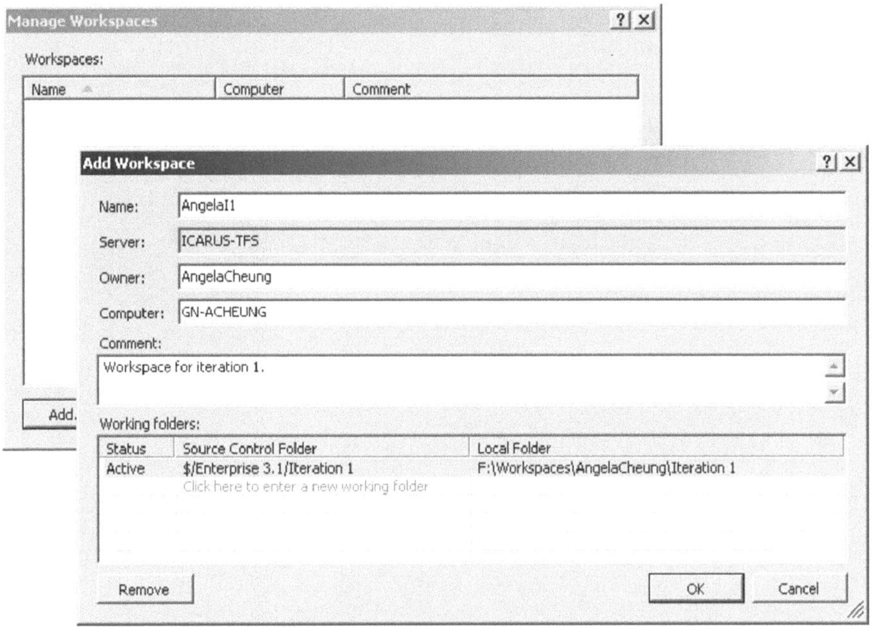

Figure 8-2. *The Add Workspace dialog box*

Angela then selects File ➤ Source Control ➤ Open from Source Control, as shown in Figure 8-3, which displays the Open from Source Control dialog box. This allows Angela to drill down through the source control structure of the team project. There is a combo box called Workspaces where she can select one of her defined workspaces, which will cause the system to get all the folders and files for the solution into the local folder defined by the workspace. Alternatively, in this dialog box Angela can click on the ellipsis and select a different location. Angela double-clicks the Iteration 1 folder in the Enterprise 3.1 team project and selects her workspace, then finds the solution file `Enterprise 3.1.sln` (Figure 8-4) and double-clicks on it. The system gets copies of all of the files and folders in the solution onto her local machine, places them in the local folder specified in the workspace, and opens the solution.

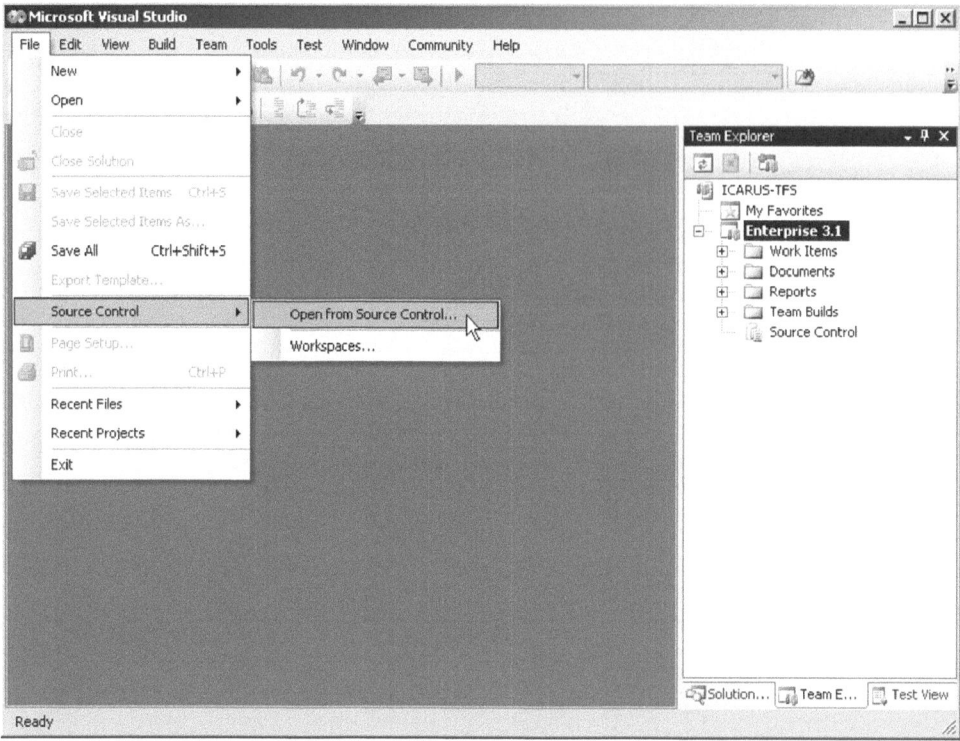

Figure 8-3. *Opening a project from source control*

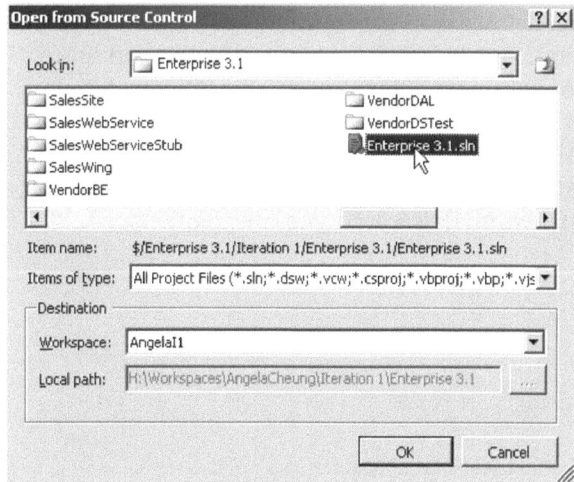

Figure 8-4. *The Open from Source Control dialog box*

At this point, let's look at three of the views that are helpful in seeing a project and its relation to source control. The familiar Team Explorer and Solution Explorer windows are shown in Figure 8-5, but there's another useful view, the Source Control Explorer, shown in Figure 8-6. This view shows you what is in the source control part of your team project, and you can view it by double-clicking on Source Control under an open team project in Team Explorer. It's very much like the view that you get of the project structure in Visual SourceSafe, and you can use it in much the same way. You can get the latest version of a file, check it out for editing, check it in, view history, apply labels, compare the TFS version with your local version, and a whole lot more. Whereas Solution Explorer shows only the solution that is open, Source Control Explorer shows what is available in the version control repository.

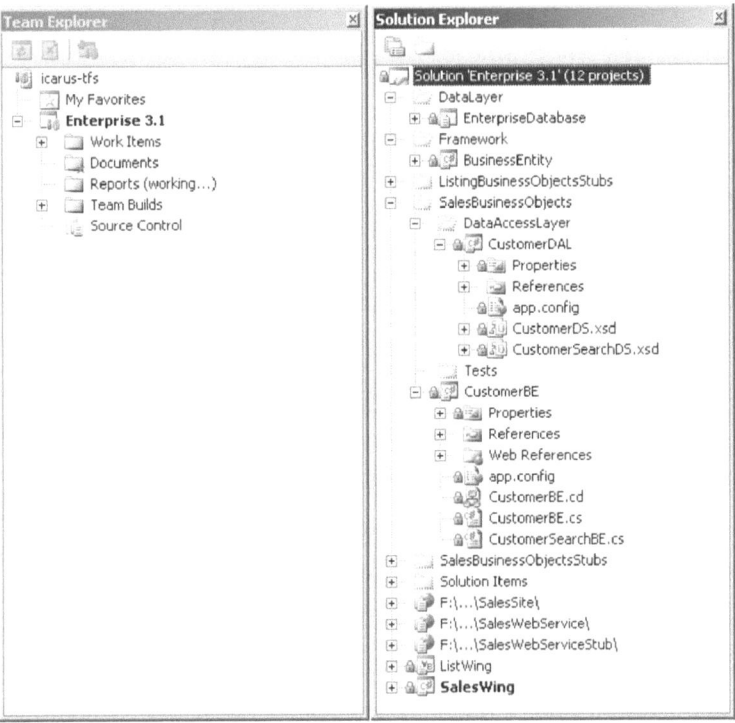

Figure 8-5. *The Team Explorer and Solution Explorer windows*

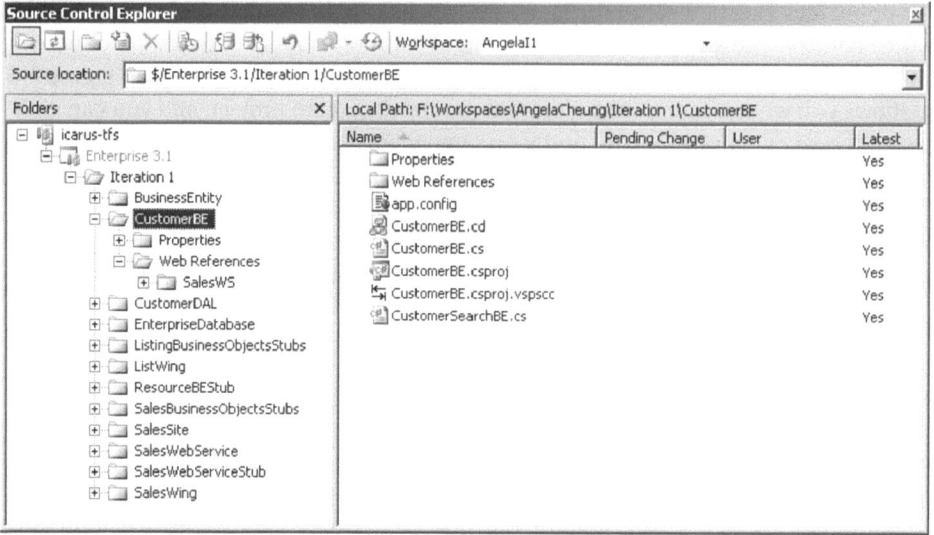

Figure 8-6. *The Source Control Explorer window*

Creating the Order Data Access Component Classes

Angela plans to create another pair of business object projects, similar to CustomerBE and CustomerDAL, to handle operations involving the order as a business entity, in which there will be various business entity classes and data access layer typed dataset classes.

Note The source code for this section is in the folder Chapter 8\Chapter8Start. Exercise 8-3 applies to this section.

Angela begins by right-clicking on the DataAccessLayer folder in the SalesBusinessObjects folder in Solution Explorer and selecting Add New Project. She selects Visual C# ➤ Windows ➤ Class Library and calls the new project OrderDAL. She deletes the automatic Class1 and changes the namespace to com.icarustravel.enterprise31.Order. The system has now added a project and its associated files, and has checked out the solution file from TFS since it needs to modify that file to add the new project. Looking at Solution Explorer, we see that all of the new files have a yellow plus (+) sign beside them, which shows that they have been added as new files and are additional to what is currently in TFS. Also we see that the Enterprise 3.1.sln file in Solution Explorer now has a red checkmark to indicate that it is checked out to Angela. Previously it showed a blue padlock. Thus, Visual Studio has automatically checked out the one file that needed to change as a result of adding the new project.

Next Angela creates a dataset called OrderDS in a similar way to the previous chapter. This typed dataset will contain all of the data required to display a particular order, including the reservations that it contains. The dataset therefore needs to contain two tables: a table called ORDER, which will contain just the one row that applies to the particular order being viewed, and a table called RESERVATION, which will contain a row for each reservation contained within the order. The TableAdapter objects in the dataset will be defined using stored procedures. There is one important difference from the CustomerDS created in the previous chapter: this OrderDS must support update of the database from the data in the dataset. To achieve this, Angela must create stored procedures to perform insert, update, and delete operations of rows in the database that will be called as required when a DataTable is saved, according to the state of each of its rows. As each TableAdapter is created, at the page in the Table Adapter Configuration wizard in which the Advanced Options button appears, it is therefore necessary to select all the options: Generate Insert, Update and Delete Statements, Use Optimistic Concurrency, and Refresh the DataTable. Angela uses the Query Builder to define the SQL for the SELECT statement, which is very simple; it just gets all of the fields from the ORDER table for a specified @ORDERID parameter—there should be just one.

```
SELECT      ID, CUSTOMERID, ORDERDATE
FROM        [ORDER]
WHERE       (ID = @ORDERID)
```

Continuing through the wizard for the ORDER table adapter, she names the four stored procedures to be generated: SELECTORDER, INSERTORDER, UPDATEORDER, and DELETEORDER. Angela clicks the Preview Script button to see what will be generated. Here's the SELECT part:

```
IF EXISTS (SELECT * FROM sysobjects WHERE name = 'GETORDER'
                                    AND user_name(uid) = 'dbo')
  DROP PROCEDURE dbo.GETORDER
GO


CREATE PROCEDURE dbo.GETORDER
(
  @ORDERID int
)
AS
  SET NOCOUNT ON;
  SELECT      ID, CUSTOMERID, ORDERDATE
  FROM        [ORDER]
  WHERE       (ID = @ORDERID)
GO
```

This simply inserts a stored procedure executing the SELECT SQL script that we just mentioned, but drops the stored proc if it already exists. The NOCOUNT ON option prevents the script from returning the number of modified rows and thus saves a little network traffic. I'll leave out the part with the DROP statement in the rest of the stored procedure listings. Here's the INSERTORDER procedure, which is created by the wizard from the original SELECT statement:

```
CREATE PROCEDURE dbo.INSERTORDER
(
  @CUSTOMERID int,
  @ORDERDATE datetime
)
AS
  SET NOCOUNT OFF;
```

```
  INSERT INTO [ORDER] ([CUSTOMERID], [ORDERDATE])
  VALUES (@CUSTOMERID,   @ORDERDATE);

  SELECT ID, CUSTOMERID, ORDERDATE FROM [ORDER]
  WHERE (ID = SCOPE_IDENTITY())
GO
```

The last SELECT results from checking the Update the Data Table option and returns
a copy of the row that was inserted. This is necessary because an identity is used to create the
value of the primary key ID field for the rows in the ORDER table, and this ID field needs to be
returned so that the rows in the ORDER table in the dataset can include the ID field.

By the way, I should say here that during the prototyping in Chapter 7, the decision to
create primary keys with database identities had not been made. Peter has now made the
decision to use incrementing identities beginning at 1000 for all primary key fields. This leaves
room for the test data scripts to insert specific primary key values below that threshold using
SET IDENTITY_INSERT (table name) ON. The test data scripts have therefore been modified
accordingly.

The SCOPE_IDENTITY() function used in the WHERE clause returns the last value of an identity element generated in the current scope, which in this case is the stored procedure. Here is
the UPDATEORDER procedure:

```
CREATE PROCEDURE dbo.UPDATEORDER
(
  @CUSTOMERID int,
  @ORDERDATE datetime,
  @Original_ID int,
  @IsNull_CUSTOMERID int,
  @Original_CUSTOMERID int,
  @IsNull_ORDERDATE datetime,
  @Original_ORDERDATE datetime,
  @ID int
)
AS
  SET NOCOUNT OFF;
  UPDATE [ORDER]
  SET [CUSTOMERID] = @CUSTOMERID, [ORDERDATE] = @ORDERDATE
  WHERE
    (([ID] = @Original_ID)
      AND ((@IsNull_CUSTOMERID = 1 AND [CUSTOMERID] IS NULL)
        OR ([CUSTOMERID] = @Original_CUSTOMERID))
      AND ((@IsNull_ORDERDATE = 1 AND [ORDERDATE] IS NULL)
        OR ([ORDERDATE] = @Original_ORDERDATE)));

  SELECT ID, CUSTOMERID, ORDERDATE FROM [ORDER] WHERE (ID = @ID)
GO
```

The complicated WHERE clause is the result of checking the Use Optimistic Concurrency
advanced option. The INSERT only occurs if the field values are the same as the original values
or are null, and they were originally null. This requires a lot of extra parameters. For instance,

there are a set of parameters prefixed by "Original_" that contain the original values read from the row by the table adapter, as well as a corresponding set of parameters of the same type without such a prefix. There is also a set of parameters of the same name and type but prefixed by "IsNull_". There will be one of these for each nullable parameter to indicate that the original value was null. Finally, the DELETEORDER procedure is

```
CREATE PROCEDURE dbo.DELETEORDER
(
  @Original_ID int,
  @IsNull_CUSTOMERID int,
  @Original_CUSTOMERID int,
  @IsNull_ORDERDATE datetime,
  @Original_ORDERDATE datetime
)
AS
  SET NOCOUNT OFF;
  DELETE FROM [ORDER]
  WHERE
    ((([ID] = @Original_ID)
    AND ((@IsNull_CUSTOMERID = 1 AND [CUSTOMERID] IS NULL)
      OR ([CUSTOMERID] =    @Original_CUSTOMERID))
    AND ((@IsNull_ORDERDATE = 1 AND [ORDERDATE] IS NULL)
      OR ([ORDERDATE] = @Original_ORDERDATE)))
GO
```

This again has all the extra code to support optimistic concurrency.

Moving now to the RESERVATION table, again the SELECT SQL is very simple; it just needs to select all of the reservation rows that have the foreign key ORDERID equal to a specified parameter, the ID of the order for which we require the reservations.

```
SELECT
  ID, RESOURCEAVAILABILITYID, ORDERID, UNITCOUNT, UNITCOST, EXTENDEDCOST
FROM RESERVATION
WHERE (ORDERID = @ORDERID)
```

However, when Angela goes through the wizard to generate the table adapter in the same way as before, she finds that it only generates the SELECT and INSERT stored procedures, which she names "GETRESERVATIONSFORORDER" and "INSERTRESERVATION". If you think about it, you can see why. The wizard does not have enough information to generate the UPDATE and DELETE stored procedures. This is because the SELECT SQL had a WHERE clause that is not based on the primary key of the table—Angela is selecting based on a foreign key relationship—so the wizard has no way of knowing which field in the set returned by the SELECT statement defines the row uniquely so that an UPDATE and a DELETE statement can be generated.

Once Angela figures this out, she decides on a plan. She will let the wizard generate these two stored procedures and then write the other two—which are trivial anyway—by hand. She can then reconfigure the table adapter to use the two handwritten ones as well as the ones that were generated.

So having completed the wizard for the RESERVATION table adapter in the same way as for the ORDER table adapter, Angela sees in Server Explorer that only GETRESERVATIONSFORORDER and INSERTRESERVATION have been created. Now she can simply go to the database project called EnterpriseDatabase, right-click on the Create Scripts folder, and select Create SQL Script. She selects Stored Procedure Script in the Add New Item dialog box, and then calls the script "DELETERESERVATION". She then writes a stored procedure along the same lines as DELETEORDER:

```
CREATE Procedure DELETERESERVATION
(
  @Original_ID int,
  @IsNull_RESOURCEAVAILABILITYID int,
  @Original_RESOURCEAVAILABILITYID int,
  @IsNull_ORDERID int,
  @Original_ORDERID int,
  @IsNull_UNITCOUNT int,
  @Original_UNITCOUNT int,
  @IsNull_UNITCOST decimal,
  @Original_UNITCOST decimal,
  @IsNull_EXTENDEDCOST decimal,
  @Original_EXTENDEDCOST decimal
)
AS
  SET NOCOUNT OFF;
  DELETE FROM [RESERVATION]
  WHERE
    (([ID] = @Original_ID)
    AND ((@IsNull_RESOURCEAVAILABILITYID = 1 AND [RESOURCEAVAILABILITYID] IS NULL)
      OR ([RESOURCEAVAILABILITYID] = @Original_RESOURCEAVAILABILITYID))
    AND ((@IsNull_ORDERID = 1 AND [ORDERID] IS NULL)
      OR ([ORDERID] = @Original_ORDERID))
    AND ((@IsNull_UNITCOUNT = 1 AND [UNITCOUNT] IS NULL)
      OR ([UNITCOUNT] = @Original_UNITCOUNT))
    AND ((@IsNull_UNITCOST = 1 AND [UNITCOST] IS NULL)
      OR ([UNITCOST] = @Original_UNITCOST))
    AND ((@IsNull_EXTENDEDCOST = 1 AND [EXTENDEDCOST] IS NULL)
      OR ([EXTENDEDCOST] = @Original_EXTENDEDCOST)))
```

This procedure deletes a row with ID field value equal to the @Original_ID parameter provided all of its fields are unchanged from their original values (whether null or not) that are passed from the calling code in the table adapter.

Angela creates UPDATERESERVATION in a similar manner with this code:

```
CREATE Procedure UPDATERESERVATION
(
  @ID int,
  @Original_ID int,
  @RESOURCEAVAILABILITYID int,
  @IsNull_RESOURCEAVAILABILITYID int,
  @Original_RESOURCEAVAILABILITYID int,
  @ORDERID int,
```

```
  @IsNull_ORDERID int,
  @Original_ORDERID int,
  @UNITCOUNT int,
  @IsNull_UNITCOUNT int,
  @Original_UNITCOUNT int,
  @UNITCOST decimal,
  @IsNull_UNITCOST decimal,
  @Original_UNITCOST decimal,
  @EXTENDEDCOST decimal,
  @IsNull_EXTENDEDCOST decimal,
  @Original_EXTENDEDCOST decimal
)
AS
  SET NOCOUNT OFF;
  UPDATE [RESERVATION] SET
     [RESOURCEAVAILABILITYID] = @RESOURCEAVAILABILITYID,
     [ORDERID] = @ORDERID,
     [UNITCOUNT] = @UNITCOUNT,
     [UNITCOST] = @UNITCOST,
     [EXTENDEDCOST] = @EXTENDEDCOST
  WHERE
    (([ID] = @Original_ID)
    AND ((@IsNull_RESOURCEAVAILABILITYID = 1 AND [RESOURCEAVAILABILITYID] IS NULL)
      OR ([RESOURCEAVAILABILITYID] = @Original_RESOURCEAVAILABILITYID))
    AND ((@IsNull_ORDERID = 1 AND [ORDERID] IS NULL)
      OR ([ORDERID] = @Original_ORDERID))
    AND ((@IsNull_UNITCOUNT = 1 AND [UNITCOUNT] IS NULL)
      OR ([UNITCOUNT] = @Original_UNITCOUNT))
    AND ((@IsNull_UNITCOST = 1 AND [UNITCOST] IS NULL)
      OR ([UNITCOST] = @Original_UNITCOST))
    AND ((@IsNull_EXTENDEDCOST = 1 AND [EXTENDEDCOST] IS NULL)
      OR ([EXTENDEDCOST] = @Original_EXTENDEDCOST)));

  SELECT ID, RESOURCEAVAILABILITYID, ORDERID, UNITCOUNT,
    UNITCOST, EXTENDEDCOST FROM [RESERVATION]
  WHERE (ID = @ID)
```

Having created the two missing stored procedures, the RESERVATION table adapter can now be reconfigured to use them. Angela goes to the OrderDS design view, right-clicks on the RESERVATION table adapter, and selects Configure. The wizard enters the page that shows Bind Commands to Existing Stored Procedures as the selected option, and Angela selects the two new stored procedures in the Update and Delete combo boxes, as shown in Figure 8-7. She then proceeds through the rest of the wizard steps as before, and the wizard generates code to use the new stored procedures. It is beyond the scope of this book to delve into what code the wizard generates and how it works, but you can view the OrderDS.Designer.cs file, which contains the partial class that defines the part of the OrderDS class that contains the automatically generated code. Any specific code that the developer adds to OrderDS is placed in a corresponding partial class in the OrderDS.cs file.

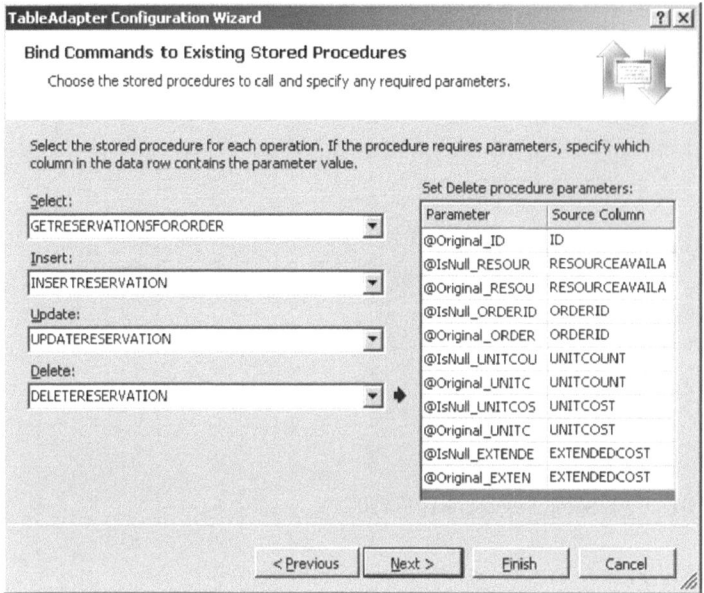

Figure 8-7. *Reconfiguring the RESERVATION table adapter*

Testing the Data Access Layer

Since in the second half of iteration 1 the team wishes to deliver code that has been formally tested, Angela needs to write some unit tests for the order data access component OrderDS class.

Note The source code for this section is in the folder Chapter 8\Exercise 3. Exercise 8-4 applies to this section.

There are a great many member functions and subclasses that are generated automatically, and unit-testing all of them may not be worthwhile. To be sure, however, that the stored procedures are working properly and that the table adapter classes are properly configured to use them, Angela must write a few simple tests. Perhaps the best classes to test, then, are the table adapters themselves: ORDERTableAdapter and RESERVATIONTableAdapter. In these classes the Fill and Update functions need to be tested to ensure that the DataTable objects passed to the Fill functions as parameters are properly populated from the database, and that the database is correctly updated from the DataTable objects passed to the Update functions. In the second case, three circumstances need to be verified: when a row is inserted, when a row is deleted, and when a row is modified.

To generate the tests, Angela opens the file containing the `ORDERTableAdapter` class by double-clicking on the class in Class view. She then right-clicks on the class name in the class declaration (Figure 8-8) and selects Create Unit Tests from the context menu. The dialog box shown in Figure 8-9 is displayed.

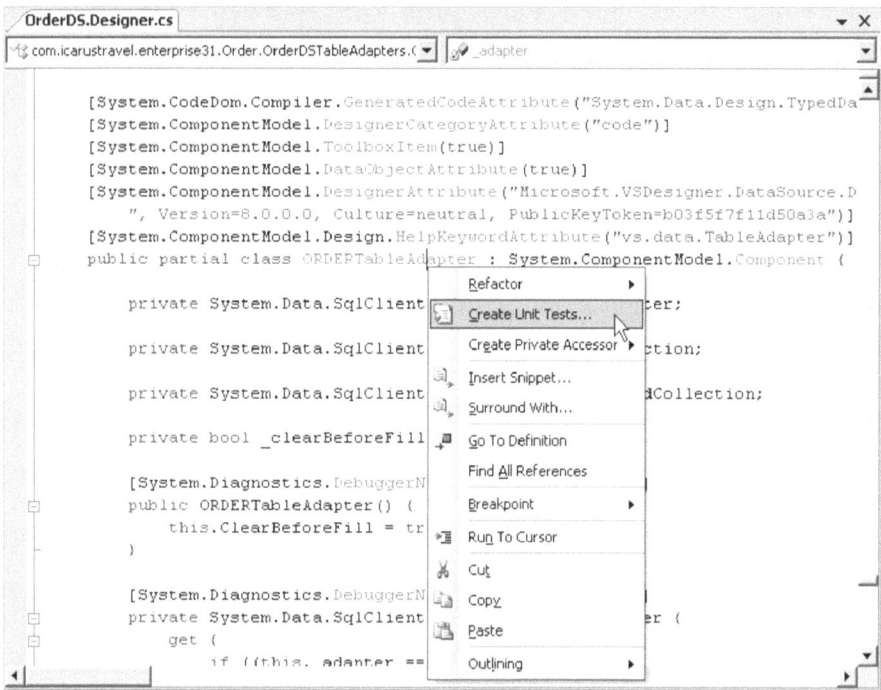

Figure 8-8. *Creating unit tests from the class definition*

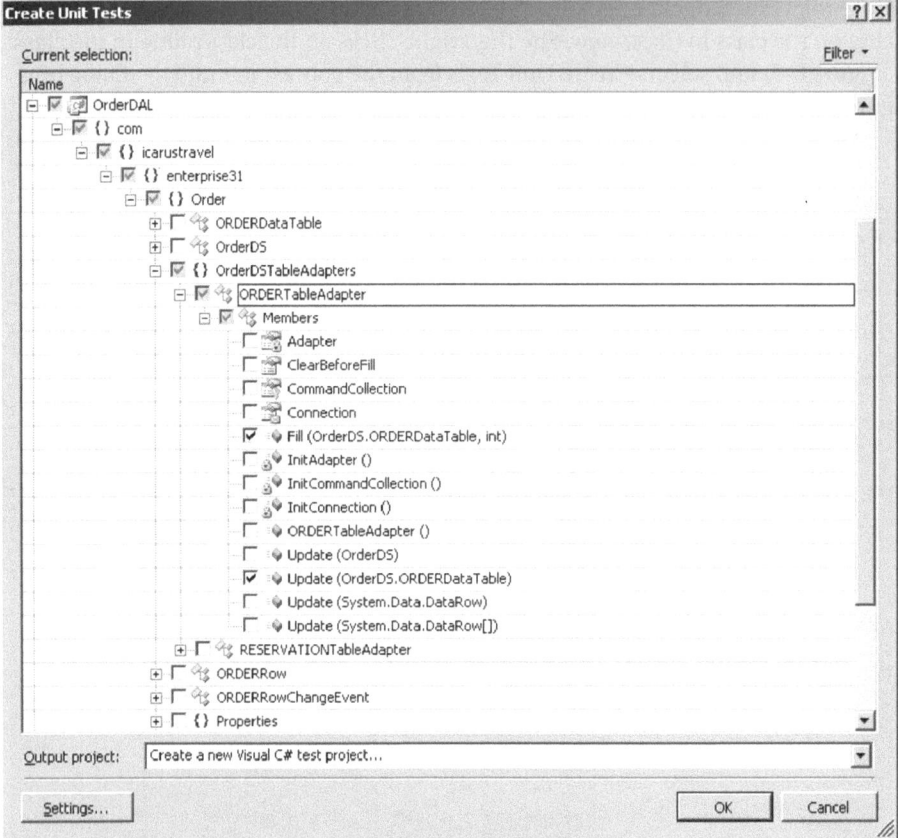

Figure 8-9. *Selecting functions for which tests will be generated*

This is actually a tree view of all the classes in the solution and is initially displayed with all the member functions checked for the chosen class, which in this case is ORDERTableAdapter. Angela only wants to generate tests for the Fill and Update member functions, and even for those, she will only test the overloads that take an object derived from DataTable such as ORDERDataTable. She therefore clears everything else, selects Create a Visual C# Test Project at the bottom of the dialog box, and clicks the Settings button to check that those are right. The Naming Settings group in the Test Generation Settings dialog box (Figure 8-10) allows Angela to define the way that the names of the files, classes, and methods are generated based on the names of the file, class, and method being tested. In the General group, there is an option to generate code that causes an inconclusive result to be returned for all tests until the developer has properly written the test code. Angela can also enable or disable generation warnings, which are warnings occurring in the unit test code generation process. The Globally Qualify All Types checkbox causes the unit test code to generate all variable declarations using globally qualified types. This can avoid ambiguity when similarly named types exist in different namespaces. Documentation comments can also be added optionally.

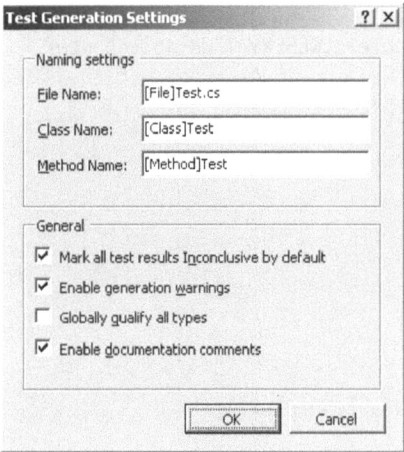

Figure 8-10. *The Settings dialog box for unit test generation*

Angela leaves the settings at the default values, returns to the Create Unit Tests dialog box, and clicks OK. She names the new project "OrderBETests" and clicks Create. The project is actually created at the top level under the solution, so Angela creates a Tests folder under the SalesBusinessObjects folder and drags the new project into it.

She then repeats the unit test generation for the RESERVATIONTableAdapter class and rebuilds the solution to make sure everything is OK. Let's have a look at the unit-test code that Team System has generated for the methods that were selected in the RESERVATIONTableAdapter class.

```
/// <summary>
///A test for Fill (OrderDS.RESERVATIONDataTable, int?)
///</summary>
[TestMethod()]
public void FillTest()
{
    RESERVATIONTableAdapter target = new RESERVATIONTableAdapter();

    OrderDS.RESERVATIONDataTable dataTable = null;
    // TODO: Initialize to an appropriate value

    System.Nullable<int> ORDERID = new System.Nullable<int>();
    // TODO: Initialize to an appropriate value

    int expected = 0;
    int actual;

    actual = target.Fill(dataTable, ORDERID);
```

```
        Assert.AreEqual(expected, actual,
    "com.icarustravel.enterprise31.Order.OrderDSTableAdapters.RESERVATIONTableAdapter."
        + "Fill did not return the expected value.");
        Assert.Inconclusive("Verify the correctness of this test method.");
    }

    /// <summary>
    ///A test for Update (OrderDS.RESERVATIONDataTable)
    ///</summary>
    [TestMethod()]
    public void UpdateTest()
    {
        RESERVATIONTableAdapter target = new RESERVATIONTableAdapter();

        OrderDS.RESERVATIONDataTable dataTable = null;
        // TODO: Initialize to an appropriate value

        int expected = 0;
        int actual;

        actual = target.Update(dataTable);

        Assert.AreEqual(expected, actual,
    "com.icarustravel.enterprise31.Order.OrderDSTableAdapters.RESERVATIONTableAdapter."
        + "Update did not return the expected value.");
        Assert.Inconclusive("Verify the correctness of this test method.");
    }
```

The first method, `public void FillTest()`, is intended to test the `Fill(dataTable, ORDERID)` function. The skeleton code that is automatically generated first creates an instance of the class under test, `RESERVATIONTableAdapter`. It then creates variables to hold the parameters to be passed to the member function to be tested and also variables to represent the expected and actual return values. The member function `Fill(dataTable, ORDERID)` is then called, and a call to the `Assert.AreEqual` function verifies the correctness of the return value. Following that, an `Assert.Inconclusive` function call has been inserted as a default, since the option in the Settings dialog box, Mark All Test Results Inconclusive by Default, was checked.

Notice that the `ORDERID` parameter of the `Fill(dataTable, ORDERID)` is of type `System.Nullable<int>`. The `Fill` function was defined by the wizard when the table adapter was created and the type `System.Nullable<int>` is a class that represents a value type, in this case `int`, that can also be assigned a null value. This is a good example of another use of generics—we used them in the previous chapter, remember—where the `Nullable` class actually takes a type parameter that specifies the type (`int`, `double`, `decimal`, etc.) of the underlying value type that the `Nullable` class represents.

There is some work to do to fill in the detail of this test. Angela must first decide what tests she will implement. To test the `Fill` function, she needs some known data in the database that the tested function can access to fill a data table, which can then be verified against the data in the database, accessing that data by a different route. This approach requires that an organized plan exist that makes this known data available in the database so the tests can be repeatable.

Of course, Angela can use her own copy of SQL Server Express Edition on her machine to provide known data, but it is very useful to be able to run the unit tests in the common build environment as well. If that approach is to be followed, there must be a common philosophy across the project from the start to make that possible. In my experience, this is something that is often neglected.

Another approach is for each developer to write the unit tests so that they stand alone; for a read case, they insert their test data into the database, run the test of the read capability, verify the data that is returned, and then clean the test data out of the database. Conversely, to test writing functionality of the code, they run the write test, verify independently that the data has been written correctly, and then clean the data out of the database. Alternatively, the read and write cases of the unit tests can be combined so that the write capabilities are tested, then the read capabilities, and finally the delete capabilities. In this way the database is left unchanged. This last idea sounds very good, but there are problems. First, this kind of "round-trip" capability may not exist in the defined functionality of the code to be tested, that is, there may be read capability but no write or delete capability. Second, the tests may fail halfway, leaving garbage data in the database that will cause the test to fail when run again, or cause subsequent tests to fail.

The unit-test capabilities of Visual Studio 2005 Team Edition allow us to perform initialization and cleanup functions at both the class and test levels in the form of commented-out code in the test skeleton:

```
//
//Use ClassInitialize to run code before running the first test in the class
//
//[ClassInitialize()]
//public static void MyClassInitialize(TestContext testContext)
//{
//}
//
//Use ClassCleanup to run code after all tests in a class have run
//
//[ClassCleanup()]
//public static void MyClassCleanup()
//{
//}
//
//Use TestInitialize to run code before running each test
//
//[TestInitialize()]
//public void MyTestInitialize()
//{
//}
//
//Use TestCleanup to run code after each test has run
//
//[TestCleanup()]
//public void MyTestCleanup()
//{
//}
```

Therefore, it is a good idea to put the initialization of the database contents and final cleanup in these methods.

Angela is the first developer to begin writing unit tests, and she has a discussion with Peter and Ron about this topic. They decide that developers will be responsible for initializing their own unit-test data in the database and for cleaning up afterward and that, if necessary, a general test support project will contain classes to do this.

Here are the test sequences that Angela defines for the `ORDERTableAdapter` class; refer to the data model in Figures 6-44 through 6-49.

Class Initialization

The class initialization writes the known, standard test data to the database that the test will access.

1. Write a single row to the RESOURCECATEGORY table.

2. Write a single row to the GEOGRAPHICREGION table.

3. Write a single row to the VENDOR table.

4. Write a single row to the RESOURCE table to represent a test resource, referencing the three previous rows.

5. Write two rows to the RESOURCEAVAILABILITY table to represent test availabilities.

6. Write a row to the ORDER table representing a test ORDER.

7. Write two rows to the RESERVATION table referencing this order to represent test reservations for the test order.

Order Fill Test Sequence

The Order Fill test verifies that the `ORDERTableAdapter` class correctly reads a known order from the standard test data in the database.

1. Create an `ORDERDataTable` data table object to be used as a parameter to the `Fill(ORDERDataTable DataTable, System.Nullable<int> ORDERID)` function.

2. Call that function, passing the data table and the ID of the test order that the class initialization sequence inserted in step 6 of the previous section.

3. Verify that the data table returned from the `Fill` function contains a single row containing the correct data for the test order.

Order Update Test Sequence

The Order Update test verifies the ability of the `ORDERTableAdapter` to write an order to the database, but first just a quick word about the `Update(ORDERDataTable DataTable)` function of the `ORDERTableAdapter`. This function updates all the rows in the database represented by the rows in `DataTable` *as necessary*. It decides what is necessary according the `RowState` property of each `DataRow` in the `DataTable`. This property contains one of these values: `Added`, `Deleted`, `Modified`, or `Unchanged`. If the state is `Unchanged`, no action at the database is necessary. If the state is `Deleted`, the Delete SQL stored procedure is called for that row. If its state is `Modified`, the

Update SQL stored procedure is called, and if its state is Added, the Insert stored procedure is called. The Update and Insert stored procedures, called on a row-by-row basis, will undoubtedly use the UPDATE and INSERT SQL statements, but the meaning of the UPDATE SQL statement is different from the Update function of the table adapter.

The test sequence is

1. Create an ORDERDataTable data table object as a parameter to the Update(ORDERDataTable DataTable) function.

2. Add an order row to that data table.

3. Call the Update function of the test ORDERTableAdapter, passing the data table.

4. Verify via an alternative route that the ORDER table in the database contains the new order with the correct data.

5. Modify the single row in the ORDERDataTable data table that was added in step 2.

6. Add a second row to the ORDERDataTable data table.

7. Call the update function of the test ORDERTableAdapter, passing the ORDER table.

8. Verify via an alternative route that the ORDER table in the database contains the first row, now modified, and that the second row was added.

9. Delete the second row in the ORDER table.

10. Call the update function, passing the data table.

11. Verify via an alternative route that the ORDER table in the database shows that the second row has been deleted but the first row still exists.

12. Delete the first order row in the ORDER table.

13. Verify via an alternative route that the ORDER table in the database shows that the first row has now also been deleted.

Class Cleanup

Class cleanup removes the standard test data that was placed in the database.

1. Remove all of the rows that were added in tables as part of class initialization.

Actually, if the test described here fails in the middle, rows written to the database by part of the test may be left in the tables. To make the test fully self-contained, this aspect needs to be considered as well. One approach is to reinitialize the database between tests, but this will make the tests take longer.

Unit-Test Design

A quick way to implement the class initialization requirements is to define a dataset that can contain table adapters to read, write, insert, and delete the test rows added to the tables upon which the operation of the test depends. This class is only required by the test project used to unit-test the classes in the OrderBE project, and so it makes sense to contain this class in that test project. Its table adapters form the "alternative route" to the database mentioned in the

Order Update Test Sequence section. Unfortunately, this class is dependent on the design of the data model outside of the OrderBE model; if that changes, this class will have to be updated. This dependency is a result of the dependencies within the data model of the ORDER table on the tables RESOURCE, VENDOR, CUSTOMER, and so on.

The code for the class initialization follows, but first a note on naming conventions. Throughout this book I use Pascal case for classes (e.g., MyOrderClass) and lower camel case for variable names such as myOrderClass for a reference to an instance of MyOrderClass. As in this example, a convenient name for an instance of a class is often obtained by dropping the case of the first letter of the class. I like that convention because you can immediately see the class to which an object reference belongs. I have used all uppercase for names of data tables in the database and in datasets (such as VENDOR). Visual Studio automatically obtains names for table adapters by concatenating the table name with the TableAdapter base class name, such as VENDORTableAdapter. Dropping the case of the first letter to give a name of vENDORTableAdapter for an instance of the table adapter is therefore in keeping with these conventions—although it does look a little odd.

```
private static bool initializationComplete = false;
private static bool cleanupComplete = true;


// Create an instance of the Test Setup dataset
protected static TestSetupDS testSetupDS = new TestSetupDS();


// Create an instance of all the adapters that are used to populate the tables
// contained in the test environment.
protected static TestSetupDSTableAdapters.GEOGRAPHICREGIONTableAdapter
  gEOGRAPHICREGIONTableAdapter
  = new TestSetupDSTableAdapters.GEOGRAPHICREGIONTableAdapter();
protected static TestSetupDSTableAdapters.RESOURCECATEGORYTableAdapter
  rESOURCECATEGORYTableAdapter
  = new TestSetupDSTableAdapters.RESOURCECATEGORYTableAdapter();
protected static TestSetupDSTableAdapters.VENDORTableAdapter vENDORTableAdapter
  = new TestSetupDSTableAdapters.VENDORTableAdapter();
protected static TestSetupDSTableAdapters.CUSTOMERTableAdapter cUSTOMERTableAdapter
  = new TestSetupDSTableAdapters.CUSTOMERTableAdapter();
protected static TestSetupDSTableAdapters.RESOURCETableAdapter rESOURCETableAdapter
  =  new TestSetupDSTableAdapters.RESOURCETableAdapter();
protected static TestSetupDSTableAdapters.RESOURCEAVAILABILITYTableAdapter
  rESOURCEAVAILABILITYTableAdapter
    = new TestSetupDSTableAdapters.RESOURCEAVAILABILITYTableAdapter();
protected static TestSetupDSTableAdapters.ORDERTableAdapter oRDERTableAdapter
  = new TestSetupDSTableAdapters.ORDERTableAdapter();
protected static TestSetupDSTableAdapters.RESERVATIONTableAdapter
  rESERVATIONTableAdapter = new TestSetupDSTableAdapters.RESERVATIONTableAdapter();


// Define variables used to contain information about the test setup environment
// in the database.  These variables can be accessed by the tests themselves
// to obtain the primary keys of the various rows.
protected static int regionId;
```

```
protected static int categoryId;
protected static int vendorId;
protected static int customerId;
protected static int resourceId;
protected static int resourceAvailability1Id;
protected static int resourceAvailability2Id;
protected static int orderId;
protected static int reservation1Id;
protected static int reservation2Id;

// The initialization function for the test class.  This function initializes all
// of the standard test data in the database.
[ClassInitialize()]
public static void OrderDSTestBaseInitialize(TestContext testContext)
{
  // Only initialize once if called several times.
  if (!initializationComplete)
  {
    // Load the test environment tables with test rows
    testSetupDS.GEOGRAPHICREGION.LoadDataRow(
      new object[] { 0, "OrderBE TestRegion1" }, false);
    testSetupDS.RESOURCECATEGORY.LoadDataRow(
                              new object[] { 0, "OrderBE TestCategory1" }, false);
    testSetupDS.VENDOR.LoadDataRow(
                              new object[] { 0, "OrderBE TestVendor1" }, false);
    testSetupDS.CUSTOMER.LoadDataRow(
                              new object[] { 0, "OrderBE TestCustomer1" }, false);

    // Update the tables in the database
    gEOGRAPHICREGIONTableAdapter.Update(testSetupDS.GEOGRAPHICREGION);
    rESOURCECATEGORYTableAdapter.Update(testSetupDS.RESOURCECATEGORY);
    vENDORTableAdapter.Update(testSetupDS.VENDOR);
    cUSTOMERTableAdapter.Update(testSetupDS.CUSTOMER);

    // Save the id values for the test rows, so they are available for the tests
    // to use.
    regionId = testSetupDS.GEOGRAPHICREGION[0].ID;
    categoryId = testSetupDS.RESOURCECATEGORY[0].ID;
    vendorId = testSetupDS.VENDOR[0].ID;
    customerId = testSetupDS.CUSTOMER[0].ID;

    // Load a test RESOURCE row, update the database and save the id value
    testSetupDS.RESOURCE.LoadDataRow(new object[]{
        0,
        "OrderBE TestResource1",
        categoryId,
        "OrderBE TestResource1 Description",
        regionId,
```

```
        vendorId
    }, false);
    rESOURCETableAdapter.Update(testSetupDS.RESOURCE);
    resourceId = testSetupDS.RESOURCE[0].ID;

    // Load two test resource availability rows, update the database and save the
    // id values
    testSetupDS.RESOURCEAVAILABILITY.LoadDataRow(
                        new object[] { 0, resourceId, DateTime.Now, 10 }, false);
    testSetupDS.RESOURCEAVAILABILITY.LoadDataRow(
                        new object[] { 1, resourceId, DateTime.Now
                                    + new TimeSpan(1, 0, 0, 0), 10 }, false);
    rESOURCEAVAILABILITYTableAdapter.Update(testSetupDS.RESOURCEAVAILABILITY);
    resourceAvailability1Id = testSetupDS.RESOURCEAVAILABILITY[0].ID;
    resourceAvailability2Id = testSetupDS.RESOURCEAVAILABILITY[1].ID;

    // Load a test order row, update the database and save the id value
    testSetupDS.ORDER.LoadDataRow(
                        new object[] { 0, customerId, DateTime.Now }, false);
    oRDERTableAdapter.Update(testSetupDS.ORDER);
    orderId = testSetupDS.ORDER[0].ID;

    // Load two test reservation rows, update the database and save the id values
    testSetupDS.RESERVATION.LoadDataRow(
        new object[] { 0, resourceAvailability1Id, orderId, 1, 100.00, 100.00 },
        false);
    testSetupDS.RESERVATION.LoadDataRow(
        new object[] { 1, resourceAvailability2Id, orderId, 2, 200.00, 400.00 },
        false);
    rESERVATIONTableAdapter.Update(testSetupDS.RESERVATION);
    reservation1Id = testSetupDS.RESERVATION[0].ID;
    reservation2Id = testSetupDS.RESERVATION[1].ID;

    initializationComplete = true;
    cleanupComplete = false;
  }
}
```

This code is tedious rather than complicated and simply uses all of the table adapters defined in the TestSetupDS to save test values in each table to the database. Since some of the entries have foreign keys referencing the earlier entries, the early entries must be updated to the database first so that their identity primary key values appear in the tables.

This class initialization code is best placed in a base class that is inherited by each test class that needs it, as in the class diagram shown in Figure 8-11. The set of TableAdapter objects (e.g., vENDORTableAdapter) created by this class for each of the tables that need to be populated to form the test database environment constitutes a "back door," or alternative route, to the database, bypassing the class under test to place test data in there and also—if needed—to read back data that has been written by a test. There is also a set of static field variables that contain the ID values for the various rows that have been created as test data, like the test order and its reservations.

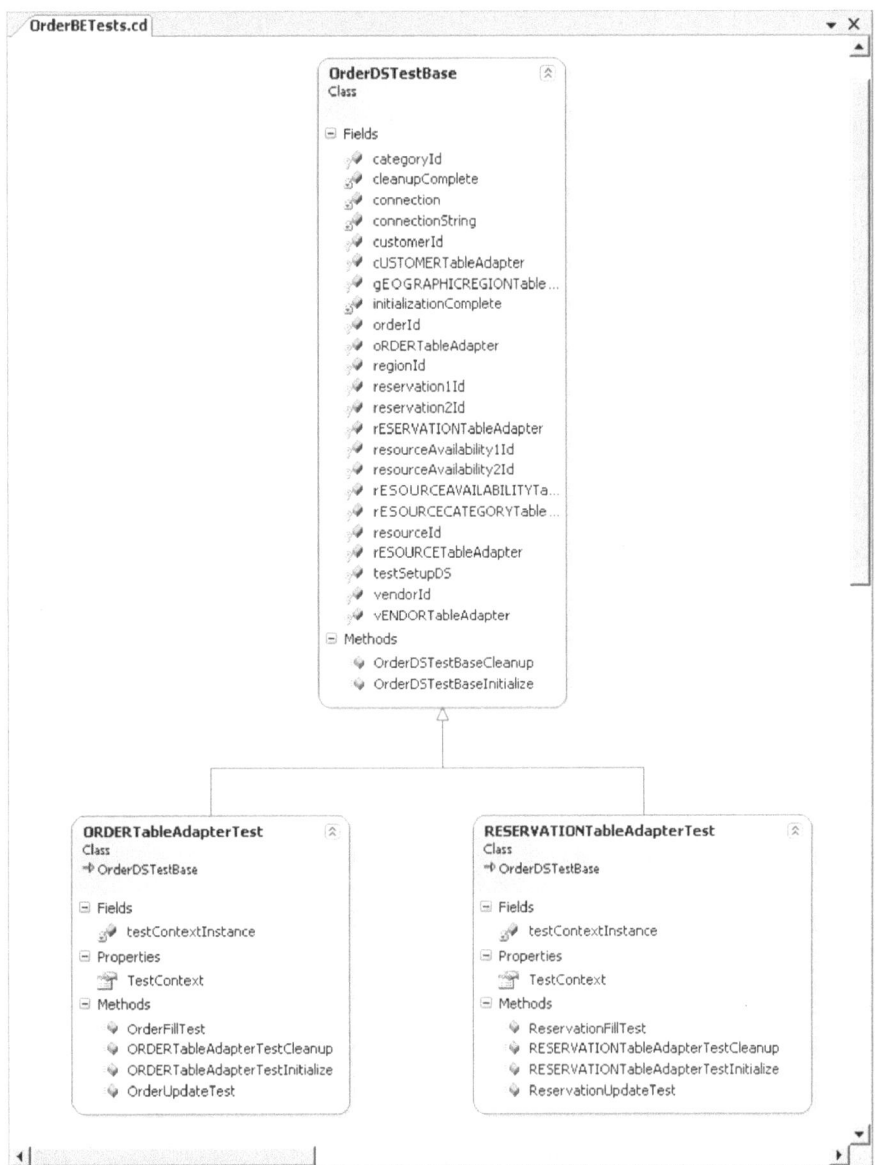

Figure 8-11. *Class diagram for the OrderBETests project*

The class initialization function creates test rows in the GEOGRAPHICREGION, RESOURCECATEGORY, VENDOR, CUSTOMER, RESOURCE, and RESOURCEAVAILABILITY tables. A test row in the ORDER table and two test rows in the RESERVATION table are also created. These are needed so that the Fill function of the ORDER and RESERVATION table adapters can be tested.

The class cleanup function simply deletes all of these rows in the order necessary to maintain referential integrity, using the same set of table adapters to write the deleted rows to the database:

```
[ClassCleanup()]
public static void OrderDSTestBaseCleanup()
{
    if (!cleanupComplete)
    {
        // Delete the test reservations
        rESERVATIONTableAdapter.Fill(testSetupDS.RESERVATION, reservation1Id);
        testSetupDS.RESERVATION[0].Delete();
        rESERVATIONTableAdapter.Update(testSetupDS.RESERVATION);

        rESERVATIONTableAdapter.Fill(testSetupDS.RESERVATION, reservation2Id);
        testSetupDS.RESERVATION[0].Delete();
        rESERVATIONTableAdapter.Update(testSetupDS.RESERVATION);

        // Delete the test order.
        oRDERTableAdapter.Fill(testSetupDS.ORDER, orderId);
        testSetupDS.ORDER[0].Delete();
        oRDERTableAdapter.Update(testSetupDS.ORDER);

        // Delete the test availabilities, and resource.
        rESOURCEAVAILABILITYTableAdapter.Fill(testSetupDS.RESOURCEAVAILABILITY,
            resourceAvailability1Id);
        testSetupDS.RESOURCEAVAILABILITY[0].Delete();
        rESOURCEAVAILABILITYTableAdapter.Update(
            testSetupDS.RESOURCEAVAILABILITY);

        rESOURCEAVAILABILITYTableAdapter.Fill(testSetupDS.RESOURCEAVAILABILITY,
            resourceAvailability2Id);
        testSetupDS.RESOURCEAVAILABILITY[0].Delete();
        rESOURCEAVAILABILITYTableAdapter.Update(
            testSetupDS.RESOURCEAVAILABILITY);

        rESOURCETableAdapter.Fill(testSetupDS.RESOURCE, resourceId);
        testSetupDS.RESOURCE[0].Delete();
        rESOURCETableAdapter.Update(testSetupDS.RESOURCE);

        // Delete the test region, category, vendor and customer.
        gEOGRAPHICREGIONTableAdapter.Fill(testSetupDS.GEOGRAPHICREGION, regionId);
        testSetupDS.GEOGRAPHICREGION[0].Delete();
        gEOGRAPHICREGIONTableAdapter.Update(testSetupDS.GEOGRAPHICREGION);

        rESOURCECATEGORYTableAdapter.Fill(testSetupDS.RESOURCECATEGORY,
            categoryId);
        testSetupDS.RESOURCECATEGORY[0].Delete();
        rESOURCECATEGORYTableAdapter.Update(testSetupDS.RESOURCECATEGORY);
```

```
        vENDORTableAdapter.Fill(testSetupDS.VENDOR, vendorId);
        testSetupDS.VENDOR[0].Delete();
        vENDORTableAdapter.Update(testSetupDS.VENDOR);

        cUSTOMERTableAdapter.Fill(testSetupDS.CUSTOMER, customerId);
        testSetupDS.CUSTOMER[0].Delete();
        cUSTOMERTableAdapter.Update(testSetupDS.CUSTOMER);

        cleanupComplete = true;
    }
}
```

Incidentally, base class [ClassInitialize()] functions do not get called automatically when the tests are run, so they need to be explicitly called from [ClassInitialize()] functions in the derived classes. When multiple tests are run, all the initialization is done before any tests are run, so it is possible that the base class [ClassInitialize()] function will be called more than once. Therefore, some protective code is needed to ensure that the static objects are initialized only once.

Unit-Test Code

I'm often unpleasantly surprised by the length of time needed to write even quite basic unit-test code. It's usually straightforward, but can require a lot of maintenance if things change. The code for the Fill and Update tests for the ORDERTableAdapter class, which Angela writes, is given next and follows the sequence described in the previous section. She writes similar tests for the RESERVATIONTableAdapter class, which you can see in the code provided with the exercises. Here is the Fill test that tests the ability of the table adapter to fill a data table of the correct type properly from the database:

```
/// <summary>
///A test for Fill (OrderDS.ORDERDataTable, int)
///</summary>
[TestMethod()]
public void FillTest()
{
    // Create an instance of the Table Adapter to be tested and a table
    //  to use as a parameter to the function to be tested
    ORDERTableAdapter target = new ORDERTableAdapter();
    OrderDS.ORDERDataTable oRDERDataTable = new OrderDS.ORDERDataTable();
    int ORDERID = orderId;

    int expected = 1;
    int actual;

    // Call the function to be tested
    actual = target.Fill(oRDERDataTable, ORDERID);

    // Verify the return value
    Assert.AreEqual(expected, actual,
```

```
        "com.icarustravel.enterprise31.Order.OrderDSTableAdapters.ORDERTableAdapter."
        +"Fill did not return the expected value.");

      // Verify the data table was populated correctly from the database
      Assert.AreEqual(testSetupDS.ORDER[0].ID, oRDERDataTable[0].ID);
      Assert.AreEqual(testSetupDS.ORDER[0].CUSTOMERID, oRDERDataTable[0].CUSTOMERID);
      Assert.AreEqual(testSetupDS.ORDER[0].ORDERDATE, oRDERDataTable[0].ORDERDATE);
    }
```

The Fill test for the order table adapter assumes that the test order is present in the database, having been written during class initialization. It calls the `Fill` function of the adapter under test, using the `orderId` value of that test order, which was saved in the base class. This value, of course, will have been initialized to the ID of the test order that the base class created. After `Fill` has been called, the field values in the table row for the test order are verified against the values in the `TestSetupDS` from which the database test environment was loaded.

The Update test is more complicated, since a sequence of order creation and modification was defined in the test sequence. Here is the code:

```
/// <summary>
///A test for Update (OrderDS.ORDERDataTable)
///</summary>
[TestMethod()]
public void UpdateTest()
{
  int newOrder1Id, newOrder2Id;
  DateTime newOrder1OrderDate, newOrder2OrderDate;

  // Create an instance of the Table Adapter to be tested and a table
  //  to use as a parameter to the function to be tested
  ORDERTableAdapter target = new ORDERTableAdapter();
  OrderDS.ORDERDataTable oRDERDataTable = new OrderDS.ORDERDataTable();

  // Define a new order in the data table.
  oRDERDataTable.LoadDataRow(new object[] { 0, customerId, DateTime.Now }, false);
  newOrder1OrderDate = oRDERDataTable[0].ORDERDATE;
  int expected = 1;
  int actual;

  // Save the new order to the database
  actual = target.Update(oRDERDataTable);

  // Verify the return value
  Assert.AreEqual(expected, actual,
    "com.icarustravel.enterprise31.Order.OrderDSTableAdapters.ORDERTableAdapter."
    + "Update did not return the expected value.");

  // Save the id value which was created from an identity in the database
  newOrder1Id = oRDERDataTable[0].ID;
```

```
// Clear the testSetupDS ORDER table and fill it using the new order id value
testSetupDS.ORDER.Clear();
oRDERTableAdapter.Fill(testSetupDS.ORDER, newOrder1Id);

// Verify that the new order has the correct fields
Assert.AreEqual(newOrder1Id, testSetupDS.ORDER[0].ID);
Assert.AreEqual(customerId, testSetupDS.ORDER[0].CUSTOMERID);
Assert.AreEqual(newOrder1OrderDate.Day, testSetupDS.ORDER[0].ORDERDATE.Day);
Assert.AreEqual(newOrder1OrderDate.Month, testSetupDS.ORDER[0].ORDERDATE.Month);
Assert.AreEqual(newOrder1OrderDate.Year, testSetupDS.ORDER[0].ORDERDATE.Year);

// Modify the date of the new order and save it for later check
oRDERDataTable[0].ORDERDATE = DateTime.Now + new TimeSpan(1, 0, 0, 0);
newOrder1OrderDate = oRDERDataTable[0].ORDERDATE;

// Add a second order and save its date for later check
oRDERDataTable.LoadDataRow(new object[] { 0, customerId, DateTime.Now
  + new TimeSpan(2, 0, 0, 0) }, false);
newOrder2OrderDate = oRDERDataTable[1].ORDERDATE;

//  Save the modified and new orders to the database via the adapter under test.
expected = 2;
actual = target.Update(oRDERDataTable);

// Verify the return value of the update
Assert.AreEqual(expected, actual,
  "com.icarustravel.enterprise31.Order.OrderDSTableAdapters.ORDERTableAdapter."
  + "Update did not return the expected value.");
newOrder2Id = oRDERDataTable[1].ID;

// Get the first order from the database via the test setup adapter (back door)
expected = 1;
testSetupDS.ORDER.Clear();
actual = oRDERTableAdapter.Fill(testSetupDS.ORDER, newOrder1Id);

// Verify that the rows are in the database
Assert.AreEqual(expected, actual,
  "com.icarustravel.enterprise31.Order.OrderDSTableAdapters.ORDERTableAdapter."
  + "Fill did not return the expected value.");

// Verify that their field values are correct
Assert.AreEqual(newOrder1Id, testSetupDS.ORDER[0].ID);
Assert.AreEqual(customerId, testSetupDS.ORDER[0].CUSTOMERID);
Assert.AreEqual(newOrder1OrderDate.Day, testSetupDS.ORDER[0].ORDERDATE.Day);
Assert.AreEqual(newOrder1OrderDate.Month, testSetupDS.ORDER[0].ORDERDATE.Month);
Assert.AreEqual(newOrder1OrderDate.Year, testSetupDS.ORDER[0].ORDERDATE.Year);
```

```
// Repeat for the second new order
expected = 1;
testSetupDS.ORDER.Clear();
actual = oRDERTableAdapter.Fill(testSetupDS.ORDER, newOrder2Id);
Assert.AreEqual(expected, actual,
  "com.icarustravel.enterprise31.Order.OrderDSTableAdapters.ORDERTableAdapter."
  + "Fill did not return the expected value.");

Assert.AreEqual(newOrder2Id, testSetupDS.ORDER[0].ID);
Assert.AreEqual(customerId, testSetupDS.ORDER[0].CUSTOMERID);
Assert.AreEqual(newOrder2OrderDate.Day, testSetupDS.ORDER[0].ORDERDATE.Day);
Assert.AreEqual(newOrder2OrderDate.Month, testSetupDS.ORDER[0].ORDERDATE.Month);
Assert.AreEqual(newOrder2OrderDate.Year, testSetupDS.ORDER[0].ORDERDATE.Year);

// Delete the second order
oRDERDataTable[1].Delete();
expected = 1;
actual = target.Update(oRDERDataTable);
Assert.AreEqual(expected, actual,
  "com.icarustravel.enterprise31.Order.OrderDSTableAdapters.ORDERTableAdapter."
       + "Update did not return the expected value.");

// Verify by the test setup adapter that it is no longer there
expected = 0;
testSetupDS.ORDER.Clear();
actual = oRDERTableAdapter.Fill(testSetupDS.ORDER, newOrder2Id);
Assert.AreEqual(expected, actual,
  "com.icarustravel.enterprise31.Order.OrderDSTableAdapters.ORDERTableAdapter."
       + "Fill did not return the expected value.");

// Verify by the test setup adapter that the first order is still there
expected = 1;
testSetupDS.ORDER.Clear();
actual = oRDERTableAdapter.Fill(testSetupDS.ORDER, newOrder1Id);
Assert.AreEqual(expected, actual,
  "com.icarustravel.enterprise31.Order.OrderDSTableAdapters.ORDERTableAdapter."
       + "Fill did not return the expected value.");

// Delete the first order
oRDERDataTable[0].Delete();
expected = 1;
actual = target.Update(oRDERDataTable);
Assert.AreEqual(expected, actual,
  "com.icarustravel.enterprise31.Order.OrderDSTableAdapters.ORDERTableAdapter."
       + "Update did not return the expected value.");
```

```
// Verify by the test setup adapter that it is no longer there
expected = 0;
testSetupDS.ORDER.Clear();
actual = oRDERTableAdapter.Fill(testSetupDS.ORDER, newOrder1Id);
Assert.AreEqual(expected, actual,
  "com.icarustravel.enterprise31.Order.OrderDSTableAdapters.ORDERTableAdapter."
  + "Fill did not return the expected value.");
}
```

Here is a brief description of the previous code:

1. An instance of the table adapter under test, ORDERTableAdapter, is created. Then an instance of ORDERDataTable is created to use as a parameter to its Update function.

2. A new row is inserted in the ORDERDataTable instance to represent a new order. The Update function is called and its return value verified.

3. The testSetupDS ORDER table is cleared and used to retrieve the new order from the database independently of the adapter under test and its stored procedures. The fields of the new order are verified.

4. The date of the first new order is modified and a second new order is added to the test ORDERDataTable instance. The Update function of the adapter under the test function is called again.

5. The two orders are verified using the same procedure with the testSetupDS ORDER table.

6. The second new order is deleted, and Update is called again on the adapter under test. The testSetupDS ORDER table is loaded to ensure that it is no longer present in the database.

7. The first new order is deleted, and Update is called again on the adapter under test. The testSetupDS ORDER table is loaded again to ensure that it has also been removed from the database.

Running the Unit Tests

Now let's see how Angela runs these unit tests. There are several ways of doing this in Visual Studio 2005 Team Edition for Developers. One approach is to use the Test View window (Figure 8-12), which you display by selecting Test ➤ Windows ➤ Test View from the main menu. Like most windows in Visual Studio 2005, you can set it to floating, dockable, or a tabbed document. I usually set it to dockable and drag it onto the right-hand group of windows so that it is tabbed in the group with Solution Explorer and Team Explorer. While I'm on the subject, I find it a good idea to customize the Standard toolbar so that it contains buttons to display most of these views (Toolbox, Properties, Server Explorer, Team Explorer, Solution Explorer, Test View, etc.) so I can quickly show or hide them. When I want the whole screen available to see code, I can close them and open them again easily, but of course you may prefer to use the keyboard shortcuts.

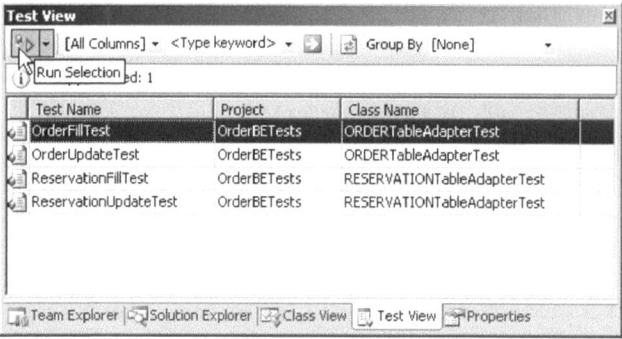

Figure 8-12. *The Test View window*

Figure 8-12 shows one format for the Test View window, but you can change it in many ways. The four tests defined so far are all in the same project, so to distinguish them Angela has customized the view in Figure 8-12 by adding the Class Name column. She has done this by right-clicking on the surface of this window and selecting Add/Remove Columns. You can also group the tests by various attributes, such as the class name, solution, project, namespace, and so forth.

Note The source code for this section is in the folder `Chapter 8\Exercise 4`. Exercise 8-5 applies to this section.

To run one or more tests, you can select them in this window, right-click, and select Run Selection or Debug Selection, or you can click the little triangle-shaped button at the top left, which also has a drop-down to select the run or debug command. You can also create new tests from here and open the Test Manager if you have Team Edition for Testers or Team Suite installed. We'll discuss Test Manager more in Chapter 9. All in all, it's a useful little window.

When you run a test from the test view, the Test Results window is displayed, as shown in Figure 8-13. This window displays the status of each test as the tests are running and reports the result as pass or fail. Failed is shown if one of the `Assert` statements fails or if the code throws an uncaught exception. Double-click on a particular test to display a detailed Test Results window, as shown in Figure 8-14.

	Result	Test Name ▼	Project	Error Message
☐	Passed	ReservationUpdateTest	OrderBETests	
☐	Passed	ReservationFillTest	OrderBETests	
☑	Failed	OrderUpdateTest	OrderBETests	Assert.AreEqual failed. Expected:<1022>, Actual:<0>.
☐	Passed	OrderFillTest	OrderBETests	

Figure 8-13. *The Test Results window*

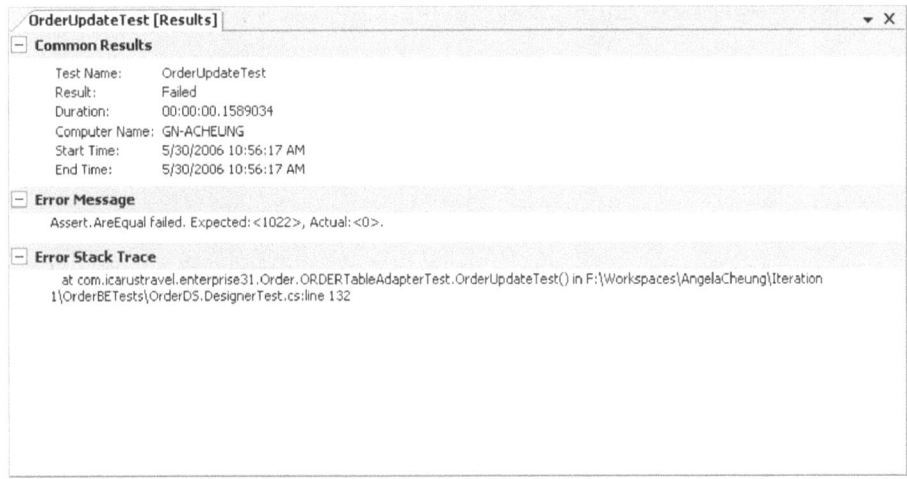

Figure 8-14. *The Test Results window*

Checking the Code into Version Control

Having reached a significant point in her development, Angela needs to check the code into TFS. Here I can mention the check-in policies that have been set up for iteration 1. Several policies can be set on the team project to restrict the check-in of modified or new code. For instance, one policy requires an error-free build, and another requires each checked-in file to be associated with a work item. So far only these two conditions have been set on the team project for iteration 1. The other check-in policies that can be applied will be considered later.

■ **Note** The source code for this section is in the folder `Chapter 8\Exercise 4`. Exercise 8-6 applies to this section.

The process of checking a large number of files into version control can be handled very well using the Pending Changes window described in Chapter 5, even though the changes here are much more complicated since quite a large number of files have been added or modified. The Pending Changes window is shown in Figure 8-15 with the source files shown in folder view, but you can also view them in flat view. Two work items represent the justification for these changes, and according to the check-in rules, Angela must associate each file with one or both of these. The files shown in Figure 8-15 selected for check-in are those that implement the Order DAC (Order Data Access Component) functionality, the `OrderDAL` project and the modified `EnterpriseDatabase` project. Most are added files, but `CreateStoredProcedures.SQL` has been modified to include new stored procedures. Angela originally generated this script from her stored procedures in the database in a similar way to Alberto's generation of the table create scripts in Chapter 6. She has now modified it for the new stored procedures supporting the `OrderDS` table adapters. Once these have been picked out as shown, Angela clicks the second button from the top on the left side to display the work items. She selects the My Work Items query to display only the work items that are currently assigned to her, as shown in Figure 8-16.

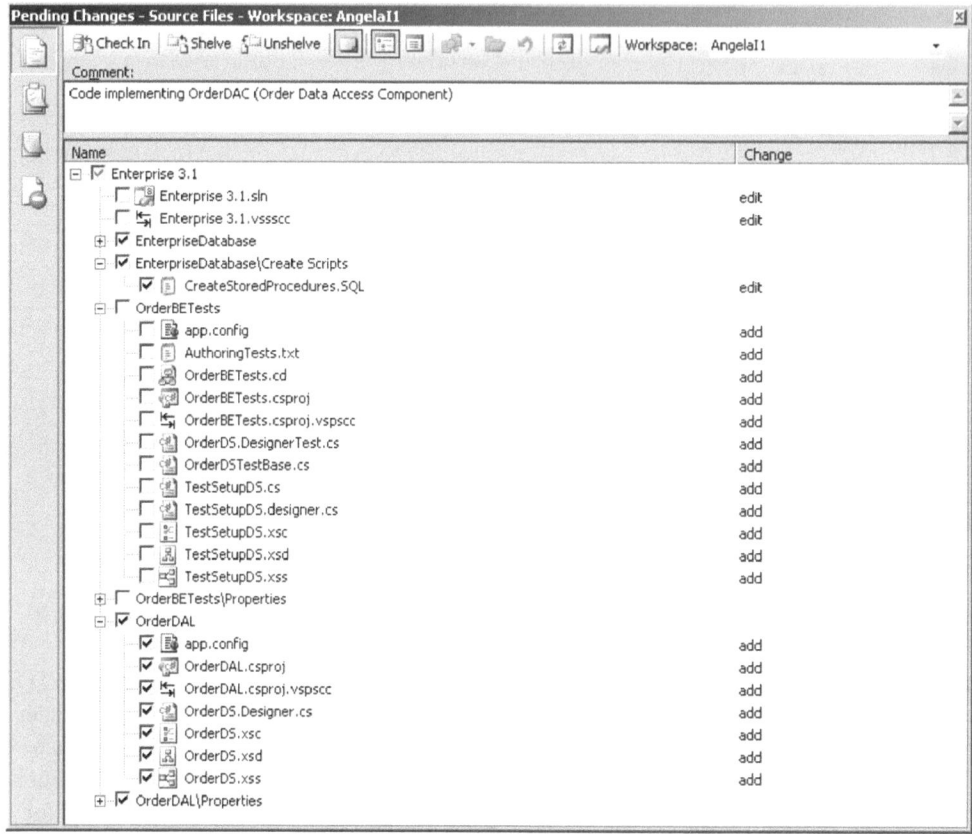

Figure 8-15. *The Pending Changes window prior to check-in of Angela's changes*

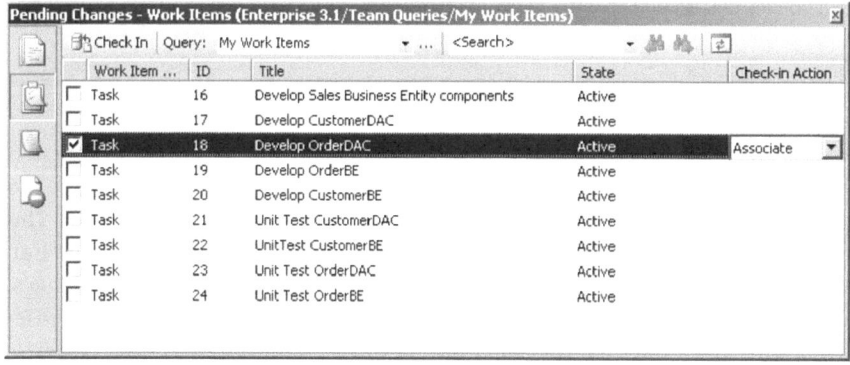

Figure 8-16. *The Pending Changes work items view with the correct work item associated with the files selected for check-in*

Angela checks the work item Develop OrderDAC, which corresponds to the work of developing the Order data access layer classes and all its stored procedures. She sees that the check-in action on the right automatically shows "Associate," the only option. This will cause the checked work item to be associated with all of the files in Figure 8-15 that were selected for check-in. Angela also clicks on the Policy Warnings button on the left to make sure there are no violations of policy that will prevent the check-in. She can now go back to the view in Figure 8-15 and click the Check In button at the top left. Although she is doing the check-in in three stages, she has arranged it so that the build will not be broken as none of the files will be included in the solution until that file is checked in, which she can do last. Each of these three stages will create a *changeset*, which is an object that is held in Team System and can be examined later. It includes a set of files and a set of work items as well as associated check-in notes and policy warnings. Various dialog boxes flash on the screen as all of the files are transferred to TFS. When the transfer completes successfully, only the pending changes in Figure 8-17 are left.

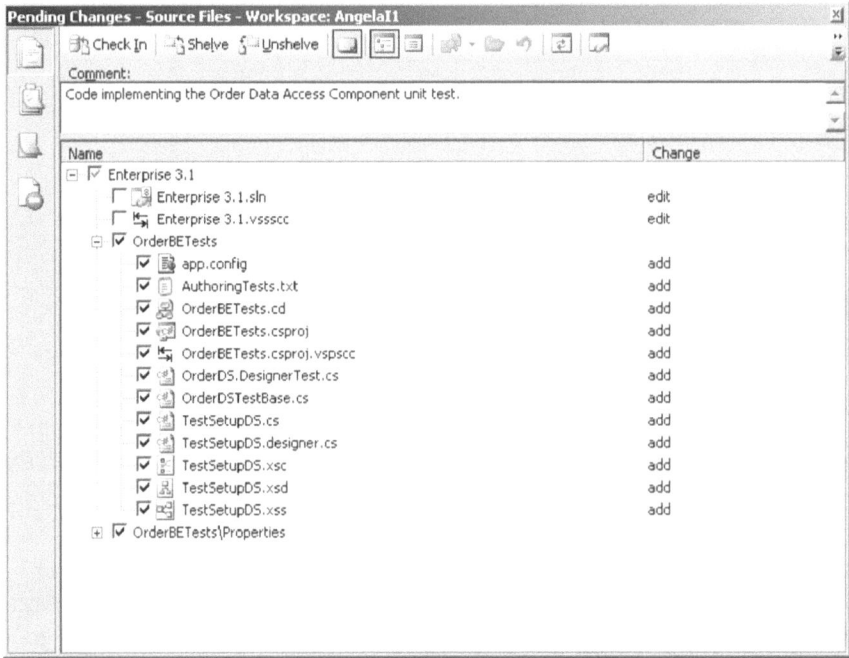

Figure 8-17. *The Pending Changes window after the first batch of files have been checked in*

Now it is time to check just the files involved in the unit-test code so that they can be added to version control and associated with the unit test work item Unit Test OrderDAC in Figure 8-16. This time, in the Work Items view of the Pending Changes window, that work item is checked and associated with the checked files in the Source Files view in Figure 8-17. After another quick check of the policy warnings screen, Angela checks in these files. Again the build will not be broken.

Lastly, the Source Files view of the Pending Changes window looks like Figure 8-18, with only the solution files left for check-in. This time Angela wishes to associate these files with two work items, as shown in Figure 8-19. After all of the code is checked in, the screen in Figure 8-18 appears blank.

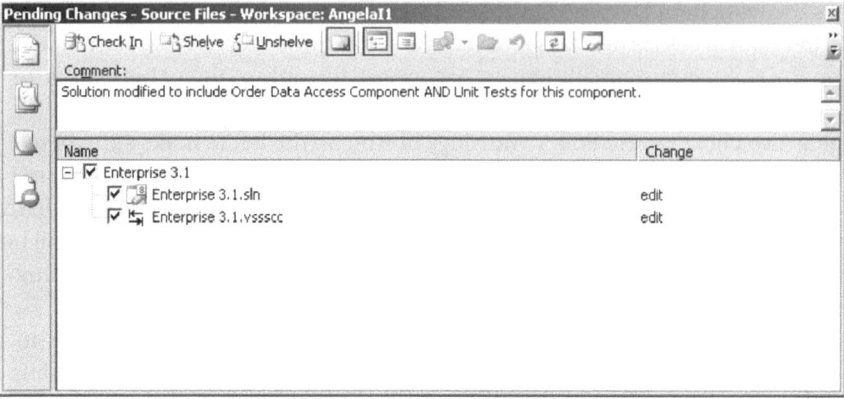

Figure 8-18. *The Pending Changes window ready for the final check-in*

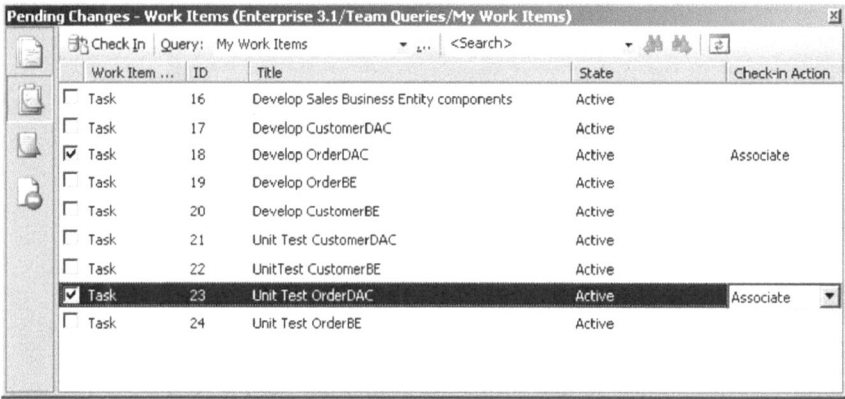

Figure 8-19. *The Pending Changes Work Items view with both the work items associated with the solution files*

We can look at the windows available in the Source Control Explorer to see the effect of these check-in operations. The rear window in Figure 8-20 is the Source Control Explorer with the entire iteration selected. The History window has been opened, which shows the change-sets for the last three check-ins that Angela has made. The detail of the latest one is displayed, and we can choose the source files, work items, check-in notes, or policy warnings (it is possible to override policy warnings and cause a check-in despite the fact that some may exist). The Work Items view is shown, and the two work items associated with the check-in of the solution file can be seen.

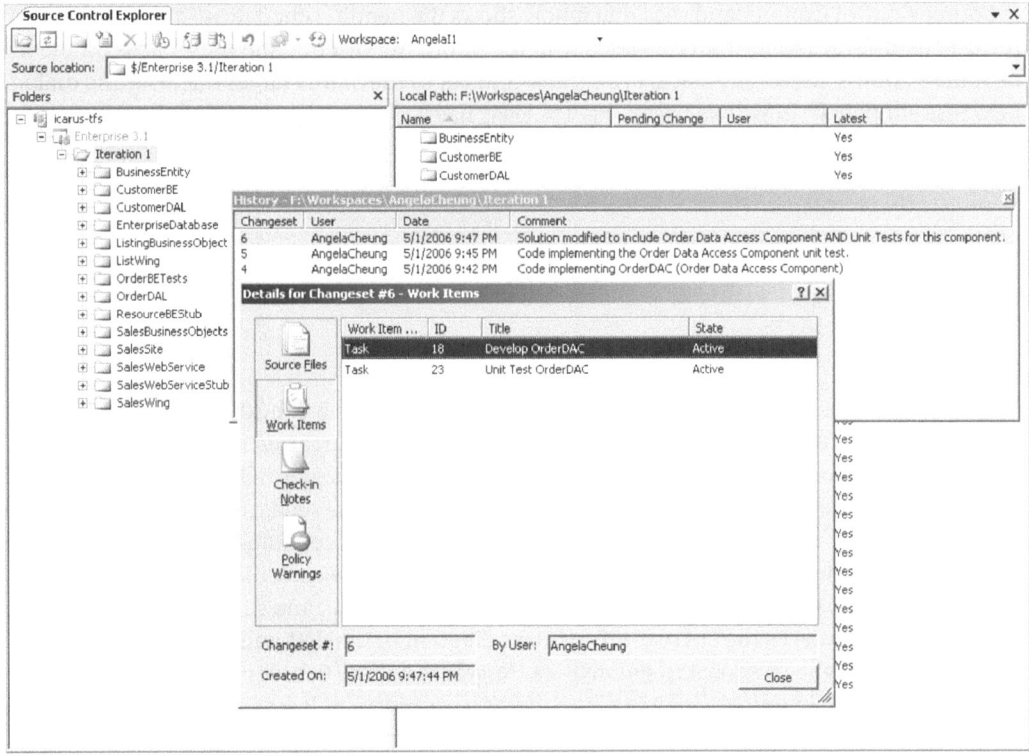

Figure 8-20. *Some Source Control Explorer windows showing the history of the three check-in operations; the detail window on the last one shows the associated work items.*

The Order Business Entity Class

Having completed the OrderDAL project and its associated classes, Angela now works on the business entity class, OrderBE. This class is similar to CustomerBE except that it needs the write capability that was not necessary in CustomerBE for iteration 1. Angela wants to create a new project called OrderBE under the SalesBusinessObjects solution folder, but this time she notices that the solution file, Enterprise 3.1.sln, has a little picture of a person to the left of it. When she hovers her mouse over it, the tooltip reads, "Checked out by someone else, or in another place." She wants to see who has it checked out, so she opens Source Control Explorer, looks at the solution file, and sees that Rahul has it checked out. She decides that he must be adding some listing business objects. Angela knows that TFS supports multiple checkout and merging upon check-in, so she goes ahead and creates the new project, and Visual Studio automatically checks out the solution file to her. Just to be sure, she looks at the Enterprise 3.1.sln file again in Source Control Explorer and sees that it now shows the pending change as `Edit, [more]` and the user as `AngelaCheung, [more]`. To see who the "more" represents, she right-clicks on the file in Source Control Explorer, selects Properties, and clicks the Status tab in the resulting dialog box. Sure enough, it shows two users; `AngelaCheung` has it checked out for edit in her workspace and `RahulSingh` has it checked out for edit in his workspace.

■**Note** The source code for this section is in the folder `Chapter 8\Exercise 6`. Exercise 8-7 applies to this section.

Angela decides to make use of the class diagram features to create the `OrderBE` class structure, so she deletes the automatic `Class1`, sets the namespace to `com.icarustravel.enterprise31.Order`, right-clicks on the `OrderBE` project, and selects View Class Diagram. Of course, there are no classes in the project yet (and Visual Studio gives a warning). She renames the class diagram in Solution Explorer to `OrderBE.cd`. She decides to try a different technique to create the new classes than the one used in the previous chapter. She opens the class diagram for `CustomerBE`, right-clicks on the tab at the top of the tabbed document section, and selects New Vertical Tab Group. Angela now sees the `CustomerBE.cd` class diagram on the left and the new `OrderBE.cd` diagram on the right, as shown in Figure 8-21. Angela drags the `BusinessEntityBE` class from the left-hand diagram onto the right. Oops—there's a warning box! It says, "One or more selected shapes could not be copied. Check to see that you have the correct project references." "Well, maybe you can't do that," thinks Angela. She was hoping that she could put the base class on the diagram and then link up her new class to inherit from it. "Wait, it says something about references—ah, that's it." She needs to add a project reference to the `BusinessEntity` project, which she would need to do if she were defining inheritance in the normal way via the code. She adds the necessary reference, then tries the same thing—and this time it works fine! She then drags a class from the Toolbox onto the drawing surface of `OrderBE.cd`, and in the New Class dialog box, leaves Access set to the default Public, leaves the Create New File option selected, and names the new file "OrderBE.cs", as shown in Figure 8-22.

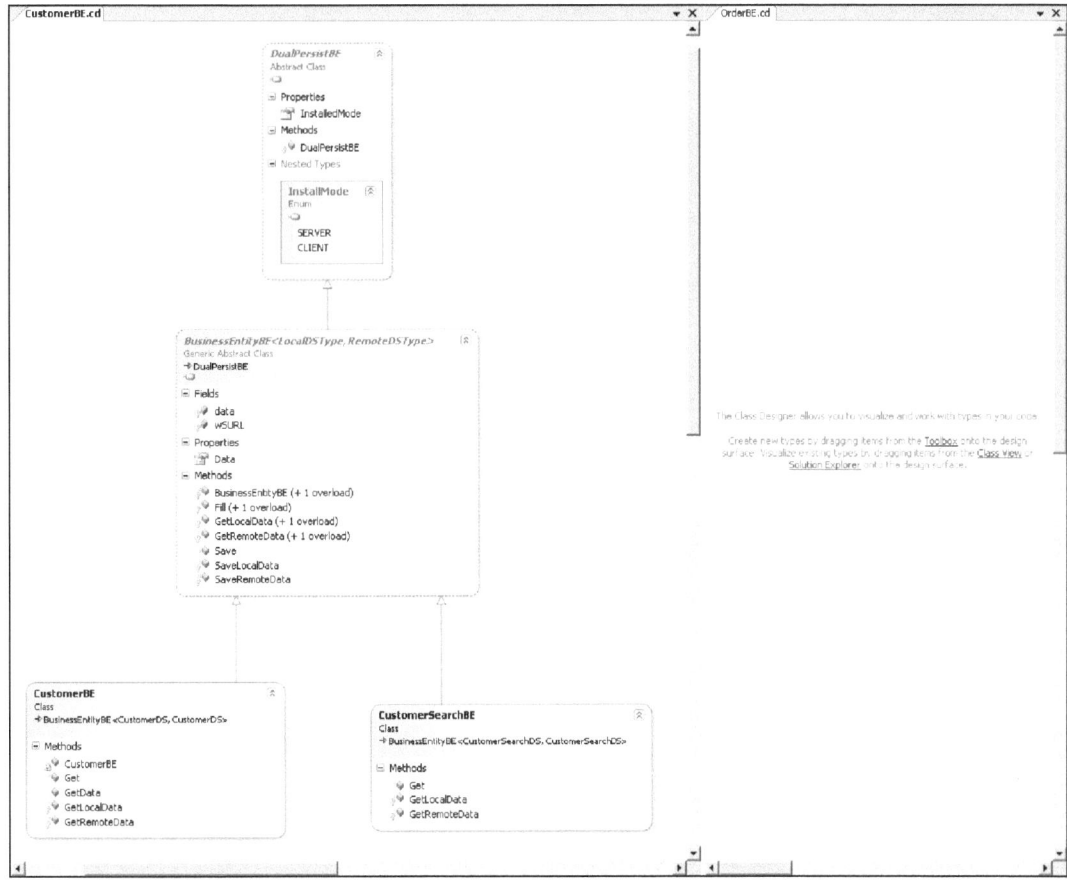

Figure 8-21. *Beginning a new class diagram for OrderBE*

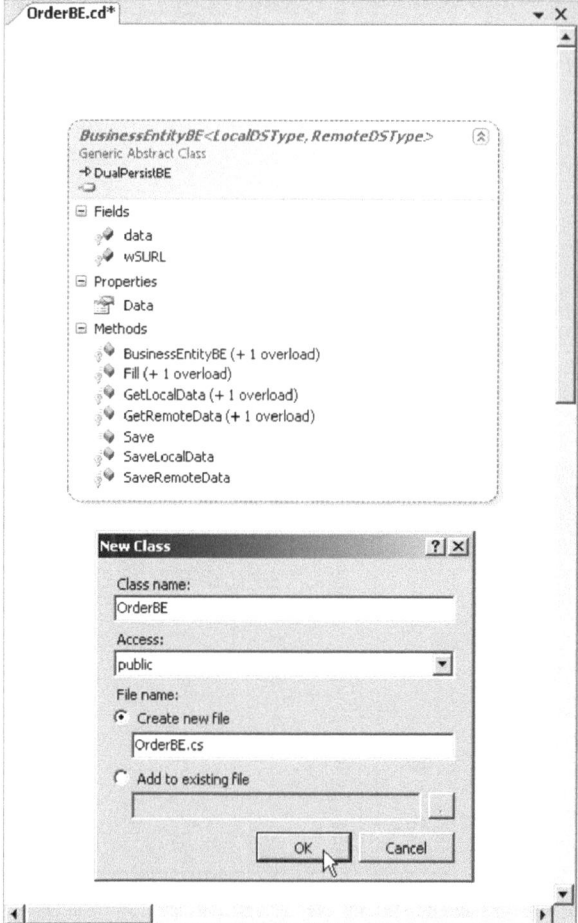

Figure 8-22. *Adding a new class to the class diagram for OrderBE*

Next Angela clicks on the inheritance symbol in the Toolbox and drags the arrow from the new OrderBE class to the copy of BusinessEntityBE on the OrderBE.cd class diagram (Figure 8-23). So far, so good. Let's look at the code that she has created:

```
using System;
using System.Collections.Generic;
using System.Text;

namespace com.icarustravel.enterprise31.Order
{
  public class OrderBE :
    com.icarustravel.enterprise31.BusinessEntity.BusinessEntityBE<object, object>
  {
  }
}
```

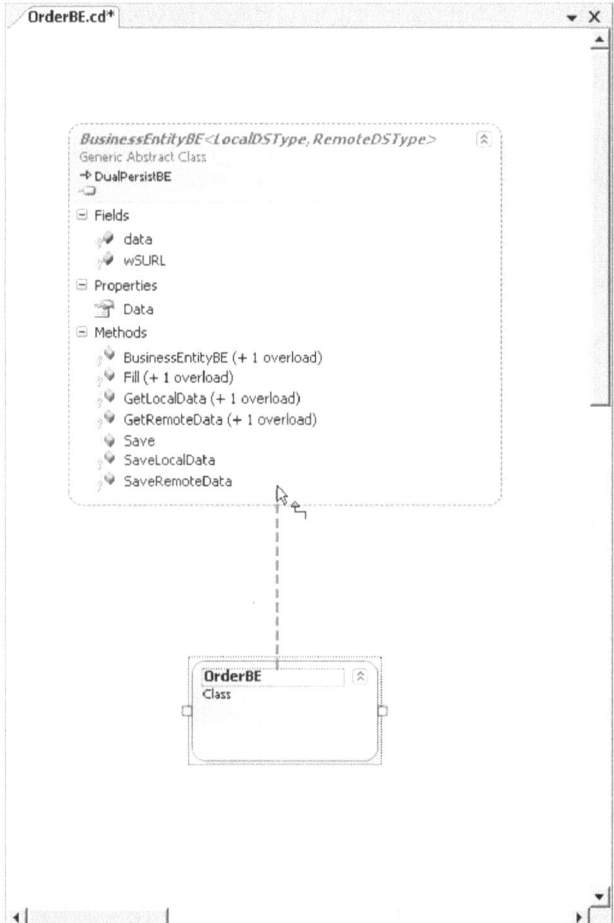

Figure 8-23. *Adding an inheritance relationship*

If I were writing this by hand, I'd probably employ a using directive rather than putting in the fully qualified class name for the base class. Also, the inheritance from the generic type has not yet been defined properly—it's just <object, object>.

Before that can be done, the SalesWebService must be updated to include the Get and Save methods. Angela does this next by opening the code for SalesWebService.cs in both the stub and the real web service and adding the web methods that will support the OrderBE business entity:

```
[System.Web.Services.WebMethod()]
public OrderDS GetOrder(string id)
{
    return new OrderDS();
}


[System.Web.Services.WebMethod()]
public void SaveOrder(OrderDS data)
{
}
```

The project SalesWebServiceStub can then be built, and Angela updates the web references to it throughout the solution.

Going back to the class diagram for the OrderBE project, Angela now clicks on the inheritance relationship between the OrderBE class and the BusinessEntityBE class. The Properties window (Figure 8-24) shows information about the base type, the derived type, and the type arguments. These default to object, and Angela must type the correct arguments, which are

com.icarustravel.enterprise31.Order.OrderDS

for the first, which is the type argument LocalDSType, and

com.icarustravel.enterprise31.Order.SalesWS.OrderDS

for the second, the RemoteDSType type argument, as shown in Figure 8-24.

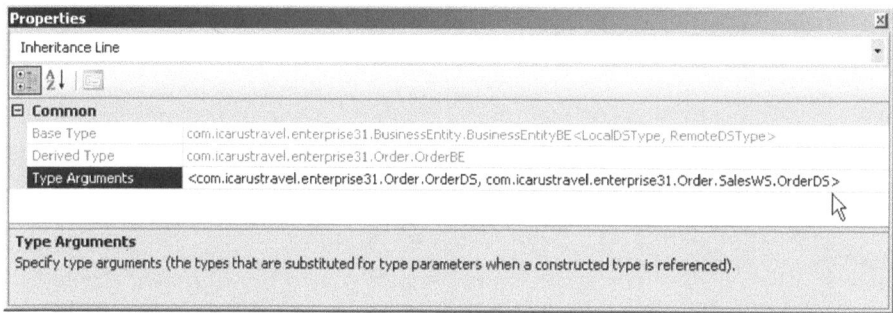

Figure 8-24. *The Properties window for the inheritance relationship between OrderBE and BusinessEntityBE on the OrderBE.cd class diagram*

Next Angela must add the Get functions and the overrides of the GetLocalData and GetRemoteData functions. She can also do this via the class diagram. The Get function will obtain a single-order entity identified by its ID value. One way to add a method on a class diagram is to right-click on the class in the OrderBE.cd diagram and select Add ➤ Method. Angela does this, then types "Get" and presses the Enter key, which inserts a member function into the class with no parameters. Clicking on the member function within the class causes the Properties window to display the properties of the member function. Inserting a member function in that way defaults it to public access and type void. Angela changes the type to OrderBE, leaves Access set to Public, sets the Static property to True, and types in summary XML documentation. The Properties window now looks like Figure 8-25.

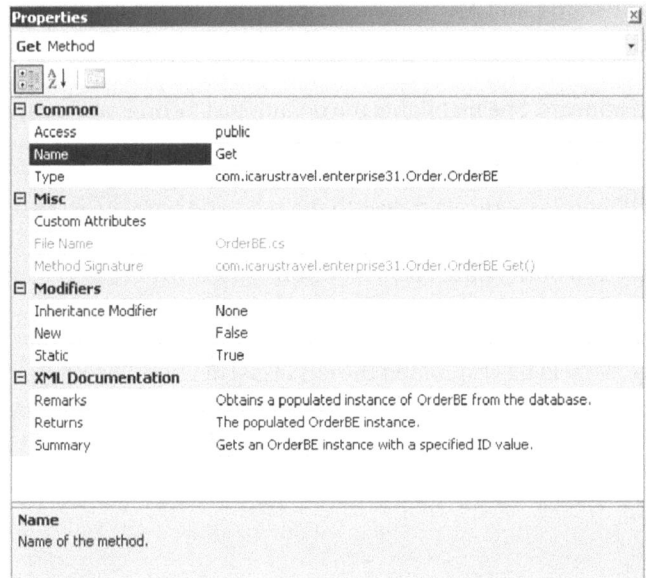

Figure 8-25. *The Properties window for a method within a class on a class diagram*

It is not possible to modify the signature of a method in the Properties window by adding parameters or from the diagram surface itself. Angela therefore right-clicks on the method and selects Class Details to display the Class Details window. As you can see in Figure 8-26, the member function is automatically selected in the Class Details window.

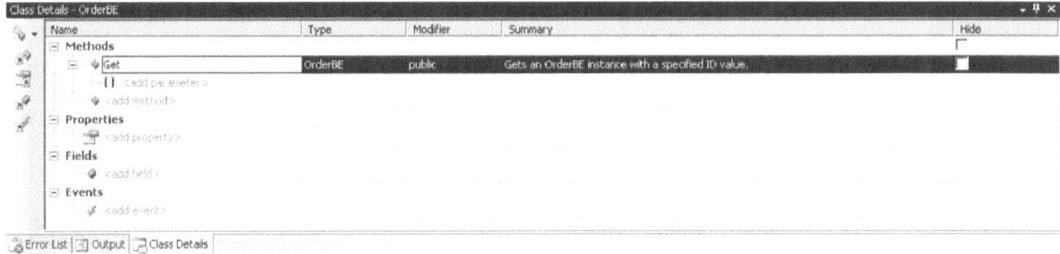

Figure 8-26. *The Class Details window. The new Get method has been expanded; no parameters are defined yet.*

You can do a great deal from this window, but Angela simply adds a single parameter to the Get function. She first expands the Get function entry by clicking on the plus sign (+) at its left, then she types the parameter name "id" into the Add Parameter field and presses Enter. To the right of that, the Type column appears. She highlights the default text "string" and types the "I" of *int* over the top. An IntelliSense drop-down appears; she makes sure *int* is selected and presses Enter. To the right of the Type field is the Modifier field, which can accept the value None, ref, out, or params—None is OK here—so Angela moves to the right and types in an XML description.

The next step is to add the overrides of the base class functions GetLocalData and GetRemoteData. Again this can be done nicely from the class diagram by right-clicking on the class OrderBE and selecting IntelliSense ➤ Override Members, which brings up the dialog box shown in Figure 8-27. As you can see, Angela has expanded the BusinessEntityBE base class and selected four member functions to override. The class does not need to override the other overloads of GetLocalData and GetRemoteData since OrderBE does not at this point implement a complex Get function with multiple parameters that qualify the instance or instances to be obtained.

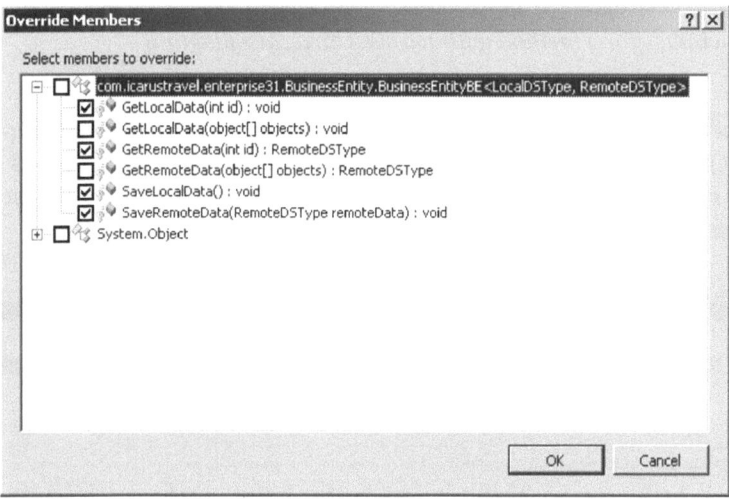

Figure 8-27. *The Override Members dialog box*

Angela now clicks OK, and Visual Studio generates the override functions. Once Angela adds some XML comments in the Class Details window, the class diagram and the Class Details window look like Figure 8-28.

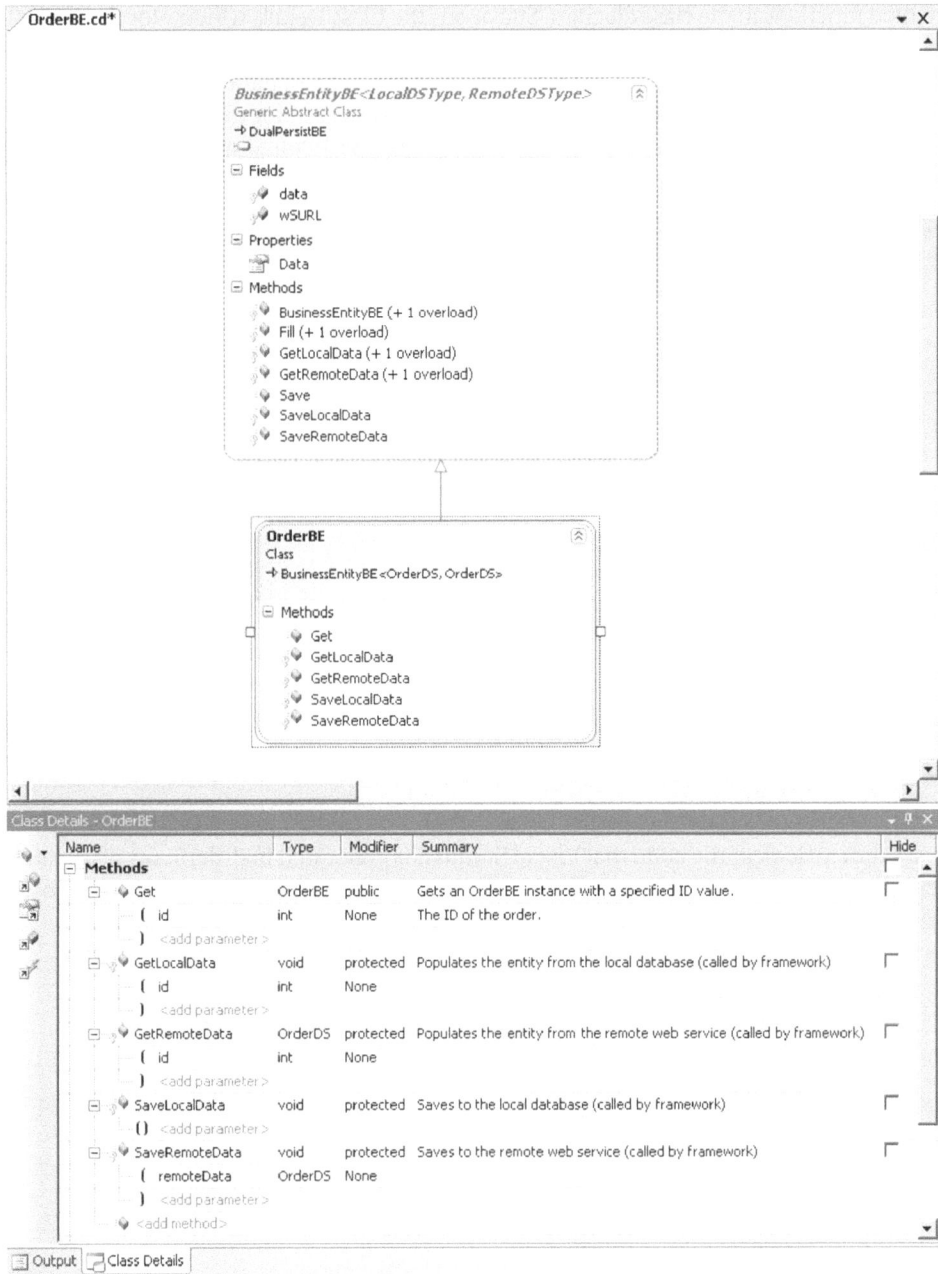

Figure 8-28. *The OrderBE class diagram and class details after all the methods have been added*

Angela must add to the OrderBE class one more method, which is needed by the
SalesSite project. She needs a function returning a DataTable object that can be allocated to
the ObjectDataSource (called ObjectDataSourceOrder), to which the GridView control in the
OrderDetails.aspx page will bind. We saw in Chapter 7 when Ed was prototyping the Sales Site
why he needed this function for the ObjectDataSource. This time, Angela uses another approach

to add method functions in the class diagram. She opens the Class Details window for the OrderBE class in the OrderBE.cd class diagram. In the Add Method field, she types the new method name "GetData"; then she specifies a type of DataTable, and adds an int id parameter and a string tableName parameter (Figure 8-29). Finally, she opens the properties for this new member function and sets the static property to True, making the new function a static function.

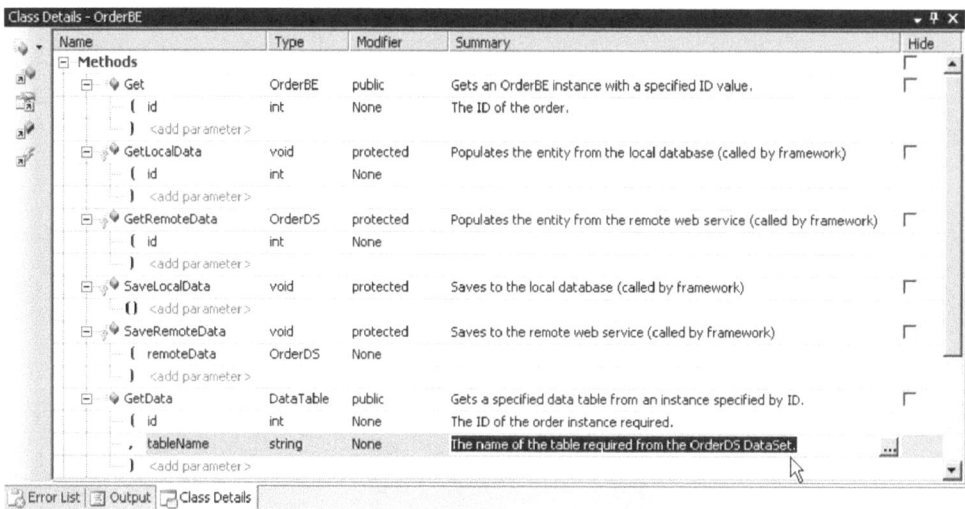

Figure 8-29. *Adding the GetData member function*

Now it's time to look at the code that Visual Studio has generated in OrderBE.cs as a result of this action—I've shortened the lines to make it fit on the printed page. Just look at all those XML comments; perhaps we will all be more encouraged to add comments when they are organized into the class diagram scheme.

```
namespace com.icarustravel.enterprise31.Order
{
  public class OrderBE
    : com.icarustravel.enterprise31.BusinessEntity.BusinessEntityBE
      <com.icarustravel.enterprise31.Order.OrderDS,
       com.icarustravel.enterprise31.Order.SalesWS.OrderDS>
  {
    /// <summary>
    /// Gets an OrderBE entity with the specified. ID value.
    /// </summary>
    /// <remarks>Obtains a populated OrderBE entity from the database with the ID
    /// value specified.</remarks>
    /// <param name="id">The identifier number of the Order.</param>
    /// <returns>The populated OrderBE instance.</returns>
    public static OrderBE Get(int id)
    {
      throw new System.NotImplementedException();
    }
```

```csharp
/// <summary>
/// Populates the entity from the local database (called by framework).
/// </summary>
/// <remarks>Contains the specific code to populate the entity object data from
/// the local database.</remarks>
protected override void GetLocalData(int id)
{
  throw new System.NotImplementedException();
}

/// <summary>
/// Populates from the remote web service (called by framework).
/// </summary>
/// <remarks>Contains the specific code to populate the entity object data from
/// the remote web service.</remarks>
protected override RemoteDSType GetRemoteData(int id)
{
  throw new System.NotImplementedException();
}

/// <summary>
/// Saves to the local database (called by framework).
/// </summary>
/// <remarks>Contains the specific code needed to save the entity to the local
/// database.</remarks>
protected override void SaveLocalData()
{
  throw new System.NotImplementedException();
}

/// <summary>
/// Saves to the remote server (called by framework).
/// </summary>
/// <remarks>Contains the specific code that saves the entity to the remote web
/// service.</remarks>
protected override void SaveRemoteData(RemoteDSType remoteData)
{
  throw new System.NotImplementedException();
}

/// <summary>
/// Returns a specified table from the entity data.
/// </summary>
/// <param name="id">The identifier number of the order.</param>
/// <param name="tableName">The name of the DataTable to return.</param>
public static DataTable GetData(int id, string tableName)
```

```
    {
      throw new System.NotImplementedException();
    }
  }
}
```

All of the member functions that Angela defined have been added to the file, each with a default throw of a NotImplementedException, and the XML comments have also been placed in the right places. There is one small problem with the code: the override functions have been given the type RemoteDSType, which is a type parameter in the base class and not a type. It is not in scope in the derived class and therefore must be replaced with the actual value of the type parameter, which is

com.icarustravel.enterprise31.Order.SalesWS.OrderDS

Also the directive using System.Data must be added at the top.

Testing the Business Entity Layer: Read Capability

Many people subscribe to the belief that units tests should be written before the code itself is written. The Icarus team prefers to prototype the system before adopting this approach, but Angela will attempt it for the business objects. Having defined the classes using the Class Designer, she will write the unit tests they must pass before implementing the code within them.

Note The source code for this section is in the folder Chapter 8\Exercise 7. Exercise 8-8 applies to this section.

Fortunately, the tests that were written for the data access layer, the OrderDAL project, have a lot of common code that can be used for the OrderBE class. To create the unit tests for the OrderBE class, Angela simply right-clicks on the class in the OrderBE.cs code and selects Create Unit Tests. If the team adopts a black-box concept, then it is not necessary to unit-test the private and protected functions of the class, so the only read functions requiring unit tests are Get(int id) and GetData(int id, string tableName). Only those functions, then, need to be checked in the Create Unit Tests dialog box. Angela sets the output project to OrderBETests so that the new test classes are created in the same project as the tests for the data access layer (Figure 8-30).

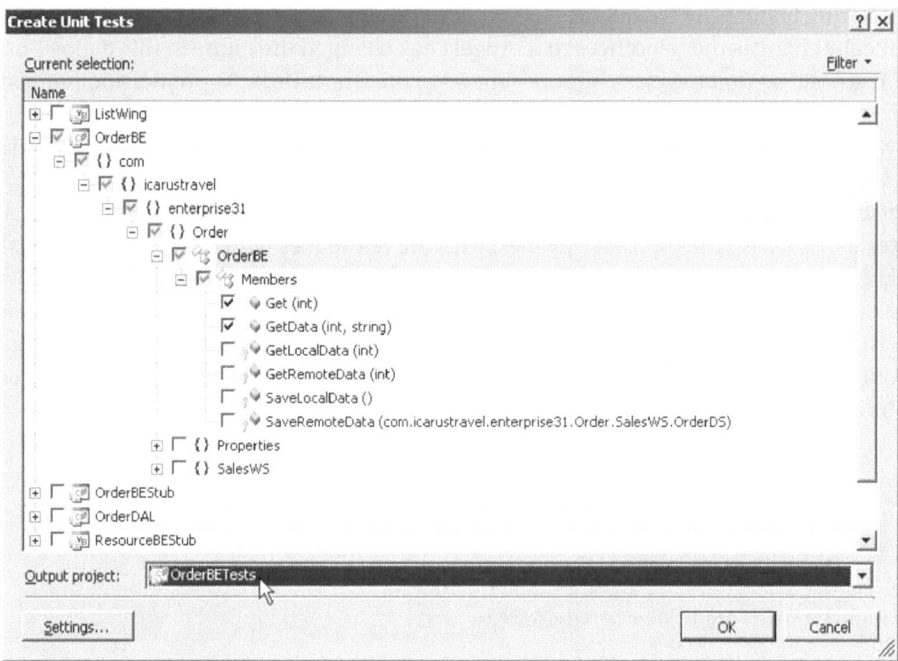

Figure 8-30. *Creating unit tests for the OrderBE business entity class*

In order to use the common unit test class OrderDSTestBase, it makes sense to rename it and move it into a file of its own. Use of this class implies that unit testing of OrderBE will be done using the database, whereas the unit test could be achieved by stubbing the data access layer. Given that the machinery already exists to set up a standard test case in the database, it perhaps makes sense to use it again.

To rename the class, Angela uses the refactoring capability in Visual Studio 2005. To do this, she goes to the class diagram for the OrderBETests project and right-clicks on the OrderDSTestBase class. She then selects Refactor ➤ Rename from the context menu, which opens the dialog box shown in Figure 8-31.

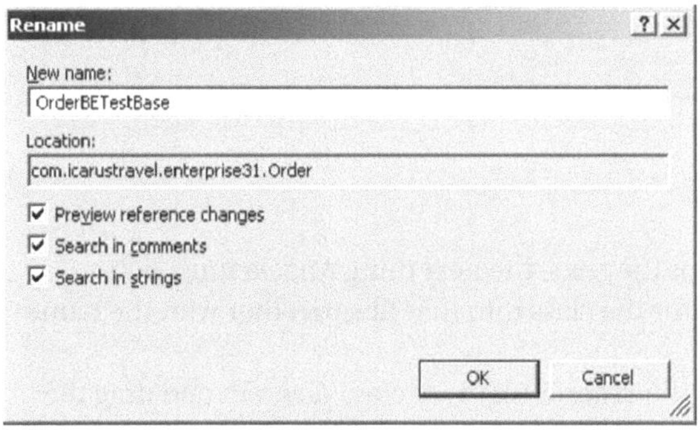

Figure 8-31. *The Rename dialog box*

The refactoring feature in Visual Studio 2005 allows us to rename an identifier in the code and automatically changes the references to it. Angela has changed the name in this dialog box to "OrderBETestBase" so that the class is more general to the whole OrderBE project and not just the data access layer portion of it. She has selected all three checkboxes in the Rename dialog box, which will cause the refactoring process to check in strings and comments as well as code and will allow Angela to preview reference changes.

The Preview Changes dialog box, shown in Figure 8-32, displays a tree-view breakdown of the references to the class OrderTestBase by files, with the references within each file marked with a checkbox. The Preview Code Changes panel of the window shows the code for the file, highlighting the references to be changed. You can examine each one by selecting it in the tree view and viewing in the lower pane, then checking it (or not) according to whether it should be changed. Comments and strings are included as well. In this case, there are only three changes and all can be accepted, so Angela clicks Apply to put the changes into effect.

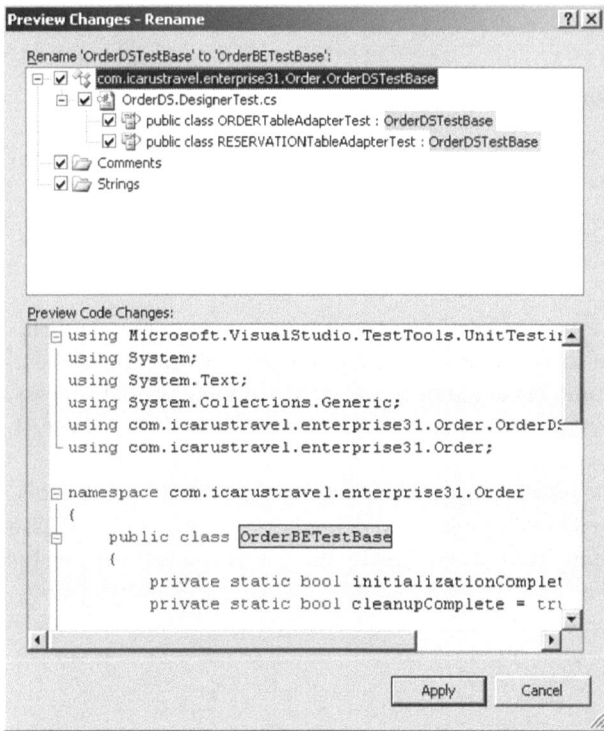

Figure 8-32. *The Preview Changes dialog box*

Once she has renamed the base class for the tests, the next thing Angela must do is rename its file. She can then copy the code for the class into that file, together with the namespace and using statements.

It is then a simple matter to go back to the OrderBETests.cd class diagram and drag the OrderBETest class from the Class View window onto the class diagram (Figure 8-33) and add an inheritance relation to make it inherit from OrderBETestBase (Figure 8-34). In Figure 8-34, the classes have been set to show less information by clicking the "Less" up arrow in the top-right corner of each one.

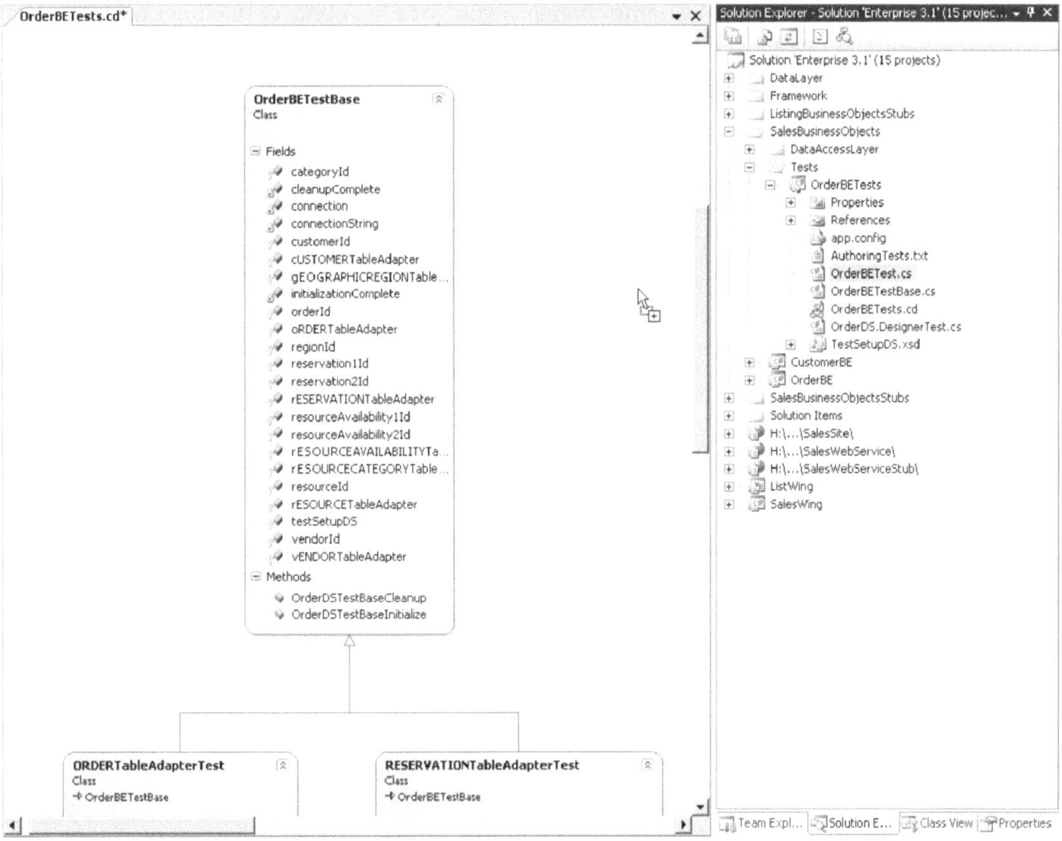

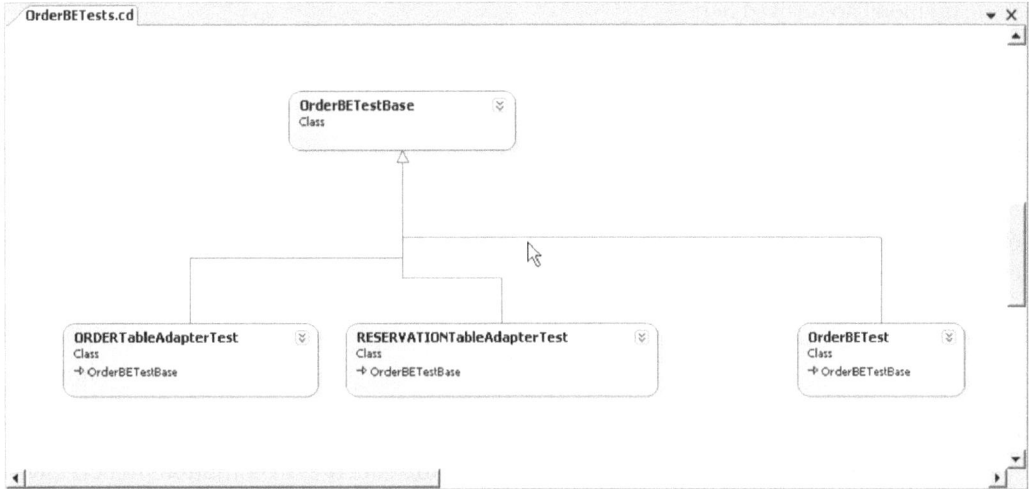

Figure 8-33. *Dragging the OrderBETest class onto the OrderBETest.cd class diagram*

Figure 8-34. *The new class diagram with OrderBETest inheriting from OrderBETestBase*

There's another way to do a name change: if you go to the name of the function and simply type a different name, a little glyph appears, which you can click to display a smart tag menu, as shown in Figure 8-35. If you select Rename with Preview, you will see the Preview Changes dialog box.

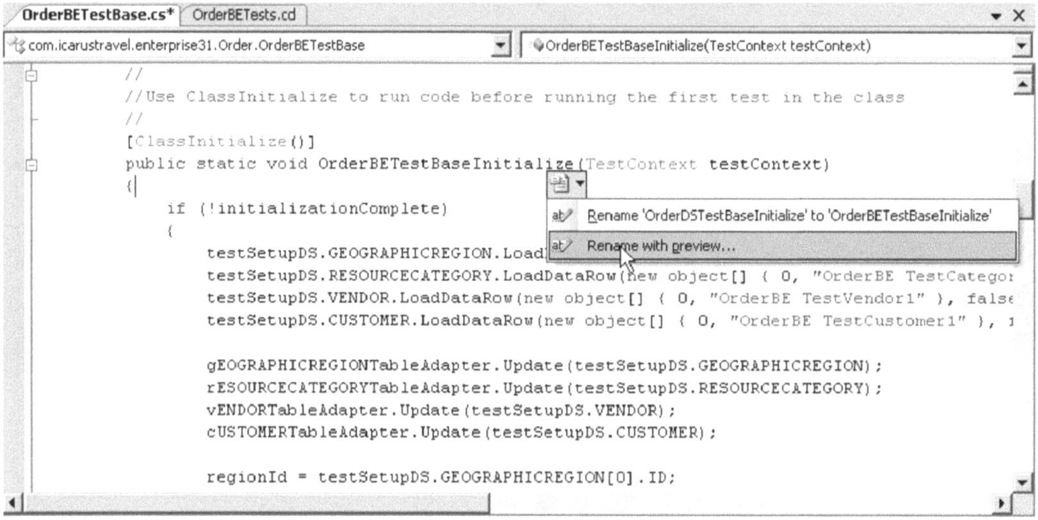

Figure 8-35. *The Rename smart tag menu*

Think back to the unit tests for the two table adapters; the class initialization used a dataset of its own called TestSetupDS with a group of table adapters to write specific test data to the database. The Fill tests on the two adapters for the ORDER and RESERVATION tables then compared the data obtained from the data tables after the Fill call with the known data. The same method can be used here.

In addition to this straightforward local database persistence test, the persistence of the business entity objects to the remote web service must also be tested. It would also be good to test the web services at the unit level, but initially, we can test the OrderBE as a black-box unit (including its model in the database) end to end by verifying its Get and Save functions in both the client and server mode of operation. Nearly all of the test code can be common between the remote and local tests; all that has to change is the setting for the static InstalledMode property of the ultimate base class DualPersistBE. You can see the tests in the file OrderBETest.cs in the exercise code for this section, since it is a bit long to reproduce in this text.

Angela completes the tests and runs them, but of course they all fail because she has written the tests before the code that implements the functionality. The only code present in the OrderBE class is the skeleton code generated by the Class Designer, which returns unimplemented exceptions from every member function. Angela must add the code for Get(int id) and GetData(int id, string tableName) functions.

The code that Angela adds to implements the static Get(int id) function first creates a new instance of OrderBE, then calls its base class function Fill(int id) to populate the new instance from the database. Here is the code:

```
public static OrderBE Get(int id)
{
    OrderBE orderBE = new OrderBE();
    orderBE.Fill(id);
    return orderBE;
//    throw new System.NotImplementedException();
}
```

The static `GetData(int id, string tableName)` calls this same `Get(int id)` function to obtain a populated `OrderBE` object. Then the table specified by name is retrieved from the `OrderBE` object's `DataSet` (actually an `OrderDS`) and returned.

```
public static DataTable GetData(int id, string tableName)
{
    return Get(id).data.Tables[tableName];
//    throw new System.NotImplementedException();
}
```

Angela also needs to complete the code for the override functions `GetLocalData(int id)` and `GetRemoteData(int id)`, which are called by the `BusinessEntityBE` base class. In `GetLocalData`, the two tables are populated from the local database using the `Fill` functions of the table adapters for the ORDER and RESERVATION tables. We must not forget that the connection string for the database is defined in the properties of the `OrderDAL` project, which are carried within the assembly and cannot be changed during install. This connection string will have to be written to the table adapters dynamically and obtained from the `App.config` of the application that uses the business entity class libraries.

```
protected override void GetLocalData(int id)
{
    new ORDERTableAdapter().Fill(data.ORDER,id);
    new RESERVATIONTableAdapter().Fill(data.RESERVATION,id);
//    throw new System.NotImplementedException();
}
```

For the `GetRemoteData`, an instance of the correct web service proxy must be created and its URL set to the value obtained from the `App.config` file. The `GetOrder(int id)` function on the `SalesWebService` returns the data for the specified order in an `OrderDS` dataset. This `GetRemoteData` function then returns this same dataset:

```
protected override SalesWS.OrderDS GetRemoteData(int id)
{
    SalesWS.SalesWebService salesWebService = new SalesWS.SalesWebService();
    if (wSURL != null)
    {
        salesWebService.Url = wSURL;
    }

    return salesWebService.GetOrder(id);
//    throw new System.NotImplementedException();
}
```

As long as the database connections in the table adapters in the `OrderDSTestBase` class match those in the `OrderDS` class and define a valid database, all the tests will now work. It is still necessary, however, to make the database connection string configurable. We will see how this is done in the next section.

Parameterizing the Database Connection and Web Service URL

When you configure a table adapter using Dataset Designer, you are asked to specify a connection string, which the designer uses to create a database connection that is added as the `Connection` property of the `TableAdapter` class. The connection string is a setting in the project that appears in the assembly and cannot be modified at install time. It remains in the assembly as a record of the connection that the developer used to *design* the tables and table adapters. When the dataset and its adapters are part of an installation of the software, this will be the default connection string, but usually it will be required to be different. There may be different security and transaction requirements; for example, the name of the host and perhaps the name of the database will be different. It is therefore necessary to provide the capability to create the connection programmatically and assign it to the `Connection` property of the table adapter just after the adapter has been created. A good way to do this is by defining an overload of the table adapter constructor that can be part of a partial class that, together with the partial class in `OrderDS.designer.cs` generated by Dataset Designer, forms the whole definition of the table adapter. Of course, you could edit the partial class that is contained in the file `OrderDS.designer.cs` and add the constructor overload there, but this is an automatically generated file, and if the table adapter is reconfigured, this file will be regenerated and the changes lost. This is a strong rationale behind the concept of partial classes, where a class can be defined in multiple places so that one part can be generated automatically and one part manually. This approach is a lot cleaner than the old methods, in which the tools automatically generated code in special places within a file, which was also edited manually.

Note The source code for this section is in the folder `Chapter 8\Exercise 8`. Exercise 8-9 applies to this section.

Angela therefore defines a constructor overload for `ORDERTableAdapter` and `RESERVATIONTableAdapter` in the `OrderDS.cs` that looks like this:

```
namespace com.icarustravel.enterprise31.Order.OrderDSTableAdapters {

    public partial class ORDERTableAdapter : System.ComponentModel.Component
    {
        public ORDERTableAdapter(System.Data.SqlClient.SqlConnection connection)
        {
            this.ClearBeforeFill = true;
            this.Connection = connection;
        }
    }
}
```

```
    public partial class RESERVATIONTableAdapter : System.ComponentModel.Component
    {
        public RESERVATIONTableAdapter(
                            System.Data.SqlClient.SqlConnection connection)
        {
            this.ClearBeforeFill = true;
            this.Connection = connection;
        }
    }
}
```

This file is automatically created if you select View Code from the right-click menu on the design surface in Dataset Designer. The constructors duplicate the automatically created default constructors, except that they receive the connection as a parameter and assign it to the Connection property of the class. The connection itself can be created earlier and used for all of the table adapters that are needed in the implementation of the Get function, like this:

```
protected override void GetLocalData(int id)
{
  System.Data.SqlClient.SqlConnection connection =
        new System.Data.SqlClient.SqlConnection(localConnectionString);
  new ORDERTableAdapter(connection).Fill(data.ORDER, id);
  new RESERVATIONTableAdapter(connection).Fill(data.RESERVATION, id);
}
```

The variable localConnectionString is static and added to the base class BusinessEntityBE. Initialization of this variable occurs at the same time as the URL variable by reading either from the App.config file or web.config according to the install mode (see the file BusinessEntityBE.cs).

The table adapters defined in OrderBETestBase do not need this treatment, since they are not defined within a class library project. The connection strings are written to the App.config file, which is used when the test is run. The settings for the test can therefore be defined in the project properties before build or can be edited in the .config file before the test is executed.

The web service URL has already been parameterized and added to the .config file for the Sales Wing application. It also needs to be added to an App.config in the OrderBETests project. Although this project is a DLL, when the tests it defines are run by Test View, the App.config file (which is called OrderBETests.dll.config in the bin\debug folder) is copied to the test directory and is opened as the .exe.config file by the ConfigurationManager.OpenExeConfiguration function in the static constructor of the BusinessEntityBE class.

Problems with Sequences of Unit Tests

Angela runs each local and remote read test individually without any problems, but when she runs even the first two together in a sequence, there is an embarrassing failure of the remote case, as shown in Figure 8-36. Angela double-clicks on the test result to review the detailed description of the test results, as shown in Figure 8-37. The window says that there is an out-of-range exception in accessing a row in a table—Angela thinks that maybe it's when the dataset for the OrderBE object is being checked in the test code for correct content.

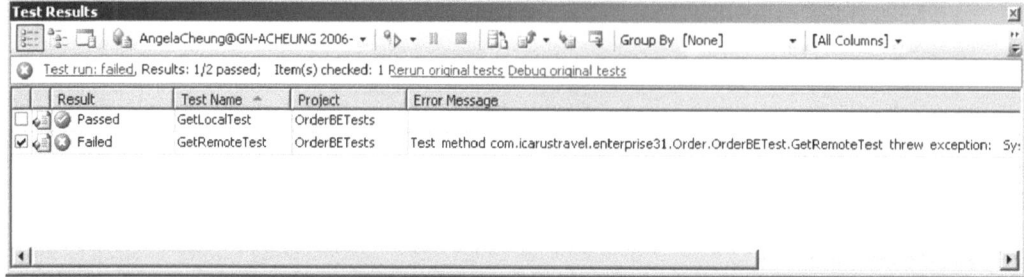

Figure 8-36. *The failure of the GetRemoteTest*

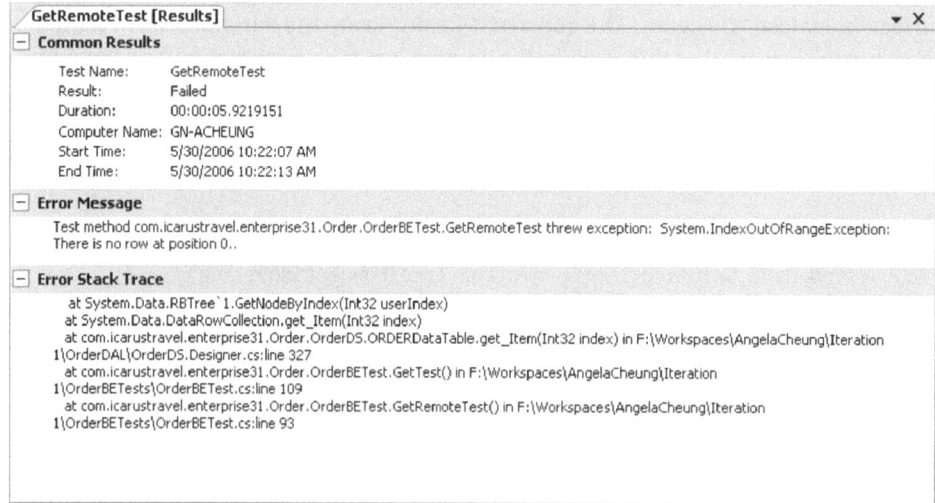

Figure 8-37. *The detailed results of the GetRemoteTest*

Angela decides to try some debugging. She sets a breakpoint at the place in the code where the second (failing) test begins, as shown in Figure 8-38. She runs the two tests by selecting them both in the Test View window and choosing Debug Selection from the right-click menu. The Test Results window shows that the first test is passed, and then the breakpoint is hit.

```
/// <summary>
///A test for Get (int)
///</summary>
[TestMethod()]
public void GetRemoteTest()
{
    com.icarustravel.enterprise31.Order.OrderBE.InstalledMode =
        com.icarustravel.enterprise31.Order.OrderBE.InstallMode.Client;

    GetTest();
}

private void GetTest()
{
    int id = orderId;
```

Figure 8-38. *Debugging the failing unit test; Angela places a breakpoint at the start of the test.*

I'm going to assume you are familiar with the basic debugging capability of Visual Studio, such as placing breakpoints in code and stepping over, stepping into, and stepping out of functions. Angela steps into the GetTest() function, into the OrderBE.Get(int id) function, and then into the Fill(int id) function in the BusinessEntityBE base class. It correctly takes the InstalledMode == InstallMode.Client path in the code:

```
protected void Fill(int id)
{
  data = new LocalDSType();

  if (InstalledMode == InstallMode.Client)
  {
    data.Merge(GetRemoteData(id));
  }
  else
  {
    GetLocalData(id);
  }
}
```

She steps into the GetRemoteData(id) function call:

```
protected override SalesWS.OrderDS GetRemoteData(int id)
{
  SalesWS.SalesWebService salesWebService = new SalesWS.SalesWebService();
  if (wSURL != null)
  {
    salesWebService.Url = wSURL;
  }

  return salesWebService.GetOrder(id);
}
```

Here she hovers the cursor over the static variable wSURL and sees that its value is null. Therefore, the proxy will be using the value of the URL that is in its configuration, which was generated when the web reference was added to the project. The value is therefore the URL of the web service stub, which returns an empty dataset. "Well, that explains the missing rows in the table," thinks Angela. "But why would the value of the static variable wSURL be null?"

The static variable wSURL gets loaded with the value from the .config file in the static constructor for BusinessEntityBE only if the install mode is set to client, so Angela places a breakpoint in the static constructor and runs the test again from the beginning. It hits the breakpoint in the static constructor, then hits the breakpoint at the beginning of the local test. When she lets it run again, it hits the breakpoint at the beginning of the second test *without going through the static constructor again.*

"Of course!" yells Angela and Charles takes off his headphones. She has been puzzling over this for a couple of hours. "Hey, Charles, when you run a set of unit tests, a static constructor in the class under test will only execute once!"

"Yes, that's right," agrees Charles in a voice that suggests that he knew all along but was waiting to be asked. "A static constructor is required to execute once between the assembly being loaded and before an instance of the class is created or any of the static variables are accessed."

Angela says nothing; she wonders if Charles really did know that. Of course, the OrderBETests assembly is loaded, and the static constructor runs before the first instance of OrderBE is created for the first test. Then, in the second test, the install mode is changed to client and the second test runs, but of course the static constructor does not execute again even though the install mode has been changed to InstallMode.Client. So the code in the static constructor for BusinessEntityBE never retrieves the settings applicable to client mode from the .config file. This is one of those annoying things that only happen in unit tests, but Angela needs to be able to run a whole sequence of tests. Indeed, they must run automatically after formal builds, as we'll see later in this chapter.

Actually Angela *did* know that static constructors only execute once, but the catch here is the way in which this fact relates to the running of a sequence of unit tests. The constructor only runs once for the whole sequence of tests.

She decides to force the code in the static constructor to run each time the install mode changes by adding an event to the base class DualPersistBE that will be fired when a mode change occurs:

```
public abstract class DualPersistBE
{
  protected delegate void OnInstallModeChangeDelegate();
  protected static event OnInstallModeChangeDelegate InstallModeChange;

  //  etc.

  private static InstallMode installedMode = InstallMode.SERVER;

  public static InstallMode InstalledMode
  {
    get { return installedMode; }
    set
    {
      installedMode = value;
      if(InstallModeChange != null)
        InstallModeChange.Invoke();
    }
  }
}
```

The code in the static constructor can then register an event handler that will call the same initialization that the static constructor currently does:

```
static BusinessEntityBE()
{
  InitializeStaticSettings ();
```

```
    DualPersistBE.InstallModeChange +=
                            new OnInstallModeChangeDelegate (OnInstallModeChange);
}

protected static void OnInstallModeChange()
{
  InitializeStaticSettings();
}

private static void InitializeStaticSettings()
{

  // Initialization of URL, connection string etc.

}
```

This fixes the problem nicely. Angela debugs a few more times to verify everything is happening in the right order, and finds that her whole sequence of unit tests now passes consistently.

What does this illustrate? Apart from reminding us about static constructors, it shows that during unit test, the class is often being used in an unnatural manner. What would be the alternative to this little trick with events?

Just then Peter walks into the cubicle and Angela explains the problem. "Maybe we could run the class under test in a different AppDomain and unload the AppDomain between each test to make sure the class starts up each time as though the program was starting," he suggests. "I haven't written the code for that, but it would be worth a try. I don't like putting in events that are only needed for unit test."

"No, it is a bit of an artificial thing to do," she agrees.

"Could you raise it as an issue, Angela? Assign it to me, and I'll try the AppDomain idea when I get a chance."

Angela goes to Team Explorer, right-clicks on the Work Items folder, and selects Add Work Item ➤ Issue from the context menu (Figure 8-39). The issue that she adds is shown in Figure 8-40. Unfortunately, Peter never did get a chance to try this idea and Angela's event mechanism stayed in the code. Perhaps you would like to investigate it.

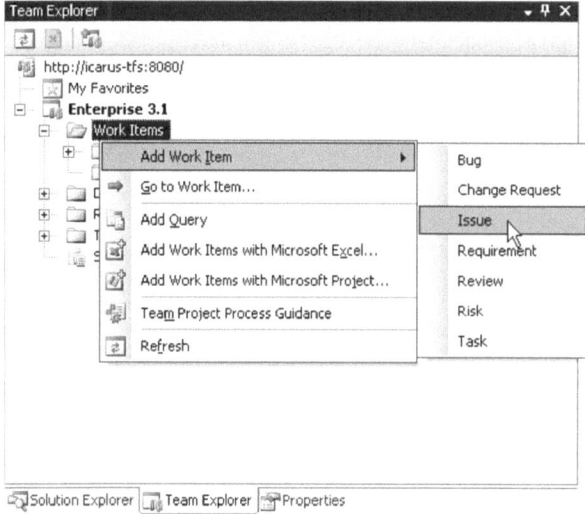

Figure 8-39. *Adding an issue as a work item to the team project*

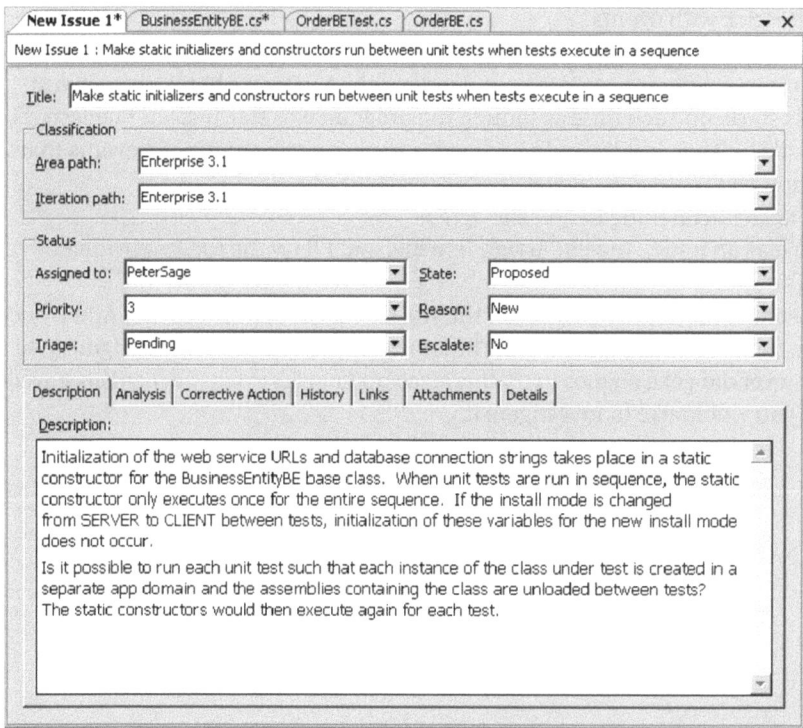

Figure 8-40. *The issue work item for the unit test sequence problem*

Testing the Business Layer: Write Capability

So far we have not discussed the write capability of OrderBE. The presentation layer must be able to save an OrderBE instance of a particular ID value that is either new or was previously obtained via the Get(int id) function. Before the save, reservations in the order may have been added, deleted, or modified and fields in them may also have changed. All of these cases will be covered by the Update function of ORDERTableAdapter and RESERVATIONTableAdapter, which will check the status of each row before calling the INSERT, DELETE, or UPDATE stored procedure. The Save() function needed on OrderBE is an instance function rather than a static one, since it will be a specific instance of the OrderBE class that will be saved.

Note The source code for this section is in the folder Chapter 8\Exercise 9. Exercise 8-10 applies to this section.

The tests for the Save() function essentially involve first calling the OrderBE.Get(int id) function to read a standard test order and return it as an OrderBE instance. The test can then make some modifications to the order and its reservations before calling its OrderBE.Save() function. These modifications must include changing order details, such as the date, as well as some of the reservation details, such as the unit count and unit cost. It is also necessary to test the capability to add a reservation and delete it. If reservations in the standard test order are deleted and then re-created, they will get new ID values and mess up subsequent tests. Therefore, the sequence must demonstrate this capability by adding a new reservation and then deleting it again. The detailed code of the tests is too long to reproduce here, but you can look at it in the exercise code for this chapter in the OrderBETest.cs file.

Of course, the tests fail until the SaveLocalData and SaveRemoteData overrides are implemented. That code for these is

```
protected override void SaveLocalData()
{
  System.Data.SqlClient.SqlConnection connection =
    new System.Data.SqlClient.SqlConnection(localConnectionString);
  new ORDERTableAdapter(connection).Update(this.data.ORDER);
  new RESERVATIONTableAdapter(connection).Update(this.data.RESERVATION);
}

protected override void SaveRemoteData(SalesWS.OrderDS remoteData)
{
  SalesWS.SalesWebService salesWebService = new SalesWS.SalesWebService();
  if (wSURL != null)
  {
    salesWebService.Url = wSURL;
  }

  salesWebService.SaveOrder(remoteData);
}
```

The first of these functions creates instances of the two table adapters using their overloaded constructors with the connection passed as a parameter. Then the Update function is called on each, passing the tables in the dataset that contain modified data.

The second function calls a new SaveOrder web method defined on SalesWebService. This web method creates an instance of OrderBE and sets its dataset equal to the dataset deserialized from the method parameter via its public Data property defined in BusinessEntityBE. The Save function is then called on the OrderBE object, which will initiate a local save on the server as described earlier.

```
[System.Web.Services.WebMethod()]
public void SaveOrder(OrderDS data)
{
  OrderBE orderBE = new OrderBE();
  orderBE.Data = data;
  orderBE.Save();
}
```

Test Coverage

The ability to determine coverage of unit tests is an important new feature of Visual Studio 2005 Team Edition. Each line of code is considered covered if the unit tests have caused it to be executed. There is no attempt to measure whether the diverse ways in which the code may behave have been covered—such as whether every possible path through the code has been executed, or whether the tests have exercised the whole range of data over which a given unit of code must work correctly.

Note The source code at the start of this section is in the folder Chapter 8\Exercise 10. Exercise 8-11 applies to this section.

Let's return to Angela, who has now finished writing the first iteration of the OrderBE business entity and a basic set of unit tests to go with it. She is now ready to use the code coverage capability to derive some measure of the degree of completeness. She must first enable code coverage for the assemblies that she wishes to study. She double-clicks on a file called localtestrun.testrunconfig, which is in the SolutionItems folder in Solution Explorer. This opens the dialog box shown in Figure 8-41, which has a large number of settings controlling test running. For the moment, Angela is only interested in the Code Coverage section, which lists the assemblies in the solution. She is responsible for OrderDAL and OrderBE, so she checks both of those assemblies.

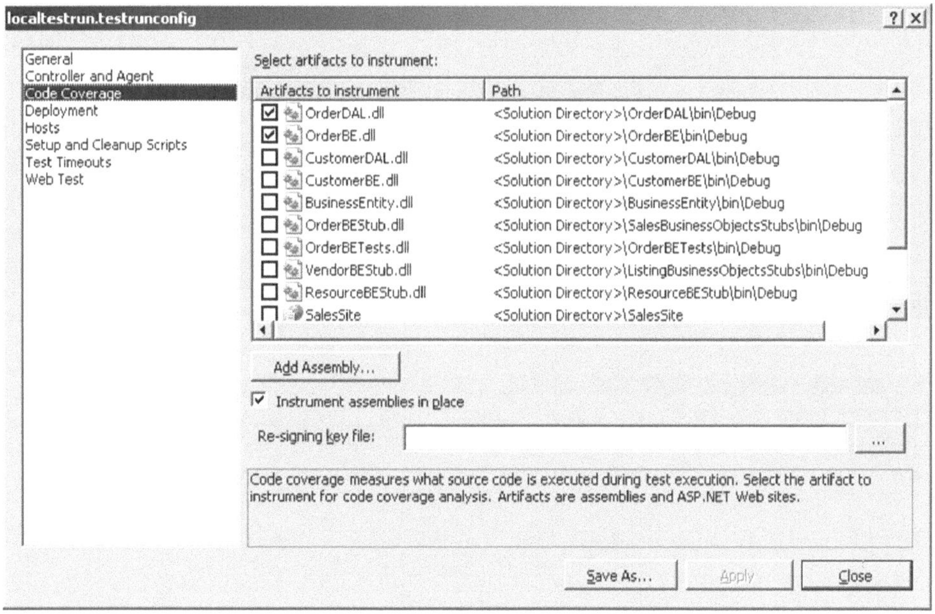

Figure 8-41. *The localtestrun.testrunconfig dialog box*

Having enabled the code coverage capability, Angela now runs her entire set of OrderBE tests and OrderDAL tests. The results in the Code Coverage Results window (Figure 8-42) reveal quite poor coverage of the OrderBE.dll assembly (only 9.2 percent), but when the results are expanded (Figure 8-43), it is clear that the code in the class OrderBE has been covered 100 percent. The poor coverage is in the SalesWS namespace (4.82 percent), which contains the SalesWebService proxy. This is automatically generated code and a good deal of it is never used, since it is not included in the design. You therefore must use this feature carefully and make sure the code that is intended to be used in the design is covered. It makes little sense to spend time testing code that is not going to be executed. But there is a philosophical point here. Suppose you design a general-purpose class that has a set of methods and then use that class in an application where only half of its methods are used. Do you spend time in the project to test all of the methods that the class exposes—because it's intended as a general component—even though not all the methods are currently used? It has to be a judgment call. If you truly want the class to be reliable as a general component, you have to test all its features, but in the case of the automatically generated web service proxy, in this case where there's never any intention to use some of the methods (such as GetOrderAsynch, for example), it's sufficient to exercise all the code that's written by the team members. Peter agrees and accepts Angela's unit tests for iteration 1 on review.

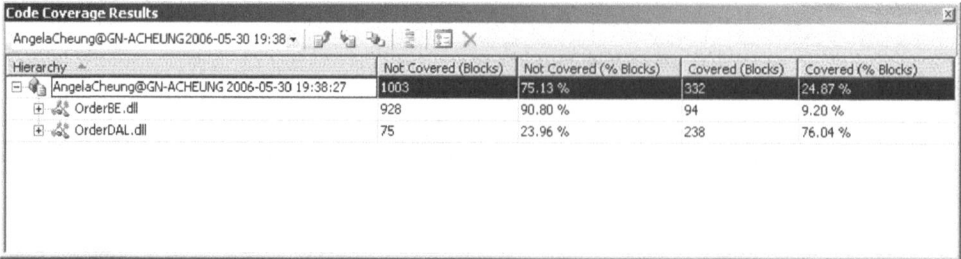

Figure 8-42. *The top-level code coverage results*

Code Coverage Results				
Hierarchy	Not Covered (Blocks)	Not Covered (% Blocks)	Covered (Blocks)	Covered (% Blocks)
AngelaCheung@GN-ACHEUNG 2006-05-30 22:09:47	1003	75.13 %	332	24.87 %
OrderBE.dll	928	90.80 %	94	9.20 %
{ } com.icarustravel.enterprise31.Order.SalesWS	928	95.18 %	47	4.82 %
{ } com.icarustravel.enterprise31.Order	0	0.00 %	39	100.00 %
OrderBE	0	0.00 %	39	100.00 %
Get(int32)	0	0.00 %	4	100.00 %
GetData(int32,string)	0	0.00 %	5	100.00 %
GetLocalData(int32)	0	0.00 %	9	100.00 %
GetRemoteData(int32)	0	0.00 %	7	100.00 %
SaveLocalData()	0	0.00 %	8	100.00 %
SaveRemoteData(class com.icarustravel.enterprise31.	0	0.00 %	6	100.00 %
{ } com.icarustravel.enterprise31.Order.Properties	0	0.00 %	8	100.00 %
OrderDAL.dll	75	23.96 %	238	76.04 %

Figure 8-43. *The Code Coverage Results window shows that the poor coverage is in the web service proxy code.*

Static Code Analysis Check-In Policy

"Hey, Angela," says Ron, looking into her cubicle. "I'm going to set up the team project so that it requires static code analysis as part of the check-in policy."

"Oh . . . right," says Angela hesitantly. "I haven't tried running those yet."

"You'll be the first then," replies Ron cheerfully. "We might as well start. At some point we need to run static code analysis on the data access layer work that you already checked in too."

"Are you going to set a testing policy for check-in as well?" she asks.

"Good point. How should we do that? We need to gradually add the tests as each piece of functionality gets checked in, and the developers will add the tests for their areas of responsibility as they go along."

"Maybe the developer adds her tests first," suggests Angela. "Then she changes the check-in testing policy to include those tests."

Ron hesitates a moment. "The trouble is, the developers don't have access to the source control team project settings—and strictly speaking they really shouldn't. To keep the developers honest, each one should write a set of unit tests and be required to run them before checking the new functionality into TFS. It's only after team leader review that the tests can be added to the check-in testing policy."

"So the check-in testing policy is more of a *regression* testing policy than a policy requiring initial tests," Angela observes thoughtfully.

"Yeah—it's really there to ensure that when a developer makes a change and checks code in, the change doesn't break the existing working baseline of functionality. So let's plan it this way. When a developer adds a new piece of functionality—or fixes a bug—it's their responsibility to write unit tests for that functionality and run them before checking the code into TFS. If it's a bug they've fixed, then they should write a new unit test that checks the fix for the bug. Then, before they can check the code into TFS, they have to run the static analysis *and* the unit tests that have been added to the check-in testing policy. Then, it's the responsibility of the test manager to add the new unit tests for the new functionality to the set of tests required to be run as part of the testing check-in policy."

"Wait," says Charles, who is listening to the conversation. "When I check in my new code that I've developed at the same time as Angela, I won't be able to run the new unit tests that Angela has added, because the version on my computer won't have them. That will be the case if I got the latest version before Angela checks in her new code and new tests."

"Yes, that *is* right, isn't it?" agrees Ron thoughtfully and hesitates before suggesting a solution. "OK, then—you'll have to do a Get Latest from TFS *before* you attempt to check anything in. That way you'll merge your new code with any changes that have gone in while you've been working on it, then make sure it all builds, and the specified check-in policy tests all run *before* you'll be allowed to check your code in."

"Right," says Charles doubtfully. "I wonder how well this merge capability will work."

"Well, let's give it a try this way and see how it goes. I'll go and explain it to everyone else. OK?"

"OK," the developers both agree.

After Ron has explained this concept to the other developers, and has sent an explanatory email to Rahul in India, he sits down at his computer to set the check-in policies. To edit check-in policies, you need to be in the project administrators group and select Team Project Settings ➤ Source Control (Figure 8-44) from the right-click menu in the team project, Enterprise 3.1, in the Team Explorer window. This displays the Source Control Settings dialog box. On the Check-in Policy tab, clicking the Add button displays the Add Check-in Policy dialog box, where you can select the check-in policies, as shown in Figure 8-45.

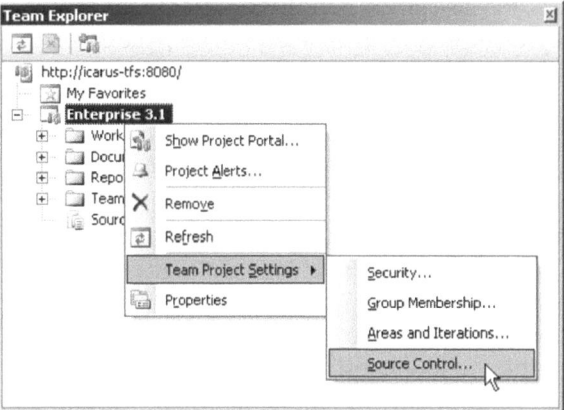

Figure 8-44. *Displaying the source control settings in Team Explorer*

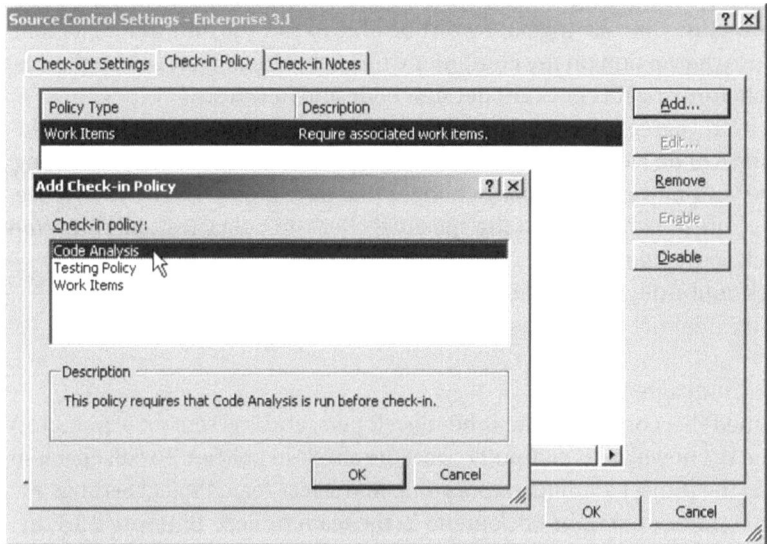

Figure 8-45. *The Add Check-in Policy dialog box*

Note The source code at the start of this section is in the folder Chapter 8\Exercise 10 since the previous exercise did not change the code. Exercise 8-12 applies to this section.

Selecting Code Analysis and clicking OK produces the dialog box shown in Figure 8-46. The Code Analysis Policy Editor lets you specify the code analysis features you want. For the moment, Ron leaves these options set at the defaults and clicks OK.

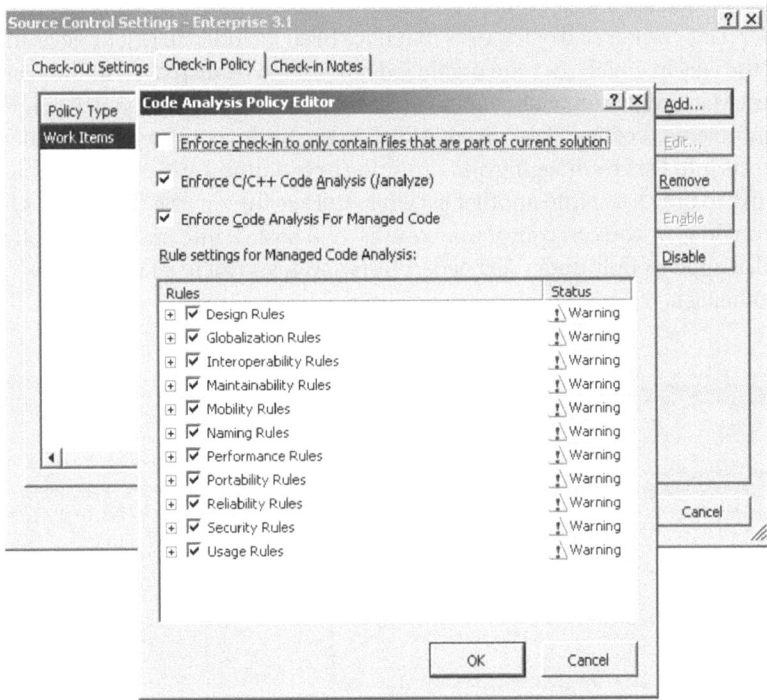

Figure 8-46. *The Code Analysis Policy Editor*

Ron then needs to set up a check-in testing policy. To do this he needs to go visit Herman, the test manager, and we need a short digression into one of the features of Team System for Testers.

Test Manager

Herman is the test manager, but *Test Manager* is also a very useful feature of Visual Studio 2005 Team Edition for Software Testers, which is not included in the Architect or Developer edition.

Note Exercise 8-13 applies to this section.

When Test Manager is opened for the first time, a file called `<solution name>.vsmdi` is created in the `SolutionItems` folder. This contains all of the tests that have been included in test projects in the solution and defines the way in which they are organized into lists to be displayed in the Test Manager window. The Test Manager window, shown in Figure 8-47, allows you to organize your tests into a hierarchical arrangement of lists. You can create lists at the top level or lists within other lists, and you can move tests into lists by dragging and dropping or by cutting and pasting. Tests can be in more than one list; to drag a test into another list while still leaving it in the first you hold down the Ctrl key while you drag, or you can copy it from one list and paste it into another. Initially, when a test is first created, it appears only under All Loaded Tests and Tests Not in a List; you can drag it from there to any other list.

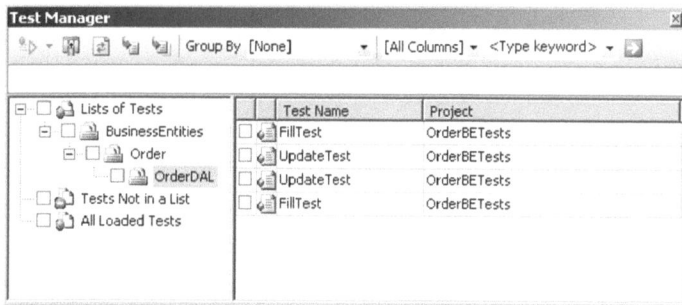

Figure 8-47. *Organizing the order business entity tests into lists in Test Manager*

Herman, at Ron's request, gets the latest version of the whole project into a workspace for himself and opens Test Manager. He then arranges the four unit tests that Angela has written for `OrderDAL` into a list at their place in the `BusinessEntities` hierarchy, as shown in Figure 8-47. All of those that test the table adapter objects directly are in the OrderDAL list, whereas those that test the `OrderBE` class will be in a different list. It will be Herman's job to keep the tests that the developers write organized properly into lists such as these and include selections from those lists in the check-in testing policy. Herman checks the new `Enterprise 3.1.vsmdi` file into source control.

Check-In Testing Policy

Ron goes back to his office, opens the Source Control Settings dialog box again at the Check-in Policy tab, and clicks the Add button. This time he selects Testing Policy and clicks OK to brings up the Testing Policy dialog box. First Ron needs to browse for a test metadata file by clicking Browse and drilling down through the source control structure on the team project, as shown in the Browse dialog box in Figure 8-48, until he finds the file called `Enterprise 3.1.vsmdi` that Herman created.

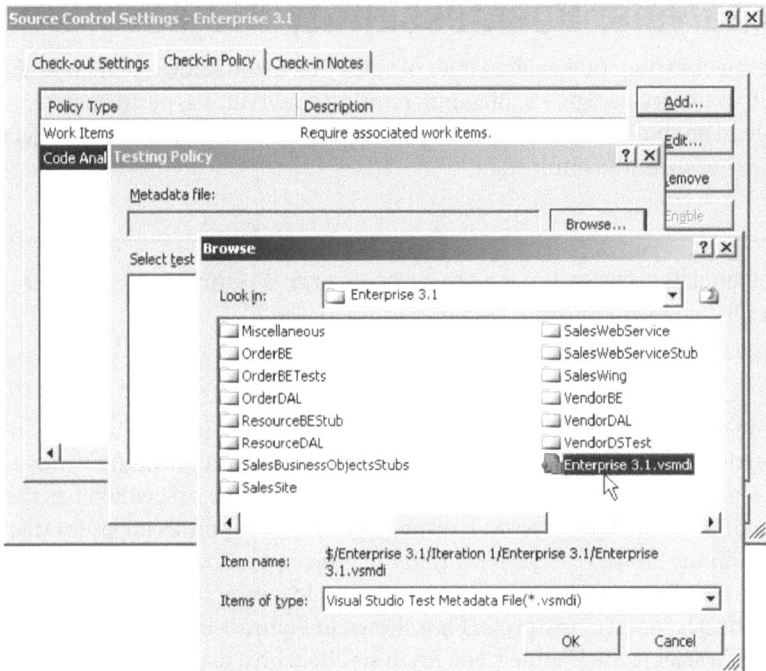

Figure 8-48. *Selecting the metadata file to allow specification of the testing check-in policy.*

Once he has selected it in the Browse dialog box and clicked OK, Ron sees the dialog box in Figure 8-49, where he selects each of the nested lists and clicks OK. Note that selecting an outer list does not automatically select the inner lists. After this is completed, three check-in policies are in effect that Angela and the other developers will have to satisfy: an associated work item, satisfactory static code analysis, and a testing policy requiring that Angela's tests of OrderDAL pass.

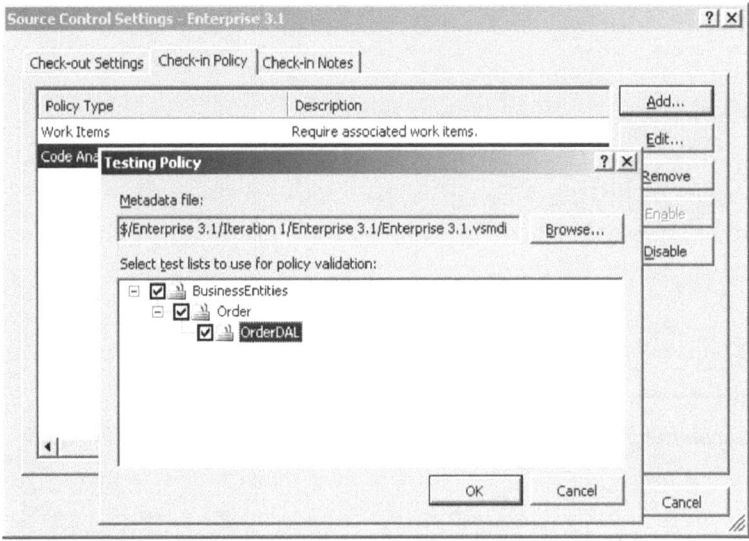

Figure 8-49. *The Testing Policy dialog box, populated from the Enterprise 3.1.vsmdi file*

Static Code Analysis: BusinessEntity Project

The static code analyzer checks your code against a set of rules that avoid known defects and poor design in areas such as library design, localization, naming conventions, performance, and security. It is possible to enable or disable rules and the technical leadership of the project needs to decide which are important to enforce.

Note The source code at the start of this section is in the folder `Chapter 8\Exercise 10` since the previous exercise did not modify any code. Exercise 8-14 applies to this section.

Now Angela has some extra work to do. Running the static code analysis is just a matter of enabling it in the properties for each project that she has developed and rebuilding those projects. She decides to start with the `BusinessEntity` project in the framework, which has the `BusinessEntityBE` and `DualPersistBE` base classes. First she opens the properties pages for that project by double-clicking on the `Properties` folder within the project, as shown in Figure 8-50. (You can also open the properties pages by choosing Properties from the right-click menu.) The properties pages for the `BusinessEntity` project are shown in Figure 8-51, with the Code Analysis tab selected. Angela selects the Enable Code Analysis checkbox, leaves all of the code analysis rules selected (but notes that here is where she can disable them), closes the dialog box, and rebuilds the `BusinessEntity` project by right-clicking on it in Solution Explorer and selecting Rebuild.

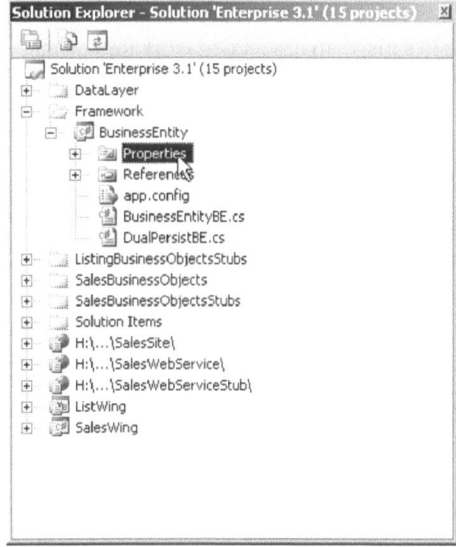

Figure 8-50. *Double-clicking on the properties folder in a project displays the properties pages for the project.*

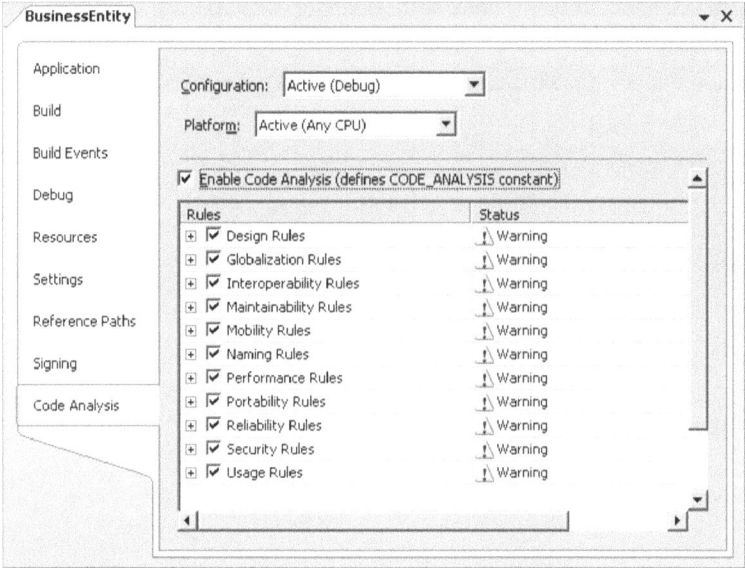

Figure 8-51. *The properties pages for the BusinessEntity project in the framework folder, with the Code Analysis tab displayed*

Angela notices that the output window shows the message "Running Code Analysis . . ." and an ominous number of extra messages flash past. After the build is complete, she displays the Error List window in Figure 8-52. "Holy mackerel, just look at all those yellow triangles!" And she thought she had done such a great job. It's 5:30 PM and she decides to go home and watch a nice movie.

The next morning Angela arrives with a set jaw and resolves to make her last stand, determined to go down fighting in the face of an overwhelming onslaught of yellow triangles. She starts at the beginning—CA2211 in Figure 8-52.

		Description ▾	File	Line	Column	Project
⚠	15	CA2211 : Microsoft.Usage : Consider making 'wSURL' non-public or a constant.				BusinessEntity
⚠	12	CA2211 : Microsoft.Usage : Consider making 'localConnectionString' non-public or a constant.				BusinessEntity
⚠	5	CA2210 : Microsoft.Design : Sign 'BusinessEntity' with a strong name key.				BusinessEntity
⚠	4	CA2209 : Microsoft.Usage : No valid permission requests were found for assembly 'BusinessEntity'. You should always specify the minimum security permissions using SecurityAction.RequestMinimum.				BusinessEntity
⚠	8	CA1810 : Microsoft.Performance : Initialize all static fields in com.icarustravel.enterprise31.BusinessEntity.BusinessEntityBE`2 when those fields are declared and remove the explicit static constructor.	BusinessEntityBE.cs	15		BusinessEntity
⚠	10	CA1800 : Microsoft.Performance : 'settingsSection', a local, is cast to type 'System.Configuration.ClientSettingsSection' multiple times in method BusinessEntityBE`2.InitialiseStaticSettings():Void. Cache the result of the 'as' operator or direct cast in order to eliminate the redundant castclass instruction.	BusinessEntityBE.cs	66		BusinessEntity
⚠	21	CA1711 : Microsoft.Naming : Rename 'com.icarustravel.enterprise31.BusinessEntity.DualPersistBE+OnInstallModeChangeDelegate' so that it does not end in 'Delegate'.	DualPersistBE.cs	9		BusinessEntity
⚠	18	CA1710 : Microsoft.Naming : Rename 'com.icarustravel.enterprise31.BusinessEntity.DualPersistBE+OnInstallModeChangeDelegate' to end in 'EventHandler'.	DualPersistBE.cs	10		BusinessEntity
⚠	1	CA1709 : Microsoft.Naming : Correct the casing of namespace name 'com.icarustravel.enterprise31.BusinessEntity'.				BusinessEntity
⚠	2	CA1709 : Microsoft.Naming : Correct the casing of namespace name 'com.icarustravel.enterprise31.BusinessEntity'.				BusinessEntity
⚠	3	CA1709 : Microsoft.Naming : Correct the casing of namespace name 'com.icarustravel.enterprise31.BusinessEntity'.				BusinessEntity
⚠	7	CA1708 : Microsoft.Naming : Change member names 'Data' and 'data' so that they differ by more than case.				BusinessEntity
⚠	20	CA1705 : Microsoft.Naming : Correct the capitalization of member name 'InstallMode.SERVER'.	DualPersistBE.cs	14		BusinessEntity
⚠	19	CA1705 : Microsoft.Naming : Correct the capitalization of member name 'InstallMode.CLIENT'.	DualPersistBE.cs	15		BusinessEntity
⚠	9	CA1051 : Microsoft.Design : Make 'data' private or internal (Friend in VB, public private in C++) and provide a public or protected property to access it.				BusinessEntity
⚠	6	CA1014 : Microsoft.Design : 'BusinessEntity' should be marked with CLSCompliantAttribute and its value should be true.				BusinessEntity
⚠	17	CA1009 : Microsoft.Design : Declare the second parameter of 'OnInstallModeChangeDelegate' as an EventArgs, or an instance of a type that extends EventArgs, named 'e'.	DualPersistBE.cs	10		BusinessEntity
⚠	16	CA1009 : Microsoft.Design : Declare the first parameter of 'OnInstallModeChangeDelegate' as an object named 'sender'.	DualPersistBE.cs	10		BusinessEntity
⚠	14	CA1000 : Microsoft.Design : Remove BusinessEntityBE`2.wSURL from 'com.icarustravel.enterprise31.BusinessEntity.BusinessEntityBE`2' or make it an instance member.				BusinessEntity
⚠	13	CA1000 : Microsoft.Design : Remove BusinessEntityBE`2.OnInstallModeChange():Void from 'com.icarustravel.enterprise31.BusinessEntity.BusinessEntityBE`2' or make it an instance member.	BusinessEntityBE.cs	41		BusinessEntity
⚠	11	CA1000 : Microsoft.Design : Remove BusinessEntityBE`2.localConnectionString from 'com.icarustravel.enterprise31.BusinessEntity.BusinessEntityBE`2' or make it an instance member.				BusinessEntity

Figure 8-52. *The attack of the yellow triangles. The warnings result from rule violations discovered by running the static code analyzer.*

Making Static Variables Non-Public

`CA 2211: Microsoft Usage : Consider making "wSURL" non-public or a constant.`

"wSURL—that's the static variable I'm using to hold the URL of the sales web service," Angela thinks. "Why should that be a problem?" Fortunately all of the code analyzer warnings are well documented, so she can paste the number CA2211 into the help index or just select that error and hit F1. "Non constant fields should not be visible," she reads.

> *"Static fields that are neither constants nor read-only are not thread-safe. Access to such a field must be carefully controlled and requires advanced programming techniques for synchronizing access to the class object. Because these are difficult skills to learn and master, and testing such an object poses its own challenges, static fields are best used to store data that does not change. This rule applies to libraries; applications should not expose any fields."*

"So what this is telling me," she deduces, "is that I should not leave that variable exposed to public use, because someone might change it and it would not be thread safe."

Angela has designed the code so that this variable is not intended to change since it is set up by the static constructor via the `InitializeStaticSettings()` method. This method is called by the constructor but also by the event delegate function for the `InstallModeChange` event. This event only occurs as a result of a change to the install mode, which only takes place during unit testing. Normally the install mode is set on start-up and stays the same, so it does not look as though there will be a threading problem. "Nevertheless, if it doesn't need to be publicly accessible I suppose it shouldn't be," she admits.

Are multiple threads likely to run through this class? Yes, definitely when an instance of the class is created by code in an `aspx.cs` file, because multiple threads are generated by Internet Information Server (IIS) to handle ASP.NET pages. Also, when the class is instantiated within the Windows Forms Sales Wing application, there may possibly be more than one thread—an extra thread perhaps running to perform background synchronization after offline working. So this could theoretically be an issue. There are several ways to satisfy this rule. One is to make the static variable private instead of protected, but then the derived classes `OrderBE` and `CustomerBE` will not be able to access it. It would be a nice idea for it to be private and not be accessible at all outside `BusinessEntityBE`—it's also not a good idea to have to write the repetitive code in each `GetRemoteData(int id)` function that initializes the URL for the web service proxy.

```
protected override SalesWS.OrderDS GetRemoteData(int id)
{
  SalesWS.SalesWebService salesWebService = new SalesWS.SalesWebService();
  if (wSURL != null)
  {
    salesWebService.Url = wSURL;
  }

  return salesWebService.GetOrder(id);
}
```

That bold code should be in the base `BusinessEntityBE` class, and maybe the line preceding it too, but only the derived class knows which web service proxy to create. Perhaps some refactoring is required here. How can it be done? One way is to make use of generics a little more and put an additional type parameter in the definition of `BusinessEntityBE` called `RemoteWSType` that will specify the type of the web service proxy to be instantiated when a web service proxy is required. The definition for `BusinessEntityBE` then becomes

```
public abstract class BusinessEntityBE<LocalDSType, RemoteDSType, RemoteWSType>
    : DualPersistBE
    where LocalDSType : DataSet, new()
    where RemoteDSType : DataSet, new()
    where RemoteWSType :
System.Web.Services.Protocols.SoapHttpClientProtocol, new()
{
  protected LocalDSType data;
```

```
private static string wSURL = null;
protected static string localConnectionString;
private RemoteWSType wsProxy = null;

protected RemoteWSType WebServiceProxy
{
  get
  {
    if (wsProxy == null)
    {
      wsProxy = new RemoteWSType();
      if (wSURL != null)
      {
        wsProxy.Url = wSURL;
      }
    }
    return wsProxy;
  }
}
```

```
// etc.
```

Here the new type parameter has been added and constrained to derive from System.Web. Services.Protocols.SoapHttpClientProtocol and to have a public parameterless constructor. Do you remember that we discussed constraints on type parameters in Chapter 7? Here Angela is using a new() constraint on the type parameter that will allow an instance of the class that it represents to be constructed using the new keyword. If the constraint were not present, the compile would fail at the line

```
wsProxy = new RemoteWSType();
```

The other constraint requiring that the class be derived from SoapHttpClientProtocol allows successful compilation of the line

```
wsProxy.Url = wSURL;
```

This is possible since SoapHttpClientProtocol defines Url as a public string type property.

The offending static variable wsURL has been made private and a new protected property WebServiceProxy of type RemoteWSType, which creates an instance of the web service proxy and initializes the its Url property. Note that the new wsProxy variable is not static to avoid possible threading issues, but, Angela thinks, if she could be sure the proxy class was thread safe, implementing it as a static variable might be a possibility. In the derived classes, the GetRemoteData and SaveRemoteData functions now cannot access wsURL and are simplified; for example, for OrderBE, the GetRemoteData and SaveRemoteData functions become

```
protected override SalesWS.OrderDS GetRemoteData(int id)
{
  return this.WebServiceProxy.GetOrder(id);
}
```

```
protected override void SaveRemoteData(SalesWS.OrderDS remoteData)
{
  this.WebServiceProxy.SaveOrder(remoteData);
}
```

The only reason now for not placing these in the base class is the fact that they call specific functions, GetOrder(id) and SaveOrder(remoteData), on the web service proxy.

There is another instance of the CA2211 error in the list that applies to the static variable localConnectionString. This can be made private as long as a property is added:

```
protected System.Data.SqlClient.SqlConnection Connection
{
  get
  {
    if (dbConnection == null)
    {
     dbConnection = new System.Data.SqlClient.SqlConnection(localConnectionString);
    }

    return dbConnection;
  }
}
```

This creates a connection if needed using the static localConnectionString and returns it. The GetLocalData and SaveLocalData functions need to change on the derived classes, for example, in OrderBE:

```
protected override void GetLocalData(int id)
{
  new ORDERTableAdapter(this.Connection).Fill(data.ORDER, id);
  new RESERVATIONTableAdapter(this.Connection).Fill(data.RESERVATION, id);
}

protected override void SaveLocalData()
{
  new ORDERTableAdapter(this.Connection).Update(this.data.ORDER);
  new RESERVATIONTableAdapter(this.Connection).Update(this.data.RESERVATION);
}
```

Notice that the same connection is still used for both calls to Update.

Well, that's knocked out two of those yellow triangles and accomplished some good refactoring. Angela runs all her unit tests again and verifies that they all pass.

Avoiding Static Constructors (CA1810)

Angela examines the list of static analysis errors. Many of them seem to be concerned with naming issues and should not be a problem, particularly with the refactoring capability of Visual Studio 2005, but she sees one that looks a bit complicated:

```
CA1810 : Microsoft.Performance : Initialize all static fields in
    com.icarustravel.enterprise31.BusinessEntity.BusinessEntityBE`3 when those
    fields are declared and remove the explicit static constructor.
    E:\Projects\Iteration1-P2\BusinessEntity\BusinessEntityBE.cs 17
```

So it doesn't like the use of a static constructor. Angela presses F1 to find the appropriate help page. Essentially it says that static constructors reduce performance since the JIT compiler has to put in various checks to determine if the static constructor has executed. Help recommends that all static fields be initialized using inline initializers.

There were two reasons why Angela used a static constructor in the design of BusinessEntityBE:

- To initialize the static variables holding the URL string for the web service and the connection string for the database.

- To attach an event delegate to the InstallModeChange event defined in the DualPersistBE base class. This event is only needed for unit testing so that the static strings defining the web service URL and the connection string are reinitialized from the .config file if the install mode changes.

The first reason can be easily got around by defining a static function that obtains the value of each .config string and is called as a static initializer when the static variable is declared. This can be applied to the wSURL and localConnectionString variables:

```
private static string wSURL = GetWSUrl();
private static string localConnectionString = GetLocalConnectionString();

// etc.

private static string GetLocalConnectionString()
{
  // Lots of code.
  return settingElement.Value.ValueXml.InnerText;
}

private static string GetWSUrl()
{
  // Lots of code.
  return settingElement.Value.ValueXml.InnerText;
 }
```

If you look at the complete listing in the example code, you'll see some duplicated code in these functions, but it only executes once at start-up, so it doesn't impact performance when the system is running.

To find an alternative that covers the second reason, let's consider why Angela coded it in this way. She needs the installMode static variable so that each class derived from DualPersistBE can check to determine if it installed on a client or server. This defaults to InstallMode.SERVER but on the client applications it is explicitly set to InstallMode.CLIENT at start-up. It would be good if this static variable were placed in the BusinessEntityBE itself instead of introducing the DualPersistBE base class. The reason for that class, though, is that since BusinessEntityBE is a generic class, each case of its type parameterization will generate a new set of static variables, and thus Angela needs a base class in which to retain this install mode information. The install mode must change during sequences of unit tests and so reinitialization is required when this happens. It is not possible to define a virtual static function; therefore, Angela cannot adjust the initialization to suit the derived class by defining a virtual `Initialize` method. This is why the event is needed.

To cause this event delegate initialization to occur at the same time as the initialization of the static variables, Angela defines a dummy variable that is initialized by a call to a static function that adds the event delegate:

```
private static bool staticEventsInitialized = InitializeStaticEvents();

// etc.

private static bool InitializeStaticEvents()
{
  DualPersistBE.InstallModeChange
      += new OnInstallModeChangeDelegate(OnInstallModeChange);
  return true;
}
```

Angela recompiles the code and checks that the unit tests still pass. In the list of static code analysis issues CA1810 no longer appears.

Do Not Declare Static Members on Generic Types (CA1000)

The use of static members on generic types is not recommended since the type parameters for the generic type must be supplied with the class name, using the angle bracket notation, each time the static member is called. This applies to public and protected members since when the member is referenced internal to the generic type, the class name is not required and the problem does not occur. This issue can therefore be solved simply by making the declaration of `OnInstallModeChange` private:

```
private static void OnInstallModeChange()
```

Types That Own Disposable Fields Should be Disposable (CA1001)

This error occurs because the class contains fields that implement the `IDisposable` interface but does not itself implement the `IDisposable` interface. The `IDisposable` interface contains one method, `Dispose()`, which may be called by a user of the class to confirm that all of the resources allocated as part of the instance of the class have been released.

A defined sequence of code must be implemented to satisfy the CA1001 rule:

```
#region IDisposable Members

protected override void Dispose(bool disposing)
{
```

```
    if (disposing)
    {
      if (this.dbConnection != null)
      {
        this.dbConnection.Dispose();
        this.dbConnection = null;
      }
    }
}

public void Dispose()
{
  Dispose(true);
  GC.SuppressFinalize(this);
}

#endregion
```

In addition the base class, `DualPersistBE` must contain a declaration of a virtual `Dispose(bool disposing)` function, something like this:

```
protected virtual void Dispose(bool disposing)
{
  if (disposing)
  {
  }
}
```

Declare Event Handlers Correctly and Should Have the Correct Suffix (CA1009, CA1710, CA1711)

This rule requires event handlers to be declared with the first parameter called sender of type object and the second of a type derived from EventArgs, usually called e. They should be named so that the name ends in "EventHandler". This error can be corrected by changing the names of the delegate at the top of DualPersistBE as shown here, together with all the references to it:

```
protected delegate void InstallModeChangeEventHandler(object sender, EventArgs e);
protected static event InstallModeChangeEventHandler InstallModeChange;
```

Use Generic Event Handler Instances (CA1003)

This rule requires that rather than defining a specific signature of event handler, the developer should use the System.EventHandler delegate, which is a generic class with a single type argument defining the type of the event arguments class. This class must be derived from EventArgs. The use of this generic delegate class means that a standard delegate can be used to represent the event handler function.

Why would you want to use your own delegate? Well, in Angela's case there's no need at all, but often you might want to pass a special set of event arguments and you might define the delegate to reference a function with those arguments. With the generic system event handler, those special arguments can be encapsulated in a special event arguments class derived from `EventArgs` and be used as the type parameter.

Anyway, the event declaration at the top of the `DualPersistBE` class is very simple and now becomes

```
protected static event System.EventHandler<EventArgs> InstallModeChange;
```

where the delegate declaration is no longer necessary and the addition of the delegate to the event is

```
DualPersistBE.InstallModeChange +=
        new System.EventHandler<EventArgs>(OnInstallModeChange);
```

So the type argument is not derived from `EventArgs`; it is the `EventArgs` type itself.

Do Not Declare Visible Instance Fields (CA1051)

Although Angela declared a property that accesses the field "data," she also declared it as protected and accessed it from the derived classes `OrderBE` and `CustomerBE`:

```
protected LocalDSType data;

public LocalDSType Data
{
  get { return this.data; }
  set { this.data = value; }
}
```

and in `OrderBE`:

```
protected override void GetLocalData(int id)
{
  new ORDERTableAdapter(this.Connection).Fill(data.ORDER, id);
  new RESERVATIONTableAdapter(this.Connection).Fill(data.RESERVATION, id);
}
protected override void SaveLocalData()
{
  new ORDERTableAdapter(this.Connection).Update(this.data.ORDER);
  new RESERVATIONTableAdapter(this.Connection).Update(this.data.RESERVATION);
}
```

Why did she do this? She thought that it was slightly more efficient to access the field variable directly than through the property accessor. This is not usually true now because of inlining, which replaces the reference to the property with the accessor code itself, so a function call is not usually carried out. Therefore, the CA1051 rule says that you should always access fields of a class by property accessor and only use the fields themselves inside that class for implementation purposes, so derived classes should use the properties the same way as an unrelated class would. This makes things a lot more consistent. To comply with this rule, it is only necessary to replace `protected` with `private` in the declaration of the `data` field in `BusinessEntityBE` and change the references to `data` to the property name `Data`.

Long Acronyms Should be Pascal Cased (CA1705)

The rule required two-letter acronyms to use uppercase and three or longer acronyms to use Pascal casing, so to adhere to this rule, Angela must change the two names `InstallMode.CLIENT` and `InstallMode.SERVER` to Pascal casing, `InstallMode.Client` and `InstallMode.Server`. Of course, Angela uses the refactoring capability (described earlier) to do this.

Assemblies Should Declare Minimum Security (CA2209)

This rule requires that assemblies communicate to administrators the minimum security permissions they require in order to execute. This can be done by declaring attributes at the assembly level. A good place to put the attributes is in the `AssemblyInfo.cs` file. The minimum possible security permission that will satisfy the rule is

```
[assembly: SecurityPermission(SecurityAction.RequestMinimum,
                                    Flags = SecurityPermissionFlag.NoFlags)]
```

so the application requests no security permissions.

Mark Assemblies with CLS Compliant (CA1014)

All assemblies should indicate whether or not they are compliant with the common language specification. The following attribute can be added to the `AssemblyInfo.cs` file to indicate this:

```
[assembly: CLSCompliant(true)]
```

Assemblies Should Have Valid Strong Names (CA2210)

Yes, they really should, so here's how Angela does it. She opens the properties pages for the project and selects the Signing tab. She clicks the Sign The Assembly checkbox to enable it, and then chooses New from the Choose A Strong Name Key File drop-down, as shown in Figure 8-53, which displays the Create Strong Name Key dialog box. She types "Enterprise3.1" as the name for the key file and adds a password—Icarus always uses the password "feathers" for development, but a strong password will be used in production.

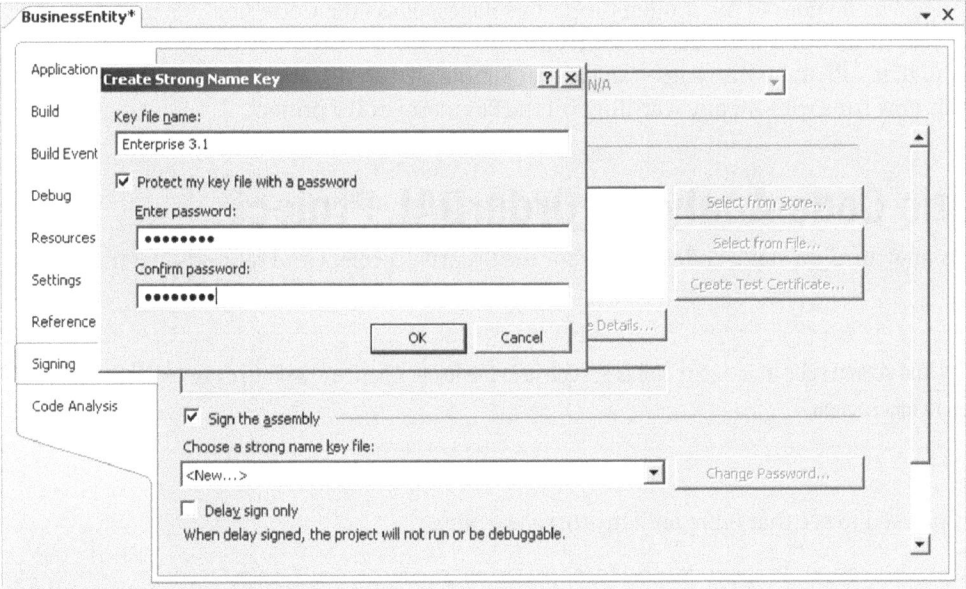

Figure 8-53. *Setting up signing*

Naming Conventions (CA1709)

Angela's got those yellow triangles on the run now; there's only four left, three of them complaining about the namespace casing:

```
CA1709 : Microsoft.Naming : Correct the casing of namespace name
    'com.icarustravel.enterprise31.BusinessEntity'
    BusinessEntity
```

Well, Icarus likes its namespaces like that I'm afraid, beginning with a lowercase reversed domain name, which is very common in the Java world. Icarus adopted this convention some years ago, so they don't want to change it. Here's an example where a rule needs to be disabled or a custom rule substituted.

To disable this rule, Angela goes to the project properties pages, clicks the Code Analysis tab, and expands the Naming Rules node. She then deselects CA1709. Ron will also need to disable the rule on the check-in policy.

Avoid Excessive Parameters on Generic Types (CA1005)

It's certainly a good idea to limit parameters to two on generic types, particularly if you are defining something like a collection class that will be used in a lot of places; doing so makes a generic class much easier to understand. However, in this case there does seem to be a need for the three type parameters and no obvious way of getting around it. So again, this rule can be disabled.

Angela again goes to the project properties pages, clicks the Code Analysis tab, expands the Design Rules node, and deselects CA1005.

And that's all of the warnings—at least for `BusinessEntityBE`. Project and static code analysis now runs without any warnings on the `BusinessEntity` project.

Static Code Analysis: OrderDAL Project

Angela now turns on static code analysis for the `OrderDAL` project and rebuilds just that project.

Note The source code at the start of this section is in the folder `Chapter 8\Exercise 14`. Exercise 8-15 applies to this section.

She is pleased to see that there are only three warnings:

```
CA2209 : Microsoft.Usage : No valid permission requests were found for
    assembly 'OrderDAL'.
    You should always specify the minimum security permissions using
    SecurityAction.RequestMinimum.
CA2210 : Microsoft.Design : Sign 'OrderDAL' with a strong name key.
CA1014 : Microsoft.Design : 'OrderDAL' should be marked with
    CLSCompliantAttribute and its value should be true.
```

To correct these, she can do the same things that she did for the `BusinessEntity` project. For CA2209, she adds the security permission attribute to the `AssemblyInfo.cs` file in the `OrderDAL` project:

```
[assembly: SecurityPermission(SecurityAction.RequestMinimum,
                                    Flags = SecurityPermissionFlag.NoFlags)]
```

and for CA1014, she adds the `CLSCompliant` attribute to the same file:

```
[assembly: CLSCompliant(true)]
```

For the CA2210, she needs to set strong naming. She can use the same key, so she copies the key that was created during the strong naming setup of the business entity from the project folder to a new folder called `Miscellaneous`, created at the top level of the solution folder. Then, when she sets up the strong naming options on the properties pages for the `OrderDAL` project, she does not need to create a new key. Instead, she uses the browse option from the Choose A Strong Name Key File to find the key in the `Miscellaneous` folder. She copies the key into the project folder and it forms part of that project.

She now rebuilds `OrderDAL` and sees no static code analysis warnings.

Static Code Analysis: OrderBE Project

Angela now turns on static code analysis for the OrderBE project and rebuilds just that project.

Note The source code at the start of this section is in the folder Chapter 8\Exercise 15. Exercise 8-16 applies to this section.

The static code analysis warnings for the OrderBE project are

```
CA1020 : Microsoft.Design : Consider merging the types defined in
    'com.icarustravel.enterprise31.Order' with another namespace.
CA1709 : Microsoft.Naming : Correct the casing of namespace name
    'com.icarustravel.enterprise31.Order'.
CA1709 : Microsoft.Naming : Correct the casing of namespace name
    'com.icarustravel.enterprise31.Order'.
CA1709 : Microsoft.Naming : Correct the casing of namespace name
    'com.icarustravel.enterprise31.Order'.
CA2209 : Microsoft.Usage : No valid permission requests were found for
    assembly 'OrderBE'.You should always specify the minimum security
    permissions using SecurityAction.RequestMinimum.
CA2210 : Microsoft.Design : Sign 'OrderBE' with a strong name key.
CA1014 : Microsoft.Design : 'OrderBE' should be marked with
    CLSCompliantAttribute and its value should be true.
```

Warning 1 simply advises that there are not enough types in the com.icarustravel. enterprise31.Order namespace. Angela does not agree since she will probably need to add more types to this namespace, so she will disable this rule in the static code analysis for this project. Warnings 2, 3, and 4 repeat the warning that the namespace is not compliant, so she will also disable those rules. Warnings 5, 6, and 7 are the same as for the OrderDAL project, and she corrects them in the same way.

Angela reruns all the unit tests, just to make sure—and they all fail! She sees a message about strong naming verification failing for every test:

```
Failed  GetLocalTest  OrderBETests  Strong name verification failed for the
    instrumented assembly
    'OrderBE, Version=1.0.0.0, Culture=neutral, PublicKeyToken=7a8cdc48fb11821c'.
    Please ensure that the right key file for re-signing after instrumentation is
    specified in the test run configuration.
```

Well, this is obviously something to do with instrumentation, and Angela remembers that she still has code coverage turned on. She double-clicks on the localtestrun.testrunconfig file in the Solution Items folder, selects the Code Coverage tab and deselects the OrderDAL.dll and OrderBE.dll assemblies in the Artifacts to Instrument list. She applies the changes, closes that dialog box, and reruns all the unit tests. Now they all pass. So what does Angela need to do since she wants to be able to do code coverage on strongly named assemblies?

Looking at the Code Coverage tab in Figure 8-54, you can see a text box named Re-signing key file. The assemblies have to be instrumented to perform the code coverage analysis when the tests are run, and strongly named assemblies must be re-signed, so Angela must specify the key here.

For the early part of the project, however, the team decides not to strongly name their assemblies. This will save some effort with passwords and the re-signing just mentioned. Angela therefore disables CA2210 disabled in static analysis and removes the strong naming from the assemblies. At least she has understood how to do it.

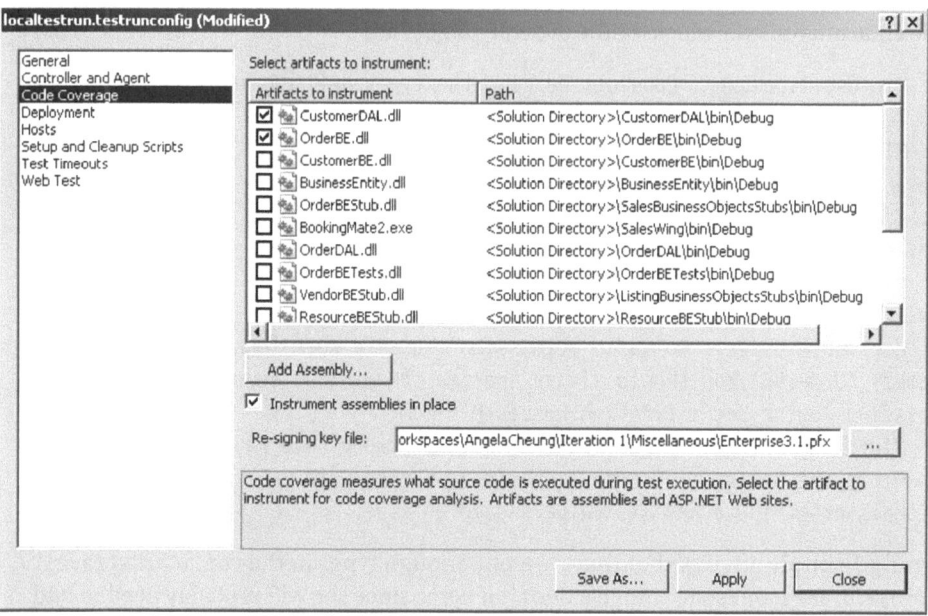

Figure 8-54. *The Code Coverage tab in the localtestrun.testrunconfig file*

Checking In OrderBE and Its Related Projects

Angela has now completed the work of developing and testing OrderBE. Surprisingly, there are a large number of files in the Pending Changes window. For example, because of the refactoring that she did, she had to make a number of changes to CustomerBE. Even the SalesWing Windows Forms application has changed automatically because of the name change to the enumeration type InstallMode.Client. That's a slight quirk with refactoring assistance; sometimes things change without you noticing. Angela has changed the SalesWebService project by the addition of the new web methods that must be supported; these methods also went into SalesWebServiceStub. Also she added the Miscellaneous folder containing the signing key.

Note The source code at the start of this section is in the folder Chapter 8\Exercise 16. Exercise 8-17 applies to this section.

As with the `OrderDAL` work, Angela separates the changes into those that were associated with the `OrderBE` development, those associated with `OrderBE` tests, and those associated with both. She then checks them in separately. She also checks in `SalesWing` separately since it has a large number of static code analysis warnings (which she is not responsible for correcting), and she needs to override the static analysis check-in condition errors.

Angela begins with the `OrderBE` and related files and associates them with the work item Develop OrderBE. Next she checks in the `OrderBETest` and related files and associates them with the work item Unit Test OrderBE. Next she checks in the solution files that are common to both of the work items and associates them both with the checked-in files.

Finally, Angela checks in the `SalesWing` project, which had some minor changes to it associated with the Develop OrderBE work item. This time the Policy Warnings tab of the Pending Changes window displays the warning shown in Figure 8-55. She checks it in anyway, and sees the dialog box shown in Figure 8-56. She selects the Override Policy Failure and Continue Checkin checkbox and types an explanation into the Reason box, that the static analysis errors were preexisting.

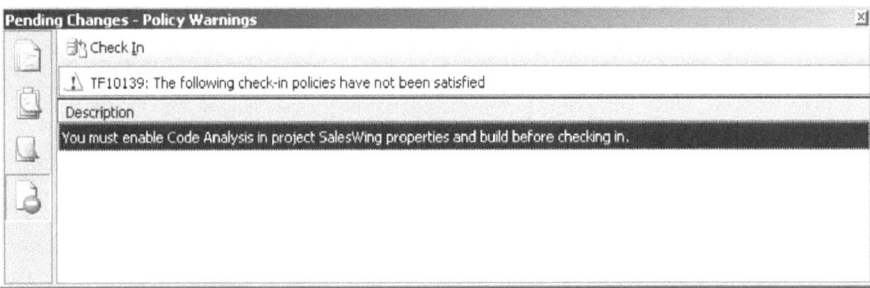

Figure 8-55. *Policy Warnings*

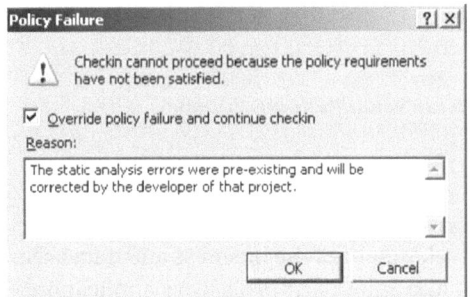

Figure 8-56. *Overriding the check-in policy warnings*

Updating the Work Items

Angela has now completed her work on four work items and can set their status to Resolved. They will require code and test review, so she has assigned them to Ron for this purpose. She double-clicks the My Work Items query in Team Explorer and updates them in the window shown in Figure 8-57.

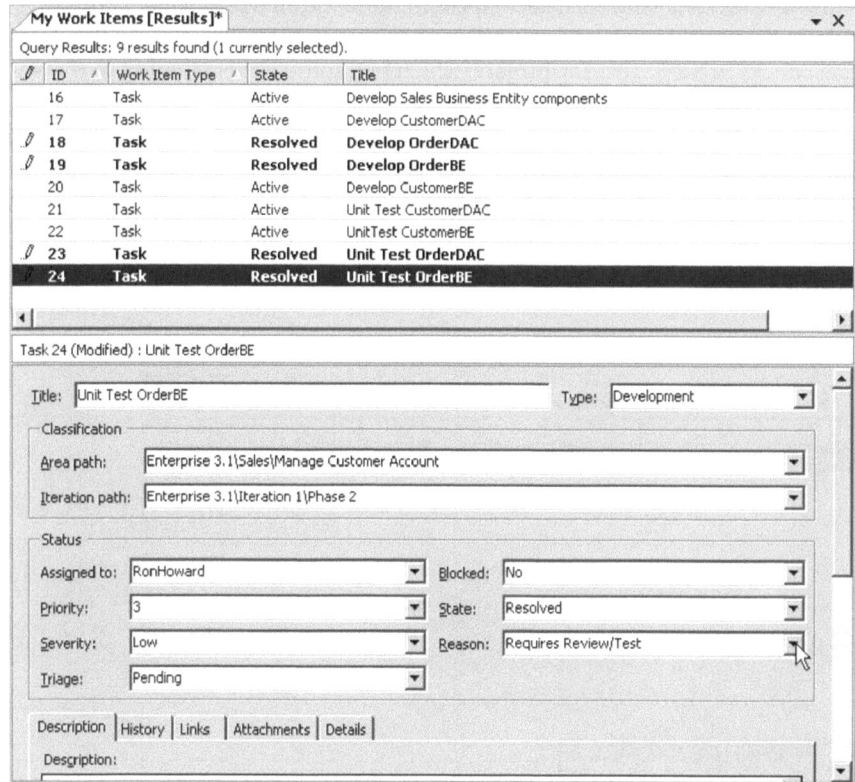

Figure 8-57. *Updating the status of the work items after development is complete*

Summary

In this chapter you have seen the detailed formal development of the business and data access layers of the OrderBE business object, which is part of the SalesBusinessObjects application.

You watched Angela create a new workspace and open the entire solution from source control. She then went on to create the datasets and table adapters for the order business entities—these hold single customer orders. She also developed unit tests for them.

You learned how to use the Pending Changes window to check in code to version control and how to associate the code with work items. Remember the concept of the changeset?

Angela used the Class Designer to develop the OrderBE business entity class. You saw the refactoring capability of Visual Studio 2005.

Ron, the team leader, decided on some check-in policies, and you learned about executing code coverage and setting sequences of tests as part of the check-in policy. We looked at the capabilities of Test Manager to organize tests into lists.

Finally, Angela faced the challenge of making her code compliant with the rules enforced by the static code analysis feature of Visual Studio 2005.

This chapter stressed formal aspects of development whereas the previous chapter emphasized prototyping. In the next chapter, we will look at how Visual Basic .NET can be used in a similar manner and then begin joining the application together.

CHAPTER 9

Integration and Functional Testing

This chapter begins with development of some more business object classes in Visual Basic .NET. It then describes integrating the business layer with the presentation applications and organizing the system-testing methods.

The Listing Business Objects Data Access Layer

While Angela works on the sales business objects, Rahul works on the ListingBusinessObjects application. ListingBusinessObjects follows the same pattern in that the classes inherit from the same base classes but are written in Visual Basic .NET. Angela has told Rahul that she needs to make some changes to the base classes BusinessEntityBE so, when this is done, he will need to obtain the latest version of those classes. You saw these changes toward the end of the previous chapter. At present, though, he has work to do in creating the typed datasets and their table adapters to access the listing data model and to load individual vendors, lists of vendors, and individual resources. Vendors and resources will need to be saved after modification, so Rahul will have to generate insert, update, and delete stored procedures as well as select procedures.

The VendorDS Dataset

The VendorDS dataset will contain table adapters that are very similar to the table adapters in CustomerDS—in particular, the CITY, STATE, and COUNTRY table adapters will be the same. Rahul sees no point in repeating all this work, so he decides to try some drag-and-drop techniques. He creates a new solution folder called ListingBusinessObjects and inside that another folder called DataAccessLayer. Within that folder he creates a Visual Basic class library project called VendorDAL. He sets the root namespace to com.icarustravel.enterprise31.Vendor and deletes the Class1 automatically generated. Then Rahul creates a dataset called VendorDS with an empty design surface. How can he use the Visual Studio design tools to copy the CITY, STATE, and COUNTRY table adapters from CustomerDAL class? He opens CustomerDS, which Angela wrote, and opens a new horizontal tab group so that he has CustomerDS open on the left and the empty VendorDS on the right, as shown in Figure 9-1.

Note The source code at this point is found in `Chapter 9\Chapter9Start`. Exercise 9-1 will help you through this section.

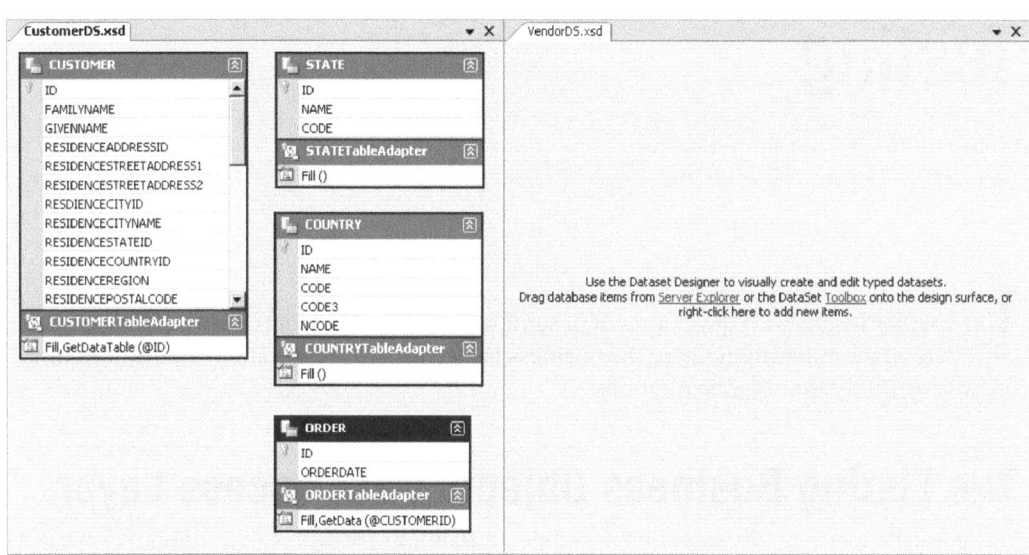

Figure 9-1. *Copying the TableAdapters from CustomerDS to VendorDS*

Rahul now selects the STATE table in the left window and drags it across to the empty design surface on the right, expecting a copy of the STATE table adapter to be placed in the new dataset. He sees a warning prompt about saving unencrypted data in the settings, to which he clicks Yes, but then he sees the dialog box shown in Figure 9-2.

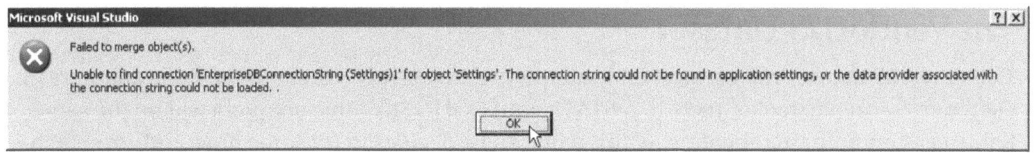

Figure 9-2. *The connection string in the application settings is missing.*

If you think about it, this is to be expected. Normally when you add a table adapter to a dataset on the design surface, the configuration wizard opens and the first thing you must do is define a connection to a database. So by just copying the table adapter, the connection does not get copied. Rahul must add a connection to the project manually rather than via the Table Adapter Configuration Wizard. To do this he opens the project properties by double-clicking on the My Project folder under the VendorDAL project in Solution Explorer (see Figure 9-3), clicks the Settings tab, and types the name "EnterpriseDBConnectionString" in the Name field of the empty property. In the Type field, he selects (Connection String) from the drop-down, and leaves the Scope field set to the default, Application. In the Value field, he clicks the ellipsis, which opens the Connection Properties dialog box shown in Figure 9-4. He selects the development database (the one on his machine), localhost\SqlExpress for the server, the authentication method (which in this case is Windows Authentication), and the name of the database. He tests the connection and clicks OK, which produces the connection string setting shown in Figure 9-5. Rahul, like the other developers on the project, is using a local copy of SQL Server Express Edition on his own machine as the database to develop and test his stored procedures and table adapters. Since the team has included the EnterpriseDatabase project, with its scripts for generating tables, stored procedures, and test data, it is easy for developers to keep their local databases up to date. Now the two tables, STATE and COUNTRY, can be dragged onto the VendorDS design surface and the data previewed to be sure they are working.

Figure 9-3. *To add a database connection to a VB project, first open the properties for the project by double-clicking on the My Project folder.*

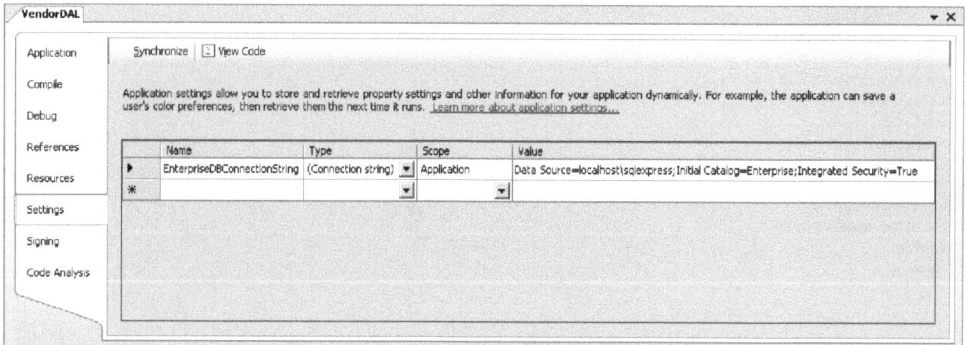

Figure 9-4. *The Connection Properties dialog box*

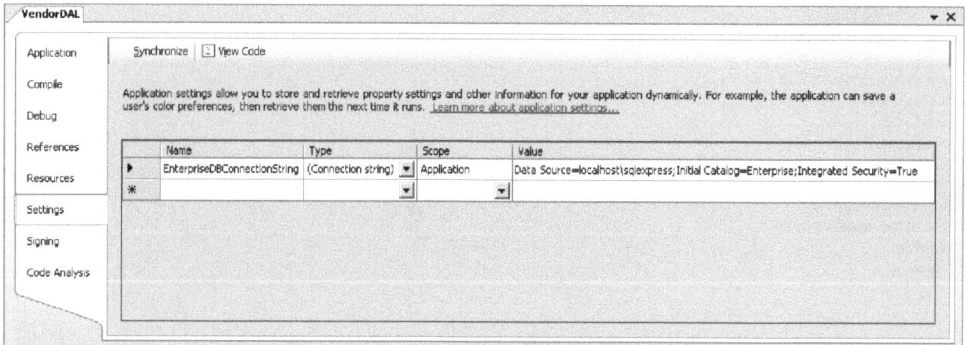

Figure 9-5. *The project properties pages for the VendorDAL project displaying the Settings tab with the new connection string defined*

The VENDOR table adapter is very similar to the CUSTOMER table adapter, but Rahul will need to change the stored procedures. He first creates a new stored procedure script in the EnterpriseDatabase database project; next he copies and pastes the SQL for the GETCUSTOMER stored procedure, changes its name to "GETVENDOR", and changes the CUSTOMER table name to "VENDOR". Then he modifies various other fields to match the fields in the VENDOR table in the VendorDS stub dataset in the VendorBEStub project in the ListingBusinessObjectsStubs solution folder.

Rahul then creates the VENDOR table adapter in the VendorDS dataset by dragging a TableAdapter from the Toolbox onto the design surface. In the pop-up configuration wizard, he selects the added database connection. Then on the next page of the wizard, he chooses the radio button Use Existing Stored Procedures. Rahul picks the GETVENDOR stored procedure for the SELECT stored procedure—leaving the others blank for now—and selects only the Fill A Data Table option. The write capability for this table adapter is not needed for iteration 1. Finally, he renames the table adapter "VENDOR".

In Chapter 7 Rahul added a RESOURCE table (to hold summary information of the resources associated with a given vendor) to the stub version of VendorDS in the VendorBEStub project. To create the real version of this data table, Rahul adds another table adapter and chooses the Create Stored Procedures option. Only a SELECT stored procedure is required since the table is read-only and serves only to populate the Resources tab of the VendorDetails control. Rahul can generate the SQL for the stored procedure by using the Query Builder to retrieve all of those rows in the RESOURCE table with the VENDORID field equal to a parameter @VENDORID, and ordered by NAME and ID fields. Only ID and NAME are required for output fields. He names the stored procedure "GETRESOURCESFORVENDOR"; the finished dataset is shown in Figure 9-6.

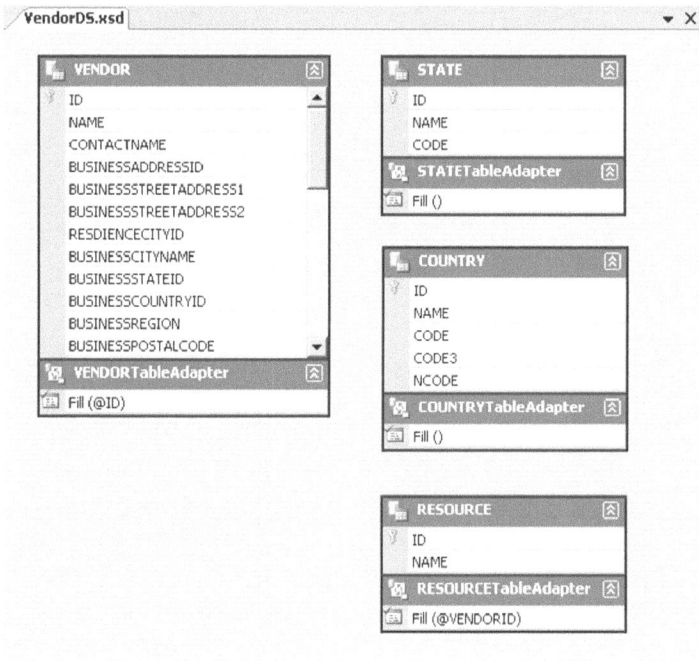

Figure 9-6. *The VendorDS dataset*

Testing VendorDS

Testing follows much the same pattern as for OrderDS. Rahul has talked to Angela about possibly having a common base class to set up the database environment. They have agreed that for iteration 1, it is easier to keep them separate, but for iteration 2 they may be able to be merged for initializing the common areas of the database test environment. It is a good idea to use common code like this where possible, since unit test code can require a great deal of maintenance, but I do not have space in this book to follow the idea further.

Unit tests must be created at the VendorDS level for the VENDORTableAdapter, STATETableAdapter, COUNTRYTableAdapter, and RESOURCETableAdapter classes. They need only the Fill function tested for iteration 1, and the results should be compared with standard database test environment data. Rahul creates the unit test project and class by right-clicking on the VENDORTableAdapter and selecting Create Unit Tests. He selects only the Fill member function and repeats this for the other three adapters. He then selects Create A New Visual Basic Test Project and names it "VendorDSTest". Visual Basic creates a class file VendorDS.DesignerTest.vb, and following a pattern similar to the testing of OrderDS, Rahul opens the class diagram (as shown in Figure 9-7) for the test project and adds a class VendorDSTestBase. He then adds inheritance relationships as shown in the figure. This will handle the common database test environment setup for the set of tests shown in the class diagram. The content of these classes is very similar to that for testing the OrderDS set of table adapters, except that there are more table adapters in this dataset, although only the Fill functions need to be tested. I described the OrderDS testing in a fair amount of detail in the previous chapter, so I won't go into that level of detail here.

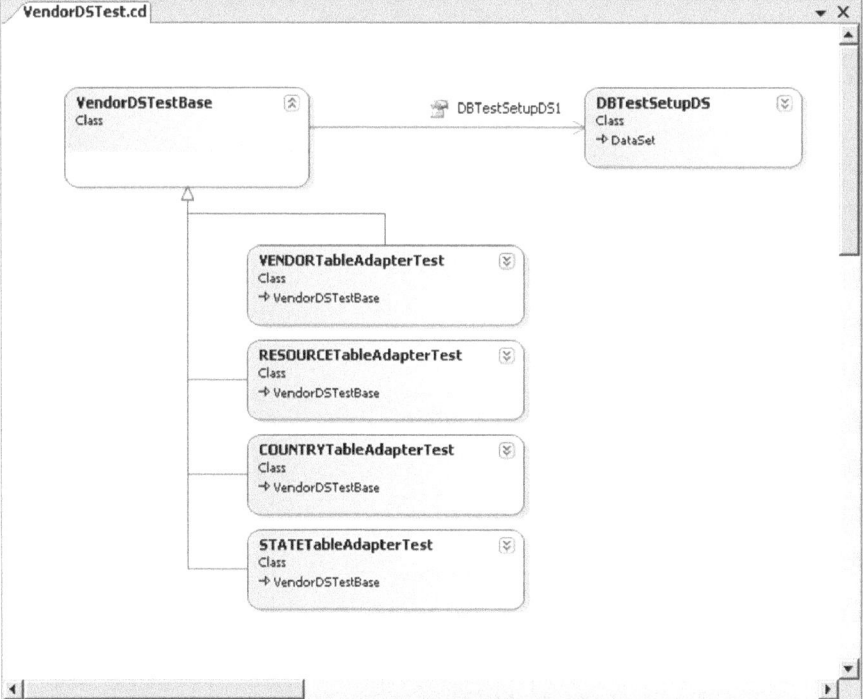

Figure 9-7. *Class diagram for the VendorDS testing project*

Note The source code at this point is found in Chapter 9\Exercise 1.

The VendorSearchDS Class

This dataset is needed to provide a list of results returned from a search of vendors based on initial letters of the ID number, business name, and contact name in a way similar to that in which customers were obtained.

Note The source code at this point is found in `Chapter 9\Exercise 1`. Exercise 9-2 will help you through this section.

The SQL stored procedure for the VENDORSEARCH data table is

```
CREATE PROCEDURE dbo.VENDORSEARCH
(
  @ID nvarchar(10),
  @NAME nvarchar(50),
  @CONTACTNAME nvarchar(50)
)
AS
  SET NOCOUNT ON;
  SELECT ID, [NAME], CONTACTNAME
  FROM [VENDOR]
  WHERE (CAST(ID AS CHAR(10)) LIKE @ID + N'%')
  AND (UPPER([NAME]) LIKE UPPER(@NAME) + N'%')
  AND (UPPER(CONTACTNAME) LIKE UPPER(@CONTACTNAME) + N'%')
  ORDER BY [NAME], CONTACTNAME
```

The VendorSearchDS table adapter in Figure 9-8 is set up to use this as an existing stored procedure. There is no write capability.

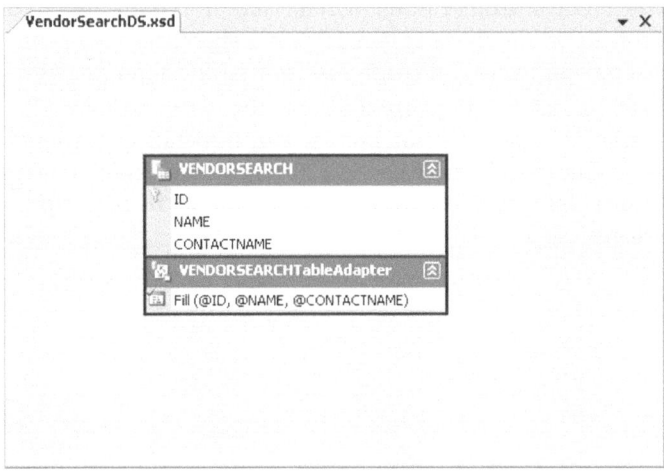

Figure 9-8. *The VendorSearchDS dataset*

The ResourceDS Class

This dataset is needed to provide details of an individual resource in tables that can be bound to fields on the Resource Detail Windows Form page in the List Wing application described in Chapter 7. It contains the following tables:

- RESOURCE table: Normally contains just one row for the resource for which details are being displayed

- RESOURCECATEGORIES table: Contains the categories to be populated into the category drop-down collection on the Resource Detail page

- GEOGRAPHICREGIONS table: Contains the regions to be populated into the region drop-down collection on the Resource Detail page

- RESOURCEAVAILABILITY table: Contains all of the resource availability entries for the resource

Rahul expects that more will be needed in this dataset in later iterations when more information about the resource will be made visible. To construct this dataset, he can use the Generate Stored Procedures option in the TableAdapter Configuration Wizard for all of the tables. For RESOURCECATEGORIES and GEOGRAPHICREGIONS, only a SELECT command is required that obtains all of the rows in the tables of the same name in the database. For RESOURCE and RESOURCEAVAILABILITY, all four types of stored procedure are required: select, insert, update, and delete. For the RESOURCE table this is straightforward, since the SELECT SQL must simply get all of the fields in the RESOURCE table in a row identified by the ID value as a parameter, and the other stored procedures will be generated from that.

However, the RESOURCEAVAILABILITY table is similar to the RESERVATION table in OrderDS in that the rows are identified by foreign key rather than by primary key. Rahul uses a slight trick here: he defines the SELECT SQL when configuring the table adapter to select the row by the primary key ID, with a parameter @ID. He completes the configuration and then edits the stored procedure that was generated for SELECT, which he called GETAVAILABILITIESFORRESOURCE. He changes the WHERE clause to select by the foreign key RESOURCEID, and changes the parameter to @RESOURCEID. He saves the stored procedure and reconfigures the RESOURCEAVAILABILITY table to make sure the code generated matches the stored procedure. If this does not work, or you don't like such tricks, you can always write the stored procedures the hard way and configure your table adapter to use the procedures you have written via the Use Existing Stored Procedures option in the wizard. The trouble is that putting in all of the code to implement the optimistic concurrency can get a bit tedious and error prone. Look back at the section "Creating the Order Data Access Component Classes" in Chapter 8 to remind yourself of what I mean by this. The finished dataset is shown in Figure 9-9.

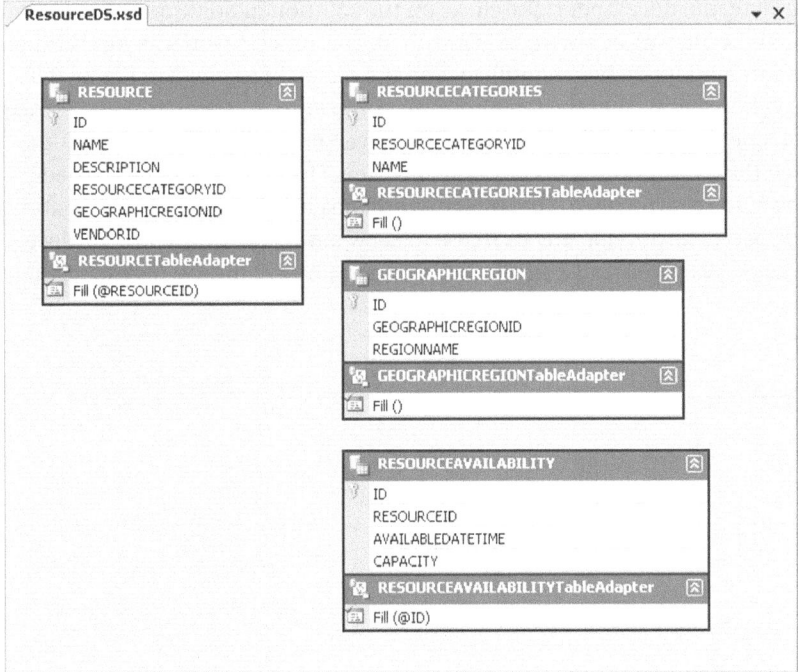

Figure 9-9. *The ResourceDS dataset*

Testing VendorSearchDS and ResourceDS

The unit testing of these datasets follows a pattern similar to the other datasets that have been tested. The details are tedious but straightforward.

Note The source code at this point is found in `Chapter 9\Exercise 2`.

Updating the Workspace

Now Rahul has completed the development and unit testing of the data access layer of `ListingBusinessObjects` and can begin work on the business object layer to produce the `VendorBE` and `ResourceBE` classes. First, he must update his workspace with the latest version of the rest of the solution, which will include the work checked in by Angela. For one thing, he will have to make sure his code does not break Angela's unit tests before he can check the DAL work into version control. Also, he needs Angela's modified base classes `BusinessEntityBE` and `DualPersistBE` before he can write the `VendorBE` and `ResourceBE` classes.

Note Exercise 7-3 will assist you with understanding this section.

To perform the update, the developer right-clicks on the solution in Solution Explorer and selects Get Latest Version (Recursive), as shown in Figure 9-10. This process works its way through all the files in the solution until it reaches a conflict when the dialog box shown in Figure 9-11 is displayed. This dialog box signals that the file under version control has been changed since the version in the developer's workspace was obtained from version control *and also* that the developer has modified the old version in his or her workspace. The changes that have been made to the version in source control need to be merged with the changes made to the version in the developer's workspace. The developer can choose to allow automatic merge to take place by clicking the Auto Merge All button, or he or she can click the Resolve button to resolve the conflicts manually.

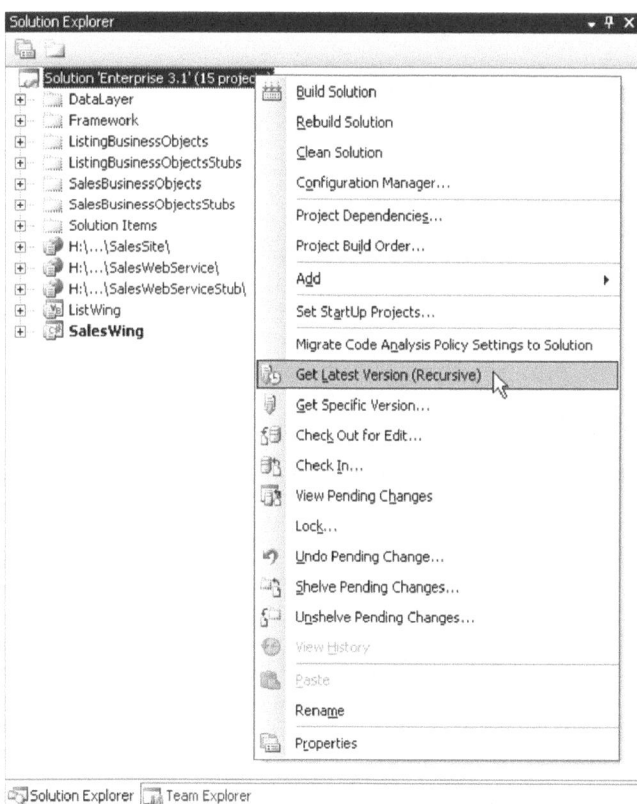

Figure 9-10. *Updating the solution with the latest files in version control*

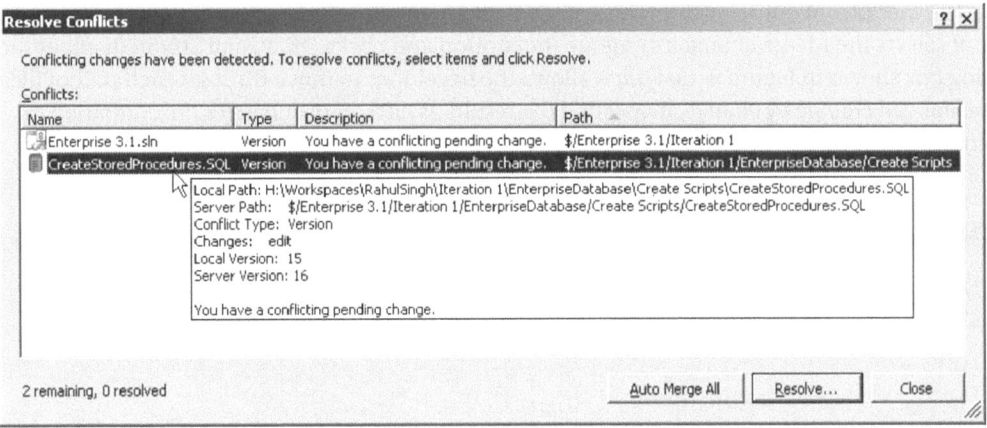

Figure 9-11. *Dialog box indicating the presence of conflicting changes*

When the developer clicks the Resolve button, Visual Studio displays the dialog box shown in Figure 9-12, which offers three choices:

1. Discard the changes in the workspace, which would delete the developer's work.

2. Discard the changes from the server, which would leave the developer's work unchanged for that file.

3. Use the merge tool to resolve the merge.

Notice that in Figure 9-12 the Merge changes for me option is disabled. This is because the CreateStoredProcedures.SQL file has internal conflicting changes that cannot be merged automatically. You can see this in Figure 9-12 where the window says that there are 17 local changes and 1 conflicting.

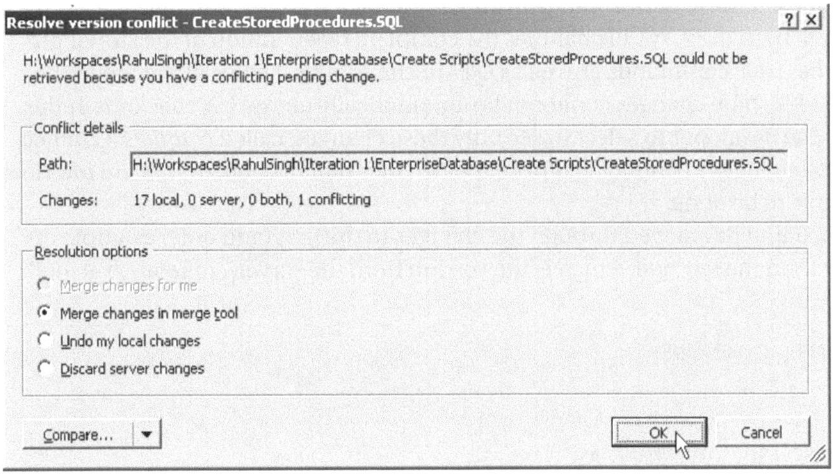

Figure 9-12. *Resolve version conflict dialog box*

The merge tool option is the safest, since it allows the developer to see what is happening. Rahul selects the Merge changes in merge tool option and clicks OK. Visual Studio displays the dialog box shown in Figure 9-13, which allows the developer to move through each pair of files to be merged change by change, inspecting the results as each of the changes are combined to form the resulting text in the lower pane.

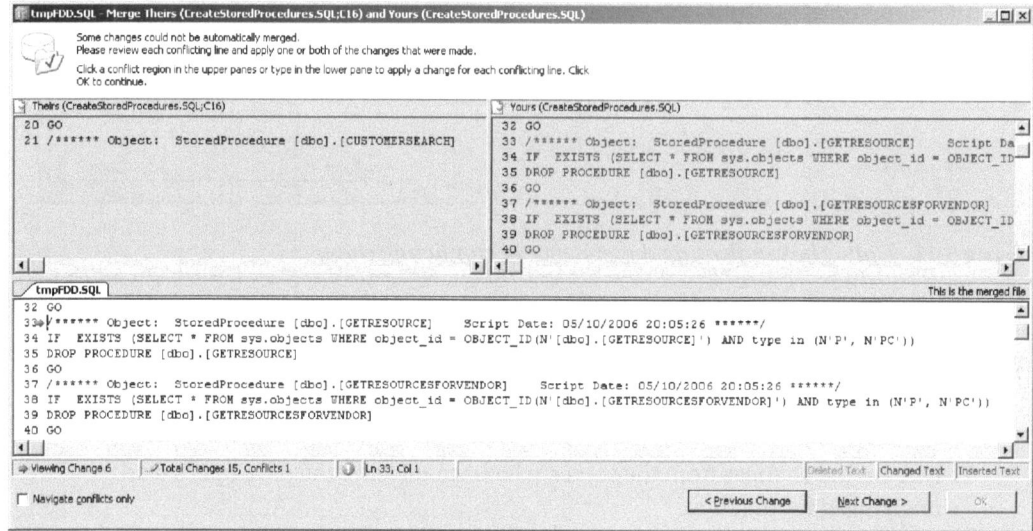

Figure 9-13. *Resolving conflicts using the merge tool*

For example, Figure 9-13 shows a change, number 6, in which the local version has had two SQL DROP commands added for the stored procedures GETRESOURCE and GETRESOURCESFORVENDOR. Rahul has made these changes to the CreateStoredProcedures.sql file as a result of adding these two stored procedures to the database. Remember that the whole CreateStoredProcedures.sql file handles the complete regeneration of the stored procedures, and so it has DROP commands as well as CREATE commands. Notice at the top of the screen, a message says some changes could not be automatically merged. A checkbox at the bottom left allows the developer to select to see only these changes, called *conflicts*. Conflicts at this point refer to changes in lines of text from the two files that overlap, or that are too close for an obvious merge to be done.

In Figure 9-14, Rahul has moved through the changes to the first (and only) example of this kind of conflict. On the left side, which is the version from the server, someone has modified the line

ORDER BY FAMILYNAME, GIVENNAME

to become

ORDER BY FAMILYNAME ASC, GIVENNAME ASC

and Rahul has modified the same line in his local version of the file to

```
ORDER BY FAMILYNAME, GIVENNAME, ID
```

So Rahul has decided that the results of a SELECT statement will be ordered by ID as well as the other two fields, but someone else—probably Angela—has added ASC to ensure that the order is ascending. The tentative merge that the system has generated has taken neither of the changes and has just left the original line of code in the pane at the bottom.

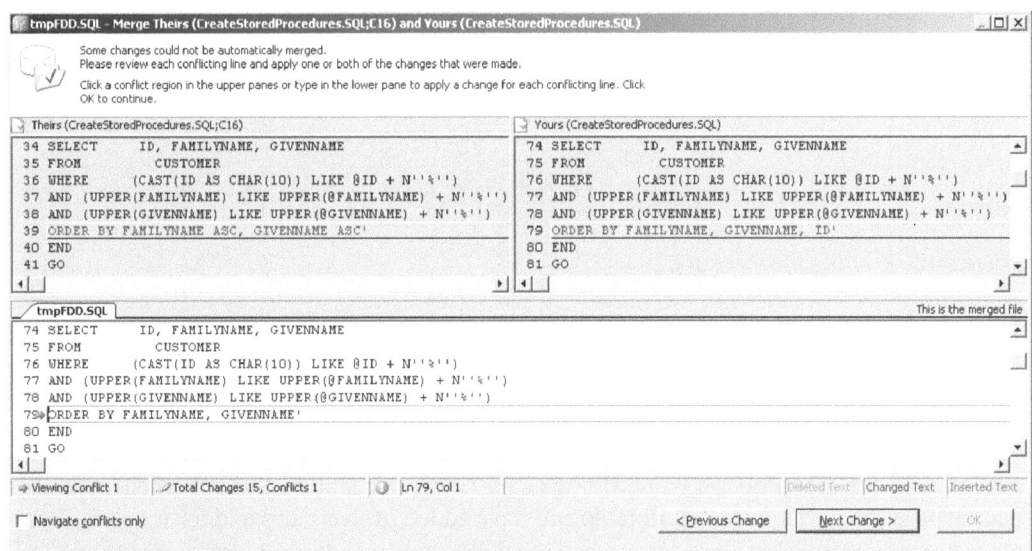

Figure 9-14. *Resolving conflicts using the merge tool*

Rahul needs to make sure both changes go into the merge. Notice that the additions in both the left and right panes appear in panels; hovering over them causes the cursor to change into a hyperlink cursor. Clicking on either of these lines causes the text to be inserted into the merged result; clicking on both puts both lines in. Alternatively, Rahul could right-click on the lines to open a context menu that allows him to put one or both additions into the merge. The context menu also contains an option to complete the merge with everything from the right or left. Rahul clicks both sides so that both of the lines are included in the merge:

```
ORDER BY FAMILYNAME, GIVENNAME, ID'
ORDER BY FAMILYNAME ASC, GIVENNAME ASC'
```

They appear one after the other in the merged result, and of course this is no good at all since it is invalid SQL. Therefore, Rahul must edit these lines manually in the merge file pane to make them look like

```
ORDER BY FAMILYNAME ASC, GIVENNAME ASC, ID ASC'
```

which makes sense and takes into account the intention of both changes. Once the text is inserted in the merged file, it can be edited using cut, paste, or typing methods. Rahul then clicks OK and sees the dialog box shown in Figure 9-15. He clicks Yes and then sees the dialog box in Figure 9-16, where he also clicks Yes.

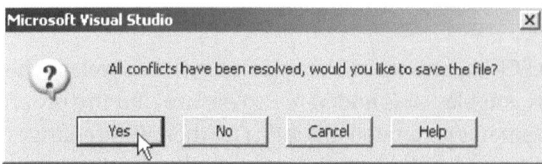

Figure 9-15. *All conflicts resolved*

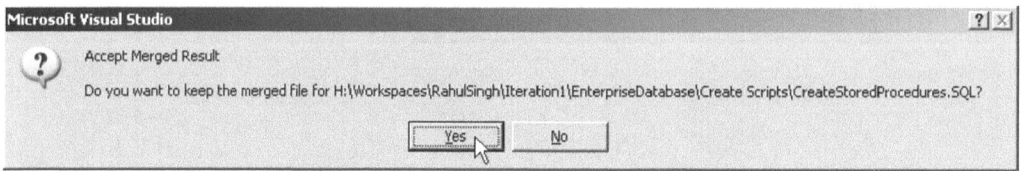

Figure 9-16. *Keeping the merged file*

One more file shows a conflict: the `Enterprise 3.1.sln` solution file. Unfortunately, there have been a lot of complicated changes to this file, both by Rahul and Angela, that have involved inserting quite a number of projects and solution folders. It is theoretically possible to merge solution files, since they are human-readable, plain-text files. For simple changes, an automatic merge will probably work. However, for complex changes, perhaps where several people have checked out the solution file and have added projects and folders, it may be better to just select Undo My Local Changes in the dialog box in Figure 9-12 for the solution file and then add the new local projects again manually as existing projects. This is what Rahul chooses to do.

■**Note** The source code at this point is found in `Chapter 9\Chapter9Merged`.

Multiple Code Checkout and Merging in TFS

Although this book describes the way in which Visual Studio 2005 Team System is used in a project and traces the fortunes of Icarus Enterprise 3.1, it is a good idea occasionally to take time out to explore an area in some depth. Checkout and merging is an important new feature of TFS, and it is a good idea to understand its principles rather than just stumble through a development hoping that it will do what is wanted. I have to say that, by and large, this feature does seem to do pretty much what you need if you just leave it alone to get on with its job!

When Merging Takes Place

Merging takes place when one version of a file updates another version of the same file. When there are conflicting changes, somebody has to decide how the conflicting changes in the two versions of the file will be reconciled so that no one's work is inadvertently lost. Multiple checkout means that two or more developers can make changes to the same file at the same time. These changes have to be reconciled by merging. Let's consider when merging takes place, and when it does not, in relation to multiple checkout. Merging also occurs in relation to branching, but we'll consider that later. For multiple checkout, merging can occur in two situations:

1. When a file in a developer workspace is updated with the latest version from TFS

2. When a developer checks in a file to TFS

Merging will not always occur, even in these cases. First consider case 1, which is the example I showed in the previous section. Four situations are possible here:

- The developer retrieved the file and did not change it, and nobody changed the file in TFS. In this case, no action is required since the developer already has the latest version.

- The developer checked out the file and modified its contents. Nobody changed the corresponding file in TFS. In this case, the developer already has the latest version and it need not be altered.

- The developer retrieved the file and modified its contents. After the developer had obtained the version, someone else checked out the file, modified it, and checked it back into TFS. Now there are two versions with conflicting modifications, and when the developer gets the latest version, they must be merged on the developer's machine so that none of the changes are lost.

- The developer retrieved the file and did not change it, but somebody else has since changed the file in TFS. In this case, you might think that the new file from TFS will simply overwrite the existing one in the developer's workspace, but instead a merge still takes place because they are considered conflicting changes.

What about case 2? These are the alternatives:

- The developer checked out a file and did not change it, and nobody else changed the file in TFS. When the developer checks the file in, no changes need to be made to the file in TFS.

- The developer checked out a file from TFS and modified it. When he or she checks it back in, it will replace the file in TFS.

- The developer checked out a file from TFS and modified it. In the meantime, someone else checked it out, modified it, and checked it back in. When the developer checks it back in, there are conflicting changes, both of which need to be preserved by a merge operation.

- The developer checked out the file from TFS and did not change it; in the meantime someone else checked it out, changed it, and checked it back in. When the developer checks it back in, his or her file is of an earlier version than that now in TFS. What happens? TFS considers them both files that need to be merged; even though the first developer made no changes, it was still checked it out and checked back in, so a merge will take place.

How Merging Takes Place

When a merge is necessary, Visual Studio displays the dialog box shown earlier in Figure 9-11, which indicates the file for which the conflict has occurred. The user can then choose either Auto Merge All or Resolve. The Auto Merge All option will merge all of the files automatically if this is possible; otherwise it will do nothing and the user will be required to click the Resolve button, which brings up the dialog box shown in Figure 9-12. An auto-merge will occur for a file if there are no "internal conflicts"—that is, conflicts within the content of the two versions of the files so that the merge tool cannot reasonably be expected to make a reliable decision about how to include both changes. If the two changes are in the same line, it will always be an internal conflict, which cannot be auto-merged. But there are other cases—if the lines are too close together, for example. In addition, if two lines were inserted into the versions of the files at the same place, the merge tool has no way of knowing which should precede the other in a combined file. Note that it is not always safe to accept auto-merging of files—if in doubt, you may find it best to view the automatic merges using the merge tool before accepting them.

Merging Groups of Files

Merging groups of files takes place when, for example, an entire project, folder, or solution is acted upon recursively, such as a user getting the latest version from TFS and putting it in a workspace or checking such a group into TFS. In such cases, files may be subject to changes because they have been edited, renamed, or deleted.

Suppose a developer checks out a file and changes its content. At the same time, another developer checks out the same file, renames it, and checks it back in. When the first developer executes a "get latest" operation from TFS, the only option available is to discard either the server changes or the local changes. It is not possible to merge a renamed file with a file of the original name.

Here's another example. A developer checks out a file and makes changes to it, but before he checks it in again another developer checks it out, deletes it, and checks in the pending change (deletion of the file). The first developer, when doing a "get latest version" operation, can either undo the local changes and therefore leave the file deleted, or restore the local file, with changes. Obviously, the latter option makes sense since there is no point in merging changes with a file and then deleting it.

The Listing Business Objects

Let's return to the work of Rahul. He now has his workspace updated with Angela's latest and greatest business entity base classes and a complete database `CreateStoredProcedures.sql` script that will create all of the latest stored procedures in his local database. He first executes that script, and then runs all of the unit tests and verifies that they pass. Now it is time to return to the listing business objects and put `VendorBE` together.

The VendorBE Class

First Rahul adds a Visual Basic class library project called `VendorBE` under the `ListingBusinessObjects` solution folder, sets the namespace, and adds a class called `VendorBE`. He then adds references to `VendorDAL` and `BusinessEntity` to the project properties at the References tab, and also adds `System.Configuration`, `System.Data`, and `System.Web.Services` as references. Next he opens the class diagram for the project, renames the class diagram `VendorBE.cd`, and drags the `com.icarustravel.enterprise31.BusinessEntity` namespace from class view onto the design surface.

Note The source code at the beginning of this section is found in `Chapter 9\Chapter9Merged`. This is the code after Rahul has updated his workspace and merged his code with Angela's changes. Exercise 9-4 illustrates the work of this section.

Rahul wants the new `VendorBE` class to inherit from the generic class `BusinessEntityBE`, so he clicks on the inheritance arrow in the Toolbox and drags from `VendorBE` up to `BusinessEntityBE`. Selecting the inheritance connector itself, he then goes to the Properties window and types "VendorDS" as the first type parameter in the inheritance, "DataSet" for the second, and "System.Web.Services.Protocols.SoapHttpClientProtocol" for the third. The last two are temporary so that the project will build. He can't add the correct ones until the `ListingWebService` project has been added. He now builds the `VendorBE` project—no problem. The class diagram now looks like the one shown in Figure 9-17. Let's have a look at the code for `VendorBE` that was generated by the work on the class diagram:

```
Public Class VendorBE
  Inherits com.icarustravel.enterprise31.BusinessEntity.BusinessEntityBE(
    Of com.icarustravel.enterprise31.Vendor.VendorDS,
    System.Data.DataSet,
    System.Web.Services.Protocols.SoapHttpClientProtocol)

End Class
```

Not much to it yet, is there?

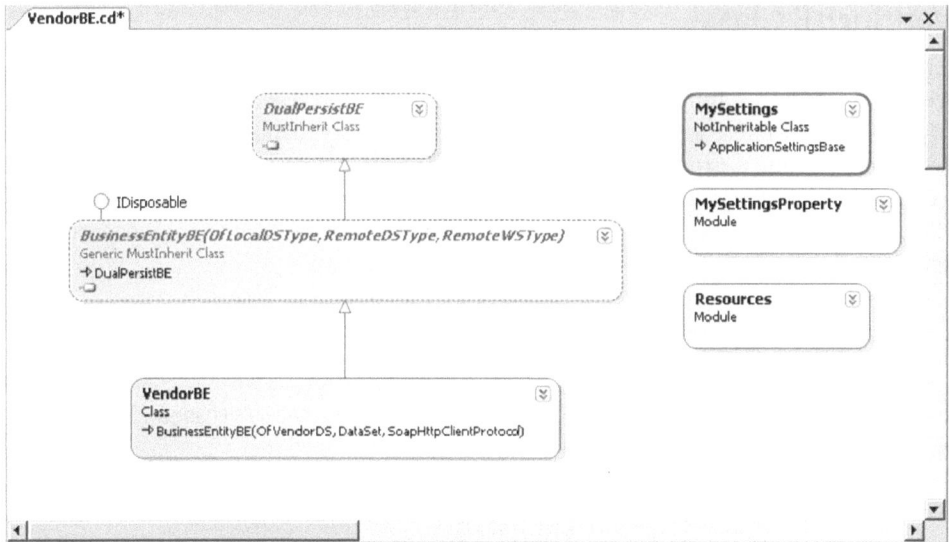

Figure 9-17. *Class diagram for the VendorBE project, VendorBE.cd*

ListingWebServiceStub

This stub and the actual web service must be implemented from the application diagram using the Implement Application command on the context menu, as shown in Figure 9-18. The service and binding namespaces in the web service provider endpoints on the applications ListingWebService and ListingWebServiceStub in the application diagram for the solution are both set to

http://webservices.enterprise31.icarustravel.com/

This time Rahul chooses Visual Basic as the language. The implementation details are shown in Figure 9-19. Of course, Rahul has to let Peter do this operation as it is only possible with the Architect edition of Visual Studio Team System.

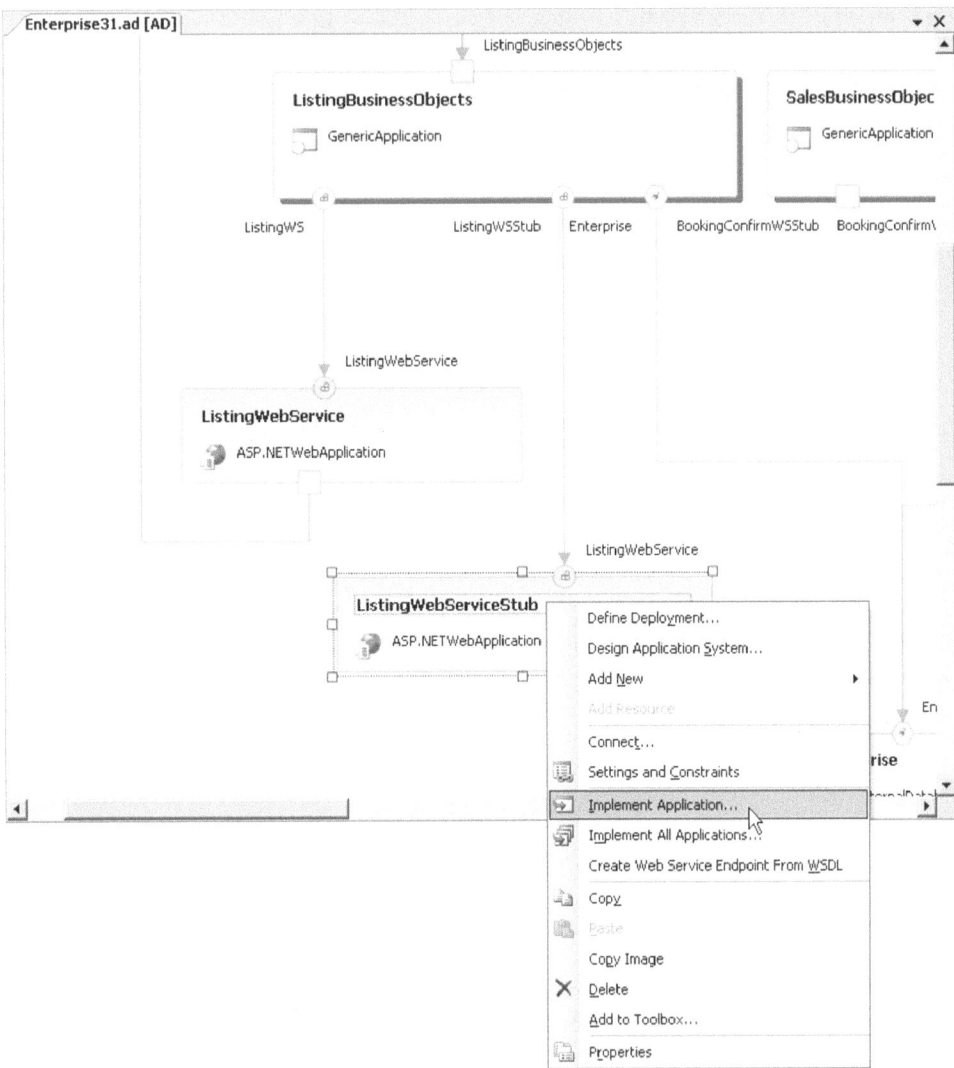

Figure 9-18. *Implementing the ListingWebServiceStub project*

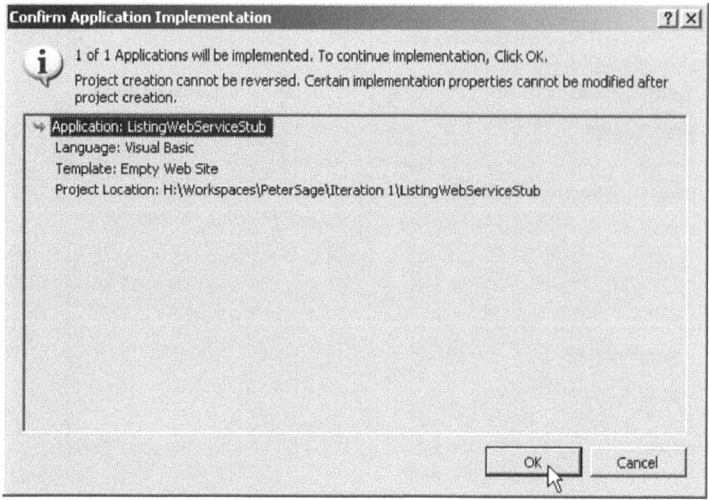

Figure 9-19. *Implementation details for the ListingWebServiceStub project*

When he has created the project in this way, Rahul adds a reference to VendorDAL and then modifies the default web service so the code looks like this:

```vbnet
Imports System.Web
Imports System.Web.Services
Imports System.Web.Services.Protocols

Imports com.icarustravel.enterprise31.Vendor

Namespace com.icarustravel.enterprise31.ListingWebService

    <System.Web.Services.WebServiceBinding(Name:="ListingWebService", _
        ConformsTo:=System.Web.Services.WsiProfiles.BasicProfile1_1, _
        EmitConformanceClaims:=True, _
        Namespace:="http://webservices.enterprise31.icarustravel.com/")> _
    <System.Web.Services.Protocols.SoapDocumentService()> _
    <System.Web.Services.WebService( _
        Namespace:="http://webservices.enterprise31.icarustravel.com/")> _
    Public Class ListingWebService
        Inherits System.Web.Services.WebService

        <WebMethod()> _
        Public Function GetVendor(ByVal id As Integer) As VendorDS
            Return New VendorDS()
        End Function
```

```
    <WebMethod()> _
    Public Sub SaveVendor(ByVal data As VendorDS)
    End Sub

End Class
```

End Namespace

In the properties for the web services, Rahul sets the Use Dynamic Ports property to false and sets the Port Numbers to arbitrary values for development purposes: 8030 for ListingWebService and 8031 for ListingWebServiceStub. Once he builds the solution, he adds a web reference in the VendorBE project to ListingWebServiceStub and sets the type parameters on the inheritance relation in Figure 9-17 to their permanent values, as shown in Figure 9-20.

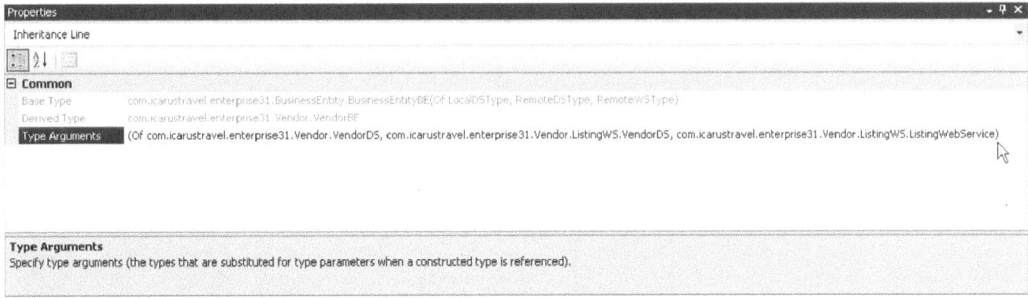

Figure 9-20. *The type parameters for the inheritance of VendorBE from BusinessEntityBE in the Properties window for the inheritance link on the class diagram*

Completing VendorBE

The next thing Rahul does is override some of the members of BusinessEntityBE. He does this on the class diagram by right-clicking on the class and selecting IntelliSense ➤ Override Members, as shown in Figure 9-21. In Figure 9-22 Rahul has selected the members to override, which includes all except the GetLocalData and GetRemoteData overloads, which take an array of objects.

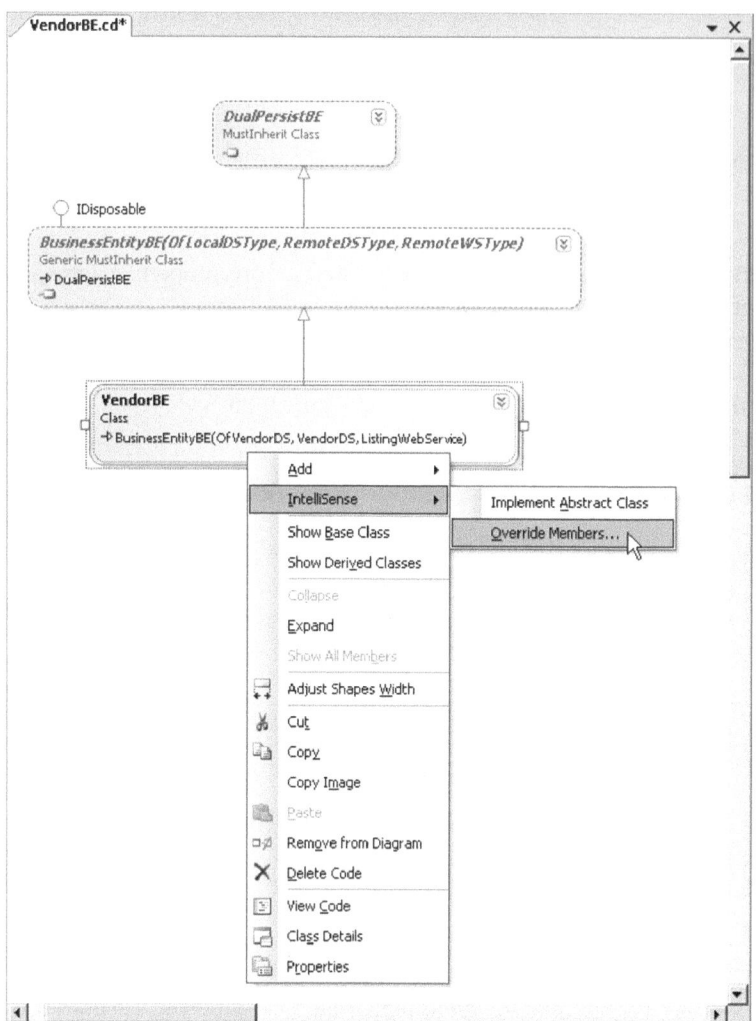

Figure 9-21. *Choosing Override Members*

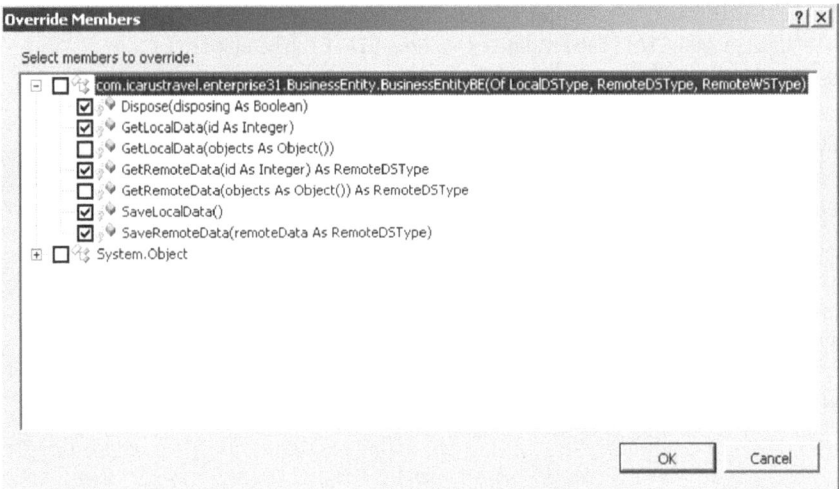

Figure 9-22. *Override members on the class diagram*

Just as Angela did in Chapter 8, Rahul must change the RemoteDSType type that has appeared in the code to the correct value of the type parameters in the GetRemoteData and SaveRemoteData functions, for example:

```
Protected Overrides Function GetRemoteData(ByVal id As Integer) As
                    com.icarustravel.enterprise31.Vendor.ListingWS.VendorDS

End Function
```

He then adds the code for the GetRemoteData and GetLocalData functions:

```
Public Class VendorBE
  Inherits com.icarustravel.enterprise31.BusinessEntity.BusinessEntityBE( _
    Of com.icarustravel.enterprise31.Vendor.VendorDS, _
    com.icarustravel.enterprise31.Vendor.ListingWS.VendorDS, _
    com.icarustravel.enterprise31.Vendor.ListingWS.ListingWebService)

  Protected Overrides Sub Dispose(ByVal disposing As Boolean)

  End Sub

  ' Override GetLocalData function.
  Protected Overrides Sub GetLocalData(ByVal id As Integer)

    ' Fill the VENDOR table
    Dim vendorTableAdapter As VENDORTableAdapter = New VENDORTableAdapter()
    vendorTableAdapter.Fill(Me.Data.VENDOR, id)

    ' Fill the RESOURCE table
    Dim resourceTableAdapter As RESOURCETableAdapter = New RESOURCETableAdapter()
    resourceTableAdapter.Fill(Me.Data.RESOURCE, id)
```

```vbnet
    ' Fill the STATE table
    Dim stateTableAdapter As STATETableAdapter = New STATETableAdapter()
    stateTableAdapter.Fill(Me.Data.STATE)

    ' Fill the COUNTRY table
    Dim countryTableAdapter As COUNTRYTableAdapter = New COUNTRYTableAdapter()
    countryTableAdapter.Fill(Me.Data.COUNTRY)
  End Sub

' GetRemoteData override
  Protected Overrides Function GetRemoteData(ByVal id As Integer) _
                        As com.icarustravel.enterprise31.Vendor.ListingWS.VendorDS
    Return Me.WebServiceProxy.GetVendor(id)
  End Function

  Protected Overrides Sub SaveLocalData()
  End Sub

  Protected Overrides Sub SaveRemoteData(ByVal remoteData _
                        As com.icarustravel.enterprise31.Vendor.ListingWS.VendorDS)
  End Sub
End Class
```

This code creates and uses instances of the table adapter classes such as VENDORTableAdapter, and they will still use their default connections to the local database that Rahul added at design time. Therefore, he must still add the constructor overload in each of these table adapters to allow the connection defined in a .config file to be used. We saw this in Chapter 8 for Angela's table adapter classes.

First the static Get function can be added (Figure 9-23), with an integer id as its only parameter, which returns an instance of VendorBE.

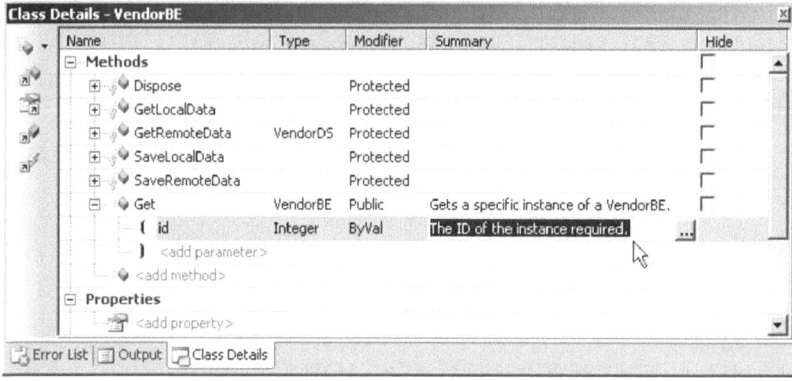

Figure 9-23. *Defining the shared VendorBE Get(int id) function in the Class Details window*

The code for this, when filled in manually, is

```
''' <summary>
''' Gets a specific instance of a VendorBE.
''' </summary>
''' <param name="id">The ID of the instance required.</param>
Public Function [Get](ByVal id As Integer) As VendorBE
    Dim vendorBE As VendorBE = New VendorBE()
    vendorBE.Fill(id)
    Return vendorBE
End Function
```

Before the project can be built, Rahul must add an `imports` statement (the equivalent of the C# `using` directive) at the top of the file:

```
Imports com.icarustravel.enterprise31.Vendor.VendorDSTableAdapters
```

Next, as we said, Rahul must manually add the constructor overloads on the table adapters that take a connection so that the database connection for each adapter can be provided from the `.config` file for the application. He right-clicks on the `VendorDS.xsd` in Solution Explorer and selects View Code. Visual Basic creates a file called `VendorDS.vb` in which Rahul can place the partial classes containing the overload constructors:

```
Namespace VendorDSTableAdapters
  Partial Public Class VENDORTableAdapter
    Inherits System.ComponentModel.Component

    Public Sub New(ByVal connection As System.Data.SqlClient.SqlConnection)
      MyBase.New()
      Me.ClearBeforeFill = True
      Me.Connection = connection
    End Sub
  End Class
End Class

' similar constructors for other table adapters for the data set.

End Namespace
```

Then the calls to the constructors in the `VendorBE.GetLocalData` function can be replaced with calls to these overloads:

```
Dim vendorTableAdapter As VENDORTableAdapter = New VENDORTableAdapter(Me.Connection)
vendorTableAdapter.Fill(Me.Data.VENDOR, id)
```

At this point Rahul suddenly realizes that he has a problem. The base `BusinessEntityBE` class includes a static function called `GetWSURL`. By the way, static functions in C# are called shared functions in VB .NET. This function gets from the application `.config` file a specified property string that is the URL for the sales web service. The problem is, Rahul's base class will need to pick up the URL string for the *listing* web service exposed by the Icarus web server, rather than the *sales* web service. When a generic base class such as this is used, the compiler will generate separate static variables for each parameterization of the base class. In other words, there will be different static variables for the BusinessEntityBE base class of VendorBE compared to that of CustomerBE. This is essential for the correct web service URL to be used, but also the static function GetWSURL must somehow pick up a differently named string for the URL from the .config file for VendorBE compared to CustomerBE.

To do this, a name is needed for the URL string property in the .config file for the executable that is obtainable from one of the type parameters of the base class. Then a different entry in the .config file can be accessed for each type parameterization of BusinessEntityBE to specify the web service URL for that case. One good way is to use the fully qualified class name of the web service type parameter, RemoteWSType, with its dots replaced by underscores. To do that, Rahul must add this statement at the top of the BusinessEntityBE class:

```
private static string uRLPropertyName =
                            new RemoteWSType().ToString().Replace('.','_');
```

This static string variable uRLPropertyName can then be used in the code that exists in the static function GetWSUrl that is called to initialize the static variable wSURL:

```
if (settingsSection != null)
{
  SettingElement settingElement =
    ((System.Configuration.ClientSettingsSection)(settingsSection)).Settings.Get(
                                                            uRLPropertyName);
  if (settingElement != null)
  {
    return settingElement.Value.ValueXml.InnerText;
  }
}
```

The entries in the App.config file for all applications using the business entity objects then become

```
<setting name="com_icarustravel_enterprise31_Order_SalesWS_SalesWebService"
    serializeAs="String">
  <value>http://localhost:8020/SalesWebService/SalesWebService.asmx</value>
</setting>
<setting name="com_icarustravel_enterprise31_Vendor_ListingWS_ListingWebService"
    serializeAs="String">
  <value>http://localhost:8030/ListingWebService/ListingWebService.asmx</value>
</setting>
```

Note The code at this stage can be found in Chapter9\Exercise 4, which is the completed code for Exercise 4.

ResourceBE Class

The development of the ResourceBE business entity class proceeds along similar lines to VendorBE. Both of these classes must also be unit-tested by Rahul using methods similar to those Angela used for OrderBE and CustomerBE. When Rahul has completed this, he will be ready to check in the resource business objects and begin working on integrating them with the List Wing façade application (Chapter 7).

Organizing the Team Build

So far I have not mentioned the very important Team Build feature in Team Foundation Server. There are two technical leaders for the Icarus team, Peter and Ron. Peter is responsible for the architectural guidance of the team and has the ultimate say on all technical aspects of the design of the software. Ron is responsible for the day-to-day running of the team and team members' ability to generate software, according to the design, in a consistent and reliable manner. It therefore falls to Ron to do most of the management of the team project in Team Foundation Server, including the setting of check-in policies, which help to achieve a level of consistency across the team. It is also Ron's job to organize the team build. Many organizations allocate a separate person for this task, called a build manager; this decision depends on the size of the team and the allocation of tasks. In Icarus's project, Peter is the technical lead; Clare is the project manager responsible for scheduling and tracking progress, so Ron has time available for the team build job, which is advantageous since he combines it with the team leadership role. The build management task is therefore placed at a central location in the project under a person with a technical knowledge of the issues, rather than given to a less technical person charged with the sometimes-frustrating task of "pulling it all together."

Note Exercise 5 covers the material in this section.

Creating a Build Type

Ron sets about establishing the team build on the Team Foundation Server for the Icarus 3.1 project. Team builds are specified by Build Types under TFS. To create a new build type, Ron right-clicks on the Team Builds folder of the project in Team Explorer and selects New Team Build Type, as shown in Figure 9-24. TFS displays the first page of the New Team Build Type Creation Wizard, as shown in Figure 9-25. On this page Ron specifies the name of the build and a description. Ron plans to have a build type for each iteration of the project.

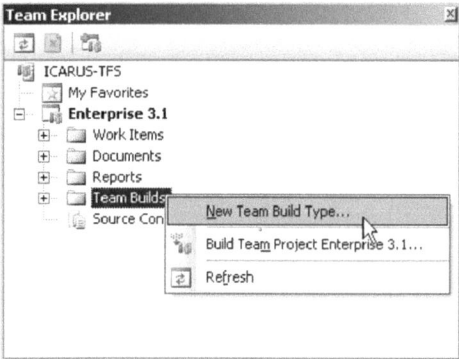

Figure 9-24. *Creating a new team build*

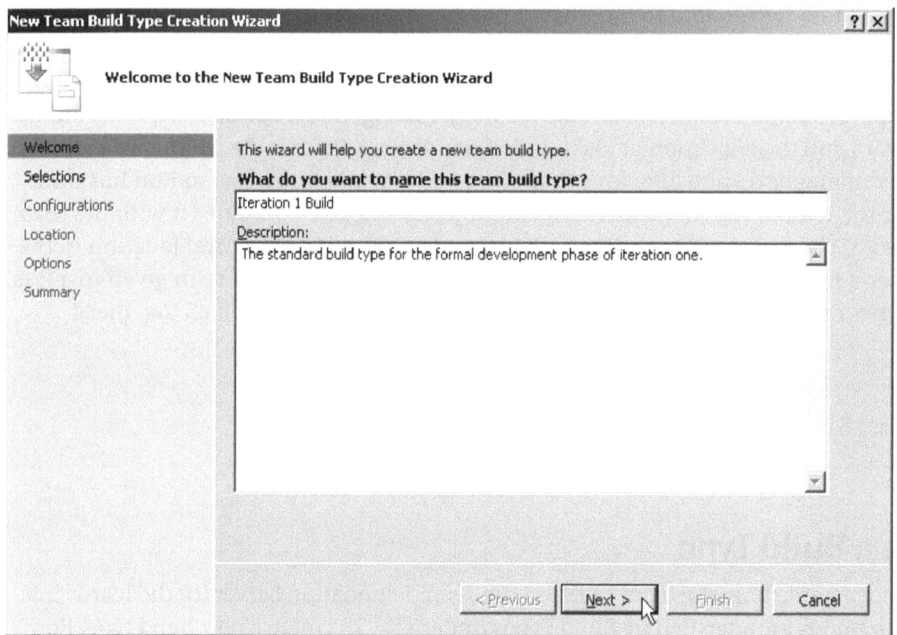

Figure 9-25. *Page 1 of the New Team Build Type Creation Wizard*

Ron clicks Next to go to the second page (Figure 9-26), which allows him to specify solutions that he wants to include in the build as well as their build order. Solutions are selected for build from workspaces, which are mappings of folders in version control to local folders on a developer's machine. Ron has created a workspace called Iteration1Build specifically for the build process, which maps the top-level folder in version control, called Iteration One, to a drive on his own machine. There is only one solution in iteration 1, so he selects it for build and clicks Next to move to the next page.

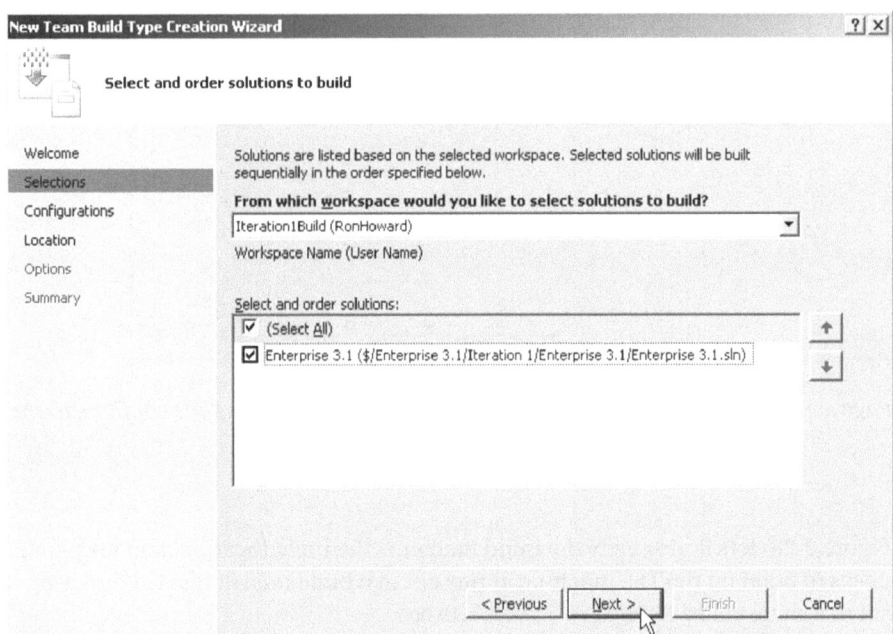

Figure 9-26. *Page 2 of the New Team Build Type Creation Wizard—specifying the solutions to include in the build*

Page 3 (Figure 9-27) allows Ron to select the configuration and platform. During iteration 1, Ron will build the debug configuration to allow debugging during testing if required. He chooses the platform Any CPU, since there will be no constraints on the choice of CPU in the Icarus servers.

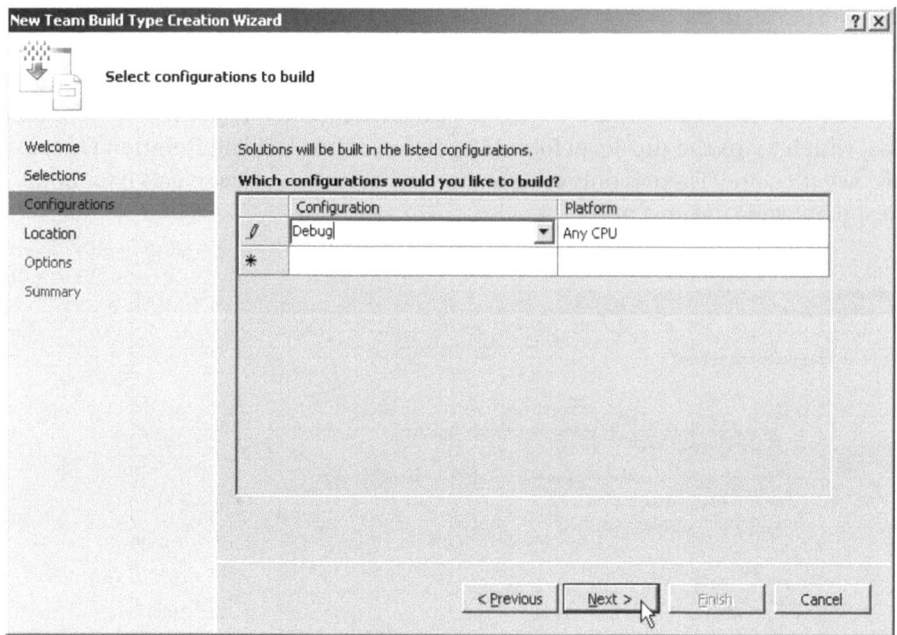

Figure 9-27. *Page 3 of the New Team Build Type Creation Wizard—specifying the configurations to build*

Page 4 (Figure 9-28) lets Ron specify the build machine, the build location, and drop location. Ron chooses to build on the TFS machine at present in a build area `H:\Builds` and drop the build result to a share called `\\ICARUS-TFS\BuildDrops`.

After clicking Next, Ron sees the Select Build Options page (Figure 9-29), which lets him specify the test and code analysis. At this stage in the project, Ron decides not to run tests or code analysis as part of the build; he knows many of the projects have not yet satisfied the requirement of static code analysis and the testing is not yet mature. Ron then clicks Next, and the wizard displays the summary page shown in Figure 9-30. Ron clicks Finish to complete the build type.

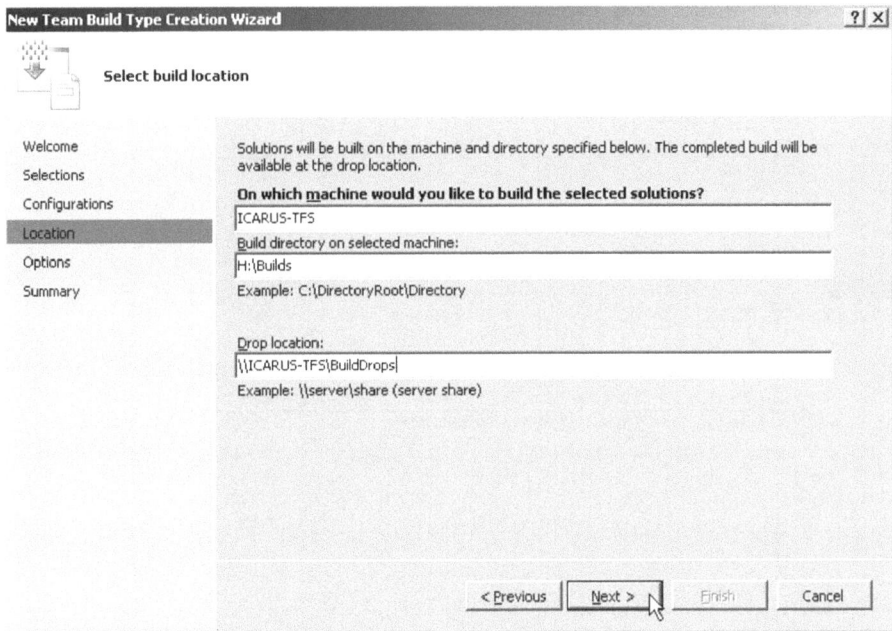

Figure 9-28. *Page 4 of the New Team Build Type Creation Wizard—specifying the build and drop locations*

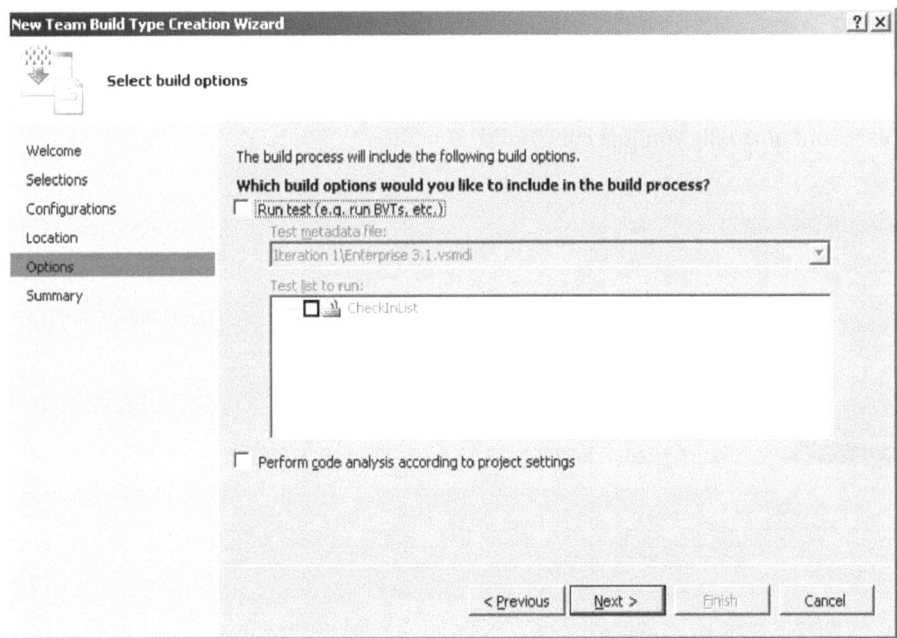

Figure 9-29. *Page 5 of the New Team Build Type Creation Wizard—specifying the build options*

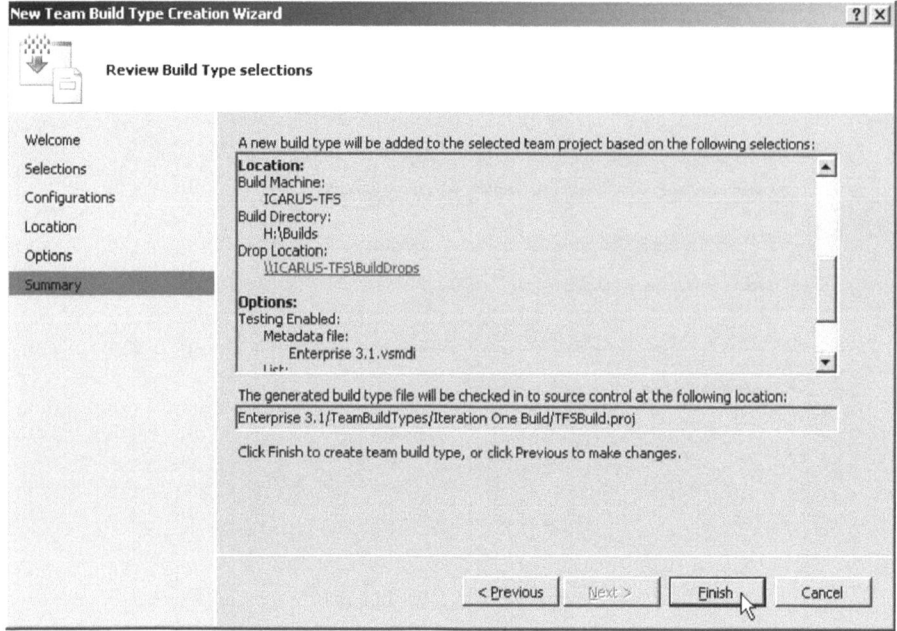

Figure 9-30. *Page 6 of the New Team Build Type Creation Wizard—summary*

Executing a Build

To execute a team build, you right-click on the build type in Team Explorer and select Build <Team project name> from the context menu, as shown in Figure 9-31. Team Explorer displays the dialog box shown in Figure 9-32. This dialog box allows you to change the build location for a special case, but normally you just click Build.

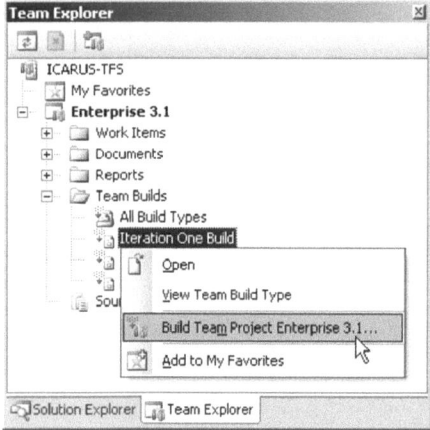

Figure 9-31. *Executing a build*

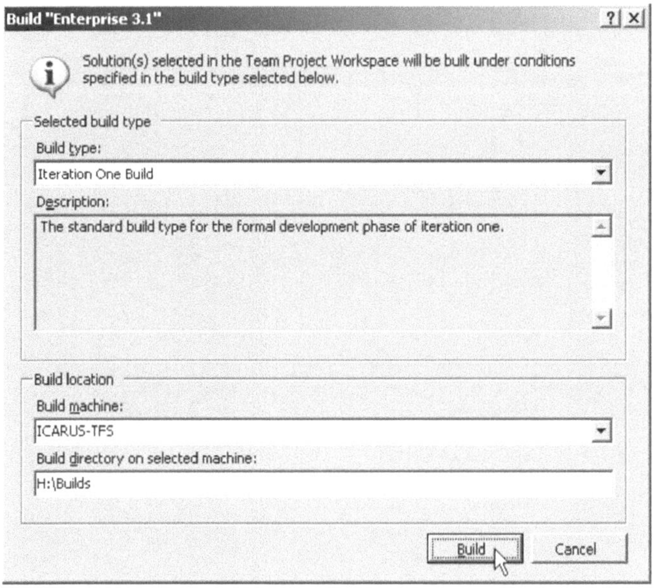

Figure 9-32. *Build "Enterprise 3.1"*

The build progress can be followed in the report shown in Figure 9-33, which updates as the build proceeds. Changesets that have occurred since the last build are associated with this build and are included in this report. Changesets are sets of files that were checked in together; they are expected to be associated with one or more work items and represent a defined piece of functionality added to the code base. The Associated Changesets node in Figure 9-33 can be expanded as shown in Figure 9-34, and individual changesets can be examined, as in Figure 9-35, to show a window similar to the Pending Changes window. With each changeset there is a set of files, visible in Figure 9-35: a set of work items that were associated with the check-in operation, a set of check-in notes, and a set of policy warnings. All of these may be viewed in the changeset window in Figure 9-35.

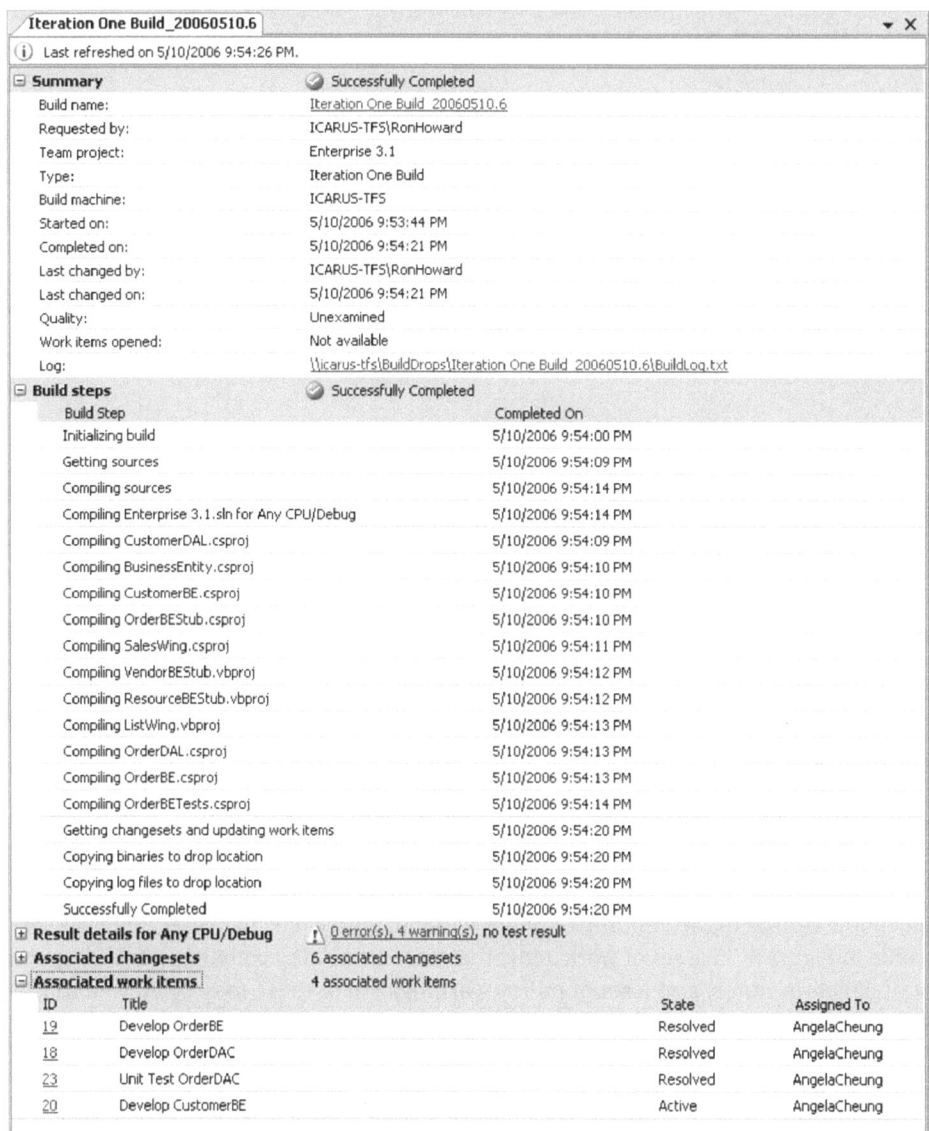

Figure 9-33. *Build report*

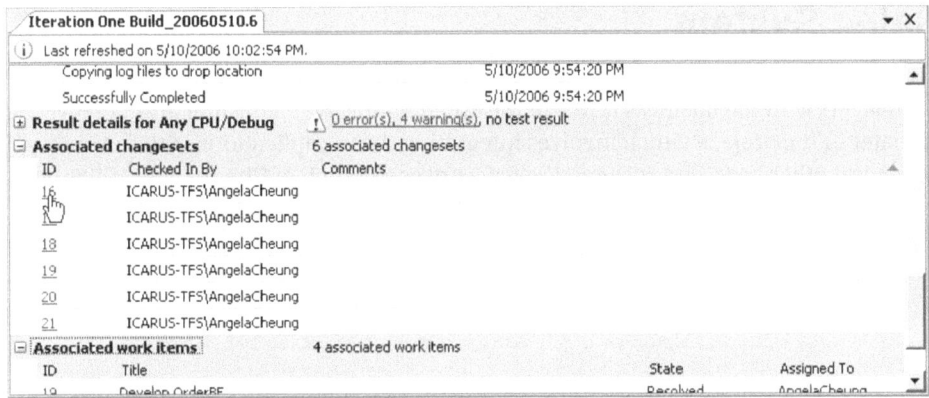

Figure 9-34. *Associated changesets*

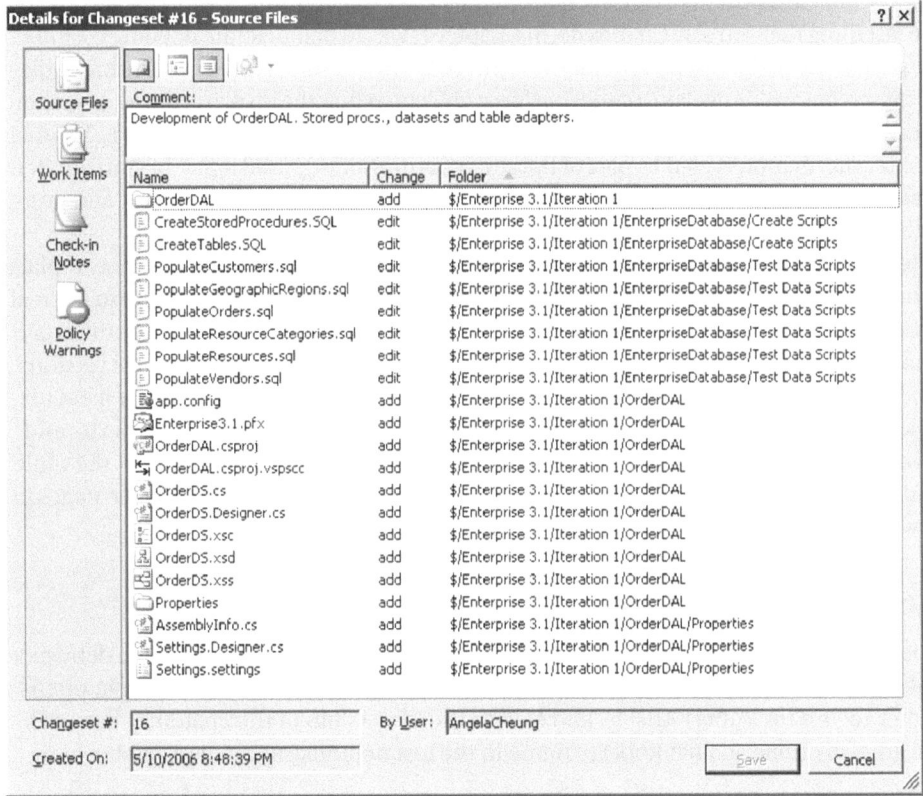

Figure 9-35. *Associated changeset 12*

The Sales System

In this section I'll describe the integration aspects of the Icarus project—the integration of the presentation layers with the business layers of the applications. We'll consider another level of integration later in the project, which involves integrating these applications with the orchestration server and other back-end systems. We have not seen much of Charles since Chapter 7, but he is proceeding with this task by taking the order and customer business entity objects and integrating them with the Sales Wing Windows Forms application that he first built for the storyboarding effort.

Note The code at this stage can be found in `Chapter9\Exercise 4`, which is the completed code for Exercise 4. Exercise 6 covers the material in this section.

Charles begins this part of the project by opening the project from TFS into his own workspace. The last thing that you saw Charles do, in Chapter 7, was to demonstrate opening customer records as part of the prototyping of iteration 1, phase 1. He now must integrate the order display and edit screens with Angela's `OrderBE` business objects so that the display, edit, and creation of orders can be tested as part of the formal delivery of the iteration 1 capability. The `SalesWing` application façade, demonstrated as part of the storyboarding effort, used a pair of stub datasets (`OrderDS` and `ReservationSelectionDS`) that were defined in the `OrderBEStub` project and populated with dummy data in the `OrderBE` class within that stub project.

To integrate the presentation screens with the business objects, Charles must now replace the reference to the `OrderBEStub` project in the `SalesWing` application with a reference to the real `OrderBE` project that Angela has written and tested. He also adds a reference to the `OrderDAL` project, since the business object and typed dataset are in different projects in the real versions (although they were in the same project in the stub). This is all there is to do—at least for the read part of the customer order capability. Provided Angela has made the `OrderDS` and `ReservationSelectionDS` the same as the ones used in the `OrderBEStub`, with all of the table names and field names the same, the real datasets should bind to the controls on the pages in the same way as the stub datasets.

Verifying the Read Behavior for Orders

It will be beneficial to run through the operation of the `SalesWing` application with the debugger to check that it is working as expected. Charles runs the application in the debugger, opens the customer record for Robert Ansley, and selects the Orders tab of the customer data control. There are two orders against Robert's name in the test demonstration data, as shown in Figure 9-36.

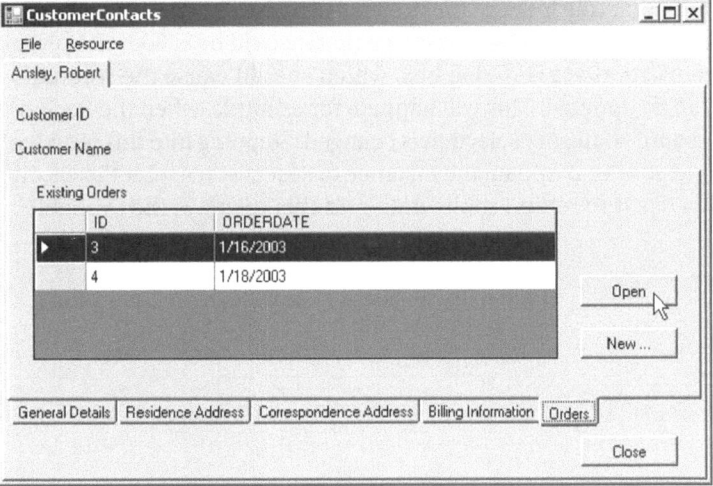

Figure 9-36. *The orders for Robert Ansley*

To begin testing the functionality that displays order detail, Charles will select one of the orders (ID = 3) and click the Open button. To trace through the code, though, he first must set a breakpoint on the event handler for the Open button, as shown in Figure 9-37. When he clicks the Open button, this breakpoint is immediately hit, and he single-steps the code as far as the call to ShowDialog() on the OrderDetail class. If you remember, the OrderDetail form is rather complicated; it has two nested custom controls, ReservationDetail and SelectedResource. There are therefore potentially three form load events that could gather data into datasets to bind to the controls, but currently nothing is being done in the middle one, ReservationDetail. Charles therefore sets breakpoints at OrderDetail_Load and SelectedResource_Load and clicks the Start Debugging button in the Standard toolbar (pressing the F5 key does the same).

```
CustomerDetails.cs                                                    ▼ X
com.icarustravel.enterprise31.SalesWing.CustomerDetails  ▼  buttonOpenOrder_Click(object sender, EventArgs e)  ▼

    private void buttonOpenOrder_Click(object sender, EventArgs e)
    {
        if (this.dataGridViewOrders.SelectedRows.Count == 1)
        {
            int selectedOrderId = (int)this.dataGridViewOrders.SelectedRows[0].Cells["ID"].Value;

            OrderDetail orderDetail = new OrderDetail();

            orderDetail.OrderId = selectedOrderId;
            if (orderDetail.ShowDialog() == DialogResult.OK)
            {
                OrderBE orderBE = new OrderBE();
                orderBE.Data = orderDetail.Data;
                orderBE.Save();
            }
        }
    }
```

Figure 9-37. *Breaking in the Open button event handler*

SelectedResource_Load is hit first (the inner of the nested user controls), and Charles steps into UpdateResourceOptions(). He designed this function so that it could be called whenever anything changed on the main OrderDetail dialog box, which should cause the resource options displayed to the user to be updated. This will happen, for example, when the Region combo box selection or the Resource Category selection is changed. Stepping into this function (Figure 9-38), we see that its purpose is to update the instance of ReservationSelectionDS on the user control, which will cause it to rebind to the data grid that displays the available resource options.

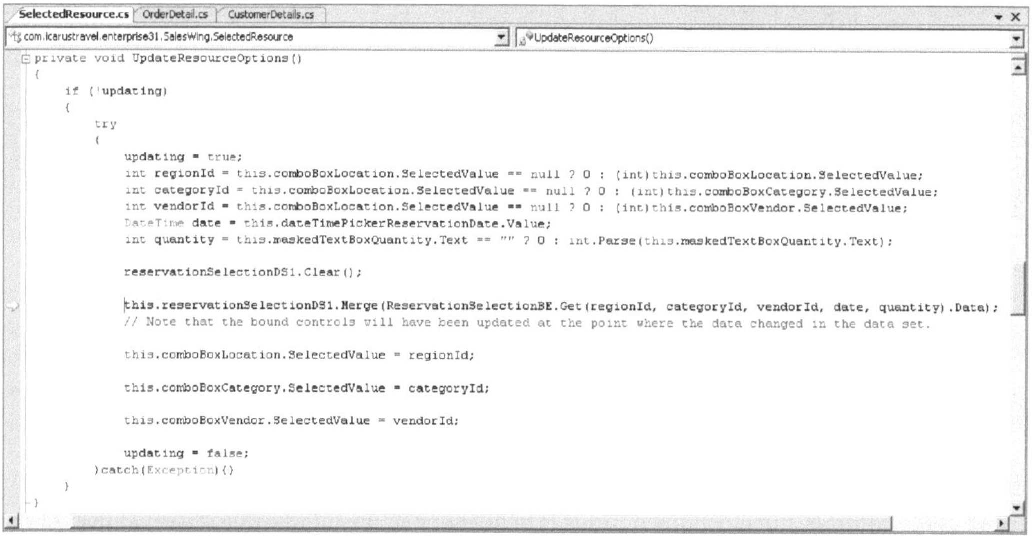

Figure 9-38. *The UpdateResourceOptions function*

There are a couple of quirks in this function. One is that it can be reentered. This is because, when the controls rebind, the change events for the combo boxes will fire and throw the code right back into this function. It therefore has the updating flag as a guard against that. The second is that all of the combo boxes—Location, Category and Vendor—will get updated when the ReservationSelectionDS is loaded with new data, so their settings (i.e., the selected item on each) need to be saved. The plan is that the vendors displayed in the Vendor combo box will be limited to those available within the selected region and category, but this has not been implemented in iteration 1.

Charles steps into the call to the Get function on ReservationSelectionBE, which is the entry point to the sales business objects, and follows it through into the Fill function on BusinessEntityBE, and then back to the GetRemoteData function on ReservationSelectionBE (Figure 9-39).

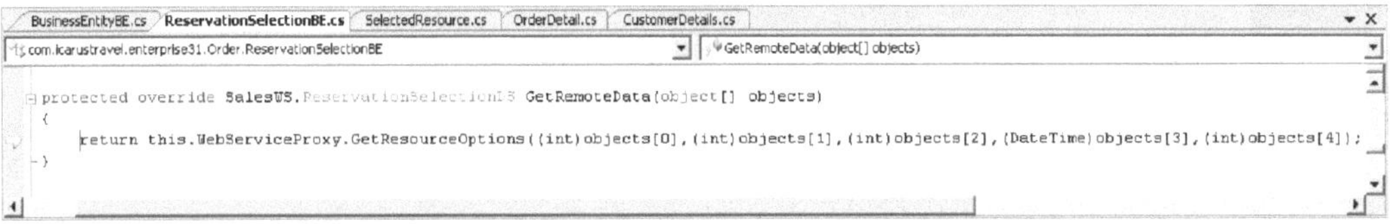

Figure 9-39. *The GetRemoteData function*

This is the standard way that all of the business entity classes work in the design. This function calls the GetResourceOptions function on the Sales web service proxy. Charles steps into the WebServiceProxy property to make sure that it is created properly, with the correct URL value from the SalesWing.exe.config file. He then steps into the web method itself. Before you can do this, you actually have to enable debugging on the web service by setting an attribute in the web.config file for the web service, as shown here:

```xml
<?xml version="1.0"?>
<configuration>
  etc.
  <system.web>
    etc.
    <compilation debug="true">
    etc.
    </compilation>
  </system.web>
  etc.
</configuration>
```

The web method (Figure 9-40) calls the same static Get method of ReservationSelectionBE on the server, which Charles also steps into and follows until the GetLocalData method is entered (Figure 9-41). Here the table adapter Fill functions are used to populate each table in the dataset.

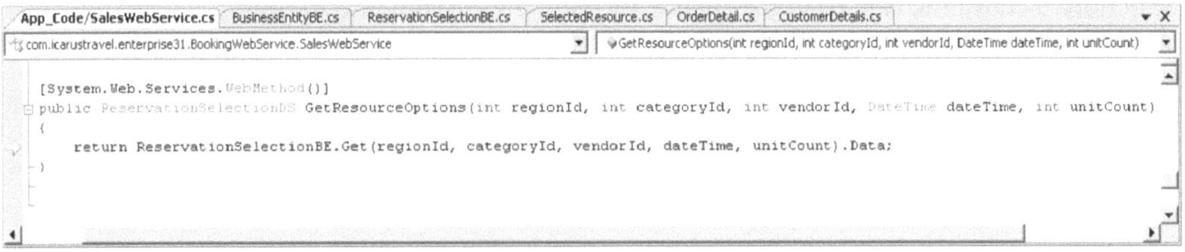

Figure 9-40. *The GetResourceOptions web method*

Figure 9-41. *The call to GetLocalData in ReservationSelectionBE on the web server*

Charles checks the connection string at this point (to make sure it is being picked up correctly from the web.config file for the web service) by highlighting this.Connection in Figure 9-41 and dragging it to the Watch 1 window (Figure 9-42). The connection string specifies the instance of SQL Server Express on his own machine and the database Enterprise, which is correct. He steps through the code until it returns to the SelectedResource_Load method, then lets it run until the OrderDetail_Load breakpoint is reached.

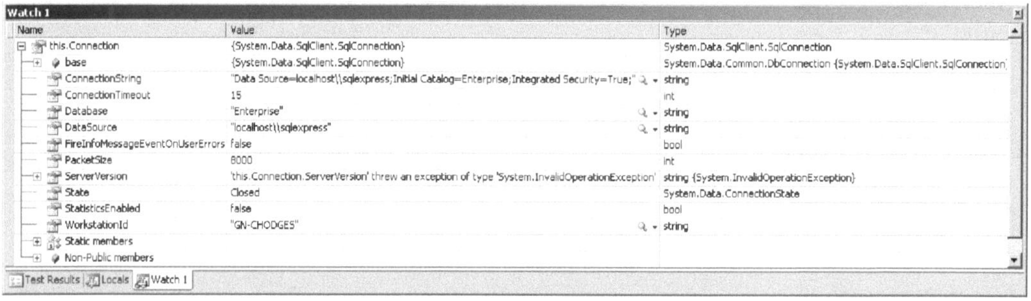

Figure 9-42. *Checking the database connection within the web service*

This time Charles steps into the OrderBE.Get method and follows the code through to the GetOrder web method call on the SalesWebService, and then into that web method (Figure 9-43), which calls the static Get(int id) method on the OrderBE class. Finally he steps down into the function to check the call to GetLocalData(), where the ORDER and RESERVATION tables are populated (Figure 9-44).

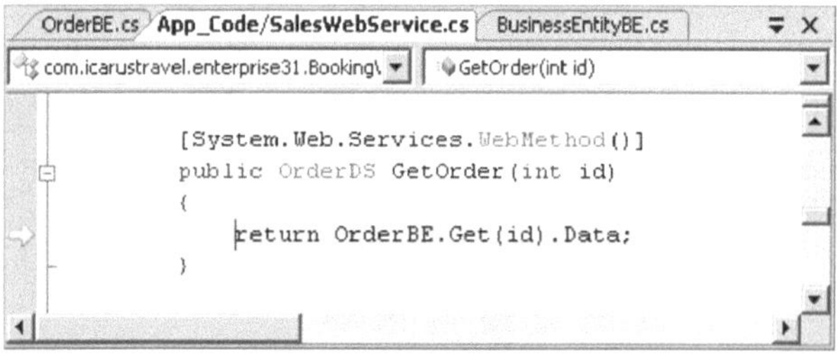

Figure 9-43. *The GetOrder web method*

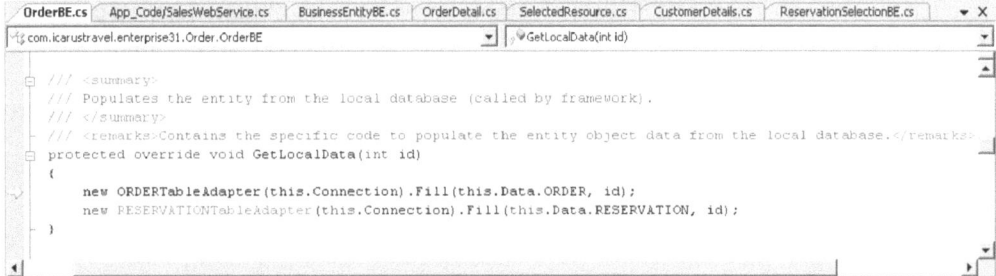

Figure 9-44. *The call to GetLocalData in OrderBE on the web server*

To summarize, the end result of this is that the instance of ReservationSelectionDS declared within the SelectedResource user control is populated and will update the controls to which it is bound. Also, the instance of OrderDS declared within the OrderDetail web form is populated and updates the controls to which it is bound on that form.

Verifying the Write Behavior for Orders

The Order Detail dialog box is shown in Chapter 6, Figure 6-10. After you've opened an order in the way just described, you can add or delete one or more reservations. You add reservations by first making selections in one or more of the Location, Category, and Vendor combo boxes, and then selecting a date and quantity. Next, you select one of the resulting options displayed in the Alternative Options DataGridView control and click the Add Reservation button. This causes the following event handler function to execute:

```
private void buttonAddReservation_Click(object sender, EventArgs e)
{
  SelectedResource.ReservationData reservationData
                                    = this.reservationDetail1.ReservationData;

  this.orderDSOrders.RESERVATION.LoadDataRow(new object[]
    {
      -1,
      reservationData.ResourceAvailabilityId,
      this.orderId,
      reservationData.VendorId,
      reservationData.ResourceId,
      reservationData.VendorName,
      reservationData.ResourceName,
      reservationData.Date,
      reservationData.Quantity,
      reservationData.UnitCost,
      reservationData.ExtendedCost
    },false
  );
}
```

This function adds a row to the RESERVATION table based on fields obtained from a property on the `ReservationDetail` control, which returns a struct based on the selected row in the `DataGridView` of resource options.

To delete a reservation, you click the Remove Reservation button on the Order Detail dialog box, which marks the corresponding row in the RESERVATION table as deleted.

When you click the OK button, the `CustomerDetails` form executes a save of the order details via the `OrderBE.Save()` function, which has already been tested in Angela's unit tests.

Verifying the New Order Functionality

Charles verifies the new order behavior by tracing through the code in a similar way as the read and write behavior.

Testing the Sales Wing Application

Visual Studio 2005 Team System does not contain the capability to generate tests for Windows Forms, but it does provide the capability to generate web tests that can be used for web forms, as you will see later in this chapter. For Windows Forms, either manual or generic tests can be used. Manual tests provide a framework of control around a manual process; generic tests provide a wrapper around some other kind of test to place it under the control of Team System. Third-party applications can be used for Windows Forms testing, such as NUnitForms (written by Luke T. Maxon), available without charge at the time of this writing from `http://nunitforms.sourceforge.net/`.

The test team at Icarus plans to investigate this option, but initially they've developed some automatic testing of the Windows Forms themselves.

A senior developer, Rob Smith, has been assigned to the test team under Herman to provide C# development experience, where tests written in C# need to be developed, and he is currently working on developing tests for the Sales Wing Windows Forms application. Various discussions have taken place between Rob and Peter about the best way for a C# program to interface with the Windows Forms in the application. They have decided to write the tests as unit tests that will create instances of each form and test the correct operation of all the controls on the form, including any user controls, right through to the database. Initially Rob will create instances of each form individually from his unit-test code, providing them with the same parameters as would be provided if an instance of a form were created by an event handler responding to a button click on another form. This initial approach does not allow sequences of navigation between forms to be tested, but Rob plans to investigate this as the next step.

To create his first test, Rob right-clicks on the Test View window and selects New Test from the context menu to display the dialog box shown in Figure 9-45. He types the name "OrderDetailDisplayTest" since this class will contain test functions that cover all aspects of the operation of the `OrderDetail` Windows Form. This is a complicated form that contains two nested user controls: `ReservationDetail` and `SelectedResource`. The `ReservationDetail` control is intended to display details about a reservation that is being arranged, with pictures and hyperlinks for a resource as well as a tab that allows search and selection of that resource by providing geographic regions, categories, and so forth. Only the tab containing this capability has been implemented for iteration 1, so only the capability of this tab currently needs testing in the `ReservationDetail` control. All of this search and select capability is encapsulated within the second user control: the `SelectedResource` control.

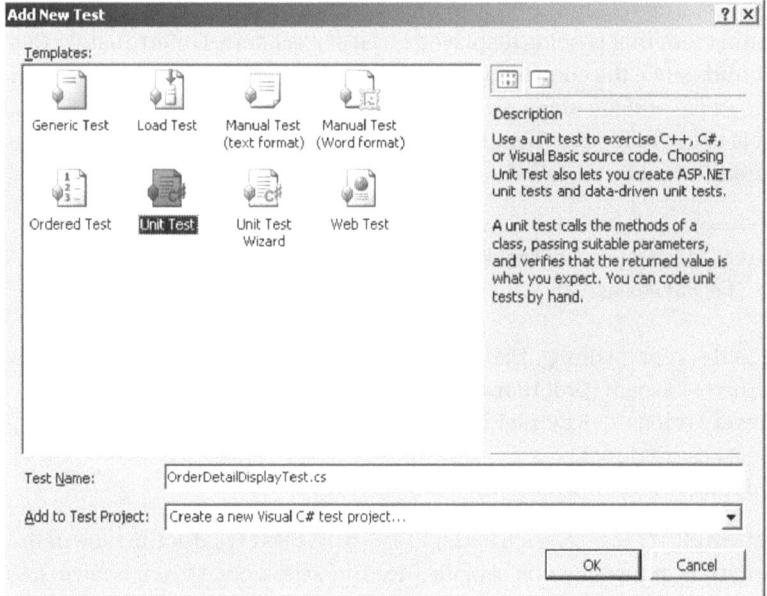

Figure 9-45. *The Add New Test dialog box*

Rob calls the new test project SalesWingTest and places it in a new solution folder called ApplicationTests, since it will consist of application-level tests designed to test parts of the complete working application. As with the unit tests that Angela wrote, it is necessary to provide some initialization to the database in the form of known rows in various tables, and this again is placed in a base class called SalesWingTestBase.

The code to create and initialize the OrderDetail form is as follows:

```
[TestMethod]
public void OrderDetailDisplayTest1()
{
  // Set DualPersistBE into client mode.
  DualPersistBE.InstalledMode = DualPersistBE.InstallMode.Client;

  OrderDetail orderDetail = new OrderDetail();
  orderDetail.OrderId = orderId;
  orderDetail.Show();

  // Code to check that the information in the controls on the form
  // matches what would be expected in the content of the database.
}
```

In the previous code, first the static variable of DualPersistBE is set to client mode. Next an instance of the OrderDetail form is created, and its OrderId property is set equal to the known ID of the order placed in the database. The Show() function is then called, which causes the class to go through the same functionality as if the user had clicked Open on the Orders tab of the CustomerDetails control. The function accesses the business layer objects and the database to populate the datasets on the form that bind to the controls.

After this action, as the comments say, the code in the test function must access the controls to check that the data within them that is being displayed is the correct data. Unfortunately, this is not quite as easy as it sounds since the controls are placed automatically in the partial class in the `OrderDetail.Designer.cs` file and are made private. There is a way to access private fields in a class, however, and that is to use reflection. Here is the code needed to obtain the `DataGridView` control at the top of the `OrderDetail` form, called `dataGridViewReservations`:

```
// ==============================================================
// Compare the text values displayed in the Reservations GridView with
// the known values in the database.

// Get the private variable representing the Reservations data grid view.
FieldInfo dataGridViewInfo = typeof(OrderDetail).GetField(
        "dataGridViewReservations", BindingFlags.Instance | BindingFlags.NonPublic);
DataGridView dataGridViewReservations =
        (DataGridView)dataGridViewInfo.GetValue(orderDetail);
```

where the call to `Type.GetField(string name, BindingFlags bindingAttr)`, for the type of the `OrderDetail` Windows Form class, returns an object of the `FieldInfo` class. Note that it is necessary in the `bindingAttr` parameter in the `GetField` function to specify that instance fields and non-public fields are to be considered: `BindingFlags.Instance | BindingFlags.NonPublic`. The `FieldInfo` object contains the ability to extract the value of the field that it represents from a specific instance of the `OrderDetail` class. `FieldInfo.GetValue(Object obj)` returns an `Object`, so it has to be cast to its known type.

Having obtained the control from the form that contains the data that he needs to check, Rob can now write a set of (rather tedious) `Assert` statements comparing the data in the `DataGridView` with what he expects, knowing what was written to the database during the class initialization:

```
// Verify the number of rows in the DataGridView is correct
Assert.AreEqual(2, dataGridViewReservations.Rows.Count);

// Verify the fields are correct in the first row
Assert.AreEqual(testSetupDS.RESERVATION[0].ID.ToString(),
    dataGridViewReservations.Rows[0].Cells["columnID"].Value.ToString());

Assert.AreEqual(testSetupDS.RESERVATION[0].ORDERID.ToString(),
    dataGridViewReservations.Rows[0].Cells["columnORDERID"].Value.ToString());

Assert.AreEqual(testSetupDS.VENDOR[0].ID.ToString(),
    dataGridViewReservations.Rows[0].Cells["columnVENDORID"].Value.ToString());

Assert.AreEqual(testSetupDS.RESERVATION[0].EXTENDEDCOST.ToString(),
    dataGridViewReservations.Rows[0].Cells["columnEXTENDEDCOST"].Value.ToString());
```

```
Assert.AreEqual(testSetupDS.RESERVATION[0].UNITCOUNT.ToString(),
    dataGridViewReservations.Rows[0].Cells["columnUNITCOUNT"].Value.ToString());

Assert.AreEqual(testSetupDS.RESERVATION[0].UNITCOST.ToString(),
    dataGridViewReservations.Rows[0].Cells["columnUNITCOST"].Value.ToString());

Assert.AreEqual(testSetupDS.RESOURCEAVAILABILITY[0].AVAILABLEDATETIME.ToString(),
    dataGridViewReservations.Rows[0].Cells
                                ["columnAVAILABLEDATETIME"].Value.ToString());

Assert.AreEqual(testSetupDS.RESOURCE[0].NAME.ToString(),
    dataGridViewReservations.Rows[0].Cells["columnRESOURCENAME"].Value.ToString());

Assert.AreEqual(testSetupDS.VENDOR[0].NAME.ToString(),
    dataGridViewReservations.Rows[0].Cells["columnVENDORNAME"].Value.ToString());
```

and so it goes on. Yuk! Each of these statements compares a field in a table of the testSetupDS dataset in the base class with a cell in a row in the data grid view for the reservations. Following this, the code in this test class obtains the DataGridView object within the SelectedResource user control and verifies that its content matches what should be obtained as resource options listed.

I'm sure with a bit of effort, there's a better way of structuring these kinds of tests. Maybe the data that's in the base class and that's written to the database could be made a bit tidier and accessible in a more intuitive manner. In this code there's a lot of coupling between the dataset in the base class and the fields of objects examined in the test class. Also the code that reflects the private variables could be encapsulated in a class instead of being repeated. Products such as NUnitForms usually define a set of classes whose job it is to access the data in Windows Forms controls. Anyway, I've tried to demonstrate the principle in this section; you can look at the entire test in the exercise code for this chapter.

The Sales Website Application

This section describes the work of integrating the Sales Site presentation layer with the business objects. It also examines the Visual Studio Team Edition for Testers features that test the website operation.

Note The code at this stage can be found in Chapter9\Exercise 6, which is the completed code for Exercise 6. Exercise 7 covers the material in this section.

Displaying Orders and Reservations

Back in Chapter 7 we followed Ed as he built the prototype web form pages for the Sales website part of the application. That façade now needs to be integrated into the sales business objects delivered by Angela and then tested. In many ways this part of the project is the most critical in terms of performance and scalability, since it is likely to receive more web traffic than the other sections of the project.

Like the integration of the Sales Wing smart client application, with the sales business objects, the task is quite simple provided the stub datasets defined in SalesBusinessObjectsStubs match the real datasets in the SalesBusinessObjects projects. Ed therefore changes the references in the SalesSite to remove OrderBEStub and add the CustomerBE and OrderBE projects. He then rebuilds the project and selects SalesSite as the start-up project and MyWings.aspx as the start page in Solution Explorer. Next, he attempts to run the sales website under the debugger. As he goes through the pages, he finds that a few field and table names were changed, which causes exceptions to be thrown. He corrects the data text fields specified in the columns for some of the DataGridView controls and manages to get the site through the correct sequence (see Chapter 6, Figures 6-11, 6-12, 6-13, and 6-14) for a customer and order already in the database.

Another change needs to be made to the set of ASP.NET forms making up the presentation layer of the sales site: to arrange for parameters to be provided in the calls that are made by the ObjectDataSource controls placed on the pages to the static GetData functions in business object classes such as CustomerBE and OrderBE. For example, when the My Orders page is entered, the ObjectDataSource bound to the GridView will call a specified member on a specified object—in this case, the GetData static method on the CustomerBE class—and it must provide a parameter that specifies the ID value of the customer. Where does this value come from? You would expect it to come from perhaps a session cookie generated when the customer authenticates, but since authentication is not included in iteration 1, Ed will leave it as a constant to be provided as a query string parameter; it's usually "2" for the test cases, which is the ID in the test data of our old friend Robert Ansley!

When the Order Detail page is displayed, a constant cannot be used since we have to see the detail for the correct order. The ID value for the order whose link on the My Orders page was clicked, needs to be passed to the static GetData function on OrderBE from the ObjectDataSource called ObjectDataSourceOrder on the Order Detail page. To do this, Ed must do two things. First, he needs to alter the GridView on the MyOrders web form so that clicking the hyperlinks in its rows navigates to a URL that includes as a parameter the ID of the order clicked. Second, he needs to make the ObjectDataSource used to retrieve the reservation rows take that parameter and pass it to the call on the OrderBE object.

You might think that Ed will need client-side scripting, but no, it is all included in the capability of the GridView web form control. He selects the GridView control on the design view of the web form MyOrders, clicks the glyph in the top-right corner, and selects Edit Columns from the smart tag menu, as shown in Figure 9-46.

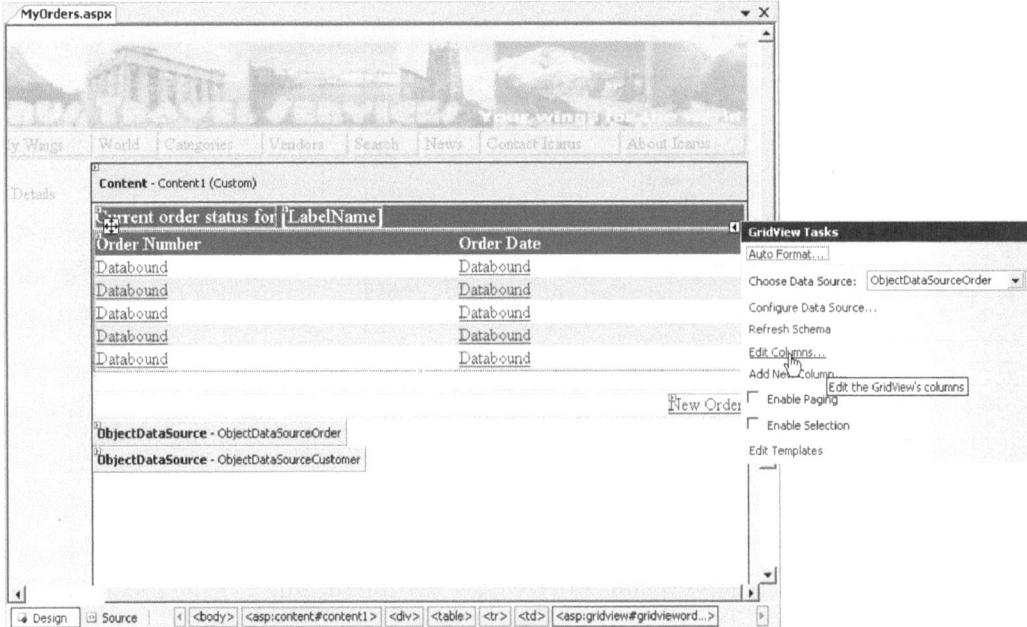

Figure 9-46. *Editing the GridView web control columns using the smart tag menu*

Team System displays the Fields dialog box, shown in Figure 9-47. Ed has defined two fields (corresponding to columns) in the `GridView` that displays the list of orders on the My Orders page. Both of them are hyperlink fields, with the displayed text bound to the object data source. Ed wants clicking on either of these, for a particular order, to take the user to the Order Detail page populated with the details for that order. Figure 9-47 shows the properties for one of these. Instead of typing a value for `NavigateUrl`, Ed has typed the following into the `DataNavigateUrlFormatString` property:

`~/OrderDetails.aspx?ORDERID={0}&CUSTOMERID={1}`

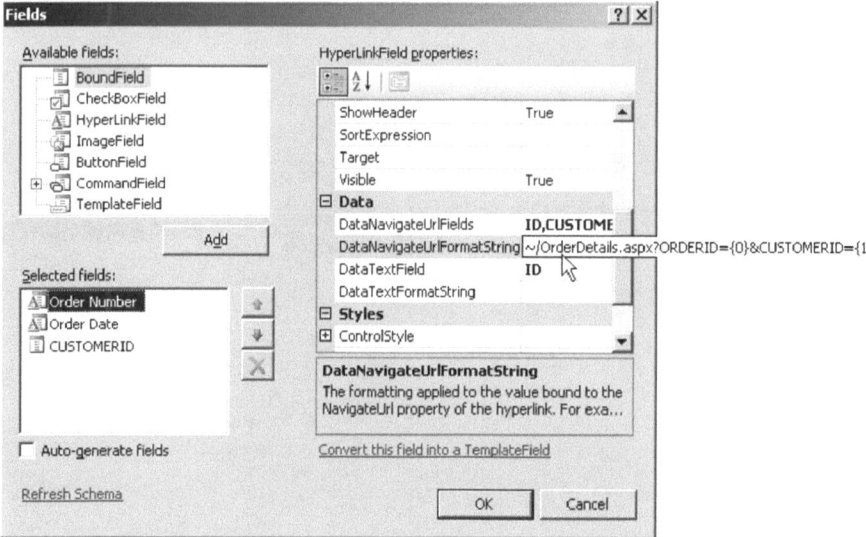

Figure 9-47. *Setting the hyperlink column in a GridView web control to add a parameter to its URL.*

This line will act as a format string to produce the URL with the addition of two parameters (indicated by {0} and {1} in the format string). The actual values that will be placed in parameters such as these are defined in the DataNavigateUrlFields property, where field names from the bound data source may be listed. In this case there are two, ID and CUSTOMERID, which will result in the replacement of the parameter {0} on each row with the value of the ID field and parameter {1} with that of the CUSTOMERID field of the ObjectDataSource that is bound to this control. Ed sets these two properties to the same values on both the Order Number and Order Date fields so that clicking on either of them will navigate to the same URL, complete with the ID of the order and the CUSTOMERID as parameters in the query string.

Now for the second thing we mentioned a few paragraphs ago—making the ObjectDataSource use the query string parameter in its call on OrderBE. To do this, Ed clicks the smart tag glyph on the top-right corner of ObjectDataSourceReservation on the Order Detail page (Figure 9-48) and selects Configure Data Source from the smart tag menu. He clicks Next until he sees the Define Parameters page in the wizard. Then Ed clicks the Show Advanced Properties link and resizes the dialog box. He selects QueryString in the Parameter Source combo box and types "ORDERID" in the QueryStringField property, as shown in Figure 9-49. He clicks Finish, builds the project, and tests it. Now the correct order details will be displayed on the Order Detail page, as required, after the user clicks an entry on the My Orders page.

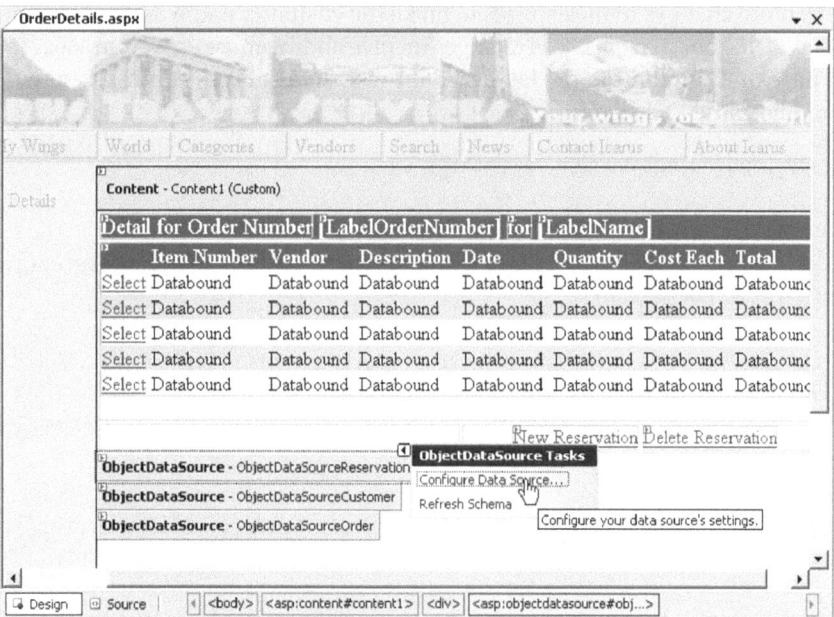

Figure 9-48. *Configuring the ObjectDataSource web control using the smart tag menu*

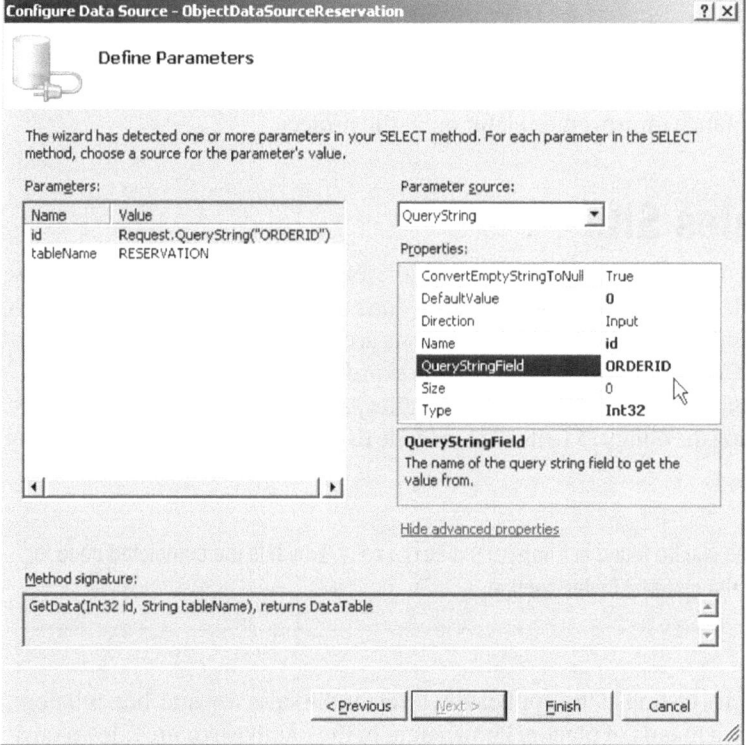

Figure 9-49. *Configuring an ObjectDataSource to use a field from the query string.*

Ed makes a few more changes to these pages to make the customer name and order numbers appear in labels at various places. These changes involve adding more ObjectDataSource controls on each page and populating the labels from these data sources explicitly in the Page_Load event handler, as in this example:

```
protected void Page_Load(object sender, EventArgs e)
{
  IEnumerator customerEnumerator =
                              this.ObjectDataSourceCustomer.Select().GetEnumerator();
  if (customerEnumerator.MoveNext())
  {
    DataRowView customerRowView = (DataRowView)customerEnumerator.Current;
    this.LabelName.Text = (string)customerRowView["GIVENNAME"]
                                  + " " + (string)customerRowView["FAMILYNAME"];
  }

  IEnumerator orderEnumerator = this.ObjectDataSourceOrder.Select().GetEnumerator();
  if (orderEnumerator.MoveNext())
  {
    DataRowView orderRowView = (DataRowView)orderEnumerator.Current;
    this.LabelOrderNumber.Text = ((int)orderRowView["ID"]).ToString();
  }
}
```

Back in Chapter 7, I mentioned that having multiple ObjectDataSource controls on the same page that access different tables of the same dataset was not very efficient. It looks as if Ed has made this problem of multiple ObjectDataSource controls a little worse, so there should be some scope for performance improvement later on in the project.

Testing the Sales Site

As explained in Chapter 1, Visual Studio 2005 Team Edition for Testers provides the capability to create a form of test called a web test. This kind of test consists of a sequence of interactions, or *requests*, of a browser with the application. The requests are recorded into a script that can be subsequently edited. Once the sequence has been recorded, you can add features to it, such as validation and data extraction. This testing capability in Team System contains a very rich set of features, including the ability to write custom code to implement additional capability.

Note The code at this stage can be found in Chapter9\Exercise 7, which is the completed code for Exercise 7. Exercise 8 covers the material in this section.

This kind of test provides testing at the application level for the sales website, but as before, it will be necessary to have a means of placing known data in the database to provide an environment against which to test. In that way, predictable results will come from the activities initiated by the sequence of browser steps. Earlier in this chapter I introduced Rob Smith, who was developing tests for the Sales Wing application. He will also be developing tests for the sales website application. Initially this work will use the web testing features "out of the box," but later Rob expects to develop various custom capability.

Web Testing Individual Pages

Rob plans to test each page individually by accessing its URL directly, providing the parameters needed in the query string, such as ORDERID, as mentioned in the previous section. In addition, he'll write tests that follow a sequence of actions to test a scenario of the application's use. Let's first look at the individual page tests.

To create a web test, Rob can either use Test View or Test Manager. Since he has Visual Studio 2005 Team Edition for Testers, he can display Test Manager, which he prefers. He clicks the New Test button on the Test Tools toolbar (Figure 9-50), which displays the Add New Test dialog box. He selects Web Test, types the name "MyOrders.webtest", and chooses to create a new C# test project called `SalesSiteTests`.

Figure 9-50. *Using the Test Tools toolbar to create a new test*

After Rob clicks OK, an Internet Explorer window opens, as shown in Figure 9-51. He types the URL of the My Orders page and clicks Go, which brings up the My Orders page, shown in Figure 9-52.

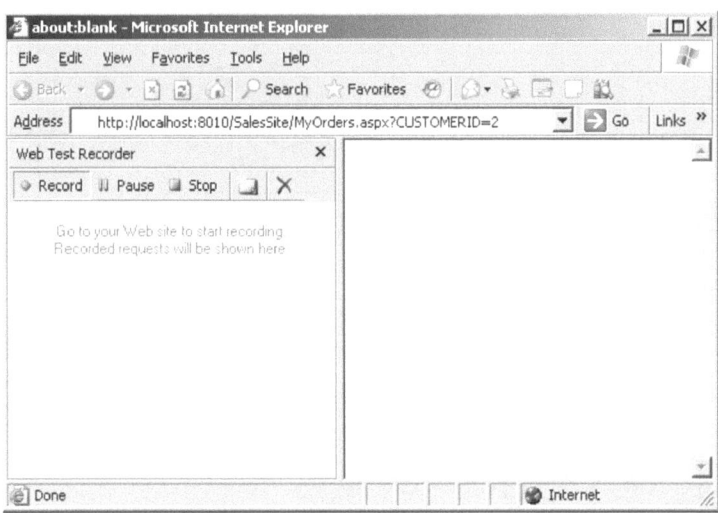

Figure 9-51. *Recording a web test sequence*

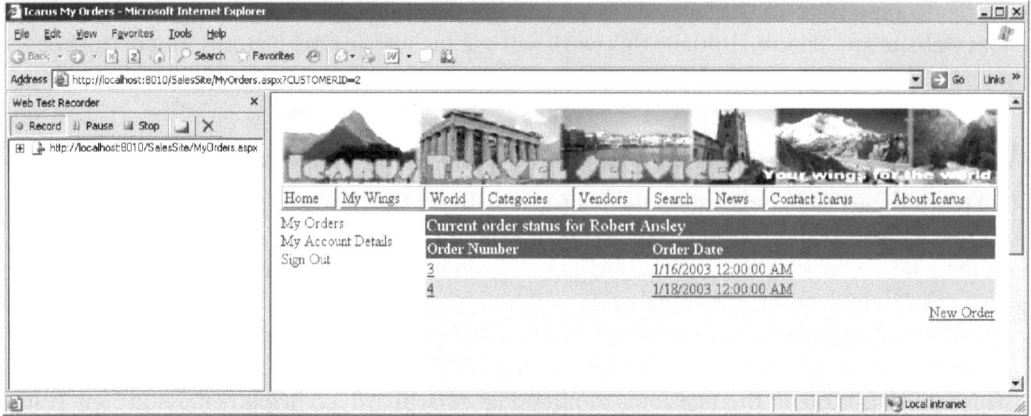

Figure 9-52. *The MyOrders.aspx page under test*

In iteration 1, there is no capability to select the customer, so the one displayed is always the same, and two orders, number 3 and 4, are displayed that Mr. Ansley has made. Simply displaying this page has tested a great deal of the functionality of the application. The first test that Rob will write will consist of just this page. He clicks the Stop button in the left pane to stop recording and looks at the simple test that he has created, shown in Figure 9-53.

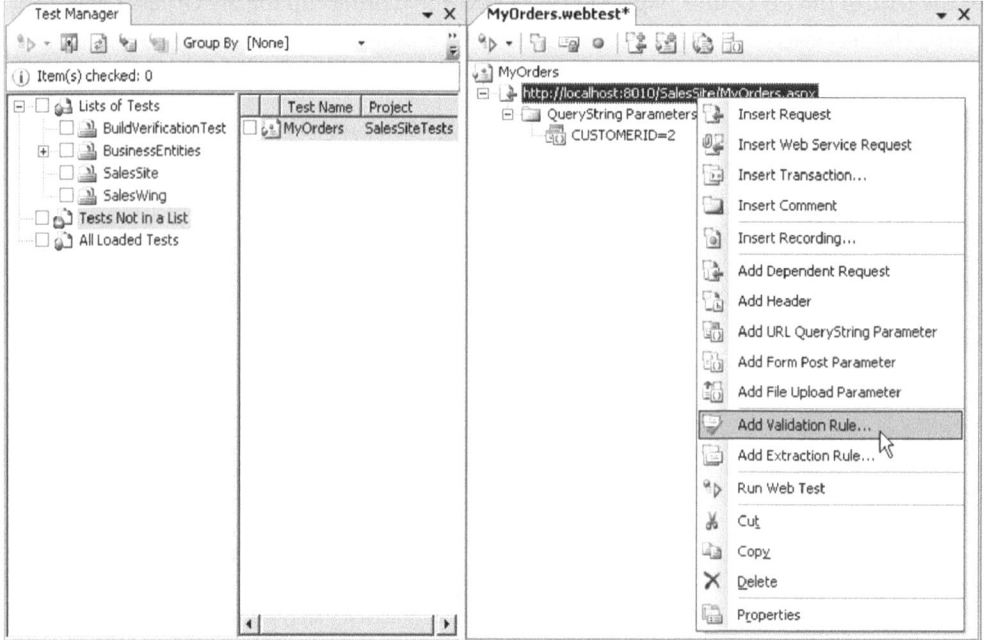

Figure 9-53. *The MyOrders.webtest*

Figure 9-53 shows the Test Manager window and the new `MyOrders.webtest` side by side in a vertical tab group. If you want to see two tabbed documents side by side like this, you right-click in the tab of the one you want to see separately and select New Vertical Tab Group from the context menu. The `MyOrders` test consists of the single request to the URL of the My Orders page. The context menu shown in Figure 9-53 displays the kind of additions that you can make to it. For this simple test, Rob must add a few validation rules that will verify that the displayed page is correct, according to the standard test data loaded into the database. Selecting Add Validation Rule from the context menu displays the Add Validation Rule dialog box, shown in Figure 9-54, where Rob has selected Find Text under Select A Rule.

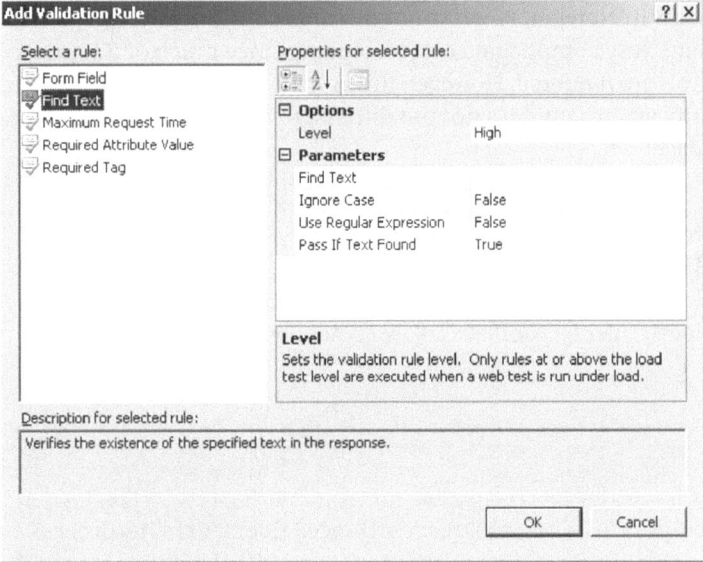

Figure 9-54. *The Add Validation Rule dialog box*

In these kinds of tests, it is not practical to verify that the graphical layout of a particular page is correct and visually acceptable—that probably has to be done manually by viewing the page and making a comparison with documented appearance. The main benefit of web tests is to verify that the web server responds correctly in the right amount of time and that the HTML returned has the correct content (particularly that the correct data is displayed). As you can see in the Add Validation Rule dialog box, we can define quite a few in-built verification checks. You can verify that

- A particular form field has a specified value.

- A particular text string exists in the response.

- The response does not exceed a maximum time.

- A specified attribute on a specified HTML tag has a required value.

- A required tag is present a minimum number of times in the response.

Rob believes he can verify that the page returns the correct data by defining a set of the Find Text type validation rules. Let's look again at Figure 9-52 and list the things that need to be verified:

- The customer name is displayed correctly.

- The number of orders is correct.

- The orders are displayed in the correct order.

- Each order has the correct order number and date.

The best way to define the text that must appear may be to use the View Source option of the browser. The source that appears in Notepad when you right-click on the browser page and select View Source always seems very complicated and forbidding since much of it is generated when the web form controls are rendered. However, this is what the browser receives and this is what the tests must verify against, and it's not too difficult to find the relevant part of the source for the My Orders page:

```
<tr>
 <td style="height: 20px; font-size: large; color: #ffffff;
   background-color: darkolivegreen;" colspan="2">
  <span id="ctl00_ContentPlaceHolder1_Label1">Current order status for </span>
  <span id="ctl00_ContentPlaceHolder1_LabelName">Robert Ansley</span> 
 </td>
</tr>
<tr>
 <td colspan="2">
  <div>
   <table cellspacing="0" border="0" id="ctl00_ContentPlaceHolder1_GridViewOrders"
                         style="height:100%;width:100%;border-collapse:collapse;">
    <tr style="color:White;background-color:DarkOliveGreen;">
      <th scope="col">Order Number</th><th scope="col">Order Date</th>
    </tr>
    <tr>
      <td><a href="OrderDetails.aspx?ORDERID=3">3</a></td>
      <td><a href="OrderDetails.aspx?ORDERID=3">1/16/2003 12:00:00 AM</a></td>
    </tr>
    <tr style="background-color:LightGreen;">
     <td><a href="OrderDetails.aspx?ORDERID=4">4</a></td>
     <td><a href="OrderDetails.aspx?ORDERID=4">1/18/2003 12:00:00 AM</a></td>
    </tr>
   </table>
  </div>
 </td>
</tr>
```

The lines of HTML code shown in bold are the ones that need to be verified, but unfortunately they will not always be laid out in such a neat manner—in fact, you probably can't assume anything about the way the HTML is arranged. Anyway, it is unlikely that the highlighted lines will be broken by <newline> characters, so five verifications corresponding to each of the highlighted strings should work. It's a pity that you can't name the validation rules—they just all appear the same under the Validation Rules folder under the request. I find it a good idea to place the Properties window to the right as a tabbed document in another vertical tab group, as shown in Figure 9-55; that way, you can quickly see what each validation rule is about by clicking on it. I am very enthusiastic about the improved docking capabilities of Visual Studio 2005. You can quickly move things around to suit a particular activity, and then after spending an hour or so working on it, you can put everything back when you've finished.

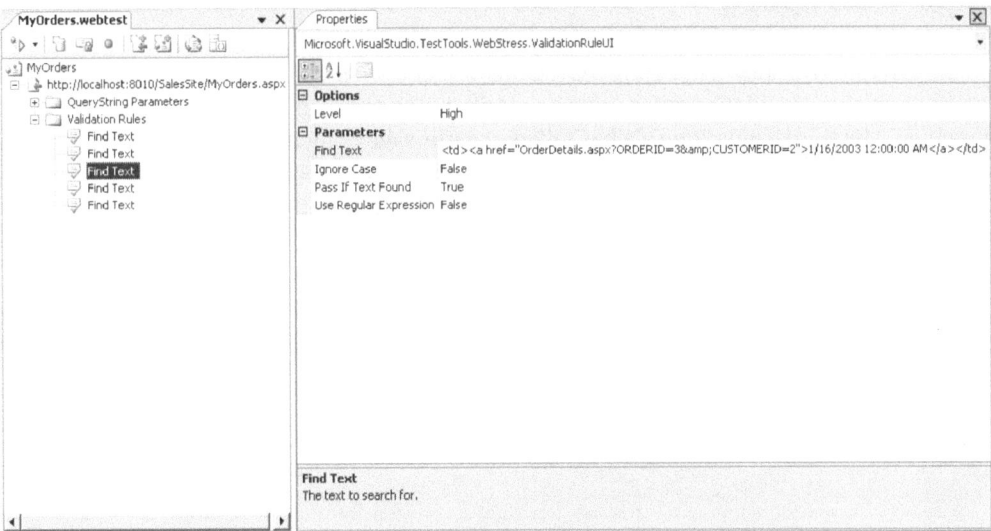

Figure 9-55. *The validation rules added to the single request in the web test*

There doesn't seem to be an obvious way of easily verifying the correctness of the order in which the entries in the list of orders are displayed. Rob could perhaps put the whole sequence of HTML, including both the orders, in a Find Text type validation rule. This however, would mean putting <newline> characters into the string (which do not appear to be allowed) as well as counting tabs and spaces. There are other options; for example, he can make the text string a regular expression, which would allow new lines, tabs, and so forth to be ignored, or he can define a custom validation rule.

For now, the five validation rules that Rob has defined seem to be a pretty reasonable test of the data on this page for iteration 1. To see this test run, Rob clicks the Run Test button at the top left of the test tabbed document, as shown in Figure 9-56.

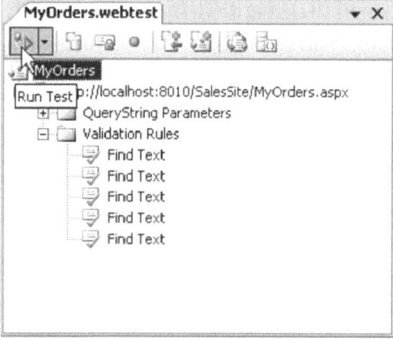

Figure 9-56. *Running a test*

The test report is shown in Figure 9-57. Oops, it failed! Well, the response page looks all right, but one of the validation rules must have failed. Rob clicks the Details tab, as shown in Figure 9-58. The third validation rule has failed; the message (which you can't quite see) says that the required text did not appear in the response. Rob could look at the response by clicking the Response tab, but he can see the problem immediately: there's an extra "9" in the *required* string where the cursor is pointing. It's not the application that's wrong but the test! Rob corrects this and runs the test again by clicking on the Click here to run again link. The test now passes.

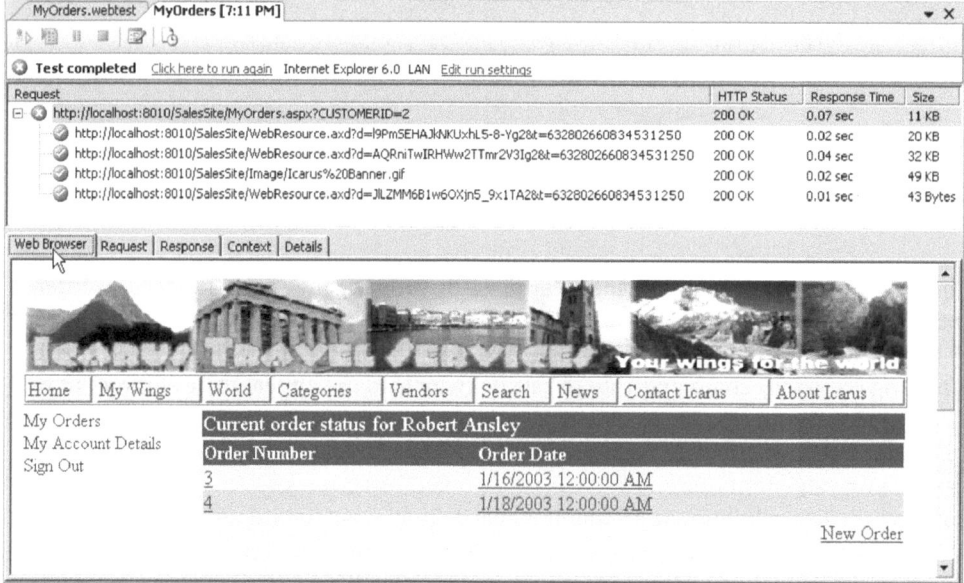

Figure 9-57. *Test report—failure!*

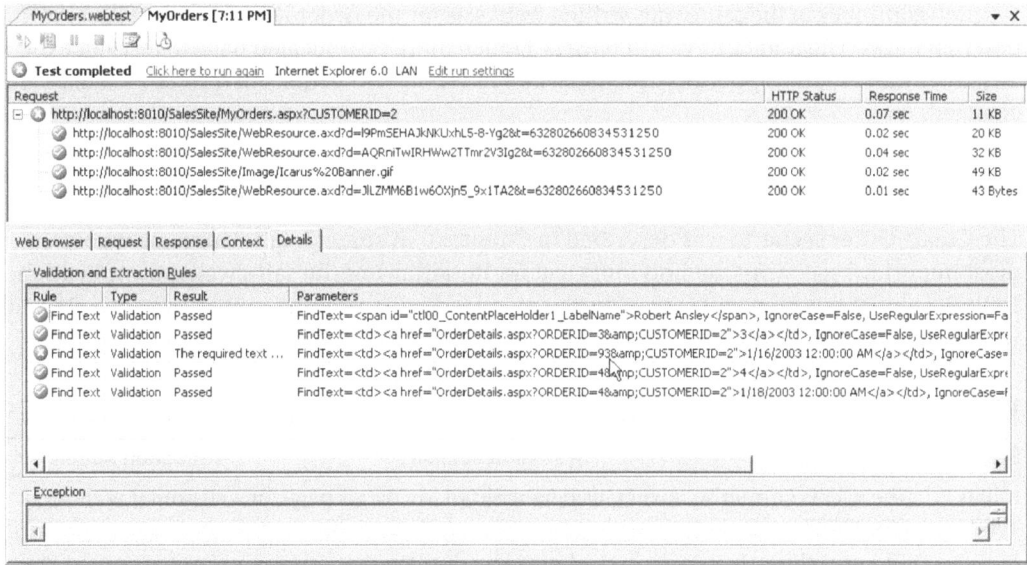

Figure 9-58. *The Details tab on the test report*

Well, that's just one small test, but it illustrates the use of web tests. Rob must write a great deal more tests, but first he places that test in the SalesSite list in Test Manager by dragging it, as shown in Figure 9-59.

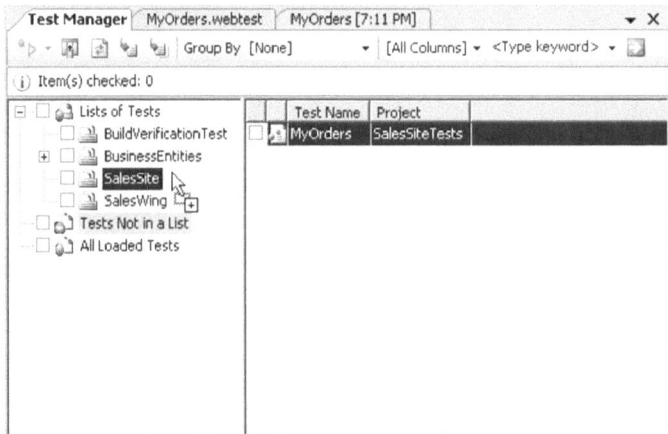

Figure 9-59. *Dragging the new test into the SalesSite list in Test Manager*

Rob continues in the same way, writing web tests for the Order Detail and Add Reservation web pages. The Add Reservation page is a much more complicated page to test since the display of the resource options is updated when the various selections in the combo boxes are changed.

Web Testing the Create Order Scenario

The Create Order scenario was described in Chapter 6 in some detail. This is probably the most important scenario that Rob must test for iteration 1 of the sales website application. Table 9-1 shows this scenario, with a fourth column added, to describe the validation rule that will be added to the request at that point.

Table 9-1. *The Create Order Web Test Scenario*

Step	User Action	System Response	Validation Action
Initial State	The user is currently viewing his personalized My Wings page for a customer without any orders.		
1.	The user clicks the My Orders link.	The system displays the empty My Orders page.	
2.	The user clicks the New Order link.	The system displays My Orders with the new order added.	
3.	The user clicks on the new order.	The system shows the Order Detail page for the new order.	
4.	The user clicks the Add Reservation link.	The system shows the Make Reservation page.	
5a.	The user selects the date on which the reservation is required in the Date date picker control. This control consists of day, month, and year drop-down lists.		
5b.	The user enters a quantity (e.g., 1) into the Quantity text box.		
5c.	The user clicks the Search button.	The system updates the Alternative Options data grid on the page to show all the resources that meet the criteria specified by the user.	Verify that all the expected resource options are present.
6.	The user selects one of the options.	The system shows the option as being selected.	
7.	The user selects one of the resources listed in the Alternative Options data grid view and clicks the Add Reservation button.	A reservation is added to the order and saved to the database. The system displays the Order Detail page modified to show a row added to the Reservations data grid.	Verify that the new reservation row is present.

The simplest way to implement this test is to first initialize the test data by running the CreateTestData.bat batch file. This batch file sets up the database so that it contains a benchmark set of customers, orders, and other data, as you have seen earlier. Then you can record a sequence following the steps in Table 9-1, which will end up leaving an order in the database. Then, if you run the test defined by the recorded sequence, it will create a second order under the customer. The problem is you must be sure which order in the list has the reservation added. To avoid this ambiguity, it is necessary to reinitialize the test data by running CreateTestData.bat each time the test is run. Then you can be sure the My Orders page will always look the same after a new order has been created.

There is another problem. When you record the sequence of steps through the pages, some of the URLs that are used for the requests will have query strings with request parameters added. The two parameters used are the CUSTOMERID and the ORDERID, so a typical URL for a request looks like

```
http://localhost:8010/SalesSite/OrderDetails.aspx?ORDERID=1000&CUSTOMERID=3
```

which is actually the URL used in the third request, as shown in Figure 9-60. This is the request that simulates clicking on the new order that has been created in the My Orders page. The request is to view the order in detail in the Order Detail page (OrderDetails.aspx).

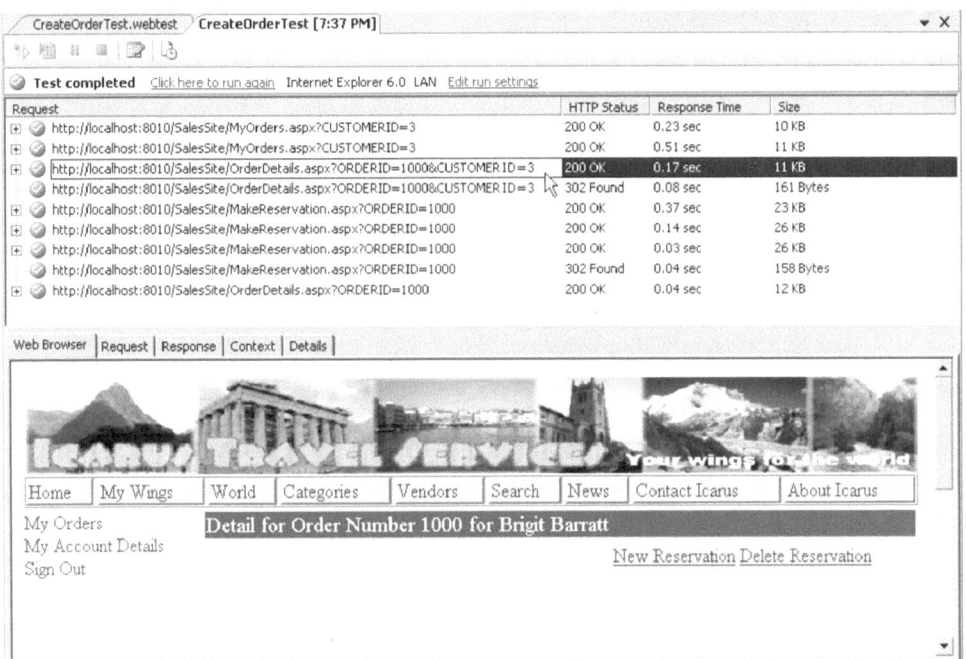

Figure 9-60. *The results of step 3 of the CreateOrder test*

Thinking back to the way the code is written, the ORDERID value of 1000 is the ORDERID field in the new row in the ORDER table of the database. This is added to the URL in that row in the GridView control on the My Orders page, as we saw earlier. The ID field in the ORDER table is an identity field, so the database generated the field's numerical value when the new order was written to the database. The identity definition of the ID field values of the ORDER table causes the values to begin at 1000 and increase by 1 each time a new row is inserted. Therefore, we won't get the same ID twice in normal operation. The command DBCC CHECKIDENT in SQL Server resets an identity; you simply set the identity seed to a new value. This might help, but for the moment let's look at another technique that has more general application in web tests.

Each step in a web test can include validation rules, but you can also include *extraction rules*. An extraction rule can be used at step 2 to extract the ORDERID field value for the new order. That value can then be used as a request parameter in a later request. You create an extraction rule by right-clicking on the step in the web test, as shown in Figure 9-61, and selecting Add Extraction Rule.

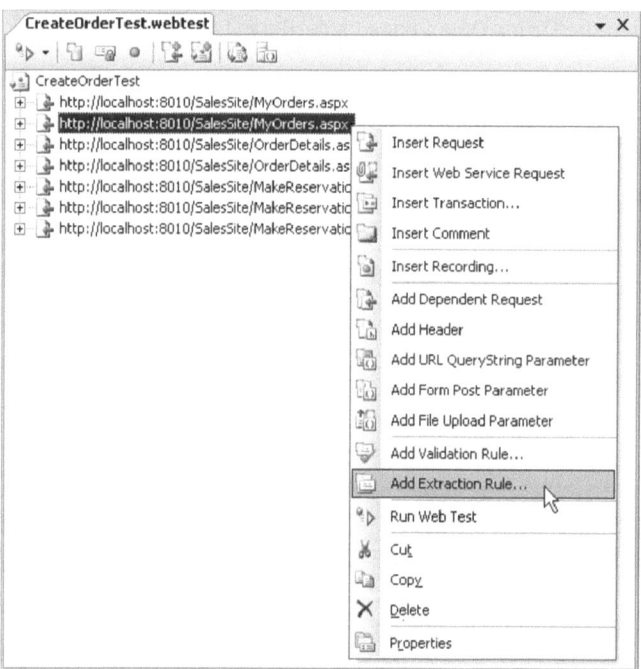

Figure 9-61. *Creating an extraction rule*

Extraction rules allow data to be extracted from the response of the application to a web request. There are various types, which follow the types of the validation rules, but in this case the simple Extract Text rule can be used to extract the ID value of the new order where it appears in the HTML response:

```
<td><a href="OrderDetails.aspx?ORDERID=1000&amp;CUSTOMERID=3">1000</a></td>
<td><a href="OrderDetails.aspx?ORDERID=1000&amp;CUSTOMERID=3">
                                          3/10/2006 3:50:48 PM</a></td>
```

It's rather difficult to use the first and last strings to identify the string that is required, but if "ORDERID=" is chosen as the first and "&" as the last, the extracted string will be "ORDERID=1000&"—which will work as the required parameter in the next HTTP request in the web test. You can specify in the rule whether to extract the first occurrence of the string defined this way or some later numbered occurrence defined by an index. As we explained earlier, you can define extractions that result in the creation of context parameters, which you can reference in later steps. In Figure 9-62, Rob has defined the extraction rule to generate a context parameter with the defined name of ORDERID, and he can bind later settings to that context parameter.

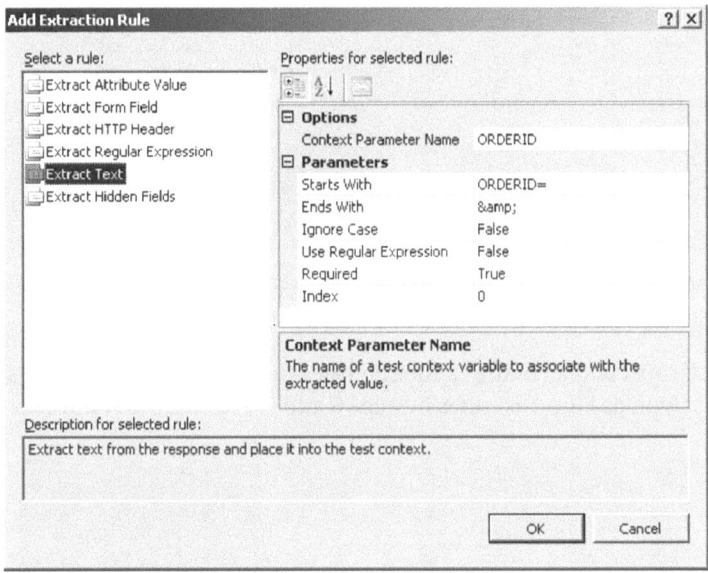

Figure 9-62. *The Add Extraction Rule dialog box*

During recording of the sequence, Visual Studio automatically generated query string parameters for each of the requests that used them by simply copying the value of the parameter at that point into the sequence. This won't work, as we have explained, so Rob changes the value of the ORDERID query string parameter so that it takes its value from the ORDERID context parameter, as shown in Figure 9-63. He does this by selecting the query string parameter in the CreateOrderTest definition in the left pane and displaying its Properties window on the right. The Value field has a drop-down from which Rob can select any of the context parameters that exist at this point in the test. Note that the string extracted is already URL encoded, since it is already a URL in an <A> tag—a happy accident—so Ron leaves the URL Encode option set to false. He must follow this procedure at every other step in the web test that uses the ORDERID, so that they all use the context parameter as opposed to the constant value.

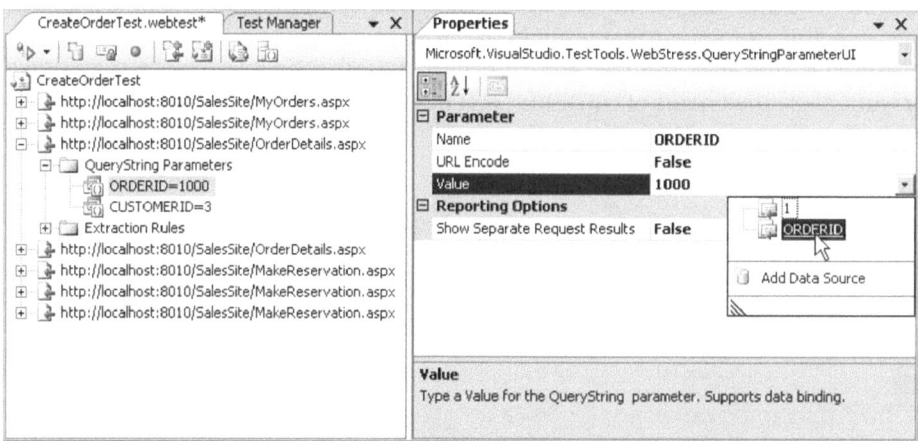

Figure 9-63. *Setting the query string parameter to use the result of an extraction rule*

To finish this web test, Rob must add all of the validation rules to satisfy the requirements included in Table 9-1. He adds them as Find Text rules in steps 5 and 7. There are no Find Text rules for the earlier steps.

Step 5c

```
Find Text: "<td>88</td><td>France</td><td>Seine River Cruises</td>
            <td>Dinner Cruise on Seine</td><td>100.00</td><td>100.00</td>"
Find Text: "<td>23</td><td>Mexico</td><td>Sachez Guest House</td>
            <td>Single Room</td><td>100.00</td><td>100.00</td>"
Find Text: "<td>49</td><td>USA</td><td>San Pedro Hotel</td>
            <td>Double Room</td><td>100.00</td><td>100.00</td>"
Find Text: "<td>62</td><td>France</td><td>Seine River Cruises</td>
            <td>Morning Cruise on Seine</td><td>100.00</td><td>100.00</td>"
Find Text: "<td>75</td><td>France</td><td>Seine River Cruises</td>
            <td>Afternoon Cruise on Seine</td><td>100.00</td><td>100.00</td>"
Find Text: "<td>88</td><td>France</td><td>Seine River Cruises</td>
            <td>Dinner Cruise on Seine</td><td>100.00</td><td>100.00</td>"
```

Step 7

```
Find Text: "<td><a>Seine River Cruises</a></td>
                    <td>Morning Cruise on Seine</td><td>4/10/2006 12:00:00
                    AM</td><td>1</td><td>100.0000</td><td>100.0000</td>"
```

In step 5c the validation rule checks that all of the entries in the Alternative Options `GridView` are present in the HTML sent to the browser. The step 7 rule verifies that the new reservation appears in the Reservations `GridView` in the order details.

Summary

In this chapter, we described integration aspects of the development of the formal part of iteration 1, and we introduced several new Team System features. In addition, you saw how the layers of the Sales Wing, List Wing, and Sales Site applications work together.

You first saw the development of the listing business objects and their datasets in Visual Basic. After Rahul had finished this VB work, he had to merge his code with Angela's. You learned how merging works when multiple checkout is permitted. Then, we described how the team build capability of Team System can be used to build the project.

You watched Charles first integrate the Sales Wing presentation application with the sales business objects and then debug the code to see that it worked correctly. Ed then integrated the Sales Site application with the same business objects. You saw how the object data source works when query string parameters must be used. Finally, you saw some examples of Team System's web tests, focusing on the sales website.

In the next chapter we'll look at using Team System to evaluate performance.

CHAPTER 10

Web and Performance Testing

This chapter examines performance testing of the Sales Site application. You'll learn how the tools available in Visual Studio 2005 Team Edition can be used to characterize and improve the performance of the application being developed by the Icarus team. While the developers move on to iteration 2, the test team continues to develop functional and performance testing of iteration 1.

Load Testing of the Sales Site

Visual Studio 2005 Team Edition for Testers provides a category of tests called *load tests* that can be created and managed under Test Manager. A load test is made up of a collection of other existing tests arranged in a defined percentage mix, and can contain any kind of test except a manual one. As well as a mix of tests, the load test can simulate a mix of users, a mix of different browsers and networks, and a load profile that can change with time. The load test can be run either on one machine or on an array of test machines organized as agents and controllers. Load tests can specify performance counters to gather as part of the test report; these counters can be gathered from the test machine or the agents and controllers, as well as from the target machine.

Load Testing of the Order Creation Scenario

In the previous chapter you followed Rob Smith as he built a test of the order creation scenario, which executed a sequence of requests to the Sales Site web application of Icarus Enterprise 3.1. To recap, the sequence was as follows:

1. Accessing the My Orders page for a specific customer

2. Creating a new order

3. Requesting the Order Detail page of the new order

4. Opening the Add Reservation page

5. Adding simple search criteria to that page and searching for resource options

6. Adding a new reservation to the order

This is a good example of the critical functionality of that site, but we cannot assume that customers will always be making new orders. Customers will very likely spend a good deal of time browsing the resources offered by Icarus before they make an order, and they will also spend some time reviewing their orders. A representative load test of the Sales Site application should therefore include a mix of tests—perhaps 70 percent browsing resources, 10 percent creating orders, and 20 percent reviewing orders. The browse capability, however, is not included in the iteration 1 functionality, so a fair test at iteration 1 might be 33 percent placing orders and 67 percent reviewing orders, so that twice as much time is spent reviewing orders as placing them.

Note The code at this point can be found in `Chapter 10\Chapter10Start`. Exercise 10-1 is relevant to this section.

Before the `AddReservation` web test defined in Chapter 9 can be used in a load test, it needs a small modification. Load tests are made up of a collection of other tests that are already defined. As I said earlier, a test in the collection can be any type of test except a manual test, but it must be able to be run repetitively. The `AddReservation` web test used an extraction rule to extract the `ORDERID` each time a new order was created, and made that value available for use in the request parameters of later requests. The extraction rule was defined as an Extract Text type of rule that defined the beginning string as "ORDERID=" and the ending string as "&". This extracted a string such as "ORDERID=1234&", which was then used as the value of the query string parameter ORDERID. This rule relies on the fact that in the HTML for the page listing the orders for a customer, the My Orders page, there is a list of orders, each of which has a URL within a hyperlink tag with the first parameter in the form `"ORDERID=1234"`.

This procedure for the extraction rule is not quite correct—you might expect the request that included the extracted value to contain something like `"ORDERID=ORDERID=1234&"`—but it did seem to work! Anyway, web tests can do better than that, and Rob will need to change the rule in any case because he needs to extract the *last order* that was added and use its `ORDERID` value in the next query string. This is because new orders will be added repetitively and always the latest order added must be the one that is opened.

There is another type of extraction rule called Extract Regular Expression, which allows you to define a regular expression that will return a string extracted from the HTML response. A regular expression such as

```
(?<=ORDERID\=).*?(?=&amp;)
```

will extract the text "2224" in the following:

```
<a href="OrderDetails.aspx?ORDERID=2224&amp;CUSTOMERID=3">
    2224</a></td><td>
<a href="OrderDetails.aspx?ORDERID=2224&amp;CUSTOMERID=3">
    3/13/2006 4:06:12 PM</a></td>
```

and will obtain that string by examining the bolded portion of text, where "ORDERID=" is the string that matches the look-back condition and "&" satisfies the look-forward condition.

However, this code still returns only the first instance of this specified ORDERID value text in the page. Better writers of regular expressions than myself may be able to write one that will return only the very last instance of this text in the HTML response, but it does not matter because there is a much more powerful way to write extraction rules. You can write *custom extraction rules* in the form of a class that inherits from a class called `Microsoft.VisualStudio.TestTools.WebTesting.ExtractionRule`. Rob decides to implement an extraction rule called `ExtractLastOrderId`. To do this, he first creates a new project as a C# class library in the ApplicationTests solution folder. He adds a reference to `Microsoft.VisualStudio.QualityTools.WebTestFramework`, defines a new class, and types in the following code:

```csharp
using System;
using System.Collections.Generic;
using System.Text;
using Microsoft.VisualStudio.TestTools.WebTesting;

namespace ExtractionRules
{
  public class ExtractLastOrderId : ExtractionRule
  {
    public override void Extract(object sender, ExtractionEventArgs e)
    {
      e.Success = false;
      string orderId = "";

      int startIndex = e.Response.BodyString.LastIndexOf("ORDERID=") + 8;

      if (startIndex != -1)
      {
        int endIndex = e.Response.BodyString.IndexOf("&", startIndex);

        if (endIndex != -1)
        {
          orderId = e.Response.BodyString.Substring(startIndex,endIndex-startIndex);

          e.WebTest.Context.Add(this.ContextParameterName, orderId);
          e.Success = true;
        }
      }

      if (e.Success)
        e.Message = "Extracted ORDERID.";
      else
        e.Message = "No ORDERID extracted.";
    }

    // Etc.
  }
}
```

This section of code simply finds the last occurrence in the entire e.Response.BodyString of the string between "ORDERID=" and "&". Once this is written and compiled, a reference to the ExtractionRules project must be added to the test project that needs to use it—in this case SalesSiteTests—and then it will appear in the left pane of the Add Extraction Rule dialog box (shown in Chapter 9, Figure 9-62). The extraction rule at step two must then be changed to use the custom extraction rule.

In addition, the capacity figure for the resource being reserved must be set artificially high (say 10,000) in the test database. This is because the logic that determines the resource options available uses the resource capacity to determine if any reservable places are available, and the available places are reduced by all the existing reservations. In a load test there may be thousands of reservations made, as the same step is repeated for a long period, so the resource cannot be allowed to run out of capacity. Once these corrections are made, the CreateOrder test can be placed in a load test.

Creating a Load Test for the Sales Site

Load tests are created like any other kind of test: from Test View, from Test Manager, from the Test toolbar, or from the Test menu.

Note The code at this point can be found in Chapter 10\Exercise 1. Exercise 10-2 demonstrates the material in this section.

Rob decides to create a load test, which he'll call SalesLoad1.loadtest. He selects Load Test in the Add New Test dialog box and places the test in the SalesSiteTests project. This starts the New Load Test Wizard, which I'll explain in some detail so that you can see the extensive features available. The first page, shown in Figure 10-1, introduces the features that the wizard will help you define. These include a load test scenario consisting of a set of tests, a load pattern, a test mix, a browser mix, and a network mix. You also define a set of counters from target computers from which you collect performance data and settings for duration and description.

Clicking the Next button moves to page 2, shown in Figure 10-2, where the scenario is given a name and the "think time" (which we'll define in a moment) may be specified. Load tests are made up of one or more scenarios. Each scenario is an encapsulation of a particular kind of workload. For example, with Icarus 3.1, home customers accessing the sales website to create and review orders might be one scenario. Home customers browsing resources without making a purchase might be another. Travel agents accessing the web services via the SalesWing application might be another. Each of these would provide separate components of the load on the web server array, the database, and the network, and might need to be tested separately. When a load test is run, only one scenario must be selected as the active scenario for that test run.

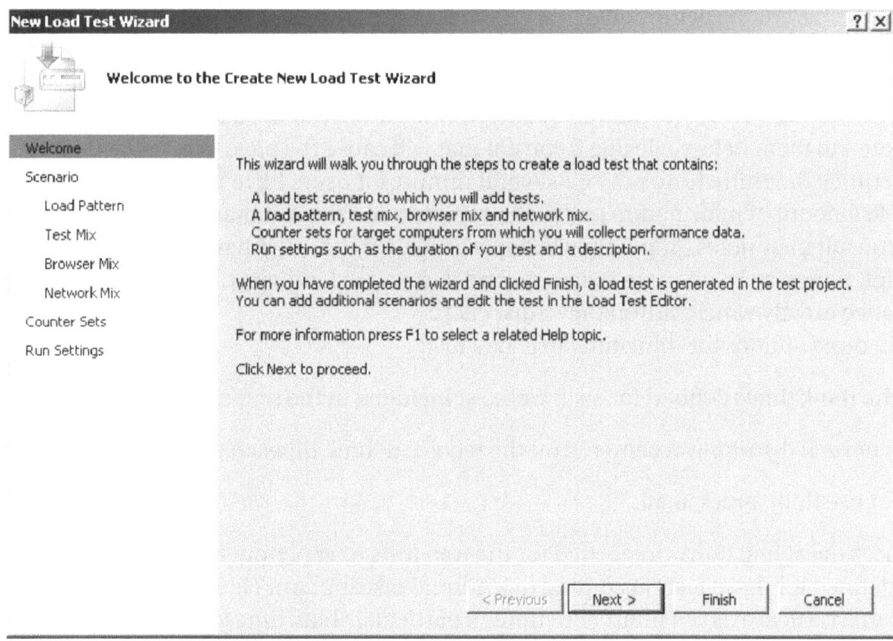

Figure 10-1. *New Load Test Wizard page 1—introductory information*

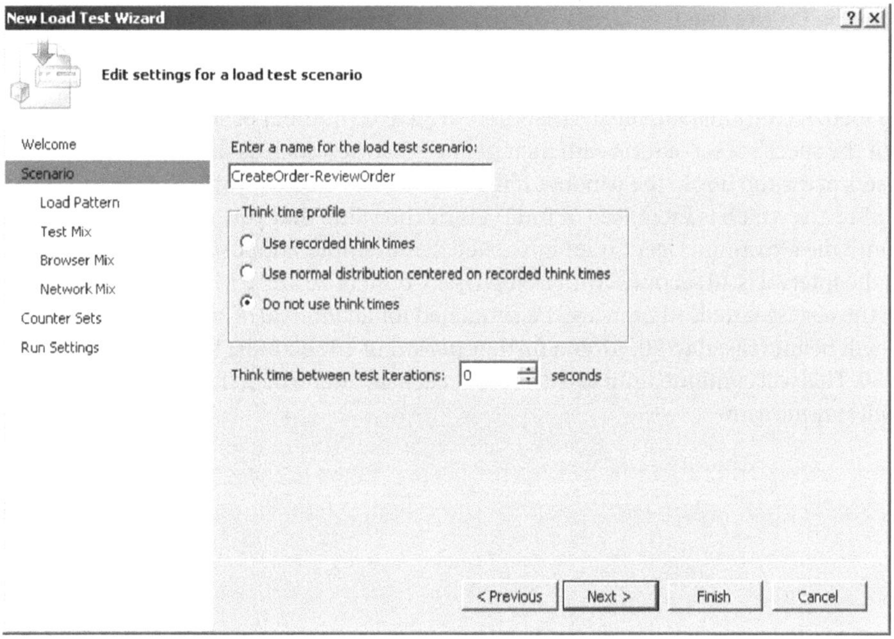

Figure 10-2. *New Load Test Wizard page 2—think times*

Think time is part of the definition of a scenario and specifies the time that elapses for each individual user between tests. It is an attempt to simulate normal human behavior. In the definition of their scenarios, web tests also allow think time to be defined between each of their steps. This simulates realistic human behavior, since users will need to look at the page that is presented to them before clicking a control that will cause the page to be posted to the server. Sometimes the think time may be several minutes if users have to read and digest a considerable amount of information and make complex decisions; it may also include time for users to consult their notes, or possibly talk to a client. On the other hand, in some simple pages the think time may be no more than a second if users are familiar with a sequence and know in advance exactly which button they must click.

There are three options for think time in a load test:

1. Use the think times defined for each web test included in the scenario.

2. Use a normal distribution centered on the recorded think times in the web tests.

3. Do not use think times at all.

Option 2 causes the actual think times used for the web tests to vary from the original think time values defined for those tests according to a normal distribution. This means that if we were to plot on a vertical axis the number of times a particular think time value occurred for a particular web test within a load test and plot the values of think time on the horizontal axis, we would see the familiar bell curve centered around the value defined in the web test for that step. If you are trying to simulate a particular working environment, think times are important, but if you are trying to stress the system as much as possible, then you might set these values to 0. Rob clicks the Do Not Use Think Times radio button so the think times will be 0 for his first test.

On the next wizard page, shown in Figure 10-3, you have the choice of specifying a constant load or a step load. A constant load means that there are a fixed number of simulated users that each carry out the specified set of tests with their defined features, such as think time. You set the number of users at the top box in the window. If the step load is selected, you can specify a starting number of users, which is increased at intervals by the value that you set in the Step User Count field until the Maximum User Count is reached. For example, suppose Start User Count is set to 10 and the interval is 10 seconds, with a Step User Count of 10 and a Maximum User Count of 200. When the test is started, 10 users will be simulated for an interval of 10 seconds and then the number will be increased to 20. After a further period of 10 seconds, the number will be increased to 30. This will continue until 200 users are reached, after which the number of simulated users will stay the same.

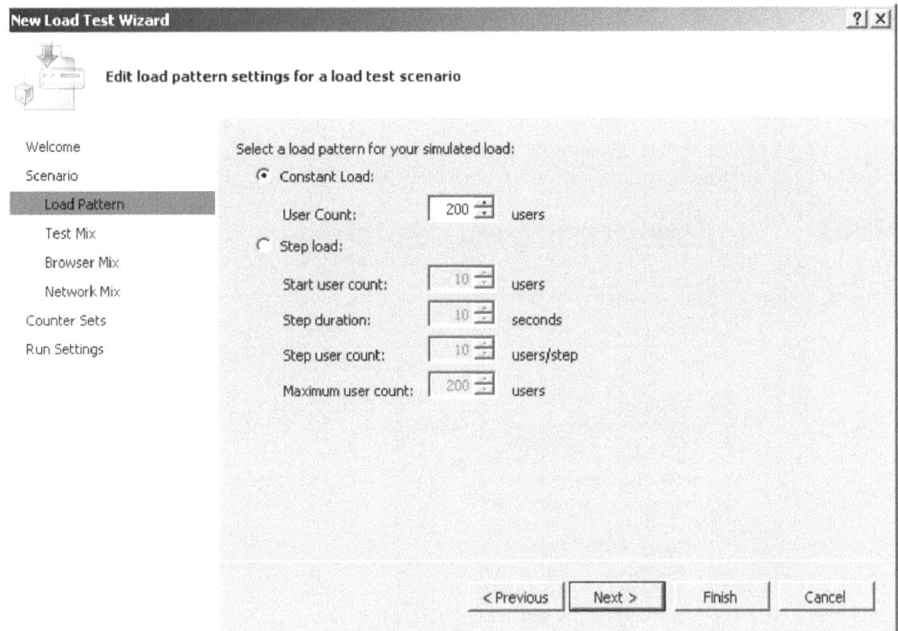

Figure 10-3. *New Load Test Wizard page 3—Constant load or Step load*

The Step load option is useful when you need to examine how the system behaves with increasing load. As the number of users increases, the values of various counters from the machines will change until eventually the system reaches a limit at which it fails to operate to its specifications. Usually this will mean that response times become longer than those that were deemed acceptable when the system was specified. In some cases it may mean that failure occurs, and the system does not respond at all or data becomes corrupted. It is very important to identify situations in which serious problems such as these occur and to take steps to overcome such problems early in the project. Remember that at the end of Chapter 4, the performance requirements of the system were specified; these are the values that need to be verified during these and later performance tests. For this particular load test, Rob sets the number of users to a constant value of 200.

Figure 10-4 shows the next page of the wizard, in which tests are added to the scenario. The wizard initially shows no tests in the scenario. To add tests you click the Add button, which displays the Add Tests dialog box, also shown in Figure 10-4. You select tests in the left pane and add them to the scenario by clicking the > button or remove them by clicking the < button. Rob adds the two web tests that he has defined, CreateOrderTest and ReviewOrderTest, and clicks OK.

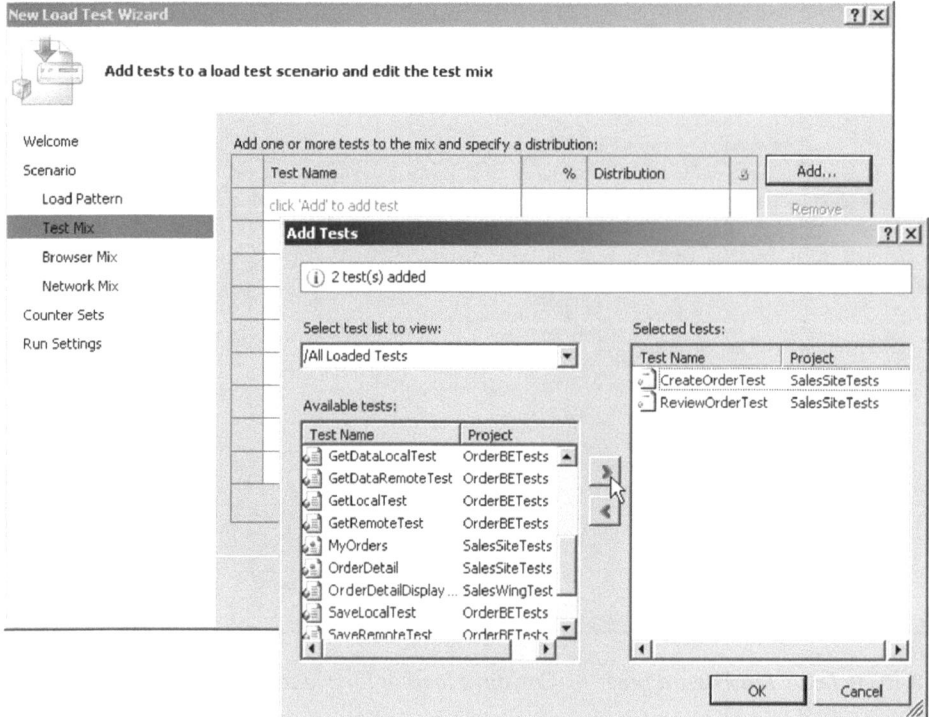

Figure 10-4. *New Load Test Wizard page 4—adding tests to the load test scenario*

In Figure 10-5, the distribution of the two tests is specified. Earlier I said that the team felt that at this stage a sales website customer was twice as likely to be reviewing their existing orders as making a new order. Rob has therefore set the distribution at 33 percent Create Order and 67 percent Review Order. These percentage values specify the *probability* that a particular virtual user will run a given test at a time when a new test is started by that user, where 0 percent indicates that a test will never be run and 100 percent indicates a certainty that it will run every time. On average we would expect to see twice as many review tests as create tests, but—like the real world—there is a small possibility that all users will decide to create an order at the same time. The unlikely *can* happen and we might expect our response times to suffer in those circumstances, but we would not want data to become corrupted.

Clicking Next takes you to page 5, shown in Figure 10-6, where you can define the browser mix. It may be that the performance of a particular application is dependent on the type of browser used, and this page gives you the option to add different browsers to the test and specify the statistical distribution of browsers among users. For example, you might decide that 80 percent of your users will work with Internet Explorer 6.0 and 20 percent with Internet Explorer 5.5. In this case there would be an 80 percent probability that a particular virtual user would use IE 6.0 and a 20 percent probability that the user would use IE 5.5. Simulated browsers are allocated to virtual users based on these probabilities when the test starts. To keep things simple, Rob selects 100 percent IE 6.0 for this test.

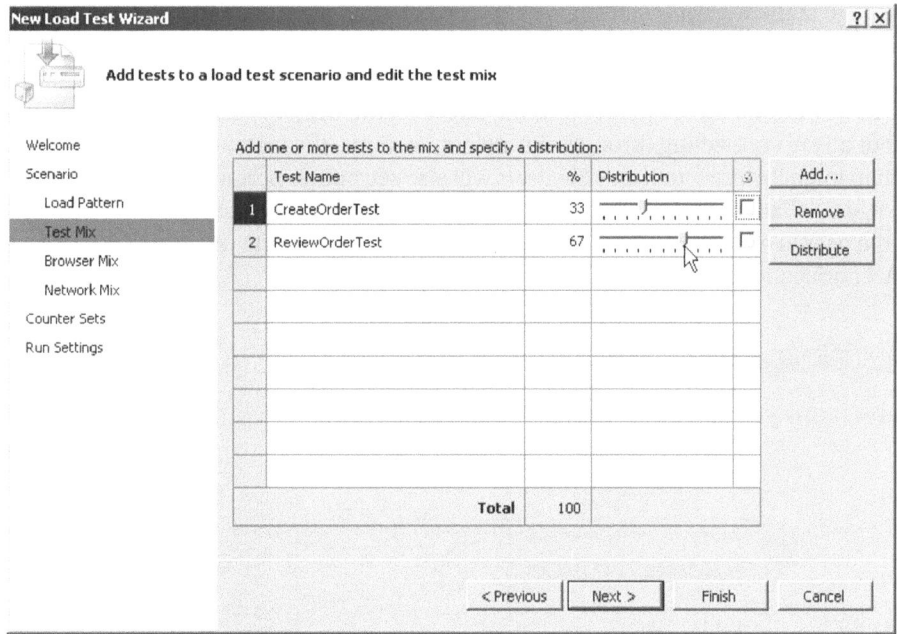

Figure 10-5. *New Load Test Wizard page 4—adjusting the distribution between the two tests*

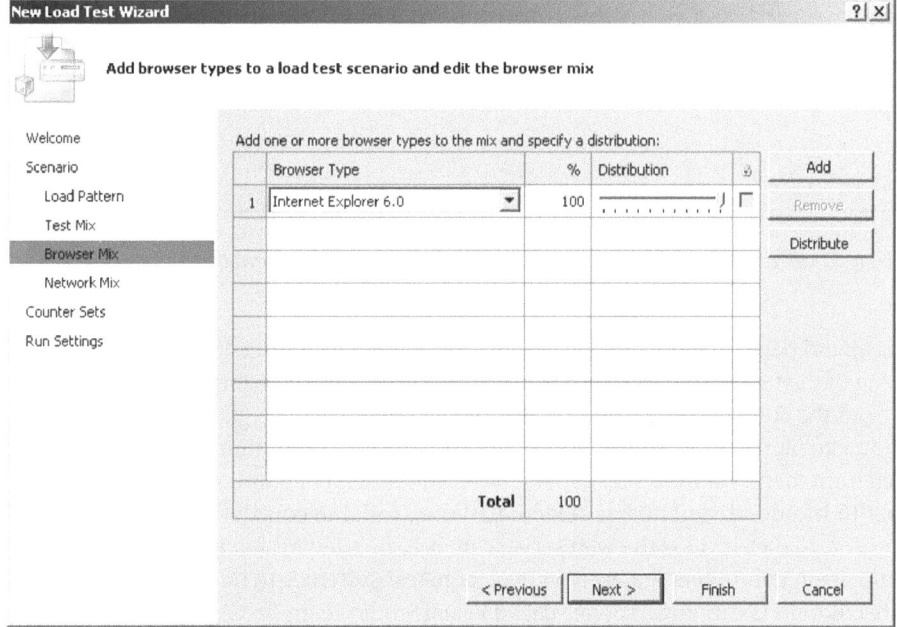

Figure 10-6. *New Load Test Wizard page 5—adjusting the distribution between browser types*

The next page of the wizard (Figure 10-7) allows you to add different network types to the test. There is a selection of network types that are available (such as LAN), different speeds of DSL connection, and dial-ups. Simulating different network connections may be important in determining both the load on the server and the effect on the user. For example, if there are many users but all are connecting through dial-up connections, the load on the server will be a lot lighter than might be expected, and the users will also see poorer performance. Such a situation could suggest changes to the design of the application, such as reducing the amount of data sent to the user in each page. For this test, Rob chooses to make the test work 100 percent through a LAN connection.

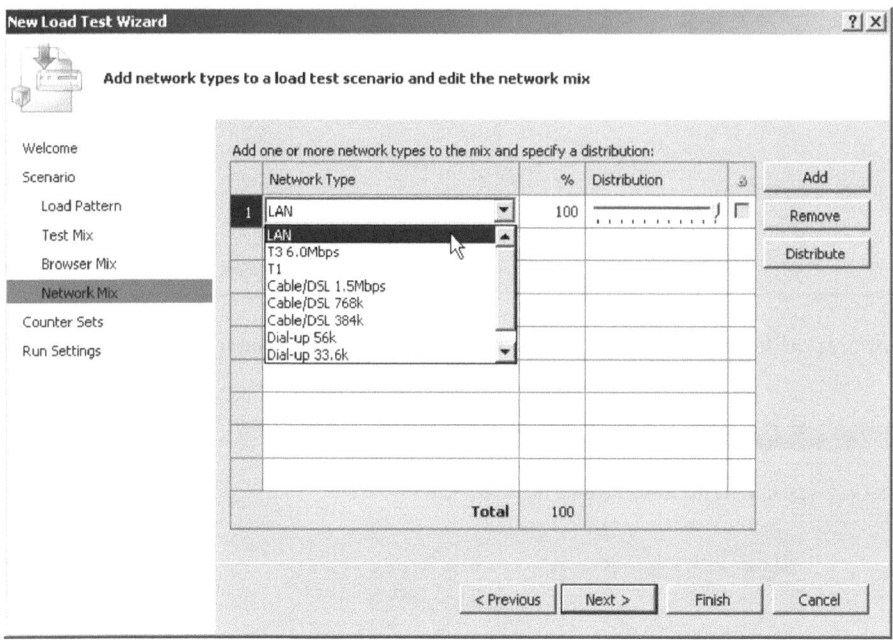

Figure 10-7. *New Load Test Wizard page 6—adjusting the distribution between network types*

The next wizard page (Figure 10-8) allows you to specify the counters to be captured during the running of the test. By default, the LoadTest and Controller categories of counter will be gathered from the control computers and the Agent category will be gathered from agent computers. You can name other computers as well and specify the counter categories that are to be obtained from them. For example, Rob has selected the server computer icarus-web-tst1 as a computer to be added, and he has selected all the available counter categories from it. The computer icarus-web-tst1 is the web server that is to be used for load testing. Controller computers and agent computers are used when a large test system is to be constructed. Agent computers are computers running a service called Visual Studio Team Test Agent. This Microsoft product is separate from TFS and Visual Studio, and acts as a source of virtual users to provide requests to the web server or array of servers under test. Controller computers run a service called Visual Studio Team Test Controller that controls the agent service instances. At present, Rob is simply planning to run the load test locally from his desktop GN-RSMITH computer, against the icarus-web-tst1 server.

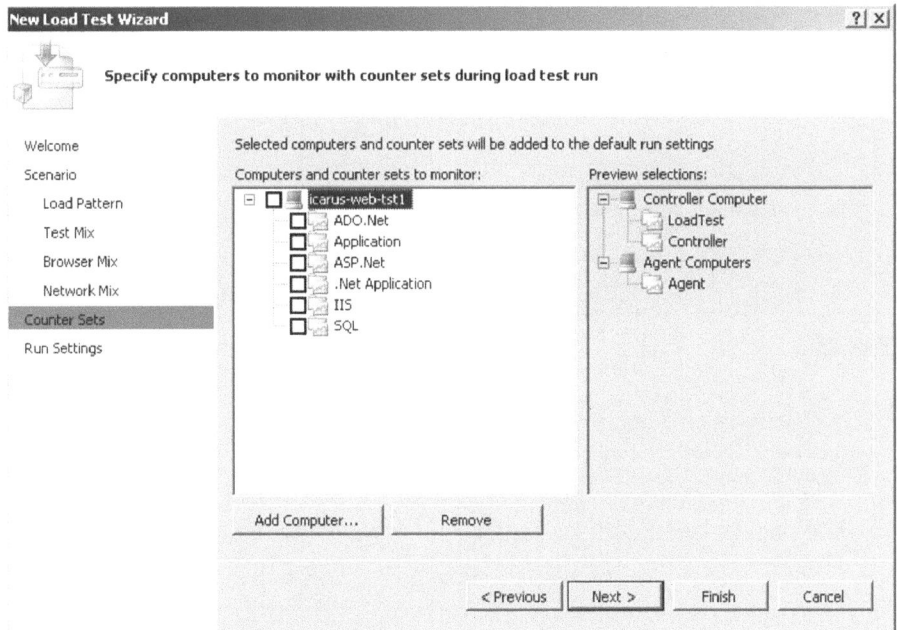

Figure 10-8. *New Load Test Wizard page 7—adding counters*

The last page of the wizard (Figure 10-9) lets you specify the timing and other settings for the load test. A warm-up period may be specified in hours, minutes, and seconds followed by a duration for the running of the actual test. During the warm-up period, the tests run in their specified manner but data samples are not recorded. Following this, the test runs for the period specified in the run duration and samples are recorded. The sampling rate is the interval between successive samples. More than one set of run settings can be specified for a load test, so some sort of description can be entered on this wizard page, which may be useful in identifying the settings to use when running the load test. You can specify the Maximum Error details option to avoid consuming a large amount of database space with an excessive number of errors. Errors that occur due to a failure of a particular web test, or other tests, are included in these details.

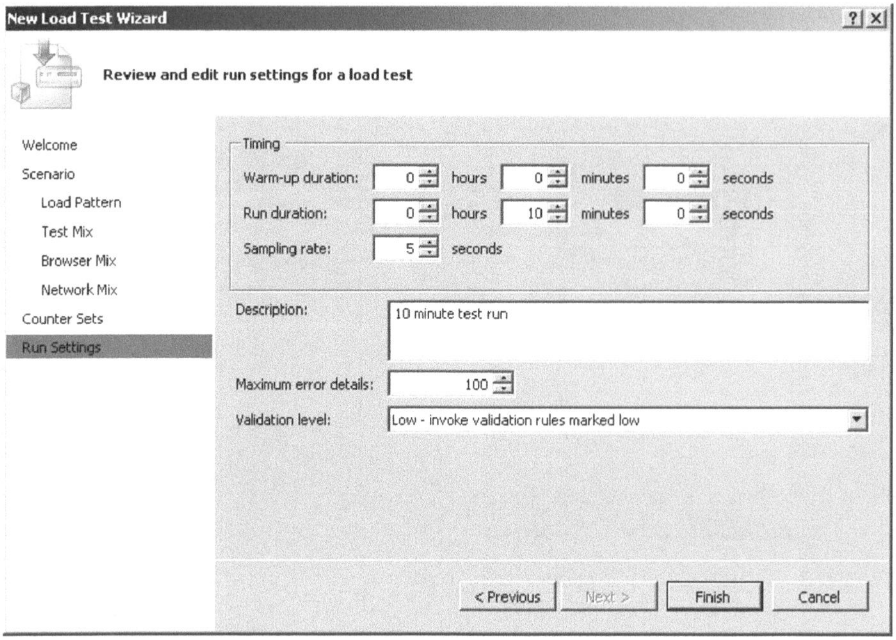

Figure 10-9. *New Load Test Wizard page 8—timing and other run settings*

Finally, on this page, you can specify the validation level for the run settings. When defining a web test validation rule, you give it a validation level of low, medium, or high. The value that you specify on this page of the wizard determines which validation rules are applied. If you set this value to Low—invoke validation rules marked low, only those validation rules marked as low level will be applied. If you set it to Medium—invoke validation rules marked medium or low, only those rules with medium or low levels will be applied. If you set the validation level of the run settings to High—invoke all validation rules, all the validation rules will be applied. This feature allows you to define a minimum set of validation rules that can be run quickly and assigned as low level, whereas you can define the more thorough validation rules, which take longer to execute, at medium or high level and leave them out of most load test runs.

Rob leaves all the settings at their defaults: zero warm-up duration, a 10-minute run, and the other settings as shown in Figure 10-9. He then clicks Finish.

The load test, as a tabbed document, is shown in Figure 10-10. As you can see, Rob has placed the Properties window also as a tabbed document to its right in another vertical tab group. All of the features of the test that Rob defined during the execution of the wizard can be modified from this page. For instance, Figure 10-10 shows that Rob has selected the scenario created by the wizard, CreateOrder-ReviewOrder, on the left so that he can view and edit the properties for that scenario on the right. If for example, Rob needs to change the test mix, he can simply click on the ellipsis to the right of the Test Mix item in the Properties window to open a dialog box called Edit Test, similar to the one shown in Figure 10-5. This dialog box allows him to adjust the probabilities of a client running a particular test.

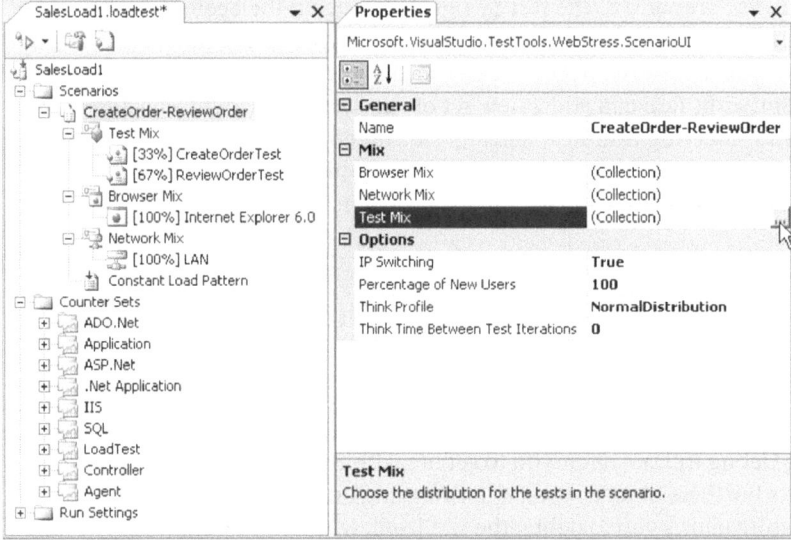

Figure 10-10. *The SalesLoad1 Load test*

Rob decides that perhaps, after all, he should define a two-minute warm-up time for the set of run settings that he defined during the wizard sequence. He can do this by clicking on the Run Settings1 entry under the Run Settings folder on the left and typing in a new value for the warm-up duration, as shown in Figure 10-11.

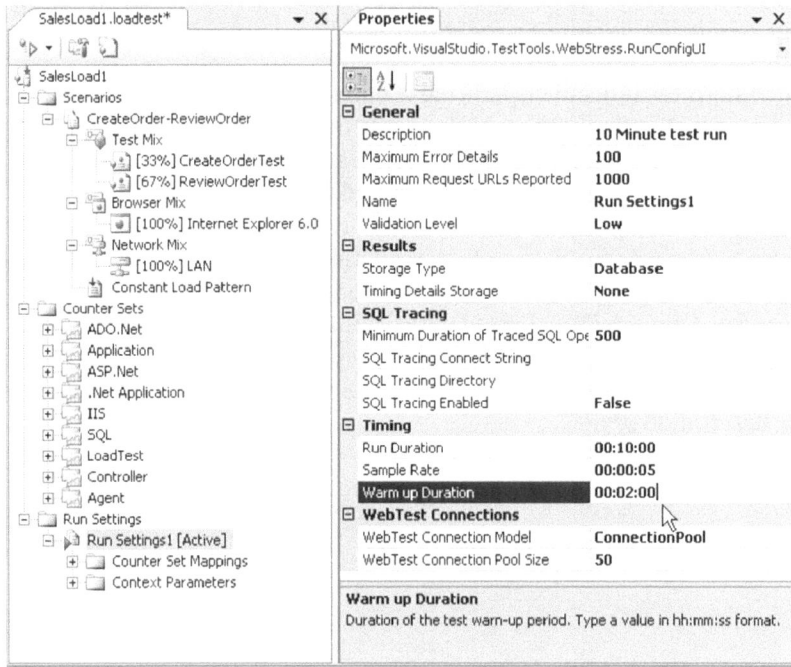

Figure 10-11. *Correcting the warm-up time setting*

Also, he can add a new scenario to the test by right-clicking on the Scenarios folder in the test document on the left of the window in Figure 10-11 and selecting Add Scenario from the context menu. This will invoke the pages dealing with a scenario definition from the wizard that we just saw. Similarly, Rob can add a new set of run settings by right-clicking on the Run Settings folder and selecting Add Run Setting. He can edit the run settings from the Properties menu. Rob can also select Manage Counter Sets from the context menu or from the toolbar within the test to redisplay the dialog box shown in Figure 10-8 and modify the counter configuration.

Running the Load Test Against the Sales Site

Having created a load test, making use of two existing web tests, Rob would now like to run it against the Sales Site application that has been installed on `icarus-web-tst1`. To do this, he simply clicks the run icon at the top-right corner of the test. There's also the option to debug the test, but choosing Debug will not allow you to set breakpoints inside the code that implements Sales Site and its business objects, even if it is running on the same machine as the test. Instead, the debug feature allows you to debug the test itself, which is very useful if you have created custom extraction or validation rules, and indeed there is also a coded version of the test that can be generated and modified. To debug the server, you would have to attach the debugger to the process that Internet Information Services (IIS) creates to perform the ASP.NET work, `w3wp.exe` on Windows Server 2003.

Note The code at this point can be found in `Chapter 10\Exercise 2`. Exercise 10-3 demonstrates the material in this section.

Clicking the run icon starts the test and displays the window shown in Figure 10-12, which is indeed a mine of information. Starting at the top left, we see the Counters pane, which contains a tree view that splits the counter information in various ways. First there is the Overall set of test counters, including those counters relating to pages and requests such as requests per second, percentage of pages meeting their goal, and average response time. Then there are counters grouped under the CreateOrder-ReviewOrder scenario that we defined. Within this the counters are grouped into the two tests, `CreateOrderTest` and `ReviewOrderTest`. Here we can see such counters as Avg. Requests/Test, Passed (or Failed) Tests/Sec, Failed Tests, Passed Tests, and so forth. There are also counters arranged under each page within each test in the Pages node, so that for the `CreateOrder` test we can view the average page time for a specific page, such as the Make Reservation page.

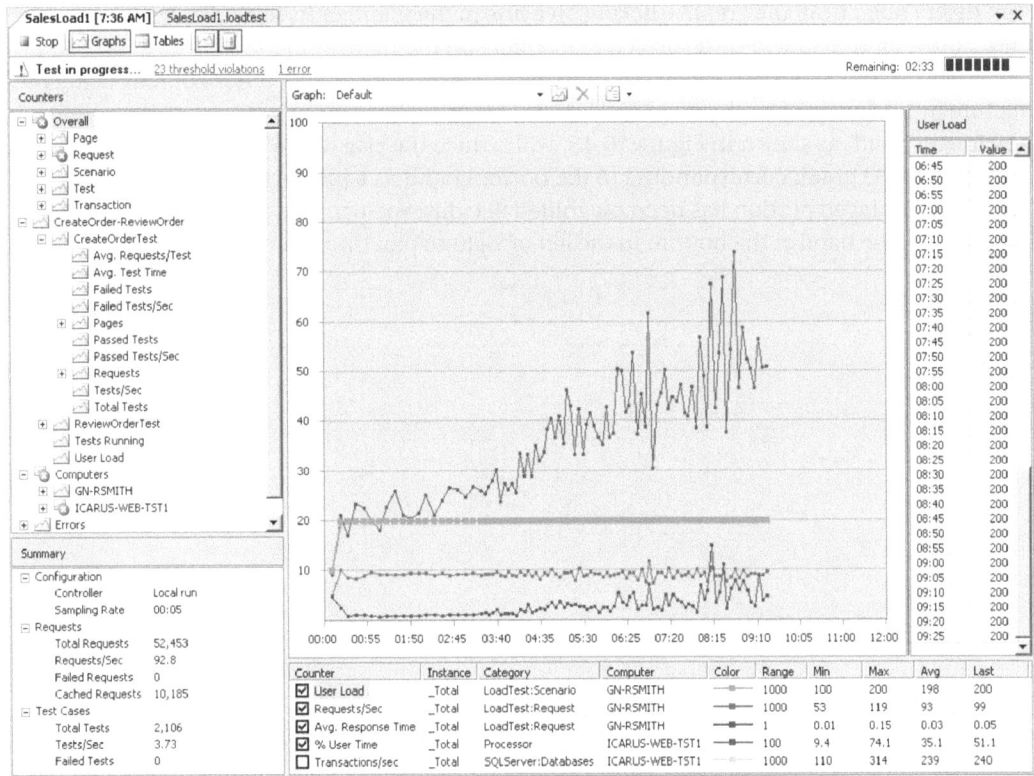

Figure 10-12. *The running SalesLoad1.loadtest*

Below this in the same tree view, we see counters organized by computer arranged under ICARUS-WEB-TST1 and the workstation that is running the test, Rob's machine GN-RSMITH. Here some of the nodes in the tree view are marked with red error buttons and some with yellow warning triangles. These symbols indicate that the values of the counters captured indicated an error or warning situation at some time during the test.

The counters can be viewed either in graphical or table form by selecting any of them in this pane and choosing Show Counter On Graph, or Show Counter On Legend, but you can also drag and drop them into the graph or legend area. The graph can become far too crowded when many counters are added, so it is useful to add additional graphs, which you can do by clicking the Add Graph button at the top of the Graph pane.

Below the Counters pane is the summary pane, which shows Configuration, Requests, and Test Cases. The configuration shows a local run—that is, running from the local computer rather than using agents—with a sampling interval of 5 seconds. Summary data such as the number of tests per second and the number of failed tests and requests is displayed.

The center and right of the screen is used for displaying either graphs or tables. More than one graph can be defined and, when displaying graphs, the display has three separate panes: Graph, Legend, and Plot Points (the last two panes are optional). You can show only one graph at a time; you select the graph for display from a drop-down at the top. As I said earlier, you can drag counters from the Counters pane to the Legend or Graph pane. Once on the Legend pane they can be displayed or hidden by selecting or deselecting the box on the left, or you can delete them from the graph. Clicking on a line in the graph or its legend entry causes the plot points for that line to be displayed in the pane on the right.

You can zoom in on a particular part of the graph and pan across it horizontally using the feature just below the Graph pane. Clicking and dragging the small block at the left or right of the longer band, as shown in Figure 10-13, will reduce the size of the band and display only that part of the graph corresponding to the bottom band as a proportion of the entire graph. Once the displayed portion has been magnified like this, you can move the displayed portion by dragging the band at the bottom to the left or right to pan through the graph.

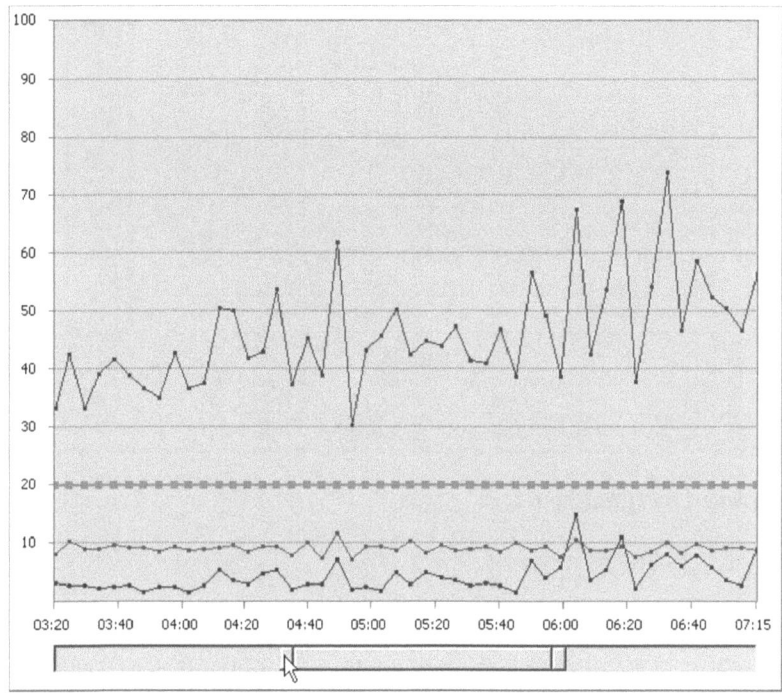

Figure 10-13. *Panning and zooming on the load test graphs*

There is another way to zoom in on a portion of the graph of interest, as Figure 10-14 shows. Here, the region of interest is highlighted on the graph by holding the left button and dragging the mouse cursor across it. When the left button is released, the graph is displayed with the highlighted portion filling the screen.

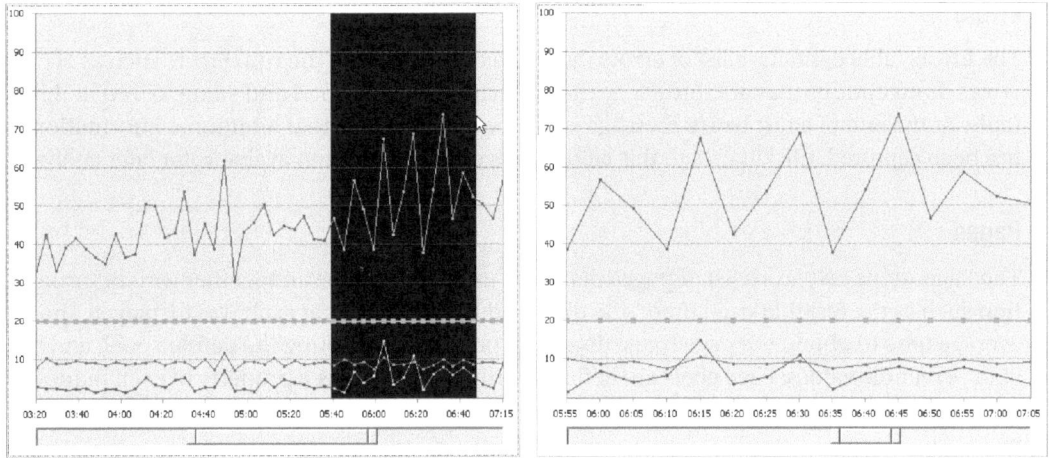

Figure 10-14. *Zooming in on a region of interest*

Instead of displaying graphs in the right portion of the window, we can choose to display tables, as shown in Figure 10-15. There is an in-built set of tables that can be displayed, as described in the next sections.

Time	Computer	Category	Counter	Instance	Message
00:00:05	ICARUS-WEB-TST1	ASP.NET	Requests Queued	systemdiag...	The value 2 exceeds the warning threshold value of 1.
00:02:50	GN-RSMITH	LoadTest:Request	Avg. Connection Wait Time	_Total	The value 0.02107477 exceeds the warning threshold value of 0.01812.
00:02:55	ICARUS-WEB-TST1	ASP.NET	Requests Queued	systemdiag...	The value 1 exceeds the warning threshold value of 1.
00:03:00	GN-RSMITH	LoadTest:Request	Avg. Connection Wait Time	_Total	The value 0.03003261 exceeds the warning threshold value of 0.02254902.
00:03:40	GN-RSMITH	LoadTest:Request	Avg. Connection Wait Time	_Total	The value 0.04015385 exceeds the warning threshold value of 0.03319663.
00:04:05	ICARUS-WEB-TST1	.NET CLR Memory	% Time in GC	_Global_	The value 14.45699 exceeds the warning threshold value of 10.
00:04:20	GN-RSMITH	LoadTest:Request	Avg. Connection Wait Time	_Total	The value 0.05672727 exceeds the warning threshold value of 0.03246853.
00:04:35	GN-RSMITH	LoadTest:Request	Avg. Connection Wait Time	_Total	The value 0.03630303 exceeds the warning threshold value of 0.02843036.
00:04:35	ICARUS-WEB-TST1	.NET CLR Memory	% Time in GC	_Global_	The value 25.20446 exceeds the critical threshold value of 25.
00:04:40	ICARUS-WEB-TST1	.NET CLR Memory	% Time in GC	_Global_	The value 10.19579 exceeds the warning threshold value of 10.
00:04:55	GN-RSMITH	LoadTest:Request	Avg. Connection Wait Time	_Total	The value 0.08795901 exceeds the critical threshold value of 0.05314706.
00:05:10	ICARUS-WEB-TST1	.NET CLR Memory	% Time in GC	_Global_	The value 19.20352 exceeds the warning threshold value of 10.
00:05:15	ICARUS-WEB-TST1	.NET CLR Memory	% Time in GC	_Global_	The value 15.90073 exceeds the warning threshold value of 10.
00:05:25	ICARUS-WEB-TST1	.NET CLR Memory	% Time in GC	_Global_	The value 10.56391 exceeds the warning threshold value of 10.
00:06:15	GN-RSMITH	LoadTest:Request	Avg. Connection Wait Time	_Total	The value 0.19031 exceeds the critical threshold value of 0.06344248.
00:06:15	ICARUS-WEB-TST1	.NET CLR Memory	% Time in GC	_Global_	The value 14.33551 exceeds the warning threshold value of 10.
00:06:30	GN-RSMITH	LoadTest:Request	Avg. Connection Wait Time	_Total	The value 0.1763684 exceeds the critical threshold value of 0.09694758.
00:06:45	ICARUS-WEB-TST1	Processor	% Processor Time	_Total	The value 82.13166 exceeds the warning threshold value of 80.
00:06:50	ICARUS-WEB-TST1	ASP.NET	Requests Queued	systemdiag...	The value 1 exceeds the warning threshold value of 1.
00:06:50	ICARUS-WEB-TST1	.NET CLR Memory	% Time in GC	_Global_	The value 21.13743 exceeds the warning threshold value of 10.
00:06:55	GN-RSMITH	LoadTest:Request	Avg. Connection Wait Time	_Total	The value 0.08054808 exceeds the warning threshold value of 0.07336275.
00:07:15	GN-RSMITH	LoadTest:Request	Avg. Connection Wait Time	_Total	The value 0.07804301 exceeds the warning threshold value of 0.07088333.
00:07:25	ICARUS-WEB-TST1	.NET CLR Memory	% Time in GC	_Global_	The value 18.57882 exceeds the warning threshold value of 10.
00:07:50	GN-RSMITH	LoadTest:Request	Avg. Connection Wait Time	_Total	The value 0.1259278 exceeds the warning threshold value of 0.07596976.
00:07:50	ICARUS-WEB-TST1	ASP.NET	Requests Queued	systemdiag...	The value 3 exceeds the warning threshold value of 1.
00:07:50	ICARUS-WEB-TST1	.NET CLR Memory	% Time in GC	_Global_	The value 25.75487 exceeds the critical threshold value of 25.
00:08:05	ICARUS-WEB-TST1	.NET CLR Memory	% Time in GC	_Global_	The value 19.45474 exceeds the warning threshold value of 10.
00:08:10	ICARUS-WEB-TST1	ASP.NET	Requests Queued	systemdiag...	The value 1 exceeds the warning threshold value of 1.
00:08:10	ICARUS-WEB-TST1	.NET CLR Memory	% Time in GC	_Global_	The value 48.21771 exceeds the critical threshold value of 25.
00:08:15	GN-RSMITH	LoadTest:Request	Avg. Connection Wait Time	_Total	The value 0.08125582 exceeds the warning threshold value of 0.04590909.
00:08:15	ICARUS-WEB-TST1	.NET CLR Memory	% Time in GC	_Global_	The value 92.77534 exceeds the critical threshold value of 25.
00:08:25	GN-RSMITH	LoadTest:Request	Avg. Connection Wait Time	_Total	The value 0.09091111 exceeds the warning threshold value of 0.05861225.
00:08:30	GN-RSMITH	LoadTest:Request	Avg. Connection Wait Time	_Total	The value 0.1650957 exceeds the critical threshold value of 0.1311434.
00:08:30	ICARUS-WEB-TST1	.NET CLR Memory	% Time in GC	_Global_	The value 18.71928 exceeds the warning threshold value of 10.
00:08:35	GN-RSMITH	LoadTest:Request	Avg. Connection Wait Time	_Total	The value 0.09937634 exceeds the warning threshold value of 0.06390551.
00:08:35	ICARUS-WEB-TST1	.NET CLR Memory	% Time in GC	_Global_	The value 13.89602 exceeds the warning threshold value of 10.
00:08:45	ICARUS-WEB-TST1	ASP.NET	Requests Queued	systemdiag...	The value 2 exceeds the warning threshold value of 1.
00:08:45	ICARUS-WEB-TST1	.NET CLR Memory	% Time in GC	_Global_	The value 24.73009 exceeds the warning threshold value of 10.
00:08:50	GN-RSMITH	LoadTest:Request	Avg. Connection Wait Time	_Total	The value 0.150883 exceeds the warning threshold value of 0.08873558.
00:08:50	ICARUS-WEB-TST1	.NET CLR Memory	% Time in GC	_Global_	The value 20.006 exceeds the warning threshold value of 10.
00:08:50	ICARUS-WEB-TST1	Processor	% Processor Time	_Total	The value 83.28313 exceeds the warning threshold value of 80.
00:08:55	ICARUS-WEB-TST1	ASP.NET	Requests Queued	systemdiag...	The value 3 exceeds the warning threshold value of 1.
00:08:55	ICARUS-WEB-TST1	.NET CLR Memory	% Time in GC	_Global_	The value 16.68467 exceeds the warning threshold value of 10.
00:09:05	GN-RSMITH	LoadTest:Request	Avg. Connection Wait Time	Total	The value 0.1817471 exceeds the critical threshold value of 0.1233333.

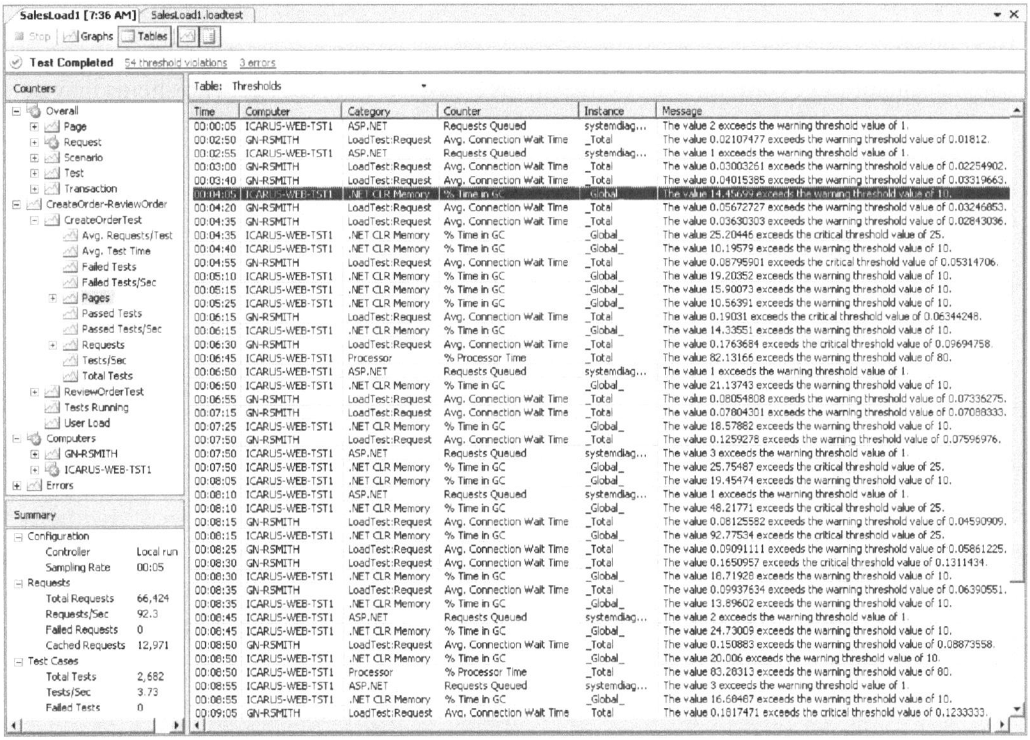

Figure 10-15. *Displaying tables instead of graphs*

Errors

The Errors table contains a list of errors that were created during the run. Errors such as HTTP errors or exceptions that are thrown by the application are retained and summarized in this table. At the end of a test run, a message is displayed indicating that additional information has been captured. Clicking Yes to this alert makes error information available for later analysis.

Pages

The Pages table displays a list of pages that were used during the run together with information such as the test that used them, the total number of times that each was displayed, the average time to obtain the page (page time), the percentage meeting the defined goal, and the 95th percentile values. Page goals are defined within a web test as a property of each request.

Requests

The Requests table contains all requests that were used during the run, including dependent requests such as JScript files and images.

Tests

The Tests table contains a list of the tests that were used during the run, with information such as total number of tests, total passed, total failed, rates of pass and fail, and so forth.

Thresholds

The Thresholds table contains a list of thresholds crossed during the run. Thresholds may be set against any counter in the Counters pane by right-clicking on the counter and selecting Add Threshold Rule from the context menu. A default set of threshold rules is automatically added to a load test. The Thresholds table contains the first 1,000 threshold violations, including the time, category, computer, counter, and a message.

Transactions

The Transactions table displays a list of transactions in the run. Transactions are a web test concept; you can link a set of page actions together to form a unit and record the time for that entire unit. For example, creating an order could be considered to be a transaction and could be defined as such when the web test is developed.

SQL Trace

The SQL Trace table contains data from the post-run analyzer available when SQL tracing was used. SQL tracing can be incorporated into a load test and can collect SQL trace data during the running of the test. This data provides information about the longest-running queries and stored procedures in the database.

Agent

The Agent table provides information broken down by agent. It is only available when tests are run with multiple agents.

Interpreting the Load Test Data

Having obtained a set of results from the load test, Rob now takes a look to see if the data is acceptable. First he looks at the data in the legend at the bottom of the display (Figure 10-16). This shows the minimum, average, and maximum values for some of the recorded variables. The user load is 200 users (as Rob specified), and the requests per second average 93. Each user has a think time of 10 seconds in both of the web tests, so we would expect maybe 20 requests per second if 200 users make a request every 10 seconds. But there are typically about four related requests for each user request for a page, so this is about right.

Note The code at this point can be found in `Chapter 10\Exercise 3`. Exercise 10-4 demonstrates the material in this section.

Counter	Instance	Category	Computer	Color	Range	Min	Max	Avg	Last
☑ User Load	_Total	LoadTest:Scenario	GN-RSMITH	—■—	1000	0	200	198	0
☑ Requests/Sec	_Total	LoadTest:Request	GN-RSMITH	—■—	1000	74	119	93	86
☑ Avg. Response Time	_Total	LoadTest:Request	GN-RSMITH	—■—	1	0.01	0.15	0.04	0.03
☑ % User Time	_Total	Processor	ICARUS-WEB-TST1	—■—	100	19.2	77.4	43.8	36.8
☐ Transactions/sec	_Total	SQLServer:Databases	ICARUS-WEB-TST1	—■—	1000	175	314	238	211
☐ Disk Transfers/sec	_Total	PhysicalDisk	ICARUS-WEB-TST1	—■—	100	2.4	11.5	5.5	5.6
☐ Disk Transfers/sec	0 C: E: F: G:	PhysicalDisk	ICARUS-WEB-TST1	—■—	100	2.4	11.5	5.5	5.6
☐ Batch Requests/sec	-	SQLServer:SQL Statistics	ICARUS-WEB-TST1	—■—	1000	140	267	202	173
☐ Requests Queued	-	ASP.NET	ICARUS-WEB-TST1	—■—	100	0	11	0	0
☐ Page Faults/sec	-	Memory	ICARUS-WEB-TST1	—■—	10000	23	1,456	420	251
☐ Disk Read Bytes/sec	_Total	PhysicalDisk	ICARUS-WEB-TST1		10000	0	9,741	369	0

Figure 10-16. *Summary data for the average response time, etc.*

The response time averages 0.04 seconds, which is well within the requirement of 5 seconds specified in Chapter 4, and the maximum is still much less than 5 seconds. The % User Time counter is the percentage of processor time on the web server that is devoted to the process and is an average of 43.8 percent with a peak of 77.4 percent. So the application appears to be performing within spec. What about the load? The specification required 10,000 users making a request at 30-second intervals, which is about equivalent to roughly 3300 users making a request every 10 seconds. This test had 200 users making a request roughly every 10 seconds, so the application needs to scale up by a factor of 16 in performance; with perfect scaling this would require 16 web servers in parallel. It seems rather optimistic to expect the application to scale that well, but Rob was running this test against a server that also runs the database, so we would expect performance to be considerably better than this when the database is moved onto another machine. In addition, there are plans to run the business objects applications on another set of machines. Also, the figures above show a response time much better than required, and the CPU is only running at 48 percent load, so the server can probably handle more traffic.

In truth, Rob has run a very superficial load test—not bad for iteration 1, but to demonstrate performance and scalability a much more realistic server arrangement will be needed with a separate database server and at least two or three parallel web servers. Also, the test will need to be run from agents to provide sufficient, consistent load on the server array.

The test shows many threshold violations. Rob clicks on the appropriate link and sees the table of threshold violations shown in Figure 10-17.

Figure 10-17. *Table of threshold violations*

The best option is this case is to click on Category to sort them by category. Having done this, Rob can list the separate types of violations, picking the worst in each case:

```
Critical: ICARUS-WEB-TST .NET CLR Memory, % Time in GC
The value 92.77534 exceeds the critical threshold value of 25.


Critical: ICARUS-WEB-TST1 ASP.NET, Requests Queued
The value 11 exceeds the critical threshold value of 10.


Critical: GN-RSMITH LoadTest:Request, Avg. Connection Wait Time
The value 0.19031 exceeds the critical threshold value of 0.06344248.


Warning: ICARUS-WEB-TST Processor, % Processor Time
The value 83.28313 exceeds the warning threshold value of 80.
```

Excessive Time in Garbage Collection

Microsoft .NET applications use a managed heap, and when objects are created using the new operator, the memory needed to hold them is allocated from the heap. The managed heap in .NET works in a contiguous manner; as memory is allocated from the heap, the pointer that indicates the next free location is simply moved up to the top of the objects allocated. Heap space that is used by objects whose references have gone out of scope is not therefore reused in the normal process of heap allocation. This is unlike the heap used in C++, where the memory is maintained in a linked list so that when memory is released, it can be linked back into the list of free blocks and be available for immediate reuse. In a short-running application, or one that has only a small amount of recycling of objects (i.e., objects being created or falling out of scope and new objects being created), the heap may never run out of space in the lifetime of the application. However, the .NET common language runtime (CLR) provides a mechanism to recycle space on the heap occupied by objects whose references have fallen out of scope. This mechanism, called *garbage collection*, kicks in automatically when the CLR determines that the available heap may be getting low. It may also be called manually. The operation of the garbage collector is very complex and quite beyond the scope of this book; however, the Icarus team will run into issues where the operation of the garbage collector needs to be understood so I must at least give a summary introduction to the issues.

The garbage collector time threshold is included by default in load tests. It is set to give a warning when the percentage of processor time spent in garbage collection rises above 10 percent and to indicate a critical situation when it rises above 25 percent. Of course, Rob can easily remove this threshold and ignore the garbage collector time, but the team would be wise to consider it, since excessive garbage collection can indicate poor use of memory in the application. The garbage collector in .NET has three levels of operation: generation 0, generation 1, and generation 2. Briefly, when objects are created they are placed in a category called generation 0 and when the garbage collector runs, it identifies all the objects in generation 0 that are unreachable from the application (we'll ignore finalizers for now). This memory space is released back into the free heap and the existing objects on the heap are compacted so that the free space is contiguous. Any objects in generation 0 that are still reachable are pushed into generation 1. If sufficient memory can be reclaimed from generation 0 objects, the garbage collector does not consider generation 1 or 2. Studies of many applications have found that newer objects tend to have shorter lifetimes and have closer relationships with each other, and compacting a portion of the heap is quicker than compacting the entire heap. This *generational* garbage collection therefore has been found effective.

Developers should be encouraged to consider garbage collection during the design of their code, and various practices that will minimize the need for it to occur are described in many books and web logs. Returning to the test results shown in Figure 10-12, we can obtain a lot more information from the set of counters on the left of the display.

Figure 10-18 shows the counters available that provide information about the .NET CLR heap management. You can see this by expanding the Computers node in the Counters pane. The most obvious one that would be useful is the % Time in GC but the Gen 0, Gen 1, and Gen 2 heap sizes might also be useful. Rob drags the % Time In GC counter onto the graph with the results shown in Figure 10-19, with a magnified portion showing the large peak that occurs in the % Time In GC value. The top line is the percentage of processor user utilization, the lowest is the response time to requests, and the middle one is the percentage of time spent in garbage collection. You can see the little yellow warning triangles that mark the threshold violations. They seem to be spread fairly uniformly throughout the latter part of the test.

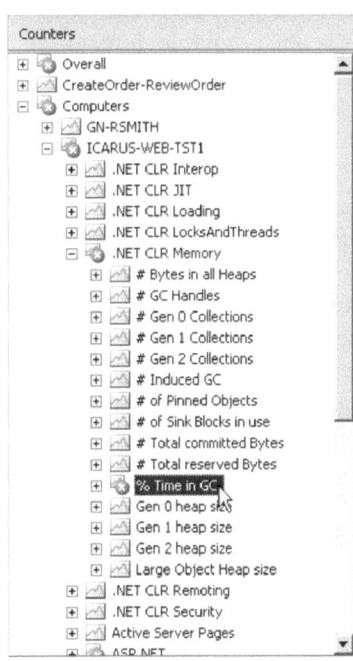

Figure 10-18. *Counters available within the category of .NET CLR heap management*

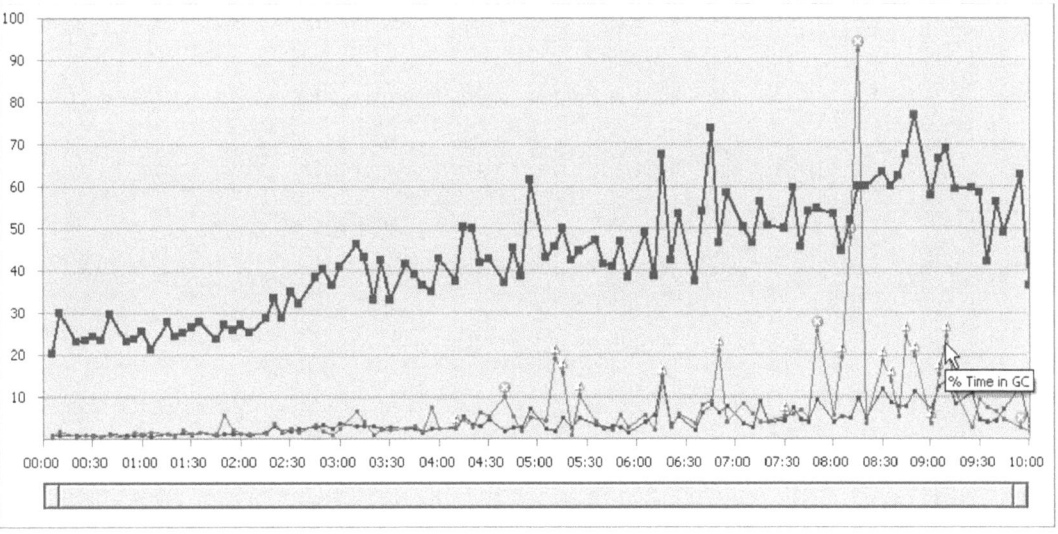

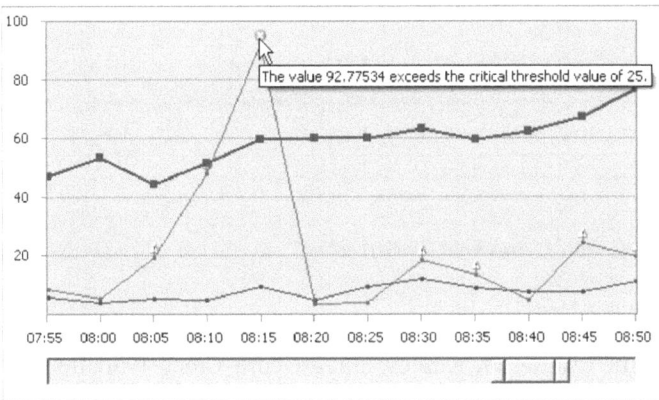

Figure 10-19. *Graph showing the percentage of time spent in garbage collection*

Unfortunately, this does not shed any light on the reason for the excessive garbage collection or the large spike. The heap size counters are shown in Figure 10-20. The one at the top is generation 0 and the lower one with the highest peaks is generation 1. Generation 2 is the lowest. Although these are not very instructive at this stage, they illustrate some of the information available.

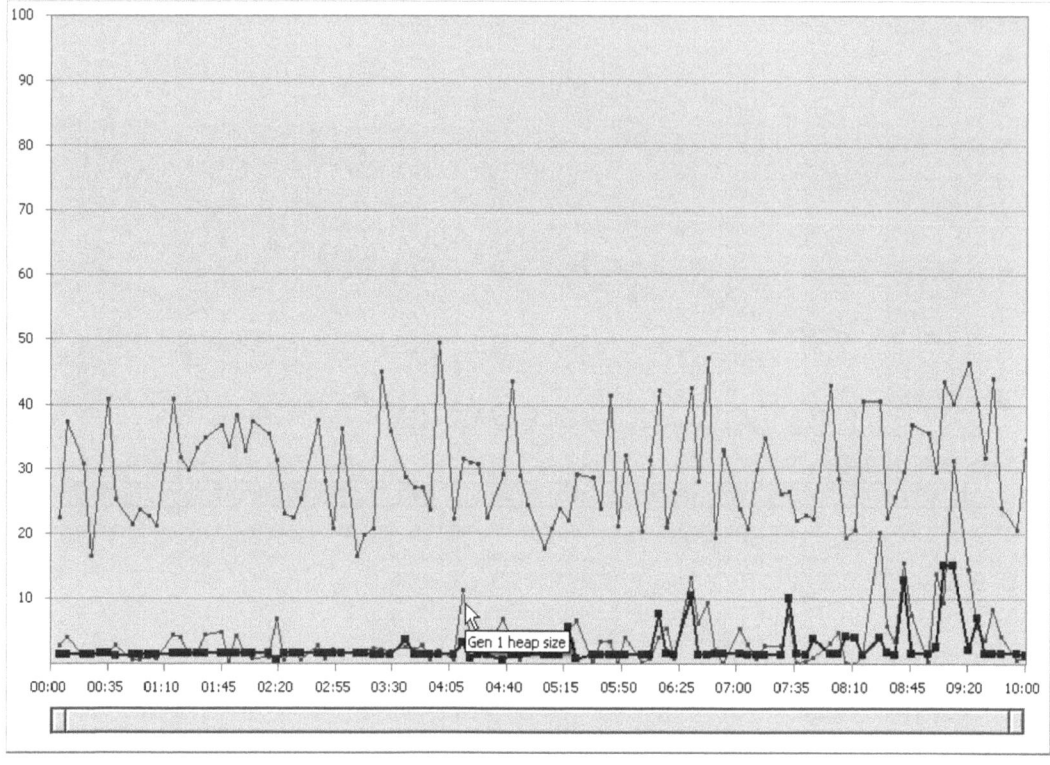

Figure 10-20. *Graph showing the Gen 0, Gen 1, and Gen 2 heap sizes*

Rob decides that the peak in GC time should be flagged as an issue, so he creates a work item by right-clicking on the test in the Test Results window and selecting Create Work Item ➤ Issue from the context menu, as shown in Figure 10-21.

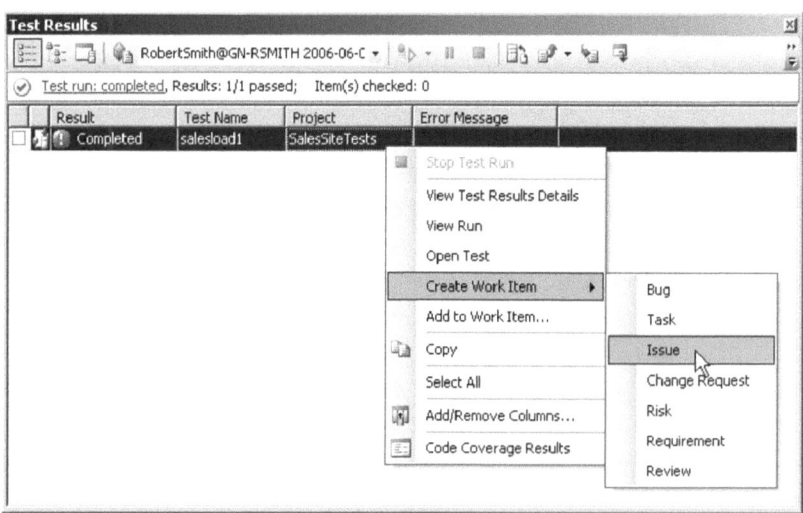

Figure 10-21. *Creating an issue work item from a test result*

Rob first is offered a chance to publish the results (Figure 10-22), which he accepts. Then a new work item is opened, which he assigns to Peter for analysis. The work item he creates is shown in Figure 10-23. Rob then returns to the Test Results window and selects Add to Work Item from the right-click context menu. He selects the work item just created as the one to which the test results should be added. Visual Studio adds the test results as an attachment to the new work item.

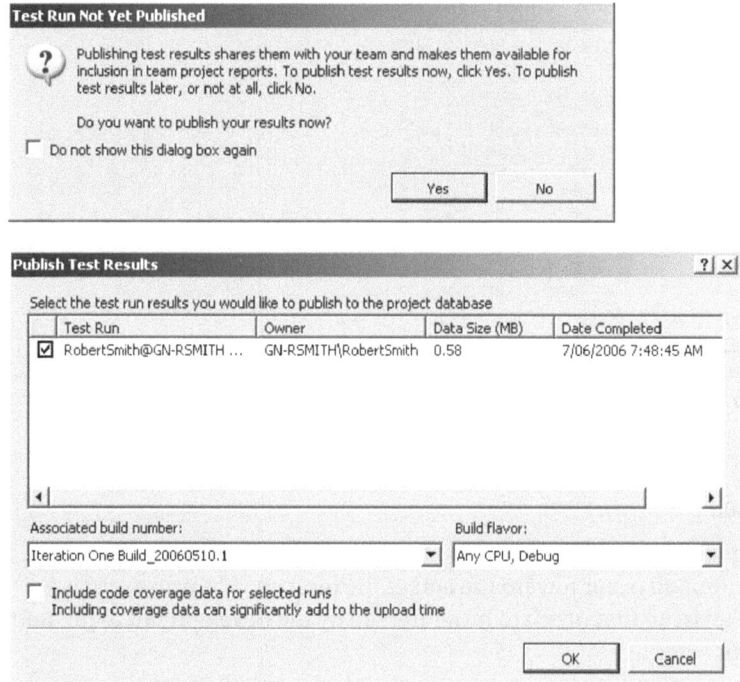

Figure 10-22. *Publishing the test results*

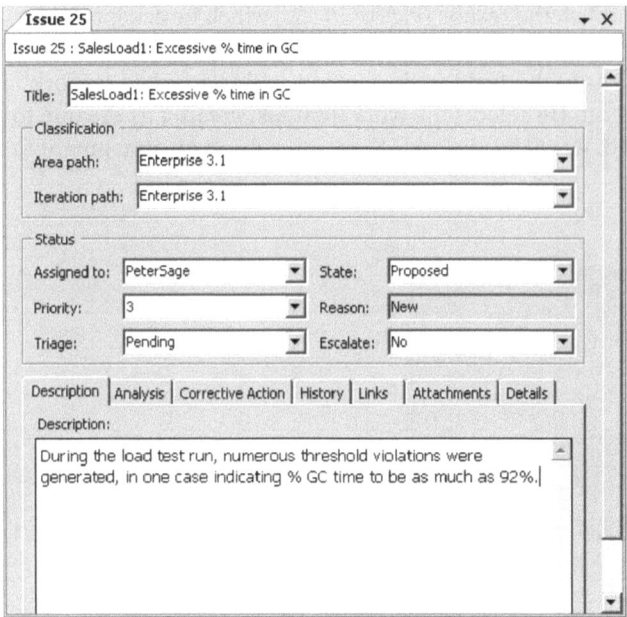

Figure 10-23. *The work item for the garbage collection time issue*

Excessive Requests Queued

Rob drags the ASP.NET Requests Queued counter onto the graph, as shown in Figure 10-24.
The critical threshold violations all occur toward the end of the test run. The cause of this is
not clear, but it is certainly an issue that needs to be addressed by the development team. Rob
writes another work item for Peter.

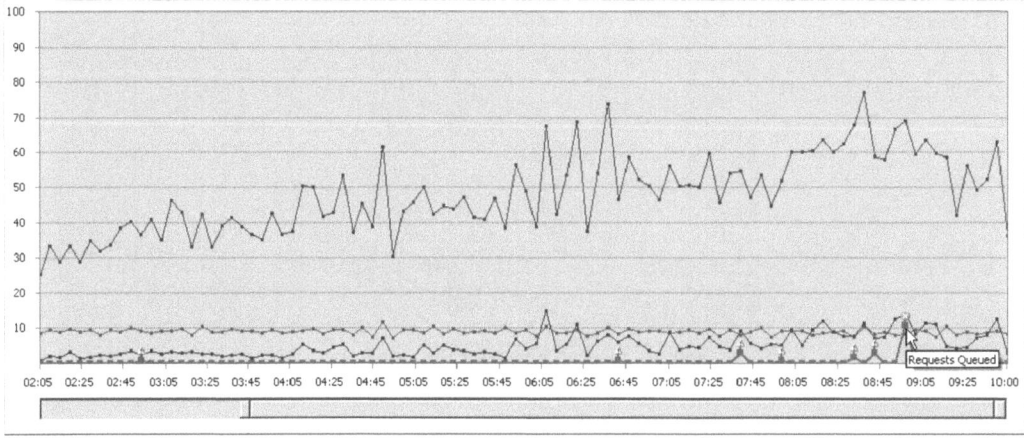

Figure 10-24. *The Requests Queued counter*

Excessive Connection Wait Time

The Avg. Connection Wait Time (Figure 10-25) has many threshold violations that worsen in the latter half of the test. Note that this is a counter from the local machine that is carrying out the tests rather than the server running the sales site. It means that, at these points in the test, the wait time for a connection to the web server goes above the threshold value. Rob mentions this in the Excessive Requests Queued work item.

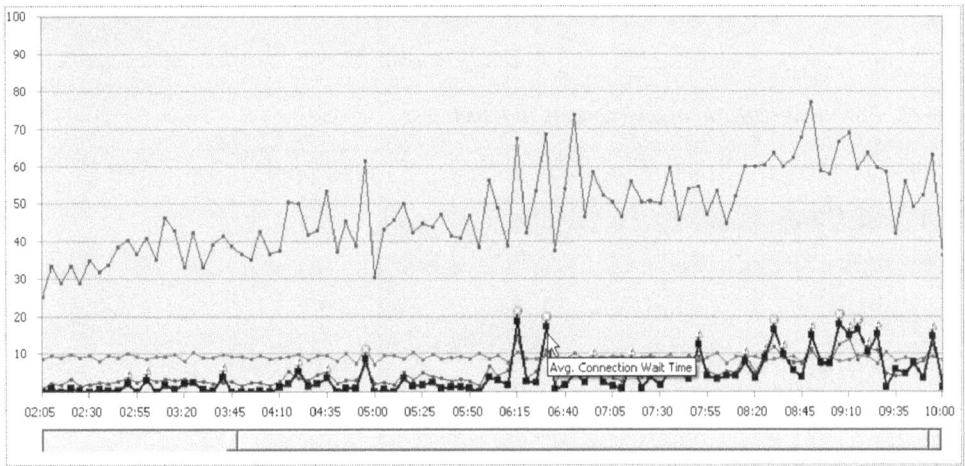

Figure 10-25. *The Avg. Connection Wait Time counter*

Parameterizing Load Tests

The web tests created in the previous chapter used URLs for the web server that were captured when the test was recorded. Often the tests will be developed running against one server and will then be required to run against a completely different server. The URL therefore must be parameterized so that it can be modified when installations on different servers are to be tested. After a web test has been recorded, you can parameterize all of the servers within the URLs by clicking the Parameterize Web Servers button. This displays a dialog box listing all of the servers used in the requests with a default context parameter name to the right (Figure 10-26). You can change the name of the context parameters or their values in the Parameterize Web Servers dialog box by clicking the Change button. In the Change Web Servers dialog box (Figure 10-27), you can choose to use either a web server with a URL or an ASP.NET development server by specifying a path to the website and a web application root.

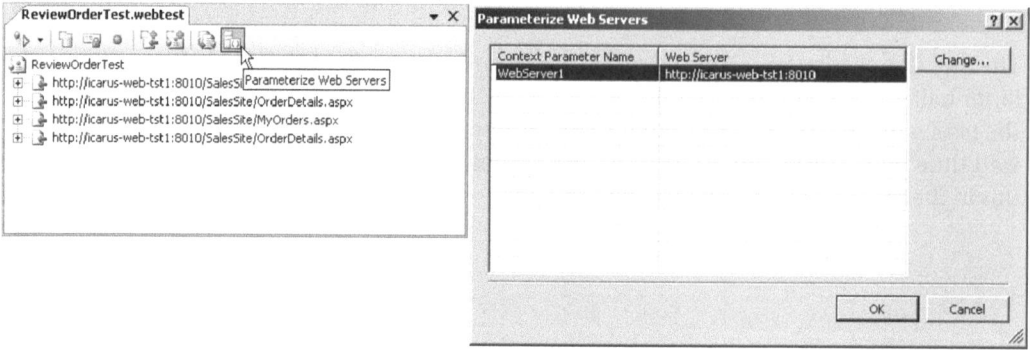

Figure 10-26. *Parameterization of web servers in a web test*

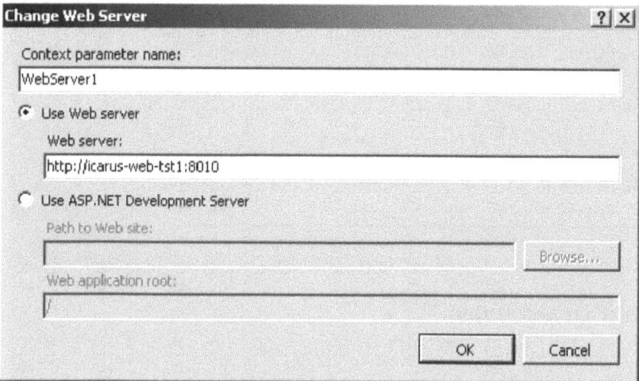

Figure 10-27. *The Change Web Server dialog box*

The important thing about context parameters is that they can also be defined in a load test. If you have several web tests included in a load test, you will want to specify the URL parameters in the load test and expect them to be used by each web test. You do this by making the parameter names for URLs in the web tests the same as in the load test, and then the value of the parameter in the load test will override the value that it was given in the web test. This is an essential feature since you do not want to have to modify the context parameter of every web test (or other test) included in a scenario of a load test. Instead, you set the value of each context parameter in the load test, and they are picked up by the web tests.

Profiling the Sales Site Scenarios

In Chapter 1, we explained that code profiling has two modes of operation: sampling and instrumentation. Sampling is a useful technique that is fairly noninvasive and gathers statistical information consisting of a collection of samples, each of which contains the name of the function that was being executed when the sample was taken. Also, the names of other functions on the stack at that instant in time are collected. A sophisticated analysis tool that comes with Visual Studio 2005 Team Edition for Developers allows this information to be explored.

Note The code at this point can be found in `Chapter 10\Exercise 4`. Exercise 10-5 demonstrates the material in this section.

In sampling mode, the idea is to obtain sufficient information to give a statistically valid picture of the areas where the code spends most of its time so that any performance tuning can concentrate on those areas. To analyze a server application, the profiler must be attached to the process running under the server and the server must be stimulated with some kind of ongoing controlled activity. In order to profile the code effectively, it is a good idea if possible to stimulate the web server in a way that concentrates on repetitively performing a fairly simple task. That way, it will be much easier to analyze the sampling data and interpret it in a manner that is helpful in identifying where code improvements can be made.

A good way to do this is to use a load test that repetitively executes one or more web tests. The web tests can be chosen to exercise the portion of the application that is to be studied and may therefore be more limited than those used in the earlier part of this chapter.

In Team System, load tests and web tests are only included with the Tester Edition, whereas code profiling is only included with the Developer Edition. In the Icarus team, Ed and Rob decide to collaborate in a profiling effort. Ed sets his machine up as a web server, with the application installed in a virtual directory, and Rob uses his machine to write the web tests and load tests to provide activity for the web server. This configuration is shown in Figure 10-28.

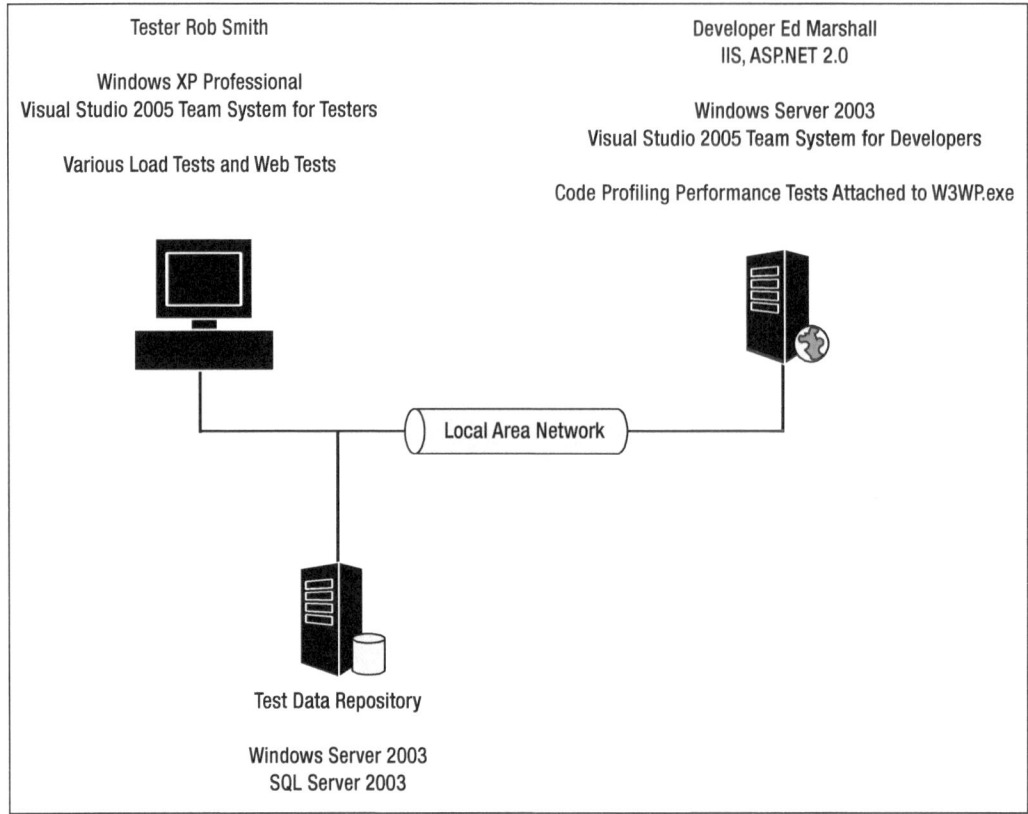

Figure 10-28. *Sales site profiling configuration*

Profiling by Sampling

To create a new performance session, Ed opens the solution on his machine and displays the Performance Explorer window by selecting View ➤ Other Windows ➤ Performance Explorer. The Performance Explorer window is initially empty. Ed clicks the New Performance Session button (as shown in Figure 10-29), which creates an empty performance session with a default name of Performance2. He then opens the properties by right-clicking on the new Performance2 performance session in the Performance Explorer and selecting Properties. There are a whole set of pages; the first, shown in Figure 10-30, allows you to select whether the performance session is to operate in sampling or instrumentation mode.

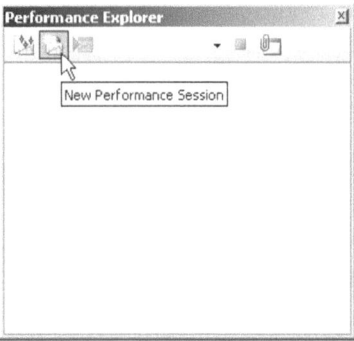

Figure 10-29. *Creating a new performance session*

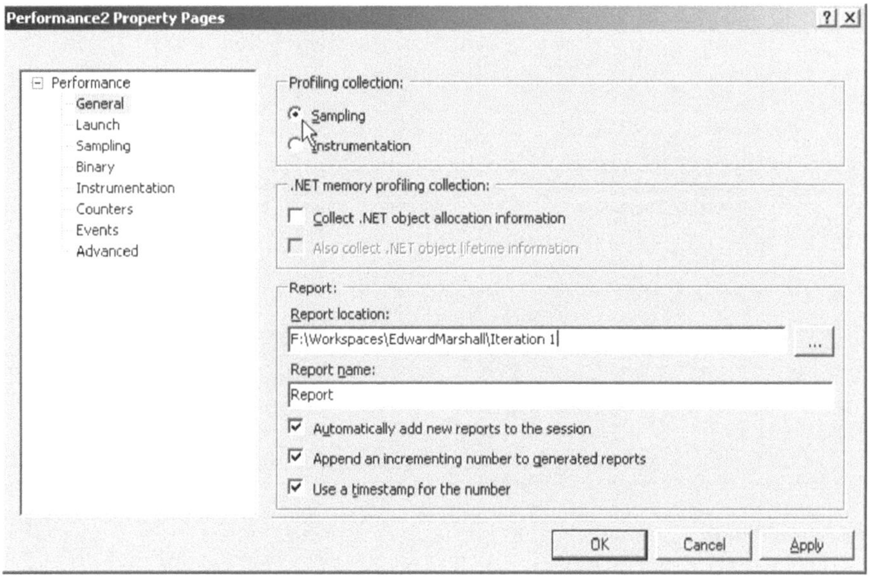

Figure 10-30. *The General properties*

Let me just elaborate on the difference between these two modes. In sampling mode the application is interrupted at predetermined intervals. At each sampling instant, the executing function is determined and the call stack is examined. A record is kept of all the functions that are detected to be executing or on the call stack at these sampling points. When a particular function is found to be executing, a number associated with that function name, called its Exclusive Sample Count, is incremented. If a particular function is found to be on the stack at the sample instant, a count associated with its name, called its Inclusive Sample Count, is incremented. I do not know how the performance sessions work internally, but I think this is a good model to have in mind when you first start looking at these numbers.

In instrumentation mode—which we'll consider in detail later—code sections, called *probes*, are added to each function so that the exact time duration of the execution of that function can be determined. Instrumentation mode is much more invasive and takes longer to set up. Ed ensures that the sampling mode is selected.

Also on the General page is an option to collect .NET memory allocation information and object lifetime information. This could certainly prove useful in examining the garbage collector issue that was discovered during load test, but for now Ed leaves that option unchecked (you will see it in use later). Also on this page Ed can specify the location in which the reports are to be stored as well as some other options, which can usually be left set to their defaults.

The Launch page (Figure 10-31) allows you to specify one or more binaries to launch. In this case the performance session is going to be attached to an already executing process, so none of these should be checked. When it is time to carry out performance profiling on the List Wing and Sales Wing Windows applications, they would be launched from settings in this page.

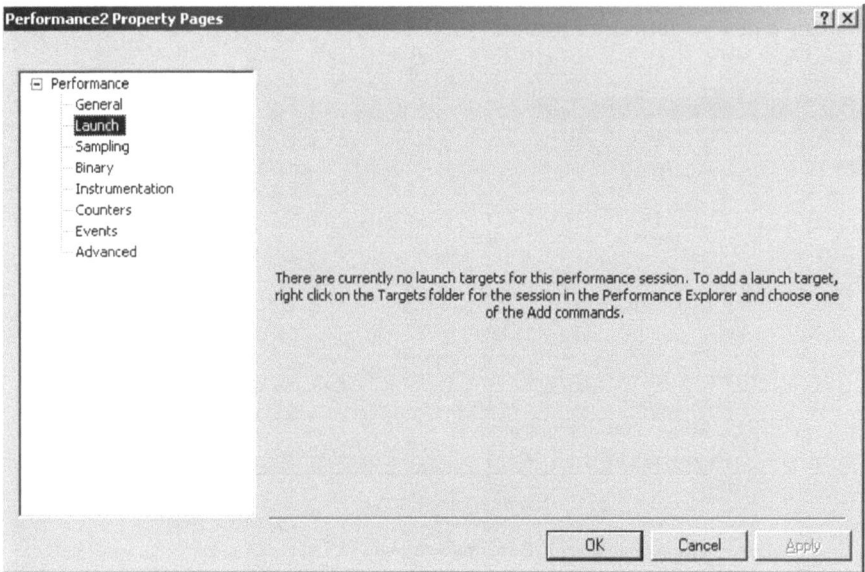

Figure 10-31. *The Launch page*

The Sampling page in Figure 10-32 allows you to select various sampling options. Sampling events can be based on a count of clock cycles, on page faults, on system calls, or on performance counters. Only performance counters associated with CPU events such as cache misses, Instruction Translation Look-aside Buffer (ITLB) misses, and so forth can be used to determine the sampling interval. There are some fascinating options here that allow you to sample the code based on events that reduce the efficiency of the CPU. You can then obtain a profile indicating where these events occur. This is a different concept from profiling to determine where the CPU spends most of its time. Ed uses the default sampling interval based on clock cycles for this performance session. The remaining properties pages do not contain features concerned with this performance session, and we can leave them alone for now.

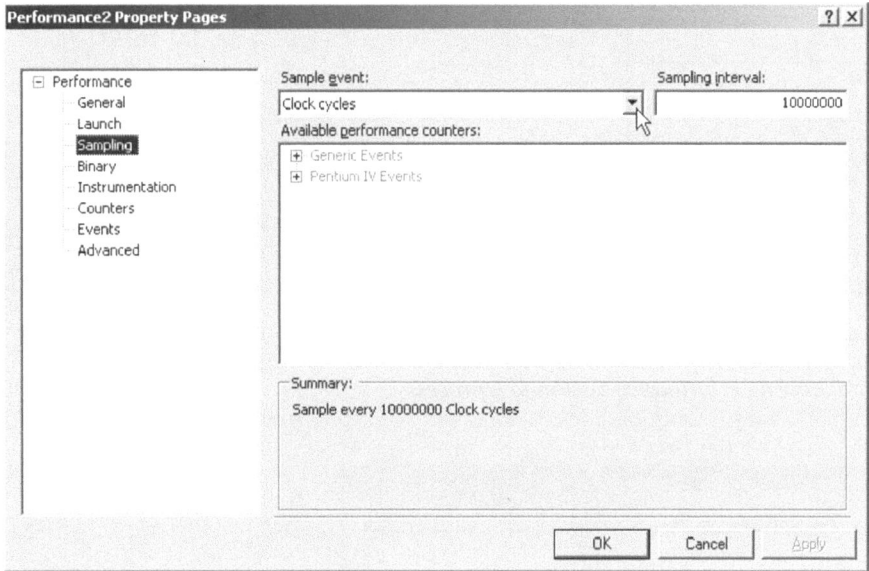

Figure 10-32. *The Sampling page*

It is also not necessary to add any target binaries to the performance session since, when the performance session is attached to the ASP.NET worker process, the binaries will be in the bin folder for the website or will be obtained from the .NET cache.

Before a performance session can be attached to a process, it is necessary to perform a bit of magic—to set up the sampling environment—but first let's see what happens if you just go ahead and attach to a process. To attach your performance session—Performance2 in this case—you must right-click on the performance session in Performance Explorer and select Attach/Detach (Figure 10-33). This will display the Attach Profiler to Process dialog box, as shown in Figure 10-34, where you need to check the Show Processes From All Users box to see the w3wp.exe process. As Figure 10-34 shows, you will see several processes with this name if there are several ASP.NET worker processes running on the machine corresponding to different websites, and it's a bit difficult to determine which you should attach to. One obvious way is to start running your load test from the test client machine; then you can look at Task Manager and see which w3wp process has all the activity, note its process ID, and select that one in the dialog box.

Figure 10-33. *Attaching a performance session to a process*

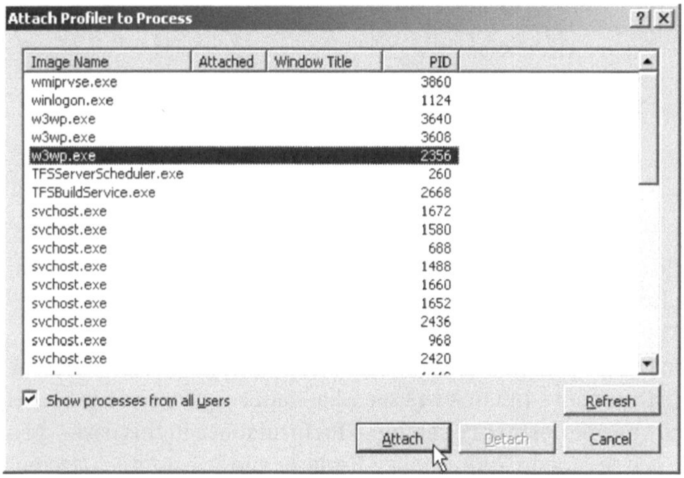

Figure 10-34. *Attach Profiler to Process dialog box*

To be exact, IIS 6.0 actually creates a new instance of w3wp for each application pool. Another more sophisticated way—which is particularly useful if you have a web server with several sites running at once—is to execute the script

```
iisapp.vbs
```

which is located in systemroot\system32. The script will return a list of processes associated with application pools in IIS 6.0, for example:

```
W3WP.exe PID: 2084   AppPoolId: SalesSite
```

Of course, to use this method you have to set the site under test—in this case the Sales Site application—under its own application pool using Internet Information Services Manager.

When you've identified the process, click the Attach button and you will see the dialog box in Figure 10-35. It is no use clicking Yes to the "Continue anyway?" question; you will not see any information for the sampling of the work process and all of the assemblies in your website. When this dialog box appears you must click No, since the profiling environment must be set up.

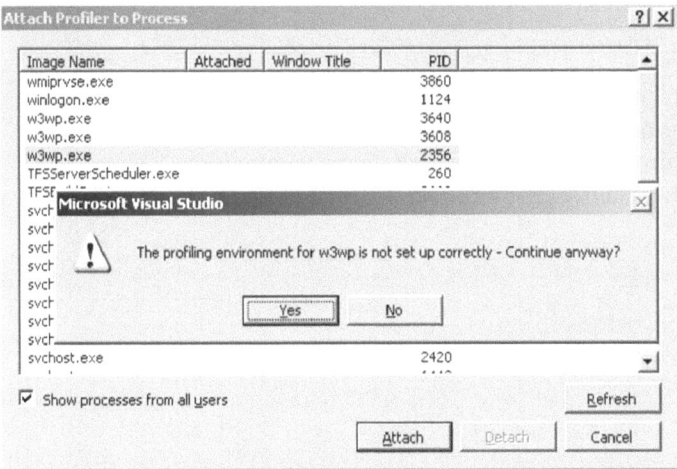

Figure 10-35. *This warning dialog box indicates that the environment variables are not set up.*

This is where you need the magic that I mentioned earlier! Open a command window and navigate to the folder that contains the Performance Monitor tools, usually

```
cd \Program Files\Microsoft Visual Studio 8\Team Tools\Performance Tools
```

Then type the following command:

```
vsperfclrenv /globalsampleon
```

and reboot the system. This action actually sets up some environment variables that allow the sampling of the W3WP.exe process to occur. Once this little adjustment is made, you can happily attach to the w3wp.exe process. Incidentally, when you have finished profiling services, you can reverse this process with the commands

```
cd \Program Files\Microsoft Visual Studio 8\Team Tools\Performance Tools
vsperfclrenv /globaloff
```

and then reboot the system again.

Note that you do not need to run this command if you are sampling an application that you launch from Visual Studio. For instance, if you choose to sample the SalesWing application by adding the Sales Wing project as a target project to a performance session, everything will work fine without the vsperfclrenv command magic. I am deliberately showing you some more interesting sampling techniques in this chapter, the sort that the Icarus project needs.

Let's return to Rob and Ed. Rob has built a load test based on a single web test being executed 100 percent of the time. The web test is called `AddReservationPage.webtest`, with the convention that all web tests ending in "Page" will test an individual page rather than navigating a sequence. Shown in Figure 10-36, the web test was produced by following a simple sequence of first going to the URL

```
http://{WebServer1}/SalesSite/MakeReservation.aspx?ORDERID=2&CUSTOMERID=2
```

and then setting the Region, Category, and Vendor drop-downs and clicking the Search button. There are no extraction rules or validation rules other than those inserted automatically during recording. Rob added a context parameter by clicking the Parameterize Web Servers button on this web test, so that he could set the web server URL in a load test that includes the web test.

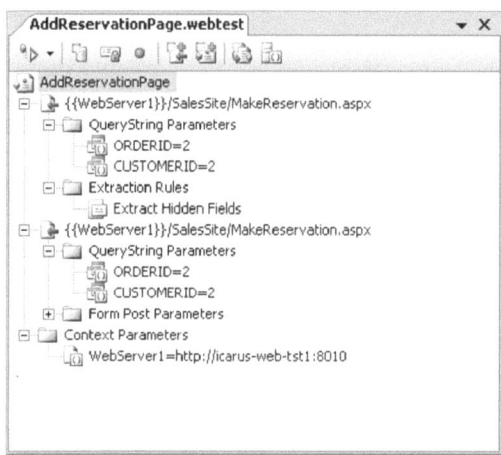

Figure 10-36. *AddReservationPage.webtest*

The details of `AddReservationPage.loadtest` are shown in Figure 10-37. No counters have been included for the server machine, there is no warm-up, and the scenario properties (not shown) are set with the Think Time option turned off and Think Time Between Test Iterations set to 0. Rob and Ed hope this will make the server do some serious work and so the samples obtained will have a greater probability of occurring when the server is in significant parts of the application, rather than just idling.

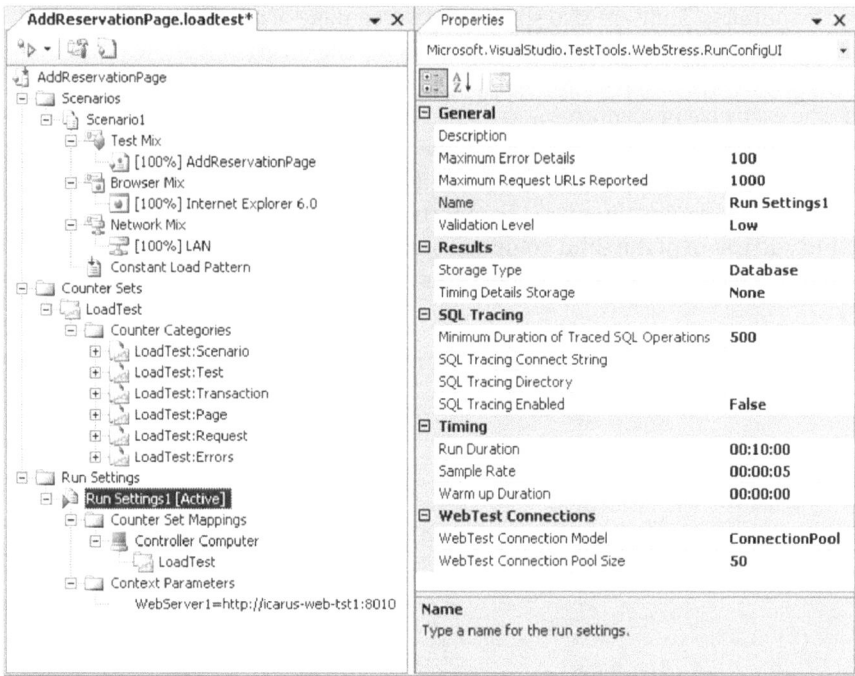

Figure 10-37. *AddReservationPage.loadtest*

Once the test has been set up in this way, Rob starts it running and waits for the graphs of response time and requests per second to stabilize. Then Ed attaches his performance session to the correct instance of w3wp.exe on the server. They allow everything to run until the load test is nearing its end, and then Ed detaches the performance session before the load test stops. The performance session automatically processes the data gathered and shows it as a report document added to the performance session, as shown in Figure 10-38.

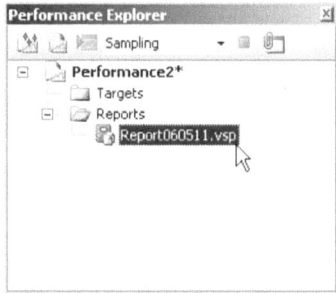

Figure 10-38. *The performance session, complete with report*

Part of the report document is shown in Figure 10-39, with the Functions tab selected. I explained earlier about the inclusive and exclusive counters; these are shown in the columns headed Inclusive Samples and Exclusive Samples on the right. The rows in the table are organized by the assemblies containing the functions, and these columns are totaled across all the functions in those assemblies. They are also shown as a percentage of all the samples in two additional columns, Inclusive Percent and Exclusive Percent. The diagram is shown with the entries ordered by decreasing inclusive percentage. This is achieved by simply clicking on that column heading. The exclusive percentages add up to 100, but of course the inclusive percentages will not, because more than one function will appear on the stack at any sample instant. To prove this you can export the report as a Comma-Separated Values (CSV) file using the Export Report option on the context menu at the report in Performance Explorer, load it into Microsoft Excel, and add a sum of the third column. You can also select multiple rows and do a copy and paste into Notepad to create a CSV file of just a small section if you need to do that.

Function Name	Inclusive Percent ▾	Exclusive Percent	Inclusive Samples	Exclusive Samples
⊞ mscorwks.dll	98.608	35.762	49714	18030
⊞ Unknown	94.129	6.714	47456	3385
⊞ webengine.dll	92.671	0.305	46721	154
⊞ System.Web.ni.dll	92.044	7.569	46405	3816
⊞ App_Web_d3_x-hlz.dll	86.167	0.061	43442	31
⊞ mscorlib.ni.dll	60.709	13.539	30607	6826
⊞ System.Data.dll	43.944	23.713	22155	11955
⊞ OrderBE.DLL	42.853	0.046	21605	23
⊞ BusinessEntity.DLL	42.693	0.058	21524	29
⊞ OrderDAL.DLL	41.880	0.635	21114	320
⊞ System.ni.dll	13.496	2.584	6804	1303
⊞ kernel32.dll	3.080	2.136	1553	1077
⊞ w3core.dll	2.315	0.768	1167	387
⊞ ntdll.dll	2.208	2.164	1113	1091
⊞ MSVCR80.dll	1.712	1.712	863	863
⊞ w3isapi.dll	1.531	0.119	772	60
⊞ w3dt.dll	1.515	0.050	764	25
⊞ W3TP.dll	1.513	0.024	763	12
⊞ App_Web_rnnlfli3.dll	1.192	0.038	601	19
⊞ IISUTIL.dll	0.910	0.553	459	279
⊞ System.Configuration.ni.dll	0.641	0.125	323	63
⊞ WS2_32.dll	0.492	0.165	248	83
⊞ msvcrt.dll	0.428	0.349	216	176
⊞ System.Transactions.dll	0.415	0.125	209	63
⊞ ADVAPI32.dll	0.383	0.190	193	96
⊞ rsaenh.dll	0.226	0.065	114	33
⊞ aspnet_filter.dll	0.224	0.034	113	17
⊞ mswsock.dll	0.192	0.121	97	61
⊞ System.Web.RegularExpressions.ni.dll	0.135	0.002	68	1
⊞ WS2HELP.dll	0.121	0.091	61	46
⊞ W3CACHE.dll	0.109	0.036	55	18
⊞ ole32.dll	0.087	0.087	44	44
⊞ HTTPAPI.dll	0.052	0.020	26	10
⊞ System.Drawing.ni.dll	0.034	0.016	17	8
⊞ System.Xml.ni.dll	0.012	0.012	6	6
⊞ RPCRT4.dll	0.008	0.008	4	4
⊞ W3COMLOG.dll	0.004	0.004	2	2
⊞ SamplingRuntime.dll	0.004	0.000	2	0

🗎 Summary	ƒx Functions	📇 Caller/Callee	📖 Call Tree	🔎 Allocation	📋 Objects Lifetime	▼

Figure 10-39. *The report document for the performance session open to the Functions tab*

Now we must look at how to analyze and interpret such a vast amount of data, remembering that the aim is to identify that part of the application where performance improvements can be made to best effect. In Figure 10-39 the Functions tab is displayed, in which the relative time in each function is represented and the functions are arranged hierarchically under the assemblies in which they are defined. For example, App_Web_d3_x-hlz.dll is the assembly that has been created in the .NET cache area by compilation of the SalesSite project source code. We can see that 86 percent of the inclusive samples are in that assembly, which means that 86 percent of the time, either a function in that assembly is executing or a function is executing in another assembly that was called by a function in that first assembly. This means that 86 percent of the time SalesSite web forms are being processed in one way or another. Now we would like to find out where in that 86 percent the most time is spent. Actually, that is very clear from the Exclusive Percent column. It is made up chiefly of time spent in System.Data.dll, mscorwks.dll, and mscorlib.ni.dll. The last two DLLs are parts of the CRE and the first DLL is database facilities. Unfortunately, the source program debug database (PDB) file for mscorwks.dll is not available so expanding it does not provide a breakdown of functions. However, breaking down mscorlib.ni.dll shows that most time is spent in functions concerned with hash tables and strings. For System.Data.dll, most inclusive time is spent in DBDataAdapter.Fill functions.

These are all functions that offer services to our application, and they are taking up processor time. But to understand why, we have to discover why our application is calling them. For example, the window in Figure 10-40 shows that System.Data.dll is exclusively taking up 23 percent of the application's time and inclusively, the Fill function is taking up 34 percent. So it looks like the Fill function is the most commonly used entry point to this assembly where much of the application's time is spent. So who calls this Fill function? I'm sure you can make a good guess—but let's use the features of the performance report to find out. In the window in Figure 10-40 you can right-click on the Fill(class System.Data.DataTable) function, as shown, and select Show Functions Calling Fill, which displays the Caller/Callee tab populated with the information required, as shown in Figure 10-41.

Function Name	Inclusive Percent	Exclusive Percent	Inclusive Samples	Exclusive Samples
⊟ **System.Data.dll**	43.944	23.713	22155	11955
System.Data.Common.DbDataAdapter.Fill(class System.Data.DataTable)	34.848	0.036	17569	18
System.Data.Common.DbDataAdapter.Fill(class Syst...	34.765	0.046	17527	23
System.Data.Common.DbDataAdapter.FillInternal(cla... [Show functions called by Fill]	34.717	0.067	17503	34
System.Data.Common.DataAdapter.Fill(class System... [Show functions calling Fill]	24.863	0.131	12535	66
System.Data.Common.DataAdapter.FillFromReader(c... [Copy]	20.464	0.016	10317	8
System.Data.Common.DataAdapter.FillLoadDataRow([Add/Remove Columns...]	17.012	0.079	8577	40
System.Data.ProviderBase.SchemaMapping.LoadData	15.689	0.137	7910	69
System.Data.DataTable.LoadDataRow(object[],bool) [Group by Module]	11.655	0.147	5876	74
System.Data.Common.DbCommand.System.Data.IDb... [Sort]	6.165	0.014	3108	7
Summary Functions Caller/Callee		Objects Lifetime		

Figure 10-40. *The Functions tab expanded to show the System.Data.dll functions*

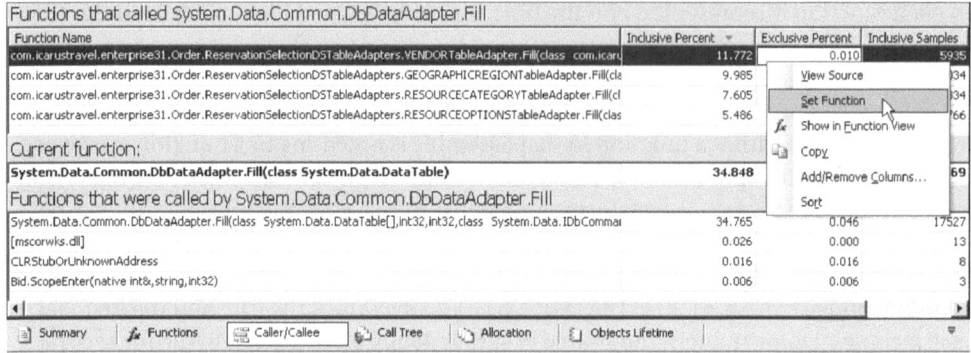

Figure 10-41. *The Caller/Callee tab showing the information for the DbDataAdapter.Fill function*

You can see that the four callers in Figure 10-41 are the Fill functions of VENDORTableAdapter, GEOGRAPHICREGIONTableAdapter, RESOURCECATEGORYTableAdapter, and RESOURCEOPTIONSTableAdapter, which were defined in the ReservationSelectDS dataset. To find out who calls the VendorTableAdapter.Fill function, we can right-click on it and again select Set Function, which will make this function take the Current Function place in the middle of the display and show its callers at the top and its callees at the bottom.

Let's first take a moment to consider what the figures mean in Figure 10-41 and the next two figures. The Caller/Callee tab shows a function in the middle (the Current Function) and all the functions called by it (the callees) below, as well as the functions that call it (the callers) above. The inclusive and exclusive samples and percent are also shown. Let's think about what these values mean in this display. When a sample is made, the stack is examined, and the Inclusive Samples column for the Current Function display shows the number of samples for which this function was found somewhere on the stack. The Inclusive Percent column gives the percentage of all samples for which this function was found somewhere on the stack.

The Inclusive Samples column in the Callers section at the top shows the number of samples for which that function was *also* on the stack, pushed on *before* the current function. The callees Inclusive Samples column shows the number of samples for which that function was also on the stack, pushed on *after* the current function. For the exclusive case a similar description applies, except that the requirement was that the current function was actually *executing* when the sample was made. This is rather tricky to get clear, but keep in mind that it's the state of the stack at the instant the sample is made that determines which counts get incremented when each sample is made.

As Figure 10-42 shows, the VENDORTableAdapter.Fill function is called by the GetLocalData function of VendorBE, as we would expect. We can see here if anything is calling this VENDORTableAdapter.Fill that we *didn't* expect. How nice to be able to identify unwelcome callers like this! We can work our way further up the call tree (not shown) until we finally see who is calling. Unfortunately, when we get up to see the callers for VendorBE.GetData we only see the assembly mscorwks.dll. It's like we know which company the call is coming from but not the person in the company who's calling us! If we try to go up further we get a huge list of every function that called any function within mscorwks.dll.

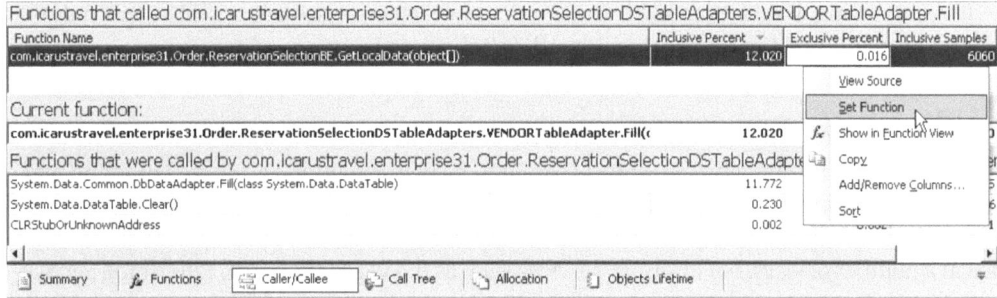

Figure 10-42. *The Caller/Callee tab showing the information for the VENDORTableAdapter.Fill function*

So what have we found out? We know that the `Fill` functions on the four table adapters in `ReservationSelectDS` are called lots of times and that they form the main entry point to the `System.Data.dll`, which either occupies *or* calls other assemblies that occupy 44 percent of the application's time. So here is where Ed should try to make some improvement. If the performance of the application is to be improved, either he must reduce the number of calls to these four table adapters, or he must reduce the time spent in each call.

We can also start somewhat at the other end by looking at `OrderDAL` as an assembly and viewing the inclusive sample percentages for the `Fill` functions by expanding the `OrderDAL` assembly, as shown in Figure 10-43. You can see that these figures are almost the same as the inclusive caller sample percentages in Figure 10-41. Why are they not exactly the same? Well, because sometimes, for example, `VendorTableAdapter.Fill` is on the stack but `DbTableAdapter.Fill` is not. This would be the case if `VendorTableAdapter.Fill` were itself executing when the sample occurred or another function that it calls was executing.

Function Name	Inclusive Percent ▼	Exclusive Percent	Inclusive Samples	Exclusive Samples
⊞ mscorwks.dll	98.608	35.762	49714	18030
⊞ Unknown	94.129	6.714	47456	3385
⊞ webengine.dll	92.671	0.305	46721	154
⊞ System.Web.ni.dll	92.044	7.569	46405	3816
⊞ App_Web_d3_x-hlz.dll	86.167	0.061	43442	31
⊞ mscorlib.ni.dll	60.709	13.539	30607	6826
⊞ System.Data.dll	43.944	23.713	22155	11955
⊞ OrderBE.DLL	42.853	0.046	21605	23
⊞ BusinessEntity.DLL	42.693	0.058	21524	29
⊟ OrderDAL.DLL	41.880	0.635	21114	320
com.icarustravel.enterprise31.Order.ReservationSelectionDSTableAdapters.VENDORTableAdapter.Fill(cla	12.020	0.016	6060	8
com.icarustravel.enterprise31.Order.ReservationSelectionDSTableAdapters.GEOGRAPHICREGIONTableA	10.231	0.010	5158	5
com.icarustravel.enterprise31.Order.ReservationSelectionDSTableAdapters.RESOURCECATEGORYTableA	7.833	0.008	3949	4
com.icarustravel.enterprise31.Order.ReservationSelectionDSTableAdapters.RESOURCEOPTIONSTableAd	5.913	0.024	2981	12
com.icarustravel.enterprise31.Order.ReservationSelectionDS..ctor()	4.140	0.004	2087	2
com.icarustravel.enterprise31.Order.ReservationSelectionDS.InitClass()	4.060	0.006	2047	3
com.icarustravel.enterprise31.Order.ReservationSelectionDS.GEOGRAPHICREGIONDataTable..ctor()	1.248	0.020	629	10
com.icarustravel.enterprise31.Order.ReservationSelectionDS.RESOURCEOPTIONSDataTable..ctor()	0.910	0.008	459	4
com.icarustravel.enterprise31.Order.ReservationSelectionDS.RESOURCEOPTIONSDataTable.InitClass()	0.728	0.030	367	15
com.icarustravel.enterprise31.Order.ReservationSelectionDS.RESOURCECATEGORYDataTable..ctor()	0.704	0.006	355	3
com.icarustravel.enterprise31.Order.ReservationSelectionDS.GEOGRAPHICREGIONDataTable.InitClass()	0.682	0.014	344	7
com.icarustravel.enterprise31.Order.ReservationSelectionDS.VENDORDataTable..ctor()	0.601	0.008	303	4
com.icarustravel.enterprise31.Order.ReservationSelectionDSTableAdapters.RESOURCEOPTIONSTableAd	0.571	0.002	288	1

Figure 10-43. *The Functions tab expanded to show the four table adapter fill functions*

It is interesting to note that more time is spent in `VENDORTableAdapter.Fill` than in the other table adapter fill functions. This is another point worth investigating.

Profiling by Instrumentation

The alternative to profiling by sampling is profiling by instrumentation, where enter and exit probes are inserted into the application's functions and report back to the instrumentation infrastructure. It is possible to instrument a variety of applications and run performance sessions in a number of ways. For example, services such as the World Wide Web Publishing Service can be profiled using a performance session of instrumentation type. It is therefore possible to profile the Sales Site application, with the assemblies of interest automatically instrumented. The site can then be stimulated using a load test. After the test is complete, the instrumentation results can be examined to obtain the times for execution of functions of interest. This tends to be a somewhat slow process because the data retrieved tends to be very extensive, but it has the advantage that the system is operating in a realistic multithreading environment—although its performance will be impaired by the addition of the instrumentation probe code itself.

Note The code at this point can be found in `Chapter 10\Exercise 5`. Exercise 10-6 demonstrates the material in this section.

Once you have carried out sampling analysis and determined areas of interest, you will want to test member functions of the business objects under very controlled conditions so that you can evaluate consistently the effects of code changes, made with the intention of improving performance. Normally the `SalesBusinessObjects` classes are instantiated as objects by the presentation layer consisting of the `SalesSite` web application project, but for instrumentation purposes it may be better to create instances of the objects from a Windows or command-line application. Rather than creating new applications, the unit tests that have already been created—and maybe some additional ones—are a good place to profile the business objects using instrumentation. Both instrumentation of `SalesSite` and the unit tests have value in a project such as Icarus's, and often the results of one technique tend to indicate further work using a different technique. Certainly, there may well be situations that occur—due to multiple threading, for example—that are better studied by instrumenting the site itself. Let's look at the instrumented unit test.

Having worked with Rob to complete a certain amount of work using sampling profiling, Ed has some ideas as to where his code might be improved. There does seem to be an excessive amount of time spent in `ResourceSelectionBE.GetDataTable`, and he'd like to reduce the number of times it is called and decrease its execution time. He therefore decides to run his unit tests using the profiler to determine the amount of time spent in `ResourceSelectionBE.GetDataTable` and its related functions. To identify the amount of time spent in this function he writes a new, very simple unit test that calls the `GetDataTable` ten times, and then exits without checking any results. He ensures that the values passed as the parameters to the function under test are realistic and result in data returned from the test database. Here is the unit-test code:

```
[TestMethod()]
public void GetResourceOptionTableTest()
{
  int regionId = 0;
  int categoryId = 0;
  int vendorId = 0;
  DateTime dateTime = new DateTime(2006,4,10);
  int unitCount = 1;

  string tableName = "RESOURCEOPTIONS";
  DataTable actual;

  for(int i=0;i<10;i++)
    actual =
com.icarustravel.enterprise31.Order.ReservationSelectionBE.GetDataTable(
                 regionId, categoryId, vendorId, dateTime, unitCount, tableName);
}
```

Developers might want to instrument a more complicated unit test, but this one will serve to examine the time spent in the GetDataTable function and allow its performance to be optimized.

To accomplish his goal Ed wants to set up a performance session that will automatically instrument the set of binaries that have been placed in the bin folder for the OrderBETests project and that will launch a selected unit test. It is no good trying to do this using the Performance Wizard since that will not list test projects, so he opens the Performance Sessions window and clicks the New Performance Session button to create a blank performance session. Next he right-clicks on the new performance session, called Performance1, and selects Properties from the context menu. On the General page he selects Instrumentation instead of Sampling, types "OrderBEUnitTest" for the report name, and closes the dialog box.

Now Ed must add some target assemblies to the performance session that he wants to examine. He right-clicks on the Targets folder beneath it and selects Add Target Binary. Again, it's no good selecting Add Target Project from the context menu because test projects are not listed, but the Add Target Binary option allows him to add any binary accessible as a file. In the Add Target Binary dialog box, Ed navigates through the project structure to the folder

OrderBETest\bin\Release

in his workspace area, as shown in Figure 10-44. He selects these assemblies:

BusinessEntity.dll
OrderBE.dll
OrderDAL.dll

Ed then clicks Open in the dialog box, which includes these binaries in the performance session.

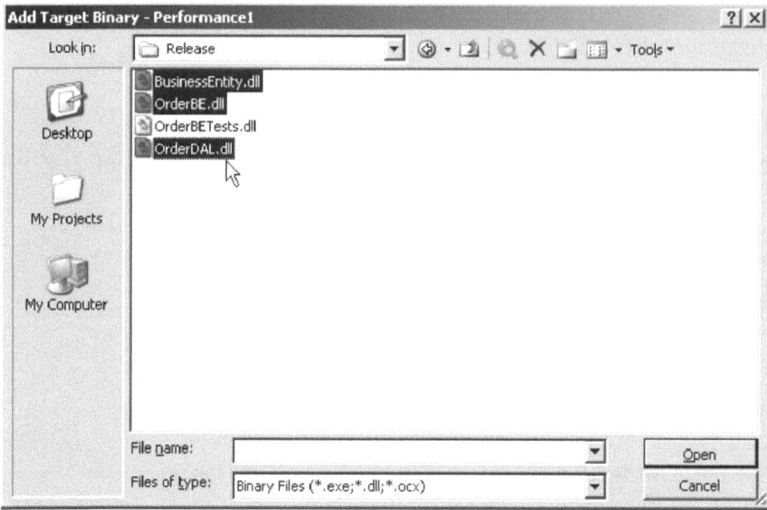

Figure 10-44. *Adding binaries to the performance session*

Just to better understand the system, right-click on Performance1 and select Launch. You will immediately see the dialog box shown in Figure 10-45. The point to remember is that a performance session controlled from the Performance Sessions window must either launch a binary executable or be attached to an existing process. Actually, only sampling performance sessions can be attached to existing processes, and since this session is an instrumentation one, it must therefore have a launch binary associated with it.

Figure 10-45. *You need a launch binary for every performance session.*

So Ed needs to add a launch binary—none of the binaries he's already added will do because they're class libraries and can't be launched. When you run a unit test from the Test View or Test Manager window, an executable supplied by Microsoft runs and calls the tests defined in your test class by reflection. What is this application? Well, it's actually called MSTest.exe and on Ed's machine it's located in the folder

E:\Program Files\Microsoft Visual Studio 8\Common7\IDE

So Ed needs to add that as one of the binaries. He does so by following the same process as before, then navigating to MSTest.exe in the Add Target Binary dialog box and clicking Open.

However, we do not need to try to instrument that binary. Going back to the Performance Explorer window, Ed must select `MSTest.exe`, right-click, uncheck Instrument on the context menu, and make sure Set as Launch is checked. You can easily see under Targets which are to be instrumented and which are to be launched: those to be instrumented are marked with green dots, and those to be executed have a green arrow (Figure 10-46). Some could legitimately have both, but not in this particular case.

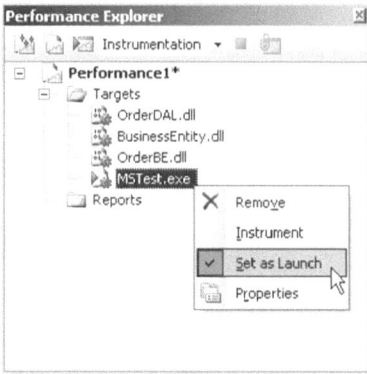

Figure 10-46. *Instrumented binaries have green dots and launch binaries have green arrows.*

Ed is almost there, but not quite—this will cause `MSTest.exe` to run but it will not tell that application which tests are to be run. To avoid confusing results, Ed would like one performance test for each unit test, so he only wants to run the test called `GetResourceOptionTableTest` in this case. This is the test we listed earlier that calls the function `ReservationSelectionBE. GetDataTable` ten times with suitable arguments. `MSTest.exe` can be run from the command line and accepts a range of command-line arguments, which are listed by the command

```
E:\Program Files\Microsoft Visual Studio 8\Common7\IDE>MSTest /?
```

The two options of use here are `/testcontainer` and `/test`:

```
/testcontainer:[file name] Load a file that contains tests. You can
  specify this option more than once to load multiple test files.
  Examples:
    /testcontainer:mytestproject.dll
    /testcontainer:loadtest1.loadtest

/test:[test name] The name of a test to be run. You can
  specify this option multiple times to run more than one test.
```

Ed right-clicks on the `MSTest.exe` binary in Performance Explorer and selects Properties. In the resulting dialog box is a text box for entering command-line arguments to the binary when it is launched. Ed types in these options:

```
/test:GetResourceOptionTableTest
    /testcontainer:"F:\Workspaces\EdwardMarshall\Iteration 1\OrderBETest\bin\Debug"
```

He enters them all on one line, separated by spaces, as shown in Figure 10-47.

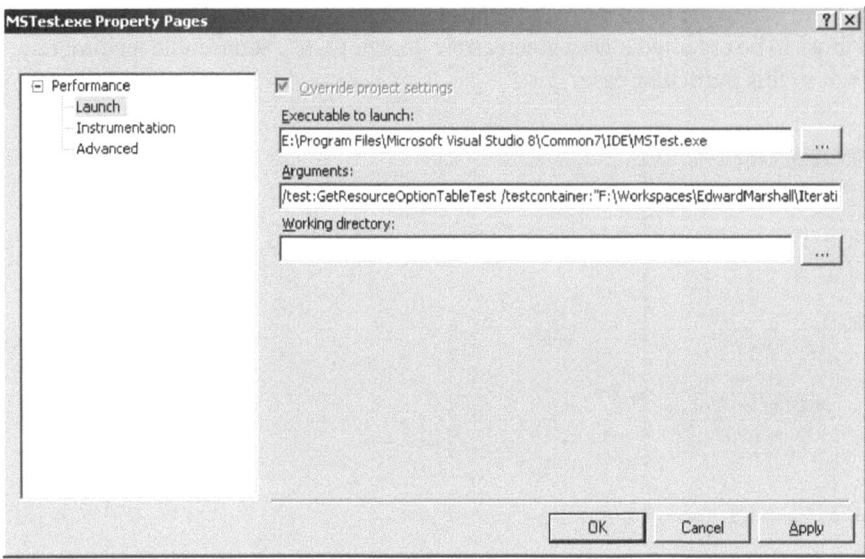

Figure 10-47. *The command-line options for the MSTest.exe launch binary*

Ed can now right-click on this performance session and select Launch. First the selected assemblies are instrumented, and then the unit test under MSTest.exe runs, gathering the output of the instrumentation probes into a report. The report's summary page appears in Figure 10-48.

Performance Report Summary

Most Called Functions

Name	Number of Calls	%
System.Type.GetTypeFromHandle	260	5.149
....Data.DataColumnCollection.Add	220	4.356
System.Data.DataColumn..ctor	220	4.356

Functions With Most Individual Work

Name	Time (msecs)	%
System.Data.DataTable.Clear	0.333839	10.249
....Data.Common.DbDataAdapter.Fill	0.243788	7.485
...tem.Data.ConstraintCollection.Add	0.215162	6.606

Functions Taking Longest

Name	Time (msecs)	%
...ocols.SoapHttpClientProtocol..ctor	636.577000	39.161
....Data.Common.DbDataAdapter.Fill	367.974674	22.637
...iguration.SettingsBase.get_Item	163.615205	10.065

Summary   Functions   Caller/Callee   Call Tree   Allocation

Figure 10-48. *Performance Report Summary for GetResourceOptionTableTest*

Figure 10-49 shows the Functions tab; the assembly `OrderBE.dll` has been expanded to show all of the functions that are called in this assembly, along with the reported timings from their instrumentation probes. The one Ed would like to study is

```
com.icarustravel.ReservationSelectionBE.GetDataTable(
                                int32,int32,int32,DateTime,int32,string)
```

This appears as the highlighted function in the list. The report shows that it has been called 10 times, as expected.

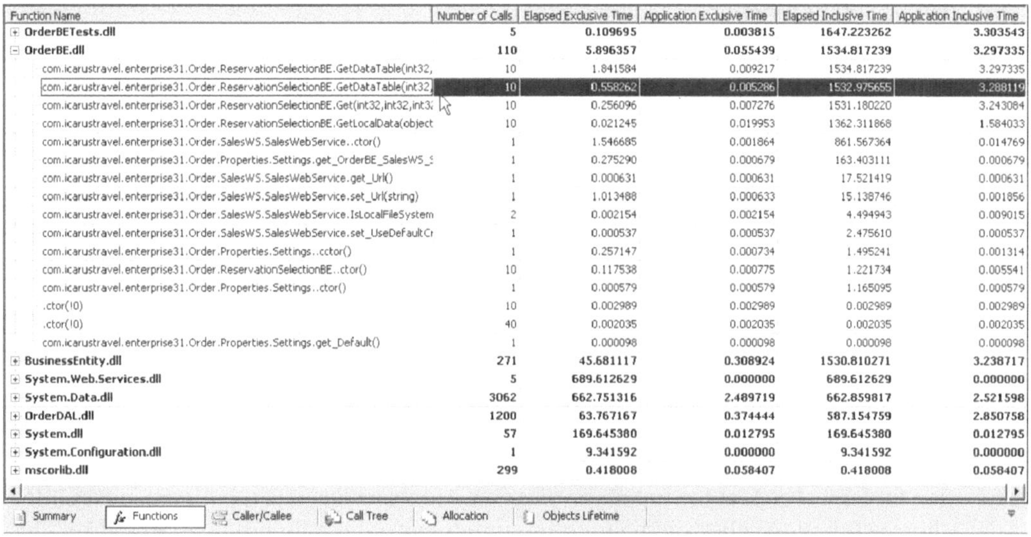

Function Name	Number of Calls	Elapsed Exclusive Time	Application Exclusive Time	Elapsed Inclusive Time	Application Inclusive Time
⊞ OrderBETests.dll	5	0.109695	0.003815	1647.223262	3.303543
⊟ OrderBE.dll	110	5.896357	0.055439	1534.817239	3.297335
com.icarustravel.enterprise31.Order.ReservationSelectionBE.GetDataTable(int32,	10	1.841584	0.009217	1534.817239	3.297335
com.icarustravel.enterprise31.Order.ReservationSelectionBE.GetDataTable(int32,	10	0.558262	0.005286	1532.975655	3.288119
com.icarustravel.enterprise31.Order.ReservationSelectionBE.Get(int32,int32,int3.	10	0.256096	0.007276	1531.180220	3.243084
com.icarustravel.enterprise31.Order.ReservationSelectionBE.GetLocalData(object	10	0.021245	0.019953	1362.311868	1.584033
com.icarustravel.enterprise31.Order.SalesWS.SalesWebService..ctor()	1	1.546685	0.001864	861.567364	0.014769
com.icarustravel.enterprise31.Order.Properties.Settings.get_OrderBE_SalesWS_S	1	0.275290	0.000679	163.403111	0.000679
com.icarustravel.enterprise31.Order.SalesWS.SalesWebService.get_Url()	1	0.000631	0.000631	17.521419	0.000631
com.icarustravel.enterprise31.Order.SalesWS.SalesWebService.set_Url(string)	1	1.013488	0.000633	15.138746	0.001856
com.icarustravel.enterprise31.Order.SalesWS.SalesWebService.IsLocalFileSystem	2	0.002154	0.002154	4.494943	0.009015
com.icarustravel.enterprise31.Order.SalesWS.SalesWebService.set_UseDefaultCr	1	0.000537	0.000537	2.475610	0.000537
com.icarustravel.enterprise31.Order.Properties.Settings..cctor()	1	0.257147	0.000734	1.495241	0.001314
com.icarustravel.enterprise31.Order.ReservationSelectionBE..ctor()	10	0.117538	0.000775	1.221734	0.005541
com.icarustravel.enterprise31.Order.Properties.Settings..ctor()	1	0.000579	0.000579	1.165095	0.000579
.ctor(!0)	10	0.002989	0.002989	0.002989	0.002989
.ctor(!0)	40	0.002035	0.002035	0.002035	0.002035
com.icarustravel.enterprise31.Order.Properties.Settings.get_Default()	1	0.000098	0.000098	0.000098	0.000098
⊞ BusinessEntity.dll	271	45.681117	0.308924	1530.810271	3.238717
⊞ System.Web.Services.dll	5	689.612629	0.000000	689.612629	0.000000
⊞ System.Data.dll	3062	662.751316	2.489719	662.859817	2.521598
⊞ OrderDAL.dll	1200	63.767167	0.374444	587.154759	2.850758
⊞ System.dll	57	169.645380	0.012795	169.645380	0.012795
⊞ System.Configuration.dll	1	9.341592	0.000000	9.341592	0.000000
⊞ mscorlib.dll	299	0.418008	0.058407	0.418008	0.058407

| 🖹 Summary | ⨍ꜝ Functions | 📇 Caller/Callee | 🗔 Call Tree | 🔍 Allocation | 🗋 Objects Lifetime |

Figure 10-49. *Functions tab of the performance report for GetResourceOptionTableTest*

Actually this function appears twice in the table. According to Microsoft, the double calls are a side effect of the profiler when there are calls between two instrumented DLLs. Since the DLLs don't know whether the outgoing calls are in an instrumented binary, they also instrument themselves to catch the return calls. So you end up seeing the function from both the calling binary and the target binary. The longer of the two values should be used for analysis.

The name and argument details of the function appear on the left, and the four columns on the right contain the *total* time spent in the function. To find the average time, you need to divide the times recorded by the number of calls, or you can select Add/Remove Columns from the context menu and add Average Time columns. The window in Figure 10-49 displays four time columns:

- **Elapsed Exclusive Time:** This is the time elapsed while the code in this function completes execution. It includes any time spent in the kernel, and time spent executing other threads and processes, but it does not include time spent in functions called by this function. It also does not include time spent in the instrumentation probes. It is therefore truly the time *elapsed* while the code in this function executes, summed over all executions of the function, as if the instrumentation were not present.

- **Application Exclusive Time:** This is the time spent actually executing the code within the function. It excludes any time spent in the kernel and executing other threads, and also excludes time spent in functions called by this function. It is summed over all executions of the function.

- **Elapsed Inclusive Time:** This is the time elapsed while the function, or any function it calls, is executing. It includes time spent in the kernel or executing other threads and processes, and it also includes time spent executing functions that are called by this one and any kernel or other thread time that occurs while those functions are executing. It does not include time spent in processing the instrumentation probes. It can therefore be described as the elapsed time between the entry to the function and its exit, summed over all executions of the function, but corrected to remove effects of the instrumentation itself.

- **Application Inclusive Time:** This is the time spent executing the code in this function and any functions called by it, summed over all executions of the function. It does not include time spent in the kernel or other tasks and processes.

These ideas should be made clear by Figure 10-50, where a thread is shown entering a function under test at A, at the top of the diagram. After a while, at B, the thread moves into a .NET library function called by the function under test, which then returns at C. Next the thread is suspended at D, and the processor executes code in the kernel until another thread in the same process executes a different function at E. Later this thread is suspended at F, and the kernel executes again until G, when a thread in a different process executes. At H, this process is suspended and the kernel executes until I, when the original thread is resumed until J, when another function in the same assembly is called from the function under test. This returns at K, and the function under test returns at L. The key at the bottom of the figure indicates which portions of the processors execution time are included in the various times presented in the profiler results. All the figures are presented in milliseconds.

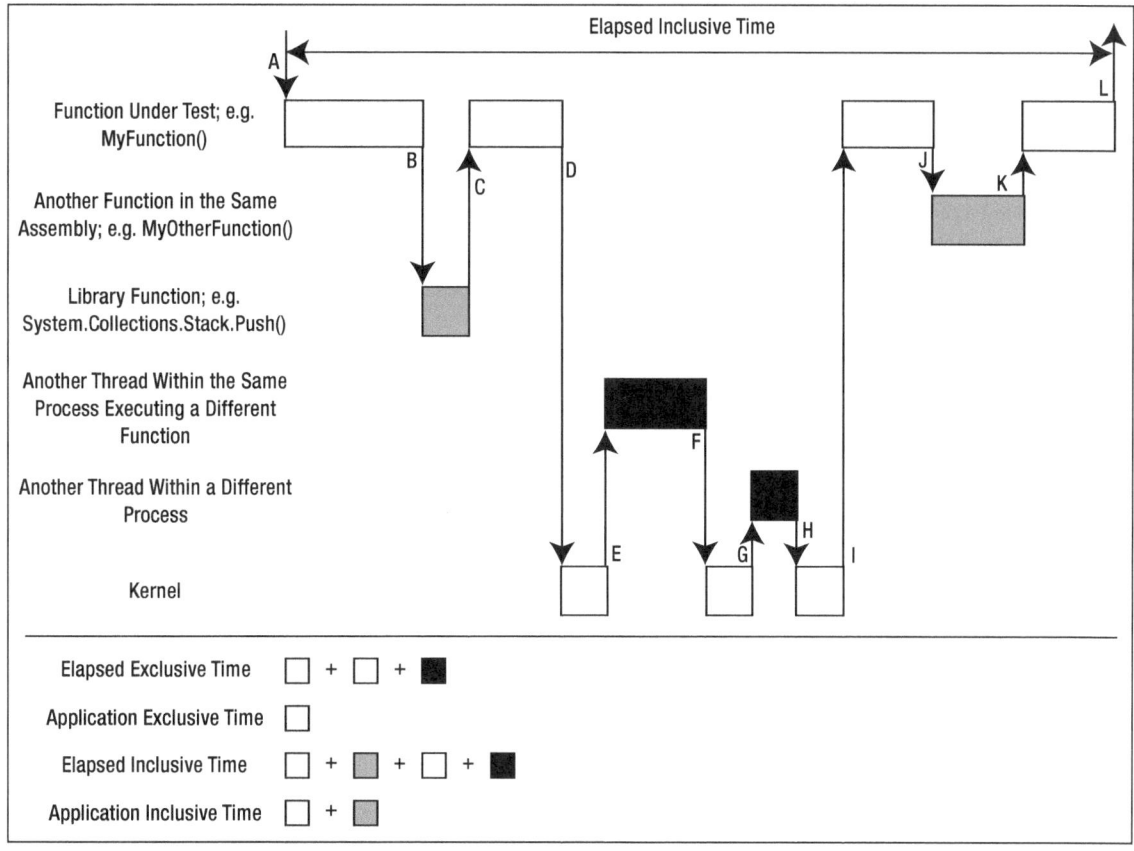

Figure 10-50. *Different time figures are recorded when profiling in instrumentation mode.*

Table 10-1 summarizes the data (correct to three significant figures) from Figure 10-49.

Table 10-1. *Time measurements for the function ReservationSelectionBE.GetTableData*

Measurement Name	Value
Elapsed Exclusive Time	0.558 ms
Application Exclusive Time	0.00529 ms
Elapsed Inclusive Time	1530 ms
Application Inclusive Time	3.29 ms

You can see that the Application Exclusive Time, even for 10 repeats of the call, is only 5.29 microseconds, whereas the 0.558 ms of elapsed exclusive time is 100 times longer. Similarly, for the inclusive times, the elapsed time is nearly 500 times longer than the Application Inclusive Time of 3.29 ms. Obviously the processor is doing a great deal of other activity while the test is executing; part of this is waiting for the database to respond. There also may be considerable paging going on, particularly if the database is on the same machine, which was the case for this test. Of course, you can probably expect an instrumented piece of software to execute much more slowly because of the time taken to execute the instrumentation probes themselves, which must gather and process the timing data as the application executes. However, according to the documentation, this time is removed from the elapsed timing figures, which is good because you want to be able to see how the code performed in the elapsed context as well as the application context without worrying about the effect of the probes. We should be able to relate *elapsed* timing observed here to the absolute performance of the system, such as the response times. These times are made up of application time components and waiting time. If, for example, the machine under test has insufficient memory, the elapsed times may be very long due to paging, as Ed may be seeing here.

At this point, Ed wants to concentrate on improving the Application Inclusive Time for the execution of the GetDataTable function.

Improving the Application Inclusive Time

A good example of using the profiler in instrumentation mode is to observe how the Application Inclusive Time of the GetDataTable function can be improved. Ed explores the functions called by GetDataTable by right-clicking on that function name and selecting Show Functions Called By GetDataTable. He then selects the called functions with the longest Application Inclusive Times and issues the Set Function command from the context menu several times to drill down to the view shown in Figure 10-51. As you can see, two callees together make up the Application Inclusive Time: the call to GetLocalData and a mysterious call to a hexadecimal address. If Ed selects Set Function from the context menu on this callee, he'll find that it is actually the constructor for ReservationSelectionDS.

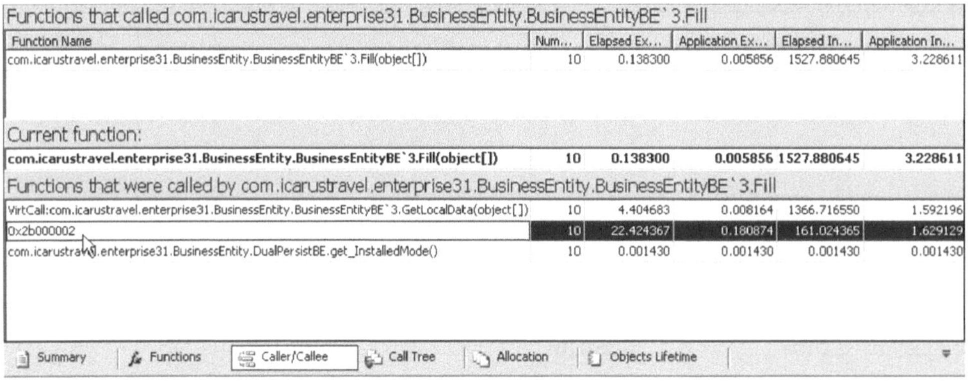

Functions that called com.icarustravel.enterprise31.BusinessEntity.BusinessEntityBE`3.Fill					
Function Name	Num...	Elapsed Ex...	Application Ex...	Elapsed In...	Application In...
com.icarustravel.enterprise31.BusinessEntity.BusinessEntityBE`3.Fill(object[])	10	0.138300	0.005856	1527.880645	3.228611

Current function:					
com.icarustravel.enterprise31.BusinessEntity.BusinessEntityBE`3.Fill(object[])	10	0.138300	0.005856	1527.880645	3.228611

Functions that were called by com.icarustravel.enterprise31.BusinessEntity.BusinessEntityBE`3.Fill					
VirtCall:com.icarustravel.enterprise31.BusinessEntity.BusinessEntityBE`3.GetLocalData(object[])	10	4.404683	0.008164	1366.716550	1.592196
0x2b000002	10	22.424367	0.180874	161.024365	1.629129
com.icarustravel.enterprise31.BusinessEntity.DualPersistBE.get_InstalledMode()	10	0.001430	0.001430	0.001430	0.001430

| Summary | Functions | Caller/Callee | Call Tree | Allocation | Objects Lifetime |

Figure 10-51. *The Caller/Callee tab at the BusinessEntityBE.Fill function showing the functions called*

Here is the code for the function BusinessEntityBE.Fill:

```
protected void Fill(object[] objects)
{
  data = new LocalDSType();
```

```
if (InstalledMode == InstallMode.Client)
{
  data.Merge(GetRemoteData(objects));
}
else
{
  GetLocalData(objects);
}
}
```

This code constructs the `LocalDSType`, which in this case is `ReservationSelectionDS`. It then calls the `GetLocalData` function. Ed notes that the call to the `ReservationSelectionDS` constructor is quite costly. Next, he right-clicks on `GetLocalData`, selects Set Function, and sees the window shown in Figure 10-52.

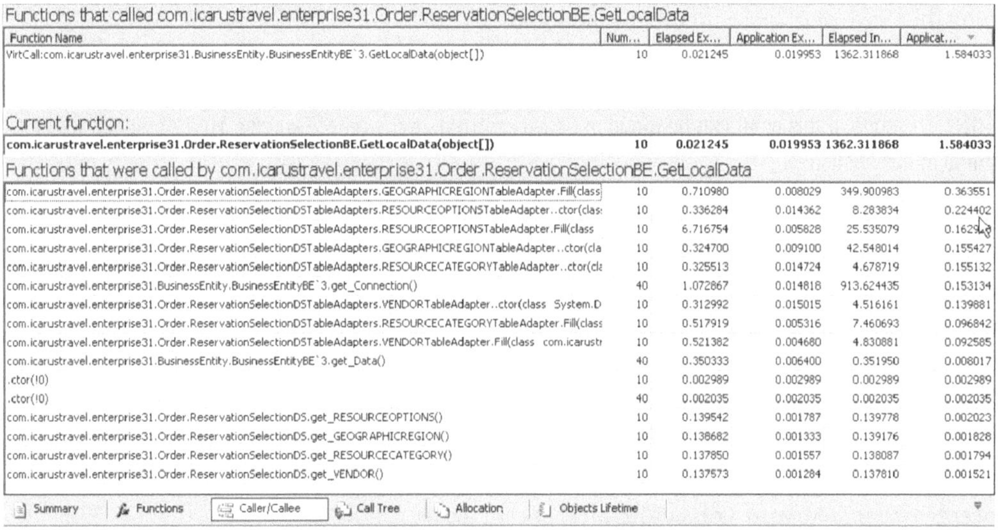

Functions that called com.icarustravel.enterprise31.Order.ReservationSelectionBE.GetLocalData					
Function Name	Num...	Elapsed Ex...	Application Ex...	Elapsed In...	Applicat...
VirtCall:com.icarustravel.enterprise31.BusinessEntity.BusinessEntityBE`3.GetLocalData(object[])	10	0.021245	0.019953	1362.311868	1.584033

Current function:					
com.icarustravel.enterprise31.Order.ReservationSelectionBE.GetLocalData(object[])	10	0.021245	0.019953	1362.311868	1.584033

Functions that were called by com.icarustravel.enterprise31.Order.ReservationSelectionBE.GetLocalData					
com.icarustravel.enterprise31.Order.ReservationSelectionDSTableAdapters.GEOGRAPHICREGIONTableAdapter.Fill(class	10	0.710980	0.008029	349.900983	0.363551
com.icarustravel.enterprise31.Order.ReservationSelectionDSTableAdapters.RESOURCEOPTIONSTableAdapter..ctor(clas:	10	0.336284	0.014362	8.283834	0.224402
com.icarustravel.enterprise31.Order.ReservationSelectionDSTableAdapters.RESOURCEOPTIONSTableAdapter.Fill(class	10	6.716754	0.005828	25.535079	0.16294
com.icarustravel.enterprise31.Order.ReservationSelectionDSTableAdapters.GEOGRAPHICREGIONTableAdapter..ctor(cla	10	0.324700	0.009100	42.548014	0.155427
com.icarustravel.enterprise31.Order.ReservationSelectionDSTableAdapters.RESOURCECATEGORYTableAdapter..ctor(cla	10	0.325513	0.014724	4.678719	0.155132
com.icarustravel.enterprise31.BusinessEntity.BusinessEntityBE`3.get_Connection()	40	1.072867	0.014818	913.624435	0.153134
com.icarustravel.enterprise31.Order.ReservationSelectionDSTableAdapters.VENDORTableAdapter..ctor(class System.D	10	0.312992	0.015015	4.516161	0.139881
com.icarustravel.enterprise31.Order.ReservationSelectionDSTableAdapters.RESOURCECATEGORYTableAdapter.Fill(class	10	0.517919	0.005316	7.460693	0.096842
com.icarustravel.enterprise31.Order.ReservationSelectionDSTableAdapters.VENDORTableAdapter.Fill(class com.icarustr	10	0.521382	0.004680	4.830881	0.092585
com.icarustravel.enterprise31.BusinessEntity.BusinessEntityBE`3.get_Data()	40	0.350333	0.006400	0.351950	0.008017
.ctor(!0)	10	0.002989	0.002989	0.002989	0.002989
.ctor(!0)	40	0.002035	0.002035	0.002035	0.002035
com.icarustravel.enterprise31.Order.ReservationSelectionDS.get_RESOURCEOPTIONS()	10	0.139542	0.001787	0.139778	0.002023
com.icarustravel.enterprise31.Order.ReservationSelectionDS.get_GEOGRAPHICREGION()	10	0.138682	0.001333	0.139176	0.001828
com.icarustravel.enterprise31.Order.ReservationSelectionDS.get_RESOURCECATEGORY()	10	0.137850	0.001557	0.138087	0.001794
com.icarustravel.enterprise31.Order.ReservationSelectionDS.get_VENDOR()	10	0.137573	0.001284	0.137810	0.001521

Summary	Functions	Caller/Callee	Call Tree	Allocation	Objects Lifetime

Figure 10-52. *The Caller/Callee tab at the ReservationSelectionBE.GetLocalData function showing the functions called*

Time is obviously spent in each of the `Fill` functions, and this is beyond Ed's control since the code was automatically written by Visual Studio as part of the dataset and table adapter generation. However, he also notes that the calls to the four constructors for the table adapters are quite costly. Certainly in this and the previous functions, numerous objects concerned with database access are constructed, and this will generate heap pressure. Ed remembers that excessive garbage collector activity was flagged in the load testing. He wonders if he could reduce the number of objects created and destroyed and therefore reduce both the execution time and the heap pressure.

Note *Heap pressure* is the rate at which memory is demanded from the heap by the application as a result of creation of objects, and is measured in bytes/second. So high heap pressure means a high rate of demand of memory from the heap. Unless our application has access to an infinite memory, high heap pressure will result in a high amount of time spent in garbage collection to recover the memory. However, heap pressure is a bit more complicated than that, since the behavior of the garbage collector may be different if one or two large objects are created as compared to a large number of small objects, even though the bytes/second demanded from the heap may be the same. In any case, if heap pressure can be reduced, our application will generally run more efficiently.

Keep in mind that each of the table adapter objects requires a connection. This connection is currently created and held as an instance field within the base class BusinessEntityBE. ADO.NET contains a mechanism called the connection pool to avoid excessive connection establishment with a database. We can therefore create connections without worrying too much since they come from the pool and are returned to the pool when they are released by calling the Close or Dispose member functions.

Note The code at this point can be found in Chapter 10\Exercise 6. Exercise 10-7 demonstrates the material in this section.

Ed theorizes that perhaps table adapters could be pooled in a similar way to connections and possibly even the dataset classes. He discusses this with Angela, who is responsible for the sales business objects. They agree that Ed will try some experiments with this idea and determine if it provides any significant improvement. Ed decides to implement four stacks of table adapters within ReservationSelectionBE. These stacks will contain table adapters of the four types required to access the database to retrieve the ReservationSelectionBE object. Here is the current code in the GetLocalData() function:

```
protected override void GetLocalData(object[] objects)
{
  new GEOGRAPHICREGIONTableAdapter(Connection).Fill(this.Data.GEOGRAPHICREGION);

  // Similar code for the other adapters
}
```

In this code, a new table adapter of the required type is created and filled from the database. Ed's new experimental code looks like this:

```
protected override void GetLocalData(object[] objects)
{
  GEOGRAPHICREGIONTableAdapter gEOGRAPHICREGIONTableAdapter =
                                    GetGEOGRAPHICREGIONTableAdapter();
  gEOGRAPHICREGIONTableAdapter.Fill(this.Data.GEOGRAPHICREGION);
  FreeGEOGRAPHICREGIONTableAdapter(gEOGRAPHICREGIONTableAdapter);

  // Similar code for the other adapters
}
```

This requires the Get and Free functions:

```
static System.Collections.Stack gRAdapterStack = new Stack();

static GEOGRAPHICREGIONTableAdapter GetGEOGRAPHICREGIONTableAdapter()
{
  Stack stackS = Stack.Synchronized(gRAdapterStack);
  if (stackS.Count > 0)
    return (GEOGRAPHICREGIONTableAdapter)stackS.Pop();
  else
    return new GEOGRAPHICREGIONTableAdapter(
                  new System.Data.SqlClient.SqlConnection(localConnectionString));
}

static void FreeGEOGRAPHICREGIONTableAdapter(
                          GEOGRAPHICREGIONTableAdapter gEOGRAPHICREGIONTableAdapter)
{
  Stack stackS = Stack.Synchronized(gRAdapterStack);
  stackS.Push(gEOGRAPHICREGIONTableAdapter);
}
```

The Get functions for each table adapter, such as GetGEOGRAPHICREGIONTableAdapter(), first synchronize the stack to make it thread safe, then extract an adapter from a stack, in this case gRAdapterStack to return, if there is at least one present. If none are left on the stack, the function creates an extra one and returns it to the caller. The Free function calls the Synchronized function to ensure thread safety and then pushes the table adapter onto the top of the stack. Theoretically there should not be more adapters created than there are threads running in w3wp.exe, but this theory would need thorough testing. For now, it is just experimental code. Ed has put together similar sets of functions for the other three adapters.

Ed tests the experimental code first with the unit test used for checking the timing. He then places the new code on the website to verify that it runs properly in a multithreading environment under the load test that was run previously, and all seems satisfactory. The results from the instrumented unit test are shown in Figure 10-53. Comparing it to Figure 10-49, you'll see that the Application Inclusive Time is now 2.69 ms rather than 3.29 ms with the original code—a reduction of just over 18 percent, which is not a dramatic reduction but certainly significant.

We can see this in more detail by looking at Figure 10-54, which is the same display as shown in Figure 10-52 but using the experimental code. Compare the time taken to call the

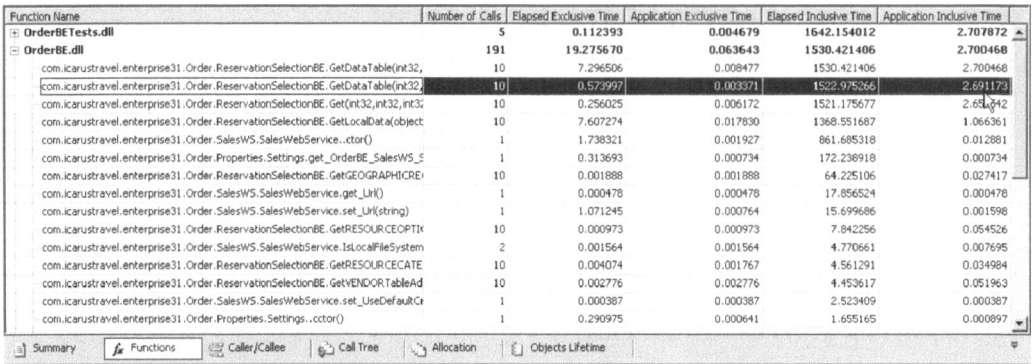

Figure 10-53. *The results for the instrumented unit test, showing the improvement after the code changes have been made to maintain a stack of table adapters*

table adapter constructors in the old design with the time taken to call the new Get and Free functions for each adapter in the new design. These figures show an obvious savings, as Table 10-2 shows.

Table 10-2. *Savings Achieved by Keeping a Stack of Table Adapters*

Adapter Name	Constructor Time	Get() Time	Free() Time	% Saving
GEOGRAPHICREGION	0.155	0.0274	0.0179	70%
RESOURCECATEGORY	0.155	0.0350	0.0220	63%
VENDOR	0.139	0.0520	0.0128	53%
RESOURCEOPTION	0.224	0.0545	0.0151	68%

Functions that called com.icarustravel.enterprise31.Order.ReservationSelectionBE.GetLocalData

Function Name	Num...	Elapsed Ex...	Application Ex...	Elapsed In...	Application In...
VirtCall:com.icarustravel.enterprise31.BusinessEntity.BusinessEntityBE`3.GetLocalData(object[])	10	7.607274	0.017830	1368.551687	1.066361

Current function:

com.icarustravel.enterprise31.Order.ReservationSelectionBE.GetLocalData(object[])	10	7.607274	0.017830	1368.551687	1.066361

Functions that were called by com.icarustravel.enterprise31.Order.ReservationSelectionBE.GetLocalData

com.icarustravel.enterprise31.Order.ReservationSelectionDSTableAdapters.GEOGRAPHICREGIONTableAdapter.Fill(class	10	0.700867	0.006945	357.417996	0.333648
com.icarustravel.enterprise31.Order.ReservationSelectionDSTableAdapters.RESOURCEOPTIONSTableAdapter.Fill(class	10	7.007736	0.007142	25.702436	0.164282
com.icarustravel.enterprise31.BusinessEntity.BusinessEntityBE`3..cctor()	1	0.040577	0.040577	884.327155	0.100611
com.icarustravel.enterprise31.Order.ReservationSelectionDSTableAdapters.VENDORTableAdapter.Fill(class com.icarustr	10	0.525557	0.004420	4.636618	0.092221
com.icarustravel.enterprise31.Order.ReservationSelectionDSTableAdapters.RESOURCECATEGORYTableAdapter.Fill(class	10	0.524527	0.004813	6.752240	0.088466
com.icarustravel.enterprise31.Order.ReservationSelectionBE.GetRESOURCEOPTIONSTableAdapter()	10	0.000973	0.000973	7.842256	0.054526
com.icarustravel.enterprise31.Order.ReservationSelectionBE.GetVENDORTableAdapter()	10	0.002776	0.002776	4.453617	0.051963
com.icarustravel.enterprise31.Order.ReservationSelectionBE.GetRESOURCECATEGORYTableAdapter()	10	0.004074	0.001767	4.561291	0.034984
com.icarustravel.enterprise31.Order.ReservationSelectionBE.GetGEOGRAPHICREGIONTableAdapter()	10	0.001888	0.001888	64.225106	0.027417
com.icarustravel.enterprise31.Order.ReservationSelectionBE.FreeRESOURCECATEGORYTableAdapter(class com.icarust	10	0.002256	0.002256	0.022064	0.022064
com.icarustravel.enterprise31.BusinessEntity.BusinessEntityBE`3.get_Data()	40	0.360831	0.013927	0.366041	0.019137
com.icarustravel.enterprise31.Order.ReservationSelectionBE.FreeGEOGRAPHICREGIONTableAdapter(class com.icarustr	10	0.001362	0.001362	0.017958	0.017958
com.icarustravel.enterprise31.Order.ReservationSelectionBE.FreeRESOURCEOPTIONSTableAdapter(class com.icarustra	10	0.002581	0.002581	0.015124	0.015124
com.icarustravel.enterprise31.Order.ReservationSelectionBE.FreeVENDORTableAdapter(class com.icarustravel.enterpri	10	0.003224	0.002063	0.021012	0.012761
com.icarustravel.enterprise31.Order.ReservationSelectionDS.get_RESOURCEOPTIONS()	10	0.139229	0.002432	0.139604	0.002807
com.icarustravel.enterprise31.Order.ReservationSelectionDS.get_RESOURCECATEGORY()	10	0.155200	0.002439	0.155554	0.002793
com.icarustravel.enterprise31.Order.ReservationSelectionDS.get_VENDOR()	10	0.144567	0.002241	0.145053	0.002727
.ctor(10)	10	0.002667	0.002667	0.002667	0.002667
.ctor(10)	40	0.001242	0.001242	0.001242	0.001242
com.icarustravel.enterprise31.Order.ReservationSelectionDS.get_GEOGRAPHICREGION()	10	0.139091	0.000846	0.139379	0.001134

| ▤ Summary | ⚞ Functions | ▦ Caller/Callee | ▤ Call Tree | ⬤ Allocation | ▥ Objects Lifetime | | ▼ |

Figure 10-54. *The Caller/Callee tab at the ReservationSelectionBE.GetLocalData function showing the functions called and their timings—after the code change*

Instrumenting Memory Allocations

Ed now turns his attention to profiling the memory allocations, an area in which Visual Studio 2005 Team Edition for Developers provides extensive support. As shown in Figure 10-55, two checkboxes in the General page for a performance session control .NET memory profiling collection: Collect .NET object allocation information and Also collect .NET object lifetime information.

Note The code at this point can be found in Chapter 10\Exercise 7. Exercise 10-8 demonstrates the material in this section.

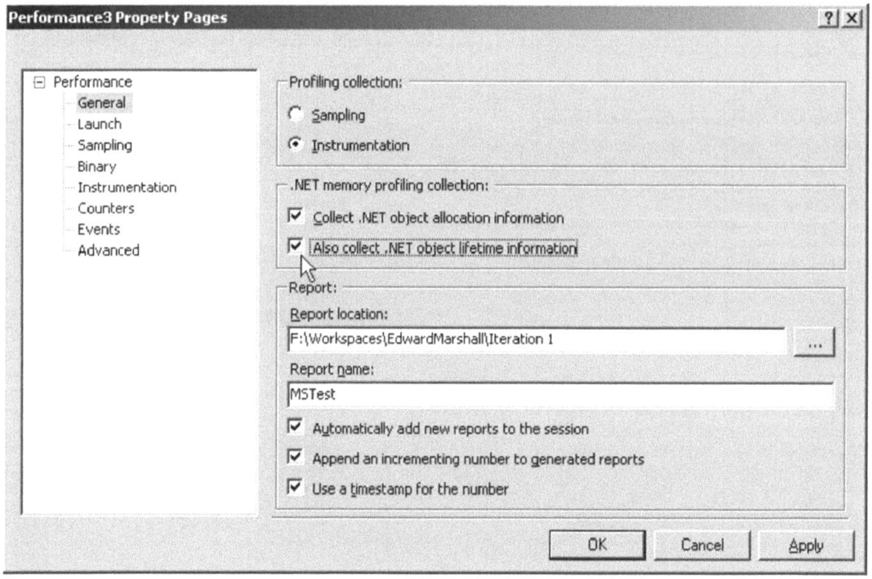

Figure 10-55. *Options for memory allocation profiling*

These options correspond to those on the Allocation and Objects Lifetime tab in the profiler report. Ed selects both of these checkboxes and reruns his performance session on the original code (before his experimental changes that have just been described). The results are shown in Figure 10-56 (displaying the Functions tab).

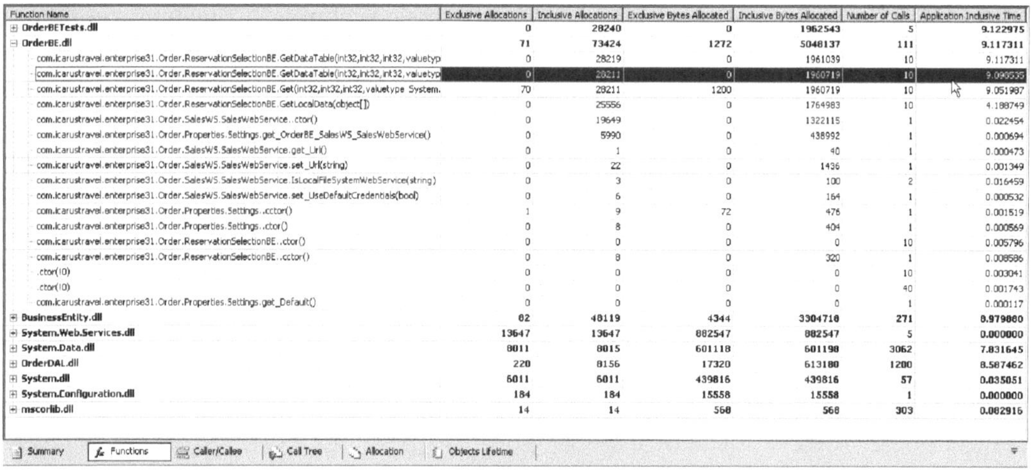

Figure 10-56. *Functions tab after memory allocation profiling (original code)*

One thing that's immediately noticeable is that the Functions tab includes a different set of columns, but you can add more by right-clicking and selecting Add/Remove Columns from the context menu. In fact, there are a variety of useful columns that I have not yet mentioned, such as average, minimum, and maximum values of the inclusive and exclusive timings discussed earlier. Also available are values such as process ID, source code filename, and source code line number, as well as the time attributed to profiling probes in either the inclusive or exclusive case for the given function. The documentation clearly defines application inclusive time to exclude time attributed to profiling probes within that function:

> *Application Inclusive Time. Calculated time for a function or summary item that excludes samples that contain transition events and time from collection probes, but includes the application time of subroutines called by the function.*

The probe overhead can be included as a column:

> *Time Inclusive Probe Overhead. The total time attributed to profiling probes in the inclusive time of the instances of this function that were called by the parent function in the call tree.*

Neither is the probe overhead included in the elapsed times. However, notice that the Application Inclusive Time for the highlighted GetDataTable function in Figure 10-56 has increased from the consistent value around 3.2 ms that was previously recorded to around 9 ms. It is not clear why this is so, but it may be due to the added instrumentation of allocations. You have to be careful not to be misled by things like this.

Figure 10-56 shows the object allocations organized by function, both exclusively and inclusively. Exclusive allocations refer to those allocations made within the function itself, and inclusive allocations refer to those made either within the function or in any function in the calling tree descending from it. Figure 10-56 shows both the number of objects allocated and the number of bytes allocated. The figures shown are the total for all calls (10 in total) to the function GetDataTable; there does not seem to be an average column available for allocations—only for times—so you have to do the division yourself!

From this view, you can drill down to examine in detail where inclusive allocations are being made by right-clicking on a function and selecting the Show Functions Called By option. For example, in the window in Figure 10-57 Ed has clicked on the Inclusive Allocations column heading to sort by descending values. He is rather surprised to see that his ResourceSelectionBE.GetDataTable function is top of the list. Remember that this function is called 10 times by the unit test, and will be the function used by an ObjectDataSource on the AddReservation.aspx page bound to the DataGridView control that lists the resource options found by a search.

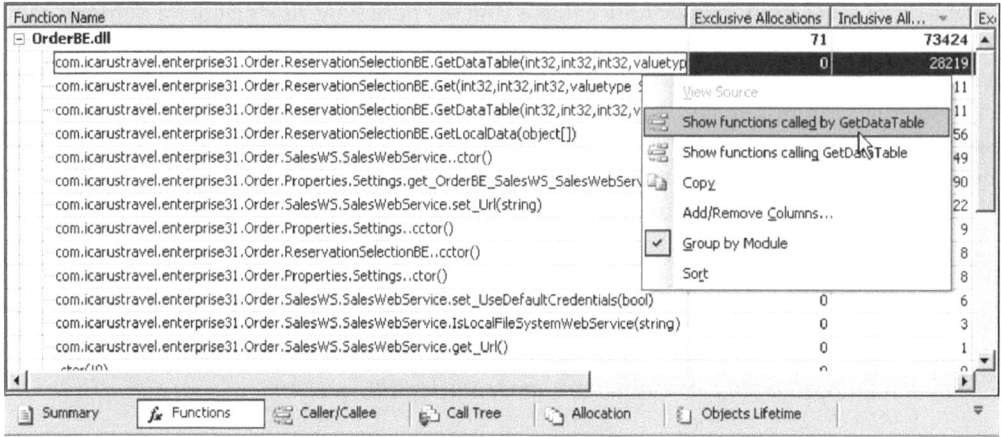

Figure 10-57. *Investigating where the large number of allocations occurs*

From the right-click menu, Ed selects Show functions called by GetDataTable. He repeats this several times, drilling down until he sees the view in Figure 10-58.

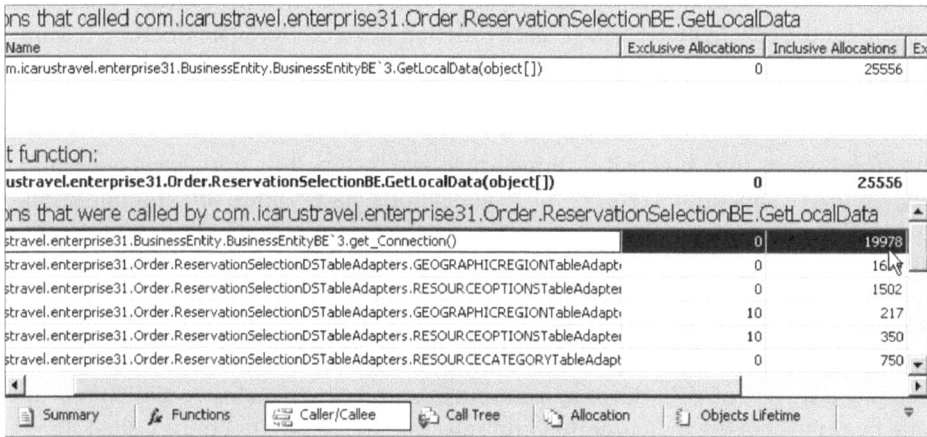

Figure 10-58. *The exclusive and inclusive object allocations in ReservationSelectionBE.GetLocalData*

This view shows the functions called by the GetLocalData(object[]) function of ReservationSelectionBE. Ed expects to see the constructors for the table adapters displaying high values—these are the ones he hopes to eliminate in his experimental code. Also, the large number of allocations in the table adapter Fill functions is no surprise, since Ed would expect them to create a lot of objects. What does surprise Ed, though, is the number of allocations occurring in the get_Connection() function. This function retrieves the Connection property of the `BusinessEntityBE` base class, which is the database connection. This will create a connection for the instance of `ReservationSelectionBE`, but surely creating a connection would not involve this many memory allocations!

Ed takes the drill-down process a bit further to see what lies beneath this property get call, and again following the path of maximum inclusive object allocations down through the call tree, he arrives at the screen shown in Figure 10-59, which reveals that the most allocations occur in a function called `BusinessEntityBE'3..cctor()`. This convention used by the profiler means the static constructor for `BusinessEntityBE`. Actually this really means all the static initializations, since there is no static constructor for `BusinessEntityBE`. As shown in the figure, Ed selects View Source from the right-click menu to display the static initializers for `BusinessEntityBE`.

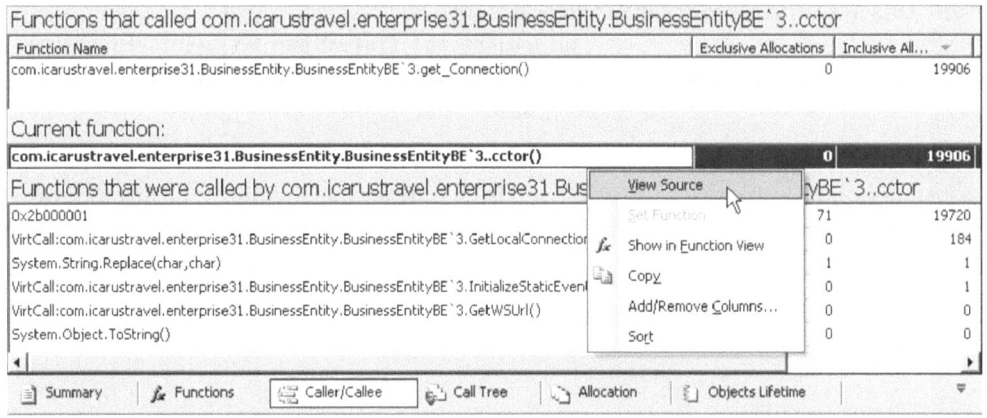

Figure 10-59. *The object allocations in the static constructor for Business Entity BE*

```
private LocalDSType data;
private static string uRLPropertyName =
                        new RemoteWSType().ToString().Replace('.','_');
private static string wSURL = GetWSUrl();
protected static string localConnectionString = GetLocalConnectionString();
private static bool staticEventsInitialized = InitializeStaticEvents();

private RemoteWSType wsProxy = null;
private System.Data.SqlClient.SqlConnection dbConnection = null;
```

He can also right-click on the unnamed 0x2b000001 function called by this static constructor and select Set Function from the context menu to see that this is actually the `SalesWebService` constructor. This is the call to new `RemoteWSType()` in the static initializer code just listed. So it is this constructor that is responsible for the largest amount of object allocations. Well, this is a surprise! Why is the code creating an instance of the web service proxy when it's working locally in this unit test?

The answer can be found in Chapter 9, where Rahul modified `BusinessEntityBE` to use the `ToString()` function result of the web service proxy class to generate the name of the URL property in the `.config` file. The class created is merely used for this purpose and goes straight out of scope after all those object allocations! This only occurs once for each parameterized type of BusinessEntityBE, but obviously Ed needs to find a better way to derive this name.

This is an example of the kind of unfortunate coding that can result in large amounts of object allocation. Even though it will only occur a few times in the application, it will still use a lot of heap space at start-up quite unnecessarily, and this problem would never have been found if the object allocation profiling had not been used.

Hey, wait a minute! Creating instances of the web service proxies is rather expensive of object allocations, so where else is the code doing this? Of course, a new instance of the web service proxy is created every time a web service is called in the GetRemoteData function in a business entity. For example, the function

```
protected override SalesWS.ReservationSelectionDS GetRemoteData(object[] objects)
{
  return this.WebServiceProxy.GetResourceOptions(
                              (int)objects[0],(int)objects[1],(int)objects[2],
                              (DateTime)objects[3],(int)objects[4]);
}
```

calls the get accessor on the WebServiceProxy property in the base class. The accessor creates a new instance of the web service proxy and retains it only for the lifetime of the instance of the class. Here is the WebServiceProxy accessor:

```
protected RemoteWSType WebServiceProxy
{
  get
  {
    if (wsProxy == null)
    {
      wsProxy = new RemoteWSType();
      if (wSURL != null)
      {
        wsProxy.Url = wSURL;
      }
    }

    return wsProxy;
  }
}
```

Ed might be able to do the same thing he did for the table adapters: create a thread-safe static stack to hold instances of the various kinds of proxy to be used whenever instances of the inheriting class are created. This approach might be expected to reduce heap pressure quite considerably.

So far we have ignored the Allocation and Objects Lifetime tabs of the performance session report. The Allocation tab lists classes by their fully qualified names; under each class the functions are listed that create one or more instances of that class. For instance, in the window shown in Figure 10-60, Ed has clicked on the header of the Total Bytes Allocated column to organize the list of classes in order of decreasing values. System.String is the class for which created instances make up the largest number of bytes allocated, amounting to over 28 percent of the total allocated during execution of the unit test. It would be nice to know where all—or most—of these instances of String are being created and why. Ed can find this out by expanding the System.String class in the window in Figure 10-60, where he can see that the biggest creator of System.String is the constructor for SoapHttpClientProtocol. To find out more, Ed can select Show Functions Calling ctor from the context menu on this row.

Type/Allocating Function	Instances	Total Bytes Allocated ▼	% of Total Bytes	
⊟ **System.String**	4957	636102	28.409	
System.Web.Services.Protocols.SoapHttpClientProtocol..ctor()	2914	445802	19.910	*View Source*
System.Configuration.SettingsBase.get_Item(string)	1036	126598	5.654	*Show in Objects Lifetime View*
System.Data.Common.DbDataAdapter.Fill(class System.Data.DataTable)	459	21072	0.941	
0x2b000001	15	1596	0.071	𝑓ₓ Show in Function View
System.Data.SqlClient.SqlConnection..ctor(string)	18	1326	0.059	Show functions called by ctor
System.Configuration.ConfigurationManager.get_AppSettings()	7	436	0.019	
System.String.Replace(char,char)	1	136	0.006	Show functions calling ctor
System.Uri.get_Host()	1	36	0.002	Copy
⊞ **System.Data.RBTree`1.Node[]**	240	248640	11.105	Add/Remove Columns…
⊞ **System.Byte[]**	566	207730	9.278	Sort
⊞ **System.Char[]**	1104	106664	4.764	
⊞ **System.Collections.Hashtable.bucket[]**	441	91560	4.089	
⊞ System.Object[]	1744	58316	2.604	

📄 Summary   𝑓 Functions   Caller/Callee   Call Tree   Allocation   Objects Lifetime

Figure 10-60. *The Allocation tab of a performance report showing the classes ordered by decreating total bytes allocated*

The result, as you can see in Figure 10-61, shows that the caller of the SoapHttpClientProtocol constructor is the SalesWebService constructor, and we already know where that is called. If we right-click on the *caller* function and select Set Function, we get right back to the display shown in Figure 10-59, and we can see that it is the static constructor of BusinessEntityBE that's creating all these strings. Therefore, we can approach the problem either from the bottom—starting with the classes being created and working up the call tree to discover the major callers—or from the top—by looking at which functions create the most objects and work down the call tree to find which objects are being created and where in the code creations are occurring.

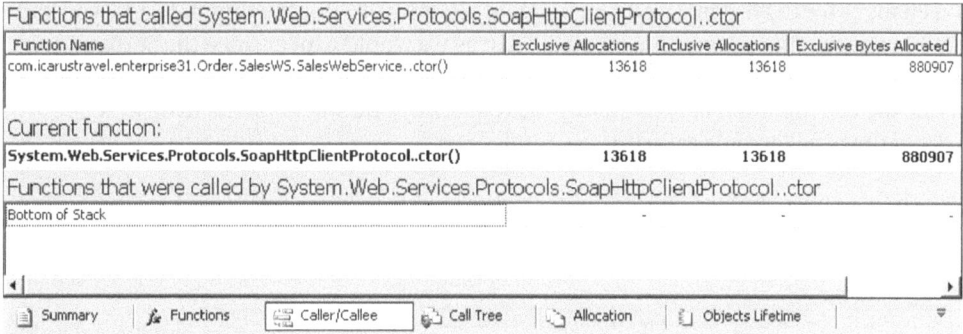

Functions that called System.Web.Services.Protocols.SoapHttpClientProtocol..ctor			
Function Name	Exclusive Allocations	Inclusive Allocations	Exclusive Bytes Allocated
com.icarustravel.enterprise31.Order.SalesWS.SalesWebService..ctor()	13618	13618	880907

Current function:

System.Web.Services.Protocols.SoapHttpClientProtocol..ctor()	13618	13618	880907

Functions that were called by System.Web.Services.Protocols.SoapHttpClientProtocol..ctor

Bottom of Stack	-	-	-

📄 Summary   𝑓 Functions   Caller/Callee   Call Tree   Allocation   Objects Lifetime

Figure 10-61. *Caller/Callee tab showing which function calls the SoapHttpClientProtocol constructor*

The rightmost tab in a performance session report is named Objects Lifetime, and it is interesting to look at System.String again from this tab, as shown in Figure 10-62. There are a lot of columns in this tab, and they can help you to better understand the behavior of your application. The count of objects collected under the three generations of their classification by the garbage collector is shown; as you can see, all but 33 of the instances of `string` are collected when the garbage collector runs at generation 0, meaning that they are short-lived objects. For any class that we are interested in on this view, such as `System.String`, we can go to the allocation view from the context menu as you see on the figure. We know that the huge number of strings created in the web service constructor will all be very short-lived. Looking back at Figure 10-60, you can see that 2,914 of the strings were created by that function. These will die in generation 0, and it is clear from Figure 10-62 that all but 33 of the rest die there as well. I do not know a way to find out exactly which function creates the 33 long-lived strings, but it could be the `SqlConnection` constructor and the function labeled 0x2b000001, which is actually the `BusinessEntityBE` static constructor, since these add up to 33, though it is not clear why all these strings should be so long lived. Perhaps they just happen to still be in scope when a garbage collection takes place and so get pushed to generation 1.

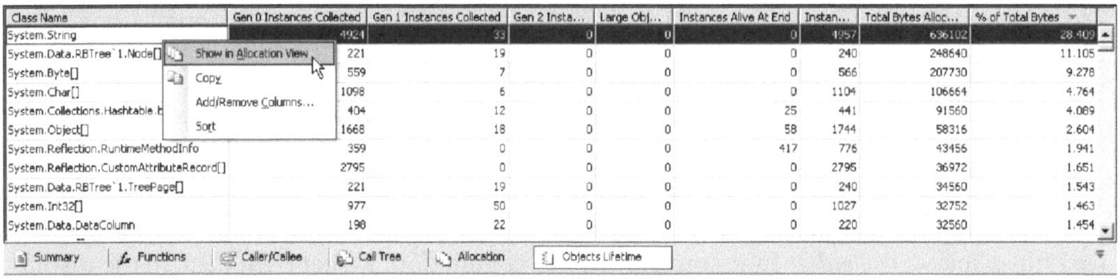

Figure 10-62. *The lifetime details of System.String, which has the most memory allocation*

The effect on memory allocation of the table adapter experimental changes needs to be verified. So Ed again performs the performance profiling, with object allocation turned on, for the code with the experimental changes in it. He looks at these same views to assess his experimental changes for the original and new code. In Figure 10-63, for the original code, you can see that 10 of each table adapter are created—just as we would expect since the `GetDataTable` function is called 10 times—and there are 360 total bytes, 36 for each. Figure 10-64 shows that all but one die at generation 0. Presumably the remaining one still happens to be in scope when the garbage collector is called.

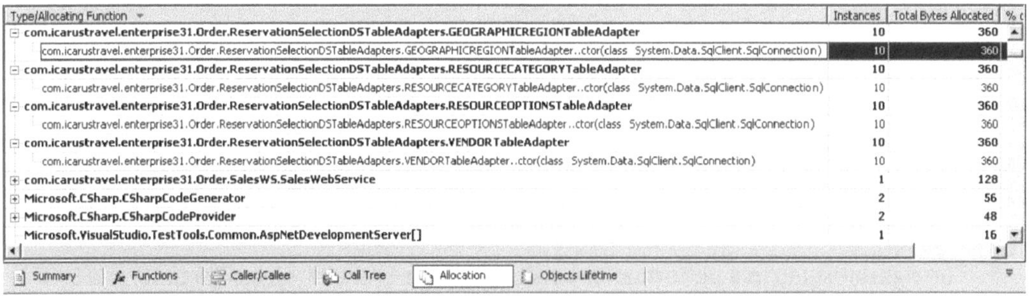

Figure 10-63. *Allocation tab showing the table adapters*

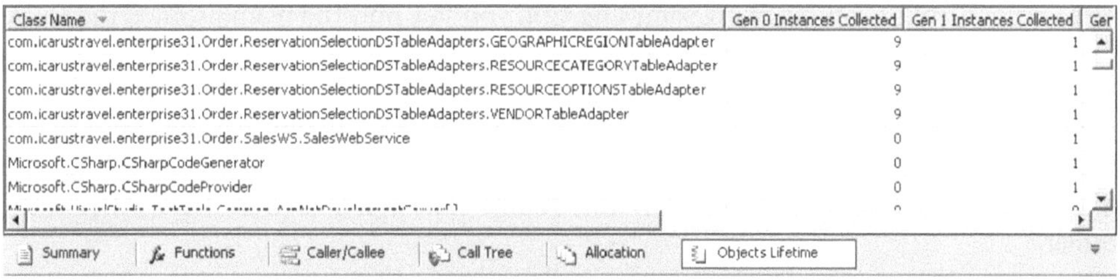

Class Name ▾	Gen 0 Instances Collected	Gen 1 Instances Collected	Ger
com.icarustravel.enterprise31.Order.ReservationSelectionDSTableAdapters.GEOGRAPHICREGIONTableAdapter	9	1	
com.icarustravel.enterprise31.Order.ReservationSelectionDSTableAdapters.RESOURCECATEGORYTableAdapter	9	1	
com.icarustravel.enterprise31.Order.ReservationSelectionDSTableAdapters.RESOURCEOPTIONSTableAdapter	9	1	
com.icarustravel.enterprise31.Order.ReservationSelectionDSTableAdapters.VENDORTableAdapter	9	1	
com.icarustravel.enterprise31.Order.SalesWS.SalesWebService	0	1	
Microsoft.CSharp.CSharpCodeGenerator	0	1	
Microsoft.CSharp.CSharpCodeProvider	0	1	
Microsoft.VisualStudio.TestTools.Common.AppNetDevelopmentContext	0	0	

Summary | Functions | Caller/Callee | Call Tree | Allocation | Objects Lifetime

Figure 10-64. *Objects Lifetime tab showing the table adapters*

Similar figures for Ed's experimental code are shown in Figure 10-65 and Figure 10-66. As expected, only one instance of each adapter is created, as is clear from Figure 10-65. In Figure 10-66 you see that the table adapters are all alive at the end of the execution of the test, since they remain accessible to the application via the static queues. So Ed's experimental changes do seem to work as expected. If more threads were running, more instances of each table adapter would be needed to supply the demand from the stacks. But in the case of a single-threaded test like this, the same table adapters are recycled—just as expected.

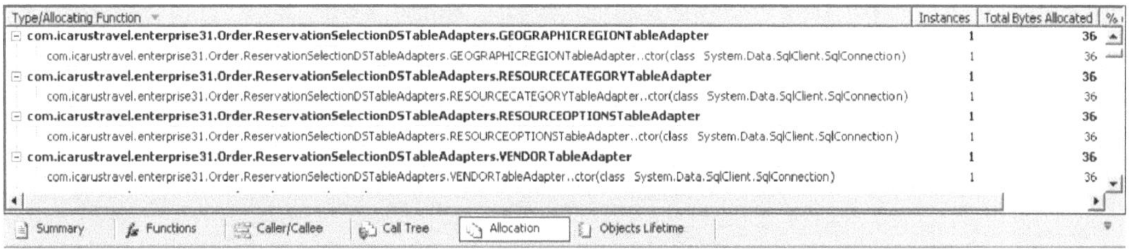

Type/Allocating Function ▾	Instances	Total Bytes Allocated	%
⊟ com.icarustravel.enterprise31.Order.ReservationSelectionDSTableAdapters.GEOGRAPHICREGIONTableAdapter	1		36
com.icarustravel.enterprise31.Order.ReservationSelectionDSTableAdapters.GEOGRAPHICREGIONTableAdapter..ctor(class System.Data.SqlClient.SqlConnection)	1		36
⊟ com.icarustravel.enterprise31.Order.ReservationSelectionDSTableAdapters.RESOURCECATEGORYTableAdapter	1		36
com.icarustravel.enterprise31.Order.ReservationSelectionDSTableAdapters.RESOURCECATEGORYTableAdapter..ctor(class System.Data.SqlClient.SqlConnection)	1		36
⊟ com.icarustravel.enterprise31.Order.ReservationSelectionDSTableAdapters.RESOURCEOPTIONSTableAdapter	1		36
com.icarustravel.enterprise31.Order.ReservationSelectionDSTableAdapters.RESOURCEOPTIONSTableAdapter..ctor(class System.Data.SqlClient.SqlConnection)	1		36
⊟ com.icarustravel.enterprise31.Order.ReservationSelectionDSTableAdapters.VENDORTableAdapter	1		36
com.icarustravel.enterprise31.Order.ReservationSelectionDSTableAdapters.VENDORTableAdapter..ctor(class System.Data.SqlClient.SqlConnection)	1		36

Summary | Functions | Caller/Callee | Call Tree | Allocation | Objects Lifetime

Figure 10-65. *Allocation tab showing the table adapters—new experimental code*

me ▾	Gen 0 Instances Collected	Gen 1 Inst...	Gen 2 Inst...	Large ...	Instances Alive At End	Ins
stravel.enterprise31.Order.ReservationSelectionDSTableAdapters.GEOGRAPHICREGIONTableAdapter	0	0	0	0	1	
stravel.enterprise31.Order.ReservationSelectionDSTableAdapters.RESOURCECATEGORYTableAdapter	0	0	0	0	1	
stravel.enterprise31.Order.ReservationSelectionDSTableAdapters.RESOURCEOPTIONSTableAdapter	0	0	0	0	1	
stravel.enterprise31.Order.ReservationSelectionDSTableAdapters.VENDORTableAdapter	0	0	0	0	1	
stravel.enterprise31.Order.SalesWS.SalesWebService	0	1	0	0	0	
CSharp.CSharpCodeGenerator	0	1	0	0	0	
CSharp.CSharpCodeProvider	0	1	0	0	0	

Summary | Functions | Caller/Callee | Call Tree | Allocation | Objects Lifetime

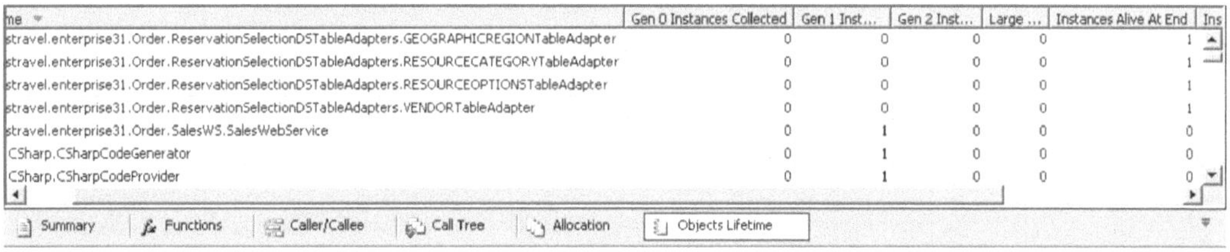

Figure 10-66. *Objects Lifetime tab showing the table adapters—new experimental code*

Summary

This chapter described initial performance profiling using both web and load tests. You saw how the results can be used to locate inefficiencies within the code.

You learned about the concept of the load test, and you saw how a simple load test is defined. The included web tests used some custom extraction rule techniques. We discussed the counter data that was obtained and what it meant.

We examined code profiling using sampling, and you saw how the team profiled the Sales Site web application. We studied the profile report to determine areas of the code needing improvement.

Finally, we explored the technique of profiling using instrumentation. We profiled a unit test for ReservationSelectionBE, one of the sales business objects used by the Sales Site application. You saw how Ed, the site's developer, tested some experimental code changes by using the profiler.

In the next chapter you will learn how to handle change and risk by using branching. We will also tackle the security requirements of the project.

Handling Change and Security Requirements

Change is a fact of life and often in the course of a project, major changes occur in the requirements. This may be for various reasons—perhaps the business climate has changed, the competition has released surprising new product news, or there are cost and schedule overruns and the project must be down scoped. For whatever reason, when a change of requirements hits a project in development, it can be very hard to control. Branching and merging can be used to reduce the impact of a change. This chapter illustrates how the branching and merging capabilities of Visual Studio 2005 Team Edition operate, and how they can be used to manage the configuration of two branches of development. Following our example of Icarus Enterprise, you will see how the team copes with and controls a major change in requirements.

Also, this chapter follows the evolving architecture and code base of the project as the security features are added. These features are aimed at providing authentication of users by username and password along with control of user access to the various entities in the system, such as customers, vendors, and orders.

The Unexpected Meeting

An unexpected team meeting has been scheduled for 10:00 Monday morning. All the team members file into the conference room and find seats.

"Nice to see you all again," says Clare amiably. "I hope everyone had a good weekend."

"I suppose that's the last one we're going to get," mumbles Peter.

"Oh, come on, Peter, it's not that bad," says Clare, rolling up her sleeves and reaching for the whiteboard marker. With an air of drama she begins to write something, but unfortunately the marker has dried up. She falters, cursing under her breath.

"Oh, here you go," Peter says grudgingly, with a reluctant smile as he hands her a good one.

"Thanks," she murmurs and writes the words "Offline Working Changes" on the whiteboard. "Well, there's been a bit of a change," she begins. "Susan has all of the details, but in effect, offline working for agents is going to be completely different. Ian's been complaining from day one—you know, Ian from Sydney—that the offline working as defined, wouldn't be any use. He's been saying that agents would not be able to make reservations for customers unless they had the whole vendor database on their machines." She looks at Susan.

"Yes," agrees Susan. "He's been saying that there's no point in only having data for resources that have already been looked at. 'What's the point of that?' he wanted to know."

"Actually he said, 'What's the bloody point of that?' I think," corrects Peter with a smirk.

"*Anyway*," says Clare, "Susan's going to explain what changes he suggested and James and William have agreed to."

"OK," says Susan and she stands up and gives a verbal summary to the team of the changes that are to be made. When she has finished, the whiteboard is covered in various colored scribbles with arrows leaping in various directions. Susan seems to keep a collection of very good markers. The salient points are as follows:

- The entire Icarus resource database will be replicated on travel agent client machines so that offline browsing will be the same as online browsing. This will not happen for permanently connected clients in the call centers, as there is to be no offline working in their case.

- The replicated resource database will synchronize with the central database automatically as a background task when a client machine is connected.

- Vendor data will not be replicated on Sales Wing client machines, except as needed to support the collection of resources.

- Customer data will be replicated onto Sales Wing client machines and offline agents will be able to make new orders for a customer as well as the Icarus call center, or the sales website. All orders made for a customer will be aggregated in the Enterprise database—in other words, merged for a given customer. Similarly, reservations made by different operators as part of a particular order will also be aggregated within that order. In the case of conflicting modifications to a reservation, the latest will win, and in the case of a deletion conflicting with a modification, again the latest will prevail.

- Offline reservations will still be provisional and will be confirmed immediately upon reconnection of an offline client, provided the resources are still available. Merging takes place at this time.

After Susan has explained these requirements, Clare takes the floor again and describes a tentative schedule in which the project will split into two branches using Team System's branching capabilities to make life easier. One branch will continue as initially planned and will develop the security features. It will also enhance the existing Sales Wing, Sales Site, and List Wing applications together with enhancements to the sales and listing business objects as needed. The Sales Status application will be started in iteration 3 as originally planned.

Meanwhile, a new branch will be started from the code as demonstrated at the end of iteration 1, and will be used to develop the database and code enhancements needed for the modified offline working capability, in particular the replication, synchronization, and merging of orders. A team of two developers with Joe Campbell as the lead will tackle this effort. Joe, an experienced C# senior developer, is a new addition to the project team.

"That way," says Clare, "we won't introduce more risk into the existing project stream, which can carry on in the same way until the new replication branch is ready to merge into the main effort."

"Sounds like a plan!" comments Peter. "Who's going to do all the extra architectural work?"

"Well," says Clare, drawing the word out, "you're going to be much more efficient, Peter."

Modified Offline Working Scenarios

Right after the team meeting, Susan and Joe begin work on a set of scenarios for the new offline working capability. They break the scenarios down into the following headings. I've listed some examples of their scenarios in the next sections.

Resource Replication Scenarios

These scenarios cover the replication of resources and their availability on client machines:

- A complete set of resources is replicated into the local database of a newly installed client.

- A modification to a resource becomes replicated on the client.

- The number of available places on the available dates is updated on the client.

- If a resource is removed from availability, this fact is replicated on the client.

Customer Synchronization Scenarios

These scenarios describe the replication of customer details on client machines:

- A new customer is added by an agent on his or her local machine while offline; when the machine is connected online again, the customer details are replicated to the Icarus central database.

- An agent makes a change to customer details when offline, and when the local machine is back online, the change is replicated into the Icarus central database.

- A new customer is added by an Icarus call center operator and access is given to a local agent. The new customer details are replicated to the agent's local machine as soon as the agent is next connected online.

- An Icarus call center operator makes a change to a customer. Replication takes place to all agents with access to that customer when their machines are connected online.

Provisional Reservation Scenarios

These scenarios describe the ability of Sales Wing to create orders when offline and confirm those orders when it is next online:

- An agent uses Sales Wing to make an order for a customer while offline by browsing the replicated database and adding suitable reservations. The order is displayed as tentative to the user.

- The agent's machine is connected online again and the Sales Wing application confirms the order with the central database by checking that the resources reserved are still available on the required dates in sufficient numbers. The order is then replicated onto the central Icarus database. A message is displayed to the user to indicate the confirmation.

- This is the same as the previous scenario, but confirmation of the tentative order is rejected because the resources have been reserved for other orders while the agent was offline. The order remains tentative.

- An agent changes an order while offline. When the agent connects again, the modifications are replicated into the central Icarus database.

- An Icarus call center operator changes an order to which an agent has access. The modifications are replicated onto the agent's local database.

- An agent makes a change to an order while he or she is offline. Meanwhile a call center operator makes a change to the same order. When the agent connects online again, the two orders are merged in a controlled manner to make one composite order. A message is displayed to the operator when the merge takes place.

Iteration 2 Change Branch: Create Solution Architecture

"Who's that shouting?" asks Joe, getting up startled from his desk at 9:15 the following Monday morning.

"I think it's Peter," says Ed, who shares his cubicle.

"WHO DID THIS?" yells Peter as the two go down the hall to look. Peter is in his office, his hands raised, staring around in disbelief. "LOOK AT IT!" he blasts.

"What's up, Peter?" ventures Angela coming up behind the others, who are staring open-mouthed at the scene. "Are you all right?"

"Of course I'm all right," says Peter, recovering himself. "But look—someone's been in here over the weekend and messed everything up. Do you think it could be sabotage?"

Angela, Joe, and Ed look around. Everything has been rearranged in a beautifully neat and tidy fashion. All Peter's papers and books have been tidied on the bookshelves. His desk has been cleared and everything has been placed in labeled trays. Ed opens Peter's filing cabinet to reveal an array of labeled folders with all Peter's technical papers arranged into categories for efficient access. Even Peter's coffee cup has been cleaned and placed on a pretty little mat.

"Peter," says Angela gently, "it's really rather nice."

"Oh, no," groans Peter. "I'll never be able to find anything anymore. Who could have done such a thing, who could possibly—"

"Actually," says another voice from the hallway, "it was me, Peter." Peter turns around to see Clare with a benevolent smile. "You'll soon get used to it," she says brightly.

Peter must perform a review of the architecture that was designed to support the offline working in Chapter 6, shown in Figures 6-22, 6-23, and 6-24, to determine what changes are needed. The original requirement was for SalesWing to operate either online or offline and use the SalesBusinessObjects application in client mode. These business objects are configured either in client or server mode when the application using them starts. In client mode, the business objects always persist to the database through the web services; in server mode, they always persist through the table adapters. In client mode the application is to detect if the client is offline and then redirect persistence to a local copy of the database, but this was not implemented in iteration 1. The project plan required that iteration 1 take account of offline working and include the design but not demonstrate it. The design was indeed included by virtue of the dual persistence business entities, but quite a lot was left out.

Resource Data Replication

The main feature of the changes introduced in the team meeting was that the entire resource database would be replicated on the client local database, enabling provisional reservations to be made of any resource offered by Icarus's vendors. This is actually a simplification as it avoids the need to update the client local database with only resources that have been browsed. Having all of the resources in the client local database would also mean replicating the VENDORS, GEOGRAPHICREGION, and RESOURCECATEGORY tables. The size of the last two will be quite small; the quality-of-service (QoS) requirements in Chapter 4 show the VENDORS table to have a maximum of 10,000 rows and the RESOURCE table a maxmium of 100,000 rows. This may not be a problem using SQL Server 2005 Express Edition, but some research will need to be done. The main problem, though, will be the ORDER and RESERVATION tables since the QoS requirements specify 50 million orders with an average of 3 line items per order. Since a line item is represented by a row in the RESERVATION table, the RESERVATION table would contain 150 million rows. The RESERVATION table is used by the stored procedure GETRESOURCEOPTIONS to determine whether enough places are available for a given resource on a particular date for it to be included in the options returned by a resource search.

Peter admits to himself that he had not completely considered this, even for maintaining the availability information for resources stored locally under the original requirements. Of course, only future entries in the RESERVATION table need to be replicated on the client, and past entries can be removed without violating referential integrity. Nevertheless, Peter feels that the availability information will have to be denormalized on the client local database as far as possible. The RESOURCE table can have up to 100,000 rows, but there will also have to be a table that shows the number of each of these resources available for each day of the year that the resource is available. This means that to hold a year's information this table will be (375 days)×(100,000 resources), which is 37.5 million rows to describe the current availability. These rows need only hold a foreign key, an integer count, and a date, but it still seems a huge number of rows to store locally on a laptop. Another approach would be to only store one row for each resource and contain a year's availability data in a field of that row itself, either as a text string of some agreed format, or a binary serialization of an array or class. This would certainly reduce the number of rows, but would it reduce the size of the database or make its access more efficient? Peter decides that he will need to experiment to determine the best approach here, and carries out a brief test on his local machine where he uses a script to load 50,000 resource entries into a table, each with a year's supply of availability entries—a total of over 18 million availability records. He finds that performance is adequate and the size of the data file is well within the specifications of SQL Server 2005 Express Edition.

Under this scheme, the offline client will need to work with a different table adapter to read the resource options from the database when creating a new reservation. The adapter will use a different GETRESOURCEOPTIONS stored procedure that will work with the denormalized resource database. The requirement to include the entire resource collection in the Client Local Database therefore does not seem to introduce any architectural change at the level of Figures 6-22, 6-23, and 6-24, but it does introduce a change to the design of the sales business objects that will impact the continuing development of the sales functionality.

Peter envisages the replication of the resource data as being carried out by a separate thread running in the SalesWing application, or possibly as a service on the client machine. Essentially, this thread will page through the resource table rows on the central database, denormalizing them as described earlier and storing them locally, either adding new rows or replacing existing local rows.

There may well be better techniques of implementing the replication needed, but time and space prevent more than a simple coded approach here. For example, SQL Server replication capability may be applicable, but it lies beyond the scope of this book, whose primary focus is Team System.

Customer Replication and Order Merge

Only customers to which a travel agent has access are to be replicated to the client local database, and the replication should be made to occur automatically by a separate thread in a manner similar to the resource replication thread. Replication occurs both ways. If a new customer is created on the local machine when it is offline, it will need to be copied to the central database. Customers present in the central database but not on the local machine need to be copied to the local machine. When the customer entries are different, the latest one overwrites the earlier one. Customer replication is not considered in this book, nor is its accompanying code considered beyond the scenario stage.

Iteration 2 Change Branch: Create Product Requirements

Peter writes a brief document describing the replication product requirements covering the following points:

- The SalesBusinessObjects application, when installed upon a remote client in support of the SalesWing application, shall be capable of working with either local or remote persistence.

- The system shall determine automatically whether or not it is connected to SalesWebService and select the correct mode.

- The system shall store customers and orders locally only for those customers for which the agent user of the installation is responsible.

- The system shall synchronize orders and customers when online by merging orders between the local copies and the copies on the Icarus central database (the Enterprise database application).

- The system shall replicate all resources from the central database with sufficient information about vendors, categories, and regions to allow search and selection of resource for the generation of new orders. This replication shall take place on a separate thread in the SalesWing application from the one responding to operator input.

- New orders created when offline shall remain tentative until confirmed by the system. A confirmation and synchronization thread shall also run in the SalesWing application that will confirm or reject tentative orders. It will synchronize order and customer information between the client local database (named ClientLocalDatabase application) and the Icarus central database (Enterprise application).

Iteration 2 Change Branch: Developing and Testing the Changes

Both changes and additions are needed to the code base to implement the resource replication behavior. Visual Studio 2005 Team Edition provides a capability called *branching* that allows a collection of files to evolve in two or more diverging paths. This can be useful when it is necessary to work on a software project code base in two independent directions without changes to one branch interfering with the work on the other. To create a branch you select groups of files or folders in version control—not an entire project or solution—in the Source Control Explorer window. Figure 11-1 shows an example. A, B, and C are three different files forming part of a solution; they may be source code, XML files, script files, documentation, or any other files that are placed under source control. A separate branch of the solution, called the side branch here, is generated to allow some experimental work to take place. File A and file B will need to be changed in the side branch compared to the main branch, but C will not be changed. Therefore, only files A and B need to be branched and the main and side branch solutions both include the common file C as well as differing versions of A and B.

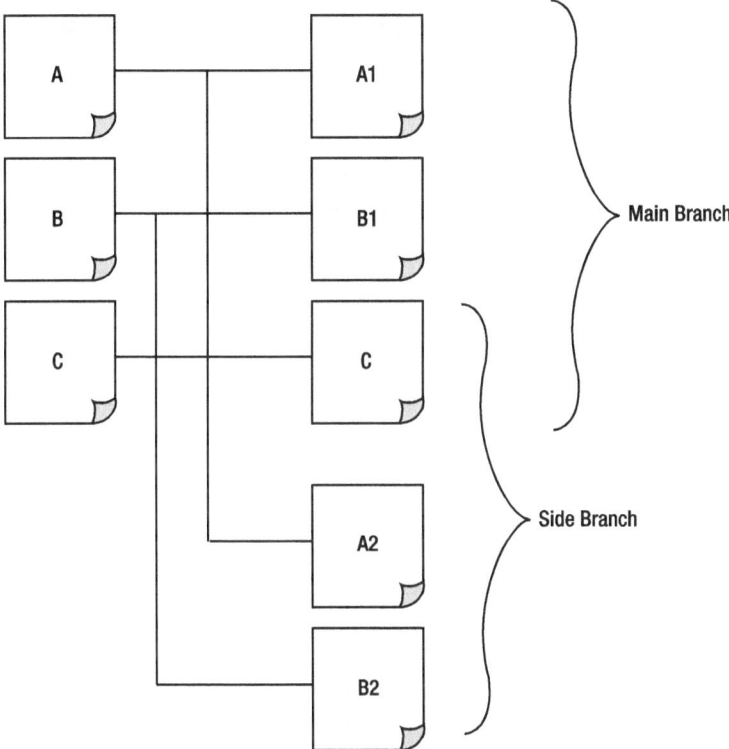

Figure 11-1. *The concept of branching*

There are various situations in which branching is of use. One example is when it is necessary to begin a new program of enhanced capability on an application, when the original code for the application must continue in production and be subject to maintenance. Major changes will probably be made to the new version branch, but bugs will be fixed on the production branch. At some point the production branch will need to be merged into the enhancements branch.

In the case of Icarus Enterprise, the new branch is to be used to let development proceed on a new area of functionality without affecting the rest of the code. Some of the code for new areas of functionality can be added without branching, since it requires only new files and does not affect existing ones. These are:

- Business entities datasets and table adapters containing the functionality needed to obtain the resource data from the server for replication.

- A new web service on the server to respond to client requests for the latest resource data.

- Business entities, datasets, and table adapters containing the functionality needed to read the resource data from the client for comparison during replication and to write the updated data back.

These new areas will not require branching because they are only used by the new offline capability. The areas of change where branching is needed are as follows:

- Add a new thread to the Sales Wing application that will perform resource replication, and run until all the resources on the client are updated from the server.

- Include, in the Sales wing application, the capability to support operations from both the local database ClientLocalDatabase and the remote SalesWebService. At the moment, the DualPersistBE base class supports client and server mode. In iteration 1, client mode always worked so as to persist the business entities via the remote web services rather than a local database. In iteration 2 it was always intended that client mode would detect whether the client was online or offline and persist to the client local database if in an offline situation. The database connection string in the App.config file would then be used to specify the local database connection. Now, as well as this ability to cope with the online or offline situation, some business entities installed in client mode will need to support both local and remote persistence *on demand*. This is so that the replication thread can read these entities from the remote database and write them to the client local database—or sometimes the other way around.

- Add the ability to detect whether or not the client is can reach SalesWebService, and cause the application to switch from online and offline mode as necessary. Note that client and server mode is a different concept from online and offline. An installation of business entities is permanently either in client or server mode according to where it is installed. Client mode business entity classes may operate in either online or offline mode according to whether or not the client has a connection to the web services.

These areas will require branching of their files since the new requirements will clash with further work along the existing stream.

Branching the Code

Joe will need to branch the SalesWing application so that he can add the capability to set up and begin the resource update thread when the application starts. He does this by opening

Source Control Explorer and selecting the solution folder in the left pane so that all of the project folders appear on the right, as shown in Figure 11-2. He then right-clicks on the project folder SalesWing, in either the left or right pane, and selects Branch from the context menu, which displays the dialog box shown in Figure 11-3.

Note The code at this point is available under Chapter 11\Chapter11Start. Exercise 11-1 should help you understand the material described in this section.

Figure 11-2. *Creating a branch for the Sales Wing application*

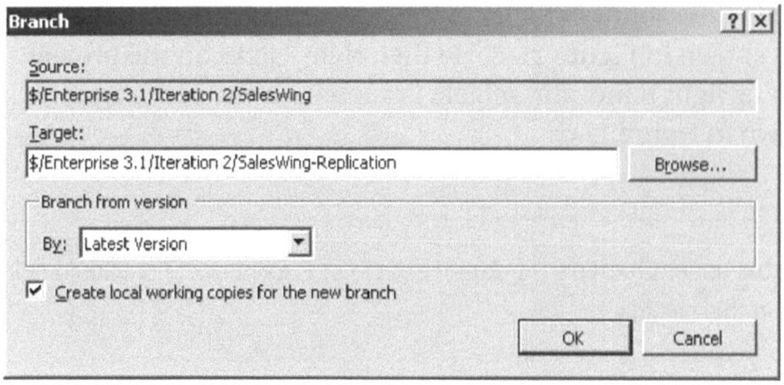

Figure 11-3. *The Branch dialog box*

A branch operation always has a source and a target; they will appear as separate named items in Source Control Explorer. This is a different concept from some other version control systems, such as Rational ClearCase, where the files have the same name and a particular branch is selected by specifying a view that includes that branch in its configuration spec. Branches can come from the latest version, a changeset, a version identified by date, a label, or the workspace version. In the Branch dialog box, you use the By drop-down to specify the source in the Branch From Version box. Latest Version is the most recent version in TFS source control. A changeset is a set of files that were checked in together, so identifying the source of the branch by changeset requires a search through changesets. Similarly, if identifying the source by label, you need to search through the defined labels for the specified items. Identifying by date requires you to enter a date via a calendar control. Choosing Workspace Version uses the versions, of the specified files or folders, in the developers workspace or folders as the source of the branch. This is a useful feature if the developer has already made changes to the files and now has to check them in onto a new branch.

Joe has not yet made any changes, so he selects Latest Version, labels the branch "SalesWing-Replication", and clicks OK. Next he needs to branch the solution file, since he will have to work with a solution file that includes the branched project rather than the original one. The branched project has the same name but is in the new branched folder called SalesWing-Replication both in the workspace and in the source code repository. Branching the solution file is also a good idea because he will need to add various projects to it that will include the replication business object classes. He can then check the solution file in without affecting other developers.

Branching is a two-step process: you make the branch and then you must check in the changes. Figure 11-4 shows the Pending Changes window when the two branches have been made. Next Joe makes sure that all the pending changes are selected and clicks the Check In button. Now the Source Control Explorer window shows both the SalesWing project and the SalesWing-Replication project as well as the two solution files, Enterprise 3.1.sln and Enterprise 3.1-Replication.sln.

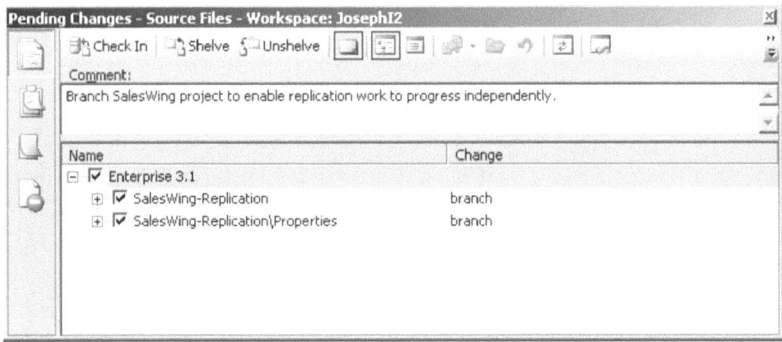

Figure 11-4. *The Pending Changes window after the branches to the solution file and SalesWing project have been made*

The solution file can then be closed and the new `Enterprise 3.1-Replication.sln` solution opened. It's now necessary to modify this new branch of the solution by removing the `SalesWing` project from the new branch, `Enterprise 3.1-Replication.sln`, and adding the `SalesWing.csproj` project in the `SalesWing-Replication` folder instead. A slight problem occurs at this point; when the `SalesWing` project is removed from the solution, any projects that reference it lose their reference. The only one in this case was `SalesWingTest`, where Visual Studio checked it out automatically from TFS and removed the reference from the project file. This must be replaced, or else the solution will not build, so a new reference to the branched `SalesWing` project must be added. To do this, Joe must first undo the pending change that has been made automatically for the `SalesWingTest` project—that is, the removal of the reference—then branch that project to form `SalesWingTest-Replication` and change the reference in the `SalesWingTest-Replication` project to point to the branched version of `SalesWing`. The entry in the `SalesWingTest-Replication.csproj` project file now points to the same project in a different folder. Of course, the branched project `SalesWingTest-Replication` must also be added to the branched solution `Enterprise 3.1-Replication.sln`.

Once this is done, Joe checks that the solution builds and then checks everything into TFS from the Pending Changes window shown in Figure 11-5. Joe actually found it necessary to add the `Enterprise 3.1-Replication.vssscc` file to source control manually, which is done by selecting a folder in Source Control Explorer and using the File ➤ Source Control ➤ Add to Source Control option on the main menu. There is also an Add Files button on the Source Control Explorer toolbar.

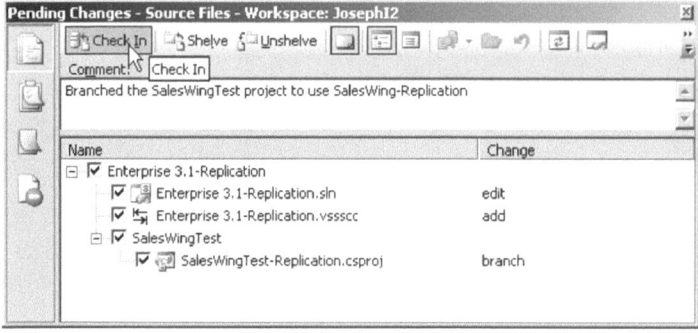

Figure 11-5. *The Pending Changes window after the changes to the solution have been made*

Now that Joe has his own branch, he can check in whenever he likes without affecting the main branch as long as he only changes files that have been branched, such as those in the SalesWing, SalesWingTest folders, or the Enterprise 3.1-Replication.sln file, or files not included in the original solution. There are various options for how the branching could have been done. In fact, since he only wants to modify the Program.cs file within the SalesWing application, he could perhaps just have branched that one file. He would then automatically receive all updates to other parts of the SalesWing application. However, he would still need to branch the SalesWing.csproj file in order to include the branched version of the Program.cs file, then he would also have to branch the solution file to include the branched project file. Even then, it would still be necessary to branch projects that reference the SalesWing project so that they could reference the branched SalesWing.csproj project file. Also, other developers might make changes to other files within SalesWing that relied on changes to the version of Program.cs on their branch—not Joe's version—and thus break his build. This would mean that he would have to fix these problems by merging in such changes, perhaps at inopportune times. Thus it is probably better to save the merging until the resource replication work is completed. The bottom line is that you have to think things out quite carefully when you use branching; it isn't an automatic process you can just assume will be right. Neither is merging, as we'll see toward the end of this chapter.

Why would you choose to create a branch rather than just let the developer work on side-line changes, using shelving perhaps instead of checking in the code? One reason is to allow several developers to work on the same branch. Another is that creating the branch formalizes the process of working on a side issue of the project. It enables team builds to take place and work items to be utilized, and brings in all the other trappings of Team System that make the project more manageable and controlled. Also, it allows formal testing of the branch code to be properly carried out and tracked with work items.

The Replication Data Access Layer Classes

Joe next adds a new solution folder to the branch of the solution on which he is working and calls it "ReplBusinessObjects". The architecture that has been agreed on requires a set of business objects that are concerned with the replication process itself, both on the server and on the client. These objects will be supported by data access layer (DAL) objects that will include datasets and table adapters similar to those that have been used before with the other business entities. Since the creation of these datasets and their table adapter classes are so familiar, they need not be discussed in detail here.

Note The code at this point is available under `Chapter 11\Exercise 1`. Exercise 11-2 should help you follow this section.

The DAL classes in the `ResourceReplSvrDAL` project provide access to the `Enterprise` database so that the server can support replication requests from clients. They only need to read data from the database; therefore, it is only necessary to define the `SELECT` stored procedures for them in their table adapters.

There are two table adapters for the `ResourceReplSvrDS` dataset: one to read a set of RESOURCE table entries and one to generate a set of rows that will indicate the current number of vacancies for a particular resource on a particular date. The rows in this second table effectively denormalize the information contained in the RESOURCEAVAILABILITY and RESERVATION tables to provide a count of the number of places available for a resource on each date.

These rows are generated by aggregation in the SQL, counting the number of reservations and calculating the number of vacancies grouped by resource and date. Both stored procedures accept a beginning and end ID parameter so that the resources can be paged through in blocks together with their vacancy rows.

The client objects in the `ResourceReplClientDAL` project read and write records to the two tables forming the Replicated Resource data model. This consists of a table called RESOURCELOCAL, identical to the RESOURCE table on the server, and a table called RESOURCEFREELOCAL that contains denormalized rows representing the number of places available on each date for each resource. `ResourceReplClientDS` contains two table adapters that read and write blocks of rows from the two tables in Figure 11-6. The stored procedures are very straightforward. The `SELECT` procedures simply read entries from RESOURCEFREELOCAL and RESOURCELOCAL for which the RESOURCEID and ID fields, respectively, are between the specified limits. The `INSERT`, `UPDATE`, and `DELETE` procedures persist individual records in a straightforward manner.

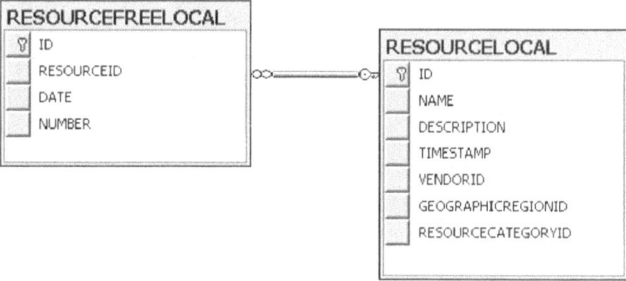

Figure 11-6. *The Replicated Resource data model on the client*

The Replication Business Objects

A business entity class called `ResourceReplSvrBE` is defined on the server. This class encapsulates, as a business entity, a block of resource replication information obtained using the datasets described in the previous section. It exposes a `GetData` function to be used by a new web service called `ClientReplWebService` that supplies the `ResourceReplSvrDS` in response to a call on its web method:

`ResourceReplSvrDS GetResourceData(int started, int endId)`

The method accepts start and end limit IDs to specify a block of resources to be retrieved.

Note The code at this point is available under `Chapter 11\Exercise 2`. Exercise 11-3 should help you follow this section.

On the client, `ResourceReplClientBE` encapsulates the logic that handles the sequencing of the resource replication on the client. This is placed within a static public function, `void UpdateClient()`, that will go through a complete update of resources on the client as well as their availability entries in the RESOURCEFREELOCAL table. It uses `ClientReplWebService` to obtain blocks of resource information from the server, and uses the table adapters in `ResourceReplClientDS` to obtain the current replicated resource entries from the client local database and return modified and new entries. This function will take a long time to execute if there are a large number of resources defined on the server; therefore, it must run as a separate thread as you will see in the next section.

`ResourceReplClientBE` and `ResourceReplSvrBE` do not inherit from `BusinessEntityBE` but contain the necessary static methods to read the web service URL (in the client case) and local database connection string from the `.config` file for the application in a manner similar to `BusinessEntityBE`. These entities are simpler because they do not have to work in both local and remote configurations.

The Replication Thread

One of the new features in C# 2.0 is called *anonymous methods*. Prior to C# 2.0, to add a delegate to an event you needed to first define a function that the delegate would represent and then create a new delegate, passing that function as an argument, and assign it as a handler for the event. For example:

```
class SomeClass
{
  public delegate void MyDelegate(string message);
  public event MyDelegate MyEvent;
  public void SomeFunction()
  {
    MyEvent = new MyDelegate(MyEventHandler1);
    MyEvent += new MyDelegate(MyEventHandler2);
    MyEvent.Invoke("Event has been fired");
  }

  void MyEventHandler1(string message)
  {
    System.Console.Out.WriteLine("Handler1:" + message);
  }
```

```
    void MyEventHandler2(string message)
    {
      System.Console.Out.WriteLine("Handler2:" + message);
    }

}
```

This code will generate the following output:

```
Handler1:Event has been fired
Handler2:Event has been fired
```

In C# 2.0 delegates can be instantiated using anonymous methods, such as

```
public void SomeFunction()
{
  MyEvent = delegate(string message)
  {
    System.Console.Out.WriteLine("Handler1:" + message);
  };
  MyEvent += delegate(string message)
  {
    System.Console.Out.WriteLine("Handler2:" + message);
  };

  MyEvent.Invoke("Event has been fired");
}
```

A delegate is a type-safe reference to a section of code, usually a function. Using anonymous methods, the code is included in the instantiation of the delegate itself rather than being written as a separate function.

Note The code at this point is available under `Chapter 11\Exercise 3`. Exercise 11-4 should help you follow this section.

We can use this technique in instantiating a thread, and Joe includes the following code in the `Program` class of the `SalesWing` application:

```
// Start the resource update thread
new System.Threading.Thread(
  delegate()
  {
    do
    {
      ResourceReplClientBE.UpdateClient();
    } while (!terminate.WaitOne(10000, false));
  }
).Start();
```

This code will start a thread that will execute the static void UpDateClient() member of the ResourceReplClientBE class, then wait for 10 seconds (10,000 milliseconds) on an EventWaitHandle called terminate. The EventWaitHandle object is declared in the static Program class and set at the end of the Main() function:

```
static class Program
{
  private static EventWaitHandle terminate =
                                new EventWaitHandle(false, EventResetMode.AutoReset);
  [STAThread]
  static void Main()
  {
    // Start the resource replication thread
    // etc. etc.

    // Application code
    // etc. etc.

    // Terminate the resource replication thread
    terminate.Set();
  }
}
```

Many developers prefer not to place the delegate code in the delegate instantiation but write it in a separate function. The anonymous method approach is convenient, however, if only a short piece of code is needed to implement the delegate and it is called in only one place.

Iteration 2 Main Branch: Security Use Cases and Scenarios

The main area of work, aside from the replication changes, that was planned for iteration 2 was the addition of authentication and authorization to the product. Security is a very important feature of the Icarus 3.1 project. For example, it would be a disaster if

- A customer was able to access another customer's account, access their personal data or view, and change their bookings. This would constitute a severe infringement of the user's privacy.

- A vendor was able to access another vendor's listings in write mode. An unscrupulous vendor could withdraw a competitor's products from sale, or alter the descriptive text.

- A travel agent could view another travel agent's customers and "poach" them, or send unsolicited advertising emails.

For reasons like these, security is included early on in the project at iteration 2. Precedence is given only to the basic operation of the software itself in iteration 1.

In Chapter 4, the Authenticate User use case appeared as an included use case of Manage Orders and Manage Customer Account, which were both part of the Sales use case, shown in Figure 4-5. It is also required in the Listings use case shown in Figure 4-10. A user must be authenticated before being permitted to access certain operations. Once a user is authenticated, they will need to be authorized before being permitted access to many items of data.

A user of the Sales Site application will not be required to be authenticated until an attempt is made to view a page that contains protected data—that is, data that requires some level of authorization. An example would be the opening of a customer record in the Sales Wing application, access to the My Orders page in the Sales Site application, or opening a vendor record in the List Wing application.

Users will be authenticated against a table of users held in the database, which will include a username and password. There will be a concept of a *privilege level*, which such users will possess, with may take the following values:

1. **None**: Home users only able to access their own accounts and orders. Vendors only able to access their own accounts and listings.

2. **Limited Privilege**: Travel agents able to access the accounts of their customers.

3. **Full Privilege**: Call center operators able to access any account.

Users of the Sales Wing and List Wing applications will be required to authenticate as soon as they start the application. Use of the Sales Wing application will always require a higher level of privilege than None since multiple customers will be viewable. List Wing, on the other hand can be used by users of any privilege level, but vendors will only see their own data.

Sales Site Scenarios

This section describes scenarios that define security requirements for the Sales Site application. These include authentication, where the user logs on to the site, and authorization, in which access to various objects in the database is controlled.

Home User Authentication

Remember Sam, the home Internet customer? In the scenario shown in Table 11-1, Sam tries to access his own list of current orders with Icarus in the My Wings page on the sales website.

Table 11-1. *The Home User Authentication Scenario Storyboard*

Step	User Action	System Response
Initial State	Sam is viewing some other part of the Icarus website (not illustrated).	
1.	Sam clicks on a My Wings link.	The browser requests the My Wings web page, but the system detects that the user is not authenticated and redirects to the Logon page. The Logon page in Figure 11-7 is displayed to the user, Sam.
2.	Sam enters his username (SamSmith10) and password (eagles22) and clicks the Logon button.	The system verifies that SamSmith10 is a user of the system and verifies that eagles22 matches the password stored on the system for Sam's account. The system redirects the browser back to the My Wings page, populated with information for the user SamSmith10, and delivers a cookie to allow subsequent access within the session without further authentication.

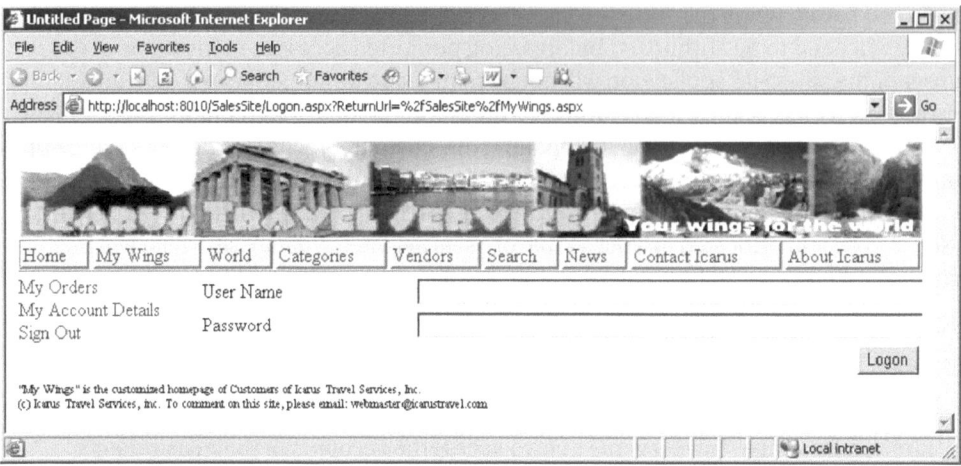

Figure 11-7. *Authentication page*

The team defines other scenarios, such as an invalid username, an invalid password, or an invalid username and password. In each case, the Logon page is returned to the browser for another attempt.

Authorized Viewing of the My Orders Page

This scenario occurs when Sam clicks on the My Orders link in the menu at the side of the My Wings page. This scenario demonstrates the ability of the system to ensure that Sam, who is authenticated as an unprivileged user, is only allowed to see information about objects in the database that he, as a user, owns. In other words, he can view only his own customer account information and his own orders.

You may think that such authorization is not necessary; the .aspx file displayed in the browser will have within it the user's ID and, when the My Orders page is requested by the browser, it will include the customer ID as a parameter in the query string. Thus, you may think that home customers can only ever see their own orders since it would be impossible for the browser to send a different customer ID. Well, this is indeed true in normal operation, but it is certainly possible for a technically knowledgeable user to modify the user ID parameter that is posted back. For example, the malicious user may not use a browser at all but a specially written program that accesses the URL, scans through a range of possible user ID values, and records the HTML returned by the server. Individuals who specialize in such attacks have a range of methods available in their repertoire. Therefore, it is very important that the server verifies access to private data independently of anything that the browser is expected to do. This scenario is shown in Table 11-2.

Table 11-2. *The MyOrders Page Authorization Scenario Storyboard*

Step	User Action	System Response
Initial State	Sam is viewing the My Wings page of the Icarus website.	
1.	Sam clicks on the My Orders link.	The browser requests the My Orders web page, and the system detects that the user is authenticated and permits viewing of it.
2.		The page is populated from the database via the sales business logic and a set of order summary rows are requested from the database. The system determines that the user SamSmith10 has no privilege but is permitted access to each order because they are owned by him.
3.		The system returns the My Orders page to the browser populated by only those orders owned by Sam.

The team also defines an error scenario in which the browser sends a request for a page with a CUSTOMERID that is not equal to the ID of the authenticated user. This scenario must return an error condition to the user.

Other Security Scenarios

The team defines the following additional security scenarios:

- Access to Order Detail page with correct CUSTOMERID and ORDERID

- Attempted access to Order Detail page with CUSTOMERID not matching authenticated user

- Attempted access to Order Detail page with correct CUSTOMERID and ORDERID not belonging to customer

- Access to Make Reservation page with correct CUSTOMERID and ORDERID

- Attempted access to Make Reservation page with CUSTOMERID not matching authenticated user

- Attempted access to Make Reservation page with correct CUSTOMERID and ORDERID not belonging to customer

- Successful Search button post from Make Reservation page

- Attempted Search button post from Make Reservation page with similar errors to previous scenarios

- Successful Add reservation to order link button post from Make Reservation page

- Attempted Add reservation to order link button post from Make Reservation page with similar errors to previous scenarios

All these scenarios need to be implemented and tested at iteration 2. It's looking complicated, isn't it? At iteration 3 the scenarios that involve creating and managing users will also need to be defined, as well as those needed to manage access of controlled objects by users, such as making customers accessible to particular travel agents or removing their accessibility.

The information about users and their accessibility must also be replicated in client local databases, so that agents can still access their customers' orders when they are offline.

Sales Wing Application Scenarios

The scenarios that the team must define for the security functionality of the Sales Wing application are somewhat different from those of Sales Site because the users will have a higher level of privilege: either Limited Privilege in the case of the travel agents or Full Privilege in the case of the call center operators.

Sales Wing User Authentication

The scenario shown in Table 11-3 occurs when the operator of the Sales Wing application first starts the application.

Table 11-3. *The Sales Wing User Authentication Scenario Storyboard*

Step	User Action	System Response
Initial State	The user is logged on to Windows XP displaying the desktop.	
1.	The operator starts the Sales Wing application.	The application is started by the system and displays a welcome screen for three seconds.
2.		The Logon dialog box is displayed to the user.
3.	The user types a valid username and password, and then clicks the Logon button.	The system records the user's ID in the application and displays the main Customer Contacts screen.

It is important to note that authentication must be carried out in the web server by exposing an authentication web service and returning a cookie to the application. Subsequent operations initiated by the Sales Wing application that call web services can then send this cookie as part of their request. Subsequent authorization of requests for actions relating to customers and orders, when the application is online, must then be carried out in the web service by identifying the user with this cookie, rather than relying on the Sales Wing application to ensure all requests are from authenticated users. When offline, the authentication must be carried out in Sales Wing to protect its local data from unauthorized access.

If the Sales Wing application were operating in online mode, and the web services relied on the Sales Wing application to perform the only authorization, it would be possible for a malicious user to substitute an application of their own making instead of the legitimate Sales Wing application and access the web services without authentication. The demanding of this strategy by the requirements team is an example of a nonfunctional security requirement on the product.

Sales Wing Authorization for Opening a Customer Record

In the scenarios in Tables 11-4 and 11-5, the user of the Sales Wing application displays a list of users using the search capability already described, by last name, first name, or ID. The customers displayed must be limited to those the user is permitted to access. There are two cases: the user has Full Privilege (Table 11-4) or the user has Limited Privilege (Table 11-5).

Table 11-4. *The Sales Wing Open Customer Authorization, Full Privilege, Scenario Storyboard*

Step	User Action	System Response
Initial State	The user is authenticated as a Full-Privilege user by Sales Wing and the Customer Contacts screen is displayed.	
1.	The operator selects the File ➤ Open Customer option from the main menu.	The system verifies that the user has full privileges and displays a list of all customers in the Open Customer dialog box.
2.	The operator types in a few letters of the last name of the required customer.	The system verifies that the user has full privileges and displays only those customers satisfying the last name filter, but otherwise does not restrict them.
3.	The operator clicks the Open button.	The system verifies that the user has full privileges and opens the customer details tab for the customer with the ID selected.

Table 11-5. *The Sales Wing Open Customer Authorization, Limited Privilege, Scenario Storyboard*

Step	User Action	System Response
Initial State	The user is authenticated as a Limited Privilege user by Sales Wing and the Customer Contacts screen is displayed.	
1.	The operator selects the File ➤ Open Customer option from the main menu.	The system verifies that the user has limited privileges and displays a list of those customers in the Open Customer dialog box for which the user has access rights.
2.	The operator types in a few letters of the last name of the required customer.	The system verifies that the user has limited privileges and displays only those customers satisfying the last name filter, and for which the user has access rights.
3.	The operator clicks the Open button.	The system verifies that the user has limited privileges and opens the customer details tab for the customer with the ID selected only if the user has access rights to the customer.

Notice that even after the list of customers has been displayed in the Open Customer dialog box, filtered by search criteria and access rights, authorization must still take place when a customer is selected and that customer's details are retrieved from the web service to populate the customer details tab in the Sales Wing application. This is because a rogue application could directly access the web service to get the customer details without going through the Open Customer dialog box. For the same reasons we previously described, when Sales Wing is operating in online mode, all the authorization must be carried out on the server rather than the client.

Other Sales Wing Scenarios

Here are some samples of the other scenarios that the team defines for the Sales Wing application:

- **Sales Wing Display Order Detail, Full Privilege**: The action when an order is opened and the order detail page must be populated and displayed.

- **Sales Wing New Order, Full Privilege**: The order detail page is opened for a new order.

- **Sales Wing Order Detail, Resource Search, Full Privilege**: A resource search is conducted for the order that is open.

- **Sales Wing Order Detail, Add Reservation, Full Privilege**: A reservation is added to the order that is open.

- **Sales Wing Order Detail, Remove Reservation, Full Privilege**: A reservation is removed from the order that is open.

- **Sales Wing Order Detail, Save Order, Full Privilege**: The open order is saved and the details persisted to the database.

All of these scenarios must be duplicated for the case of the user having limited privilege; the orders and customers must then be limited to those for which the user has access. The scenarios must also be duplicated for both online and offline mode. In online mode, the user must be authorized to carry out the desired action at the web service level using a cookie to identify the user. The web service will then determine the user's privilege level and access rights over customers and orders. Authorization must be satisfied for any request for action that involves retrieving data relating to the order, or modifying the order.

Iteration 2 Main Branch: Create Application Architecture

Peter and his senior developers must undertake the Create Solution Architecture task as soon as the storyboarding of the security scenarios has moved to a point where sufficient information is available. Obviously, by the time iteration 2 starts, the architecture is already established and, if the long-term planning was correct, it should only need adjustment to accommodate the new scenarios discussed in the previous section. Two areas of the architecture will need modification: the data model and the business entity design.

ASP.NET Membership and Role Management

ASP.NET 2.0 provides new capability for handling membership and roles together with a set of ASP.NET logon controls. The membership features make it very easy to add validation and storage of user credentials to a website. The membership information can be automatically stored in SQL Server, Active Directory, or an alternative data store. The membership capability of ASP.NET 2.0 integrates this information with Forms Authentication to provide complete logon capability for a site and facilitates password maintenance and user management. The Role Management feature in ASP.NET 2.0 can be used with the membership features to authorize users to view different pages and files according to their role membership. If you are implementing any sort of security system for a website, you should study these features in detail to see if they provide what you need, or whether they can be customized to provide the features you want.

The Icarus system described in this book, however, is much more than just a website with login and authorization-controlled access to certain pages. The security is required not only to control access to the website and the various pages, but also to control access on a record-by-record basis to individual tables via the business entity objects. For example, access to orders must be authorized on the basis of ownership or granted access, and order access depends on the user's privilege level. Collections of orders must be generated for display that are filtered on a basis of these authorization criteria. In addition, the same authentication and authorization scenarios must apply to access from the Sales Wing and List Wing Windows Forms applications via the web services. For these reasons, the architectural team chose not to use ASP.NET Membership and Role Management. However, you may find that you can utililize certain features to implement parts of a complex security system such as the one described in this book. So you should study ASP.NET Membership and Role Management before deciding to build your own system.

Data Model

The data model must include all of the information needed to both authenticate users and authorize them for requested action. The next sections show the data model that Peter and his team agree upon for iteration 2. The key point is that the model must contain the information needed to implement the security scenarios. The program logic to implement security is yet to be placed in an appropriate part of the architecture. Various places are available: the client applications, the presentation layer, the business layer, or the data layer.

Controlled Objects

Controlled objects are rows in a table that have protected access. Each row in any table that is a controlled object will also have a row in the CONTROLLEDOBJECTS table, shown in Figure 11-8. The purposes of this table are to provide a primary key to which access entries can point (as described later) and to provide space for any data fields required in the future that are common to all controlled objects. Customers, orders, vendors, and resources are controlled objects, and each row in any of their corresponding tables has a related row in the CONTROLLEDOBJECTS table. The rows in the CONTROLLEDOBJECTS table are referenced by foreign keys in the other four tables in Figure 11-8.

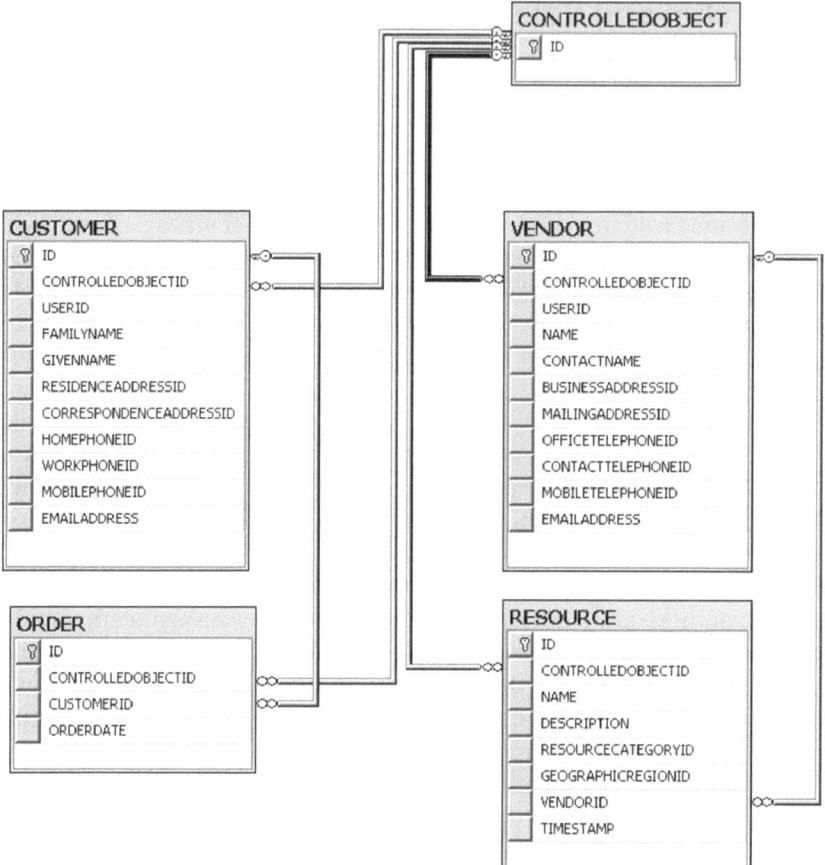

Figure 11-8. *Controlled objects in the security data model*

User Table

All users of the system will have an entry in the USER table, shown in Figure 11-9, containing the user's ID number, username, authentication password, and privilege level ID. Users may also be customers or vendors, and all customers or vendors are users; thus there is a row in the USER table for each row in the CUSTOMER table and also for each row in the VENDOR table. A foreign key in the VENDOR and CUSTOMER table points to a row in the USER table. There are also users who are agents or Icarus employees who have a row in the USER table but no row in either the VENDOR or CUSTOMER table. The primary key values in the USER table match the foreign key values in access entries, as described next.

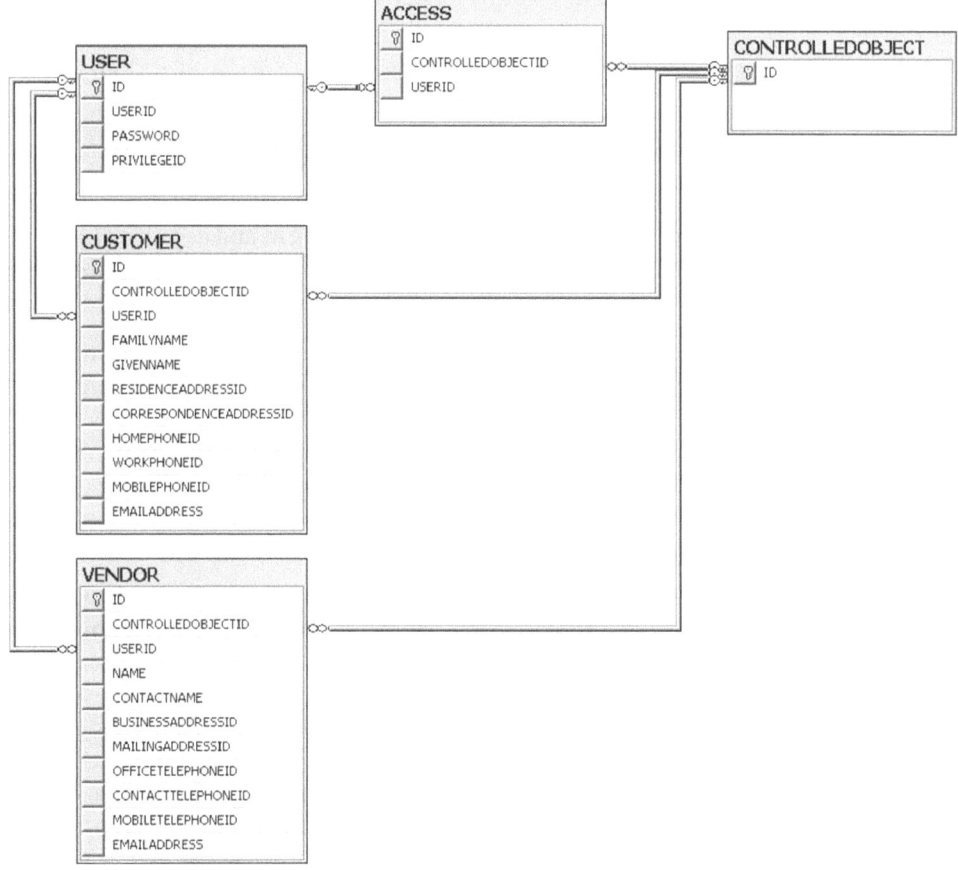

Figure 11-9. *Users and access in the security data model*

Authorization Ownership and Authorization Access

A controlled object has an *ownership* relationship with one user. The accessing user is the owner in the following cases:

- If the object being accessed is the row in the CUSTOMER table that represents an accessing customer user.

- If the object being accessed is the row in the VENDOR table that represents an accessing vendor user.

- If the object being accessed is an order belonging to an accessing customer user.

- If the object being accessed is a resource belonging to an accessing vendor user.

A user with authorization privilege equal to NONE, as described in the next section, may still access all controlled objects that have an ownership relationship with the user.

A controlled object has an *access* relationship with a user if there is a row in the ACCESS table that has its CONTROLLEDOBJECTID foreign key pointing to the controlled object's row in the CONTROLLEDOBJECT table and its USERID foreign key pointing to the user's row in the USER table.

Authorization Privilege

A user must be allocated one of three levels of authorization privilege:

- **None**: The user is only permitted access to controlled objects with which he or she has an ownership relationship. An example is a customer logging in and accessing his or her own orders and customer details, or a vendor accessing that vendor's own listings or account details.

- **Limited**: The user is permitted access to controlled objects only when the user has an access relationship with those objects. Once the user has access to an object, access to that object is full and complete. There is no read-only or similar limited access.

- **Full**: The user has full access to all controlled objects.

Security Business Logic

As we discuss the detailed design of the security implementation, you can refer back to the application diagrams in Chapter 5, Figure 5-18, and Chapter 6, Figure 6-23. This section summarizes the logic that is required in business entity classes that represent controlled objects in the database. Instances of business entity classes may represent either a single business entity, such as an order or customer, or a collection of entities, such as "all of the orders belonging to a particular customer," "all of the resources belonging to a particular vendor," or "all the resources that meet a specified set of criteria in a search." If the individual entities in either the single or multiple case are controlled objects, then only those accessible to the authenticated user must be populated into the business entity object.

Part of the architecture creation involves deciding how to place and organize the security business logic and how it will interact with the rest of the system to implement the scenarios described earlier. Choices that come to mind are

1. Perform tests in the presentation layer aspx.cs code-behind pages and in the Windows Form classes to determine whether a user is permitted to perform the action desired and to limit the instances of controlled objects included in displayed collections.

2. Perform tests in the business entity classes to limit information that is returned to these presentation layer classes.

3. Perform these tests in the base classes of the business entities to try to achieve some reuse of the code.

4. Perform tests in the stored procedures to determine which data, if any, should be returned to populate a business entity.

Option 1 can seem attractive, particularly when multiple operations are possible from a particular page and the settings of various controls are needed in the security decision. However, it is usually not a good idea to place security logic in these pages since the same logic is often needed in more than one page in a particular presentation. Also for this project, there are multiple presentations. Both the web services and the website use the same business objects. The same business objects are also used by the `SalesWing` and `ListWing` Windows applications to access their local databases. Finally, as you know, the security logic *must* be implemented on the server, so it cannot be placed in the presentation layer made up of the `SalesWing` and `ListWing` Windows Forms applications.

Options 2 and 3 are attractive because they collect the logic involved with business entity security along with the rest of the business logic and allow reuse in the various parts of the entire application. It is efficient to place those parts of the security logic that are common to all business entities in the base class. One problem with this approach, though, is that the way the access control logic is applied will very likely be dependent on the type of business entity being populated, particularly in the case of collection entities, such as those returning the results of a search.

Option 4 also encapsulates the security logic in a reusable place and has the advantage of reducing network traffic between the business layer and the database. For example, if a collection is being returned, then it makes a lot of sense to return only entities in the collection that are accessible to the user, rather than returning all entities and then removing inaccessible ones from the collection. Also, the ownership and access information is there in the database, and if joins can be easily performed in the stored procedures across those tables to return only accessible entities, it is not necessary to separately access the database to retrieve the authenticated user's privilege, ownership, and access information.

The downside of option 4 is that the stored procedures can become complicated and difficult to maintain, document, and debug. It is usually not a good idea to implement decision-making logic in SQL; instead, place it in C# or VB code and use SQL only for the retrieval of data from tables.

Given that, it appears that the security logic will likely be spread between options 2, 3, and 4 in an effort to keep the logic as encapsulated as possible with clear and simple interfaces between the different sections. The devil is invariably in the details, and the exact separation of the logic between these sections will likely depend on the individual business entity cases. Nevertheless, we can make a few further generalizations concerning the best split for single and multiple entities.

Single Entity Operations

Controlling access to a single entity seems to be quite simple. Either access is allowed and the entity is returned populated, or access is prohibited and either `null` is returned from a function in the business logic, or an exception is thrown. Because of the performance impact of throwing and catching exceptions, it is usually not a good idea to use the exception mechanism as a part of the business logic if that logic is to be used frequently. However, Peter does not expect access to individual entities to be denied by the security system in normal operation; the user will always access an item by choosing from a previously displayed list, and if the user was not permitted access, those items would not appear in the list. So single-entity access prohibitions in Enterprise 3.1 are likely to arise rarely, either as a result of misuse or perhaps as a result of listed entities becoming *stale*—that is, an entity that was accessible when the list containing it was returned is no longer accessible when the user attempts to view its detail.

Therefore, in the single-entity case it may be possible to place the security check in the business entity and thus make use of the data model to provide access information, such as the user's privilege level and whether access is provided to the entity according to the contents of the tables. The available information will be used by the business entity class to determine if the user has the right to request the particular action, and an exception will be thrown if access is to be denied. The following information is available to the business entity:

- User ID number from the user's authenticated cookie—available in the entity class

- The ID of the entity for which the action is required—available in the entity class

- Whether the controlled object is owned by the user—available from the database

- Whether the user has access to the controlled object—available from the database

- The authorization privilege level of the user—available from the database

The logic to implement the check should therefore be quite simple and with a bit of luck might go into a base class such as `BusinessEntityBE`.

Entity Collection Operations

Operations performed on a collection entity such as the `CustomerSearchBE` class described in Chapter 7 involve retrieving a collection of rows in one or more tables from the database. Together, these rows define the collection of entities encapsulated in the entity object. It makes a great deal of sense in this case to only return rows corresponding to accessible entities from the database. To do this, you can pass the ID of the user in a parameter to the stored procedure and include checks of ownership privilege and access rights in the procedure. Unfortunately, these criteria, when mixed in an already complicated set of inner and outer joins, can make the stored procedure far more complicated. Therefore, it may be better to perform the select operation in two stages in the stored procedure, thus allowing the database to optimize the operation. It may even be better to return all rows and perform a second select operation in the dataset object when it is present in the business entity class. You may need to experiment to find the best compromise.

Iteration 2 Main Branch: Create Product Requirements

Peter writes a fairly brief security requirements document summarizing the required behavior of the system, as he has designed it, to implement the scenarios described earlier. Its requirements are summarized as follows:

- The concept of a user shall be implemented by the product with a username and password.

- Only users defined within the system may access the system. The system shall require authentication by username and password to allow access to the Sales Site and to the Sales Wing and List Wing Windows applications.

- The product shall support the concept of a controlled object with limited accessibility.

- Controlled objects may have one owner: a user who shall always have access to it.

- Controlled objects and users may be related by access lists. All users who have an access list entry linking them to a controlled object shall have access to that object.

- Users shall have an access privilege level. Users with no privileges shall only have access to controlled objects owned by them. Users with Limited Privilege will have access to those objects to which they have access links. Users with Full Privilege shall have access to all controlled objects.

- There are various kinds of controlled objects. Orders, Customers, Vendors, and Resources are examples of controlled objects. Users are not necessarily controlled objects unless they are also Customers or Vendors.

- Only Full Privilege users shall be able to modify the access links or privilege levels of other users.

Iteration 2 Main Branch: Developing and Testing Authentication and Authorization

This section describes first the design of the code implementing the authentication and authorization logic. Authentication is the capability of an operator to provide a username and password and be recognized as a valid user of the system. Authorization is the capability of the system to limit access of authenticated users only to certain data.

Authenticating the Sales Site Client

Angela has been asked to work on the changes necessary for the business entities to support security. She begins by opening the `Enterprise 3.1.sln` solution (not `Enterprise 3.1-Replication.sln`, which is Joe's replication branch) from source control and verifying that it builds.

Angela reads the documentation on Forms Authentication. Customers accessing the sales website need to be authenticated before any of the restricted pages are accessed. Forms Authentication can easily be used for this purpose and is a well-known technique. To switch on Forms Authentication, you need to create the following entries in the `web.config` file:

```
<configuration>
  <system.web>
    ...
    <authentication mode="Forms">
      <forms loginUrl="Logon.aspx" name=".ASPXFORMSAUTH" defaultUrl="MyWings.aspx">
      </forms>
    </authentication>
    <authorization>
      <deny users="?"/>
    </authorization>
    ...
  </system.web>
</configuration>
```

Note The code at this point is available under `Chapter 11\Exercise 4`. Exercise 11-5 should help you follow this section.

The `<authentication>` tag selects Forms mode and the `loginUrl` attribute in the `<forms>` tag defines the URL to which the browser is to be redirected when the session is unauthenticated. Normally the user is returned to the original URL after authentication. The `defaultUrl` is the URL to which the user is returned after authentication if the URL originally accessed by the user is invalid. The `<authentication>` tag allows or denies users access to various subdirectories, or in this case the entire site. "`?`" is a wildcard meaning all unauthenticated users. The entries shown here cause redirection of unauthenticated (anonymous) users attempting to access any page in the site to `Login.aspx`.

Once the users have been sent to this URL, the page must authenticate the user by allowing a username and password to be entered. For test purposes, Angela puts together a simple login page with two text boxes and a Login button. The event handler for the button click is

```
protected void ButtonLogon_Click(object sender, EventArgs e)
{
  int userId = UserBE.Authenticate(
                           this.TextBoxUserName.Text, this.TextBoxPassword.Text);
  if (userId >= 0)
  {
     FormsAuthentication.RedirectFromLoginPage(userId.ToString(), false);
  }
}
```

Here you see a new business entity called `UserBE`. It is very similar to the other business entities in that it has a corresponding `UserDAL` project in the data access layer that defines a `UserDS` with a table adapter. The adapter will allow read and write access to the USER table in the database. The business entity also supports a static member function:

```
public static int Authenticate(string username, string password)
```

This function creates an instance of `UserBE`, determines whether the user exists and whether the password matches the one stored in the database, and returns the ID of the user. The function returns -1 if authentication fails. The call to `RedirectFromLoginPage` is standard forms authentication and gives the browser an authentication ticket and redirects it back to the page at which it started. If that page is invalid, the browser will be directed to the default page set in the `<authentication>` tag described earlier in this section. The ticket will contain the user ID from the database, that is, the primary key in the USER table. In each subsequent authenticated access in the session, this user ID will be available in the current HTTP context, which is obtained as a static property of the `HttpContext` class. Its `User` property returns an object implementing `IPrincipal`, from which the `string` parameter `userId.ToString()` shown earlier in the call to `RedirectFromLoginPage` can be recovered:

```
string userIdString = HttpContext.Current.User.Identity.Name;
```

Angela makes some changes to the BusinessEntityBE class so that this user ID string is picked up in the constructor and made available in database accesses to determine authorization of access to controlled objects.

Authenticating at the Web Service Access

The need to authenticate at the web service access has been described earlier so that only bona fide instances of the SalesWing application with users authenticated by that system can access the SalesWebService. Some discussion of the architecture has taken place, and the team has agreed that the Icarus web services will not rely on the integrity of local authentication.

■ **Note** The code at this point is available under Chapter 11\Exercise 5. Exercise 11-6 should help you follow this section.

To understand this, imagine a scheme where a new user started the SalesWing application and logged in and was authenticated against the USER table replicated in the local database. Remember that data from the USER table will need to be replicated locally to allow users to be authenticated when the client is offline. Following this scheme, when this user accessed, say a customer, then the SalesWing client could send an encrypted user ID value signed with a certificate to prevent tampering en route. The web service then would not have to verify the user's username and password, but would accept the ID as being validly authenticated locally. The problem with this is that there is nothing to stop a local user with rights over the local database from tampering with the data and modifying the stored passwords. Encryption mechanisms are available that could conceivably prevent this, but the team decides that the web services will always authenticate users. Thus, the client application must supply a username and password to the server, the same pair that the user entered when logging into the system.

Microsoft Web Services Extensions 3.0 provides the capability needed to implement such a scheme, and the team plans to use this scheme later in the project. For iteration 2, however, since none of the developers have the time to perform the necessary research, Angela, implements a simple scheme where the username and password are passed as parameters in each web service call. This at least allows the end-to-end authentication and authorization to be tested.

Implementing Authorization

To begin implementing the authorization aspects of security, Angela must add the additional features of the data model that are defined in the security architecture. These features consist of the additional tables USER, CONTROLLEDOBJECT, and ACCESS, together with their relationships, as shown earlier in Figures 11-8 and 11-9.

■ **Note** The code at this point is available under Chapter 11\Exercise 6. Exercise 11-7 should help you follow this section.

It will also be necessary to add the CONTROLLEDOBJECTID foreign keys to the CUSTOMER, VENDOR, ORDER and RESOURCE tables to allow those tables to reference their entry in the CONTROLLEDOBJECT table. The primary keys in the CONTROLLEDOBJECT table can be generated using an identity field, but the value generated must be retrieved using the ScopeIdentity() function; that way, it can be placed in the foreign key CONTROLLEDOBJECTID fields in these four tables. For example, Angela modifies the stored procedure INSERTORDER to read

```
ALTER PROCEDURE dbo.INSERTORDER
(
  @CUSTOMERID int,
  @ORDERDATE datetime
)
AS
  SET NOCOUNT OFF;
  INSERT INTO [CONTROLLEDOBJECT] DEFAULT VALUES;
  INSERT INTO [ORDER] ([CONTROLLEDOBJECTID], [CUSTOMERID], [ORDERDATE])
  VALUES ( SCOPE_IDENTITY(), @CUSTOMERID, @ORDERDATE);
  SELECT ID, CUSTOMERID, ORDERDATE FROM [ORDER] WHERE (ID = SCOPE_IDENTITY())
```

The last line in this stored procedure returns the fields from the new row to update the dataset row that was the origin of the inserted data from the table adapter. This return of inserted data is needed because the ID field is an identity field and its values are generated by the database. Angela also modifies the DELETEORDER stored procedure so that it deletes the entry in the CONTROLLEDOBJECT table as well as the row in the ORDER table.

Single-Entity Authorization

Single-entity authorization limits to authorized users, the read and write access to single entities, such as the details for a specific customer. To implement the read case, Angela changes the GETCUSTOMER stored procedure to the following:

```
ALTER PROCEDURE dbo.GETCUSTOMER
(
  @ID int,
  @USERID int,
  @HASACCESS int output,
  @ISOWNER int output,
  @USERPRIVID int output
)
AS
  SET NOCOUNT ON;
  SET @HASACCESS = (SELECT COUNT(ACCESS.ID)
  FROM
  ACCESS, CUSTOMER
  WHERE ACCESS.USERID = @USERID
  AND ACCESS.CONTROLLEDOBJECTID = CUSTOMER.CONTROLLEDOBJECTID
  AND CUSTOMER.ID = @ID);
```

```
SET @ISOWNER = (SELECT COUNT(*)
FROM
CUSTOMER
WHERE CUSTOMER.USERID = @USERID AND CUSTOMER.ID = @ID);
SET @USERPRIVID = (SELECT [USER].PRIVILEGEID FROM [USER]
WHERE [USER].ID = @USERID);
/* Original Code */
```

This change allows passing of the user ID in the procedure call, and the return of a count of any ACCESS rows, a flag indicating ownership, and the user privilege level. This is all of the information needed to determine whether the user is authorized to access the customer details. The determination can be done in the CustomerBE code using this information returned by the stored procedure:

```
protected override void GetLocalData(int id)
{
  new COUNTRYTableAdapter(Connection).Fill(this.Data.COUNTRY);
  new STATETableAdapter(Connection).Fill(this.Data.STATE);
  new ORDERTableAdapter(Connection).Fill(this.Data.ORDER, id);
  System.Nullable<int>
    privilegeId = -1,    // For returned User Privilege level
    hasAccess = -1,      // For returned access count
    isOwner = -1;        // Is Owner flag
  new CUSTOMERTableAdapter(Connection).Fill(
    this.Data.CUSTOMER, // CUSTOMER data table
    id,                 // Customer ID
    this.userId,        // User ID
    ref hasAccess,      // Returned Access Count
    ref isOwner,        // Returned Owener flag
    ref privilegeId);   // Returned user privilege ID

  // Verify access rights
  switch (privilegeId)
  {
    case 0:              // Access rights = None
      if (isOwner == 0)
        throw new Exception("Security Access Violation");
      break;
    case 1:              // Access rights = Limited
      if (hasAccess <= 0 && isOwner == 0)
        throw new Exception("Security Access Violation");
      break;
    case 2:              // Access rights = Full
      break;
  }
}
```

In this modified `GetLocalData(int id)` function, the call to `CustomerTableAdapter.Fill` has been modified to include the user ID and the return integer variables `hasAccess`, `isOwner`, and `privilegeId`. If the privilege level is None, the customer that's being retrieved must be owned by the user. If the privilege level is Limited, either at least one access entry must exist connecting the user with the controlled object entry corresponding to the customer *or* the customer must be owned by the user. If the privilege level is Full, access is unconditional. The variables `privilegeId`, `hasAccess`, and `isOwner` are of type `System.Nullable<int>` (see Chapter 8), which is a generic class that represents a value type (in this case `int`) that can also be assigned a null value. This logic could easily have been placed in the stored procedure as an alternative, but the main thing is that only one call to the stored procedure is required to obtain all of the information. Placing the logic in the class is in line with our goal of not putting decision-making logic in stored procedures.

When Angela has coded more of the security functionality—in particular for `CustomerSearchBE`, which is an entity collection—she will determine if this logic can be placed in the `BusinessEntityBE` base class.

Multiple-Entity Authorization

As we stated earlier, when a collection of entities is to be returned, it makes much more sense to pass the user ID to the stored procedure and place some extra joins and conditions as shown here:

```
ALTER PROCEDURE dbo.CUSTOMERSEARCH
(
  @ID nvarchar(10),
  @FAMILYNAME nvarchar(50),
  @GIVENNAME nvarchar(50),
  @USERID integer
)
AS
  SET NOCOUNT ON;
  SELECT CUSTOMER.ID, FAMILYNAME, GIVENNAME
  FROM CUSTOMER,
  -- Security Code------
  ACCESS
  ---End Security Code-
  WHERE (CAST(CUSTOMER.ID AS CHAR(10)) LIKE @ID + N'%')
  AND (UPPER(FAMILYNAME) LIKE UPPER(@FAMILYNAME) + N'%')
  AND (UPPER(GIVENNAME) LIKE UPPER(@GIVENNAME) + N'%')
  -- Security Code------
  AND ACCESS.CONTROLLEDOBJECTID = CUSTOMER.CONTROLLEDOBJECTID
  AND ACCESS.USERID = @USERID
  ---End Security Code-
  ORDER BY FAMILYNAME, GIVENNAME
```

The bold lines indicate the code added to implement the authorization. The table called ACCESS is added to the list of tables, and two conditions are added so that rows are only returned if *both* of the following are true:

- An entry exists in the ACCESS table with its CONTROLLEDOBJECTID foreign key point-ing to the same entry in the CONTROLLEDOBJECT table as the entry in the CUSTOMER table.

- That same access entry has its USERID field pointing to the entry in the USER table cor-responding to the parameter @USERID.

So rows are only returned for customers who have an access link to the user (who would probably be a travel agent). A further modification is needed to this stored procedure to allow for when the user has full privileges or when the user is the customer. The stored procedure then can be written as follows:

```
ALTER PROCEDURE dbo.CUSTOMERSEARCH
(
  @ID nvarchar(10),
  @FAMILYNAME nvarchar(50),
  @GIVENNAME nvarchar(50),
  @USERID integer
)
AS
  SET NOCOUNT ON;
  SELECT CUSTOMER.ID, FAMILYNAME, GIVENNAME
  FROM
  [USER], CUSTOMER
  LEFT JOIN
  ACCESS
  ON ACCESS.CONTROLLEDOBJECTID = CUSTOMER.CONTROLLEDOBJECTID
  WHERE (CAST(CUSTOMER.ID AS CHAR(10)) LIKE @ID + N'%')
  AND (UPPER(FAMILYNAME) LIKE UPPER(@FAMILYNAME) + N'%')
  AND (UPPER(GIVENNAME) LIKE UPPER(@GIVENNAME) + N'%')
  AND [USER].ID = @USERID
  AND (ACCESS.USERID = @USERID OR [USER].PRIVILEGEID = 2
  OR CUSTOMER.USERID = @USERID)
  ORDER BY FAMILYNAME, GIVENNAME
```

This works well, but is much more difficult to understand. In addition, the security code is now completely intermeshed in with the rest.

There is a great deal more work to be done on security, including taking care of the write case for customers, where again the authorization code can be build into the INSERT, UPDATE, and DELETE stored procedures for a table adapter. Also, the team needs to add the authoriza-tion code for the other controlled object tables, VENDOR, RESOURCE, and ORDER, both in their read and write cases.

At this point, the team has arrived at an implementation that minimizes the traffic between the business tier and the data tier and also minimizes the number of stored procedure calls in handling a business transaction. As I have said before, to achieve the very best results in per-formance and scalability, other splits of functionality between the business tier and the database could be considered. For example, the privileges check could be done during authentication, stored in the user's cookie, and then one of three stored procedures could be called according to the user's privilege level. This would simplify the stored procedures with minimal effect on performance.

Managing Users

I won't discuss in detail the work done by Charles and Angela during iteration 2 in implementing user management as part of security. Essentially there are screens in the SalesWing application that allow users to be added to the system and to permit their privileges and access links to be set up. These screens are not needed on the SalesSite application since they are used for adding agent and call center operator users. The screens use the UserBE class and utilize bound controls and object data sources in a similar manner to the customer screens.

Merging the Branches, Iteration 3: Replication and Main Functionality

At the end of iteration 2, the change branch in which the replication of resources on client machines has been developed is to be merged into the main track (to which security capability has been added). Earlier, in Chapter 9, when I talked about merging files in which independent changes had been made by two or more developers, I explained that merging two branches was another example of when the merge process of files takes place. In the merge operation, either a new file is created by merging two existing files, or a new folder full of files is created by merging all the files from two existing folders. There are special cases during a folder merge, as described in Chapter 9, when files have been deleted or renamed.

Note The code at this point is available under Chapter 11\Exercise 7. Exercise 11-8 should help you follow this section.

Ron is going to perform the merge operation. He begins by defining a workspace called RonI2, mapping the top folder in the project, Iteration 2, to a suitable location on his own drive. Then he opens Source Control Explorer, right-clicks on the top-level folder, and selects Get Latest. Several projects have been branched and the content of their files on the branches will be different. Also a number of projects have been added. The branched project with the most differences is likely to be SalesWing. So Ron begins by selecting the replication version of that project folder, called SalesWing-Replication. He then right-clicks and selects Merge, as shown in Figure 11-10.

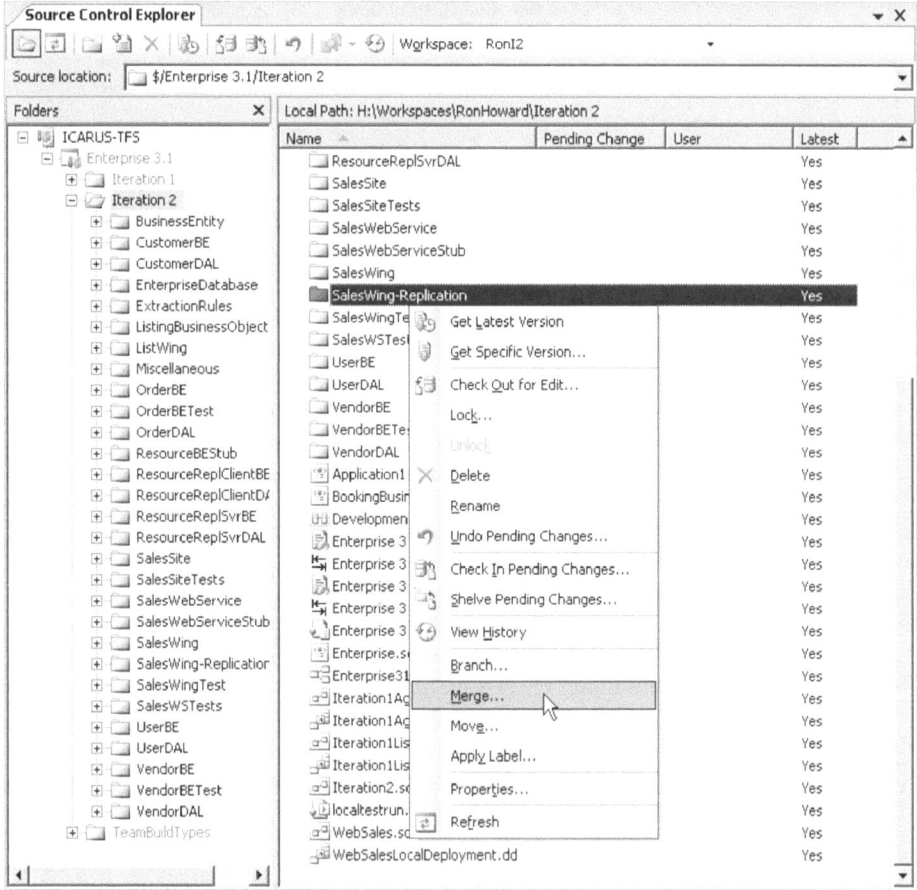

Figure 11-10. *Beginning the merge of the SalesWing development tracks*

The Source Control Merge Wizard appears, as shown in Figure 11-11. Notice that Ron's action has automatically selected the *source* of the merge to begin the operation, which will mean that the source branch for the merge in the top text box will be prepopulated with SalesWing-Replication. If the Source Branch entry is not correct, you can use the Browse button to find the correct source branch. After the merge, all the files and folders in the *source* branch will be unchanged, but the files in the *target* branch may contain changes, depending on how the files differ between the two. The idea is that the source branch is merged into the target branch, but the source branch still remains and work may continue on it. The two branches do *not* merge and become one, and further merges can be done later if more changes are made to the source branch. Indeed, at this point, the replication work is far from complete, and Joe will continue to work on it. Merging can also go the other way; the replication branch could accept the latest changes from the main branch. Joe will need the latest changes from the rest of the team before he continues to develop the replication branch.

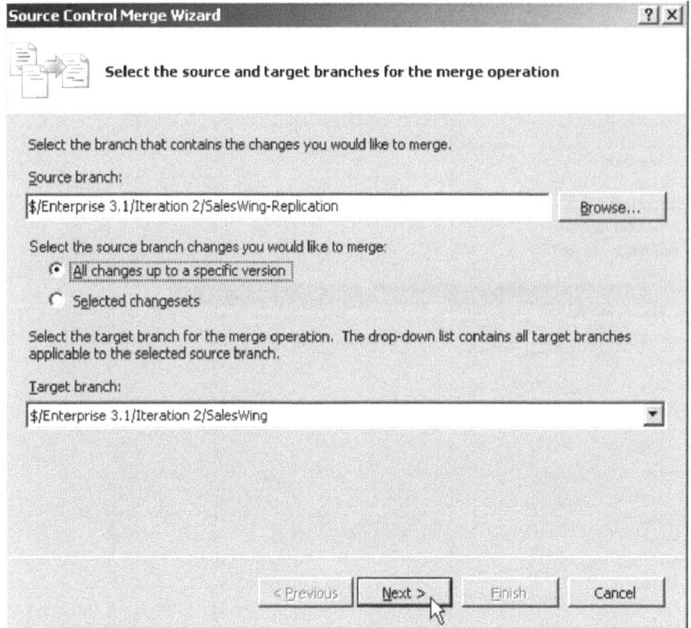

Figure 11-11. *Selecting the source and target branches*

In the wizard, Ron can select to merge all the changes up to a specified version (the default option as shown) or he can merge only specific changesets. If you are concerned about messing up the stability of the destination branch, you can take changesets a few at a time. When the project is in the consolidation track and most of the changes relate to bug fixes, the changesets will be associated with definite work items and the merge can be done bit by bit, with some smoke tests run in between stages.

Ron must also select the target branch; the drop-down displays only branches that exist for this folder—in this case, there's only one and it's already selected as the default. Ron leaves the options shown in Figure 11-11 and clicks Next.

Figure 11-12 shows the next wizard page, which lets you select the versions of the source code items. At this point, Ron has chosen to merge all changes *up to a specified version*. On this page, he selects that version. He may define it by changeset, by data, by label, as the latest version, or he may select the version currently in his workspace as the source of the merge. (Depending on which version you select, other options will appear on this page that let you specify the changeset, date, or label.) Keep in mind that defining the latest version by changeset is not the same as selecting only specified changesets. Ron selects Latest Version from the Version Type drop-down and clicks Next.

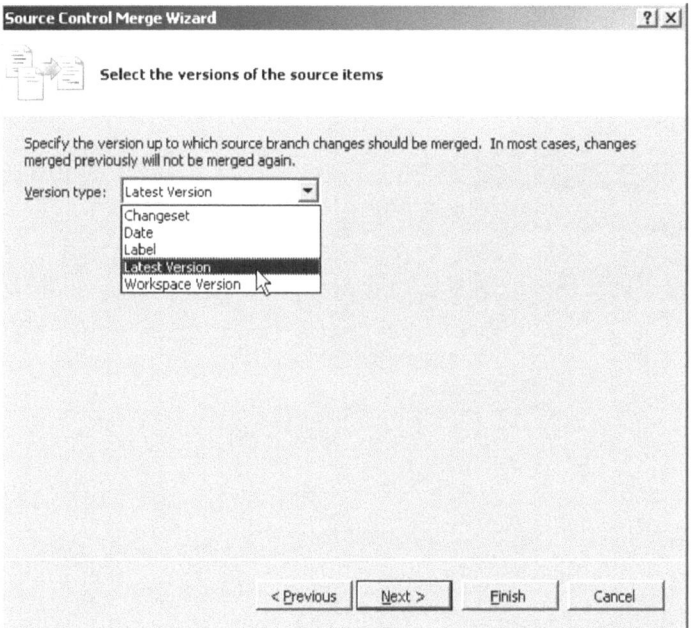

Figure 11-12. *Selecting the versions to be merged*

The final screen of the wizard (Figure 11-13) appears, and Ron clicks Finish. The merge now takes place. As shown in Figure 11-14, there are two files with conflicting changes. This means that changes have been made to these files on both the main branch and the replication branch. There may be other files where conflicts do not occur, and the latest file will have been taken in those cases. The conflicts for these two files need to be resolved. In this case, Ron chooses to resolve them one at a time. He starts by selecting the Program.cs file and clicking the Resolve button.

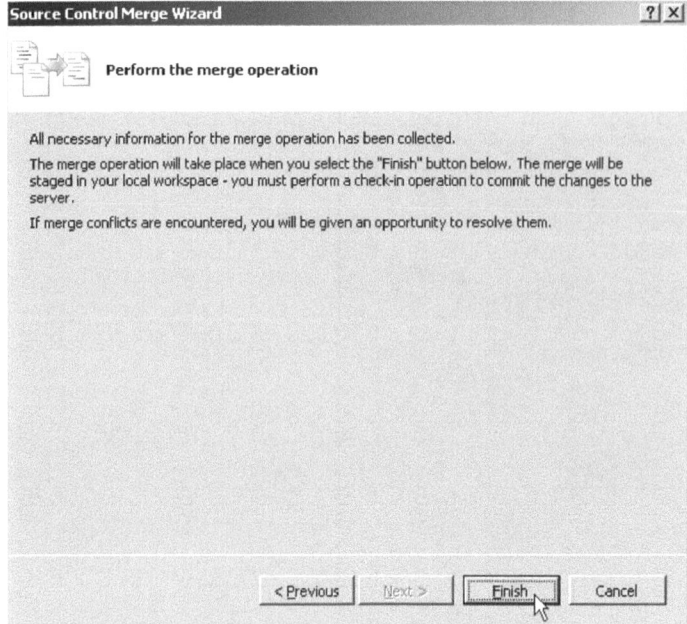

Figure 11-13. *The summary screen*

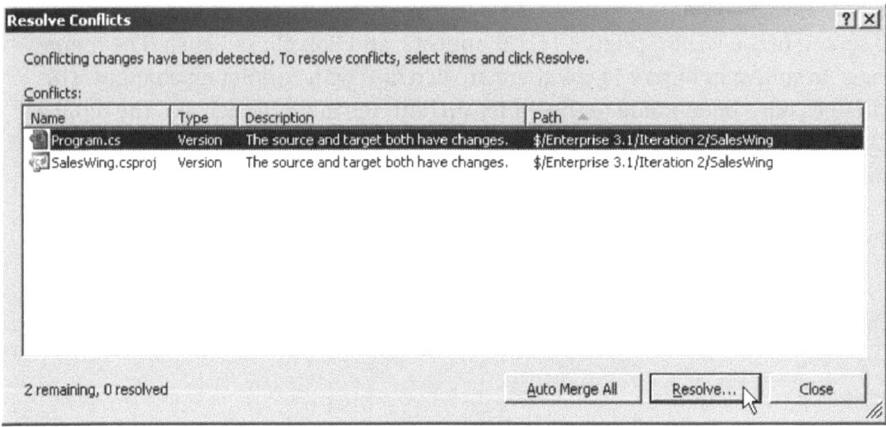

Figure 11-14. *Files that have conflicting changes*

Figure 11-15 shows the choices available. There are two conflicting changes, and here we must remember the distinction between *file conflicts* in Figure 11-14 and *internal conflicts*; conflicting changes in Figure 11-15 refer to internal conflicts. Recall from Chapter 9 that an internal conflict is one between changes within a file where there is no obvious automatic resolution. Since there are conflicting changes in this case, Ron cannot just select Merge changes for me (that option is automatically disabled), so he selects Merge changes in merge tool and clicks OK.

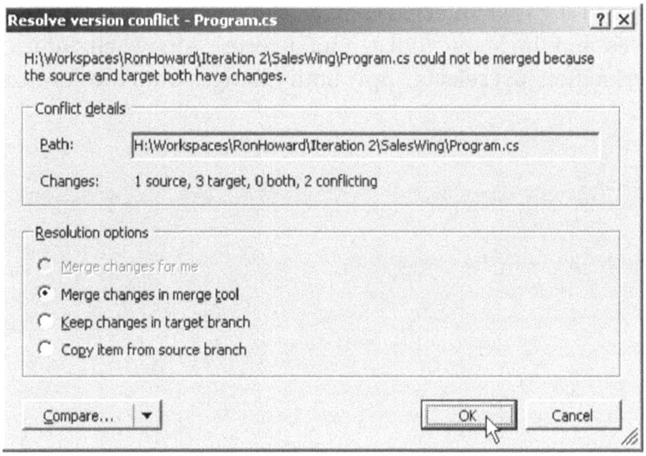

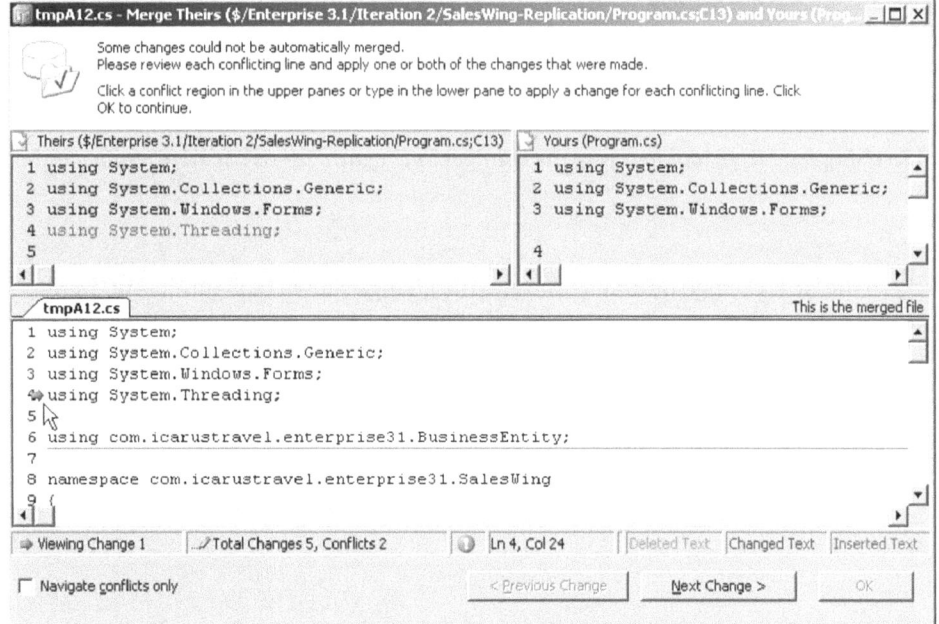

Figure 11-15. *Choices in resolving the conflicts*

The first change is shown in Figure 11-16. It is not an internal conflict, so the merge tool can make a decision unaided. The SalesWing-Replication\Program.cs file on the left has a using directive—using System.Threading—which is not in the SalesWing\Program.cs file on the right. The merge tool has already added the extra directive in the merged file underneath, and Ron accepts this and clicks the Next Change button.

Figure 11-16. *Using the Merge tool to merge the conflicts in Program.cs—the using directives*

The next change, shown in Figure 11-17, is an internal conflict. Here the conflict is trivial, involving some added `using` directives, and the Merge tool cannot determine in which order to put them. It really does not matter, so Ron just selects Apply Both Changes from the context menu so that they are both added.

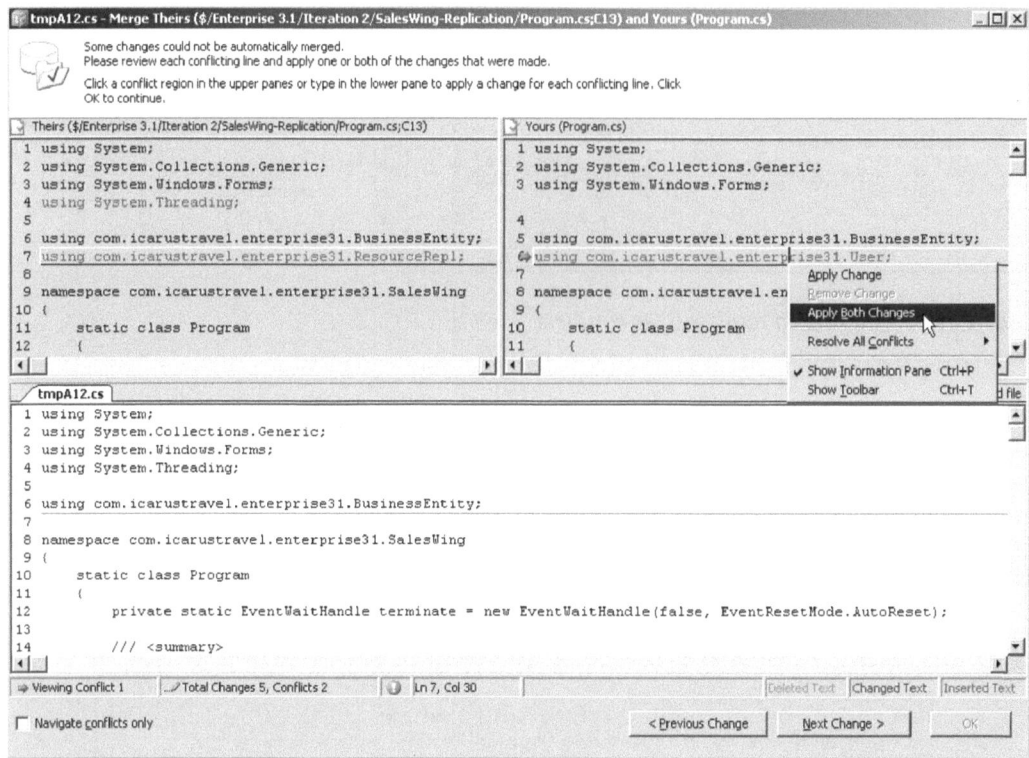

Figure 11-17. *Using the Merge tool to merge the changes in Program.cs—a trivial internal conflict*

Ron clicks the Next Change button to move to the change shown in Figure 11-18. Here there is no internal conflict; a new `EventWaitHandle` has been declared and initialized in the `SalesWing-Replication\Program.cs` file that does not conflict with any change in the `SalesWing\Program.cs` file. The line has been automatically added to the merged file below. The next change, shown in Figure 11-19, has a nonconflicting change in the file `SalesWing\Program.cs` on the right, where some new variables have been declared.

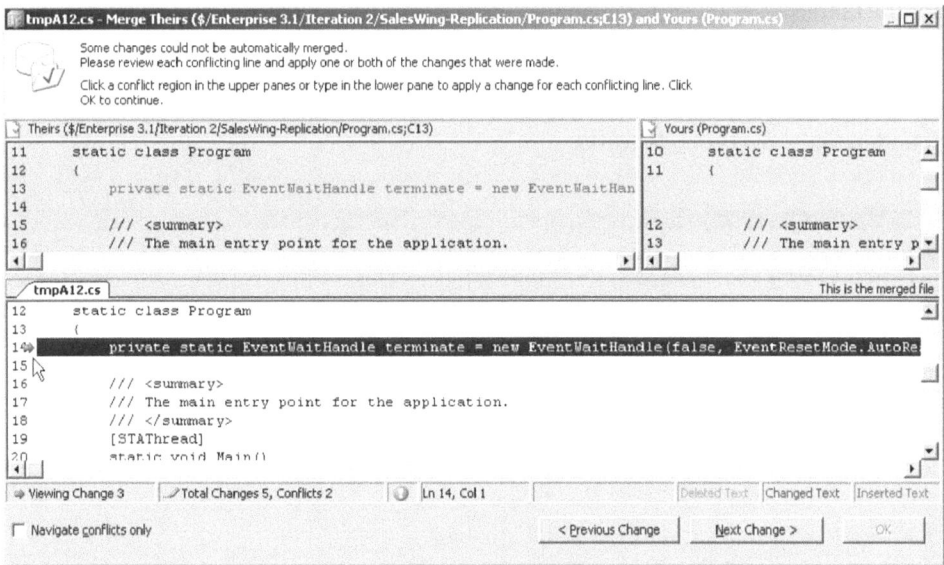

Figure 11-18. *Using the Merge tool to merge the changes in Program.cs—a trivial internal conflict. A nonconflicting change appears in the file on the left.*

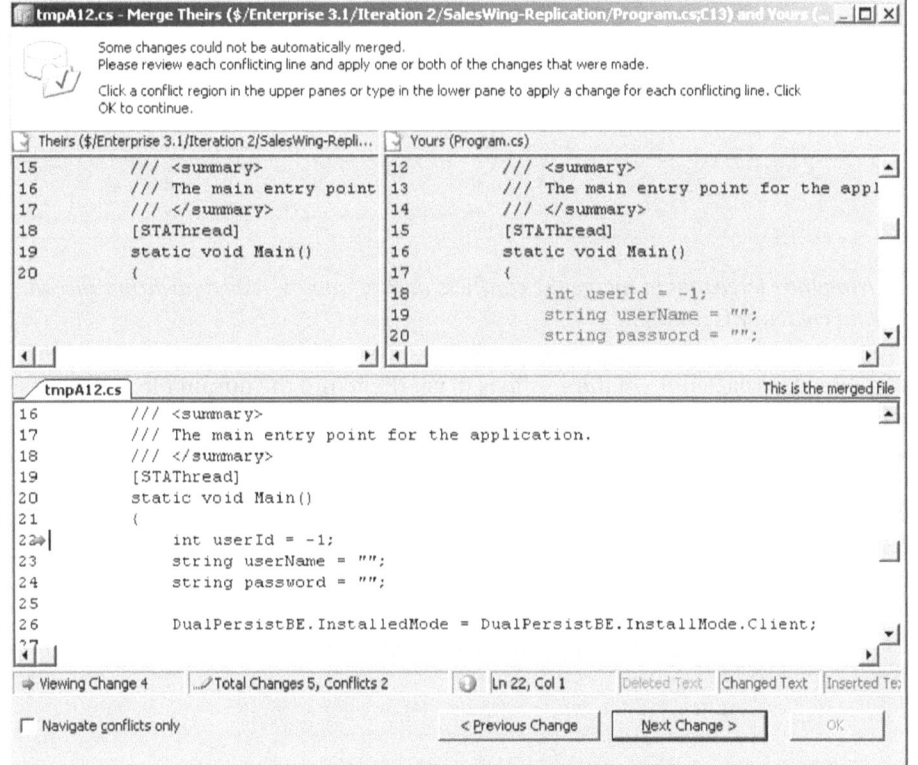

Figure 11-19. *Using the Merge tool to merge the changes in Program.cs—a trivial internal conflict. A nonconflicting change appears in the file on the right.*

So far the merge is very easy, but when Ron clicks Next Change again, he sees the intermingled group of conflicts shown in Figure 11-20. Ron now has to get Angela and Joe involved to determine how to merge the code. It's no good simply clicking both of the conflicts; otherwise the code that is generated will be completely wrong. Ron cannot do this himself as he does not understand how the code works.

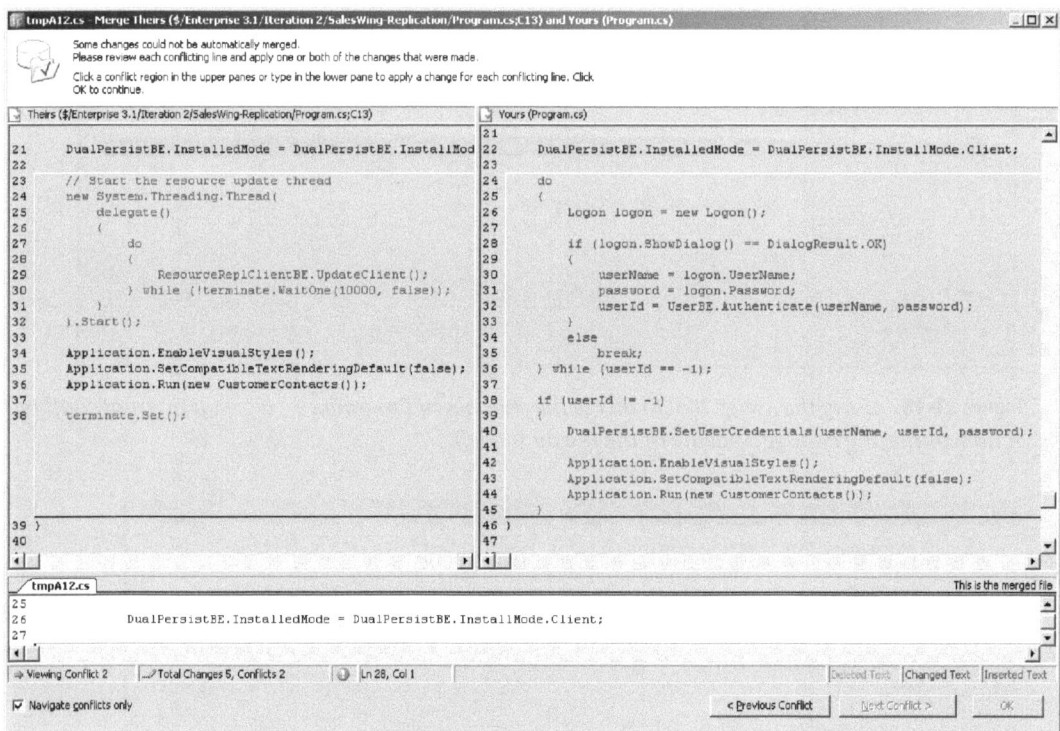

Figure 11-20. *Using the Merge tool to merge the conflicts in Program.cs—the replication thread and the login and credentials storage*

In the end, Ron does click both of the conflicts to get them into the output file, interspersing them with some blank lines. Then Angela corrects the file by editing in the output window, with Joe looking over her shoulder. The resulting code looks like this:

```
DualPersistBE.InstalledMode = DualPersistBE.InstallMode.Client;
Application.EnableVisualStyles();
Application.SetCompatibleTextRenderingDefault(false);
do
{
  Logon logon = new Logon();
```

```
  if (logon.ShowDialog() == DialogResult.OK)
  {
    userName = logon.UserName;
    password = logon.Password;
    userId = UserBE.Authenticate(userName, password);
  }
  else
    break;
} while (userId == -1);

if (userId != -1)
{
  DualPersistBE.SetUserCredentials(userName, userId, password);

  // Start the resource update thread
  new System.Threading.Thread(
    delegate()
    {
      do
      {
        ResourceReplClientBE.UpdateClient();
      } while (!terminate.WaitOne(10000, false));
    }
  ).Start();
  Application.Run(new CustomerContacts());
  terminate.Set();
}
```

The resource update thread must not start until the user has been authenticated by the display of the Logon dialog box and the call to UserBE.Authenticate(username, password). Once this conflict is resolved, there are no more changes, and Ron clicks OK. He sees a couple of prompts asking him whether he wants to save the file and accept the result; he clicks Yes to both. The Program.cs file no longer appears in the Resolve Conflicts window.

Finally, Ron needs to merge the SalesWing.csproj file. This merge turns out to be easy. As shown in Figure 11-21, there is an internal conflict in the file where two project references have been added. In this case, the order does not matter, and Ron can just click both of them. Often, however, merging project and solution files is not at all easy unless you are aware of their syntax. It is often safer to add files to a project file, or adjust project settings manually, rather than to attempt to merge project files with complicated conflicting changes. Even if the changes do not conflict, unless you understand the syntax, accepting an automatic merge may cause errors. This also applies to solution files.

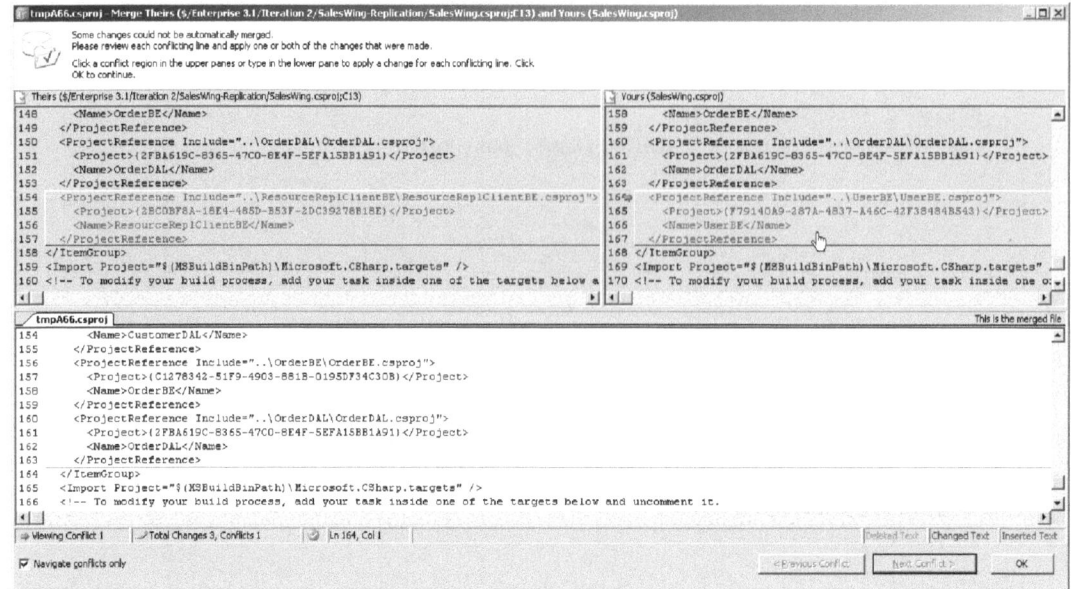

Figure 11-21. *Using the Merge tool to merge the conflicts in SalesWing.csproj. Here two project references have been added and the order does not matter.*

After all of the saves have been done, the merge of SalesWing is now complete. Ron attempts to build the solution and finds an error because the referenced assembly ResourceReplClientBE is not in the solution. Of course, Joe was working with a solution that was also branched. Should he attempt to merge the solution file? There are five projects that are not in the main-branch solution: ResourceReplClientBE, ResourceReplSvrBE, ResourceReplClientDAL, ResourceReplSvrDAL, and ClientReplWebService. Ron decides that merging the solution file in the Merge tool is too difficult and adds these five projects to the solution manually. He builds the entire solution and runs a quick smoke test of SalesWing and SalesSite. He also verifies that the replication thread is running properly.

Incidentally, the SalesWingTest project was also branched by Joe, but this does not have to be merged. At the moment it is only needed to allow Joe's branch to build and for the test to be run for his branch. If Joe makes any changes to SalesWingTest, perhaps to test the replication features, it will then need to be merged with the main branch.

Great, but one thing remains to be done. Remember that the merged set of files is present only on Ron's machine; the merge results have not yet been placed in TFS. The Pending Changes window shown in Figure 11-22 displays the files that have changed. Enterprise 3.1.sln has changed because the five replication projects have been added. Enterprise 3.1.vsssscc has not actually changed but was checked out automatically. The other two files under SalesWing are ones that were merged using the Merge tool. Ron makes sure that all of the files are checked and then clicks the Check In button. A progress box flashes onto the screen, the progress bar slides across, and everything is done.

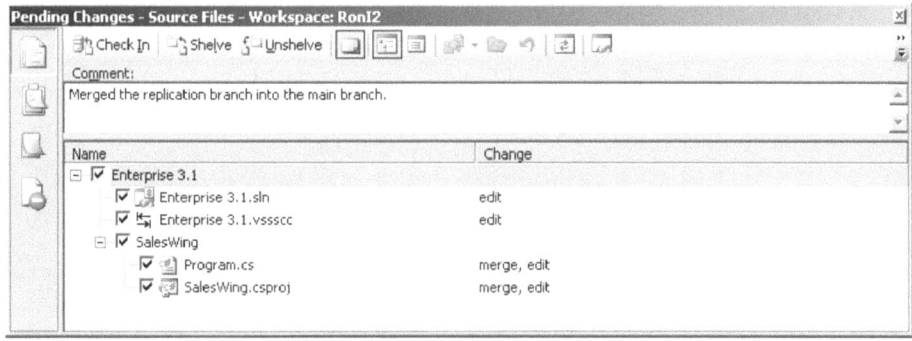

Figure 11-22. *The Pending Changes window after the merge operation and the manual additions of the replication projects to the solution*

Summary

This chapter has concentrated on how a project can respond to a fairly significant change of requirements by developing along two separate branches, one analyzing and implementing the change, the other working in the original direction. Team System supports this well with the concept of branching and merging.

First, we examined the scenarios for the changed requirements and the architecture and design changes needed. Next, you learned about the branching of code in Team System and saw how the developer branched some files within the solution to allow the replication branch to proceed independently of the main branch. The chapter went on to describe the development of the new replication capability on the replication branch.

Next, we watched and discussed progress along the main branch of the project where Angela designed and coded some of the security features, such as authentication and authorization.

Finally, you learned how to merge one branch into another as the team leader merged the replication work into the main branch.

In the next chapter, we will look particularly at the management and control aspects of the development in its advanced stages and watch the detailed use of these Team System features as they are used to control and track progress.

CHAPTER 12

Managing Iterations: Moving Toward Completion

In the previous chapters, we've examined requirements definition, architectural design, coding, and tests, with a focus on the features in Team System that support these activities. This chapter will be devoted to the organizational aspects of adding increasing functionality to the evolving system. We join the management team at the beginning of iteration 4.

Planning Iterations 4 and 5

Susan describes the backlog of scenarios at the beginning of iteration 4. It contains those areas that have been defined as part of the requirements for the project in Chapter 4 but that have not yet been implemented. They can be summarized as follows:

- Resource browsing and search capability, or the ability for a home customer or travel agent to browse through the resource catalog or search for keywords, and then make an order by navigating from the description page of a resource of interest to a new order page, with a reservation of that resource automatically added to the new order.

- Offline working—customer and order synchronization. The ability to synchronize customer details and customer order details held in the Client Local Database for a travel agent with the Icarus Enterprise database and resolve any conflicting changes.

- Integration of the Sales Site and Sales Wing applications with the payment server and the asynchronous back-end applications via the orchestration server.

- Integration of the List Wing application with the payment server and the asynchronous back-end applications via the orchestration server.

- Advanced scenarios for List Wing, including the ability to add visual information (called "Visual Resource Details") about resources, web pages, etc.

- Scenarios relating to the Sales Status application.

"You're right—adding the offline synchronization scenarios at this point does follow quite nicely," says Peter halfway through the iteration 4 planning meeting. "But I do think we should keep it on a separate branch until the end of this iteration."

"But then we really should bring the two branches together, don't you think?" presses Ron. "That way, we can move along one track as the project moves to consolidation."

"I do think at that point we need team focus on one path for consolidation," adds Clare. Peter and Susan both nod in agreement. "But for the moment we've still got two branches going," she continues. "You *are* doing regular merges, though, Ron?"

"Oh, yes," confirms Ron firmly. "Once a feature is shown to work and is reliable, I merge it from the replication branch into the main branch. And Joe regularly takes other functionality into his replication branch—at least at the end of each iteration. That's how iterations 2 and 3 worked."

"We adopt each offline feature into the main branch once it's become lower risk," says Peter. "We kind of have a high-risk branch—and a low-risk branch."

"But we still don't really know if this whole offline working concept is totally viable," argues Clare. "And we won't know for sure until these synchronization scenarios are proven to work. So theoretically," she frowns, "we could have to pull it all out again! Should we have kept it separate and not done this staged merge?"

"If we had done that, the final merge would have been a real mess!" claims Ron strongly.

"Yes, I suppose," admits Clare reluctantly. "Anyway it's too late now—we're well down that path, and it does seem to be working out so far."

This discussion indicates how branching can often be a compromise. Figure 12-1 illustrates how it is being used to develop separately the replication and synchronization for offline working. At the end of each iteration, the code is merged both ways as each feature of the offline functionality is completed. The diagram shows three stages of the offline functionality: the resource replication, the offline working of business entities, and the Customer/Order synchronization. The diagram also shows—for the benefit of readers—how the chapters in this book cover the work. Many chapters were devoted to the iteration 1 work, since this was such a critical part of the project. Chapter 11 showed some parts of iterations 2 and 3 in considerable detail. In this chapter you will see selected portions of the work undertaken in iterations 4, 5, and 6 in a lot less detail, but with more attention to using the work item tracking capability of Team System.

In the remainder of the meeting, the management team decides to include in iteration 4 the following groups of scenarios:

- List Wing—Visual Resource Details

- Sales Wing and Sales Site—Resource browsing and searching, new order creation, and reservation from browse

- Sales Status—Various new reporting facilities

They also decide to allocate the scenario groups for iteration 5:

- Listing business objects—Back-end integration

- Sales business objects—Back-end integration

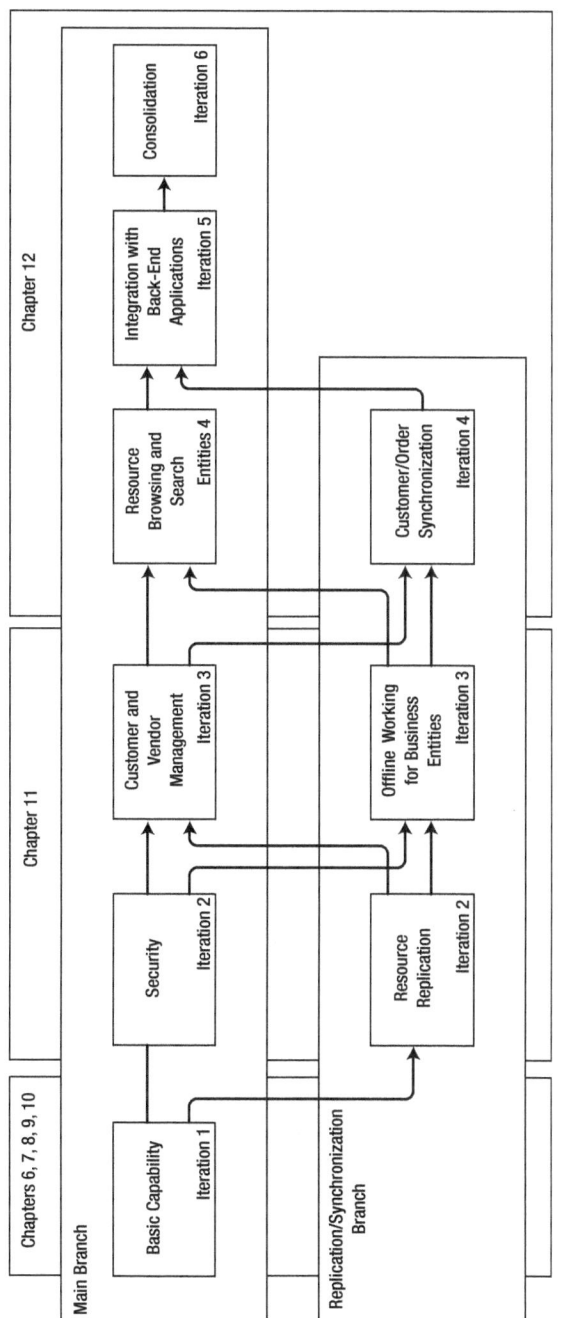

Figure 12-1. *The branching used for offline working during iterations 2, 3, and 4*

Iteration 4

Iteration 4 begins on Thursday, August 3, 2006, and follows the same plan as the other iterations: an analysis phase followed by a formal development phase.

Planning the Iteration

Clare begins by opening Microsoft Project and adding the same tasks that you saw in iteration 1:

- Create Iteration Plan
- Prioritize Scenarios
- Write Scenarios
- Storyboard Scenarios
- Create Product Requirements
- Create Solution Architecture

There are also a couple of tasks to represent the formal development and test:

- Develop and Unit Test
- Application Test

Note Exercise 12-1 demonstrates the content of this section.

She does this by opening Microsoft Project on her machine and selecting Team ➤ Choose Team Project to connect to the ICARUS-TFS server and the Enterprise 3.1 project. She then types in the names of the tasks and sets the other required Work Item Type column to "Task". She then clicks Publish. Next she sets the Area Path field to \Project\MasterSchedule\Iteration4, which is a special area path that she has included in the project to hold project tasks that are not related to a functional area of the requirements (you saw this at the end of Chapter 3). Then Clare sets the Iteration Path field to \Iteration 4 and publishes again. Keeping these general tasks separate from those that will relate specifically to functional areas of the project will help in using the reporting capabilities of Team System to accurately visualize the status of the remaining work. Clare lays out the schedule of the tasks as shown in Figure 12-2.

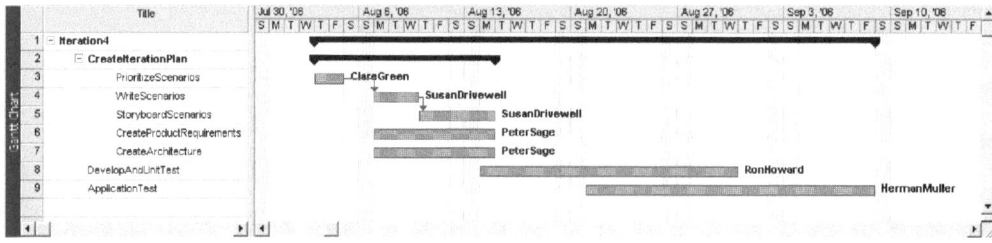

Figure 12-2. *Schedule for iteration 4*

The overall task, called Iteration4, is the original iteration as defined in Chapter 3; it contains the architecture and code development tasks. The Application Test task, however, extends beyond the end of the iteration so that the testers are still continuing with iteration 4 while the developers have moved on to work on the design of iteration 5. Comparing Figure 12-2 with Figure 3-24 in Chapter 3, the overall Iteration4 task therefore extends beyond what was planned in Figure 3-24. It now allows for the overlapping of iterations as the requirements team begins on the next iteration while the testers are working on the current one. There will be other tasks to add to this schedule once the scenarios have been determined. These will include the tasks of analyzing the scenarios to convert them to product requirements, developing and unit-testing the implementation code, and testing the scenarios at the application level.

Defining the Scenario Work Items

In performing the Prioritize Scenarios task, Susan, Clare, Peter, and Ron, with some help from Angela and Charles, decide on the list of top-level scenarios to implement in this iteration.

Note Exercise 12-2 demonstrates the content of this section.

Broadly the list is as follows:

- Scenarios involved in navigating the resource catalog via geographic, category, and alphabetic methods.

- Scenarios that display the Visual Resource Details page from within the catalog and allow a new order to be created from there.

- Scenarios that describe adding visual resource descriptive detail to catalogued resources using the List Wing application.

- Synchronization of orders made while the Sales Wing client was offline, and that are therefore classified as *tentative*, with the Enterprise database. Tentative orders may be either confirmed by this action or remain tentative.

Next, Susan, Angela, and Charles write and storyboard the Sales Wing and Sales Site scenarios. The resource catalog navigation scenarios were described quite fully in Chapter 4, and are similar for the Sales Site and for the Sales Wing application. The Order Synchronization scenarios are more complex and Susan, Angela, and Joe determine the details of these. For example, the Confirm Offline Order scenario storyboard is shown in Table 12-1.

Table 12-1. *The Order Confirmation Scenario Storyboard*

Step	User Action	System Response
Initial State	An agent's computer has been working online for long enough for the resource replication thread to complete the update of resources on the agent's machine.	
1.	The agent exits the Sales Wing application.	
2.	The agent disconnects from the Internet.	
3.	The agent starts the Sales Wing application while still disconnected from the Internet.	
4.	The agent opens a customer and clicks on the Orders tab for the customer.	
5.	The agent clicks on the New Order button.	The system shows the Order Detail dialog box for the new order.
6.	The agent sets some desired criteria for a resource.	The system shows several possible resources, having searched from the Client Local Database.
7.	The agent selects a suitable resource and clicks the Add Reservation button.	The system adds the resource as a reservation included in the order.
8.	The agent clicks OK on the Order Detail page.	The system saves the order in the Client Local Database and returns to the Customer Details page, displaying the new order in the Orders tab indicated as tentative by a checkbox on the right showing the checked state.
9.	The agent exits from the application.	
10.	The agent connects to the Internet.	
11.	The agent starts the Sales Wing application.	The system begins the background thread that attempts to confirm all tentative orders.
12.		The system verifies that the resources required by the order made by the agent offline are still available on the required date(s) and in the required numbers. The system saves the tentative order as a confirmed order to the Icarus central database, just as if the agent had made the order online.

There are many variations on this scenario that the team documents. One case is when the resources are no longer available in the quantities required on the date required. In this case the confirmation is rejected and the order remains tentative.

Other scenarios involve more than one reservation included in an order. There are scenarios in which all of the reservations are available, and the whole order can be confirmed, but in other scenarios one or more of the resources are not available and the whole order therefore remains tentative.

There are also scenarios in which the Internet connectivity is disconnected while the application is running, in some cases while an order is being created. For instance, the search in the Order Details page may take place while the user is online, but the user may be disconnected before the order is saved. In this case the order must be saved as tentative and no errors or inconsistencies must arise.

The scenarios to be included in iteration 4 are shown in Figure 12-3. Only the most basic are included for the order synchronization.

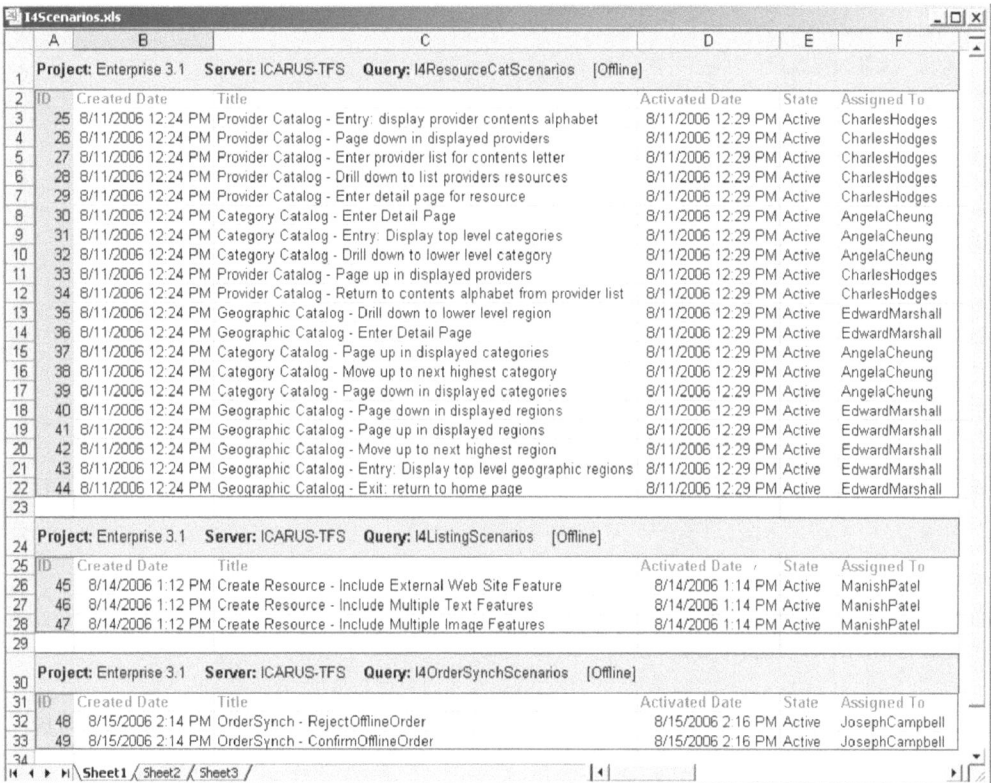

Figure 12-3. *The iteration 4 scenarios*

Defining the Analysis Tasks

The developers involved in the storyboarding of the scenarios will begin to analyze these new customer requirements and convert them into product requirements during the storyboarding process. In fact, the group, including Susan, Angela, and Charles, meets to discuss the storyboards, but in the times that they are working alone, Angela, Joe, and Charles start to develop some tentative code and put together their design. This work forms the analysis tasks that precede the formal coding and unit testing of the implementation of these new scenarios. To manage the iteration effectively, Clare adds these tasks to the project. They are shown in Figure 12-4, with ID 50, 51, and 52. The AnalyzeOrderSynchScenarios task shown in detail at the bottom of the figure has been given to Joe.

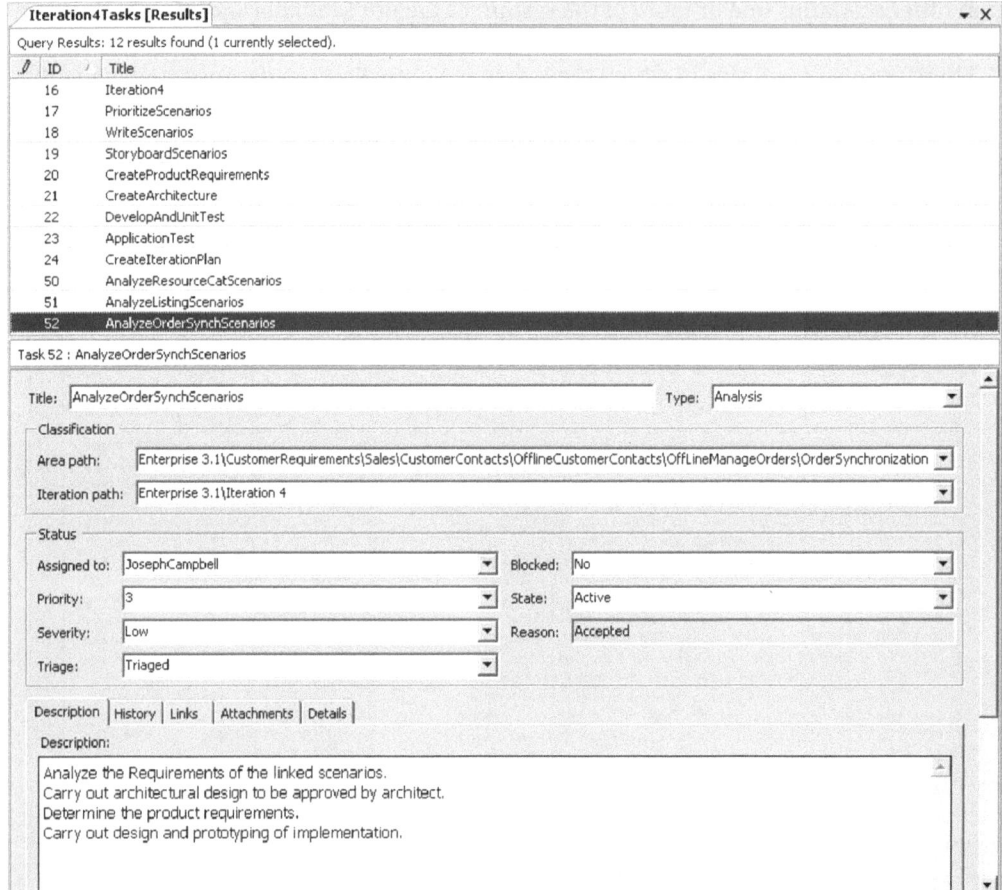

Figure 12-4. *The tasks included in iteration 4 so far, including the three analysis tasks at the top and details for Task 52 at the bottom*

Figure 12-5 shows the same screen with the Links tab selected. Clare has added links to the two scenario work items. As Joe carries out this task and designs the changes to the code base, he must ensure that both of these scenarios are implemented. Clare's new schedule for iteration 4 is shown in Figure 12-6.

Clare saves this as a Microsoft Project (MPP) file and then takes both of her schedule MPP files—the one in Figure 12-2 and the one in Figure 12-6—and drags them from My Documents to the Iteration4 folder she has created in Team Explorer (under Documents/Project Management), as shown in Figure 12-7. Notice that it's sometimes convenient to make Team Explorer a floating window to move files. These documents are now available to be viewed by other members of the team. If you do not like drag and drop, you can right-click on one of the document folders in Team Explorer and select Upload Document. This allows you to navigate to the file on your machine and select it for upload.

Iteration4Tasks [Results]   ▾ ✕

Query Results: 12 results found (1 currently selected).

𝟘	ID	Title
	16	Iteration4
	17	PrioritizeScenarios
	18	WriteScenarios
	19	StoryboardScenarios
	20	CreateProductRequirements
	21	CreateArchitecture
	22	DevelopAndUnitTest
	23	ApplicationTest
	24	CreateIterationPlan
	50	AnalyzeResourceCatScenarios
	51	AnalyzeListingScenarios
	52	AnalyzeOrderSynchScenarios

Task 52 : AnalyzeOrderSynchScenarios

Title: AnalyzeOrderSynchScenarios   Type: Analysis

Classification

Area path: Enterprise 3.1\CustomerRequirements\Sales\CustomerContacts\OfflineCustomerContacts\OffLineManageOrders\OrderSynchronization ▾

Iteration path: Enterprise 3.1\Iteration 4

Status

Assigned to: JosephCampbell   Blocked: No

Priority: 3   State: Active

Severity: Low   Reason: Accepted

Triage: Triaged

Description | History | Links | Attachments | Details |

Link Type	Description	Comments	Open
Related Workitem	Requirement 48: OrderSynch - RejectOfflineOrder	Implement Scenario	Add...
Related Workitem	Requirement 49: OrderSynch - ConfirmOfflineOrder	Implement Scenario	Edit...
			Delete

Figure 12-5. *The task details showing links to the related scenario work items.*

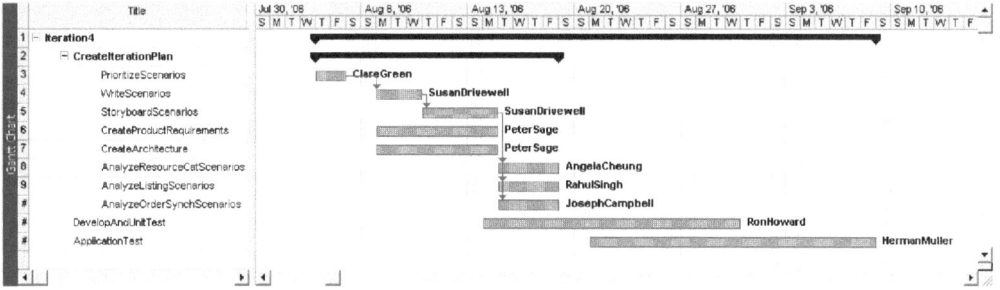

Figure 12-6. *The iteration 4 schedule, with the analysis tasks added*

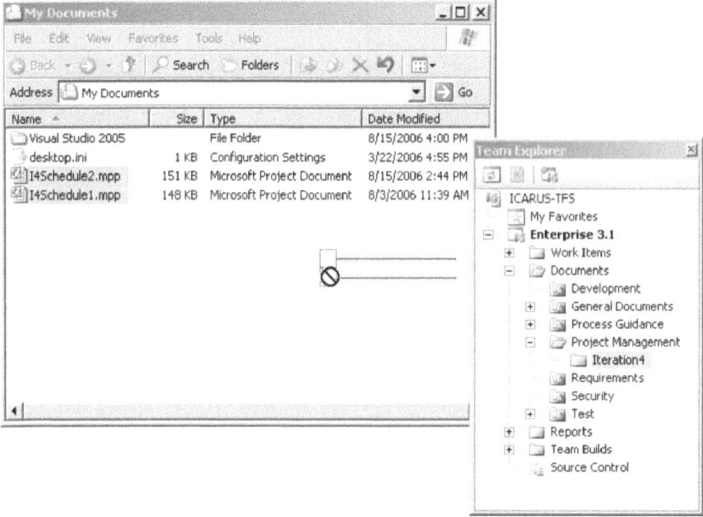

Figure 12-7. *Uploading the documents by dragging and dropping into Team Explorer*

Reporting Capability

One of the features of Visual Studio 2005 Team Edition that I have not yet discussed is its reporting capability. A set of reports is provided by default in a team project; these projects are available in the Team Explorer window, as shown in Figure 12-8. You can open any of these reports by double-clicking on them in the Team Explorer window, or you can access them from the team portal by clicking Reports in the side menu of the home page.

■**Note** Exercise 12-3 demonstrates the content of this section.

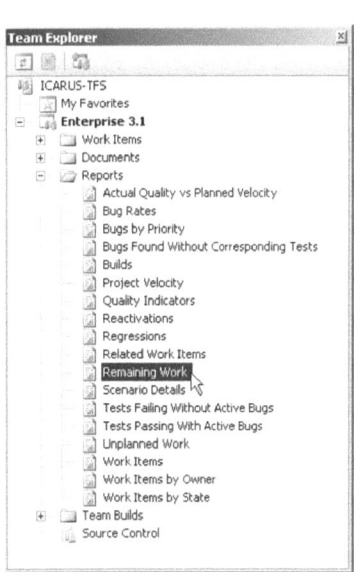

Figure 12-8. *The reports available in the Team Explorer window*

A good example to view at this point in the iteration is the Remaining Work report shown in Figure 12-9, which consists of a graph with the number of work items in a specified category that are active, plotted against time on the horizontal axis. At the top of the report a set of drop-down controls allows the displayed report to be limited to specific iterations and project areas, work item types, and a definite start date and end date. In this way the work progress can be viewed as it changes with time in a particular part of the project. By viewing several of these reports for different project areas, the project manager can see at a glance which areas are proceeding quickly and which are lagging behind.

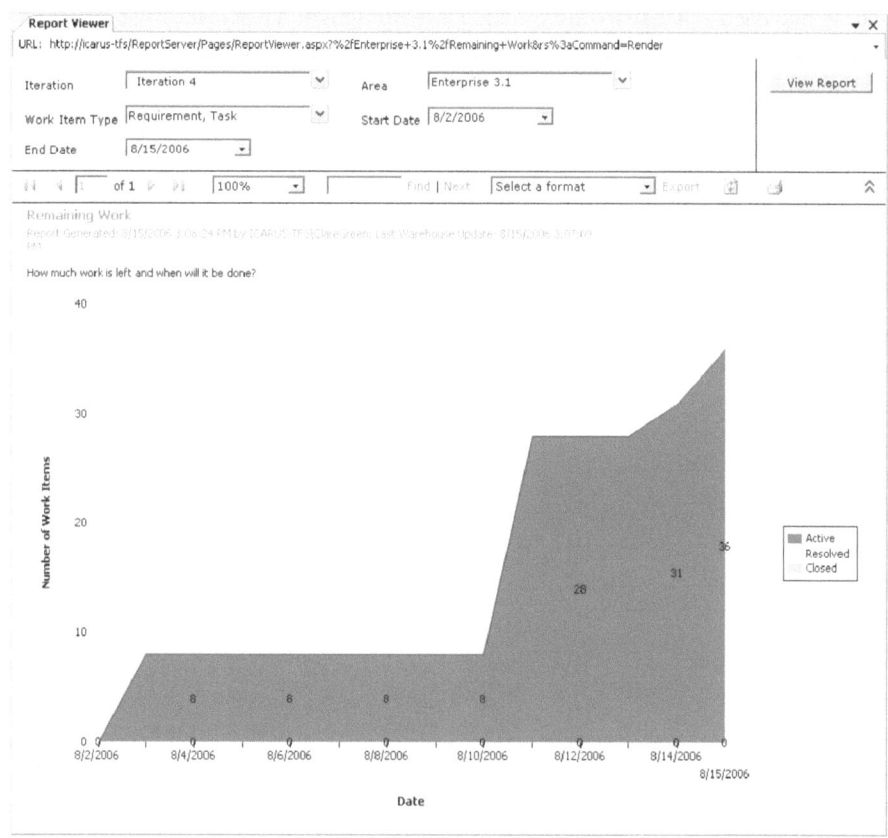

Figure 12-9. *The Remaining Work report*

The example in Figure 12-9 includes both Requirement and Task type work items and so represents a measure of the work that remains to be done at a particular point in time. The only requirements added here are scenarios, but other kinds of requirements could be included. Translating this into a measure of the time taken to complete the remaining work is another matter entirely, and depends on the length of time likely to be taken to complete the remaining scenarios and tasks. It could be that one remaining task takes a huge amount of time to complete, but this would indicate a poor division of work and a lack of sufficient analysis during task definition. This reminds us again of the discussion at the beginning of Chapter 6, where it was agreed that analysis and prototyping had to be undertaken before the development tasks could be estimated with any confidence. Figure 12-9 shows an increase in the remaining work during the early part of the iteration as Clare and Susan add tasks and scenarios. Later in this chapter we will see this work being completed.

Another report worth viewing at this stage is the Work Items by Owner, shown in Figure 12-10. This report shows the work items arranged under their owners, with the remaining hours and other information listed for each. In Figure 12-10 only the work items of type Task have hours against them since the hours were allocated when the iteration schedule was laid out by Clare. So far the work items of type Scenario have not yet had hours allocated to them, since this is an outcome of the analysis tasks that have been given to the developers. For example, when Joe has completed his analysis of the order synchronization scenarios, he should be able to give an estimate of the time that each will take to implement. Development and test tasks will be created for each scenario; these will contain estimates of hours required and the number of hours completed and the time remaining. In this case, the scenarios themselves need not have hours allocated to them since they may not appear on schedules. There are certainly other ways to use the work items in a given project, and the team should adopt a convention early in the process to ensure consistency.

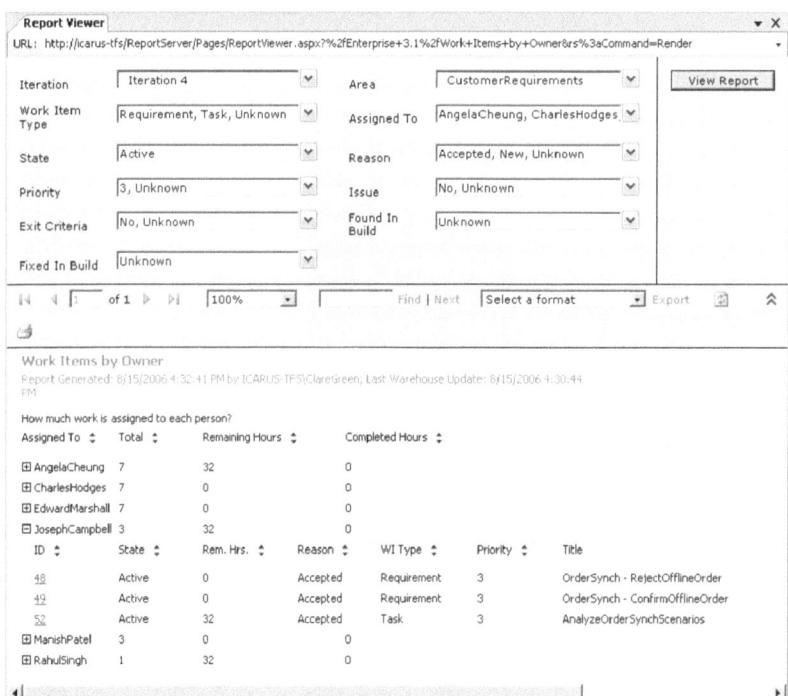

Figure 12-10. *The Work Items by Owner report*

Analyzing the Scenarios and Defining the Development Tasks

Peter works with Joe to define the product requirements and the architecture in support of the order synchronization scenarios.

Note Exercise 12-4 demonstrates the content of this section.

Some key features of the design in support of these scenarios were added during iteration 3:

- The base class `DualPersistBE` was changed to support an online/offline flag that is exposed as a static property for all business entities derived from this class.

- This flag is used by the `Fill` and `Save` functions in the `BusinessEntityBE` base class to cause persistence to and from the Client Local Database (local persistence) when the business entity class is operating in the offline mode.

- The local connection string setting is used by the entity when in client mode to specify the connection to the local database. This is the same string that is used by the entity when in server mode.

- A separate thread (which polls the server) is used to determine whether the server is reachable. If the server is not reachable, the client will be placed in offline mode and the online/offline flag is used to indicate this.

Further design features are to be introduced in iteration 4:

- The `BusinessEntityBE` class will be modified to include overloaded `Fill` and `Save` functions that allow the call to these functions to force either a local or remote persistence fill or save. This will allow the order synchronization function to read an order from the local database and save it to the remote database as part of the confirmation process.

- When orders are saved, the `SAVERESERVATION` or `INSERTRESERVATION` stored procedure will verify that the resource being reserved is available on the date and quantity required, and will fail if that is not true.

- The failure of a `SAVERESERVATION` or `INSERTRESERVATION` call will be detected in the `SaveLocal()` function of `OrderBE` and will abort the save of the entire order.

- The save of all of the reservations and the order itself will be included in a transaction so that the entire transaction fails if a reservation cannot be made due to nonavailability of any resource to be reserved.

- This transactional order save will be used both in online order saves to catch an optimistic concurrency type failure, and will also be used to save orders to the Icarus central database during the order synchronization process.

The product requirements for the Browse Resource Catalog scenarios are much more straightforward. They mainly concern business entity classes added to the Listing business objects that provide collections of resources obtained in various situations when navigating through the resource catalogs. The collections will be bound to `DataGrid` controls to provide the lists of regions, categories, vendors, and resources displayed during the browse capability described in Chapter 4. These business entity classes operate in local or remote mode in the same manner as the other business entities and permit the navigation of the catalogs in either online or offline mode. Several new functions are to be added to the Listing web service to support remote access to the catalog browsing. These business entities will be used by both the Sales Wing application and the Sales Site (ASP.NET) application to provide browsing of the catalogs.

The third area of new scenarios—the resource listing—provides for the capability to add a detail page for the resource that will be displayed to the customer in the form of sets of images and text. Again a set of business entity classes included in Resource Business Objects will support this capability together with Windows Forms added to the List Wing application.

Order Synchronization Tasks

As a result of the analysis, the team creates new development tasks that together will implement the scenarios included in the iteration. Let's take a closer look at those concerned with the order synchronization scenarios.

1. Modify the `OrderBE` class to operate in local or remote mode on demand. This is needed for order synchronization.

2. Develop the `OrderConfirmSetBE` business entity, which represents a set of tentative orders that require confirmation and will be read-only persisted from the Client Local Database. `OrderConfirmSetBE` will also contain the member functions that carry out the order synchronization actions in reading each tentative order from the Client Local Database and writing it to the Icarus Enterprise database.

3. Unit-test the `OrderConfirmSetBE` class. Verify that this class performs its function of orchestrating the order synchronization process. The class will have one or more member functions that will be called by the order synchronization thread to perform synchronization of the tentative set of orders. Unit tests will be written to perform this action and added to the code base.

4. Develop `OrderConfirmSetDS`. This data access layer component will be needed by the `OrderConfirmSetBE` class to carry out the read persistence of tentative orders in the local database.

5. Unit-test `OrderConfirmSetDS`. Verify the operation of this dataset and its table adapter(s) using unit tests, which are added to the code base.

Joe adds the above five tasks as part of performing the analysis of the scenarios. They begin as proposed tasks and are then supported by attached analysis documents, containing information similar to what has been described earlier. Joe therefore advances these tasks to the Investigation Complete stage. These task work items also have estimated hours and links to the scenario work items that they will implement. Joe uses Visual Studio to add these tasks; the first one is shown in Figure 12-11. He assigns all the tasks to Ron, who in turn will reassign them to developers once they receive architectural and team lead approval. They are approved by Peter and Ron and then become active tasks assigned to developers for completion.

Later Ron looks at the list of tasks in Excel using a query that shows just the development tasks that are in the proposed state. He uses one of his own queries from the My Queries folder in Team Explorer (Figure 12-12). Ron has added extra columns using the Column Options dialog box, which is visible in Figure 12-12.

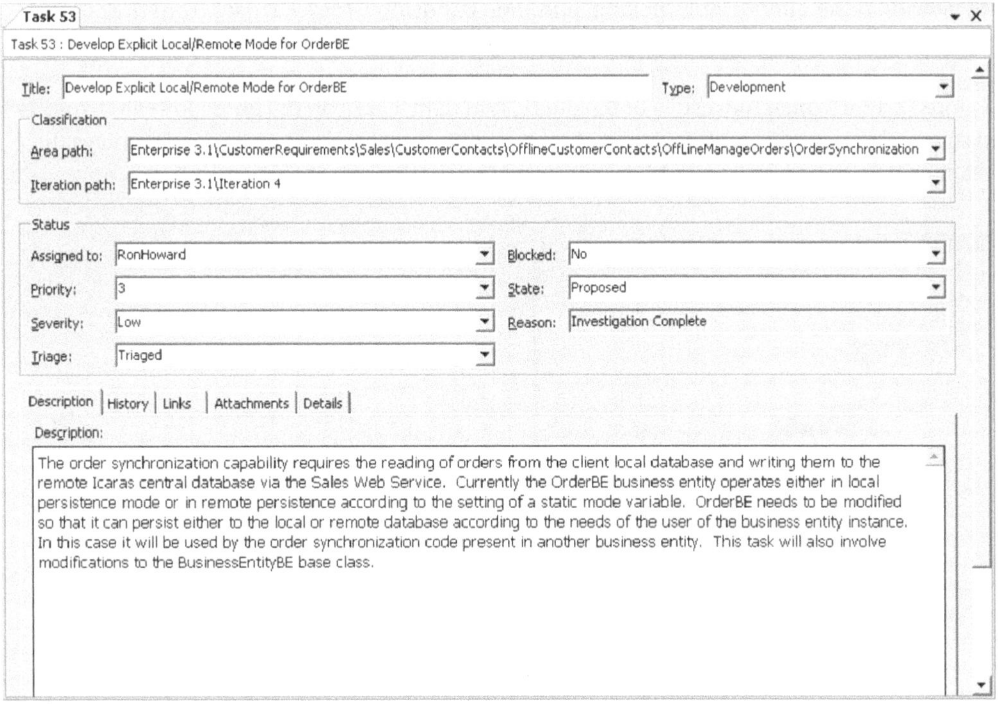

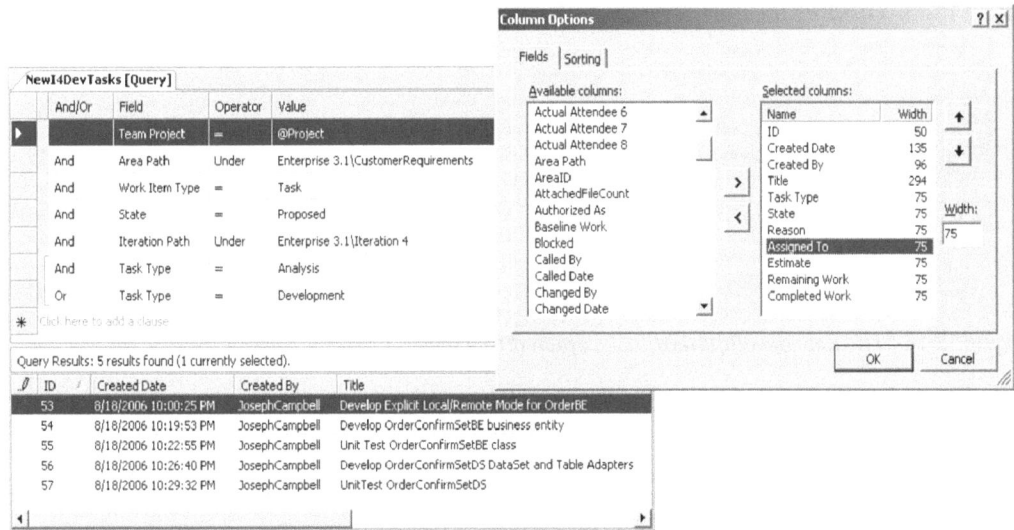

Figure 12-11. *The development task: Develop Explicit Local/Remote Mode for OrderBE*

Figure 12-12. *Ron's query for retrieving the proposed development tasks*

Notice that this query uses grouped clauses to specify a condition that either the task type will be Analysis *or* it will be Development. Grouped clauses are clauses that would be enclosed within parentheses if the query was written as a Boolean expression, and are created by selecting both clauses in the query, right-clicking, and then choosing Group Clauses from the context menu. These grouped classes are indicated as such by a bracket that appears to the left of the logical expressions Task Type = Analysis, Task Type = Development in the main query displayed in Figure 12-12. To open the results of the query, Ron right-clicks on the query in Team Explorer and selects Open in Microsoft Excel, as shown in Figure 12-13. Excel opens and displays the spreadsheet shown in Figure 12-14.

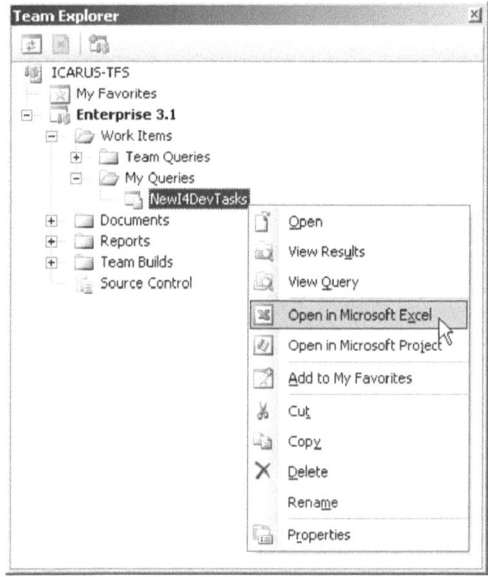

Figure 12-13. *Opening the work items from a query in Microsoft Excel*

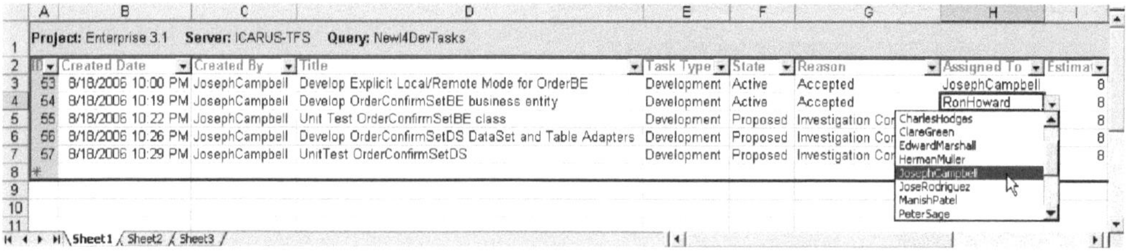

Figure 12-14. *The new development tasks opened in Excel*

Figure 12-14 shows the development task work items added by Joe as a result of his analysis of the order synchronization scenarios. There are also development task work items (not shown) that have been added by the other developers involved in the analysis of the scenarios. Ron looks at these, and after discussing the architecture in a review meeting with Peter and the developers, he approves them. To do this he changes the state from Proposed to Active, sets the Reason fields to Accepted, and assigns each one to the developer who will do the work—in this case back to Joe again.

Ron can now use this information to update Clare's published schedule for iteration 4; the schedule is available on TFS in the project management documents. He right-clicks on the document in Team Explorer and selects Edit, as shown in Figure 12-15. Microsoft Project opens the document.

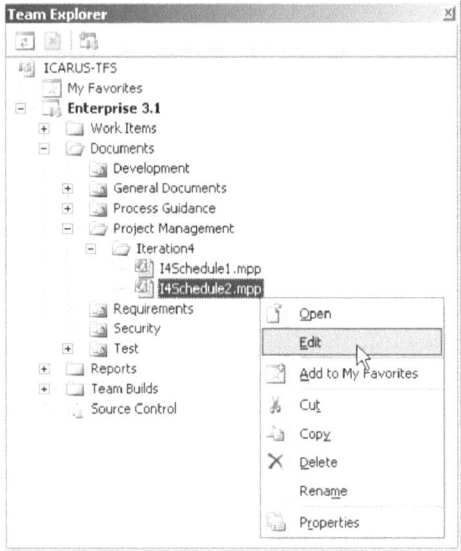

Figure 12-15. *Opening the iteration 4 schedule from Team Explorer*

Ron now wants to update this schedule to include the tasks that Joe and the other developers have created as a result of their analysis of the new scenarios. To do this he clicks the Get Work Items button in the Team toolbar and selects the Iteration4Tasks query in the Get Work Items dialog box (Figure 12-16). He ensures that all of Joe's development tasks are checked and clicks OK. Microsoft Project then displays the updated project (Figure 12-17), where the tasks have been added at the bottom.

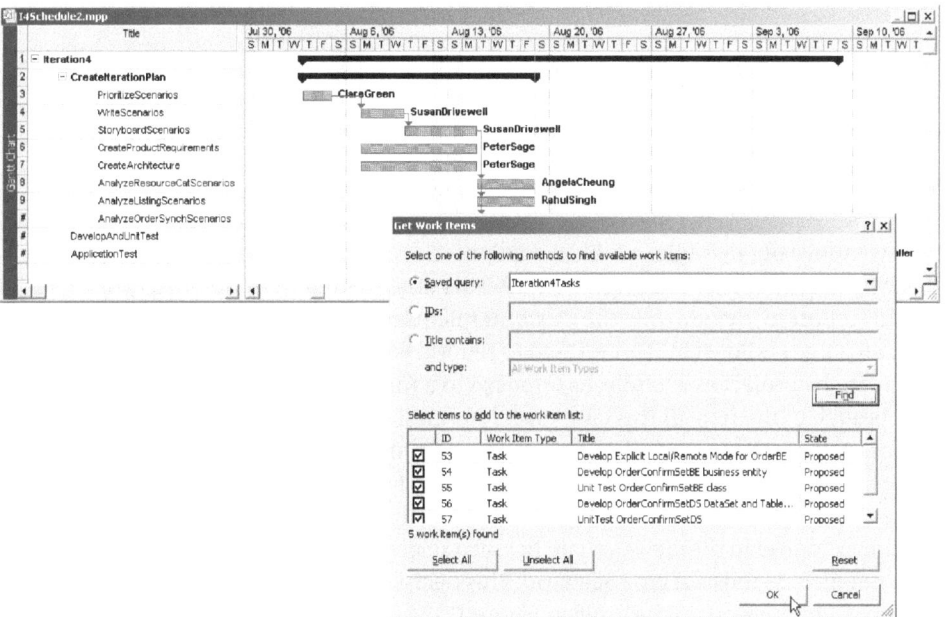

Figure 12-16. *Getting more tasks for the iteration 4 schedule*

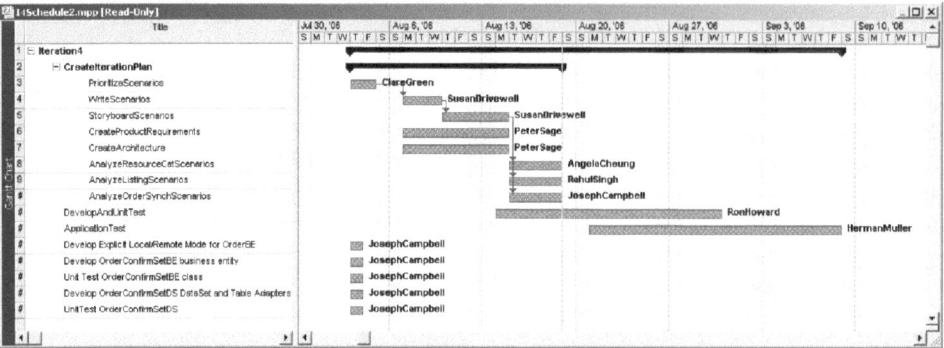

Figure 12-17. *The development tasks added but not scheduled*

Notice that Joe estimated one day for each and these figures from the Details tab of the work item have been used by Project to determine the length of the tasks. Now Ron drags the new tasks to a position in the list under the Develop and Unit Test task, which includes all of the development work. He then indents them so that the Develop and Unit Test task becomes a summary task, and lays out the schedule how he thinks Joe will probably carry out the tasks. The result is shown in Figure 12-18.

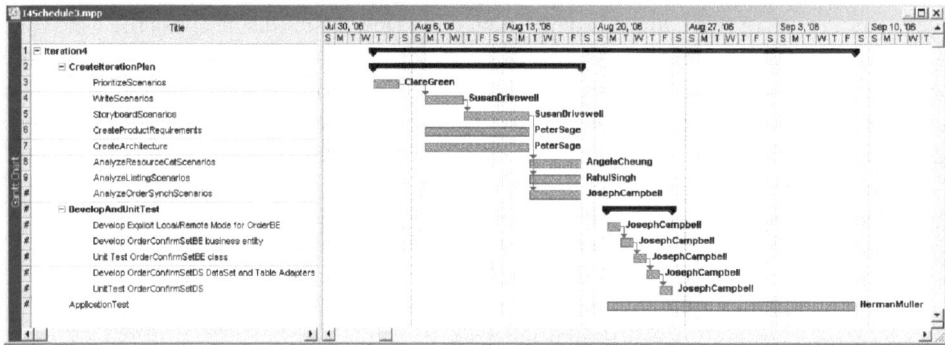

Figure 12-18. *The development tasks added and scheduled*

Before we move on, let's take a look at some of the reports that are available now. The remaining work report is shown in Figure 12-19. This time Clare has set the Area drop-down at the top of this report to include only the Customer Requirements area and everything below it. The project area tree is shown in Figure 12-20 to remind you of its structure. Note that the tasks concerned with the project as a whole, as opposed to a functional area of it, were placed under the Project branch of the tree, in this case under Iteration4. So by selecting just the Customer Requirements area for the report, Clare has removed from the report the more general project work (such as the summary tasks, like Plan Iteration, and the general project tasks, like Create Architecture). She could narrow the view further by selecting just the Sales or Listing areas in the Area drop-down control in the viewer. Clare has also selected to display only work items of type Task and to not include those of type Scenario. This decision depends on which work items you think best represent the work of the project. Figure 12-21 shows these selections. These reports can all be exported from the report viewer in various formats; in fact, Figure 12-19 was generated by exporting the report in TIFF format.

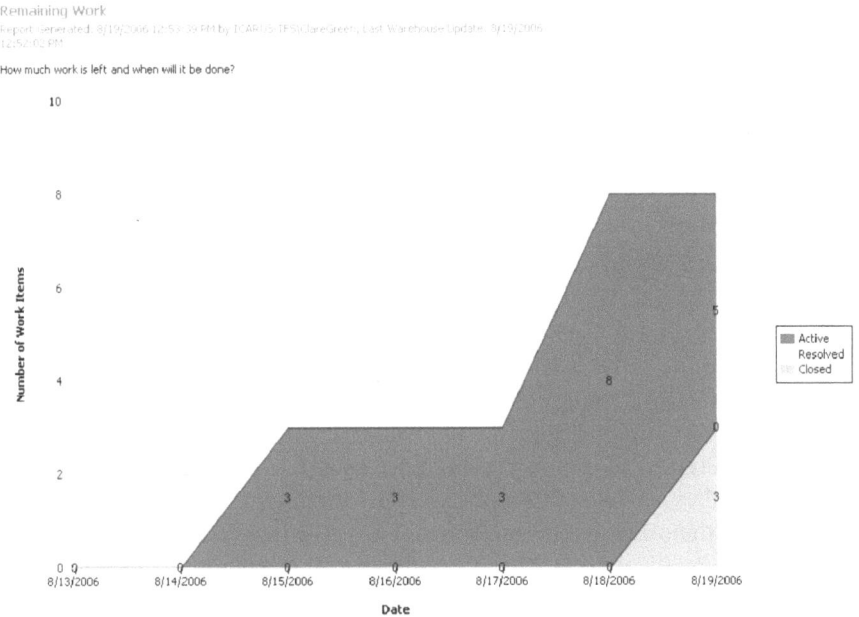

Figure 12-19. *Remaining work in the Customer Requirements area after the analysis tasks have been completed and the development tasks added*

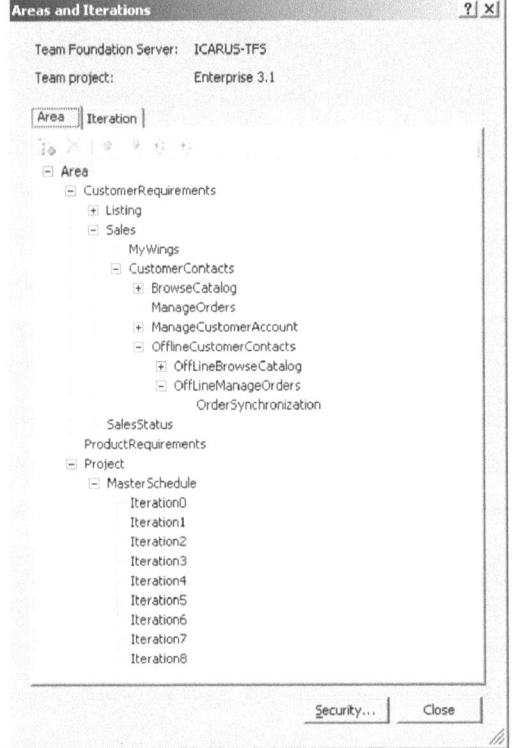

Figure 12-20. *Project area tree*

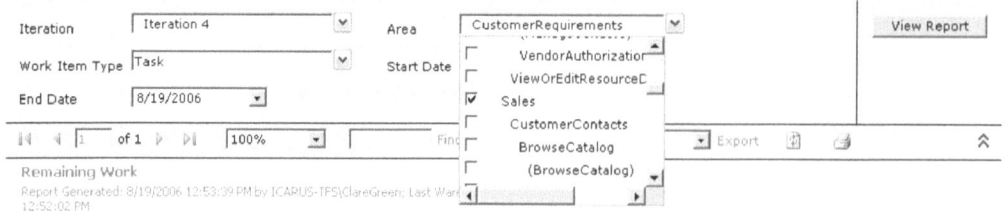

Figure 12-21. *Selecting the required project area for the report*

You can drill down in this report by clicking on an area within the graph. For example, clicking on the area showing the active work items will display another report, Work Items by State, filtered to show just the work items in the active state, as shown in Figure 12-22. This graph can also be obtained by double-clicking the Work Items by State report in Team Explorer; in that case, by default it will show the report broken down by all work item states that exist in the project. Just for variety, I've exported this report in PDF format and displayed it in Adobe Acrobat Reader 6.0. It's worth noting that even when the document is exported in this format you can click on the work item ID numbers that are embedded URL links and, provided TFS is still accessible, drill down further to look at individual work items. Of course, you may not want readers of this document to obtain any more information than you are giving them, so you need to set up security properly on the WorkItemTracking website of TFS. Access to reports is controlled within the Visual Studio Team Explorer window and directly by the SQL Server 2005 Reporting Services security settings.

Adobe Acrobat - [Work Items by State.pdf]

File   Edit   Document   Tools   View   Window   Help

Work Items by State
Report Generated: 8/19/2006 1:20:43 PM by ICARUS-TFS\ClareGreen;   Last Warehouse Update: 8/19/2006 1:18:49 PM

How many active, resolved and closed work items do we have?

State	Total	Remaining Hours		Completed Hours
Active	5	40		0

ID	Assigned To	Rem. Hrs.	Reason	WI Type	Priority
53	JosephCampbell	8	Accepted	Task	3
54	JosephCampbell	8	Accepted	Task	3
55	JosephCampbell	8	Accepted	Task	3
56	JosephCampbell	8	Accepted	Task	3
57	JosephCampbell	8	Accepted	Task	3

1 of 2   8.5 x 11 in

Figure 12-22. *Work items by state, obtained by clicking on the active graph area in Figure 12-19*

Clicking on a work item ID, such as link 53 in Figure 12-22, will navigate to the report shown in Figure 12-23, which shows all the information about the work item very tidily and also allows navigation to other work items by following further links.

Figure 12-23. *Detailed report for Task WorkItem ID 53, obtained by following the link from the first work item in Figure 12-22*

I'll mention one more report before I move on in following the work of the iteration: the Work Items by Owner report shown in Figure 12-24. The report is shown as an Excel document which I obtained by first double-clicking on the report name in Team Explorer and then setting the drop-down controls:

Iteration: Iteration 4

Area: Customer Requirements

Work Item Type: Task and Scenario types

I left the other settings at their defaults. I then exported the report by setting the format type to Excel and clicking the Export link button. You can see from the report that Joe (JosephCampbell) is responsible for two scenarios and five tasks (the development tasks described earlier). All except the scenarios, for which no hours were allocated, show the full remaining 8 hours per task since Joe has yet to begin them.

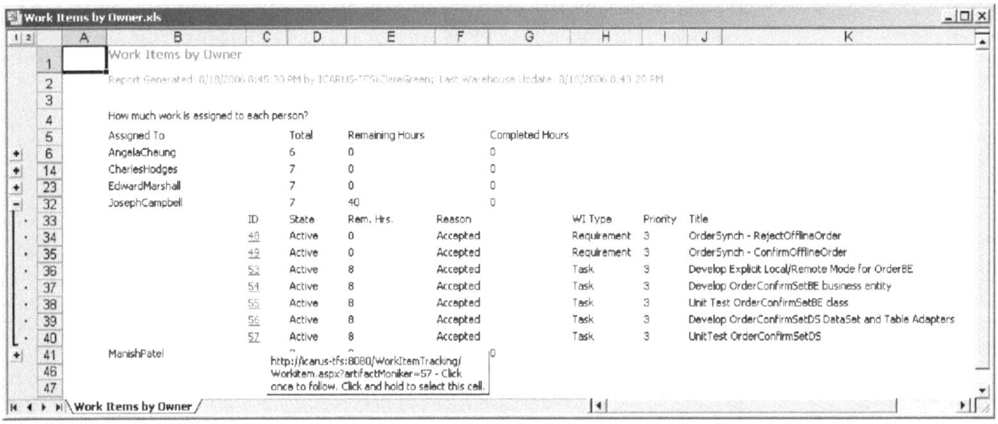

Figure 12-24. *Work Items by Owner exported to Excel*

Code Completion and Check-In

Since this chapter concentrates on organizational aspects, I will only briefly describe the code that Joe develops. You can look at the accompanying exercise code to understand it better.

Note The code that is developed in the section is available under `Chapter 12\OrderSynchCode`.

Joe begins his work by adding the `OrderConfirmSetBE` class to the `OrderBE` project. This class of business entity is not a dual persistence entity, like `OrderBE` for example, since it represents the set of orders existing in the Client Local Database that are tentative and therefore need to be confirmed. This is the first instance of a single persistence entity to have arisen in the project, so it makes sense to put this idea on a consistent footing by adding a base class in the framework to handle it. Single persistence entities have no need to read a web service URL, but they need a specific dataset class and they need to read the local database persistence string. Joe therefore defines a new class in the framework called LocalPersistBE and derives the OrderConfirmSetBE from it, as shown in Figure 12-25.

Figure 12-25. *Class structure of OrderConfirmSetBE, a LocalPersist business entity*

The derived class overrides GetLocalData to create an instance of the table adapter class needed to populate this object from the Client Local Database. The other main function of this class is the static ConfirmTentativeOrders(), which creates an instance of the class, populates it, and calls its member function ConfirmOrders().

```
public static void ConfirmTentativeOrders()
{
  try
  {
    OrderConfirmSetBE orderConfirmSetBE = new OrderConfirmSetBE();
    orderConfirmSetBE.Fill();
    orderConfirmSetBE.ConfirmOrders();

  } catch(Exception ex)
  {
    string exStr = ex.Message;
  }
}
```

The catching of the exception is for debugging purposes only at present, but proper exception handling must be added to the project in a later iteration.

The job of the `ConfirmOrders()` function is to iterate through the order entries listed in the `OrderConfirmSetBE` instance and read each order from the Client Local Database and from the Icarus Enterprise database, if it exists. It must then merge the reservations in the two orders before writing the result back to the Icarus Enterprise database. If an order corresponding to the one from the Client Local Database does not exist in the Enterprise database, a new one must be created. The code needed to read and write the individual orders is already included in `OrderDS`, but `OrderBE` needs the ability to select explicitly either local or remote persistence in order for the `ConfirmOrders()` function to be able to work. For example, the following function is added to `BusinessEntityBE`:

```
public void SaveRemote()
{
  if (OnlineMode)
  {
    RemoteDSType remoteDS = new RemoteDSType();
    remoteDS.Merge(this.data);
    SaveRemoteData(remoteDS);
  }
}
```

When Joe is satisfied that this code is working correctly, he checks in all of the pending changes, associating them with the work items shown in Figure 12-26. The work that has been done on the three tasks implements the scenario with ID 49, OrderSynch – ConfirmOfflineOrder scenario, but does not yet implement the ID 48 scenario, since Joe has not yet added the capability to reject an order synchronization action if the resources are not available. So Joe checks scenario 49 and sets the Check-in Action column to Resolve. The code that is being checked in is also associated with tasks 53, 54, and 56, so he checks those tasks as well and notes that the Check-in Action is set to Associate. The explicit local and remote working for the `OrderBE` business entity has been achieved, and the two tasks that implement the `OrderConfirmSetBE` and its persistence have been done. These three tasks together implement scenario 49.

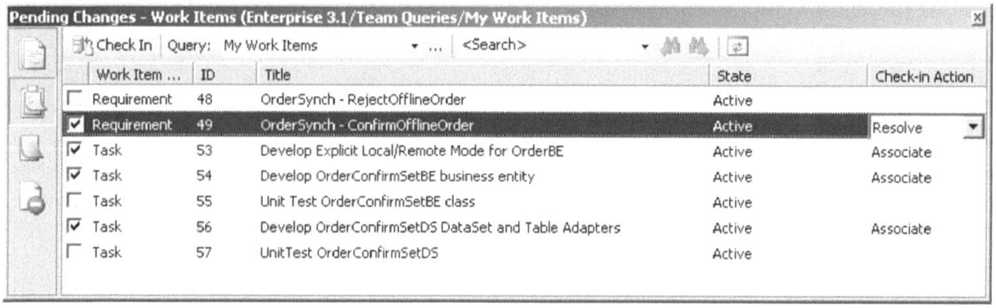

Work Item ...	ID	Title	State	Check-in Action
☐ Requirement	48	OrderSynch - RejectOfflineOrder	Active	
☑ Requirement	49	OrderSynch - ConfirmOfflineOrder	Active	Resolve
☑ Task	53	Develop Explicit Local/Remote Mode for OrderBE	Active	Associate
☑ Task	54	Develop OrderConfirmSetBE business entity	Active	Associate
☐ Task	55	Unit Test OrderConfirmSetBE class	Active	
☑ Task	56	Develop OrderConfirmSetDS DataSet and Table Adapters	Active	Associate
☐ Task	57	UnitTest OrderConfirmSetDS	Active	

Figure 12-26. *Pending Changes window—associating the changeset with work items*

As a result of the check-in action, Joe notes that the state of scenario 49 has automatically been changed to Resolved. He assigns the task to Herman Muller for further assignment to one of the testers and saves it so that it appears as shown in Figure 12-27. The History tab, visible in Figure 12-27, shows the progress of this scenario from its creation by Susan to its resolution by Joe's changeset 6 and assignment to Herman.

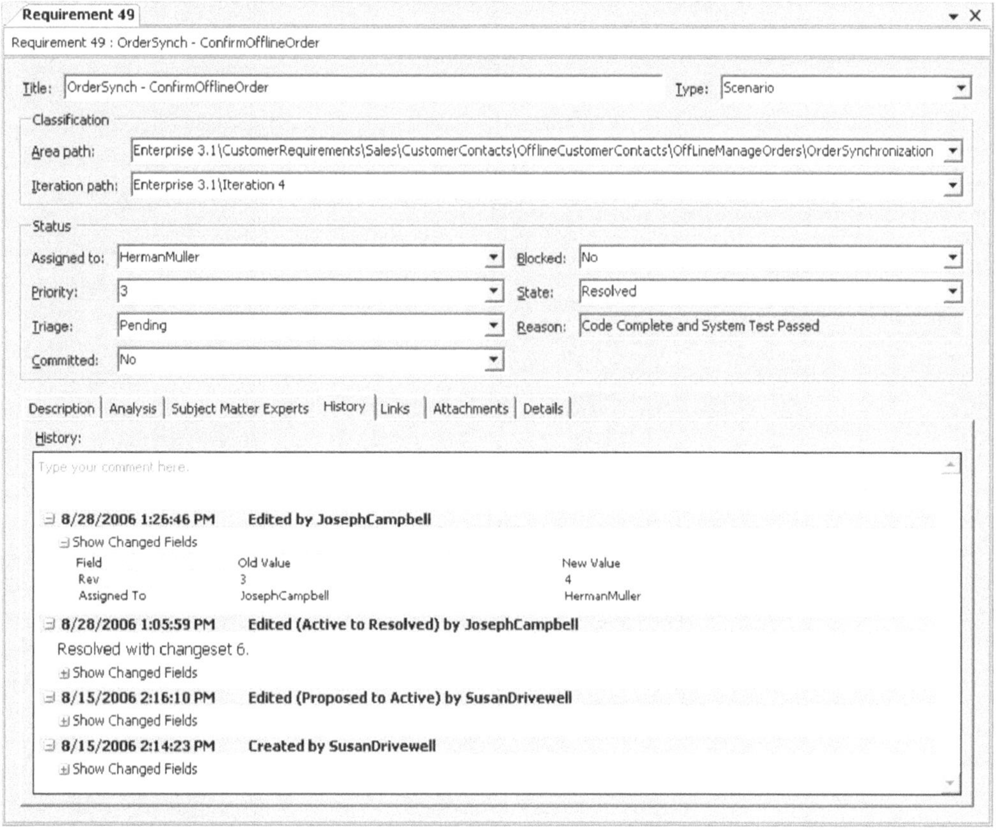

Figure 12-27. *Scenario 49 after the check-in*

Figure 12-28 shows the Links tab. As you can see, Joe has selected the link to changeset 6 and clicked the Open button to display the Changeset window. In particular, you can see that all of the files implementing the OrderConfirmSetDS and its table adapters are included in the changeset.

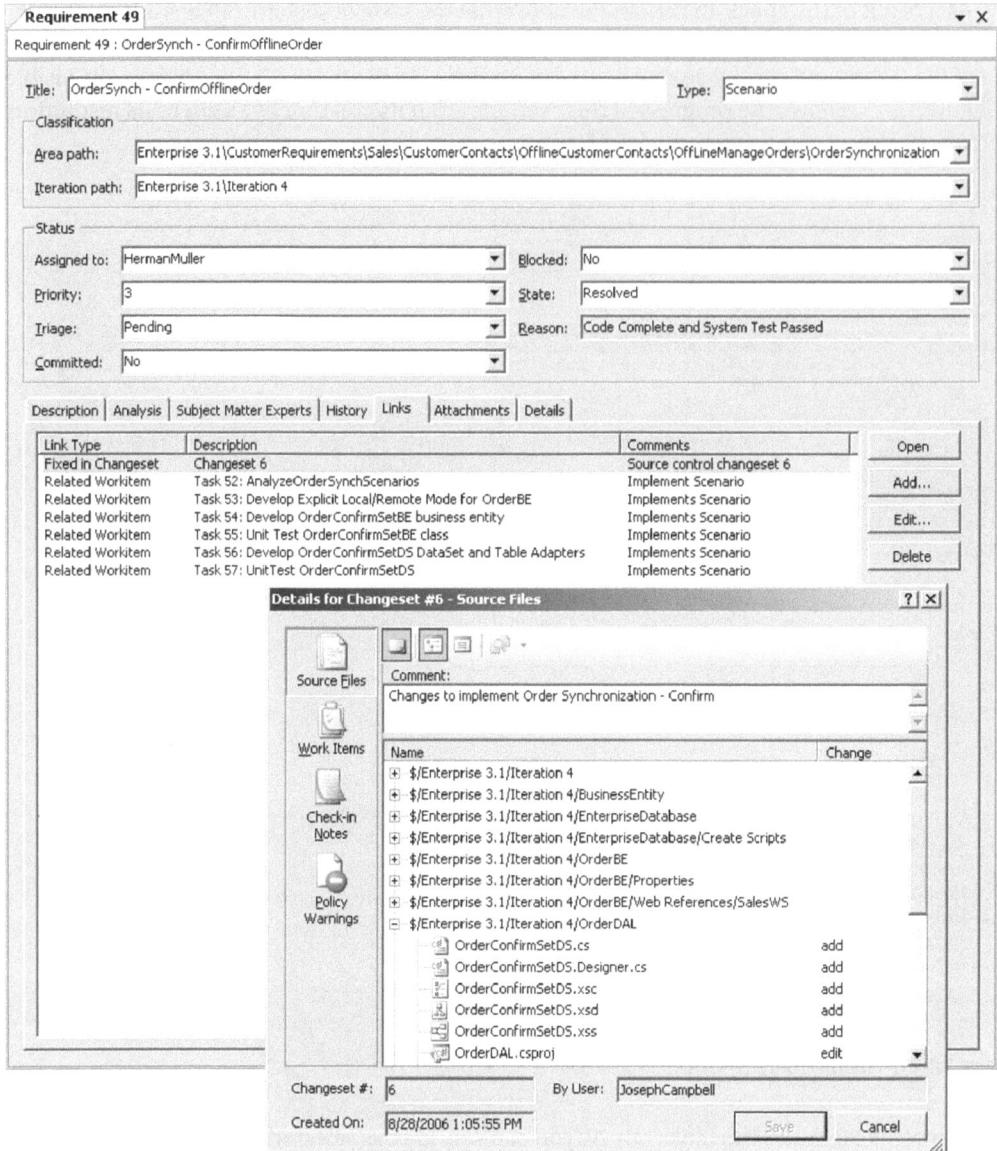

Figure 12-28. *Scenario 49 after the check-in, showing the linked changeset*

The next day the other developers with scenarios allocated to them, Angela, Charles, Ed, and Manish, check in their completed code. The following day, Joe completes the unit-test tasks and checks in the code associated with that. He sets his four development tasks to complete, and sets the remaining work to 0 and completed work to 8 hours for each task before saving them.

End of the Development Phase—Checking the Status

Ron opens Visual Studio and creates a new workspace with a suitable local folder on his machine. He selects File ➤ Source Control ➤ Open from Source Control to retrieve the solution from the source control and verifies that it builds without errors. He builds both the main branch and the replication branch. Ron then creates a team build for the iteration, including both solutions, and performs a team build to ensure that all is well.

Clare and Ron then take a look at various project reports to determine the status of the project. It's Wednesday, August 30, and that's when, according to the schedule in Figure 12-17, the development work of iteration 4 is due to be completed. At this point, the plan says that the developers will begin iteration 5 and the testers will continue the work of testing iteration 4 until September 8. Figure 12-29 shows the Remaining Work report on this date, including Requirements and Tasks under the Customer Requirements project area and iteration 4.

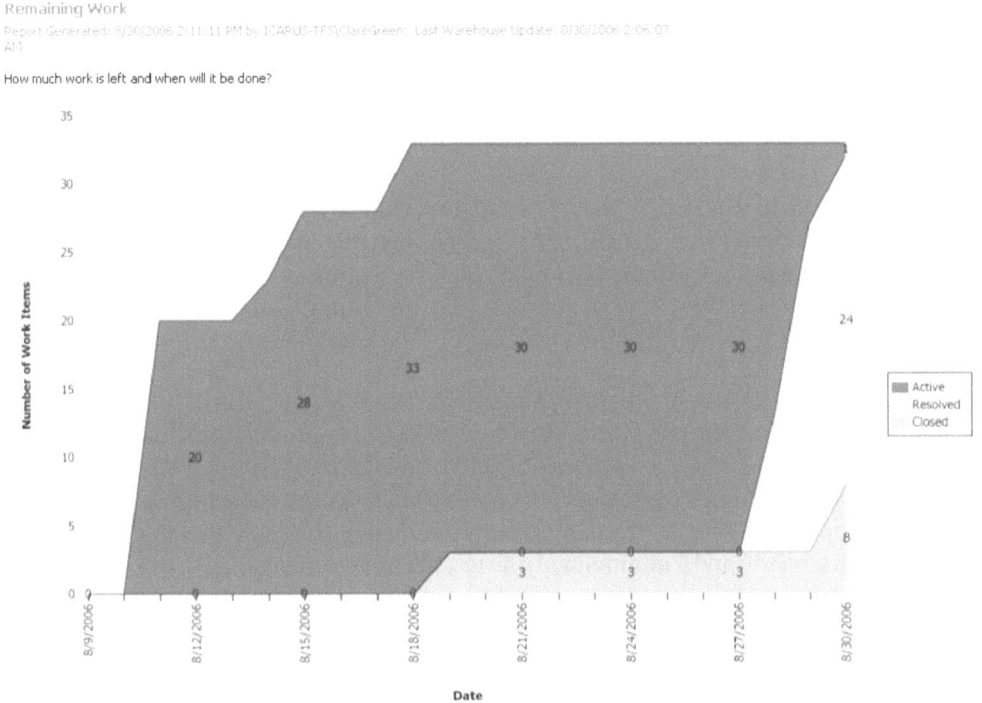

Figure 12-29. *The remaining work at the end of the development part of iteration 4*

"Hey, it's looking pretty good, isn't it?" says Clare. The Active area at the top (reddish brown on the screen) has shrunk to almost nothing and the Closed area at the bottom (green on the screen) has increased a bit, and the resolved area in the middle has expanded rapidly. Clicking on the Closed area opens the Work Items by State reports and shows that the closed work items are the development tasks 50–57 assigned to Joe (which he has closed). The work items in the Resolved area are all the scenarios 25–49 that were assigned to various developers and have been marked as Resolved when the code was checked in.

Clare looks closer at the graph on her laptop in the meeting room and frowns. "Why doesn't the yellow area come right up to the top?" she asks Ron. "In fact, I think I can see a little figure one there."

She clicks on the Active area, and sure enough Figure 12-30 shows that things are not *quite* as good as they first thought. One scenario concerned with order synchronization is still active:

the one that describes rejection of a tentative order because the resources are no longer available. This is shown as assigned to JosephCampbell, and Joe is called to explain. He explains that he had difficulty designing the code to implement this and he needs to experiment with it before being able to trust a particular approach. Clare and Ron reluctantly agree to defer this scenario to iteration 5.

Work Items by State
Report Generated: 8/30/2006 2:27:34 PM by ICARUS-TFS\ClareGreen; Last Warehouse Update: 8/30/2006 2:27:08 PM

How many active, resolved and closed work items do we have?

State ↕	Total ↕	Remaining Hours ↕		Completed Hours ↕			
⊟ Active	1	0		0			
ID ↕	Assigned To ↕	Rem. Hrs. ↕	Reason ↕	WI Type ↕	Priority ↕	Title	
48	JosephCampbell	0	Accepted	Requirement	3	OrderSynch - RejectOfflineOrder	

Figure 12-30. *This scenario remains unresolved at the end of iteration 4.*

Ron later opens the scenario in Team Explorer and changes its state to Proposed and a reason of Postponed but leaves it assigned to Joe. The graph of remaining work in Figure 12-29 would then show 0 active work items. It's time to plan the testing effort.

Planning the Test Effort

Earlier in this book, you saw in-depth examples in which the testing features of Visual Studio 2005 Team Edition for Testers were used to verify various areas of the product capabilities. In this and the next chapter, I plan to spend more time on the relationship between the test tasks and the development tasks through the interaction of scenarios, tasks, tests, and bugs, as well as their tracking and reporting. Generally speaking, it's not a bad plan to assume that there will be one test task for each scenario and a minimum of one test per scenario. Since a scenario is a defined sequence of steps through an interaction with the product (a path through a use case actually), then there cannot be variations in a scenario due to multiple branch possibilities in the sequence. Each path that arises from differing branches is a different scenario. Nevertheless, there is often a need for more than one test per scenario since it is usually desirable to exercise a scenario with varying data. We must also remember that a scenario is a unique sequence but doesn't necessarily correspond to a unique path through the code, since the path may depend on data. The Icarus project will assume one task called Write Tests and one called Run Tests for each scenario, but those tasks may each involve more than one test.

Using Excel, Herman enters the test tasks for all the scenarios that have been resolved in iteration 4. He first goes to the project portal home page, in this case `http://icarus-tfs/sites/Enterprise3.1/default.aspx`, and then clicks the Documents and Lists option in the top menu bar. Next, he clicks the Requirements folder and then the Iteration 4 folder, to arrive at the screen shown in Figure 12-31.

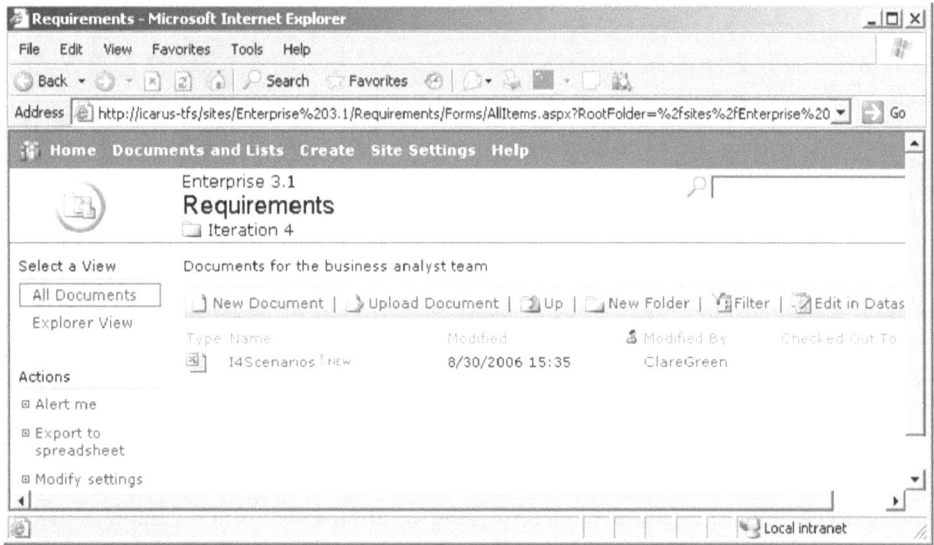

Figure 12-31. *The contents of the Requirements/Iteration 4 document folder on the project portal*

Clicking on the I4Scenarios document opens it in Excel, producing the spreadsheet shown in Figure 12-3. Herman wants to add a set of test tasks, one for each scenario, and he can use this spreadsheet as a temporary place in which to enter them. He first clicks the New List button on the Team toolbar and selects Input List in the New List dialog box; you can have more than one list in a spreadsheet. This new list will become the list of test tasks. Then, with the new list area in the spreadsheet selected, he clicks the Choose Columns button on the Team toolbar, selects Task in the Work Item Type drop-down, clicks Add Required, and clicks OK. Then he copies and pastes all of the title fields from the scenarios into the Title field in the new list, and sets the Work Item Type field to Task and the Task Type field to Test. Then he copies those fields all the way down. Default values for the rest of the fields are set automatically, but Herman sets the Iteration Path field to Iteration 4 and the Area Path field to the same values as the corresponding scenario. This copy-and-paste trick has saved him a lot of typing!

The resulting spreadsheet is shown in Figure 12-32. We compressed it a bit to show all the fields, but the main thing is that the area paths and titles are the same as for the scenarios. These work items are only distinguished from the scenarios by the fact that the work item type is Task and the task type is Test.

Project: Enterprise 3.1   Server: ICARUS-TFS   Query: [None]

ID	Title	Work Item Typ	State	Reas	Assigned	Area Path	Bloc	Exit C	Issue	Iteration P	Prio	Sever	Task Typ	Triage
	Category Catalog - Drill down to lower level category	Task	Propos	New	HermanM	\CustomerRequirements\S	No	No	No	Iteration 4	3	Low	Test	Pending
	Category Catalog - Enter Detail Page	Task	Propos	New	HermanM	\CustomerRequirements\S	No	No	No	Iteration 4	3	Low	Test	Pending
	Category Catalog - Entry: Display top level categories	Task	Propos	New	HermanM	\CustomerRequirements\S	No	No	No	Iteration 4	3	Low	Test	Pending
	Category Catalog - Move up to next highest category	Task	Propos	New	HermanM	\CustomerRequirements\S	No	No	No	Iteration 4	3	Low	Test	Pending
	Category Catalog - Page down in displayed categories	Task	Propos	New	HermanM	\CustomerRequirements\S	No	No	No	Iteration 4	3	Low	Test	Pending
	Category Catalog - Page up in displayed categories	Task	Propos	New	HermanM	\CustomerRequirements\S	No	No	No	Iteration 4	3	Low	Test	Pending
	Create Resource - Include External Web Site Feature	Task	Propos	New	HermanM	\CustomerRequirements\Li	No	No	No	Iteration 4	3	Low	Test	Pending
	Create Resource - Include Multiple Image Features	Task	Propos	New	HermanM	\CustomerRequirements\Li	No	No	No	Iteration 4	3	Low	Test	Pending
	Create Resource - Include Multiple Text Features	Task	Propos	New	HermanM	\CustomerRequirements\Li	No	No	No	Iteration 4	3	Low	Test	Pending
	Geographic Catalog - Drill down to lower level region	Task	Propos	New	HermanM	\CustomerRequirements\S	No	No	No	Iteration 4	3	Low	Test	Pending
	Geographic Catalog - Enter Detail Page "	Task	Propos	New	HermanM	\CustomerRequirements\S	No	No	No	Iteration 4	3	Low	Test	Pending
	Geographic Catalog - Entry: Display top level geographic regions	Task	Propos	New	HermanM	\CustomerRequirements\S	No	No	No	Iteration 4	3	Low	Test	Pending
	Geographic Catalog - Exit: return to home page	Task	Propos	New	HermanM	\CustomerRequirements\S	No	No	No	Iteration 4	3	Low	Test	Pending
	Geographic Catalog - Move up to next highest region	Task	Propos	New	HermanM	\CustomerRequirements\S	No	No	No	Iteration 4	3	Low	Test	Pending
	Geographic Catalog - Page down in displayed regions	Task	Propos	New	HermanM	\CustomerRequirements\S	No	No	No	Iteration 4	3	Low	Test	Pending
	Geographic Catalog - Page up in displayed regions	Task	Propos	New	HermanM	\CustomerRequirements\S	No	No	No	Iteration 4	3	Low	Test	Pending
	OrderSynch - ConfirmOfflineOrder	Task	Propos	New	HermanM	\CustomerRequirements\S	No	No	No	Iteration 4	3	Low	Test	Pending
	OrderSynch - RejectOfflineOrder	Task	Propos	New	HermanM	\CustomerRequirements\S	No	No	No	Iteration 4	3	Low	Test	Pending
	Provider Catalog - Drill down to list providers resources	Task	Propos	New	HermanM	\CustomerRequirements\S	No	No	No	Iteration 4	3	Low	Test	Pending
	Provider Catalog - Enter detail page for resource	Task	Propos	New	HermanM	\CustomerRequirements\S	No	No	No	Iteration 4	3	Low	Test	Pending
	Provider Catalog - Enter provider list for contents letter	Task	Propos	New	HermanM	\CustomerRequirements\S	No	No	No	Iteration 4	3	Low	Test	Pending
	Provider Catalog - Entry. display provider contents alphabet	Task	Propos	New	HermanM	\CustomerRequirements\S	No	No	No	Iteration 4	3	Low	Test	Pending
	Provider Catalog - Page down in displayed providers	Task	Propos	New	HermanM	\CustomerRequirements\S	No	No	No	Iteration 4	3	Low	Test	Pending
	Provider Catalog - Page up in displayed providers	Task	Propos	New	HermanM	\CustomerRequirements\S	No	No	No	Iteration 4	3	Low	Test	Pending
	Provider Catalog - Return to contents alphabet from provider list	Task	Propos	New	HermanM	\CustomerRequirements\S	No	No	No	Iteration 4	3	Low	Test	Pending

Figure 12-32. *The iteration 4 test tasks ready to be published to TFS. This is a new list area in a spreadsheet made by copying and pasting from the scenarios spreadsheet for iteration 4.*

Herman publishes the temporary spreadsheet to TFS, without saving it locally, and then writes a query called I4Tests. This query will return the iteration 4 tests and is similar to the previous queries. He creates a new spreadsheet and a new list, selecting the I4Tests query in New List dialog box. He then assigns the test tasks to members of his team and sets them all to the Active state. Herman then opens the latest version of the iteration 4 schedule from the project portal in Microsoft Project, adds the tasks from the I4Tests query, and lays out a schedule. This is shown in Figure 12-33 (not all of the large list of Resource Catalog test tasks are visible). Notice that when this schedule was refreshed from TFS, the names disappeared from the development and unit test tasks. This is because those tasks have been marked as Closed and so are not assigned to anyone. It is a good idea to keep copies of your evolving schedule as .mpp files separately on the project portal because sometimes when you refresh it from TFS, changes like this can be a surprise.

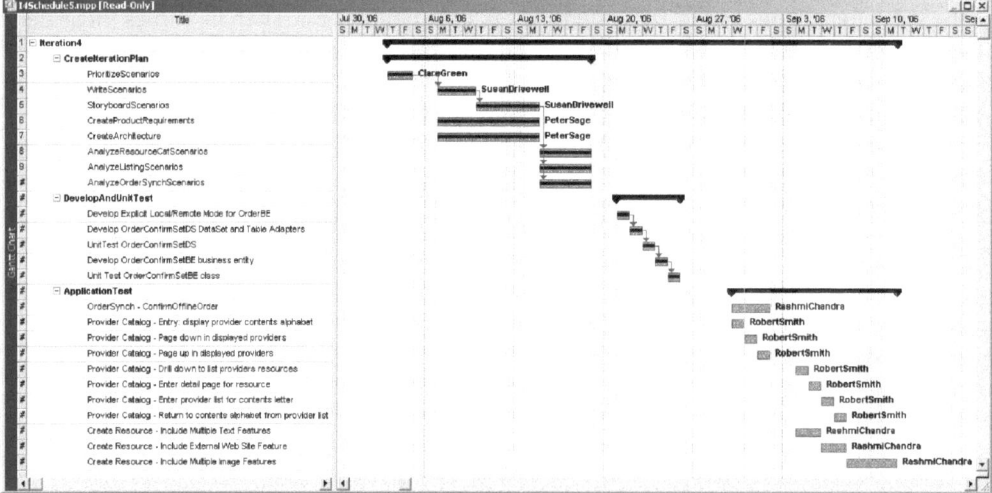

Figure 12-33. *The testing schedule for iteration 4*

Manual Testing

So now the testing phase of iteration 4 is under way and the requirements and development team can begin iteration 5. Before we look at that activity, let's examine a few of the tests.

Note Exercise 12-5 illustrates the content of this section.

Many of the tests that verify the new browse catalog functionality, at least via the sales web site, will be web tests. The tests of the Sales Wing and List Wing Windows Forms applications are mainly manual, although a few coded tests have been written by Rob Smith (Chapter 9). Rob's tests are particularly useful for regression testing some of the areas of functionality that were developed early in the project. I treated web tests quite extensively in Chapters 9 and 10, but so far I have not given you the chance to see the Icarus team demonstrating manual tests in action.

Rashmi Chandra, a member of the test team in India, has been allocated the task of testing the scenario, where tentative orders made offline using the Sales Wing application are confirmed when the application is connected online. There is another scenario, which was postponed to iteration 5, in which the tentative order is rejected. Rashmi is going to define a manual test for this rather complex situation, so she begins by opening her installation of Visual Studio 2005 Team Edition for Testers and displaying the Test Manager window. She creates a new test by clicking the New Test button in the Test toolbar, which displays the Add New Test dialog box. She selects Manual Test (Word Format) and types the name of the test. From the Add To Test Project drop-down she selects an existing project, OfflineTests, which contains tests for the offline features of the product (Figure 12-34). Finally, she clicks OK, and Microsoft Word opens, displaying a template manual test document.

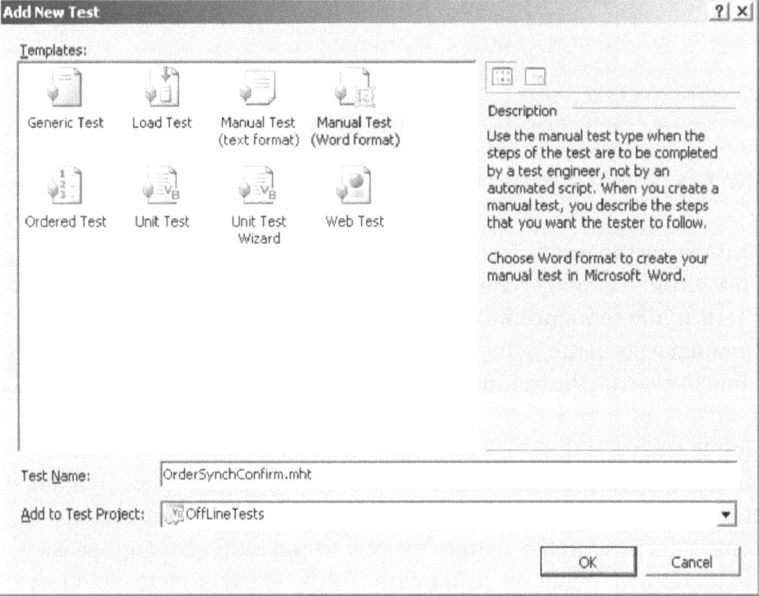

Figure 12-34. *Creating a new manual test*

Rashmi writes the title of the test, a brief background of the application functionality that is being tested, and then completes the table with instructions for each step of the manual test and the required response, where applicable. The complete test is displayed in Figure 12-35.

Test Title
Order Synchronization, Confirm New Tentative Order

Test Details
This test verifies that an order made when the Sales Wing application is offline and stored in the client local database as tentative, is confirmed when the Sales Wing application is connected online again.

Test Target
The Sales Wing application can operate online and offline. The term "Online" means that it is connected via a network to the Sales Web Service provided by Icarus. The term "Offline" means that no network connectivity exists between the application and the Sales Web Service. When online, the application replicates resource data and resource availability data in its client local database. Customer data is also replicated in the client local database for those customers that are clients of the agents that use the particular installation of the Sales Wing application.
When Sales Wing is offline orders may be made or modified and are held in the client local database as tentative orders. When Sales Wing is again connected online, those tentative orders are written via the Sales Web Service to the Icarus Enterprise database and in that way become confirmed.

Test Steps

Step No.	Step Description	Expected Result
1	Connect the Sales Wing client on-line and run the Sales Wing application long enough for the resource data to become replicated.	
2.	Close the Sales Wing application.	
3.	Take the Sales Wing client off-line.	
4.	Start the Sales Wing application.	
5.	Open a known customer and create a new order.	
6.	Add two reservations to the order.	
7.	Save the Order.	The order is saved and the Tentative checkbox is checked.
8.	Exit the Sales Wing Application.	
9.	Connect the Sales Wing client on-line.	
10.	Start the Sales Wing application.	
11.	Wait one minute, then open the same customer and observe the list of orders.	The order that was added in step 5 exists and the Tentative checkbox is unchecked.
12.	Open the order and verify that the reservation details are correct.	Both of the reservations are the same as was entered in step 6.

Revision History

Author	Change Description	Time/Date modified
Rashmi Chandra	Initial version	August 30, 2006

Figure 12-35. *The completed text for the OrderSynchConfirm manual test*

To run the test, Rashmi selects the test in Test View (or Test Manager) and clicks the Run Selection (Run Checked Tests in Test Manager) button. There may be web tests, unit tests, or other types of automatic tests in the sequence mixed up with the manual tests, and an alert box warns that there are manual tests in the sequence. When a manual test is reached, another alert box warns that it is time to execute the manual test. When the tester clicks OK, she sees the screen in Figure 12-36.

It is now the tester's job to carry out the steps described in the document displayed in the lower window and determine, according to the specified criteria, if the test has passed or failed.

To record this fact, the tester clicks either the Pass or Fail radio button at the top and enters suitable reasons for the decision in the Comments box. When either Pass or Fail is selected, the Apply button is enabled. When the tester clicks Apply, she completes that test. Other manual or automatic tests in the sequence may need to execute before the sequence ends, but the pass or fail result appears immediately in the Test Results window for each manual test when Apply is clicked.

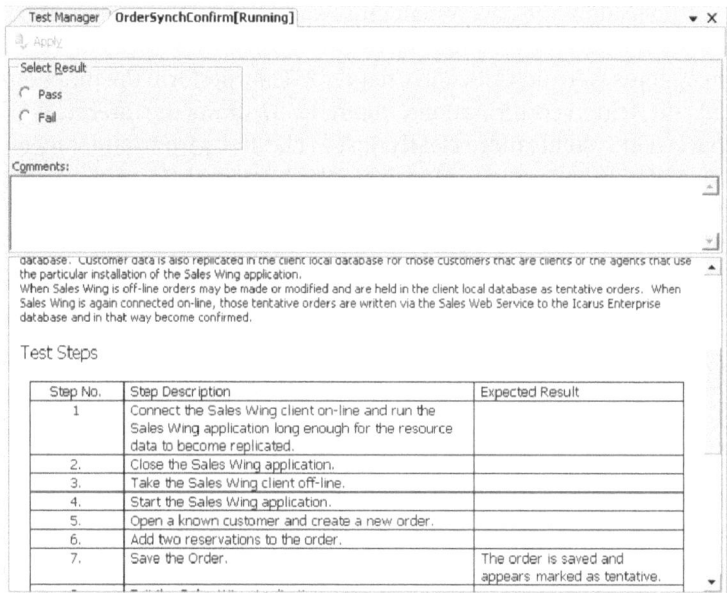

Figure 12-36. *Running the OrderSynchConfirm manual test.*

Iteration 5

Clare is surprised to hear sounds of other people as she enters the office on Saturday to try to catch up on the work of planning iteration 5. There is shouting and cheering. It sounds like some kind of sports event is taking place.

Rahul is visiting again and rounding a corner she sees him bowl a perfect leg spin delivery to Charles who appears to be playing the part of batsman. There is a loud THWACK and the cricket ball flies toward her office. She hears a clunk and a delicate tinkling sound, which she suspects is the Royal Doulton bone china coffee mug that she brought back from her visit to England. "You're not supposed to actually *hit* it, Charles!" she hears Peter yell.

"What are you doing!" she shouts in shocked surprise. "Don't tell me you're playing CRICKET!"

Then she notices Peter, who looks embarrassed and is holding a video camera connected to his laptop. He clears his throat. "No—we're not *exactly* playing cricket—no, not really. "

Clare is almost speechless. "Then what exactly *are* you doing?" she stammers.

Rahul is completely unfazed as he stares in intense concentration at the screen of Peter's laptop. He absently hands the cricket ball to Clare so he can work better with the keyboard. "I think it is now right, Peter," he says. "We have simulated the turbulent effects to an accuracy of plus or minus 10 percent."

"Actually, Clare," says Peter very slowly and deliberately, "we're conducting a systems integration test."

Interfacing with Back-End Systems

The main thrust of iteration 5 is to be back-end integration. This means integration of the new applications with the existing Icarus back-end systems that currently work with the old front-end applications. The two back-end applications the new system must work with are the orchestration service (and its downstream systems) and the payment service.

The existing downstream systems were described in Chapter 2. They perform the functions of accounting as well as email and written confirmations. Figure 12-37 shows the interfaces between the front-end and back-end systems more clearly. Just to clarify, by front-end, I mean those systems that are customer facing: the Resource Manager, Sales Manager VB 6 applications, and the ASP sales site. The payment service, orchestration service, and the services that it deals with are the back-end systems, together with the Enterprise database. *Downstream* services refers to the document and email services to which the orchestration service directs messages. I have used a block diagram in Figure 12-37 rather than an application diagram because I want to indicate how the interfacing occurs between the systems. I have shown the DCOM and Microsoft Message Queue (MSMQ) parts of the system as separate blocks.

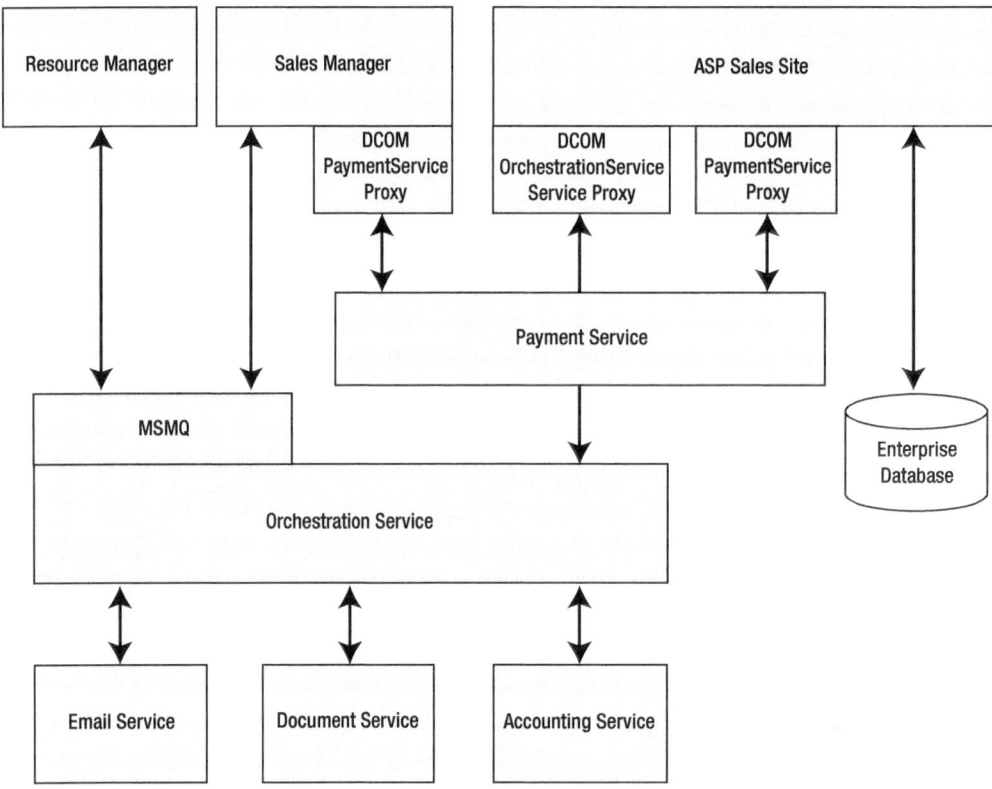

Figure 12-37. *The interfaces with the existing back-end systems*

Chapter 2 described Peter's investigations into the existing architecture and indicated that the orchestration service had at least two methods by which documents could be delivered to it. The ASP sales site application deals with it via a DCOM component, and in this case the COM server is hosted on the orchestration server and a proxy exists on the client. The proxy exposes specific methods to the ASP page; those methods (which execute on the orchestration server) generate XML messages that form the input to the BizTalk 2000 orchestration. Peter assumes that the original architect at Icarus used the COM server to avoid having to generate

XML documents from the ASP scripting. The interface between the VB 6 Sales Manager and Resource Manager applications are designed to place the XML message strings into a message queue implemented on the orchestration server using MSMQ.

Back-End Scenarios

The scenarios that need to be implemented involving the back-end systems are grouped as follows. Remember that these are interactions that are in addition to those with the Enterprise database.

Sales Scenarios

During the Storyboard Scenarios task for this iteration, the requirements group arrives at a set of sales scenarios:

- **Online payment scenarios:** These include actions that happen during the online generation of a new order by the new Sales Site or Sales Wing applications. They may occur as a result of a new order or modification to an existing order and involve synchronous interaction with the payment service.

- **Order confirmation payment scenarios:** These are similar to the above but occur as a result of order synchronization confirmation when a new or modified order has been created by the Sales Wing application when offline and the order is being confirmed automatically by that application when it is again online.

- **Customer credit scenarios:** These occur when an order has been modified or canceled and a refund is due to the customer. This also involves interaction with the payment service.

- **Order confirmation scenarios:** These occur when an online order is being processed at the last stage (after payment) in order to generate email or printed confirmation of a customer's order.

- **Invoice scenarios:** These occur when an order is placed by the Sales Wing or Sales Site application and the customer elects to pay by check. In this case an email or paper invoice is generated, and the customer's ledger account is debited by the total cost of the order.

- **Vendor commission scenarios:** These scenarios occur when a sale is made and commission must be credited to the vendor's account.

Listing Scenarios

We can also summarize the listing scenarios that the team defines:

- **New vendor scenario:** A new vendor is accepted. A letter of introduction is sent by email or printed mail, confirming the business relationship and terms. A ledger account is established.

- **New or modified listing scenario:** A vendor modifies a listing, either directly or via an operator using the List Wing application. This modification may involve price, availability, or informational details. Email and printed confirmations of the changes are generated.

Back-End Interface Architecture

Thinking about the diagram in Figure 12-37, Peter decides that he is not justified in carrying forward to the Enterprise 3.1 project both the MSMQ and DCOM methods of interfacing with the orchestration service. Instead, he decides to use the MSMQ approach and abandon the COM components. He remembers that modifications to orchestration service are under way by Icarus to expose the orchestration service as a web service. Once this is available, the .NET code forming the MSMQ interface can be replaced by a web service proxy. The payment service, on the other hand, has only the DCOM interfacing available, so Peter will have to develop a simple COM Interop wrapper and access the existing DCOM payment component from his new code. The new system is simpler in that the interfacing with the payment COM component only needs to happen in the Sales Business Logic application. The MSMQ interfacing with the orchestration service needs to occur in the Sales Business Logic and Listing Business Logic applications, but there is no duplication of code since the two business logic applications have different needs of the orchestration service. This is much simpler than the existing system where back-end interfacing is scattered through the ASP pages on the Sales Site, and again underlines the importance of separating business logic from presentation features. Figure 12-38 shows the new architecture.

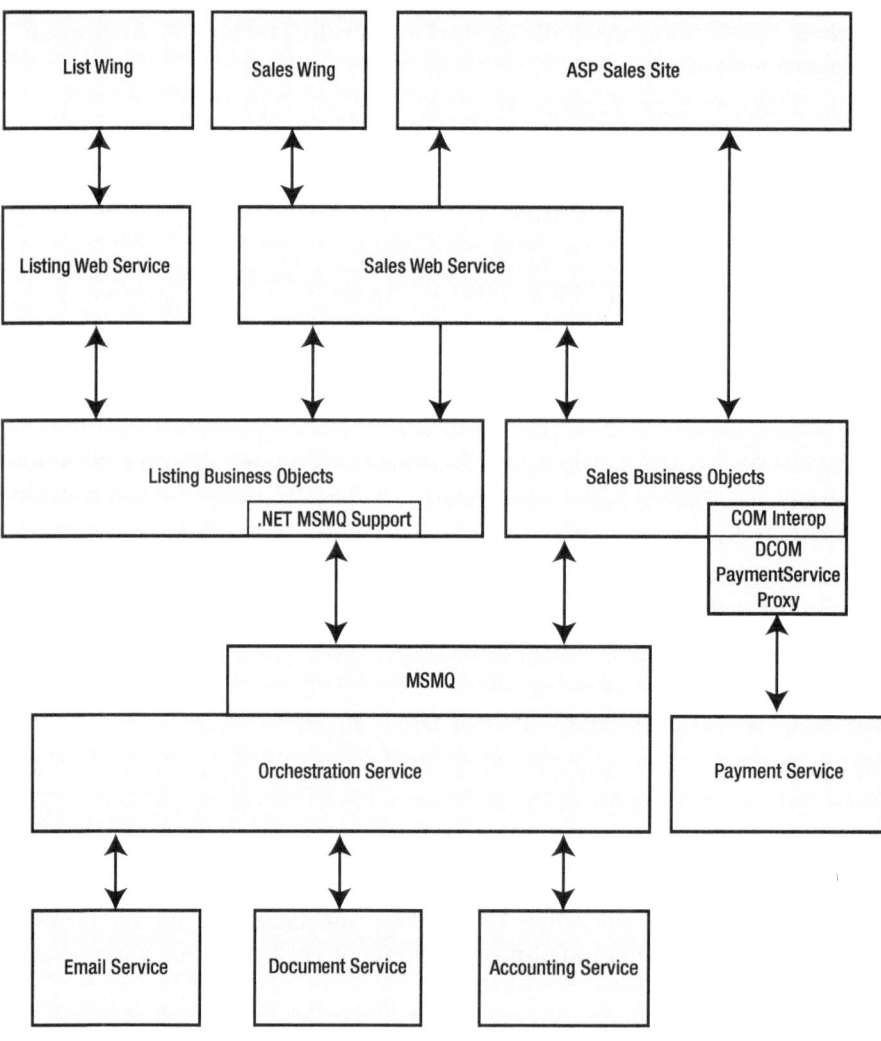

Figure 12-38. *The interfaces with the existing back-end systems*

Planning Iteration 5

The planning prototyping and testing of iteration 5 proceeds in much the same way as iteration 4. First the general tasks like Plan Iteration, Write Scenarios, and Create Architecture, are defined. Then the specific tasks that arise out of the analysis of the scenarios by the developers are defined. There is little value in repeating techniques that I've already shown in detail for iteration 4. Instead, I will use the remainder of this chapter to reveal the coding techniques used to interface with the existing DCOM and MSMQ systems.

Developing the DCOM Interface

The payment server is a COM server written in Visual Basic 6 that is installed on the payment system host shown in Chapter 2, Figure 2-22. The host runs Windows 2000 and the COM server is installed under COM+ services. Its most important function is

```
Public Function MakePayment(
    creditCardNumber As String, expiryDate As Date, nameOnCard As String) As String

' Code implementing the Make Payment function

End Function
```

It has been exported as an MSI file called PaymentCOMServer.MSI, which enables a DCOM proxy to be installed on any client machine by simply installing that MSI. It is very easy to use COM+ services to generate an MSI file that will install a DCOM proxy on a client machine. Selecting the context menu option in Figure 12-39 starts a wizard that provides the option to generate this MSI file.

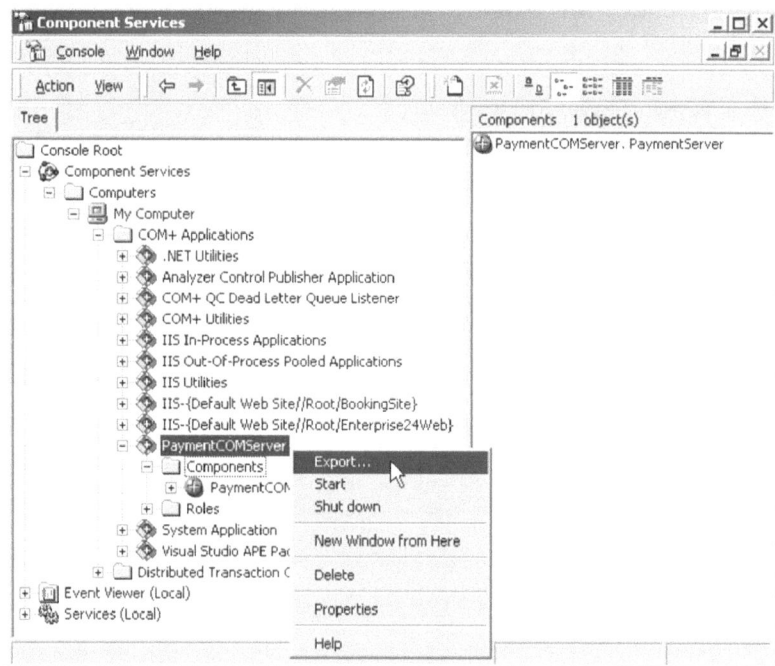

Figure 12-39. *Using COM Services in Windows 2000 to export an installed COM component*

The COM proxy will expose the same methods defined in the COM component itself but will accept calls to the methods, marshal the parameters, and pass them over the network to the machine that hosts the real COM server. That machine will hold a pool of the required type of COM objects, and on receiving a request will unmarshal the parameters and pass them to the same call on the real COM component, allocated to the client, from the pool. The return value of the function is passed back through the same marshaling process. You can think of marshaling as being similar to .NET serialization in that it is just a means of sending objects over a network. In the existing system, instances of PaymentServer, the COM object that encapsulates the payment capability, are created and called in VB 6.0 using code something like this:

```
Dim paymentServer1 As paymentCOMServer.PaymentServer
Set paymentServer1 = CreateObject("PaymentCOMServer.PaymentServer")
Result = paymentServer1.MakePayment(
                            "1234 1234 1234 1234", DateTime.Now, "A. N. Other")
```

Fortunately, for simple DCOM components like this one that are registered on the development machine by running the MSI mentioned earlier, it is very easy to use the COM Interop capabilities of .NET. We simply add the COM component as a reference in the project, choosing it from those listed in the COM tab on the Add Reference dialog box. A .NET assembly, in this case Interop.PaymentComServer.dll, will be generated that wraps the calls to the DCOM server and allows the new operator to be used to create instances and members to be called. IntelliSense is also supported.

Similar test code written in C# looks like this:

```
PaymentCOMServer.PaymentServerClass paymentServer = new PaymentServerClass();

string ccNum = "1234 1234 1234 1234";
DateTime expiryDate = DateTime.Now;
string nameOnCard = "A. N. Other";

this.textBoxResult.Text = paymentServer.MakePayment(
                                    ref ccNum, ref expiryDate, ref nameOnCard);
```

Developing the MSMQ Interface

As in the Icarus legacy system, Microsoft Message Queue is added to a Windows 2000 machine using Add/Remove Windows Components in the Add/Remove Programs Control Panel applet. Once installed, queues are created and managed using Computer Management (Figure 12-40). These applets are similar in Windows XP Professional so that it is a straightforward matter to set up test queues on a developer machine. Security settings will also need to be specified by the developers in order to verify that security will work properly when integrating with the production system.

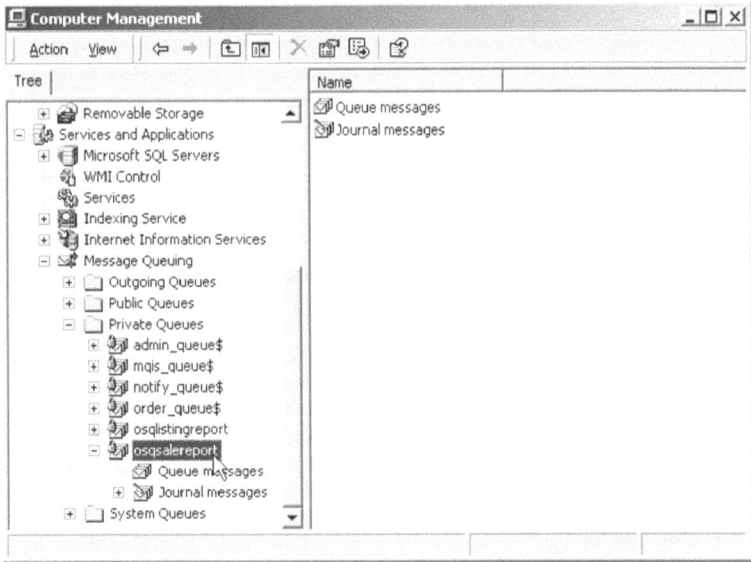

Figure 12-40. *Managing message queues via Computer Management*

To interface with the messaging queues on the existing orchestration server, classes within the System.Messaging namespace can be used. The existing messages that the orchestration service accepts are defined using XML Schema Definition (XSD) files and Peter plans to generate XML files that will be compatible with these schemas by serializing classes using the XmlMessageSerializer class. For example, Peter carries out some tests using the following code:

```
public struct Reservation
{
  public int ResourceAvailabilityID;
  public int UnitCount;
  public decimal UnitCost;
  public decimal ExtendedCost;

  public Reservation(int resourceAvailabilityID, int unitCount,
                                      decimal unitCost, decimal extendedCost)
  {
    ResourceAvailabilityID = resourceAvailabilityID;
    UnitCount = unitCount;
    UnitCost = unitCost;
    ExtendedCost = extendedCost;
  }
}
```

```
public class SaleReportOSQ
{
  public int CustomerID;
  public string CustomerName;
  public Reservation[] Reservations;

  public SaleReportOSQ() { }
  public SaleReportOSQ(
    int customerID, string customerName, Reservation[] reservations)
  {
    CustomerID = customerID;
    CustomerName = customerName;
    Reservations = reservations;
  }
}

Reservation reservation1 = new Reservation(1, 10, (decimal)100.0, (decimal)1000.0);
Reservation reservation2 = new Reservation(1, 5, (decimal)100.0, (decimal)500.0);
SaleReportOSQ saleReportOSQ = new SaleReportOSQ(
                2, "A. N. Other", new Reservation[] { reservation1, reservation2 });

MessageQueue salesReportsOSQ = new MessageQueue(QUEUE_FORMAT_NAME);
salesReportsOSQ.Formatter = new XmlMessageFormatter(
  new string[] { "OSQTest.Reservation", "OSQTest.SaleReportOSQ" });
salesReportsOSQ.Send(saleReportOSQ, "Sale 1");
salesReportsOSQ.Close();
```

The task of writing the code that will generate the XML to match the existing schema requirements has been allocated to Charles for iteration 5. He faces a considerable amount of work to ensure that XML messages generated in this manner are compatible with the existing schema. To accomplish this, Charles must write the OrchestrationServiceStub, as described in Chapter 5, and must verify the XML received at the stubs against the schema obtained from the existing system.

Summary

In this chapter you saw the progress of iterations 4 and 5 of the Icarus Enterprise 3.1 project, with emphasis on the process of managing and reporting progress through the use of scenario and task type work items.

The team wrote the scenarios for iteration 5 and entered them into Team System via Excel. Clare evolved a project plan for the iteration, starting with the overall tasks, and extended the plan with the analysis tasks and then the development and test tasks. You learned how the reporting features of Team System can be used to indicate progress, remaining work, and the status of work items.

We summarized the design features implementing the new scenarios. You saw how the development progress of the scenarios was tracked by Team System. We also introduced the manual testing features of Team System, and provided an example of a manual test to verify a complex piece of the system capability.

Finally, we summarized the design approach in integrating the new system with the legacy back-end systems using DCOM and MSMQ.

The next chapter will concentrate again on using Team System to manage activities, this time as the team moves through the consolidation track of the project and concentrates on finding and correcting defects.

CHAPTER 13

Tracking and Correcting Defects

In this chapter I will concentrate on the testing of the Icarus 3.1 system, which is almost complete, as well as on the detection of defects and their tracking through the process of triage, analysis, corrections to code, and retest. You will see in the first part of this chapter the detailed progress of a defect through Team System. Team System assigns the work item representing a defect the less formal name of *bug*, so I will use that term from this point on.

Discovering Bugs

Bugs are discovered by either formal or informal testing. As I've said before, both are important and complementary. Formal tests establish a baseline of known behavior and quality, in terms of the adherence of the code base to implementing requirements as interpreted by a set of test cases. There is a danger that the code becomes tuned to only those test cases and operates extremely well within that domain but demonstrates defects when used in ways that are expected but that are not covered by a test case. Of course, if the test cases verify all the scenarios and the set of scenarios represent the complete requirements on the product, the job is done—by definition. The danger is that, in a complex product, the set of scenarios never becomes rich enough, and when real users start working with the product, they discover situations that were never envisaged initially. MSF CMMI recognizes this danger in its three core ideas:

Partner with customers.

Quality is everyone's business every day.

Make deployment a habit.

These are all statements that encourage an evolving perception of what the product must do to be acceptable. As customers learn more about the product as it moves through development, they become increasingly aware of the variety of situations that might occur. If everyone considers quality every day, developers and testers will take note of aspects of behavior that do not seem to quite make sense. Instead of ignoring them in favor of concentrating on an established set of tests and no more, the mechanism should exist within the project for such peculiarities to be documented and become issues and perhaps eventually tests. I once worked at a company where I was horrified to discover that the testers were the only ones permitted to enter defects into the tracking system. It was not my job as a developer to find bugs; when I happened to discover a bug in the middle of fixing another, unrelated bug, there was no mechanism for me to enter the new bug into any system that would ensure it was not forgotten. I could either correct it immediately or report it to one of the testers and hope that they would interrupt their work to make a new defect report. As it turned out, there was no test that would have detected this bug, and so the testers could not record it; in the end I fixed it unofficially. This is an example of inefficient demarcation of responsibilities that goes against the idea of quality being everyone's business every day!

Let me immediately qualify this by saying that of course some control is needed to prevent people from misplacing priorities and spending too much time correcting minor defects that would be better left to a new release. It is better that the *casual tester* has the means of recording the observed anomaly so that it can go through the proper process of classification and prioritization—*triage*, as you'll see later—so that priorities can be assigned effectively. Let me also repeat that it's not just functions—it's performance and other QoS requirements like security and safety, too.

Let's now follow the discovery and correction of a typical bug.

Running a Manual Test and Discovering a Bug

In the previous chapter you saw Rashmi write a manual test to verify one of the basic scenarios relating to the offline working capability required for the system. The test verified the basic ability of the system to allow an order to be made using the Sales Wing application offline and for that order to be confirmed when the Sales Wing application was next connected online. That was only one of many manual tests that Rashmi wrote to test this functionality. As an example of the detection and processing of a bug within Team System, we can look at another manual test, as defined in Figures 13-1 and 13-2.

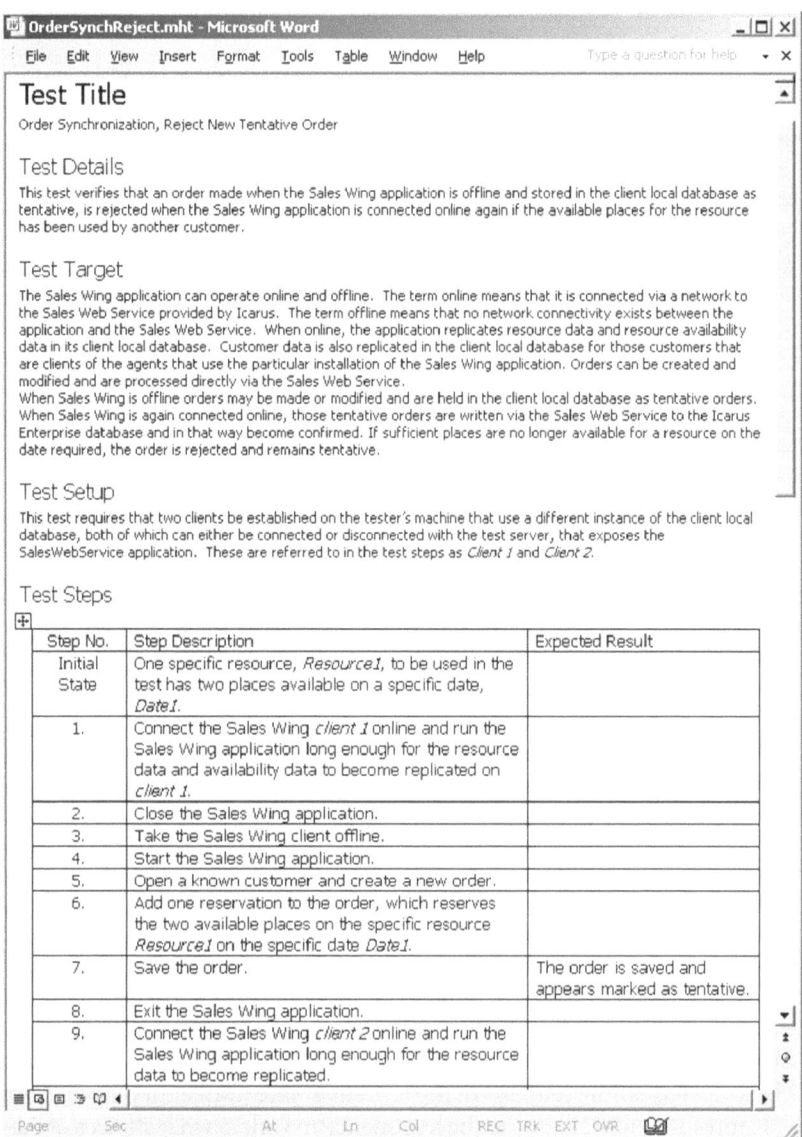

Figure 13-1. *Offline order rejection manual test*

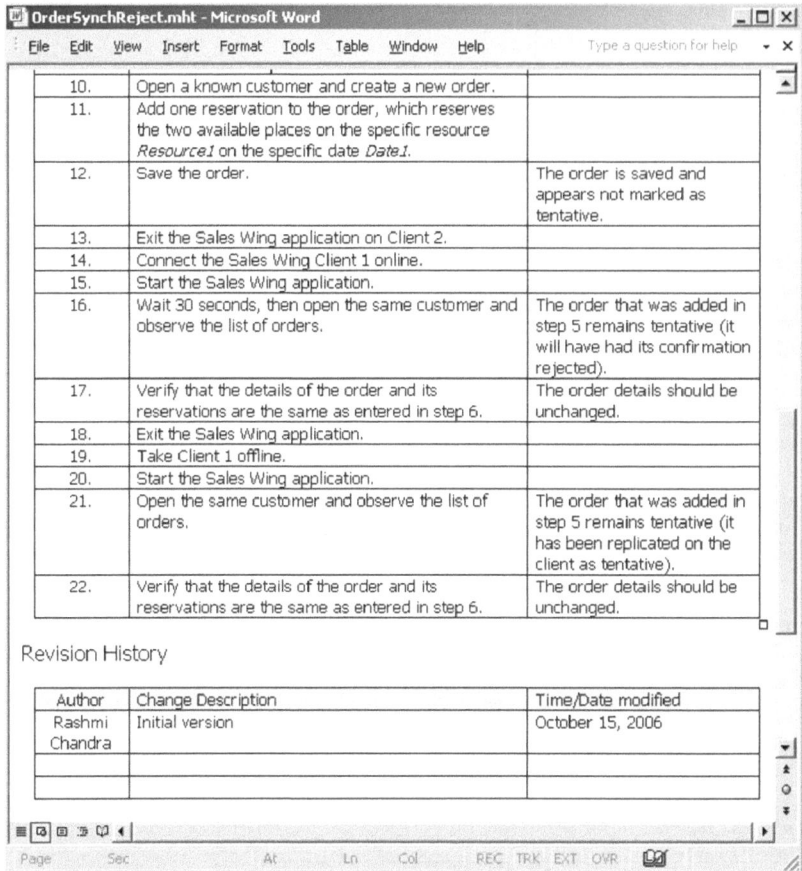

10.	Open a known customer and create a new order.	
11.	Add one reservation to the order, which reserves the two available places on the specific resource *Resource1* on the specific date *Date1*.	
12.	Save the order.	The order is saved and appears not marked as tentative.
13.	Exit the Sales Wing application on Client 2.	
14.	Connect the Sales Wing Client 1 online.	
15.	Start the Sales Wing application.	
16.	Wait 30 seconds, then open the same customer and observe the list of orders.	The order that was added in step 5 remains tentative (it will have had its confirmation rejected).
17.	Verify that the details of the order and its reservations are the same as entered in step 6.	The order details should be unchanged.
18.	Exit the Sales Wing application.	
19.	Take Client 1 offline.	
20.	Start the Sales Wing application.	
21.	Open the same customer and observe the list of orders.	The order that was added in step 5 remains tentative (it has been replicated on the client as tentative).
22.	Verify that the details of the order and its reservations are the same as entered in step 6.	The order details should be unchanged.

Revision History

Author	Change Description	Time/Date modified
Rashmi Chandra	Initial version	October 15, 2006

Figure 13-2. *Offline order rejection manual test, continued*

This test verifies the ability of the order synchronization part of the system to reject some orders made when the Sales Wing application is offline. This happens when Sales Wing is again connected online if the resource no longer has available capacity. In this case, the order that was marked as tentative when created offline remains in the tentative state until either modified or deleted by an operator. Figures 13-1 and 13-2 describe a sequence in which two instances of the client application are installed on the test client machine, both using different instances of the Client Local Database. Both of these client instances connect to the same instance of the Sales Web Service and Client Replication Web Service, which for test purposes run under the ASP.NET Development Server. The ASP.NET Development Server starts when a solution using web services is started in the debugger, but in this test it is required that the web services be started and stopped manually. The ASP.NET Development Server can easily be started in a .bat file using these commands:

```
start /B
E:\WINDOWS\Microsoft.NET\Framework\v2.0.50727\WebDev.WebServer.EXE
/port:8040
```

```
/path:"H:\Workspaces\Administrator\Chapter 13 Begin\ClientReplWebService"
/vpath:/ClientReplWebService

start /B
E:\WINDOWS\Microsoft.NET\Framework\v2.0.50727\WebDev.WebServer.EXE
/port:8020
/path:"H:\Workspaces\Administrator\Chapter 13 Begin\SalesWebService"
/vpath:/SalesWebService
```

These commands need to each be placed on one line in the .bat file. The ports are arbitrary fixed values, which must match those defined for the various web service URLs in the App.config file for the SalesWing project. The App.config file becomes SalesWing.exe.config when the application is deployed in the two places on the test machine. The two .config files will also contain different values for the database connection strings so that two client installations are simulated.

In step 1 of the test, the first client, Client 1, is placed online and started and left connected for enough time for the client replication thread to complete at least one pass. This ensures that the resources, available capacity, vendors, geographic regions, resource categories, local customers, and their orders and reservations have been replicated on the client. The term *local customers* refers to customers to which the agent using the client installation has access under the security features.

After the application has been stopped and the client taken offline, the application is started again in step 4 and a new order is created offline in steps 5, 6, and 7. Figures 13-3 and 13-4 show the new order that has been created offline as a result of steps 5, 6, and 7.

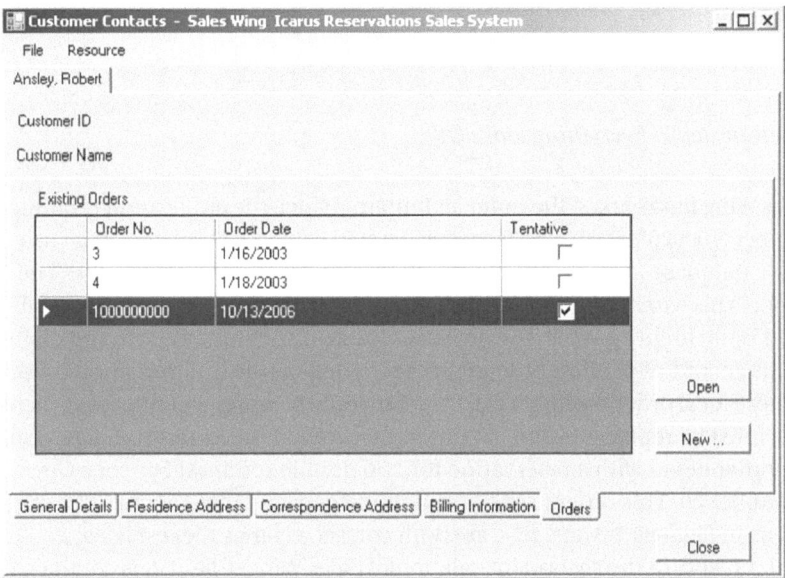

Figure 13-3. *Results of step 7—the information looks OK.*

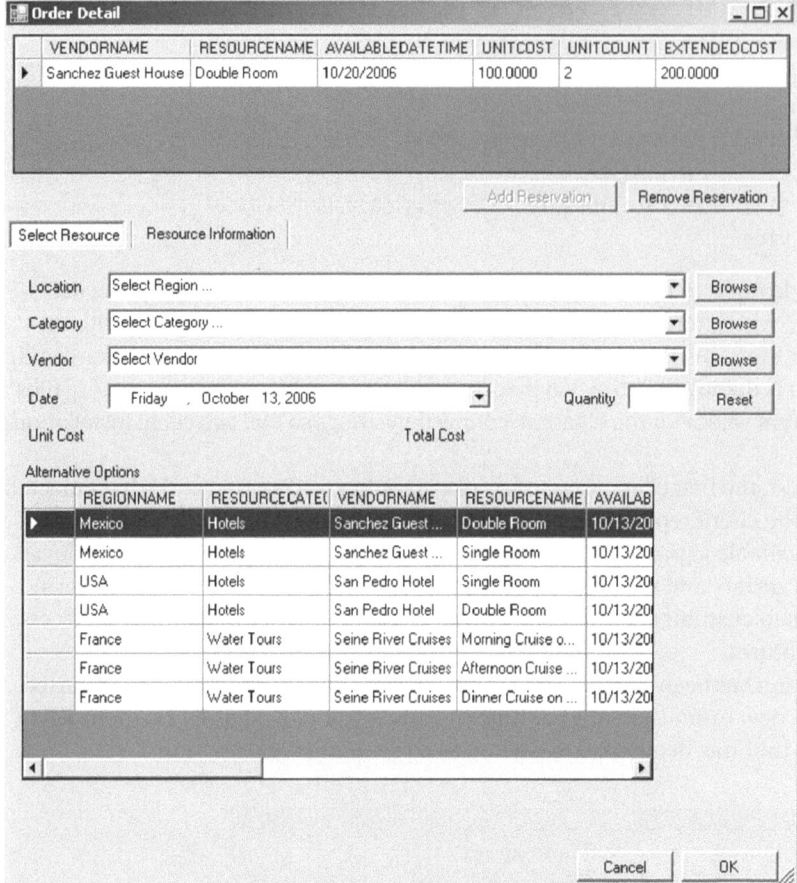

Figure 13-4. *Order details at step 7. Everything looks OK.*

In Figure 13-3 Sales Wing has marked the order as Tentative since the application is offline. A temporary order number (1000000000) has also been generated, which is above the range used by the Icarus Enterprise database and is unique only within the Client Local Database. The temporary order number is necessary because order numbers are the primary key in the ORDER table and are generated by an identity. When the client is offline, the identity runs in the Client Local Database and thus generates a different sequence from that on the Enterprise database on the Icarus server. These local order numbers will therefore only be unique on the local client machine and therefore must be replaced when the order is written to the Enterprise database. Figure 13-4 shows the order detail with a reservation for two double rooms at Sanchez Guest House in Mexico on October 20. This order uses the remaining capacity that Sanchez can offer on that date. The screens in Figure 13-3 and 13-4 are both correct as far as the test goes.

Next, in steps 9, 10, 11, and 12 the second installation of Sales Wing, Client 2, is connected online and creates an identical order while online. The results look similar to those in Figures 13-3 and 13-4 except that the order is made for a different customer, Brian Bennett, and because the Client 2 installation of Sales Wing was online when the order was made, it is not marked as Tentative and is given a permanent order number (1000) from the identity sequence in the Enterprise database (Figure 13-5).

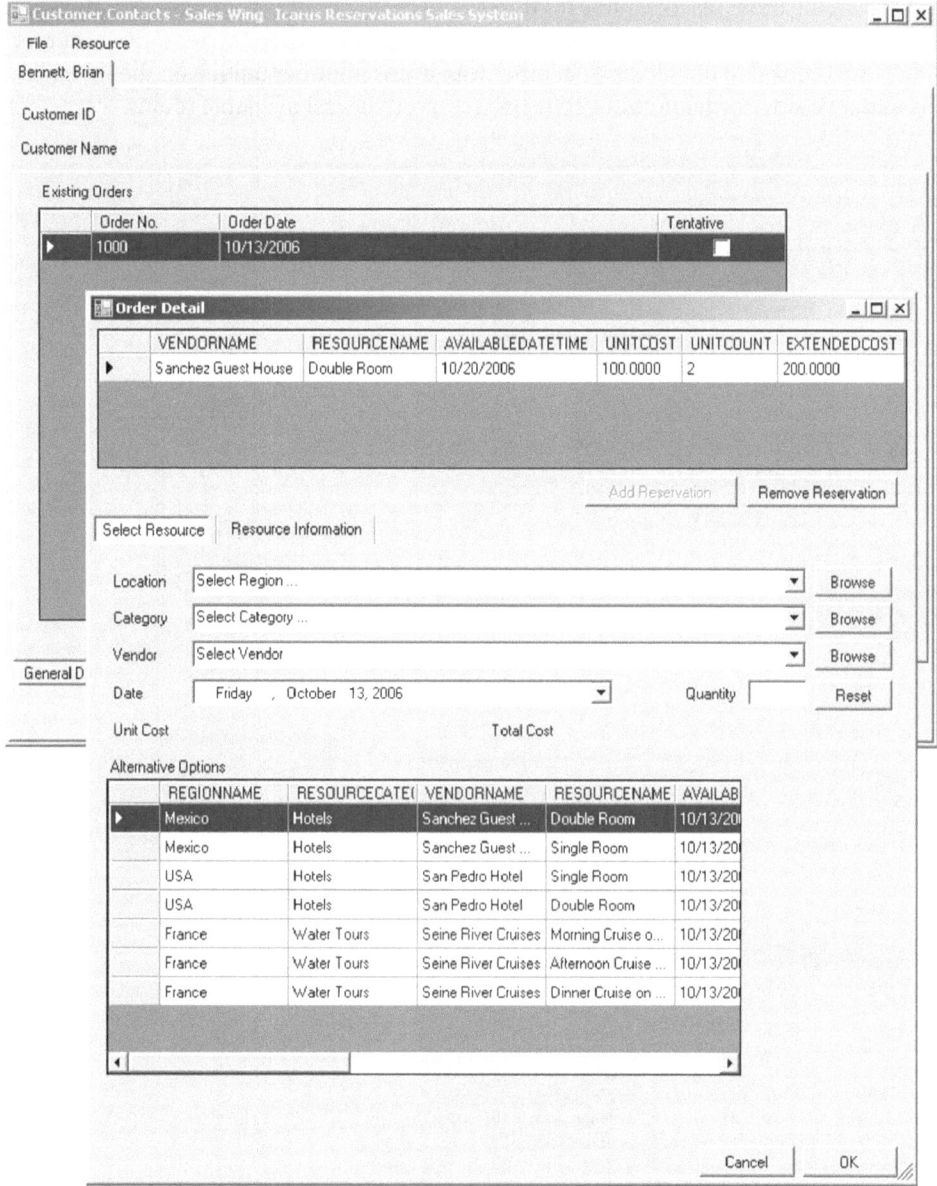

Figure 13-5. *Order details at step 13—again, everything looks OK.*

In steps 14, 15, 16, and 17, the Client 1 installation is connected online and started. A period of time is allowed to let the synchronization thread attempt to synchronize the orders, and then the Customer Details Orders tab and the new order are displayed as shown in Figure 13-6. The order is still shown as Tentative, since the order made by Client 2 used up the remaining capacity of Sanchez Guest House on that date. The order made offline by Client 1 was rejected as required by the test. The figure also shows the open Order Details dialog box, which displays the details of the order that was made and that has now been copied to the Enterprise database and given a permanent order number. Remember from Figure 13-3 order numbers 3 and 4 already existed.

Number 1000 was the order placed online for the second customer, Brian Bennett. Number 1001 was therefore the next available order number that was allocated when the tentative order for Robert Ansley was copied to the server. That order was given a number unique on the server, but it remains tentative since order number 1001 had reserved the last available rooms.

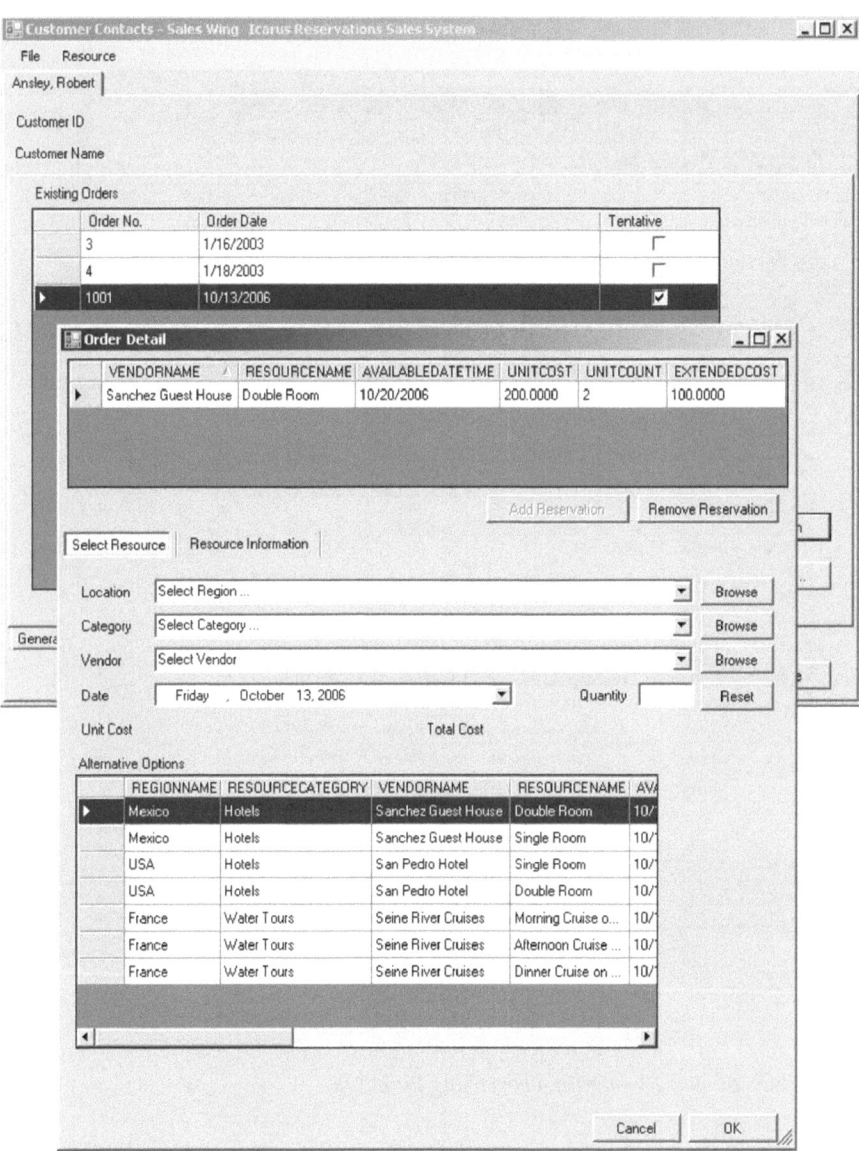

Figure 13-6. *Order details at step 17—there's a problem here.*

Unfortunately, the dialog box in Figure 13-6 shows a problem. Look at the reservation entry at the top of the Order Detail dialog box. The unit cost should be 100.00 dollars and the extended cost 200.00 since two rooms are reserved. This is correct in Figure 13-5 for Brian Bennett's order, but in Figure 13-6 the costs have been transposed, with the unit cost shown as 200.00 and the extended cost shown as 100.00. This is an obvious bug; somehow during the synchronization process these two figures have become switched. It looks like the developer (it was Joe!) was so careful to verify that the Tentative check box was set correctly in this rather complex situation that he neglected to verify that the figures were correct. Well, it's a mistake anyone can make. Actually, there is a second bug here since the unit cost and extended cost in the Order Detail dialog box are shown to four decimal places rather than the usual two places for money, but this is less important than getting the values correct.

Rashmi notes the main bug in the space provided for comments in the manual test page and continues with the test through steps 18, 19, 20, 21, and 22. Figure 13-7 shows the results at step 22; strangely enough, here they are OK.

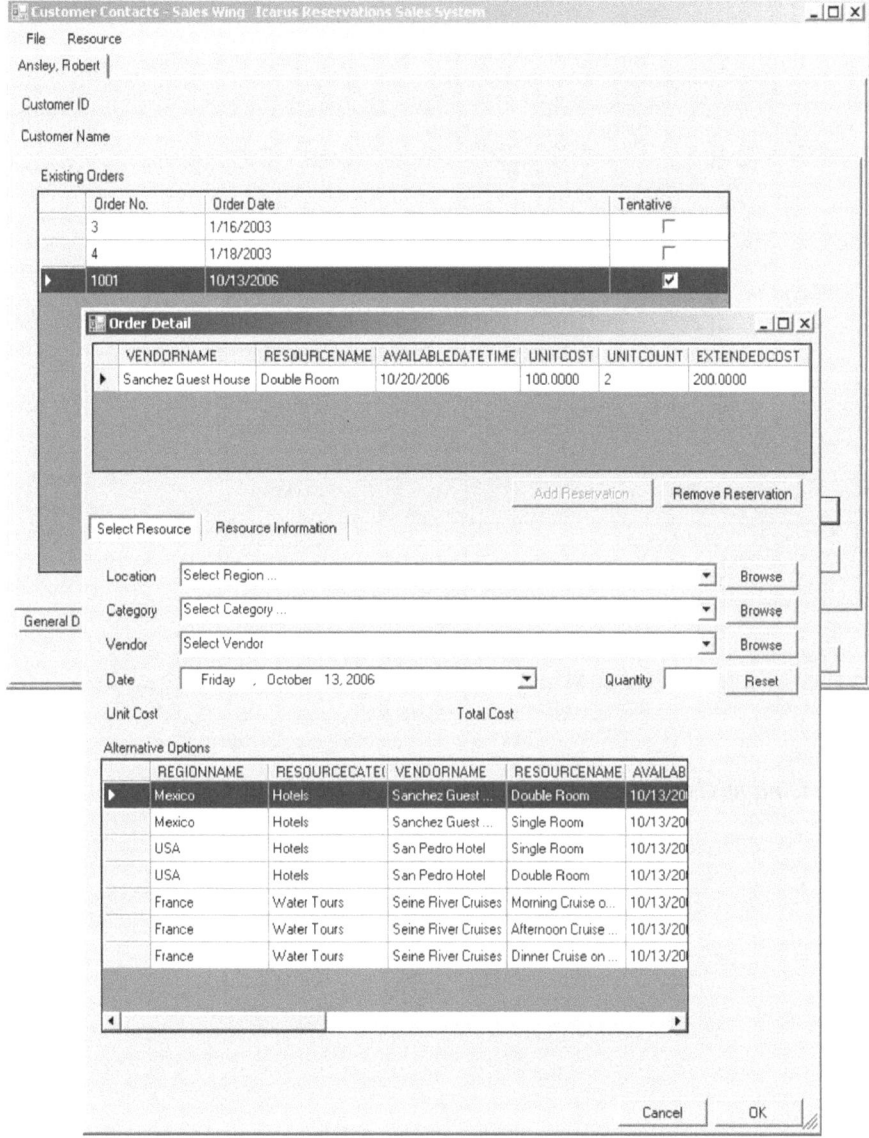

Figure 13-7. *Order details at step 22—everything looks OK.*

Figure 13-8 shows the page displayed when this manual test is being run. Rashmi has added text in the Comments section to explain why the test failed. At completion she checks the Fail radio button and then clicks the Apply button. The Test Results window now shows a test run containing just this one test that has failed. To ensure that this failure leads to corrective action Rashmi right-clicks on the test and selects Create Work Item ➤ Bug from the context menu (Figure 13-9). First she is given the option to publish the test run, which she needs to do so that it will be visible to other team members. Then a new bug type work item is created and Rashmi completes the information, as shown in Figure 13-10. On the Attachments tab she adds a screen shot of the dialog box showing the failed step, as in Figure 13-6, and Visual Studio adds the XML file containing all of the test run details automatically.

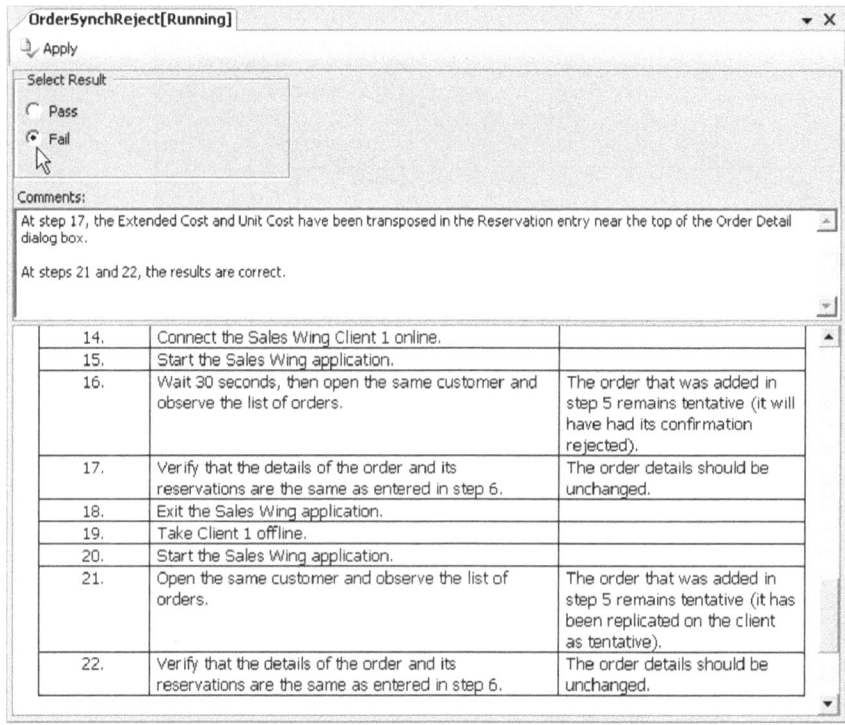

Figure 13-8. *The test window visible when running the manual test*

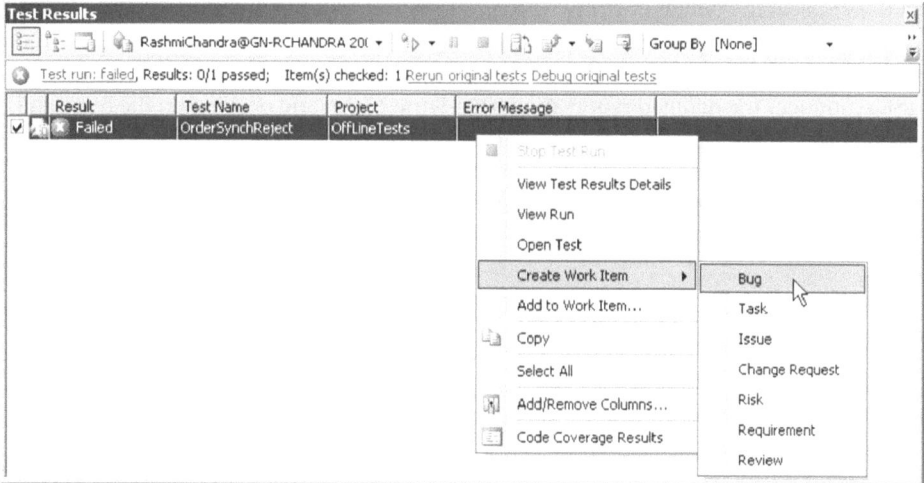

Figure 13-9. *Creating a new Bug type work item*

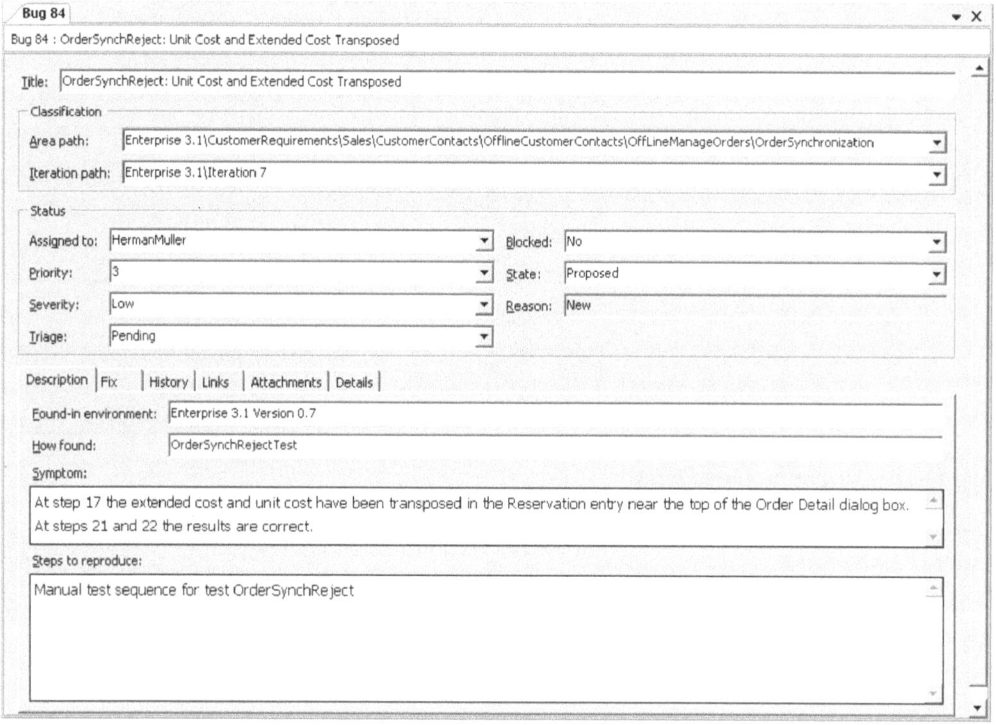

Figure 13-10. *The new Bug work item*

Rather than look at the details of the work item in Team Explorer, we can see all the contents together on the project portal, starting with the Work Items report, shown in Figure 13-11, which is set to include only iteration 7 Bug type work items in the Proposed state. Clicking on the hyperlink for bug 84 produces the detailed report shown in Figure 13-12, and clicking on the hyperlinks in that report will open test details or the attachments as shown.

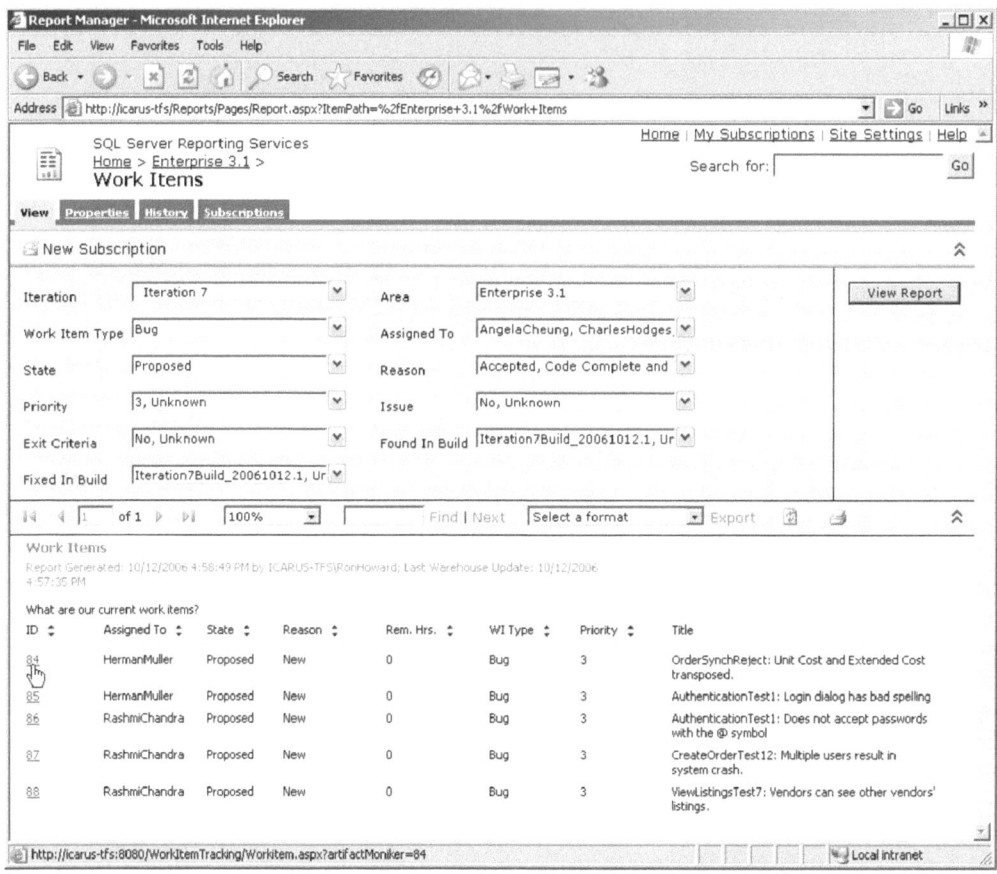

Figure 13-11. *Current proposed bugs*

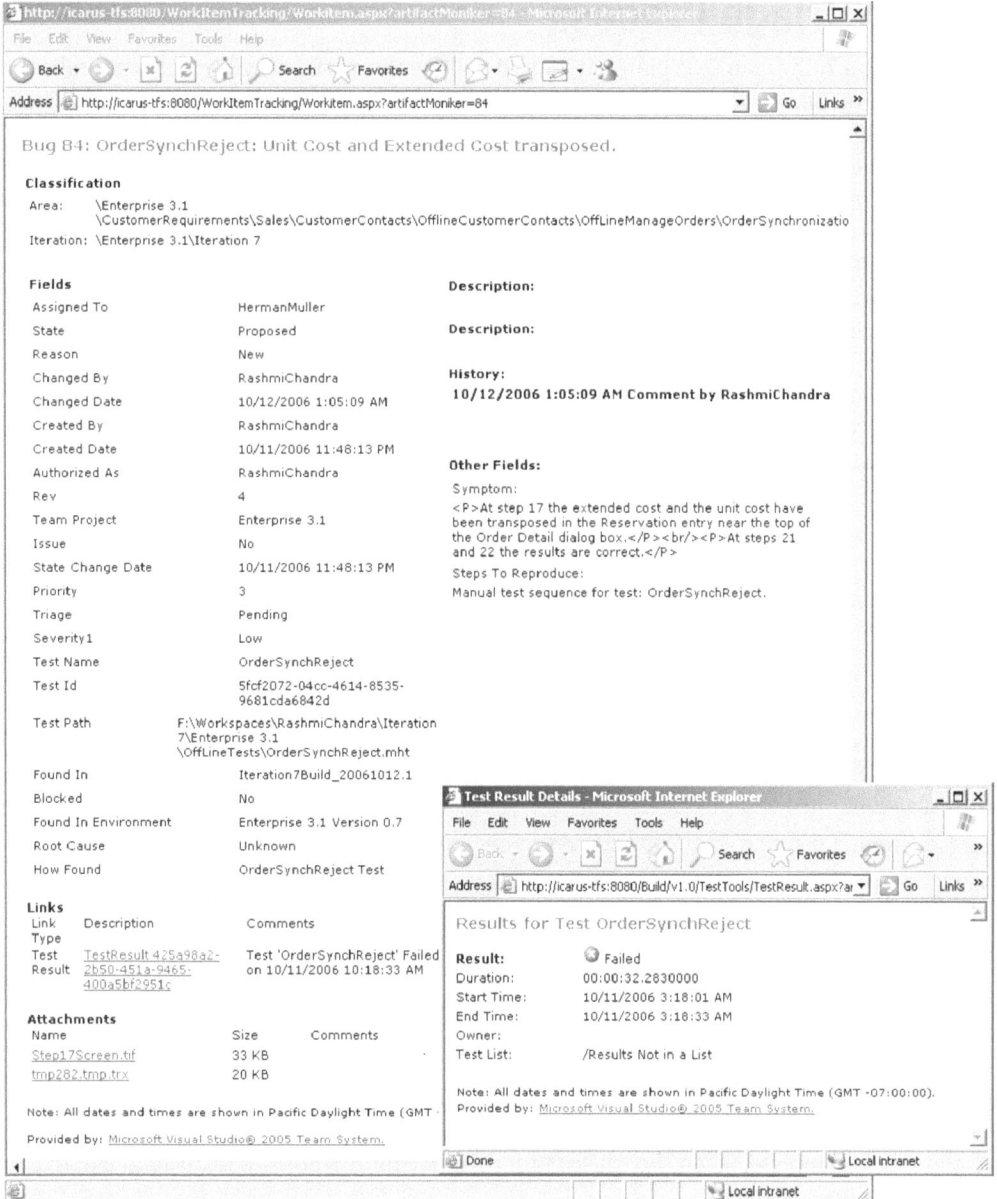

Figure 13-12. *Details of the Bug work item for the OrderSynchReject test failure*

The Bug Triage Process

During iteration 7, the team has planned to hold daily sessions of a triage team (often called a Change Control Board, or CCB), which consists of Clare, Herman, Peter, Ron, and Susan. Their job throughout the project has been to review change requests and defects, and then determine the action to be taken for each one. In iteration 7, most of the features are now complete and their job as a group is to make decisions about bugs that have been reported by the test team.

The term *triage* is borrowed from the medical profession, where it means to make an initial assessment of a group of patients to determine the priorities and place them in groups to receive the most appropriate action, taking into account their condition, the availability of resources, and how those resources can be best utilized. The aim is to achieve the best outcome for the largest number of patients. So it is with software bugs—some will be classified as needing a quick bandage from a junior member of the team; others can be classified as walking wounded that can wait their turn behind the more pressing problems; some will be so serious as to require immediate attention by perhaps the whole team; and finally, a few will be hopeless cases that must be abandoned to their fate. Table 13-1 summarizes the options available for each Bug work item.

Table 13-1. *Possible Disposition of a Bug at Triage*

Action	New State	Reason
Allocate to the development team to be fixed.	Active	Approved
Allocate to the development team or requirements team for investigation.	Active	Investigate
Defer it to another iteration.	Closed	Deferred
Reject it.	Closed	Rejected

Figure 13-13 is a state transition diagram for a bug. A newly discovered bug is entered as a work item of type Bug, in the Proposed state with the Reason value set automatically to New. It remains in the Proposed state until the triage process occurs, which has the four possible outcomes listed in Table 13-1, resulting in transition to Active (Reason Approved), Active (Reason Investigate), Closed (Reason Deferred) or Closed (Reason Rejected). In the case of the transition to Active (Reason Investigate), the bug will return to the Proposed state when the investigation is complete, when the triage team will have more information available to make a further decision.

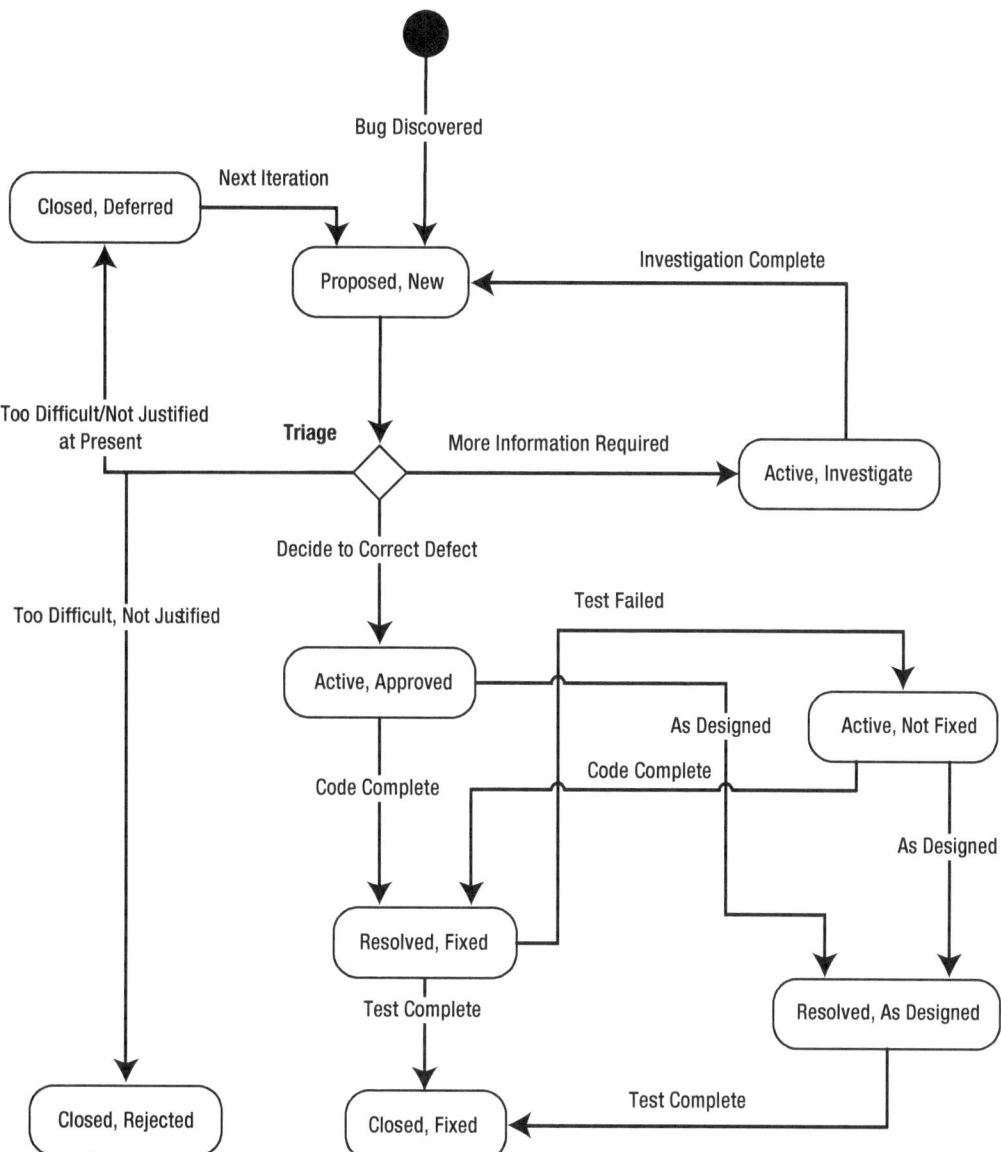

Figure 13-13. *The possible state transitions of a Bug type work item*

The Active (Reason Approved) state is where the coding occurs to correct the defect. When this is complete, the developer will transition it to the Resolved state, allocating it to the tester who authored the bug for verification of the fix. When the test is complete, the tester will transition it to the Closed state, with the Reason Fixed. In some cases, the tester will find that the bug still exists and will transition it back to Active (Reason Not Fixed), reassigning it to the developer. Sometimes the developer will find that the reported bug is actually exhibiting designed behavior and transition it to Resolved (Reason As Designed), in which case the tester will probably modify the test before passing it and transitioning it to Closed (Reason Fixed).

In a work item of type Bug there are Severity and Priority fields that need to be determined during triage. The Severity field is a measurement of the impact of the existence of the bug on the usefulness of the software. If a bug causes the software to crash every 10 minutes, with loss of all the data, it is obviously a bug whose correction is critical to the success of the project. The priority field is usually decided at triage and represents the priority attached to it once it has been transitioned to the Active state.

There is another important property of the bug in triage, which is a measure of the difficulty and risk involved in correcting the problem. This difficulty/risk property can sometimes be determined during triage, but often will need to be determined by an investigative phase. Once the severity and the difficulty/risk have been determined, the triage team can make a judgment to either activate the bug with Reason Approved, defer the bug, or reject it. When the bug is approved, it must be given a priority, again based on the severity and difficulty.

Figure 13-14 indicates the way in which the Severity field value and the difficulty and risk values attributed to a bug affect the decision to be made as to its disposition. The severity of the bug is plotted horizontally, with increasing severity to the right, the zero on the axis corresponding to a perfectly working product. The Difficulty and Risk axis indicates increasing difficulty of correcting the bug in the upward direction. Of course, such a diagram cannot be quantitatively precise and only serves to indicate the way the triage team should organize their thinking.

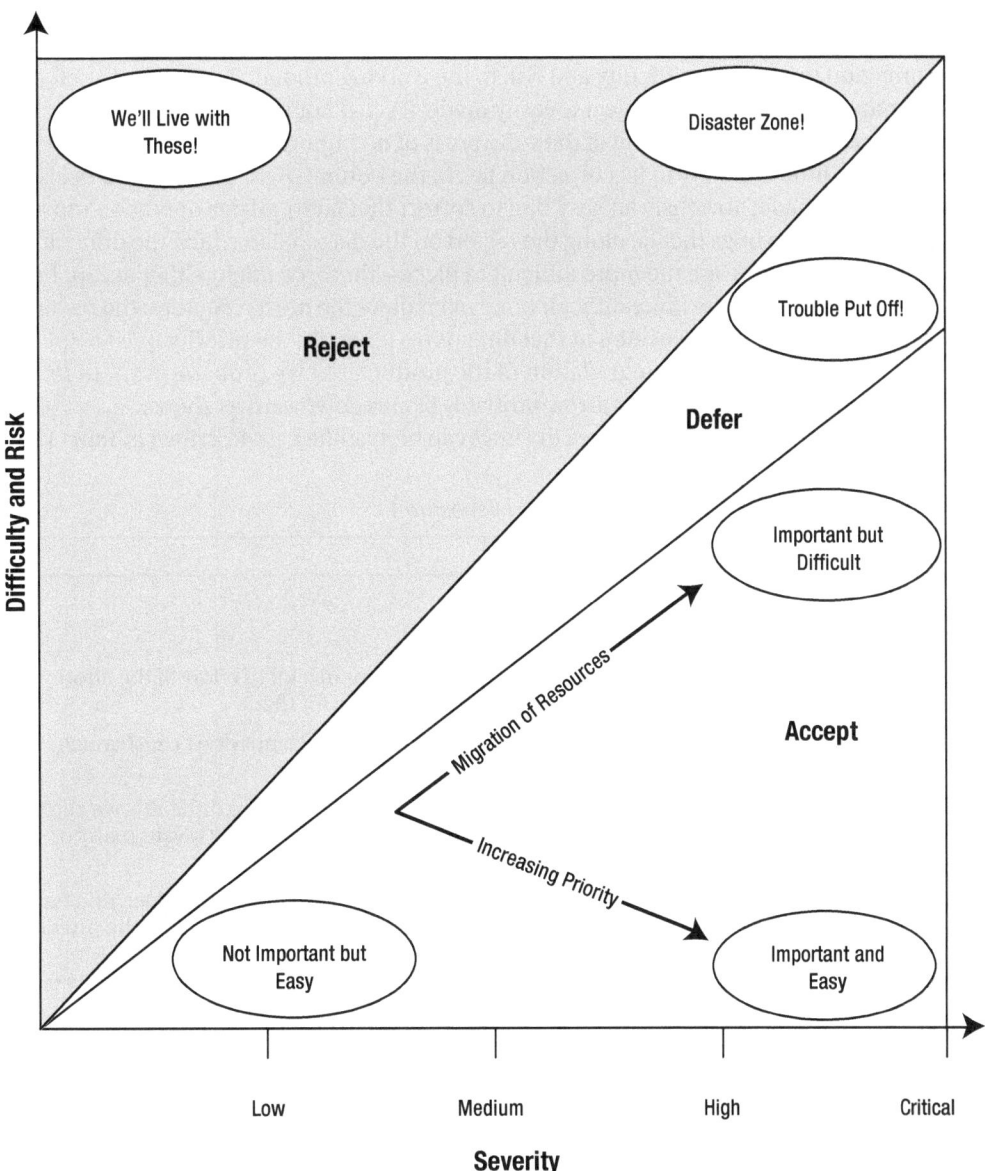

Figure 13-14. *The factors affecting the disposition of a bug at triage*

Generally speaking, there will be thresholds on the diagram that demarcate the regions in which we accept, defer, or reject a bug or a change. Thus, a bug that has low severity and whose correction poses great difficulty and risk to the working product lies in the top-left corner of the graph and a decision to reject is easily made; it's just not worth the effort and risk to fix a bug whose effect on the working of the software is of no importance. A bug that is very severe but poses little difficulty in its correction lies in the bottom-right corner and a decision to accept is easily made; obviously an easy bug to correct that badly affects operation must be fixed right away. Those bugs that lie along the region on the diagonal in which the difficulty is comparable to the severity are the more difficult to place—those we might either accept or defer. If they are accepted, the more difficult ones will require the most resources; the resources arrow shows resources being allocated in that direction. Generally, the priority must be placed on those that cause the greatest degradation of the product, but we probably want to fix the easy-critical ones first, so the priority arrow probably slopes downward as shown.

The ellipses on the diagram show how the bugs can be classified, as described in Table 13.2.

Table 13-2. *Classification of Bugs and Probable Disposition*

Classification	Action
Not important but easy	Fix them, but low priority.
Important and easy	Fix them, at high priority.
Important but difficult	Fix them, at medium priority, but put in a lot of effort. If the effort is not available, it might be better to defer them.
We'll live with these!	These are too difficult and dangerous to fix, but don't cause much trouble. Just leave them.
Trouble put off!	These are going to need fixing, but they are more difficult—we can't put them off for too long. They are a worry; we don't want many of these!
Disaster zone!	These are impossible to fix within the schedule and budget, and have a serious effect on the product. Any of these indicate that the project is heading for failure. Let's hope there are none of them!

Returning to the progress of the bug authored by Rashmi, at the triage meeting all agree that it is indeed a defect and should be accepted with a severity of High with a priority of 3, the highest. Obviously the software could not be used if the extended cost and unit costs were in error in this manner. Nobody can see much difficulty arising from the fixing of this bug—it is probably a simple coding error and Ron suggests that it be assigned to Joe, who did the original coding. It is so assigned and its State is set to Active, Reason Approved.

Regarding the other bugs for consideration (Figure 13-11), some are approved and assigned to developers, but two, 87 and 88, are assigned for investigation. These are both critical bugs and rather worrying at this stage in the project. The team is concerned that they might be difficult to correct, so some investigation is justified before approving them for coding. The list of bugs that have been assigned is shown in Figure 13-15, which is the same report as Figure 13-11 but requested after the assignments have been made.

Figure 13-15. *The assigned bug work items on October 13, 2006*

Investigating the Bug

Joe arrives at 9:00 Monday morning, October 16, and runs his MyActiveBugs query to see if he had any bugs assigned to him on Friday. There's just one. "Unit Cost and Extended Cost transposed," he reads. "But only on the server database, not on the client local database, and only when it's rejected," he notices. Well, this is going to need some careful debugging through the code to see what's really happening.

After a little thought, Joe decides that he does not need to set up two clients to produce an equivalent situation to that described in the test that has failed. He can use a single installation of the Sales Wing program that connects to the Sales web service also hosted on his machine using a copy of the Icarus Enterprise database on his machine as well. The Sales Wing client application will use a different database on his machine acting as the Client Local Database. That way he can adjust the values of the availability figures on the two databases so that an order can be created offline but is rejected when the application is reconnected online.

Joe first sets up the Client Local Database so that there are two spare places at Sanchez Guest House on October 20, 2006, by setting the data table entries for the RESOURCEFREELOCAL table on the Client Local Database to look like Figure 13-16.

ID	RESOURCEID	DATE	NUMBER
1	1	10/20/2006 12:00:00 AM	2
2	1	10/21/2006 12:00:00 AM	8
3	1	10/22/2006 12:00:00 AM	10
4	1	10/22/2006 12:00:00 AM	10
5	1	10/24/2006 12:00:00 AM	10

Figure 13-16. *The RESOURCEFREELOCAL table data rows on the Client Local Database on Joe's machine just prior to creating an offline order*

Sanchez Guest House has a RESOURCEID of 1, so it is the first entry in the table in Figure 13-16 that indicates the number of places available on the specified date of October 20. Remember that this table would have been updated last time the client machine was connected to the ResourceReplWebService and the entries in its NUMBER column are the total capacity, reduced by all the places reserved on that date when the replication to the client last occurred. Next Joe goes through the sequence of creating an offline order, just like steps 4, 5, 6, and 7 of the test that failed in Figure 13-1, and verifies at each step that the Unit Cost and Extended Cost figures are correct. He notes that, in the Orders tab of the Customer Details dialog box, the new order is marked as Tentative and upon opening the Order Detail dialog box, he sees that all is correct.

Next he wants to see exactly what happens when the client is again connected online, so he opens the solution in Visual Studio and sets a breakpoint at the point in the UpdateClient() function in ResourceReplClientBE class that is not reached until the client is found to be online, shown in the upper part of Figure 13-17. While the ClientReplWebService is unreachable, an exception will be thrown, which is caught and results in OnLineMode being set continually to false. Only if an exception is not thrown during the access of the ClientReplWebService will the breakpoint be reached at the point where the OnLineMode is set to True.

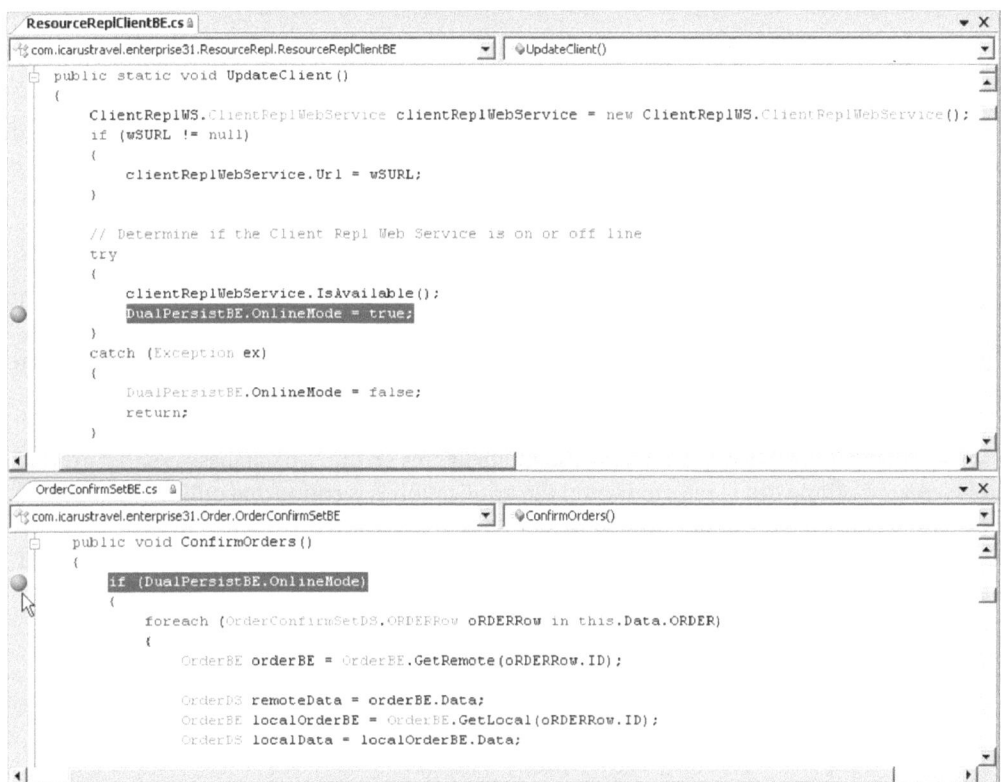

Figure 13-17. *The initial breakpoints set by Joe, before connecting the client online*

Note It is normally bad practice to use the throwing of an exception as part of the normal flow of a piece of code, because throwing an exception takes quite a lot of processing time. In this case, however, it is a quick way of determining if the URL is reachable and is placed at the beginning of a thread function that only executes once every 10 seconds. It is also occurring on the client so it does not affect other users. Nevertheless, a better way of detecting whether the URL is reachable should probably be found.

Joe also sets a breakpoint at the start of the `ConfirmOrders()` function in the `OrderConfirmSetBE` class, shown in the lower part of Figure 13-17. The code will not allow this function to be called in the `ConfirmOrders` thread until the `OnLineMode` flag has been set to true.

Visual Studio provides the capability to attach the debugger to a process that is already running outside of Visual Studio. Joe would like to begin debugging the Sales Wing client application while it is still running. He does this by selecting the Attach to Process option from the Debug menu and then selecting the `SalesWing.exe` process, as shown in Figure 13-18.

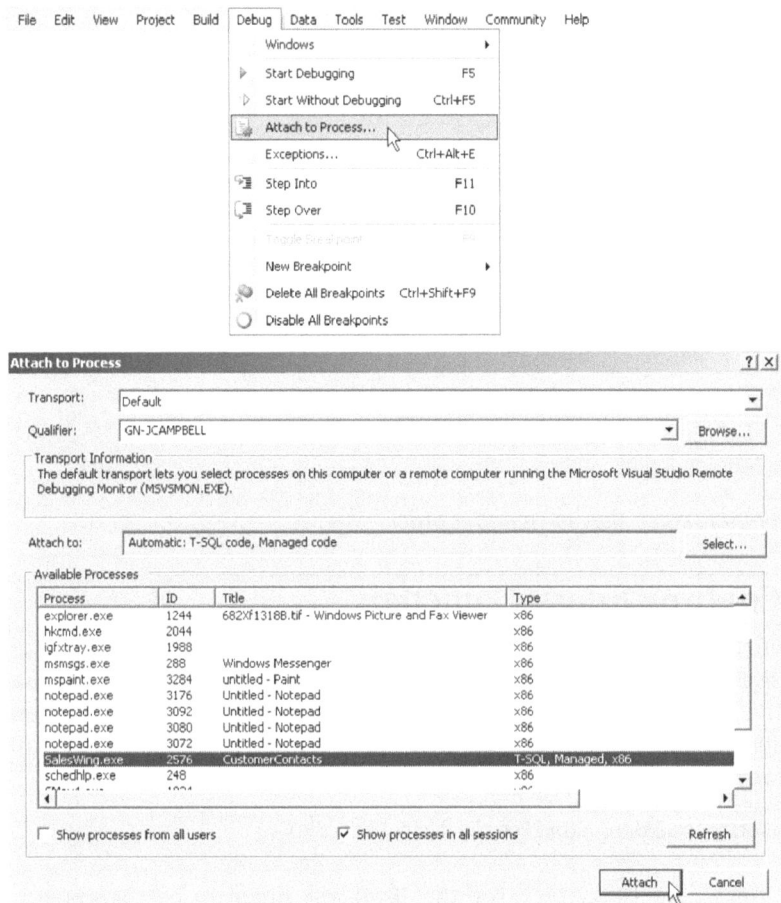

Figure 13-18. *Attaching to the running SalesWing.exe process*

None of the breakpoints are hit as the web services are not yet running on Joe's machine. (Note that the automatic startup of the ASP.NET Development Server must be prevented.) As soon as the two web services ClientReplWebService and SalesWebService are started manually, Joe expects the breakpoint in the ConfirmOrders() function to be hit; the function will proceed to write the tentative orders in the instance of OrderConfirmSetBE to the SalesWebService for confirmation or rejection.

First the breakpoint in UpdateClient is hit as the ClientReplWebService is discovered to be accessible again. Joe presses the run key (F5) to wait until the breakpoint in ConfirmOrders() is hit. He expects the new tentative order to be discovered as a new order, not existing on the server yet, and so he places a breakpoint at the location shown in Figure 13-19 and presses F5 again to find that the new breakpoint is immediately hit.

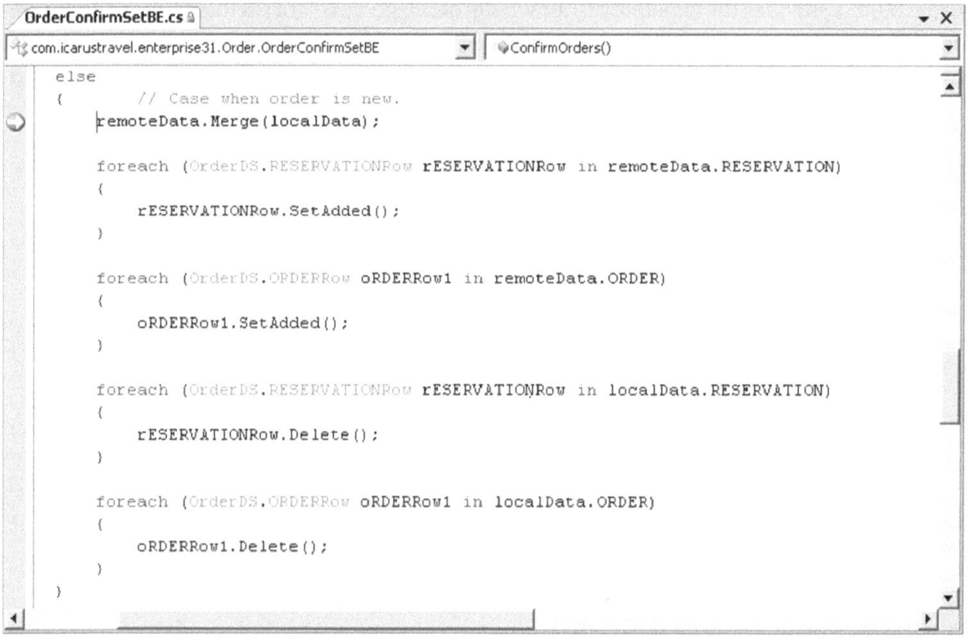

```
else
{           // Case when order is new.
    remoteData.Merge(localData);

    foreach (OrderDS.RESERVATIONRow rESERVATIONRow in remoteData.RESERVATION)
    {
        rESERVATIONRow.SetAdded();
    }

    foreach (OrderDS.ORDERRow oRDERRow1 in remoteData.ORDER)
    {
        oRDERRow1.SetAdded();
    }

    foreach (OrderDS.RESERVATIONRow rESERVATIONRow in localData.RESERVATION)
    {
        rESERVATIONRow.Delete();
    }

    foreach (OrderDS.ORDERRow oRDERRow1 in localData.ORDER)
    {
        oRDERRow1.Delete();
    }
}
```

Figure 13-19. *The breakpoint to catch the new tentative order*

Debugging the ConfirmOrders() Function

The ConfirmOrders() function cycles through all of the orders on the client that are marked as tentative and distinguishes between those orders that do not exist on the server and those that already exist but are tentative, either because they have always been rejected for confirmation or they have been modified offline. The following code determines whether a tentative order on the client is new or already exists on the server:

```
foreach (OrderConfirmSetDS.ORDERRow oRDERRow in this.Data.ORDER)
{
    // Get an OrderBE object from the server for the ID of the order to be confirmed.
    // (It may not exist)
```

```
OrderBE orderBE = OrderBE.GetRemote(oRDERRow.ID);
OrderDS remoteData = orderBE.Data;

// Get the OrderBE object with the same ID from the Client Local Database.
OrderBE localOrderBE = OrderBE.GetLocal(oRDERRow.ID);
OrderDS localData = localOrderBE.Data;

// Does the order exist on the server?
// If so there will be one row in the ORDER table.
if (remoteData.ORDER.Count == 1)
{    // Case when order already exists on server.

  // Code needed to confirm an existing tentative order
}
else
{    // Case when order is new.

  // Code needed to confirm a new tentative order
}

  // Other action after order confirmation
}
```

This code should be clear from the comments. The member function ConfirmOrders() of the OrderConfirmSetBE class makes use of the OrderBE class to confirm each order. It first obtains an instance from the server identified by the ID of the order to be confirmed and then obtains the same order from the client. If the order does not exist on the server, the number of rows in the ORDER table of its dataset will be zero.

The code following this breakpoint handles new orders. The dataset obtained from the local version of the OrderBE object is called localData and contains the new tentative order. The code merges this with the remoteData dataset obtained from the remote OrderBE object, which is not present on the server. The code then sets all of the Order and Reservation rows to the Added state, and then deletes all of the rows for the tentative order in the local dataset, both in the ORDER and the RESERVATION tables.

There is nothing here likely to transpose the fields, so Joe quickly steps through this code. He then reaches the code that saves the new order to the SalesWebService and saves the local version of the order with its rows deleted. This deletion of the local order is conditional on a successful save to the server.

```
orderBE.SaveRemote();

if (orderBE.SaveStatus == OrderSaveStatus.SaveOK)
{
  localOrderBE.SaveLocal();
}
```

Joe decides to execute this and then check the contents of the server and local databases to see that they are correct. After execution of the SaveLocal function he looks at the ORDER and RESERVATION tables in the server database, as shown in Figure 13-20.

ORDER: Query(g...ss.Enterprise) ▾ ✕

ID	CONTROLLEDOBJECTID	CUSTOMERID	ORDERDATE	TENTATIVE
1	300	1	1/12/2003 12:00:00 AM	NULL
2	301	1	1/14/2003 12:00:00 AM	NULL
3	302	2	1/16/2003 12:00:00 AM	NULL
4	303	2	1/18/2003 12:00:00 AM	NULL
1000	1000	2	10/16/2006 12:00:00 AM	True
NULL	NULL	NULL	NULL	NULL

◄◄ ◄ | 5 of 5 | ▶ ▶| ▶ (▣)

RESERVATION: Q...ss.Enterprise) ▾ ✕

ID	RESOURCEAVAILABILITYID	ORDERID	UNITCOUNT	UNITCOST	EXTENDEDCOST
1	1	1	1	100.0000	100.0000
2	2	1	1	100.0000	100.0000
3	10	2	1	100.0000	100.0000
4	11	2	1	100.0000	100.0000
5	1	3	1	100.0000	100.0000
6	2	3	1	100.0000	100.0000
7	10	4	2	100.0000	200.0000
8	11	4	2	100.0000	200.0000
1000	20	1000	2	100.0000	200.0000
NULL	NULL	NULL	NULL	NULL	NULL

◄◄ ◄ | 9 of 9 | ▶ ▶| ▶ (▣)

Figure 13-20. *The ORDER and RESERVATION tables on the server after the ConfirmOrders() function has completed*

This looks correct, since the new order has been placed on the server and given a new order number 1000 with the Tentative field set to True as there will not be enough resource availability for it to be confirmed. A row has been added in the RESERVATION table with the foreign key field ORDERID set to 1000, and the values of the UNITCOST and EXTENDED cost fields are correct; they have not been swapped.

No problems so far. Joe expects at this point that the tentative order will have been deleted on the client, so he checks the Client Local Database ORDER table and confirms that this is so. Next he expects the tentative order on the server to be replicated onto the client with the new ID number, so he places a breakpoint at the beginning of the section of the UpdateClient() function of the ResourceReplClientBE class so that he can follow the replication process in detail. Joe presses F5 to let it run to that point. He then steps through the code until he comes to the loop in the following code snippet that handles each order for the customer obtained from the server. He steps around the loop until the order ID matches that shown in the server database for the new tentative order. The line of code with the Select function call determines if a row exists in the Client Local Database with the same ID as in the server database; since this is a new row, he expects the // New order action path to be taken.

```
for (serverIndex = 0;
            serverIndex < orderReplSvrDS.ORDERCOLLECTION.Rows.Count; serverIndex++)
{
```

```
int iD = orderReplSvrDS.ORDERCOLLECTION[serverIndex].ID;

OrderReplClientDS.ORDERRow[] rows =
                    (OrderReplClientDS.ORDERRow[])orderReplClientDS.ORDER.Select(
                                        "ID = '" + iD.ToString() + "'");
if (rows.Length > 1)
   throw new Exception("Internal Error: Excessive rows in client resource table.");

if (rows.Length == 1)
{
   // Modified order action
}
else
{
   // New order action
}
}
```

Joe continues to single-step through this code, verifying that the `// New order action` path is followed and the new order and its reservation are correctly written to the Client Local Database. At this point the rows are correct in both the server and client local databases. Joe gets a strong cup of coffee. What *is* going on here?

Having found no problem so far, Joe resolves to continue debugging the `ConfirmOrders()` function, and places a breakpoint at its beginning to see what happens when it is called subsequent to the first attempt to confirm the tentative order. This time, as the code loops to deal with each tentative order on the client, Joe sees that it finds an existing order with a matching ID on the server database. This is expected since the order has already been copied to the server during the rejected confirmation attempt. The client is again attempting to synchronize the order as, having been rejected, it is still marked as Tentative on the client. This synchronization will update the server with any changes to the client and also reattempt confirmation. The code is the same as was listed at the start of this section, but this time it is the action for the existing order that is executed. Joe single-steps through the code, which first updates the order data and then updates the set of reservations belonging to the order. For each reservation in the client version of the order, it either updates a reservation if it already exists or adds a new reservation. There is code later in the `ConfirmOrders()` function to delete any reservations on the server that no longer exist on the client.

Joe steps through until he comes to the highlighted lines. Ah, there's the problem! Somehow the statements copying the UNITCOST fields and EXTENDEDCOST fields have become switched, probably as a result of some copy-and-paste action during coding.

```
foreach (OrderDS.RESERVATIONRow rESERVATIONRow in localData.RESERVATION)
{
   OrderDS.RESERVATIONRow[] reservationRows =
      (OrderDS.RESERVATIONRow[])remoteData.RESERVATION.Select(
                                      "ID = '" + rESERVATIONRow.ID.ToString() + "'");
   if (reservationRows.Length == 1)
   {
      // Case when reservation exists and may have been modified
```

```
      reservationRows[0].EXTENDEDCOST = rESERVATIONRow.UNITCOST;
      reservationRows[0].UNITCOST = rESERVATIONRow.EXTENDEDCOST;
      reservationRows[0].UNITCOUNT = rESERVATIONRow.UNITCOUNT;
   }
   else
   {
      // Action to add a new reservation
   }
}
```

This sort of mistake is easily made when repetitive code is written to assign fields in dataset objects to fields in other dataset objects. This code would only have executed when a tentative order existed in the Client Local Database and also on the server, which is a situation that only occurs when an order has been rejected and remains tentative on the server and is replicated as tentative on the client. In such circumstances, the order is copied to the server each time the ConfirmOrders() function executes. With this bug, the two fields will be transposed each time the order is copied. When the order is replicated back to the client, it will be replicated in the transposed state and the fields switched back again when the ConfirmOrders() function runs again. Thus the version on the server and client would be expected to flip between the correct and transposed state each time these two functions execute. It was apparently just chance that caused the tester to observe the correct value on the client and incorrect value on the server; the results could have been the opposite way around, correct on the server and incorrect on the client.

Fixing the Bug

Fixing this bug is obviously going to be a simple matter! Joe opens the file OrderConfirmSetBE.cs and makes the code correction, which automatically checks it out. The two highlighted lines earlier now become

```
reservationRows[0].EXTENDEDCOST = rESERVATIONRow.EXTENDEDCOST;
reservationRows[0].UNITCOST = rESERVATIONRow.UNITCOST;
```

He goes to the Pending Changes window, selects the Work Items tab, and associates the changes to be checked in with the bug that he has fixed, as shown in Figure 13-21. Joe then selects the file for inclusion in the changeset, as shown in Figure 13-22, and clicks the Check In button.

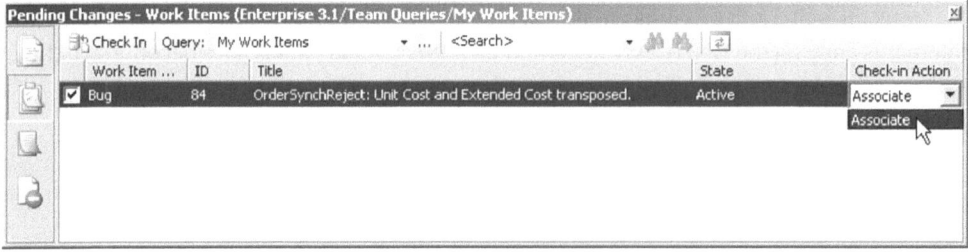

Figure 13-21. *Checking in the changes for the bug fix—associating the work item*

Pending Changes - Source Files - Workspace: JosephI7
Check In
Shelve
Unshelve
Workspace: JosephI7
Comment:
Check In
Bug fixed, one code change.
Name
Change
Folder
OrderConfirmSetBE.cs
edit
F:\Workspaces\JosephCampbell\Iteration 7\Enterprise 3.1\OrderBE

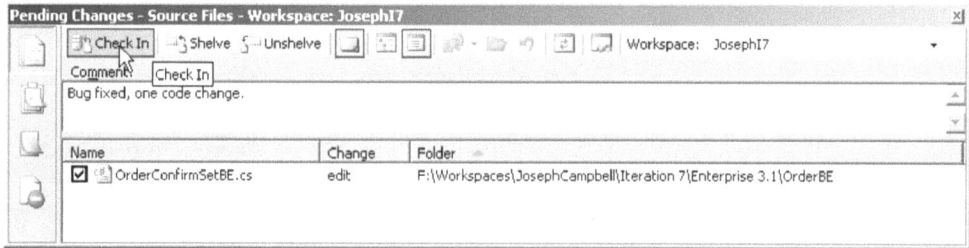

Figure 13-22. *Checking in the changes for the bug fix—checking in the file*

Joe then opens the bug work item 84 and completes some details of the fix, changing State to Resolved and Reason to Fixed. Then he assigns it back to Rashmi for retesting, as shown in Figure 13-23. Just as a check he clicks on the Links tab and opens the linked changeset (Figure 13-24). Yes, the files are correct—just the one—and he verifies the changes are there by right-clicking on the file and selecting Compare ➤ With Previous Version. Here he can see the changes that went into the file on a line-by-line basis.

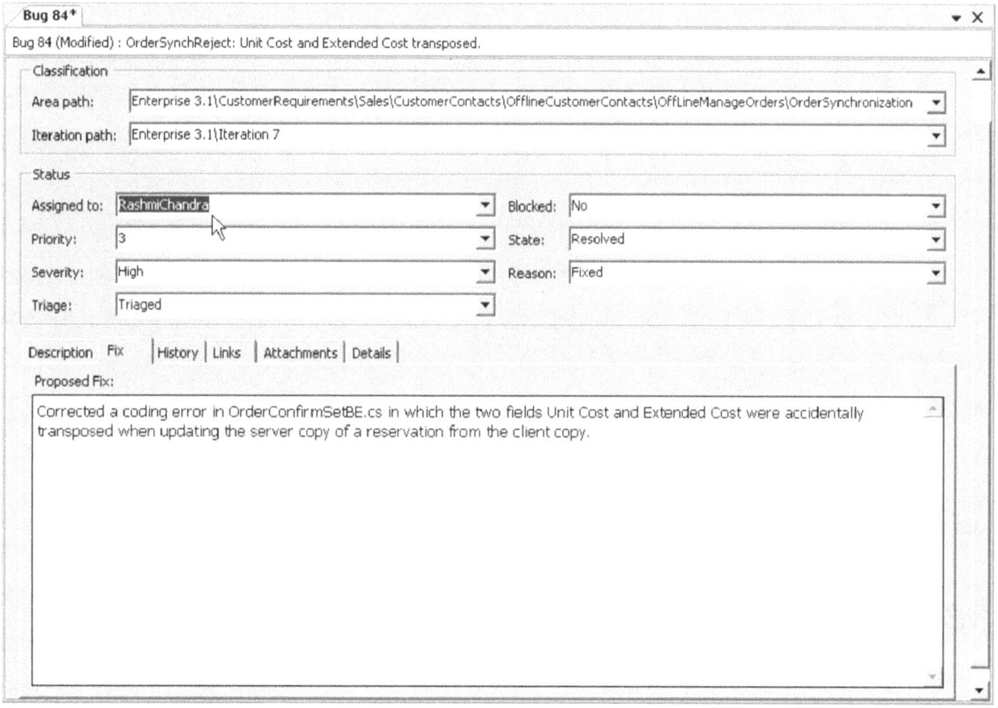

Bug 84*
Bug 84 (Modified) : OrderSynchReject: Unit Cost and Extended Cost transposed.
Classification
Area path: Enterprise 3.1\CustomerRequirements\Sales\CustomerContacts\OfflineCustomerContacts\OffLineManageOrders\OrderSynchronization
Iteration path: Enterprise 3.1\Iteration 7
Status
Assigned to: RashmiChandra
Blocked: No
Priority: 3
State: Resolved
Severity: High
Reason: Fixed
Triage: Triaged
Description
Fix
History
Links
Attachments
Details
Proposed Fix:
Corrected a coding error in OrderConfirmSetBE.cs in which the two fields Unit Cost and Extended Cost were accidentally transposed when updating the server copy of a reservation from the client copy.

Figure 13-23. *Checking in the changes for the bug fix—completing the work item*

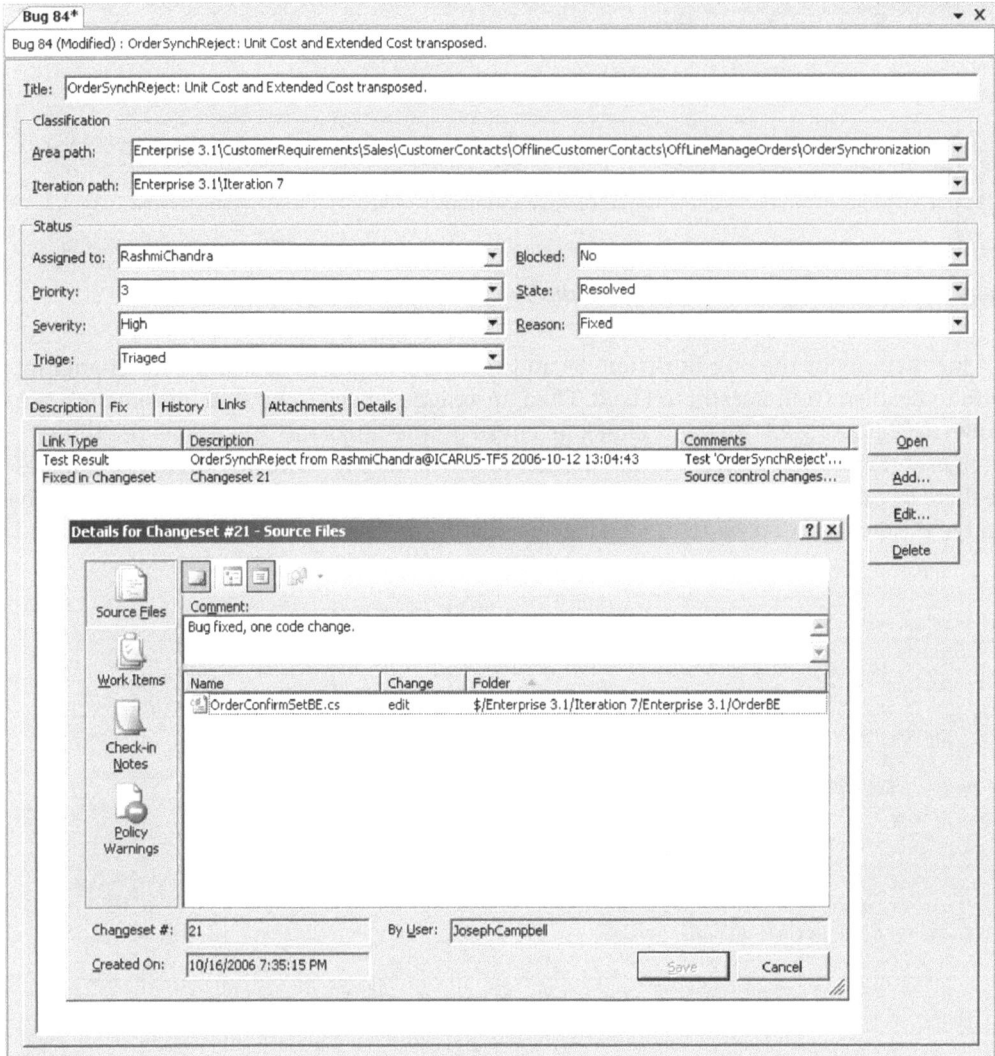

Figure 13-24. *Checking in the changes for the bug fix—viewing the changeset*

The Daily Build

Ron performs the daily build every morning between 9:00 and 10:00. First he routinely checks the history of the entire code base by displaying the Source Control Explorer window, right-clicking on the root of the code base, iteration 7, and selecting History from the context menu. This displays the history as shown in Figure 13-25. The team is keeping each iteration in a different folder in source control, and the Administrator entry at the start of the iteration was the addition of the code base from iteration 6 to form the starting point for this iteration. Changeset 19 will be Rashmi checking in her latest test, and the rest will be the developers fixing bugs.

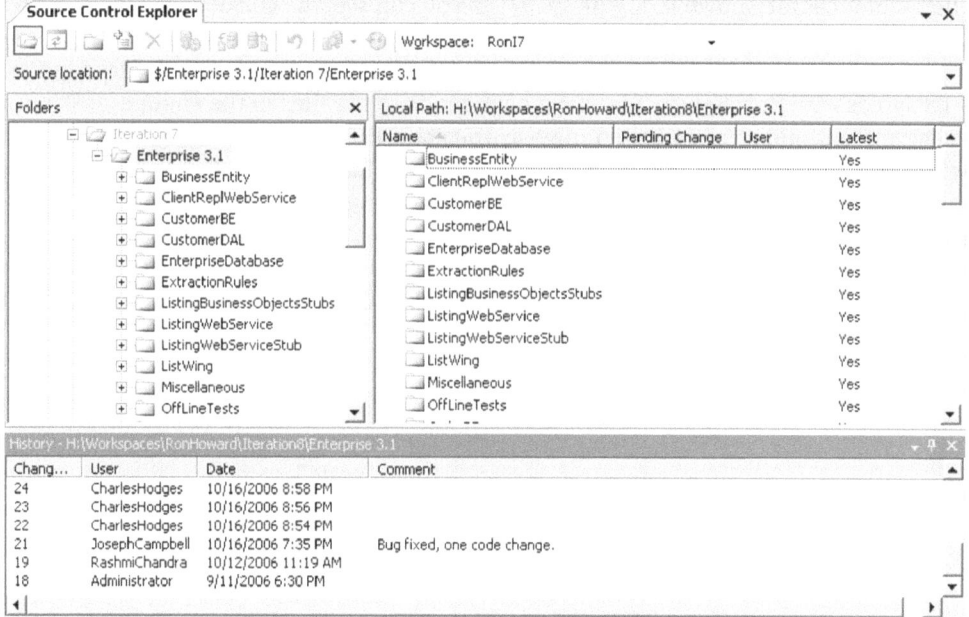

Figure 13-25. *Looking at the history before doing the daily build*

Ron reviews each of these changesets by double-clicking on each changeset in the history and viewing the changeset details, which show the files that have been changed. He looks at the changes in the files by right-clicking on the files in the changesets and selecting Compare ➤ With Previous Version from the context menu, as shown in Figure 13-26.

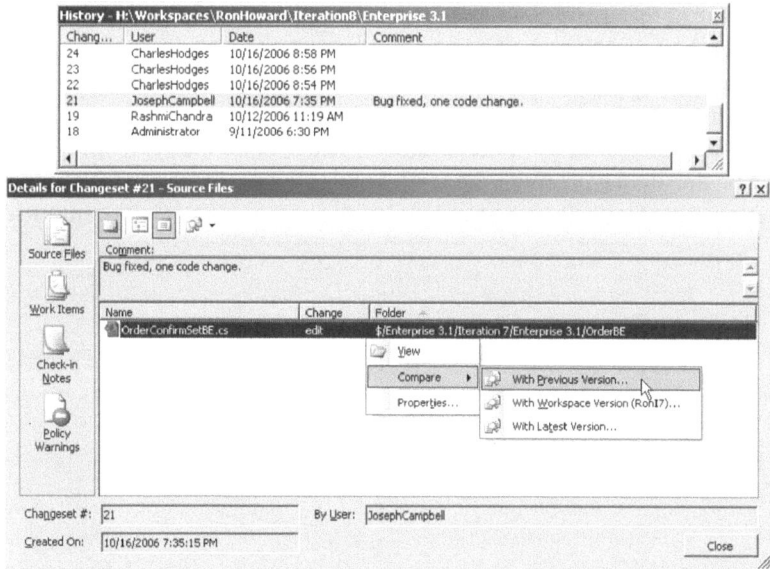

Figure 13-26. *Viewing the changeset details and selecting a comparison with the previous version*

The differences are shown in Figure 13-27. As you can see, the correction of the simple error is properly done. In the changeset window shown in Figure 13-26, Ron can also click on the work items and verify that the bug work item has been filled out correctly and that the description of the fix agrees with the changes that have been made to the files in the changeset. This is the review process, and it can be as thorough as you choose. For a complex bug, it is difficult for the reviewer to completely understand exactly how the bug has been fixed and to be sure that the fix is complete and does not disrupt other functionality. Nevertheless, in a project where no expense is to be spared to achieve the highest quality, the review can be very thorough. Once the reviewer is satisfied, and Ron simply verifies that the changes all look related to the bug and seem reasonable, he clicks on the Check-in Notes tab of the Changeset dialog box and adds his reviewer's comments.

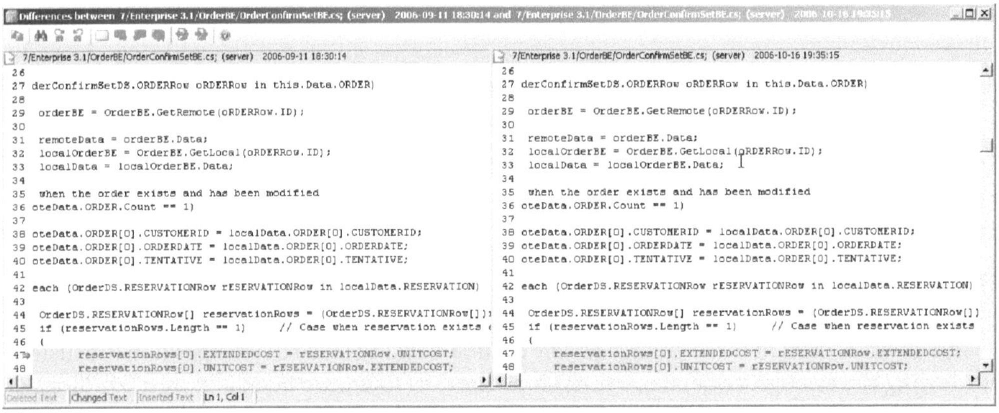

Figure 13-27. *Comparison with the previous version—looking at Joe's changes for approval*

Once Ron has reviewed all of the changesets, he is ready to begin the build, using the build type already defined for the iteration. He starts the build by right-clicking on the build type in the Team Explorer window and selecting Build Team Project Enterprise 3.1. He clicks Build in the resulting Build dialog box and waits until the build is complete. In the build report (Figure 13-28), the associated changesets and associated work items appear. The list of builds can always be viewed by double-clicking on the build type under the Team Builds folder in Team Explorer. When a build is made, Team System automatically applies a label to the solution and all its contents.

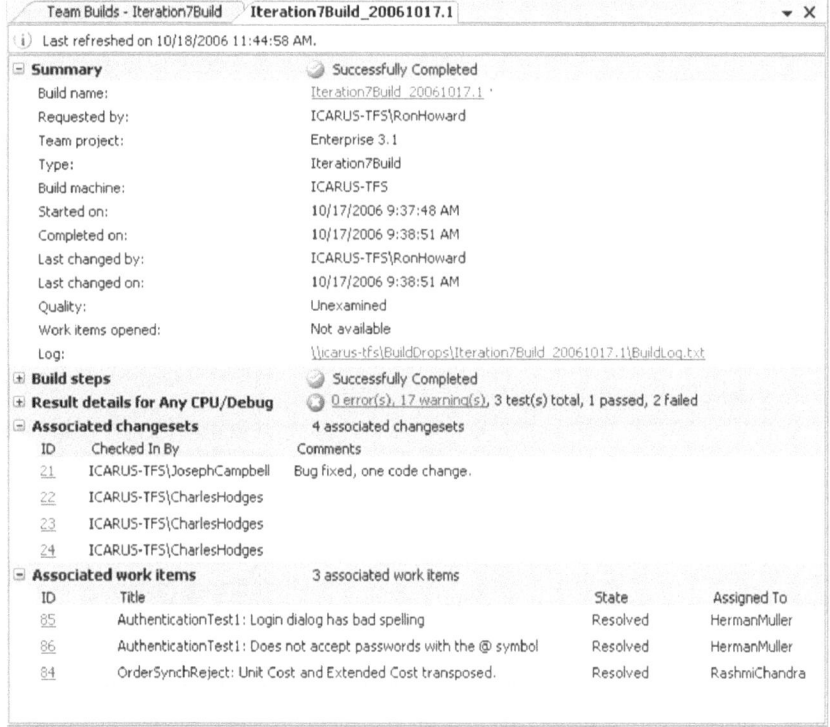

Figure 13-28. *Build report for the daily build of October 17, 2006*

Testing the Bug Fixes

There is now a set of fixes in the new daily build for Rashmi and the other testers to verify. For example Bug 84 that was resolved by Joe needs to be verified by the tester as having been corrected. Rashmi runs through the same manual test, and sees that now everything is correct, so she opens the bug work item 84 by double-clicking on the Resolved Bugs query in the Team Queries folder in Team Explorer. She selects bug 84 from the list and changes State to Closed as shown in Figure 13-29. The Reason field automatically changes to Fixed.

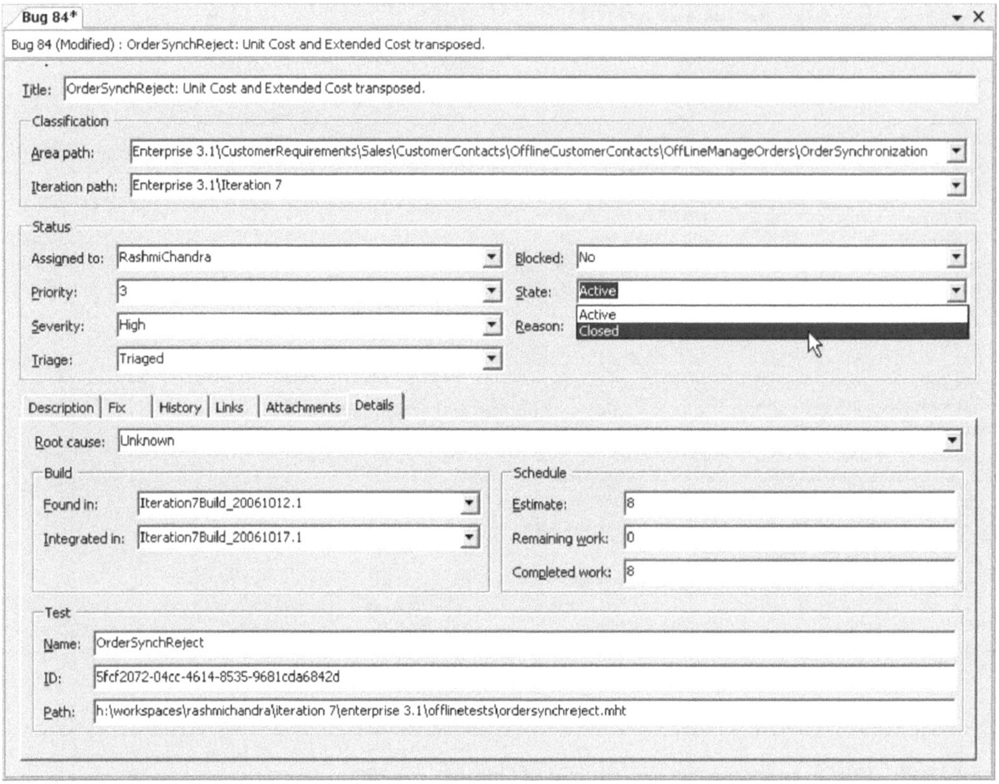

Figure 13-29. *Marking the bugs as closed, once the tester has verified the fix*

We haven't looked at the Details tab on this bug yet and, in Figure 13-29, you can see that the Found In and Integrated In builds are shown. Rashmi selected the Found In build identifier when she created the bug, but Team System automatically entered the Integrated In build when Ron performed the build that contained code associated with this bug work item. Joe manually filled in the Estimate, Remaining Work, and Completed Work fields, but Team System added the Test information at the bottom automatically when Rashmi created the bug from a test result, as shown in Figure 13-9.

If you haven't had enough of bug 84, you can look at the history of its rise to notoriety and inglorious defeat in Figure 13-30. The bug has followed the standard route through Figure 13-13. Scanning the events from bottom to top in Figure 13-30, we see first its creation and subsequent editing by Rashmi on October 12—the edit would have been when she added the screen shot as an attachment. Then on October 13 at the triage meeting it was approved and changed from Proposed to Active by Ron. Later on October 16, after Joe had found and corrected the code error, it was associated with the changeset containing the modified file. This happened automatically during the check-in action depicted in Figures 13-21 and 13-22 as a result of the association made in Figure 13-21. Then, a little while later on the same date, Joe completed the details on its work item screen by changing its State setting to Resolved and adding some notes about the fix. Then on October 17, Ron ran the build, which included this bug type work item, and the bug was automatically updated to show that it was fixed in that team build. Finally on October 17, Rashmi reran the test and verified the fix, changing the State setting of the bug to Closed and setting the Reason option to Fixed.

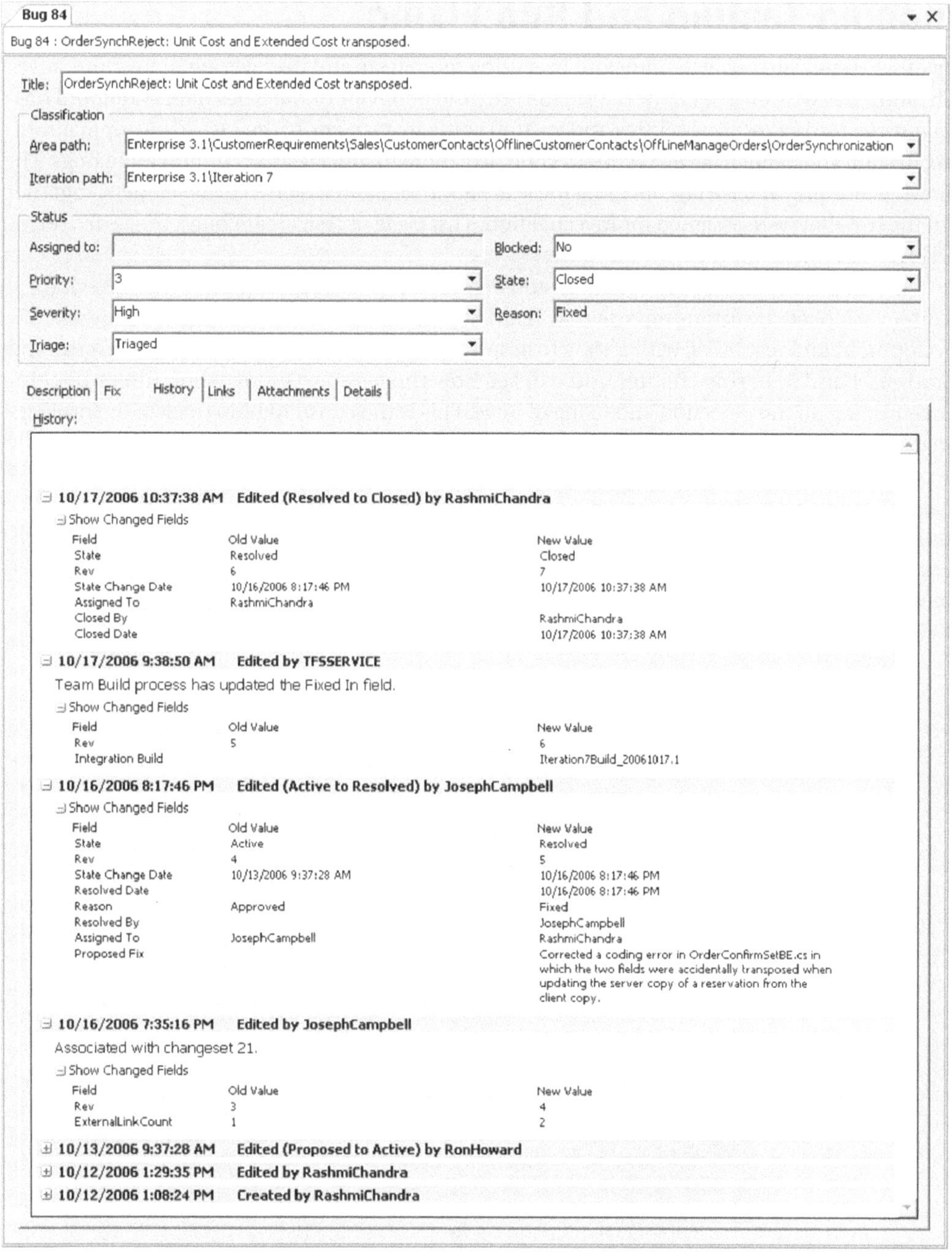

Figure 13-30. *The rise and fall of bug 84*

Herman assigns the other two resolved bugs, numbers 85 and 86, to another tester, Sahana, working with Rashmi for verification of their fixes. She finds that these have all been properly corrected and changes their State to Closed and Reason to Fixed.

Ongoing Testing and Bug Fixing

The other testers are busily writing and executing more tests and discovering many more bugs. Rob Smith has written a set of web tests to verify the behavior of the Sales Site, and Rahul has taken some testing responsibilities and written some tests to verify the List Wing application. Also, Rashmi and Sahana have executed a good deal more manual tests and found more bugs. The following morning in the triage meeting these are approved and assigned to developers, together with the two that were assigned for investigation. This cycle of test, create bugs, triage, fix, retest, and close continues for the next few days.

On October 24, Clare, Ron, Herman, and Peter meet to review progress. In the previous chapter we looked at various reports that Team System can produce showing the progress of development and test tasks, with a view to assessing the development as it proceeded through iterations 4 and 5. In this chapter you will see how those reports look when the project is concentrating on the detection and fixing of bugs. This is the consolidation track of the project, and it is important to follow things like bug rates and code churn to get a measure of how quickly the project is reaching a stable state. First, the group looks at the Remaining Work report filtered to show just bug work items in iteration 7. You can see this in Figure 13-31, where the top shaded area shows the number of active bugs as they vary with time, the area below shows the resolved bugs, and the bottom area represents the closed bugs. Clare can click on the Active area to see which bugs are still outstanding and who is responsible for them, as shown in Figure 13-32.

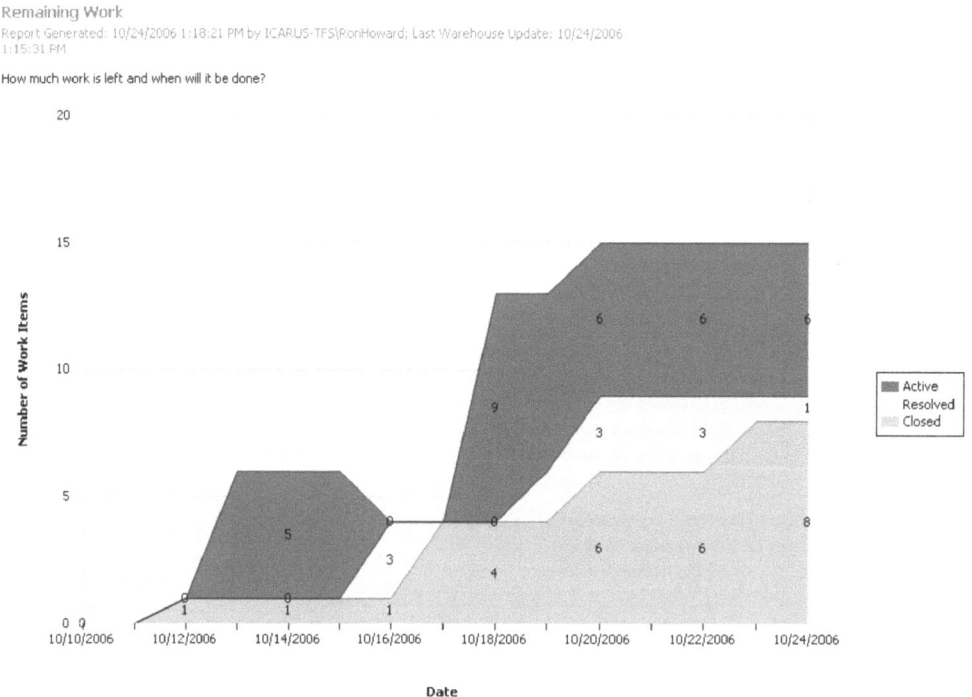

Figure 13-31. *Remaining work on October 24 2006, filtered to show only iteration 7 bugs in the offline order area*

Work Items by State
Report Generated: 10/24/2006 1:23:46 PM by ICAPUS-TFS\RonHoward; Last Warehouse Update: 10/24/2006 1:21:32 PM

How many active, resolved and closed work items do we have?

State ⇕	Total ⇕	Remaining Hours ⇕	Completed Hours ⇕			
⊟ Active	6	12	0			
ID ⇕	Assigned To ⇕	Rem. Hrs. ⇕	Reason ⇕	WI Type ⇕	Priority ⇕	Title
90	JosephCampbell	4	Approved	Bug	2	ResourceReplTest1: Resource Availability on client has incorrect value.
93	JosephCampbell	8	Approved	Bug	2	OrderSynchReject4: Wrong behavior with deleted reservation.
94	JoseRodriguez	0	Approved	Bug	2	OrderSynchReject2: Wrong behavior with added reservation.
95	JoseRodriguez	0	Approved	Bug	3	OrderSynchConfirm3: Wrong behavior with modified unit count.
96	EdwardMarshall	0	Approved	Bug	3	CreateOrderTest2: Order List Was Incorrect
97	EdwardMarshall	0	Approved	Bug	3	CreateOrderTest3: Reservations were incorrectly ordered.

Figure 13-32. *Active bugs on October 24, 2006*

It looks like Ed and Jose have finished the work since there are zero remaining hours, but they may have just forgotten to enter a value in this field on the work item. If you are going to use these figures, you must be quite strict in getting the team members to complete them. Another useful graph is the Bug Rates graph. An example is shown in Figure 13-33, for just the Customer Management testing, which is the work of one developer and tester.

This graph has three lines. The upper one (it would appear red on your screen) with the square plot points gives the current number of bugs in the Active state plotted for each day in the chosen range. The line with the round plot points (yellow on the screen) gives the number of new or reactivated bugs on each day. This represents a *rate* of discovery of bugs and gives the number of bugs discovered per day. The line with the diamond-shaped points (green on the screen) shows the bugs resolved in each day. Again, this is a *rate* graph giving the rate of fixing bugs measured in bugs fixed per day. For the mathematically inclined, the time derivative of the Active value at any point in time is obviously equal to the New and Reactivated graph minus the Resolved graph. It is clear from this graph that the project is proceeding in the right direction. The New and Reactivated line, although rather erratic, certainly has a downward trend and the resolved curve is averaging around one or two bugs per day. Why is the New and Reactivated graph so erratic? Probably this is because the testers are not running many tests per day because they are busy designing and writing tests; thus there tends to be a group of bugs found on one day and then nothing for two or three days.

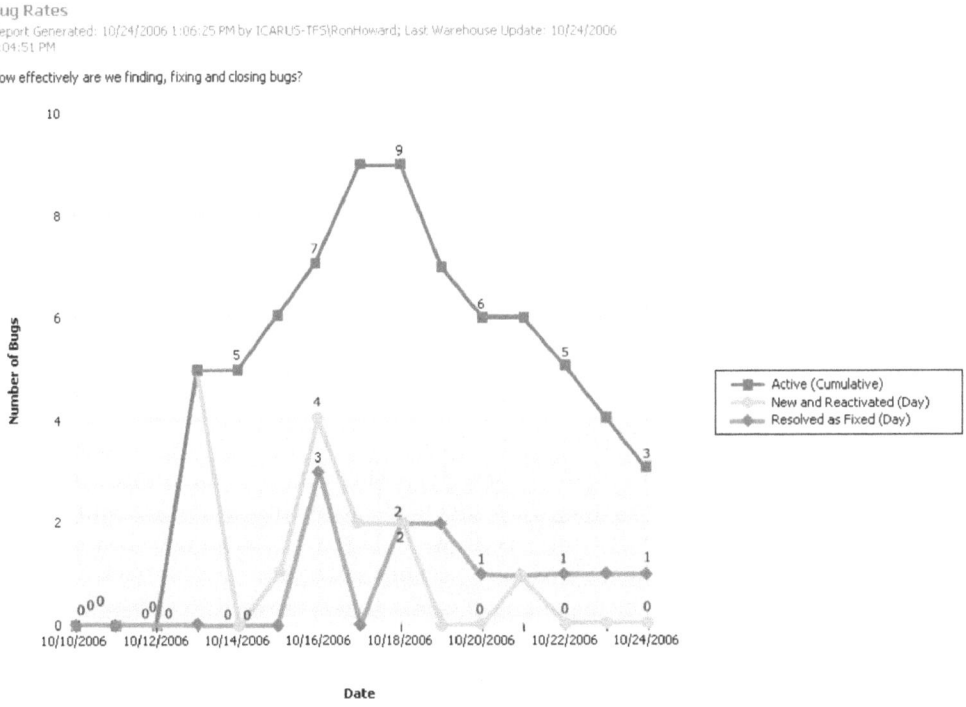

Figure 13-33. *Bug Rates on October 24, 2006, for the customer management area*

The Quality Indicators graph is another useful graph to see the trend of the project. An example is shown in Figure 13-34, again for just the customer management area, the work of one tester. It shows a set of quality indicators plotted against time; on each day the following set of indicators is plotted:

- Code Churn: The number of lines in the code base that change due to check-ins on the given date.

- Active Bugs: The number of bug work items currently in the Active state on the given date.

- Percentage Code Coverage: If code coverage is enabled for unit tests, this is the percentage of code coverage for unit tests in the latest test run on or before the given date.

- Tests Passed: The number of tests passed in the latest test run on or before the given date.

- Tests Inconclusive: The number of tests inconclusive in the latest test run on or before the date.

- Tests Failed: The number of tests failed in the latest test run on or before the given date.

Looking at this graph in Figure 13-34, we can see that the total number of tests executed each day rises to 4, then 13, then 16. During the period in which four tests are being executed each day, initially they all fail; then on October 15, one test passes and on October 16, two tests pass. By October 17, the number of tests is increased to 13 and 5 are passing. Then from October 19 onward 16 tests are run each day with a gradual day-by-day increase in the tests passed. So again this looks promising. Extrapolating the Active Bugs curve, we can estimate that the bugs in this area will be fixed in another three days.

What about code churn—that's the line with the square plot points that peaks up to 22 on October 17. From then on it shows a downward trend, meaning that the lines of code modified with each changeset is reducing. Again this is proceeding in the right direction. It looks as though the quality of this area of the project is steadily improving. The tests on this graph do not include code coverage, so that value stays at zero all the time.

Clare, Peter, Herman, and Ron look carefully at these graphs for different areas of the project and also the corresponding graphs for total project.

"I can't help wondering if we are really testing this product thoroughly enough," says Peter. "We are only executing 16 tests for customer management. That does not seem enough somehow."

"Well, we are testing all of the scenarios that were defined," says Herman.

"You mean you have only one test for each scenario?" asks Peter. "Are there any multiuser scenarios?"

"There were none defined," Herman points out.

"What about thread safety and transactions and other multiuser issues?"

"No, we are just testing basic functional scenarios—create a user, modify a user—things like that."

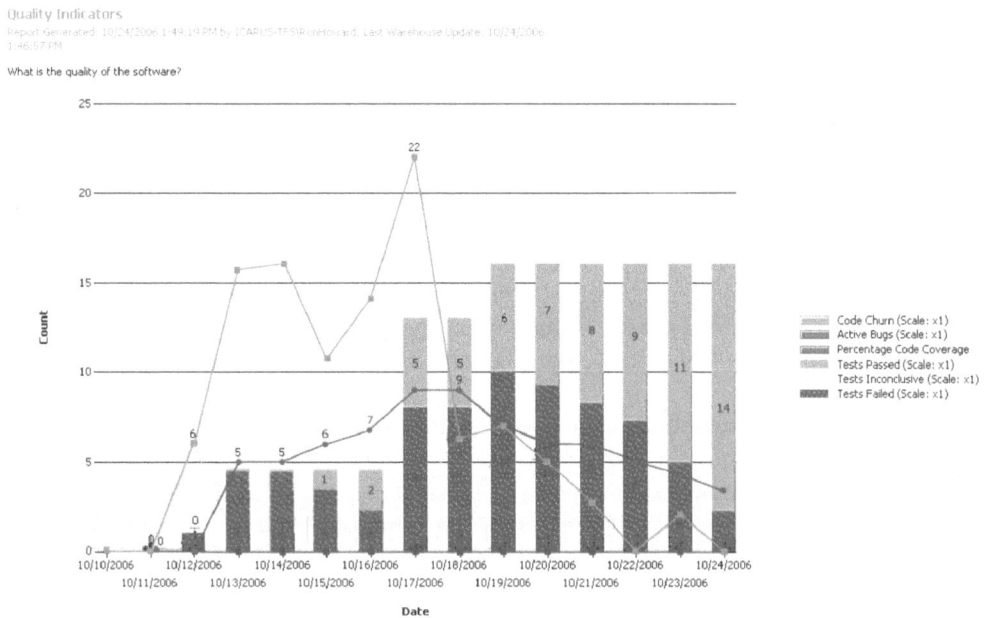

Figure 13-34. *Quality indicators on October 24, 2006, for the customer management area*

"Well, I'm really worried," Clare adds with a very serious look at Peter. "This is a very critical project for Icarus, you know, Herman. This has got to work as soon as we install it." She looks at Peter again. "Peter, what about performance?"

"We've been too busy with all the changes to offline working, frankly," he explains. "I was going to get Angela working on performance testing, but she and Joe have just been too busy sorting out all this order synchronization complication. To be honest I wish that had never happened!"

"Well, Icarus did press that change on us," admits Clare. She sighs deeply. "I think we have to give testing the absolute priority for iteration 8. Some of the developers that we were going to let go onto other projects need to work hard on writing more tests for a few weeks."

"So we're all going to be testers now," says Ron brightly.

"That's what's needed," agrees Peter.

So the testing effort has been a little underestimated. The quality indicators look good, but everyone knows that not enough tests are being carried out. It takes a long time to write tests, and there are many creative ways that the system needs to be exercised if the risk of deployment is to be minimized. Right at the start Icarus management made it clear that success with this project could be make or break Icarus, so the team cannot afford to deploy a partially tested product. The Team System reporting tools have clearly indicated the number of tests that are being carried out, and now the team needs to increase that number and still keep those quality indicators moving in the right direction.

"We must get everyone focused on quality now," says Clare.

"Yeah, we've got to really concentrate on stressing the product in all kinds of ways—multiuser, multithread—all those kinds of things," adds Peter.

"Let's organize a team meeting to get everyone focused on the same goal then," says Clare as they leave the meeting.

Everybody's a Tester

The next morning on Wednesday all the developers and testers file into the conference room for a full team meeting. Clare explains in very serious terms that the testing is not far enough along and that although product quality is good, it needs to have more diverse and thorough testing.

"We've thought of a plan," she reassures them. "For the next month we are all going to be testers, and we are going to be imaginative testers."

"What we want to do," says Peter, "is have everyone think of as many ways that they can to try to break the product. Install the product on your machine and try everything you can think of."

"Then when you find something wrong," continues Ron, "write down the scenario carefully and Herman's people will make it into a test."

"We want you to also work in pairs, and try to see what happens in multiple-user situations," adds Peter. "At the same time, I'm going to work with Herman and Rob Smith to develop some really thorough load tests that will verify the functionality under load when IIS is generating lots of threads."

There is general agreement all around the room. Most people feel that the complexity of the product has increased and were uncertain of its behavior. There is a good deal of relief that testing is going to be handled more thoroughly.

Summary

In this chapter you had a glimpse of the consolidation phase of the project in iteration 7, which is the second from last. You also saw the execution of a manual test for a complex piece of functionality and the creation of a bug as a work item.

We then discussed the triage process for bugs, and you followed the progress of the same bug through to its assignment to a developer. The developer debugged the code in detail to find and correct the cause of the bug, and we traced the process of correcting and retesting the bug in Team System.

You learned about the charts available from Team System for tracking progress in testing, the finding of bugs, and their correction. We discussed the relationship of these charts to the evolution of the product quality. Finally, we stressed the importance of having sufficient tests of a diverse nature and getting everyone on the team involved in product quality.

In the next and final chapter, you will see the completion of testing and deployment of the product, along with some final thoughts about the project.

CHAPTER 14

Releasing the Product

This chapter traces the final stage in the Icarus project in which the software moves through the release stages and ultimately to deployment.

The Process Guidance

MSF CMMI describes the release process in the Release a Product work stream process guidance page, which you can see on your team portal or download from Microsoft. We will look at how the activities in this work stream relate to the project and the team and how the technologies in Visual Studio 2005 can be used to assist in carrying them out. Later we will examine some of the steps in detail.

Establish a User Acceptance Test (UAT) Environment

The Establish a User Acceptance Test (UAT) Environment activity consists of determining the equipment required for user acceptance test and then commissioning it prior to the beginning of the test. In this project, after UAT, the UAT hardware system will become the staging system to allow any issues to be resolved prior to production rollout.

Earlier in this book we mentioned that only two versions of the orchestration server existed at Icarus: the production and staging environments. For user acceptance testing, it will be necessary to verify that the new software written for `SalesBusinessObjects` and `ListingBusinessObjects` works correctly with the `OrchestrationServiceStub` and `PaymentServiceStub`. During the staging period after UAT, integration will take place with `OrchestrationService` and its back-end services, `EmailService`, `DocumentService`, and `AccountingJournalService`, shown in Chapter 5, Figure 5-18. This will be done using the Icarus staging orchestration server. During the latter part of iteration 7, the team has been testing this capability using the `OrchestrationServiceStub`, also shown in Figure 5-18. Peter and another member of the development team will travel to Icarus to install the release candidate on the UAT/Staging environment. All members of the team are very busy with the final bug fixing work that is occupying the team during iteration 8 as they move toward a release candidate.

They hope that the system can be installed very quickly on the UAT/Staging environment. Peter plans to use the deployment design features of Visual Studio 2005 Team Edition for Architects to model the UAT/Staging environment as a logical data center and verify deployment. He designs this UAT data center fairly early and delivers a detailed specification to Icarus so that the technicians can install the operating system and support software correctly. From the logical point of view, the UAT data center is identical to the production data center; the features of the environment that are represented by the settings of the logical servers in the data center diagram are the same. These features include the operating systems, .NET versions, and the IIS settings—we discussed all three of these in Chapter 5. The only difference between the production and staging environments will be scale; the production environment uses more servers in the array hosting the sales website and web services.

Later in this chapter you will see how Peter designs the staging/production logical data center, revises the application diagrams for the new system, and verifies deployment.

Establish Validation Guidelines

The user acceptance tests themselves were written by Susan and her assistants during each iteration after the storyboarding of the scenarios had taken place. Before user acceptance testing takes place, however, it is necessary to establish some guidelines as to which tests should be included. Also, the procedures must be established for running the tests, recording the results, and accepting or rejecting the release candidate according to the results.

Select Release Candidate

Often companies define various types of release called alpha, beta, release candidate, gold release, and so forth. The alpha and beta releases are usually partially functioning versions of the product given to potential customers for evaluation purposes. I have not mentioned these releases earlier, but in line with the concept of maintaining customer involvement, the team at Guru's Nest has delivered a set of beta releases beginning at iteration 4 to allow evaluation of the evolving feature set and ad hoc testing by Icarus. The release candidate will be the release that is installed for UAT, and after UAT will be a candidate to become the gold, or production, release.

We ended the previous chapter with the team resolving to make a final push for more thorough testing. As the team moves through iteration 7, finding and correcting bugs using more and more searching tests, each daily build can be evaluated against the system test reports. As the latest date for release to UAT approaches, a build for which the test results are acceptable can be named as a release candidate. You might expect that this would be the last build to come from the team, but occasionally this might not be the case. The release candidate will probably still have unresolved bugs, but the severity of the bugs will be low enough to be acceptable in release.

Create Rollout and Deployment Plan

The rollout and deployment plan will consist of a set of tasks entered into Team System. It will address the following issues for the Icarus project:

- Installation of the web servers with the web service and web site applications, and installation of the application servers with the `SalesBusinessObjects` and `ListingBusinessObjects` applications

- Installation of the ClickOnce install manifests so that `SalesWing` and `ListWing` clients can be installed from the servers

- Assistance to call center operators as they install `List Wing` and `Sales Wing` applications from servers, together with their component applications `SalesBusinessObjects` and `ListingBusinessObjects`

- Installation of the `SalesStatus` applications on selected administrator machines

- Installation of the `Enterprise` database and migration of the data

- Training of help desk for agents and vendors, and support staff, field maintenance or operations staff, and end users

Clare will be responsible for making this plan and for allocating the resources to it and coordinating with the various people at Icarus to determine the scheduling and availability of customer resources.

User Acceptance Testing, Analyze User Acceptance Test Results, Accept Product for Release

A description of these three tasks appears in the process guidance. Clare is planning that Ian from Trendy Travel in Australia participate in the UAT via a virtual private networking (VPN) connection and that William and James provide operators from their groups. Achilles, a member of World Wide Chef's staff from Athens, will also participate. Icarus is regarding the acceptance of the product by Trendy Travel and WWC as essential to the success of the UAT.

Package Product

Later in this chapter, you will learn how to use Visual Studio 2005 features to package the various parts of the entire product for installation on both the production and UAT/Staging environment.

Execute Rollout Plan

Team System can be used to track the execution of the plan and to gain experience for future projects.

Create Release Notes

Release notes will be published after completion of the plan.

Planning the User Acceptance Testing and Rollout

Using Microsoft Project, Clare generates tasks and publishes them to TFS, where she uses Team Explorer to assign them to senior members of the team. She lays out the schedule in the Gantt chart shown in Figure 14-1.

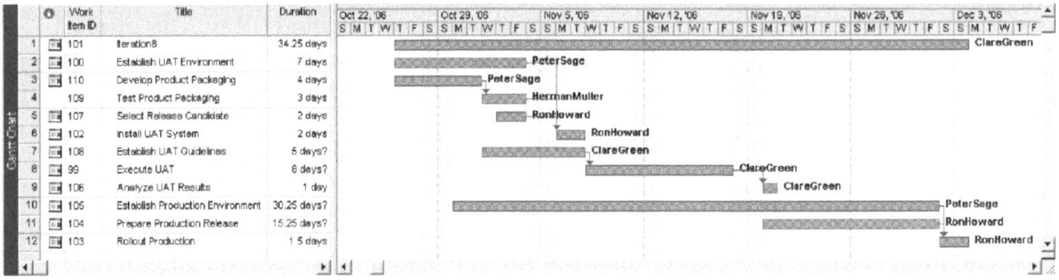

Figure 14-1. *Schedule for the rollout and deployment*

Iteration 8 has been extended to include the rollout itself, which has been put back to December 2 and 3 to avoid the Thanksgiving weekend. The early part of iteration 8 will be taken up with final testing and bug fixing before a release candidate can be selected—the Select Release Candidate task. During this early stage, Peter, together with Angela and Charles, will decide on the product packaging. This task consists of deciding how to package the files that need to be installed for the various component applications making up the distributed application so that they can be easily and reliably installed on the servers and workstations making up both the UAT/Staging environment and the production environment. Both these environments will be physical implementations of the logical data center called Icarus Global Data Center (see Chapter 5).

Peter's other task early in iteration 8 is to supervise the establishment of the UAT/Staging environment. The UAT environment will be constructed at Icarus prior to installation of the UAT system by Ron and Peter, and Peter must supply specifications based on his original design for the logical data center so that the machines and their connections can be configured correctly and the correct platform software installed, such as operating systems and .NET runtime.

Once the product packaging has been developed—and we will look at this in a little more detail later—it must be tested by Herman's team, following installation instructions that Peter's team must also produce.

Around the same time, Ron, who is performing the usual daily builds and participating in the daily triage session described in the previous chapter, will work with that group (Clare, Herman, Peter, Ron, and Susan) to determine a suitable release candidate, to promote to the version to be installed on the UAT environment.

Once the packaging, UAT environment, and release candidate are ready, Ron will create installation media, and he and Peter will fly to Icarus and install the UAT system.

The user acceptance tests were written for each scenario during the implementation of that scenario, but Susan has a task to put together guidelines for performing the UAT prior to its commencement. These guidelines need to be approved by both Icarus and Guru's Nest management well before UAT begins, since the scope of UAT needs to be understood by all concerned, particularly the testers, to avoid delays and misunderstandings that could jeopardize the rollout date. Nevertheless, the process guidance for MSF CMMI makes it very clear that the purpose of UAT "is not to validate that the release candidate conforms to the specification (customer requirements in the shape of scenarios and qualities of service) but to agree that the release candidate delivers what the market needs." This is a nice thought, but obviously those who must approve the product at UAT must have been sufficiently involved early on, so that the product's specification *does* match the market needs. Although Susan will write the document containing the UAT guidelines, Clare has overall responsibility of the task since it must be agreed on by the various stakeholders at Icarus and Guru's Nest.

Eight days have been allowed in Clare's schedule for UAT with the understanding that, if necessary the intervening weekend can be used. Peter gloomily foresees a lot of disrupted sleep for many team members since the Australians and Europeans will be working in their time zones! Much of the responsibility for testing the Sales Wing and List Wing applications has, in fact, been delegated to Trendy Travel and World Wide Chefs, and this is an example of Icarus, as well as Guru's Nest, taking the idea of partnering with customers very seriously.

Peter's other task during most of the iteration is to work with the infrastructure people at Icarus to establish the production environment, which is another physical implementation of the logical Icarus Global Data Center put together in Chapter 5.

Once the UAT is complete, a task is added to determine its result, that is, whether or not the release candidate is acceptable. Then two weeks have been allowed to prepare the release version. The same release media used for UAT can, and should be, used for production release, but there will probably be issues to tidy up involving URLs and connection strings in configuration files. Also, this period can be a buffer in case UAT overruns or more bugs are found. After UAT, the hardware configuration becomes the staging system, allowing preproduction testing and resolution of any remaining issues.

The rollout to production is scheduled to take place on the weekend of December 2 and 3!

Designing the UAT/Production Logical Data Center and Verifying Deployment

Here we see how Peter draws the final application, system, and deployment diagrams. Quite a lot has changed since Chapter 5 and it will be helpful to draw the concepts together again in diagrams.

The Final Production and UAT Application

As one of the tasks to be carried out as the project moves toward deployment, Peter reviews his application diagram, which has evolved from the one designed for iteration 1 (see Chapter 6, Figure 6-23). If you remember, Figure 6-23 was a rewrite of the one shown in Chapter 5, Figure 5-18, and contained only the iteration 1 functionality. It also took account of the changes to the way in which the business logic component applications, SalesBusinessObjects and ListingBusinessObjects, were to be used. In Chapter 6 you saw how these business applications were designed so that they could exist on the logical server, in the secure zone, and also on the clients, both with SalesWing and ListWing. We did not look very much at the offline aspects of the ListWing application, but the same principle holds for that application as well as the SalesWing application.

Figure 14-2. *Final Icarus Enterprise 3.1 production application diagram*

Figure 14-2 shows the final version of the application as it exists at iteration 8. At the top are the three client applications: an ordinary web browser, WebBrowser, and the two Windows Forms applications ListWing and SalesWing. ListWing interacts with the ListingBusinessObjects application shown lower in the diagram, and SalesWing interacts with both ListingBusinessObjects and SalesBusinessObjects.

SalesWing will need to create business objects of classes such as OrderBE and CustomerBE, as explained in Chapters 6 and 7. It will also need to create instances of classes in ListingBusinessObjects such as VendorBE, ResourceBE, and others to retrieve data to support the Resource Catalog browse capability described in Chapter 4. Space in this book has prevented a detailed discussion of the design of these classes and how they interact with the SalesWing and SalesSite applications, but you can imagine that there has been a lot of communication between Charles, Ed, and Rahul as these issues are resolved. ListWing will need to create business objects that are instances of classes such as ResourceBE and VendorBE to support its job of managing vendors and resources. The data access layers for these classes such as OrderDS and CustomerDS are included within the applications as defined on these diagrams; thus in Figure 14-2, SalesBusinessObjects and ListingBusinessObjects both interact with two external database applications, ClientLocalDatabase and Enterprise. Both of these interactions are not used simultaneously by any instance of these applications as is clear from the system diagrams that follow.

Interactions are also shown between the SalesBusinessObjects and ListingBusinessObjects applications and the corresponding SalesWebService and ListingWebService. These interactions will only be used by the instances of the business object applications on the clients, as again will be clear from the system diagrams. The web service stubs are shown in Figure 14-2, but these will appear in none of the production or UAT system diagrams.

The SalesBusinessObjects and ListingBusinessObjects applications also are shown to interact with the OrchestrationService; SalesBusinessObjects also interacts with PaymentService. It will only be the instances on the servers that have these connections together with a connection to the Enterprise database.

Finally in Figure 14-2, you can see that the applications concerned with replication are also shown: the ClientReplWebService, the ClientReplBusinessObjects, and the ServerReplBusinessObjects. You may be surprised that there is no connection between the SalesWing and ListWing applications and the ClientReplBusinessObjects, when the ClientReplBusinessObjects are obviously part of both the installed Sales Wing and List Wing systems. This is because, in Figure 14-2, the SalesWing application now represents only the Windows Forms application executable. The SalesBusinessObjects and ReplBusinessObjects are indeed loaded by that executable, but the replication thread runs completely independently once it is started.

The Sales Wing and List Wing Systems

Figure 14-3 shows the Sales Wing system to be deployed during UAT and in production, which consists of an instance of five applications selected from the application diagram in Figure 14-2. Keep in mind that the Sales Wing system—the application as the user sees it—is larger than the SalesWing application. Remember that systems are ways in which a distributed application is configured for use and includes a selection of one or more instances of applications chosen for the application diagram. The SalesWing Windows Forms application communicates with an instance of SalesBusinessObjects and an instance of ListingBusinessObjects that each persist instances of their business object classes to and from the instance of the `ClientLocalDatabase` that is also included in the system. The business object applications also make use of their `SalesWS` and `ListingWS` connections to the web services, which terminate on connection points to the external world at the bottom of the diagram. An instance of the `ClientReplBusinessObjects` application is also included in this system and has connections from its `ClientReplWebService` connection to the outside world and also a connection to the `ClientLocalDatabase` application. This allows it to go about its work of updating various entities in the client local database from the Icarus Enterprise database. In the system diagrams that follow, the Sales Wing and List Wing *systems* have the same names as the smaller `SalesWing` and `ListWing` applications. To avoid confusion I'll always add the word *system* when necessary.

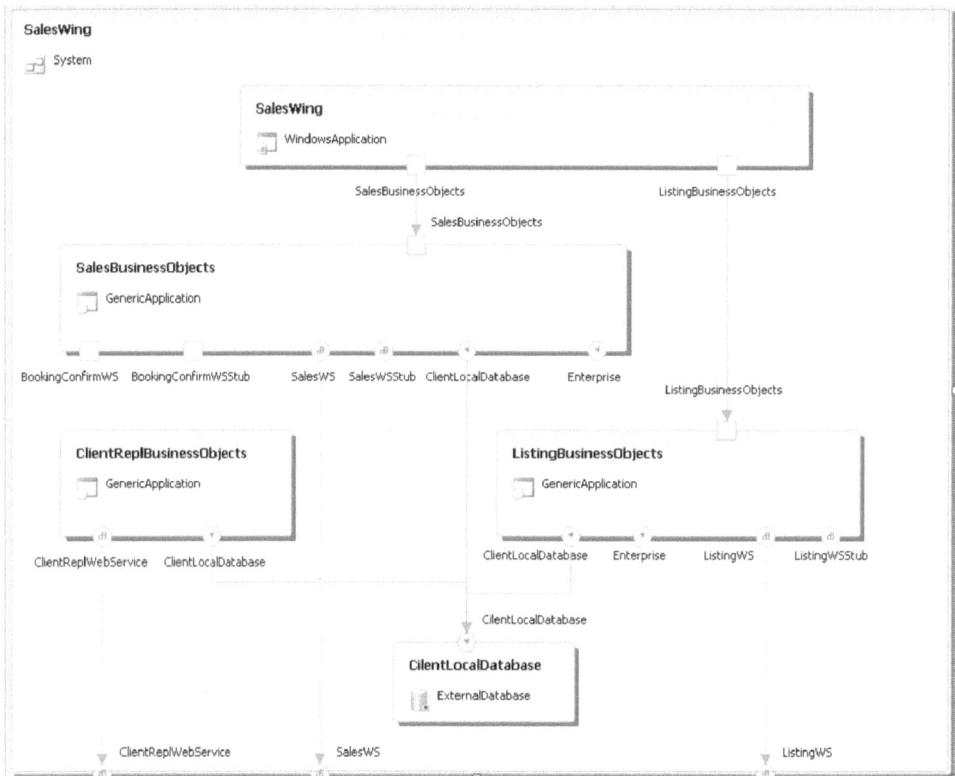

Figure 14-3. *Production and UAT system diagram for the Sales Wing application*

There is a different configuration of Sales Wing that will be installed in the Icarus call centers, called `SalesWingInternal`, which is shown in Figure 14-4. This system does not include the `ClientLocalDatabase` or the `ClientReplBusinessObjects` applications, since call center operators will always be online.

Figure 14-5 shows the production List Wing system, consisting of an instance of the `ListWing` Windows Forms application together with an instance of `ListingBusinessObjects` and `ClientLocalDatabase`. This arrangement enables the List Wing system to do its offline work. Addition of the connections from the `ListingWebService` endpoint on the `ListingBusinessObjects` application to a proxy endpoint at the edge of the system provides for its online operation where that connection will be connected to an instance of `ListingWebService` on the Icarus server.

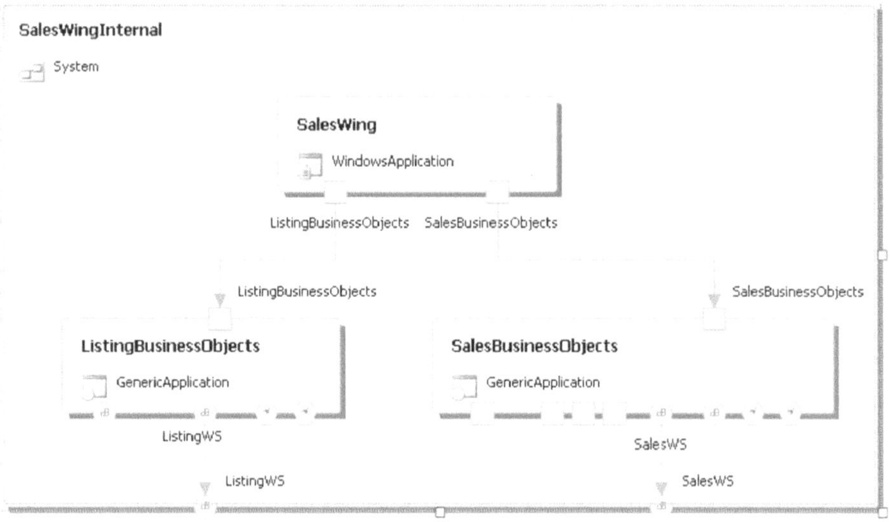

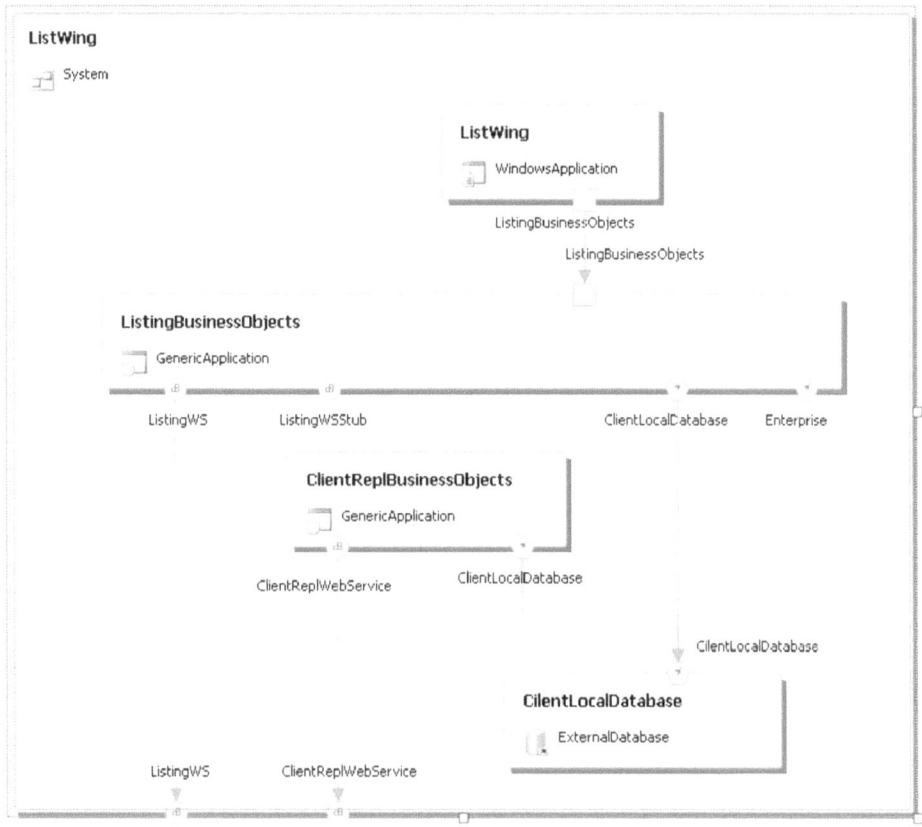

Figure 14-4. *Production and UAT system diagram for the call center Sales Wing application*

Figure 14-5. *Production and UAT system diagram for the List Wing application*

There is also an instance of `ClientReplBusinessObjects`, which connects to the `ClientLocalDatabase` instance. The `ClientReplWebService` proxy endpoint allows the listing web service to replicate vendors and their resources locally.

For the admin client machines within Icarus, used by the vendor administrators, the version of List Wing called `ListWingInternal` will be installed (not shown). This does not have the `ClientLocalDatabase` or `ClientReplBusinessObjects` since these machines will always be online.

The Icarus Presentation System

The presentation system is made up of the `EnterpriseBusinessLogic` system and instances of the web services and `SalesSite`, as shown in Figure 14-7. The `EnterpriseBusinessLogic` system itself is shown in Figure 14-6; it is similar to that in Chapter 5, Figure 5-20, but includes the addition of the `ServerReplBusinessObjects` application, which did not become part of the design until iteration 2. Initially, in this system the `OrchestrationService` and `PaymentService` application will be replaced by the `PaymentServiceStub` applications shown in Figure 14-2. The presentation system in Figure 14-7 includes two instances each of the `SalesWebService` and `ListingWebService`: one to service the intranet and one the Internet. A single instance of `SalesSite` services the home customers on the Internet.

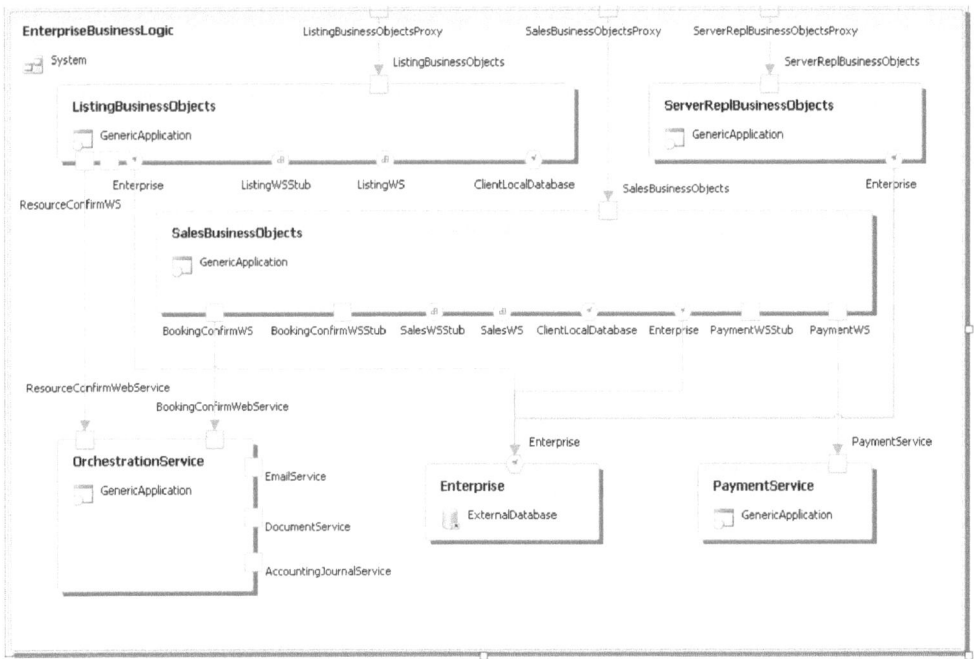

Figure 14-6. *Production and UAT system diagram for business logic*

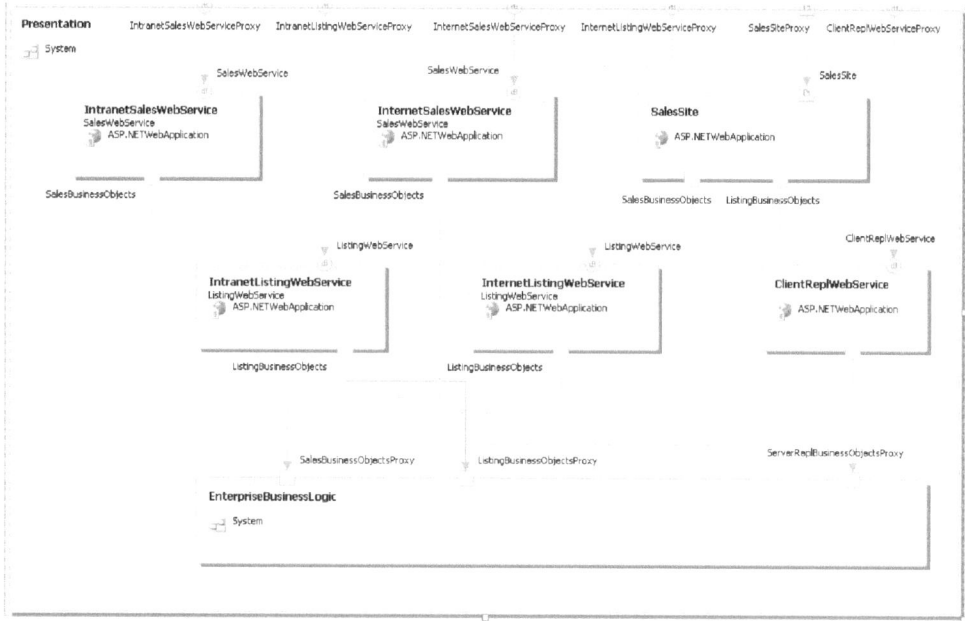

Figure 14-7. *Production and UAT system diagram for presentation*

The User Acceptance Test System

Figure 14-8 shows the UAT system, which includes the Presentation system with two instances of the SalesWing *system*, two of the ListWing *system* and one of the WebBrowser application. One instance of the SalesWing and ListWing systems is deployed on the Icarus intranet and the other instance of the same pair on the Internet. The Internet instances of the SalesWing and ListWing systems are at Trendy Travel in Australia and World Wide Chefs in Athens, respectively, so that staff at those sites can participate in the UAT.

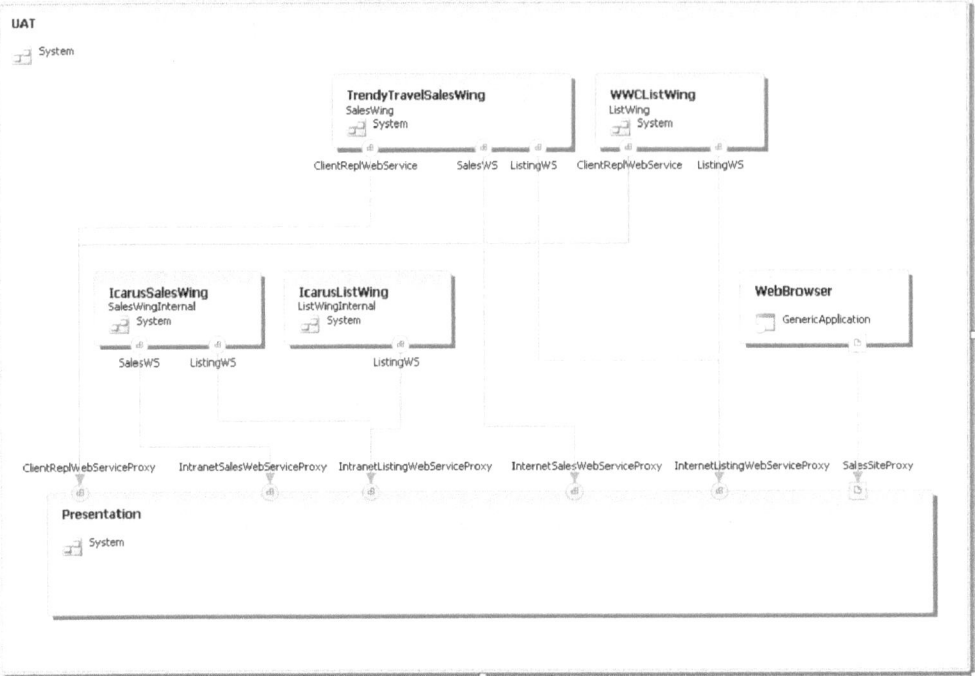

Figure 14-8. *User acceptance test system*

Deployment of the UAT System

Peter designs a data center for UAT using the Data Center Designer. This represents a trimmed-down version of the production data center in Chapter 5, Figure 5-39, but there is another set of changes. The travel agent and vendor client machines are represented in Figure 14-9 as zones, such as the TrendyTravelClient and WWCClient, in which a DatabaseServer logical server prototype is included. This is because database applications using the ExternalDatabase prototype have implicit constraints (explained in Chapter 5) that prevent an ExternalDataBase prototype application from being deployed on a WindowsClient prototype logical server. As we explained in Chapter 6 when we talked about developers' machines as zones, the servers within are *logical* servers and in effect are implemented physically by one machine.

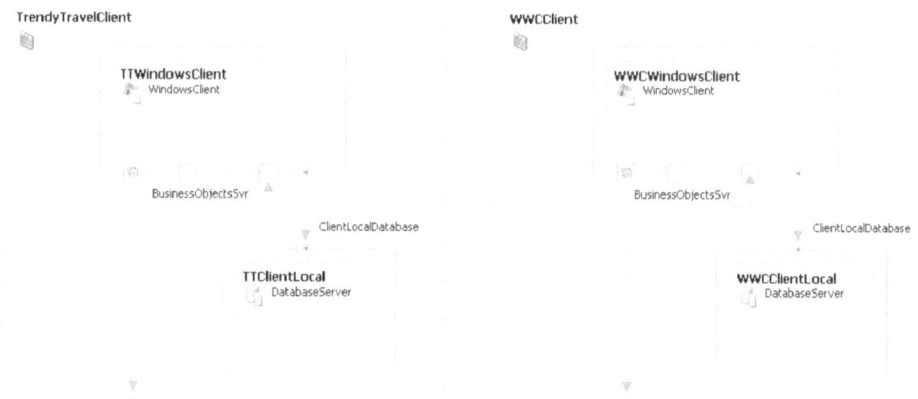

Figure 14-9. *Logical data centers for the Sales Wing and List Wing client applications*

Another trick needs to be added, seen in Figure 14-9. A straight `WindowsClient` logical server prototype will not be able to host the `SalesBusinessObjects` and `ListingBusinessObjects` applications since they need a `GenericEndpoint` prototype implementing the .NET Remoting protocol (see Figure 5-39 again). This can be done by adding a `GenericServerEndpoint` and a `GenericClientEndpoint`, with the .NET Remoting protocol joining them. This makes it look as though the `TTWindowsClient` and `WWCWindowsClient` applications both serve and consume the business objects via these endpoints. In the case of the client applications, these business objects are not remoted at all, but loaded into the same app domain by the `SalesWing` and `ListWing` applications when they start up.

Figure 14-10 shows the UAT system deployment diagram, which Peter uses to model the deployment that he will perform at Icarus prior to the start of the UAT. One difference between this diagram and the production deployment is that the production logical data center will include zones; the high security zone, the Internet, and intranet peripheral zones and the various client zones, as shown in Figure 5-39. In the UAT deployment most of the UAT machines are placed in the `IcarusDevelopmentNetwork` zone, which is part of the `AdminZone` in Figure 5-39. This zone has limited-bandwidth Internet access so that the client machines used by the UAT personnel at Trendy Travel and World Wide Chefs can access the web services via a VPN.

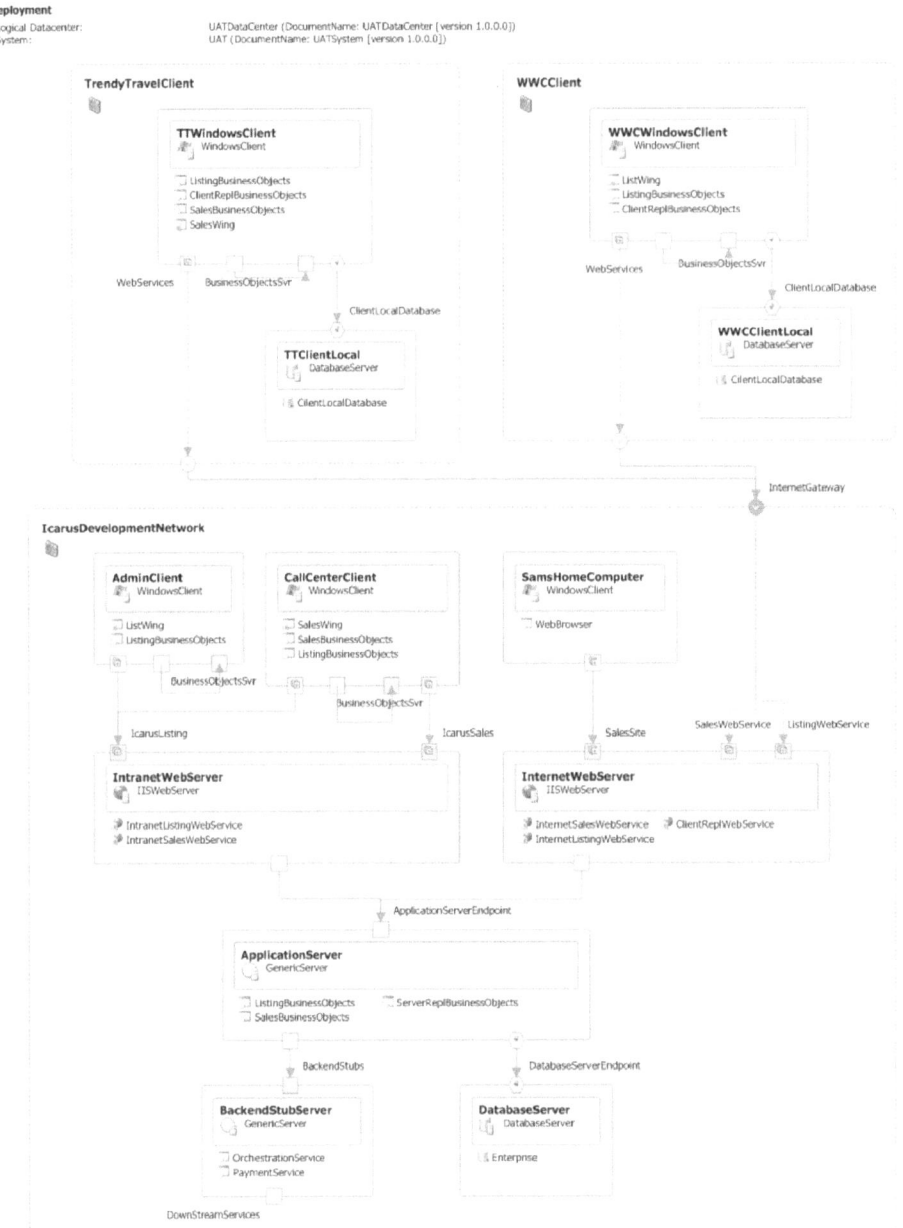

Figure 14-10. *The user acceptance test deployment diagram*

The admin client and call center client within Icarus's development zone uses the
SalesWingInternal and ListWingInternal configuration of the Sales Wing and List Wing
systems, that is, without ClientLocalDatabase and replication. These therefore can use
simpler logical server configurations—just simply a WindowsClient prototype—with the addition
of the BusinessObjectSvr endpoint and its corresponding client endpoint described earlier.

There are two logical servers of the IISWebServer prototype; each hosts instances of SalesWebService and ListingWebService, but the one connected to the Internet also hosts ClientReplWebService. A single logical server of the GenericServer prototype called ApplicationServer hosts all the business objects applications: SalesBusinessObjects, ListingBusinessObjects, and ServerReplBusinessObjects. A machine is also provided to host the Enterprise database and another to host the OrchestrationService and PaymentService, which will be deployed in stub form for initial testing.

Deployment of the Production System

Peter also generates a new production logical data center diagram, which is very similar to Figure 5-39. The difference is that the WWCWindowsClient and the TTWindowsClient logical servers will look exactly like those in Figure 14-9. Also, all the CallCenterClient instances will look like the CallCenterClient in Figure 14-10, with the same applications deployed, including those at Chennai, UK, and Hong Kong. The AdminClient instances will also look like those in Figure 14-10, with the same applications. Remember that only the Sales Wing and List Wing systems at travel agents and vendors will have the full configuration, including the ClientReplBusinessObjects and ClientLocalDatabase to enable offline working.

Designing the Product Packaging

This section describes the Package Product task in the process guidance. Designing the product packaging here means more than designing a box, and it is an important part of the architecture that Peter must address.

Deployment Projects

Peter creates a solution folder called Deployment in which to create deployment projects for the solution. He needs to create deployment projects that will make deployment of each part of the distributed application simple and consistent. Visual Studio 2005 supports a number of different kinds of deployment projects: Setup Project, Web Setup Project, Merge Module Project, Setup Wizard, CAB Project, and Smart Device CAB Project. We'll only consider here the ones relevant to the project.

A Web Setup Project is intended to install a web application on a web server. This type of setup project can be used to install the web services SalesWebService, ListingWebService, and ClientReplWebService. It can also be used to install the SalesSite application.

The business layer projects SalesBusinessObjects, ListingBusinessObjects, and ServerReplBusinessObjects can be installed using a Setup Project. This type of project essentially copies a defined set of files to an application folder on the target machine.

Installation of the Sales Wing and List Wing applications will be best accomplished using the ClickOnce type of deployment so that Travel Agents and Vendors can easily install the applications on their own machines over the Internet. In discussing these applications we strictly mean the *systems* as in Figures 14-3 and 14-5, but remember way back in Chapter 5 I mentioned that applications contain other applications—here's an example. We have to call the thing we provide to the agents and vendors an *application*, even though it's actually a system constructed from bits of a larger application.

CallCenterClient and AdminClient machines can also be installed in the ClickOnce manner, but the Icarus IT department may want to be able to install standard machines for a call center using *disk imaging*. In this process, a standard disk image is provided for a call center machine and an application such as Symantec Ghost or Acronis True Image is used to quickly copy an image to each machine as they are rolled out. Icarus will be rolling out the new application to an existing set of machines and will probably install the new Sales Wing and List Wing applications on machines alongside existing applications. Peter plans to provide a CD-ROM disc to allow installation of each call center machine, but he also has to coordinate with Icarus's IT support group as they are currently investigating remote client deployment options.

Table 14-1 summarizes the type of deployment project chosen for each component application of the entire Icarus Enterprise 3.1 distributed application.

Table 14-1. *Deployment Projects for Each Application within the Entire Icarus Enterprise 3.1 Application*

Application	Type of Deployment
Sales Wing (external)	ClickOnce deployment (manual install of SQL Server Express)
List Wing (external)	ClickOnce deployment (manual install of SQL Server Express)
Sales Wing (internal)	Visual Studio 2005 Setup Project
List Wing (internal)	Visual Studio 2005 Setup Project
Sales Status (internal)	Visual Studio 2005 Setup Project
Sales Site	Visual Studio 2005 Web Setup Project
Sales Web Service	Visual Studio 2005 Web Setup Project
Listing Web Service	Visual Studio 2005 Web Setup Project
Client Replication Web Service	Visual Studio 2005 Web Setup Project
Sales Business Objects	Visual Studio 2005 Setup Project
Listing Business Objects	Visual Studio 2005 Setup Project
Server Replication Business Objects	Visual Studio 2005 Setup Project
Enterprise Database	SQL scripts and instructions to DBA

Client Deployment: ClickOnce

ClickOnce deployment is very simple to set up when a solution is open in Visual Studio 2005. To make an application available for installation, you right-click on the project (in this case SalesWing or ListWing in Solution Explorer) and select Publish, which displays the dialog box shown in Figure 14-11. Here you can specify a location at which to publish the application so that prospective users may install it. You can choose a disk path, a file share, an FTP server, or a website. If you publish it to a website, FTP location, or a file share, the application will immediately be available for installation from that location by anyone who has access to that location.

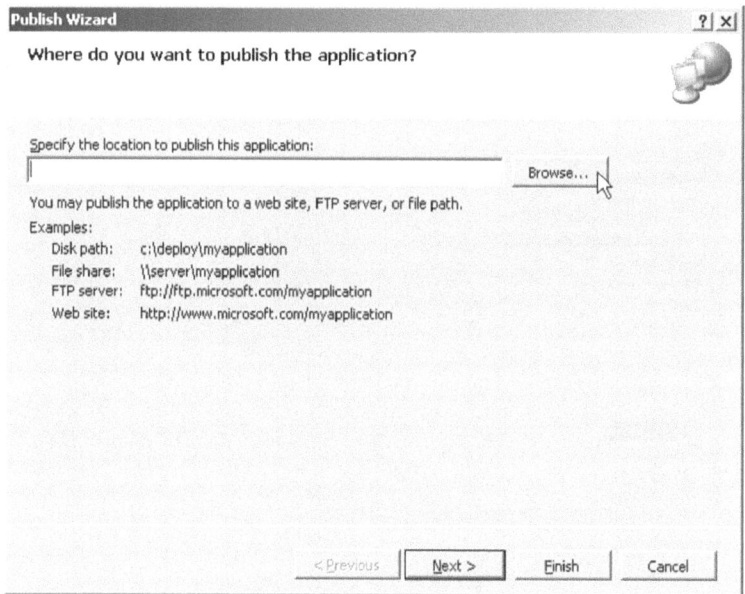

Figure 14-11. *Publishing an application for ClickOnce installation*

In this case, Peter does not want to make the application immediately available for installation. Instead, he wants to produce the files that can be *later* installed on an Icarus website as part of the deployment of the entire distributed application. This will make the Sales Wing application available for agents to install. Peter certainly does not have access at this time to that very secure location.

He therefore uses Windows Explorer to create an additional folder under the SalesWing folder in his workspace called ClickOnce where he plans to create all the files that need to be deployed on the web server to publish the application. He will have to remember to add this to source control.

Continuing with the Publish Wizard in Figure 14-11, Peter clicks Browse to open the dialog box in Figure 14-12. He selects File System and finds and selects the ClickOnce folder under SalesWing in his workspace as shown, then clicks Open. In Figure 14-11, clicking Next displays the next page in the wizard, shown in Figure 14-13.

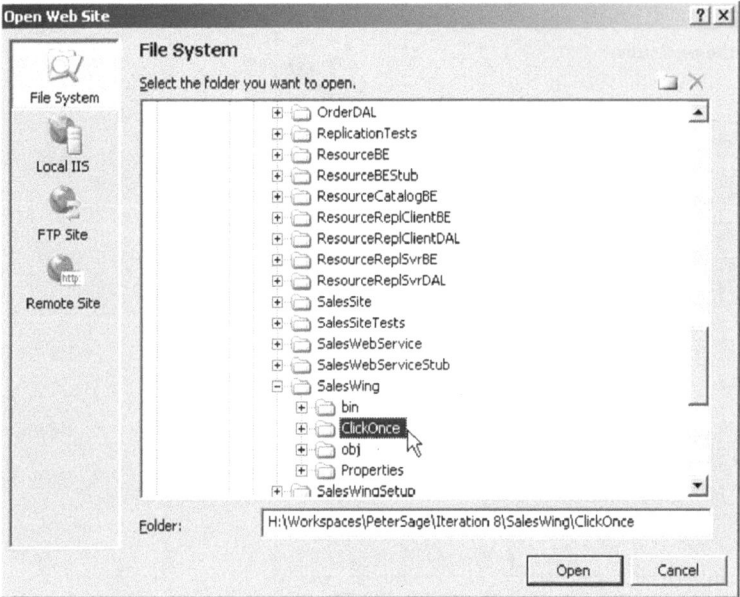

Figure 14-12. *Selecting the publish location*

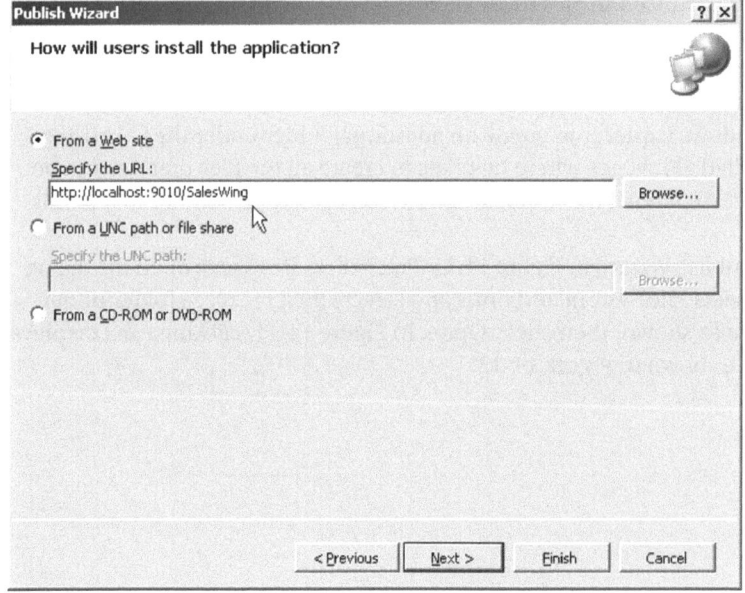

Figure 14-13. *Specifying the method of installation*

Once Peter specifies a file location in which to publish the Sales Wing application, the wizard then asks by what method it will eventually be published: website, file share, or CD-ROM or DVD-ROM. This page allows the Publish Wizard to generate the correct files. Peter knows that the application will be installed from an Icarus website, but he does not yet know the exact URL. He therefore sets up a deployment site on his own machine with SalesWing and ListWing virtual folders. He sets the port for the website as an arbitrary 9010. When he has published the application to a file folder the XML files generated will contain this URL as the "codebase" property of the deployment provider, so for the real deployment of the ClickOnce files, this will need to be changed in the XML files. However, at the present time Peter simply wants to test his deployment process, so he clicks the Browse button and picks out the website he has set up and the SalesWing virtual directory. Clicking Next displays the page shown in Figure 14-14, which allows offline availability to be determined. Once the Sales Wing application is installed, it needs to be able to run offline, so Peter clicks the Yes option and then clicks Next. The idea of online/offline here is a ClickOnce concept, which need not concern us further, but the Sales Wing application must obviously run when the client machine is disconnected from the Internet. On the last wizard page, a summary, he clicks Finish. This creates a set of files called a manifest in the ClickOnce folder under the SalesWing project. Creating a ClickOnce install like this will include the assemblies referenced by the SalesWing project, so the installed Sales Wing application will be the system shown in Figure 14-3 as we require—with the exception of ClientLocalDatabase, which will still need to be installed manually.

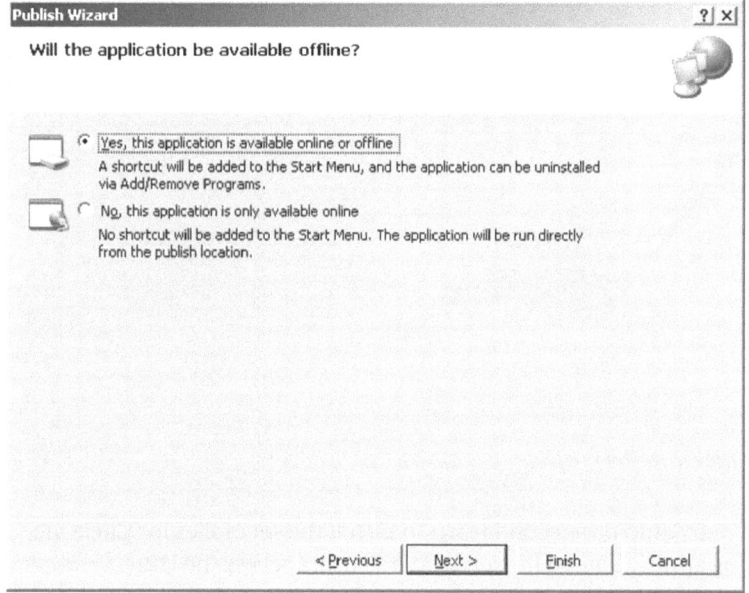

Figure 14-14. *Determining whether the ClickOnce application will be available offline*

Next Peter wants to create another setup project that will enable the manifest files to be installed on the installation website (temporarily localhost:9010/SalesWing) when the entire Icarus Enterprise 3.1 application is deployed. To do this, he creates a Web Setup project from the Add New Project dialog box and calls it "ClickOnceApplications". Once he clicks OK in that dialog box, Visual Studio creates the project and opens the window shown in Figure 14-15.

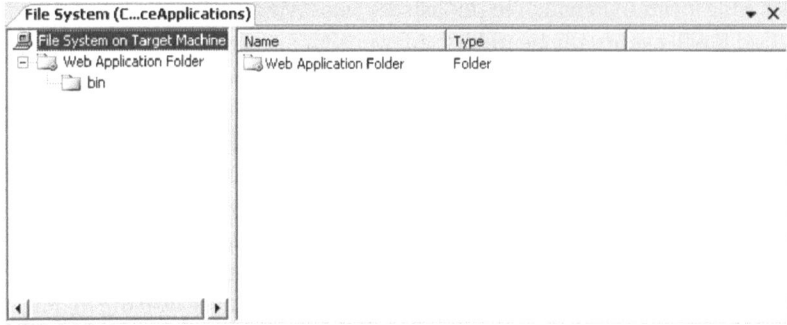

Figure 14-15. *A Web Setup deployment project*

Essentially this kind of project consists of a set of folders, each containing files or project output, that correspond to the folders that will be created on the target machine when the installation takes place. There are many more features available than just these for controlling the installation process and taking account of variations. In this case Peter wants to install a specified group of files in a virtual directory on a web server—that's all there is to it. He can delete the folder called bin on the left by right-clicking on it and selecting Delete. Then he adds a web folder called SalesWing and one called ListWing and simply drags all of the files and subfolders from the ClickOnce folder into the SalesWing folder, as shown in Figure 14-16.

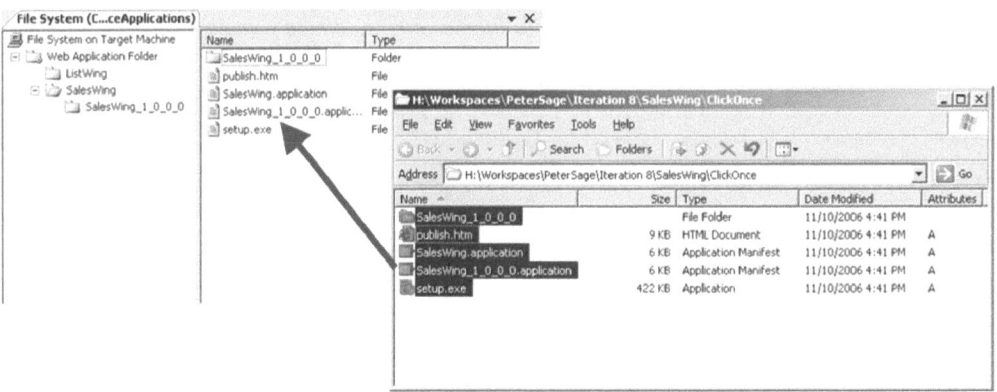

Figure 14-16. *Dragging the files into the project*

Now he can build the Web Setup project and run it to install the set of files for ClickOnce installation of the Sales Wing application on his server. When users access the URL

http://localhost:9010/SalesWing/publish.htm

the application displays the install page shown in Figure 14-17. This is the page the travel agents will see when they visit Icarus's site to install the application. Peter still needs to figure out how the agents will install the ClientLocalDatabase component application of Sales Wing—perhaps this can be done by scripts or included in the ClickOnce install. You can think about this!

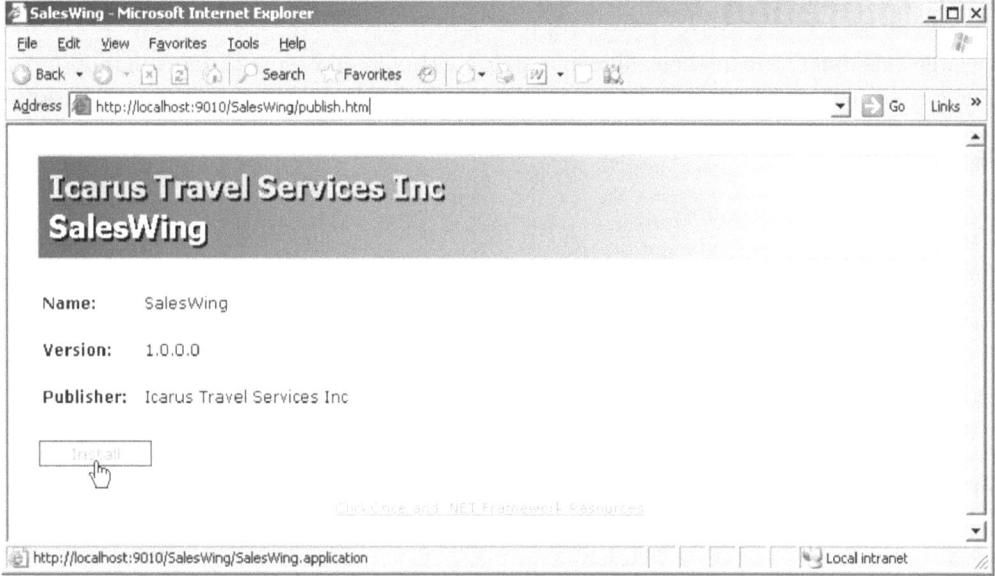

Figure 14-17. *The install page for the SalesWing application*

Setup Projects for the Rest of the Applications

According to Table 14-1, Peter must develop setup projects for the rest of the component applications, using either the Setup Project or Web Setup Project option. Each will include the files necessary for the application being installed. Usually it is sufficient to select the project output for the chosen project, say SalesWebService, in which case the dependencies and the web.config files will be included as well. The same rule applies to the business objects projects like SalesBusinessObjects.

In my experience, there is a great deal of detailed work involved in building installers, whether using Visual Studio 2005 or products such as Install Shield (Install Shield Software Corporation) or Wise (Wise Solutions). Providing the capability to customize the .config files is one complication. In the case of Enterprise 3.1 there are many .config files, including those for the SalesWing and ListWing projects, as well as the web.config files for SalesWebService, ListingWebService, ClientReplWebService, and SalesSite. The business objects projects are to be run on application servers accessible to the web services and SalesSite via .NET Remoting. For these assemblies their connection strings are obtained programmatically from the web.config files of their clients. So connection strings need to be set in the .config files for all applications at install time. Similarly, the web service URLs used by the smart client applications need to be set up when the ClickOnce manifests are deployed on the installation website.

Setup projects contain rich capabilities, such as dialog boxes that are displayed to the user at install time to provide these kinds of features. One of Peter's developers will need to use these capabilities to complete all of the install details. Space in this book prevents any further discussion of these interesting techniques.

Data Migration

One large area that I have not been able to treat in this book is the work of data migration. This is the responsibility of Alberto and the Icarus DBA; it is their job to write scripts that will perform a number of very important tasks in migrating data from the old SQL Server 2000 system to the new database:

- Migrate all of the vendors.

- Migrate the resources.

- Migrate the customers.

- Migrate the orders and reservations.

The team agrees that only orders that have reservations in the future will be migrated, but all vendors, resources, and customers need to be moved. The data migration has been tested over a period of weeks leading up to the "go live" date for the whole application, and the new application has been tested against the migrated data to ensure its integrity.

How It All Happened

In this section we see the installation of the UAT system, the performance of the UAT, and the deployment and production test.

Installing the UAT System

On the afternoon of Sunday, November 5, Peter and Ron fly to Icarus's headquarters to begin installation of the UAT configuration of the application. On Monday they install all of the applications on the servers, including the ClickOnce manifests for Sales Wing and List Wing. Alberto has been there most of the previous week migrating the data from production, since it has been agreed that the production data will be used for the UAT. Ron installs the internal version of Sales Wing on the two client machines to be used inside Icarus. Aside from a couple of connectivity problems due to a firewall being configured incorrectly by Icarus's support team, all goes very well. Clare and Peter have done their planning very well. The first part of the UAT from the point of view of World Wide Chefs and Trendy Travel is to install their smart client applications using the ClickOnce install.

At the present time, it is necessary to install SQL Server Express on the clients manually, which is a big disadvantage, but Clare has convinced Icarus to accept this in view of the changes in offline working.

The User Acceptance Test

Much of the work during UAT falls to Susan, who spends a great deal of time providing guidance to the testers. It is a laborious process as all the tests are manual. During the night, Trendy Travel and World Wide Chefs are performing their tests and Susan's assistant, Linda Brown, takes over and answers questions from overseas using MSN Messenger.

There are 38 issues discovered during the UAT. Twenty-eight of them match up with known minor bugs that are to be accepted at rollout and fixed within three months under warranty.

The other 10 are indeed new issues, and 2 are considered serious. The 10 issues were all discovered by people using the system in ways that were not envisaged. Peter and Ron accept responsibility for investigating the two serious issues. During the last week Peter spends two whole days debugging on the staging system and finally finds a very subtle threading issue. Ron works with Alberto on the other problem, and at last Alberto discovers a transactional issue with a stored procedure.

Everyone is very relieved. Now all is ready for the rollout.

Go-Live Weekend

The rollout team on the weekend of December 2 consists of Clare, Peter, Ron, Angela, and Alberto, together with the support personnel from Icarus who perform most of the actual install. Again, Alberto has successfully migrated the database onto new machines running SQL Server 2005 during the previous week, but he must do a final migration after the system is shut down at 2:00 Saturday morning. Icarus has gone to a great deal of trouble to email all of their vendors and customers to inform them of the shutdown, so a successful first attempt at go-live is most important.

At 3:00 AM Saturday Alberto and Icarus's DBA begin a complete data migration. This goes without any trouble as it has been rehearsed previously, but it is a slow process and takes until 2:00 that afternoon!

In parallel with this effort, Peter sits with the Icarus folks as they install the business object applications on the bank of four application servers. At the same time Ron works with another Icarus technician to begin installing the web servers with the Sales Site application. There are four servers to install; by the time they have finished they join Peter and Angela for a late lunch. Angela has been installing clients; she has completed 20 and is very bored!

After lunch, together they tackle the web servers that will handle the intranet and Internet web service installations. Angela gratefully hands over the client install job to one of the Icarus people, who completes the other 25 that afternoon. There are three web servers for the Internet and two for the intranet, and one of the intranet servers refuses to install. Peter finds that someone at Icarus has set one of the websites to .NET 1.1 instead of 2.0. By 6:00 PM the servers are installed and the team goes out to dinner and retires early to their hotel. There will be an early start Sunday morning as they begin the production testing.

Sunday morning at 7:30 production testing begins using a web browser client, an instance of Sales Wing and List Wing. The team from Guru's Nest are now joined by testers from Icarus, drawn from the administrative staff. The production test is a much simplified version of the user acceptance test that must be completed Sunday. At this point, all the systems are up and running, but the system is disconnected from the Internet by the disabling of the gateway. Production testing goes on all morning; then after a break for lunch testing continues most of the afternoon. By 4:35 PM it is complete. There *are* a few issues, 27 in fact, but of these 19 were known minor issues that are to be corrected during the first three months. Of the eight new issues, six of them are put down to network issues and one of the Icarus support team replaces a router connecting the secure zone to the intranet peripheral zone. After a great deal of discussion—two hours in fact—the other two issues turn out to be a result of operator error.

At 8:00 PM the technicians reconnect the main router that connects the Internet and the frame relay WAN and the application goes live!

A cheer echoes around the room as they watch the activity of the servers begin to ramp up as real customers start to use the system.

"There's the first order!" shouts Alberto, who is looking at the database.

There is not much to do now, and the team sits around chatting for half an hour before going out for a late dinner. Tomorrow morning they're all getting a plane home. What a weekend! What a project!

Debriefing and Wrap-Up

You and I have nearly reached the end of this book, and we'll soon bid goodbye to the people from Icarus and the team from Guru's Nest. Clare has been speaking to another customer and in a while she will be telling them all about a new project. It will give them plenty to think about.

But let's reflect on this project and the treatment I have given it. What were its strong and weak points? Has it used Visual Studio Team System effectively? What areas have I as the project scribe left out, which you as the reader should study for yourself?

Requirements and Business Case

The offline working features have tended to dominate the requirements, since they are probably the most novel and difficult to specify. I wonder whether this makes a great deal of business sense. Travel agents will probably deal with other companies besides Icarus, and I doubt that most would want to make the commitment to include a large database on their local machine, particularly a laptop computer. Indeed, another business issue is how agents would handle reservations with other companies similar to Icarus. In many ways an agent would probably want a smart client application that would deal with several listing agents such as Icarus. Certainly the smart client needs to be small and lightweight, and the ClickOnce deployment is a huge advantage. Having to deploy even SQL Server Express Edition on their local machines is bound to cause a maintenance problem for the agents.

Architecture

Has the Icarus team made good use of the architectural features of Team System? Peter has used the distributed system designers quite extensively both to design the system at the high level and to model its deployment in the early planning stages. He used the distributed system designers again at each iteration to model the evolving application, and to simulate its deployment in the development and test logical data centers. At the end of the project he used the designers to confirm the design of the UAT and production systems and the deployment of both systems.

Peter used the implementation feature of the Application Designer to generate the basic applications for the website, web services, and smart client applications. At the end of the project, the applications on the diagram were automatically updated from the settings included in the code.

It seems that many of the advantages of using application diagrams are lost when generic applications are used since there is then no coupling between the implementing code and the application depicted on the diagram. This could be improved by the use of custom applications created using the System Definition Model (SDM) SDK. It is a pity that the team did not have time to explore the use of these features.

Development and Unit Test

The plan to include an analysis and prototyping phase and then a formal development phase in each iteration seems to have been a good one. This plan allowed the developers to experiment with the new features of Visual Studio 2005, ASP.NET 2.0, and C# 2.0—features such as generics, master pages, partial classes, and datasets. Even if you adopt a test-driven code philosophy during the formal development, this prototyping phase seems to be essential. In the later iterations, when the framework is firmly in place, the formal development of some features could perhaps begin right away. Even so, features such as security are novel enough to require prototyping. Performance is another consideration where prototype evaluation at an early stage is important.

The team could have separated the prototyping effort more cleanly from the formal development effort. The iterations could then be overlapped a little more so that the architectural/prototyping group would be moving on to the next iteration while the formal development group was "finishing" development of an iteration.

In their unit-test approach, the team included the database in units to be tested. The unit test then verified a "column" of functionality from the level of the database to the table adapters, the business entities, or the user interface itself. This is appropriate when the business entities have mainly a persistence functionality and there is little more to be tested. In Chapters 8 and 9 we saw exactly that. There was little point in trying to test the business entities such as `OrderBE` and `VendorBE` by building table adapter stubs to test just the business entity class alone, as there was very little functionality in that class. The main things that could be at fault were the table adapters and stored procedures as well as their multiuser features, such as transactions and security aspects. We did not see the unit tests that Icarus wrote for transactions and security, but these would have been difficult and important.

We also did not see the unit testing of the cost calculation functionality that was built within `OrderBE` to calculate the unit cost and extended cost for each reservation. The cost calculation functionality took account of various discounts as well as currency conversion, and testing the functionality independently of the database would have been useful. But then the database is important here, too, since the pricing model information would have been included in the resource data model. Space in this book prevented us from exploring that aspect of the project.

Application Testing and Deployment

The application testing of the product consisted of load testing, web testing, and specially written unit tests that tested the Windows Forms applications. There was also a significant number of manual tests that verified the subtle behavior required in the offline working requirements. This seems to be a good use of Team System testing features.

General Comments About the Book

I could have made this book much longer! I have tried to include something on all aspects of the use of Visual Studio Team System in a realistic project. The scope is very broad, but I do think that developers and architects gain from an understanding of areas such as project management, testing, and deployment. I have devoted a lot more time to the requirements, architecture, and prototyping than to the testing part of the project; there is much more to be learned about web and load testing. For instance, you could spend a good deal of time studying the way in which different kinds of applications behave when load testing parameters such as test mix, browser mix, and network mix are varied.

Generic tests were not explored in this book. Perhaps the brief outline of the tests applied to the Windows Form applications Sales Wing and List Wing user interface could be placed under the generic test framework. You could explore this idea. Remember also that load tests can include unit tests and generic tests, so by the use of unit tests, load testing can be applied—not just to the website, but also to the Windows Forms applications and, via load tests that include unit tests, to different subsections of the system.

I have devoted a lot of time to requirements—the scenarios in Chapter 4, the storyboards in Chapter 6, and the scenarios in Chapter 11 are quite detailed. I justify this by saying that Team System is very much about process; you have to choose a process for every team project. I chose to write about MSF for CMMI Process Improvement, and I have shown how that process can be applied. Understanding the development of requirements through writing scenarios is vital to employing such a process effectively. Indeed, in exploring this aspect, I was surprised a little by the number and complexity of the scenarios that need to be included in this kind of project. The work of defining and testing these should never be underestimated.

I could not treat the later iterations in any degree of thoroughness when describing the code; I have tried to show some key features leaving the rest to your imagination. I have not written the entire code for the project—such an amount of work would be beyond the ability of one developer! So if you feel that Icarus's system will not work in reality, you may well be correct. But how would *you* change it? What would you design differently? If I have stimulated your thoughts and encouraged your criticism, then I have succeeded in my aims.

Epilogue

We meet the team for the last time at their favorite local restaurant where they are enjoying an end-of-project dinner. Peter has forgiven Clare for his office makeover and they are engaged in a detailed conversation about another project. Charles has presented her with a very nice new replacement coffee mug.

Rahul, Charles, Ed, and Ian are engaged in an animated discussion about the flight characteristics of various ball shapes. Ed and Ian seem to be more concerned with the flight of ellipsoidal shaped balls, whereas Charles advocates the larger round ball, but after a couple of beers the talk turns more to comparison of Aussie "footy" and American football, with numerous interjections by Charles on the merits of soccer as the only pure version of the ancient and noble game.

Suddenly Clare's cell phone rings. "Clare Green speaking," she says and listens attentively for a few moments. "So you want the simulation package as well then..." she says; it is obviously a business call.

Rahul looks up, puzzled. He glances at Peter, who smiles knowingly. Clare continues to speak for a while longer, then hangs up.

She is trying hard to suppress her excitement, "You tell them, Peter," she chuckles.

Peter clears his throat dramatically. "Fellow team members!" he begins with an air of deliberate pomposity. "I'd like to tell you about our next project." He pauses, looking around with relish at the dramatic effect. "We are going to be developing a training system for the sports industry. One of its features will be a ball flight simulator—"

"I'm not selling it to England!" interjects Rahul suddenly, with a look of abject horror.

"No way, mate!" agrees Ian, "we want the ashes back in Australia."

"It's all right, guys," says Peter in a mock soothing voice. "Why don't you tell them, Susan?"

Susan and Angela have been talking quietly with William Fairways all evening. "OK," says Susan. "William has a business interest in a company based in Palm Springs and they are going to fund us to develop a training system that will help people learn to play golf."

Index